The Legal Environment of Business

10th edition

Roger E. Meiners
University of Texas at Arlington

Al. H. Ringleb
Consortium International MBA

Frances L. Edwards
Clemson University

SOUTH-WESTERN
CENGAGE Learning

Australia · Brazil · Japan · Korea · Mexico · Singapore · Spain · United Kingdom · United States

The Legal Environment of Business
Tenth Edition
Meiners Ringleb Edwards

VP/Editorial Director: Jack W. Calhoun

Editor in Chief: Rob Dewey

Acquisitions Editor: Steve Silverstein

Sr. Developmental Editor: Jan Lamar

Marketing Manager: Jennifer Garamy

Technology Project Manager: Rob Ellington

Sr. Content Project Manager: Cliff Kallemeyn

Sr. Art Director: Michelle Kunkler

Production Technology Analyst: Adam Grafa

Sr. First Print Buyer: Kevin Kluck

Production and Composition: Pre-Press PMG

Cover and Internal Designer: Craig Ramsdell/
Ramsdell Design

Cover Image: © Mark Gibson/Getty Images, Inc.

© 2009, 2006 South-Western, a part of Cengage Learning

ALL RIGHTS RESERVED. No part of this work covered by the copyright herein may be reproduced, transmitted, stored or used in any form or by any means graphic, electronic, or mechanical, including but not limited to photocopying, recording, scanning, digitizing, taping, Web distribution, information networks, or information storage and retrieval systems, except as permitted under Section 107 or 108 of the 1976 United States Copyright Act, without the prior written permission of the publisher.

For product information and technology assistance, contact us at
Cengage Learning Academic Resource Center, 1-800-423-0563

For permission to use material from this text or product,
submit all requests online at **www.cengage.com/permissions**
Further permissions questions can be emailed to
permissionrequest@cengage.com

Library of Congress Control Number: 2007942187
ISBN 13: 978-0-324-65436-3
ISBN 10: 0-324-65436-7

South-Western Cengage Learning
5191 Natorp Boulevard
Mason, OH 45040
USA

Cengage Learning products are represented in Canada by
Nelson Education, Ltd.

For your course and learning solutions, visit **academic.cengage.com**

Purchase any of our products at your local college store or at our
preferred online store **www.ichapters.com**

Printed in the United States of America
1 2 3 4 5 6 7 11 10 09 08 07

To Terry L. Anderson,
Whose original scholarship, diligent efforts, and good cheer
are reflected in his abilities as a scholar and a teacher. His
great respect for nature in his beloved Montana has made a
lasting contribution.

R.E.M.

Brief Contents

Preface xvii

Part 1: Elements of Law and the Judicial Process   2

1. Introducing the Modern Environment of Business, Law, and Ethics   4
2. The Court Systems   24
3. Trials and Resolving Disputes   48
4. The Constitution: Focus on Application to Business   75
5. Criminal Law and Business   102

Part 2: Elements of Traditional Business Law   124

6. Elements of Torts   126
7. Business Torts and Product Liability   150
8. Real and Personal Property   176
9. Intellectual Property   200
10. Contracts   222
11. Domestic and International Sales   252
12. Negotiable Instruments, Credit, and Bankruptcy   281
13. Business Organizations   310
14. Agency and the Employment Relationship   338

Part 3: The Regulatory Environment of Business   366

15. The Regulatory Process   368
16. Employment and Labor Regulations   388
17. Employment Discrimination   419
18. Environmental Law   447
19. Consumer Protection   475
20. Antitrust Law   503
21. Securities Regulation   530
22. The International Legal Environment of Business   554

Appendices   579

A. Legal Research and the Internet   579
B. Case Analysis and Legal Research   583
C. The Constitution of the United States of America   589
D. The Uniform Commercial Code (Excerpts)   601
E. National Labor Relations Act (Excerpts)   617
F. Title VII of Civil Rights Act of 1964 (Excerpts)   621
G. Americans with Disabilities Act (Excerpts)   624
H. The Antitrust Statutes (Excerpts)   626
I. Securities Statutes (Excerpts)   630

Glossary 634
Index 661

Contents

Preface   xvii

Part 1: Elements of Law and the Judicial Process   2

Chapter 1: Introducing the Modern Environment of Business, Law, and Ethics   4

Law and the Key Functions of the Legal System   5
International Perspective: Chad: A Third-World Country Tries to Create a Legal System   7
Sources of Law in the United States   7
Lighter Side of the Law: Creative Common Law   13
Classifications of Law   13
Ethics and Business   15
International Perspective: Sources of Law in Japan   16
Issue Spotter: OK to Grease Palms?   17
Lighter Side of the Law: Our Values   17
Cyber Law: Online Ethics and Legal Compliance   18
Issue Spotter: Putting Ethics into Practice   18
International Perspective: Does Regulation Improve Business Ethics?   19

Summary   *21*
Terms to Know   *21*
Discussion Question   *21*
Case Questions   *22*
Ethics Questions   *22*
Internet Assignment   *23*

Chapter 2: The Court Systems   24

The Court Systems   25
The Federal Courts   26
International Perspective: The French Court System   28
The State Courts   30
Lighter Side of the Law: Tough Justice: Shoot 'Em or Flush 'Em   31
Jurisdiction   31
Lighter Side of the Law: Being a Judge Makes Me Sick?   32
International Perspective: London's Commercial Court   33
Cyber Law: The Long Arm of the Internet   34

Issue Spotter: Can Your Firm Be Reached?   36
Relations between the Court Systems   37
Venue   43
Lighter Side of the Law: Justice Can Have a Bite to It   43

Summary   *44*
Terms to Know   *45*
Discussion Question   *45*
Case Questions   *45*
Ethics Question   *47*
Internet Assignment   *47*

Chapter 3: Trials and Resolving Disputes   48

Basic Trial Procedures   49
Lighter Side of the Law: The Legal Magic of Spell Check   53
Lighter Side of the Law: The Dog Ate My Summons   57
Lighter Side of the Law: You Got Me There, Counselor!   59
Lighter Side of the Law: Why Alabama Courts Are Ranked Forty-Eighth in the Nation   61
Lighter Side of the Law: Shortest Decision by an Appeals Court?   62
Arbitration   63
International Perspective: German Trial Procedure   63
Issue Spotter: Are There Limits on the Terms of Arbitration?   65
Negotiation   66
Cyber Law: International Arbitration and Mediation of Domain Name Disputes   67
Mediation   68
International Perspective: Global Acceptance of Arbitration   68
Innovative Forms of ADR   70
Lighter Side of the Law: Can't Get Good Help These Days   70

Summary   *71*
Terms to Know   *72*
Discussion Question   *73*
Case Questions   *73*
Ethics Question   *74*
Internet Assignment   *74*

Chapter 4: The Constitution: Focus on Application to Business 75

The Commerce Clause   76
Lighter Side of the Law: Great Constitutional Moments   79
The Taxing Power   82
Issue Spotter: Unconstitutional Business Activity?   83
International Perspective: Freedom of Speech   84
Business and Free Speech   84
Cyber Law: Freedom of Speech on the Net   86
Lighter Side of the Law: Freedom of Bark but Not
Burn in Ohio   88
International Perspective: Freedom of Commercial
and Political Speech Abroad   89
Other Key Parts of the Bill of Rights   89
Cyber Law: No Right of Privacy in Chat Rooms   92
Fourteenth Amendment   94
Lighter Side of the Law: Drop That Fry! Hands over
Your Head!   96

  Summary   98
  Terms to Know   99
  Discussion Question   99
  Case Questions   99
  Ethics Question   101
  Internet Assignment   101

Chapter 5: Criminal Law and Business 102

Crime   103
Crime Categories   103
Lighter Side of the Law: You Mean It Isn't Usual
Police Practice?   104
Prosecution of Crimes   105
Defenses   106
Evidence   107
Prosecution   108
White-Collar Crime   110
Lighter Side of the Law: Maybe the Client Will
Not Suspect Anything   111
International Perspective: Interpol   113
Issue Spotter: What to Do When the Feds Show Up?   113
Cyber Law: Should Criminals Be Let Near the Internet?   114
International Perspective: White-Collar Crime in
Other Nations   116
Sentencing Guidelines and Compliance   116

  Summary   118
  Terms to Know   119
  Discussion Question   119
  Case Questions   119
  Internet Assignment   120
  Pulling It Together   122

Part 2: Elements of Traditional Business Law 124

Chapter 6: Elements of Torts 126

Torts and the Legal System   127
Negligence-Based Torts   127
International Perspective: Tort Liability in France   128
Lighter Side of the Law: Watch Me Dance!   131
Issue Spotter: Effective Liability Releases   133
Intentional Torts against Persons   135
Issue Spotter: Dealing with Drunks   136
Issue Spotter: Dealing with the Elderly
and their Heirs   141
Lighter Side of the Law: Teaching Torts in Law
School   143
Lighter Side of the Law: I Will Be a Billionaire for
Sure After This   144
Issue Spotter: Say Good Things About a
Good Employee?   145
Cyber Law: Tort Liability for Internet Servers   146
International Perspective: Libel in Foreign Courts   146

  Summary   147
  Terms to Know   148
  Discussion Question   148
  Case Questions   148
  Ethics Question   149
  Internet Assignment   149

Chapter 7: Business Torts and Product Liability 150

Tort Law and Business   151
Issue Spotter: Hiring Employees from Competitors   156
Product Liability   157
International Perspective: Is Japan Really Different?   157
Lighter Side of the Law: Well, It Didn't Look Safe
to Me!   159
Issue Spotter: Understanding Product Problems   160
Lighter Side of the Law: I'm from the FBI; I Know
the Law   162
Lighter Side of the Law: Never Enough Ways to Warn   166
Issue Spotter: A Way to Reduce the
Damage?   168
Lighter Side of the Law: Extra Careful: Winning
Warning Labels   168
International Perspective: European-American
Product Liability: Same Law, Different Procedures   169

  Summary   171
  Terms to Know   172

Discussion Question 173
Case Questions 173
Ethics Question 174
Internet Assignment 174

Chapter 8: Real and Personal Property 176

Real Property 177
International Perspective: Insecure Property Rights 179
Lighter Side of the Law: The Tenants Who Would Not Go Away 183
International Perspective: Americans Crossing into Mexico for Land 184
Public Control of Real Property 186
Issue Spotter: Would Tighter Leases Help? 187
Torts against Property 188
Issue Spotter: Protecting Company Property 191
Lighter Side of the Law: Protect Your Assets 192
Torts against Property Owners 192
Issue Spotter: Duties to Elderly Customers 194
Lighter Side of the Law: Wildlife Gone Wild 194
Issue Spotter: Protecting Customers' Kids 195

Summary 196
Terms to Know 197
Discussion Question 197
Case Questions 197
Ethics Question 198
Internet Assignment 199

Chapter 9: Intellectual Property 200

Lighter Side of the Law: Don't Step on His Estate's Velvet Shoes 201
Trademarks 201
Issue Spotter: Establishing Your Name 201
International Perspective: Costs of Counterfeiting 203
Cyber Law: Who Owns and Controls Domain Names? 204
Issue Spotter: Knock Off the Knock-Offs? 208
Lighter Side of the Law: Our Garbage Disposals Would Not Do That! 209
Copyright 209
Issue Spotter: Fair Sharing of Information? 212
Patents 213
Lighter Side of the Law: Why Many Patents Are Overturned When Challenged 213
International Perspective: Patent Differences 215
Trade Secrets 215
Issue Spotter: Protecting Valuable Information 217

Summary 218
Terms to Know 219
Discussion Question 219

Case Questions 219
Ethics Question 221
Internet Assignment 221

Chapter 10: Contracts 222

Contract Law 223
Elements of a Contract 223
Lighter Side of the Law: Listener Beware 225
Lighter Side of the Law: You Aren't So Beautiful, to Me… 231
International Perspective: Problems Enforcing Contracts 233
Issue Spotter: Are You Due a Commission? 238
Cyber Law: Digital Signatures and Contracts 239
Issue Spotter: Liars' Contest? 239
Performance, Discharge, and Breach of Contracts 240
Issue Spotter: Do You Have to Eat the Loss? 242
Remedies 243
International Perspective: Contracting with the Japanese 244
Lighter Side of the Law: Me, Read the Rules? 246

Summary 248
Terms to Know 249
Discussion Question 249
Case Questions 249
Ethics Question 251
Internet Assignment 251

Chapter 11: Domestic and International Sales 252

Introduction to the UCC 253
Forming a Sales Contract 256
International Perspective: How to Assure Foreign Buyers of Product Quality 259
Issue Spotter: Gouge the Wholesaler 262
Performance and Obligations 262
Sales Warranties 264
Issue Spotter: How Much Advice Should Retailers Give? 266
Lighter Side of the Law: Does It Come with a Warranty? 267
Remedies and Damages 268
International Sales 271
Issue Spotter: What Law Applies, and Where, to Your Contract? 272

Summary 275
Terms to Know 277
Discussion Question 277
Case Questions 277

Ethics Question   279
Internet Assignment   280

Chapter 12: Negotiable Instruments, Credit, and Bankruptcy   281

Negotiable Instruments   282

Lighter Side of the Law: Bounce My Check, Will You?   284

International Perspective: Mixing Religion and Finance   287

Credit   288

Credit with Security   290

Issue Spotter: Helping a Dream?   290

Lighter Side of the Law: So, Do We Write This Off as a Bad Loan?   291

Issue Spotter: Lean on a Lien?   298

Bankruptcy   299

Issue Spotter: Credit for the Bankrupt?   301

International Perspective: Bankruptcy Efficiency around the World   303

Lighter Side of the Law: Home Sweet Home   305

Summary   305
Terms to Know   307
Discussion Question   307
Case Questions   307
Ethics Question   309
Internet Assignment   309

Chapter 13: Business Organizations   310

Sole Proprietorships   311

Partnerships   311

International Perspective: Small Is Not So Beautiful in Japan   313

Limited Partnership   314

Issue Spotter: Brotherly Love?   315

Corporations   316

Lighter Side of the Law: Your Honor, I'll Turn Rocks into Gold   319

Lighter Side of the Law: Mad at Each Other? Sue the Insurance Company   322

International Perspective: Abuses of Shell Corporations from Afar   322

Limited Liability Companies   323

Key Organizational Features   324

Issue Spotter: Keeping Things in Order   327

Other Business Organizations   328

International Perspective: The Difficulty of Starting a Business   329

Franchises   329

International Perspective: The Road to Riches?   331

Cyber Law: Offering Franchises on the Internet   334

Summary   334
Terms to Know   335
Discussion Question   335
Case Questions   335
Ethics Question   337
Internet Assignment   337

Chapter 14: Agency and the Employment Relationship   338

Agency Relationships   339

Lighter Side of the Law: Is Slavery an Employment Relationship?   343

Cyber Law: Computer Abuse by Employees   348

The Essential Employment Relationship   350

International Perspective: Principals and Agents under a Civil-Law System   350

International Perspective: Flexibility in Labor Markets   354

Lighter Side of the Law: Don't Rat Out Your Boss   355

Tort Liability for Employers and Principals   357

Issue Spotter: Can You Be Too Encouraging to Employees?   358

Issue Spotter: Use of Company Cars   358

Lighter Side of the Law: Who, Him? Must Be an Independent Contractor   360

Summary   360
Terms to Know   361
Discussion Question   361
Case Questions   361
Ethics Question   363
Internet Assignment   363
Pulling It Together   364

Part 3: The Regulatory Environment of Business   366

Chapter 15: The Regulatory Process   368

Administrative Agencies   369

Lighter Side of the Law: Give Us All Your Imported Goods So We Can "Protect" Consumers 370

Administrative Law   370

Enforcing Rules   374

Cyber Law: Do Old Regulations Apply to New Forms of Competition?   374

Issue Spotter: Contest a Regulatory Order?   377

Judicial Review   378

International Perspective: Administrative Agencies in Japan   379

Lighter Side of the Law: Regulators Protecting Consumers?   380

Controls on Agencies 383
Summary *384*
Terms to Know *385*
Discussion Question *385*
Case Questions *385*
Ethics Questions *386*
Internet Assignment *387*

Chapter 16: Employment and Labor Regulations 388

Public Policy Limits to At-Will Employment 389
Lighter Side of the Law: Good Reasons Not to Come to Work 391
Substance Abuse 391
Issue Spotter: What Attitude toward Drinking and the Office? 392
Issue Spotter: How Does an Employer Handle an Employee Who Flunks a Drug Test? 393
Worker Health and Safety 394
Lighter Side of the Law: Heal My Sensitive Heart 396
Workers' Compensation 397
Issue Spotter: Reducing Risks and Improving Looks 400
Lighter Side of the Law: Donuts Are Not Healthy 401
Family and Medical Leave 401
General Regulation of Labor Markets 402
Issue Spotter: How Do You Count Hours for Telecommuters? 405
Major Labor Relations Acts 405
Lighter Side of the Law: Rules Are Rules 406
The National Labor Relations Board 407
Unionization 408
International Perspective: The Power of German Unions 409
Issue Spotter: Moves to Help Keep Unions Out 411
Collective Bargaining 411
Cyber Law: Employee Blogs 413
Summary *415*
Terms to Know *416*
Discussion Question *416*
Case Questions *416*
Ethics Question *417*
Internet Assignment *418*

Chapter 17: Employment Discrimination 419

Origins of Discrimination Law 420
Title VII of the 1964 Civil Rights Act 420
International Perspective: EEOC Impact on Global Operations 423
Lighter Side of the Law: A New Protected Class? 423
Cyber Law: Your E-mail Is Your Boss's E-mail 424

Bringing a Charge of Discrimination 427
Lighter Side of the Law: Modify Your Body in Private 429
Issue Spotter: Effective Sexual Harassment Policy 433
Issue Spotter: Dealing with Discrimination Complaints 435
Affirmative Action 437
International Perspective: Employment Discrimination in Europe and Japan 438
Disability Discrimination 438
Lighter Side of the Law: Addicted to Not Working? 439
Issue Spotter: Accommodating Disabilities 442
Lighter Side of the Law: Get the Women Out of My Classes 443
Summary *443*
Terms to Know *444*
Discussion Question *444*
Case Questions *444*
Ethics Question *446*
Internet Assignment *446*

Chapter 18: Environmental Law 447

Environmental Regulation 448
Pollution and the Common Law 449
Clean Air Act 451
International Perspective: Industrialization Brings Environmental Problems to China 455
Clean Water Act 456
Issue Spotter: Does Obeying EPA Regulations Eliminate Litigation? 458
Land Pollution 461
Lighter Side of the Law: Environmental Harmony 463
Lighter Side of the Law: Honor Your Local Superfund Site 464
Species Protection 465
Lighter Side of the Law: Protect Truly Rare Species 465
Issue Spotter: Picking a Sweet Spot 467
Global Environmental Issues 468
International Perspective: Exporting Hazardous Waste 469
Summary *471*
Terms to Know *472*
Discussion Question *472*
Case Questions *472*
Ethics Question *474*
Internet Assignment *474*

Chapter 19: Consumer Protection 475

The FDA: Food and Drug Regulation 476
Lighter Side of the Law: Food Fraud Everywhere 478
International Perspective: Drug Controls and Uncontrols 479

Issue Spotter: How Much Can You Hype Health
Supplements? 481

The FTC and Consumer Protection 481

Lighter Side of the Law: Protecting Consumers 483

International Perspective: Foreign Advertising
Regulation 487

Issue Spotter: How Aggressive Can You
Be in Advertising? 487

Cyber Law: Regulating Cyberspace Advertising 488

Lighter Side of the Law: Make Granny Pay More 489

Consumer Credit Protection 490

International Perspective: Credit Around the World 494

Issue Spotter: Dealing with Customer Records 495

Lighter Side of the Law: Watch Who You
Nickel and Dime 496

Issue Spotter: How Should You Handle
Unpaid Accounts? 497

    Summary *500*
    Terms to Know *501*
    Discussion Question *501*
    Case Questions *501*
    Ethics Question *502*
    Internet Assignment *502*

Chapter 20: Antitrust Law **503**

Antitrust Statutes 504

Monopolization 507

Lighter Side of the Law: Didn't We Just Sue Them
Eighty Years Ago? 510

Horizontal Restraints of Trade 511

Cyber Law: B2B Antitrust Concerns 512

Lighter Side of the Law: We're Lawyers, and We're
Here to Help You 516

Issue Spotter: Share and Share Alike 517

Vertical Restraint of Trade 517

International Perspective: European Antitrust 522

Lighter Side of the Law: Give Us What We Want,
or We Will Throw a Tantrum 523

The Robinson–Patman Act 523

Issue Spotter: Who Do You Sell What to,
and for How Much? 525

    Summary *526*
    Terms to Know *527*
    Discussion Question *527*
    Case Questions *528*
    Ethics Question *529*
    Internet Assignment *529*

Chapter 21: Securities Regulation **530**

The Elements of Securities 531

What Is a Security? 532

Cyber Law: Securities Offerings on the Web 533

Issue Spotter: What Are You Selling? 534

Offering Securities to Investors 534

Issue Spotter: Can New Start-Up Firms Issue Securities? 537

Regulation of Securities Trading 537

Lighter Side of the Law: Triple Your Money Overnight! 538

Securities Fraud 539

Lighter Side of the Law: The Pay Is Okay, but the
Food Is Terrible 543

Insider Trading 543

The Investment Company Act 545

International Perspective: European Approaches to
Insider Trading 546

Issue Spotter: Can You Exploit the Gossip? 546

The Investment Advisers Act 547

Lighter Side of the Law: Public Servants 548

Stock Market Regulation 548

    Summary *550*
    Terms to Know *551*
    Discussion Question *551*
    Case Questions *551*
    Ethics Question *552*
    Internet Assignment *553*

**Chapter 22: The International Legal
Environment of Business** **554**

International Law and Business 555

U.S. Import Policy 557

Issue Spotter: Starting an Import Business 559

Issue Spotter: Where to Produce? 561

Lighter Side of the Law: A Bargain—Only $29.35 for a
Razor Blade! 562

Business Structures in Foreign Markets 563

International Perspective: Controlling International
Pirates 564

Foreign Corrupt Practices Act 564

International Contracts 567

Issue Spotter: Making the Deal Stick 572

International Dispute Resolution 572

Lighter Side of the Law: You Yanks Are
Too Old for Us Hip Brits 573

    Summary *574*
    Terms to Know *575*
    Discussion Question *575*
    Case Questions *575*
    Ethics Question *577*
    Internet Assignment *577*
    Pulling It Together *578*

Appendices

A. Legal Research and the Internet   579
B. Case Analysis and Legal Research   583
C. The Constitution of the United States of America   589
D. The Uniform Commercial Code (Excerpts)   601
E. National Labor Relations Act (Excerpts)   617
F. Title VII of Civil Rights Act of 1964 (Excerpts)   621
G. Americans with Disabilities Act (Excerpts)   624
H. The Antitrust Statutes (Excerpts)   626
I.   Securities Statutes (Excerpts)   630

Glossary   **634**

Index   **661**

Table of Cases

The principal cases are in bold type. Cases cited or discussed in the text are roman type. References are to pages. Cases cited in principal cases and within other quoted materials are not included.

281 A.2d 435 Ct. App., D.C. (1971)	362
8182 Maryland Assoc. L.P. v. Sheehan	336

A

Abbott Labs v. Gardner	381
Akin v. Ashland Chemical	170
Allstate Insurance v. Ginsberg	149
Altamaha Riverkeepers v. City of Cochran	473
Amdahl v. Lowe	250
American Civil Liberties Union of Georgia v. Miller	86
American Geophysical Union v. Texaco	220
American Mining Congress v. EPA	473
Anglin v. Barry	250
Armstrong v. Food Lion	359
Asahi Metal Industry Co. v. Superior Court of California	122
Aspen Skiing Company v. Aspen Highlands Skiing Corporation	528
Association of Washington Business v. State of Washington, Department of Revenue	372
Atkinson v. City of Pierre	**190**
Audi AG v. D'Amato	205
Austin v. Michigan Chamber of Commerce	86
Axelson v. McEvoy-Willis	258
Azar v. Lehigh Corp.	173

B

Babbitt v. Sweet Home	466
Baccus Imports v. Dias	82
Badger v. Paulson Investment Co.	362
Banco Nacional de Cuba v. Sabbatino	576
Bane v. Ferguson	336
Barrett v. Mt. Brighton, Inc.	149
BASF v. United States	558
Baughn v. Honda Motor Co.	22
Baxter v. Ford Motor	160
BCB Anesthesia Care v. Passavant Memorial Area Hospital	528
Beacon Mutual Ins. v. OneBeacon Ins.	220
Beal Bank, SSB v. Biggers	292
Bearden v. Wardley	347
Beattey v. College Centre of Finger Lakes	46
Bennett Enterprises v. Domino's Pizza	337
Bigelow v. Virginia	86
Birklid v. Boeing	417
Blimka v. My Web Wholesalers, LLC	**36**

Board of Trustees of the State University of New York v. Fox	88
Boggs v. Somerville Bank and Trust	308
Bolser Enterprises v. Arizona Registrar of Contractors	382
Bolton v. Scrivner	446
Boomer v. Atlantic Cement Company	451
Bose Corp. v. Consumers Union	88
Bouchat v. Baltimore Ravens	220
Bradkin v. Leverton	247
Braswell v. United States	91
Broadcast Music, Inc. v. CBS	514
Brogan v. U.S.	119
Brookshire Food Stores v. Allen	198
Brown v. Soh	390
Brown v. Swett and Crawford of Texas	**312**
Buckeye Check Cashing v. Cardegna	74
Burger King v. Rudzewicz	45
Burke v. McKee	248
Burlington Industries v. Ellerth	431
Butters v. Vance International	576

C

Caley v. Gulfstream Aerospace Corp	**230**
Callison v. City of Philadelphia	402
Campisi v. Acme Markets, Inc.	**193**
Carrel v. National Cord and Braid	170
Caterpillar Tractor Co. v. Hulvey	73
Center for Biological Diversity v. Marina Point Development Associates	467
Central Hudson Gas and Electric Corporation v. Public Service Commission of New York	**87**
Cerminara v. California Hotel and Casino	148
Chamber of Commerce v. Dept. of Labor	386
Chamblee v. Grayco	198
Charlotte Chambers v. Dakotah Charter	45
Chemical Manufacturers Assn. v. NRDC	473
Chemical Waste Management v. Hunt	80
Chiarella v. United States	544
Chiodini v. Fox	198
Chisholm and Company v. Bank of Jamaica	576
Chrysler Credit Corp. v. Keeling	307
Chung v. New York State Racing Assn.	307
Chuway v. National Action Financial Service	498

Cincinnati v. Discovery Network 100
Cipollone v. Liggett Group, Inc. 22
Citibank v. Pitassi 308
Citizens Bank of Maryland v. Strumpf 308
City of Philadelphia v. Fleming Companies 552
City of Skagway v. Robertson 100
City of Winder v. Girone 198
Clark County School District v. Breeden 445
Clorox Company Puerto Rico v. Procter
   and Gamble 502
Club Italia Soccer and Sports Organization,
   Inc. v. Charter Township of Shelby, Michigan 97
**Club Italia Soccer and Sports Organization,
   Inc. v. Charter Township of Shelby,
   Michigan** **97**
Coelho v. Posi-Seal International 354
Coffee Beanery v. Albert **332**
Collins v. Barker 197
Commonwealth Edison v. Montana 100
Community Television Services v. Dresser 278
Connelly v. Hyundai Motor Co. 174
**Consolidated Edison Company v.
   Public Service Commission of New York** **85**
Cooper Tire & Rubber v. Mendez **54**
Copenhaver v. Berryman 251
Cosgrove Distributors, Inc. v. Haff 336
Costello v. Capital Cities Communications 148
Covalt v. High 335
Crawford v. Williams 173
Creech v. Roberts 46
Crest Ridge Construction v. Newcourt **256**
Critical Mass Energy Project v. Nuclear
   Regulatory Comm. 386

D

Daanen v. Cedarapids 244
Dana v. Boren 349
Davis v. Baugh Industrial Contractors, Inc. **12**
Davis v. Michigan Dept. of Treasury 82
DCS Sanitation Management v. Castillo **235**
Denney v. Reppert 249
Denny v. Radar Industries 62
Derry v. Peek 152
Deutchland Enterprises v. Burger King 337
DiMercurio v. Sphere Drake Insurance PLC 576
Dirks v. Securities and Exchange Commission 544
Dixon v. U.S. 122
Doe v. Cahill 146
Donovan v. Dewey 385
Dow Chemical v. United States 375
Dr. Miles Medical v. John D. Park and Sons 517
Dura Pharmaceuticals v. Broudo 552
Dushkin v. Desai 173

E

E. I. duPont deNemours v. Christopher 221
Eastman Kodak v. Image Technical Services 522
Eaton v. Englecke Manufacturing 251
Edwards v. Direct Access 45
EEOC v. J.B. Hunt Transport 446

Effron v. Sun Line Cruises 576
Equal Employment Opportunity Comm. v. Dial Corporation 434
Erichsen v. No-Frills Supermarkets of Omaha **194**
Erie Railroad Co. v. Tompkins **40**
Ernst and Ernst v. Hochfelder 551
Espinoza v. Farah Manufacturing 422
Estate of Witlin 336
Ex parte Kia Motors America, Inc. 46

F

F.T.C. v. Ruberoid Company 369
Federal Trade Commission v.
   Cyberspace.com LLC 484
Feist Publications v. Rural Telephone Service Co. 210
First English Evangelical Lutheran Church of
   Glendale v. Los Angeles County 101
First National Bank of Boston v. Bellotti 84
Fisher v. Monsanto 174
Flanigan v. Prudential Federal Savings and Loan 355
Foley v. Interactive Data 355
Folsom v. Great Atlantic & Pacific Tea Co. 73
Force v. Ford Motor **166**
Fordyce Bank and Trust v. Bean Timberland 295
Fox v. MCI Communications 389
Freeman v. San Diego Association of Realtors 513
Friedman v. So. Cal. Permanente Medical Group 445
FTC v. Febre 483
FTC v. Indiana Federation of Dentists 516
FTC v. Procter and Gamble 511
Fuerschbach v. Southwest Airlines **137**

G

Gardner v. Loomis Armored 389
General Electric Supply v. Republic Construction 251
Georgia v. Tennessee Copper Company 449
Gibbons v. Ogden 77
Gleason v. Taub 197
Goldberg v. Florida Power and Light **131**
Goldberg v. Sweet 83
Grams v. Milk Products 270
Greenman v. Yuba Power Products **161**
Greenslade v. Chicago Sun-Times 424
Gretillat v. Care Initiatives 440
Griffith v. Clear Lakes Trout 260
Grosjean v. First Energy 445
Grossman v. Novell 552
Guardian Industries v. NLRB 417
Guz v. Bechtel National 356

H

Hardcore Concrete, LLC v. Fortner Insurance Services 341
Harris v. Forklift Systems 425
Hart Enterprises Intl. v. Anhui Provincial Import
   and Export 279
Hartwig Farms v. Pacific Gamble Robinson 278
Harvey v. Veneman 373
Heckler v. Chaney 386
Hector v. Watt 120
Heintz v. Jenkins 497

Henningsen v. Bloomfield Motors 160
Hicklin Engineering v. R.J. Bartell 216
Hinson v. N&W Construction Company 231
Hormel Foods v. Jim Henson Productions 220
Huaiyin Foreign Trade Corp v. United States 550
Huffman and Wright Logging Co. v. Wade 198
Huggins v. Citibank, N.A. 149
Hughes v. Oklahoma 80
Hunter Mining v. Management Assistance, Inc. 362

I

Impastato v. DeGirolamo 334
In re Darby 330
In the Matter of Kmart Corporation 304
International Airport Centers v. Citrin 348
International Shoe Company v. Washington 35
International v. Jartran 487
Invention Submission v. Rogan 376
Iowa Mold Tooling Co. v. Teamsters Local Union No. 828. 417
Ironite Products Co. v. Samuels 318

J

Jacob & Youngs v. Kent 251
James v. Bob Ross Buick 142
Japan Line, Ltd. v. County of Los Angeles 83
Johnson v. University Health Services 529
Jordan v. Earthgrains 335
Juarez v. CC Services 399

K

Kassbaum v. Steppenwolf Productions 220
Kassel v. Consolidated Freightways Corp. 100
Katzenbach v. McClung 77
Kau Kau Take Home No. 1 v. City of Wichita 197
Kelo v. City of New London, Connecticut 90
Koh v. Inno-Pacific Holdings, Ltd. 46
Kohl v. U.S. 186
Krumme v. Moody 308

L

L&L Doc's v. Florida Division of Alcoholic Beverages and Tobacco 237
Lack v. Wal-Mart Stores 445
Latta v. Kilbourn 313
Lawler v. American Airlines 149
Leavitt v. Monaco Coach 279
Lee v. R & K Marine 267
Leegin Creative Leather Products v. PSKS 519
Leichtman v. WLW Jacor Comm. 148
Lightle v. Real Estate Commission 153
Little v. Liquid Air Corp. 174
Logan v. D.W. Sivers 245
Lor-Mar/Toto v. Constitution Bank 283
Lovelades Harbor v. United States 460
Lujan v. Defenders of Wildlife 381

M

M/S Bremen v. Zapata Off-Shore 575
Machinchick v. PB Power 430

Macon-Bibb County Planning and Zoning v. Vineville Neighborhood 187
MacPherson v. Buick Motor Company 158
Main Central Railroad Co. v. Brotherhood of Maintenance of Way Employees 73
Marquette v. Norcem 278
Marshall v. Barlow's 90, 395
Marshall v. Gipson Steel 220
Mary Kinser v. Gehl Company 175
Massachusetts v. Environmental Protection Agency 470
Matrix Group Limited v. Rawlings Sporting Goods 154
Mazetti v. Armour 160
McCray v. U.S. 100
McCulloch v. Maryland 76
McCune v. Myrtle Beach Indoor Shooting Range 134
McDonald v. Santa Fe Trail Transportation 421
MDM Group Associates v. CX Reinsurance Company 155
Metro-Goldwyn-Mayer Studios v. Grokster 211
Meyers v. Meyers 363
Meyers v. National Detective Agency 362
Miller v. Pilgrim's Pride Corporation 42
Miner v. Fashion Enterprises 326
Mitchell v. Gonzales 132
Morales v. Trans World Airlines 80
Moran v. Sims 180
Mount Sinai Hospital v. Jordan 250

N

National Labor Relations Board v. Joseph Macaluso, Inc. 73
National Society of Professional Engineers v. United States 528
NBA v. Williams 528
Nederlandse Draadindustrie NDI B.V. v. Grand Pre-Stressed 279
Nedlloyd Lines B.V. v. Superior Court 576
New Hampshire Motor Transport Assn. v. Town of Plaistow 100
New York City Transit Authority v. Beazer 101
New York Times v. Tasini 221
New York v. Burger 90
Newsom v. Thalhimer Brothers 148
Nielsen v. Gold's Gym 185
Nintendo of America v. Dragon Pacific 221
Nollan v. California Coastal Commission 93
North River Homes v. Bosarge 279
Northern Pacific Railway Co. v. United States 507
Northern Pacific Railway Company v. United States 521
Northwestern States Portland Cement Co. v. Minnesota 82
Norton v. Caremark 363
NRDC v. EPA 473
Nutraceutical Corp. v. Von Eschenbach 478
Nystrom v. Trex Company 214

O

Occhionero v. Edmundson 362
Oil Co. v. Khan 519

Old Island Fumigation v. Barbee 171
Oncale v. Sundowner Offshore Services 426
Origins Natural Resources Inc. v. Kotler 220
Ortho Pharmaceutical v. Heath 501

P

Paranzino v. Barnett Bank 74
Parish v. ICON **164**
Parker v. Glosson **227**
Parr v. Woodmen of the World Life
    Insurance 445
Pasquantino v. U.S. 116
Patterson v. Rohm Gesellschaft **174**
People v. Salas **105**
Pepsico v. Coca-Cola 529
Peterson v. Beck 197
Pfennig v. Household Credit Services 502
Philip Morris USA v. Williams **95**
Phillips v. Budget Rent-a-Car Systems 149
Phillips v. Grendahl 502
Pic-A-State Pa. v. Reno 100
Plancarte v. Guardsmark 362
Police v. Suders 432
Polk v. BHRGU Avon Properties 250
Polygram v. 32–03 Enterprises 277
Powell v. Washburn **182**
Public Citizen v. Mineta 386

Q

Qualitex v. Jacobson Products 221
Quasem Group, Ltd. v. W.D. Mask Cotton 279
Quill Corp. v. North Dakota 82
Quinones v. Houser Buick 445

R

R. Williams Construction v. Occupational Safety
    and Health Review Commission 395
Ray v. Citigroup Global Markets 541
Regina v. Dudley and Stephens 22
Rene v. MGM Grand Hotel 446
Reno v. American Civil Liberties Union 86
Repetti v. Sysco Corp. 352
Republic Tobacco v. North Atlantic Trading ... **144**
Responsible Economic Development v. S.C.
    Department of Health
    and Environmental Control 460
Reynolds v. Ethicon Endo-Surgery **141**
Reynolds v. Ozark Motor Lines 416
Risdon Enterprises, Inc. v. Colemill Enterprises ... 46
Ritter v. Custom Chemicides 149
Robinson v. Government of Malaysia 577
Rose v. Sheehan Buick 218
Rowan v. Tractor Supply 417
Roy B. Taylor Sales v. Hollymatic 529
Rubinstein v. Collins 552
Russell v. Kinney Contractors **139**
Russell-Vaughn Ford v. Rouse 198
Rust v. Kelly 336
Rylands v. Fletcher 170

S

S.E.C. v. Monarch Funding Corp. 119
Schenck v. U.S. 84
Schlosser v. Fairbanks Capital 502
Schuchmann v. Air Services Heating and Air Conditioning ... 490
SEC v. SG Ltd. 552
ServiceMaster of St. Cloud v. GAB Business Services ... 308
Shapero v. Kentucky Bar Association 88
Sierra Club v. Mississippi Environmental Quality
    Permit Board **454**
Sierra Club v. Morton 384
Sindell v. Abbott Laboratories 168
Skinner v. Railway Labor Executives' Association ... 90
Smith v. Kulig **189**
Sony v. Universal City Studios 211
Sonzinsky v. U.S. 82
South-Central Timber Development v. Wunnicke ... 81
Southern Idaho Pipe and Steel v. Cal-Cut Pipe and Supply ... 277
Southern Railway Co. v. Arizona 79
Southland Corp. v. Keating 73
Spanish Broadcasting System of Florida v. Clear
    Channel Communications 507
Spur Industries v. Del Webb Development 472
Squish La Fish v. Thomco Specialty Products ... **129**
Standard Oil v. United States 509
Stanley Smith & Sons v. Limestone College 250
State Farm v. Campbell 101
States v. Lourdes Hospital 148
Sterling v. Velsicol Chemical 473
Stewart v. Federated Department Stores 194
Storetrax.com v. Gurland **320**
Strahs v. Tovar's Snowplowing, Inc. 198
Swierkiewicz v. Sorema 428
Swift v. Tyson 40
Synergy Gas v. NLRB 417

T

T. W. Oil v. Consolidated Edison 278
Tanks v. GCRTA 417
Tatum v. State of Florida 120
Teague v. Bakker 551
Telebrands Corp. v. Federal Trade Commission ... **486**
The Vons Companies v. Seabest Foods 46
Thomas v. Resort Health Related Facility 74
Todd v. Exxon Corporation **515**
Todd v. Societe Bic 174
Town Center Shopping Center v. Premier
    Mortgage Funding **344**
Transatlantic Financing v. U.S. 251
Treibacher Industrie, A.G. v. Allegheny Technologies ... **274**
Two Pesos v. Taco Cabana 208

U

U.S. Search, LCC v. U.S.Search.Com Inc. 220
U.S. Securities and Exchange Commission
    v. Ginsburg **544**
U.S. Steel v. Fortner Enterprises 521
U.S. v. Bajakajian 93
U.S. v. Farraj 120

U.S. v. Hsu 119
U.S. v. Jolivet 120
U.S. v. Kahriger 82
U.S. v. Mead Corp. 558
U.S. v. Prosperi 120
U.S. v. S.C. Recycling and Disposal 473
U.S. v. TIC Investment 473
U.S. v. V-1 Oil Co. 100
U.S. v. Virginia 97
U.S. v. Yang **217**
United Auto Workers v. Johnson Controls 22
United Fire and Casualty v. Acker 308
United Housing Foundation v. Forman 551
United States Gypsum v. National Gypsum 221
United States v. Baker Hughes 511
United States v. Brandt **20**
United States v. El Paso Natural Gas 511
United States v. Johnson **536**
United States v. King **567**
United States v. LaGrou Distribution Systems **477**
United States v. Paradise 438
United States v. Rutherford 501
United States v. Seeger 422
United States v. Stanley **19**
United States v. Syufy 528
United States v. Trenton Potteries 512
United States v. United States Gypsum 514
United States v. Young **107, 117**
Utah Pie Co. v. Continental Baking Co. 529

V

Valiant Steel v. Roadway Express 250
Velten v. Robertson 362

Vermeulen v. Worldwide Holiday 363
Virginia State Board of Pharmacy v. Virginia
    Citizens Consumer Council 86

W

Wal-Mart Stores v. Samara Brothers 208
Ward v. Rock Against Racism 84
Waremart Foods v. NLRB 417
Wassell v. Adams 135
Weisgram v. Marley Co. 73
West Lynn Creamery v. Healy 100
Weyerhaeuser Co. v. Ross–Simmons Hardwood
    Lumber Co. 529
**Weyerhaeuser v. Ross-Simmons
    Hardwood Lumber** **524**
Whalen v. Union Bag and Paper **450**
White Cap Industries v. Ruppert 362
Wickard v. Filburn 77, 78
Wild v. Brewer 101
Wilk v. AMA 528
Williams v. Briggs 174
Williamson v. Amrani 501
Wise v. Mead 444
Woeste v. Washington Platform Saloon
    and Restaurant 173
Wygant v. Jackson Board of Education 446
Wyoming v. Oklahoma 80

Z

Zeran v. America Online 146
Zimmerman v. D.C.A. at Welleby, Inc. 173
Ziva Jewelry v. Car Wash Hq. 198

Preface

Courses on the legal and regulatory environment of business provide important background for students preparing for a variety of careers. One faces legal, social, political, and ethical issues in any profession. Most are simple situations that can be handled with common sense, but in many situations ignorance of the principles of law can result in problems.

This textbook presents the legal environment from the perspective of the professional non-lawyer. Few students who take this course will become lawyers, and most will take few additional classes. This course is the opportunity to learn key points of the law from the standpoint of a working professional.

We have received excellent feedback from professors and students who have used the nine previous editions of this book and have pointed out both its shortcomings and its strong points. We have taken these comments into account in preparing this edition to make the book even more helpful and practical as we study the complex legal environment that businesses face in an increasingly international setting.

Basic Organization

A one-semester course in the legal environment of business faces the problem of determining what to cover in such a short time. It is like a physician giving a one-semester course to teach students what they need to know about medicine—so many topics, so little time. There is agreement that the key elements of the legal system must be covered. This is done in Part One of the book, Elements of Law and the Judicial Process. Part Two, Elements of Traditional Business Law, reviews the major areas of the common law (broadly defined) that apply to business. Part Three, The Regulatory Environment of Business, covers the major regulatory laws that managers are likely to face and reviews major points of international business law.

Key Features

Edited Cases

A primary way to learn law is to read real cases that the courts had to resolve. Each major case presented in the text has the background facts and legal proceedings summarized by the authors under the label **Case Background.** Then the court's holding, legal reasoning, and explanation of the law as it applies to the facts at hand are presented from the published opinion in the words of the judge in the **Case Decision.** Since most decisions are long, we present only the key portions of the holding. Material that has been deleted is indicated by asterisks (***) when there is a large deletion and by periods (...) for shorter deletions. Finally, **Questions for Analysis** are offered for the reader to consider or for class discussion (answers are provided in the *Instructor's Resource Guide*).

Issue Spotters

About sixty Issue Spotters are scattered throughout the text. Each briefly presents a business situation that requires application of legal elements just covered in the text. These challenges are a way for students to self-test their retention and ability to reason as they apply newly learned principles to practice. They also remind readers that the material learned in this course is practical to everyday issues in business (answers are provided in the *Instructor's Resource Guide*).

International Perspectives

These discuss how similar aspects of the law are handled in other countries. As globalization reaches more businesses, managers must know how to deal with different legal systems and cultures. This feature makes clear that the rules of the game are different in other nations and that managers must be prepared to resolve problems in a complex legal environment.

Cyberlaw

This feature presents short discussions of application of the law to developments arising from the information age. E-commerce and e-mail mean legal issues for the courts to resolve as they apply legal principles to never-before-heard-of ways of doing business, transmitting information, and communicating with friends and strangers.

Lighter Side of the Law

These add a light touch to the topic at hand by discussing an actual case or unusual legal situation. While law and business are serious, odd things happen that remind us that trouble can come from very unexpected places, that the results of the legal process can be surprising, that scoundrels are among us, and that truth can be stranger than fiction.

Summary

The text of each chapter is summarized in bullet format that provides a quick review of the major points of law and the major rules covered and serves as a self-test of points that will be covered in examinations.

Terms to Know

After the Summary, there is a list of key terms from the chapter. You should know what they mean as they are an important part of the vocabulary and substance of the concepts covered in the chapter. Besides being in the chapter, and explained in there, each term is defined in the Glossary in the back.

Discussion Question

Every chapter has one question for general discussion that picks up on major ideas from the chapter. The purpose is to make sure you understand the concepts of the chapter well enough to be able to discuss a topic that was covered and should be expanded upon.

Case Questions

Most problems are solved, but some end up in court where judges decide the resolution based on legal principles. Real case problems are summarized in each case question. Using the knowledge from the chapter, and maybe some instinct about how a court is likely to resolve a dispute, try to decide which party to a dispute is likely to prevail and why. Some of the questions are answered online at http://academic. cengage.com/blaw/meiners the others are answered in the *Instructor's Resource Guide*. These cases can also be discussed in class or used as a study tool.

Ethics Question

Each chapter has an ethics question that poses a problem related to the legal area covered in the chapter. Remember that ethical issues are different than legal issues, so we go beyond legal reasoning in considering the problem.

Internet Assignment

As discussed in Appendix A, Legal Research on the Internet, there are lots of legal resources now available online. The Internet Assignments at the end of the chapters point you to a specific source related to the chapter and may ask you to go to some sites to locate answers to specific questions to you become more familiar with such sites. These questions, and the Appendix, were prepared by Andrew Dorchak, Internet law librarian at Case Western School of Law. Questions are answered in the *Instructor's Resource Guide.*

Pulling It Together

At the end of the three major sections of the text several case questions are posed that bring together more than one legal issue covered in more than one chapter. Many situations involve more than one legal issue, so the cases here serve as a refresher to go back to earlier chapters and pull in concepts covered there along with legal principles covered in another chapter.

Glossary

At the back of the book is a list of about a thousand key terms covered in the text. While they were covered in the text when they first appeared in substantive use, the terms are defined here too to help give you a clear understanding of a legal concept that has a specific application in law.

Appendices

Besides Legal Research on the Internet, Appendix A, already mentioned, Appendix B covers Case Analysis and Legal Research. It explains the structure of court opinions and how they are often briefed by law students and lawyers to give a short summary of a complex matter. The case reporter system and other major legal resources are also reviewed. Appendix C is the full text of the United States Constitution. Appendices that follow give key excerpts from major statutes, including the Uniform Commercial Code, the National Labor Relations Act, Title VII of the Civil Right Act of 1964, the Americans with Disabilities Act, Antitrust Statutes, and Securities Statutes.

New to This Edition

The tendency in textbooks is to keep packing in more material—adding new information as changes occur. Over the years, this can make books unmanageable. We reduced the coverage of material that students can do without, recognizing that only so many pages and topics can be covered in one class. In paring down the material, we hope to enhance the learning of key concepts.

Our reviewers convinced us that the text needed to be focused more on practical aspects of basic legal rules. Therefore, in this edition, some of the legal detail has been eliminated, such as exceptions that are uncommon or occur in only a few states. We focus on the basic nuts and bolts and use business examples. Three quarters of the major cases in the text are new to this edition. The cases focus on practical situations in ordinary business that students can best relate to and are realistic in a business career. The holdings are straightforward application of the law to the facts. There is more attention to business law and less focus on legal theory.

We have added a new chapter to this edition, Chapter 5, *Criminal Law and Business*. This chapter covers the elements of criminal law and process. Many federal and state statutes provide criminal penalties for so-called white-collar crimes that a review of criminal processes is increasingly relevant. Specific attention is given to mail fraud and other major statutes that we see frequently arise in criminal litigation related to the business sector.

The chapter on administrative law has been moved from the first part of the book to the last section of the book, where it serves to introduce regulatory law. Chapter 15, *The Regulatory Process*, gives an overview of administrative procedures common to the multiple areas of substantive statutory law that follows in subsequent chapters.

Chapter 14, *Agency and the Employment Relationship*, reviews the elements of agencies and then integrates principles of agency law as they relate to the basics of the employment relationship, making clear the common law basis of employment. In all chapters, we approach the law from the standpoint of a business practitioner in an "average" business who have practical problems to handle.

Ancillaries

Students and instructors can access the book *Companion Site* at http://academic. cengage.com/blaw/meiners. For students, the web site offers answers to selected chapter-ending Case Questions, an *Interactive Quiz* with multiple choice questions for each chapter in the text, links to the URLs mentioned in the text, and *Case Updates*. For instructors, the site provides downloadable supplements.

- The *Study Guide* has been revised by text author Roger Meiners. To aid students in their study of the legal environment of business, it includes a chapter summary and outline, multiple-choice and true-false questions, and a test on the key terms included in the chapter. Answers to the questions are included in an appendix at the end of the *Study Guide*.
- The *Instructor's Resource CD-ROM:* Includes the *test bank*, *Instructor's Resource Guide*, *ExamView*, and *PowerPoint*.
- An electronic *Instructor's Resource Guide* (available on IRCD and companion website) has been revised. As before, it answers all questions in the book. It also provides a detailed outline of each chapter, summarizing the content of the text, including all cases. The instructor can refer quickly to this guide to remember the points the students have covered in the text. The guide also provides numerous additional summarized cases that the instructor can use to illustrate key points of law. Additional material, such as more discussion of certain points and examples of the law in practice, is provided as lecture and discussion enhancements.
- The updated electronic *Test Bank* (available on IRCD and companion website) has more than 6,000 questions and is available on ExamView, which is a computerized testing software program. Most questions are referenced to the main text page. More questions based on fact have been added to test critical thinking ability.
- A set of *PowerPoint* slides keyed to the text are available.

New to this edition, *WebTutor ToolBox* is available to those adopters who wish to use it. Preloaded with content and available via a free access code when packaged with this text, *WebTutor ToolBox* pairs all the content of this text's rich Book Companion Web Site with sophisticated course management functionality. You can assign materials (including online quizzes) and have the results flow automatically to your grade book. *WebTutor ToolBox* is ready to use as soon as you log on—or you can customize its preloaded content by uploading images and other resources, adding weblinks, or creating your own practice materials. Students only have access to student resources on the web site. Instructors can enter an access code for password-protected Instructor Resources.

West's Business Law Digital Video Library Featuring more than sixty segments on the most important topics in Business Law, West's Business Law Digital Video Library helps students make the connection between their textbook and the business world. Four types of clips are represented: 1) **Legal Conflicts in Business** features modern business scenarios; 2) **Ask the Instructor** clips offer concept review; 3) **Drama of the Law** presents classic legal situations; and 4) the newest addition to Business Law Digital Video Library, **LawFlix**, features segments from widely recognized modern-day movies. Together these clips bring Business Law to life. Access to West's Business Law Digital Video Library is free when bundled with a new text. Access to the Business Law Digital Video Library is available in an optional package with a new text at no additional cost. If Business Law Digital Video Library access did not come packaged with your textbook, it can be purchased online at academic.cengage.com/blaw/dvl. For more information about this product, visit http://digitalvideolibrary.westbuslaw.com.

Acknowledgments

The authors thank the adopters and reviewers from around the country who sent helpful comments and materials for the ninth edition. Much of the credit for the improvements belongs to them. The reviewers for this edition include:

Michael Elia
University of Phoenix

James G. Frierson
East Tennessee University

Ken Galvin
Robert Morris College

Bob Hamill
Indiana Wesleyan University

Laura Henry
Robert Morris College

Jack E. Karns
East Carolina University

Paul Klein
Duquesne University

William J. McDevitt
St. Joseph's University

Vanessa Paskaitis
University of Phoenix

Neal Phillips
University of Delaware

The authors also extend thanks to the professionals in business, law, and government who assisted in making this textbook as up-to-date and accurate as possible.

Finally, we thank the editors and staff of West Educational Publishing Co. In particular, we thank the sales representatives who continually give us valuable information on the day-to-day perceptions of the textbook—information provided by the instructors and students who are using it. We thank Bob Dreas, whose diligence and determination got us through the production process on schedule. Special thanks also goes to our developmental editor, Jan Lamar, who tolerates us with good humor. The efforts of our publisher, Rob Dewey, and editor, Steve Silverstein, who both manage huge tasks, are much appreciated.

We welcome and encourage comments from the users of this textbook—both students and instructors. By incorporating your comments and suggestions, we can make this text an even better one in the future.

Roger E. Meiners
Al H. Ringleb
Frances L. Edwards

The Legal Environment of Business

10th edition

PART 1: Elements of Law and the Judicial Process

OVERVIEW

Part One reviews the major components of the legal system and provides the framework for understanding the material presented in the other two parts of the book. Just as people in business must understand the elements of accounting, finance, management, and marketing, it is important that they also know how the legal environment plays a critical role in the way business and the economy function. Law changes as the structure of business changes, as social pressures produce changes in political policy that are reflected in the rules under which business operates, as the ethical expectations of business increase, and as the economy becomes more interwoven in international operations.

The chapters in this part review the major components of the legal system: the origins of law, constitutional law, the role of law in society and business, the structure and functioning of the court system, the use of alternative forms of dispute resolution, and the key elements of criminal law as it applies to business. This serves as a structural background for the rest of the text, which reviews substantive laws that impact business.

Getty Images

Chapter 1: *Introducing the Modern Environment of Business, Law, and Ethics*
The legal, social, and ethical pressures that people in business face today in a complex, international political economy are discussed in the context of the origins of our legal system. The focus is on the purposes, sources, and structure of law and the legal system in the context of the modern economy.

Chapter 2: *The Court Systems* The structure and power of our federal and state court systems are reviewed, followed by a discussion of how a case gets to a court and what powers the courts have over the parties to a case and its resolution.

Chapter 3: *Trials and Resolving Disputes* The steps in litigation—from the time a party files a complaint, through the stages of litigation, the forms of relief possible, and the appeals process—are discussed. Most business disputes are not taken to court but to alternate dispute resolution. The key aspects of arbitration and mediation are reviewed.

Chapter 4: *The Constitution: Focus on Application to Business* The constitutional limits on government actions, especially with respect to business matters, are covered. Congress has nearly unlimited power to regulate and tax, but some protections are provided for civil liberties against an over-reaching state.

Chapter 5: *Criminal Law and Business* Many statutes provide the possibility of criminal penalties being imposed for violations that may involve persons in business capacities. The processes are reviewed as are key statutes that specifically target certain actions in business.

Introducing the Modern Environment of Business, Law, and Ethics

Chapter 1

Getting a job and beginning to build a career after college are major challenges. Afraid of being left jobless, some people take less-than-ideal jobs, which sometimes turn out better than expected. On the other hand, some people take what seem to be great jobs but soon discover otherwise.

It is not uncommon for recruiters to puff up the qualities of a position. A job billed as "character-building" may be one of unending stress. One advertised as having a "team working environment" can mean people jammed in small cubicles. One person reports that while being recruited he was shown a nice office and introduced to his supervisor, whom he liked very much. But when he arrived for work, he was stuck in a back room, the likeable supervisor was gone, replaced by someone he could not stand, and the assignments given were not of the quality discussed.

Suppose that happens to you. Can you sue the recruiter who hired you? Can you sue the company that hired you? Do you have the right to demand a better office? What is your legal status in the situation? These are some of the legal issues in business that we will explore.

In the situation just posed, the employee probably has little choice but to keep the job as is or leave. The employer is unlikely to have violated any legal obligation. But what about the ethical obligation to be honest with current and potential employees? Is overstating the quality of a position unethical, even if it is not in violation of the law? This is another aspect of the modern business environment.

Business is complex. Ethical, legal, social, political, and international issues all impact company operations. As Exhibit 1.1 indicates, whether your field is human resources, banking, advertising, or software development, you must be familiar with a wide range of subjects to have the skills needed to be aware of possible problems and to recognize potential opportunities that someone with a limited view would be likely to miss. This book, which focuses on the legal environment of business, helps to fit one large piece into the complicated puzzle that is the business world.

The study of the legal environment of business begins with an overview of the nature of law and the legal system. Composed of law from several sources, the legal environment is influenced by the needs and demands of the business community, consumers, and government. This chapter provides an understanding of the functions of law in society, the sources of U.S. law, and the classifications of law. It then considers some major ethical issues that play a role in the modern environment of business. ∎

Getty Images

Exhibit 1.1 Overview of a Business's Legal Environment

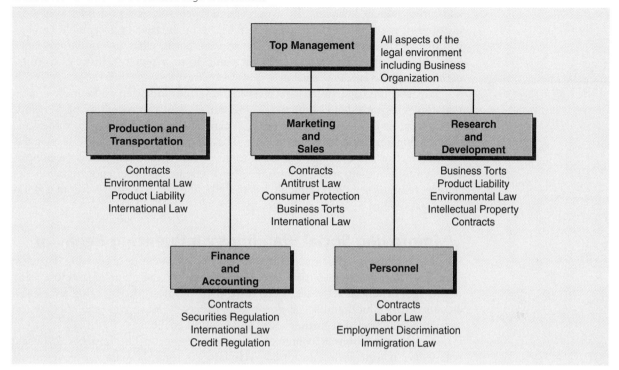

Law and the Key Functions of the Legal System

In the legal environment of business, *law* refers to a code of conduct that defines the behavioral boundaries for business activity. There is no precise definition of law. Law is an abstract term but has long meant the same general thing. According to *Justinian's Institutes*, a summary of Roman law published in 533 in Constantinople, "The commandments of the law are these: live honorably; harm nobody; give everyone his due." A century ago Oliver Wendell Holmes, a legal scholar and Supreme Court justice, offered the following definition:

> Law is a statement of the circumstances, in which the public force is brought to beaar . . . through the courts.

In his 1934 book, *Growth of Law*, the jurist Benjamin N. Cardozo defined law as follows:

> A principle or rule of conduct so established as to justify a prediction with reasonable certainty that it will be enforced by the courts if its authority is challenged.

Consider these modern definitions from *Black's Law Dictionary*, an authoritative legal dictionary:

1. Law, in its generic sense, is a body of rules of action or conduct prescribed by [the] controlling authority and having binding legal force.
2. That which must be obeyed and followed by [members of a society] subject to sanctions or legal consequences is a law.

Thus, law may be viewed as a collection of rules or principles intended to limit and direct human behavior. By enforcement, such rules or principles provide a measure of predictability and uniformity to the boundaries of acceptable conduct within a society. Nations have both *formal rules*, that is, what are commonly called laws, and *informal* or *implicit* rules that come from a society's history, customs, commercial practices, and ethics.

Law and the legal system serve several key roles in society. The most important functions include: 1) influencing the behavior of the members of a society, 2) resolving disputes within the society, 3) maintaining important social values, and 4) providing a method for social change. The International Perspective feature discusses the efforts in the nation of Chad to develop a legal system that is meaningful to its citizens and attractive to business development. Its experience, which is not unique, reminds us of how difficult it is to do business in a country without a workable legal system.

Improving Social Stability by Influencing Behavior

The legal system is a major social institution that helps define acceptable behavior. The law limits activities that are detrimental to the "public interest" and encourages beneficial activities. The law restricts business practices that are viewed as outside the ethical and social norms of a society. At the same time, the law can encourage practices that further social and political goals.

The laws in different countries reflect social norms. The business of raising and selling marijuana in Amsterdam (Holland) is legal, because the government decided that legalizing marijuana would reduce crime in the drug trade and make it less likely that people would use harsh, illegal drugs, such as heroin. In the United States, selling marijuana is illegal and can be punished by long prison terms, but the production and sale of alcoholic beverages is legal in most of the country. In Saudi Arabia, people have been executed for being involved in the alcohol business.

Conflict Resolution

Another important function of the law is dispute resolution. Disagreements are inevitable, since societies are made up of people with differing desires and values. Karl N. Llewellyn, a legal theorist, states:

> What, then, is this law business about? It is about the fact that our society is honeycombed with disputes. Disputes actual and potential, disputes to be settled and disputes to be prevented; both appealing to law, both making up the business of law.... This doing of something about disputes, this doing of it reasonably, is the business of law.

A formal mechanism for the resolution of disputes is the court system, which is used for resolving *private disputes* between members of society and *public disputes* between a person and the government. Our court system is intended to provide a consistent mechanism for resolving disputes. As we will see in Chapter 3, businesses are increasingly turning to conflict resolution outside of the courts.

Social Stability and Change

A society is shaped by its values and customs. It is not surprising, then, that law plays a role in maintaining the social environment. Honesty and integrity are reflected by the enforceability of contracts, respect for other people and their property is reflected in tort and property law, and some measures of acceptable behavior are reflected in criminal laws.

Getty Images

INTERNATIONAL PERSPECTIVE

Chad: A Third-World Country Tries to Create a Legal System

Chad is in north central Africa. It is three times the size of California, has a population of ten million people, and has an effective per capita income of about $1,500 per year.

Chad must develop a legal system more attractive to the world business community and outside investors. No commonly accepted rule of law exists. Chad's citizens do not like to use the court system, because judges often receive orders from the governing authority on how to decide cases, or they take bribes. Disputes are often resolved by an unauthorized system of "courts" established by the police and military authorities. Formal law is often in conflict with the customs of ethnic and religious groups and so is largely ignored. The lack of a predictable legal system is a significant deterrent to the development of the country's commercial base.

To help resolve these difficulties in the legal system, Professor Louis Alcoin recommended the following:

Reform the court system to improve dispute resolution with emphasis on ensuring that judges are independent of the governing authority. Establish a separate court to be used only to resolve commercial disputes. Write and publish the civil and commercial codes. Reform the areas of enforcing judgments, business registrations, the investment code, property law, government contracts, and banking. Publish new legislative acts with the understanding that none would take effect until they are published. In undertaking these legal reforms, include laws that reflect the country's customs and traditions to the extent appropriate.

In the absence of reforms, the country will not overcome the barriers to development that result from the lack of a reliable or respected legal system.

Consider gay relationships. Until recent years, gay partners could be subject to criminal prosecution for their actions. Now the discussion has turned to whether such relationships can have the same status as traditional marriages. Some contend that legalizing same-sex marriages would be destructive to the structure of society; others argue that it would be stabilizing.

The legal system provides a way to bring about changes in "acceptable" behavior. For example, to help alter behavior, laws restrict race discrimination in decisions to hire, promote, or discharge a worker. In the past, race discrimination was an accepted norm of social and business behavior. Attitudes changed, and such behavior is no longer legally acceptable. Next we turn to the sources of law and how law is created.

Sources of Law in the United States

The U.S. Constitution creates the branches of government—each of which has the ability to make law. Congress—the legislative branch of government—uses its constitutionally granted powers to create what is often referred to as the *fourth branch* of government, that is, administrative agencies. Similarly, state constitutions determine the structure of government within a state, establish legal procedures, and create various rights and restrictions. Federal and state courts play a major role in interpreting and enforcing laws.

Constitutions

A *constitution* is the fundamental law of a nation. It establishes and limits the powers of government. Other laws are created through a constitution. The U.S. Constitution (Appendix C) allocates the powers of government between the states and the federal government. Powers not granted to the federal government are retained by states or are left to the people.

The U.S. Constitution

The U.S. Constitution is the oldest written constitution in force in the world. It sets forth the general organization, powers, and limits of the federal government. Specifically, the Constitution creates the legislative, executive, and judicial branches of the U.S. government.

This division in governmental power is referred to as the *separation of powers*. It arose out of a fear of the founders of this country that too much power might become concentrated in one governmental branch. The separation of powers means that each branch of government has functions to perform that can be checked by the other branches. The government structure that has developed is illustrated in Exhibit 1.2.

The U.S. Constitution is law that is supreme over state or federal laws that go beyond what the Constitution permits. According to Article VI:

> This Constitution, and the Laws of the United States which shall be made in Pursuance thereof; and all Treaties made, or which shall be made, under the Authority of the United States, shall be the supreme Law of the Land; and the Judges in every State shall be bound thereby, any Thing in the Constitution or Laws of any State to the Contrary notwithstanding.

State Constitutions

The powers and structures of all state governments are based on written constitutions. Like the federal government, state governments are divided into legislative, judicial, and executive branches. The constitutions specify how state officials are chosen and removed, how laws are passed, how the court systems run, and how finances and revenues are paid and collected. Each state constitution is the highest form of law in a state. Some state constitutions, unlike the U.S. Constitution, are very long and filled with details, because amending state constitutions is often much easier than changing the U.S. Constitution.

Legislatures and Statutes

Congress and the state legislatures are the sources of *statutory law*. Statutes or legislation include much of the law that significantly affects business behavior. For example, in 1972, Congress enacted the Clean Water Act. It sets standards for water quality for the nation and grants the Environmental Protection Agency the authority to adopt regulations that would make the goals of the statute effective. Similarly at the state level, every state legislature has passed statutes to regulate the insurance industry, usually accomplished with the help of a state insurance commission.

Federal courts may review statutes passed by Congress to ensure that they do not violate the U.S. Constitution. The courts in each state may review statutes passed by their legislature to ensure that they do not violate the constitution of the state or of the United States. If a state legislature passes a statute that violates the U.S. Constitution, and a state court does not strike down the statute, the statute may be stricken by a federal court.

United States Congress

Article I, Section 1, of the U.S. Constitution provides that all power to make laws for the federal government is given to Congress, a legislature consisting of a Senate and a House of Representatives. Of the thousands of pieces of legislation proposed

Exhibit 1.2 The Government of the United States

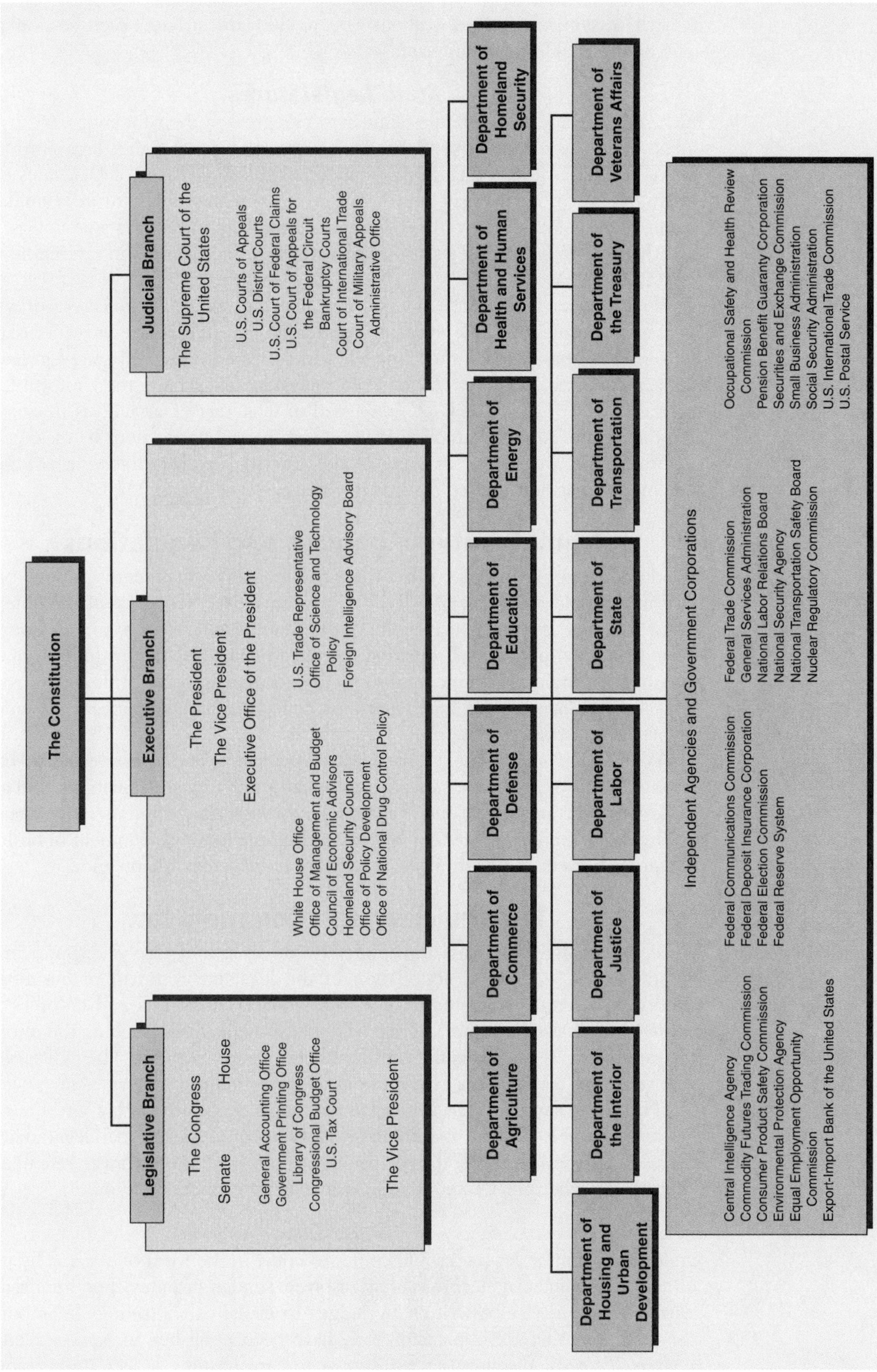

The Constitution

Legislative Branch

The Congress

Senate　　House

General Accounting Office
Government Printing Office
Library of Congress
Congressional Budget Office
U.S. Tax Court

The Vice President

Executive Branch

The President
The Vice President

Executive Office of the President

White House Office
Office of Management and Budget
Council of Economic Advisors
Homeland Security Council
Office of Policy Development
Office of National Drug Control Policy

U.S. Trade Representative
Office of Science and Technology
　Policy
Foreign Intelligence Advisory Board

Judicial Branch

The Supreme Court of the
United States

U.S. Courts of Appeals
U.S. District Courts
U.S. Court of Federal Claims
U.S. Court of Appeals for
　the Federal Circuit
Bankruptcy Courts
Court of International Trade
Court of Military Appeals
Administrative Office

Department of Agriculture
Department of Commerce
Department of Defense
Department of Education
Department of Energy
Department of Health and Human Services
Department of Homeland Security
Department of Veterans Affairs

Department of the Interior
Department of Justice
Department of Labor
Department of State
Department of Transportation
Department of the Treasury

Department of Housing and Urban Development

Independent Agencies and Government Corporations

Central Intelligence Agency
Commodity Futures Trading Commission
Consumer Product Safety Commission
Environmental Protection Agency
Equal Employment Opportunity
　Commission
Export-Import Bank of the United States

Federal Communications Commission
Federal Deposit Insurance Corporation
Federal Election Commission
Federal Reserve System

Federal Trade Commission
General Services Administration
National Labor Relations Board
National Security Agency
National Transportation Safety Board
Nuclear Regulatory Commission

Occupational Safety and Health Review
　Commission
Pension Benefit Guaranty Corporation
Securities and Exchange Commission
Small Business Administration
Social Security Administration
U.S. International Trade Commission
U.S. Postal Service

Note: This chart shows only the more important federal agencies that affect business agencies of the government.

in each session of Congress, about 200 to 300 are enacted each session after approval by the House and Senate.

State Legislatures

Each state has lawmaking bodies similar to Congress in their functions and procedures. With the exception of Nebraska, all states have a two-part legislature containing a House of Representatives (sometimes called a House of Delegates or an Assembly) and a Senate. The lawmaking process in state legislatures is similar to the procedure followed by the Congress. However, in some states voters may directly propose or enact legislation through the voting process in referendums or initiatives.

The National Conference of Commissioners on Uniform State Laws works with lawyers, law professors, the business community, and judges (see www.nccusl.org). For over a century, it has drafted "model" laws for consideration by state legislatures. Some are ignored, but others have been widely adopted, such as the Uniform Commercial Code (UCC). The UCC, discussed in Chapters 11 and 12, is designed to ease the legal relationship among parties in commercial transactions by making laws uniform among the states. Another "model" law adopted by 35 state legislatures is the Uniform Partnership Act, covered in Chapter 13.

Administrative Agencies and Regulations

An administrative agency is created when the legislative or executive branch of the government delegates some of its authority to an agency. Congress or the state legislature enacts a law that specifies the duties of the agency. For example, Congress created the Environmental Protection Agency to enact regulations to flesh out the goals of environmental statutes and to be the primary enforcer of those laws. Similarly, all states have created state environmental agencies to help create and enforce state environmental regulation.

With congressional delegation, administrative agencies can exercise broad powers to enact regulations, supervise compliance with those regulations, and adjudicate violations of regulations. Regulations flowing from administrative agencies are among the important sources of law affecting the legal environment of business. The procedures of administrative agencies are discussed in Chapter 15.

The Judiciary and Common Law

The common law—law made and applied by judges as they resolve disputes among private parties—is a major foundation of the legal environment of business. In addition to making the common law, the judiciary interprets and enforces laws enacted by legislative bodies. As we will see, some statutes, such as the antitrust laws, are not precise and require significant court interpretation. The judiciary also reviews actions taken by the executive branch and administrative agencies.

The oldest source of law in the United States, the common law dates to colonial times, when English common law governed most internal legal matters. To maintain social order and to encourage commerce, the colonists retained the common law when the United States became an independent nation.

Case Law

Under the common law, a dispute comes to court in the form of a *case*. The judge follows earlier judicial decisions that resolved similar disputes. For hundreds of years now, the decisions written by judges to explain their rulings in important cases, and some not-so-important cases, have been published in books called *case reporters*. To settle disputes that are similar to past disputes, judges study recorded cases for guidance in their decisions *precedent*, that can be applied to the facts of new cases under consideration.

To settle unique or novel disputes, judges create new common law. New laws, however, are based on the general principles suggested by many previously reported decisions. Since common law is state law, there are some differences across the states in the interpretation of common-law principles, but the judges in one state often look to cases from other states to help resolve disputes that do not have clearly established principles within a state.

Doctrine of **Stare Decisis**

The practice of deciding new cases by referencing previous decisions is the foundation of the English and American judicial processes. The use of precedent in deciding present cases forms a doctrine called *stare decisis*, meaning "to stand on decided cases." Under this doctrine, judges are encouraged (but not forced) to stand by precedents. According to Judge Richard Posner:

> Judge-made rules are the outcome of the practice of decision according to precedent (stare decisis). When a case is decided, the decision is thereafter a precedent, i.e., a reason for deciding a similar case the same way. While a single precedent is a fragile thing . . . an accumulation of precedents dealing with the same question will create a rule of law having virtually the force of an explicit statutory rule.

Value of Precedent

Stare decisis is useful for several reasons. First, consistency in the legal system improves the ability to plan business decisions. Second, as a rule is applied in many disputes involving similar facts, people become increasingly confident that the rule will be followed in the resolution of future disputes. Finally, the doctrine creates a more just legal system by neutralizing the prejudices of individual judges. If judges use precedent as the basis for decisions, they are less influenced by their personal biases.

Changes in Society

An advantage of dispute resolution through the common law is its ability to change with the times. Although most cases are decided on the basis of stare decisis, judges are not prohibited from changing legal principles if conditions warrant. As changes occur in technology or in social values, the common law evolves and provides new rules that better fit the new environment. A judge may modify or reverse an existing legal principle. If that decision is appealed to a higher court for review, the higher court may accept the new rule as the one to be followed.

In recent years, there have been rapid changes in the ways we can communicate with one another. While the mail dominated in the past, businesses now use faster communications systems to be competitive. E-mail often replaces the old method of personally signed documents. The law adapts to accept new communication methods. In the case that follows here, we see an example of a state high court changing the common law to conform better to the way business is done today.

Introducing Court Cases Like all cases presented in this book, the *Davis* case begins with its legal citation. There were several parties to the case on both sides, but the citation only refers to the lead plaintiff, who brought the suit, and the first defendant named in the suit. Then we see where the decision comes from and the reporter citation. The decision was issued by the Washington Supreme Court in 2007. It is published in volume 150 of the *Pacific Reporter* (P), which is in its third series, and the case begins on page 545. We follow with a description of the facts determined at trial, which are summarized by the textbook authors. Then we move to the court decision, an explanation of the law, and legal reasoning. The judge who authored the decision for the court is named, we quote from the decision, and we finish with some questions.

Davis v. Baugh Industrial Contractors, Inc.
Supreme Court of Washington
150 P.3d 545 (2007)

Case Background *Glacier Northwest hired Baugh Industrial Contactors to build a processing facility that included a system of underground pipes. Three years later, Glacier suspected a leak in a pipe. It assigned an employee, Alan Davis, to uncover the leak, which he did. While he was down in a hole dug to get to the pipes, a concrete wall collapsed, killing him. While the pipes were supposed to last 100 years, it is likely they had been damaged when installed, resulting in a leak. Tami Davis, Alan's daughter, sued Baugh and others, contending their negligent work practices were the cause of Alan's death.*

The trial court called superior court *held for Baugh and dismissed the suit. Under the traditional common law rule, the contractor was not liable for such an accident, so the risk of liability was on the property owner, Glacier. This decision was appealed and reviewed by the Washington high court.*

Case Decision Chambers, Justice

* * *

Under the completion and acceptance doctrine, once an independent contractor finishes work on a project, and the work has been accepted by the owner, the contractor is no longer liable for injuries to third parties, even if the work was negligently performed. Historically, after completion and acceptance, the risk of liability for the project belonged solely to the property owner. This court has not addressed this doctrine in over 40 years and, in the meantime, 37 states have rejected it. Under the modern ... approach, a builder or construction contractor is liable for injury or damage to a third person as a result of negligent work, even after completion and acceptance of that work, when it was reasonably foreseeable that a third person would be injured due to that negligence.

We join the vast majority of our sister states and abandon the ancient Completion and Acceptance

Doctrine. We find it does not accord with currently accepted principles of liability....

The Completion and Acceptance Doctrine is also grounded in the assumption that if owners of land inspect and accept the work, the owner should be responsible for any defects in that accepted work. While this assumption may have been well founded in the mists of history, it can no longer be justified. Today, wood and metal have been replaced with laminates, composites, and aggregates. Glue has been replaced with molecularly altered adhesives. Wiring, plumbing, and other mechanical components are increasingly concealed in conduits or buried under the earth. In short, construction has become highly scientific and complex. Landowners increasingly hire contractors for their expertise and a nonexpert landowner is often incapable of recognizing substandard performance. ...

We conclude that the Doctrine of Completion and Acceptance is outmoded, incorrect, and harmful and join the modern majority of states that have abandoned it in favor of the [modern] approach [holding a builder or contractor liable for injury due to negligent work]. We reverse the superior court order ... and remand for further proceedings in keeping with this holding.

Questions for Analysis

1. The court rejected the common law rule concerning completion and acceptance that had been in effect until this decision and ordered a new trial. What was the key reason for that decision? How does the new rule affect liability?

2. A judge on the court dissented from the decision. Explaining his opposition to the decision of the majority, he said this change in the law should have been done by the legislature in a statute, not the court. What are the practical problems with such a view?

Getty Images

LIGHTER SIDE OF THE LAW
Creative Common Law

An 18-year-old high school student in California "earned" over $1 million in a stock scam. When the federal authorities busted his operation, charged him with securities fraud, and made him repay his earnings, he was also booted off his high school baseball team.

   He then sued his high school for $50 million. The basis of his suit was that he had planned to be a major league baseball player, but now that he could not play on his high school team, he could not perform in front of baseball scouts who would draft him into the pros.

Source: *True Stella Awards*

The Executive

In addition to being the one who signs (or vetoes) bills passed by Congress, the president is another source of law. The president creates law by issuing *executive orders*, requiring federal agencies to do certain things within the president's scope of authority, such as an order to give preference to buying recycled products or to restrict financial transactions by suspected terrorist organizations.

   The president can also influence how administrative agencies undertake their duties and responsibilities. One administration may not pursue environmental, antitrust, or international trade regulation as strongly as another administration. Thus, some industries or individual companies may face a more hostile legal environment under one administration than under another.

International Sources of Law

Companies doing business in other countries face additional laws. A firm doing business in another country is subject to its laws. Other sources of international law affecting business include the laws of individual countries; the laws defined by treaties, which are international agreements, and trade agreements among countries; and the rules enacted by multinational regional or global entities, such as the World Trade Organization.

   Article II, Section 2 of the U.S. Constitution requires approval by two thirds of the Senate before a treaty agreed to by the president becomes binding on the U.S. Treaties of significance to business include the United Nations Convention on Contracts for the International Sale of Goods, which can govern the sale of goods between parties from different countries (discussed in Chapter 11), and the United Nations Convention on the Recognition and Enforcement of Foreign Arbitral Awards, which assists in the enforcement of arbitration clauses in international contracts. Treaties and other laws particular to the international legal environment are discussed in Chapter 21 and at various points in other chapters.

Classifications of Law

The organization of law can be thought of in several ways, such as whether it originated from a constitution, a legislative body, or the judiciary. It is common to classify law on the basis of whether it is: 1) public or private, 2) civil or criminal, or 3) procedural or substantive. Laws usually fall into more than one classification. For example,

Exhibit 1.3
Examples of Public and
Private Law

Public Law	Private Law
Administrative Law	Agency Law
Antitrust Law	Contract Law
Bankruptcy Law	Corporation Law
Constitutional Law	Intellectual Property Law
Criminal Law	Partnership Law
Environmental Law	Personal Property
Labor Law	Real Property
Securities Regulation	Tort Law

the sale of car insurance is affected by private law (a contract between the company and the buyer) and public law (state regulation of insurance). A violation of state law could result in civil or criminal penalties for an insurance seller.

Public and Private Law

Some examples of public and private law are provided in Exhibit 1.3. *Public law* concerns the legal relationship between members of society—businesses and individuals—and the government. Public law includes statutes enacted by Congress and state legislatures and regulations issued by administrative agencies.

Private law sets forth rules governing the legal relationships among members of society. It helps to resolve disputes and to provide a way for the values and customs of society to influence law. Private law is primarily common law and is enforced mostly through the state court systems. Unlike public law, which at times makes major changes in legal rules, private law tends to be quite stable and changes slowly.

Civil and Criminal Law

When a legislative body enacts a law, it decides whether the law is to be civil, criminal, or both. Unless a statute is designated as criminal, it is considered civil law. Examples of civil and criminal law are provided in Exhibit 1.4.

Criminal law concerns legal wrongs or crimes committed against the government. As determined by federal or state statute, a crime is classified as a *felony* or

Exhibit 1.4
Examples of Civil and
Criminal Law

Civil Law	Criminal Law
Contract Law	**Misdemeanor Offenses**
Auto Repairs	Assault and Battery (Simple)
Buying Airline Tickets	Disturbing the Peace
Forming a Business	Larceny (Petit)
Sale of Clothing	Public Intoxication
House Insurance	Trespass
Tort Law	**Felony Offenses**
Assault and Battery	Burglary
Defamation	Homicide
Invasion of Privacy	Larceny (Grand)
Medical Malpractice	Manslaughter
Trespass	Robbery

a *misdemeanor*. A person found guilty of a criminal offense may be fined, imprisoned, or both. To find a person guilty of a crime, the trial court must find that the evidence presented showed *beyond a reasonable doubt* that the person committed the crime. The severity of punishment depends in part on whether the offense was a felony or a misdemeanor. Generally, those offenses punishable by imprisonment for more than a year are classified as felonies. Misdemeanors are generally less serious crimes, punishable by a fine and/or imprisonment for less than a year. We will discuss this in detail in Chapter 5.

Civil law is concerned with the rights and responsibilities that exist among members of society or between individuals and the government in noncriminal matters. A person or business found liable for a *civil wrong* may be required to pay money damages to the injured party, to do or refrain from doing a specific act, or both. In finding the wrongdoer liable, the jury (or the judge in a nonjury trial) must find that the *preponderance of the evidence* favored the injured party.

Substantive and Procedural Law

Substantive law includes common law and statutory law that define and establish legal rights and regulate behavior. *Procedural law* determines how substantive law is enforced through the courts by determining how a lawsuit begins, what documents need to be filed, which court can hear the case, how the trial proceeds, and so on.

A criminal case, for example, must follow criminal procedural law. The appropriate appellate procedure must be followed when a lower-court decision is appealed to a higher court for review. Similarly, agencies enforcing administrative laws and regulations must follow appropriate procedures. While most of our focus will be on substantive law, it is important to keep in mind that proper procedure must be followed by all participants in the formal legal system. Examples of substantive and procedural law are provided in Exhibit 1.5.

Ethics and Business

The public image of business has been slipping for decades. According to a poll conducted in 1966, 55 percent of the American people had a "great deal of confidence" in American business executives. In recent years, that percentage has dropped to about 20 percent. Surveys indicate that confidence in business leaders is low—especially with regard to honesty and ethical standards. (Confidence in political leaders and institutions is even lower.)

One possible explanation is that ethical standards have fallen. After all, 75 percent of college students admit to some form of cheating and 79 percent of employees admit to pilfering supplies from their workplace, and 44 percent admit

Substantive Law	Procedural Law
Antitrust Law	Administrative Procedure
Contract Law	Appellate Procedure
Criminal Law	Civil Procedure
Environmental Law	Court Orders
Labor Law	Criminal Procedure
Securities Regulation	Rules of Evidence

Exhibit 1.5
Examples of Substantive and Procedural Law

INTERNATIONAL PERSPECTIVE

Sources of Law in Japan

Japan is a member of the civil-law family of nations. It adopted much of the German civil-law legal system in the late 1800s to be more attractive to Western businesses. Like its civil-law counterparts, Japan's basic source of law is its codes. In contrast to common-law systems where many basic laws are developed by judges, civil-law codes are enacted by the government—in Japan, the *Diet,* or national parliament. The codes arrange categories of law in an orderly and comprehensive way. In Japan, these are the Civil Code; the Commercial Code; the Penal Code; and procedural codes, such as the Code of Criminal Procedure and the Code of Civil Procedure.

To illustrate, under common law judges have developed rules in tort law imposing liability for intentional and negligent acts that inflict harm. Article 709 of the Japanese Civil Code is similar. It states:

A person who violates intentionally or negligently the right of another is bound to make compensation for damages (for injuries to the person, his liberty, or reputation as well as his property) arising therefrom.

The Japanese courts apply codes very strictly. The application of a code provision to a dispute is influenced by past applications, particularly those of the highest courts. Because the Japanese rely more on informal dispute resolution, many parts of the codes have not been litigated. In such situations, Japanese lawyers rely on interpretations of the codes by legal scholars. If no specific code provision applies to a dispute that has arisen, the court may look to traditions in reaching a decision, or it may apply a code provision intended to apply to another type of dispute. Through this process—and the enactment of new code provisions by the Diet—Japan's civil-law legal system adjusts to social, economic, and technological changes.

Getty Images

to lying about their work history to make themselves more attractive to employers. Unethical and illegal behavior is not confined to some executives at Enron or WorldCom; such instances are noteworthy because of the size of the financial damage done. But such behavior is not new. A study by a professor at Indiana University in 1939 showed that the 70 largest firms in the United States had suffered, since their founding, an average of 14 adverse legal decisions for reasons ranging from financial fraud to false advertising.

Whether or not ethics have declined, legislation to address issues of corporate dishonesty has mushroomed, accompanied by a cultural expectation that companies will reform. Public anger at real or perceived problems in business helps explain jury attitudes that produce huge verdicts against companies. A survey by the Minority Corporate Counsel Association found anti business sentiment at an all-time high, regardless of age, race, or sex. Most people believe that companies hide the truth about the dangers of their products and destroy documents that could get the companies in trouble.

We will return to the issue of corruption in international business in the final chapter of the book, but we note here that not all ethical problems arise only from bad behavior within organizations in an effort to dupe investors or customers. Corruption within governments induces businesses to pay bribes to get things done.

More indirectly, campaign contributions by businesses and business leaders are a part of the political economy in which we operate. Most contributions are legal, but the suspicion of influence peddling is always present. If you do not contribute, maybe your firm will get passed by in the billions in contracts that are awarded each year under the direction of political leaders. To get along, you have to go along. The issue then becomes, who regulates the regulators?

Getty Images

ISSUE SPOTTER
OK to Grease Palms?

You are hired as a construction supervisor by a firm specializing in multi story offices. Such construction requires visits by city building inspectors, who must sign off on certain work completed before a permit is issued to begin the next stage. Other supervisors let you know that the inspectors are used to being slipped $100 to $500, depending on the level of permit being issued. You get repaid by a petty cash fund that is largely for this purpose. What are your options?

Perceptions of Ethics and Responses

In response to declining public image and real internal problems, most corporations have written codes of ethics. In a study several years ago, Professor William Frederick found that corporations with codes of ethics were cited for legal infractions by federal regulatory agencies more frequently than corporations without codes. In corporations making a special effort to improve corporate ethics by placing more people purported to have a socially conscious perspective on their boards of directors, relatively little change in the corporate culture was found.

LIGHTER SIDE OF THE LAW
Our Values

Respect: We treat others as we would like to be treated ourselves. We do not tolerate abusive or disrespectful treatment. Ruthlessness, callousness, and arrogance don't belong here.

   Integrity: We work with customers and prospects openly, honestly, and sincerely. When we say we will do something, we will do it; when we say we cannot or will not do something, then we won't do it.

Source: *Enron 1998 Annual Report*

Getty Images

From Codes to Compliance

Ethics codes matter little unless there is a serious effort to ensure compliance within an organization. Ethics and legal requirements become blended in compliance codes. To be effective, such codes require diligent enforcement by management. According to the Department of Justice (DOJ), the existence of an effective corporate *compliance program* is a key factor in the agency's decision whether to prosecute an organization or to recommend leniency to a court when a legal problem arises. This will be discussed more in Chapter 5.

   The U.S. Sentencing Guidelines, which list punishment requirements for various crimes, state that a company found guilty of violating a law could have its fines reduced by as much as 95 percent if it is found to have a strong compliance program in place. A good ethics/compliance program can also result in a civil proceeding rather than a criminal prosecution of legal violations. Prevention is less costly than a cure. A survey of over 3,000 workers in 2005 found 69 percent had received ethics training at work, a significant increase compared to earlier surveys. Before we move on to cover specific areas of law in this book, we will first consider the issue of ethics.

CYBER LAW

Online Ethics and Legal Compliance

The evolution of the Internet has meant changes in the law, as we will see at various points in the text. It also means new ethical challenges—but also some opportunities.

Software now allows employers to monitor every keyboard click an employee makes. This is criticized as an invasion of privacy. Is it wrong for an employee to send personal e-mails? Is that really any different from chatting for a few minutes with a co-worker? On the other hand, since employers can be sued for sexual harassment if obscene e-mails are passed around or if pornographic Web sites are accessed from company computers,

managers have good reason to monitor employees' Web site visits and to keep copies of all e-mail transmissions. They can also watch for breaches in security.

Many companies have employees take legal and ethics training online. It is a cost-effective way to make sure employees are informed about employment discrimination, payoffs, conflicts of interest, and other matters that can spell big trouble for businesses. Employees may also be tested online regarding their knowledge of law and ethics. Many employers find online training more effective than gathering people in auditoriums for instruction, where they may tune out the information presented.

Getty Images

Ethics and Morals: Definitions and Applications

When considering standards of behavior, a distinction can be made between morals and ethics. The term *morals* refers to generally accepted standards of right and wrong in a society. The term *ethics* refers to more abstract concepts that might be encountered in the study of the standards of right and wrong in philosophy and theology. For purposes of our practical discussion of business, the terms *morals* and *ethics* are interchangeable.

ISSUE SPOTTER

Putting Ethics into Practice

A large chain of stores gives all employees a brief pamphlet called *Business Conduct Guide*. It states that everyone in the company should be "guided by the highest ethical and legal standards." It then gives brief guidance on a number of legal issues. For example:

Antitrust: We must compete vigorously and fairly in the marketplace using our independent judgment to make the best decisions for the Company.
Credit: We must provide accurate disclosure of credit terms and meet all requirements relating to fair credit reporting and equal credit opportunity.

Employees are told to report violations either to their supervisor or to the Chief Financial Officer of the company. Is this likely to be part of an effective ethics/compliance program? Can sales clerks relate to these issues?

Getty Images

Morals and ethics should not be confused with etiquette or good manners. Since statements about either can use terms such as *should* or *ought*, this confusion is tempting. A person may say, "You should not slurp your soup," but that concerns good manners, not moral or ethical behavior. Morals and ethics are more important than etiquette.

INTERNATIONAL PERSPECTIVE

Does Regulation Improve Business Ethics?

The financial scandals have been a reason for expanded securities regulation. The drug trade has resulted in increased control of money transfers. When problems arise, there is usually a call for increased government regulation to prevent future problems.

All nations have regulations and bureaucracy. But the wrong kind of regulation, especially when coupled with a corrupt bureaucracy, stifles business and reduces economic opportunities for ordinary people. The World Bank report, *Doing Business,* notes that the more regulation a country has, the more corruption it is likely to have and the lower its standard of living.

The World Bank gives some examples. To start a small business in Indonesia, an entrepreneur must wait an average of six months for permits. In the United Arab Emirates, trying to collect payment from a customer who will not pay requires 27 procedures taking almost two years. In India, bankruptcy procedures take an average of ten years. The Countries that regulate business the most include Bolivia, Burkina Faso, Chad, Costa Rica, Guatemala, Mali, Mozambique, Paraguay, the Philippines, and Venezuela. The countries that regulate the least include Australia, Canada, Denmark, Hong Kong, Jamaica, the Netherlands, New Zealand, Singapore, Sweden, and the United Kingdom.

Good regulation requires ethics in government. In many countries, regulation simply provides a legal excuse

Getty Images

Ethics and the Law Compared

Moral and ethical statements should not be confused with rules of law, although the two overlap. The fact that an action is legal does not mean that it is moral and ethical. As explained by David Skeel of the Pennsylvania Law School and Willian Stuntz of Harvard Law School in an article, "Good morals inspire and teach; good law governs. When the roles are confused, law ceases to rule and discretion rules in its place."

Just as legality does not always mean morality, illegality does not always imply immorality. The fact that an action is illegal does not necessarily mean it is immoral or unethical. If the speed limit is 65 mph, is it unethical to go 68 mph? The moral status of the civil rights activities of the 1960s is not settled by the fact that some of those activities were illegal. In his *Letter from Birmingham Jail*, Martin Luther King, Jr., said, "I can urge [people] to disobey segregation ordinances, for the [ordinances] are morally wrong."

Laws designed to restrict opportunities for minorities were common before the civil rights movement. The moral force used to oppose those laws was a key reason many of the laws were stricken and segregation declared illegal. However, some laws remain on the books that restrict economic opportunities.

United States v. Stanley
United States Supreme Court
483 U.S.669 107 S.Ct.3054 (1987)

Case Background *Stanley was an Army sergeant who volunteered in 1958 to participate in a program he was told would test the effectiveness of protective clothing against chemical warfare. The volunteers, unknown to them, were given doses of LSD. The Army wanted to test the effects of that drug. For years afterward, Stanley suffered hallucinations, memory loss, and periods of incoherence; he could not* *work well, and on occasion would "awake from sleep at night and ... violently beat his wife and children, later being unable to recall the entire incident." Stanley left the Army in 1969 and was divorced. In 1975, the Army contacted him and asked him to cooperate in a study of the long-term effects of LSD on "volunteers" from the 1958 test. That was the first time Stanley knew he had been given the drug.*

continues

Stanley sued the Army for compensation, but the claim was denied. Stanley then filed suit under the Federal Tort Claims Act. The district court ruled for the government because Stanley "was at all times on active duty and participating in a bona fide Army program during the time the alleged negligence occurred. . . . [T]he government is not liable under the Federal Tort Claims Act for injuries to servicemen where the injuries arise out of or are in the court of activity incident to service." The court of appeals upheld this judgment. Stanley appealed.

Case Decision   Scalia, Justice.

* * *

The Constitution explicitly conferred upon Congress the power . . . "[t]o make Rules for the Government and Regulation of the land and naval Forces," U.S. Const. Art. I, §8, cl. 14, thus showing that "the Constitution contemplated that the Legislative Branch have plenary control over rights, duties, and responsibilities in the framework of the Military Establishment. . . ."

[The dismissal of Stanley's claim was upheld; he had no case under the Federal Tort Claims Act or under the laws written by Congress concerning the rights of members of the Armed Forces.]

* * *

Justice Brennan . . . dissenting in part.

In experiments designed to test the effects of lysergic acid diethylamide (LSD), the Government of the United States treated thousands of its citizens as though they were laboratory animals, dosing them with this dangerous drug without their consent. One of the victims, James B. Stanley, seeks compensation from the Government officials who injured him. The Court holds that the Constitution provides him with no remedy, solely because his injuries were inflicted while he performed his duties in the Nation's Armed forces. If our Constitution required this result, the Court's decision, though legally necessary, would expose a tragic flaw in document. . . .

Before addressing the legal questions presented, it is important to place the Government's conduct in historical context. The medical trials at Nuremberg in 1947 deeply impressed upon the world that experimentation with unknowing human subjects is morally and legally unacceptable. The United States Military Tribunal established the Nuremberg Code as a standard against which to judge German scientists who experimented with human subjects. Its first principle was:

"1. *The voluntary consent of the human subject is absolutely essential".*

"The duty and responsibility for ascertaining the quality of the consent rests upon *each individual* who initiates, directs or engages in the experiment. *It is a personal duty and responsibility which may not be delegated to another with impunity." United States* v. *Brandt* (The Medical Case), 2 Trials of War Criminals Before the Nuremberg Military Tribunals Under Control Council Law No. 10, pp. 181–182 (1949) (emphasis added).

The United States military developed the Code, which applies to all citizens—soldiers as well as civilians. . . .

Having invoked national security to conceal its actions, the Government now argues that the preservation of military discipline requires that Government officials remain free to violate the constitutional rights of soliders without fear of money damages. What this case and others like it demonstrate, however, is that Government officials (military or civilian) must not be left with such freedom. . . .

* * *

[Brennan argued that Stanley should be allowed to sue the officers who conducted the experiments, but not the U.S. government.]

Questions for Analysis

1. A report issued by Congress expressed outrage at what had happened. Besides express outrage, what else could Congress have done?

2. Brennan would give Stanley the right to sue the people in charge of the experiment but not the right to sue the government. Details of the legal rules aside, is that decision more moral than the one to give Stanley no cause of action?

Should the courts uphold laws that produce immoral results? In the *Soldano* case we saw a moral problem caused by a legal rule that affects decisions of private citizens. What about statutes that produce immoral results? If the statutes do not violate constitutional rights, the courts tend to leave them alone. Otherwise, judges become legislators. Consider the ethical aspects of the issues raised in the *Stanley* case.

Summary

- The modern environment of business means that managers in all firms face a variety of ethical, legal, social, political, and international issues that make business increasingly complex.
- *Law* is a collection of principles and rules that establish, guide, and alter the behavior of members of society. Rules include both the formal rules (law) of society and the informal rules as dictated by customs, traditions, and social ethics.
- Law and the legal system serve important functions in an orderly society. Law helps to define acceptable behavior. To ensure order, the legal system provides a formal means through which disputes can be resolved. The law maintains the important values of a society. Finally, the legal system provides a way to encourage changes in social consciousness.
- Sources of law include the U.S. and state *constitutions*, Congress and the state legislatures, the judiciary branch, the executive branch (the president at the federal level and the governors at the state level), state and federal administrative agencies, and multiple sources that form the international legal environment of business.
- Judge-made or *common law* is the original source of law in this country. This system encourages judges to use prior decisions, or *precedents*, for guidance in deciding new disputes. The doctrine of *stare decisis* helps give consistency to case law.
- Law can be classified on the basis of whether it is public or private, civil or criminal, or substantive or procedural.
- The public image of business and of other institutions has declined. Dishonesty is believed to be more prevalent than it was in years past. To overcome real and perceived problems, the business community is encouraging codes of ethics, and firms are enforcing *compliance programs*.
- The terms *ethics* and *morals* are generally interchangeable. These terms should not be confused with statements about etiquette or good manners or with rules of law.

Terms to Know

You should be able to define the following terms:

constitution, 7	reasonable doubt, 15	ethics, 18
precedent, 11	civil law, 15	law, 21
stare decisis, 11	preponderance of the evidence, 15	common law, 21
criminal law, 14	substantive law, 15	compliance programs, 21
felony, 14	procedural law, 15	
misdemeanor, 15	morals, 18	

Discussion Question

1. Should the common-law maxim "Ignorance of the law is no excuse" apply to an immigrant who does not speak English?

Case Questions

1. Consider the following factual situation taken from an English judge's decision in 1884: The crew of an English yacht . . . were cast away in a storm on the high seas . . . and were compelled to put into an open boat belonging to the said yacht. That in this boat they had no supply of water and no supply of food. . . . That on the eighteenth day . . . they . . . suggested that one should be sacrificed to save the rest. . . . That next day . . . they . . . went to the boy . . . put a knife into his throat and killed him then and there; that the three men fed upon the body . . . of the boy for four days; that on the fourth day after the act had been committed the boat was picked up by a passing vessel, and [they] were rescued, still alive. . . . That they were carried to the port of Falmouth, and committed for trial . . . That if the men had not fed upon the body of the boy they would probably not have survived to be so picked up and rescued, but would within the four days have died of famine. That the boy, being in a much weaker condition, was likely to have died before them. . . . The real question in this case [is] whether killing under the conditions set forth . . . be or be not murder. [*Regina* v. *Dudley and Stephens*, 14 Queens Bench Division 273 (1884)] Is it murder? Was the action immoral?

2. We know that smoking is a serious health hazard. Should cigarette manufacturers be liable for the serious illnesses and untimely deaths caused by their products, even though they post a warning on the package and consumers voluntarily assume the health risks by smoking? [*Cipollone* v. *Liggett Group, Inc.*, 505 U.S. 504, 112 S. Ct. 2608 (1992)]

   ✓ **Check your answer at http://academic.cengage.com/blaw/meiners**

3. Two 8-year-old boys were seriously injured when riding Honda mini trail bikes provided by their parents. The boys were riding on public streets and ran a stop sign when they were hit by a truck. One boy was not wearing a helmet. The bikes had clear warning labels on the front stating that they were only for offroad use. The owner's manual was clear that the bikes were not to be used on public streets and that riders should wear helmets. The parents sued Honda. The supreme court of Washington said that there was one basic issue. "Is a manufacturer liable when children are injured while riding one of its mini trail bikes on a public road in violation of manufacturer and parental warnings?" Is it unethical to make products like minibikes that will be used by children, when we know accidents like this will happen? [*Baughn* v. *Honda Motor Co.*, 727 P.2d 655 Sup. Ct., Wash., (1986)]

4. Johnson Controls adopted a "fetal protection policy" that women of childbearing age could not work in the battery-making division of the company. Exposure to lead in the battery operation could cause harm to unborn babies. The company was concerned about possible legal liability for injury suffered by babies of mothers who had worked in the battery division. The Supreme Court held that the company policy was illegal. It was an "excuse for denying women equal employment opportunities." Is the Court forcing the company to be unethical by allowing pregnant women who ignore the warnings to expose their babies to the lead? [*United Auto Workers* v. *Johnson Controls*, 499 U.S. 187 (1991)]

   ✓ **Check your answer at http://academic.cengage.com/blaw/meiners**

Ethics Questions

1. The federal tax code is riddled with special-interest loopholes. Most of these exist because firms and trade associations lobby Congress and provide campaign support to members of Congress to gain special favors to individual firms or industries. Is it ethical for firms to seek special privilege?

2. Migrant farm workers are at the bottom of our employment force and quality-of-life standards. They work very hard, do not make much money, and often live in miserable conditions. You run a large vegetable farm operation that hires migrant workers an average of four weeks per year. You pay the going wage rate for the workers, who rent dumps to live in while they work in your area before moving north. Do you have an

ethical responsibility to pay more than the market wage so that these workers can live in better conditions? Do you have a responsibility to provide housing to the workers you employ? If you pay above-market rates, your profits could fall, and you could even go out of business. Assuming these to be facts, what responsibilities do you think you have?

3. The ABC Company has been supplying widgets to your XYZ Company for many years. The widgets are needed in the production of gidgets. ABC has always been a fair company to deal with. When problems have arisen, ABC has usually resolved them to your satisfaction. Now the LMN firm from Shanghai has approached you, saying it will provide widgets to you for 30 percent less than you were paying ABC. ABC tells you that there is no way it can cut its prices and, if you cut it off, it will have to pare back production so that 50 people will be fired. Should you stick with ABC to protect American jobs? What other considerations may be involved?

Internet Assignment

http://uscode.house.gov
http://www4.law.cornell.edu/uscode/
http://www.uscourts.gov
http://www.ussc.gov/
http://www.ussc.gov/general/USSCoverview.pdf

The national agencies of the federal judicial administration consist of the following:

(a) The Judicial Conference of the United States (28.U.S.C. Section 331),
(b) The Administrative Office of the U.S. Courts (28 U.S.C. Sections 601–612),
(c) The Judicial Councils of the Circuits (28 U.S.C. Section 332),
(d) The Judicial Conference of the Circuits (28 U.S.C. Section 333),
(e) The U.S. Sentencing Commission (28 U.S.C. Sections 991–998).

These agencies have a significant impact on the federal legal landscape. For example, recommendations of the Judicial Conference of the United States ordinarily become law with very few, if any, changes made by the legislature. Understanding the federal courts' operations requires some knowledge of the functions of judicial agencies.

1. Find the U.S. Code section associated with (a) through (c), using the official U.S. government Web site.
2. Find the U.S. Code section associated with (d), using the Legal Information Institute Web site.
3. According to the Federal Judiciary home page (FAQs), how many courts of appeals are there?
4. According to the Federal Judiciary home page, how many district courts are there?
5. According to the U.S. Sentencing Commission Web site (Overview), what two factors do the sentencing guidelines take into account?

The Court Systems

Chapter 2

Folley's Metal Fabrication of California advertises and sells its products in several western states. Its products are all manufactured in California. If a customer in Arizona buys a Folley's product after seeing a Folley's advertisement, and is then injured using it, can that injured customer bring the lawsuit to the Arizona state court systems for resolution? Must the dispute be decided in a California state court, because the business is located in that state? Or would such a dispute be decided in the federal court system? Does the law of Arizona or California apply? In any dispute, parties must understand and resolve these questions before they can effectively use our court system.

This chapter provides an overview of the American court system and discusses how a party who has suffered a legal wrong can seek relief in the courts. In their operations, businesses may face disputes with competitors, suppliers, customers, and government agencies. Many problems are resolved by the parties with no serious disruption in business relationships or activities. A significant number, however, require resolution in our court system through civil litigation.

A business that has a civil dispute going to litigation must first determine, with the help of an attorney, which court has the power and the authority to decide the case. That is, which court has the jurisdiction to take the case for resolution? Today, many businesses operate in several states and often in several countries. As a consequence, the choice of the appropriate court may not be clear, or the parties may be in a position to choose between appropriate courts. ∎

Getty Images

The Court Systems

The federal court system was created in response to the following declaration in the U.S. Constitution:

> The judicial Power of the United States shall be vested in one supreme Court and in such inferior Courts [courts subordinate to the Supreme Court] as the Congress may from time to time ordain and establish.

Over many years, the federal court system developed into a three-level system. It consists of the U.S. district courts, the U.S. courts of appeals, and the U.S. Supreme Court. Each court has its own role within the federal court system. Since the 13 original states had courts before the federal system was created, they have the oldest court systems. The two systems have evolved to have many similarities.

Federal Judges

Federal judges are nominated by the president and confirmed by a majority vote in the U.S. Senate. Since the Constitution guarantees federal judges the right to serve "during good behavior," they enjoy a lifetime appointment. Judges below the Supreme Court level retire at age 70, but may remain on "senior status" and still hear cases. There are about 1,200 federal judges. According to the Constitution, federal judges may be removed from office only if the Congress impeaches them for treason, bribery, or other high crimes and misdemeanors. The impeachment process includes the actual impeachment (indictment) by the House of Representatives, followed by a trial before the Senate. If at least two thirds of the senators vote for removal, the judge is removed from office. This happens only rarely; only four federal judges in history have been removed.

While Congress may change the structure of the federal court system, it may not reduce a judge's salary or term of office once an appointment has been made. The writers of the Constitution gave federal judges job security, because they wanted to guarantee that judges would be independent and free from the pressure of politics.

State Judges

State judges are chosen by a variety of methods, as Exhibit 2.1 shows. They are elected, appointed, or chosen by a method that mixes the election and appointment processes. In several of the states with the mixed system, the state bar association has a committee to recommend qualified attorneys for the bench. The governor then appoints a judge from its list. The judge selected then serves until the next election, at which time the public is asked to vote *for* or *against* him. This system for selecting judges is referred to as the *Missouri System.*

In contrast to the position enjoyed by federal judges, most state judges serve for a fixed term, whether they are appointed or elected. Terms range from one year for judges in some Midwestern states to a 14-year term for judges in New York. Massachusetts and New Hampshire appoint judges to serve until they reach age 70; only Rhode Island provides a lifetime term of office.

Some observers claim that appointed judges are of higher average quality than elected judges. Others claim that elected judges work harder than appointed judges. There is statistical evidence that in states with elected judges, the average awards in tort cases are larger and out-of-state companies are treated worse than in states with appointed judges.

Exhibit 2.1   Selection Methods for Appeals Court and Trial Court Judges

Merit selection by nominating commission and governor	Governor (G) or legislature (L) appointment	Elections by party	Non-partisan elections	Combined merit selection and other methods
Alaska	California (G)	Alabama	Arkansas	Arizona
Colorado	Maine (G)	Illinois	Georgia	Florida
Connecticut	New Jersey (G)	Louisiana	Idaho	Indiana
Delaware	New Hampshire	Michigan	Kentucky	Kansas
Hawaii	(G)	Ohio	Minnesota	Missouri
Iowa	South Carolina (L)	Pennsylvania	Mississippi	New York
Maryland	Virginia (L)	Texas	Montana	Oklahoma
Massachusetts		West	Nevada	South Dakota
Nebraska		Virginia	North Carolina	Tennessee
New Mexico			North Dakota	
Rhode Island			Oregon	
Utah			Washington	
Vermont			Wisconsin	
Wyoming				

Source: American Judicature Society

Judicial Immunity

Under the *doctrine of judicial immunity*, a judge is absolutely immune from suit for damages for judicial acts. This immunity applies even when the judge acts maliciously. Without this rule, judges could fear being sued by parties unhappy with their judicial decisions. As a result, judges would lose their ability to be independent decision makers. By protecting judges from such suits, judicial immunity serves to keep judges unconcerned about the relative power of parties who appear in court.

Organization of the Court Systems

Both state and federal court systems have lower courts of *original jurisdiction*, where disputes are first brought and tried, and courts of *appellate jurisdiction*, where the decisions of a lower court can be taken for review. In both systems, the courts of original jurisdiction are trial courts. One judge presides. The court's principal function is to determine the facts in the dispute and to apply the appropriate law to those facts in making a decision, or judgment. As we discuss in the next chapter, the jury is responsible for deciding the facts in a case; if there is no jury in a case, the judge decides the facts.

Appellate courts are concerned with errors in the application of the law and making sure proper procedure was followed at the trial court proceeding. Normally three judges review decisions at the appeals court level. Five or more judges are used in the highest appellate state courts, the state supreme courts. The basic structure of the American court system is illustrated in Exhibit 2.3. While we focus more on federal courts here, the majority of litigation occurs in state courts.

The Federal Courts

The Constitution intends for the judiciary in the United States to have significant independence from the other branches of government as part of the system of checks and balances. This is quite unlike most countries, where judges are civil servants who tend to have less independence than judges in the United States enjoy. While some state judges are in political positions, as we will discuss, federal judges, once on the bench, are quite independent.

Federal District Courts

As the trial courts of the federal system, U.S. district courts are the courts of original jurisdiction in the federal system. The district courts are the only courts in the system that use juries. Most cases involving questions of federal law originate in these courts. The geographical boundaries of a district court's jurisdiction does not cross state lines. Thus, each state has at least one federal district court; the more populated states are divided into two, three, or—as in California, New York, and Texas—four districts. In addition, there are federal district courts in the District of Columbia, Puerto Rico, Guam, and the Virgin Islands.

Federal Appellate Courts

U.S. courts of appeals may review federal district court decisions. Established in 1891, the U.S. courts of appeals are the intermediate-level appellate courts in the federal system. There are 12 courts of appeals, one for each of the 11 circuits into which the United States is divided and one for the District of Columbia. The division of the states into circuits and the location of the U.S. courts of appeals are presented in Exhibit 2.2.

The U.S. courts of appeals exercise only appellate jurisdiction. If either party to the litigation is not satisfied with a federal district court's decision, it has the *right* to

Exhibit 2.2 The Federal Judicial Circuits

appeal to the court of appeals for the circuit in which that district court is located. The Fourth Circuit U.S. Court of Appeals in Richmond, Virginia, for example, will hear appeals only from the federal district courts in the states of Maryland, North Carolina, South Carolina, Virginia, and West Virginia. The one exception is the U.S. government, which does not have the right to appeal a verdict in a criminal case.

The U.S. courts of appeals assign three-judge panels to review decisions of the district courts within their circuits. They also review orders of federal administrative agencies when a party appeals the final decision of a regulatory agency. As a practical matter, because it is so difficult to obtain review by the U.S. Supreme Court, the courts of appeals make the final decision in most cases.

Specialized Federal Courts

Although the U.S. Supreme Court, courts of appeals, and district courts are the most visible federal courts, there are a few important courts with limited or special jurisdiction within the federal court system. These courts differ from other federal courts in that their jurisdictions are defined in terms of subject matter rather than by geography.

The most prominent of these courts is the Court of Appeals for the Federal Circuit. Although its territorial jurisdiction is nationwide, its subject-matter jurisdiction is limited to appeals from the U.S. district courts in patent, trademark, and copyright cases and in cases where the United States is a defendant; appeals from the U.S. Court of Federal Claims and the U.S. Court of International Trade; and the review of administrative rulings of the U.S. Patent and Trademark Office.

U.S. Supreme Court

The U.S. Supreme Court is the highest court in the country, as we see in Exhibit 2.3. Created by the U.S. Constitution, the Supreme Court is primarily an appellate review court. Cases reaching the Court are usually heard by nine justices, one of whom is the Chief Justice. The term of the Court begins, by law, on the first

---

INTERNATIONAL PERSPECTIVE

The French Court System

Like most European countries, France is a civil-law country—its legal system is based on written (code) law rather than on judge-made common law. The structure of the French system appears similar to that of the U.S. federal court system. The French system consists of a supreme court (*cour de cessation*), a court of appeals (*cour d'appel*), and a court of general jurisdiction (*tribunal d'instance*).

The appellate process in France is considerably different from that in the United States. In contrast to the powers held by the U.S. Supreme Court, the *cour de cessation* does not have the authority to pronounce judgment. Rather, it has power either to reject an appeal or to invalidate a decision and return the case to the court of appeals for reconsideration.

In the event the appeal is rejected, the proceedings are finished. If, on the other hand, the decision of the *cour d'appel* is invalidated, that court then reconsiders the case before a five-judge panel. However, the judges are not bound by the higher court's determination of the law as they would be in the United States. They may either accept or reject it. They may also consider new facts.

If the case is then appealed a second time to the *cour de cessation*, the case is heard by a panel of 25 judges. If this appeal is rejected, the proceedings end; if the *cour d'appel* decision is invalidated, the case is returned to it for reconsideration. On the second appeal, however, the judges of the *cour d'appel* must follow the higher court's decisions on points of law.

Getty Images

Exhibit 2.3 The Court Systems

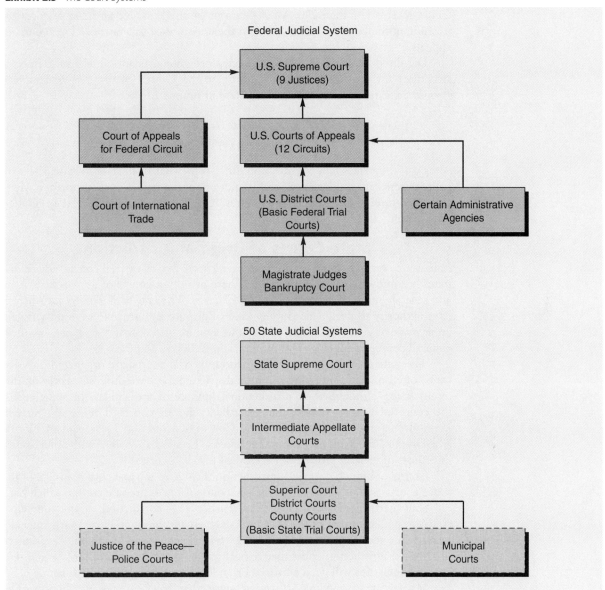

Monday in October and continues as long as the business of the Court requires. The Court sits in Washington, D.C.

As an appellate court, the Supreme Court may review appeals from the U.S. district courts, the U.S. courts of appeals, and the highest courts of the states. In rare instances, such as in a dispute between two state governments, the U.S. Supreme Court has *original and exclusive jurisdiction*. Although Congress may change the Court's appellate jurisdiction, it cannot change the Court's original jurisdiction conferred upon it by the Constitution.

Appellate review is normally obtained by petitioning the court for a *writ of certiorari*. Appeals to the Supreme Court are at the Court's discretion. The members of the Court determine which cases they wish to review; at least four justices must agree to review a case. If that does not happen, the decision of the lower court becomes final. Although it receives thousands of such petitions each term, the Court accepts less than 200. Most petitions granted involve an issue of constitutional importance or a conflict between the decisions of two or more U.S. courts of appeals.

Despite differences in substantive law, foreign courts are often similar in basic structure, but not in procedure, to those in the United States. *The International Perspective* feature looks at the court system in France.

The State Courts

Although the names and organization differ somewhat from state to state, the state court systems are similar in general framework and jurisdictional authorities. Many are three-level systems and many states have local courts of special or limited jurisdiction.

State Courts of Original Jurisdiction

Each state court system has courts of *original jurisdiction*, or trial courts, where disputes are initially brought and tried. There are often courts of *general jurisdiction* and several courts of *limited* or *special jurisdiction*. The courts of general jurisdiction have authority to decide almost any kind of dispute and are able to grant virtually every type of relief. In many states, the amount in controversy, however, must generally exceed a specific amount, typically $2,000 to $5,000.

The state courts of general jurisdiction, or trial courts, are organized into districts, often on the county level. These district courts have different names in different states, although their jurisdictional limitations are similar. In some states, the courts of general jurisdiction are called superior courts. The same courts in Pennsylvania and Ohio are called the Courts of Common Pleas, and in Florida and Oregon, the Circuit Courts. In Kansas, Louisiana, Maine, and other states, the courts of general jurisdiction are called district courts.

Courts of limited or special jurisdiction include municipal courts, justice of the peace courts, and other more specialized courts (such as probate courts, which handle only matters related to wills and trusts). The jurisdiction of the municipal courts is similar to that of the district courts, except that municipal courts typically hear claims that involve less money. Litigants not satisfied with the decision of the limited-jurisdiction court may appeal to the court of general jurisdiction. On appeal, the parties will get a new trial or, in legal terminology, a *trial de novo*.

Many states provide *small claims courts* that have limited jurisdiction. The amount in controversy in most small claims courts must not exceed $5,000 ($7,500 in California). Subject matter includes debts, contract disputes, warranty claims, personal injuries, and security deposits. Small claims courts are particularly good for collecting small debts, because procedure is much less formal, and representation by an attorney is not necessary and usually is not permitted. Small claims courts are a much faster and less expensive forum than the district courts. Most state courts have Web sites to guide you through the procedure.

State Courts of Appellate Jurisdiction

Every judicial system allows the review of trial court decisions by a court with *appellate jurisdiction*. Generally, a party has the right to appeal a judgment to at least one higher court. When a court system contains two levels of appellate courts, appeal usually is a matter of right at the first level and at the discretion of the court at the second. These courts have different names in different states, such as District

Courts of Appeal in Florida and Appellate Division Courts in New York. The most common issues reaching the highest court in a state typically involve the validity of a state law, the state constitution, or a federal law as it is affected by a state law. A party seeking further review from the highest state court may seek review from the U.S. Supreme Court, but that is rarely granted.

LIGHTER SIDE OF THE LAW
Tough Justice: Shoot 'Em or Flush 'Em

Bay County Florida Judge Hauversburk, dealing with a felony parole violation, announced that he was "locked and loaded." He told the defense attorney to let his client know that "if he does anything that I see as a threat to me or anybody in this courtroom, then I'm going to fire first and ask questions later."

Broward County Florida Judge Schapiro had a device that made a sound like a toilet flushing when he pushed a button. He pressed it after asking one attorney, "Do you know what I think of your argument?"

Both judges were disciplined and ordered to get counseling.

Source: *National Law Journal*

Getty Images

Rules of Civil Procedure

From the moment the *plaintiff—the* party who claims to have suffered an injury that the law can remedy—brings an action, a lawsuit is governed by detailed procedural rules. These force the parties to define the issues in the dispute. The rules also control how the parties to the dispute—the plaintiff and the *defendant* (the party who allegedly injured the plaintiff)—present evidence and arguments in support of their positions.

Although the states are free to develop their own procedural rules, most have adopted the *Federal Rules of Civil Procedure* or rules similar to them. The Federal Rules, which have been modified over the years, were developed by an advisory committee appointed by the U.S. Supreme Court, and they became effective in 1938. The Federal Rules govern the procedure of the litigation process, including the pleadings, discovery, trial procedures, and relevant motions. Note that these rules govern only civil litigation; somewhat different procedures are used in criminal and administrative litigation.

The Federal Rules of Civil Procedure are contained in the United States Code, Title 28. In addition to establishing trial procedural rules, Title 28 establishes the organization of the federal courts, judicial agencies, and important rules governing jurisdiction and venue. This chapter concentrates on jurisdiction and the organization of the court system. Chapter 3 examines trial procedures and processes.

Jurisdiction

The literal meaning of the term *jurisdiction* is "the power to speak of the law." A court's jurisdiction defines the limits within which it may declare, administer, or apply the law. The limitations imposed upon a court by a constitution, and the statutes that created it, determine what kinds of disputes it may resolve, depending on who the parties to a case are.

When a plaintiff files a lawsuit, the correct court must be chosen to resolve the dispute. While there are a number of courts, the plaintiff's choices are limited to the court or courts having appropriate jurisdiction. The plaintiff must select a court that has both:

1. Subject-matter jurisdiction
2. Personal jurisdiction over a) the person of the defendant or b) the property of the defendant

If a court should rule in a particular case and it is later determined that jurisdiction was lacking, the judgment of that court will be declared null and void upon appeal. Without jurisdiction a court cannot exercise authority.

Subject-Matter Jurisdiction

Subject-matter jurisdiction is created by a constitution or a statute regarding the types of disputes a court can accept to resolve. It might include requirements on the amount in controversy or restrictions on the legal area a court can hear. For example, state statutes might restrict disputes in district (trial) courts to civil cases involving more than $2,000, or they might require that all cases involving wills be heard by a probate court. That is, the state legislature places limitations on the subject-matter jurisdiction of various courts.

LIGHTER SIDE OF THE LAW
Being a Judge Makes Me Sick?

A California judicial board fact-finding panel held that Los Angeles judge Patrick Murphy was not entitled to 400 days of paid sick leave he had claimed. Murphy claimed his illnesses included a phobia of sitting in judgment. Apparently to help heal himself, while being paid $130,000 a year as a judge, he enrolled full-time in a medical school in the Caribbean.

Source: *National Law Journal*

Getty Images

Subject-Matter Jurisdiction in the Federal Courts

Under the U.S. Constitution, the federal courts may hear only those cases within the judicial power of the United States. That is, federal courts have the judicial power to hear cases involving a *federal question:*

> The judicial Power shall extend to all Cases . . . arising under this Constitution, the Laws of the United States, and Treaties made, or which shall be made, under their Authority. . . .

This includes cases based on the relationship of the parties involved:

> [The judicial Power shall extend] to all Cases affecting Ambassadors, other public Ministers and Consuls . . . to Controversies between two or more States;—between a State and Citizens of another State;—between Citizens of different States . . . and between a State, or the Citizens thereof, and foreign States, Citizens or Subjects.

When federal jurisdiction is based on the parties involved, most of the litigation is generated 1) by cases in which the United States is a party to the suit or 2) by cases involving citizens of different states. The purpose for allowing federal jurisdiction when a dispute arises between citizens of different states—referred to as *diversity-of-citizenship* jurisdiction—is to provide a neutral forum for handling such disputes.

INTERNATIONAL PERSPECTIVE

London's Commercial Court

When international contracts are signed, the parties can specify how future disputes will be resolved, including the choice of a court. If a court is not agreed upon initially, parties can agree at the time of a dispute where to resolve the matter. The Commercial Court in London is a popular forum; many of its cases involve parties from more than one country.

Formed in 1895, the court is often chosen because London is a major business city, most firms have assets in the U.K. that the court can control, and the judges are all experienced in commercial matters. Over 1,000 cases are filed each year; about a quarter of them actually go to trial. Most are complex business matters, such a reinsurance, banking, or commodity trading. Smaller and less complex cases are assigned to the London Mercantile Court, and cases involving shipping disputes go to the Admiralty Court.

Each trial is handled by one judge; there is no jury. Trials usually occur within a year and are finished rather quickly; the losing party pays the winner's attorney fees. Since English courts are respected, their judgments are likely to be enforced in other countries, and the remedies used by the court have been innovative and relevant to commercial matters.

Getty Images

State courts might be biased in favor of their own citizens and against "strangers" from other states or countries. To obtain *diversity jurisdiction*, there must be total diversity among the parties. That is, all parties on one side of the lawsuit must have state citizenship different from the parties on the other side of the lawsuit. To establish federal jurisdiction in a diversity case, the parties must also show two things: (1) that they are from different states and (2) that the *amount in controversy* (the sum the plaintiff is suing the defendant for) is more than $75,000. In cases involving questions of federal law, there is no dollar amount requirement.

Personal Jurisdiction

Once it is established that the court has subject-matter jurisdiction, the plaintiff must meet the personal jurisdiction requirements. A court's jurisdictional authority is generally limited to the boundaries of the state in which it is located. Territorial jurisdiction usually does not become an issue, unless the defendant is not a resident of the state in which the plaintiff wishes to bring the lawsuit. In such a case, the plaintiff must determine how to bring the defendant—or the defendant's property—before the court.

Jurisdiction over the Person

A court's power over the person of the defendant is referred to as *in personam jurisdiction*. The defendant is served with a *summons*, a notice of the lawsuit (see Exhibit 2.4). That is, after selecting the appropriate court, the plaintiff must properly notify the defendant of the action filed by *service of process*. The summons directs the defendant to appear before the court to defend against the plaintiff's allegations. The court will issue a *default judgment* against a defendant who fails to appear.

Service of process is usually achieved by *personal service*. The summons is delivered to the defendant by the plaintiff, the plaintiff's attorney, a private process server, or a public official, such as a sheriff or a U.S. marshal. If the defendant cannot be located, courts allow the limited use of substituted service, such as publication of the pending lawsuit in a newspaper. The U.S. Supreme Court has emphasized that substituted service must be reasonably calculated to alert the defendant of the action.

Exhibit 2.4
A Typical Summons

United States District Court
for the
Southern District of California

Civil Action, File Number **80151**

Elena Gori
Plaintiff

v.   Summons

Tom Eyestone
Defendant

To the above-named Defendant:

You are hereby summoned and required to serve upon *Carol Chapman,* plaintiff's attorney, whose address is *3620 San Felipe, San Diego, California,* an answer to the complaint which is herewith served upon you, within 20 days after service of this summons upon you, exclusive of the day of service. If you fail to do so, judgment by default will be taken against you for the relief demanded in the complaint.

Gloria Hernandez
Clerk of Court

[Seal of the U.S. District Court]
Dated 2/5/09

Jurisdiction over Out-of-State Defendants

If both parties to a lawsuit are residents of the same state, the courts of the state clearly have jurisdiction over both persons. But if the defendant is a resident of another state, obtaining jurisdiction can be more difficult. The most obvious method

CYBER LAW

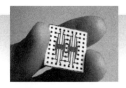

The Long Arm of the Internet

Sales on the Internet allow a business nationwide opportunities. When does a Web site advertiser become subject to jurisdiction in other states, when a buyer wishes to sue the online seller? As often happens with new areas of law, various courts issued conflicting decisions initially, but the legal standards have become more settled.

In general, personal jurisdiction is appropriate when the defendant has engaged in business in a state. So, Amazon.com, which does active business in every state by selling directly online, is subject to jurisdiction of courts in every state.

Jurisdiction is not appropriate when the defendant's contact with the forum state is only informational. Even if the Web site is interactive, if it is only informative, no jurisdiction is created. Similarly, if a Web site provides information about sales, allows customers to download order forms, and provides an e-mail address for inquiries, that is not enough to subject the defendant to jurisdiction.

The one area that is still a bit unclear is how much activity must occur with residents in a state for the Web seller to become subject to jurisdiction. In one case, when a seller sold one low-cost item to one buyer in a state, that was held not to be active business, especially since the contact was initiated by the buyer. In another case, the Utah supreme court held that if an out-of-state company sent one spam e-mail to a Utah resident, there was no jurisdiction in Utah courts.

Getty Images

CHAPTER 223A. Jurisdiction of Courts of the Commonwealth over Persons in Other States and Countries

Section 3. A court may exercise personal jurisdiction over a person, who acts directly or by an agent, as to a cause of action in law or equity arising from the person's

(a) transacting any business in this commonwealth;

(b) contracting to supply services or things in this commonwealth;

(c) causing tortious injury by an act or omission in this commonwealth;

(d) causing tortious injury in this commonwealth by an act or omission outside this commonwealth, if he regularly does or solicits business, or engages in any other persistent course of conduct, or derives substantial revenue from goods used or consumed or services rendered in this commonwealth;

(e) having an interest in, using, or possessing real property in this commonwealth;

(f) contracting to insure any person, property, or risk located within this commonwealth at the time of contracting.

[The remainder concerns divorce, alimony, and child custody issues.]

Exhibit 2.5
Long-Arm Statute: General Laws of Massachusetts

for obtaining in personam jurisdiction over nonresident defendants is to serve them with process while they are within the state. The nonresident defendant need only be passing through the state to be legally served with a summons.

While it would seem as if defendants could avoid lawsuits by staying out of state, often the court can still exert jurisdiction. If the defendant committed a wrong, such as causing an automobile accident, within the court's territorial boundaries, or has done business within the state, the court can exercise jurisdiction under the authority of the state's *long-arm statute* (see Exhibit 2.5). A long-arm statute is a state law that permits a state's courts to reach beyond the state's boundaries for jurisdiction over nonresident defendants.

Jurisdiction over Out-of-State Business Defendants

Long-arm statutes are aimed primarily at nonresident businesses. Do business defendants receive less favorable treatment by courts when it comes to jurisdiction than do individual defendants? Juries tend to be more hostile to business defendants, viewing them as more powerful, wealthy, and unfair, an entity against whom the state's citizens need protection. True or not, courts primarily have jurisdiction over a corporation in the following three situations:

1. The court is in the state in which the corporation was incorporated.
2. The court is in the state where the corporation has its headquarters or its main plant.
3. The court is in a state in which the corporation is doing business.

While the first two points are obvious, the third basis for jurisdiction—doing business in a state—has been subject to constitutional scrutiny by the U.S. Supreme Court. In reaching out-of-state corporate defendants, states rely upon long-arm statutes. As Exhibit 2.5 demonstrates, those statutes often list "transacting any business" in the state as a basis for jurisdiction. According to the Supreme Court in *International Shoe Company* v. *Washington* (66 S.Ct. 154, 1945), a state's long-arm statutes must identify certain *minimum contacts* between the corporation and the state where the suit is being filed to qualify as transacting business.

Getty Images

ISSUE SPOTTER
Can Your Firm Be Reached?

You work for a Florida real estate development firm, GoldenShores. Many clients are people who come from the New York area to retire or to have a second home. To increase marketing, a colleague suggests sending e-mails to potential clients advertising property for sale and offering a 5 percent discount to any buyers who respond to the e-mail and eventually buy property. New York requires real estate agents who offer property for sale to be registered in the state of New York. Your colleague says that this requirement does not apply to your company, as it is located in Florida and only sells property in Florida. He claims it does not matter if the state of New York likes the advertisements or not; it cannot come after GoldenShores. Is that right?

In the *Blimka* case, we see an example of long-arm jurisdiction being established in state court over a company from another state doing business over the Internet.

Blimka v. My Web Wholesalers, LLC
Supreme Court of Idaho
152 P.3d 594 (2007)

Case Background *My Web Wholesalers, a small company in Maine, used the Internet to do business around the country. It made offers on its Web site but did not distribute e-mails to customers who did not request information.*

Blimka, an Idaho resident, discovered My Web when surfing the net. He called My Web to discuss bulk merchandise offered on the Web site. DePalma, a My Web manager, agreed to sell Blimka 26,500 pairs of jeans for a total of $20,935. Blimka wired the money to My Web. When a shipment of 16,000 pairs of jeans arrived, Blimka called My Web to complain that the jeans were not of the quality discussed.

Blimka sued My Web and DePalma for fraud, a tortious act in state court in Idaho. Defendants were properly served in Maine, but did not respond to the complaint, so the district court issued a judgment against My Web and DePalma. Defendants filed a motion for relief from the judgment, claiming it was void for lack of personal jurisdiction. The district court held that it had personal jurisdiction. Defendants appealed.

Case Decision Jones, Justice

* * *

This case concerns the exercise of personal jurisdiction by an Idaho court over nonresident defendants, a small Maine-based company and its manager, who utilized the Internet to advertise and conduct business on a national scale.

* * *

The proper exercise of personal jurisdiction over non resident defendants by an Idaho court involves satisfying two criteria: First, the court must determine that the non resident defendant's actions fall within the scope of Idaho's long-arm statute. Second, the court must determine that exercising jurisdiction over the non resident defendant comports with the constitutional standards of the Due Process Clause of the U.S. Constitution. . . .

Blimka alleges that the defendants directed misrepresentations to him in Idaho via electronic means and that he sustained injury when he took delivery of the jeans in Idaho, only then learning that they had been misrepresented. . . .

In this case, the allegedly fraudulent representations were directed at an Idaho resident and the injury occurred in this state. Thus, we hold that Blimka's allegation of fraud was sufficient to invoke the tortious acts language of [the long-arm statute] with respect to both defendants.

Next, the defendants contend that their contacts with Idaho were insufficient under the Due Process Clause of the U.S. Constitution to permit personal jurisdiction in this case. The Fourteenth Amendment to the U.S. Constitution permits a state to exercise personal jurisdiction over a non resident defendant when that defendant has certain minimum contacts with the state such that the maintenance of the suit does not offend "traditional notions of fair play and substantial justice."

Where an Idaho resident alleges that a defendant in Maine intentionally directed false representations to, and caused injury in, Idaho that resident need not travel to Maine to pursue his or her claim against the perpetrator of the fraud. The defendants' actions satisfy minimum contacts with respect to the fraud allegations.

Additionally, because the defendants purposefully directed their allegedly false representations into Idaho, the exercise of personal jurisdiction is presumed not to offend traditional notions of fair play and substantial justice. Idaho has an ever-increasing interest in protecting its residents from fraud committed on them from afar by electronic means. . . .

In sum, neither the Idaho long-arm statute nor the Due Process Clause precluded the district court from exercising personal jurisdiction over the defendants and entering a binding judgment against them in this case. As a result, the district court's decision to deny the defendants' motion for relief from judgment was not an abuse of that court's discretion and will not be disturbed by this Court. . . .

We hold that the acts of the defendants were sufficient to subject them to the jurisdiction of the Idaho courts for the purpose of this litigation. The decision of the district court is affirmed. Blimka is awarded attorney fees and costs on appeal.

Questions for Analysis

1. The Idaho high court held that Idaho courts did have jurisdiction over an out-of-state seller who misrepresented goods sold over the Internet. Does this mean most Internet-based sellers are subject to jurisdiction in every state where they do business?
2. Why did My Web not move the case from Idaho state court to federal court?

Jurisdiction Based upon Power over Property

When a court cannot obtain jurisdiction over the person of the defendant, it still may have authority to establish jurisdiction based on the existence of the defendant's property within the state.

In Rem *Jurisdiction*

In lawsuits based on a dispute over property, a court in the state where the property is located has jurisdiction to resolve claims against that property—whether the property owner is there or not. The court is said to have *in rem* jurisdiction. Property in an *in rem* proceeding can include tangible property, such as real estate and personal property, and intangible property, including bank accounts and stocks.

Quasi in Rem *Jurisdiction*

A court has *quasi in rem* jurisdiction when a defendant's property in a state is attached to secure payment for an unrelated matter. For example, suppose Paris Hilton owes AutoBody of Nevada $8,000 for painting her low rider. Unable to collect from Hilton, AutoBody sues her. AutoBody cannot serve Hilton personally with process because she lives in California. AutoBody discovers that Hilton has property in Nevada. AutoBody sues to attach, or seize, the property to satisfy the debt. The court bases its jurisdiction on the fact that Hilton owns property in the state. The court is said to have *quasi in rem jurisdiction*, and the decision it renders binds the parties. As in an *in rem* proceeding, the property can be either tangible or intangible.

Relations between the Court Systems

The jurisdiction relationships between state and federal court systems are illustrated in Exhibit 2.6. Some disputes can be resolved only in the state courts, some

Exhibit 2.6
Jurisdiction Relationships
between Court Systems

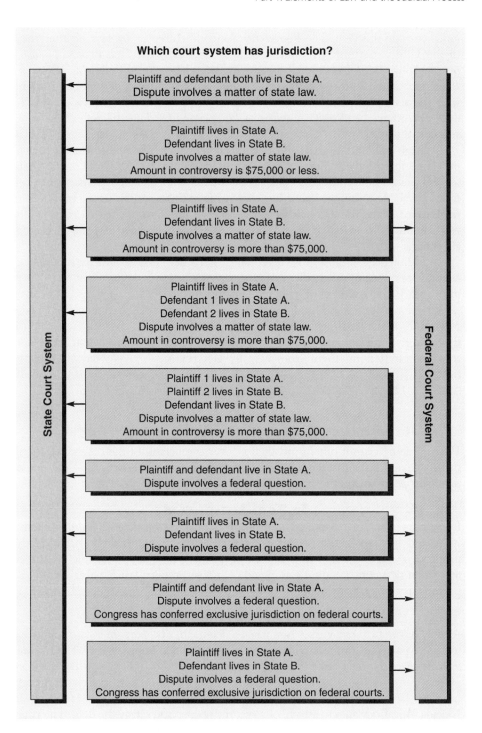

Exhibit 2.6
Jurisdiction Relationships
between Court Systems

disputes only in the federal courts, and some disputes in either the federal or the state court systems.

Exclusive Jurisdiction

Courts in the federal system have *exclusive jurisdiction* over certain disputes. State courts do not have subject matter jurisdiction over these cases and so may not try them. Congress usually specifies by statute matters over which the federal courts have exclusive jurisdiction. For example, federal courts have exclusive jurisdiction in cases involving federal crimes, bankruptcy, patents, and copyrights.

Similarly, state courts have exclusive jurisdiction over disputes such as divorce, adoption, and other matters controlled by the state government. A state government may confer exclusive jurisdiction on its courts as long as it does not infringe on the supremacy of federal law. If a plaintiff seeks relief for such a state matter in a federal court, the case would be dismissed for lack of jurisdiction. The plaintiff would need to refile the case in the appropriate state court.

With exclusive jurisdiction, the court hearing the case—whether a federal court or a state court—applies its procedural rules and follows its substantive law. If the court with jurisdiction is a state court in California, for example, it follows California procedural rules and applies the laws of the state of California. If the court is a federal court, it follows federal rules of procedure and applies federal law.

Concurrent Jurisdiction

As Exhibit 2.6 illustrates, both the federal and the state court systems have jurisdiction in some disputes. When both systems have the power to hear a case, *concurrent jurisdiction* exists. In such cases, where the case is heard usually depends on which court the plaintiff picks. As Exhibit 2.6 also illustrates, both systems may have jurisdiction when either of the following is the case:

1. There is diversity of citizenship and the amount in controversy exceeds $75,000.
2. The dispute involves a federal question and Congress has not conferred exclusive jurisdiction on the federal courts.

Federal Question Jurisdiction

The concurrent jurisdiction of the two court systems is understandable in cases where there is diversity of citizenship. An out-of-state defendant may worry that the state courts in the plaintiff's state might be biased in favor of the plaintiff. The rationale for state courts to exercise jurisdiction in federal question cases has been explained by the Supreme Court. The court has noted that concurrent jurisdiction has long existed.

However, Congress may hold that state courts do not have jurisdiction over a particular matter of federal law. That is, Congress provides that federal courts have exclusive jurisdiction over an area of law, or Congress provides exclusive jurisdiction "by unmistakable implication from the legislative history, or by a clear incompatibility between state-court jurisdiction and federal interests." In such cases, only the federal court system has jurisdiction over the case. If a plaintiff seeks relief for such a matter in a state court, the case would be dismissed for lack of jurisdiction.

Concurrent Jurisdiction and Removal

When concurrent jurisdiction exists, the plaintiff may bring suit in either the state court or the federal court system. If the plaintiff chooses the state court system, the defendant has the right to have the case removed to a federal court based on diversity of citizenship. This right of removal is intended to protect out-of-state defendants from state courts that might be biased in favor of their own citizens.

A plaintiff considers several issues when deciding which court system best suits her legal needs. For example, the rules of procedure in federal and state courts may be different, and the plaintiff's attorney may be more familiar with (and more successful using) one set of rules than the other. Also, local politics may be an issue for state judges. The plaintiff can do little to prevent the defendant from removing the case to the federal court if the defendant has the right to do so. However, if the plaintiff volunteers to file suit in the defendant's home state court, then the defendant cannot move the case to federal court.

Applying the Appropriate Law in Federal Court

When there is diversity of citizenship, and the case is in federal court, the central question becomes, which body of substantive law should the court apply to resolve the dispute—federal law or state law?

Suppose that Rich Boy and Unk were involved in a dispute and Rich Boy sued Unk in California. If both were from California, the case would be tried in a California state court, and California law would be applied to resolve the dispute. However, if Unk was from Florida and Rich Boy was from California and the amount in controversy exceeded $75,000, the dispute could be decided by a federal court because of diversity of citizenship. If the issue in dispute was governed by statutory law, federal and California courts would apply the same law—the statutory law of California—and the outcomes very likely would be the same. But what would happen if the case involved common-law issues? Would a federal court and a state court hearing similar cases reach different decisions? This is what used to happen in the United States until the Supreme Court decided the landmark 1938 case of *Erie* v. *Tompkins*.

In *Erie* v. *Tompkins*, the Supreme Court overturned an old Supreme Court case, *Swift* v. *Tyson* (1842) and held that except in matters governed by the federal Constitution or by acts of Congress (statutes), federal courts must apply state law. Thus, federal judges must apply both a state's common law and a state's statutory law when deciding diversity-of-citizenship cases. The federal court, however, follows federal procedural law.

Erie Railroad Co. v. Tompkins
United States Supreme Court
304 U.S.64, 58 S.Ct.817 (1938)

Case Background *Tompkins was injured on "a dark night" by something protruding from a passing freight train owned by Erie Railroad Company, as Tompkins stood next to the tracks in Pennsylvania, He claimed the accident occurred because of negligent operation of the train. Tompkins was a citizen of Pennsylvania, and Erie was a company incorporated in New York. Tompkins (the plaintiff) brought suit in federal district court.*

Erie argued that the court, in deciding the case, should apply the law of Pennsylvania. Under Pennsylvania law, Tompkins was a trespasser, and Erie would not be liable for his injuries. Tompkins argued that because of diversity of citizenship, federal common law should apply. Under federal common law, Erie could be liable for Tompkins's injuries.

The trial court agreed with Tompkins, and the jury awarded him $30,000 in damages. The decision was affirmed by the court of appeals. Erie appealed to the U.S.

Supreme Court, arguing that in diversity-of-citizenship cases, federal courts must apply the appropriate state law.

Case Decision Brandeis, Justice.

* * *

First. *Swift* v. *Tyson* held that federal courts exercising jurisdiction on the ground of diversity of citizenship need not, in matters of general jurisprudence, apply [the common law] of the state as declared by its highest court; that they are free to exercise an independent judgment as to what the common law of the State is—or should be. . . .

Second. Experience in applying the doctrine of *Swift* v. *Tyson* had revealed its defects. . . . Diversity of citizenship jurisdiction was conferred [by the Constitution] to prevent discrimination in state courts against those not citizens of the State. *Swift* v. *Tyson* introduced grave discrimination by non-citizens against citizens. It made rights enjoyed under the [state's common law] vary according to whether enforcement was sought in the state or in the federal court.... Thus, the doctrine rendered impossible equal protection of the law. In attempting to promote uniformity of law throughout the United States, the doctrine had prevented uniformity in the administration of the law of the State.

* * *

Third. Except in matters governed by the Federal Constitution or by Acts of Congress, the law to be applied in any case is the law of the State. And whether the law of the State shall be declared by its Legislature in a statute or by its highest court in a decision is not a matter of federal concern.... Congress has no power to declare substantive rules of common law applicable in a State.... And no clause in the Constitution purports to confer such a power upon the federal courts.

* * *

Fourth. The defendant contended that by the common law of Pennsylvania ... the only duty owed to the plaintiff was to refrain from willful or wanton injury.... The Circuit Court of Appeals ... declined to decide the issue of state law. As we hold this was error, the judgment is reversed and the case remanded to it for further proceedings in conformity with our opinion.

Reversed.

Case Note The concept of federal common law in diversity-of-citizenship cases was ended. Hence, Pennsylvania law applied and Tompkins was a trespasser and Erie was not liable for his injuries.

Questions for Analysis
1. Why had the decision in *Swift* v. *Tyson* prevented uniformity in the administration of state law?
2. After Erie, which court's procedural law must be applied in a diversity-of-citizenship case?

Applying the Appropriate Law in State Court

When a state court hears a case involving incidents that took place in more than one state or entirely in a different state, a conflict-of-law problem may arise. The court determines whether its own law or the law of another state should be applied. To help courts in such situations, states have enacted statutes that provide conflict-of-law rules. Some general *conflict-of-law* rules that affect businesses are presented in Exhibit 2.7.

Conflict-of-law, or choice-of-law, rules vary according to the nature of the dispute. In contract cases, for example, the traditional rule is that the law of the state in which the contract was made determines the interpretation of the contract. In tort cases, the general rule is that courts apply the law of the place where the tort occurred. However, the rules are not always simple. Courts evaluate the interests of the states involved in a dispute. The state with the most *significant interest* in the case would be the state whose law would be applied.

States do not all use the same rules, but they tend to be quite similar. They try to account for the interests of parties in the fair resolution of the dispute, for the

Substantive Law Issue	Apply State Law
Contract Disagreement	From state in which contract was formed or in which contract was to be performed or most significantly affected by the contract or designated in the contract
Liabillity Issues Arising from Injury	From state in which injury occurred
Workers' Compensation	From state of employment or in which injury occurred

Exhibit 2.7
Conflict-of-Law Rules Frequently Affecting Businesses

interests of the governments in the effective application of laws and the policy rationales upon which they are based, and for the benefits that result from the ability of citizens to predict the legal consequences of their actions. The following case discusses how a court goes about applying choice-of-law rules to a dispute.

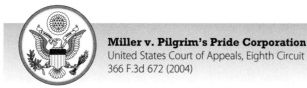

Miller v. Pilgrim's Pride Corporation
United States Court of Appeals, Eighth Circuit
366 F.3d 672 (2004)

Case Background *Pilgrim's Pride (PP) hired Simmons Mill to build a bin on top of a feed mill at a PP facility in Arkansas. There was no written agreement. While working on the project, Applewhite, a Simmons' employee, was killed when a roof on which he was working at the PP facility gave way under him.*

Simmons, a Texas company, fulfilled its obligations to Applewhite's heirs under the Texas workers compensation laws. His heir, Miller, then sued PP, claiming the death was caused by PP's negligence. PP provided an out-of-court settlement for Miller to end the claim. PP then sued Simmons in federal district court in Arkansas to seek indemnification, or repayment, for the money paid to Miller. Simmons asked the court to dismiss the suit filed by PP.

The district court held that Texas law should govern PP's claim. Texas law prohibits a claim for indemnification, unless the parties had a written agreement that required one party to indemnify the other. The court dismissed PP's claim. PP appealed, contending that Arkansas law, not Texas law, should govern the case.

Case Decision Bowman, Circuit Judge

* * *

A district court applies the law of the forum state when exercising its diversity jurisdiction. In this case, the parties agree that Arkansas' choice-of-law doctrines govern the matter, but disagree as to the outcome of the application. For its part, the district court applied the five-factor balancing test that the Arkansas Supreme Court has adopted, and held that Texas law applied. We agree that Texas law governs the merits of this suit. . . .

The Arkansas Supreme Court has adopted … Leflar's five-factor approach to deciding choice-of-law questions. Arkansas has not, however, altogether discarded the more traditional approach represented by the *lex loci delicti* [the law of the place of the wrong] rule. Accordingly, we must consider the *lex loci delicti* rule within the framework of the five Leflar factors: "(1) predictability of results; (2) maintenance of inter-

state and international order; (3) simplification of the judicial task; (4) advancement of the forum's governmental interests; and (5) application of the better rule of law." In our view, the question of which State's law should be applied turns on the fourth factor. . . .

The first of the five Leflar factors is predictability of results. . . . Because this suit does stem from an accident, and because the laws of Texas and Arkansas would yield substantially the same result, this factor does not weigh heavily in the balance.

The second and third factors, maintenance of interstate and international order and simplification of the judicial task, are not at issue here. . . .

The fourth factor, advancement of the forum state's governmental interests, is the crucial factor in this case. The traditional *lex loci delicti* rule is a reflection of an older attitude, which held that forum states had an interest in retaining jurisdiction over, and applying their laws to, suits arising from acts within their jurisdiction so as to insure that injuries to their citizens were redressed. Arkansas' adoption of the Leflar approach without discarding this traditional rule shows that this interest is still applicable, but does not control the outcome. Moreover, the adoption of the Leflar factors indicates that in this age of global commerce, Arkansas' governmental interests are not fully defined by the narrower *lex loci delicti* rule. As we already have noted, Applewhite was a resident of Texas and was compensated under Texas's workers compensation law. If the deceased employee were an Arkansas resident, the State of Arkansas would clearly have a vested interest in the application of the whole of its workers compensation scheme to the proceedings in order to fully vindicate the rationale behind its laws. As the case exists now, we can see no state interest that would be advanced by applying Arkansas, as opposed to Texas, principles of indemnification. Rather, it is in Arkansas's interest to have the case decided by applying Texas law in order to vindicate Texas's interest in having its workers compensation scheme applied in a uniform manner. . . .

Finally, we have noted that the fifth factor, application of the better rule of law, does not reflect a subjective judicial preference for one state's more or less elegant law, but is aimed at avoiding the application of unfair or archaic laws. . . .

Having decided that Texas law should govern this case, we have little trouble concluding that the District Court did not err when it granted Simmons's . . . motion to dismiss. . . .

For the reasons stated, the decision of the District Court is affirmed.

Questions for Analysis

1. The courts held that Texas law, not Arkansas law, would govern the decision in this case. Since the accident occurred in Arkansas, why did its law not control?

2. Why was the case in federal court in Arkansas instead of in state court in Arkansas or Texas?

Venue

A lawsuit must be brought in a court having proper venue. On the basis of fairness, state statutes generally provide that a lawsuit be brought in a court located in the county in which either the plaintiff or the defendant lives. Similarly, the defendant can be sued in a federal court only in a district where either the defendant or the plaintiff lives or where the dispute arose.

LIGHTER SIDE OF THE LAW

Justice Can Have a Bite to It

When West Virginia judge Troisi became irritated with a rude defendant, he stepped down from the bench, took off his robe, and bit the defendant on the nose. A report prepared for the state supreme court found that the judge frequently lost his temper in court. Troisi resigned and pleaded no contest to battery charges. He spent five days in jail and was put on probation. After he was released, he yelled at a court clerk who had testified against him. That violated his probation, so it was back to jail for six months. "Mr. Troisi just doesn't get it," said Judge Recht.

Source: *National Law Journal*

Getty Images

Change of Venue

In some controversial or well-publicized cases, defendants request a *change of venue* from the court where the plaintiff filed the case. In such cases, defendants worry that because of the publicity surrounding their case, they will be unable to get a fair trial. Once such fairness requirements are met, the court selected has jurisdiction and venue.

Forum Non Conveniens

Closely related to venue is the doctrine *forum non conveniens* (the forum is not suitable). A party asks the court to dismiss the case and transfer it to another court, even though the original court has jurisdiction, because there is another, more convenient court that could hear the case. When considering the motion, a court considers where the actions related to the case took place, where the witnesses are located, whether the parties will be unfairly burdened by using a particular court, and whether problems of conflicts of law might be avoided by transferring the case.

Summary

- Civil litigation involves the use of law and the legal process to resolve disputes among businesses, individuals, and governments. Litigation through the court systems provides a means of resolving disputes without the need to resort to force.
- Most U.S. judges are attorneys. It is their responsibility to uphold the legal system's reputation for honesty and impartiality. Federal judges are nominated by the president and confirmed by the Senate. They enjoy lifetime employment once appointed. State judges are variously appointed and elected, depending upon state procedures.
- The court system is made up of the *state court systems* and the *federal court system.* Most courts follow the *Federal Rules of Civil Procedure* to govern the important procedural aspects of the litigation process.
- In the study of the court system, the most basic notion is the concept of jurisdiction. The term *jurisdiction* means "the power to speak of the law." A court must have jurisdiction to hear and resolve a dispute. A court's jurisdiction is divided into two basic categories: *subject-matter jurisdiction* and *personal jurisdiction.*
- Subject-matter jurisdiction is a constitutional or statutory limitation on the types of disputes a court can resolve. Typical subject-matter constraints include minimum requirements on the amount in controversy in the dispute and restrictions on the types of disputes the court has authority to resolve.
- The jurisdiction of a court varies according to its position in the court system and which court system it is in. Courts of *original jurisdiction* in the federal and the state court systems are *trial courts.* They have authority to hear virtually any kind of dispute and provide any kind of relief. Courts with *appellate jurisdiction* have the power to review cases decided by courts below them. Most state court systems and the federal court system have two levels of *appellate courts.* The highest appellate court in the federal system is the U.S. Supreme Court.
- The federal court system has limited subject-matter jurisdiction. The federal courts are limited by the U.S. Constitution to cases involving a *federal question* or *diversity of citizenship,* where the amount in controversy exceeds $75,000. The state court systems can hear most disputes, including federal question cases where Congress has not limited jurisdiction to the federal court system.
- In addition to meeting the subject-matter jurisdictional requirements of a court, the parties—the plaintiff and the defendant—must meet personal jurisdictional requirements of the court. A state court's personal jurisdiction is generally limited to the boundaries of its state.
- Personal jurisdiction normally is not an issue, unless the defendant is not a resident of the state in which the plaintiff wants to bring the action. Jurisdiction of the court over the defendant is obtained by personal *service of process.* For out-of-state defendants, however, the court may need to exercise jurisdiction under authority of the state's *long-arm statute.* Generally, the plaintiff must show that the out-of-state defendant is transacting business or has some other interest in the state.
- When the court is unable to establish its jurisdiction through personal service on the defendant, the court may be able to establish *in rem jurisdiction* over property owned by the defendant that is located within the state.
- The federal courts in diversity-of-citizenship cases must apply the appropriate state common and statutory law.
- In state court cases, when the incident in question took place in another state, the court must look to the forum state's *conflict-of-law* or *choice-of-law,* rule to determine what substantive law will apply to resolve the dispute.

Terms to Know

You should be able to define the following terms:

Missouri System, 25

doctrine of judicial immunity, 26

original jurisdiction, 26

appellate jurisdiction, 26

general jurisdiction, 30

special jurisdiction, 30

trial de novo, 30

plaintiff, 31

defendant, 31

jurisdiction, 31

subject-matter jurisdiction, 32

diversity jurisdiction, 33

summons, 33

service of process, 33

default judgment, 33

in rem jurisdiction, 37

quasi in rem jurisdiction, 37

exclusive jurisdiction, 38

diversity of citizenship, 40

conflict-of-law, 41

lex loci delicti, 42

venue, 43

forum non conveniens, 43

personal jurisdiction, 44

long-arm statute, 44

Discussion Question

1. Judges in many nations are trained for their offices in law school. They are hired into the judicial system and work their way up through that system. In the United States, there is no special training to be a judge; it is an honor bestowed, usually on senior attorneys, or it is an office one runs for in some states. What advantages might the other system have over the U.S. method?

Case Questions

1. Burger King (BK) is headquartered in Miami. Its franchise contracts are governed by Florida law. Rudzewicz had a Michigan franchise that was not doing well. BK cancelled the franchise and told Rudzewicz to vacate the restaurant. Rudzewicz refused and kept running it. BK filed suit in federal court in Florida, claiming that Rudzewicz was in breach of contract. Rudzewicz claimed that the Florida federal court did not have jurisdiction, because he was a Michigan resident and the restaurant was in Michigan. The district judge held that under Florida's long-arm statute, the contract Rudzewicz signed made him subject to litigation in Florida. The court of appeals reversed, ruling that fairness did not allow jurisdiction in Florida. What would you think the Supreme Court held? [*Burger King* v. *Rudzewicz*, 105 S. Ct. 2174 (1985)]

2. Charlotte Chambers and other South Dakota residents chartered a bus in South Dakota from Dakotah Charter, a South Dakota corporation, to attend a Tae Kwon Do tournament in Arkansas. While en route from South Dakota to Arkansas, the bus stopped in Missouri. Chambers fell on the steps in the bus and broke her ankle. She sued, claiming that Dakotah failed to maintain the bus in a safe condition. Dakotah contended that the plaintiff's carelessness caused her injury. Which law should apply to the case—the law of South Dakota, where the contract was made; Missouri, where the injury occurred; or Arkansas, where the contract was ultimately to be performed? [*Charlotte Chambers* v. *Dakotah Charter*, 488 N.W.2d 63 Sup. Ct., S.D. (1992)]

   ✓ Check your answer at http://academic.cengage.com/blaw/meiners

3. Edwards received unsolicited faxes from Direct Access in violation of the Federal Telephone Consumer Protection Act, which makes it illegal to send unsolicited faxes. Edwards, a Nevada resident, sued Direct, not a Nevada resident, in state court in Nevada for damages allowed under the law. Direct contended that the suit could not be filed in state court, because it concerned federal law, so Nevada courts did not have jurisdiction. Is that correct? [*Edwards* v. *Direct Access*, 124 P.3d 1158 Sup. Ct., Nev. (2005)]

4. Vons of California sells meat to fast-food restaurants. Some meat tainted by *E. coli* bacteria was bought by Washington State Jack-in-the-Box restaurants. Jack-in-the-Box customers who ate the meat suffered serious illness, and several died. Vons sued the owners of

two Jack-in-the-Box franchises in California court, seeking repayment for money it was forced to pay to the food-poisoning victims. Vons claimed that Jack-in-the-Box did not cook the meat properly. The franchise owners responded that the California court did not have personal jurisdiction over them based on insufficient contacts with the state. The owners had assigned their rights to run the restaurants to third parties, who operated the restaurants. Thus, the link between the harms caused by improper cooking and the relationship of the franchise owners to California was too remote. The franchise agreements were signed in California and were governed by California law. The contracts between the Jack-in-the-Box owners and the operators were signed in Washington State. Is there a sufficient connection between the owners and the restaurants, operators to the state of California to allow the court to exercise jurisdiction? [*The Vons Companies v. Seabest Foods*, 37 Cal.App.4th, 1090 Ct. App., Cal. (1995)]

✓ **Check your answer at http://academic.cengage.com/blaw/meiners**

5. An accident in Florida killed three of the four members of a family from Alabama who were riding in their Kia automobile that had been bought in Alabama. Suit was filed in Alabama state court against Kia by the survivor of the accident. Kia requested that the trial be moved to Florida on the ground of *forum non–conveniens*, because almost all of the witnesses were in Florida. Was that motion reasonable? [*Ex parte Kia Motors America, Inc.*, 2003 WL 21040313 Sup. Ct., Ala. (2003)]

6. Beattey was a resident of Indiana who was attending college in New York. He was driving in the Bahamas on vacation when he was struck by a vehicle driven by an employee of College Centre, a New York-based school with an operation in the Bahamas. Beattey was flown to Florida for treatment of his injuries, but he died by the time the plane landed in Florida. Beattey's parents sued College Centre in a state court in Florida. The accident was the fault of the College Centre driver, so his employer, College Centre, was liable. College Centre argued that the law of the Bahamas should be applied, in which case its liability would be quite limited. The trial court held that Bahamian law would apply. The Beatteys appealed, arguing that New York law should apply because the defendant was a company based in New York. Which law seems most likely to apply? [*Beattey v. College Centre of Finger Lakes*, 613 So.2d 52 Ct. App., Fla. (1992)]

✓ **Check your answer at http://academic.cengage.com/blaw/meiners**

7. Koh, a California resident, won a judgment in California of $240,000 against Inno-Pacific, a Singapore company, but Inno-Pacific did not pay the judgment. Koh discovered that the company had an interest in land in Washington State, so he filed suit in Washington to seize the property to satisfy his judgment. The trial court in Washington dismissed the suit, because it lacked personal jurisdiction over Inno-Pacific. Koh appealed. On what basis could the Washington court have jurisdiction? [*Koh v. Inno-Pacific Holdings, Ltd.*, 54 P.3d 1270 Ct. App., Wash. (2002)]

8. Colemill, a South Carolina company, bought an airplane from Southeastern Flight Services, a Georgia company. The deal included a maintenance package that required Southeastern to keep the plane in top operating condition. Shortly after the purchase, the plane crashed, killing all on board. There was evidence that the aircraft had been defectively manufactured and improperly maintained. The plane was manufactured in Michigan and maintained in Georgia; the crash occurred in South Carolina. In a wrongful death action brought in Georgia, which state's law will apply? [*Risdon Enterprises, Inc. v. Colemill Enterprises*, 324 S.E.2d 738 Ct. App., Ga. (1984)]

9. Ruth Creech, an Ohio resident, filed an action for malpractice against the City of Faith Hospital of Tulsa, Oklahoma. The claims arose out of injuries suffered while Creech was a patient at the hospital in Tulsa. Creech had heard of it through the *Expect a Miracle* television program featuring Oral Roberts. Broadcast nationally, the program invited people to come to the hospital for treatment. The case was tried in federal court in Ohio. The court found for Creech. The hospital appealed on the ground that the federal court could not exercise jurisdiction over them under the Ohio long-arm statute. They contended that they did not have sufficient minimum contacts with Ohio to confer jurisdiction. Do you think the court's exercise of jurisdiction reasonable? [*Creech v. Roberts*, 908 F.2d 75 6th Cir. (1990)]

Ethics Question

1. Should judges consider the social consequences of their decisions? What if the case involves an individual who has committed a hideous crime, and the judge is being asked to release the individual on a "technicality"?

Internet Assignment

http://www.uscourts.gov/allinks.html
http://www.findlaw.com/casecode/index.html#federal
http://www.law.emory.edu/FEDCTS/
http://pacer.psc.uscourts.gov/

The Internet can be an important source of federal court opinions. Since 1995, many federal circuit courts have released their opinions via the Internet. PACER allows low-cost access to court opinions and docket information from federal district and bankruptcy courts.

Search the first three Web sites, and explain in one or two sentences which site you prefer for finding federal court opinions. Are the opinions of the district court closest to your home available via the Internet? If so, when did the service start? Does your circuit court allow keyword searching? Why might PACER, despite its $.08 per page charge, be useful?

Trials and Resolving Disputes

Chapter 3

When Barbara Fong's software company, Gnof, was sued by unhappy stockholders who lost money when stock prices dropped, it is possible that the case was settled out of court. As in other areas of litigation, suits brought by shareholders are often settled or dropped before trial. Of all civil cases filed in court, about 90 percent are resolved before a judgment is entered at trial.

Why resolve a suit out of court? Experienced lawyers can make pretty good estimates of the outcome of most cases that go to trial, so they can recommend resolution that heads off costly litigation. Cases that are litigated consume more hours of attorneys' time, and time of company personnel are more likely to need expert witnesses. Fong would rather concentrate on her business than spend days preparing for a deposition and, later, for possible testimony at trial.

Trials involving businesses can be costly and uncertain. Some involve complex facts that require extensive evidence, including mountains of business records. Trials often require testimony by managers and high-priced experts, and there is good evidence that juries tend to be less sympathetic to businesses than to individuals.

Over time, due to the expense, time, and uncertainty of litigation, *alternative dispute resolution (ADR)* has become ever more common. Courts and Congress encourage the use of arbitration, mediation, and negotiation to settle disputes, and parties often find these preferable to litigation. In this chapter we will first discuss litigation and then the alternatives. ■

Getty Images

Basic Trial Procedures

A distinctive element of our judicial system is that it is an *adversary system of justice.* It requires the parties to represent themselves and to argue their positions before a court. The responsibility for bringing a lawsuit, shaping its issues, and presenting evidence rests upon the parties to the dispute.

Courts play a small role in establishing the facts of a case. Unlike in many countries that use a system of inquiry run by judges, judges in the United States do not investigate the parties or the facts of a case. Instead, the court applies legal rules to the facts that the parties establish. This section discusses the major procedural rules governing the civil litigation process.

Pleadings Stage

As we discussed in the last chapter, to begin a lawsuit, the plaintiff must determine which court has subject-matter jurisdiction and jurisdiction over the parties to the dispute. The plaintiff gives notice to the defendant by *service of process*, including a *summons*, an example of which is in Exhibit 2.4.

Along with the summons, the plaintiff serves the defendant with the first of the *pleadings*, commonly called the *complaint*. Pleadings are the formal statements made to the court by the parties to a case that list their claims and defenses. The complaint is a statement that sets forth the plaintiff's claim against the defendant. As illustrated in Exhibit 3.1, the complaint contains statements:

- alleging the essential facts necessary for the court to take jurisdiction.
- of the facts necessary to claim that the plaintiff is entitled to a remedy.
- of the remedy the plaintiff is seeking.

Exhibit 3.1 is quoted from a complaint filed in federal court in New York. Billionaire casino owner Steve Wynn owns a lot of highly valued artwork, including a painting by Pablo Picasso, which he bought for $48.4 million in 1997. He claimed to have a contract to sell it for $139 million, one of the highest prices ever received, when he managed to poke a hole in the painting. The painting was repaired, but the deal was called off, because the value decreased due to the damage. Wynn claimed the value fell by $54 million, and that it should be covered by his insurance policy issued by Lloyd's of London; but they were not keen to pay. As you see, the complaint lays out the bare facts, legal issues, and remedy sought. We will return to this complaint in several future chapters, as it relates to several areas of law.

Responses to the Complaint

Following the service of the plaintiff's complaint, the defendant must file an answer. If the defendant does not respond, the court will presume the claims of the plaintiff are true and grant the plaintiff's requests. Depending on the circumstances, the defendant may file 1) a motion to dismiss, 2) an answer with or without an affirmative defense, or 3) a counterclaim.

Motion to Dismiss

A *motion to dismiss* by the defendant asks the court to dismiss the case because it does not have jurisdiction over either the subject matter of the dispute or the defendant's person. The defendant may also file a *motion to dismiss for failure to state a claim* or a *demurrer* (some states do not use the term *demurrer*; they use only the term *motion to dismiss*). This is an assertion that even if the facts asserted are true, the injury claimed by the plaintiff is one for which the law furnishes no remedy.

Exhibit 3.1   Excerpt from Actual Complaint

United States District Court Southern District of New York

07 CV 202

Stephen and Elaine Wynn
Plaintiffs
—against—   Complaint
Lloyd's, London and Certain Underwriters at
Lloyd's, London
Defendants

Plaintiffs, by and through its attorneys Buchanan Ingersoll & Rooney PC, by way of its complaint and against the Defendants, alleges as follows:

The Parties

1. Plaintiffs, Stephen and Elaine Wynn ("Wynn" or "Plaintiffs") are individuals who are citizens of the State of Nevada.

2. Defendant, Lloyd's, London ("Lloyds") is an underwriting company with a principal place of business located at 1 Lime Street, London EC3M 7HA, United Kingdom.

3. ... Certain Underwriters at Lloyd's, London ("Certain Underwriters," and together with Lloyds, the "Defendants")....

Jurisdiction and Venue

5. This Court has jurisdiction over this action pursuant to 28 U.S.C. § 1332(a)(1), in that the matter in controversy exceeds the sum of $75,000, exclusive of interest and costs, and is between citizens of the State of Nevada and citizens or subjects of a foreign country.

6. Venue in this District is proper under 28 U.S.C. § 1391(a)(2), since a part of the events giving rise to the claim occurred in this judicial district, and a part of the policy proceeds that are the subject of the action relates to the restoration of the damaged painting situated in this judicial district, and defendants.

7. Venue is further appropriate in this district under 28 U.S.C. paragraph 1391(a)(1), as the Defendants reside and/or conduct business in this district.

Statement of Facts

8. At all relevant times mentioned herein, Plaintiffs are individuals involved in, among other things, the buying, selling and collecting of artwork.

9. At all relevant times mentioned herein, Defendants were and are engaged in the business of underwriting specialized insurance coverage, including but not limited to, providing insurance coverage on artwork.

10. On or about June 8, 2006, Plaintiffs and Defendants entered into an insurance policy ... for all risks of physical loss or damage for the coverage of fine arts....

18. On or about September 30, 2006, while demonstrating the painting to colleagues and friends, plaintiff and insured, Stephen Wynn, unintentionally placed a tear in a Picasso painting titled "Le Reve" owned by the Plaintiffs.... The painting is admittedly covered under the Agreement.... [Lloyd's was notified; the painting went to New York for inspection, repair and appraisal.]

25. By letter dated November 3, 2006, Plaintiffs notified the Defendants that the post-restoration market value will be approximately $85 million dollars....

30. ... Defendants have not submitted the appraisers' reports and continue to wrongfully withhold from Plaintiffs such reports.

31. Plaintiffs are therefore entitled to receive Defendants' appraisal reports, which will reveal the Defendants' appraised depreciated value of the restored painting....

Count I Declaratory Judgment

36. The Plaintiffs therefore, respectfully request that this Court issue a declaratory ruling directing Defendants to provide the Plaintiffs with an appraisal report or initial damages assessment so the appraisal process set forth in the Policy can timely take place....

Count II Breach of Covenant of Good Faith and Fair Dealing

39. The Defendants breached their implied covenant of good faith and fair dealing by reasons, among other things, intentionally, knowingly, willfully, unreasonably, recklessly, arbitrarily, frivolously and/or maliciously:

   a. Failing to render a sincere and substantial performance of their obligations under the Agreement;

   b. Arbitrarily, recklessly and frivolously refusing to provide either an appraisal report or a post restoration value on the restored painting....

40. By virtue of the foregoing, Plaintiffs have suffered loss and damage. Wherefore, Plaintiffs respectfully request that this Court enter an Order:
   a. Directing Defendants to provide a copy of their appraisal reports to the Plaintiffs;
   b. Directing Defendants to provide the Plaintiffs with a post restoration value of the Painting in furtherance of settlement;
   c. Awarding Plaintiffs all consequential losses resulting from the Defendants' breach of the covenant of good faith and fair dealing;
   d. Granting Plaintiff's attorneys' fees and costs; and
   e. Granting Plaintiffs such other and further relief as the Court deems just and proper.

Dated: New York, New York
    January 10, 2007

Buchanan Ingersoll P
Barry I. Slotnick, Esq, (BS-1398)
Attorney for Plaintiffs
One Chase Manhattan Plaza, 35th Floor
New York, New York 10005

Answer

If the defendant's motion to dismiss is denied or if the defendant does not make such a motion, the defendant must file an *answer* with the court. In this pleading, the defendant denies the allegations made by the plaintiff; otherwise a judgment is entered for the plaintiff.

In answering a complaint, the defendant may admit to the plaintiff's allegations but may assert additional facts that should result in the action being dismissed. Called an *affirmative defense*, the defendant admits to the facts claimed by the plaintiff but offers additional facts he asserts constitute a defense—a legal excuse—to the plaintiff's complaint. The defendant could admit to being in a car accident involving the plaintiff but could assert that the claim is now barred by the statute of limitations; that is, the plaintiff waited too long to file suit. Other examples of affirmative defenses include self-defense, assumption of risk, contributory negligence, and other defenses we will study later.

Counterclaim

Besides denying the plaintiff's allegations in an answer, the defendant can assert a claim against the plaintiff. The defendant's claim is a *counterclaim* and may be based on the same events that the plaintiff bases the complaint on. The counterclaim is a complaint by the defendant, and the plaintiff must respond to it just as the defendant responded to the original complaint.

Reply

Any new matters raised by the defendant's answer are automatically taken as denied by the plaintiff. When the defendant files a counterclaim, the plaintiff may answer with a *reply*, which is an answer to the counterclaim. We see these steps outlined in Exhibit 3.2.

Discovery Stage: Obtaining Information before Trial

After the pleadings, litigation enters the discovery stage. The parties use various legal tools to obtain evidence about the dispute. The attorneys are interested in gathering information from the opposing parties and their witnesses and experts. The process of obtaining information is known as *discovery*. The Federal Rules of

Exhibit 3.2
Stages of a Typical Civil
Lawsuit

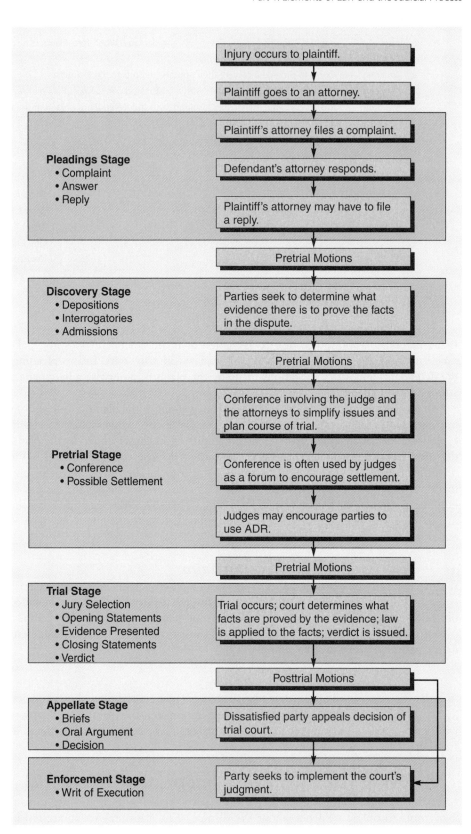

Civil Procedure and the corresponding state procedural rules set down the guidelines for the discovery process.

Purpose of Discovery

Discovery serves several functions. Years ago, disputes moved from the pleadings directly to the trial stage. As a result parties had little information about the specific evidence the other party was going to use. The evidence presented could catch the opposing party by surprise—a "trial by ambush." The discovery process now prevents surprises by giving the parties access to each others' information.

Discovery also preserves evidence of witnesses who might not be available at the time of the trial, as well as the testimony of witnesses whose memory may fade over time. Finally, by allowing both parties the opportunity to learn what evidence would be available at trial, discovery encourages pretrial settlements. Parties can assess the strengths of both sides and estimate what a reasonable settlement would be. Most cases are settled, but if the case goes to trial, discovery narrows the issues so the trial can focus on the important questions in the case. Notice in Exhibit 3.1 how there is a laundry list of claims. If the case goes to trial, it will be narrowed down to specifics.

Tools of the Discovery Process

The discovery rules offer several ways to get information from an opposing party: depositions, written interrogatories, orders for production of documents, requests for admissions, and orders for a mental or physical examination. According to the Federal Rules of Civil Procedure, a party seeking information must select a discovery tool that is not "unduly burdensome" to the other party. In practice, parties can force out nearly any information related to the legal issues. The opposing party cannot refuse to comply just because compliance is time consuming or costly.

Depositions and Interrogatories A principal discovery tool is the *deposition*—the sworn, in-person testimony of a witness recorded by a court reporter. The person whose deposition is taken, perhaps an eyewitness to an accident or an expert witness expected to provide testimony at trial, may be questioned by attorneys from both sides.

LIGHTER SIDE OF THE LAW

The Legal Magic of Spell Check

California attorney Arthur Dudley prepared a brief for an appeals court case. The term *sua sponte*, which means "on its own motion," appeared five times. When he ran spell check, it replaced *sua sponte* with "sea sponge." He did not notice, but the judges did.

One line in the brief now read: "It is well settled that a trial court must instruct sea sponge on any defense." Other lawyers told him he invented a new defense: the sea sponge duty to instruct.

Source: *www.law.com*

Getty Images

The deposition is useful to find information relevant to the dispute, including leads to other witnesses or documents. It may be used at trial to impeach, or challenge, a witness who attempts to change his story at the trial. The deposition of a witness who is unavailable at the time of the trial may be allowed in place of live testimony.

Written *interrogatories* are questions submitted by a party to a case to the other party, or a witness, or another person with relevant information. The party receiving the interrogatories prepares written answers, usually with the aid of an attorney, and signs them under oath. Although the interrogatories lack the face-to-face spontaneity of a deposition, they can require the party to provide information from her records and files—the kind of information not carried in one's head.

Expert Witnesses Many trials involving businesses use expert witnesses to help establish facts critical to a case, such as the value of lost profits, the costs to a victim of an accident, or the scientific evidence of harm from a product. These witnesses usually have their deposition taken before trial so that the other side knows the essence of their testimony and can prepare questions for trial.

There have been abuses by experts who want to please their clients and overstate the case by inflating damages or asserting harm to exist based on reasoning contrary to general scientific opinion. The Supreme Court has instructed courts to exclude evidence that is not reliable and is contrary to scientific standards. The Court has held that when expert testimony is critical to a case but is rejected because it is not scientifically sound, then it is proper to grant summary judgment to the defendant and not allow another trial on the matter. The Court does not want to encourage parties to use hired guns who provide evidence that is not credible.

We see an example of faulty expert testimony in the *Cooper Tire* case.

Cooper Tire & Rubber v. Mendez
Supreme Court of Texas
204 S.W. 3d 797 (2006)

Case Background *Mendez was driving a minivan with six passengers when a rear tire made by Cooper Tire lost its tread. Mendez lost control and rolled the minivan. Four passengers were killed. Mendez and two others survived. Examination of the tire showed that a nail had punctured it. The survivors sued Cooper for product defect. A jury awarded over $11 million in damages; the appeals court affirmed. Cooper appealed.*

Case Decision Willett, Justice

* * *

To establish proof of a manufacturing defect that caused the tread separation, plaintiffs relied on the expert testimony of Richard Grogan.... The theory presented ... was that the tire failed because the "skim stock" was contaminated with hydrocarbon wax at the plant where it was manufactured, causing the belts to separate. "Skim stock is a specially formulated rubber compound that coats the steel belts in a steel-belted radial tire and through vulcanization holds them together." Cooper Tire complains that the testimony ... was inadmissible....

Expert testimony is admissible if (1) the expert is qualified, and (2) the testimony is relevant and based on a reliable foundation....

Richard Grogan conceded that he is not a chemist, an engineer, or a tire designer. He obtained an ordinary national certificate, the British equivalent of a high school diploma, and holds no post-secondary degrees. He does not consider himself an expert in accident reconstruction. He worked for many years for the Dunlop Tire Company in England, in its technical department, tire examination lab, and technical service section, where he examined tires including tires that had failed. He left Dunlop in 1980. He has taught courses ... on tire failures. In 1987 he published a book entitled *An Investigator's Guide to Tire Failures*. This book was revised and expanded in 1999. He has also written many articles on tire failures.

Grogan opined that the tire separated because the skim stock was contaminated.... He testified that the tread separation did not originate at the nail hole, because he detected "polishing" in other portions of the tire's layers, indicating that the separation started elsewhere. He described his observation of polishing at one point in his testimony as seeing "how the rubber has been removed from the cords and then left quite bright and clean.". . . Grogan also offered reasons that the tire did not fail due to the nail, excessive vehicle weight, under-inflation, or ordinary wear.

Assuming that Grogan was generally qualified to testify on the subject of tire failures, he presented a theory of wax contamination that was unreliable and should not have been admitted.

The only publication Grogan could cite as supporting his theory was his own book's support for the proposition that liner marks are indicative of poor adhesion. . . .

The record is devoid of proof that Grogan's theory has achieved such general acceptance. There is no evidence of a general acceptance in the scientific community that wax contamination is a cause of tire belt or tread separations, or that liner marks and polishing are accepted as proof of such a theory. . . .

[Chemical engineer] Herzlich and two other Cooper Tire experts, Jerry Leyden, a chemist and former tire compounder, and Jean Hoffman, the chief chemist at the plant where the tire was manufactured, testified that wax migration is a normal, expected, and well-understood phenomenon, that it occurs during the manufacture and throughout the life of the tire, and that wax migration was not indicative of a defect. . . .

Grogan offered no theory as to how the tire could be used for 30,000 miles, and suffer a nail puncture at some point, without failing if wax was improperly deposited on the skim stock during the manufacturing process and the tire was defective when it left Cooper Tire's plant. . . .

* * *

In summary, Grogan presented a novel theory of a manufacturing defect that did not . . . meet the reliability standard we have established for the admission of expert testimony. Failure to meet this standard means that his testimony was legally no evidence of a manufacturing defect or a defect that caused the tire failure. . . .

In these circumstances we hold that plaintiffs' attempts to eliminate other possible causes for the tire failure were legally insufficient to establish a manufacturing defect.

We reverse the judgment of the court of appeals, and render judgment in favor of Cooper Tire.

Questions for Analysis

1. The Texas high court held that the expert testimony relied upon by the plaintiffs to establish their case was not reliable. Why did the court not order a new trial?

2. The jury believed the expert testimony presented for plaintiffs. Why did their judgment not stand?

Generally, the party requesting the order specifies the exact type of mental or physical examination desired and the time, the place, and the specialists who are to conduct it.

Sanctions for Failing to Respond to a Discovery Request Under the rules of civil procedure, judges have broad powers to impose sanctions against a party who fails to comply with discovery requirements. If a party fails to comply with the requirements, of, say, a deposition, the requesting party can make a motion to the judge to force compliance. If the party does not comply with a court order, the court may order a *default judgment* granting victory to the other party or find the noncomplying party in *contempt of court* and order the party to jail or impose a fine. For example, one federal judge fined Wal-Mart $18 million for having "a corporate policy" of frustrating discovery and withholding evidence in numerous cases.

Orders for the Production of Documents An order for the production of documents allows a party access to information in the possession of the other party. The kinds of information that are often sought are medical bills, business records, letters, and repair bills. The party seeking the information usually has the right to inspect, examine, and reproduce. Businesses have an obligation to maintain company records in a coherent manner, so they may be accessed in case of a lawsuit.

Failure to do so may result in sanctions by the court and even a judgment for the opposing party. If a trade secret or other confidential information is involved, a company can get a *protective order* to ensure confidentiality. The court may impose severe sanctions, or penalties, on a party found to have violated a protective order.

Requests for Admissions Either party can serve the other with a written request for an admission of the truth in matters relating to the dispute. Requests are used to settle facts about which there are no real disputes. That eliminates the need to establish such matters at trial. For example, in a contract dispute over the price of a product, one party may ask the other to admit that deliveries were made according to the terms of the contract. If admitted, these facts need not be proven at trial.

Mental and Physical Examinations When the physical or mental condition of a party is an issue, the court may be asked to order that party to submit to an examination. Because of concerns for privacy, the party requesting the order must show a greater need for the information than in requests for other forms of discovery.

Discovery: Impacts on Business

Discovery can impose significant costs on businesses. Firms can be forced to endure the expense and the disruption, while managers answer questions and produce documents. In one regulatory dispute between Ford Motor and the Federal Trade Commission, it cost Ford $4 million just to copy required documents. The burdens are heavy when executives have to take time to prepare for and provide a deposition. In disputes involving technical matters or significant detail, a deposition may take two weeks or more.

It is not uncommon for the chief executive of a corporation to get a subpoena requesting that he appear for a deposition. In most cases, the information sought is in the hands of subordinates. Courts protect executives if the purpose of a deposition is to harass them, but their participation is not uncommon. This disruption of business is one more reason out-of-court settlement is likely.

Summary Judgment

At the close of discovery, either party may move for a *summary judgment*. The Federal Rules of Civil Procedure state, in Rule 56(c), that summary judgment "shall be rendered . . . if the pleadings, depositions, answers to interrogatories, and admissions on file, together with affidavits, if any, show that there is no genuine issue as to any material fact and that the moving party is entitled to judgment as a matter of law." That is, a party asks the judge to apply the law to the facts and resolve the dispute. If the motion is granted, the case is over or the judgment may apply to only some issues, which are eliminated, and the trial proceeds on the remaining issues. For example, in the Cooper Tire case, the trial court should have granted summary judgment in favor of the defendant due to a lack of credible evidence by the plaintiffs.

Pretrial Stage

Either party or the court may request a *pretrial conference*. These commonly held conferences normally involve the attorneys and the judge. The conferences often simplify the issues and plan the course of the trial. To ensure more efficient trials, judges may get the parties to drop certain parts of the case and focus on the key issues. Also at pretrial conferences, judges often encourage the parties to reach an out-of-court settlement.

Trial Stage

After discovery is complete, if there has been no dismissal, summary judgment, or settlement, the dispute is set for *trial*. In many court systems, the trial calendar is quite long. Delays of two or three years before a noncriminal case comes to trial are not uncommon.

The Jury

The Sixth and Seventh Amendments to the U.S. Constitution, as well as state constitutions, provide for the right to a *jury* in certain cases. In criminal cases, there is a right to a jury trial. In the federal court system, this right is guaranteed if the amount in controversy exceeds $20 and is a common-law claim. Most state court systems have similar guarantees, although the minimum amount in controversy may be higher. There is no right to a jury trial when a private plaintiff requests an equitable remedy, rather than money damages, or in civil cases in which the government seeks non-criminal penalties for violating federal law.

Decision to Use a Jury The right to a jury trial does not have to be exercised. If a jury is not requested, the judge determines the true facts in the dispute and applies the law to resolve it. The judge's temperament, the complexity of the evidence, and the degree to which the emotions of the jury are likely to affect the judgment affect decisions to request a jury trial.

Selection of the Jury Jury selection begins when the clerk of the court sends a notice instructing citizens to appear for jury duty. The people called are in a jury pool.

LIGHTER SIDE OF THE LAW
The Dog Ate My Summons

Trying to avoid jury duty is common. The Harris County (Houston, Texas) District Court clerk compiled the following list of excuses offered by jury duty dodgers:

"I have to feed my bird during the day."

"I take care of three cats during the day."

"I have to pee—a lot."

"I shot holes in my daughter's boyfriend's car."

"My wife killed someone."

"I had something removed from my head this morning."

Source: *National Law Journal*

Getty Images

The process used to select jury members is called *voir dire*. Depending upon the court, either the judge or the attorneys conduct voir dire. The purpose is to determine whether a prospective juror is likely to be so biased that he or she could not reach a fair decision based on the evidence presented. Attorneys are allowed a limited number of challenges that permit them to reject prospective jurors without stating a reason why. Juries traditionally involve a panel of 12 persons, but in many states, panels of fewer than 12—frequently six—are used.

The Trial

Although judges have some freedom to change the structure of a trial, most follow the general order summarized in Exhibit 3.3. Jury and nonjury trials are handled in much the same way, but they have a number of procedural differences. In nonjury trials, the judge may put more limits on the attorneys' opening statements and closing arguments. The following discussion details the steps involved in a typical jury trial.

Exhibit 3.3
Summaries of Typical Jury
and Nonjury Trials

Jury Trial	Nonjury Trial
1. The selection of a jury	1. Plaintiff's opening statement
2. Plaintiff's opening statement	2. Defendant's opening statement
3. Defendant's opening statement	3. Plaintiff's presentation of direct evidence
4. Plaintiff's presentation of direct evidence	4. Defendant's presentation of direct evidence
5. Defendant's presentation of direct evidence	5. Plaintiff's presentation of rebuttal evidence
6. Plaintiff's presentation of rebuttal evidence	6. Defendant's presentation of rebuttal evidence
7. Defendant's presentation of rebuttal evidence	7. Defendant's final argument
8. Opening final argument by the plaintiff	8. Plaintiff's closing argument
9. Defendant's final argument	9. Judge's deliberation and verdict
10. Plaintiff's closing argument	
11. Instruction to the jury	
12. Jury deliberation and verdict	

Opening Statements After the jurors have been sworn in, both attorneys make *opening statements*. The attorneys tell the jury what the crucial facts are and how they will prove that those facts support their position. Opening statements are often limited to 20 minutes. The plaintiff's attorney normally presents the first statement.

Presentation of Direct Testimony Following the opening statement, the plaintiff's attorney calls witnesses. The plaintiff has the burden of proving that his claims are correct. Each witness is first questioned by the plaintiff's attorney on *direct examination*. The defendant's attorney then examines that witness on *cross examination*. Cross examination may be followed by *redirect examination* by the plaintiff's attorney and then by *re-cross examination* by the defendant's attorney. The judge controls the length and the course of these examinations.

Closing Arguments Before the case goes to the jury, the attorneys each present a *closing argument*. They summarize the evidence for the jury in a manner most favorable to their case. As in the opening statement, the judge limits the amount of time available to the attorneys for their closing arguments.

Instructions to the Jury Before the jury retires to deliberate and reach a verdict, the judge gives the jury *instructions*, or *charges*. In the instructions, the judge tells the jury the applicable law, summarizes the facts and issues of the dispute, and states which of the parties has the *burden of persuasion*. After the instructions, the jurors are placed in the custody of the *bailiff* or other court official, who will see that they remain together and that there is no misconduct.

Reaching a Verdict The jury deliberates to reach an agreement and find for the plaintiff or the defendant. In a civil trial, the parties must prove their contentions to the jury by a *preponderance of the evidence*. If jurors are unable to reach a unanimous decision, the jury is said to be *hung*, and a new trial before a different jury may be necessary. The jury is discharged and a *mistrial* declared.

Because of the cost and delay associated with a new trial, judges are reluctant to allow hung juries. Although many jurisdictions require a unanimous jury decision, some states allow verdicts in civil disputes to be less than unanimous, such as 10 of 12 jurors.

After the jury has reached a verdict, the verdict is read in court by the foreman of the jury or by the judge or the clerk of the court. The judgment is then entered. In some cases, the jury deliberates a second time to determine damages to be awarded if they find for the plaintiff.

LIGHTER SIDE OF THE LAW

You Got Me There, Counselor!

The editor of the Massachusetts Bar Association's Lawyers Journal has a collection of courtroom bloopers by lawyers when questioning parties at trial. Among them:

"Were you present when your picture was taken?"

"Are you qualified to give a urine sample?"

"Did he kill you?"

"Were you alone or by yourself?"

"How many times have you committed suicide?"

Source: *Wall Street Journal*

Getty Images

Motions for a Verdict

The parties may ask the judge to issue a favorable verdict that makes jury deliberation unnecessary. Most common is a *motion for a directed verdict* or *a motion for judgment as a matter of law*. These are the same thing; different jurisdictions use different terms. After the cases have been presented, but before the case goes to the jury, a party may request that the court enter a judgment in its favor, because there is not legally sufficient evidence on which a jury could find for the other party. The defense is more likely to prevail on such a motion. That is, the judge holds that the plaintiff failed to provide sufficient grounds, even if what is claimed is true, to be able to win a verdict.

Similarly, after a jury returns a verdict, the losing party may make a *motion for judgment as a matter of law* or a *motion for judgment notwithstanding the verdict*. The judge is asked to hold that there were not legally sufficient grounds to support the jury's verdict and to either overturn the entire verdict or a portion of it.

Remedies in Civil Litigation

A plaintiff brings a civil suit seeking a remedy from the court. A *remedy* is the way a right is enforced or how a violation of a right is compensated or prevented. The remedies awarded by courts in civil disputes are classified as either *equitable remedies* or *monetary damages*. Most cases are for monetary damages, but in some cases a remedy in equity is more appropriate. Exhibit 3.4 summarizes the remedies available in civil litigation.

Monetary Damages

If a court finds that a party has suffered a legally recognized harm, monetary damages may be awarded. The general categories of monetary damage awards are *compensatory*, *punitive*, and *nominal*.

Compensatory Damages Compensatory damages are intended to give injured parties enough money to restore them to the economic position they were in before the injury, or to cover the costs incurred because of the injury. These are the most common monetary damages. Compensatory damages may be awarded for loss of time and money, pain and suffering, injury to reputation, and mental anguish.

Exhibit 3.4 Equitable Remedies and Monetary Damages

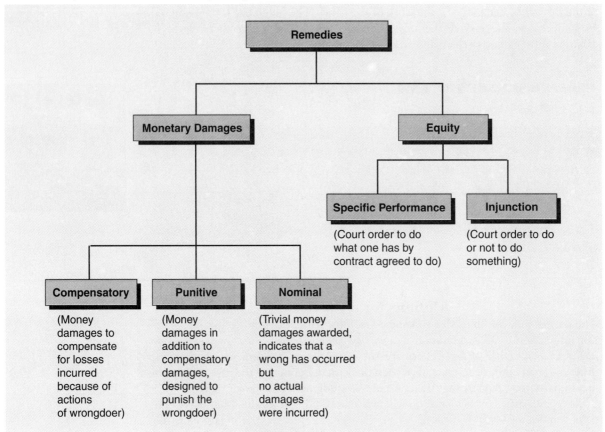

Suppose Beyoncé contracts to appear in a movie for $500,000. If Beyoncé refuses to appear, and Paramount must pay Mary J. Blige $800,000 to appear instead, Paramount may be entitled to $300,000 in compensatory damages from Beyoncé. In Chapter 10 on contracts, we will review more issues involved in compensatory damages.

Punitive Damages When the wrongdoer's actions are particularly reprehensible, or when the defendant's conduct is willful or malicious, the court may award the injured party *punitive* or *exemplary damages* in addition to compensatory damages. These may be awarded in some tort cases, as we will see in Chapters 7 and 8. Punitive damages are to punish the wrongdoer and discourage others from similar conduct.

An Atlanta jury awarded $4.24 million in compensatory damages to a family whose teenage son was killed when his General Motors pickup truck erupted in flames after being broadsided by a drunk driver. The jury also "sent a message to General Motors" to fix the gasoline tanks it determined were the cause of the death— in the form of an additional $100 million in punitive damages. As we will see in Chapter 4, the Supreme Court has reviewed some of the constitutional issues related to punitive damages.

Nominal Damages If a plaintiff suffers a legal wrong but has not suffered actual damages to person or property, or if the damages are considered trivial by the court, the court may award *nominal damages.* The plaintiff may recover as little as one dollar.

Equitable Remedies

The courts recognize that there are times when monetary damages are not practical or effective. Money may not be relevant, or the defendant may not be solvent yet could do certain things to help rectify a wrong. Using the broad powers of equity that courts have, they have developed *remedies in equity* that can be imposed when remedies at law, such as monetary damages, are inadequate.

Specific Performance In equity, courts can order *specific performance* as a remedy and require the offending party to do what had been promised. This remedy may apply in contract cases, when monetary damages would not be adequate or the subject matter is unique. If the owner of a unique piece of land has a contract to sell the land and then changes her mind, a court may order her to perform as promised and transfer title to the land to the buyer for the promised payment. Specific performance is more likely when the subject matter is land or rare properties, such as art, antiques, or even baseball cards, because such items may be unique and irreplaceable, or because the other party may have incurred substantial expense in expectation of the deal.

Courts rarely order someone to perform personal services. Suppose Beyoncé agreed to appear in a Paramount movie, but then refused. A court would not order Beyoncé to appear, because courts do not want to become involved in supervising services, such as making sure that Beyoncé acts well and to Paramount's satisfaction. Courts also do not want to force people into involuntary servitude, doing work they do not want to do. Monetary damages are more appropriate.

LIGHTER SIDE OF THE LAW

Why Alabama Courts Are Ranked Forty-Eighth in the Nation

The state of Alabama sued ExxonMobil, claiming the company underpaid the state for natural gas royalties. An Alabama jury held that Exxon owed the state $64 million in royalties and then tacked on $12 billion in punitive damages. One juror said he voted for that amount because the state needed the money. The U.S. Chamber of Commerce ranks Alabama, West Virginia, and Mississippi courts as the worst in the nation.

Source: *San Francisco Chronicle*

Getty Images

Injunction An injunction is a court order directing a person to do something, to not do something being planned, or to stop doing something. Injunctions can be temporary or permanent. In a *temporary injunction*, the court imposes conditions on the activities of the alleged wrongdoer until the rights of the parties have been determined or the wrongdoer makes changes in the activity to make them acceptable. In a *permanent injunction*, the rights of the parties have been determined, and the court found that the activities damage the rights of the injured party and that they cannot be modified to satisfy the court.

Suppose Obama decides to store chemical wastes on his farm. His neighbor may ask the court for a temporary injunction stopping Obama from doing that until the harmful effects on the neighborhood can be determined.

Temporary injunctions are much more common than permanent injunctions. A temporary injunction halts a possibly bad practice, giving the court time to hear arguments about the matter. A permanent injunction is only to be granted, the Supreme Court has explained, when the plaintiff shows that 1) it has suffered irreparable injury; 2) remedies at law, such as monetary damages, are inadequate to compensate for the injury; 3) considering the balance of hardships between the parties, the remedy in equity is warranted; and 4) the public interest would not be injured by use of a permanent injunction.

Appellate Stage

The decision in a case may be appealed if one of the parties believes an *error of law* was made during the trial. The parties cannot appeal the factual determinations made at the trial. However, bases for appeal include failure by the trial judge to admit or exclude certain evidence, improper instructions being given to the jury, and the granting or denying of motions to dismiss the case. Appellate courts ensure that the trial court judge correctly applied the law.

Arguments before Appeals Courts

The parties present their arguments to the appellate court through *written briefs* and *oral arguments*, which discuss the law, not the facts in the case. Usually, three judges hear an appeal. The appellate court has authority to review any ruling of law by the trial judge. It has the power to *affirm*, *reverse*, or *modify* the judgment of the trial court. The decision of the appellate court is the one that receives the majority vote of the judges.

LIGHTER SIDE OF THE LAW

Shortest Decision by an Appeals Court?

In *Denny* v. *Radar Industries*, the Michigan Court of Appeals disposed of the appeal with this published opinion:

"The appellant has attempted to distinguish the factual situation in this case from that in [an earlier case]. He didn't. We couldn't." Affirmed.

Source: *184 N.W.2d 289 (1970)*

Getty Images

Decisions by Appeals Courts

An appellate court's majority decision is referred to as the court's written or *majority opinion*. This opinion gives the legal rationale for the court's decision. It also provides guidance to judges and attorneys for the resolution of similar disputes. A court may also issue a *concurring opinion*, one written by a judge who agrees with the majority decision but for a different reason, or a *dissenting opinion*, written by a judge who disagrees with the decision of the majority. While concurring and dissenting opinions may influence future thinking about the dispute, the majority decision decides the case and has the force of law.

When the appeals court's majority opinion agrees with the trial court's decision, the court has *affirmed* that decision. When the majority opinion disagrees with the trial court, the appellate court's decision *reverses* the trial court's decision. The appellate court may also affirm the decision but *modify* it in some way—for example, by reducing the damages awarded by the trial court. In such situations, the appeals court is likely to *remand* the case—return the case—to the trial court for retrial. The trial court must then retry the case, in part or in whole, taking into account the appellate court's ruling.

Enforcement Stage

After a trial, if no appeal is taken or if no further appeal is available, the *judgment*, or decision, of the court becomes final. The same dispute cannot be considered again in that or any other forum. It is *res judicata*—a thing decided by judgment.

The judgment may be a monetary award to the plaintiff, a declaration of the rights between the parties, or an order prohibiting some activity. When the defendant wins, the judgment generally does not involve an award of money. It states that the defendant is not responsible for the plaintiff's injuries. In some instances, the court may require that the losing party pay the other party's legal expenses, but usually each side is responsible for their own costs.

Enforcing Judgments

When the plaintiff recovers a damage award and the defendant does not pay, the plaintiff can seek a *writ of execution*. The writ is a court order to an official, such as the sheriff, to seize the property of the defendant to satisfy the judgment. Courts may order *garnishment* of a debtor's property, which usually involves an order for a certain amount of the debtor's paycheck to be paid on a regular basis to the judgment winner.

Although obtaining a writ of execution to enforce a judgment may be easy, it is often difficult to collect a judgment. If a party does not have valuable property to seize, or if the losing party flees the jurisdiction taking his property with him, or hides property out of the country, it may be nearly impossible for the plaintiff to collect a judgment. In other cases, the losing party, by stalling or otherwise failing to comply with the writ of execution, makes it difficult and costly for the plaintiff to collect. This is one of the many complexities of the litigation process that cause parties to use alternative forms of dispute resolution.

Arbitration

If you have a checking account or a credit card, most likely you have agreed to an arbitration agreement, even though you may not have read the details of the

---

Getty Images

INTERNATIONAL PERSPECTIVE

German Trial Procedure

The rules governing trial procedures can vary substantially from country to country. In Germany, trials are conducted much differently from trials in the United States. Perhaps most striking to U.S. observers is the fact that judges in Germany play a much more active role in the trial process than do American judges. In Germany, civil procedure is governed by rules called the Zivilprozessordnung (ZPO). Under these rules, the judge holds hearings to gather evidence to help him reach a decision in the case. The trial progresses informally (compared to trials in the United States) through these hearings.

In the United States, the role of the judge is usually limited to applying the law to the facts of the case. In Germany, the judge decides the facts of the case and then applies the law to those facts. The judge, not the lawyers, decides which witnesses to call. The judge, not the lawyers, interrogates the witnesses and records their testimony. Judges may ask questions only about the evidence that the parties to the case present themselves. And what is presented is much more limited than what is typically presented at U.S. trials. This is so because German courts

contract when you signed up for the account. Many contracts contain arbitration clauses that obligate the parties to the contract to submit disputes to arbitration, not litigation.

Arbitration is the most widely recognized form of alternative dispute resolution (ADR). It is a process similar to litigation in which two or more persons agree to allow a neutral person or panel to resolve a dispute. The advantages of using a neutral expert, called an *arbitrator* or *arbiter*, are twofold: 1) the arbitrator is mutually agreed upon by the parties and has the trust of both parties; and 2) because the arbitrator is usually an expert in the subject matter, less time is needed to educate her about the dispute, which usually results in a faster resolution of the matter.

In the *Federal Arbitration Act (FAA)*, Congress states in the strongest terms that agreements to arbitrate must be upheld. A "written provision in any . . . contract evidencing a transaction involving commerce to settle by arbitration a controversy thereafter arising out of such contract or transaction . . . shall be valid, irrevocable, and enforceable, save upon such grounds as exist at law or in equity for the revocation of any contract" (9 U.S.C. §2). If a party tries to avoid arbitration, the courts are instructed by the FAA to compel and enforce arbitration.

Similarly, most states have adopted the *Uniform Arbitration Act (UAA)*, which has provisions very similar to those in the FAA. States that have not adopted the UAA have laws that are similar. These laws strongly uphold the integrity of the arbitration process.

There are frequent challenges in court to arbitration awards, but the courts uphold the vast majority of arbitration decisions.

The Arbitration Process

It is common for parties to provide for arbitration of future disputes by inserting an arbitration clause in a contract, such as this standard arbitration clause:

> Any controversy or claim arising out of or relating to this contract, or the breach thereof, shall be settled by arbitration administered by the American Arbitration Association under its Commercial Arbitration Rules, and the judgment on the award rendered by the arbitrator(s) may be entered in any court having jurisdiction thereof.

Similarly, parties to a dispute not already covered by an arbitration clause may agree to submit the dispute to arbitration. Arbitration begins when a party files a *submission* to refer a dispute to arbitration. If you go to the Web site of the American Arbitration Association (www.adr.org) you can see forms used to submit a dispute to arbitration. The time in which a dispute must be filed is usually much shorter than the time in which a lawsuit must be filed. Some commercial arbitration clauses require that cases must be filed within a couple of months of the claim or the right to contest the matter is lost.

Selection of Arbitrators

When a case goes to court, the parties to the case may have no control over who the judge will be. Under arbitration, the parties agree on who the arbitrator will be, or they agree to a selection method under the arbitration rules specified in their arbitration agreement. Most matters are arbitrated by one arbitrator, but panels of three arbitrators are not unusual.

Arbitrators are often attorneys, but that is not a general requirement. Rather, arbitrators are required to be impartial, which means that they must avoid conflicts of interest and should uphold the integrity of the arbitration process as spelled out in codes of ethics for arbitrators. Since arbitration is common in many areas, such as labor disputes, the parties usually insist upon arbitrators with experience in the field. Arbitration associations help ensure the quality of the arbitrators, as the associations want to maintain a reputation for quality dispute resolution. Hence, arbitrators often have more expertise in their case area than do most judges, who may hear certain kinds of cases rarely.

Hearing Procedure

Arbitration associations have rules that guide participants and arbitrators. For example, JAMS alternate dispute resolution service (www.jamsadr.com) requires parties to cooperate in good faith in the "voluntary, prompt, and informal exchange of all non privileged documents . . . relevant to the dispute immediately upon commencement of the Arbitration." If a party does not comply with document requests, the arbitrator may order compliance. There is no power to find a party in contempt, as a judge may do, but an arbitrator can order the uncooperative party to pay fees, compensation, and expenses. In practice, since the arbitrator determines the award in the matter, failure to comply may result in loss of a case.

The hearing is normally a closed-door proceeding conducted like a trial but without a trial's restrictive procedural rules. For example, the manner in which evidence can be presented in an arbitration hearing is generally less rigid. Since the arbitrator is an expert in the field, he is less likely to be persuaded by improperly presented evidence.

ISSUE SPOTTER

Are There Limits on the Terms of Arbitration?

As a manager at WeLuvPets, you wish to keep down the cost of possible litigation that arises from unhappy former and current employees. You draw up a contract that all new employees must sign as a condition of employment. It says that any and all employment disputes, including claims made under laws against discrimination in employment, will be subject to binding arbitration. It also stipulates that WeLuvPets will choose the arbitrator and that both parties to the dispute will pay one-half of the costs of arbitration. Is the agreement binding on all who sign it? Are all the conditions you put in the arbitration agreement sensible?

Getty Images

The Award

After the hearing, the arbitrator reaches a decision, called an *award*, which is usually given within 30 days. The award is usually in writing. However, the arbitrator need not state the legal basis of the decision unless the parties have requested that they be provided and are willing to pay for that extra work.

The arbitrator makes on award based on application of law to the evidence presented. Besides deciding if one party owes the other party cash, goods, or something else, the arbitrator decides how the parties will split her fee and the administrative fees. In some arbitration, the arbitrator does not construct an award but chooses between the claims of the two parties. For example, under the rules regarding salary disputes in Major League Baseball, the arbitrator picks either the salary requested by the player or the salary offered by the baseball team.

Arbitrators have wide latitude in making awards. For example, in a case involving a claim by a stockbroker against his former employer, an arbitration panel of the National Association of Securities Dealers ordered the employer to pay $2.7 million in compensatory damages and $25 million in punitive damages. The panel also ordered the company to eliminate "defamatory" materials from the broker's records. The panel held that the employer engaged in "reprehensible conduct" in smearing the broker's name after he was fired. While only a small percentage of arbitration cases involve punitive damages, arbitrators have the authority to order them paid when warranted.

Appealing the Award

Just as parties who lose in court may be dissatisfied, parties who lose in arbitration may want to carry the matter further. Errors of fact or law by an arbitrator are not reviewable by the courts. According to the Federal Arbitration Act, there are four grounds for overturning an award:

1. The award was obtained by corruption or fraud.
2. There was evidence of partiality or corruption by an arbitrator.
3. An arbitrator was guilty of serious procedural misconduct, such as refusing to hear relevant evidence, that prejudiced the rights of a party.
4. An arbitrator exceeded his power, and an award was made on a subject not relevant to the proceeding.

Under the doctrine of *res judicata*, the final judgment on the merits of a case by a court prevents an issue from being relitigated. This doctrine also applies to arbitration awards. While this doctrine has a few limitations in arbitration cases, in general, an arbitration award is final, and the matter cannot be litigated again or appealed. This point is worth repeating: once arbitration is agreed to, it is very rare to be allowed to reject it in favor of litigation.

Voluntary and Compulsory Arbitration

Most arbitration is voluntary. The parties submit their dispute to an arbitrator for a decision rather than go to court. This agreement can occur at the time of a dispute or, more commonly, as part of a contract that preceded the dispute. Labor contracts between a union and an employer and employment contracts often include arbitration requirements. Many commercial contracts include standard terms about arbitration. Most stockbrokers and banks require their customers to sign a contract stating that in the event of a dispute over their account the matter will be arbitrated. Many insurance contracts require arbitration of disputes. Hence, arbitration is a common feature in modern contracts.

Public Sector Employment

Many states require compulsory arbitration for some or all public sector employees. Police officers, firefighters, and public school teachers may not be permitted to strike. Public employees, usually through their unions, and their employers, often must arbitrate the terms of employment: wages, hours, and working conditions. When such arbitration is mandatory, legislation usually requires the awards to have a written record and decision, so it is clear that the awards are supported by the evidence.

Negotiation

The least formal form of ADR is *negotiation;* it is almost always voluntary and, unlike arbitration, has no mandatory procedure, but there can be legal consequences for lying. Negotiation occurs when parties decide to settle a matter between themselves; the use of lawyers or representatives is not required but is common.

Getty Images

CYBER LAW

International Arbitration and Mediation of Domain Name Disputes

The global use of domain names means that they must be unique to be effective in the server system. The World Intellectual Property Organization (WIPO), as part of its function to establish international rules for trademarks and other forms of intellectual property, has a domain name dispute resolution service that protects the integrity of country code top-level domains (such as .mx for Mexico) and for generic top-level domains (gTLDs), such as .edu for education.

WIPO, headquartered in Geneva, Switzerland, has a Uniform Dispute Resolution Policy (UDRP) that deals with problems such as cybersquatting. Parties can go to the WIPO Arbitration and Mediation Center (http://arbiter.wipo.int) for dispute resolution. Experts from many countries are available to handle disputes. Most are law professors or lawyers who specialize in this area of law. If only one panelist is requested to settle a dispute, the fee for one to five domain names included in a complaint is $1,500; the fee is $3,000 if three panelists are requested. Such resolution has the advantage of global acceptance of the results. Over a thousand disputes a year are submitted to the Center.

Negotiation has risen in popularity in recent years. Over 4,000 major firms have signed a pledge to the CPR Institute for Dispute Prevention and Resolution to seek ADR. The firms subscribed to the following statement:

> In the event of a business dispute between our company and another company, which has made or will then make a similar statement, we are prepared to explore with that other party resolution of the dispute through negotiation or ADR techniques before pursuing full-scale litigation. If either party believes that the dispute is not suitable for ADR techniques, or if such techniques do not produce results satisfactory to the disputants, either party may proceed with litigation.

Issues in Negotiation

Whenever people bargain for something, they are engaged in negotiation. Many contracts are formed after negotiation. A negotiated settlement of a dispute is usually a contract that, like other contracts, is enforced by the courts. When parties enter into negotiation, it is often with the intention of making a deal, that is, looking forward to forming a contract.

Stages of Negotiation

While the steps of negotiation may be much the same in all situations, negotiation in a dispute involves parties at odds with one another. Since the parties to the dispute are unlikely to be experienced negotiators and may be influenced by their anger about what has happened, negotiation to settle a dispute is often handled by an attorney or other experienced person.

The first stage of negotiation involves studying the issues. A party should: gather facts and relevant information and not rely personal opinions; understand the weak points; consider the objectives of negotiation; know the law that would be applied to the situation if litigated; know the alternative routes that can be taken; and decide how to handle the negotiation process, such as whether the parties to the dispute will be present.

Next, the parties must exchange information. At this point, the style of the negotiator plays a role. Some negotiators are combative "tough guys," while others are thoughtful problem solvers in their approach. In either case, the negotiator must know what information to present, such as an offer to settle.

Most negotiators expect to compromise. Some concessions are planned in advance to help get the parties closer to a realistic settlement. Since the courts encourage negotiation, settlement offers presented in negotiation may not be used as evidence in court. If a negotiation is properly handled, almost nothing said in the negotiation can be used in court later, if the negotiation fails. The fact that a negotiation that fails will not come back to haunt a party in court encourages the integrity of the process. If an agreement is reached, it is usually spelled out in writing and becomes a contract that can be enforced in court. The courts have a policy of enforcing negotiated settlements.

Mediation

Unlike negotiation, where the parties to a dispute or their representatives meet to try to settle a matter, in *mediation* a third party—the *mediator*—is always used to help the parties to a dispute try to reach a solution by coming to an acceptable agreement. Unlike arbitration, where the arbitrator imposes an award on the parties, the mediator cannot impose a decision but can only help resolve a conflict.

The American Arbitration Association suggests the following provision be included in contracts:

> If a dispute arises out of or relates to this contract or the breach thereof and if the dispute cannot be settled through negotiation, the parties agree first to try in good faith to settle the dispute by mediation administered by the American Arbitration

INTERNATIONAL PERSPECTIVE

Global Acceptance of Arbitration

International business contracts usually contain arbitration clauses. Over 100 nations have signed the United Nations Convention on the Recognition and Enforcement of Foreign Arbitral Awards, which binds signatory nations to uphold the validity of arbitration awards. The gap between the formal law and local legal reality has often been large.

Although China signed the Convention, Chinese courts had a reputation for not enforcing arbitration decisions. For example, one non-Chinese company won an award for $4.9 million in arbitration at the Swedish Chamber of Commerce. The Shanghai company that lost did not pay. When the foreign firm sued in court in China to enforce the award, the courts refused to enforce the arbitration decision. China's supreme court has recently held that lower courts in China could not reverse arbitration awards without its permission.

India has also had a reputation as a country where foreign awards are hard to enforce through Indian courts. The government of India adopted the Indian Arbitration Act to encourage the use of arbitration. Indian courts cannot review the merits of foreign arbitration unless the party has substantial proof of bias or the award otherwise violates public policy.

Thousands of international disputes go to arbitration each year. The American Arbitration Association's International Centre for Dispute Resolution handles about 700 cases a year involving billions of dollars in claims. The International Chamber of Commerce's International Court of Arbitration handles a similar number of disputes. The increased acceptance of arbitration by courts around the world facilitates the expansion of global business by helping ensure enforcement of contracts.

Getty Images

Association under its Commercial Mediation Rules before resorting to arbitration, litigation, or some other dispute-resolution procedure.

Mediation is commonly used to resolve disputes that start out in the courts. Many federal and state courts require that mediation be attempted before trial or at least offered as an alternative. Surveys indicate that attorneys prefer to go to mediation rather than to arbitration when pressured to go to ADR.

Mediation is also often used to help resolve labor disputes. The Federal Mediation and Conciliation Service was established to help unions and employers bargain to a contract. Mediation is also commonly used to help resolve marital problems and, if not successful, to set the terms of divorce. In such cases, mediation is a voluntary process that helps avoid litigation.

The Mediator

Some states do not have requirements about who may serve as a mediator, but most people want a person trained or experienced in mediation. Some states or courts require those offering their services as mediators to be trained professionals. The law in Massachusetts states:

> A "mediator" shall mean a person not a party to a dispute who enters into a written agreement with the parties to assist them in resolving their disputes and has completed at least thirty hours of training in mediation and who either has four years of professional experience as a mediator or is accountable to a dispute resolution organization . . . or one who has been appointed to mediate by a judicial or governmental body. (M.G.L.A. ch. 233 §23C)

The Society of Professionals in Dispute Resolution is an organization that helps to train and govern the credentials of mediators (see www.acrnet.org). The Society identifies the skills that a mediator should possess and the steps that should be taken in proper mediation. Those who offer their services as mediators and fail to act in a professional manner may be subject to liability by a party to the dispute unhappy with the outcome.

Mediation Process

When agreed upon by both parties, a mediator may review the issues to prepare to handle the matter. The mediator explains the process involved and makes clear that he is a neutral party. The mediator collects information, outlines the key issues, listens, asks questions, observes the parties, discusses options, and encourages compromise. If successful, the mediator helps draft an agreement between the parties that settles the dispute. The agreement is an enforceable contract and, therefore, settles the matter.

A standard part of the mediation process is an agreement by the parties to maintain confidentiality. Nothing said in the mediation can be made public or be used in court as evidence if mediation should fail and a suit follows. Regardless of what the parties agree upon, there is a presumption in law that information revealed during negotiation or mediation should not be used in evidence. To encourage honesty in negotiation and mediation, most discussions are privileged, and mediators cannot be required to testify later in court. Some states, including Colorado, have made this a firm rule by statute:

> Mediation proceedings shall be regarded as settlement negotiations, and no admission, representation, or statement made in mediation not otherwise discoverable or obtainable shall be admissible as evidence or subject to discovery. In addition, a mediator shall not be subject to process requiring the disclosure of any matter discussed during mediation proceedings. (Colo. Rev.Stat. 13-22-307)

Creative Business Use of Mediation

One party cannot force another party to enter into mediation, but experience indicates that offers to mediate, even though not binding, can resolve many problems and thereby reduce litigation and the bad press that can go with it. For example, Ford Motor has a mediation program through which a mediator can offer solutions to consumers' complaints without costly litigation. Consumers must first discuss complaints with their dealer and local district office. If a problem is not resolved, a complaint may be filed with the Ford Consumer Appeals Board. The board's decision is binding on Ford and dealers but not on consumers, who retain all rights to legal remedies. Ford has learned that the process, in addition to solving most complaints that reach this level, encourages dealers to be more responsive to consumer problems.

Innovative Forms of ADR

Negotiation, mediation, and arbitration are the oldest and most established forms of ADR, but parties are free to agree upon other forms that allow them to settle their dispute in a peaceful manner. Some forms of ADR have been invented by private parties, while others have been implemented by courts and private parties looking for ways to reduce the time and costs of litigation and reduce the burdens imposed on the taxpayer-supported judicial system. The Alternative Dispute Resolution Act of 1998 directs every federal court to implement a dispute-resolution program, but Congress has not funded this mandate. Nevertheless, state and federal courts have experience with ADR. Judges almost always press parties to negotiate a settlement, and many courts have formal mediation or other ADR programs. One innovative example follows.

LIGHTER SIDE OF THE LAW
Can't Get Good Help These Days

Attorney Toby Wilkinson was appointed by the court to represent Texas death-row inmate Daniel Acker. Wilkinson filed a writ of *habeas corpus* to challenge the legality of Acker's imprisonment, and he was paid $22,270 for his work. But the writ turned out to be mostly copied from an earlier letter Acker had written the judges himself, including the line: "I'm just about out of carbon paper. As soon as I get some more typing supplies I have about 30 more errors I want [noted] in my appeal."

The Texas Court of Criminal Appeals denied the writ.

Source: *Austin American-Statesman*

Getty Images

Summary Jury Trial

A *summary jury trial* is the jury equivalent of a minitrial. It generally takes place after discovery has been completed and when it appears that a case will not be settled before trial.

The summary trial begins with the selection of advisory jurors who do not know that the trial is not binding. A judge or magistrate usually presides. Each side is given a short time to summarize its case. Presentations are limited to evidence admissible at trial, including depositions, discovered documents, expert reports, and other discovery material. Witnesses usually do not participate. After the presentations, the judge gives the jury instructions on the law. The jury then reaches its decision. The judge then meets with the parties to discuss the decision and encourage settlement.

If one or both parties are not satisfied with the result of the summary trial, which usually takes one day, they may still take the dispute to a full trial. Nothing learned at the summary trial may be used as evidence at trial. However, the federal and state courts that use the process report a high rate of success.

Expanding the Use of ADR

Congress has encouraged the use of ADR, originally in the Federal Arbitration Act and recently in the Judicial Improvements Act and the Administrative Dispute Resolution Act. States have been changing their rules of civil procedure to encourage the use of ADR techniques. The objective is to reduce the costs and delays associated with the state and federal court systems. An executive order issued by the president in 1996 expanded the use of binding arbitration by federal agencies. Many government agency Web sites list a variety of ADR processes available, as government and business both attempt to reduce the amount of costly traditional court litigation.

Summary

- The American legal system is an adversary system of justice. The responsibility for bringing and presenting a lawsuit rests upon the litigants. The system reflects the belief that truth is best discovered through the presentation of competing ideas.
- Litigation begins with pleadings. The plaintiff must notify the defendant by service of process that a complaint has been filed with a court. The defendant must answer the complaint with a motion to dismiss, a defense, or a counterclaim, or the plaintiff wins by default. The plaintiff may respond to the defendant's answer with a reply.
- Before trial, the discovery process allows the parties to gather evidence. Depositions or interrogatories may be taken from both the parties and the witnesses. The discovery process allows parties to know what the trial is to be about so that few surprises arise. Gathering evidence may cause the parties to settle the case as the likely outcome becomes clear.
- At most trials, the defendant has the right to ask for a jury trial. Attorneys discuss with clients the advisability of a jury trial or a trial where the judge hears and determines the entire matter. When a jury is used, it is the finder of fact.
- At trial, after opening statements by both parties, the plaintiff presents witnesses and evidence to prove the facts of her case. Witnesses are questioned by both sides. After the cases have been stated, either party can request that the judge give a directed verdict to end the case. In most cases, the matter goes to the jury after closing arguments and instructions by the judge. The jury determines the facts of the case and applies the law as explained by the judge.
- The remedies awarded by the courts in resolving civil disputes include monetary damages and equitable relief. Monetary damages include compensatory, punitive, and nominal damages. Equitable remedies include specific performance and injunctions.
- A party unhappy with the result may appeal the decision. The court of appeals reviews the case to determine whether any errors were made in the application of the law to the facts as they were determined by the judge or jury. The court of appeals may affirm, reverse, or modify the trial court's decision.

- Plaintiffs winning judgments are responsible for attempting to collect the judgment, which is difficult if the defendant leaves the state or has few assets. The plaintiff may have to return to the court to obtain orders to force compliance with the judgment. A writ of execution allows the property of the defendant to be seized to satisfy the judgment.
- Arbitration is the most formal ADR process. A decision to enter into arbitration is a binding contract. The parties who agree to arbitration choose an arbitrator, a neutral party who arbitrates the dispute and issues a binding decision, called an award, much like a judge resolves a case.
- Arbitration hearings are run much like a trial, but the rules of evidence are not as strict. Each side presents its case to the arbitrator and may call witnesses and experts to testify. An arbitrator's award need not be justified in writing. Appeals of awards to the courts are rarely successful, because the parties have agreed to be bound by the decision. Unless fraud or other misconduct by the arbitrator can be shown, the courts are very unlikely to intervene.
- Arbitration is often a standard part of employment contracts, insurance and commercial sale contracts, and agreements with stockbrokers.
- Negotiation is the least formal kind of ADR. The parties deal directly with each other or do so through attorneys or other agents who represent them in confidential discussions to resolve a matter. The parties exchange information, make offers, compromise, and move toward a formal settlement.
- Mediation is a more structured form of negotiation; a neutral mediator helps the parties come to a resolution of a dispute. A mediator must be agreed upon by both parties. A mediator gets the parties to agree on a process, explains the rules, gathers information, outlines key issues, talks to and listens to the parties, suggests options, encourages compromise, and may help draft an enforceable settlement. Mediation is usually confidential.
- Summary jury trials are used by some state and federal courts to encourage parties to settle before trial. A brief, nonbinding trial with a jury is held. The decision that results from the summary trial usually leads to a settlement, as the parties have good insight about how the case would be resolved after a regular, more costly, trial.

Terms to Know

You should be able to define the following terms:

alternative dispute
   resolution (ADR), 48

adversary system, 49

pleadings, 49

complaint, 49

motion, 49

demurrer, 49

answer, 51

affirmative defense, 51

counterclaim, 51

deposition, 53

voir dire, 57

burden of persuasion, 58

directed verdict, 59

damages, 59

punitive or *exemplary damages*, 60

nominal damages, 60

remedies in equity, 61

specific performance, 61

injunction, 61

dissenting opinion, 62

res judicata, 63

writ of execution, 63

arbitration, 64

award, 65

negotiation, 66

mediation, 68

summary jury trial, 70

Discussion Question

1. In many aspects of business, a manager can choose to include an arbitration or mediation clause to govern disputes, such as with customers and employees, or can leave that out and use litigation. What are the pros and cons of such alternatives in regular business practice?

Case Questions

1. Bonnie Weisgram died from smoke inhalation during a fire in her home. Her son, Chad Weisgram, sued Marley, the maker of a heater, claiming it was defective and caused the fire. At trial, Weisgram offered expert witness testimony to prove that the heater was defective. Marley objected that the testimony was unreliable and therefore inadmissible, but the judge overruled the objections; the jury found for Weisgram. The appeals court held that the testimony of Weisgram's expert was not scientifically sound. The appeals court directed a judgment for Marley, holding that there were no grounds for a new trial. Weisgram appealed; does he have a good reason for a new trial? [*Weisgram* v. *Marley Co.*, 120 S. Ct. 1011 (2000)]

   ✓ Check your answer at http://academic.cengage.com/blaw/meiners

2. Hulvey was injured while operating a Caterpillar forklift. He sued Caterpillar for his injuries. Hulvey lost, but the decision was set aside because of juror misconduct. Caterpillar appealed the decision to set aside the verdict of the jury. Hulvey claimed that the verdict should be set aside because one of the jurors, Olmstead, was an attorney who "swayed" the other jurors with his knowledge of the law. Olmstead made derogatory comments about people who file personal injury suits, noting that despite his claims of pain, Hulvey could sit in a chair at court for long periods of time. Should the appeals court uphold the decision concerning juror misconduct? Should courts inquire into the discussion in the jury room? [*Caterpillar Tractor Co.* v. *Hulvey*, 353 S.E.2d 747 Sup. Ct., Va., (1987)]

3. Folsom was injured while unloading potatoes at A&P's warehouse. He sued A&P, alleging that the company was responsible for his injuries. At the close of a two-and-a-half-day trial, the jury deliberated 35 minutes and found for A&P. Folsom alleged jury misconduct because of short deliberation and moved for a new trial. Is it ok for a jury to resolve a case so quickly? [*Folsom* v. *Great Atlantic & Pacific Tea Co.*, 521 A.2d 678 Me. (1987)]

   ✓ Check your answer at http://academic.cengage.com/blaw/meiners

4. A franchise agreement between the parent company franchisor and the franchisees who operated 7-Eleven stores said that any dispute between the franchisor and franchisees would be settled by arbitration. A franchisee sued the franchisor in state court, claiming that some actions of the franchisor were in violation of state law concerning franchises. The state supreme court ruled that the issues covered by the state law could be tried in state court and did not have to go to arbitration. What did the U.S. Supreme Court hold about the choice between arbitration and litigation? [*Southland Corp.* v. *Keating*, 465 U.S. 1 (1984)]

5. An employer and a union disputed what happened at an arbitration hearing. The employer challenged the arbitration award in federal court and subpoenaed the arbitrator to testify about what happened at the arbitration at which he presided. Could the arbitrator be required to testify? [*Main Central Railroad Co.* v. *Brotherhood of Maintenance of Way Employees*, 117 F.R.D. 485 U.S. Dist. Ct., Me. (1987)]

6. Mediator Hammond assisted in negotiations between a union and a company. After mediation, the union declared that an agreement had been reached. The employer denied that an agreement had been reached and refused to sign the union contract. The union filed an unfair labor practice complaint with the National Labor Relations Board. The company claimed that it had the right to call the mediator as a witness in the unfair labor practice complaint. Could the mediator be called to give testimony in the case? [*National Labor Relations Board* v. *Joseph Macaluso, Inc.*, 618 F.2d 51 9th Cir., (1980)]

   ✓ Check your answer at http://academic.cengage.com/blaw/meiners

7. People who borrowed money from Buckeye Check Cashing signed an agreement that included a clause requiring any dispute to go to arbitration. Suit was filed by some customers against Buckeye claiming their service violated the lending laws of Florida, which would make the agreement invalid. The Florida high court held that because the legality of the contract was in question, the matter had to go to court for review, not arbitration. Do you think that ruling was upheld on review by the U.S. Supreme Court? [*Buckeye Check Cashing* v. *Cardegna*, 126 S. Ct. 1204 (2006)]

8. Thomas sued his former employer for racial, sexual, and national origin discrimination in violation of two civil rights laws. During pretrial negotiations, the employer offered Thomas his job back "without prejudice," meaning that it would not affect some of his claims in the lawsuit, such as for mental distress, but if he returned to work, he could not claim he was owed back wages from the date from which he could have started working. Thomas refused the offer. The employer asserted that it should have the right to present testimony to the jury about its offer that was rejected. Thomas said that the negotiations were completely confidential and there could be no testimony. Who was right? [*Thomas* v. *Resort Health Related Facility*, 539 F.Supp. 630 U.S. Dist. Ct. E.D.N.Y., (1982)]

✓ Check your answer at http://academic.cengage.com/blaw/meiners

9. Paranzino claimed she deposited $200,000 in a bank but was given a receipt for only $100,000, but she did not notice the mistake until later. She sued the bank, but attended court-ordered mediation. The mediation required parties to sign a confidentiality agreement. At mediation, the bank offered $25,000 to settle the matter. Paranzino rejected that and called the newspaper to explain the details of the story. This violated the confidentiality agreement. What can be done in such a case? [*Paranzino* v. *Barnett Bank*, 690 So.2d 725 Ct. App., Fla. (1997)]

Ethics Question

1. Because litigation is so costly, many firms settle suits that they are quite sure they would win if litigated. It is cheaper to settle for $10,000 or $50,000 than to consume management time and litigation fees. While it is unethical to bring dubious suits that are largely intended to extract a settlement, is it ethical for firms to settle such cases rather than spend additional resources and defeat such suits?

Internet Assignment

http://judiciary.house.gov/Printshop.aspx?Section=1
http://www.law.cornell.edu/rules/frcp/
http://www.law.cornell.edu/rules/fre/
http://www.law.cornell.edu/rules/frcrmp/

Rules of court play an important part in legal proceedings. For example, the Federal Rules of Civil Procedure govern both the trial process and the pretrial discovery process, often allowing parties to settle a civil dispute before going to trial. Rules of evidence control what can or cannot be admitted into trial, such as hearsay evidence, Rules of criminal procedure ensure a fair, impartial proceeding.

Browse the Web sites listed above. Note especially which ones seem more official and which ones seem more current. Answer the following questions, based on the official government Website:

1. Which federal rule of civil procedure governs the availability of interrogatories to parties?
2. Which federal rules of evidence deal with hearsay evidence?
3. What is the hearsay evidence rule, and what are the first five exceptions to it?
4. What are the four elements of discovery and inspection in the arraignment and preparation of a criminal trial?

The Constitution: Focus on Application to Business

Chapter 4

George Washington presided over a convention in Philadelphia in 1787, at which the Constitution of the United States was drafted. The Constitution became effective in March 1789, when it was ratified by the legislatures in 9 of the 13 original states. It is composed of the preamble and seven Articles. The preamble reads:

> We the People of the United States, in Order to form a more perfect Union, establish Justice, insure domestic Tranquility, provide for the common defence, promote the general Welfare, and secure the Blessings of Liberty to ourselves and our Posterity, do ordain and establish this Constitution for the United States of America.

The Articles of the Constitution are:

    I. Composition and powers of Congress
   II. Selection and powers of the president
  III. Creation and powers of the federal judiciary
  IV. Role of the states in the federal system
   V. Methods of amending the Constitution
  VI. Declaring the Constitution to be supreme law of the land
 VII. Method for ratifying the Constitution

The Constitution was amended almost immediately. The concern was that there was not enough protection for individual rights. In 1791, the first 10 amendments—the *Bill of Rights*—were ratified by the states after having been approved by the First Session of Congress. A proposed amendment must be passed by a two-thirds vote in the House and Senate and then be ratified by three fourths of the state legislatures. An amendment may also be proposed by two thirds of the state legislatures by calling for a constitutional convention, the results of which must be ratified by three fourths of the state legislatures; but that has never happened. The Constitution is reprinted in Appendix C.

All citizens and businesses are affected by the Constitution. Court rulings about the rights of people accused of crimes draw the most popular attention. Supreme Court interpretation of the rights of the accused and of other constitutionally protected rights changes over time. The Court has reversed itself on major constitutional issues over the years, reading the same words in an opposite manner. Some would say this means the Court is political; but it may reflect changes in technology, social values, economic conditions, and political realities. ∎

Getty Images

The Commerce Clause

While all parts of the Constitution have application to business and to individuals, certain provisions have a particular impact on business. In that respect, perhaps the most important part of the Constitution is Article I, Section 8: "The Congress shall have Power ... To regulate Commerce with foreign Nations, and among the several States...." Known as the *commerce clause*, these words have been interpreted to give Congress the power to enact most of the federal regulation of business. When combined with the necessary and proper clause, this gives Congress tremendous regulatory power.

The Necessary and Proper Clause

The Constitution lists specific congressional powers (including collecting taxes, regulating commerce, and providing for national defense). At the end of the list, clause 18 of Article I, Section 8, gives Congress power "to make all Laws which shall be necessary and proper for carrying into Execution the foregoing Powers and all other Powers vested by this Constitution in the Government of the United States, or in any Department or Officer thereof." This is called the *necessary and proper clause*.

McCulloch *v.* Maryland

Chief Justice Marshall gave a broad reading to the necessary and proper clause in 1819 in *McCulloch* v. *Maryland* (17 U.S. 316). In that case, the state of Maryland questioned whether Congress had the right to establish a national bank, since banking was not a power of Congress specified in the Constitution. The Supreme Court upheld the constitutionality of the bank under the necessary and proper clause. The Court held that the clause expands the power of Congress:

> 1st. The clause is placed among the powers of Congress, not among the limitations on those powers.
>
> 2nd. Its terms purport to enlarge, not to diminish the powers vested in the government. It purports to be an additional power, not a restriction on those already granted.

Over the years, the Supreme Court has upheld most federal statutes as necessary and proper, even if the subject of the legislation could not have been contemplated when the Constitution was written. For example, the Court upheld a federal statute limiting liability that would arise from nuclear accidents as necessary and proper to achieve the government's objective of encouraging the development of private nuclear power plants. The authors of the Constitution knew nothing about nuclear power, the Internet, or other things that Congress would deal with eventually.

Federal Supremacy

Another key point made in the *McCulloch* decision is that when the federal government has the power to act under the Constitution, its actions are supreme; that is, they take precedence over the actions of other governments. The state of Maryland argued that even if the federal government had the right to establish a national bank, the state could impose taxes on it, as it did on other banks. The Court struck down the Maryland tax as in violation of Article VI, Paragraph 2, the *supremacy clause:* "The Constitution, and the Laws of the United States ... shall be the supreme Law of the Land; and the judges in every State shall be bound thereby...." If Congress did not want Maryland to tax a bank created by Congress, Maryland could not do so because, so long as they are constitutional, federal laws are supreme over state laws.

Defining "Commerce among the Several States"

Although most federal regulation of business evolved in the last century, Congress has had broad regulatory powers since the early days of the Republic. In 1824, Chief Justice Marshall established some of the basic guidelines of the commerce clause in *Gibbons* v. *Ogden* (22 U.S. 1). He held that commerce among the states means *interstate commerce*, that is, business that concerns more than one state. Further, Justice Marshall held:

> What is this power? It is the power to regulate; that is, to prescribe the rule by which commerce is to be governed. This power, like all others vested in Congress, is complete in itself, may be exercised to its utmost extent, and acknowledges no limitations other than are prescribed in the Constitution.

Power over Interstate Commerce Is Extensive

Just because the effect of a business on interstate commerce is small does not mean that the business is exempt from extensive federal regulation, if Congress so desires. In a landmark case in 1942, *Wickard* v. *Filburn* (317 U.S. 111), the Supreme Court upheld detailed control of the market for wheat. Filburn had a small farm in Ohio. According to the U.S. Department of Agriculture, which was authorized by Congress to set the price of wheat and tell every farmer how much wheat they could grow, Filburn produced 239 bushels of wheat more than he was allowed. He was fined $117 and ordered not to plant more than he was told.

Filburn protested that the law was unconstitutional, because he should be free to plant crops on his land and furthermore, he used the wheat he grew on his farm to feed his chickens and dairy cows and to make bread for his family, so there was no effect on interstate commerce. The Court held that although Filburn's effect on the market for wheat was "trivial," it was still subject to federal control. Since "home-consumed wheat would have a substantial influence on price and market conditions," Congress could regulate its price and the quantity allowed grown by every farmer. Hence, almost all commerce is defined as *interstate commerce*.

In the *Katzenbach* v. *McClung* decision, the Court used the commerce clause to extend nondiscrimination requirements of the 1964 Civil Rights Act to local businesses.

Katzenbach v. McClung
United States Supreme Court
379 U.S. 294 85 S.Ct. 377 (1964)

Case Background *Ollie's Barbecue was a restaurant in Birmingham, Alabama, owned by McClung. It had 220 seats for white customers. Although most employees were black, black customers were allowed to buy food only at a take-out window. The Department of Justice (Attorney General Katzenbach) sued the restaurant for violating Title II of the 1964 Civil Rights Act, which prohibits racial segregation in places of public accommodation. This includes restaurants that offer "to serve interstate travelers of [if] a substantial portion of the food which it serves... has moved in interstate commerce." McClung contended* *that since his customers were local, not traveling interstate, he should be exempt from the law. The government noted that half of the food McClung bought came from out of state, which was enough to make the business interstate.*

The distict court held for McClung and refused to enforce the Act. The government appealed directly to the supreme Court.

Case Decision Clark, Justice.

* * *

continues

Much is said about a restaurant business being local but "even if appellee's activity is local and though it may not be regarded as commerce, it may still, whatever its nature, be reached by Congress if it exerts a substantial economic effect on interstate commerce." *Wickard* v. *Filburn.*

This Court has held time and again that this power extends to activites of retail establishments, including restaurants, which directly or indirectly burden or obstruct interstate commerce.

* * *

Confronted as we are with the facts laid before Congress, We must conclude that it had a rational basis for finding that racial discrimination in restaurants had a direct and adverse effect on the free flow of interstate commerce. Insofar as the sections of the Civil Rights Act here relevant are concerned, Congress prohibited discrimination only in those establishments having a close tie to interstate commerce, that is, those, like McClung's, serving food that has come from out of the State. We think in so doing that Congress acted well within its power to protect and foster commerce in extending the coverage of Title II only to those restaurants offering to serve interstate travelers or serving food, a substantial portion of which has moved in interstate commerce.

The absence of direct evidence connecting discriminatory restaurant service with the flow of interstate food, a factor on which tha appellees place much reliance, is not, given the evidence as to the effect of such practices on other aspects of commerce, a crucial matter.

The power of Congress in this field is broad and sweeping; where it keeps within its sphere and violates no express constitutional limitation it has been the rule of this Court, going back almost to the founding days of the Republic, not to interfere. The Civil Rights Act of 1964, as here applied, we find to be plainly appropriate in the resolution of what the Congress found to be a national commercial problem of the first magnitude. We find in it no violation of any express limitations of the Constitution and we therefore declare it valid.

The judgment is therefore reversed.

Questions for Analysis

1. Might the Court have found that the Civil Rights Act did not apply to a local restaurant if the restaurant could show that all of its food was produced in the state?

2. Suppose evidence showed that when restaurants were required to integrate, they often closed their doors and refused to do more business, Does this go against the argument that the law improves interstate commerce?

Federal and State Regulatory Relations

The legal environment contains many state and federal laws and regulations. As Exhibit 4.1 illustrates, the responsibility for regulating a particular activity may be the responsibility of a state governing body or a federal governing body, or it may be shared by state and federal governments. Federal environmental regulation, for example, requires the Environmental Protection Agency to set national pollution control standards. Given the federal standards, state environmental regulators must then set specific requirements to be met within a state.

States often legislate on a matter on which Congress has legislated. When can state law exist along with federal law? Federal regulation takes precedence over state regulation, so state regulations may not contradict or reduce the standards imposed by federal law. States also may not enact laws that burden interstate commerce by imposing restrictions on businesses from other states.

In some areas, such as postal authority, Congress ruled that the states may not regulate at all. States may not pass laws in such areas, even if the laws do not contradict federal laws. States may add their own rules to strengthen the impact of a federal rule, so long as the rules do not conflict with the intent of the law and do not impede interstate commerce. For example, states may pass air pollution

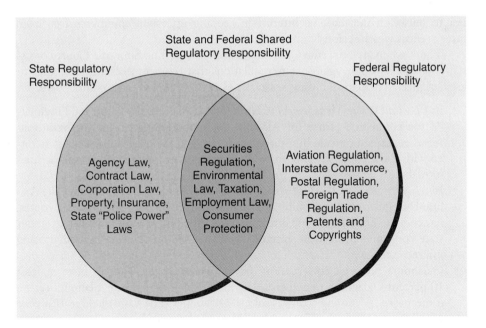

Exhibit 4.1
State and Federal
Regulatory Responsibilities

State and Federal Shared
Regulatory Responsibility

State Regulatory
Responsibility

Federal Regulatory
Responsibility

Agency Law,
Contract Law,
Corporation Law,
Property, Insurance,
State "Police Power"
Laws

Securities
Regulation,
Environmental
Law, Taxation,
Employment Law,
Consumer
Protection

Aviation Regulation,
Interstate Commerce,
Postal Regulation,
Foreign Trade
Regulation,
Patents and
Copyrights

regulations to apply to their industries that are stricter than the federal air pollution rules. However, unless specifically allowed by Congress, states may not pass rules less strict than the federal rule. In some areas, such as insurance, Congress has authorized states to regulate the business within state borders.

LIGHTER SIDE OF THE LAW
Great Constitutional Moments

Arkansas required trucks to have straight mudflaps. Illinois required trucks to have mudguards that "contour the rear wheel, with the inside surface being relatively parallel to the top 90 degrees of the rear and 180 degrees of the whole surface.... and must be installed not more than 6 inches from the tire surface ... and must have a lip or flange on its outer edge of not less than 2 inches." Trucks on interstate highways could be ticketed in either state for having the wrong flap.

The Supreme Court held that the Arkansas flaps were more common and so, "the heavy burden which the Illinois mudguard law places on the interstate movement of trucks and trailers seems to us to pass the permissible limits of safety regulations."

Source: *Bibb* v. *Navajo Freight Lines*, 79 S.Ct. 962

Getty Images

When State Law Impedes Interstate Commerce

In 1911, the Supreme Court, in *Southern Railway Co.* v. *Arizona* (222 U.S. 20), had to consider Arizona regulations that required trains to be shorter in Arizona than in other states for "safety considerations." The effect of the Arizona requirement was to impede interstate commerce. At the Arizona border, trains had to be shortened.

The Supreme Court struck down the Arizona law. Chief Justice Stone said, "The decisive question is whether in the circumstances the total effect of the law as a safety measure in reducing accidents and casualties is so slight or problematical as not to outweigh the national interest in keeping interstate commerce free from interferences which seriously impede it."

There are many Supreme Court cases in this area. The Supreme Court consistently takes a hard line against state regulations that restrict interstate commerce or are designed to help local businesses at the expense of out-of-state competitors:

- In *Chemical Waste Management* v. *Hunt* (504 U.S. 334), the Court held it violated the commerce clause for Alabama to impose a higher fee for hazardous waste generated outside the state than it charged for hazardous waste generated within the state, when both were disposed at commercial disposal facilities in Alabama.
- In *Morales* v. *Trans World Airlines* (504 U.S. 374), the Court held that the Airline Deregulation Act prohibits the states from regulating airline rates, routes, or services. Therefore, state attorneys general could not sue the airlines under state consumer protection statutes when they claimed airline fare advertising injured consumers.
- Oklahoma required coal-burning power plants in the state to burn at least 10 percent Oklahoma-mined coal. Wyoming challenged the regulation, because it meant less Wyoming coal was sold to Oklahoma. The Court held in *Wyoming* v. *Oklahoma* (502 U.S. 437) that the Oklahoma law was discriminatory and interfered with interstate commerce.

The states have a legitimate interest in protecting public health, safety, and other public policies. When such goals are the reason for a state law, the regulation chosen must be designed to achieve its legitimate interest with minimal impact on interstate business. The *Hughes* decision concerns little fish but was used by the Court to lay out the three steps still used today to guide evaluation of state regulations that affect interstate commerce.

Hughes v. Oklahoma
United States Supreme Court
441 U.S. 322 99 S.Ct. 1727 (1979)

Case Background *To protect minnows that live in state waters, Oklahoma prohibited shipping or selling minnows out of state. Hughes was convicted of transporting minnows from Oklahoma to Texas. He bought the minnows from a dealer licensed to do business in Oklahoma. If the minnows had been captured and sold within the state, it would have been legal. It was illegal to take the fish across the state line. The Oklahoma Supreme Court upheld the statute and Hughes's conviction as constitutional for Oklahoma's interest in protecting its natural resources. Hughes appealed.*

Case Decision Brennan, Justice.

* * *

We turn then to the question whether the burden imposed on interstate commerce in wild game by [the Oklahoma law] is permissible under the general rule

articulated in our precedents governing other types of commerce. Under the general rule, we must inquire (1) whether the challenged statute regulates even-handedly with only "incidental" effects on interstate commerce, or discriminates against interstate commerce either on its face or in practical effect; (2) whether the statute serves a legitimate local purpose; and, if so, (3) whether alternative means could promote this local purpose as well without discriminating against interstate commerce. The burden to show discrimination rests on the party challenging the validity of the statute, but "when discrimination against commerce . . . is demonstrated, the burden falls on the State to justify it both in terms of the local benefits flowing from the statute and the unavailability of nondiscriminatory alternatives adequate to preserve the local interests at stake." Furthermore, when considering the purpose of a challenged statute, this Court is not bound by "the name, description, or characterization given it by the legislature or the courts of the State," but will determine for itself the practical impact of the law.

[The Oklahoma law] on its face discriminates against interstate commerce. It forbids the transportation of natural minnows out of the State for purposes of sale, and thus "overtly blocks the flow of interstate commerce at the State's borders." Such facial discrimination by itself may be a fatal defect, regardless of the State's purpose, because "the evil of protectionism can reside in legislative means as well as legislative ends." At a minimum such facial discrimination invokes the strictest scrutiny of any purported legitimate local purpose and of the absence of nondiscriminatory alternatives.

Oklahoma argues that [its law] serves a legitimate local purpose in that it is "readily apparent as a conservation measure." The State's interest in maintaining the ecological balance in state waters by avoiding the removal of inordinate numbers of minnows may well qualify as a legitimate local purpose. We consider the States' interests in conservation and protection of wild animals as legitimate local purposes similar to the States' interests in protecting the health and safety of their citizens.

* * *

Far from choosing the least discriminatory alternative, Oklahoma has chosen to "conserve" its minnows in the way that most overtly discriminates against interstate commerce. The State places no limits on the numbers of minnows that can be taken by licensed minnow dealers; nor does it limit in any way how these minnows may be disposed of within the State. Yet it forbids the transportation of any commercially significant number of natural minnows out of the State for sale. [Its law] is certainly not a "last ditch" attempt at conservation after nondiscriminatory alternatives have proved unfeasible. It is rather a choice of the most discriminatory means even though nondiscriminatory alternatives would seem likely to fulfill the State's purported legitimate local purpose more effectively.

[This decision] does not leave the States powerless to protect and conserve wild animal life within their borders. Today's decision makes clear, however, that States may promote this legitimate purpose only in ways consistent with the basic principle that "our economic unit is the Nation," and that when a wild animal "becomes an article of commerce ... its use cannot be limited to the citizens of one State to the exclusion of citizens of another State."

Reversed.

Questions for Analysis

1. The Court held that the Oklahoma law unfairly discriminated against interstate commerce. How could the state have designed a regulation to achieve the same result, protecting minnows, that would not harm interstate commerce?

2. Suppose Oklahoma got other states to agree to a restriction on the shipment of minnows to help other states protect their resources. Would that be a reasonable compromise?

Imitation not Allowed

The states may not copy federal regulations if such imitation inhibits interstate commerce. Consider the following situation. Congress has long required that timber removed from federal lands in Alaska may not be shipped out of state unless processed in Alaska. Unprocessed logs could not be shipped out of Alaska; they had to be cut into boards first. The state of Alaska imitated the federal rule, requiring that timber cut on state lands be processed in the state before shipment out of state.

The Supreme Court struck down the state law in *South-Central Timber Development* v. *Wunnicke* (467 U.S. 82). "Although the Commerce Clause is by its text an affirmative grant of power to Congress to regulate interstate and foreign commerce, the Clause has long been recognized as a self-executing limitation on the power of the States to enact laws imposing substantial burdens on such commerce." That is, although Congress could impose such a requirement on timber, the state could not do so, unless authorized by Congress. Congress may regulate interstate commerce, but the states have much more limited powers.

The Taxing Power

Congress is given the power to "lay and collect Taxes, Duties, Imposts, and Excises" by Article I, Section 8, Clause 1, of the Constitution. Although this text does not cover tax law (since it is a complex topic requiring specialized courses), keep in mind that taxation is a potent tool of regulation. Taxes can be used for more than raising revenue to pay for government services. They can deter and punish certain behavior. For example, a tax may be tied to a requirement to keep detailed records about goods subject to the tax. This way, goods such as explosives, firearms, drugs, and liquors can be kept under close federal supervision.

Federal Taxation

The Supreme Court rarely questions the constitutionality of federal taxing schemes. In 1937, the Court noted in *Sonzinsky* v. *U.S.* (300 U.S. 506):

> Inquiry into the hidden motives which may move Congress to exercise a power constitutionally conferred upon it is beyond the competency of courts.... We are not free to speculate as to the motives which moved Congress to impose it, or as to the extent to which it may operate to restrict the activities taxed.

The Court has upheld taxes on illegal gambling and illegal drugs. This makes it easier for the government to prosecute people involved in illegal activities. If the income from such activities is reported, the government has evidence of illegal dealings. If the income is not reported and money is found, then the tax laws have been violated. As the Court held in *U.S.* v. *Kahriger* (345 U.S. 22), "the power of Congress to tax is extensive and sometimes falls with crushing effect on businesses."

State Taxation

The Constitution protects interstate commerce from discriminatory state taxes. As the Court ruled in *Northwestern States Portland Cement Co.* v. *Minnesota* (358 U.S. 450):

> A State cannot impose taxes upon persons passing through the state or coming into it merely for a temporary purpose.... Moreover, a State may not lay a tax on the "privilege" of engaging in interstate commerce.... Nor may a State impose a tax which discriminates against interstate commerce either by providing a direct commercial advantage to local business ... or by subjecting interstate commerce to the burden of "multiple taxation."... States, under the Commerce Clause, are not allowed "one single tax-dollar worth of direct interference with the free flow of commerce."

Consider the following cases in which the Supreme Court reviewed state taxing schemes to decide whether they interfered with interstate commerce:

- The state of Hawaii imposed a 20 percent tax on all alcoholic beverages except for local products. The Court struck this down (*Baccus Imports* v. *Dias*, 468 U.S. 263), holding that the tax imposed on alcoholic products had to be the same regardless of origin.
- Michigan exempted from state income taxes the retirement benefits paid to state employees. The state taxed all other retirement income, such as retired federal government employees' benefits. The Supreme Court struck this down in *Davis* v. *Michigan Dept. of Treasury* (489 U.S. 803) as discriminatory. State income taxes must apply equally to all retirement benefits.
- In *Quill Corp.* v. *North Dakota* (504 U.S. 298), state sales taxes imposed on out-of-state firms doing mail-order business with North Dakota residents were

stricken as a violation of the commerce clause. Mail-order firms that do not have a physical presence in the state may not be taxed.

- Illinois imposed a 5 percent tax on all long-distance calls to or from the state. If a taxpayer can show that another state has billed the call, the Illinois tax is refunded. This tax was held not to violate the commerce clause in *Goldberg* v. *Sweet* (488 U.S. 252) because it satisfies a four-part test of the constitutionality of state tax schemes. The tax:

1. applies to an activity having a substantial nexus (connection) with the state.
2. is fairly apportioned to those inside and outside the state.
3. does not discriminate against interstate commerce.
4. is fairly related to services provided by the state.

Getty Images

ISSUE SPOTTER
Unconstitutional Business Activity?

Your company, an auto parts maker in Michigan, belongs to the Michigan Industrial Alliance (MIA), a trade association that lobbies on behalf of its members' interests in the state and federal legislatures. The MIA has succeeded in getting influential members of the Michigan legislature to propose legislation that would exempt auto parts produced in Michigan from sales tax, while auto parts brought to Michigan from other states or foreign countries would be subject to the tax. The legislation was designed to encourage auto manufacturers in Michigan to buy more auto parts made in Michigan.

Should your company support this lobbying activity in the legislature? Is it likely to succeed if the bill becomes law?

Apportioning State Tax Burden

The Supreme Court has held that business income may be taxed by the states as long as they use formulas that account for the intrastate share of interstate commerce.

The apportionment issue generates a lot of litigation, because firms often have manufacturing and distribution facilities in many states and purchase inputs from many sources. It is difficult to know how to assign the various costs to the different portions of an operation—different accounting techniques produce different results. The federal courts are concerned with whether the tax imposes greater burdens on transactions that cross state lines than on those that occur entirely within a state.

State Taxes May Not Impede Foreign Trade

Although Congress has nearly unlimited taxing power, the states may not interfere with interstate commerce through their taxing schemes. Further, since the Constitution gives Congress the power to regulate international trade, as it does interstate commerce, the states may not interfere with international commerce.

The Supreme Court emphasized that point in *Japan Line, Ltd.* v. *County of Los Angeles* (441 U.S. 434). Several California cities and counties imposed a property tax on cargo-shipping containers owned by Japanese companies. The containers were used only in international commerce on Japanese ships. The California taxes were imposed on the containers in the state during loading and unloading. The Supreme Court held the tax to be unconstitutional. The commerce clause reserves to Congress the power over foreign commerce. Foreign commerce may not be subject to state taxes, or the states could regulate foreign trade.

INTERNATIONAL PERSPECTIVE

Freedom of Speech

In the United States, there are very few restrictions on what the media may investigate and publish. There is a long tradition of media attempts to uncover bad deeds by public officials. Unless a statement is published about a person that the publisher knew was false and harmful, there is little that the subject of a critical report can do in response. Suits against the media for defamation, or attempts by the government to prevent publication of sensitive material, are rarely successful.

In the rest of the world, there are more restraints on speech. In the United Kingdom, it is quite common for politicians to sue the media successfully for defamation. In many European countries, books asserted to contain hateful material may not be published. In Belgium, journalists must reveal their sources of information.

Hans Tillack, a reporter for a leading German magazine, *Die Stern,* was arrested in Brussels in 2004, all his files were seized, and he was not allowed access to a lawyer. What was he accused of doing? Publishing articles alleging that many members of the European Parliament engage in fraud by collecting pay when they are not working. The rest of the media said little about the matter, but one Danish member of European Parliament said: "The practice of the EU [European Union] is to stop those who reveal fraud, instead of stopping the fraud."

Getty Images

Business and Free Speech

The First Amendment restricts congressional control of *freedom of speech:* "Congress shall make no law . . . abridging the freedom of speech. . . ." This right is not absolute. As Justice Holmes said in *Schenck* v. *U.S.* (249 U.S. 47), "The most stringent protection of free speech would not protect a man in falsely shouting fire in a theatre and causing a panic." The Constitution prohibits laws "abridging the freedom of speech," but it does not prohibit all laws restricting communication. For example, as the Supreme Court noted in *Ward* v. *Rock Against Racism* (491 U.S. 781), the City of New York could require a city sound technician to be present to regulate the volume at which music was played at an outdoor concert, but the technician could not control the content of the sound.

Do commercial speech (advertisements) and political statements by corporations about public issues deserve the same freedoms? In both cases, the parties are trying to convince some people about something—to buy soap or to support a political program. The Constitution does not distinguish between the two kinds of speech, but traditionally there have been more restrictions on commercial speech than on political speech by business.

Business and Political Speech

The Supreme Court has emphasized the right of businesses to speak out on political issues. In 1978, the Court struck down a Massachusetts law that prohibited corporations from making contributions that could influence certain political issues. In *First National Bank of Boston* v. *Bellotti* (535 U.S. 765) the Court noted that "The freedom of speech . . . guaranteed by the Constitution embraces at the least the liberty to discuss publicly and truthfully all matters of public concern without previous restraint or fear of subsequent punishment. . . ."

The Court soon followed this decision with the *Consolidated Edison* decision. In the case, the Court explained the three-part test that restrictions must pass to be allowed to regulate such speech. This is still the key test used today.

Consolidated Edison Company v. Public Service Commission of New York
United States Supreme Court
447 U.S. 530 100 S.Ct. 2326 (1980)

Case Background *Consolidated Edison inserted material in favour of nuclear power in the monthly bills sent to its electricity customers. The Public Service Commision of New York ruled that Consolidated Edison could not discuss its opinions on controversial issues of public policy it its bills.*

The New York Court of Appeals upheld the Commission's prohibition. Consolidated Edison appealed. The issue is whether the First Amendment of the Constitution is violated by the Commission's order to prohibit the inclusion in electric bills of inserts discussing public policy issues.

Case Decision Powell, Justice

* * *

The Commission's ban on bill inserts is not, of course, invalid merely because it imposes a limitation upon speech. We must consider whether the State can demonstrate that its regulation is constitutionally permissible. The Commission's arguments require us to consider three theories that might justify the state action. We must determine whether the prohibition is (1) a reasonable time, place, or manner restriction, (2) a permissible subject-matter regulation, or (3) a narrowly tailored means of serving a compelling state interest. . . .

A restriction that regulates only the time, place or manner of speech may be imposed so long as it's reasonable. But when regulation is based on the content of speech, governmental action must be scrutinized more carefully to ensure that communication has not been prohibited "merely because public officials disapprove the speaker's views."

* * *

The Commission does not pretend that its action is unrelated to the content or subject matter of bill inserts. Indeed, it has undertaken to suppress certain bill inserts precisely because they address controversial issues of public policy. The Commission allows inserts that presents information to consumers on certain subjects, such as energy conservation measures, but it forbids the use of inserts that discuss public controversies. The Commission . . . justifies its ban on the ground that consumers will benefit from receiving "useful" information, but not from the prohibited information. The Commission's own rationale demonstrates that its action cannot be

upheld as a content-neutral time, place, or manner regulation. . . .

The First Amendment's hostility to content-based regulation extends not only to restrictions on particular viewpoints, but also to prohibition of public discussion of an entire topic. . . .

To allow a government the choice of permissible subjects for the public debate would be to allow that government control over the search for political truth.

* * *

Where a government restricts the speech of a private person, the state action may be sustained only if the government can show that the regulation is a percisely drawn means of serving a compelling state interest. . . .

Where a single speaker communicates to many listeners, the First Amendment does not permit the government to prohibit speech as intrusive unless the "captive" audience cannot avoid objectionable speech.

Passengers on public transportation or residents of a neighborhood disturbed by the raucous broadcasts from a passing soundtruck may well be unable to escape an unwanted message. But customers who encounter an objectionable billing insert may "effectively avoid further bombardment of their sensibilities simply by averting their eyes." The customer of Consolidated Edison may escape exposure to objectionable material simply by transferring the bill insert from envelope to wastebasket.

* * *

Reversed.

Questions for Analysis
1. The court held the company could discuss controversial political issues. Should a distinction be drawn between political speech paid for by private persons and that paid for by customers who may not want the speech? The political inserts in this case were paid for by Con Ed customers who buy electricity.
2. Would you distinguish between speech that address issues and corporate political speech that endorses particular candidates for office?

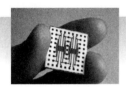

Getty Images

CYBER LAW

Freedom of Speech on the Net

Georgia passed a statute making it a crime for "any person … knowingly to transmit any data through a computer network … for the purpose of setting up, maintaining, operating, or exchanging data with an electronic mailbox, home page, or any other electronic information storage bank or point of access to electronic information if such data uses an individual name … to falsely identify the person." That is, there could be no anonymous communications.

In *American Civil Liberties Union of Georgia* v. *Miller* (977 F. Supp. 1228), the federal court issued an injunction preventing Georgia from enforcing the statute. Statutes that regulate speech must be narrowly tailored to survive First Amendment challenges. The Georgia statute was too sweeping in its coverage to stand.

Similarly, the Supreme Court, in *Reno* v. *American Civil Liberties Union* (117 S.Ct. 2329), struck down the Communications Decency Act of 1996. While the supposed intent of the law was to restrict pornography for children on the Web, the court held that the act went too far in restricting First Amendment rights; it was like "burning the house to roast the pig."

An example of a legitimate restriction comes from *Austin* v. *Michigan Chamber of Commerce* (494 U.S. 652). In that decision, the Supreme Court allowed states to prohibit the use of general corporate money for supporting or opposing political candidates. The compelling government interest that allows this regulation is the desire to eliminate distortions caused by corporate spending for this purpose out of general corporate funds, as opposed to corporate spending for this purpose that comes from corporate money that has been set aside for specific political purposes.

Business and Commercial Speech

The modern *commercial speech* doctrine first came about as restrictions on advertising were attacked as anticompetitive. Some commercial speech restrictions violated antitrust laws, but most such restrictions also violated the rights of sellers of legal products and services to inform citizens of the availability and merits of their goods. This trend began in the 1970s.

In 1975, in *Bigelow* v. *Virginia* (421 U.S. 809), the Supreme Court reversed the conviction of a Virginia newspaper editor who published ads about the availability of low-cost abortions in New York City. A Virginia law prohibited publications from encouraging abortions. The Court held that speech that is related to legal products or services has value in the marketplace of ideas.

The following year, in *Virginia State Board of Pharmacy* v. *Virginia Citizens Consumer Council* (425 U.S. 748), the Court struck down a Virginia law prohibiting the advertising of prices of prescription drugs. "It is clear … that speech does not lose its First Amendment protection because money is spent … as in a paid advertisement. . . ." The Board of Pharmacy argued that the restrictions on advertising were needed to protect the public from their ignorance about drugs. The Court rejected that, holding, "that people will perceive their own best interests if only they are well enough informed, and that the best means to that end is to open the channels of communication rather than to close them."

While commercial speech that is not truthful may be regulated (unlike political speech), the Court finds little justification for extensive controls on truthful commercial speech. In the *Central Hudson Gas and Electric* decision, the Court established a four-part test that must be met to justify restrictions on commercial speech. This is the leading case on this issue.

Central Hudson Gas and Electric Corporation v. Public Service Commission of New York
United States Supreme Court
447 U.S. 557, 100 S.Ct. 2343 (1980)

Case Background *The winter of 1973–1974 was difficult because of the Organization of Petroleum Exporting Countries (OPEC) oil embargo and shortages of natural gas. The Public Service Commission of New York ordered electric utilities in New York to end all advertising that "promotes the use of electricity." The order was based on the commission's finding that New York utilities might not have enough power to meet all customer demands for the winter. The Commission declared all promotional advertising contrary to the national policy of conserving energy. It offered to review any proposed advertising that would encourage energy conservation. The New York high court upheld the constitutionality of the Commission's regulation. The utility appealed to the Supreme Court.*

Case Decision Powell, Justice

* * *

The Commission's order restricts only commercial speech, that is, expression related solely to the economic interests of the speaker and its audience. . . . The First Amendment, as applied to the States through the Fourteenth Amendment, protects commercial speech from unwarranted government regulation. Commercial expression not only serves the economic interest of the speaker, but also assists consumers . . . in the fullest possible dissemination of information. In applying the First Amendment to this area, we have rejected the "highly paternalistic" view that government has complete power to suppress or regulate commercial speech. "People will perceive their own best interests if only they are well enough informed and . . . the best means to that end is to open the channels of communication, rather than to close them . . ." Even when advertising communicates only an incomplete version of the relevant facts, the First Amendment presumes that some accurate information is better than no information at all.

Nevertheless, our decisions have recognized "the 'common-sense' distinction between speech proposing a commercial transaction, which occurs in an area traditionally subject to government regulation and other varieties of speech.". . . The Constitution therefore accords a lesser protection to commercial speech than to other constitutionally guaranteed expression. The protection available for particular commercial expression turns on the nature both of the expression and of the governmental interests served by its regulation.

The First Amendment's concern for commercial speech is based on the informational function of advertising. Consequently, there can be no constitutional objection to the suppression of commercial messages that do not accurately inform the public about lawful activity. The government may ban forms of communication more likely to deceive the public than to inform it, to commercial speech related to illegal activity.

If the communication is neither misleading nor related to unlawful activity, the government's power is more circumscribed.

* * *

In commercial speech cases . . . a four-part analysis has developed. (1) At the outset, we must determine whether the expression is portected by the First Amendment. For commercial speech to come within that provision, it at least must concern lawful activity and not be misleading. (2) Next, we ask whether the asserted governmental interest is substantial. If both inquiries yield positive answers, (3) we must determine whether the regulation directly advances the governmental interest asserted, and (4) whether it is not more extensive than is necessary to serve the interest.

We now apply this four-step analysis for commercial speech to the Commission's arguments in support of its ban on promotional advertising.

The Commission does not claim that the expression at issue is inaccurate or relates to unlawful activity. . . .

The commission offers two state interests as justifications for the ban on promotional advertising. The first concerns energy conservation. Any increase in demand for electricity—during peak or off-peak periods—means greater consumption of energy. The Commission argues . . . that the State's interest in conserving energy is sufficient to support suppression of advertising designed to increase consumption of electricity. In view of our country's dependence on energy resources beyond our control, no one can doubt the importance of energy conservation. Plainly, therefore, the state interest asserted is substantial.

* * *

We come finally to the critical inquiry in this case: whether the Commission's complete suppression of speech ordinarily protected by the First Amendment is no more extensive than necessary

continues

to further the State's interest in energy conserva- tion. The Commission's order reaches all promo- tional advertising, regardless of the impact of the touted service on overall energy use. But the ener- gy conservation rationale, as important as it is, cannot justify suppressing information about elec- tric devices or services that would cause no net increase in total energy use. In additional, no showing has been made that a more limited re- striction on the content of promotional advertising would not serve adequately the State's interests.

* * *

Reversed.

Questions for Analysis

1. Since the Court found that the state had a substantial interest in the subject in question (electricity conservation), why did it find the ad restrictions to be unconstitutional? What part of the four-part test was not met?
2. Suppose the Commission had said that only advertising designed to promote energy conser- vation was allowed. Would that have met the Supreme Court test?

LIGHTER SIDE OF THE LAW
Freedom of Bark but Not Burn in Ohio

Gilchrist was charged with taunting a dog, when he barked at a police dog sitting in an unat- tended police car. He argued that he was not taunting but rather engaging in "unrestrained late-night enthusiasm." Besides, the dog barked first. An Ohio appeals court upheld dismissal of the charges.

Another Ohio appeals court held that burning a rainbow flag at a gay pride parade was not protected speech, because the burners did not obtain a burn permit first. Requiring such a permit is "unquestionably within the city's constitutional power."

Source: *State of Ohio v. Gilchrist; City of Columbus v. Meyer*

Getty Images

The Supreme Court has ruled that First Amendment rights are violated by re- strictions on advertising for professional services, such as by lawyers or doctors. In *Shapero* v. *Kentucky Bar Association* (468 U.S. 881), the Court held that the state bar association violated the First Amendment by prohibiting lawyers from soliciting business by sending truthful letters to prospective clients known to face possible legal action. If an attorney engages in misleading or deceptive solicitation practices, the attorney may be punished by the bar for doing so, but the bar may not act as a barrier to truthful commercial speech.

The Court further discussed the regulation of commercial speech in *Board of Trustees of the State University of New York* v. *Fox* (492 U.S. 469). The standard for judging commercial speech regulation is one that is "not necessarily perfect but rea- sonable" and one "narrowly tailored to achieve the desired objective." The basis of the regulation must be a substantial state interest in controlling an undesirable activi- ty, balanced against the cost imposed by the restrictions. When regulations are chal- lenged, the state bears the burden of justifying restrictions on commercial speech.

Freedom to Criticize

Freedom of speech can mean that a business is criticized. The Supreme Court upheld this right in *Bose Corp.* v. *Consumers Union* (466 U.S. 485). A report in *Con- sumer Reports* was critical of the quality of a stereo speaker made by Bose. Bose sued, claiming product disparagement.

Getty Images

INTERNATIONAL PERSPECTIVE

Freedom of Commercial and Political Speech Abroad

Most nations, even democratic countries with a tradition of personal freedom, impose more restrictions on speech than the United States.

Consider incidents involving Internet commercial and political communications. A French court ordered Yahoo! to block French Internet users from having access to auctions selling Nazi artifacts, such as a German uniform from World War II. The court, noting that the sale of such items is illegal in France, ruled that Yahoo! must block access to such products or face a fine of 100,000 francs ($13,000) a day. Yahoo!, knowing that it is nearly impossible to make such blocks effec-

tive, removed such items from its auction site. This would be the equivalent of the U.S. government prohibiting the sale of Osama bin Laden artifacts in the United States.

The highest court of Germany upheld a prison sentence for an Australian citizen who posted information on a Web site based in Australia that denies that the Holocaust occurred. Denying the Holocaust is banned as hate speech. The German high court held that it had jurisdiction over this violation of German law. This would be the equivalent of the U.S. Supreme Court upholding a conviction of an Iranian citizen who posted material on an Iranian Web site claiming that the World Trade Center terrorist attacks never happened.

The Supreme Court held that for a public figure, such as a corporation selling products, to recover damages for a defamatory falsehood, the trial court must find clear and convincing evidence that there was actual malice in publishing a knowing or reckless falsehood. Since actual malice was not shown in this case, the suit was dismissed. This principle applies to Internet-based speech. At least two federal appeals courts have held that Web sites dedicated to mocking or posting negative opinions about a business are protected speech.

Other Key Parts of the Bill of Rights

The Bill of Rights contains the first ten amendments to the Constitution. Some amendments, while providing important rights for citizens, have little special impact on business. Most of the rest of the amendments, numbered 11 through 27, also have no special impact on business, although we will see that the Fourteenth Amendment has important consequences. No amendment was written specifically to address a business issue. Some just happen to have an impact on the legal environment of business.

Unreasonable Search and Seizure

The Fourth Amendment reads: "The right of the people to be secure in their persons, houses, papers, and effects against unreasonable searches and seizures, shall not be violated, and no Warrants shall issue, but upon probable cause. . . ." Most cases arising under this amendment are criminal and concern the proper method of search and seizure of suspected criminals and evidence. Searches by government agents to help enforce regulations that may result in criminal charges are subject to limits. In Fourth Amendment cases, key issues are whether proper search and seizure procedures were used by government authorities and whether a person has a constitutionally protected reasonable expectation of privacy.

Limits on Searches and Inspections

If a government inspector shows up at a business to inspect the premises or search company records for some purpose related to the law being enforced by the inspector, does the business have to allow admission? Not without a warrant in many instances, the Supreme Court held in *Marshall* v. *Barlow's* (436 U.S. 307). In that case, an inspector for the Occupational Safety and Health Administration (OSHA) arrived at Barlow's plant in Idaho and asked to search the work areas. Barlow asked the inspector if he had a warrant. He did not. Barlow refused him admission to the plant unless he got a warrant. OSHA asked the Court to require businesses to admit inspectors to conduct warrantless searches.

The Court refused, saying that warrantless searches are generally unreasonable and that this rule applies to commercial premises as well as homes. The government argued that if inspectors had to obtain warrants, businesses would have time to hide safety and health defects on worksites. The Court responded:

> We are unconvinced ... that requiring warrants to inspect will impose serious burdens on the inspection system or the courts, will prevent inspections necessary to enforce the statute, or will make them less effective. In the first place the great majority of businessmen can be expected in normal course to consent to inspection without warrant; the Secretary (of Labor) has not brought to this Court's attention any widespread pattern of refusal.

As the Court predicted, most businesses allow warrantless searches; the requirement to obtain a warrant when demanded is not burdensome, nor has it much affected law enforcement.

Warrantless Searches

Warrantless searches are allowed for "closely regulated" businesses. For example, in *New York* v. *Burger* (482 U.S. 691), the Supreme Court held the state could impose warrantless searches on auto junkyards. They are closely regulated, because they become chop shops for stolen vehicles and parts. The Court noted that the government had a "substantial" interest behind the regulatory scheme (to reduce auto thefts), and the warrantless inspections were necessary to make the regulatory scheme work. Those who run junkyards know that a condition of their being licensed to have such an operation is that they must submit to warrantless searches of the grounds as outlined in the state statute.

Gathering Evidence

Evidence improperly gathered by law enforcement officials violates Fourth Amendment rights regarding search and seizure and may not be used in court under the *exclusionary rule*. Generally, this means that evidence gathered from a home or business without a warrant was improperly obtained and cannot be used. Businesses have fewer constitutional rights in this respect than persons in their homes.

In *Skinner* v. *Railway Labor Executives' Association* (489 U.S. 602), the Court approved warrantless searches of railroad employees involved in train accidents or safety violations. The searches consist of blood, breath, and urine tests for evidence of alcohol or drugs. These searches do not violate the Fourth Amendment, because they are in a "closely regulated" industry, are based on compelling public interest in safety, and may be used only in specific situations. The employees know they are subject to this requirement, so the limited invasion of privacy is acceptable.

Self-Incrimination

The Fifth Amendment protects individuals against *self-incrimination:* "No person shall be ... compelled in any criminal case to be a witness against himself." This protection applies to persons, not to corporations. Although corporate executives cannot be made to testify against themselves, business records that might incriminate the corporation—and executives—must be produced, since such records are not protected by the Fifth Amendment.

That corporations are not due the same Fifth Amendment protection as are individuals was noted by the Supreme Court in *Braswell* v. *United States* (487 U.S. 99). Braswell was president and sole shareholder of a corporation. Claiming Fifth Amendment privilege against self-incrimination, he refused to produce company records ordered under a federal grand jury subpoena. The Court rejected this claim, holding that the corporation was an entity not protected by the Fifth Amendment; hence, Braswell had to produce corporate records, even though the records might incriminate him.

Just Compensation

The Fifth Amendment states, "... nor shall private property be taken for public use, without just compensation." Termed the *just compensation or takings clause*, it requires governments to pay for property a government requires someone to sell because public officials determine that the property should be used for some specific purpose, such as for the construction of a highway, school, or military base.

Such use of *eminent domain* is common. The power of governments to condemn private property for such public uses is ancient. Compensation is based on fair market value. While some property owners are not happy about being forced to move, the relatively small amount of litigation over the values paid for property indicates that the compensation is usually adequate.

Eminent Domain as Development Aid

More controversial is the use of eminent domain to take private property for other private parties. A common economic development tactic is for a city to use its power to piece together land desired by a private party, who promises to build a facility, shopping center, or higher-valued homes on property than currently exists on the land. If the private developer must deal with sellers individually, the process can take longer and will be more costly than if the government forces sales at existing market prices. Cities like the new development, as it means higher tax revenues and more residents. To avoid the claim that property is being transferred from one private party to another, a 99-year lease from the government to the developer is often used. The practice was legal in some states and illegal in others. The Supreme Court set off a national discussion of the issue when it handed down the *Kelo* decision.

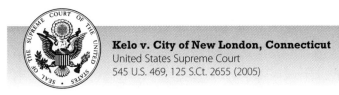

Kelo v. City of New London, Connecticut
United States Supreme Court
545 U.S. 469, 125 S.Ct. 2655 (2005)

Case Background *The City of New London wanted to encourage development. It worked on a plan to piece together property along a riverfront to be used for upscale housing, a new shopping center, and a facility for the Pfizer Company. Some homeowners refused to sell, including Suzette Kelo, who prized her waterfront home, and Wilhelmina Dery, who was born in her home in 1918 and lived there her entire life. The City then used its power of eminent domain to buy the property and provide it to the developers. The homeowners protested that this taking violated the "public use"*

provision of the Fifth Amendment. The Connecticut courts held the taking as proper. Homeowners appealed.

Case Decision Stevens, Justice

* * *

The trial judge and all the members of the Supreme Court of Connecticut agreed that there was no evidence of an illegitimate purpose in this case. Therefore ... the City's development plan was not
continues

adopted "to benefit a particular class of identifiable individuals."

On the other hand, this is not a case in which the City is planning to open the condemned land—at least not in its entirety—to use by the general public. Nor will the private lessees of the land in any sense be required to operate like common carriers, making their services available to all comers. But although such a projected use would be sufficient to satisfy the public use requirement, this "Court long ago rejected any literal requirement that condemned property be put into use for the general public." . . . The disposition of this case, therefore, turns on the question whether the City's development plan serves a "public purpose."

* * *

For more than a century, our public use jurisprudence has wisely eschewed rigid formulas and intrusive scrutiny in favor of affording legislatures broad latitude in determining what public needs justify the use of the takings power.

Those who govern the City were not confronted with the need to remove blight . . . but their determination that the area was sufficiently distressed to justify a program of economic rejuvenation is entitled to our deference. The City has carefully formulated an economic development plan that it believes will provide appreciable benefits to the community, including—but by no means limited to—new jobs and increased tax revenue. . . . Because that plan unquestionably serves a public purpose, the takings challenged here satisfy the public use requirement of the Fifth Amendment. . . .

Petitioners contend that using eminent domain for economic development impermissibly blurs the boundary between public and private takings. Again, our cases foreclose this objection. Quite simply, the government's pursuit of a public purpose will often benefit individual private parties.

* * *

The judgment of the Supreme Court of Connecticut is affirmed.

Questions for Analysis

1. The Court upheld the use of eminent domain to further private economic development. Does this mean any government can force one private landowner to sell so that another private party who wants the land can get it?
2. Why would government favor such actions when local property owners oppose it?

While governments have always been required to pay for property taken for public use, what if regulation takes all or most of the value of property? Local governments, where most land-use requirements are determined, have broad powers to change zoning and land-use requirements without paying compensation, even though the value of the land is affected by changes in land-use rules. When new rules reduce property values, must the government compensate property owners?

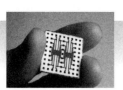

CYBER LAW
No Right of Privacy in Chat Rooms

An FBI agent monitored online chat rooms to uncover distribution of child pornography. He would enter the chat rooms, so his user name was seen, but he would not participate. Based on the agent's observations, Charbonneau was accused of distributing child pornography to contacts made in the chat room. Charbonneau contended that this method of collecting evidence violated his Fourth Amendment right to a reasonable expectation of privacy.

A federal court held that the evidence collected was good. "The expectation of privacy in E-mail transmissions depends in large part on both the type of E-mail sent and recipient of the E-mail." Messages sent to a chat room, unlike personally addressed E-mails, lose their privacy, so the evidence may be used against him.

More than one court has held this to be the rule.

Source: *U.S. v. Charbonneau* (979 F.Supp. 1177); *U.S. v. Dietz* (452 F.Supp. 2d 611)

Getty Images

Regulatory Takings

A 1987 Supreme Court decision, *Nollan* v. *California Coastal Commission* (483 U.S. 825), addressed compensation in case of changing land-use rules. The Nollans wanted to tear down their house and build a larger one on their beach property in Ventura, California. The Coastal Commission said that their permit would be granted only if they agreed to allow the public an easement (access) to the private land that was their backyard. The high-tide line determines the lot's oceanside boundary. The Coastal Commission wanted the public to have the right to use what had been the Nollans' backyard—above the high-tide line—along the beach.

The Supreme Court held that the takings clause of the Fifth Amendment had been violated. The state could not tie a rebuilding permit to an easement (land use) that it would have to pay for if it simply imposed the easement. "California is free to advance its 'comprehensive program,' if it wishes, [of increased beach access] by using its power of eminent domain for this 'public purpose,' but if it wants an easement across the Nollans' property, it must pay for it."

As a rule, the regulatory takings cases indicate that the destruction of property value must be almost complete for compensation to be due. If a regulation reduces the value of some property by, say, 60 percent, it is very unlikely that compensation is due. That is not an uncommon result of a change in zoning laws or a rule that eliminates the ability of a company to produce a particular product.

Right to Trial

The Sixth Amendment addresses the right of persons to trial by jury in criminal cases. The Seventh Amendment provides for the right to jury trial in common-law cases. Although the law is well established about the constitutional right to jury trial in criminal cases and common-law cases, what about cases in which a business is charged with a violation of a statute that regulates the business? If the charge is criminal, the right to request a jury trial remains. What if the charge is civil?

If the only question at trial arises under a statute that may impose civil penalties, such as money fines or an injunction, no right to jury trial exists. Because civil penalties are imposed by statute, there is no constitutional right to trial on such matters.

Excessive Fines

The Eighth Amendment is most famous for its restriction on "cruel and unusual punishments," but it also holds that no *excessive fines* may be imposed. As large jury awards have become more common in recent years, defendants have questioned whether the Eighth Amendment offers protection against huge punitive damage awards. As we will see in the Leatherman case, the Supreme Court has applied the Eighth Amendment through the Fourteenth Amendment to limit excessive punitive damages.

The claim of excessive fines also has been raised in suits that allow the government to press for large damages. For example, when illegal drug dealing occurs on private property, the property may be confiscated. Even if the property is worth a thousand times what the drugs were worth, this has generally been held not to be an excessive fine in violation of the Eighth Amendment, so long as the fines are part of a rational and consistent scheme to deter certain behavior.

A restriction imposed on forfeiture arose in the Supreme Court case, *U.S.* v. *Bajakajian* (118 S.Ct. 2028). The Bajakajians were leaving the country with $357,144 in cash. The money was legally earned; they were taking the money to repay relatives who had given them money to start their business. While it was legal to take the money out of the country, the Bajakajians failed to report that they were leaving with more than $10,000. Government agents seized all the money, contending that it could be kept because it was an "instrumentality" of the crime committed. The Court held that the forfeiture was an "excessive fine" in violation of the Eighth Amendment, as it was grossly disproportional to the seriousness of the offense.

Fourteenth Amendment

When we were discussing the First Amendment and *Central Hudson Gas and Electric*, the Supreme Court noted that "The First Amendment, as applied to the States through the Fourteenth Amendment, protects commercial speech from unwarranted government regulation." That is, the Fourteenth Amendment is the key constitutional tool to force state governments to abide by the protections offered in the Constitution, including the First and Fifth Amendments, among others. Before that time, unless similar protections were offered in a state constitution, such liberties might not have applied in instances of actions by state and local governments.

The Fourteenth Amendment holds, in part, "No State shall ... deprive any person of life, liberty, or property, without due process of law; nor deny to any person within its jurisdiction the equal protection of the laws." This amendment has been a powerful device for extending federal constitutional guarantees to the states and preventing states from passing laws that diminish federal constitutional protections.

The Fourteenth Amendment, which was passed after the Civil War to try to prevent Southern states from passing laws to reinstitute some aspects of slavery, has two key provisions concerning substantive and procedural law: the *due process clause* and the *equal protection clause*. Substantive due process comes into play whenever the courts review the ability of the government to restrict the freedoms of life, liberty, or property. Equal protection comes into play when the courts are called upon to review a classification of persons that has been established by a government.

Bringing suit under the Fourteenth Amendment is made easier by Section 1983 of Chapter 42 of the United States Code (42 USC § 1983). As you can see here, it provides broad language for suit, and many are brought under it:

> Every person who, under color of any statute, ordinance, regulation, custom, or usage, of any State or Territory or the District of Columbia, subjects, or causes to be subjected, any citizen of the United States or other person within the jurisdiction thereof to the deprivation of any rights, privileges, or immunities secured by the Constitution and laws, shall be liable to the party injured in an action at law, suit in equity, or other proper proceeding for redress, except that in any action brought against a judicial officer for an act or omission taken in such officer's judicial capacity, injunctive relief shall not be granted unless a declaratory decree was violated or declaratory relief was unavailable.

While this is a sweeping statement, the Supreme Court holds that fundamental liberty interests are deeply rooted in this Nation's history and tradition and require a "careful description" of the asserted fundamental liberty interest. That is, courts are not to call any freedom that someone would like to assert a protected liberty interest.

Due Process

In general, due process claims can be stated two different ways: First, due process is violated when the state infringes on fundamental liberty interests without narrowly tailoring that infringement to serve a compelling state interest. Second, due process is infringed when state action either shocks the conscience or offends judicial notions of fairness and human dignity.

Suppose a state prohibited all persons from making or selling tobacco products in the state. A challenge to the law could be based on due process. The person claiming he or she should be allowed to make, consume, or sell tobacco products would claim that the Fourteenth Amendment was violated because the substance of the law, not the procedures used to enforce the law, restricted the freedom of persons in the state without a constitutional rationale. When governments restrict the rights of citizens, unless a fundamental constitutional liberty is at stake (would that include access to tobacco products?), the law needs to relate rationally to a legitimate government interest, such as public health, to satisfy due process requirements.

Most due process cases involve protection of individual liberties, but the constitutional standard also extends to businesses, when governments go beyond the discretion they are ordinarily allowed. The Philip Morris case that follows is an example of due process being applied in a business context. As the Supreme Court notes, when a constitutional issue is at stake, the courts are to review the matter with great care.

Philip Morris USA v. Williams
United States Supreme Court
127 S.Ct. 1057 (2007)

Case Background *Jesse Williams died from smoking-related lung cancer. His wife sued Philip Morris, which made his favorite cigarette. She claimed the company knowingly and falsely led him to believe that smoking was safe. The jury awarded $821,000 in compensatory damages and $79.5 million in punitive damages. The Oregon high court upheld the award. Philip Morris appealed.*

Case Decision Breyer, Justice

* * *

Philip Morris pointed out that the plaintiff's attorney had told the jury to "think about how many other Jesse Williams in the last 40 years in the State of Oregon there have been.... In Oregon, how many people do we see outside, driving home ... smoking cigarettes? ... In light of this argument, Philip Morris asked the trial court to tell the jury that ... "you are not to punish the defendant for the impact of its alleged misconduct on other persons, who may bring lawsuits of their own in which other juries can resolve their claims...." The judge rejected this proposal and instead told the jury that "punitive damages are awarded against a defendant to punish misconduct and to deter misconduct," and "are not intended to compensate the plaintiff or anyone else for damages caused by the defendant's conduct."

* * *

This Court has long made clear that "punitive damages may properly be imposed to further a State's legitimate interests in punishing unlawful conduct and deterring its repetition." At the same time, we have emphasized the need to avoid an arbitrary determination of an award's amount. Unless a State insists upon proper standards that will [control] the jury's discretionary authority, its punitive damages system may deprive a defendant of "fair notice ... of the severity of the penalty that a State may impose," it may threaten "arbitrary punishments,"... and, where the amounts are sufficiently large, it may impose one State's (or one jury's) "policy choice," say as to the conditions under which (or even whether) certain products can be sold, upon "neighboring States" with different public policies....

In our view, the Constitution's Due Process Clause forbids a State to use a punitive damages award to punish a defendant for injury that it inflicts upon nonparties or those whom they directly represent, *i.e.*, injury that it inflicts upon those who are, essentially, strangers to the litigation. For one thing, the Due Process Clause prohibits a State from punishing an individual without first providing that individual with "an opportunity to present every available defense."...

For another, to permit punishment for injuring a nonparty victim would add a near standardless dimension to the punitive damages equation. How

continues

many such victims are there? How seriously were they injured? Under what circumstances did injury occur? The trial will not likely answer such questions as to nonparty victims. The jury will be left to speculate. And the fundamental due process concerns to which our punitive damages cases refer—risks of arbitrariness, uncertainty and lack of notice—will be magnified...

We therefore conclude that the Due Process Clause requires States to provide assurance that juries are not asking the wrong question, *i.e.*, seeking, not simply to determine reprehensibility, but also to punish for harm caused strangers.

* * *

We vacate the Oregon Supreme Court's judgment and remand the case for further proceedings not inconsistent with this opinion.

Questions for Analysis

1. The Court held that the huge punitive damage award was improperly issued by the jury, as it believed it was punishing the cigarette company for all injuries it had caused. Why did the court hold it improper for juries to do that?

2. Suppose the jury was instructed to only consider punitive damages for Williams and awarded the same amount. Would that be an unconstitutional violation of due process?

LIGHTER SIDE OF THE LAW
Drop That Fry! Hands over Your Head!

12-year-old Ansche Hedgepeth was arrested for eaing French fries at a Washington, D.C. subway (Metro) station in clear violation of the rules. She was searched, put in handcuffs behind her back, and had her shoelaces removed until she was released to her mother several hours later. She sued for violation of equal protection.

She lost. "There is no fundamental right to freedom from physical restraint in cases where probable cause for arrest is present."

Source: *Hedgepeth v. Washington Metro Area Transit,* 284 F.Supp.2d 145

Getty Images

Equal Protection

The Fourteenth Amendment, as previously noted, says, "No state shall ... deny ... the equal protection of the laws." The *equal protection* clause has come to mean that governments must treat people equally. However, equal protection does not extend to all government activities. Some actions by government that discriminate are held to tougher standards than others.

Going back to our example concerning state limits on tobacco, suppose a state passed a law prohibiting people under age 25 or over age 65 from making, consuming, or selling tobacco products. A challenge to the law would be brought by someone under age 25 or over age 65 claiming that the equal protection clause of the Fourteenth Amendment is violated. That is, persons in those age groups belong to the class of persons affected by the law, which they claim is constitutionally wrong because it creates a class that suffers a loss of freedom. To uphold such a law that classifies persons, the court must find a valid governmental interest, such as public health because people under 25 may have higher addiction rates than older people who have access to tobacco, and to keep down expenditures on health care for people over age 65, who are in the Medicare program. While it may be rational to have age restrictions on access to tobacco, there could be no such rationale for restrictions on tobacco based on race or sex.

Government action that discriminates on the basis of race is held to a standard of strict scrutiny. Hence, government programs that discriminate are not likely to meet a Fourteenth Amendment challenge unless there is a compelling state interest. This meant, of course, that "Jim Crow" laws that discriminated against minorities were stricken as unconstitutional.

State classifications based on sex are also subject to scrutiny. To be allowed to stand, such laws must substantially relate to important government objectives and provide "exceeding persuasive justification," as the Supreme Court held in the 1996 case, *U.S.* v. *Virginia*. It held that the state of Virginia violated the equal protection clause by excluding women from the Virginia Military Institute.

Claims of violations of due process and equal protection are strongest when they involve sex or race discrimination, but these constitutional protections are due all persons, including businesses. However, when a business claims it has suffered an injury to its protected rights, the review will not be as strict as when it involves an individual, as we see in the *Club Italia* case.

Club Italia Soccer and Sports Organization, Inc. v. Charter Township of Shelby, Michigan
United States Court of Appeals, Sixth Circuit
470 F. 3d 286 (2006)

Case Background *The company Soccer City contacted the Township of Shelby about the development and construction of soccer facilities on town property. The town authorized it to conduct environmental tests on the land and to submit a formal development proposal. After finding a suitable site, Soccer City submitted a formal proposal.*

Club Italia, a non profit organization, got a copy of Soccer City's proposal from the town, complained about the bidding process, and expressed an interest in submitting a proposal. The town board voted to accept other proposals, giving interested parties three weeks to submit bids. Club Italia did not submit a bid in the time allowed, so the town gave the contract to Soccer City, the only bidder.

Club Italia sued the town, claiming the bidding procedure violated the Due Process and Equal Protection Clauses, as made actionable under 42 U.S.C. § 1983. The district court granted the town summary judgment; Club Italia appealed.

Case Decision Clay, Circuit Judge

* * *

The Due Process Clause of the Fourteenth Amendment prohibits states from "depriv[ing] ... any person of life, liberty, or property, without due process of law." In essence, Plaintiff's due process claim is that, as a prospective bidder, Plaintiff had a property or liberty interest in the opportunity to bid and it was

denied that interest without due process of the law. In other words, Plaintiff claims Defendant's bidding regulations denied Plaintiff its procedural due process rights under the Fourteenth Amendment.

The right to procedural due process "requires that when a State seeks to terminate [a protected] interest ... it must afford 'notice and opportunity for hearing appropriate to the nature of the case' before the termination becomes effective." Importantly, procedural due process rights are only violated when a *protected* liberty or property interest is denied without adequate hearing. Thus, in order to succeed on this claim, Plaintiff must show (1) that it was deprived of a *protected* liberty or property interest, and (2) that such deprivation occurred without the requisite due process of law. . . .

While this class of liberty interests is intentionally broad, it should not be viewed as a catchall category to support any and all due process violations. The Due Process Clause cannot be used to execute a judicial coup over the handling of government contracts under the guise of protecting liberty interests. Rather, a state actor's decision to deny a plaintiff a single contract only amounts to a restraint on business when those "actions ... preclude [Plaintiff] from entering into other contracts with the State, [or] besmirch [Plaintiff's] good name."

continues

In the present case, Defendant's decision to award the challenged contract to Soccer City instead of Plaintiff did not besmirch Plaintiff's name, nor did it preclude Plaintiff from entering into any other contracts with the state. This decision affected only the instant contract. . . . Plaintiff has failed to allege the deprivation of a liberty interest.

Property interests are not created by the Constitution but "by existing rules or understandings that stem from an independent source such as state law rules or understandings that secure certain benefits and that support claims of entitlement to those benefits." According to this Court, a constitutionally protected property interest in a publicly bid contract can be demonstrated in two ways. A bidder can either show that it actually was awarded the contract and then deprived of it, or that, under state law, the County had limited discretion, which it abused, in awarding the contract.

It is clear from the record that Plaintiff is unable to make either of the requisite showings. Plaintiff does not argue that it was ever awarded, or even considered for, this contract because it was unable to even submit a bid. Further, it is undisputed that there was no external factor that limited Defendant's discretion in awarding this contract. The bidding regulations Defendant enacted were entirely self-imposed. . . .

Plaintiff asserts that the "invitation to compete" created a property interest in the right to bid itself, so there existed a protected property interest. While we agree that this is the proper inquiry, we are unpersuaded by Plaintiff's argument. . . .

Since Plaintiff is unable to allege that it was deprived of a liberty or property interest protected by the Due Process Clause, we need not reach the question of whether the plaintiff was afforded the requisite procedural due process. Therefore, we conclude that Plaintiff's due process claim was properly dismissed.

* * *

Accordingly, this Court affirms the order of the district court because, while Plaintiff has standing, it fails to state a claim based upon either due process or equal protection.

Questions for Analysis

1. The court found that there was no violation of due process or equal protection in how the contract was issued, but Club Italia claims its rights were injured, because it only had three weeks to submit a complex bid, which was not realistic. Why was that not a violation of due process?
2. Since courts give more careful study to claims made based on race or sex discrimination, suppose Club Italia was a minority-owned firm. Would that have gotten more sympathy from the court?

Summary

- The commerce clause and the necessary and proper clause give Congress nearly unlimited discretion to regulate and tax business. Unless a statute specifies that certain businesses are exempt, regulations apply to all, since even local (intrastate) business has been held to affect interstate business.
- States may impose regulations that do not conflict with federal regulations or may impose regulations in areas in which Congress gives them specific regulatory authority, but states may not impose burdens on interstate commerce. Numerous state regulatory and taxing schemes have been limited because they violate the commerce clause of the Constitution.
- The taxing power of the federal government is nearly unlimited. Taxes may be used for purposes other than just to raise revenues. They may be discriminatory or used to regulate and may be punitive in nature. The Supreme Court rarely questions the taxing schemes of Congress. State taxing schemes may not discriminate against interstate or international commerce.
- Commercial speech is afforded a high level of First Amendment protection. Businesses have the right to participate in political discussion whether or not it concerns an issue that directly affects business.

- Restrictions on commercial speech are subject to constitutional guidelines concerning strong public necessity. Truthful speech about lawful activities may be regulated only if the regulation would advance a substantial governmental interest and the regulation is no more extensive than is necessary.

- Since companies have Fourth Amendment guarantees against unreasonable searches and seizures, law enforcement authorities can be required to obtain warrants for most inspections. The main exception is in the case of closely regulated industries. The business sensibility of requiring an inspector to obtain a warrant for a routine inspection is dubious.

- Companies may not withhold documents or testimony requested by prosecutors on the grounds that the evidence might incriminate the company; only individuals may invoke that Fifth Amendment right. Efforts to evade the requirement to testify by holding corporate evidence out of the country will not necessarily work.

- When government agencies prevent property from being used in a legitimate manner because of long, unjustified procedural delays, or if agencies impose rules that substantially change the property value, compensation may be sought under the just compensation clause of the Fifth Amendment.

- The Supreme Court has held that large damage awards—(including punitive damages)—by juries against businesses do not violate the Eighth Amendment protection against excessive fines, nor do they violate Fourteenth Amendment due process clause protections of fair play and substantial justice.

- The due process clause of the Fourteenth Amendment has been used to extend constitutional protections to matters subject to state regulation. Economic regulations must be shown to be related to a legitimate government interest, such as public safety. The clause is also used to ensure fairness in law enforcement procedures.

- The equal protection clause of the Fourteenth Amendment is used to protect individuals from suffering a loss of freedom from state laws that discriminate against a class of persons, when there is no compelling governmental interest in the law, such as public health or safety.

Terms to Know

You should be able to define the following terms:

commerce clause, 76	self-incrimination, 90	excessive fines, 93
necessary and proper clause, 76	just compensation or takings clause, 91	due process clause, 94
interstate commerce, 77		equal protection clause, 94
commercial speech, 86	eminent domain, 91	

Discussion Question

1. Congress requires, via the Internal Revenue Service, that you report to the IRS any income from illegal activities, such as drug dealing. If you report the income, you reveal your illegal activities. If you do not report the income and the dealing is discovered, you can be charged with income tax evasion. Does this violate the Fifth Amendment? If not, why not?

Case Questions

1. Many states prohibit their lottery tickets from being sold out of the state, so Pic-A-State would have its agents buy lottery tickets in various states and hold them there; someone in

Pennsylvania would buy a claim on the tickets held in the other states. Congress passed a law prohibiting interstate transmission of lottery ticket information to be used for lottery ticket sales. Pic-A-State, which was being put out of business, challenged the law as unconstitutional. Was it correct? [*Pic-A-State Pa.* v. *Reno*, 76 F.3d 1294 3rd Cir. (1996)]

2. Plaistow, New Hampshire, passed an ordinance prohibiting truck traffic during late-night hours at a truck terminal loading and unloading facility. It did so to reduce noise and fumes for the benefit of town residents. The truck terminal had been in operation several years. Most of the trucks came five miles from an interstate highway to change loads. The truckers contested the regulation as a restriction on interstate commerce and maintained that regulating an area (interstate trucking) subject to federal regulations was illegal. Were the truckers right? [*New Hampshire Motor Transport Assn.* v. *Town of Plaistow*, 67 F.3d 326 (1st Cir., 1995)]

3. The state of Iowa had a statute limiting to 55 feet the length of trucks on its highways. This made it illegal for commonly used double-trailer trucks 65 feet long to use Iowa highways. The shippers had to either use shorter trucks or go around the state. Iowa justified the regulation on the basis of safety on the highways, and because the bigger trucks caused more damage to its highways. Was this regulation constitutional? [*Kassel* v. *Consolidated Freightways Corp.*, 450 U.S. 662 (1981)]

4. When margarine was invented, it cut into the butter market. The dairy lobby begged Congress for help and got it in the form of a federal tax on margarine of one quarter of a cent per pound on white margarine and ten cents per pound on yellow margarine. Obviously, since people were used to yellow butter, white margarine was unattractive and less competitive. This discriminatory tax on margarine, especially yellow margarine, was challenged. What resulted? [*McCray* v. *U.S.*, 195 U.S. 27 (1904)]

✓ Check your answer at http://academic.cengage.com/blaw/meiners

5. Montana imposed a tax on coal that ran as high as 30 percent of its value. The tax generated as much as 20 percent of all state revenues. Since over 90 percent of the coal was shipped to other states, the tax was mostly borne by non-Montanans in higher utility prices. Was this tax constitutional? [*Commonwealth Edison* v. *Montana*, 453 U.S. 609 (1981)]

6. Massachusetts imposed a tax on all milk sold in the state. The tax proceeds, collected by the state, were distributed to dairy farmers in Massachusetts. Milk buyers who bought milk from out-of-state dairies contested the tax as unconstitutional for interfering with interstate commerce. Were they correct? [*West Lynn Creamery* v. *Healy*, 114 S.Ct. 2205 (1994)]

✓ Check your answer at http://academic.cengage.com/blaw/meiners

7. The City of Skagway, Alaska, adopted an ordinance to curb aggressive sales tactics aimed at pedestrians and tourists and to preserve the historic character of the town. It restricts person-to-person solicitation activities to enclosed structures or to areas containing at least 200 square feet of vending space. Some tour operators, who solicited customers on the street, contested the ordinance as a violation of the First Amendment. The trial court held that the ordinance was too broad in scope. The city appealed. Is the ban in violation of commercial speech rights? [*City of Skagway* v. *Robertson*, 143 P.3d 965 Sup. Ct., Alaska (2006)]

8. The city of Cincinnati, for reasons of the safety and appearance of its streets and sidewalks, would not allow new racks on public property that distributed "commercial handbills" (free newspapers and advertising papers). Regular newspapers were allowed to have racks. The publishers of the free circulars sued the city for violating their First Amendment rights. Did they win? [*Cincinnati* v. *Discovery Network*, 113 S.Ct. 1505 (1993)]

✓ Check your answer at http://academic.cengage.com/blaw/meiners

9. Under the Hazardous Materials Transportation Act, the Secretary of Transportation regulates the transportation of hazardous materials. The regulatory scheme includes warrantless, unannounced inspections of property and records involved in transporting hazardous materials. A propane gas dealer contested the constitutionality of surprise, warrantless inspections of its transport facilities. The government sued to force such inspections. Was that position upheld? [*U.S.* v. *V-1 Oil Co.*, 63 F.3d 909 9th Cir. (1995)]

10. Albert Wild was served a summons by the Internal Revenue Service to appear and testify about the tax records of Air Conditioning Supply Company, of which Wild was owner and president. He appeared but refused to produce the records, claiming Fifth Amendment protection against self-incrimination. The IRS wanted to force him to produce the records of the company. Could they do so? [*Wild* v. *Brewer*, 329 F.2d 924 9th Cir. (1964)]

    ✓ **Check your answer at http://academic.cengage.com/blaw/meiners**

11. A church owned land in a rural area that it used as a recreation area for disabled children. A fire in the area destroyed vegetation, allowing flooding to occur. To protect public safety, the county adopted an ordinance prohibiting any new building in the area until it determined what to do. The church request to rebuild was denied for six years while the county pondered what the building code, if any, should be for the area. The church sued for loss of use of the land. Could it recover under the just compensation clause of the Fifth Amendment? [*First English Evangelical Lutheran Church of Glendale* v. *Los Angeles County*, 482 U.S. 304 (1987)]

12. Campbell caused an accident in which another person was killed. His insurance company, State Farm, refused to pay claims related to the accident and took the case to trial, where Campbell and State Farm lost. State Farm paid the entire judgment, but Campbell sued the company for bad faith and emotional distress. The jury awarded him $1 million in compensatory damages and $145 million in punitive damages. The Utah supreme court upheld the award. State Farm appealed to the U.S. Supreme Court. Would the punitive damages stand? [*State Farm* v. *Campbell*, 123 S., Ct. 1513 (2003)]

13. The New York City Transit Authority ruled that methadone users, who are usually recovering from heroin addiction, would not work for it in any job capacity. The district court held that this violated the equal protection clause by unfairly excluding methadone users, even from jobs that were not safety sensitive, such as drivers. The Transit Authority appealed to the Supreme Court. Was there a violation of the equal protection clause? [*New York City Transit Authority* v. *Beazer*, 440 U.S. 568 (1979)]

Ethics Question

1. A firm subject to OSHA inspections requires an OSHA inspector, who shows up unexpectedly one day, to get a warrant before engaging in the search. The firm owner knows that the inspector is a genuine inspector and that there is no question that the warrant to search will be issued. However, requiring the inspector to get the warrant takes half a day of the inspector's time (which is paid for by taxpayers). Is it ethical to bar such inspections?

Internet Assignment

http://www.archives.gov/national-archives-experience/characters/constitutiion.html
http://www.law.cornell.edu/anncon/
http://www.findlaw.com/casecode/constitution/
http://confinder.richmond.edu/

Search Google for *constitution* and *site:archives.gov*. Restricting the search to the Web site *archives.gov* will allow you to access an official version of the Constitution of the United States. The texts of the constitutions of many of the countries of the world are also readily available on the Internet. The Internet, however, may not the best source for scholarly analysis of constitutional law issues. While some annotations to the U.S. Constitution are available for free on the Internet, the print version of the *United States Code Annotated* containing the U.S. consitution and related annotations comprised four bound volumes and over 2250 pages, as of 2007, Careful scholarly research is best performed using books and researched databases licensed by your institution's library.

Criminal Law and Business

Chapter 5

Scott Levine owned Snipermail, a Florida company that distributed Internet ads to e-mail addresses. Through his business, Levine had access to certain Acxiom databases. Acxiom provides data management services for companies for marketing and other business purposes. Levine went beyond his authorized access and collected data including names, telephone numbers, addresses, e-mail addresses, and detailed demographics on a large number of people. He did not use the data to steal from anyone, but sold it to a company to use in an ad campaign.

Levine was charged with several crimes: unauthorized access to data, access device fraud, and obstruction of justice. At trial, a friend of Levine's, a police officer, testified that Levine helped many people and was not violent. He thought Levine should not go to prison "because of addresses and e-mails and phone numbers." Friends argued that he should be given home detention, not prison time. The Secret Service argued that the Internet and cyberspace should be free from cybercrime. The judge ruled that, due to Levine's actions, Acxiom lost $850,000, and sentenced him to eight years in prison plus three years probation. Levine is forbidden access to encryption devices. ∎

Getty Images

Crime

Scott Levine violated laws passed by Congress that make it a criminal offense to break into secured computer databases. It is a new version of old criminal laws regarding physically breaking into property belonging to another, which can also lead to prison time. Congress and state legislatures decide which acts will be held to be criminal offenses, that is, ones for which the accused may be sent to prison. Hence, we have a federal criminal code and a criminal code in each state.

A *crime* may be a positive or negative act that violates a penal law; that is, it is an offense against a state or the federal government. According to *Black's Law Dictionary*, a crime is "any act done in violation of those duties which an individual owes to the community, and for the breach of which the law has provided that the offender shall make satisfaction to the public." What crimes are and what punishments there may be is determined by statutes passed by federal and state legislatures, within limits set by federal and state constitutions.

As discussed in Chapter 1, we distinguish between *civil law* and *criminal law*. Civil law concerns civil and private rights and remedies. That is, some laws passed by legislatures are declared to be civil in nature. The government enforces those laws, at the federal, state, or local level, but there are no criminal penalties. Violations of civil statutes result in fines or orders to do or not do something, but not jail time. Private rights are enforced by common-law actions, when private parties bring suit, usually regarding torts, contracts, or property law. These are not criminal actions either, as only the government can bring criminal charges.

Crime Categories

Upon being found by a court to have committed a crime, that is, to be *convicted*, the range of possible punishments is set out in the statute that declared the matter to be criminal. Some crimes may be punished by death, but most are punishable by imprisonment and/or by paying a fine. Because of a crime, one may be removed from public office and may be disqualified from holding office or voting in public elections.

Crimes and *misdemeanors* are technically the same thing, but in practice, a crime represents a more serious offense than a misdemeanor. A *felony* is a serious crime. In many states, a crime declared to be a felony may be punished by more than a year in prison. That is the definition used in the *Model Penal Code* adopted by the American Law Institute. That Code has been adopted in part by a majority of the states.

In the federal criminal code, and in many states, felonies are listed in classes (Class A, Class B, etc.) or in degrees (first degree, second degree, etc.) to denote the seriousness of a criminal charge. For example, first degree murder is the most serious. It is a murder that has been planned or that was committed with extreme cruelty. Second degree murders are not premeditated and generally receive smaller punishments.

Manslaughter, which may be voluntary or involuntary, is an unlawful killing committed recklessly or under the influence of extreme mental distress. A killing done in the "heat of passion" may be declared manslaughter, subject to lesser punishment, than a murder.

Similarly, other crimes may have different degrees or classes of severity.

Types of Felonies

Exhibit 5.1 shows the actual number of crimes, which are generally classified as crimes against persons or against property. Note that the number of crimes reported

Exhibit 5.1
Number of Crimes
Reported in the U.S. (2005)

Total Violent Crimes	**1,390,695**
Murder and Manslaughter	16,692
Forcible Rape	93,934
Robbery	417,122
Aggravated Assault	862,947
Total Property Crimes	**10,166,159**
Burglary	2,154,126
Larceny-theft	6,776,807
Motor vehicle theft	1,235,226

Source: Bureau of Justice Statistics

varies quite a bit compared to the actual number of incidents. Most murders and vehicle thefts are reported, but many rapes are not. Violent crimes are ones where physical force is used: murder, rape, armed robbery, and assault and battery. Such crimes generally carry the most severe penalties. Crimes against property include burglary and theft, which includes receipt of stolen goods. *White-collar crimes*, discussed more below, include nonviolent crimes committed by corporations or individuals. Embezzlement, bribery, fraud, and violations of federal and state laws regulating business, such as securities laws, generally fall into this category. Victimless crimes are criminal acts in which no other party is immediately involved, such as possession of illegal drugs.

Lesser Criminal Offenses

Misdemeanors generally are classified as crimes that are to be punished by less than one year in prison. Many are punished by fines, but not jail time. As is the case with felonies, a combination of jail time and fines may be imposed. One may also be ordered to forfeit property; vehicles used to transport illegal drugs are often forfeited to the state. Many states classify misdemeanors by their level of severity—class A, B, and C. The term petty offense may also describe misdemeanors in some jurisdictions.

At the local level of government, ordinances may be enacted. They are the equivalent of municipal or county statutes. The powers of local governments are determined by state law. Their ordinances usually deal with zoning, building regulations, and local safety issues. In most instances, they may be punished only by fine or by jail time, much like a misdemeanor.

LIGHTER SIDE OF THE LAW
You Mean It Isn't Usual Police Practice?

Summers, a McDonald's manager, got a call from someone pretending to be a police officer, who told her that her employee, 18-year-old Ogborn, was suspected of stealing a customer's purse. The caller told Summers to strip search Ogborn, which she did, taking her clothes away from her in a back room. While in the room, she was forced to have sex with Summers' fiancé, Nix.

Nix was sentenced to five years imprisonment for sexual abuse and unlawful imprisonment. Summers, who called off the engagement, was convicted of misdemeanor unlawful imprisonment. The judge gave her one year probation. Summers said it is McDonald's fault for not warning her about strip-search hoax phone calls and that she was a victim too. She sued McDonald's for $31 million in damages in civil litigation.

Source: *The Courier-Journal*, Louisville, Kentucky.

Getty Images

Prosecution of Crimes

Legislatures decide what will be criminal offenses. Government agencies charged with enforcing the laws decide who will be charged with committing crimes. Prosecutors, after receiving reports from the police or other investigators, may decide whether or not to bring charges. Since all law-enforcement agencies have limited resources, not all claims of crimes are investigated or result in charges being brought. Further, this is where politics and personal preference can come into play. Prosecutors can avoid charging favored parties with crimes or bring lesser charges against them, but may go hard after parties who have fallen out of favor. While we want unbiased prosecution of crimes, it is not a perfect process.

To be convicted of a crime, it must be shown that 1) the accused committed the illegal act, and 2) that there was necessary intent or state of mind to commit the act. When one commits a criminal act, they perform a wrongful deed, an *actus reus.* That is the physical part of the crime—the guilty act. That fact must be established at trial. There must also be *mens rea;* this is the criminal intent that must be established, the "guilty mind" or showing of wrongful purpose in the criminal act committed. If these are present, so that it is shown that the defendant caused the act involved, then guilt can be established. In the *Salas* case, we see a discussion of the right of the defendant to raise the issue of knowledge of a violation as a defense.

People v. Salas
Supreme Court of California
127 P.3d 40, 37 Cal.4th 967 (2006)

Case Background *Salas ran a number of partnerships formed to buy property for development. He and his employees called numerous people, asking if they would like to invest in the partnerships. The state investigated and brought criminal charges for selling unregistered securities in violation of state law. Defendants admitted that the partnership interests were securities that had not been registered. However, they claimed they believed the partnership interests were exempt from registration.*

The trial court instructed the jury that this good faith belief was irrelevant to criminal culpability and defendants were convicted. The appeals court reversed, holding that guilty knowledge—meaning either knowledge of the security's nonexempt status or criminal negligence in failing to determine its status—is an element of the crime of selling an unregistered security. The trial court erred when it failed to instruct the jury in that manner. That decision was appealed.

Case Decision Kennard, Justice

* * *

Depending upon the crime, a requirement of guilty knowledge may mean that defendants are innocent unless they know the facts making their conduct criminal. In other cases, it is sufficient that the defendants either know those facts *or* were criminally negligent in failing to know them. ["In every crime or public offense there must exist a union, or joint operation of act and intent, or criminal negligence."] Defendants here do not argue that a violation of [the securities law] requires that the seller actually knew that the security he sold should have been registered; however, they contend that criminal liability requires that a seller of securities either knew the security was not exempt from registration or was criminally negligent in failing to know. The Attorney General, on the other hand, argues that a seller is guilty if he "willfully"—that is, intentionally—sells an unregistered security, without regard to whether the seller knew or should have known that the security should have been registered....

[We] hold that a defendant is not guilty of the crime of selling an unregistered security . . . if there is

continues

a reasonable doubt whether the defendant knew the security was not exempt from regulation or was criminally negligent in failing to know that the security was not exempt.

* * *

Under the so-called rule of convenience and necessity, "the burden of proving an exonerating fact may be imposed on a defendant if its existence is "peculiarly" within his personal knowledge and proof of its nonexistence by the prosecution would be relatively difficult or inconvenient." . . .

This analysis applies here. A defendant's knowledge or lack of knowledge of the exempt status of the securities is a fact peculiarly within the defendant's personal knowledge. What steps, if any, the defendant took to determine whether the security is exempt often will also be a fact peculiarly within the defendant's knowledge. There is no unfairness or hardship in requiring the defendant to assume the burden of presenting evidence of the facts on which he or she relies. . . .

We hold that lack of knowledge that a security is not exempt (or criminal negligence) is an affirmative defense, on which the trial court must instruct only if the defendant presents enough evidence to raise a reasonable doubt. Consequently, the prosecution will not

have to prove that a defendant lacked a good faith belief in every one of the numerous grounds for exemption; it need only address the evidence the defense presented to raise a reasonable doubt as to the defendant's good faith.

* * *

Given [Salas'] self-proclaimed awareness of the exemption requirements, his total control over [operations], his admitted personal supervision of records related to investors, and his involvement in conversations with investors, the evidence that Salas was criminally negligent in not knowing that there were [violations of securities laws] was overwhelming. . . .

[The conviction of Salas stands, but not that of his employees, who should have been allowed to raise an affirmative defense regarding their knowledge of the law.]

Questions for Analysis

1. The court held that there is a right to raise an affirmative defense about lack of knowledge of securities law, so why was the conviction of Salas upheld?
2. Why would the court use a different standard for employees than for Salas, the boss of the operation?

Criminal acts need not be planned; they may be based on negligence. *Criminal negligence* as explained by *Black's Law Dictionary,* is "a degree of carelessness amounting to a culpable disregard of rights and safety of others." That is, it is criminal conduct that is not intentional, but is wrongful because one failed to act with the reasonable care that is expected under the circumstances. For example, if someone gets drunk and drives the wrong way down a highway and kills a person in an accident, there may be guilt for negligent homicide or manslaughter. There was no intent to kill the person who was the victim, but the act showed a disregard for the safety of others and violated the obligation to be prudent in our actions. A driver knows, or should know, that reckless driving, drunk or not, can lead to death or injury.

Defenses

If proper procedure is not followed in a criminal case, prosecution will not be successful. If a crime is not prosecuted within the time set by the *statute of limitations,* then the state loses the right to bring suit. That time varies by crime. For unsolved murders, it may never end. The statute of limitations may *toll;* that is, the clock stops running under certain circumstances, such as if one has fled the country to avoid prosecution.

There are, of course, specific defenses that may be raised in criminal cases. These include *intoxication* and *insanity,* but in practice these defenses rarely succeed.

In some violent crimes cases the claim of *self-defense* may be made. The defendant admits to the use of physical force but argues it was justifiable to protect himself against another person. Conviction may be avoided also if one can show that law enforcement authorities set up a trap to lure someone into a crime they had no intention of committing. While it is legitimate to spring traps on criminals, *entrapment* can be a successful defense.

When a person is arrested on suspicion of a crime, they must be read their *Miranda rights*. This refers to a Supreme Court opinion in 1966 that held that under the Constitution, persons accused of a crime, or held in suspicion of a crime, must be informed of their right to remain silent, as provided by the Fifth Amendment, their right to be represented by counsel, and must be told that statements they make can be used as evidence against them.

Evidence

While evidence in civil trial must be properly gathered and presented, the standards in criminal trials are more strict. The state gathers the evidence in criminal cases. It must be shown that the evidence was gathered, handled, and presented properly. If not, the evidence is excluded and the entire prosecution may fail. Hence, defendants pay close attention to procedural aspects of criminal trials and the quality of the evidence and the procedures surrounding the evidence.

To obtain evidence, law enforcement authorities may search property and seize documents and other physical items that they think may be relevant. As discussed in the chapter on Constitutional law, the Fourth Amendment protects us against improper search and seizure. It violates our privacy interests to have our person and property subject to unjust searches. If evidence is gathered improperly, then it may not be used at trial under the *exclusionary rule*. A huge number of cases turn on this issue, and the Supreme Court has cases that address some aspect of search and seizure every year.

Before authorities may search property or persons and seize evidence, unless they are in "hot pursuit" of a suspected criminal, a warrant must be obtained first. A *warrant* is issued by a judge or appointed magistrate who, in the name of the state, authorizes an officer to search for and seize any property, often called personal "effects," that may be evidence of a crime. To obtain the warrant, the law enforcement officials must show *probable cause* to the judge. That means that they have reasonable grounds, based on their knowledge to date, to believe that a person should be searched or arrested. The *Young* case discusses a search incident.

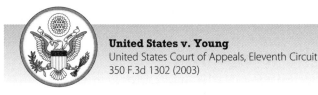

United States v. Young
United States Court of Appeals, Eleventh Circuit
350 F.3d 1302 (2003)

Case Background *Under Internal Revenue Service (IRS) regulations, federal taxes on gasoline and diesel fuel do not apply to sales of fuels for marine use. Marinas that sell tax-free fuel must obtain a "637 certificate" from the IRS. Young obtained a certificate for his business, a marine retailer in Marco Island, Florida. The IRS believed Young never used the fuel for marine purposes, but sold it in cash* *deals to truck stops and service stations that should have bought fuel that had paid federal taxes.*

The IRS believed that Young shipped his sale proceeds by Federal Express, which agreed to let the IRS x-ray packages shipped by Young. Packages were found to contain large amounts of cash. Based on the x-rays, the IRS obtained a warrant to seize and open Young's packages,
continues

which did contain cash. At trial, Young moved to suppress that evidence, because the IRS did not obtain a warrant to x-ray the packages originally. The trial court rejected that motion and Young was convicted. He appealed.

Case Decision Fay, Circuit Judge

* * *

The Federal Express packages were "effects" in the context of the Fourth Amendment, and therefore defendants presumptively possessed a legitimate expectation of privacy in their contents. . . .

However . . . every Federal Express airbill utilized by defendants [states] "We may, at our option, open and inspect your packages prior to or after you give them to us to deliver."

* * *

No reasonable person would expect to retain his or her privacy interest in a package shipment after signing an airbill containing an explicit, written warning that the carrier is authorized to act in direct contravention to that interest. Federal Express told its customers two things: (1) do not ship cash, and (2) we may open and inspect your packages at our option. As a matter of law, this simply eliminates any expectation of privacy. We affirm the district court's finding that Young did not have any legitimate expectation of privacy in the packages x-rayed by the IRS agents. . . .

Young assumed the risk that Federal Express might consent to a search. When Federal Express did consent, Young's Fourth Amendment rights were not offended.

Affirmed

Questions for Analysis

1. The IRS could x-ray the FedEx packages without a warrant, but if the FedEx notice did not say anything about contents being subject to search, would the IRS have been allowed to x-ray the packages without a warrant?
2. Suppose Young had been carrying a briefcase filled with cash and was driving along the highway in Florida. Could an IRS agent stop him and inspect the briefcase?

Prosecution

Suppose you have an employee you are sure has been stealing from your store. You call the police to report this matter. Since the person suspected of a crime is not caught red-handed in the act, there is no immediate arrest, as would be the case if the police caught someone breaking into your store at night. If law enforcement authorities, after reviewing your evidence, decide to bring criminal charges against your employee, certain steps are followed, with some variation from place to place.

Your evidence would be considered by a prosecuting attorney. More evidence might be requested, and the prosecutor's office might do its own investigation. Assuming the prosecutor agrees to go forward, a determination would be made as to what kind of charges to bring—misdemeanor or felony. In some instances a grand jury is used to review potential felony cases. The grand jury determines probable cause. It is uncommon for a grand jury not to issue an *indictment* when so requested by a prosecutor.

Arraignment

When criminal charges are filed, the accused is usually arrested by the police based on a warrant. In many non violent matters, a date is set by which the accused must surrender to the court, rather than have the police take the person into custody. The suspect is "booked" at the police station, photographed, fingerprinted, and searched. The matter is entered on the police record, and the accused must be allowed the chance to contact a lawyer. There will be a court appearance called an *arraignment*, at which time the district attorney gives the accused a copy of the criminal charges. The appearance may be before a judge or a magistrate, and the defendant may plead guilty, no contest (*nolo contendere*), or innocent.

If the judge allows the matter to proceed, the accused is usually released and ordered to appear once a court date is set. In some cases, the defendant will have to post bail to be released prior to trial. Violent criminals who pose a threat to the community, or those who pose a threat of taking off before trial, may be held without bail; or bail may be set so high that it is unlikely to be met.

In many misdemeanor cases, there may be a settlement conference to save court time. The attorneys attempt to resolve the matter without trial, but under the supervision of a judge. If there is no agreement, then trial is scheduled.

In felony cases, the judge decides at the arraignment whether there is sufficient evidence to proceed or if the matter should be reduced to a misdemeanor or dismissed. In practice, most cases proceed based on the charges brought by the state. If a trial date for the felony charges is set, there is likely to be an attempt to obtain a *plea bargain* to save the time, cost, and uncertainty of a trial. A plea bargain allows the matter to be settled under supervision of a judge, by having the defendant plead guilty to the charges, plead to a lesser charge, or plead no contest in exchange for punishment specified in an agreement with the prosecutor. Most criminal law matters are settled this way.

Trial

If there is a trial, the government attorney, often a district attorney, presents the prosecution's case. Both sides have opening statements and then present their cases. As noted above, all evidence must have been properly gathered and handled to protect the rights of the accused. As the store owner, you would be likely called to testify about the matter. In this case, you would be both a victim and a witness, but the charge of, say, embezzlement, is a crime against the state. That is why most criminal cases are called something like *State* v. *Clinton* or *People* v. *Bush*. If the employee stole money from your business, you could sue the employee for the common law tort of conversion, but that is a separate legal matter from the criminal case brought by the state.

As discussed in Chapter 1, to be convicted in a criminal case, the defendant must be found guilty "beyond a reasonable doubt." That means the evidence fully satisfies and convinces the court to a moral certainty. The facts presented at trial must, by virtue of their value when subjected to study, prove guilt.

If the jury finds the accused innocent, that is the end of that criminal matter. The rule against double jeopardy prevents a defendant from being tried a second time for the same crime. If the jury cannot agree on a verdict, then a mistrial may be declared. At that point, it is up to the prosecutor to decide if time and resources will be invested in another trial, if the matter will be dropped, or if lesser charges will be filed. If the defendant is found guilty, depending on the severity of the charges and the criminal history of the defendant, there may be prison time, jail time, probation, fine, and/or restitution to the victim.

Event Occurs
   Law enforcement authorities notified, respond, investigate; arrest may occur
Reports Filed
   Prosecutor evaluates matter; may dismiss, order arrest, or issue warrant
   Charges filed seeking conviction; more evidence gathered
   Arraignment—Indictment Read
   Settlement, Dismissal or Trial

Exhibit 5.2
General Steps in Criminal Procedure

White-Collar Crime

Google the term *white-collar crime* and you will get more than a million hits. The term is reputed to have originated in 1939, when used in a speech to mean a "crime committed by a person of respectability and high social status in the course of his occupation." Today it probably refers to any criminal activity for financial advantage that occurs in the course of business. A person need not be of "high social status" to commit white-collar crime. What is a crime has expanded greatly over the years, as more things have been declared criminal activities and penalties have been stiffened. The FBI estimates that such crimes cause economic losses of at least a third of a trillion dollars a year. While most cases are against individuals, corporations can be subject to prosecution. Many areas are covered by federal and state statutes that can impose criminal liability for violations.

This is a list of the major areas of white-collar crime that can result in criminal convictions. Some areas of law will be covered in detail later in the text; others are only mentioned here.

Antitrust Under the Sherman Act and Clayton Act (2004), prison terms may be imposed on those involved in price fixing and certain other anti competitive practices, and such terms can be as long as 10 years. Antitrust prosecutions have increased in recent years as indicated by this statement from the Department of Justice:

> Anticompetitive conduct by criminal cartels—such as price fixing, bid rigging, and procurement fraud—remains the highest enforcement priority of the Antitrust Division. For the fiscal year ending on September 30, 2006, the Division obtained criminal fines totaling $473,445,600, representing a 40 percent increase over FY 2005, and filed 33 criminal cases, many involving multiple defendants. Fiscal Year 2006 yielded 5,383 jail days imposed for price fixing, bid rigging, obstruction, fraud, and related anticompetitive conduct.

Bankruptcy Fraud This is committed when a person or corporation hides or lies about assets in bankruptcy proceedings. It also applies when creditors are given false information, or when illegal pressure is applied to bankruptcy petitioners.

Bribery This usually concerns the offer of or taking of money, goods, services, or other things of value to influence official actions or decisions.

> U.S. Code Section 201. Bribery of public officials and witnesses . . .
>   (b) Whoever—1) directly or indirectly, corruptly gives, offers or promises anything of value to any public official or person who has been selected to be a public official, or offers or promises any public official or any person who has been selected to be a public official to give anything of value to any other person or entity, with intent—(A) to influence any official act . . . 2) being a public official or person selected to be a public official, directly or indirectly, corruptly demands, seeks, receives, accepts, or agrees to receive or accept anything of value personally or for any other person or entity, in return for: (A) being influenced in the performance of any official act. . . .

For example, a member of Congress from California was sentenced to over eight years in prison in 2006 for taking cash in exchange for legislative favors.

Counterfeiting The copying of a genuine item without authorization, especially when it is passed off for the genuine item. It applies to illegal copying of currency, most of which happens outside of the country, as well as to copying designer clothing and other products.

Credit Card Fraud The unauthorized use of a credit card to obtain goods, services, or cash. The Federal Trade Commission gives some common examples:

1) A thief goes through trash to find discarded receipts or carbons and then uses your account numbers illegally. 2) A dishonest clerk makes an extra imprint from your credit or charge card and uses it to make personal charges. 3) You respond to a mailing asking you to call a long distance number for a free trip or bargain-priced travel package. You're told you must join a travel club first, and you're asked for your account number, so you can be billed. The catch: Charges you did not make are added to your bill, and you never get your trip.

Computer and Internet Fraud This often includes credit card fraud or other unauthorized access to financial accounts, as well as unauthorized use of computers and computer files and sabotage of computers. See U.S. Code, Title 18, Sections 1029, 1030, 1362, 2511, 2701-03.

LIGHTER SIDE OF THE LAW
Maybe the Client Will Not Suspect Anything

Attorney Boylan was hired by a client to sue a dealership about a defective car. The client paid him $2,500 for his services. He told the client he got a settlement for $733,000 but was waiting on the money.

When no money ever appeared, the client complained, and Boylan was arrested on criminal fraud charges. The prosecutor was mystified as to why Boylan made up such a huge figure, which could only excite his client.

Source: *Hartford Courant*, Hartford, CT.

Getty Images

Economic Espionage This is the theft or misappropriation of valuable business information, such as a trade secret. Information may be taken from or by a person or a business. As the U.S. Code indicates, the penalties are harshest when such activities involve foreign businesses.

§ 1831. Economic espionage (a) In General—Whoever, intending or knowing that the offense will benefit any foreign government, foreign instrumentality, or foreign agent, knowingly—1) steals, or without authorization appropriates, takes, carries away, or conceals, or by fraud, artifice, or deception obtains a trade secret; 2) without authorization copies, duplicates, sketches, draws, photographs, downloads, uploads, alters, destroys, photocopies, replicates, transmits, delivers, sends, mails, communicates, or conveys a trade secret ... shall ... be fined not more than $500,000 or imprisoned not more than 15 years, or both.

Embezzlement When someone is in a position of trust with money or other valued property, and they take it for their use, they have embezzled. A number of federal and state laws could apply in such cases.

Environmental Law Violations Most federal and state statutes that regulate water, air, and land provide for the possibility of criminal conviction for harming the environment. The Environmental Protection Agency states

The criminal enforcement program has successfully prosecuted significant violations across all major environmental statutes, including: data fraud cases (e.g., private laboratories submitting false environmental data to state and federal environmental agencies); indiscriminate hazardous waste dumping that resulted in serious injuries and death; industry-wide ocean dumping by cruise ships; oil spills that caused significant damage to waterways, wetlands, and beaches; international smuggling of CFC refrigerants that damage the ozone layer and increase skin cancer risk; and illegal handling of hazardous substances such as pesticides and asbestos that exposed children, the poor, and other especially vulnerable groups to potentially serious illness.

While the EPA collects significant fines, its primary settlement goal is to force additional spending, running in the billions of dollars per year, on new pollution reduction measures. It averages 300 criminal prosecutions per year, resulting in 150 to 200 years of prison and jail time imposed on defendants.

Financial Fraud Federal regulatory agencies oversee banks and other financial institutions. Those firms and their employees are subject to potential criminal liability for fraud in loans, financial documents, mortgages, and other abuses.

Government Fraud Various laws govern contracts with public agencies for the provision of supplies and for construction. Besides billing for goods not delivered and double billing, agencies must watch to be sure they are not delivered inferior goods. Fraud laws also apply to federal payment programs, including farm subsidies, public housing, and educational programs. After hurricane Katrina hit New Orleans, there were dozens of convictions for fraud in collecting benefits intended for victims.

Healthcare Fraud Since one in every six dollars in the United States is spent on health care, and most of that is through government agencies or insurance companies, various laws apply to deal with problems of over billing and other scams by hospitals, doctors, ambulance services, laboratories, pharmacies, and extended-care facilities.

Insider Trading According to the Securities and Exchange Commission:

> The securities laws broadly prohibit fraudulent activities of any kind in connection with the offer, purchase, or sale of securities. These provisions are the basis for many types of disciplinary actions, including actions against fraudulent insider trading. Insider trading is illegal when a person trades a security while in possession of material nonpublic information in violation of a duty to withhold the information or refrain from trading.

It is not only company heads who may be convicted of insider trading: business professors can be, too. In 2005, Roger Blackwell, a professor of marketing at Ohio State University, was convicted of 14 counts of insider trading, conspiracy, and obstructing an SEC investigation into trading in the securities of Worthington Foods with information he gained while a member of the company's board of directors.

Insurance Fraud Insurance companies can engage in fraud by charging higher rates than allowed by state regulators, but most fraud is by policy holders who lie about the condition of their property to get lower rates or who pad their claims.

Mail Fraud Since a lot of fraud is committed by mailing materials that help create a fraud, this is a common basis for the government to prosecute those involved in some sort of trickery. According to U.S. Code, Title 18, Section 1341:

> Whoever, having devised or intending to devise any scheme or artifice to defraud, or for obtaining money or property by means of false or fraudulent pretenses, representations, or promises, or to sell, dispose of, loan, exchange, alter, give away,

Getty Images

INTERNATIONAL PERSPECTIVE

Interpol

Interpol is the largest international police organization with 184 member nations. It works to encourage cross-border police cooperation and to combat international crime. Each member nation has a National Central Bureau that is the contact point with the international body.

Interpol plays a major role in the investigation of international criminal activities, such as the drug trade. Since money laundering is key to the drug trade, Interpol devotes significant efforts to helping track the flow of funds from illegal activities. Similarly, it helps track funds used in international terrorism.

In business related areas, Interpol focuses on intellectual property crime, such as counterfeiting and piracy of trademarks, patents, and copyrights. Such illegal trades are estimated to be between 5 to 7 percent of global trade: over a half-trillion dollars.

In the last decade, Interpol has worked more on the problem of fraud involving credit and debit cards in international transactions. It also assists in Internet issues, because many viruses are global, and illegal trade in such things as child pornography is often international. As business becomes increasingly global, and the cost of communication continues to fall, international cooperation in dealing with criminal matters will become ever more important.

distribute, supply, or furnish or procure for unlawful use any counterfeit or spurious coin, obligation, security, or other article, or anything represented to be or intimated or held out to be such counterfeit or spurious article, for the purpose of executing such scheme or artifice or attempting so to do, places in any post office or authorized depository for mail matter, any matter or thing whatever to be sent or delivered by the Postal Service... shall be fined under this title or imprisoned not more than 20 years, or both. If the violation affects a financial institution, such person shall be fined not more than $1,000,000 or imprisoned not more than 30 years, or both.

This statute is wide-reaching. For example, in one case a businessman obtained more than $100 million worth of contracts from the City of Chicago by claiming his companies were minority or woman-owned, so he had a better chance to win contracts. He did all work properly under the contract, but when it was revealed that he lied about the ownership status of his companies, he was convicted of mail fraud, because he had sent materials containing false information. That was held to be the "scheme or artifice" that violated the statute. He was sentenced to 10 years in prison.

Getty Images

ISSUE SPOTTER
What to Do When the Feds Show Up?

The managers at your organization think things have been run properly. But one day federal investigators inform the company that an investigation has begun into possible illegal practices that could lead to assorted charges against the company and managers in the related part of the organization. Maybe no laws have in fact been broken, or maybe someone has been up to something that could in fact be a real problem. What is the proper course of action to take?

Money Laundering Just as the mails are often used in the commission of a crime, so too is money. Hiding the truth about the origins of money is called *money laundering*.

If one is engaged in illegal activities, such as drug dealing, there is still an obligation to report the income from transactions to the government for tax purposes. To avoid charges of income tax evasion, and to report a legitimate source for such income, drug money may be laundered by creating a paper trail that claims a legitimate business origin for the money. Section 1956 of Title 18 is entitled "Laundering of Monetary Instruments." It states:

> Whoever, knowing that the property involved in a financial transaction represents the proceeds of some form of unlawful activity, conducts or attempts to conduct such a financial transaction, which in fact involves the proceeds of specified unlawful activity . . . with the intent to promote the carrying on of specified unlawful activity; or . . . knowing that the transaction is designed in whole or in part . . . to conceal or disguise the nature, the location, the source, the ownership, or the control of the proceeds of specified unlawful activity . . . shall be sentenced to a fine of not more than $500,000 or twice the value of the property involved in the transaction, whichever is greater, or imprisonment for not more than 20 years, or both.

In 2005, 762 defendants were convicted of money laundering by the Treasury Department. The average prison time was over five years. In similar cases brought under bank secrecy laws, over 300 people were convicted and given average prison sentences of 42 months.

Racketeer Influenced and Corrupt Organizations (*RICO*) Act Congress passed RICO in 1970. Its intent was to provide an extra weapon against organized crime, especially the Mafia. Lawyers realized that the Act allows civil claims to be brought by any person injured in their business by a RICO violation. A successful RICO claim automatically receives triple actual damages plus costs and attorneys' fees. The financial windfall available under RICO inspired legal creativity. Civil claims, such as common-law fraud, were portrayed as criminal wrongs, which allowed filing a civil RICO action.

RICO's broad application was the result of Congress' inclusion of mail and wire fraud as crimes upon which a RICO claim could be brought. The federal courts have limited the scope of RICO in the civil context. As a result, civil litigants must jump many barriers before they can expect the financial windfall available under RICO. It is one of the most complicated and unpredictable areas of the law. RICO is rarely applied to the Mafia, but is used in suits against persons, businesses, political protest groups, and terrorist organizations.

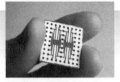

CYBER LAW

Should Criminals Be Let Near the Internet?

People with a criminal history of sex crimes are often restricted as to where they can live, and people are put on notice where they do live as part of an effort to reduce the likelihood of further attacks. What about those who use the Internet for criminal purposes? Should they have restricted access to the Web?

The Internet is used for child pornography, fraud, linking drug dealers together, and other illegal purposes. While those convicted of crimes involving children or child pornography have restricted access to the Internet or use it only with supervision, such as review of usage, the courts have only begun to explore the constitutionality of restricting Internet use by persons convicted of financial crimes. Chief Justice Roberts has indicated that some restrictions could be valid if reasonably related to a defendant's illegal actions. As in all areas of law, courts must balance constitutional liberties against the threat posed by those who engage in illegal activities.

Getty Images

Securities Fraud While insider trading gets a lot of press, securities fraud in the form of market rigging, theft from accounts of clients of securities firms, and other violations of securities laws are much more common. The chapter on securities regulation will cover various aspects of the requirements imposed on professionals in the securities industry.

Tax Evasion The Internal Revenue Service devotes significant resources to tracking down persons and businesses that fail to file tax returns, fail to report all of their income, or overstate their expenses. All are illegal. The federal tax code states:

> Any person who willfully attempts in any manner to evade or defeat any tax imposed by this title or the payment thereof shall, in addition to other penalties provided by law, be guilty of a felony and, upon conviction thereof, shall be fined not more than $100,000 ($500,000 in the case of a corporation), or imprisoned not more than five years, or both, together with the costs of prosecution.

While most investigations are settled without litigation, each year hundreds of persons are imprisoned for tax fraud. Major problem areas include fraud by tax preparers; 109 were sentenced to prison in 2006. That year, 115 people were sentenced to prison for fraud in the construction industry, often for not reporting income; 83 people in the health care industry were sentenced to prison: and 56 people from the restaurant industry were sent to prison, mostly for pocketing cash and not reporting the income, but some for hiding money from drug deals.

Telephone and Telemarketing Fraud According to the Department of Justice:

> Telemarketing fraud is a term that refers generally to any scheme to defraud in which the persons carrying out the scheme use the telephone as their primary means of communicating with prospective victims and trying to persuade them to send money to the scheme. When it solicits people to buy goods and services, to invest money, or to donate funds to charitable causes, a fraudulent telemarketing fraud operation typically uses numerous false and misleading statements, representations, and promises, for three purposes: 1) *To make it appear that the good, service, or charitable cause their telemarketers offer to the public is worth the money that they are asking the consumer to send.* 2) *To obtain immediate payment before the victim can inspect the item of value they expect to receive.* 3) *To create an aura of legitimacy about their operations, by trying to resemble legitimate telemarketing operations, legitimate businesses, or legitimate government agencies.*

Fraud committed on the Internet is essentially the same and is also subject to criminal prosecution. The Justice Department notes that it is "any type of fraud scheme that uses one or more components of the Internet—such as chat rooms, e-mail, message boards, or Web sites—to present fraudulent solicitations to prospective victims, to conduct fraudulent transactions, or to transmit the proceeds of fraud to financial institutions or to others connected with the scheme."

Wire Fraud This is much like mail fraud and telephone or Internet fraud. If there is any electronic communication involved in illegal activities, it is the basis of federal prosecution for an activity that traditionally would have been subject only to state prosecution. Now either federal or state authorities can prosecute for a wide range of activities. U.S. Code, Title 18, Section 1343 provides:

> Whoever, having devised or intending to devise any scheme or artifice to defraud, or for obtaining money or property by means of false or fraudulent pretenses, representations, or promises, transmits or causes to be transmitted by means of wire, radio, or television communication in interstate or foreign commerce, any

Getty Images

INTERNATIONAL PERSPECTIVE

White-Collar Crime in Other Nations

Senior executives in the United States, such as the heads of Enron and WorldCom, were given long prison terms for activities that get lumped under the title white-collar crime. These cases get attention and raise concerns about bad behavior at the top of the corporate chain.

There is good reason to suspect that law enforcement in the United States is tougher than it is elsewhere. In Korea, Japan, and most European nations, close ties between government and business cause many illegal financial activities to be overlooked or treated mildly. A slap on the wrist has been the usual "punishment." That may be changing as international capital markets demand greater accountability. Investors do not like being duped.

Breaking with the tradition of ignoring white-collar crime in Korea, the long-time chairman of Hyundai Motor Company was found guilty of embezzlement and fraud. In Japan, where punishment of executives has been rare and the government has kept such matters secret, the head of a successful Internet company, Livedoor, was given a prison term for stock fraud. In Germany, the prominent Siemens company has undergone a long criminal probe involving huge bribes paid around the world to get business. All countries have laws against white-collar crime; enforcement is another matter.

writings, signs, signals, pictures, or sounds for the purpose of executing such scheme or artifice, shall be fined under this title, or imprisoned not more than 20 years, or both. If the violation affects a financial institution, such person shall be fined not more than $1,000,000, or imprisoned not more than 30 years, or both.

The sweeping nature of such statutes is seen in the Supreme Court case, *Pasquantino* v. *U.S.* (125 S. Ct. 1766), where Americans bought liquor in the United States and smuggled it into Canada for resale to avoid high Canadian taxes. The real violation was of Canadian tax law, but since electronic communications were used to engage in illegal activities that originated in the United States, two people were sent to prison for five years each.

Sentencing Guidelines and Compliance

The Sentencing Guidelines are a controversial aspect of federal criminal law. Congress mandated that the courts be given clear rules about what sentences are to be imposed by judges for criminal law violations (see www.ussc.gov for details). Punishment is reduced under the Sentencing Guidelines when a company has a program in place to help ensure that problems do not happen within the organization. But if problems do happen, the existence of a program can be significant. Justice Department guidelines for effective compliance programs require:

1. Compliance standards and procedures that are reasonably capable of reducing the prospect of criminal conduct
2. High-level persons within the organization to have overall responsibility to oversee compliance with standards and procedures
3. Effective communication of standards and procedures to all employees and agents, such as by training
4. Reasonable steps to achieve compliance with standards by monitoring and auditing the program
5. Consistent enforcement of standards
6. When offenses do occur, reasonable steps to respond to the problem and to prevent further such offenses

Some companies have formed compliance committees to look for evidence of proper activities within the organization that go beyond the traditional accounting and financial reporting concerns of audit committees. Hiring an outsider to be on the committee can bring a fresh perspective. Some companies use whistleblower hotlines to encourage employees to anonymously report possible problems. If these are designed properly, they can aid in the compliance effort. However, some European countries, such as France, prohibit such hotlines, contending that those who are accused of improper behavior have a right to know who complained. So companies with international operations will have to be careful about such hotlines.

When sentencing guidelines were first proposed, there were supporters, because some judges were "too easy" on criminals; others thought some judges were "too tough" on criminals, and it was argued that it was unfair for the same crime to result in wide variations in punishment from court to court. The Guidelines standardize sentencing. Judges have some leeway, but not nearly the discretion they previously had, and some judges have refused to comply with the Guidelines. The Supreme Court has held that the Guidelines are advisory rather than mandatory. Nevertheless, the argument over the Guidelines can be expected to continue, as there are a number of challenges to their constitutionality. Proper application of the Guidelines is a common issue in appeals, as the *Young* case shows.

United States v. Young
United States Court of Appeals
Eighth Circuit 413 F.3d 727 (2005)

Case Background *Young, a cattle rancher, and McConnell, an accountant, were involved in several business entities in the cattle business for over a decade. They solicited funds to invest in their cattle operations, representing to clients and banks that they had more assets than they actually did.*

When the price of cattle fell in 2001, the scheme collapsed, and Young and McConnell closed their businesses and filed bankruptcy. They claimed to own over 343,000 head of cattle, when in fact they owned only 17,000. Their investors lost $147 million, and banks lost $36 million. Only $16 million was recovered.

After they were indicted, they cooperated with government investigators. They entered into plea agreements, admitting to mail fraud, making false statements, and other violations. Applying the Guidelines, Young was sentenced to 108 months in prison and McConnell to 87 months. They appealed, contending that the Guidelines had been applied too harshly, so their sentences should be reduced. Their sentences had been "enhanced" under the Guidelines, because they endangered the solvency of financial institutions. Defendants contended that they had no knowledge of that possibility.

Case Decision Hansen, Circuit Judge

* * *

[Defendants' sentences] are well below the applicable statutory maximum; indeed, they are not even one third of the maximum. . . .

We . . . reject any assertion that it was not foreseeable to the appellants that their fraudulent actions would jeopardize the safety and soundness of banks with which they were not directly involved. One group of investors, who obtained at least part of its funding from Elkhorn Valley Bank, lost over $30 million from the appellants' scheme. Given this level of investing, it was reasonably foreseeable to the appellants that their investors would be borrowing money from banks and using the cattle purportedly bought from the appellants as collateral for the loans. In fact, the investors' banks . . . performed inspections of the appellants' operations and cattle in an effort to ensure the security of the collateral backing the loans made to the appellants' investors. The appellants well knew that the consequences of their fraud extended well beyond their own banks and their individual investors. . . .

Affirmed

continues

1. The appeals court affirmed the sentences and noted that they could have been much heavier. Assuming the same size loss occurred, why would the penalty be greater if such a fraud threatened the solvency of a bank?

2. Defendants were guilty of mail fraud and other violations. Why would they be convicted on multiple counts, rather than just one count for their illegal activity? Is that just piling on more punishment for the same event?

Summary

- Crimes are actions that violate a law of the federal or state government that has been declared to be enforceable by criminal penalties. Most crimes are matters of state law.
- Felonies are more serious crimes for which prison may be imposed. Misdemeanors are lesser crimes that usually are punishable by less than a year in jail or a fine.
- For a person to be convicted of a crime, the person must have committed a wrongful act, or *actus reus*, and must have had the necessary intent or state of mind, or *mens rea*, to commit the crime.
- Criminal acts need not be intentional; they may be based on negligence, a careless disregard of the rights and safety of others, which is a violation of our duty to act with reasonable care.
- A criminal case must be prosecuted during the statute of limitations or the state loses its opportunity. Other defenses include entrapment—when the state has tricked someone to commit a crime that would not otherwise have occurred—and a failure to allow the defendant to exercise constitutional rights, such as be made aware of Miranda rights.
- In criminal cases evidence must be handled with special care to ensure that it has not been tainted. If not treated properly, it will be excluded from trial.
- Unless a person is caught in the act of committing a crime, there is usually a warrant issued for arrest. Judges or magistrates issue arrest warrants based on presentation of probable cause by law enforcement officials.
- When a person is arrested, there will be an arraignment before a judge or magistrate to read the charges. In serious cases, there may be a grand jury used to issue an indictment. Parties may plead guilty, no contest, or not guilty.
- Most cases, especially misdemeanors, are settled by pleas without a trial. Judges must approve plea bargain agreements. If there is a trial and the jury finds the defendant innocent of the charge, there may not be another trial on that charge.
- White collar crimes include a wide range of actions where persons or corporations are accused of violating federal or state statutes that concern the abuse of business processes.
- Areas in which white collar crimes occur include: antitrust, bankruptcy fraud, bribery, counterfeiting, credit card fraud, computer and internet fraud, economic espionage, embezzlement, environmental law, financial fraud, government fraud, healthcare fraud, insider trading, insurance fraud, mail fraud, money laundering, securities fraud, tax evasion, telephone and telemarketing fraud, and wire fraud.
- Congress has imposed Sentencing Guidelines to tell judges the ranges of sentences to be imposed for various crimes. The Supreme Court has held these to be advisory, and they remain controversial, because they cut into the traditional powers of judges to determine punishment in crime cases.

- Companies that have taken active steps to ensure compliance with various legal duties can lessen punishment in case a problem does arise. Lesser charges may be filed, and the penalty for violations may be lighter, if the company is shown to have a reasonable compliance program in place.

Terms to Know

You should be able to define the following terms:

felony, 103	miranda rights, 107	bribery, 110
white-collar crimes, 104	exclusionary rule, 107	mail fraud, 112
misdemeanors, 104	probable cause, 107	money laundering, 113
actus reus, 105	indictment, 108	RICO, 114
mens rea, 105	arraignment, 108	wire fraud, 115
criminal negligence, 106	*nolo contendere*, 108	
statute of limitations, 106	plea bargain, 109	

Discussion Question

1. Proof in criminal cases must be "beyond a reasonable doubt" for there to be a conviction. Is such a high standard likely to lead to many guilty defendants getting off?

Case Questions

1. Brogan answered falsely when IRS and Department of Labor agents asked if he had received cash or gifts from a company whose employees were represented by the union in which he was an officer. Brogan was convicted on federal bribery charges and for making a false statement within the jurisdiction of a federal agency. He appealed, contending that false statements to federal investigators does not include mere denials, which are protected by the Fifth Amendment, because it holds that a person cannot be forced to testify against himself. Did Brogan have a right to use the Fifth Amendment in this situation? [*Brogan* v. *U.S.*, 118 S. Ct. 805 U.S. Supreme Court (1998)]

2. Hsu was indicted, following an FBI sting, for violating the Economic Espionage Act by conspiring to steal corporate trade secrets regarding an anti cancer drug. The defense requested a copy of the trade secret documents at stake. The government contended that the defense did not need access to the documents except under supervision of the judge. The defense maintained that constitutional and procedural requirements of criminal prosecutions dictate full access to the documents, so the defense of legal impossibility could be established—that Hsu could not steal trade secrets that did not exist. District court agreed with the defense; government appealed. Must the defendant be allowed full access to trade secrets that are a key part of a case? [*U.S.* v. *Hsu*, 155 F. 3d 189 3rd Cir. (1998)]

   ✓ Check your answer at http://academic.cengage.com/blaw/meiners

3. The SEC filed civil charges against Bertoli for securities violations. The action was stayed while Bertoli was tried and convicted of criminal charges related to the matter. He was sentenced to 78 months in prison and fined $100,000. The SEC then moved for summary judgment on the civil suit based on findings of fact in the criminal case. The district court granted summary judgment for the SEC and permanently enjoined Bertoli from associating with anyone in the securities industry. Bertoli appealed, contending that the first trial, the criminal one, was distinct from the second, civil, suit brought against him. Is that correct? [*S.E.C.* v. *Monarch Funding Corp.*, 192 F.3d 295 2nd Cir. (1999)]

4. Jolivet was convicted of mail fraud, money laundering, and conspiracy in connection with an insurance fraud scheme she carried out with her husband. Fraudulent documents were provided to insurance companies to extract settlements for auto accidents that never occurred. She appealed the conviction, contending that she was not guilty of money laundering, because she never hid the funds that were taken improperly. Money laundering is when someone disguises illegally obtained money by running it through another business or bank to hide the origins. Was Jolivet correct? [*U.S.* v. *Jolivet*, 2000 WL 1364207 8th Cir. (2000)]

    ✓ **Check your answer at http://academic.cengage.com/blaw/meiners**

5. Hector was prosecuted following police seizure of 80 pounds of drugs from his airplane. The seizure was held to be unlawful, the evidence was suppressed, and the suit against Hector was dismissed. He then sued the government officials involved in his arrest and prosecution to recover $3,500 in bail-bond expenses, $23,000 in attorney's fees, and $2,000 in travel costs. The district court held that he could not recover the costs incurred during the criminal prosecution. Hector appealed. Can he recover those costs? [*Hector* v. *Watt*, 235 F.3d 154 3rd Cir. (2000)]

6. Prosperi, a Florida attorney, represented Donovan's investments, which included Amaretto, a company organized in the Netherlands Antilles and owned by Donovan. According to the government, Prosperi began stealing millions from Donovan in 1987. He was convicted of various violations, including counterfeiting. He created counterfeit certificates of deposit (CDs) that purported to be from J.P. Morgan for the purpose of fooling Donovan. Prosperi appealed the conviction for counterfeiting. The trial judge acquitted him on that count, accepting his contention that the counterfeit CDs looked nothing like the real thing. The government appealed, contending that the counterfeits do not have to look genuine. Who would you think is correct? [*U.S.* v. *Prosperi*, 201 F.3d 1335 11th Cir. (2000)]

    ✓ **Check your answer at http://academic.cengage.com/blaw/meiners**

7. Farraj was a paralegal at a law firm that represented plaintiffs in a suit against tobacco companies. Plaintiffs' lawyers prepared a trial plan over 400 pages long that included strategy, deposition summaries, and lists of exhibits intended to be used. Farraj, accessing the plan on secure computers at the law firm, e-mailed 80 pages of the plan to the defense attorneys and offered to sell them the entire plan. The FBI was brought in to pose as a defense attorney to arrange the purchase. The agent met with Farraj, who was then arrested. He was charged with transporting stolen property across state lines. Farraj moved to have the charge dismissed, contending that the content of an e-mail is not "property." He contended that he transmitted information, not goods. Do you think that position correct? [*U.S.* v. *Farraj*, 142 F.Supp.2d 484 S.D. N.Y. (2001)]

8. Tatum ran a pawn shop. Police became suspicious of one of Tatum's employees, Newton, who was engaged in illegal fencing activities with known burglars. Undercover detectives gained Newton's confidence and sold him and Tatum some jewelry. Evidence was presented at trial that Tatum knew or should have known that the jewelry was stolen. He was convicted of violating the Racketeer Influenced and Corrupt Organizations (RICO) Act for conspiring to deal in stolen property. He was sentenced to seven and one-half years in prison. His criminal intent was based on his and Newton's dealings with the undercover officers during the sting operation. Tatum appealed. What do you think the rule is? [*Tatum* v. *State of Florida*, 857 So.2d 331 Dist. Ct. App., Fla. (2003)]

Internet Assignment

http://sentencing.typepad.com/ (Sentencing Law and Policy)
http://www.confrontationright.blogspot.com/ (the Confrontation blog)
http://ohiolegalblog.blogspot.com (Ohio Legal Research Blog)
http://www.ssrn.com/
http://www.bepress.com/

Compare the Sentencing Law and Policy blog to the Confrontation blog. What features do you like about each? Why is each of these blogs more credible than a hypothetical Joe's Criminal Law blog?

Search the Internet to see if you can find a blog dedicated to legal research in your state. Note: Some law-related blogs are called *blawgs*.

If you are able to access the Social Science Research Network or the Berkeley Electronic Press, search for articles related to white-collar crime. Even if you do not have access to the full text of these articles, you can at least find the names of scholars and articles being published in this area of law.

Pulling It Together

We have covered a number of key concepts in Chapters 1 through 5; so here we consider some cases that bring in legal issues from more than one area for you to identify. Part I of the text reviewed the key elements of the legal system—the sources and roles of law, the structure of the legal system, the court system, alternate dispute resolution, the Constitution as it applies to business, and criminal law. Here we consider cases that overlap more than one area, so we can see the interconnection of multiple areas of law.

1. Jurisdiction and Constitutional Law

A Japanese company, Asahi, sold parts to a Taiwanese company that then sold finished products in the United States. One of the products, claimed to be defective, injured a consumer who sued the Taiwanese company in state court in California. The company settled the case and then sued Asahi in a California state court. The Taiwanese company contended that the part Asahi had sold it in Taiwan was the cause of the defect in the product. Can the Taiwanese company make Asahi appear in court in California? What constitutional issues would be involved in such a jurisdictional question? [*Asahi Metal Industry Co.* v. *Superior Court of California*, 480 U.S. 1026 (1987)]

2. Due Process and Criminal Law

Dixon bought guns at gun shows while she was under indictment for a felony. She made false statements on the applications to buy the guns. She was indicted and convicted of receiving a firearm while under indictment and for making false statements. She admitted that she bought the guns and lied, but said she did it because her boyfriend threatened to kill her or hurt her daughters if she did not buy the guns for him. She appealed, contending due process had been violated, because the judge did not agree with her claim that her defense— that she acted under duress—should be held to a preponderance of the evidence standard, while the government should have to prove beyond a reasonable doubt that she did not act under duress. Instead, the trial judge said both positions on duress would be held to a preponderance of the evidence standard. Did the trial court violate her Fourteenth Amendment due process rights? [*Dixon* v. *U.S.*, 126 S. Ct. 2427 (2006)]

Getty Images

PART 2: Elements of Traditional Business Law

OVERVIEW

Common-law rules evolved over centuries as judges and juries responded to changes in business and social norms. The common law is the traditional basis of private legal relationships that dominate the business legal environment. While the common law evolved differently than the major codes of other nations, the basic elements of how private relationships are governed are similar around the world. Over the years, the common law has been modified and codified in various statutes and regulations.

These chapters review the core topics of what traditionally has been called *business law*. This part of the law concerns the rights and obligations of parties to each other in business formation and in various working relationships.

Contracts, especially those formed in domestic and international sales of goods, are a key part of business relationships. To make contracts work, credit is often extended, and various forms of negotiable instruments are often used. We begin by studying tort law: the common-law obligations and rights we have to protect the sanctity of each others' persons and property. We also study the law of property itself: physical property and—of rapidly growing importance—intellectual property.

Getty Images

Chapter 6: *Elements of Torts* Torts, legal wrongs for which remedies may be sought, provide common-law protection for our persons and our property. The two major branches of tort law, *negligence* and *international torts*, are covered.

Chapter 7: *Business Torts and Product Liability* This chapter focuses on torts that are peculiar to business. Of all the possible torts that may arise, the one area that has changed rapidly and involves the most money is that of product liability.

Chapter 8: *Real and Personal Property* Real property, such as land and buildings, and personal property, such as computers and clothing, have long been among the most valuable assets of many people and business. The law in this area dates back hundreds of years.

Chapter 9: *Intellectual Property* Increasingly, the major contribution of business comes in the form of intellectual property—trademarks, copyrights, patents, and trade secrets—created by mental activity. These assets are subject to common-law rules strengthened by federal statutes.

Chapter 10: *Contracts* Business relationships are based on contracts. This chapter considers the key elements the courts look for when a contract is contested to determine the rights and obligations that may have been created.

Chapter 11: *Domestic and International Sales* The Uniform Commercial Code dominates the law of sales in the United States, so we see how these rules can differ from traditional contract law, and we see how the rapidly growing area of international sales is often governed by particular contract rules.

Chapter 12: *Negotiable Instruments, Credit, and Bankruptcy* Most business contracts involve payment by one of the common forms of negotiable instruments that evolved over time to facilitate exchange. Similarly, businesses often grant credit, which can have a variety of terms and, at times, can be associated with the difficult problem of bankruptcy.

Chapter 13: *Business Organizations* Businesses are a set of contracted obligations. The major forms of business, including partnerships and corporations, are arrangements that evolved to suit the needs of parties doing business. The range of organizational opportunities for businesses is explored.

Chapter 14: *Agency and the Employment Relationship* Parties have freedoms and responsibilities under the law of agency to arrange business affairs in many ways among principals and agents. Employment law is built upon agency principles, and a range of possible relationships may be formed.

Elements of Torts

Getty Images

Chapter 6

Involvement in litigation is distressing to most business operators, but fear of tort suit may be the worst of all. Other areas of law are more predictable and more likely to be controllable. Tort suits tend to arise from unexpected instances that involve momentary carelessness or bad behavior. Talk on your cellphone to a customer while making a delivery and you might cause an accident by carelessly running a stop sign. Your mistake makes you responsible for damages that could be catastrophic. Leave a wet spot on the floor of your store and you could be responsible for a customer who falls and breaks a hip. Become furious at the stupid mistakes of an employee that cause you to lose valuable business and you might do something foolish that could result in a rash of suits for your actions.

The biggest jury verdict in history was a tort case. In 1984, Pennzoil agreed to buy a large share of Getty Oil. Texaco, knowing of the agreement, offered more money for Getty and got Getty's owners to refuse Pennzoil's offer in favor of Texaco's. Pennzoil then sued Texaco for the common-law tort of inducement of breach of contract. A Houston jury awarded Pennzoil $10.5 billion in damages. Texaco did not have that much cash and could not raise it, so a settlement of about one-third the verdict was agreed upon. While the dollars in that case are huge we see the same point in many tort cases—juries often place a high value on the enforcement of legal rights.

Like other parts of the common law, the law of torts evolves through case decisions that reflect social values, community standards, and the way we deal with each other in the current environment. Common law tort cases go back centuries. In recent years, tort law has become a major issue for business; tort liability is a significant expense, and some claim that tort judgments bear little relation to reality. ∎

Torts and the Legal System

Tort has many definitions. The word is derived from the Latin *tortus*, or twisted, and it means "wrong" in French. Although the word faded from common use years ago, it has acquired meaning in the law. A *tort* is generally defined as a civil wrong, other than a breach of contract, for which the law provides a remedy. Tort is a breach of a duty owed to another that causes harm. That is, liability is imposed for conduct that unreasonably interferes with the interests of another.

Business and Torts

As we are about to review, torts are classified on the basis of how harm is inflicted: *negligently*, *intentionally*, or *without fault* (*strict liability*). Regardless of how a tort is classified, businesses become involved in a tort action in one of three ways: 1) a person is harmed by the actions of a business or its employees, 2) a person is harmed by a product manufactured or distributed by the business, or 3) a business is harmed by the wrongful actions of another business or person. The principles of tort law covered in this chapter are applicable to persons in everyday life, but the focus is on business applications. Chapter 7 discusses torts that are specific to business. Chapter 8 discusses torts that are specific to property.

Role of Tort Law

Many accidents result in personal injury and property damage. To have a legal action in tort, the injury suffered by a person or property must legally be the consequence of the actions of another. In a tort action, the party whose interests have been injured sues the party allegedly responsible.

As discussed in Chapter 1, one act may result in both a criminal case and a tort case. For example, O. J. Simpson was tried by the state of California for murder but was found not guilty. In a tort suit that followed, based on the same incident, he was held responsible for assault and battery. The criminal case is brought by the government against the alleged wrongdoer for violating a rule imposed by the legislature. The victim of the crime is a witness in a criminal case. The criminal case does not provide compensation to the injured party. The victim is the plaintiff in the tort suit, hiring an attorney to sue for compensation for injuries wrongfully inflicted by the defendant (the accused criminal in the criminal case). In practice, it is not common for there to be both a criminal case and a tort case evolving from the same incident, since most criminals do not have enough assets to be worth suing in tort.

While most criminal acts, especially violent ones, involve a tort, most torts do not involve criminal acts. The rules vary from state to state, but the principles are similar across the states. Tort law is private law. It is intended, as the Alaska Supreme Court has said, to place an injured party "as nearly as possible in the position he would have occupied had it not been for the defendant's tort." In a small percentage of tort suits, punitive damages are awarded in addition to compensation for injury. Punitive damages are intended to punish the defendant financially for malicious behavior and to send a message that such behavior will not be tolerated.

Negligence-Based Torts

Torts based on *negligence* protect people from harm from others' unintentional but legally careless conduct. As a general rule, we have a duty to conduct ourselves in all situations so as not to create an unreasonable risk of harm or injury to others.

Persons and businesses that do not exercise due care in their conduct will be liable for negligence in a wide range of torts if the following elements can be shown by an injured party:

1. The wrongdoer owed a duty to the injured party (often known as the *duty of ordinary care*).
2. The duty of care owed to the injured party was breached through some act or omission on the part of the wrongdoer (often this breach itself is termed "negligence").
3. There is a causal connection between the wrongdoer's negligent conduct and the resulting harm to the injured party.
4. The injured party suffered actual harm or damage recognized as actionable by law as a result of the negligent conduct.

Negligence is conduct—an act or *omission*, which is a failure to act—by a person or business that results in harm to another to whom the person owes a duty of care. If conduct creates an *unreasonable risk of harm* to others, such conduct may be termed negligent even though there was no intent to cause harm. In contrast to an intentional tort, in negligence the harmful results of a person's conduct are not based on an intended invasion of another person's rights or interests. Thus, the person who intentionally runs over another person while driving has committed the intentional tort of battery. A person who unintentionally runs over another while driving carelessly may have committed a tort of battery based on negligence.

Duty of Care

In determining whether a person's conduct is negligent, that is, whether it violates the duty of care in any given situation, the law applies a standard of reasonableness. The standard is usually stated as *ordinary care* or *due care* as measured against the conduct of a hypothetical person, called the *reasonable person*.

The reasonable person represents a standard of how persons in the relevant community ought to behave. If the person is a skilled professional, such as a doctor, financial consultant, or executive, the standard is that of a reasonably skilled, competent, and experienced person who is a qualified member of that profession. In determining whether a person's conduct was negligent, the question is, what would

---

INTERNATIONAL PERSPECTIVE

Tort Liability in France

In France, as in other code nations, a wrongdoer's liability is established in the Civil Code. In general, the Civil Code makes a wrongdoer liable for damages that result from his or her negligence. In particular, the Civil Code specifically permits recovery for economic loss arising from negligent conduct (quasi-delit). The only limitations on damages are that they must be the immediate and direct consequence of the tort.

The wrongdoer's liability, however, is conditioned on finding the specific elements of the tort. The tort must be

defined in the Civil Code, which is more restrictive than the general, common-law standards.

First, the harm—either physical or economic—must be specific and certain. Second, there must be a finding of fault on the part of the negligent party, the U.S. doctrine of strict liability in tort is not present to any significant extent in the French system. Third, there must be a finding of causality, and the courts use the notion of *proximate cause*. Finally, the extent of the harm and the recoverable loss is determined by a judge and not by a jury.

Getty Images

a reasonable, qualified person have done under the same or similar circumstances? If the conduct was not that of a reasonable person in the eyes of the jury or the judge, the person has failed the reasonableness test and has acted negligently.

The reasonableness standard, or the reasonable person standard, is a theoretical concept in law. It describes a person who acts in a reasonable manner under the circumstances. Although the law does not require perfection, errors in judgment must be reasonable or excusable under the circumstances, or negligence will be found. In a professional relationship, a mistake can result in a suit for negligent misrepresentation. It may be a careless, unintended error, but it does harm. If a loss occurs, liability may be borne by the party who failed to provide the services expected. In the *Squish La Fish* case, we see an example of bad information causing a small firm to suffer a huge loss.

Squish La Fish v. Thomco Specialty Products
United States Court of Appeals, Eleventh Circuit
149 F.3d 1288 (1998)

Case Background *Squish La Fish holds a patent on a plastic device called "Tuna Squeeze" that squeezes oil and water from cans of tuna. A distributor ordered two million units. Squish hired ProPack to affix each Tuna Squeeze to preprinted cardboard "point of purchase" cards for display in stores. ProPack brought in Thomco to advise it as to the kind of adhesive to use to make the Tuna Squeeze stick to the cardboard. The Thomco representative recommended a 3M adhesive called Extra High Tack Adhesive Transfer and said that the adhesive would easily wash off of the Tuna Squeeze in warm water. ProPack and Squish relied on Thomco's advice.*

After 8,600 units had been produced, it was discovered that the adhesive would not wash off of the Tuna Squeeze and the distributor was not happy with the results. The adhesive was replaced with two-sided tape, but the distributor wanted a guarantee that the product would be delivered on time and that there would not be adhesive problems. Squish could not make the promise because there were problems finding a good adhesive. The distributor canceled the contract.

Squish sued Thomco for negligent misrepresentation. The district court granted summary judgment for Thomco; Squish appealed.

Case Decision Cohill, Senior District Judge

* * *

The Georgia Supreme Court adopted the "negligent misrepresentation exception" from the *Restatement (Second) of Torts* §522 (1977). Under this now well-established rule,

One who supplies information during the course of his business, profession, employment, or in any transaction in which he has a pecuniary interest has a duty of reasonable care and competence to parties who rely upon the information in circumstances in which the maker was manifestly aware of the use to which the information was to be put and intended that it be so used. This liability is limited to a foreseeable person or limited class of persons for whom the information was intended, either directly or indirectly.

The elements of this cause of action have recently been formulated as follows: (1) the negligent supply of false information to foreseeable persons, known or unknown; (2) such persons' reasonable reliance upon that false information; and (3) economic injury approximately resulting from such reliance.

* * *

We find that the district court committed an error of law when it failed to acknowledge that Squish La Fish's indirect reliance, through ProPack, on Thomco's alleged representations concerning the . . . adhesive, were sufficient to bring the company within the negligent misrepresentation . . . rule. . . .

Applying the three-part test for negligent misrepresentation to the facts before the district court, it is clear that Squish La Fish, as the manufacturer of the product being affixed by Thomco's adhesive, was a foreseeable user of Thomco's representations concerning that adhesive. The parties dispute the remaining two prongs of the analysis: whether any false

continues

information was conveyed about the adhesive's removability, and whether Squish La Fish indirectly relied upon any such information. The record shows that disputed issues of material fact remain for trial as to both issues.

* * *

Reversed and remanded.

Questions for Analysis

1. The appeals court held that Thomco could be liable for negligent misrepresentation to Squish La Fish. Did Thomco intend to mislead Squish about the adhesive used in the packaging?
2. Would it seem a good defense for Thomco to say that Squish and ProPack should have tested the adhesive before going into production?

Causation

A basic element of a tort in negligence is a *causation* between one party's act and another's injury. For a party to have caused an injury to another and be held negligent, the act must have been the cause in fact and the proximate cause of the other's injury.

Res Ipsa Loquitur

In some cases the plaintiff states a case that is so obvious that the doctrine of *res ipsa loquitur*—"the thing speaks for itself"—applies. It does not always mean the plaintiff wins the case, but the showing is strong enough to prevent dismissal of the claim without further examination.

Suppose K-Fed is walking down the street when a car jumps the curb and runs over him. He has suffered an injury, and it is certainly not his fault. He sues the driver. There is good reason to suspect that it is the fault of the driver, or perhaps mechanical failure in the car that caused the car to run off the road on its own. In any event, K-Fed's suit for negligence in tort can plead *res ipsa loquitur*. It is enough to get the suit going in court, because the cause of the accident is with another party and is likely to result in a judgment for the plaintiff. But most cases are not so simple and require more to be shown.

Cause in Fact

Cause in fact is established by evidence showing that a defendant's action or inaction is the actual cause of an injury that would not have occurred but for the defendant's behavior. Courts express this in the form of a rule commonly referred to as the *but for* or *sine qua non* rule. That is, the injury would not have occurred *but for* the conduct of the tortfeasor. Suppose a hotel has a pile of trash, stored improperly, that catches fire and causes a person in the hotel to die from smoke inhalation. Failure to attend to the trash was the failure by the defendant hotel to take steps to protect its guests. A hotel's failure to install a proper fire escape, for example, is not the cause in fact of the death of a person who suffocated in bed from smoke. The person would have died regardless of whether the hotel had a proper fire escape.

Proximate Cause

In most jurisdictions, the injured party must prove that the defendant's act was not only the cause in fact of the injury but also the proximate cause or legal cause of the injury. *Proximate cause* limits liability to consequences that bear a reasonable relationship to the negligent conduct. Consequences that are too remote or too far removed from negligent conduct will not result in liability.

A person's act may set off a chain of events and injuries that were not *foreseeable*. The principal cause in fact of the Great Chicago Fire of 1871 that destroyed much of the city may have been Mrs. O'Leary's negligent conduct of leaving an oil lamp in the barn for her cow to kick over but no court would hold her liable for the full consequences of her initial act. The chain of events must be foreseeable, as the high court of Florida discusses in the *Goldberg* case.

LIGHTER SIDE OF THE LAW
Watch ME Dance!

Megan Zacher was with friends drinking at Calico Jack's Cantina for a birthday celebration. Calico had a "Shake It Like Shakira" contest with a top prize of $250. Zacher got on top of a bar to dance (or shake) and fell off, suffering an injury that required surgery.

She sued Calico Jack's for negligence. Her lawyer said the bar owners should have known the contest was "dangerous and likely to lead to injury."

Source: *Associated Press*

Getty Images

Goldberg v. Florida Power and Light
Supreme Court of Florida
899 So.2d 1105 (2005)

Case Background *A storm in Pinecrest, Florida, caused an electric line to fall. A homeowner called Florida Power and Light (FPL) about the downed line. Six FPL trucks came to the scene, as did a police officer. The FPL repair crew told the officer they had things under control and he could leave. When repairing the line, the crew turned off power in the area, which turned off a traffic signal. The crew was aware the signal was off but did nothing about it.*

The Goldbergs were driving in the main stream of traffic, which was proceeding under the turned off light. A car coming from a side street tried to get into the line of traffic and caused an accident in which the Goldberg's daughter was killed. They sued FPL for negligence by breaching their duty to control traffic at the intersection.

The jury found FPL negligent and awarded $37 million in damages. The trial judge reduced damages to $10 million. The appeals court reversed, holding FPL was not negligent. The cause of the accident was the driver who entered into the traffic, not the fact the traffic signal was out. The Goldbergs appealed.

Case Decision Lewis, Justice

* * *

The determination of the existence of a duty of care in a negligence action is a question of law. "The duty element of negligence focuses on whether the defendant's conduct foreseeably created a broader 'zone of risk' that poses a general threat of harm to others." A duty may arise from multiple sources: "(1) legislative enactments or administration regulations; (2) judicial interpretations of such enactments or regulations; (3) other judicial precedent; and (4) a duty arising from the general facts of the case." The present case falls within the fourth category—the duty, if it exists, would arise from the general facts of the case. . . .

The trial court determined that FPL had a common-law duty to warn of the hazardous situation it created when the company intentionally terminated the flow of power which rendered the traffic signal inoperable. . . .

We agree that the facts of this case establish that FPL's actions created a foreseeable zone of risk encompassing the motorists utilizing the intersection . . . and gave rise to a legal duty to warn motorists of the hazardous condition it created by deactivating the traffic signal. . . .

continues

Under the facts of this case, it is perfectly reasonable to conclude that FPL owed a duty to warn affected motorists of the danger created and posed by the inoperable traffic signal. The evidence presented at trial indicated that to satisfy a reasonable standard of care would have required FPL to notify the police department, place road flares, direct traffic, or take some other precautions reasonably necessary to alert and protect the safety of passing motorists. Having performed none of these even elementary precautionary measures, FPL breached its duty. . . .

The issue of proximate cause is generally a question of fact concerned with "whether and to what extent the defendant's conduct foreseeably and substantially caused the specific injury that actually occurred." This Court has stated that "harm is 'proximate' in a legal sense if prudent human foresight would lead one to expect that similar harm is likely to be substantially caused by the specific act or omission in question." The proper question is whether the individual's conduct is "so unusual, extraordinary or

bizarre (i.e., so 'unforeseeable') that the policy of the law will relieve the [defendant] of any liability for negligently creating this dangerous situation." In this Court's words, "The law does not impose liability for freak injuries that were utterly unpredictable in light of common human experience." Where reasonable persons could differ as to whether the facts establish proximate causation, the issue must be left to the fact finder. . . .

For the foregoing reasons, we quash the . . . decision of the Third District Court of Appeal and remand the case for reinstatement of the initial district court decision.

Questions for Analysis

1. The court held that FPL was negligent for not foreseeing that having the traffic light turned off could cause an accident. But FPL did not cause the accident, a driver did. Why should FPL be liable?

2. If FPL is liable, why should it be responsible for such large damages?

Various state supreme courts have restated proximate cause in terms similar to the *Goldberg* case. The Missouri court has held that the duty owed by the plaintiff to the defendant "is generally measured by whether or not a reasonably prudent person would have anticipated danger and provided against it. . . ." The New Mexico court explained: "A duty to the individual is closely intertwined with the foreseeability of injury to *that individual* resulting from an activity conducted with less than reasonable care. . . ." And the Texas court stated that "before liability will be imposed, there must be sufficient evidence indicating that the defendant knew of or should have known that harm would eventually befall a victim."

Substantial Factor

Proximate cause has been criticized as difficult to understand and apply. The California Supreme Court, in *Mitchell* v. *Gonzales* (819 P.2d 872), joined some other states in replacing the *proximate cause rule* in negligence actions in favor of the *legal cause rule*, which uses the *substantial factor test*.

The substantial factor test states: "A legal cause of injury is a cause which is a substantial factor in bringing about the injury." That is, as the Pennsylvania Supreme Court has explained, the jury is asked to determine whether a defendant's conduct "has such an effect in producing the harm as to lead reasonable men to regard it as a cause, using that word in the popular sense." As Exhibit 6.1 indicates, defendants could be liable even if their negligent behavior was only one factor contributing to an injury, so long as it was found to be a substantial factor.

Intervening Conduct

One issue in determining proximate cause is the possibility of *intervening conduct*. Even if negligence occurred, if the causal connection to the resulting harm is broken by an intervening act or event, there is a *superseding cause*. If the causal

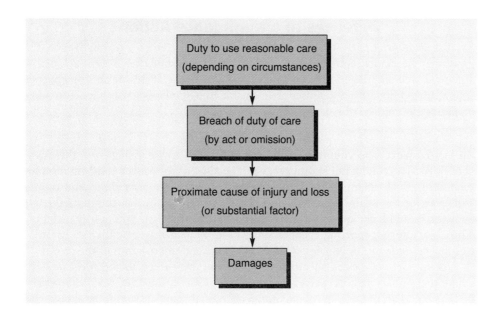

Exhibit 6.1
Elements of Negligence

relationship between the defendant's act and resulting harm is broken by the intervening act, which was unforeseeable under the circumstances, the defendant will likely not be liable.

Go back to the *Goldberg* case. What about the driver who hit the Goldberg car? Was that not intervening conduct that caused the accident? That was what FPL argued. Allowing the light to go out may have been negligent, but the other driver was the primary cause of the accident. The court rejected that, holding that "whether there exists an intervening and superseding cause is primarily a question of fact... left to the fact finder." There, the jury held it did not relieve FPL of liability.

Suppose Diddy Construction has dug a ditch across a sidewalk to lay some pipe. When the workers quit for the night, they left the ditch uncovered and did not place any warnings. That night, if Pink shoves Jay-Z into the ditch and Jay-Z is hurt, Pink's act is intervening conduct that relieves Diddy of liability. However, suppose Jay-Z had accidentally fallen into the ditch at night and was drowning, because the ditch was filled with rainwater. Frierson dives into the ditch to save Jay-Z and Frierson drowns. Diddy Construction will be liable to Jay-Z and Frierson. Because *danger invites rescue*, the common law holds the negligent party responsible for the losses suffered by those who attempt to save people who are in danger as the result of the torts of others.

ISSUE SPOTTER
Effective Liability Releases

You help run a resort that in the winter offers snowtubing. Patrons pay to slide down a snow hill on an inflated tube. Since they can fall off or run into each other and get hurt, you have them sign a liability release that says they will not sue the resort if they get hurt while snowtubing. Is such a release sufficient? What if they claim the injury was due to the negligence of the resort? Will the liability release protect your company against successful litigation that could bankrupt the resort?

Getty Images

Defenses to a Negligence Action

Even if an injured party has established the required elements of negligence, the party may be denied compensation if the defendant establishes a *valid defense*. As a general rule, any defense to an intentional tort is also available in a negligence action. In addition, other defenses are available to defendants in negligence actions, including assumption of risk and comparative negligence.

Assumption of Risk

An injured party who voluntarily assumed the risk of harm arising from the negligent or reckless conduct of another may not be allowed to recover compensation for such harm. Such action by the injured party is called *assumption of risk* and creates a defense for the negligent defendant. The defense requires that the injured party knew or should have known of the risk and that the risk was voluntarily assumed. Thus, spectators at sporting events such as baseball games assume the risk for injuries that result from the usual playing of the game and the reaction of the crowd.

Assumption of risk is an affirmative defense, as we see in the *McCune* case, where there was a liability waiver or *exculpatory clause*. It must be specifically raised by the defendant to take advantage of it. When established, assumption of risk usually bars the plaintiff from recovery, even if the defendant was negligent.

McCune v. Myrtle Beach Indoor Shooting Range
Court of Appeals of South Carolina
612 S.E.2d 462, 364 S.C.242 (2005)

Case Background *McCune, her husband, and friends played paintball at the Myrtle Beach Indoor Shooting Range. She used a protective face mask provided by the Range. Before she played, she signed a general liability waiver that released the Range from liability from all known or unknown dangers, for any reason, with the exception of gross negligence on the part of the Range.*

While playing, she complained that the mask did not fit well. She said it restricted her range of vision. At one point, the mask caught on the branch of a tree, lifting it off her face. She was hit in the eye by a paintball and blinded. She sued the Range for negligence for not providing a mask that would fit better and give better protection. The trial court granted summary judgment in favor of the Range. McCune appealed.

Case Decision Beatty, Justice

* * *

McCune maintains the trial court erred in granting summary judgment to the Range on the basis of the exculpatory language in the release of liability signed by McCune. McCune asserts she did not anticipate the harm that was inflicted or the manner in which it occurred. Additionally, she contends the failure of the

equipment was unexpected and she could not have voluntarily assumed such a risk. We disagree.

As an initial matter, we must determine whether this is a case involving express assumption or implied assumption of the risk. Express assumption of the risk sounds in contract and occurs when the parties agree beforehand, "either in writing or orally, that the plaintiff will relieve the defendant of his or her legal duty toward the plaintiff."

"Express assumption of risk is contrasted with implied assumption of risk which arises when the plaintiff implicitly, rather than expressly, assumes known risks. As noted above, implied assumption of risk is characterized as either primary or secondary. Primary implied assumption of risk is but another way of stating the conclusion that a plaintiff has failed to establish a prima facie case [of negligence] by failing to establish that a duty exists. Secondary implied assumption of risk, on the other hand, arises when the plaintiff knowingly encounters a risk created by the defendant's negligence."

In the instant case, we are confronted with a defense based upon McCune's express assumption of the risk. She signed a release from liability prior to participating in the paintball match. The courts of South Carolina have analyzed express assumption of the risk cases in terms of exculpatory contracts. . . .

An exculpatory clause . . . is to be strictly construed against the party relying thereon. An exculpatory clause will never be construed to exempt a party from liability for his own negligence "in the absence of explicit language clearly indicating that such was the intent of the parties." . . .

The agreement was voluntarily signed and specifically stated: (1) she assumed the risks, whether known or unknown; and (2) she released the Range from liability, even from injuries sustained because of the Range's own negligence. It is clear McCune voluntarily entered into the release in exchange for being allowed to participate in the paintball match.

Additionally, she expressly assumed the risk for all known and unknown risks while participating and cannot now complain because she did not fully appreciate the exact risk she faced. . . .;

Accordingly, we hold the trial court properly determined the release signed by McCune was sufficient to release the Range from all liability in this incident. Therefore, the decision of the trial court is affirmed.

Questions for Analysis

1. The court held that because of the liability waiver, the defendant was released from liability even if the defendant had been negligent. Why would it be allowed even in the case of negligence?
2. Do you think McCune appreciated the risks involved? Would she have put herself in such danger if she had known she may have been blinded?

Comparative Negligence

Under *comparative negligence*, which replaced an old rule called *contributory negligence*, damages are reduced by the percentage of the injuries caused by the plaintiff's own negligence.

For example, in *Wassell* v. *Adams* (865 F.2d 849), a woman opened the door to her hotel room in the middle of the night after she heard a knock on it. She was assaulted by an unknown person. The jury found both the hotel and the woman to be negligent. The hotel was held responsible for 3 percent of the injury that occurred; the woman was 97 percent responsible. When the negligence is compared this way, the damages are allocated by percent of responsibility. Here, the damages were $850,000, so the woman recovered three percent of that sum from the hotel; she was responsible for the rest. Many states have a rule that if the plaintiff is 50 percent or more responsible, no recovery is allowed.

Intentional Torts against Persons

Some tort liability is based on the intent of a defendant to interfere with the protected interests of a plaintiff. *Intentional torts* are classified on the basis of the interests the law seeks to protect: personal rights and property rights. We first review intentional torts against persons and then look at intentional torts against property. The law imposes a greater degree of responsibility on *tortfeasors*, persons who commit torts, for intentional acts that harm protected interests than for unintentional or negligent acts. As Justice Holmes said, it is the difference between kicking a dog and tripping over a dog. In both cases, the dog gets kicked, but one case is intentional, while the other case is careless.

Establishing Intent

Several elements establish the legal requirement of *intent*. First is the state of mind of the defendant, which means that the person knew what he was doing. Second is

Exhibit 6.2
Terms of an Effective
Liability Waiver

A liability waiver is more likely to be upheld if:

1. Disclaimer is placed in a prominent place in the document.
2. The print size is larger than surrounding print (courts do not like fine print).
3. Disclaimer, in all capital letters, or in bold, or in some color different from other print.

Include such key terms as:

I knowingly and freely assume all risks, known and unknown, even if arising from negligence of the seller.

I hereby release and hold harmless the seller with respect to any and all injury, disability, death, loss, or damage.

I have read this release of liability and assumption of risk agreement, fully understand its terms, understand that I have given up substantial rights by signing it, and sign it voluntarily without any inducement.

[Signature and date]

that the person knew, or should have known, the possible consequences of his act. Third is knowing that certain results are likely to occur.

While these elements are tied together, there may be legal differences between act, intent, and motive. To be liable, a defendant must have acted; that is, there must have been voluntary action. An act is to be distinguished from its consequences. Intent is the fact of doing an act, such as firing a gun. The motive—why the person wanted to fire the gun—is legally distinct. If Britney fires a gun into a crowd of people, that is a wrongful act for which she may be held liable regardless of her motives. For her to say that she had no bad motive—that when she fired the gun she really wished no one would be hurt—does not relieve her of liability. Under tort law, she acted voluntarily. She is presumed to have intended the consequences of her act, or should have known what the consequences could be, and so is responsible for them.

Intentional torts are based on *willful* acts that invade protected interests. Intentional torts occur when a jury finds that, under the circumstances, a reasonable person would have known that harmful consequences were likely to follow from the act. Intent matters much less than the act of invading the interests of another person. Even in cases in which the defendant did not have a bad motive (e.g., defendant was playing a trick), if the tortfeasor intended to commit the act that inflicted injury on another, the willful intent would be present for tort liability. Next we review the major categories of torts.

ISSUE SPOTTER
Dealing with Drunks

You have a convenience store. In the evenings, it is not uncommon for people to come in who seem to have had a bit too much to drink. They pick up a six-pack of beer and buy gasoline. Should you refuse to sell them beer and gas? Can you be liable if you do sell them what they want, and they go out and plow into someone while driving? What sort of policy should you have?

Getty Images

Assault

Assault is intentional conduct directed at a person that places the person in fear of immediate bodily harm or offensive contact. The protected interest is freedom from fear of harmful or offensive contact. Actual contact with the body is not necessary. For example, pointing a gun or swinging a club at a person can constitute an assault. The requirement of "fear" is satisfied if a reasonable person under the same or similar circumstances would have apprehension of bodily harm or offensive contact. An essential element of this tort is that the person in danger of harm or injury must know of the danger of suffering a battery and be apprehensive of its threat. If, for example, a person points a gun at another while the other person is sleeping, there is no assault, because there was no fear of harm while sleeping.

Battery

Battery is an unlawful touching, which is intentional physical contact without consent. The protected interest is freedom from unpermitted contact with one's person. Even if the contact does not cause actual physical harm, it is unlawful if it would offend a reasonable person's sense of dignity. This is the case in many batteries that occur in the workplace that involve inappropriate sexual contact. There may be no physical battering, but the contact is impermissible. The following case involves a joke at work not taken well.

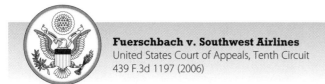

Fuerschbach v. Southwest Airlines
United States Court of Appeals, Tenth Circuit
439 F.3d 1197 (2006)

Case Background *Fuerschbach worked as a customer service representative for Southwest Airlines at the Albuquerque airport. The airline prides itself on being a "fun-loving, spirited company." It is common for new employees, when they successfully complete a probationary period, to be subject to a prank to celebrate the event. Some pranks have been elaborate, and Fuerschbach was aware that one might be pulled on her.*

Her supervisor had been subject to a mock arrest once, and thought it was fun, so she set one up for Fuerschbach. Supervisors got two Albuquerque police to come and pretend to arrest Fuerschbach at work. The officers approached her at the ticket counter, told her she had outstanding warrants against her, and told her she was under arrest. They handcuffed her. She began to cry, so the officers took her to the back, where other employees jumped out and yelled "congratulations for being off probation." The handcuffs were removed so a little party could begin. But Fuerschbach could not stop crying and was eventually sent home. She saw a psychologist who said she suffered from post-traumatic stress disorder.

Fuerschbach sued everyone connected with the event on numerous grounds, including assault and battery. The district court granted summary judgment for defendants. Fuerschbach appealed.

Case Decision Lucero, Circuit Judge

* * *

Fuerschbach's claim of assault and battery by [the police officers] survives summary judgment.... For there to be an assault, there must have been an "act, threat, or menacing conduct which causes another person to reasonably believe that he is in danger of receiving an immediate battery." Battery occurs when an individual "acts intending to cause a harmful or offensive contact with the person of the other or a third person, or an imminent apprehension of such a contact, and ... an offensive contact with the person of the other directly or indirectly results." The district court granted the defendants' motion for summary judgment, finding that the officers did not intend to

continues

cause an offensive contact, but rather that "the officers were courteous and professional," and that in any
event, placing an individual in handcuffs is not an offensive contact.

Any bodily contact is offensive "if it offends a
reasonable sense of personal dignity." Viewing the
evidence in the light most favorable to Fuerschbach,
a jury could conclude that the officers' actions offended a reasonable sense of personal dignity. A jury
could find that placing a person's hands in position to
be handcuffed, handcuffing the individual, and then
leading the individual to walk 15 feet offends a reasonable sense of personal dignity.

Moreover, the officers' demeanor is not proba-
tive of their intent to cause an offensive contact. Nor
is the officers' intent merely to pull a prank on
Fuerschbach an excuse. The record reveals that the
officers intended to touch Fuerschbach's arms, to
place her arms in position to be handcuffed, and to
then handcuff her tightly, thus intending to cause an
offensive contact. Viewing the evidence in the light
most favorable to Fuerschbach, the officers intended
to cause an offensive contact with Fuerschbach's person and did cause an offensive contact. Accordingly,
we reverse the district court's grant of summary judgment to the officers on Fuerschbach's assault and battery claim.

[Note: Some other claims were allowed to go forward, some were denied. Fuerschbach could only
make a workers' compensation claim against Southwest, as there was no intent by anyone at the airline to
harm her, and the actions involved occurred at work.]

Questions for Analysis

1. The appeals court held that Fuerschbach could
   sue the officers for assault and battery. The officers clearly did not mean to harm her; it was a
   joke. Why could they be liable?
2. Would you suppose Fuerschbach continued to
   work for Southwest?

Assault and Battery

Assault and battery are often the same, although they are separate offenses in some
states. The principal distinction is the difference between the requirements of
apprehension of an offensive physical contact for an assault and of actual physical
contact for a battery. The two torts may exist without each other. An individual
may strike another who is asleep, for example, thus committing battery but not
assault. On the other hand, an individual may shoot at another and miss, thereby
creating an assault but no battery. In common discussion, and in some states, the
term *assault* is used to cover assault and battery.

Defenses

There are situations in which assault and battery are permitted. A person accused
of a tort may have a *defense*, a legally recognized justification for the actions, that
relieves the defendant of liability. Common defenses are consent, privilege, self-
defense, and defense of others and of property. These defenses can be used in any
tort but are most common in cases of assault and battery.

Consent occurs when the injured party gave permission to the alleged wrongdoer to interfere with a personal right. Consent may be either expressed or implied
by words or conduct. An example of consent in battery includes voluntary participation in a contact sport, such as boxing or football.

A *privilege* can give immunity from liability. It can excuse what would have
been a tort had the defendant not acted to further an interest of social importance that deserves protection. For example, breaking into a burning store to save
someone trapped inside would not be trespass because of the privilege to save
someone.

Self-defense is a privilege based on the need to allow people who are attacked to
take steps to protect themselves. The force allowed is that which a reasonable person may have used under the circumstances. A person may take a life to protect his

Assault
Battery
False Imprisonment or False Arrest
Emotional or Mental Distress
Invasion of Privacy
Defamation: Libel and Slander

Exhibit 6.3
Major Categories of
Intentional Torts Against
Persons

own life, but the measures used in self-defense should be no more than are needed to provide protection. If an attacker has been stopped and made helpless, a person has no right to inflict a beating at that point.

Similarly, *in defense of others* or *in defense of property*, one may use force reasonable under the circumstances. If someone is being threatened with an attack, other persons have a privilege to defend the victim by using force. We have the right to defend our property to keep others from stealing or abusing it, but again, the force used must be reasonable under the circumstances. Since the law places a higher value on human life than on property, it is unlikely that killing or inflicting serious bodily injury on someone invading property will be allowed. It is not reasonable to shoot a person stealing a DVD player from a store.

False Imprisonment

The tort of *false imprisonment*, or false arrest, is the intentional holding or detaining of a person in violation of a protected interest in freedom from restraint of movement. The detention need not be physical; verbal restraints, such as threats, may be the basis of an action for false imprisonment.

One employer was successfully sued for keeping an employee in an office for an hour, accusing her of stealing, while a security guard stood by. She probably could have walked out, but in such situations, people tend to submit to those in positions of authority. Hence, discussions should be professional, to the point, and not threatening. In the *Russell* case we see what happens when the line is crossed.

Russell v. Kinney Contractors
Appellate Court of Illinois, Fifth District
795 N.E.2d 340, 342 Ill.App.3d 666 (2003)

Case Background *Kinney Contractors advertised that it was taking job applications from workers in various construction crafts. Russell and other workers who belonged to a construction union went to apply. Kinney did not want union workers. When the workers arrived at Kinney's offices, they walked through an open gate and headed to the office to submit applications. Kinney closed the gate behind the workers, blocking the exit, and called the police, claiming they were trespassing. When the police arrived, the workers were let out.*

The workers sued Kinney for false imprisonment, contending they were on Kinney property for a legitimate purpose and that they had been held without reasonable cause. The trial court, called circuit court, *dismissed the suit, holding that it was a labor dispute subject to jurisdiction of the National Labor Relations Board (NLRB) under the National Labor Relations Act (NLRA), which deals with unfair labor practices. The court held it was not a common-law tort matter for state courts. Russell appealed.*

continues

Case Decision Chapman, Justice

* * *

[This case] requires the weighing of the federal interest of maintaining a uniform body of rules addressing labor disputes and the interests of states in protecting its citizens from harmful or inappropriate conduct....

The tort of false imprisonment, in and of itself, does not constitute an unfair labor practice under the NLRA. Though the NLRB might find that the alleged tortfeasor violated [the NLRA] in intentionally imprisoning the individuals ... the NLRB would look only to the coercive nature of the act as it relates to the plaintiffs' employment rights. The indignity, humiliation, and disgrace allegedly suffered by the plaintiffs would not be a relevant consideration of the NLRB, and it is not empowered to award damages or other relief, whereas state remedies would attempt to compensate the plaintiffs in an effort to make them whole. We ... are concerned that the NLRB could not grant the individual plaintiffs effective relief for the injury they have allegedly suffered and would thereby deny them their right to redress for an otherwise actionable wrong....

False imprisonment is an action that requires the plaintiff to establish that his or her personal liberty was unreasonably or unlawfully restrained against his or her will and that the defendant caused or procured the restraint and actually or legally intended the restraint. Here ... the state court deciding the plaintiffs' false imprisonment common law tort claim would focus on issues different from those central to the unfair labor practice claim [under the NLRA]....

For the foregoing reasons, the judgment of the circuit court dismissing the plaintiffs' complaint for lack of subject matter jurisdiction is reversed, and the cause is remanded.

Questions for Analysis
1. The appeals court held that the workers could sue for false imprisonment. Since the workers were never touched, could they have a successful claim?
2. How does that legal claim differ from the claim they may have under the National Labor Relations Act?

Shoplifting

Businesses face false imprisonment suits from the detention of suspected shoplifters. It is not uncommon for a suspected shoplifter who is innocent to sue the business for false imprisonment. Most states have antishoplifting statutes, which provide businesses with an affirmative defense to a charge of false imprisonment for detaining a shoplifter. The store must have reasonable cause to believe the person has shoplifted, and the person must be delayed for a reasonable time and in a reasonable manner.

Infliction of Emotional Distress

The tort of *infliction of emotional distress*, or *mental distress*, involves conduct that is so outrageous that it creates severe mental or emotional distress in another person. The protected interest is peace of mind. This cause of action protects us from conduct that goes way beyond the bounds of decency, but not from annoying behavior, petty insults, or bad language. Many states also provide compensation to third parties based on emotional distress. For example, a Louisiana court provided compensation for emotional distress to a woman who found her comatose husband being chewed on by rats while in bed at a hospital.

Bill collectors, landlords, and insurance adjusters are often involved in emotional-distress suits. Badgering, late-night phone calls, profanity, threats, and name calling lay the groundwork for potential emotional distress suits. Employers have been sued for the distress suffered by employees, as the *Reynolds* case discusses.

ISSUE SPOTTER
Dealing with the Elderly and their Heirs

Your company runs assisted care facilities. Most of your clients are elderly people in poor health. Most of your clients die within two years of entering a facility. Unfortunately, some of the clients never have visitors. They seem to have no relationships with any family members, but you know that legally they have heirs. If they provide no information about whom to contact in the event of an emergency or death, their body is cremated. You have heard of instances when a family member suddenly appears after a death and is irate that the family was not contacted. Suits for emotional distress, negligence, and other torts have been filed. How should you handle this matter to cover your legal obligations? What is your ethical obligation?

Getty Images

Reynolds v. Ethicon Endo-Surgery
United States Court of Appeals, Eighth Circuit
454 F.3d 868 (2006)

Case Background *Reynolds started work in 1999 as a sales representative for Ethicon. In 2002 she was assigned to a new division, selling medical equipment for bariatric weight-loss surgery. She was based in Sioux Falls, South Dakota, and covered sales in the region. Soon after she began that assignment, the company reviewed the sales territories and determined that the Sioux Falls region was weak.*

A week after Reynolds told Burns, her supervisor, that she was pregnant, he met with her and told her the Sioux Falls office would be closed and offered her the Louisville office or a severance package. She was later also offered the St. Louis office. Several weeks later, Reynolds suffered a miscarriage. She blamed it on the elimination of her position so soon after she became pregnant. When she refused to transfer or take the severance package, she was fired.

She sued Burns and Ethicon for infliction of mental distress. The district court entered summary judgment for defendants. Reynolds appealed.

Case Decision Benton, Circuit Judge

* * *

Reynolds also asserts that Ethicon and Burns are liable for intentional infliction of emotional distress (IIED) for informing her about the elimination and relocation in a distressing manner. She claims that Burns, knowing she was pregnant . . . let her believe the purpose of their . . . meeting was to review her performance. Instead, Burns then notified Reynolds about the elimination of her territory and possible relocation. As a result of Burns' conduct, Reynolds asserts she suffered a miscar-

riage and sought treatment for depressive symptoms, all proximately caused by the stress she endured.

Under South Dakota law, the elements of intentional infliction of emotional distress are: (1) an act by defendant amounting to extreme or outrageous conduct; (2) intent on the part of the defendant to cause plaintiff severe emotional distress; (3) the defendant's conduct was the cause in-fact of plaintiff's injuries; and (4) the plaintiff suffered an extreme disabling emotional response to defendant's conduct.

In South Dakota, following the *Restatement (Second) of Torts*, "the conduct necessary to form intentional infliction of emotional distress must be 'so outrageous in character, and so extreme in degree, as to go beyond all possible bounds of decency, and be regarded as atrocious and utterly intolerable in a civilized community.'" . . .

The facts of this case do not support the tort.. . . While termination from a job may be upsetting, this does not in itself constitute extreme or outrageous conduct. . . .

The judgment of the district court is affirmed.

Questions for Analysis
1. The appeals court held Reynolds had no grounds to sue for infliction of mental distress. Does she have grounds for any other tort?
2. Did the employer have an obligation to be more careful in how Reynolds was treated due to her pregnancy?

Invasion of Privacy

The concept behind the tort of *invasion of privacy* is a person's right to solitude and to be free from unwarranted public exposure. The tort may be committed in a number of ways:

1. The use of a person's name or picture without permission (which can make advertisers and marketing companies liable)
2. The intrusion into a person's solitude (illegal wiretapping or searches of a residence; harassment by unwanted and continual telephoning)
3. The placing of a person in a false light (publishing of a story with serious misinformation)
4. The public exposure of facts that are private in nature (such as public disclosure of a person's drug use or debts)

While we often think of invasion-of-privacy cases involving the rich and famous, in fact most such cases come about from more ordinary situations as the *Bob Ross Buick* case indicates.

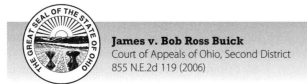

James v. Bob Ross Buick
Court of Appeals of Ohio, Second District
855 N.E.2d 119 (2006)

Case Background *James worked at a Mercedes dealership owned by Bob Ross Buick (BRBI). In 2002 James was named sales representative of the year. None of the sales representatives met sales quotas established for 2003. James was fired in January, 2004. Soon after, BRBI sent batches of letters to customers who had worked with James, encouraging them to shop for Mercedes. The letters were addressed as if they were from James, and an administrative assistant at BRBI signed James's name to the letters.*

James became aware of the letters, when a number of former clients told him they had received them. He sued for misappropriation of his name, a form of invasion of privacy. The trial court granted summary judgment in favor of BRBI. James appealed.

Case Decision Wolff, Judge

* * *

The tort of invasion of privacy includes four separate torts: "(1) intrusion upon the plaintiff's seclusion or solitude, or into his private affairs; (2) public disclosure of embarrassing private facts about the plaintiff; (3) publicity which places the plaintiff in a false light in the public eye; and (4) appropriation, for the defendant's advantage, of the plaintiff's name or likeness."

The forgery of the signature of another is a recognized variant of the tort known generally as invasion of privacy. More specifically, forgery amounts to the appropriation of the name or likeness of another. Ohio has adopted the tort of misappropriation of the name or likeness of another. . . .

The [Ohio] Supreme Court has distinguished "the mere incidental use of a person's name and likeness, which is not actionable, from appropriation of the benefits associated with the person's identity, which is." The court cited with approval the *Restatement of the Law 2d, Torts* (1965), Section 652C, including the portion regarding the incidental use of name or likeness. That portion reads:

"The value of the plaintiff's name is not appropriated by mere mention of it, or by reference to it in connection with legitimate mention of his public activities; nor is the value of his likeness appropriated when it is published for purposes other than taking advantage of his reputation, prestige, or other value associated with him, for purposes of publicity. No one has the right to object merely because his name or his appearance is brought before the public, since neither is in any way a private matter and both are open to public observation. It is only when the publicity is given for the purpose of appropriating to the defendant's benefit the commercial or other values associated with the name or the likeness that the right of privacy is invaded."

In our view, BRBI's conduct cannot reasonably be viewed as the incidental use of James's name. [BRBI employees] stated in their affidavits that, pursuant to BRBI policy, batches of these form letters were printed out on a daily basis and given to the salespeople to sign and mail to their assigned customers to maintain a relationship with them. James's name was signed to correspondence that was sent to his former clients at BRBI. In this context, his name clearly had a commercial value, as personal letters are used to induce future sales to customers who have established a client relationship with the dealership.

* * *

The monetary benefit that BRBI received as a result of its wrongful use of James's name is an appropriate (although not exclusive) measure of James's actual damages. . . . BRBI could have benefited from the use of James's name. Accordingly, upon remand, James may seek nominal, compensatory, and, if appropriate, punitive damages at trial. . . .

[Reversed and remanded.]

Questions for Analysis

1. The appeals court held that James did have a claim for a kind of invasion of privacy based on the misappropriation of his name. What value would there be in a company using the name of a sales representative?
2. What would the damages likely be in such a case? What might make them higher or lower?

Defenses

In addition to common-law protection, some states have statutes to recognize a right to privacy. In either case, the right to privacy is largely waived when a person becomes a public figure, such as an entertainer, a politician, or a sports personality. In addition, the publication of information about an individual taken from public files and records does not constitute an invasion of privacy.

Getty Images

LIGHTER SIDE OF THE LAW
Teaching Torts in Law School

Denise DiFede was attending a class on torts at Pace University's law school. She alleged that her professor used her as a tort demonstration by pulling her chair away from her as she prepared to sit down, She fell and injured her back. Claiming the incident was "outrageous, shocking, and intolerable, exceeding all reasonable bounds of decency," she sued the school for $5 million.

Source: *Reuters*

Defamation

The tort of *defamation* is an intentional false communication that injures a person's reputation or good name. If the defamatory communication was spoken, *slander* is the tort. If the communication was in the form of a printing, a writing, a picture, or a radio or television broadcast, the tort is *libel*. The elements that must be shown to exist for both torts to be actionable are:

1. Making a false or defamatory statement about another person
2. Publishing or communicating the statement to a third person
3. Causing harm to the person about whom the statement was made

LIGHTER SIDE OF THE LAW
I Will Be a Billionaire for Sure After This

Warner Books published *TrumpNation: The Art of Being The Donald* by a veteran *New York Times* reporter. The book asserts that Trump is worth less than a billion dollars, not the multiple billions he claims, and that The Donald is not the crafty businessman he asserts to be.

Trump sued Warner and the author for $5 billion in compensatory and punitive damages for making "false and malicious statements" about him, his family, and his business dealings. Furthermore, the book was "terribly written."

Source: *Forbes*

Some statements are considered *defamation per se.* That is, they are presumed by law to be harmful to the person to whom they were directed and therefore require no proof of harm or injury. Statements, for example, that a person has committed a crime or has engaged in shady business activities can be defamatory per se.

Defamation does not only include damage to the reputation of a person; it can involve damage to the good name of a business. Therefore companies must be careful about what they say about competitors and their products, as the *Republic Tobacco* case illustrates.

Republic Tobacco v. North Atlantic Trading
United States Court of Appeals, Seventh Circuit
381 F.3d 717 (2004)

Case Background *Republic and North Atlantic (NA) compete in the market for premium roll-your-own (RYO) cigarette papers, tobacco, and related products. Republic makes Job, Top, and Drum brands; NA makes Zig-Zag brand, the number-one seller for decades. The companies are market leaders and fight hard for market shares.*

NA sent existing and potential customers two letters critical of Republic. The first attacked the integrity of Republic's business conduct and claimed a display box used for its products violated a patent and trademark held by NA. The letter stated NA had sued Republic for that. One company dropped Republic after getting the letter. But NA held no patent or trademark on the display box and had not sued Republic. NA sent another letter saying it was suing Republic for antitrust violations, which was true. The letter said Republic engaged in "unfair competition" and "deceptive trade practices" among their antitrust violations. Republic sued NA for defamation. The trial court held for Republic and awarded $3.36 million in damages. The jury also awarded punitive damages, which the trial judge reduced from $10.2 million to $4.08 million. NA appealed.

Case Decision Flaum, Chief Judge

* * *

A defamatory statement is one that "tends to cause such harm to the reputation of another that it lowers that person in the eyes of the community or deters third persons from associating with him." To make out a defamation claim under Illinois law, the plaintiff must show "that the defendant made a false statement concerning him, that there was an unprivileged publication to a third party with fault by the defendant, which caused damage to the plaintiff."

Defamatory statements may be actionable *per se* or actionable *per quod.* Illinois courts have recognized four categories of statements that are considered defamatory *per se:* (1) words that impute the commission of a crime; (2) words that impute infection with a loathsome disease; (3) words that impute an inability to perform or a want of integrity in the discharge of duties of office or employment; or (4) words that prejudice a party, or impute lack of ability, in his or her trade, profession, or business. If a statement qualifies as defamatory *per se* (the theory upon which Republic solely relies), it is unnecessary for a plaintiff to demonstrate actual damage to reputation. Rather, statements that fall within these *per se* categories are thought to be so obviously and materially harmful to the plaintiff that injury to its reputation may be presumed. In contrast, with a *per quod* action, in order to recover the plaintiff must plead and prove that it sustained actual damage of a pecuniary nature...

A number of common law privileges and defenses exist that may shield a defendant from liability for making an otherwise defamatory statement... First, a statement that does not contain any verifiable facts (as some call, "an opinion") is not actionable under Illinois law... Second, substantial truth is a complete defense to an allegation of defamation... Third, under Illinois law, publication of defamatory matters in a report of an official proceeding that deals with a matter of public concern is privileged as long as the report is accurate and complete... Fourth, Illinois law confers a privilege upon "statements made within a legitimate business context." Under this rule, "a statement is conditionally privileged when the defendant makes it (1) in good faith; (2) with an interest or duty to be upheld; (3) limited in scope to that purpose; (4) on a proper occasion; and (5) published in a proper manner only to proper parties."

* * *

North Atlantic concedes that it has no trademark and held no patent on the display boxes; and it follows that there was no patent or trademark violation. Moreover [at the time it wrote the first letter] it had filed no lawsuit...

If we interpret the words according to the meaning that they were intended to convey to the reasonable reader, it is clear that they are both false and defamatory. [Both letters are defamatory]...

We conclude that a ... damage award of $1 million is ... appropriate in this case... While the evidence supports the jury's determination that North Atlantic acted with the requisite malice to justify punitive damages, the nature and enormity of North Atlantic's wrong does not justify a $10.2 million award, or even a $4.08 million award. We therefore further reduce the punitive damage award to $2 million....

Questions for Analysis

1. The appeals court agreed that NA defamed Republic by telling customers Republic may have violated the law and engaged in bad business practices. Why should customers care? Why would Republic lose business?

2. NA did sue Republic, claiming antitrust violations. Should that not protect it from suit for defamation?

Getty Images

ISSUE SPOTTER

Say Good Things About a Good Employee?

Jeff was a good employee. He was laid off three years ago when business conditions forced the company to release 20 percent of the workforce. Since then, he has worked for another firm, but you know he has been looking for a better job. Jeff has listed you as a reference. A company interested in hiring Jeff has asked for a letter of recommendation. Your firm generally does not provide such letters because of the possibility of being sued. But you feel that you can write a positive letter about Jeff, which would help a good person who was a loyal employee. Should you write the letter? Can there be a downside to writing a positive letter?

Workplace Defamation

Most defamation suits come about from former employees suing for negative statements made about them by their ex-boss. As a result, many companies have a policy of providing no information about job performance, good or bad, for current or

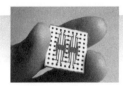

CYBER LAW
Tort Liability for Internet Servers

Internet users do things that are illegal or violate the rights of others. Are the Internet servers liable? In general, no, so long as they were not aware of, or had no reason to be aware of, the improper activity occurring on their system.

In *Zeran* v. *America Online* (129 F.3d 327), a federal appeals court held that America Online (AOL) cannot be sued for tort liability for a defamatory message that an AOL user sent. The sender may be liable, but AOL was not.

However, if a site contains defamatory material, the host of the site may be required to provide the identity of the party who posted the material. The Delaware high court held, in *Doe* v. *Cahill* (884 A.2d 451) that First Amendment protections extend to anonymous Internet speech, but not if it is defamatory. When defamatory statements are posted, the victim of the statements has the right to obtain the identity of Doe, the otherwise anonymous defendant.

past employees to outsiders who inquire about performance. When managers talk about the negative aspects of an employee's performance, they must remember that if the information is spread to those who do not have a business reason to know the information, then the company is more likely to be exposed to tort liability. An employer does have the right to share negative information for business purposes to people within an organization who should know why someone was fired or involved in some other negative event that has consequences for the company and is useful information for other employees.

Defenses

Truth and privilege are defenses to an action for defamation. If the statement that caused harm to a person's reputation is in fact the truth, some states hold that truth is a complete defense regardless of the purpose or intent in publishing the statement. *Truth* is an important defense in a defamation suit.

Depending on the circumstances, three privileges—absolute, conditional, and constitutional—may be used as a defense to a defamation action. *Absolute privilege* is an immunity applied in those situations where public policy favors complete freedom of speech. For example, state legislators in legislative sessions, participants in judicial proceedings, and government executives in the discharge of their duties have absolute immunity from liability resulting from their statements.

INTERNATIONAL PERSPECTIVE
Libel in Foreign Courts

Many countries do not have constitutional freedom of speech. The news media in the United States can communicate defamatory material about public officials or persons of legitimate public interest as long as the material is provided without actual malice. In the United Kingdom, the news media do not have this extensive privilege. Plaintiffs need show only that the defamatory statement was communicated and that their reputation was damaged. To avoid liability, a defendant must demonstrate that the statements made were true or that they had been made either in court or in Parliament.

As a result of this difference in the law of defamation, a number of U.S. communications companies—including Time, NBC, and Dow Jones—have found themselves in foreign courts, especially in the U.K. defending against defamation suits. Although the broadcasts in question may have originated in the United States and may have been republished in the foreign country without the consent of the U.S. company, the company will not be relieved of liability on that basis alone.

A *conditional privilege* eliminates liability when the false statement was published in good faith and with proper motives, such as for a legitimate business purpose. Businesses have a privilege to communicate information believed to be true. Individuals have a conditional privilege to publish defamatory matter to protect their legitimate interests, such as to defend their reputation against defamation by another.

As discussed in Chapter 4, the First Amendment to the Constitution guarantees freedom of speech and freedom of press. This *constitutional privilege* protects members of the press who publish "opinion" material about public officials, public figures, or persons of legitimate public interest. This privilege is lost if the statement was made with *actual malice*, that is, the false statement was made with reckless disregard for the truth, as in The *Republic Tobacco* case.

Summary

- Tort law concerns legal wrongs inflicted by one party on another by interfering with an interest protected by common law. Tort law changes over time as social values, technology, and business practices change. The primary purpose is to compensate the injured party and to put the burden on the tortfeasor.
- Tort liability for negligence arises when the duty of ordinary care—the care expected of a reasonable person under the circumstances—to another person is breached, usually by an act that is the proximate cause, or substantial factor of harm, to the other person.
- For a tort to be established, it must be shown that the act or failure to act on the part of the defendant was the cause in fact of the injury sustained. When the causation is obvious, the doctrine of *res ipsa loquitur* applies. After the cause is shown, then proximate cause in the logical sequence of events leading to the injury must be established. Liability may be avoided if some intervening conduct by another party becomes the superseding cause of the injury that occurred.
- A defendant in a negligence case may pose a defense of assumption of the risk on the part of the plaintiff. The plaintiff knew or should have known the risk, or may have accepted it by signing a liability waiver. There may also be a comparison of the behavior of the plaintiff and defendant by the rule of comparative negligence.
- Intentional torts are based on willful misconduct that invades the rights of another and causes injury. The rights can be the rights of persons to be safe and secure in their person or in their property. Wrongdoers will be expected to pay damages to compensate for injuries.
- Intentional interference with personal rights includes assault, when a person is placed in fear of bodily harm or offensive contact; battery, or unlawful physical contact without consent; false imprisonment, which is detaining someone within boundaries against his or her will; emotional distress, caused by outrageous conduct; invasion of privacy, which is a violation of a person's right to be free from unwanted exposure; defamation, or false communication that injures a person's reputation, including slander and libel; and malicious prosecution, or the unjustified use of the law to injure another.
- Defenses raised in tort lawsuits include that of truth in defamation cases; consent, or that the plaintiff had approved of the interference that led to injury; privilege, or that the defendant had a right to take the actions now challenged, including self-defense in case of assault; inflicting injury on another to defend someone else being attacked; and physically defending property. Force used should be no more than is reasonable under the circumstances. The law places a higher value on human life than on property.

Terms to Know

You should be able to define the following terms:

tort, 127	superseding cause, 132	false imprisonment, 139
strict liability, 127	assumption of risk, 134	emotional distress, 140
negligence, 127	exculpatory clause, 134	invasion of privacy, 142
proximate cause, 128	comparative negligence, 135	defamation, 143
res ipsa loquitur, 130	assault, 137	slander, 143
cause in fact, 130	battery, 137	libel, 143
sine qua non, 130	consent, 138	
substantial factor test, 132	privilege, 138	

Discussion Question

1. Are most accidents and injuries covered by tort law?

Case Questions

1. Ahron Leichtman, an antismoking advocate, was invited to appear on a radio talk show in Cincinnati to discuss smoking on the day of the Great American Smokeout. While he was in the studio, another talk show host lit a cigar and repeatedly blew smoke in Leichtman's face. Leichtman sued the radio station for battery. Did he have a case? [*Leichtman* v. *WLW Jacor Comm.*, 634 N.E.2d 697 Ct. App., Ohio (1994)]

2. Charlotte Newsom worked as a cashier at a store. One day she was told to report to the manager's office, where she was accused by two security staff members of stealing $500. She denied stealing the money. The meeting lasted two hours. The security staff asserted to have evidence of theft, although Newsom constantly denied the claim. Whenever Newsom stated that she wanted to leave, the staff told her she would be arrested for theft if she left. Finally, Newsom wrote a statement about the matter, denying the charge. She was fired on the spot and left the store. Did she have a case for false imprisonment? [*Newsom* v. *Thalhimer Brothers*, 901 S.Wd.2d 365 West. Dist. Ct.App., Tenn. (1994)]

   ✓ Check your answer at http://academic.cengage.com/blaw/meiners

3. When States was operated on at a hospital, an IV was put in her right arm to administer anesthesia. After the surgery, her arm, which had been fine before, was seriously damaged. What doctrine can States invoke against the parties involved in providing the surgery and anesthesia? [*States* v. *Lourdes Hospital*, 792 N.E.2d 151 Ct. App., NY (2003)]

4. A patron at a casino in Nevada got into a fight with another customer. The bouncer went to throw out the patron and got into a fight with him. The bouncer took the patron to a back room to photograph him (they keep photos of troublemakers), which resulted in another fight in which the patron suffered injury to his arm. What torts could the patron bring against the casino? What defences may work for the casino. [*Cerminara* v. *California Hotel and Casino*, 760 P.2d 108 Sup. Ct., Nev. (1988)]

   ✓ Check your answer at http://academic.cengage.com/blaw/meiners

5. Jerry Katz, a politician, stated that he would not raise taxes if elected. The local newspaper supported Katz, who won the election. At his first board meeting, Katz moved to raise taxes. His actions prompted an editorial that began, "Jerry Katz is a liar. He has lied to us in the past, and he will lie to us in the future." Katz sued the newspaper. What would that action be, and what would be the likely result? [*Costello* v. *Capital Cities Communications*, 505 N.E.2d 701 App. Ct., Ill. (1987)]

6. After Scarfo quit working for Ginsberg, she claimed that he subjected her to unwelcome sexual conduct and sued him for battery, emotional distress, and invasion of privacy. Florida uses the same categories of invasion of privacy as discussed in the chapter. Does

Scarfo potentially have a claim? [*Allstate Insurance* v. *Ginsberg*, 863 So.2d 156 Sup. Ct., Fla. (2003)]

✓ **Check your answer at http://academic.cengage.com/blaw/meiners**

7. Huggins's identity was stolen by an unknown person, who used it to obtain credit cards from various banks in Huggins's name. Huggins suffered the grief of cleaning up the identity theft. He sued the banks and credit card companies for negligence for issuing credit cards without more verification of the identity of the applicant and for failing to adopt other policies to prevent successful identity theft. Do the banks have a duty to protect potential victims of identity theft from imposter fraud? [*Huggins* v. *Citibank, N.A.*, 585 S.E.2d 275 Sup. Ct., S.C. (2003)]

8. A mother and her son were killed when an American Airlines plane hit their house in New York. The father and surviving children, who were not home at the time of the accident, sued for mental distress. The airline moved to dismiss the claim. Will dismissal most likely be granted? Why? [*Lawler* v. *American Airlines*, 450 F.Supp.2d 432 S.D. NY (2006)]

✓ **Check your answer at http://academic.cengage.com/blaw/meiners**

9. Barrett was injured when he struck a snowboard rail while he was skiing at a ski resort. He sued the resort for negligence for failure to warn of the presence of the snowboard rail. The resort owner moved to have the suit dismissed, but the trial court and court of appeals refused that motion. Resort owner appealed. Was there likely to be negligence? [*Barrett* v. *Mt. Brighton, Inc.*, 712 N.W.2d 154 Sup. Ct., Mich. (2006)]

10. A person stole a car from a car rental agency. The police spotted the stolen car and gave chase. The driver hit another car, seriously injuring that driver. The person who stole the car fled and was not caught. The injured person sued the rental agency for negligence for not keeping tighter control of their vehicles. Is there likely to be a case? What issues arise? [*Phillips* v. *Budget Rent-a-Car Systems*, 2007 WL 420240 Ct. App., Ill. (2007)]

11. Tomato growers in Tennessee bought a product called Frostguard from a California company. The company claimed the product would protect tomatoes from the harmful effects of frost. The growers applied Frostguard as directed but suffered substantial crop losses as a result of a frost. They sued the maker of Frostguard for negligence in advertising. Could they win such a tort action? [*Ritter* v. *Custom Chemicides*, 912 S.W.2d 128 Sup. Ct., Tenn. (1995)]

Ethics Question

1. Businesses have become more aggressive at suing publications that report negative news about them or make negative comments. A cigarette company sued CBS for interviewing a disgruntled former executive; an infomercial producer sued *Forbes* for $420 million for a negative article about infomercials, and ABC paid $15 million and made on-the-air apologies to settle a suit by two tobacco companies for $10 billion for a report about "spiking" cigarettes with nicotine. It has been claimed that such suits are primarily to deter the media from negative reporting. Since the suits have possible merit, there is no malicious prosecution, but the use of the law seems to be mostly strategic—to discourage the media from being critical of company practices. Is this a defensible business tactic?

Internet Assignment

http://www.law.com
http://www.lectlaw.com
http://www.abanet.org

According to the dictionary available at Law.com, what are the elements of a tort action? Give the URL for the topic of *tort* available at the 'Lectric Law Library'. Name four journal titles published by the ABA's Tort Trial and Insurance Practice section. When might you use one of these titles while researching a torts issue?

Getty Images

Business Torts and Product Liability

Chapter 7

There is no such thing as a "business tort," but many torts involve businesses as defendants, and some torts, in practice, involve only businesses. This chapter focuses on the areas of tort law that are of particular concern to business. About 5 percent of all civil suits are tort actions, but the money involved in some tort cases draws attention to this area of law. Consider some statistics about tort cases from several years ago:

- Plaintiffs win about 52 percent of personal injury suits and 41 percent of product defect suits.
- The median award in product liability suits has been about $400,000.
- The median award in personal injury suits is over $60,000.
- Ten percent of personal injury suit awards are for over $1 million.
- The average jury award for a rape on business property is $1.8 million.
- The median jury award for paraplegia is $6.5 million.

Defendants who expect to be found liable usually settle out of court. Since little information is available about such settlements, the magnitude of tort litigation is not known. ∎

Tort Law and Business

As seen in Chapter 6, there are several categories of intentional torts. Those torts occur when the tortfeasor is found to have intended to invade a protected interest and the tortfeasor knew, or should have known, of the consequences of the act that resulted in an injury.

Other torts are based on negligence, which is carelessness in a legal sense. When we fail to act the way we are obligated to behave and, as a result, others suffer an injury, we can be held liable. Persons in business are presumed to have a level of expertise that holds them to a higher level of care than is expected of a nonprofessional in the same situation.

While businesses may be defendants in suits for assault, such actions are not as peculiar to business as are the tort actions covered in this chapter. These actions mostly involve only business, and are the cases that most concern business, and tend to be big-dollar cases. As we will see, many suits involve both claims of intentional tort and claims of negligence. Plaintiffs make as many claims in one case as they can. As we will study later in the chapter, other cases involve strict liability in tort.

Costs of Tort Litigation

Each year about one-half million lawsuits involving tort claims are filed in our nation's court systems, most in state courts. As Exhibit 7.1 illustrates, compensation for injured parties—the main purpose of tort law—accounts for less than half of the total cost. The costs of tort litigation, both the process itself and the damages paid, have prompted concern about the ability of the court system to effectively and efficiently compensate innocent parties who are injured.

The cost of the tort system is difficult to calculate. One widely cited study estimates an average annual cost of $260 billion per year from 2004 through 2006. About two thirds of that involves business. Business organizations have lobbied Congress to impose federal statutory limits on tort damages. They claim that many of the awards are excessive or unjustified and that the cost is making American business less competitive in international markets, because most nations have fewer tort cases and less generous damage awards. We look next at areas of tort law that

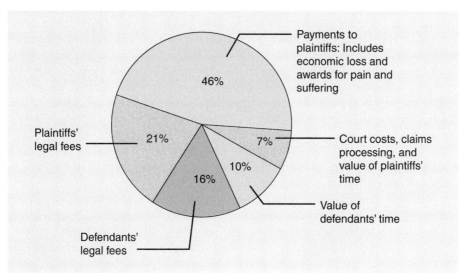

Exhibit 7.1
The Distribution of Tort Litigation Costs

Source: *Institute for Civil Justice*, RAND Corporation

tend to be peculiar to business and, in the case of product liability, involve massive sums of dollars.

Fraud

When a person suffers an injury (most injuries we study here are financial, not physical) due to deliberate deception, there may be a tort of *fraud, misrepresentation, fraudulent misrepresentation,* or *deceit.* When this issue arises in a business relationship, there is often a breach of contract or some other tort issue present. Fraud is a broad concept and may be held to be an intentional tort or to be a tort based on negligence. In the last chapter, we looked at negligent misrepresentation. Here we consider the more serious change of fraud. As we noted before, a claim of misrepresentation or fraud is very common in litigation.

Intentional Misrepresentation or Fraud

When misrepresentation is an intentional tort, there must be proof, as the House of Lords expressed in a famous case in 1889, "that a false representation has been made 1) knowingly, or 2) without belief in its truth, or 3) recklessly, careless whether it be true or false" (*Derry* v. *Peek*, 14 A.C. 337 at 374). While misrepresentation is a common-law rule subject to different interpretations, as the law has evolved, the following key elements generally have been agreed upon to establish fraud or intentional misrepresentation:

1. A material misrepresentation of a fact: false important information was passed.
2. *Scienter*, or intent to defraud: the defendant knew there was a misrepresentation of information being passed.
3. Intent to induce reliance: the defendant wanted the plaintiff to believe the falsehood.
4. Justifiable reliance by the plaintiff on the misinformation: the plaintiff had good reason to believe the misrepresentation offered by the defendant.
5. Relationship between the parties: the plaintiff and defendant were engaged in some relationship that created a legal obligation.
6. Causation: a logical link existed between reliance on the misstatement and the losses that were then suffered by the plaintiff.
7. Damages: losses were suffered by the plaintiff due to reliance on the fraud.

As with other torts, the relationship of the parties can be significant in determining whether legal responsibility is created. If a stranger walking down the street tells you to invest all of your money in Cool Video Company stock, you will not have a cause of action against the stranger when all of your money is lost when the company collapses, because there is no justification to believe a stranger about such a decision, nor is there a business relationship—it was just friendly, stupid advice. But if your stockbroker tells you to invest all of your money in Cool Video Company stock and tells you it is a safe, sure investment, when she knows it is a highly risky venture and she is getting kickbacks for sending clients to invest in the stock, then your reliance may be justified. She and her employing company may well be responsible for your losses when the company goes broke.

Fraud or intentional misrepresentation comes up in a wide variety of circumstances in business. It is a claim frequently added to a suit for breach of contract, because damages for an intentional tort have a chance of including punitive damages, which contract damages alone do not allow. While swindles are easily understood to fall into this category, overly aggressive behavior by a real estate agent trying to ensure a house sale can fall into this category.

Lightle v. Real Estate Commission
Supreme Court of Alaska
146 P.3d 980 (2006)

Case Background *Lightle, a real estate agent in Anchorage, listed a house for sale by the Leighs. The Williamses made an offer to buy the house, and the offer was accepted, conditional on their obtaining a mortgage. Later, another realtor had a client, Seeley, who was interested in the house. Lightle said the house was available as "the first offer was dead." Seeley made an offer that the Leighs accepted. Believing she had a deal on the house, Seeley canceled her existing lease, switched over the utilities, and rented a truck to move. Unknown to Seeley, Lightle wrote on her offer that it was a back-up contract only if the Williamses could not get financing, which was still in process.*

Seeley found out, rescinded her offer, demanded her deposit back, and filed a claim against the Alaska Real Estate Commission's real estate surety fund, a state-administered fund to compensate people who lose money in real estate transactions due to fraud. The Commission heard the case and held that Lightle committed fraudulent misrepresentation. It awarded Seeley damages and suspended Lightle's real estate license. Lightle appealed, but the decision was upheld by the superior court, which acts as an appeals court for Commission decisions. Lightle appealed again.

Case Decision Bryner, Chief Justice

* * *

Alaska follows the *Restatement* (Second) of Torts on what constitutes an intentional or fraudulent misrepresentation. As described in the *Restatement*, the elements of fraudulent misrepresentation are: (1) a misrepresentation of fact or intention, (2) made fraudulently (that is, with "scienter"), (3) for the purpose or with the expectation of inducing another to act in reliance, (4) with justifiable reliance by the recipient, (5) causing loss....

As used in the *Restatement*, the word "fraudulent" refers "solely to the maker's knowledge of the untrue character of his representation. This element of the defendant's conduct frequently is called 'scienter.'" Under Section 526 of the Restatement, [a] misrepresentation is fraudulent if the maker (a) knows or believes that the matter is not as he represents it to be, (b) does not have the confidence in the accuracy of his representation that he states or implies, or (c) knows that he does not have the basis for his representation that he states or implies....

The *Restatement* defines this requirement of a "purpose to induce" action as follows:

> One who makes a fraudulent misrepresentation is subject to liability to the persons or class of persons whom he intends *or has reason to expect to act or to refrain from action in reliance upon the misrepresentation*, for pecuniary loss suffered by them through their justifiable reliance in the type of transaction in which he intends or has reason to expect their conduct to be influenced....

Lightle ... [said] that the prior deal "is dead," that Seeley's offer had been accepted, and that "the house is yours"... Lightle made a partial disclosure that failed to reveal facts that "might have affected the recipient's conduct in the transaction in hand."...

For these reasons, we affirm the superior court's ruling upholding the commission's decision.

Questions for Analysis
1. The court held that Lightle committed fraud by not telling the truth about the contract status of the house. Did he intend to deceive the buyer?
2. Since Lightle was the representative of the sellers, the Leighs, why should he have any obligation to the buyer, Seeley?

Interference with Contractual Relations

One of the more common business torts is *intentional interference with contractual relations*. The basis of the claim is that the injured business's contractual relations were wrongfully interfered with by another party. The elements of this tort, which is illustrated in Exhibit 7.2 are 1) the existence of a contractual relationship between the injured business and another party, 2) that was known to the wrongdoer, who, 3) intentionally interfered with that relationship.

Exhibit 7.2 Example: Tort of Interference with a Contract

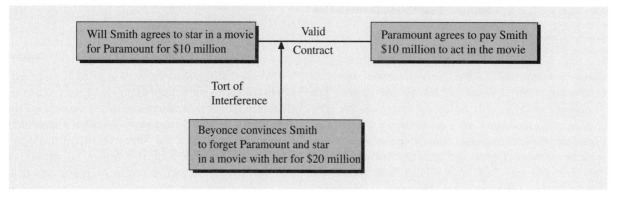

When a wrongdoer intentionally causes another party to break a good contract, the motive does not matter. The point is that breaking the contract is done to benefit the tortfeasor. This causes injury to the party who suffers the breach of contract. The party who suffers the breach may sue both the party who breached the contract for breach and the wrongdoer for the tort of interference with the contract. The *Matrix* case discusses the elements of this kind of tort.

Matrix Group Limited v. Rawlings Sporting Goods
United States Court of Appeals, Eighth Circuit
477 F.3d 583 (2007)

Case Background *Matrix, a Florida company, makes bags for sporting equipment. Rawlings, a Delaware company, makes sporting equipment. In 1996, they contracted for Matrix to have an exclusive license to use Rawlings' trademark in producing, marketing, and selling equipment bags, and the license would continue so long as certain conditions, including sales criteria, were satisfied. The parties agreed not to compete against each other in that market. In 2003, K2 acquired Rawlings as a subsidiary and also acquired Worth, a competitor to Matrix in the sports-bag market. Soon after, Rawlings terminated the agreement with Matrix.*

Matrix sued Rawlings for breach of contract and sued K2 for tortious interference with a business relationship, which is the issue of concern here. The district court held for Matrix, and the jury awarded $8.65 million in damages. Rawlings and K2 appealed.

Case Decision Murphy, Circuit Judge

* * *

The elements of a claim for tortious interference with a business relationship under Florida law are (1) the existence of a business relationship, (2) the defendant's

knowledge of that relationship, (3) the defendant's intentional and unjustified interference with that relationship, and (4) damage to the plaintiff as a result of the breach of the relationship. At trial there was testimony that K2 was aware of the contract between Rawlings and Matrix and its provisions and that president Parish of Rawlings had discussed a key letter from Matrix president Orloff with K2's general counsel. That letter had warned Rawlings that K2's plan to consolidate the Rawlings and Worth sales forces would breach the contract. Because K2 nonetheless went ahead with consolidation, the jury was entitled to infer that K2 "intended to procure a breach of the contract." Purposely causing a breach of contract is an "improper means" of interference, and using improper means to interfere with a business relationship constitutes unjustifiable interference. The jury was entitled to find from the evidence that K2 had used improper means of interference and that it had intentionally and unjustifiably interfered with the license agreement....

Damages for breach of contract and tortious interference are not coextensive, and a jury may award damages under both claims. Matrix's expert witness testified that it suffered a total of $12,797,893 in damages, but the damages which the jury awarded against both Rawlings and K2 totaled only $8,650,000. The jury's aggregate award was thus well within the bounds of the evidence presented at trial, and a jury may rationally allocate damages "between the two different causes of action, one for breach of contract, and one for tort."...

The acts committed by Rawlings and those committed by K2 were different. While Rawlings breached the contract by improperly terminating Matrix ... K2 ordered the sales forces of Worth and Rawlings to consolidate, thus causing a breach of the license agreement's noncompete clause. The jury apparently intended to apportion damages between

the defendants for these separate acts. In light of these points, and K2's failure to raise the issue in timely fashion, we conclude that the damages awarded against K2 should be affirmed....

Questions for Analysis

1. The appeals court agreed that K2 committed a tort by causing a breach of the contract between Rawlings and Matrix. Since Rawlings broke the contract, and was liable for breach of contract, why should there also be a tort claim against K2?

2. How could Rawlings and K2 have gotten out of the contract with Matrix?

Interference with Prospective Advantage

Similar to the tort of interference with contractual rights is the tort of *interference with prospective advantage*, also called *interference with prospective economic advantage* and *interference with prospective contractual relationship*. Businesses devise countless schemes to attract customers, which is a good part of competition, but it is a tort when a business attempts to improve its place in the market by interfering with another's business in an unreasonable and improper manner.

An employee of Oprah's Hot Threads, for example, cannot be positioned at the entrance of U2 Runners Sportswear to tell customers to go to Oprah's. Such conduct is predatory behavior. If the behavior of the defendant is merely competitive and not predatory in nature—for example, the defendant is so effective in advertising that customers are drawn from the losing business—the courts do not find improper interference.

Many of the cases in this area arise when a seller refuses to sell to another party any longer, making it impossible for that party to do business with its clients. In particular, there have been many suits brought by insurance agencies when the insurance companies have refused to continue to provide them insurance policies, thereby causing them to lose current and prospective customers. That is the situation in the *MDM Group* case.

MDM Group Associates v. CX Reinsurance Company
Colorado Court of Appeals
165 P.3d 882 (2007)

Case Background *MDM is an insurance broker that developed a program for insuring ski resorts against the risk that the number of paying ski days during a ski season would fall below a certain minimum. CX and others agreed to write policies starting in the 1997–1998 ski season. The*

policies generated premiums of $550,000. MDM received a commission of 12.5 percent. In the 1999–2000 year, premiums were up to $3 million, but due to poor snow that year, many ski days were lost, and the resorts filed many claims. CX resisted, resulting in negotiations, mediation,

continues

and litigation that resulted in $23 million in claims payouts. As it had the right to do, CX stopped issuing policies.

MDM sued CX for intentional interference with prospective business relations, contending CX had handled the ski resort claims improperly and in bad faith, thereby causing them to not renew their policies and causing MDM to lose renewal commissions. MDM claimed it was a rapidly growing area of insurance, so it lost the opportunity to sell policies to other clients who were interested in the insurance. The jury awarded MDM $6.75 million in damages. CX appealed.

Case Decision Casebolt, Judge

* * *

Colorado recognizes the tort of intentional interference with prospective business relations. As set forth in the *Restatement* (Second) of Torts § 766B (1979):

> One who intentionally and improperly interferes with another's prospective contractual relation … is subject to liability to the other for the pecuniary harm resulting from loss of the benefits of the relation, whether the interference consists of (a) inducing or otherwise causing a third person not to enter into or continue the prospective relation or (b) preventing the other from acquiring or continuing the prospective relation.

While the existence of an underlying contract is not required for this tort, there must be a showing of improper and intentional interference by the defendant that prevents the formation of a contract between the plaintiff and a third party. Interference with "another's prospective contractual relation" is tortious only if there is a reasonable likelihood or reasonable probability that a contract would have resulted.

> However, a defendant cannot be liable for interference with its own contract: It is impossible for one party to a

contract to maintain against the other party to the contract a claim for tortious interference with the parties' own contract. Neither party is a stranger to the contract. Each party has agreed to be bound by the terms of the contract itself, and may not thereafter use a tort action to punish the other party for actions that are within its rights under the contract.

To the extent, therefore, that MDM is asserting a claim against CX for tortiously interfering with a contract between itself and CX, such a claim may not be maintained.

It logically follows, as well, that MDM cannot maintain an action against CX for tortious interference with *any* contract to which CX is a party.…

Accordingly, MDM cannot assert tortious interference as to the insurance contracts between CX and the insured ski resorts.… Nor can MDM assert a claim against CX for prospective contractual relations if CX were expected to be a party to that contract.…

The judgment is reversed … and the case is remanded with directions to enter judgment for CX.

Questions for Analysis

1. The appeals court held that MDM could not prevail over CX in a claim for tortious interference with prospective advantage, because CX had the right to stop issuing insurance policies. Since there were buyers who wanted to get the policies from MDM, and it could no longer provide them, why was that not interference by CX?
2. CX apparently behaved in bad faith in paying insurance claims, as the ski resorts had to sue to collect on the policies. Why would that not affect the decision in this case?

ISSUE SPOTTER

Hiring Employees from Competitors

When opening a new office in a new city for your company, a quick way to get qualified employees who know the market is to bid away people now working for competitors. What legal issues in tort could arise in that regard? What precautions should you take if you use this strategy?

Getty Images

Product Liability

Product liability is a general term applied to an area of the law that is primarily tort law but also involves some contract law and statutory law. This concerns the liability that producers and sellers of goods have to those injured by a product. Since some cases involve thousands of people and billions of dollars, product liability gets a lot of media attention and is controversial. Major companies have been bankrupted by product liability decisions. The primary political issue is whether the law has become so strict in assigning liability to producers that the legislature should intervene and set limits on liability. The evolution of the common law of product liability over the past century reflects how the law changes as technology and expectations about safety and responsibility change.

Consumer Products and Negligence

A century ago, the rule was that a manufacturer was liable for injuries caused by defects in its products to parties with whom the manufacturer had a contractual relationship. The term *privity of contract* refers to the relationship that exists between contracting parties. It is essential to a contract case that *privity*, a legal relationship, exist between the parties. Since consumers rarely bought products directly from manufacturers, there often was no privity between consumer and producer. Producers were effectively isolated from liability for most product-related injuries.

Rule of Caveat Emptor

Injured parties who did not have privity of contract with the manufacturer of the defective products operated under the rule of *caveat emptor*, which means "let the buyer beware." According to the U.S. Supreme Court, the rule of caveat emptor "requires that the buyer examine, judge, and test [the product] for himself." Thus, a consumer without privity took the risk that a product was safe. If a product was not safe and there was an injury, the burden fell on the consumer.

INTERNATIONAL PERSPECTIVE

Is Japan Really Different?

Some politicians want legislation to restrict tort litigation. Japan is often cited as an example of where there is less litigation and fewer lawyers. This is claimed to make Japan more cost competitive than the United States, where tort cases are claimed to be out of control.

The United States has 25 times more lawyers per person than Japan, because the government of Japan allows only between 300 and 500 new attorneys each year. However, Japanese universities produce 50 percent more legal specialists per person than do American universities. These Japanese "nonlawyers" do all legal work except represent clients in court for a fee. Although the nonlawyers are not called lawyers, they are paid to do what Americans call legal work.

A study of fatal traffic accidents in Japan by American and Japanese law professors found that the American and Japanese tort systems are not that different. The systems are organized differently, but the results are much the same. Japanese plaintiffs win a higher percentage of tort liability suits than do American plaintiffs. Payments to Japanese plaintiffs are close to those given to American plaintiffs in similar suits. A close examination makes the actual operation of the two tort systems look more alike than is often claimed.

Getty Images

Negligence in Tort

The privity rule often left innocent, injured consumers without any remedy. In response to the harsh result the rule could impose, the courts began to recognize exceptions. Then, in 1916, in the famous *MacPherson* decision, New York struck down the privity rule and held a manufacturer liable in tort for negligence for a product-related injury. This case is still good law today.

MacPherson v. Buick Motor Company
Court of Appeals of New York
217 N.Y. 382, 111 N.E. 1050 (1916)

Case Background *Buick produced cars and sold them to dealers. MacPherson bought a new Buick from a dealer in New York. The wheels on MacPherson's Buick were made by another company for Buick. Soon after he bought the car, one of the wheels collapsed, causing an accident that injured MacPherson, who sued Buick. His suit against Buick traditionally would have been barred because of lack of privity; that is, Buick sold the car to the dealer, who in turn sold it to MacPherson. The dealer had a contract with MacPherson but was not responsible for the defect. Nevertheless, the lower courts ruled for MacPherson, finding Buick liable in tort for injuries caused by the defect. Buick appealed to the highest court in New York.*

Case Decision Cardozo, Justice

* * *

One of the wheels was made of defective wood, and its spokes crumbled into fragments. The wheel was not made by the defendant; it was bought from another manufacturer. There is evidence, however, that its defects could have been discovered by reasonable inspection, and that inspection was omitted. There is no claim that Buick knew of the defect and willfully concealed it.... The charge is one, not of fraud, but of negligence. The question to be determined is whether the defendant owed a duty of care and vigilance to anyone but the immediate purchaser.

* * *

If the nature of a thing is such that it is reasonably certain to place life and limb in peril when negligently made, it is then a thing of danger. Its nature gives warning of the consequences to be expected. If to the element of danger there is added knowledge that the thing will be used by persons other than the purchaser, and used without new tests, then, irrespective of

contract, the manufacturer of this thing of danger is under a duty to make it carefully. That is as far as we are required to go for the decision of this case. There must be knowledge of a danger, not merely possible, but probable. . . . We are dealing now with the liability of the manufacturer of the finished product, who puts it on the market to be used without inspection by his customers. If he is negligent, where danger is to be foreseen, a liability will follow.

* * *

We think the defendant was not absolved from a duty of inspection because it bought the wheels from a reputable manufacturer. It was not merely a dealer in automobiles. It was a manufacturer of automobiles. It was responsible for the finished product. It was not at liberty to put the finished product on the market without subjecting the component parts to ordinary and simple tests. Under the charge of the trial judge, nothing more was required of it. The obligation to inspect must vary with the nature of the thing to be inspected. The more probable the danger the greater the need of caution.

* * *

The judgment should be affirmed.

Questions for Analysis
1. The court held Buick liable in tort for negligence in manufacturing a product with a danger. Buick argued that it should not be liable' because it did not make the wheels. Why not make the injured party sue the producer of the defective part?
2. Buick argued that this was the only wheel out of 60,000 sold that had been shown defective. Should 1/60,000 be sufficient to establish negligence?

Manufacturers must produce products using proper care to eliminate foreseeable harm, or risk being found negligent in tort if a consumer is injured by a defective product. The rule originating with *MacPherson*, and adopted in every state, provides that

> The manufacturer of a product is liable in the production and sale of a product for negligence, if the product may reasonably be expected to inflict harm on the user if the product is defective.

A manufacturer is required to exercise *reasonable care* under the circumstances in the production of its product. Liability may be imposed on a manufacturer for negligence in the preparation of the product—for failing to inspect or test the materials, for below-normal-quality workmanship, or for failing to discover possible defects. Defects must be revealed even if the manufacturer becomes aware of them after the sale of the product. Reasonable care must also be taken in presenting the product to the public—through advertisements or other promotions—to avoid *misrepresentation*. If a causal connection can be established between the failure of the manufacturer to exercise reasonable care in any of these areas and an injury suffered by a consumer, liability based on negligence for damages may be imposed on the manufacturer. Producers are responsible for damages inflicted in such cases and punitive damages may be added.

LIGHTER SIDE OF THE LAW
Well, It Didn't Look Safe to Me!

Robert Jones of Adel, Georgia, bought Liquid Fire drain cleaner. Thinking that the bottle the product came in did not look safe enough, he poured the contents into another container. That container leaked, causing Liquid Fire to run onto his legs and resulting in "extensive, excruciating burns." Jones sued Liquid Fire because its container, which did not leak, did not appear to be safe.

Source: *Atlanta Constitution*

Getty Images

Strict Liability Under Contract Law

Negligence in tort did not resolve some product-related injury cases. Injured parties had a hard time showing that manufacturers had not exercised reasonable care in the production of their product. The *strict liability* doctrine resolved this by holding manufacturers liable to consumers injured by defective products even though the manufacturer exercised all reasonable care. Thus, the injured party is not required to attack the reasonableness of the conduct of the manufacturer, but rather focuses on problems with the product.

Strict liability was first applied to product-related injuries through a warranty theory under contract law. Later, the adoption of strict liability in tort by the American Law Institute in the authoritative *Restatement (Second) of Torts* helped spur the adoption of strict liability in tort. We now have a mix of contract law and tort law applying to products.

Strict liability under contract law is based on the relationship between the injured party and the manufacturer because of the existence of a *warranty*. Warranty is based upon a manufacturer's assurance that a product will meet certain quality and performance standards. Such warranties may be either express or implied.

Strict Liability Based on Implied Warranty

The first application of the doctrine of strict liability for defective consumer products was in the area of food and drink. For example, in a 1913 case from Washington State, *Mazetti* v. *Armour* (135 P. 633), the court held "a manufacturer of food products … impliedly warrants his goods when dispensed in original packages." Consumer injury caused by defective food or drink is a breach of *implied warranty* of safety, and the manufacturer is strictly liable for the injury.

The Supreme Court of New Jersey later extended implied warranty of safety to other consumer products. In *Henningsen* v. *Bloomfield Motors* (161 A.2d 69), the New Jersey court held the manufacturer of an automobile strictly liable to the purchaser's wife for her injuries, when the brakes failed and an accident occurred, on the basis of an implied warranty of safety.

ISSUE SPOTTER

Understanding Product Problems

Your company makes products that are sometimes involved in consumer injuries. What would you suggest doing with respect to managing the information about defects so that the company can better understand its products' problems and address them more quickly? Is these a systematic way to deal with the problem?

Getty Images

Strict Liability Based on Express Warranty

Strict liability under contract law is also applied in cases in which a manufacturer makes an *express warranty* about its product to consumers. Manufacturers often advertise quality or performance characteristics of their products. When such claims become part of the bargain between a manufacturer and a consumer, the manufacturer is held to have a duty of performance as to that representation.

Strict liability based on express warranty does not require that injured consumers have purchased the product directly from the manufacturer. The courts have long allowed the consumer to sue the manufacturer, not the retail dealer. Injured consumers are not required to prove fault, because the law requires manufacturers to guarantee the truthfulness of their representations. *Misrepresentation* about a product may be the basis for strict liability in tort.

For example, back in 1932, Ford was found liable for failing to provide a shatterproof windshield on a car. As a result, a driver lost an eye when a rock hit the windshield and the glass shattered (*Baxter* v. *Ford Motor*, 12 P.2d 409). The contract for sale did not say the car had a shatterproof windshield, but Ford advertised that the car had that safety feature. The court held the advertisement created an express warranty of safety that Ford breached when it failed to provide the safety glass. An express warranty was a part of the contract in the sale of the car because of the advertising promise made to consumers, so product liability was imposed in the contract.

Strict Liability in Tort

Strict liability is still imposed under contract law. This can be the basis for a strong liability suit. However, the plaintiff can be faced with the problem of showing a warranty existed. In response to such difficulties, the courts simplified the legal basis for injured plaintiffs by adopting the rule of *strict liability in tort*. The Supreme Court of California was the first court to adopt a general rule of strict liability in tort in product injury cases.

Greenman v. Yuba Power Products
Supreme Court of California
59 Cal.2d 57, 27 Cal.Rptr. 697, 377 P.2d 897 (1963)

Case Background *Greenman's wife bought him a Shopsmith—a power tool that could be used as a saw, drill, and wood lathe. Greenman had studied material about the product and asked his wife to buy it. Two years later, while Greenman was using the machine, a piece of wood suddenly flew out of the machine and sturck him on the forehead, inflicting serious injuries.*

Greenman sued the manufacturer, Shopsmith, and the retail dealer, Yuba Power, alleging breaches of warranties and negligence. The verdict in Greenman's favor against Shopsmith was appealed.

Case Decision Traynor, Justice

* * *

Plaintiff introduced substantial evidence that his injuries were caused by defective design and construction of the Shopsmith. His expert witnesses testified that inadequate set screws were used to hold parts of the machine together so that normal vibration caused the tailstock of the lathe to move away from the piece of wood being turned, permitting it to fly out of the lathe. They also testified that there were other more posititve way of fastening the parts of the machine together, the use of which would have prevented the accident. . . .

A manufacturer is strictly liable in tort when an article he places on the market, knowing that it is to be used without inspection for defects, proves to have a defect that causes injury to a human being. Recognized first in the case of unwholesome food products, such liability has now been extended to a variety of other products that create as great or greater hazards if defective.

* * *

The purpose of such liability is to insure that the costs of injuries resulting from defective products are borne by the manufacturers that put such products on the market rather than by the injured persons who are powerless to protect themselves. Sales warranties serve this purpose fitfully at best. . . . Implicit in the machine's presence on the market, however, was a representation that it would safely do the jobs for which it was built. Under these circumstances, it should not be controlling whether plaintiff selected the machine because of the statements in the brochure, or because of the machine's own appearance of excellence that belied the defect lurking beneath the surface, or because he merely assumed that it would safely do the jobs it was built to do. It should not be controlling whether the details of the sales from manufacturer to retailer and from retailer to Greenman's wife were such that one or more of the implied warranties of the sales act arose. "The remedies of injured consumers ought not to be made to depend upon the intricacies of the law of sales." To establish the manufacturer's liability it was sufficient that plaintiff proved that he was injured while using the Shopsmith in a way it was intended to be used as a result of a defect in design and manufacture, of which plaintiff was not aware, that made the shopsmith unsafe for its intended use.

* * *

The judgment is affirmed.

Questions for Analysis
1. The court adopted the rule of strict liability in tort. What is the advantage of this compared to strict liability imposed on the basis of implied warranty in contract?
2. Would strict liability be imposed on the manufacturer if a friend of Greenman's had used the machine and was hurt while using it?

Section 402A

The author of the *Restatement (Second) of Torts*, the American Law Institute, adopted a strict liability in tort rule in product injury cases similar to that imposed in *Greenman*. This helped bring about nationwide acceptance of the strict liability in tort rule. The *Restatement*'s strict liability in tort rule is found in Section 402A:

(1) One who sells any product in a defective condition unreasonably dangerous to the user or consumer, or to his property, is subject to liability for physical harm thereby caused to the ultimate user or consumer, or to his property, if

(a) the seller is engaged in the business of selling such a product, and

(b) it is expected to and does reach the user or consumer without substantial change in the condition in which it is sold.

(2) The rule stated in Subsection 1) applies although

(a) the seller has exercised all possible care in the preparation and sale of his product, and

(b) the user or consumer has not bought the product from or entered into any contractual relation with the seller.

While this is still the law in most states, as we see next, the standard appears to be evolving.

LIGHTER SIDE OF THE LAW
I'm from the FBI; I Know the Law

FBI Special Agent Clymer jumped the curb with his pickup and was found in it, passed out drunk—his blood alcohol was 0.306—after it caught fire, along with an empty bottle of rum. Police pulled him from the vehicle.

Clymer claims he stopped along the road to make a call, had the pickup in Park, then "somehow lost consciousness"; and the truck "somehow produced a heavy smoke that filled the passenger cab." He sued Chevy and the Chevy dealer who sold him the truck for selling him a defective vehicle.

Source: *Las Vegas Review-Journal*

Getty Images

Restatement (Third) of Torts *on Products Liability*

The American Law Institute's (ALI) definition of strict liability in Section 402A of the *Restatement (Second) of Torts* has been the leading rule adopted by most states to define liability for product-related injury. Experience with the rule over the years has led to the ALI writing a new standard for product defect cases in its newer *Restatement (Third) of Torts*. As usually happens, state supreme courts consider new expressions of the law and often gradually adopt them. Section 2 of the *Restatement (Third) of Torts* expresses a key part of product liability as follows:

Section 2. Categories of Product Defect A product is defective when, at the time of sale or distribution, it contains a manufacturing defect, is defective in design, or is defective because of inadequate instructions or warnings. A product:

(a) contains a manufacturing defect when the product departs from its intended design even though all possible care was exercised in the preparation and marketing of the product;

(b) is defective in design when the foreseeable risks of harm posed by the product could have been reduced or avoided by the adoption of a reasonable alternative design by the seller or other distributor, or a predecessor in the commercial chain of distribution, and the omission of the alternative design renders the product not reasonably safe;

(c) is defective because of inadequate instructions or warnings when the foreseeable risks of harm posed by the product could have been reduced or avoided by the provision of reasonable instructions or warnings by the seller or other distributor, or a predecessor in the commercial chain of distribution, and the omission of the instructions or warnings renders the product not reasonably safe.

This is not a great change from the *Restatement (Second)*, but the newer version focuses on what it calls "risk–utility balancing." That is, some products cannot be made safe. Gasoline is explosive. That is a risk, but if it were to be made so it could not explode, its utility would be lost. So the courts consider the reality of technology, costs, and use in practice.

The *Restatement (Third)* also encourages courts to move away from the distinction between negligence and strict liability. The focus is on functionality, not traditional categories, so all producers are expected, given the risks and utility of their products, to meet the standard expressed in Section 2 of the *Restatement (Third)*. Change in legal standards by state courts takes time. Iowa's Supreme Court has expressly adopted the newer version of product liability; others are exploring the matter. It will not cause a great change in the impact of the law in practice, because the kinds of cases will remain much the same. This is what we turn to now.

Primary Areas of Product Liability Law

We will refer to this as *strict liability in tort*, as that is still the most common way to discuss liability for defective products, although *Restatement (Third)* just calls this *product defect law*. In either case, the chain of events needed to establish liability in tort is outlined in Exhibit 7.3. There are three key areas: 1) a defect in the product from manufacturing; 2) the manufacturer failed to warn the consumer of risks of use or of known hazards in certain uses of the product; and 3) the product had a design defect in it that could have been avoided. There is another huge area that is unique, involving products that produce latent injuries that may not become known for years. We consider each of these areas in turn.

Manufacturing Defect

This area is straightforward, so we will spend little time on it. It is what the law was clearly intended to address: someone buys a new toaster, plugs it in, and is electrocuted. There was a defect in the product from the manufacturing stage. Consumers

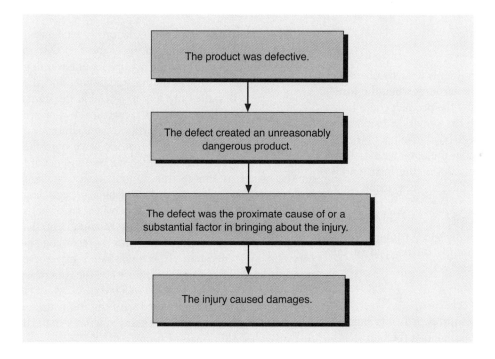

Exhibit 7.3
Elements of Strict Liability or Product Defect Law

The product was defective.

The defect created an unreasonably dangerous product.

The defect was the proximate cause of or a substantial factor in bringing about the injury.

The injury caused damages.

do not expect such defects and will be compensated for them. Both the second and third *Restatement*, make clear that liability is to be imposed. It is the other areas, which we will study in more detail, that cause more problems in applying the law.

Failure to Warn

A manufacturer's *failure to warn* consumers of dangers involved in the use of a product, or to instruct consumers about proper procedures in using a product, has long been actionable. That is, the defect in the product is in the failure to warn, not necessarily in the product itself. Failure to warn falls under a wide variety of circumstances, from failure to give information about specific dangers, to failure to issue added warnings about problems that become known after a product has been in use for some time, to failure to give special emphasis to the biggest dangers posed by a product. In the *Parish* case we see an analysis of the failure to warn claim under the standards of *Restatement (Third) of Torts*.

Parish v. ICON
Supreme Court of Iowa
719 N.W.2d 540 (2006)

Case Background *Parish was jumping on a backyard trampoline, made by Jumpking, that was surrounded by a safety net, called a* fun ring, *made by ICON. He did a back somersault but landed on his head and was rendered a quadriplegic. He sued ICON and Jumpking for failure to warn of the dangers involved in using the products. The district court granted summary judgment for the manufacturers; Parish appealed.*

Case Decision Larson, Justice

* * *

Under the *Restatement*, a product is defective because of inadequate instructions or warnings when the foreseeable risks of harm posed by the product could have been reduced or avoided by the provision of reasonable instructions or warnings by the seller or other distributor, or a predecessor in the commercial chain of distribution, and the omission of the instructions or warnings renders the product not reasonably safe. Restatement § 2(c).

The trampoline in this case, and its surrounding fun ring, together provide numerous warnings. Three warnings are placed permanently on the pad of the trampoline and advise the user:

Warning
Do not land on head or neck.
Paralysis or death can result, even if you land in the middle of the trampoline mat (bed).

To reduce the chance of landing on your head or neck, do not do somersaults (flips).
Only one person at a time on trampoline.
Multiple jumpers increase the chances of loss of control, collision, and falling off.
This can result in broken head, neck, back, or leg.
This trampoline is not recommended for children under 6 years of age.

These warnings also include nationally recognized warning symbols cautioning against those activities. During manufacture, Jumpking also places one warning on each of the eight legs of the trampoline, and the design is such that the only way to assemble the trampoline is to have these warnings facing out so they are visible to the user. Jumpking further manufactures two printed (nonpictorial) warnings that are sewn onto the trampoline bed itself. It also provides a warning placard for the owner to affix to the trampoline that contains both the pictorial warning and the language regarding safe use of the trampoline, and it provides an owner's manual that contains the warnings as found on the trampoline, as well as additional warnings regarding supervision and education. It is undisputed that these warnings exceed the warnings required by the American Society for Testing and Material (ASTM)....

Warnings are also provided with the fun ring.... The fun ring comes with a separate owner's manual that provides additional warnings.

The *Restatement* recognizes that users must pay some attention for their own safety:

> Society does not benefit from products that are excessively safe—for example, automobiles designed with maximum speeds of 20 miles per hour—any more than it benefits from products that are too risky. Society benefits most when the right, or optimal, amount of product safety is achieved. *From a fairness perspective, requiring individual users and consumers to bear appropriate responsibility for proper product use prevents careless users and consumers from being subsidized by more careful users and consumers, when the former are paid damages out of funds to which the latter are forced to contribute through higher product prices. Restatement* § 2 comment (a) (emphasis added). . . .

We conclude that a reasonable fact finder could not conclude that the defendant's warnings were inadequate, and we affirm the district court's summary judgment on that claim.

Affirmed.

Questions for Analysis

1. The Iowa high court held that there was no failure to warn of the dangers of a trampoline, so the maker was not liable for injuries suffered by a user. Could it be that the dangers of such a product are such that it should simply be banned, because it is too dangerous and simply cannot be made safe?
2. The plaintiff here was an adult; would it be different if a small child, who would be less likely to pay attention to the warnings, had been injured?

Manufacturers must warn of possible dangers in the use, storage, and handling of their products. For example, although household cleansers are dangerous and not intended for consumption, manufacturers know that adults often leave such products in places where children might get them. Thus, liability may be imposed for not warning people sufficiently of such dangers and for not taking steps to reduce possible tragedies, such as by using containers that are not attractive to children, using hard-to-remove caps, and putting danger labels or symbols on the containers. How far does the failure-to-warn liability in tort extend? The outside limits of the application are illustrated by the following cases:

- A Pennsylvania court found a gun manufacturer that failed to warn users of damage to hearing from long-term exposure to gunfire was liable for injuries.
- The Supreme Court of Alaska upheld a verdict against a diet food producer that failed to provide adequate warnings about using the adult diet food as baby food. Because the food was safe for dieting adults but not for infants, the company should have stated so on its product.
- The high court of New York held liable the producer of a commercial pizza dough roller machine for injuries suffered by a worker who stuck his hands in the machine when he tried to clean it. Although the machine had a safety switch to be used when cleaning the machine, the worker had turned off the switch so he could stick his hands in the machine. The manufacturer failed to warn when it did not clearly explain the dangers of turning off the switch.
- A jury in a federal court ordered Johnson and Johnson to pay $8.85 million to a man who had a liver transplant, because years of drinking alcohol and taking Tylenol had destroyed his liver. Johnson and Johnson had not warned Tylenol users that liver damage could occur in regular drinkers who took regular doses of Tylenol.

Design Defects

Unlike defective product cases, *design defect* cases are not concerned with a product that has been poorly manufactured and causes an injury. Rather, such cases focus on the determination of whether an injury to users could have been prevented by designing the product differently. In that regard, consider the following design defect cases:

- In a Washington State case, a worker received $750,000 for the loss of a leg. While repairing a machine, coworkers had removed a metal plate from the top of the machine. When they finished, the workers failed to replace the metal plate and covered the machine with cardboard. The plaintiff later walked on what he thought was the metal plate, as was customary, and fell into the machine. The court held that a design defect had allowed the machine to be able to run when the metal plate was removed.
- A restaurant employee was seriously burned when he tried to retrieve something that fell out of his shirt pocket and into a commercial French fryer machine. The D.C. Circuit Court of Appeals held that a jury could find that a safer alternative design of the machine was possible, in which case it could impose liability.
- A child pushed the emergency stop button on an escalator, causing a person to fall and be injured. The Seventh Circuit Court of Appeals ruled that it was a design defect both to make the button red, because that color is attractive to children, and to place the button so that it was accessible to children.

LIGHTER SIDE OF THE LAW
Never Enough Ways to Warn

Para-Chem produced an "All Weather Outdoor Adhesive" to glue down outdoor carpeting. Among the warnings on the can were "Do Not Use Indoors" and "Extremely Flammable."

Two professional carpet installers used the adhesive to put carpet in a basement. It ignited, causing an explosion that burned them badly. A jury awarded them $8 million. The appeals court upheld the verdict, holding the warning insufficient, because they did not say the fumes were "explosive."

Source: *Falkner* v. *Para-Chem*, 2003 WL 21396693 (Ohio)

The court in the *Force* case discusses the *consumer-expectation test* and risk-utility test that are often used in design defect cases.

Force v. Ford Motor
District Court of Appeal of Florida, Fifth District
879 So.2d 103 (2004)

Case Background *Force was driving a Ford when he was hit head-on by another vehicle. He was wearing his seatbelt and shoulder harness but sustained a severe head injury. He sued Ford and Mazda for product defect, contending that the shoulder harness was designed defectively and did not protect him as well as it should have. The jury held for the defendants. Force appealed.*

Case Decision Monaco, Judge

* * *

Mr. Force proposed that standard jury instruction PL 5, which is based on section 402A of the *Restatement (Second) of Torts*, be given to the jury verbatim. That instruction, as it applies to the facts of this case, reads as follows:

A product is defective if by reason of its design the product is in a condition unreasonably dangerous to the user and the product is expected to and does reach the user without substantial change affecting that condition.

A product is unreasonably dangerous because of its design if [the product fails to perform as safely as an ordinary consumer would expect when used as intended or in a manner reasonably foreseeable by the manufacturer] [or] [the risk of danger in the design outweighs the benefits].

The first parenthetical of the second paragraph is known as the consumer-expectation test. The second parenthetical is called the risk–utility test. . . .

The jury returned a zero verdict. This appeal ensued. Mr. Force seeks reversal because the trial court did not instruct the jury on the consumer-expectation test as expressed in PL-5. . . .

Under the consumer-expectation theory a product is defectively designed if the plaintiff is able to demonstrate that the product did not perform as safely as an ordinary consumer would expect when used in the intended or reasonably foreseeable manner. Essentially, this test relies on deductive reasoning to conclude that the product is defective. Under the risk–utility theory a product is defectively designed if the plaintiff proves that the design of the product proximately caused the plaintiff's injuries and the defendant fails to prove that on balance, the benefits of the design outweigh the risk of danger inherent in the design. . . .

Ford and Mazda argue with some force that the consumer-expectation test cannot be applied to design defect claims involving complex products, in general, and seatbelts in particular. Their argument is summed up by the following passage from the appellees' answer brief:

Perhaps the most significant problem with the consumer-expectations test is that an ordinary consumer of a complex product like an automobile "simply has 'no idea' how it should perform in all foreseeable situations, or how safe it should be made against all foreseeable hazards.". . .

We conclude that there may indeed be products that are too complex for a logical application of the consumer-expectation standard. We leave the definition of those products to be sorted out by trial courts. With respect to seatbelts, however, we believe that the cases finding that they may be tested by the consumer-expectation standard are better reasoned and more persuasive. Accordingly, inasmuch as the jury instruction requested by Mr. Force accurately stated the applicable law, and the evidence supported the giving of the instruction, and the instruction was necessary to resolve the issues properly, we hold that Mr. Force was entitled to submit his case to the jury on both the risk–utility test and the consumer-expectation test, and, therefore, reverse and remand for a new trial.

Questions for Analysis

1. The appeals court held that Force had the right to have the jury apply both the consumer-expectation and the risk–utility tests to his claim. What difference do you see between those tests?

2. Is it likely, as Ford argued, that members of a jury cannot understand the engineering details of the construction of complex products?

Unknown Hazards

The largest dollar volume and greatest number of product liability cases are based on *unknown hazards* or latent defects—dangers that were not known or not fully appreciated at the time the product was manufactured. Since the hazard associated with the product may not be learned for years, neither the producer nor the consumer may be able to prevent injury.

Tens of billions of dollars have been awarded in tens of thousands of claims (often joined as class actions) involving the health effects of asbestos, injuries caused by IUDs, and damage caused by drug side effects that did not appear for years. The single largest area of litigation for unknown hazard has involved asbestos. Companies in the asbestos industry, of which dozens have filed for bankruptcy-court protection, have devoted about $100 billion to help resolve litigation, which has been proceeding for more than thirty years. Although more than 300,000 plaintiffs have agreed to settlements, many more have not reached resolution. How to deal with a huge number of injured parties, all with large claims that sometimes involve generic products, has been a struggle for the courts.

Getty Images

ISSUE SPOTTER
A Way to Reduce the Damage?

Your company makes large machines used by businesses and consumers. Regardless of the quality of the construction of the machines, accidents happen that kill or injure people. Is there a strategy the company can adopt to reduce the costs of dealing with the litigation that results?

Market Share Liability One approach in mass torts arose in a California Supreme Court case, *Sindell* v. *Abbott Laboratories* (607 P.2d 924). It pioneered the notion of *market share liability* or *enterprise liability*. This arose in response to suits filed involving the daughters of women who had taken DES (diethylstilbestrol) during pregnancy. DES is responsible for cancer in the reproductive systems of (now adult) daughters of women who took DES before it was banned. Because DES was produced by many companies and was taken decades ago, plaintiffs could not identify the manufacturer of the drug taken by their mothers. The California court allowed plaintiffs to sue all drug manufacturers who marketed DES and said that those manufacturers would share liability according to their share of the market for the drug. This approach has not been used in many other case areas.

LIGHTER SIDE OF THE LAW
Extra Careful: Winning Warning Labels

M-LAW sponsors an annual Wacky Warning Label Contest. Recent winners include:

On a washing machine: Do not put any person in this washer.
On a baby stroller: Remove child before folding.
On a cell phone: Don't try to dry your phone in a microwave oven.
On the Yellow Pages: Please do not use this directory while operating a moving vehicle.
On a gas tank: Never use a lit match or open flame to check fuel level.

Source: *www.mlaw.org/wwl/*

Getty Images

Joint and Several Liability Other courts have rejected the market share liability terminology but have held that plaintiffs could sue any or all manufacturers and that the manufacturers could bring in other manufacturers as defendants so they would share the liability. This is the more traditional *joint and several liability* rule, which has been abolished in some states, that allows any defendant to be held responsible for all damages. These cases usually become complex class-action suits that may be under court supervision for years, allowing benefits to be paid to claimants on a formula-like basis out of a large pot of money from numerous companies.

Defenses in Product Liability Suits

Strict liability and the rule of negligence hold manufacturers to a high standard of product safety. This does not mean absolute liability. Manufacturers are not liable if the consumer has engaged in improper activity that increases the risk of injury. Most courts recognize product misuse and assumption of risk as defenses in product-related injury cases. Some other defenses to tort actions were discussed in Chapter 6. The rules vary somewhat from state to state, and regulations may also affect liability.

Getty Images

INTERNATIONAL PERSPECTIVE

European-American Product Liability: Same Law, Different Procedures

Product liability law for the 25 members of the European Union is governed by the Product Liability Directive adopted in 1985 and modified a bit since. Member states, most of which are civil-law nations, interpret the Directive through their own civil codes; but gradually the differences are shrinking, as the EU moves to a uniform standard.

The Directive adopted "liability without fault" for defective products, which is much like strict liability in tort. Liability is assigned to the primary producer of a finished good or to the maker of a component part that is defective. The plaintiff must show the causal connection between the defect and the damage suffered. It reads very much like Section 402A of the *Restatement (Second) of Torts.*

One big difference between the United States and the EU is the defense in the EU that a producer is not liable when "the state of scientific knowledge at the time when he put the product into circulation was not such as to enable the existence of the defect to be discovered." That eliminates the unknown hazards suits, such as DES and asbestos. Even more important, there is little product liability litigation in Europe due to procedural differences: no-contingency-fee cases, many more limits on discovery, a "loser pays" rule, no punitive damages, and no juries.

Product Misuse

If it can be shown that the product was misused, combined with another product to make it dangerous, used in some improper and unforeseen manner, or not maintained properly, the negligence of the consumer may preclude recovery for damages. As we saw before, the courts compare the negligence the plaintiff contributes to a situation to the fault of the defendant.

In one case, the court barred recovery by plaintiffs who were injured when the blowout of a fairly new tire was shown to be caused by plaintiff overinflating the tires. The court noted, "To hold otherwise would be to convert a strict liability cause of action into one of absolute liability." In another case, drunkenness by a consumer was held to have led to product misuse that resulted in injury.

Assumption of Risk

As we saw in the last chapter, one may consent to assume risk. Playing contact sports and engaging in many other activities that can lead to injury are voluntary choices that include a chance of injury. Certain consumer products are unavoidably dangerous, such that so long as the risks are understood, consumers are presumed to accept the bad with the good. Medicinal drugs are understood to be inherently dangerous. Most have known side effects about which physicians and consumers should be informed, but we must accept the fact that given the current state of scientific knowledge, these beneficial products cannot be made safer.

Another class of goods, which are more controversial, are products such as tobacco and alcohol that inflict well-known undesirable side effects. If a person smokes cigarettes for 40 years and contracts lung cancer, should the cigarette producer be liable? If a person drinks large quantities of alcohol for years and develops cirrhosis of the liver, should the liquor industry be liable? In general, the courts have said no; the persons using the cigarettes and alcohol know of the risks involved and should bear the costs. It is not hard to imagine the impact on the liquor and cigarette industries if they were held liable for health problems believed to be associated with the use of their products.

Sophisticated User Defense and Bulk-Supplier Doctrine

These defenses usually apply in business settings. *The bulk-supplier doctrine* holds that when a supplier sells a product to an intermediary in bulk, the supplier can discharge its duty to warn the ultimate users if it provides adequate instructions to the distributor next in line, or determines that the intermediary party is adequately trained in the use of the product. The bulk supplier has a duty to take reasonable steps to insure that its buyer is knowledgeable and equipped to provide warnings to the ultimate users, but it does not have to police the details of what is done as the product continues down the chain of use.

Similarly, the *sophisticated user defense*, as the Massachusetts high court explains, relieves a manufacturer of liability for failing to warn of a product's characteristics or dangers when "the end user knows or reasonably should know of a product's dangers" (*Carrel* v. *National Cord and Braid* 852 N.E.2d 100). This is similar to the more traditional *open-and-obvious doctrine*—no warning is needed when the danger is obvious.

For example, in *Akin* v. *Ashland Chemical* (10th Cir., 156 F.3d 1030), employees at Tinker Air Force Base in Oklahoma sued several suppliers of chemicals to the Air Force for toxic tort arising out of exposure to chemicals. The appeals court upheld the dismissal of the case. "Because of the wealth of research available, the ability of the Air Force to conduct studies, and its extremely knowledgeable staff, we find that the Air Force easily qualifies as a 'knowledgeable purchaser' that should have known the risks involved with low-level chemical exposure. Employees of the Air Force are also deemed to possess the necessary level of sophistication, so that defendants had no duty to warn the Air Force or its employees of the potential hazards."

Statutory Limits on Liability

Various laws are specifically designed to limit potential tort liability:

- Worker compensation statutes usually make that program the exclusive remedy for injured workers, unless an intentional tort was involved.
- Federal regulations that prescribe maximum allowable radiation exposure levels set the standard of care upon which liability is based.
- As government contractors, manufacturers of products made to government specifications are generally immune from product liability.
- Products that must follow federal regulations regarding label requirements, including warnings of possible injuries, may not be subject to common-law failure-to-warn actions. Such defenses are limited.
- State laws may specify limits on liability, such as Colorado's statutory limits on the liability of ski resorts for injuries suffered by skiers.

Ultrahazardous Activity

Long before the development of strict liability for defective products, the common law had developed a rule of strict liability for injuries resulting from *ultrahazardous activity*. This rule, which is in effect in most states, goes back to the 1868 British case, *Rylands* v. *Fletcher*. The *Restatement of Torts* defines such activity as one that "necessarily involves a risk of serious harm to the person, land, or chattels of another, which cannot be eliminated by the exercise of the utmost care" and "is not a matter of common usage."

This rule has applied to such things as blasting with explosives, allowing chemicals to seep into water supplies, crop dusting, and transporting chemicals in a city. Actually, most of these activities are not all that uncommon, but they are ultrahazardous. The party in charge of such acts is generally responsible for whatever happens. For instance, in *Old Island Fumigation* v. *Barbee* (604 So.2d 1246), Old Island fumigated two of the three buildings in a condominium complex. Old Island was told that the third building was sealed from the other two, but, in fact, it was not, and residents of the third building were made ill. Even though the opening that let the fumes into the third building was a mistake made by the architect or contractor who built the buildings, the court of appeals held against Old Island. Because fumigation is an ultrahazardous activity, Old Island was liable for injuries "regardless of the level of care exercised in carrying out this activity." The negligence of other parties is irrelevant to the imposition of liability in such cases.

Does Product Liability Need Reform?

We started the chapter by noting the big dollars that can be involved in tort suits. The numbers can be high, but injuries can produce medical expenses in the millions of dollars. While we hear of juries who award massive sums, most of those startling figures are greatly reduced or thrown out by the trial judge or by the appeals court.

Does a costly tort system make American firms less competitive than foreign firms? Not likely, as any company selling products in the United States must meet the same liability standard. The high standard of safety that has evolved becomes the standard for products marketed in much of Europe and Japan, since markets are increasingly global. Chinese companies, wanting increased access to world markets, have had to improve production quality to meet the high standards demanded in wealthy nations.

What has been called a "tort crisis" has abated in recent years as the Supreme Court has cracked down on massive punitive damage awards and doubtful expert testimony. There has also been reform legislation from Congress, to make class-action suits more difficult, and state laws that have capped liability for certain damages. Tort payouts, which had been growing rapidly since the 1970s, may have stabilized. Between 2004 and 2006, the growth seemed to have stopped. This might have been due to a slowing of the growth of asbestos-related suits, which have consumed close to $100 billion in damages over a couple decades.

Tort litigation involving companies will continue to be a flashpoint in the law, as injured people will seek relief from what they see as heartless companies not caring about ordinary people. On the other side, firms subject to dubious suits will feel wronged as they devote resources to fending off deep-pocket tort litigators. In the middle are the courts, attempting to continue to craft a set of fair rules for all.

Summary

- Misrepresentation, or fraud, is a general category of tort that can be intentional or based on negligence. When intentional, it must be shown that there was an intent to provide misleading information to convince someone to do something they would not have otherwise, and that the party had good reason to rely on the deceit, which was then the cause of a loss suffered.
- The tort of interference with contractual relations occurs when ongoing contractual deals are wrongfully and knowingly interfered with by another party who wants the existing contract to be broken.
- Interference with prospective advantage, or prospective economic advantage, is an unreasonable interference in another party's business dealings so as to prevent an ongoing relationship from succeeding.
- The rule of negligence in tort dominated product liability the first half of the twentieth century. Still good law, it requires producers to take the care of a

reasonable person when making products to prevent foreseeable injury. The reasonable person is held to the skill of an expert in the industry.

- Strict liability for defective products began in contract law based on implied warranty inferred by the courts from a review of the parties' dealings or based on express warranty about the quality of a product.

- Strict liability in tort became widely accepted after the 1963 *Greenman* decision in California. Section 402A of the *Restatement (Second) of Torts* imposes strict liability on the manufacturer when a "product in a defective condition unreasonably dangerous to the user or consumer or to his property" is sold. Besides a flaw in the product at the time of manufacture, strict liability is imposed for failure to warn of hazards in using the product and defects in the design of the product that make it less safe than it should be.

- The newer *Restatement (Third) of Torts*, Section 2, regarding product defects, moves away from a distinction between strict liability and negligence. In assigning liability, it encourages the use of a risk—utility analysis for products that are defective at the time of manufacture due to poor design or due to failure to warn of dangers.

- Many strict liability suits have concerned unknown hazards, such as those associated with asbestos, where the danger did not become known until many years later. When claims of thousands of persons exceed all funds of defendants, the claims may be joined for settlement. When many companies have made the same product, they may be held jointly and severally liable, potentially requiring all producers to pay compensation.

- A defense that may be raised in product liability suits is negligence by the user, which can include product misuse. There also can be assumption of risk by the consumer, especially for products, such as medicinal drugs, that are beneficial but have unavoidable side effects and products, such as tobacco and alcohol, that are legal but have bad effects. Producers do not have to constantly warn sophisticated buyers, such as producers, about all dangers in products.

- Strict liability in tort has long been imposed on those who engage in ultrahazardous activities, such as using explosives, and on those who handle unusually dangerous substances, such as toxic chemicals. If the party involved in the ultrahazardous activity causes an injury to an innocent party, regardless of the degree of care taken to prevent harm, liability is imposed.

Terms to Know

You should be able to define the following terms:

fraud, 152

intentional misrepresentation
   or fraud, 152

scienter, 152

intentional interference with
   contractual relations, 153

interference with prospective
   advantage, 155

privity of contract, 157

caveat emptor, 157

reasonable care, 159

strict liability, 159

implied warranty, 160

express warranty, 160

failure to warn, 164

design defect, 165

consumer-expectation test, 166

unknown hazards, 167

joint and several liability, 168

sophisticated user defense, 170

Discussion Question

1. Refer to Section 402A of the *Restatement (Second) of Torts:* What does "the seller is engaged in the business of selling such a product" mean? Who is excluded by this? What does "it is expected to and does reach the user or consumer without substantial change in the condition in which it is sold" mean? What situations does this cover? What is the difference between the idea that the rule applies although "the seller has exercised all possible care in the preparation and sale of his product" and the rule of negligence? What does "the user or consumer has not bought the product from or entered into any contractual relation with the seller" mean?

Case Questions

1. The buyers of residential property mistakenly believed that the 3.5 acres of land included the well attached to the house, which they later found out was not on the property. The previous owner and the real estate agent had pointed out the well, but had not stated that it was on the property. The buyers did not examine the existing survey of the property, nor did they order a new survey done, either of which would have shown that the well was not on the property. Did the buyers have a basis for a suit for fraud? [*Crawford* v. *Williams*, 375 S.E.2d 223 Sup. Ct., Ga. (1989)]

2. Fourteen "disciples" of yoga guru Amrit Desai worked for Desai at his large "retreat center for holistic health and education," some for as long as 20 years. The disciples had given Desai much of their wealth and worked for him for very low wages as they attempted to follow his teachings of poverty and chastity. They sued Desai for fraud when they allegedly discovered that Desai had huge quantities of cash and assorted sexual relations over many years. Could this be the basis for a fraud action to recover for lost wages and donations? [*Dushkin* v. *Desai*, 18 F.Supp.2d 117 D. Mass. (1998)]

   ✓ Check your answer at http://academic.cengage.com/blaw/meiners

3. Zimmerman bought a condo at Winding Lake II. After moving in, she experienced dampness and mildew on interior walls. The builder's efforts to remedy the situation proved fruitless. Zimmerman and other occupants stationed themselves in front of the sales office to the condo complex and carried signs and talked to passersby. One sign read: "Open House, See Mildew, Feel Dampness, No Extra Charge." Several prospective buyers left without visiting the sales office. No new units were sold. The company sued Zimmerman and others who participated. What will be the action alleged and likely result? [*Zimmerman* v. *D.C.A. at Welleby, Inc.*, 505 So.2d 1371 Dist. Ct. App., Fla. (1987)]

4. Florida land developer Lehigh would show prospective buyers Lehigh Acres and have the buyers stay at its motel. Competitor Azar would watch for the buyers, contact them at the motel, tell them that under federal law they had three days to cancel any contract with Lehigh, and then show them less expensive property that he was selling. Lehigh wanted a court order to keep Azar away from its customers, because Azar was interfering with business relationships. Will the court tell Azar to stay away? [*Azar* v. *Lehigh Corp.*, 364 So.2d 860 Dist. Ct. App., Fla. (1978)]

   ✓ Check your answer at http://academic.cengage.com/blaw/meiners

5. Woeste ate raw oysters at a restaurant and died a week later from the bacteria *Vibrio vulnificus.* The bacteria naturally occur in oysters from warm water. *Vibrio* has no effect on most people, but people with a weak immune system—as Woeste had due to Hepatitis C and cirrhosis of the liver—are susceptible. The restaurant menu warned of the danger of eating raw oysters, especially for persons with "chronic illness of the liver," but Woeste ordered without reading the menu warning. His estate sued the restaurant, and the Texas company that harvested the oysters, for negligence and strict liability. Would they have a good case? [*Woeste* v. *Washington Platform Saloon and Restaurant*, 836 N.E.2d 52 Ct. App., Ohio (2005)]

6. Many crimes involve the use of cheap handguns. Producers and sellers of such handguns know that some of these guns will be used in crimes by the purchaser of the gun or by a criminal who steals the gun. Could the producers and retailers of such handguns be held liable for the injuries suffered by persons shot during a crime? That is, could such a producer be held strictly liable or negligent for selling a "defective" product in that one of its known end uses is crime? [See *Patterson* v. *Rohm Gesellschaft*, 608 F.Supp. 1206 N. D.Tex. (1985)]

   ✓ Check your answer at http://academic.cengage.com/blaw/meiners

7. A five-year-old boy was killed when riding in the front seat of a car without a seatbelt, when an accident occurred that caused the airbag to deploy. The jury found that the airbag was "overly aggressive" and so held the car maker liable. Hyundai appealed, contending that the cause of death was the failure to have the boy in a seatbelt as required by state law. Should that defense have been allowed? [*Connelly* v. *Hyundai Motor Co.*, 351 F.3d 535 1st Cir. (2003)]

8. A four-year-old child used a Bic lighter to start a house fire that killed a 2-year-old. The lighter had a warning: "KEEP OUT OF REACH OF CHILDREN." The dead child's parents sued Bic for strict liability due to inadequate warning and because the lighter was unreasonably dangerous. What was the result? [*Todd* v. *Societe Bic*, 21 F.3d 1402 7th Cir. (1994)]

   ✓ Check your answer at http://academic.cengage.com/blaw/meiners

9. Two experienced welders were working inside a barge. A gas hose leading to the welding torch developed a leak that the workers apparently could not smell because of "nasal fatigue" from having inhaled so much gas. One worker lit a cigarette, igniting the gas, killing both workers. The workers' heirs sued the gas and gas hose producers in strict liability. Was either company liable? [*Little* v. *Liquid Air Corp.*, 37 F.3d 1069 5th Cir. (1994)]

10. A 3-year-old child turned on the hot water in a bathtub. His 11-month-old sister climbed into the tub and was severely burned before being rescued by her mother. The child died from the burns. The mother sued the hot water tank maker for installing a thermostat that allowed the water to reach 170 degrees, which was the industry standard. Is that a design defect? [*Williams* v. *Briggs* 62 F.3d 703 5th Cir. (1995)]

11. Ralph Fisher died from brain cancer apparently caused by exposure on the job to polychlorinated biphenyls (PCBs) that Monsanto manufactured and sold to Fisher's employer, Westinghouse, which used PCBs in making electrical transformers. PCBs were known to be highly toxic. Fisher's estate claimed that Monsanto should be held liable either for negligence or in strict liability for failure to warn Fisher of the dangers involved. What defense would Monsanto have? [*Fisher* v. *Monsanto*, 863 F.Supp. 285 W.D., Va. (1994)]

Ethics Question

1. Various industries have lobbied for legislative restrictions on tort liability. For instance, the nuclear power industry has long been protected by a statute that limits its upper-dollar liability in the event of a serious accident that is much lower than the potential losses from such an accident. Also, the industry cannot be held liable in tort for radiation releases so long as federal guidelines are not exceeded. Many companies in other industries would like similar protection. Is it ethical to seek statutory limits on liability? Is it ethical for legislators to grant such protection? What limits would be acceptable?

Internet Assignment

Using the Internet, answer this question:

Sloan Stamping is in the business of making car parts for the automobile industry. In order to retool for a new line of SUV's called the Luxuria, Sloan purchased a new stamping machine from McGraw Machines and immediately placed it into operation. To make new parts,

Sloan employees were required to place metal forms into the machine and then pull a hand lever to stamp the parts. The machine was not equipped with either a hand guard or any other recognized safety features to prevent operator injuries.

Three months into production with the machine, a Sloan employee was badly injured when he pulled the hand lever before removing his other hand from the machine. While recovering from his injuries, this employee and his wife sued Sloan for an employer intentional tort and McGraw for strict product liability, claiming that the machine was sold in a defective condition, which was unreasonably dangerous.

How can the employee prove that the machine was defectively designed? Will reliance on feasible alternative designs, which were safer, insure the employee's recovery at trial? See the following authority on strict product liability claims:

Mary Kinser v. *Gehl Company*, http://www.kscourts.org/ca10/cases/1999/07/98-3152.htm

Getty Images

Real and Personal Property

Chapter 8

Humpty Dumpty sat on a wall
Humpty Dumpty had a great fall
All the King's horses
And all the King's men
Couldn't put Humpty together again

Nursery rhyme dating to 1600s

What was Humpty's legal capacity on the wall? Was he sitting on his own wall? Was he pushed from the wall? Was the wall the property of another person? Was he a guest who was permitted to be on the wall, or did he ignore his host's notice to stay away from the wall? Did he have a legal right to be on the property where the wall was located, or was he a trespasser? Who is responsible for the costs of Mr. Dumpty's health care or, if the fall was fatal, is the property owner liable to his heirs? Little children need not think about these issues, but property owners have good reasons to be concerned about the safety of people who are on their property. Shoppers who fall and suffer injuries on business property often sue business owners.

Here we begin our study of the law of property—the oldest part of the common law—focusing on its application to business. Property refers to various rights that are guaranteed and protected by the government. That includes things visible and invisible—tangible and intangible—that have value. This chapter focuses on real property: things that are immovable, such as land; and personal property: things that are movable, such as furniture and clothing (traditionally called *chattel*). We consider ownership of property, in the many forms it can take, the legal basis for controls on private property imposed by governments and the liability that may rest with property owners when accidents happen on their property. ■

Real Property

Real property refers to land; things under the land, such as oil and minerals; and things solidly attached to the land, such as buildings and trees. At law, *property* is a legally protected expectation of being able to use a thing for one's advantage. That is, it is not the physical existence of property that matters so much as the right to use property for one's purposes. If someone has a right to use a piece of land however she likes, or if she has a right to use the land only for certain purposes, her expectations about the land change because of her legal interest in it. For example, if you have land that is found to contain a rare plant protected under the Endangered Species Act (discussed in Chapter 17), how you may use the land will be limited by regulations concerning protection for the plant.

The review of tort law was concerned mostly with personal interests protected by the law. *Property interests* differ from personal interests in that property refers to physical things, such as land and objects, in which one can have a recognized interest against other persons. That is, a person has the right to deny others the use of the "things" in which he has an interest. As we will see, tort law is often used to protect interests in property. Contract law is used to make arrangements with others about the use of property.

Historial Origins

Some of the terms that describe the law regarding real property appear a bit peculiar, because the terms and concepts come from the common law as developed in England from the twelfth to the sixteenth centuries. While some terms are old, some of the law has changed greatly over the years. As we will see, the common law has been modified by statutory law, although many of the statutes primarily provide procedures for enforcing common-law property rules. Next we look at some of the traditional elements of property law.

Deeds and Titles

Ownership of land is evidenced by various documents. The deed and the title are among the most important. A *deed* is the primary way to transfer ownership interests in property. Deeds are in writing and transfer title from the current property owner to the new owner. They identify the original owner(s), describe the land, identify the new owner(s), and state that ownership is being transferred, possibly subject to certain conditions.

Different types of deeds are used in different states and for different purposes. Here we mention only a few of the most common. A *quitclaim deed* is a deed of conveyance that passes whatever interests the grantor had in the property. This might not provide any assurance of good title to the property; it may only terminate the interest of the previous possessor of the property. The rights conveyed by such a deed vary from state to state. In contrast, a *warranty deed* is a deed that explicitly promises that a good, clear title to the property is being conveyed by the grantor.

The *title*, which comes from receipt of a valid deed, is the means by which the owner of property has legal possession of the property. It is the formal right of ownership. A clear title means that no other persons can claim ownership. Titles may be held by one or more persons or by a business. Titles to land are recorded by state officials, usually at the county level. Title recording provides a public record of who owns what and of limitations or claims on titles, such as the claim that mortgage lenders often hold on real estate.

Fee Simple

The law often refers to one's interest or legal rights in real property as an *estate*. According to the *Property Restatement*, an estate is "an interest in land which (a) is or may become possessory and (b) is ownership measured in terms of duration." That is, one may have possession of land now or may have the right to take possession of land at some point in the future. There are time limits on the length of ownership. Ownership may be for life, which is uncertain in length, but one cannot take property to the grave—one's interests in an estate must pass to other persons.

The most common form of real property ownership is *fee simple* or *fee simple absolute*. Fee simple means the right to exclusive possession of a particular piece of land for an indefinite time, as well as the right to dispose of the land as the owner pleases. Most real estate in the United States is in fee simple, meaning it may be inherited, transferred to others, or sold in part or in whole and, in general, it is the strongest form of real property control.

Traditionally, ownership in fee simple was said to extend to the skies, but air travel limited that concept. Ownership is also said to extend "to the center of the earth," meaning fee simple ownership includes the right to minerals and oil under the land. Those assets, like other features of land, can be sold or rented separately from the main piece of property. Subsurface *mineral rights* are often legally separated from ownership of the surface land.

Forms of Ownership

Most property is held in the name of more than one person. It may also be in the name of a business. While we commonly use the word "tenant" to mean a person who rents property, at law the word "tenant" has a broader meaning. It refers to one who possesses lands by any kind of right or title, whether in fee simple or for a limited period of time. When we consider the ownership of property, different forms of tenancy are commonly used.

A *tenancy in common* is a form of ownership in which each tenant (owner) has an undivided interest in the property. Suppose Angelina Jolie and Halle Berry each contribute half the money to buy a piece of property they own equally. They are said to have a *tenancy in common*. If Jolie dies, her interest in the property passes to her estate or to the heirs she has named; it does not go to Berry.

It is usual for married couples or partners to own property in the form of a *joint tenancy*. This is a purchase of property by two or more persons who have the same interest in the undivided possession of property. The primary difference from the tenancy in common is that in a joint tenancy, there is a right of survivorship, which means that if one owner dies, the ownership rights pass to the other owner.

The law places few restrictions on the forms used to hold property. For example, one may grant a *life estate* in a piece of property that gives a person the right to be a *tenant for life*. This may be done so that a family member has the right to occupy a piece of property until their death, at which point title to the property passes to the heirs who have been named by the owner of the property.

Evolving Property Law: Condominiums

While property law is old in origin, it adapts to changes in society. Condominiums were not seen much before the 1960s, but the fee simple estate applies to such living arrangements. Each living space in a building may be owned in fee simple (with numerous conditions attached), yet the land the building sits on, as well as common areas such as elevators and lobbies, is held in common—for the benefit of the condo owners—by another person or business. To help adapt property law to such arrangements, all states have statutes that simplified the legal process of having condos and other modern living arrangements consistent with traditional property law.

Servitudes

Servitudes are limitations or requirements about the use of property. Servitudes attach to the estate or property itself and impose certain use limits on the owner of the property. The most important forms of servitudes are easements and covenants.

Easements

An *easement* is a right to enter land owned by another and make certain use of it or to take something from land. An easement is not ownership or right of possession of an estate but a "burden" on another person's estate; that is, the right to use it for some purpose without payment. The document that creates an easement is much like a deed: it explains the use of certain property that is conveyed from the property owner to the easement holder.

Positive easements allow the easement holder to go on the estate for certain purposes. A *negative easement* would be giving up a right that the owner of an estate would normally have, such as agreeing with the Nature Conservancy to preserve and protect certain rare plants that exist on the property. One may also give or sell someone the right to remove valuable things from one's estate, such as oil, minerals or trees; this right may be referred to as a *profit*.

Unless the easement is for a set time, it will be attached permanently to the property. As with ownership arrangements, parties are generally free to agree upon any kind of easement they wish. Almost all homes have easements for utilities and for public sidewalks. Once an easement is granted, the property owner may not interfere with it unless the easement holder agrees. That is, the sidewalk may not be blocked or removed, and if a gas line needs to be dug up for repair, the gas company has the right, doing as little damage as possible, to dig up the yard to get to the pipe.

Easements are often sold to a neighbor who needs the use of someone else's property. If Ben buys twenty acres in the woods and the property is behind Nancy's land, which faces the road, to have access to his property, Ben must get an

Getty Images

INTERNATIONAL PERSPECTIVE

Insecure Property Rights

In the United States, property ownership is clear. Land is owned by a private party or by the government. There are few disputes over title to land, and no one would think of building a house on land unless clear title was assured. But in much of the world, rights to property are muddled and highly political. Hernando de Soto, head of a think tank in Peru, studied land ownership in several nations. He found that most farmers do not own the land they farm and that city dwellers do not own the land under their houses.

In the Philippines, only one third of agricultural land has clear title and only 43 percent of dwellings have clear title. In Peru, 81 percent of farmed land is not owned; only

half the urban dwellings are on titled land. The poorest nation in the Western Hemisphere is Haiti, where 97 percent of farm land is not owned and 68 percent of urban dwellings are in the "informal" sector. In Egypt, 92 percent of urban dwellings are on "unowned" land, as are 83 percent of all farms.

De Soto attributes the persistence of poverty in such countries to the inability of most people to have the chance to capitalize on the value they have put into their farms and houses. Without secure property rights, economic progress may be enjoyed mostly by the minority who live in the formal economy that we recognize as critical to global commerce.

Source: *The Mystery of Capital* (Basic Books)

easement from Nancy to build a road across her property. It is obviously a good idea to get needed easements to property settled before buying such property.

Adverse Possession

Peculiar forms of property use or possession are called *easement by prescription* and *adverse possession*. This is what is called a *hostile* use of another person's land; that is, someone who has no right to occupy or use an estate does so without permission. The use may be in the form of an easement, such as driving across another's property regularly, or may be actual possession, such as building a house and living on another's property. In such cases, the user of the property may obtain a legally recognized easement, such as the right to continue driving across the land, or may even obtain title to the land on which the house is built, so long as taxes have been paid.

The general conditions needed for adverse possession are that it must be

1. Actual: the adverse user in fact uses or possesses the property in question.
2. Open: the use or possession must be visible so that the owner is on notice.
3. Hostile: the use or possession is without permission of the owner.
4. Exclusive: the use or possession is not shared with others who also have no right to use the property.
5. Continuous: the use or possession must go on without major interruption for as much time as required by law to obtain the easement by prescription or title by adverse possession.

All states have rules, called *statutes of limitation*, for the number of years the adverse possession must occur before it becomes a legally protected possession. State law varies on the time required, from 5 to 20 years. Issues involving prescriptive easement and adverse possession are seen in the *Moran* case.

Moran v. Sims
Court of Appeals of Mississippi
873 So.2d 1067 (2004)

Case Background *Sims owned property surrounded by the Morans. His deed was recorded in 1985, but the property had been in his family for over 50 years. He built a home in 1991. The property was accessed by a driveway across the property bought by the Morans in 1996. Sims asked the court to grant him an easement. The trial court held that Sims had a prescriptive easement that allowed use of the driveway on the Morans' property. They appealed.*

Case Decision Southwick, Presiding Judge

* * *

An easement may be acquired by ten years possession.... Prescription occurs if there is ten years of use that is open, notorious, and visible; hostile; under a claim of ownership; exclusive; peaceful; and continuous and uninterrupted. Permission from the record

title owner will make the use permissive and not adverse....

The elements for a prescriptive easement will be examined individually.

a. Open, notorious and visible At trial, Sims testified that he had used the driveway running across Moran's property since he purchased the parcel in 1985.... Among the testimony was from a school bus driver who testified that he had driven the bus down the driveway to pick up children in 1956–1957.... This was sufficient under this factor.

b. Hostile Moran argues that Sims and his predecessors had implied permission to use the property. That allegedly is proved by the fact that the owners of the land across which the driveway ran never objected to his use. A prescriptive easement cannot originate from a permissive use of land because it would not be hostile. However, the absence of an objection is not the equivalent of consent.

Here, there was no evidence that Sims or his predecessors had permission to use the driveway. Consent may be inferred from evidence, but it will not be presumed in the absence of evidence.... Consent must be shown. Here it was not.

c. Claim of ownership Sims presented testimony which showed a claim of ownership, including the fact that he purchased gravel for the driveway. There was testimony on that from the person whom Sims hired to deliver and spread the gravel. This element was properly established.

d. Exclusive "Exclusive" use does not mean that no one else used the driveway. Exclusivity here means that the use was consistent with an exclusive claim to the right to use. There was evidence that the driveway was used by the Sims family and those whom they implicitly permitted to do so. The Sims' home was the only home located on the driveway.

e. Peaceful Sims testified that there was no controversy concerning the driveway prior to Moran's purchase of property. There was no evidence of a dispute with prior owners. By the time that Moran complained, the period of prescription had long since run.

f. Continuous and uninterrupted for ten years Sims recorded the deed to his property in 1985. His family had owned the property for at least fifty years before. During this time, the driveway had been in use. That is ten years, and more.

The elements of adverse possession were sufficiently proven....

Affirmed.

Questions for Analysis

1. The appeals court held that Sims did have an easement by prescription across the Moran's property. Sims asked them to give it to him, but they would not. Why not?
2. The Morans did not own the property for the ten years during which Sims used the driveway. Why did Sims not have to wait ten years?

Covenants

A *covenant*, or a *covenant running with the land*, is not a legal interest in an estate but may be thought of as a contract with an estate. Most often, covenants are restrictions that attach to the deed when a home is sold. Of course, only people can bind property to promises. Estates cannot form promises, but the agreement made in a covenant "runs" with the land. That is, the covenant is a binding obligation that goes with property when it is transferred to a new owner, who must abide by the covenant.

Most covenants impose a benefit on an estate; otherwise, why would many people agree to them? The most common forms are residential subdivision covenants; for example, only single-family homes are allowed, every home must be at least 2,000 square feet, no prefabricated homes are allowed, no dog kennels are allowed, no businesses may operate from a home, and homes must be painted pastel colors. Such covenants ensure certain attributes to a subdivision that the owners of the homes think desirable. Covenants in conflict with public policy are not enforceable. For example, years ago some covenants prohibited the sale of homes to members of racial minorities.

Assuming no violation of public policy, such as race discrimination, covenants are generally enforced by the courts. Changing them can be difficult, because that may require getting everyone affected by the covenants to agree to a change. In practice, covenants are often a critical tool in developing real estate, because they set the rules for the character of the development. But later, when rules are violated, enforcement is dubious, because it means a homeowner or group of homeowners must band together and use their resources to enforce the rules. That means suing your neighbors, which is unpleasant and costly. That happened in the *Powell* case, in which a group of property owners sued to enforce the original covenants. In such cases, the courts interpret restrictions in a manner consistent with the wishes of the purpose for which they were imposed.

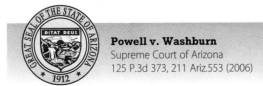

Powell v. Washburn
Supreme Court of Arizona
125 P.3d 373, 211 Ariz.553 (2006)

Case Background *In 1988, Washburn, a real estate developer, recorded the Declarations of Covenants, Conditions, and Restrictions (CC&Rs) for Indian Hills Airpark, an aviation-related planned community. By reference, they incorporated the La Paz County zoning ordinances. At that time, zoning permitted only three residential uses in a subdivision: mobile or manufactured homes, constructed homes, and hangar-houses (homes incorporating an airplane hangar). In 1996, the County amended its ordinances to permit the use of recreational vehicles (RVs) as residences.*

In 2002, Powell and others sued Washburn, requesting an injunction to prohibit the use of RVs, which some residents were using, as residences within the Airpark. The trial court held that the CC&Rs did not permit RVs as residences. The appeals court reversed. That decision was appealed.

Case Decision Ryan, Justice

* * *

A deed containing a restrictive covenant that runs with the land is a contract. The interpretation of a contract is generally a matter of law. . . .

In Arizona, the traditional rule has been that when a restrictive covenant is unambiguous, it is enforced so as to give effect to the intent of the parties. . . .

To this end, the *Restatement* recommends that

(a) servitude should be interpreted to give effect to the intention of the parties ascertained from the language used in the instrument, or the circumstances surrounding creation of the servitude, and to carry out the purpose for which it was created. . . .

We adopt the *Restatement* approach for interpreting restrictive covenants ... § 4.1 of the *Restatement* is consistent with long-standing Arizona case law holding that enforcing the intent of the parties is the "cardinal principle" in interpreting restrictive covenants. . . .

The *Restatement's* approach mirrors the contemporary judicial trend of recognizing the benefits of restrictive covenants. . . .

Applying the principles of the *Restatement*, we conclude that although the CC&Rs neither expressly prohibit nor permit RVs as residences, the plain intent and purpose of the restrictions was to limit residences in the Airpark to mobile or manufactured homes, constructed homes, or hangar-homes. We base this conclusion on the language used in the CC&Rs and the purpose for which the restrictions were created. . . .

For the foregoing reasons, we vacate the decision of the court of appeals and affirm the trial court's judgment.

Questions for Analysis

1. The Arizona high court held that RVs violated the covenants. Although they were allowed by the county, they were not to be allowed as residences in the development. Since the county rules changed, why did the covenants not change?

2. Suppose a majority of the residents of the Airpark wanted to allow RVs. Would that control the decision?

Landlord and Tenants

When we rent property, it is called a *leasehold*. The property may be owned in fee simple by the landlord, but that is not necessary to create a leasehold with a tenant. A *tenant* is a party with possessory rights for a fixed time period or at will as agreed upon. That is, the lease gives the tenant certain rights to occupy and use the property. The tenant has possession of the estate; the landlord has the right to reclaim the estate after the lease ends. Unless prohibited by the leasehold, the tenant may lease all or a portion of the property to a subtenant.

Getty Images

LIGHTER SIDE OF THE LAW
The Tenants Who Would Not Go Away

Teeman rented an apartment in New York in 1968. She subleased the apartment to the Levys in 1977, year-by-year, intending to return to the city after she had helped her ailing parents. Teeman told the Levys in 1985 that the lease would not be renewed and that she was returning. The Levys refused to vacate and began a series of lawsuits, court motions, and appeals to keep control of the apartment.

The Levys ignored court orders to vacate. Finally, in late 1999, an appeals court upheld the Levys' ejection, calling their many legal tactics "abject nonsense couched as legal argument." The court ordered them to pay Teeman's legal fees and $8,000 in sanctions to the Lawyers' Fund for Client Protection because of their "reprehensible" actions.

Source: *Levy v. Carol Management*, 698 N.Y.S.2d 226 (1999)

Leases

A *lease* is an agreement that creates a leasehold out of an estate and contains conditions, such as how much rent is to be paid and what restrictions have been placed on the use of the property. All leases are subject to a large body of statutory and common law that sets boundaries on what is legal in a leasehold and on how a dispute about any issue is to be resolved.

Many states have adopted all or part of the Uniform Residential Landlord and Tenant Act, a statute designed to modernize and clarify standard terms of leases. Although state laws may require certain terms, in general, the courts want leases to:

1. Identify the parties
2. Describe the premises (address or legal description of the property) being leased
3. State how long the lease is to be in effect
4. State how much rent is to be paid

Note that a lease does not have to end at a specific date but can go from month to month. Most leases also specify who is responsible for utility bills, when and where the rent is to be paid, the terms of a damage deposit, and the tenants' responsibility for wear and tear of the property.

Rights of a Tenant

A tenant has a legal interest in the property rented and has the right of possession during the term of the lease. Other parties may be kept out of the property, including the landlord, with some exceptions. The landlord has a privilege to enter the premises to make needed repairs. Leases often state that the landlord has the right to enter the property to inspect it or to show it to future tenants, but there is no general right to pop in anytime the landlord wants.

If a landlord fails to make essential repairs in a timely manner, such as keep the air conditioning working during the summer, or otherwise allows the premises to be uninhabitable, there may be "constructive eviction." In such cases, the landlord has broken the lease, and the tenant has the right to terminate the tenancy, leave, and, in some cases, sue to recover costs incurred by the untimely move.

Duties of a Tenant

A tenant has the right to use the property but not to abuse it by making changes that will affect the property beyond the lease term. Abuse can come from negligence,

Getty Images

INTERNATIONAL PERSPECTIVE

Americans Crossing into Mexico for Land

Millions of Americans own second homes, and many look to Mexico as a warm-weather destination for that investment. It is estimated that a million American citizens live in Mexico, and the number is rising quickly. Real estate prices on the Yucatan peninsula doubled in five years due to the American push.

Mexican property law is complex. Foreigners are allowed to own land only in certain locations; elsewhere, they can hold the property in trust, *fideicomiso,* which gives a right to use the land for 50 years. A number of foreigners have "bought" land in Mexico, presuming the law

of title to be much like in the United States, but found out differently. Over 200 American "homeowners" were evicted from a luxury development on the Baja coast, after a court held against the developer in a title dispute.

Just as in the United States, good local counsel is important. Many Mexican attorneys are fluent in English and can guide clients through the complexities of using a *notario* and other steps unfamiliar under American law. Title registries in Mexico are not as reliable as in the United States, so independent reviews are desirable. Due diligence in real estate is always a good idea; how it is performed varies greatly from country to country. U.S. law does not apply.

a careless failure to prevent damage from problems such as a leaking pipe, or careless damage by a tenant; or abuse may take the form of *waste,* which is the intentional destruction or removal of valuable property, such as trees, from the premises. A tenant may not be a nuisance to neighbors and may not engage in illegal activities on the premises.

Most landlord–tenant leases are straightforward. Fifteen states have adopted all or part of the Uniform Residential Landlord and Tenant Act proposed by the National Conference of Commissioners on Uniform State Law. Such statutes set many background standards for landlords and tenants that cannot be evaded, making detailed leases not as necessary as they otherwise might be. Lease agreements for business spaces are different.

Commercial Leases

Commercial leases are often drafted by the lessor's legal department based on state law requirements and experience with previous tenants. They tend to be long, because they cover many issues, so legal expertise is needed. The description of leased space is often defined by terms used by the Building Owners and Managers Association (BOMA; see www.boma.org). For example, the square footage leased may be called *gross leasable* or *net leasable,* both acceptable BOMA terms, but they mean different things. In multiple-tenant buildings, the lease often includes some building common areas, such as a share of building entryway, hallways, and restrooms. This usually adds 10 percent or more to the area leased.

The lease identifies the lessor and lessee; the legal description of the property (including square footage); rent; additional payment, such as "net," which are typically the percent of the space leased in relationship to property taxes, utilities, and insurance. In addition to the "nets," common-area maintenance charges may be added for lighting, cleaning, parking lot maintenance, and such. When rent includes these additional charges, it is referred to as "gross rents."

Additional terms cover security deposits; use of the property, which is usually specific; maintenance and repair responsibilities; how alterations, including structural changes, will be handled; right to sublease; early termination provision; insurance; responsibility for attorney's fees; prohibitions on hazardous substances; right of inspection; taxes; utilities; what signage will be allowed; liability waivers; damage provisions; what happens in case of eminent domain, forcing relocation; subordination to mortgage; and dispute resolution.

As we see in the *Gold's Gym* case, many commercial properties are shell buildings. Leases may use terms such as a "grey shell" without interior finish or a "vanilla shell" with four finished walls, heating and cooling, a restroom, and suspended ceiling. Depending on negotiations, the lease or a separate agreement will grant a "tenant allowance," an amount per square foot for interior finishes. Alterations must be approved by the landlord. Failure to write the lease properly can result in problems, as we see in the next case.

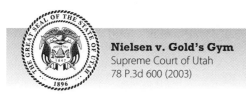

Nielsen v. Gold's Gym
Supreme Court of Utah
78 P.3d 600 (2003)

Case Background *Peterson signed a preprinted commercial lease agreement with Nielsen to lease the "premises" in a "strip mall at 1341 E. Center, Spanish Fork, UT," to be used as a "health club and gym" for three years at $0.85 annually per square foot. Nielsen was still constructing the building at the time the lease was signed. A contractor then told Peterson it would cost $168,000 to improve the building shell to be ready for the gym. Peterson went back to Nielsen to discuss who would pay for the interior improvements. When an agreement could not be reached, Peterson walked away and Nielsen leased to another party.*

Nielsen sued for $112,000 in damages for breach of contract for having to rent the space for less than Peterson had agreed. The trial court held the lease to be unenforceable for lack of agreement to the nature and extent of the property to be leased. Nielsen appealed.

Case Decision Wilkins, Justice

* * *

In this case, the building shell itself was still under construction when the lease was signed. Uncontroverted trial testimony establishes that the contractor had not completed the floor of the building shell because he anticipated that tenant improvements would require modification to the original building plans for plumbing and electrical configurations. Nor were the roof and walls completed. This renders the question of payment even more important, because it is not clear from the lease who was required to pay for those tenant-based modifications to the building shell. Furthermore, there was no evidence at trial concern-

ing industry customs ro standards, or any other extrinisic evidence that would aid the court in determining responsibility for payment. Finally, even Nielsen notes that the cost of improvements "would have consumed more than half of the total rents over the three-year term of the lease," constituting a significant portion of the overall costs associated with the lease. While payment for tenant improvements is by no means an essential term in every commercial lease agreement, the facts of this case persuade us that it was an essential part of the bargain to be reached here.

We uphold the trial court's legal determination that the lease agreement was ambiguous due to missing terms, specifically, those terms governing payment of tenant improvements. The trial court's interpretation of the contract after finding ambiguity was not challenged on appeal; thus, we also uphold the trial court's ruling that the contract was unenforceable for lack of mutual assent as to the essential terms governing which party was to pay for tenant improvements. The judgment of dismissal is affirmed.

Questions for Analysis
1. The Utah high court held that no commercial lease was ever formed, because key terms to the lease were never set. Given that the building was still under construction, how could they have set all these details?
2. Why did the court not make the lease work or assign the appropriate costs of the construction to the parties?

Public Control of Real Property

Many statutes modify the common law. Some statutes make property law operate more smoothly by providing offices for the registration of titles to private property, for listing loans taken out against property, and for noting claims made against property—(often called *liens*)—that are filed by people who assert they are owed money by the property owner, such as for failure to pay for putting a new roof on a house. Governments also have strong powers over the use of private property. Most important are the power of eminent domain and the broad police powers that include such things as control of property by zoning rules. That is what we review next.

Eminent Domain

Governments at all levels may use tax dollars to buy private property, or they may use their power of *eminent domain* to condemn property to force the sale of property or to force the granting of an easement. Eminent domain is the power to take private property for public use without the consent of the owner. As the Supreme Court noted in 1875 in *Kohl* v. *U.S.* (91 U.S. 367), "The right of eminent domain always was a right at common law. It was not a right in equity, nor was it even the creature of a statute. The . . . right itself was superior to any statute." That is, it comes from the right of the government as sovereign to control property for its purposes.

The Fifth Amendment states that "private property" shall not "be taken for public use, without just compensation." Governments are allowed to force a property owner to give up title to part or all of his land or to force a property owner to give an easement on the land for some public purpose. Governments must pay compensation, which is generally determined by statutes that allow "fair market value" for the property interests taken.

While governments have long condemned property to use it for building a school, a road, or for some other public purpose, a major issue has arisen in recent years over the use of eminent domain to benefit a private party. When a business wishes to locate in a particular place, it may face the problem that some property owners may refuse to sell or will sell only at very high prices. To encourage business location, governments, especially at the local level, have used their power of eminent domain to allow a private party to get specific property at fair market value and not have to bargain with current property owners. As we saw in the *Kelo* case in Chapter 4, the Supreme Court holds this practice to be a legitimate use of eminent domain.

Police Powers

Eminent domain is government taking of land, but government also controls private land use by regulation. Except for environmental regulations, most land regulation is done at the state and local level. This is generally called the *police power* to regulate behavior to protect or promote the "general welfare." While the general welfare usually means health or safety, in practice it means very general power to control private use of property.

Often the key issue is not whether there is such a power to regulate but whether government must provide compensation when land-use controls reduce property values. No one questions that when the government takes property by eminent domain it must pay for the property. But in general, even when the government greatly reduces the value of property by regulation, compensation might not be due. As we saw in Chapter 4, the Supreme Court has declared that when almost all value of property is destroyed by regulation, it is protected by the Fifth Amendment rule of just compensation. But when regulation causes property to lose part of its value, compensation is rarely provided, so long as the government can show a rational reason for the police power that caused the economic damage and show that there was no violation of due process with respect to the injured property owner.

ISSUE SPOTTER
Would Tighter Leases Help?

As manager of an apartment complex, you know that a nontrivial number of tenants not only make a mess that is not covered by their damage deposit, but some stop paying rent so they must be evicted. You win the eviction battles, but they incur some legal fees and, since the tenants do not have resources and often leave town, you lose the rent for a couple months, too. What can you do to reduce your losses? Can you write leases that will be more effective at making the tenants pay?

Getty Images

Zoning

Governments have long mandated controls on land use. Over 200 years ago, regulation stated that dangerous businesses, such as gunpowder factories, and stinky businesses, such as slaughterhouses, must be located away from residential areas. In more recent times, *zoning* has become the primary method of local land control. Zoning rules commonly limit building height and size, require green areas, set population density limits, decide what kinds of buildings and businesses can be built where, and set numerous rules about the quality and type of construction that must be used. So long as such regulations do not violate a provision of the Constitution, such as free speech, or violate due process rules, the zoning rules are likely to be upheld, as we are in the *Macon-Bibb* case. After the case, we turn to issues that arise when parties become involved in tort actions involving property.

Macon-Bibb County Planning and Zoning v. Vineville Neighborhood
Court of Appeals of Georgia
462 S.E.2d 764, 218 Ga.App.668 (1996)

Case Background *The Zoning Commission rezoned some property so a developer could build a shopping center. A residential area, known as Vineville, bordered the 10 acre piece of land. Some residents opposed to the development joined together and sued the commission. The trial court held that the neighborhood association had standing to challenge the zoning action and found that the Commission had abused its discretion in approving the rezoning application. The developer and Commission appealed.*

Case Decision Blackburn, Judge

* * *

In order to challenge on the merits a decision of a governing authority to rezone, plaintiffs must show special damages under the substantial interest-aggrieved citizen test. . . .

There are two steps to standing: First, that a person claiming to be aggrieved must have a substantial interest in the zoning decision and second, that this interest be in danger of suffering some special damage or injury not common to all property owners similarly situated. . . .

The mere increase in traffic congestion adjacent to one's property as the result of improvements erected
continues

on nearby property, and the attendant inconvenience resulting therefrom, which are damages suffered alike by all property owners similarly situated, does not give to one individual such a substantial interest in the decision of the [Zoning Commission] permitting the improvement as to authorize an appeal therefrom. Such an inconvenience is a condition incident to urban living. It is merely the result of normal urban growth and development. To hold that such an inconvenience would give to any resident or property holder of an urban area the right to override the decisions of boards of zoning appeals any time such property owner or resident disagreed with such decision would be a dangerous precedent to establish. It would result in materially slowing, if not completely stopping, the inevitable and necessary growth of large modern cities.

Under these circumstances, the trial court's finding that the Association had standing to challenge the decisions of the Zoning Commission upon evidence of substantial damage to a substantial interest was clearly erroneous . . .

The trial court's decision . . . is reversed.

Questions for Analysis

1. The appeals court held that the neighbors affected by the change in zoning could not sue to challenge the Zoning Commission decision. What would have been needed to get standing to challenge such a decision?

2. Suppose the neighbors could show the change in zoning would reduce the value of their homes; would that give them standing to challenge?

Torts against Property

Some wrongs do not harm people but do harm their property or property interests. Property refers to *real property*, such as land; *personal property;* or a person's possessions; and *intellectual property*, such as trade secrets. We discuss intellectual property in Chapter 9; here we review the torts that interfere with the right to enjoy and control one's property. Tort actions that may be initiated for intentional violations of the property rights of another include trespass to land, nuisance, trespass to personal property, conversion, and misappropriation.

Trespass to Land

The tort of *trespass to land* is an unauthorized intrusion by a person or a thing on land belonging to another. If the intruder intended to be on another's property, it is irrelevant if the intruder mistakenly thought she owned the land or had permission to be on it. It is not necessary for the property owner to demonstrate actual injury to the property. For example, shooting a gun across another's property may be a trespass to land despite the fact that no physical damage occurs. Landowners have a right of peaceful enjoyment of their property. If, however, a person enters another's property to protect it from damage or to help someone on the property who is in danger, that is a defense against the tort of trespass to land.

The original idea of possession of land included dominion over a space "from the center of the earth to the heavens." A trespass could be committed on, beneath, or above the surface of the land. That rule is much more relaxed today. An airplane flying over a property owner's airspace does not create an action in trespass so long as it is flying at a reasonable altitude.

In general, unless we invite people on to our property, they are trespassers and we have no obligation to protect them against accidents, as the *Smith* case discusses.

Smith v. Kulig
Supreme Court of North Dakota
696 N.W.2d 521 (2005)

Case Background *Kulig owns a building with businesses on the ground floor and apartments on the second floor. The street door to the apartments is kept locked so only tenants and their guests have access. At the back of the building is a fire escape. The tenants were told not to use the fire escape unless there was an emergency. "No trespassing" signs were posted on the fire escape. Smith was visiting Wolf at his apartment in the building. Apparently, Smith went on to the fire escape, some bolts that attached it to the wall came out, and Smith fell to his death. His estate sued Kulig. The trial court dismissed the suit, holding Smith to be a trespasser. The holding was appealed.*

Case Decision Maring, Justice

* * *

The word "trespasser" is legally defined as a person who enters or remains upon premises in possession of another without a privilege to do so created by the possessor's consent, either express or implied....

Here, the trial court found the fire escape on the back side of Kulig's building contained *no trespass* signs, as did the doors leading to and from the fire escape.... The court also found that the ladder to the fire escape had a no trespassing sign mounted on it.... The court found that Smith was a trespasser on the premises, because Smith did not have a right to use the fire escape as an entry or exit to the building and there was no emergency situation which would reasonably require him to have used it for that purpose ... the *no trespassing* signs on the property negated any implied consent upon which Smith could claim to have been a lawful occupant of the premises while using the fire escape in contravention of the warnings against such use....

An occupier of premises owes no duty to a trespasser other than to refrain from harming the trespasser in a willful and wanton manner until such time as the trespasser's presence in a place of danger becomes known, at which point the occupier's duty is to exercise ordinary care to avoid injuring him.

Thus, a landowner does not owe a duty to a trespasser other than to refrain from harming the trespasser in a willful and wanton manner. We, therefore, conclude the court did not err in applying the willful and wanton conduct standard of liability under the circumstances of this case....

With respect to trespassers, a landowner is not under any affirmative duty to give a trespasser warning of concealed perils, although, by the exercise of reasonable care, the owner might have discovered the defect or danger which caused the injury. The person in charge only owes a duty to not knowingly or willfully expose a trespasser to hidden danger or peril.... In this case, there is no evidence that Kulig knew or had reason to know the fire escape was in a dangerous condition....

We affirm the judgment dismissing the wrongful death action with prejudice.

Questions for Analysis
1. The North Dakota high court held the landlord had no duty to protect trespassers from dangers on the property. Since Smith was a guest of Wolf, a tenant, why was he a trespasser?
2. The fire escape was in poor condition and may have collapsed if people had used it in case of a fire. Why was that not a failure by the landlord to exercise due care?

Nuisance (Private and Public)

The common law of torts recognizes two kinds of nuisance: private nuisance and public nuisance. A *private nuisance* is an activity that substantially and unreasonably interferes with the use and enjoyment of land. The interference may be physical, such as vibration, the destruction of crops, or the throwing of objects upon the land. The interference may cause discomfort or a health risk from pollution, odors, excessive noise, dust, or noxious fumes. A nuisance may include offensive conditions on neighboring land that injures the occupants' mental peace through the problems those conditions create or threaten to create, or simply through their offensive nature. Most people would find, for example, that the use of the house next door for drug deals is upsetting to their mental peace while in their own houses.

Common-law nuisance actions have been useful for challenging environmental damage. In fact, nuisance actions have challenged virtually every major industrial activity that causes some form of pollution, as we will see in Chapter 18.

A *public nuisance* is an unreasonable interference with a right held in common by the general public. A public nuisance usually involves interference with the public health and welfare. For example, an illegal gambling establishment, bad odors, and the obstruction of a highway would be grounds for a public nuisance action. In addition to having the common law, states have statutes that define various activities as being public nuisances.

Whether an action creates a private or a public nuisance depends upon who is affected by it. The pollution of a well by a factory, for example, is a private nuisance if it interferes only with the rights of landowners living next to the plant. The suit will be brought by those landowners against the owners of the plant. However, if the pollution hurts the public water supply, it is a public nuisance. In such circumstances, the legal representative of the community, such as the county attorney, will bring the action on behalf of the citizens against the polluters.

Nuisance actions can be based on enforcement of statutes or common-law standards, as the court notes in the *Atkinson* case.

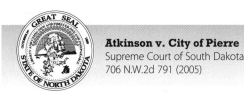

Atkinson v. City of Pierre
Supreme Court of South Dakota
706 N.W.2d 791 (2005)

Case Background *Tour Ice has produced ice at its plant in the business district of Pierre for years. Trucks pick up the ice and distribute it throughout a large area. The business is in compliance with city ordinances regarding proper operations. Atkinson moved into an apartment across the street from the ice plant. Getting nowhere with complaints to Tour Ice or the city, she sued both for nuisance, contending the noise level from operations was higher than she should have to tolerate. The trial court held for defendants. Atkinson appealed.*

Case Decision Konenkamp, Justice

* * *

Atkinson argues that the "inaction by the City of Pierre towards the noise created by Tour Ice is palpably unreasonable." She maintains that the business should be declared a nuisance. Its operation, Atkinson asserts, unreasonably violates, invades, and interferes with her private use and enjoyment of her leasehold interest in her apartment.

A claim for nuisance may be brought under statutory or common-law nuisance theories. Nuisance

is defined in SDCL [South Dakota Civil Law] 21–10–1:

> A nuisance consists in unlawfully doing an act, or omitting to perform a duty, which act or omission either: (1) Annoys, injures, or endangers the comfort, repose, health, or safety of others; (2) Offends decency; (3) Unlawfully interferes with, obstructs, or tends to obstruct, or renders dangerous for passage, any lake or navigable river, bay, stream, canal, or basin, or any public park, square, street, or highway; (4) In any way renders other persons insecure in life, or in the use of property.

In SDCL 21–10–3, the Legislature differentiates between public and private nuisances: "A public nuisance is one which affects at the same time an entire community or neighborhood, or any considerable number of persons, although the extent of the annoyance or damage inflicted upon the individuals may be unequal. Every other nuisance is private." Available remedies against nuisances are: "(1) A civil action; (2) Abatement; and (3) in cases of public nuisance only, the additional remedy of indictment or information as prescribed by statute and rules relating thereto."

The *Restatement Second of Torts* sets forth the common-law elements required to establish a private nuisance cause of action. . . . Under the *Restatement*, the following conduct gives rise to a claim of nuisance:

> One is subject to liability for a private nuisance if, but only if, his conduct is a legal cause of an invasion of another's interest in the private use and enjoyment of land, and the invasion is either (a) intentional and unreasonable, or (b) unintentional and otherwise actionable under the rules controlling liability for negligent or reckless conduct, or for abnormally dangerous conditions or activities. . . .

Mayor Dennis Eisnach of the City of Pierre . . . confirmed that no other complaints from any other residents around the ice facility were filed. . . .

SDCL 9–29–13 provides: "Every municipality shall have power to declare what shall constitute a nuisance and prevent, abate, and remove the same." Within a city's express authority is the implied power to declare what shall not constitute a nuisance. We cannot say that the city's refusal to declare Tour Ice's operation a nuisance was palpably unreasonable. Moreover, we can find no error in the courts refusal to declare the business a private nuisance. . . . Affirmed

Questions for Analysis

1. The South Dakota high court affirmed that the noise from the business operation was not legally a nuisance. What other course of action can Atkinson take?

2. Why should the position taken by the city on this issue matter to the court?

Trespass to Personal Property

The intentional and wrongful interference with possession of personal property of another without consent is a *trespass to personal property*. An important element in this tort is that someone has interfered with the right of the owner to exclusive possession and enjoyment of personal property. Liability usually occurs when the trespasser damages the property or deprives the owner of the use of the property for a time. However, if the interference with the personal property of another is warranted, there is a defense to the trespass. Many states have statutes that allow motel operators to hold the personal property of guests who have not paid their bills.

ISSUE SPOTTER
Protecting Company Property

At your office, employees often walk out with assorted supplies. Pencils and paper clips are cheap, but the cost of pens, staplers, reams of paper, and more expensive items can quickly add up. Multiply this amount by the number of employees, and losses can be significant. Can a company have a policy informing employees that taking supplies is theft of company property and will make them subject to dismissal? Does the company need to notify the employees that it is theft, or should they know? How should these losses be handled? As you think about this, remember that theft by employees causes larger losses than theft by non employees.

Getty Images

Conversion

The tort of *conversion* is an intentional and unlawful control or appropriation of the personal property of another. In contrast to trespass on personal property, conversion requires that the control or appropriation so seriously interferes with the owner's right of control that it justifies payment for the property. Several factors are considered in determining whether the interference warrants a finding of conversion: the extent of dominion or control, the duration of the interference, the damage to the property, and the inconvenience and expense to the owner. As with trespass to land, mistake is not a defense to conversion.

Generally, one who wrongfully acquires possession of another's personal property—by theft, duress, or fraud—is said to have committed the tort of conversion. In most court systems, a bona fide purchaser (a good-faith purchaser who thought the seller was the rightful owner of the property) is liable for conversion if the property was purchased from a thief, but this rule has a number of exceptions.

Misappropriation

Some forms of intellectual property, including trademarks and trade secrets, which are valuable and protected from revelation to others, are protected by tort law from *misappropriation* or *theft* by others. We will discuss intellectual property in detail in Chapter 9 and we will see that some statutes specify the damages that may be had when such property is taken by others without permission. As with other forms of property, owners may sue those who invade their property rights for damages and may ask a court to issue an injunction against further unauthorized use of the property. Next we turn to a common tort action filed against property owners.

LIGHTER SIDE OF THE LAW

Protect Your Assets

Chen knew that his dog bit his neighbor, Liu, on the hand and caused a serious injury. Knowing he could be liable for medical expenses, while Liu was in the hospital, Chen and his wife moved their house, hoping they would not be found and forced to pay. Police were able to follow the trail anyway.

Source: *China Daily News*

Getty Images

Torts against Property Owners

Remember Humpty Dumpty? Did he have a cause of action against the wall owner? It depends on several factors. Was Humpty invited to sit on the wall or was he a trespasser? If he was committing a trespass by sitting on the wall, then the owner of the wall owed him no duty of care, other than not to take steps that could cause him to suffer an injury. If Humpty had been invited to a party, and during the party decided to sit on the wall, then the property owner would not be liable to Humpty unless the owner was aware of some danger about sitting on the wall and failed to tell Humpty about it. The many principles we have discussed come together for businesses in what is generally called *premises liability*.

Premises Liability

There are many cases involving slip-and-fall. The customer of a business, presumed by law to be invited to be on the premises in order to shop, suffers an injury due to slipping on a wet or icy spot. The general rule is that the owner of the property has a duty to keep the premises reasonably safe under the circumstances. Customers are not trespassers; they are invitees welcome on business property. For example, if it is raining and water seeps into the front of the store, the property owner has a duty to try to limit the slips that could occur by mopping the area, putting down an extra doormat, and perhaps a warning sign, but customers are also expected to use common sense in such conditions. If a danger is obvious, people have a duty to protect themselves from it. What if the danger is not so obvious? If a patron is injured, will the property owner be liable? That issue is discussed in the *Campisi* case.

Campisi v. Acme Markets, Inc.
Superior Court of Pennsylvania
915 A.2d 117 (2006)

Case Background *A blind employee who worked at an Acme grocery store was walking to the back to the store, using his white aluminum guide cane. Campisi was walking down another aisle, around a corner, and tripped over the cane, suffering injuries. She sued Acme for premises liability based on negligence. The jury awarded $115,000 in damages. The trial judge granted Acme judgment notwithstanding the verdict. Campisi appealed.*

Case Decision Kelly, Judge

* * *

There is no dispute over causation and damages in this negligence claim; the parties dispute only whether a legal duty to warn existed. . . . The duty owed to a business invitee is the highest duty owed to any entrant upon load. The landowner is under an affirmative duty to protect a business visitor not only against known dangers but also against those which might be discovered with reasonable care. In determining the scope of duty property owners owe to business invitees, we have relied on *Restatement (Second) of Torts* § 343, which provides:

> A possessor of land is subject to liability for physical harm caused to his invitees by a condition on the land, if but only if he: (a) Knows or by the exercise of reasonable care would discover the condition, and should realize that it involves an unreasonable risk to such invitees, and (b) should expect that they will not discover or realize the danger, or will fail to protect themselves against it, and (c) fails to exercise reasonable care to protect them against the danger.

An invitee must demostrate that the proprietor deviated from its duty of reasonable care owed under the circumstances. Thus, the particular duty owed to a business invitee must be determined on a case-by-case basis. . . . *Restatement* Section 343A provides that no liability exists when the dangerous condition is known or obvious to the invitee unless the proprietor should anticipate the harm despite such knowledge . . .

Appellant's argument, that customers would be more cautious if stores posted a sign indicating the presence of a blind employee, is specious at best. In effect, Appellant attempts to establish a legal duty owed by Acme to her by shifting attention away from her own responsibilities as an invitee and claiming instead that the employee's handicap alone created the risk of harm. . . . Whether the hazard is a shopping cart that suddenly just out, a customer's foot, or someone's cane, customers must constantly be on alert for obstacles when exiting a grocery store aisle. The likelihood of danger further increases when a customer rounds the corner of an aisle directly toward the end of the adjacent aisle, as Appellant did here. Thus, we would consider a **customer's** duty of ordinary care to include looking for obstacles before exiting an aisle. . . .

We conclude that even if employment of the blind increases the risk of an accident such as Appellant's, such a risk does not overcome a customer's responsibility to avoid the known and obvious dangers present upon exiting a grocery store aisle. The trial court properly found that Appellant failed to prove the existence of Acme's legal duty to her. Accordingly, we affirm the court's order reversing the jury's verdict and entering judgment for Acme.

Questions for Analysis
1. The appeals court held that the patrons of a store have a duty to watch for hazards that can cause them to fall, including the cane of a blind person. What would be an example of a hazard that would be more likely to be the fault of the store?
2. Would posting a sign telling patrons there is a blind person working at the store be likely to make it safer for the customers and the worker?

ISSUE SPOTTER
Duties to Elderly Customers

The number of persons over age 65 will double in the coming decades. More patrons at businesses will be frail, have poor balance, weak eyesight, and other aging-related issues. For example, the Metropolitan Opera in New York was sued when an elderly patron fell and injured another patron in the fall. To avoid claims of negligence when falls and other problems occur, what changes may need to be made in business operations?

Getty Images

Premises liability may also occur when a business does not provide sufficient security to help prevent crimes from occurring on its property. For instance, in a 1995 Supreme Court of Connecticut case, *Stewart* v. *Federated Department Stores* (662 A.2d 753), the court upheld a $1.5 million verdict in favor of the heirs of a woman who was robbed and murdered in the parking garage of a Bloomingdale's department store. The store was found negligent for not having a security guard on duty. The store was in a high-crime area and other customers had been robbed in the garage.

LIGHTER SIDE OF THE LAW
Wildlife Gone Wild

Meckler walked out of a Tiffany jewelry store to go to her car, when she was attacked by a squirrel that "attached itself to her leg." The suit against Tiffany's notes that "while frantically attempting to escape from the squirrel and detach it from her leg, [Meckler] fell and suffered severe injuries." As a result, she "will in the future endure pain and suffering in body and mind."

The suit contends Tiffany's was negligent for failing "to warn the plaintiff of the squirrel's presence" and that they "encouraged the squirrel to remain on the premises by feeding and caring for the squirrel, despite the dangerous conditions that arose from allowing said animal to remain on the premises."

Source: *cbs2chicago.com*

Getty Images

Commercial property cannot provide protection against every criminal act that may occur, but property owners cannot ignore crime problems that may be in the area, as the *Erichsen* case discusses.

Erichsen v. No-Frills Supermarkets of Omaha
Supreme Court of Nebraska
246 Neb.238, 518 N.W.2d 116 (1994)

Case Background *Erichsen went grocery shopping at No-Frills one morning. When she returned to her car, she was assaulted, beaten, robbed, and dragged over one mile hanging from the car of her assailant, suffering serious injuries. She sued No-Frills and the owner of the shopping center for negligently failing to warn her of criminal activity, and for failing to protect her from criminal activities that were foreseeable because of ten criminal events within a 16-month period. The trial court held that defendants did not violate a duty of care to Erichsen. She appealed.*

Case Decision Lanphier, Justice

* * *

We have adopted the rule regarding landlord liability to business invitees, as set forth in *Restatement (Second) of Torts* § 344 (1965). [It] provides:

> A possessor of land who holds it open to the public for entry for his business purposes is subject to liability to members of the public while they are upon the land for such a purpose, for physical harm caused by the accidental, negligent, or intentionally harmful acts of third persons or animals, and by the failure of the possessor to exercise reasonable care to (a) discover that such acts are being done or are likely to be done, or (b) give a warning adequate to enable the visitors to avoid the harm, or otherwise to protect them against it.

Comment *f.* to § 344 makes it clear that the owner of the property is not an insurer of the land or the visitor's safety while on it. However, liability will be found under certain circumstances:

> Since the possessor is not an insurer of the visitor's safety, he is ordinarily under no duty to exercise any care until he knows or has reason to know that the acts of the third person are occurring, or are about to occur. *He may, however, know or have reason to know, from past experience, that there is a likelihood of conduct on the part of third persons in general which is likely to endanger the safety of the visitor, even though he has no reason to expect it on the part of any particular individual.* If the place or character of his business, or his past experience, is such that he should reasonably anticipate careless or criminal conduct on the part of third persons, *either generally* or at some particular time, he may be under a duty to take precautions against it, and to provide a reasonably sufficient number of servants to afford reasonable protection. (Emphasis supplied.)

We have interpreted the *Restatement* and have held that a landlord is under a duty to exercise reasonable care to protect his patrons. Such care many require giving a warning or providing greater protection where there is a *likelihood* that third persons will endanger the safety of the visitors. . . .

This court has denied relief where the appellant based his or her allegations of negligence on a single act of violence. In those cases, we held that one incident did not, under the facts presented in those cases, constitute sufficient notice to make the criminal acts sued upon reasonably foreseeable. However . . . a duty to undertake reasonable precautionary measures will be imposed on the landlord when there is a sufficient amount of criminal activity to make further criminal acts reasonably foreseeable. . . .

We find that appellant has alleged sufficient facts in her petition to overcome the demurrer of appellees. The cause is therefore remanded for further proceedings consistent with this opinion.

Questions for Analysis

1. The Nebraska high court held it was for the jury to determine if the store violated its duty to take more precautions to protect patrons against criminal attack. Why should this store do any more than any other store?
2. Can a store afford to have full-time security guards? Is that required in cases such as this one?

ISSUE SPOTTER
Protecting Customers' Kids

As a manager of a department store, you know that it is not uncommon for kids to run around in the store with little adult supervision. Some kids have been hurt when they run into display cabinets. The edges of the cabinets are sharp and hard. Kids have gashed themselves, requiring trips to the emergency room for stitches. While most customers have not asserted that the store should be liable for the uncontrolled behavior of their kids, some have. Given that this happens at least several times a year, should the store take extra steps to protect itself from possible liability? What sort of steps could be taken?

Getty Images

Summary

- Property law is the oldest part of the common law. It focuses on real property, which is land, houses, and things attached to the land; and personal property, which is movable property, such as furniture, books, and cars. The owners of property have legal interests or rights in property. Property rights are limited by common law and by statutes that restrict the use of property.

- Written deeds are used to transfer ownership interests in real property. Many forms of deeds exist that provide different levels of assurances of the quality of ownership rights being provided. Titles to property, which constitute the formal right of ownership, are passed by deeds.

- The strongest form of ownership of real property is fee simple, which is how most real estate in the United States is held. When more than one party owns real estate, it is often held in a tenancy in common, where the parties have an undivided interest that passes to their heirs on death; or it may be in a joint tenancy, which is also an undivided interest, but the other owner has a right of survivorship. Few restrictions are placed on the forms of ownership people choose to use.

- Servitudes are restrictions or requirements imposed on the use of property, most commonly easements and covenants. Such legal rights are held to run with the land, as they usually stay in place when title to property passes. Most easements grant the right to another party to enter property for some purpose, such as to have access to power lines. Covenants are often used in real estate developments to impose requirements on the design of houses and characteristics of the property that must be maintained.

- Real estate may be leased to tenants for any terms the parties agree on so long as it does not conflict with state law. Any details not covered in a lease fall under state landlord–tenant law. The parties have obligations. Tenants may not abuse the property, and landlords must make certain key repairs in a timely manner and must not invade the privacy of the tenants.

- Leases for commercial property tend to be highly specific on many details about the property. Unlike most residential leases, which are often governed by state landlord–tenant statutes, commercial leases are determined by the parties to the bargain and so require care by the parties to the transaction.

- Governments have the power of eminent domain. It allows them to condemn private property and take it for public use, so long as fair market value compensation is paid to the owners. Destruction of substantial property value by regulations such as zoning is generally not compensable. A controversial form of eminent domain in recent years is the use of eminent domain to turn the property over to a private party for profitable use.

- Intentional torts against property include trespass, or the unauthorized intrusion on the land of another, and nuisance, which is a substantial and unreasonable interference with the right of persons to use and enjoy their property. A nuisance may be private, in which case a property owner sues, or public, when many people suffer from the interference and a public attorney acts on their behalf.

- Other intentional torts include trespass to personal property, which is wrongful interference with the right of persons to use their property in a lawful manner, and conversion, which is the unlawful appropriation (theft) of the personal property of another person.

- Property owners may be sued for premises liability by those they have invited to come on their property, such as store customers. If the property owner has been negligent in maintaining the condition of the property and that negligence violates the duty of ordinary care that results in an injury, liability may be imposed. Liability may arise from failure of a property owner to provide reasonable security against criminal attacks.

Terms to Know

You should be able to define the following terms:

deed, 177	easement by prescription, 180	zoning, 187
title, 177	adverse possession, 180	private nuisance, 189
tenancy in common, 178	covenant, 181	public nuisance, 190
life estate, 178	leasehold, 182	trespass, 191
servitude, 179	liens, 186	conversion, 191
easement, 179	eminent domain, 186	premises liability, 192

Discussion Question

1. A century ago, the common law regarding landlords and tenants held the tenant responsible for major repairs to residences, such as roof repairs. Over the years, the common law changed to put such responsibility on the landlords. Why did the law evolve in that direction? What factors may have brought about the change?

Case Questions

1. Peterson operated a private golf course in Sioux Falls, South Dakota. In 1964, Peterson sold property adjoining the golf course, including a restaurant and parking lot, to AL. The parking lot was used by the golfers on Peterson's golf course and by restaurant patrons. In 1978, AL sold the property containing the parking lot to VBC. Peterson had always maintained the parking lot. In 1992, VBC demanded Peterson pay rent for the use of the parking lot by the golfers. Peterson sued, claiming title to the parking lot by adverse possession. Is Peterson right? [*Peterson v. Beck*, 537 N.W.2d 375 Sup. Ct., S.D. (1995)]

2. The Gleasons owned a large piece of property. Part of it was subject to a public drainage easement. Taub went into the drainage area with a bulldozer and removed 16,000 cubic feet of dirt to use as fill on other land. The Gleasons sued him for trespass. He defended that he had a right to go on the public easement and, furthermore that his dirt removal improved the drainage in the easement. Who would you think correct? [*Gleason v. Taub*, 180 S.W.3d 711 Ct. App.,Tx. (2005)]

3. A KFC restaurant was on a major street in town until the city redesigned the road, leaving the KFC at the end of a dead-end road, which caused business to fall. The KFC owners sued the city for inverse condemnation—a taking of their property by reducing the value of it. Can they demand compensation for this loss of value? [*Kau Kau Take Home No. 1 v. City of Wichita*, 135 P.3d 1221 Sup. Ct., Kan. (2006)]

   ✓ Check your answer at http://academic.cengage.com/blaw/meiners

4. Collins has a farm used to raise horses and cattle. It is surrounded by property owned by Barker. Large quantities of weeds grew on Barkers property and, when dry, would tumble onto Collins' property. So many weeds blew, they covered the fences and filled the water tanks, making the water undrinkable by the livestock. What can Collins sue Barker for, and do you think he has a case? [*Collins v. Barker*, 668 N.W.2d 548 Sup. Ct., S.D. (2003)]

5. Fox rented a house from Chiodini, but before he moved in, he noticed exposed electrical wiring in the basement, so he refused to move in. City inspectors confirmed a code

violation and Chiodini fixed the wiring a month after the lease was to start. By that time, Fox had moved elsewhere. Since Chiodini was willing to begin the lease the day the wiring was fixed, did Fox break the lease by refusing to move in? [*Chiodini* v. *Fox*, 207 S. W.3d 174 Ct. App., Mo. (2006)]

✓ Check your answer at http://academic.cengage.com/blaw/meiners

6. Smith, a sales rep for Ziva, left $850,000 in jewelry in the trunk of his car when he took it to a car wash to be cleaned. Smith watched the entire procedure, to make sure no one opened the trunk, but while it was being dried, someone jumped in the car, took off, and stole the jewelry. He sued the car wash for allowing the theft of his personal property. While the car wash had possession of his car, was it responsible for the jewelry? [*Ziva Jewelry* v. *Car Wash Hq.*, 897 So.2d 1011 Sup. Ct., Ala. (2004)]

7. While Rouse was looking at new cars at a dealership, he gave his car keys to a sales rep so that his car could be examined for its trade-in value. When Rouse decided to leave without buying, the keys were hidden from him—supposedly lost—for about a half hour. The sales rep thought this was a joke. Rouse sued and was awarded $5,000 in punitive damages. What was the tort claimed? Would the damages be allowed on appeal? [*Russell-Vaughn Ford* v. *Rouse*, 206 So.2d 371 Sup. Ct., Ala. (1968)]

✓ Check your answer at http://academic.cengage.com/blaw/meiners

8. The basement of the Girone home was flooded with raw sewage that overflowed from a city sewer line. Walking across the odorous floor, Mrs. Girone slipped and fell, breaking her hip. She sued the city for negligent maintenance of the sewage line and for trespass. The city contended she was negligent for not being more careful walking on the slippery floor. Who won? [*City of Winder* v. *Girone*, 462 S.E.2d 704 Sup. Ct., Ga. (1995)]

9. Members of Earth First! demonstrated in a forest against logging. Several protestors chained themselves to logging machinery owned by a private company. Logging operations had to be ceased for a day because of the protest and occupation of machinery (which was not damaged). What cause of action does the logging company have against the protesters? [*Huffman and Wright Logging Co.* v. *Wade*, 857 P.2d 101 Sup. Ct., Ore. (1993)]

✓ Check your answer at http://academic.cengage.com/blaw/meiners

10. Strahs, age 84, slipped on an icy spot in the parking lot of a drugstore, fell, and broke her hip. She sued the drugstore and the company that was under contract to keep the parking lot plowed for snow. While it had been plowed, there were icy spots remaining in the parking lot. Did she have a good case against either of those parties? [*Strahs* v. *Tovar's Snowplowing, Inc.*, 812 N.E.2d 441 Ct. App., Ill. (2004)]

11. Chamblee rented an apartment from Grayco. One day, when walking from her apartment to her car, she left the sidewalk, cut across the grass, and tripped over an exposed drainage pipe and suffered injuries. She sued Grayco for negligence in premises liability. Does she have a case? [*Chamblee* v. *Grayco*, 596 S.E.2d 683 Ct. App., Ga. (2004)]

12. Allen slipped and fell on a grape that was on the floor at a grocery store. No one saw the accident and no one is sure how the grape ended up on the floor. The manager claimed that the area had been recently checked to make sure it was clean. A jury awarded Allen $10,000 for her injuries. The store appealed. Does the verdict hold? [*Brookshire Food Stores* v. *Allen*, 93 S.W.3d 897 Ct. App., Tx. (2002)]

Ethics Question

1. A real estate development sells houses with a covenant that prohibits the sale to buyers under the age 55 so as to discourage children from living in the area. The covenant may even prohibit children from being permanent residents of the area; they can come as visitors but not residents. Is that sort of restriction ethically acceptable?

Internet Assignment

http://lawyers.findlaw.com
http://www.martindale.com

The "invisible" or "deep" web refers to information, often included within databases, which is not easily accessible by Internet search engines. Internet databases may also offer advanced search features, such as limiting a search by location. Two major directories of attorneys, *West's Legal Directory* and *Martindale-Hubbell Law Directory*, are available in searchable databases on the Internet. Use each database to find attorneys in your area who specialize in real estate transactions in your state. Noting the differences in the practice areas covered by each database, which database may be better if your issue involved a zoning problem? How about a problem with a property lease?

Intellectual Property

Chapter 9

Almost everyone gets offers of software at very low prices. Suppose you accept such an offer and, by doing so, save quite a bit of money buying software that you install on the fourteen computers at your company. Where did that software come from? Do you have proper licensing? No. This can be a poor move if the authorities charge you with illegal use of software that was pirated or illegally copied. While students might not worry much about getting caught with illegal software, it is a serious problem for a business, possibly involving fines and the cost of legal defense, as well as possible public exposure of the company's illegal act and damage to the company's reputation.

Reputation, or how others view you—also called *goodwill*—is one part of intellectual property. *Intellectual property* is created by intellectual effort, not by physical labor. It is often called *intangible property*, because it may be invisible, impossible to hold, and harder to value than the physical property we discussed in Chapter 8. For many firms, intellectual property is far more valuable than the real property owned by the company. Today, intellectual property is more important than it was in the agriculture-based economy in which land was the most important asset. It has been estimated that the brand names owned by Coca-Cola are worth over $65 billion.

In this chapter, we will look at the four major forms of intellectual property:

- Trademarks
- Copyrights
- Patents
- Trade secrets

The common law has a long tradition of providing protection for intellectual property, and the Constitution expresses its importance: Article I, Section 8, authorizes Congress "To promote the Progress of Science and useful Arts, by securing for limited Times to Authors and Inventors the exclusive Right to their respective Writings and Discoveries." Today, the Commissioner of Patents and Trademarks issues about 190,000 patents annually—half to Americans and half to foreigners—and registers about 150,000 new trademarks. The Copyright Office registers more than 600,000 copyrights annually.

Just as the common law protects real property, it also works with various statutes to protect intellectual property by allowing property owners to sue in case of *infringement*. That is, wrongful, unauthorized use of intellectual property in violation of the owner's rights is the basis for a tort action. When intellectual property is infringed upon, damages may be awarded to the property holder and an injunction against further unauthorized use may be issued. This protection has been enhanced by various statutes. How important is protection of intellectual property? The U.S. government estimates that counterfeit and fraudulent use of intellectual property costs business tens of billions of dollars a year. ■

Getty Images

Getty Images

LIGHTER SIDE OF THE LAW

Don't Step on His Estate's Velvet Shoes

A bar in Houston was named Velvet Elvis, which was also a trademark. Among its decorations was a large, black velvet portrait of the king of rock and roll, Elvis Presley. The bar was advertised as a "monument to the excesses of American culture."

Unamused, Elvis Presley Enterprises of Memphis sued, demanding that the owner remove the name Elvis and commercial representations of Presley. It contended that the decorations are trademark infringements and violate the Presley Enterprise publicity rights to Elvis, just as it requires Elvis impersonators to obtain licenses.

Velvet Elvis won round one. The judge held that customers would not be misled into thinking that the club was associated with Elvis Presley Enterprises. Presley won round two when the appeals court reversed in its favor and issued an injunction against the use of the mark "The Velvet Elvis." There was a likelihood of confusion, especially since Presley runs an Elvis-theme nightclub in Memphis.

Source: *National Law Journal* and *Elvis Presley Enterprises* v. *Capece,* 141 F.3d 188.

Trademarks

A *trademark* is a commercial symbol—a design, logo, phrase, distinctive mark, name, or word—that a manufacturer prints on its goods so they can be readily identified in the marketplace. We often recognize them as brand names, such as Nike. Other producers may not legally imitate genuine trademarks. Since companies spend large sums so consumers will recognize and trust their products, the common law has long recognized the right to protect this property. This common-law protection was made a part of federal law by the *Lanham Act.* Federal trademark law allows trademarks to be registered if they are distinctive and nonfunctional. As long as the owner continues to use and protect the trademark, the trademark's exclusive use can be perpetual.

Traditionally, trademark protection was created by priority of use. The first person to use a symbol in a business or geographic area has the right to stop others from using the same or very similar trade symbol in that business or area. The Lanham Act allows a person to register a symbol with the Patent and Trademark Office in Washington, D.C. The Trademark Revision Act allows nationwide claim to a mark from the moment it is registered, so long as sincere intent exists to use the symbol in commerce.

Getty Images

ISSUE SPOTTER

Establishing Your Name

As an increasing amount of business is done by the Internet, a company's domain name is critical. While established companies have theirs, what if you have a new company or a small company that has never had one? How do you go about getting a good name?

The advantages of registration of trademarks with the U.S. Patent and Trademark Office, rather than relying only on common-law protection of trademarks, include the following:

1. Nationwide notice of the trademark owner's claim
2. Legal presumption of the registrant's ownership of the mark in the event of a dispute
3. Federal court jurisdiction, if desired
4. Forming the basis for obtaining registration in other nations
5. Filing the registration with U.S. Customs Service to help prevent importation of foreign goods that infringe on the trademark

Registration

The registration process, which can be done online, includes payment of a fee ($375 paper or $325 electronic submission for each class of goods using a mark); submission of a copy of the mark, called a specimen; a description of the goods that will use the mark; and a declaration that, to the best of the applicant's knowledge, the mark does not conflict with other marks (see http://www.uspto.gov).

The applicant is responsible for searching existing trademarks to make sure there is no confusion or infringement with existing marks. A trademark examiner reviews the request to make sure the mark does not conflict with existing marks, is not descriptive, and does not claim too much coverage. That is, if you are trademarking a word for a brand of perfume, you cannot register the word *perfume*, because that is the generic term for that product. If the word *Charlie* is registered as a trademark for perfume, other people may be allowed to use the word in other contexts, such as Charlie's Motel.

Registration is good for ten years, after which it must be renewed. You can make sure people know a mark is protected by stating "Registered in U.S. Patent and Trademark Office" or by using the circle-R (®). You also see the symbol "TM," which puts people on notice but is not specified in the Lanham Act. However, lack of notice that a mark is a trademark does not mean the owner of the mark is not due legal protection for the mark. International protection of trademarks is encouraged by the International Bureau of the World Intellectual Property Organization by the Madrid System (http://www.wipo.int/madrid).

Classifications of Trademarks

Trademarks are classified as arbitrary and fanciful, suggestive, descriptive, or generic (see Exhibit 9.1).

Arbitrary and fanciful are most favored by the courts, because they are inherently distinctive (fanciful), like made-up names such as Exxon or Reebok, or they are names not related to the product (arbitrary), such as Black and White for a Scotch whiskey and Apple for computers.

Exhibit 9.1
Types of Trademarks

Arbitrary and Fanciful	Suggestive	Descriptive	Generic (No Longer Trademarks)
Polaroid	Orange Crush	Raisin Bran	Trampoline
Lexus	Roach Motel	Holiday Inn	Nylon
Virginia Slims	Dairy Queen	Musky (perfume)	Thermos
Ivory (soap)	Passion (Perfume)	Yellow Pages	Shredded Wheat
Clorox	Coppertone	After Tan	Zipper

INTERNATIONAL PERSPECTIVE

Costs of Counterfeiting

The World Customs Organization estimates that counterfeit goods generate more than $500 billion in sales a year, including $200 billion in the United States. Much of that money represents sales lost by owners of intellectual property (IP) rights from goods produced illegally.

The European Union estimates that, due to the loss of revenues and sales to counterfeiters—most located in China and other countries with dubious IP enforcement practices—120,000 jobs in the United States and 100,000 jobs in Europe have been lost. Some of the goods are traded openly; the makers of upscale handbags estimate that 90 percent of such items listed on eBay are fakes.

Fake sunglasses are one thing; the real problem is far more dangerous. Counterfeit medical drug sales are common around the world. Those taking such drugs receive no benefit and may even be harmed by the unknown substance. In San Diego, weak baby formula was sold with counterfeit labels, which could have caused allergy and nutrition problems in infants. Aircraft parts, including screws, are very expensive, because they must meet strict standards. Counterfeit parts have been found to have infiltrated even military supplies, endangering aircraft and helicopter crews.

Congress toughened criminal penalties through the Stop Counterfeiting in Manufactured Goods Act of 2006. European nations have also cracked down; Google was ordered to pay $400,000 to Louis Vuitton for allowing fake Vuitton goods to be advertised on Google. Firms invest in detectives to uncover counterfeit trade routes. They sue vendors and landlords who rent space to those who are clearly selling knockoffs. It is a complicated, sophisticated market with much at stake.

Getty Images

Suggestive marks hint at the product, such as Chicken of the Sea for canned tuna. They are due legal protection, but establishing that can be more difficult than if the mark is arbitrary and fanciful.

Descriptive marks are not as favored by the law and must be shown to have acquired customer recognition to be allowed protection. Examples of successful descriptive marks are Bufferin for aspirin with acid buffering and Holiday Inn for hotels.

Generic marks are words that are common and do not refer to products from a specific producer. Some words that were once trademarks have become generic or unprotected marks: *thermos* for vacuum-insulated bottles, *aspirin* for acetylsalicylic acid, and *escalator* for moving stairways.

Most colleges have trademarks for their name or employ a distinctive use of letters in their name and for their sports team name and mascot. Collegiate Licensing is a licensing agent for many universities and the manufacturers that make clothing and various items with university logos. This allows colleges to collect royalties from and control the use of their trademarks so that the trademarks are not used in ways the colleges do not approve.

Extent of Coverage

Trademarks, service marks, and other marks cannot claim too much. For example, if you go to the Trademark Office Web site, http://www.uspto.gov, and search for the Nike Shox trademark, you will see that Nike claims that combination of two words for watches and sports bags, among other goods. The listing shows the address of the company in Beaverton, Oregon, and gives the serial number assigned to Nike Shox (78406612), as well as other serial numbers that indicate other registrations by Nike. It also notes that the trademark is live.

Trademarks that are dead or abandoned are listed. For example, the word *Shox* was once claimed for "edible film strips in coffee, tea, mint, citrus, soda, candy, and ice

Getty Images

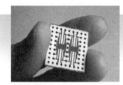

CYBER LAW

Who Owns and Controls Domain Names?

The International Corporation for Assigned Names and Numbers (ICANN) is in charge of preserving the operational stability of the Internet (see www.icann.org). The Department of Commerce granted domain-name system (DNS) control away from the United States to the global community. ICANN works with governments to coordinate the top-level domain (TLD) system, such as *.com,* and it decides on additional TLDs. For example, in 2007, it refused to allow the TLD *.xxx,* which was desired by "adult" material Web site operators.

ICANN does not issue individual domain names but does accredit firms that meet its standards for proper registry of domain names. The ICANN site lists accredited registrars. If a firm violates the rules, it loses its ability to register names. ICANN does not control spam and other problems; those issues are left to national law and Internet servers.

The World Intellectual Property Organization (see www.wipo.int) handles about half of the disputes over domain names—about 2,000 a year. That many more are handled by a couple of other organizations accredited by ICANN to resolve disputes, including the National Arbitration Forum in the United States. Hence, the law of domain names is global, and it is largely handled by private organizations and arbitration. Individual disputes may end up in court, but such cases represent a small share of the legal issues that need to be resolved.

cream flavors" by a California company, but the company no longer claims the mark, so the mark is listed as dead. Other marks are listed that once used the word Shox but are now dead, such as a water purification unit produced by an Alabama company.

The term Shox is used for other products, so Nike does not claim wide ownership of the term. For example, Shox is the trademark for the Louisville Ladder Group that makes plastic supports for ladders; it is also a mark for the Entempo Sdn Bhd Corporation of Malaysia, which uses it for "cushioning and protecting disk drives and sensitive electronic and electromechanical devices." While Nike Shox may be the most famous use of the term *Shox,* other companies use the word Shox as their mark, or part of their mark, for other lines of products.

Trademark protection applies to a wide range of creative property other than the names of products. Trademark law applies to titles of movies, advertising slogans, titles of comic books, and fictional characters, such as Batman. This allows the producers of highly popular movies and cartoon characters to license use of the names, such as Star Wars, which shows up in toys and premiums at fast-food restaurants.

Infringement, Dilution, and Cybersquatting

The extent of trademark protection depends on how well known a mark is and whether a similar mark could be confused with the original mark. The holders of marks must actively protect them, or they will be presumed to have been given up, as happened to marks that became generic.

Infringement occurs when a seller causes confusion about the origins of a product by improper use of a trademark. If a company other than Reebok makes and sells shoes using that famous name, there is infringement; consumers will be confused, thinking the shoes to be genuine Reebok, even if the shoes are not copies of genuine Reebok-brand shoes. Similarly, if a company sells shoes called *Rebok,* while not identical, that too would cause confusion. So essentially it is stealing the good name of another. The Lanham Act specifically allows suit for infringement.

Dilution is another violation of trademark rights. The Trademark Dilution Act of 1995 expanded the rights of famous and distinctive trademarks under the

Lanham Act. This right was strengthened more by the Trademark Revision Dilution Act of 2006, which holds that

> The owner of a famous mark that is distinctive, inherently or through acquired distinctiveness, shall be entitled to an injunction against another person who, at any time after the owner's mark has become famous, commences use of a mark or trade name in commerce that is likely to cause dilution by blurring or dilution by tarnishment of the famous mark, regardless of the presence or absence of actual or likely confusion, of competition, or of actual economic injury.

If a company were to sell guitars under the name Reebok, that would be dilution. No one would think the guitars to be Reebok athletic wear, but they may presume Reebok has gotten into other product lines, thereby diluting the strength of the mark.

Cybersquatting occurs when a trademark is used improperly in a domain name. It is restricted by the Anticybersquatting Consumer Protection Act, which prevents a Web site from capturing value from another's trademark. So to use the name reebokshoes.com without permission from Reebok would be cybersquatting.

Defenses in all of these situations include: 1) fair use, such as to mention a mark in comparative advertising; 2) noncommercial uses, such as parody or editorial commentary; and 3) news reporting or educational use, such as using the word Reebok here. In the *Audi* case that follows, we see a discussion of all of these points (which is why the case is long) and the standards set by the statutes and courts in applying the law when disputes arise.

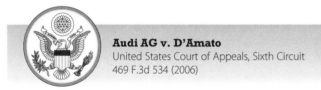

Audi AG v. D'Amato
United States Court of Appeals, Sixth Circuit
469 F.3d 534 (2006)

Case Background *D'Amato registered the domain name www.audisport.com. He sold goods and services with Audi logos. His site used various Audi trademarks. He claimed to have permission from a salesman at an Audi dealership to use the marks. Even if he did, Audi dealerships have no right, by contract, to grant any use of Audi trademarks. Audi's Web site sells assorted goods with the Audi name and logo on it. Audi sued D'Amato for infringement, dilution, and cybersquatting of its famous trademarks: Audi, Quattro, and the Audi four-ring logo. The district court held for Audi and issued a permanent injunction against D'Amato, his Web site, and domain name. He appealed.*

Case Decision Martin, Circuit Judge

* * *

Under both common law and federal law, "a trademark is a designation used 'to identify and distinguish' the goods of a person." Under the Lanham Act, we use the same test to decide whether there has been trademark infringement, unfair competition, or false designation of origin: the likelihood of confusion between the two marks. D'Amato argues that the district court's finding of a likelihood of confusion should be reversed, because Audi did not offer evidence demonstrating *actual* confusion. However, although proof that the buying public was actually deceived is necessary in order to recover *statutory damages* under the Lanham Act, only a "likelihood of confusion" must be shown in order to obtain *equitable relief*, which is at issue in this appeal.

We have held that in determining whether there is a likelihood of confusion, the following eight factors should be considered: (1) strength of plaintiff's mark; (2) relatedness of the goods; (3) similarity of the marks; (4) evidence of actual confusion; (5) marketing of channels used; (6) degree of purchaser care; (7) defendant's intent in selecting the mark; and (8) likelihood of expansion in selecting the mark....

In light of these factors, we agree with the district court's conclusion that there was a likelihood of confusion....

continues

D'Amato contends that any proof of consumer confusion is rebutted by a disclaimer on his Web site, which stated, "This page is not associated with Audi GmbH or Audi USA in any way." First, such a disclaimer does not absolve D'Amato of liability for his unlawful use of marks identical to Audi's trademarks. In addition, as we stated in [another case]:

> An infringing domain name has the potential to misdirect consumers as they search for Web sites associated with the owner of a trademark. A disclaimer disavowing affiliation with the trademark owner read by a consumer after reaching the Web site comes too late. This "initial interest confusion" is recognized as an infringement under the Lanham Act.

Further, any effect this disclaimer had in reducing confusion would likely be negated by the statement on the Web site contending that there was a "signed agreement" with Audi.

D'Amato also defends his actions on the ground that his "Web site merely had hyperlinks to goods (hats and shirts)"… and that such "hyperlinks create no liability for [him]." However, even if D'Amato's intention was in fact noncommercial (which it does not appear to be), the issue is whether his actions had a commercial *effect*. We have stated that "the proper inquiry is not one of intent…. If consumers are confused by an infringing mark, the offender's motives are largely irrelevant." Even "minimal" advertisements constitute use of the owner's trademark in connection with the advertising of the goods, which the Lanham Act proscribes.…

Even when we construe the facts in a light most favorable to D'Amato, Audi has shown that there is a clear likelihood of confusion based on D'Amato's use of the Audi Trademarks.…

Dilution law, unlike traditional trademark infringement law … is not based on a likelihood of confusion standard, but only exists to protect the quasi-property rights a holder has in maintaining the integrity and distinctiveness of his mark. We use a five-point test to determine whether a plaintiff will succeed in a federal dilution claim. Audi must show that its trademark is (1) famous and (2) distinctive, and that D'Amato's use of the mark (3) was in commerce, (4) began after Audi's mark became famous, and (5) "caused dilution of the distinctive quality" of Audi's mark.

It is clear from the record that Audi's trademarks, on which Audi has spent millions of dollars and which are known worldwide, satisfy the first two factors. Further, because the Web site sold merchandise, e-mail subscriptions, and advertising space, all with Audi's logo,

the third factor is satisfied. The fourth factor is met, as there is no dispute that www.audisport.com came after the Audi trademarks. As for the fifth element—whether the junior mark dilutes the senior mark—the Supreme Court has noted that "direct evidence of dilution such as consumer surveys will not be necessary if actual dilution can reliably be proven through circumstantial evidence—the obvious case is one where the junior and senior marks are identical."…

The Anticybersquatting Consumer Protection Act (ACPA) was enacted to curb "the proliferation of cybersquatting—the Internet version of a land grab." With respect to a famous mark, ACPA provides that a person will be civilly liable when he or she has a bad faith intent to profit from the mark, and "registers, traffics in, or uses a domain name that … is identical or confusingly similar to or dilutive of that mark."

In order to prevail under the ACPA, a plaintiff must show that a defendant's use of a domain name was done in bad faith. ACPA provides a list of nine nonexclusive factors which a court should consider in determining whether a defendant acted in bad faith:

> (I) the trademark or other intellectual property rights of the person, if any, in the domain name;
>
> (II) the extent to which the domain name consists of the legal name of the person or a name that is otherwise commonly used to identify that person;
>
> (III) the person's prior use, if any, of the domain name in connection with the bona fide offering of any goods or services;
>
> (IV) the person's bona fide noncommercial or fair use of the mark in a site accessible under the domain name;
>
> (V) the person's intent to divert consumers from the mark owner's online location to a site accessible under the domain name that could harm the goodwill represented by the mark, either for commercial gain or with the intent to tarnish or disparage the mark, by creating a likelihood of confusion as to the source, sponsorship, affiliation, or endorsement of the site;
>
> (VI) the person's offer to transfer, sell, or otherwise assign the domain name to the mark owner or any third party for financial gain without having used, or having an intent to use, the domain name in the bona fide offering of any goods or services, or the person's prior conduct indicating a pattern of such conduct;
>
> (VII) the person's provision of material and misleading false contact information when applying for the registration of the domain name, the person's intentional failure to maintain accurate contact information, or the person's prior conduct indicating a pattern of such conduct;

(VIII) the person's registration or acquisition of multiple domain names which the person knows are identical or confusingly similar to marks of others that are distinctive at the time of registration of such domain names, or dilutive of famous marks of others that are famous at the time of registration of such domain names, without regard to the goods or services of the parties; and

(XI) the extent to which the mark incorporated in the person's domain name registration is or is not distinctive and famous....

We affirm the judgment of the district court.

Questions for Analysis

1. The court affirmed that D'Amato engaged in infringement, dilution, and cybersquatting with respect to Audi's marks. Since his Web site stated that he was not affiliated with Audi, why did that not protect him? How could Audi be harmed?
2. Why does the law focus on marks that are distinctive and famous?

Counterfeiting

Counterfeiting of trademarks means the copying or imitating of a mark without authority to do so. It usually means the passing off of goods as if they were original. Hence, marks owned by universities, Major League Baseball, and well-known companies such as Nike and Disney must be protected by their owners. Levi's has seized millions of pairs of counterfeit pants. Not only are profits lost to counterfeiters, but also, since counterfeit goods are usually low quality, consumers might think the trademarks do not represent quality, and the reputation of the owner can suffer.

Note that even if people are told that the counterfeit goods are counterfeit—so that no one is being fooled—the trademark has still been counterfeited. For example, Ferrari makes very expensive cars with distinctive body designs. Ferrari sued companies that made fiberglass imitations of its car bodies that could be placed on car frames. Even though everyone knew the bodies were not Ferrari, and there was a name other than Ferrari on the bodies, the distinctive design of Ferrari was held to be a trademark that could be protected against imitations.

Private Enforcement

The Lanham Act allows private parties to obtain search-and-seizure orders to grab counterfeit goods. Private investigators often do this for companies such as Rolex that have imitations sold on the market that damage the value of their trademark. The investigator provides a U.S. Attorney with evidence of the existence and location of the counterfeit goods. The U.S. Attorney may take action directly, but usually approves the private party going to a judge to obtain a warrant. The party shows up unannounced at the location of the goods with a police officer, searches the premises, and seizes any counterfeit goods. The goods may be used as evidence in a civil suit for damages, but often no suit is brought if the person with the goods cooperates in providing leads to their origins.

Trade Dress

A commercial symbol also protected by trademark law and the Lanham Act is *trade dress*, which has been given more attention in recent years, although it is often not registered. Trade dress concerns the "look and feel" of products and of service establishments. This includes the size, shape, color, texture, graphics, and even certain sales techniques of products. This has been applied to many products, such as teddy bears, luggage, greeting cards, romance novels, and folding tables.

Getty Images

ISSUE SPOTTER
Knock Off the Knock-Offs?

Your company makes high-dollar leather products, such as purses, briefcases, and carrying bags. The company has a well-known logo that is on all the products. Knock-off versions of the product are produced in China and sold by street vendors in the United States and in stores in other countries. At times, the imitation products end up in stores in the United States. What steps can you take to protect your trademark? Should you ignore it, since customers generally know the real thing from the knock-off?

The Supreme Court supported a trade dress claim in *Two Pesos* v. *Taco Cabana* (112 S. Ct. 2753). One Mexican-style restaurant could not copy its competitor's decor, which included distinctive exterior decorations and interior design. Trade dress that is "inherently distinctive" is protected under the Lanham Act and by common-law principles concerning unfair competition.

The Supreme Court further refined the standards for trade dress in *Wal-Mart Stores* v. *Samara Brothers* (120 S. Ct. 1339). The Court held that Wal-Mart had not infringed on Samara's designs of children's clothing when it had produced its own clothing with designs similar to those sold by Samara. To receive protection, trade dress must be distinctive and must have *secondary meaning*. That is, the primary significance of the mark or trade dress is to identify the source of the product, rather than the product itself. A design, such as children's clothing, is not inherently distinctive so as to earn protection under the Lanham Act, unless it is identifiable by consumers as to the source. Samara did not have that level of recognition.

Other Marks

The Lanham Act also recognizes service marks. These marks, denoted by *SM*, apply to services, such as Jiffy Lube, rather than to goods; but the law is the same as it is for trademarks. Service marks apply to services such as advertising, insurance, hotels, restaurants, and entertainment. For example, the International Silk Association uses the motto "Only silk is silk." That is a service mark. Burger King is a trademark. The phrase "Home of the Whopper" is a service mark that is owned by Burger King.

A *certification mark* is any word, symbol, device, or any combination of these that is used, or intended to be used, in commerce to certify regional or other geographic origin ("Made in Montana"). It may also signify the type of material used, mode of manufacture, quality, accuracy, or other characteristics of someone's goods or services, or that the work was performed by members of a union ("Union Made in the USA") or another organization.

A trademark or service mark that is used in commerce by members of a cooperative, an association, or other collective group or organization is a *collective mark*. This includes a mark that indicates membership in a union, an association, or other organization.

Trade Names

A *trade name* is the name of a company or a business. Some products, such as Coca-Cola, have the same trademark as the trade name of their producer. Trade names cannot be registered under the Lanham Act, but they are protected by the common law. About half of the states allow trade names to be registered, but the rule is that trade name protection belongs to the first to use the name in a given area of business. The general rule is that the first to use the name in a particular business in a geographic area has the ownership right to the name.

Protection applies to the areas in which the name has meaning; national protection of the name cannot be claimed unless there might be confusion. For example, because Coca-Cola operates and is known worldwide, no one may use the trade name in any business, such as by opening a Coca-Cola Motel. Even though Coca-Cola is not in the motel business, its name is protected in all uses. Because the name Coca-Cola has tremendous goodwill value, the company could license its use to motel operators. Usage of the good name of the company is thus prohibited without the company's permission. For example, Rollerblade, Inc., has been careful to protect its name from becoming the generic term for in-line skates.

LIGHTER SIDE OF THE LAW
Our Garbage Disposals Would Not Do That!

On the NBC television program *Heroes,* which dramatizes "ordinary people who discover they possess extraordinary abilities," an episode showed a cheerleader stick her hand into a running kitchen sink garbage disposal. The hand came out a mess, but was instantly healed.

An InSinkErator brand garbage disposal was used on the program. Its name was visible on the top ring of the disposal, if one watched very carefully. The maker, Emerson Electric, sued NBC for trademark infringement and dilution because the scene implied a "dangerous design for a food-waste disposer." NBC said there was no basis for the suit, but that it would edit out the name in rebroadcasts.

Getty Images

Goodwill

It is the reputation of a firm that gives value to trademarks and other such forms of intellectual property. This is a prized asset of many firms. The trademarks Coke and Coca-Cola are far more valuable assets than the real property owned by the Coca-Cola Company. When firms have created such value, and have gained the trust of many customers, it is called *goodwill*.

Goodwill is the benefit or advantage of having an established business and secured customers. When a business is sold, the real property assets, such as buildings and equipment, can be evaluated precisely, as they can be replicated in the market. However, the sale price must also take into account the value of the goodwill that a business has established. Two businesses may have identical physical operations, but perhaps only one has an excellent reputation and strong customer base; that is goodwill, and it is a major intangible asset. It is often closely tied to trademark or brand name. When a trademark or other form of intellectual property suffers an injury, damage estimates must include the loss of profits due to damage to the trade name, or goodwill, of the firm.

Copyright

Copyrights are rights of literary property as recognized by law. They are intangible assets that are held by the author or owner for a certain time period. More than 600,000 items are copyrighted each year. About half are books and other written works; the other half are musical compositions. Copyrights existed for many years at common law and were supplemented by federal statutes. Copyrights are easy to obtain and the legal protection is strong.

The Copyright Act of 1976 (amended several times since) created statutory protection for all copyrightable works. It protects an original expression automatically from the time it is fixed in a tangible medium of expression—printed, sung, used in a computer, or whatever form expression takes. The length of copyright protection depends on when the work was produced, as Congress has changed the terms of protection numerous times. Most copyrighted materials in the United States now have the same protection term: the life of the author plus 70 years, as is the case in the European Union. For works for hire, such as material written by employees of a company, the copyright is 95 years from the date of publication.

The Copyright Act gives a copyright owner five exclusive rights over copyrighted works:

1. The right to reproduce the work
2. The right to publish or distribute the work
3. The right to display the work in public
4. The right to perform the work in public
5. The right to prepare derivative works based on the original work

The 1990 amendment added what are called *moral rights*, which include the right of the author to have proper attribution of authorship and to prevent unauthorized changes in or destruction of an artist's work.

Copyrighted work must be original. You cannot copyright a 200-year-old song, because you did not create it; the song is in the public domain and may be used, performed, or reproduced by anyone. The Supreme Court noted that copyrighted works must be original in *Feist Publications* v. *Rural Telephone Service Co.* (111 S. Ct. 1282), in which one company copied the white-page telephone listings of another company. The Court ruled that there is nothing original in listing telephone user names, addresses, and phone numbers alphabetically; it is "devoid of even the slightest trace of creativity." Public facts not presented in an original manner cannot obtain copyright protection. There must be an original element in the work.

Registration

Copyright registration is simple (see http://www.copyright.gov). Fill out a registration form from the Copyright Office (a part of the Library of Congress) in Washington, D.C.; send two copies of the copyrighted work; and pay a $45 fee. The Copyright Office simply records the registration; it does not check to make sure that the material is in fact original or that all the information provided is accurate. That is, unlike patents, copyrights are not issued by the government; it is only a registration process effective the day receives it. Registration provides important evidence of copyright ownership in the event of an infringement suit, and it is required for federal court to have jurisdiction in copyright cases. A notice of copyright consists of the circle-C (©), the year of first publication, and the name of the copyright owner. Notice is not required but is encouraged by the Copyright Act, because it helps provide proof of ownership in case of a dispute.

Infringement and Fair Use

We have all made copies of copyrighted works without getting permission. Is that illegal infringement? Not if the copying is considered *fair use*. The Copyright Act allows use of original material "for purposes such as criticism, comment, news reporting, teaching, … scholarship, or research." If copying is not authorized or fair use, it is infringement. When considering whether a use is fair, the courts apply four factors:

1. The purpose and character of the copying (for commercial use or for nonprofit educational use)
2. The nature of the copyrighted work
3. The extent of the copying
4. The effect of the copying on the market for the work

In the 1984 Supreme Court case, *Sony* v. *Universal City Studios* (104 S. Ct. 774), the fact that VCR owners may copy copyrighted television programs for personal use was held to be covered by the fair-use exception. Sony, the maker of VCR players, could not be sued for infringement by VCR users. However, it is not proper for publishers to publish works in manners not anticipated by original contracts with authors. In *New York Times* v. *Tasini* (121 S. Ct. 2381) the Supreme Court held that it was copyright infringement for electronic databases, such as Lexis/Nexis, to publish previously published stories online if the print versions bore copyrights. Since the authors had agreed to paper publication, "reprinting" in electronic media without permission of the authors was infringement.

While most of copyright law is quite clear, the area that remains to be settled, and which now generates a lot of litigation, is file sharing via the Internet. Napster was shut down for supporting copyright infringements by providing the service that allowed copyrighted songs to be shared without paying royalties. People immediately began to search for alternative methods of file sharing. The Supreme Court considered some similar issues in the *Grokster* case.

Metro-Goldwyn-Mayer Studios v. Grokster
Supreme Court of the United States
125 S.Ct. 2764 545 U.S.913 (2005)

Case Background *Grokster and StreamCast provided software to allow computer users to share electronic files through peer-to-peer networks that communicate directly with each other, rather than through central servers, as in the case of Napster. Users shared music and video files, including those owned by copyright holders, including MGM. They sued for copyright infringement, contending that Grokster knowingly and intentionally distributed software to enable users to infringe copyrighted works in violation of the Copyright Act. Grokster did not directly copy works but made it possible for others to violate copyrights. The district court and appeals court held for Grokster, ruling that distributing the software did not make Grokster liable for infringement committed by use of the software. MGM and other copyright owners appealed.*

Case Decision Souter, Justice

* * *

MGM and [others] fault the Court of Appeals's holding for upsetting a sound balance between the respective values of supporting creative pursuits through copyright protection and promoting innovation in new communication technologies by limiting the incidence of liability for copyright infringement. The more artistic protection is favored, the more technological innovation may be discouraged; the administration of copyright law is an exercise in managing the trade-off.

The tension between the two values is the subject of this case, with its claim that digital distribution of copyrighted material threatens copyright holders as never before; because every copy is identical to the original, copying is easy, and many people (especially the young) use file-sharing software to download copyrighted works….

continues

The argument for imposing indirect liability in this case is, however, a powerful one, given the number of infringing downloads that occur every day using StreamCast's and Grokster's software. When a widely shared service or product is used to commit infringement, it may be impossible to enforce rights in the protected work effectively against all direct infringers, the only practical alternative being to go against the distributor of the copying device for secondary liability on a theory of contributory or vicarious infringement.

One infringes contributorily by intentionally inducing or encouraging direct infringement, and infringes vicariously by profiting from direct infringement while declining to exercise a right to stop or limit it. Although "the Copyright Act does not expressly render anyone liable for infringement committed by another," these doctrines of secondary liability emerged from common-law principles and are well established in the law …

We … hold that one who distributes a device with the object of promoting its use to infringe copyright, as shown by clear expression or other affirmative steps taken to foster infringement, is liable for the resulting acts of infringement by third parties.… Mere knowledge of infringing potential or of actual infringing uses would not be enough here to subject a distributor to liability. Nor would ordinary acts incident to product distribution, such as offering customers technical support or product updates, support liability in themselves. The inducement rule, instead, premises liability on purposeful, culpable expression and conduct, and thus does nothing to compromise legitimate commerce or discourage innovation having a lawful promise.…

Both companies communicated a clear message by responding affirmatively to requests for help in locating and playing copyrighted materials.…

Here, the … record is replete with other evidence that Grokster and StreamCast … acted with a purpose to cause copyright violations by use of software suitable for illegal use.…

In addition to intent to bring about infringement and distribution of a device suitable for infringing use, the inducement theory of course requires evidence of actual infringement by recipients of the device, the software in this case. As the account of the facts indicates, there is evidence of infringement on a gigantic scale, and there is no serious issue of the adequacy of MGM's showing on this point in order to survive the companies' summary judgment requests. Although an exact calculation of infringing use, as a basis for a claim of damages is subject to dispute, there is no question that the summary judgment evidence is at least adequate to entitle MGM to go forward with claims for damages and equitable relief.…

There is substantial evidence in MGM's favor on all elements of inducement, and summary judgment in favor of Grokster and StreamCast was error. On remand, reconsideration of MGM's motion for summary judgment will be in order.

The judgment of the Court of Appeals is vacated, and the case is remanded for further proceedings consistent with this opinion.

Questions for Analysis

1. The Supreme Court held Grokster liable for enabling copyright infringement in violation of the Copyright Act. What damages could it pay for millions of files that it enabled to be copied?
2. Under this rule, why is it not illegal to write any software that enables copying of files that are copyright protected?

ISSUE SPOTTER
Fair Sharing of Information?

Your company makes electrical components for jet engines. The engineers who do the designing subscribe to a number of electrical engineering journals. The subscriptions are quite expensive, so they order one subscription of each journal and make copies of articles to give to all the engineers who might be interested. Is this copying fair use, since it is for educational purposes, or could it be copyright infringement that could lead to trouble? How should this practice be handled?

Getty Images

Patents

A *patent* is a grant from the government to an inventor for "the right to exclude others from making, using, offering for sale, or selling" the invention for twenty years after the inventor files a patent application. Unlike other forms of intellectual property that have common-law roots, patents are purely statute based. According to patent law, a person who "invents or discovers any new and useful process, machine, manufacture, or composition of matter, or any new and useful improvement thereof, may obtain a patent." A *process* generally means an industrial or technical process, act, or method. *Manufacture* refers to articles that are made by manufacturing, and *composition of matter* relates to chemical compositions and other mixtures of ingredients. For something to be *useful* means the invention must have a use and be operative, not just be a theory. Most patents are *utility patents*, the kind just described, but there are also design patents for original and ornamental designs for manufactured articles and plant patents for new varieties of plants.

Key conditions for an invention to be patented are originality and novelty. The statute states that an invention cannot be patented if "(a) the invention was known or used by others in this country, or patented or described in a printed publication in this or a foreign country, before the invention thereof by the applicant for patent," or "(b) the invention was patented or described in a printed publication in this or a foreign country or in public use of no sale in the country more than one year prior to the application for patent in the United States." That means that even if the inventor is the first to describe the invention or to show it in public, if a patent application is not filed within one year of publication, the right to a patent is lost.

A major advantage of patents is the strong protection provided. For the life of the patent, its owner has the right to exclude all others from making or using the patented invention. For example, Polaroid won a billion-dollar judgment against Kodak for infringement on its instant camera and film patents. However, the patent process has drawbacks. The application process is technical, expensive, and time-consuming. The approval process usually takes about two years, and about half of all patent applications are approved.

LIGHTER SIDE OF THE LAW
Why Many Patents Are Overturned When Challenged

The Patent Office awarded patent number 6,368,227: Method of swinging on a swing. Here is the abstract from the PTO Web site: "A method of swinging on a swing is disclosed, in which a user positioned on a standard swing suspended by two chains from a substantially horizontal tree branch induces side to side motion by pulling alternately on one chain and then the other".

This was awarded to Steve Olson, age 7, who reportedly excelled at swinging on a swing.

Source: U.S. Patent and Trademark Office

Getty Images

Eighteen months after a patent application is made that contains all the details, it is made public. That means competitors can gain a lot of valuable information even before a patent is issued. As a result, inventors prefer to use trade secrets for some innovations. More than 100 years ago, the Coca-Cola company decided to keep the formula for Coke a secret. Had it obtained a patent instead, the formula could have been used by anyone after about 1907. Some firms use a combination of trade secrets and patents to protect their innovations.

The Federal Circuit Court of Appeals has primary responsibility for reviewing patent cases. Patents may be stricken when challenged if the court determines that the patent office did not apply the proper standards when issuing a patent. If the court upholds a patent that is challenged, then the patent holder has a good chance of recovering damages from a party accused of infringing on the patent. In the *Nystrom* case, the court discusses the kind of issues that must be considered when reviewing patent validity.

Nystrom v. Trex Company
United States Court of Appeals, Federal Circuit
374 F.3d 1105 (2004)

Case Background *Nystrom runs a two-truck, two-man lumber yard. He received patent number 5,474,831 (the '831 patent). It is for "A board for use in constructing a flooring surface for exterior use [such as a deck] … manufactured to have a … convex top surface which sheds water and at the same time is comfortable to walk on.…" Nystrom sued Trex for infringing the '831 patent. Trex is a large manufacturer of exterior decking planks made from composites of wood fibers and recycled plastic. A key part of their defense was that their planks are not cut from logs. The district court held key parts of the patent invalid and dismissed Nystrom's claim. He appealed.*

Case Decision Linn, Circuit Judge

* * *

The district court construed the world "board" in independent claim 1 to mean a "piece of elongated construction material made from wood cut from a log."…

Nystrom argues that "board" in claim 1 is not limited to conventional wood boards that are cut from a log. He argues that the claim language "board" does not contain a description of the material from which the board is composed and the claim should not be so limited.…

Trex responds that the ordinary meaning of "board" is a piece of sawn lumber.…

In construing claims, the analytical focus must begin and remain centered on the language of the claims themselves.… The ordinary and customary meaning may be determined by reviewing a variety of sources, including the claims themselves; dictionaries and treatises; and the written descriptions, drawings, and prosecution history.…

While some dictionaries define "board" solely in reference to its material composition, not all dictionaries are so constrained.…

An examination of the written description and other claims of the '831 patent reveals that Nystrom did not disclaim boards made from materials other than logs. Indeed, in the written description, Nystrom described the invention as "a decking board".… This is consistent with the ordinary and customary meaning and supports a broader construction than that adopted by the district court.…

In light of our prior construction of "board" as encompassing materials made not only from wood but from other rigid materials as well, we find no reason to limit the phrase "manufacturer to have" in claim 1 to woodworking techniques.… As used in the claim [it] means that the convex top surface is shaped by manufacturing. This claim means exactly what it says, and the district court erred in limiting it to the manufacturing steps used to shape wood.…

In light of the foregoing … construction of the claim terms … the district court's grant of summary judgement of noninfringement cannot stand and is here by reversed.

Questions for Analysis
1. The appeals court upheld the patent as valid. What is the rationale for requiring that all the details of a patent be revealed to the public?
2. Should the court take into account the commercial success of a patented product when considering a challenge to a patent?

Getty Images

INTERNATIONAL PERSPECTIVE

Patent Differences

The World Intellectual Property Organization (WIPO) encourages intellectual property (IP) protection around the world and has encouraged IP laws to become more alike to avoid duplication costs and create consistency in standards. Important differences still remain.

In Europe, unlike the United States, patents may not be obtained for surgery or therapy methods, or for new plants or animal varieties, and there are more patent restrictions on software than in the United States.

In the United States an inventor may disclose an invention to the public up to one year prior to filing for a patent, while in Europe there may be no disclosure prior to filing.

A co-owner of a United States patent has the right, unless otherwise agreed, to exploit the patent fully, including licensing it. In Japan, all co-owners of a patent must agree to how it will be exploited. In Europe, the law varies from country to country.

In Japan, unlike in Europe and the United States, employees who create patentable inventions on the job must receive compensation by employers according to the value of the patent. In one case such compensation was $180 million, so choosing where to do research involves important patent law considerations.

Despite the move to patent laws that are more alike, and the Patent Cooperation Treaty, valuable products are still patented in dozens of countries at once, costing hundreds of thousands of dollars.

Trade Secrets

Coca-Cola has kept a valuable secret—the formula for Coke—for more than 100 years. Businesses have many *trade secrets*, and tort law Protects such information. The *Restatement(2d) of Torts* defines such information as follows: "A trade secret may consist of any formula, pattern, device, or compilation of information which is used in one's business, and which gives him an opportunity to obtain an advantage over competitors who do not know or use it." Information such as the Coke formula could have been patented. Other proprietary information, such as computer software, could be copyrighted, but firms may prefer to keep the information secret. Some information may not be eligible for patent or copyright protection but is still a valuable secret.

Information is a trade secret if

1. it is not known by the competition.
2. the business would lose its advantage if the competition were to obtain it.
3. the owner has taken reasonable steps to protect the secret from disclosure.

If the owner of a trade secret has taken reasonable steps to protect secret information, and it is stolen by a competitor—either by the abuse of confidence of an employee or by trespass, electronic surveillance, or bribery—the courts can provide relief to the injured business in the form of damages and an injunction against further use of the secret.

Generally, businesses with trade secrets protect themselves by having employees agree in their employment contracts not to divulge those secrets. The classic example of a theft of a trade secret involves an employee who steals a secret and then uses it in direct competition with the former employer or sells it to a competitor for personal gain.

That is what is claimed to have happened in the *Hicklin* case, in which the court discusses what belongs to the employee and what belongs to the employer.

Hicklin Engineering v. R.J. Bartell
United States Court of Appeals, Seventh Circuit
439 F.3d 346 (2006)

Case Background *For seven years, Bartell worked as an independent contractor for Axi-Line Precision, a division of Hicklin that designs and makes testing equipment for vehicle transmissions. Bartell quit working for Axi-Line and formed a competing business that sells transmission testing equipment. Hicklin sued for violation of Wisconsin's Uniform Trade Secrets Act. The judge held for Bartell. Hicklin appealed.*

Case Decision Easterbrook, Circuit Judge

* * *

Bartell did not promise to avoid future competition with Axi-Line. Nor did he promise in writing not to use his drawings and ideas for any other entity. The district court concluded that this means that Bartell may do as he pleases with any information that Axi-Line furnished him, plus whatever he developed on his own.... As an independent contractor, Bartell presumptively owned his work product. He was free to sell engineering solutions to Axi-Line on either an exclusive or a nonexclusive basis, just as lawyers may sell their legal solutions to clients on an exclusive or nonexclusive basis. In the absence of an agreement, nonexclusivity is the norm.

Thus a lawyer who develops a new form contract, securities indenture, or tax shelter when working for Client X may reuse the language when dealing with Client Y, or may publish the language in a treatise for all to see and emulate, unless he has promised X to keep silent. A software programmer, working as an independent contractor for Client Z, who develops a novel way to organize a database, may reuse the source code for another client's project, unless he promises otherwise. Norms of the trade might reverse this presumption, but Hicklin has not proffered any evidence that a mechanical engineer's human capital or knowledge, built up when working for a client, belong to that client rather than the engineer.

Things are otherwise when the client rather than the independent contractor develops the information. Then the client presumptively owns the data, and the contractor may use it only with the client's consent....

The law of trade secrets follows the same approach to ownership, both in general and in Wisconsin. So Bartell did not acquire any rights in Axi-Line's trade-secret data just because he used those data in the performance of his duties.

Would the record permit a reasonable jury to find that Bartell knew that Axi-Line treated at least some of the data it provided as trade secrets? It would. The information's nature—dimensions, materials, and tolerances on the parts used to make dynamometers and other equipment—is one reason. Many of these details (especially materials and tolerances) would be hard to obtain by reverse engineering. Axi-Line's safeguards, of which Bartell knew, are another reason. The firm took standard precautions, such as perimeter fences, excluding unescorted visitors, and keeping data under lock and key. Bartell himself suggested to Axi-Line that certain plans (which Bartell had converted from hand-drawn blueprints to computer-assisted-design models) bear confidentiality legends, and Axi-Line told Bartell to include appropriate legends in his CAD models. Even bearing the legend, these detailed models (and printouts made from them) were not shown to customers or competitors.

From Bartell's knowledge, and the norm that a client's information remains its property after an independent contractor has worked with the data, a reasonable jury could infer that Bartell implicitly agreed to use the data for Axi-Line's benefit rather than his own. Wisconsin does not require an express, written contract of confidentiality.... And breach of an implicit promise to hold information for the client's sole benefit in turn violates the Trade Secrets Act....

On remand the parties and trier of fact will need to separate Axi-Line's contributions (which Hicklin owns) from Bartell's (which he owns), determine which of Axi-Line's data are trade secrets, ascertain whether Bartell recognized that these data are confidential, pin down the use that Bartell made of those trade secrets, and if necessary decide whether Wisconsin law permits such a use. If Hicklin prevails on these issues, the district court will have to select an appropriate remedy....

The judgment is vacated and the case is remanded for proceedings consistent with this opinion.

Questions for Analysis

1. The appeals court held that Bartell could be found to have taken trade secrets from Hicklin, if any of Hicklin's trade-secrets are found in Bartell's products. Why did Hicklin not have Bartell sign a trade secret agreement? Would that have mattered?

2. If Bartell did all of the engineering work for Hicklin, then could he still be liable for theft of trade secret?

ISSUE SPOTTER
Protecting Valuable Information

At many companies, employees carry valuable information in their heads. At a sales-based organization, sales representatives know many of the clients and their volume of purchases of various products. If the representatives leave to go to work for a competitor, that information, which can be a trade secret, is carried out the door with them. If you are a manager in such a company, what steps can you take to try to prevent the exploitation of such information when the sales representatives leave?

Getty Images

Economic Espionage

While trade secrets are based on common law and generally enforced by tort litigation claiming misappropriation or other violations of a trade secret or secrecy agreement, in some cases the government will intervene. The trade Economic Espionage Act of 1996 contains a provision concerning theft of commercial trade secrets: "Whoever, with intent to convert a trade secret that is related to or included in a product that is produced for or placed in interstate or foreign commerce to the economic benefit of anyone other than the owner thereof, and intending or knowing that the offense will injure any owner of that trade secret" is subject to prosecution. Punishment for an individual can be as high as ten years in prison, and fines up to $5 million may be levied against firms.

The *Yang* case illustrates the application of this statute. Note that the case also helps us understand what is involved in a criminal conspiracy.

U.S. v. Yang
United States Court of Appeals, Sixth Circuit
281 F.3d 534 (2002)

Case Background *Lee, a native of Taiwan, worked in research for Avery, an adhesives manufacturer. When Lee was visiting Taiwan, he was approached by Yang and his daughter about providing information to their Taiwanese adhesives company. Lee agreed and was paid $25,000 per year for confidential information from Avery about new products. When the arrangement was uncovered, the FBI con-* *fronted Lee, who agreed to participate in a sting operation to help arrest and prosecute Yang. When the Yangs visited the United States, Lee met with them and discussed confidential information. The meeting was filmed. The Yangs were arrested, convicted, and fined $5 million. They appealed, contending the materials used in the sting operation were not actual trade secrets, so they could not have violated the law.*

continues

Case Decision Batchelder, Circuit Judge

* * *

[The Economic Espionage Act] provides:

(a) Whoever, with intent to convert a trade secret that is related to or included in a product that is produced for or placed in interstate or foreign commerce, to the economic benefit of anyone other than the owner thereof, and intending or knowing that the offense will injure any owner of that trade secret, knowingly

[steals, copies, buys such information, or conspires with others to do so, may be fined up to $5 million and imprisoned for up to 10 years]....

Because [under the Model Penal Code] the defendant's guilt turns on the "circumstances as he believes them to be," the court held that the government was not required to prove that what the defendant sought to steal was in fact a trade secret, but only that the defendant believed it to be one....

The Yangs' conspiracy to steal the trade secrets in violation of [The Economic Espionage Act] was completed when, with the intent to steal the trade secrets, they agreed to meet with Lee in the hotel room and they took an overt act towards the completion of the crime, that is, when the Yangs went to the hotel room. The fact that the information they conspired to obtain was not what they believed it to be does not matter, because the objective of the Yangs' agreement was to steal trade secrets, and they took an overt step toward achieving that objective. Conspiracy is nothing more than the parties to the conspiracy coming to a "mutual understanding to try to accomplish a common and unlawful plan," where at least one of the conspirators knowingly commits an overt act in pursuit of the conspiracy's objective. It is the mutual understanding or agreement itself that is criminal, and whether the object of the scheme actually is as the parties believe it to be, unlawful is irrelevant....

We affirm the judgments of conviction.

Questions for Analysis

1. The appeals court held that the Yangs conspired to buy information they believed to be trade secrets, which is a criminal offense. How could Avery prove the information involved was secret?
2. Do you think the fine, with no prison time, is sufficient to discourage such activity?

Summary

- Intellectual property is usually intangible property, which is legally protected property created mostly by mental effort. The scope of interests in intellectual property is determined by a mix of common law and statutory law that restricts infringement by others.
- Trademarks are designs, logos, distinctive marks, or words that manufacturers put on their goods for identification by consumers. At common law, the first producer to use a mark in a given area establishes priority of use. Under the Lanham Act, marks may be registered with the Patent and Trademark Office. Rights to a mark continue for as long as the mark is used and protected.
- The strongest trademarks are arbitrary and fanciful, which includes made-up words or real words applied to a product not related to the word as commonly used. Suggestive marks that hint at the kind of product are also provided strong protection. Less protection is available for descriptive marks, where the mark implies the good. Generic marks are words that were once protected trademarks but were lost as a result of lack of protection and common usage.
- Trade dress is trademark law applied to the look and feel of a product, such as a distinctive color or design. Service marks are the same as trademarks but apply to services instead of goods. Trade names are business names and are protected in the market in which the business is recognized.
- Goods that are sold pretending to be genuine trademarked goods are counterfeits and are illegal. It is also a violation of trademark law to infringe on a mark by using it improperly or by using a version of the mark that is so close to the

original that it could cause confusion in the market. Infringement usually is attacked for drawing sales away from the original mark holder. Similarly, dilution of marks is prohibited. Rules against dilution protect the integrity and distinctiveness of the mark by prohibiting their use in unrelated markets without permission.

- Copyrights allow exclusive control over original written works, musical compositions, art, and photography. Control extends to reproduction, publication, displays, performances, or derived works. While copyright exists at common law, registration under the Copyright Act provides clear evidence of ownership and is good for 70 years plus the life of the creator.

- While copyright ownership is based on the common law, the Copyright Act specifies a fair use defense to avoid a charge of infringement. The factors the courts consider in ruling on fair use include: 1) the purpose and character of the copying; 2) the nature of the copyrighted work; 3) the extent of the copying; and 4) the effect of copying on the market for the original work.

- Patents are exclusive statutory grants to protect an invention, design, or process that is genuine, useful, novel, and not obvious. Protection runs for 20 years from the time of patent application, which reveals to the public all details about the innovation.

- Trade secrets are formulas, patterns, devices, or compilations of information used in business that give an economic advantage over competitors who do not have the information. They are protected by tort law from theft. Trade secret owners must take reasonable steps to protect the information from disclosure, including obtaining employee agreements not to reveal the information.

- The Economic Espionage Act makes it a federal criminal offense to steal a trade secret and give it or sell it to another in commerce for economic benefit.

Terms to Know

You should be able to define the following terms:

goodwill, 200	counterfeiting, 207	fair use, 210
intellectual property, 200	trade dress, 207	patent, 213
intangible property, 200	secondary meaning, 208	utility patent, 213
infringement, 200	certification mark, 208	trade secrets, 215
trademark, 201	collective mark, 208	economic espionage, 217
Lanham Act, 201	trade name, 208	
dilution, 204	copyrights, 209	

Discussion Question

1. Garden Company sells wheelbarrows under the name Garden Wheelbarrow. Its sales are not doing well around the country. In an effort to achieve greater standing in the industry, Garden claims the trademark "Wheelbarrow's Wheelbarrows" for its wheelbarrows. If no one else has used that mark before, can Garden claim it?

Case Questions

1. U.S. Search, LLC sued U.S. Search.com, Inc. claiming infringement of its trademark. U.S. Search, LLC claimed first use of U.S. Search. It had not registered the mark, but filed a request with the Trademark Office for registration and also sued, demanding that U.S. Search.com, Inc. not be allowed to have continued use of its registered mark 1-800-US Search. The Trademark Office would not register the mark and the district court held

against U.S. Search, LLC, so it appealed. Does it have a good case against U.S. Search.com and 1-800-US Search? [*U.S. Search, LCC v. U.S.Search.Com Inc.*, 300 F.3d 517 4th Cir. (2002)]

2. Kassbaum, professionally known as Nick St. Nicholas, was a member of the rock band Steppenwolf from 1968 to 1971. He filed a complaint in federal court seeking a declaration that he is not barred from referring to himself as "a former member of Steppenwolf." At the request of Steppenwolf Productions, the district court dismissed his complaint. Kassbaum appealed. Can he refer to himself in that manner? [*Kassbaum v. Steppenwolf Productions*, 236 F.3d 487 9th Cir. (2000)]

3. Beacon Mutual Insurance Company sold insurance in Rhode Island under its name and also under the marks Beacon Insurance and The Beacon. It uses a lighthouse logo. A competitor changed its name to OneBeacon Insurance Group and used a lighthouse logo. Beacon sued OneBeacon for infringement. What claims could it make, and do you think will prevail? [*Beacon Mutual Ins. v. OneBeacon Ins.*, 376 F.3d 8 1st Cir. (2004)]

✓ Check your answer at http://academic.cengage.com/blaw/meiners

4. GSI is a steel fabricator—a contractor that makes steel components for construction projects. Scott Marshall worked for GSI as an estimator—he determined how much GSI could bid on a project and still earn a profit. Scott asked his brother, Alan, to write a program to help him with estimates. Alan did and was not paid for his work. Scott used the program while he worked at GSI. When Scott left GSI, he and Alan tried to market a new version of the program to sell to project estimators. GSI sued, contending that the key elements of the bid estimation process in the program were stolen from GSI by Scott and were a trade secret. The trial court enjoined the brothers from marketing the program; they appealed. Who owns the program? [*Marshall v. Gipson Steel*, 806 So.2d 266 Sup. Ct., Miss. (2002)]

5. Origins Natural Resources owns the trademark Origins. It has been used on a few clothing items over the years, but is primarily used on a successful line of cosmetics that are sold nationally. Origins filed for an injunction barring Kotler from using the trademark Natural Origins on a line of upscale women's clothing, contending that it was infringement and diluted the value of the Origins trademark. Should Origins receive the injunction? [*Origins Natural Resources Inc. v. Kotler*, 2001 WL 492429 S.D. NY (2001)]

✓ Check your answer at http://academic.cengage.com/blaw/meiners

6. Bouchat is an amateur artist. When he heard that Baltimore was to obtain a football team, the Ravens, he designed a possible logo for the team and faxed his design to the team. Soon after, the Ravens unveiled their logo, a raven holding a shield, which Bouchat believed was his design. He contacted a lawyer, who obtained copyright registration for Bouchat's design and then sued the Ravens for infringement. The jury found that the shield design was Bouchat's. The trial judge refused to overturn the verdict. Does the verdict stand? [*Bouchat v. Baltimore Ravens*, 241 F.3d 350 (4th Cir. (2001)]

7. Hormel is the maker of SPAM luncheon meat, trademarked since 1937. SPAM is a distinctive, widely recognized name. Over $5 billion worth of SPAM has been sold over the years. Hormel sued Jim Henson Productions for trademark infringement for using a Muppet character "Spa'am" in its *Muppet Treasure Island* movie. "Spa'am is the high priest of a tribe of wild boars that worships Miss Piggy as its Queen Sha Ka La Ka La.… Henson hopes to poke a little fun at Hormel's famous luncheon meat by associating its processed, gelatinous block with a humorously wild beast." The district court denied Hormel's request for an injunction against the name Spa'am. Did Hormel win on appeal? [*Hormel Foods v. Jim Henson Productions*, 73 F.3d 497 Cir. (1996)]

✓ Check your answer at http://academic.cengage.com/blaw/meiners

8. Scientists employed by Texaco routinely photocopied articles in scientific journals to enhance their knowledge in their areas of specialization. Publishers of the journals sued Texaco, claiming that such copying infringes their copyrights. Texaco defended by saying that this was fair use. Who wins? [*American Geophysical Union v. Texaco*, 37 F.3d 881, 2d Cir. (1994), order amended and superseded 60 F.3d 913, 2d Cir. (1994)]

9. Qualitex makes press pads used in dry cleaning and laundry establishments. It is well known in the industry and always made its products in a special shade of green gold. A competitor, Jacobson, began to use a similar shade on its own press pads. Qualitex registered its color as a trademark and sued Jacobson for trademark infringement for using the same color in its products. Does Qualitex have a good claim? [*Qualitex* v. *Jacobson Products*, 115 S. Ct. 1300 (1995)]

✓ **Check your answer at http://academic.cengage.com/blaw/meiners**

10. An American company imported video game cartridges from China that were pirated from the copyrighted originals made by Nintendo. The counterfeit copies also were sold with the Nintendo name on them. What laws have been violated, and what are the damages? [*Nintendo of America* v. *Dragon Pacific*, 40 F.3d 1007 9th Cir. (1994)]

11. United States Gypsum developed a new putty to use on walls and ceilings to cover cracks. A key ingredient in the compound was a silicon product made by another company. The patent application did not list that as an ingredient in the putty. A competitor started to make and sell the same putty and the two companies ended up in court. Could USG win for patent infringement? [*United States Gypsum* v. *National Gypsum*, 74 F.3d 1209 Fed. Cir. (1996)]

12. Defendant flew his plane over a chemical plant being built by duPont and took numerous photos of the construction. Although the plant was guarded on the ground from outsiders, it was not guarded from aerial inspection. The photographs revealed a lot about secret processes. Defendant said that if duPont cared, it would have covered the construction site. Does duPont have a legitimate trade secret action against the photographer? [*E. I. duPont deNemours* v. *Christopher*, 431 F.2d 1012 5th Cir. (1970)]

Ethics Question

1. Poor countries assert that patented drugs are too expensive for most of their people to afford. The issue became especially noteworthy over drugs for AIDS sufferers in Africa. Monthly drug expenses are above average total income levels. Countries have been changing their drug laws to eliminate patent rights in certain cases. Do drug companies have an ethical duty to sell their products for the lowest possible price? Should countries abolish patent protection for drugs?

Internet Assignment

http://www.uspto.gov
http://www.loc.gov

The United States Patent and Trademark Office administers the laws relating to patents and trademarks and advises the Secretary of Commerce, the President, and the Administration on patent, trademark, and copyright protection, as well as trade-related aspects of intellectual property. It provides searchable databases for patents and trademarks.

1. What is the trademark (word mark) associated with registration number 78046114? Who applied for it?
2. What is the phone number for the Patent and Trademark Depository Library in Austin, Texas?
3. What is the field code for primary examiner in the Patent Full Text and Image Database?
   The Library of Congress, among its many services, hosts the Copyright Office. This Office has publications, application forms for copyright registration, links to copyright law, and an online catalog of copyright records going back to 1978.
4. According to the Copyright Office at the Library of Congress, what are the two principle international copyright conventions?

Contracts

Chapter 10

A customer sends an inquiry by e-mail to your electronics distribution company. The customer asks if there is a quantity discount for ordering more than 10 flat-screen, 50-inch Samsung plasma HD television sets. The customer service representative responds that yes, there is a 5 percent discount off the list price of $149.99 per television for orders of 10 or more. The customer immediately responds by e-mail: "Great, I will take 10 of the 50-inch, flat-screen Samsung LCD televisions at $149.99 each, less the 5 percent discount." The customer gives a credit card number and also offers to send a check. The sales rep who receives this response notices that the previous rep accidentally typed $149.99 instead of the correct price of $1,499.99 per television. The second rep sends a message to the customer apologizing for the mistake and notes the correct price, offering it with a 5 percent discount. The customer demands the televisions at $149.99, less 5 percent, noting that the sets were offered to him at that price in writing, and he accepted that price in writing. "We have a contract," he says. Is there a contract? Do questions and responses by e-mail count as "writing"? Does your company have to absorb the loss? Can you tell the customer there was no contract, or must you offer an alternative special deal?

Pricing mistakes are only one issue that can arise in the daily business of making contracts with customers and suppliers. Whether it is buying gas at the pump with a credit card, a meal at a drive-through window, or a tuxedo that needs alterations, the transactions are all contracts.

The *law of contracts* evolved in commerce over the centuries. There are specific rules that involve the creation of a contract. The *freedom of contract*, which is a hallmark of the law, means that there are also responsibilities imposed on parties who commit to binding relationships. Here we study the key elements of the creation of contracts and the rights and duties that accompany common-law contracts. ■

Getty Images

Contract Law

Contract law is primarily state common law. It has developed through decades of judicial opinions that have resolved virtually every kind of contract dispute. When English courts began to resolve contract disputes in the early 1800s, they made express reference to the law merchant (*lex mercatoria*), which were commercial rules that merchants devised over centuries of doing business across national boundaries. Hence, contract law reflects real business experience. Today, the *Restatement (2d) of Contracts* is an authoritative document that provides a summary of the common law of contract.

Contract law that comes from the courts is modified by various statutes. Of particular importance is Article 2 of the *Uniform Commercial Code (UCC)*, a statute adopted by the states that applies to sales of goods. The UCC was designed to promote uniformity of the laws relating to commercial sales of goods. The next chapter studies the role of that law.

Definition of a Contract

Sir William Blackstone, a famous English jurist, defined a *contract* as "an agreement, upon sufficient consideration, to do or not to do a particular thing." Modern definitions center on a *promise*, the element common to all contracts. Section I of the *Restatement (2d) of Contracts* defines a contract as "a promise or a set of promises for the breach of which the law gives a remedy, or the performance of which the law in some way recognizes as a duty." It defines a promise as "a manifestation of the intention [of a party] to act or refrain from acting in a specified manner."

A contract, then, is the legal relationship that consists of the rights and duties of the agreeing parties growing out of promises. Contract law governs the enforceability of that relationship.

Not all promises are enforceable contracts. A promise may be binding (contractual) or nonbinding (noncontractual). For a promise to be binding and enforceable, it must meet the essential requirements of a contract. If a party fails to perform a nonbinding promise, contract law will not provide a remedy. This makes clear the need to meet the requirements of a contract when parties want their exchange of promises to be legally binding.

Contracts may be created by formal writing or oral discussions, or they may be inferred by the actions of the parties. A contract is an *express contract* if there is a written or oral expression of intent by the parties to enter into a legally binding agreement. A contract is an *implied contract* if it arises from the actions rather than the expressions of the parties. That is, given the way the parties have acted with respect to each other, the court infers that a contract exists. The essence of a contract is illustrated in Exhibit 10.1, regardless of whether the contract is express or implied.

Elements of a Contract

A contract gives parties confidence that bargained-for exchanges will be enforceable. This section discusses the basic elements necessary for a bargain to form a valid contract. While many contracts consist of standardized forms, the basic elements of a contract are constant: agreement, consideration, legal capacity to contract, lawful subject matter, and genuine consent to the contract (see Exhibit 10.2). In addition, compliance with the Statute of Frauds may be necessary.

Exhibit 10.1
Essence of a Contract

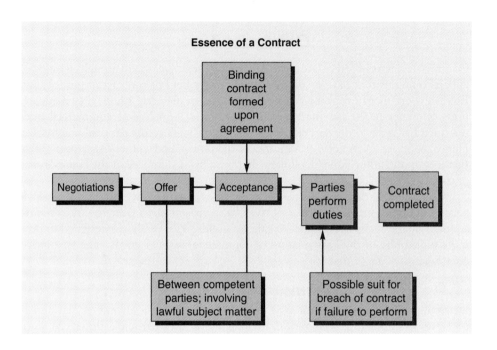

Exhibit 10.1
Essence of a Contract

Offer and Acceptance

The essence of a contract is a legally binding agreement, that is, a mutual understanding between the parties as to the substance of the contract. This agreement between the parties is reached through a process of *offer* and *acceptance*.

The Offer

An *offer* is a promise to do something or to refrain from doing some specific thing. As defined in the *Restatement (2d) of Contracts*, "An offer is the manifestation of willingness to enter into a bargain, so made as to justify another person in understanding that his assent to that bargain is invited and will conclude it." The party making an offer is called the *offeror* or *offerer*; the *offeree* is the party to whom the offer is made.

You offer to obligate yourself through a contract. Since the offeror is allowing the offeree the opportunity to create a binding promise by making a valid acceptance of the offer, the offeror controls the terms of the offer. To be an effective offer, three requirements must be met:

1. There must be a clear intent by the offeror to become contractually bound.
2. The basic terms and conditions of the offer must be clear and certain.
3. The offer must be properly communicated.

Exhibit 10.2
Key Elements of a Contract

A.	Offer and Acceptance: An Agreement
B.	Consideration
C.	Contractual Capacity
D.	Legality
E.	Genuine Consent

Manifestation of Intent To make an offer, the offeror must have the intent to be bound to the contract, and that intent must be clearly expressed or manifested. *Preliminary negotiations* are not offers but are invitations to negotiate or to make an offer. Dickering with a salesperson about the price of a car is negotiation, not an offer.

A person's intent is tested by an objective standard. The court decides from the evidence whether a reasonable person familiar with the business being transacted would be justified in believing an offer had been made. If, under the circumstances, the court decides that intent was lacking, a contract could not be formed. For example, if Shakira says, "I would like to sell my car for $5,000," there is no offer to sell that allows Sean Paul to form a contract by saying, "Sold. I will pay you $5,000."

Many things that are stated as being for sale are not definite offers that can be accepted to create a contract. For example, when a jacket worn by Paris Hilton is put on the auction block, unless otherwise stated, it is an invitation for people to submit offers on the jacket. If no offers are high enough, the owner of the jacket can withdraw it.

Similarly, most advertisements are regarded as invitations for others to submit offers to buy. If a catalog lists a particular model of laser printers for $299.99 each, it is likely that if you order one, the order will be accepted and a contract formed. But the seller listing the printers for sale can reject offers to buy, as ads are usually considered to be requests for offers to buy, rather than offers themselves. No seller wants to give up profitable sales, but if inventory is not adequate, offers by customers to buy will be rejected, unless they are willing to wait for the next shipment from China.

Definite Terms and Conditions Not every tiny detail of an offer must be present for it to be a valid offer. If you order a computer by mail order, the contract does not have to say the computer will be properly packed for shipment; that is presumed. Under the common-law rule, terms of an offer must be sufficient so that each party's promises are reasonably certain. An offer that has unclear major terms, or is missing important terms, cannot be the basis for a contract. Sometimes the courts supply missing terms if they are minor, so that the offer does not fail for *indefiniteness*. That prevents a party from backing out of a contract after the fact, claiming that there never was an offer, because some trivial point was not clear.

LIGHTER SIDE OF THE LAW
Listener Beware

The band Creed had to defend itself in court in Chicago when an unhappy fan sued the band because it gave, in his opinion, a crummy concert. Judge Flynn held for Creed: "You can't bring a lawsuit against a band for sucking."

Trying a new angle of attack, an attorney filed a class action for breach of contract on behalf of 172 named plaintiffs. They claimed they were defrauded because they paid $75 for tickets to a concert that was billed as presenting full sets by Limp Bizkit, Linkin Park, and Metallica. Limp Bizkit left the stage after 17 minutes, so it failed to deliver the full set as promised, claimed the plaintiffs.

Source: *National Law Journal*

Getty Images

Exhibit 10.3
Legal Effect of Offer
and Acceptance
Communications

Communication	Time Effective	Legal Effect
By Offeror		
1. Offer	When received by offeree	Offeree has the power to accept
2. Revocation	When received by offeree	Ends offeree's power to accept
By Offeree		
1. Rejection	When received by offeror	Terminates the offer
2. Counteroffer	When received by offeror	Terminates the offer
3. Acceptance	When sent by offeree	Forms a contract

Communication of the Offer Exhibit 10.3 summarizes the timing of communication of offer and acceptance. An acceptance requires *knowledge of the offer* by the offeree. The case of a person who finds and returns a lost dog, and later learns of a reward, is an example of an offer failing for lack of communication. Because the communication of the offer occurred after the act of acceptance (getting the dog to its owner), a proper acceptance did not take place. A contract cannot be formed by accepting an unknown offer.

Terminating an Offer

Termination of an offer can occur by the action of the parties or by the operation of law. The parties can *terminate* an offer by withdrawing it (by the offeror), rejecting it (by the offeree), or through lapse of time (by the inaction of the offeree).

An *option contract* is different because it is a binding promise to keep an offer open for a specified period of time. For example, one may pay $100 to have an option to buy a house for $200,000 any time in the next five days. The offer to sell the house may not be withdrawn during that time.

Termination by the Parties Offerors can terminate most offers by withdrawing an offer before it has been accepted by the offeree. The withdrawal of the offer by the offeror is a *revocation*. To be effective, the revocation must be communicated to the offeree before acceptance. An offer can state that it must be accepted within a designated time period. The end of that time period terminates the offer.

After an offer has been made, the offeree can create a contract by accepting the offer or can terminate the offer by rejecting it. One important form of rejection is a *counteroffer*, a proposal by the offeree to change the terms of the original offer. For example, if Johnny Depp offers to buy Brad Pitt's old laptop computer for $500, and Pitt says that he will sell it for $600, a counteroffer has been made. The original offer by Depp is terminated by the counteroffer. That is, by making a counteroffer, Pitt became the offeror and Depp became the offeree.

Finally, an offer may terminate through *lapse of time*. If an offer does not state a specific time for acceptance, the passage of a reasonable length of time after the offer has been made will terminate it. What is reasonable depends upon the circumstances. An offer to buy stock in a company at a set price terminates by lapse of time almost immediately, while an offer to sell a building expires after a longer time. It depends on the normal practices of the businesses involved.

Termination by the Operation of Law An offer that terminates by operation of law through *intervening illegality* occurs when a court decision or legislation makes an offer illegal after it has been made. Suppose Lindsay Lohan has an Internet-based business that offers to take bets on college football games. Congress then enacts a law forbidding gambling by Internet. Lohan's offer to take bets is terminated by an intervening illegality.

An offer also terminates by law if the *subject matter is destroyed.* Suppose Hayek offers to sell Duff her car. Before Duff accepts Hayek's offer, the car is wrecked in an accident. The offer terminated when the accident occurred.

The *mental or physical incapacity or death of the offeror or the offeree* also terminates an offer by operation of law. An offer is terminated because the person does not have the mental capacity to enter into a contract; or physical limitations, such as a severe injury, may make a party unable to perform a contract that requires certain skills. Similarly, an offeror or offeree who dies cannot execute a contract. If you agree to buy a home from a seller who dies before the transaction is completed, the deal is off, as the home now belongs to the heirs, who did not agree to the sale.

The Acceptance

In contract law, *acceptance* is an offeree's expression of assent or agreement to the terms of an offer. In most contracts, this means the offeree accepts by making a promise in exchange for the original promise. To be effective, an acceptance must be unconditional, unequivocal, and properly communicated. A supposed acceptance that lacks one of these elements will generally not bring about a binding contract.

Generally, contracts are called *bilateral contracts* when there is an exchange of promises. For example, you say to a friend, "I will sell you my car for $2,000"; he responds, "Fine, I will pay that." In some states, certain contracts are referred to as *unilateral contracts* when there is acceptance by *performance.* For example, your neighbor says to you, "I will pay you $30 to mow my lawn." You say nothing in response, but the next day you mow the lawn—so the offer was accepted by performance. Such contracts are valid whether they are called unilateral or bilateral.

Must Be Unconditional An offeree must accept an offer as presented by an offeror. In effect, the acceptance must be the *mirror image* of the offer. The common-law rule is that a supposed acceptance that adds conditions to the original offer is a counteroffer. By changing the terms of the offer, or not following the rules set for acceptance, there is not unconditional acceptance; the offeree rejects the offer. Failure of the parties to clearly agree is seen in the *Parker* case.

Parker v. Glosson
Court of Appeals of North Carolina
641 S.E.2d 735 (2007)

Case Background *Douglas and Sandy Glosson offered to sell 36 acres that included a truck shop, warehouse, and office. Douglas Glosson and Parker agreed on terms and signed the agreement. Sandy Glosson did not sign and the deal fell through. Parker sued for breach of contract. He requested specific performance—an order to sell the property—or damages. The trial court dismissed the suit. Parker appealed.*

Case Decision Stroud, Judge

* * *

"The elements of a claim for breach of contract are (1) existence of a valid contract and (2) breach of the terms of that contract." No contract is formed without an agreement to which at least two parties manifest an intent to be bound. Mutual assent is an "essential element" of every contract....

There is no meeting of the minds, and, therefore, no contract, when "in the contemplation of both parties ... something remains to be done to establish contract relations." This rule has been described as "too well established to require the citation of

continues

authority." Thus, if negotiating parties impose a condition … on the effectiveness of their agreement, no contract is formed until the condition is met. Likewise, when negotiating parties make it clear that they do not intend to be bound by a contract until a formal written agreement is executed, no contract exists until that time.

Here, clause 13 of the Agreement for Purchase and Sale of Real Property [the Agreement] expressly provides "this agreement shall *become an enforceable contract* when a *fully executed* copy has been communicated to both parties." (Emphasis added.) From this language, we conclude that the sellers did not intend to sell, and the buyer did not intend to buy, until the Agreement was signed by all parties. The parties identified as "Sellers" at the top of the first page of the Agreement are Douglas Glosson and Sandy Glosson; however, only Douglas Glosson has signed on the "Seller" signature lines at the end of the Agreement. Because Sandy Glosson has not signed the Agreement, the Agreement is not "fully executed"

and, therefore, no contract has been formed between the parties as a matter of law.

The reason for holding the instrument void is that it was intended that all the parties should execute it and that each executes it on the implied condition that it is to be executed by the others, and, therefore, that *until executed by all it is inchoate and incomplete and never takes effect as a valid contract, and this is especially true where the agreement expressly provides, or its manifest intent is, that it is not to be binding until signed….*

Affirmed.

Questions for Analysis

1. The appeals court held that no contract ever came into existence, so there could be no breach of contract. Why was Douglas Glosson's signature not enough?

2. The parties apparently did agree to all relevant terms, but then Sandy Glosson backed out. Should she have the right to do that after agreeing?

Must Be Unequivocal Acceptance must be unequivocal or definite. Suppose an offeree receives an offer to buy a car for $10,000. If the offeree says "I see" or "What a good idea," either expression fails the unequivocal test. There is no acceptance.

While the words "I accept" are a clear acceptance, any words or conduct expressing the offeree's intent to accept an offer is an effective acceptance. When negotiations take place, much is expressed in words and conduct that is not a rejection or acceptance. In such cases, the courts look (as in the *Parker* case) at the offeree's expressions to determine whether a reasonable person would consider them as an acceptance of the offer.

As a general rule, silence is not acceptance because it is not unequivocal. It could mean yes or no. However, the past business dealings of the offeror and the offeree may allow silence by the offeree to be acceptance. For example, if a company has serviced a copier for a customer every month for several years, there does not need to be an express statement every month that copier service is desired.

Must Be Properly Communicated The final requirement of acceptance is that it is properly communicated. Three factors can be important in meeting this requirement: 1) the method of acceptance, 2) the timeliness of acceptance, and 3) in some cases, performance as acceptance. Exhibit 10.4 summarizes the elements of offer and acceptance.

The general rule in communicating an acceptance is that any reasonable method is adequate. Problems arise when the offeror authorizes one way to communicate acceptance, but the offeree uses another. If, for example, the offeror requires that acceptance be made by a signed letter, a response by telephone will

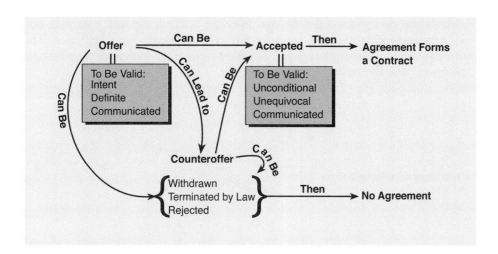

Exhibit 10.4
Alternative Results in the
Contracting Process

not create an acceptance. If no method of acceptance is specified, the offeree may use any reasonable means to communicate. The safest approach is to use the method used by the offeror in communicating the offer.

The timeliness of acceptance is important, especially when the value of goods or services being offered changes rapidly. To deal with time problems, the courts created the general rule that if the method of acceptance is reasonable under the circumstances, the acceptance is effective when it is sent.

Consideration

Consideration is something of value or something bargained for in exchange for a promise; that is, both parties to a contract get something and give up something. It is the element of a contract that keeps it from being a gift. If consideration is absent, neither party can enforce the promise or agreement.

The traditional rule is that an exchange is consideration if it creates a legal detriment to the *promisee* (the party to whom a promise is made) or a legal benefit to the *promisor* (the party making a promise). A *legal detriment* is an act, or a promise to act, or the refraining from an action, such as giving up a legal right. For example, if you are hit by a careless driver and accept an out-of-court settlement of $20,000, you give up the right to sue in court for damages. A *legal benefit* to the promisor exists when the promisor acquires some legal right through the promisee's act, promise to act, or refraining from doing some act.

Consideration requires either a legal detriment to the promisee or a legal benefit to the promisor, although both usually occur at the same time. Suppose Def Jam buys a watch from SwissWatch for $100. Def Jam suffers a legal detriment (gives up the right to keep $100) in exchange for a benefit (the watch). SwissWatch suffers a legal detriment (gives up the watch) in exchange for a benefit ($100). As the following case illustrates, courts use this *detriment-benefit test* to determine whether there is consideration for a contract.

Adequacy of Consideration

For the most part, courts do not inquire into the *adequacy of consideration* given in a contract. The bargaining is the responsibility of the parties to the contract. Even if one party bargains poorly, and the values of the items to be exchanged are very unequal, the courts generally do not interfere. Courts support contracts that are bargained for, even if the consideration is not related to market value. The main concern for the courts is to see that there was a trade of mutual promises and obligations as discussed in the *Caley* case.

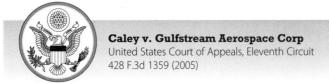

Caley v. Gulfstream Aerospace Corp
United States Court of Appeals, Eleventh Circuit
428 F.3d 1359 (2005)

Case Background *Gulfstream adopted a dispute resolution policy (DRP). It mailed the policy to all employees. It said the DRP would be the only procedure to resolve disputes between Gulfstream and employees. It would begin in two weeks and would be "a condition of continued employment." If an employee continued to work at Gulfstream, then they accepted the DRP as a condition of employment. A group of employees sued, contending that there was no contract, so the DRP could not be enforced. The district court held for Gulfstream. The employees appealed.*

Case Decision Hull, Circuit Judge

* * *

1. Offer The plaintiffs argue that the DRP does not constitute an "offer." We disagree. "An offer is the manifestation of willingness to enter into a bargain, so made as to justify another person in understanding that his assent to that bargain is invited and will conclude it." *Restatement (Second) of Contracts*, §24. The DRP clearly states that it is a contract, establishes the terms of the contract, and explains the means of accepting the contract. Thus, the DRP plainly constituted an offer....

2. Acceptance The plaintiffs also contend that they cannot be deemed to have accepted the terms of the DRP simply by their continued employment, even though the DRP expressly provides that continued employment is the proper means of acceptance. However, we agree with the district court that the employees accepted the DRP through continued employment....

"An offer may be accepted... either by a promise to do the thing contemplated therein, or by the actual doing of the thing." However, "the offer must be accepted in the manner specified by it; and if it calls for a promise, then a promise must be made; or if it calls

for an act, it can be accepted only by the doing of the act."...

By specifying the manner of acceptance as continued employment and announcing that the DRP was a condition of employment, the DRP and accompanying letter plainly set forth two options for Gulfstream employees: (1) continue in employment, thereby accepting the DRP, or (2) terminate employment. Thus, given these two options, the employees remaining in Gulfstream's employ after notice of the DRP was an unambiguous act of acceptance of the DRP....

3. Consideration The plaintiffs next argue that the arbitration agreement is unenforceable because there is no "bargained for consideration" for their relinquishment of trial rights. They argue that the employees got nothing in return.

This argument is unavailing. Georgia law provides that mutual promises and obligations are sufficient consideration to support a contract. Here, the plaintiffs received reciprocal promises from Gulfstream to arbitrate and be bound by arbitration in covered claims. In addition, the DRP provides that Gulfstream will pay the arbitration and mediation costs. These promises constitute bargained-for consideration....

Affirmed.

Questions for Analysis

1. The appeals court held that continued employment was evidence of acceptance of the offer and employment was consideration. Since the employees were already working, why was there consideration? Was there a change in anything?

2. If the case had come out the opposite, how could an employer change the terms of the working arrangement (contract)?

LIGHTER SIDE OF THE LAW
You Aren't So Beautiful, to Me…

The Pandeys, from India but living in Massachusetts, were worried that their son, Panjul, 37, would not find a suitable wife. Their friends the Giris, also from India but living in Maryland, said that their niece in India would be a good match.

After much discussion, the Pandeys flew to India to meet the girl. They were "extremely shocked to find" the bride "was ugly… with protruded bad teeth, and couldn't speak English to hold a conversation." Unlike Panjul, who they assert is "handsome," the girl is "homely and unsuitable."

Because of the broken social contract, the Pandeys sued the Giris for fraud. Although they had given the Giris no money, they demanded $200,000 in damages. The complaint also noted that Mr. Giri acted like "a big shot in a different class."

Source: *Springfield Republican*

Getty Images

Enforceable Promises without Consideration

Circumstances exist where consideration for a promise is not required by the courts for the promise to be enforceable. The doctrine used by the courts is called *promissory estoppel* (or *detrimental reliance*). The rationale for the doctrine is that it will avoid an injustice due to the promisee's reasonable reliance on the promisor's promise.

Under the doctrine, the promisor is *estopped* (prevented) from denying a promise. The *Restatement (2d) of Contracts* explains promissory estoppel this way: "A promise which the promisor should reasonably expect to induce action or forbearance on the part of the promisee … and which does induce such action or forbearance is binding if injustice can be avoided only by enforcement of the promise." We see an application of this doctrine in the *Hinson* case, which also notes that oral promises can be the basis of a contract.

Hinson v. N&W Construction Company
Court of Appeals of Mississippi
890 So.2d 65 (2004)

Case Background *N&W Construction prepared a bid for the Mississippi Job Corps Center (MJCC) to build a kitchen facility at a training center. In preparing the bid, N&W received oral bids from several plumbing contractors. Hinson quoted $92,000 as his bid for the plumbing job. The next-lowest plumbing subcontractor bid was $139,000. N&W used Hinson's bid in preparing its general contracting bid for the whole project.*

N&W was the low bidder and was awarded the MJCC contract. N&W notified Hinson that he was needed to do the plumbing work when construction began. Hinson refused the job. N&W had to hire the next-lowest bidder and pay an additional $47,000 to get the plumbing work done.

N&W sued Hinson on the basis of promissory estoppel. The trial court granted summary judgment to N&W and awarded $47,000 in damages. Hinson appealed.

Case Decision Irving, Justice

* * *

The doctrine of promissory estoppel has been stated as follows:

> An estoppel may arise from the making of a promise, even though without consideration, if it was intended that the promise should be relied upon and in fact it was relied upon, and if a refusal to enforce it would be

continues

virtually to sanction the perpetuation of fraud or would result in other injustice.

A review of the undisputed facts of this case and the evidence submitted by the parties to N&W's motion for summary judgment ... clearly indicate that the circuit court correctly granted N&W's motion for summary judgment on the theory of promissory estoppel.....

Hinson admits that he provided a verbal quote to N&W in the amount of $92,000 for plumbing work on the building....

Hinson testified that he reviewed the plans and specifications for the building, worked on his quote for approximately a week, and was satisfied with his price of $92,000....

Moreover, Hinson does not dispute that N&W used his quote for the plumbing work in its bid for the building contract.... Hinson later explained ... that he refused to do the plumbing work.... "I just had a lot of other jobs going."...

Affirmed.

Questions for Analysis

1. The appeals court held there was an enforceable promise. Since Hinson did not sign a contract and never received any payment from N&W, should Hinson be responsible? Why did N&W not get an agreement in writing?

2. Since the next bid was 50 percent higher than Hinson's, is it likely that Hinson's bid was poorly done, and that he would have suffered a big loss had he done the work?

This is not a rule imposed lightly by the courts, because they do not want to impose obligations that were not really agreed to. Promissory estoppel also arises in some cases of promises to charities. Suppose an art museum is raising $50 million for an expansion. It collects promises from various donors, but none of the money is collected until there are enough promises to make the project feasible and construction begins. Once that happens, if a donor backs out, the courts may rule that promissory estoppel applies, and the gift must be made; because the building contract was entered into on reliance of the donation being made.

Capacity to Contract

One element of a contract is *contractual capacity*, or legal ability, to create a contract. The term *capacity* refers to a party's ability to perform legally valid acts, acquire legal rights, and incur legal liabilities. Generally, minors, intoxicated persons, and the insane have limited capacity to contract. A party claiming incapacity has the burden of proving it.

Most people have complete capacity to contract. If a person, perhaps as a result of mental disability, does not have capacity to contract, a contract entered into is not enforceable. If a person has *partial capacity*, the contract is enforceable unless the person with partial capacity exercises the right to disaffirm the contract. Contracts created by those with partial capacity are voidable.

Void and Voidable Contracts

A contract that does not exist at law, and so cannot be enforced, is a *void contract*. A contract is void if it concerns an illegal subject matter, such as a contract to sell cocaine. Disputes over such matters will not be accepted by the courts.

A *voidable contract* is when one party to the contract has the right to avoid a legal obligation. As we discuss below, this is the case with some contracts entered into by minors or persons with limited mental ability. If a person is so stoned when he makes a contract that he does not know what he is doing, then, not having had the capacity to contract, he may later have the right to have the contract declared voidable. A contract is also voidable if there is fraud involved in making the contract. The victim of the fraud can accept the contract and make it valid, or not.

Minors

A *minor* is a person under the legal age of majority. The traditional age of majority was 21, but all states have statutes that set the age at 18 for most contracts and younger for some. The general rule is that a minor may enter into contracts but the contracts are voidable at the option of the minor. A company that contracts with a minor may find itself with relatively few rights if the minor disaffirms the contract. If a minor has received benefits, such as a 16-year-old buying a car on credit and driving it for six months, *restitution* must be paid for the value of the benefit received.

After a minor reaches the age of majority, the person may *ratify* contracts made while a minor. Ratification may be expressed through words, writing, or implied by conduct, such as continued use of a car. There are some contracts that minors may not disaffirm. Enlistment contracts to join the Army and marriage contracts are *nonvoidable contracts*. Some states have statues that do not allows minors to disaffirm other contracts, such as for insurance, educational loans, medical care, and bank account agreements.

Legality

For a contract to be valid, its subject matter must be *lawful*. A contract will be illegal and unenforceable if its subject matter violates a state or federal statute, or the common law, or is contrary to public policy. The terms *illegal bargain* and *illegal agreement*, rather than illegal contract, may be more proper because contract by definition refers to a legal and enforceable agreement.

Illegal Agreements

Promises that violate the law are illegal agreements that the courts will not recognize, regardless of the intent of the parties. Deals for prohibited drugs, such as

INTERNATIONAL PERSPECTIVE

Problems Enforcing Contracts

A study by the World Bank looked at the problem of enforcing a contract in countries around the world. Lack of both effective contract law and honest, efficient judicial enforcement in poor countries discourages foreign firms from investing in those countries or doing business there.

The study assumed one business refused to pay another business money that it owed for a transaction, and suit had to be brought to enforce the contract. The study examined the following variables in many countries: 1) the number of procedures mandated by law that are required to file a contract case and take it through the court system; 2) the average number of days to complete the legal process from service of process to trial and enforcement; and 3) the cost of a legal action as a percent of the value of the debt that is in dispute.

Country	Number of Procedures	Time (days)	Cost (percentage of debt)
Canada	17	346	12.0
China	31	292	26.8
Germany	30	394	10.5
India	56	1,420	35.7
Mexico	37	415	20.0
United Kingdom	19	229	16.8
United States	17	300	7.7

The United States is no paragon of efficiency, but the cost of legal action is relatively low, compared to most countries. If contract enforcement is too long, too costly, or too complex, ordinary people are unlikely to be able to integrate it into the way they do business.

Source: *http://rru.worldbank.org/doingbusiness*

Getty Images

cocaine, are illegal agreements, as are other contracts to engage in criminal activities. State law controls some activities, such as gambling. Hence, gambling contracts are often illegal, and the person who won an illegal wager cannot seek help from the courts. Some states have limits on interest rates that can be charged on certain loans; charges above the maximum allowed are called *usury* and are illegal. When a court is asked to enforce a contract, and it finds it to be in violation of law, it may strike the entire bargain as unenforceable or strike the part of the bargain that concerns illegal subject matter.

Unenforceable Contracts

Some contracts were legal and enforceable when they were made, but a change in the law makes them unenforceable. For example, suppose a company agreed to sell a shipload of wheat to the government of Iran. While the shipment is at sea, the U.S. government declares that no U.S. firms may trade with Iran. The contract at that point becomes *unenforceable* under U.S. contract law, even if it is seen as legal in Iran. The seller must end the effort to sell the goods or face prosecution for trying to fulfill a contract about a matter that is now illegal.

Contracts Contrary to Public Policy

Some contracts are unenforceable because their subject matter is *contrary to public policy*. Some contracts may not violate any particular statute yet may injure public welfare. Some contracts that courts have held to be contrary to public policy are exculpatory agreements, unconscionable contracts, and contracts in restraint of trade.

Exculpatory Agreements An *exculpatory agreement* releases one party from the consequences brought about by wrongful acts or negligence. An example is an employment contract stating that the employee will not hold the employer liable for any harm to her caused by the employer while on the job. With such a clause, the employer is no longer concerned about being sued for intentional torts. Such clauses generally violate public policy and are not enforceable.

Unconscionable Contracts The courts usually do not concern themselves with the fairness of a bargain struck by contracting parties. But in some cases, if a contract is grossly unfair to an innocent party, the courts, in equity, will not enforce it. These are called *unconscionable contracts* and occur when one of the parties, being in a strong position, takes advantage of the other party. The stronger party convinces the other party to enter into a contract contrary to his well-being. Such agreements may violate public policy and may not be enforceable.

Contracts in Restraint of Trade Contracts that restrain trade or unreasonably restrict competition are considered contrary to public policy and are not enforced by the courts. Part of the common law on this subject became part of modern antitrust law, discussed later in the text.

Even if a contract does not violate a statute, it still may be an unenforceable restraint of trade. A *covenant not to compete*, for example, may be unenforceable if it does not meet certain guidelines. These usually arise in contracts for the sale of a business and for employment. The employee (or seller) agrees not to compete with the employer (or buyer).

Suppose you buy a restaurant. You do not want the previous owner to move across the street and open up a new restaurant in competition with you, so the sale is likely to have a provision that the former owner will not open a restaurant within five miles for three years. Such restrictions are usually upheld if reasonable. A restriction on national competition would not make sense in a case like this, but local restrictions would.

More controversial, and an area in which state law varies quite a bit, are restrictions on competition by former employees. In states where such restrictions can be legal, many employers have employees sign an agreement not to work for a competitor, or go into competition against the employer, for a certain length of time after leaving. For example, when a senior sales manager left Nike to go to work for Reebok, the court held a one year, noncompete agreement in the athletic footwear market was enforceable. In the *Castillo* case, we see such a restriction fail.

DCS Sanitation Management v. Castillo
United States Court of Appeals, Eighth Circuit
435 F.3d 892 (2006)

Case Background *DCS is a Delaware company with its main office in Ohio and operations in 13 states. It cleans food processing plants, including a Tyson Foods plant in Dakota City, Nebraska. Castillo and other employees signed noncompete agreements with DCS that stated: "For a period of one year following the date of termination of employment for any reason, I will not directly or indirectly engage in, or in any manner be concerned with or employed by any person, firm, or corporation in competition with [DCS] or engaged in providing contract cleaning services within a radius of one-hundred (100) miles of any customer of [DCS]...." Ohio law governed the contract.*

When DCS lost its contract at the Tyson plant to a competitor, the competitor hired Castillo and other former DCS employees to do much the same work as before. DCS sued the employees for breach of contract. The district court held for Castillo. DCS appealed.

Case Decision Riley, Circuit Judge

* * *

The district court properly concluded Ohio has no substantial relationship to the parties or the transaction, and Nebraska has a greater material interest in the Agreements.

In Nebraska, if a court determines a noncompete agreement is unreasonable, the court will not reform the noncompete agreement in order to make it enforceable. Contrary to the Nebraska courts' approach, Ohio courts are empowered to reform overly broad or unreasonable noncompete agreements to make them reasonable. The district court correctly recognized that because Nebraska courts expressly

have rejected judicial reformation of noncompete agreements, application of Ohio law would violate a fundamental policy of Nebraska law....

Having concluded Nebraska law applies, we now turn to whether the noncompete agreements are valid under Nebraska law. Pursuant to Nebraska law, a noncompete agreement is valid if it is (1) "not injurious to the public," (2) "not greater than is reasonably necessary to protect the employer in some legitimate interest," and (3) "not unduly harsh and oppressive on the employee." "An employer has a legitimate business interest in protection against a former employee's competition by improper and unfair means, but is not entitled to protection against ordinary competition from a former employee." A noncompete agreement "may be valid only if it restricts the former employee from working for or soliciting the former employer's clients or accounts with whom the former employee actually did business and has personal contact."...

We conclude the district court properly held the noncompete agreements were overbroad and unenforceable. The district court recognized the noncompete agreements prohibit the former employees from, directly or indirectly, being concerned in any manner with any company in competition with DCS, and from providing contract cleaning services within one hundred miles of any entity or enterprise "having business dealings" with DCS, including attorneys, accountants, delivery services and the like. The breadth of the noncompete agreements effectively put the former employees out of the cleaning business within an extensive region.

continues

We hold the district court did not err in concluding Nebraska courts would not enforce such overly broad noncompete agreements....

Therefore, we affirm the well-reasoned judgment of the district court.

1. The appeals court struck down the noncompete agreement. Does this mean all such agreements in Nebraska are unenforceable?
2. What difference might it have made had Ohio law applied?

Reality and Genuineness of Consent

Freedom of contract is based on the right of individuals to freely enter into the bargains of their choice. Under some circumstances, however, a person may enter into an agreement without knowing key information about the transaction. Without knowledge, there is no *reality of consent* or *genuine consent* by the parties, and the contract may be void.

A *unilateral mistake* occurs when one party to a contract enters into it with false information or accidentally makes an error in a significant matter. If, for example, a contract to buy a house says the price is $20,000, when the buyer knows it should be $200,000, the contract cannot be enforced at the lower price because of the mistake made in typing the contract. In general, if the other party should have known of the error, it cannot be enforced to allow one to profit from a simple error.

Statutory Exceptions

Some statutes deal with high-pressure selling techniques by door-to-door salespeople. These "home solicitation" statutes allow contracts to be voided if the buyer entered into the contract under pressure by a salesperson. For example, the Federal Trade Commission's Cooling-Off Rule allows buyers in door-to-door sales with a value over $25 to void the contract in writing within three business days.

Fraud and Misrepresentation

A person who "agrees" to a contract due to *fraud, misrepresentation, duress,* or *undue influence* has the right to disaffirm the contract because there was not genuine consent. Duress occurs when someone is "forced" to sign a contract; that is, the contract is made because of a threat that gave no sensible way out. In the case of undue influence, a person enters into a contract because they are so dominated by another person, or have so much trust in that person that they are subject to improper persuasion. This happens sometimes to elderly people who rely on a trusted caretaker.

Fraud A contract induced by fraud may be rescinded. If the contract is rescinded before any losses are incurred, then there is not likely to be a cause of action for damages. As we saw in Chapter 7, it is possible that the person who committed the fraud may be sued in tort. But this is such a common issue that we cover it again here. If there is a tort, then the injured party may be able to also sue for punitive damages. To establish common-law fraud, the injured party must show that:

1. There was a *misstatement* of an important or *material* fact; that is, false information was presented as fact in the making of the contract. The misstatement must be about a key fact relevant to the contract. Unrelated misstatements, such as claiming that Abraham Lincoln was president during World War I, cannot be the basis of fraud. Hyping a product—such as by saying "This is the most fun computer game ever invented" is not sufficient to indicate an intent to defraud.
2. There must be *scienter* or intent to defraud; that is, the party wanted to mislead the other party and intentionally deceived him. Scienter means that the court

finds that there is something rotten about the deal about which the seller could not be ignorant.

3. The seller must know, or have reason to know, that the statement she is making is false. If you sell your car, which you bought used, and you believe that the mileage is correct, when in fact the odometer had been turned back by the person who owned it before you, then you do not know you are not telling the truth.

4. The recipient of the false information must justifiably rely on that information in making the decision to go ahead with the deal. If a seller tells you false information intending to deceive you, but you are not fooled and you go ahead with the deal anyway, there is no fraud. Similarly, if you believe information that you should know to be false, such as a claim that the engine in a car is made out of gold, there is no justifiable reliance.

5. There must be *privity* between the parties; that is, they must have been in a contractual arrangement. A third party observing fraud cannot sue.

6. There must be *proximate cause*. The fact that there was false information that caused the contract to be formed must be related to losses that were suffered for there to be a cause of action for damages.

7. There must be *damages* that were caused by the fraud. That is, even if there is fraud in the making of a contract, if there are no damages that result, there should be no award.

We see several of these issues in the *L&L Doc's* case.

L&L Doc's v. Florida Division of Alcoholic Beverages and Tobacco
District Court of Appeal of Florida, Fourth District
882 So.2d 512 (2004)

Case Background *Leuders and Latte formed L&L and bought Doc's Saloon in Fort Lauderdale from Carlbob for a $125,000 promissory note. The note was secured by the business and the liquor license. Doc's had slot machines in it. Soon after, the police arrested Latte for engaging in illegal gambling for having the slots. L&L defaulted on paying the note, so Carlbob, owned by Dressel, sued L&L claimed Dressel engaged in fraud by representing that the slots were a good source of revenue, when in fact they were illegal. Further, Dressel had cheated on liquor taxes by illegally refilling bottles to avoid liquor taxes. The trial court held for Carlbob. L&L appealed.*

Case Decision Shahood, Judge

* * *

The issue in this appeal is whether or not, as a matter of law, there was a fraudulent misrepresentation with regard to whether the transaction included the transfer of the slot machines. The buyers acknowledge that the sales contract clearly did not include the slot machines, but assert that they are nevertheless entitled to recovery, because Dressel made them believe they could continue to use the slot machines and generate revenue from them. They argue that their status as "recent, unsophisticated immigrants" supports their position that Dressel exploited their "lack of sophistication" and ignorance of the fact that slot machines are illegal.

Without admitting that there was a misrepresentation, seller argues that, in any event, the buyers were not justified in relying upon a misrepresentation, which they knew or should have known, with the exercise of some diligence, was false. We agree. Buyers' ignorance of the law is not excused simply because they are not from this country.... publication in the Laws of Florida or the Florida Statutes gives all citizens constructive notice of the consequences of their actions (ignorance of the law is no excuse).... The fact that gambling may be legal in the buyers' respective countries is irrelevant. Moreover, even if the slot machines and the revenues gained from them had been a subject of the contract, buyers would still have no action on the contract because such activity is

continues

illegal (agreements in violation of public policy are void and unenforceable).

Consequently, with respect to all issues raised, we affirm the trial court's entry of summary judgment and final judgment in favor of Dressel.

Affirmed.

Questions for Analysis

1. The appeals court affirmed that, because both parties engaged in fraud, it would not intervene in the matter. Why did the court not undo the sale of the bar, because there was fraud involved?
2. Why is ignorance of the law no excuse?

ISSUE SPOTTER
Are You Due a Commission?

You work in commercial real estate, and you have a contract to sell a dry cleaning business. Your contract with the seller lasts six months. It says that if the seller sells the business to anyone you brought as a contact within one year after the expiration of your contract as a real estate agent for the seller, you are owed a commission. The business does not sell, and your contract as an agent for the seller ends. Eighteen months later, you see that the seller sold the business to a buyer that you had brought to the seller when you were the seller's agent. Do you have a claim for a commission? Has the seller committed fraud against you?

Getty Images

Misrepresentation Misrepresentation and fraud are similar and often occur together. But there can be misrepresentation that does not reach the level of fraud. Misrepresentation requires a false statement to significantly influence the making of a contract. As we saw in tort law, a false statement can be made in innocent ignorance, or it can be intentional. If a false statement is made innocently, the contract may be voidable if the misstatement was material, or key, to the decision to make the contract and the value of the contract. If the misrepresentation of a material fact is intentional, then there is fraud by one party that will be grounds for rescinding a contract.

Contracts in Writing and the Statute of Frauds

Contracts do not have to be in writing to be enforceable. Written contracts are a good idea, because they are difficult to deny and courts prefer written documents over conflicting oral claims. Some contracts, however, must be evidenced by a writing to be enforceable. Such contracts are subject to the *Statute of Frauds*, which evolved from a 1677 English statute called "An Act for the Prevention of Frauds and Perjuries." The purpose is to prevent parties from claiming that a contract existed when in fact it did not. To reduce such fraud, the statute requires that for certain contracts to be enforceable, they must be in writing.

States have statutes similar to the English act. Most states have several types of contracts that are covered by the Statute of Frauds and that must be evidenced in writing to be enforced by a court in the event of a dispute:

1. Contracts for the sale of real property (land)
2. Contracts that cannot be performed within one year
3. Promises to pay the debt of another, including the debts of an estate
4. Promises made in consideration of marriage

Sufficiency of the Writing

For a writing to be *sufficient* under the Statute of Frauds, it must give the material terms of the contract and be signed by at least the defendant. Courts usually

Getty Images

CYBER LAW
Digital Signatures and Contracts

The Electronic Signatures in Global and National Commerce Act (E-Sign) became part of federal law in 2000. It is based on the Uniform Electronic Transactions Act, which had been adopted by most states. The purpose of E-Sign is to leave the substance of contract law unchanged, but to be neutral about the use of technology in creating contracts.

E-Sign removes obstacles to the use of electronic media in contract formation. A valid signature includes any "electronic sound, symbol, or process, attached to or logically associated with a contract or other record and executed or adopted by a person with the intent to sign the record." The primary impact of the law is in internal business record keeping, such as employee timesheets, business-to-business (B2B) transactions that tend to be more complex than consumer transactions, and business-to-government dealings, such as compliance with regulatory procedures over the Internet.

As in the days when written signatures dominated contracts, the authenticity of a "signature" is still critical. Companies such as Verisign provide SSL certificates to guarantee Internet Security. Signatures also include such things as the PIN number used at an ATM machine. The law does not dictate the technology that must be used for a signature to be accepted as genuine, since such technology continues to evolve.

require the writing to have the names of the parties, the consideration offered, the subject matter of the contract, and other material terms.

However, confirmations, invoices, e-mails, sales orders, and even checks may satisfy the sufficiency of the writing requirement. Without a necessary writing, the alleged contract is unlikely to be enforced.

Parol Evidence Rule

Negotiations often come before contracts. The parties may exchange e-mails or other communications before signing the actual contract. Parties may omit from the final contract some terms agreed upon in negotiations. In a later lawsuit, the parties may disagree about those terms.

The *parol evidence rule* restricts the use of oral statements in a lawsuit, when the evidence is contrary to the terms of a written contract. Oral evidence cannot contradict, change, or add terms to a written contract. Oral or parol evidence may be introduced when the written contract is incomplete or ambiguous; when it proves fraud, mistake, or misrepresentation; or when the parol evidence explains the written instrument through previous trade usage or course of dealing.

ISSUE SPOTTER
Liars' Contest?

You go to look at new cars at a dealership that is having a sale. You like one particular vehicle. The salesperson tells you that the sale ends today and the cars are going fast, so you better buy now. You are not sure. She says that to guarantee that you get the sale price, you must sign a contract today and make a down payment of $500. But, she says, she knows you are not ready to commit, so she will hold the contract and check for you for three days while you decide for sure. If you decide not to buy, you get your money back and the contract is torn up. You have nothing to lose. You sign the contract and give a check for $500. Two days later you call to say you have decided not to buy; the dealer says there is a signed contract, and you lose your $500 if you back out. Can you explain to the judge what happened and get your money back?

Getty Images

Performance, Discharge, and Breach of Contracts

Eventually contracts end. When the obligations have been *performed*, the contract is terminated or *discharged*. Just as there are rules to govern the creation of contracts, there are rules to govern the performance and discharge of contracts. Many of the various ways in which a contract can be discharged are summarized in Exhibit 10.5.

Performance

Most contracts come to an end by the complete *performance* of the parties' obligations under the contract. Contracts may be for one sale or for a long-term provision of a service. If a contract is to be completed over time, such as for Night Staff to clean the offices in BigBank's office building for two years, once Night Staff has done the cleaning for two years and BigBank has paid, the contract terminates. No further obligation is owed by either party.

Substantial Performance

Suppose Microsoft delivers a computer program written specifically for H-P. The product is delivered on time, but a couple of minor bugs in the program are discovered. Has Microsoft performed its obligation so that H-P must pay, or is there a lack of performance such that H-P may refuse or can sue Microsoft for breach of contract? In most contracts, *substantial performance* means that the contract basically

Exhibit 10.5   Discharge of a Contract and Its Effects on the Parties

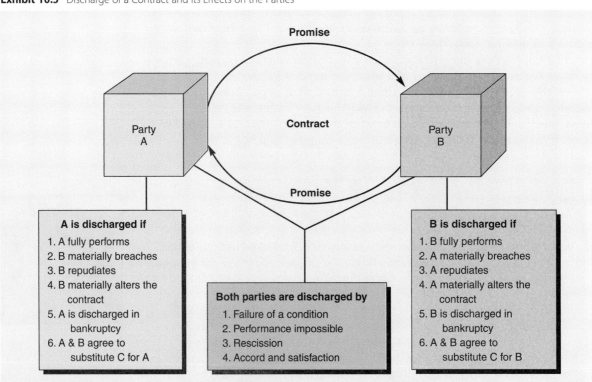

has been fulfilled and payments must be made. The parties are expected to act in *good faith*. Refusing to pay when almost all of the contract was properly completed would not be acceptable. H-P could delay final payment to Microsoft until the bugs were worked out, but there is no justification to rescind the agreement for lack of performance. Of course, if H-P incurs costs due to the bugs, Microsoft is liable for those damages. The difference between a breach where there has been substantial performance and a *material breach* (significant breach) of contract can be a judgment call, so if a party wants to make sure things will be done to perfection, that must be made clear in the contract.

Assignment and Delegation

A contract may be performed by a third party. A transfer of contract rights to another party is *assignment;* a transfer of contractual duties to a third party is a *delegation.* Many contracts are for services (duties) that cannot be assigned. Shaquille O'Neal cannot delegate his duty to play for the Miami Heat to any other person. If a dentist has agreed to cap your teeth, you cannot assign your right to have your teeth capped to someone else. However, many contracts are capable of being assigned or delegated to third parties.

For example, if H-P contracted with Microsoft to develop some software for H-P, unless prohibited in the contract, Microsoft may delegate some of the software creation to a company that does contract work for it. When that company delivers the software, Microsoft can then integrate it into the final product it delivers to H-P. As another example, if Night Staff has contracted to provide cleaning services for BigBank for two years, it may assign the contract to another cleaning company, unless the contract prohibits that, perhaps for security reasons. Night Staff is liable for problems that arise due to poor performance by the other company, but such assignments are not uncommon.

Third-Party Beneficiaries

A *third-party beneficiary* is a party who is not part of an original contract who acquires rights under the contract. This happens mostly in credit contracts. For example, suppose Sting loans Bono $5,000. In consideration for the loan, Bono promises to pay $5,000 to Diddy, to whom Sting already owes $5,000. If Bono fails to pay Diddy, then Diddy may sue Bono to collect the $5,000, even though Diddy and Bono did not enter into a contract. Diddy is a third-party beneficiary of the contract between Sting and Bono.

Discharge by Breach

When a party to a contract does not perform as required, there is a *breach of contract.* If one party prevents or hinders the other party to a contract from performing her duties, then a breach occurs. The party injured by the breach may be entitled to a remedy (discussed in the next section). To determine the remedy that may be provided, the court will look at the extent of the breach.

Material Breach

If the performance provided by a party is substantially less than the requirements of the contract, there is a *material breach.* Suppose Microsoft fails to deliver the program to H-P on time, or that it delivers seriously defective software. As a result, H-P cannot deliver its computers. H-P would have a cause of action against the breaching party, Microsoft, for damages. It would be discharged from its performance promised under the contract. It would not have to accept delivery of the defective program or accept the correct version if it arrived too late to be useful.

Anticipatory Breach

Before the performance of a contract takes place, an *anticipatory breach*, or *repudiation*, occurs if one party indicates inability or lack of desire to perform the contract. Sometimes the breaching party will not volunteer that it is going to breach, but the fact that the contract will not be performed becomes clear. If Microsoft was scheduled to ship the program to H-P by August 1, but H-P learns on July 25 that all copies of the program were destroyed by a hacker at Microsoft, H-P does not have to wait until August 1 to look for replacements, once it knows Microsoft cannot deliver on time. Depending on the terms of the contract, H-P may be able to sue Microsoft for costs it incurred due to failure to deliver on time.

Discharge by Agreement of the Parties

Just as parties have the freedom to contract, they are also free to agree to modify or to terminate their obligations under the contract. *Discharge by agreement* between the parties can take various forms. Among the most important are rescission, novation, and accord and satisfaction.

Rescission

A *rescission* occurs when both parties agree that the contract should be terminated without performance. A rescission discharges the obligations of both parties under the contract. For example, Avon contracted with Sears to sell cosmetics at Sears stores. Sears decided to cancel the deal and paid Avon $20 million to agree to terminate the arrangement. The parties agreed to rescind, or cancel, the contract.

Novation

In a *novation*, all the parties agree to discharge one party from the contract and create a new contract with another party, who becomes responsible for the discharged party's performance. Suppose J. Lo was contracted to star in a movie, but decides she does not want to. She asks Beyonce if she would like the part instead. If the movie studio agrees on that replacement, then the new agreement is a novation, and J. Lo is released from liability for not doing the movie.

ISSUE SPOTTER

Do You Have to Eat the Loss?

At the start of the chapter, we posed the problem of the sales rep who e-mailed the wrong price information to a customer, who replied that he wanted the LCD televisions for the misquoted price of $149.99 that should have been $1,499. All the terms of the contract were in place except for the misquoted price. Is there a contract, or can the seller tell the customer there is no deal without facing the likelihood of successful litigation against the sales company?

Accord and Satisfaction

Another way parties may agree to discharge their duties to one another under a contract is through *accord and satisfaction*. An *accord* is an agreement by the parties to offer and accept some performance different from that originally bargained for. *Satisfaction* is the actual performance of the new obligation. The original obligation is discharged when the new consideration is provided.

Suppose Spielberg owes DiCaprio $1,000. If Spielberg offers to direct a movie for DiCaprio in place of paying him the $1,000, and DiCaprio accepts, then there is an accord. If Spielberg then directs a movie for DiCaprio, there is accord and satisfaction. The new consideration discharges the original claim. Had Spielberg failed to direct a movie, then DiCaprio could still have sued him for the $1,000, because there was no satisfaction of the accord.

Discharge by Impossibility, Impracticability, or Frustration

The doctrine of *discharge by legal impossibility* is used to end the obligations to a contract when an event occurs that makes performance impossible. *Impossibility* occurs when a party who was to provide services dies or is incapacitated, a law is passed making performance of the contract illegal, or the subject matter of the contract is destroyed (a house you wanted to buy burns down before the deal is done). Impossibility discharges the obligations of the parties to the contract.

An extension of impossibility is *impracticability* or *frustration*. The *Restatement (2d) of Contracts* holds, at §262, that impracticability may be applied because of "extreme or unreasonable difficulty, expense, injury or loss...." The term means more than unexpected difficulty and cost. The concept may be applied to wartime shortages, crop failures, or loss of needed supplies due to international embargos. Courts generally expect at least partial performance, even if full performance is excused by impracticability.

Remedies

Parties to contracts usually perform their obligations. Still, thousands of disputes must be resolved every year. There is a basic premise that after a breach, innocent parties should be placed in the economic position they would have enjoyed had the contract been performed. If, however, the circumstances are such that the legal remedy of monetary damages is inadequate, the court may grant the injured party an appropriate equitable remedy. The major classes of remedies available are presented in Exhibit 10.6.

Damages

The most common remedy for breach of contract is monetary damages. The party who suffered from a breach seeks a judgment for lost profits and for other expenses particular to the breach. A variety of damage awards are used by the courts, including compensatory, expectancy, liquidated, nominal, and special damages.

Economic Loss Rule

The *economic loss rule* means that when a breach of contract does not include a tort, such as injury to persons, the damages only relate to economic losses suffered from a breach. As the Wisconsin supreme court explained, the "application of the economic loss doctrine to tort actions between commercial parties is generally based on three policies ... 1) to maintain the fundamental distinction between tort law and contract law; 2) to protect commercial parties' freedom to allocate economic

Monetary Damages	Equitable Remedies
Compensatory Damages	Specific performance
Expectancy Damages	Injunction
Liquidated Damages	Restitution
Nominal Damages	Reformation
Special Damages	

Exhibit 10.6
Contract Remedies

risk by contract; and 3) to encourage the party best situated to assess the risk of economic loss." (*Daanen* v. *Cedarapids*, 573 N.W.2d at 846).

Because the damages should only be related to lost profits and costs incurred due to a breach, which require accounting evidence and specific calculations, not punitive damages or mental distress awards, it is common to try to assert that a tort occurred in a breach of contract case. Look back at the complaint in the *Wynn* v. *Lloyd's* case early in Chapter 3. There is a claim the defendant acted "intentionally" and "maliciously." This is an effort to try to wriggle a tort into the case in an effort to obtain higher damages.

Calculating Damages

Suppose you arrange for Yo La Tengo and Ghostface Killah to appear together at a concert. Kind of odd, but you think it is a great idea. They will each get 20 percent of the gate, plus $10,000 each guaranteed, plus all revenues from CD and t-shirt sales. The concert arena will hold 6,000 fans; average ticket price will be $25, so revenues will be $150,000 if you sell out, of which $80,000 will go to the performers. The concert hall charges a flat $40,000 to host the show. That would leave you $30,000. You get local radio stations to hype the concert for free. A week before the concert, both artists cancel for no good reason. The arena charges you a $2,000 cancellation fee. You have sold 3,000 tickets that must be refunded. You sue the performers for breach of contract.

You win, but what are the damages? First, you have the market value of your time spent, say 200 hours. What is your usual wage rate? At $20 an hour, it would be a $4,000 "cost" you incurred by devoting time to the event's planning. Each ticket costs $1 printing and mailing cost, so there is $3,000, plus the $2,000 arena fee, or $9,000 in direct costs incurred. Those are costs covered by *compensatory* or *actual damages*. These damages, in contract cases, are to allow the party suffering the breach to recover costs incurred due to relying on the promise of the other party. What about lost profits? If you only sold 3,000 tickets, there would have been no profit, so you could not claim *expectancy damages*. These damages are to cover the profits you reasonably expected to make if the contract had been fulfilled. It looks like you would have lost a lot more money than if they had not cancelled.

INTERNATIONAL PERSPECTIVE

Contracting with the Japanese

A typical U.S. view is that a contract defines the rights and responsibilities of the parties and seeks to cover all possible contingencies. The traditional Japanese view is that a contract is secondary in a business transaction; business is an ongoing relationship, with both parties committed to the pursuit of similar objectives. Consequently, relationships, not contracts, are negotiated in Japan.

Major concepts are negotiated in Japan, but the minute details that are more common in a contract in the United States are often not included. As a result, Americans are often somewhat uncomfortable due to the lack of specificity. Some Japanese accept more details in a contract, knowing it is what Americans expect. But brief and flexible contracts are preferred. Contracts are often viewed as agreements to be refined as circumstances change. Long legal agreements drafted by the other party are likely to be viewed with suspicion. Relationships should take precedence over formal rights and obligations, and problems can be resolved by compromise.

Japanese contract-negotiating teams are often larger than American teams. The Japanese group may excuse itself during a session so members can discuss an issue among themselves. Strong statements such as "That would not work," are likely to be seen as rude. They work for a consensus within the team and the company. Negotiations may proceed slowly. The Japanese do not appear to operate with the urgency typical of Americans' because they wish to develop the basis of a lasting relationship.

Getty Images

However, if you could show that most tickets for a concert are usually sold in the last week, and selling out was likely, then you would have suffered lost profits and should collect expectancy damages. What about the fact that you cannot sleep nights worrying about this and feeling that your career as a concert promoter has been ruined? Too bad; there is no recovery for mental distress or some other tort. It was a business deal gone bad; the rule is to stick to measurable costs.

We see a discussion of damage issues in the *Logan* case.

Logan v. D.W. Sivers
Court of Appeals of Oregon
207 Or.App. 231, 141 P.3d 589 (2006)

Case Background *In early 2003, Logan sold a piece of property for $3.9 million. She could avoid paying taxes on the gain in value of the property, under section 1031 of the tax code, if she bought another piece of property of equal or greater value. To get the tax break, Logan had to identify another property within 45 days and then execute the purchase within 180 days. If not, she would pay taxes of $919,652 on the gain. She found a piece of property owned by Sivers and worked out a deal. But before the purchase was completed, Sivers sold the property to another party. It was too late for Logan to identify other property to buy, and she had to pay the taxes.*

Logan sued Sivers for breach and for the losses she suffered. The jury found for her and awarded her $919,652. The judge overturned the verdict, holding that Sivers was not responsible for the tax liability. Logan appealed.

Case Decision Rosenblum, Judge

* * *

Plaintiff brought this action for breach of contract against defendant, seeking expectation damages as well as consequential damages arising from plaintiff's tax liability. A jury awarded plaintiff the consequential tax losses but not the expectation damages....

Because the jury awarded only the consequential damages that plaintiff sought—that is, the damages that she incurred as a result of her tax liability—we consider only the propriety of that award.

A plaintiff may recover damages for breach of contract if the damages are (1) caused by the breach, (2) foreseeable, and (3) not too speculative.

As to causation, defendant argues that the only losses that can be caused by a breach of a contract to negotiate are out-of-pocket expenses incurred in the negotiations. It contends that the tax losses awarded by the jury were not caused by its breach....

The court instructed the jury that, if it found that defendant breached the contract, then it was to

decide whether the breach caused the loss and, if it did cause the loss, how much money should be paid. The court told the jury that it could award money for those damages that arise naturally and necessarily from the breach of contract and would place plaintiff in the same position as if the contract had not been breached. The jury returned a special verdict that answered four questions. The last two questions involved damages. One question asked, "Was plaintiff damaged as a result of defendant's breach?" The jury answered, "Yes." The last question asked, "What are plaintiff's damages?" The jury filled in $919,652....

As to whether the damages were foreseeable, defendant argues that the damages here were not within the reasonable contemplation of the parties.... According to defendant, no reasonable fact finder could conclude that plaintiff's tax losses were either the natural and probable result of the breach or within the reasonable contemplation of the parties.

We disagree. The rule that damages must be foreseeable "does not require that the defendant should have had the resulting injury in contemplation or should have promised either impliedly or expressly to pay therefore in case of breach."...

Whether damages are foreseeable is a question of fact for the jury. The jury here found that plaintiff's damages were foreseeable, and there is evidence to support that finding. Plaintiff adduced evidence that her broker told defendant's president that plaintiff was a "motivated 1031 buyer" and that she was on a short timeline with her section 1031 exchange. There is also evidence that defendant's president was acquainted with the rules and timelines governing section 1031 exchanges and that he understood the term "1031 buyer" to mean someone who had already sold property and is looking for replacement property that can be acquired within section 1031's strict timelines. That evidence supports the jury's finding that

continues

reasonable people in the position of the parties would have foreseen plaintiff's damages as a natural result of the breach. We therefore reject defendant's argument that the damages were not foreseeable as a matter of law....

Reversed and remanded with instructions to reinstate the jury's verdict.

Questions for Analysis

1. The appeals court held that Logan could recover, as damages, the tax liability she suffered due to the breach. Why could she not recover expectancy damages?

2. Why did Sivers argue that it should not be liable for the tax liability?

Liquidated Damages

Liquidated damages are an amount specified in the contract to be paid in the event of breach. Liquidated damages are not allowed if the court finds that they are so excessive that they actually impose a *penalty*. That is, the damages specified in the contract must be reasonably related to actual losses that could be suffered. For example, if an office building is supposed to be completed by May 15 for occupancy, the contract may require the builder to pay liquidated damages of $1,000 per day after May 15 until the building is ready. But the contract could not call for "damages" of $1 million per day; that would be a penalty, which is against public policy.

LIGHTER SIDE OF THE LAW
Me, Read the Rules?

Struna bought 52 lottery tickets with the same numbers on each. The top prize was $100,000 for a winning ticket, but the lottery rules hold that the maximum any one person can win in a drawing is $1 million, so when Struna's number won, he got $1 million, not the $5 million he expected.

He sued Convenient Food Mart, where he bought the tickets, for fraud, because the clerk did not tell him the terms of the lottery contract, which were printed on the ticket. The jury awarded him $250,000 in compensatory damages and $1.1 million in punitive damages.

The appeals court threw out the judgment.

Source: *Struna v. Convenient Food Mart*, 828 N.E.2d 647 (Ct. App., Ohio)

Getty Images

Nominal Damages

When a plaintiff has suffered a breach of contract but has not suffered a measurable economic loss, a court may award *nominal damages*. The amount of recovery to the injured party may be as little as a dollar, but attorney fees and court costs may also be awarded. Such awards can be important, because proof of breach may be related to other legal issues.

Punitive Damages

Punitive or *exemplary damages* are usually awarded when the wrongdoer's conduct has been willful or malicious and fraud was involved, bringing in tort issues. They punish the wrongdoer by allowing the plaintiff to receive relief beyond compensatory or expectancy damages.

Mitigation of Damages

When a breach of contract does occur, the injured party is required to take reasonable efforts to *mitigate*, or lessen, the losses that may be incurred. When Yo La Tengo and Ghostface Killah decided not to show for the concert, you had to stop work on it, take the steps necessary to call it off, and refund money to those who bought tickets. You could not keep incurring new costs by selling more tickets in the hope that they might change their minds and come after all. Once there is a clear breach, business as usual must resume.

Equitable Remedies

If money damages are inadequate to compensate for the injury caused by a breach of contract, or if they do not resolve the problem properly, *equitable remedies*, such as specific performance or an injunction, may be available. These remedies are available to injured parties only at the discretion of the court. They generally will not be granted where an adequate damage remedy exists, or where enforcement would impose a great burden to the defendant.

Specific Performance

Specific performance is an order by the court requiring the party who created the wrong to perform the obligations promised in the contract. The remedy is granted for breach of a contract when the payment of money damages is inadequate. Contracts for the sale of a particular piece of real property (land) or of a unique good, such as a piece of art, are the types of contract in which specific performance may be granted by the courts. Courts will not order people to perform personal service, to do some particular job, because it would be involuntary servitude. That is, a court would not force Ghostface Killah and Yo La Tengo to appear at a concert and perform. Damages would be imposed instead.

Injunction

As with the remedy of specific performance, the remedy of injunction is allowed when the payment of damages does not offer a satisfactory substitute for the performance promised. An *injunction* is an order by the court that requires a party to perform or to refrain from performing certain acts. Suppose a partnership agreement stated that a partner who quits to go into business for herself will not compete against the partnership for three years. If a partner quits the partnership to start a new competing firm, the payment of damages may be an inadequate remedy for the partnership. The court, through the granting of an injunction, may order the departed partner not to compete with the partnership.

Restitution

The remedy of *restitution* may be used to prevent unjust enrichment. That is, if one party has unjustly enriched himself—received a benefit not paid for—at the expense of another party, the court can order payment to be made or the goods involved to be returned. Closely related to this is the idea of quasi contract.

Quasi Contracts

A *quasi contract* is not a contract. The courts created the concept of quasi contract to give relief to innocent parties, or to prevent injustice, even though no true contract exists. In the words of New York's highest court in *Bradkin* v. *Leverton*, 309 N.Y.S.2d 192:

> Quasi contracts are not contracts at all.... The contract is a mere fiction, a form imposed in order to adapt the case to a given remedy.... Briefly stated, a quasi-contractual obligation is one imposed by law where there has been no agreement or expression of assent, by word or act, on the part of either party involved. The law creates it, regardless of the intention of the parties, to assure a just and equitable result.

A quasi contract, also called *quantum meruit*, is used by the courts to avoid injustice. Something of value has been provided but there was no contract, such as a doctor providing emergency medical assistance to an injured child without first getting permission of the parents, or a contract was not completed. For example, in *Burke* v. *McKee* (304 P.2d 307), a contractor had promised to clear 80 acres of land. He quit when he finished half the work, due to a dispute with the landowner. The owner refused to pay unless the contractor finished all the work. The court ordered the contractor to be paid the value of the work done to the point at which he quit. Although the contract was not completed, the landowner was not to get the value of the work for nothing, as that would be *unjust enrichment*. He could hire another contractor to finish the job at no higher cost.

Summary

- Basic to the law of contracts is freedom of contract. However, because of public policy goals, state and federal laws place some restrictions on the kinds of contracts businesses can enter into.
- Contract law is basically common or judge-made law. The *Restatement of Contracts* is an authoritative document providing a summary of the common law of contract, which is quite consistent across the states.
- A contract is a promise or set of promises that creates an agreement between parties. It creates legal rights and duties enforceable under the law.
- Under the common law, enforceable contracts have several elements in common:

  1. There must be an agreement (offer and acceptance).
  2. The parties to a contract must provide consideration.
  3. The parties must have the legal capacity to contract.
  4. The subject matter of the contract must be legal.
  5. The consent of the parties must be genuine.

- An offeror has the right to terminate an offer without warning, before it is accepted, unless there was an option granted, which is a contract in itself, giving the offeree a certain time in which to decide. If an offer is not specifically ended, it is presumed to end in a reasonable time given usual practices in that area of business.
- Acceptance of an offer must be clear and, to be effective, must not make changes in the terms offered. When an offeree makes changes to an offer, a new offer has been created. If an offeror states that acceptance must follow a specific form, such as signing a piece of paper, then that must be done for acceptance to be effective.
- Consideration is something of value bargained for in an exchange. The courts do not care much about the "fairness" of an exchange, only that there has been a voluntary exchange of mutual promises to give something of value. A legal detriment exists for both parties to the contract, so it is not a gift.
- A promise that falls short of meeting the terms of a contract may still be held to be enforceable under the doctrine of promissory estoppel. That occurs when a promise is made that the other party can reasonably rely upon in their decision making.
- Parties to a contract must have capacity to contract, meaning they must be of legal age and not suffering from a disability that precludes their understanding the matter. The subject matter of a contract must be legal for the courts to be

willing to consider enforcement; deals for subjects that are illegal by statute, or that violate public policy, will not be recognized.

- Consent must be genuine; no force or duress may be used. The claim that consent was given due to fraud or fraudulent misrepresentation is common; a party was tricked into a deal that would not have been made had the other party been truthful. This can fall into tort law, which allows room for greater damages, including punitive damages.

- Some contracts must be in writing to fulfill requirements of the Statute of Frauds. They include contracts for the sale of land and real property, promises made in consideration of marriage, contracts that cannot be completed within one year, and promises to pay the debt of another.

- Contracts may be discharged, or terminated, in several ways: by performance, through a breach by one or both of the parties to the contract, by the impossibility of performance, by operation of law, or by mutual agreement of the parties.

- In the event of a breach of contract, the injured party may ask the court for relief. Most common are money damages to compensate for expenses incurred and for lost profits. The injured party has a responsibility to minimize losses from the breach. The courts can also provide equitable relief, such as specific performance, in certain cases.

Terms to Know

You should be able to define the following terms:

express contract, 223	exculpatory agreement, 234	accord, 242
implied contract, 223	fraud, 236	impossibility, 243
offer, 224	Statute of Frauds, 238	economic loss rule, 243
option contract, 226	parol evidence rule, 239	expectancy damages, 244
acceptance, 227	assignment, 241	liquidated damages, 246
bilateral contract, 227	delegation, 241	specific performance, 247
unilateral contract, 227	breach of contract, 241	injunction, 247
consideration, 229	discharge, 242	quasi contract, 247
promissory estoppel, 231	rescission, 242	*quantum meruit*, 248
usury, 234	novation, 242	

Discussion Question

1. Jones walks into a grocery store, puts 50 cents down on the counter, and says, "A Coke please." Under contract law, what has just occurred? If the grocery store owner hands him a Coke and takes the 50 cents, what type of contract has been agreed upon?

Case Questions

1. Three armed men robbed the First State Bank of Kentucky of more than $30,000. The Kentucky Bankers Association provided and advertised a reward of $500 for the arrest and conviction of the bank robbers. The robbers were later captured and convicted. The arresting officers and the employees of the bank who provided important information leading to the arrest have all claimed the reward. Is there a contract between these parties and the Bankers Association? [*Denney* v. *Reppert*, 432 S.W.2d 647 Ct. App., Ky. (1968)]

2. Polk listed property to sell with a real estate agent. Avon made an offer and the two parties went back and forth on terms. When Polk rejected an offer from Avon, Avon then accepted an earlier offer from Polk and gave a $25,000 deposit check to cinch the deal. Polk refused to sell. Avon sued, claiming there was a contract or, at a minimum, an option contract formed by the deposit check. Is there a contract? [*Polk* v. *BHRGU Avon Properties*, 946 So.2d 1120 Dist. Ct. App., Fla. (2006)]

   ✓ Check your answer at http://academic.cengage.com/blaw/meiners

3. Barry hired Anglin to produce engineering drawings for work Barry was doing at a brewery. Anglin said it would charge "street" rates for the work, which meant $35 an hour for regular work, $40 an hour for overtime work, and $45 an hour for its time. Barry gave Anglin a "purchase order" for the work, but no rate was specified. Barry paid bills for two months, but then quit paying. Barry insisted that the work be done, but constantly complained about the rates and did not pay bills for four months. Anglin sued for $98,618, the amount it was due for work at the "street" rate. Barry claimed there was no contract, because there was no meeting of the minds about the rate to be paid. Who prevails? [*Anglin* v. *Barry*, 912 S.W.2d 633 Ct. App., Mo. (1995)]

   ✓ Check your answer at http://academic.cengage.com/blaw/meiners

4. At the end of a two-year lease, landlord and tenant discussed a new lease. The tenant sent a letter to the landlord stating that it would pay rent of $1,800 per month and that "all other terms and conditions of the [original] lease, including taxes, insurance, utilities, etc., shall remain the same." The letter also said that it was to be advised "by confirmation letter if the terms of the two-year lease extension are acceptable to [the lessor]." The lessor never responded. The tenant paid rent for a couple months, then moved out. The landlord sued for breach, claiming there was an oral agreement evidenced by the letter from the tenant; the tenant claimed there was no contract. Who is correct and why? [*Valiant Steel* v. *Roadway Express*, 421 S.E.2d 773 Ct. App., Ga. (1992)]

   ✓ Check your answer at http://academic.cengage.com/blaw/meiners

5. Mary Lowe, in the presence of her son, David, and Allen Amdahl, wrote: "January 26, 1987. I, Mary Lowe, in the presence of David Lowe received from Allen Amdahl $1.00 in cash binding the sale of my farm (of 880 acres) for the amount of $210,000 with final payment due Nov. 1, 1989. Terms of Agreement have been mutually agreed to by both parties. Contract drawn up as soon as possible." She signed this statement, and David Lowe witnessed it. Amdahl wrote on the back of the paper a payment schedule but did not sign the paper. When he returned with a formal contract, Lowe refused to sign. Amdahl sued. Was there an enforceable contract? [*Amdahl* v. *Lowe*, 471 N.W.2d 770 Sup. Ct., N.D. (1991)]

6. Rose, a minor, purchased a new car from Sheehan Buick for $5,000. Rose later, while still a minor, elected to disaffirm the purchase and notified Sheehan of her decision. She also requested a full refund of the purchase price. Sheehan refused, and Rose brought an action to invalidate the contract and to seek a refund of the purchase price. What will be the likely result? [*Rose* v. *Sheehan Buick*, 204 So.2d 903 Fla. App. (1967)]

   ✓ Check your answer at http://academic.cengage.com/blaw/meiners

7. To help in a fund raising drive for a hospital, Burt gave a pledge for $100,000 that provided, "In consideration of and to induce the subscription of others, I promise to pay to Mount Sinai Hospital of Greater Miami, Inc. the sum of $100,000 in ten installments." Burt made two installment payments of $10,000 each before his death. The hospital filed a claim for the unpaid balance against his estate. Is this a contract for which the estate is now liable? [*Mount Sinai Hospital* v. *Jordan*, 290 So.2d 484 Sup. Ct., Fla. (1974)]

8. Smith contracted to build a gymnasium for Limestone College. About the time the building was finished, an "extraordinarily heavy rainfall" caused the sewer system to back up into the gymnasium, doing damage that cost Smith $37,000 to repair. Smith billed the city sewer system for the work done. The city refused to pay, claiming there was no contract. Smith claimed an implied contract existed; was he right? [*Stanley Smith & Sons* v. *Limestone College*, 322 S.E.2d 474 Ct. App., S.C. (1984)]

9. Copenhaver put pay washers and dryers in an apartment complex owned by Berryman. With four years to run on the contract, Berryman kicked Copenhaver out. Within six months, Copenhaver had put all equipment back into service in other locations. He sued for compensatory damages for the cost of moving and for profits he lost over the rest of the four years of the contract. What damages is he owed? [*Copenhaver v. Berryman*, 602 S.W.2d 540 Ct. App., Tex. (1980)]

10. A builder constructed a house according to plans provided by the owner. The contract specified that only Reading brand pipe was to be used in the plumbing. After the house was completed, the owner discovered that another brand of pipe had been used. The owner refused final payment and demanded that the pipe be replaced with Reading pipe, which would have involved major reconstruction. Evidence at trial was that the two brands of pipe were of the same general quality. Did the owner have to make final payment, or did the pipe have to be replaced? [*Jacob & Youngs v. Kent*, 129 N.E. 889 Ct. App., N Y (1921)]

11. GE contracted to provide kitchen appliances for an apartment complex for $93,500. Several months later, GE discovered that a mathematical error had been made in the bid and that the bid should have been for an additional $30,150. GE demanded rescission of the contract. Did it get it? [*General Electric Supply v. Republic Construction*, 272 P.2d 201 Sup. Ct., Ore. (1954)]

12. Employer Engelcke Manufacturing asked one of its employees, Eaton, to design electronic plans for Whizball, a game it planned to produce and sell. Eaton said he thought he could do the job after work for about $1,500. During the next year, the project became more complicated, and Eaton devoted substantially more time to it than had been expected. Engelcke said it would pay him for his work. When the project was mostly done, Engelcke fired Eaton and refused to pay him, because the electronic plans were not completed. Engelcke claimed Eaton breached an express contract and that it got nothing of value. Was there a contract? Could there be damages? [*Eaton v. Englecke Manufacturing*, 681 P.2d 1312 Ct. App., Wash. (1984)]

13. Transatlantic agreed to ship a load of wheat from the United States to Iran for $305,842. While the ship was enroute, a war caused the Suez Canal to be closed. Transatlantic had to turn around and sail all the way around Africa to get to Iran. It sued for the additional $44,000 it cost to go the extra distance. Could it collect? [*Transatlantic Financing v. U.S.*, 363 F.2d 312 D.C. Cir. (1966)]

Ethics Question

1. You would probably not think of paying $1,000 for a $300 refrigerator, but it happens, especially when low-income people with little education sign contracts to buy appliances or furniture on time payments. Since many of these contracts have high interest rates and numerous penalties for late payments, a buyer can wind up paying many times the market value of the goods if the contract is carried to completion. Because many low-income customers do not make payments on time or quit making payments, some businesses justify the exorbitant terms, because the high returns from some customers offset the high default rate from others. Is this an ethical selling practice? Is there another way to handle the situation?

Internet Assignment

http://www.law.cornell.edu/wex/index.php/Contracts
Explain why it may be more effective to find background information on contracts law using Wex instead of your favorite Internet search engine.
Find the URLs for all topics covered by Wex.

Domestic and International Sales

Chapter 11

As a food broker, you fulfill orders that retailers place with food processors. You specialize in knowing who has what and how to get it delivered in a timely fashion by trucking companies you trust. Mostly you rely on reputation, rather than contracts, in your dealing with vendors. You know many of the sellers, buyers, and truckers, and they know you. There is little time for formal contracting. Most of the work is done informally on the phone and by e-mail.

There are few transaction costs and no need for lawyers drawing up contracts. If you sent a contract to a client you have dealt with for a long time, the client would probably wonder what was up. But things can go wrong with this approach. For example, a truck makes a delivery in July from Cleveland to Phoenix and arrives Friday night. The buyer thought the load would arrive on Monday, so it sits over the weekend. A half-million dollars worth of food is spoiled. Who is responsible for the bill? Did the trucker promise to cover such losses? As the broker, you bought and resold the food, picking up a commission in the middle; so are you stuck, or will the buyer suffer the loss? If you have a contract with each party, what does it say? What if you do not have a contract?

These are the kinds of issues addressed in this chapter on the sale of goods under the *Uniform Commercial Code (UCC)*. *Article 2* of the UCC governs the law of commercial sales. Since buying and selling goods is the primary activity of many commercial enterprises, it is not surprising that the law of sales is an important part of the legal environment of business. This chapter provides an overview of the law of sales in Article 2 of the UCC. It considers the nature of sales contracts under the UCC and the requirements the UCC places upon merchants. The chapter then examines some key aspects of international commercial sales. ■

Getty Images

Introduction to the UCC

The Uniform Commercial Code is the law that governs many contracts for the sale of goods. That is, the UCC does not apply to the sale of services, real estate, or professional services. Like the common law of contract, commercial law is primarily state, not federal, law.

History of Commercial Law

Commercial rules governing trade—"codes"—existed more than 2,000 years ago in Greece. Over a thousand years later, in medieval Europe, merchants developed rules governing trade issues, such as sales, payment, insurance, and shipping. These were known as the *lex mercatoria* or *law merchant*. This was sales law that applied to transactions in different countries. For example, a fourteenth-century merchant who sold cloth would be likely to use the same rules if the sale took place in London, England; Marseilles, France; or Prague, Bohemia. Merchants themselves, rather than governments, generally enforced this law.

By the eighteenth century, judges in England began to incorporate the customary law merchant into the common law of England to resolve contract disputes. As the economy developed during the nineteenth century, so too did commercial law. As new technologies emerged—railroads, steam ships, telegraphs—commercial law evolved to accommodate the changing needs of merchants.

In the early twentieth century, each state in the United States had a different, but related, set of commercial laws. One of the costs of doing business in different states was dealing with somewhat different rules. Some legal scholars and people in business decided it would be efficient to have a more consistent set of rules for commercial transactions.

The National Conference of Commissioners on Uniform State Laws and the American Law Institute began drafting a commercial law. In the 1950s, the groups presented the Uniform Commercial Code to the states. Every state adopted most of the UCC, although Louisiana has not adopted Article 2. Over the years, the UCC has been modified to reflect changes in the way businesses operate. Exhibit 11.1 notes the major sections of the UCC.

Article Number and Title	Coverage
1: General Provisions	Purpose of the UCC; general guidance and definitions
2: Sale of Goods	Applies to sales and leases of goods
3: Negotiable Instruments	Use of checks, promissory notes, and other financial instruments
4: Bank Deposits and Collections	Rights and duties of banks and their clients
5: Letters of Credit	Guaranteed payment by a bank that extends credit on behalf of a client
6: Bulk Transfers	Sales of a large part of a company's material
7: Warehouse Receipts, Bills of Lading, and Other Documents of Title	Papers proving ownership of goods geing shipped
8: Investment Securities	Rights and duties related to stock or other ownership interests
9: Secured Transactions	Sales in which seller holds a financial interest in goods sold

Exhibit 11.1
The Articles of the Uniform Commercial Code

Application of the UCC

We refer here to the "model" UCC and cite specific sections (§) of it. Some states modified the UCC somewhat when it was made part of state law. The UCC's purpose is "to simplify, clarify and modernize the law governing commercial transactions" (§1–102).

This chapter primarily concerns Article 2 of the UCC, which deals with the sale of goods. When does the UCC apply, rather than the common law of contracts? It applies when "the item involved is movable and is not money or an investment security" (§2–102). Examples of movable goods include wristwatches and computers. Land is not movable, nor are houses. Article 2 covers the sale of *goods*, not services, so, for example, if you contract with a lawyer to represent you, that would be under the common law of contracts.

Despite all the lawyers who draft contracts and all the business students who have taken courses such as this one, many contracts fail to state what law governs a contract. Also, there may be more than one contract in place at the same time. These issues may not matter unless there is a dispute, at which point it can make a difference if the UCC or the common law governs.

Suppose, as often happens, a contract is for a mix of goods and services and the contract does not specify common law or UCC. Which law governs a dispute? The rule is to look to whether goods or services dominate the contract. If the contract is for $180,000 total and, in breaking it down, the court sees that $70,000 covers the costs of goods and $100,000 is for services such as installation and maintenance, then the value of the services dominate, so the common law governs.

Goods, Merchants, Sales, and Titles under the UCC

Goods

The UCC defines *goods* as "all things (including specially manufactured things) which are movable at the time of identification to the contract for sale" (§2–105 [1]). In other words, the subject matter of a *sales contract* is not considered a good under Article 2 unless it is movable and tangible. A good is *movable* if it can be carried from one location to another. So real estate does not come under Article 2. A good is *tangible* when it has a physical existence; that is, it can be seen and touched. Thus, services and intangible interests—such as stocks, bank accounts, patents, and copyrights, which are called *intangible* forms of personal property—are not goods under Article 2. A contract involving such items would be governed by the common law of contracts or possibly by another part of the UCC.

Merchants

Section 1–203 holds all parties who enter into an Article 2 sales contract to a standard of *good-faith* dealing. Good-faith dealing is defined by UCC §1–201 as "honesty in fact in the conduct or transaction incurred." Article 2 places a high duty of conduct on merchants, who are treated differently from members of the public, because they have business expertise. A merchant is recognized by §2–104 as a person who

1. regularly deals in goods of the kind involved in the transaction,
2. by occupation presents himself as having knowledge or skill specialized to the transaction, or
3. employs an agent who holds herself out as having particular knowledge or skill about the goods involved.

Sales

Article 2 applies to contracts for the *sale* of goods. A sale occurs when there is a "passing of title from the seller to the buyer for a price" (§2–106[1]). Hence, the sale must involve the *title* to goods being passed. The title represents the legal rights to ownership of a thing, such as a car or a computer. If legal title does not pass, there has not been a sale under the UCC. Article 2 does not apply to the lease of goods, such as the lease of a car, but most states have adopted Article 2A, a Code article dealing with certain leases of personal property.

Titles

How do we determine who holds title to goods? We look to UCC §2–401. A person may hold legal title to a good if 1) the good exists, and 2) the good has been identified—such as by the serial number on a car—to the contract, meaning that the seller has specified which goods are being sold to the buyer. Then §2–401 allows title to be passed however the parties see fit. For example, the UCC would allow title to pass in any of the following situations, if that is what the parties bargain for, as determined by contract language, custom, or past practices:

Exhibit 11.2 Offer and Acceptance: Comparing the UCC and the Common Law of Contracts

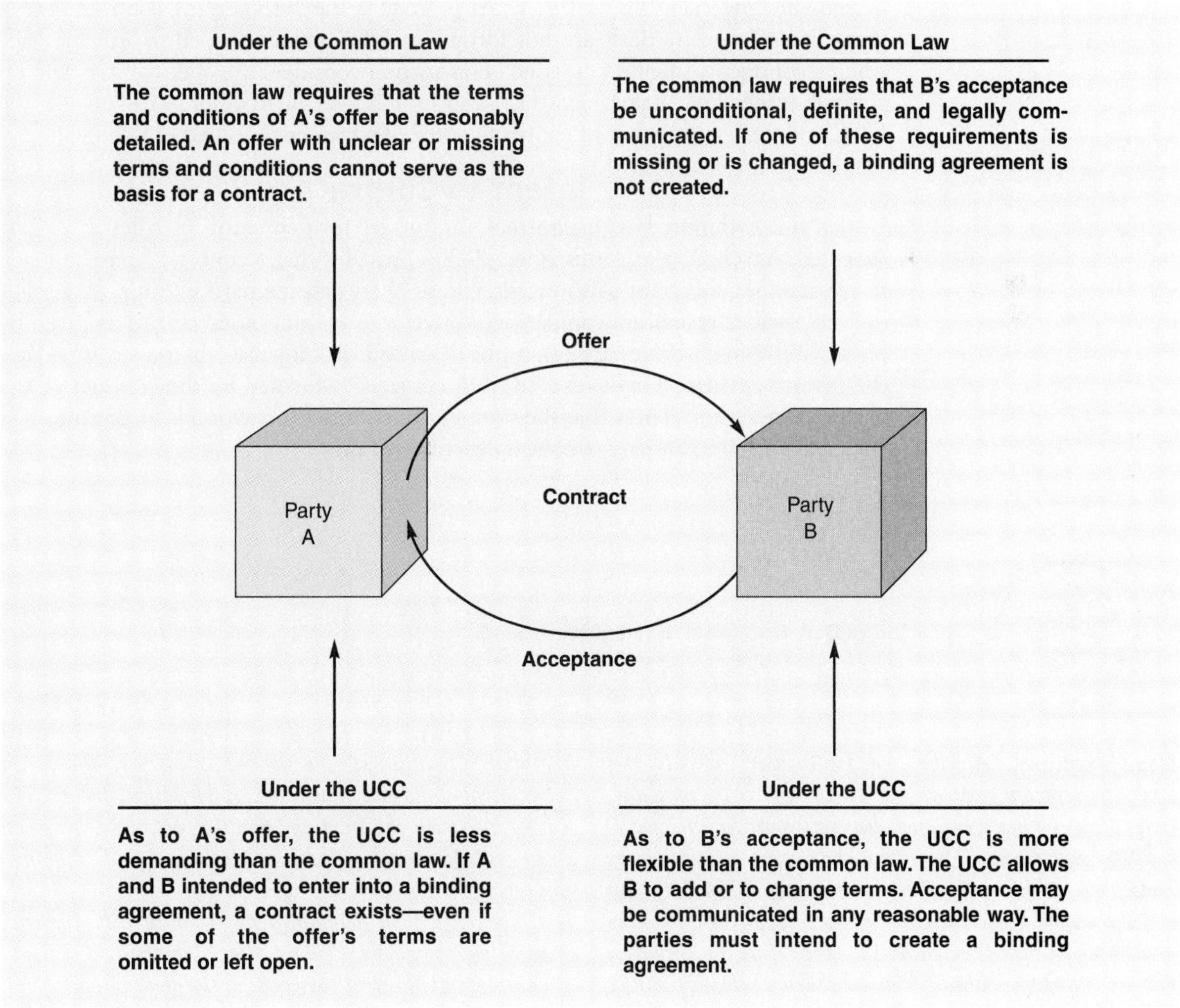

Under the Common Law

The common law requires that the terms and conditions of A's offer be reasonably detailed. An offer with unclear or missing terms and conditions cannot serve as the basis for a contract.

Under the Common Law

The common law requires that B's acceptance be unconditional, definite, and legally communicated. If one of these requirements is missing or is changed, a binding agreement is not created.

Offer

Contract

Party A

Party B

Acceptance

Under the UCC

As to A's offer, the UCC is less demanding than the common law. If A and B intended to enter into a binding agreement, a contract exists—even if some of the offer's terms are omitted or left open.

Under the UCC

As to B's acceptance, the UCC is more flexible than the common law. The UCC allows B to add or to change terms. Acceptance may be communicated in any reasonable way. The parties must intend to create a binding agreement.

- When the goods arrive for shipment at a port
- When the goods arrive at the buyer's warehouse
- When the goods leave the seller's warehouse
- When the goods are halfway between the seller's factory and the buyer's warehouse

If the parties disagree about whether or not title passed, or they failed to specify when title passed, then the courts look to §2–401, which states that 1) title passes to the buyer when the seller completes all her obligations regarding delivery of the goods; or 2) title passes to the buyer when the seller delivers the title documents, if the goods did not have to be moved.

If a seller "sells" stolen goods, then good title does not pass to the buyer (§2–403). For example, if someone steals a computer from a university and sells the computer to a buyer who does not know it is stolen, and then the university finds the stolen property, it gets it back. A thief has no title, or void title, and so cannot pass good title.

Forming a Sales Contract

Contracts are governed by the common law of contracts unless the UCC changes or modifies the rule. The UCC tends to reduce the formality of contract law. It recognizes that many deals are not formal, so UCC rules are used to "fill the gap" when a contract is silent on an issue. This section considers the effect of Article 2 on contract principles. As you read this, keep in mind the basic differences between the UCC and the common law of contracts, some of which are outlined in Exhibit 11.2.

Intent to Contract

Under the common law, a contract cannot be formed until an offer is clearly accepted. Article 2 relaxes this rule; §2–204 provides that a contract "may be made in any manner sufficient to show agreement" between the parties. Suppose a seller delivers various restaurant supplies to a buyer's restaurant based on orders given by phone and e-mail. Prices are often not discussed or known to the buyer, who pays the invoice by mail. Under the UCC, a contract is formed by the conduct of the parties. It does not matter that the moment of contract formation is uncertain.

In the *Crest Ridge* case, we see an example of this.

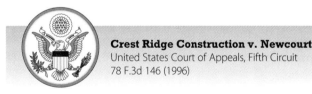

Crest Ridge Construction v. Newcourt
United States Court of Appeals, Fifth Circuit
78 F.3d 146 (1996)

Case Background *John and Joe Brower worked for a large construction company but set up their own company, Crest Ridge. They were awarded a subcontract on a job to provide wall panels. They wanted to use panels made by Newcourt, which gave them a quote of $758,000, but issued the contract in the name of the company the Browers used to work for. They cleared up that issue, and made a few amendments, which changed the price to $760,000. The contract stated it was "subject to credit department*

approval." Because it was a new company, the credit department could not find much information about Crest Ridge, but over the next six months, detailed discussions about specifications of panels continued and shipment was set.

Newcourt then demanded payment in full. Industry practice was payment 45 days after shipment, so the subcontractor could present the goods to the general contractor, who would pay the bill. Because of the cancellation, Crest

Ridge had to find another supplier at a higher price to fill the order. It sued Newcourt. The jury awarded $70,214 in damages. Newcourt appealed.

Case Decision Higginbotham, Circuit Judge

* * *

Newcourt argues that the phrase "subject to credit department approval" illustrated that it never agreed to extend credit to Crest Ridge and thus that its demand of payment up front constituted no breach of contract....

The jury heard evidence sufficient to allow it to conclude that Newcourt and Crest Ridge formed a contract. The UCC provides that "a contract for the sale of goods may be made in any manner sufficient to show agreement, including conduct by both parties which recognizes the existence of such a contract." Newcourt and Crest Ridge exchanged a price quotation and a purchase order, documents the construction industry considered to have binding effect. Moreover, the parties' conduct illustrated that they thought they had a deal.... [For six months] the parties engaged in an extended exchange designed to clarify the details of the project. Newcourt itself provided material samples, three revisions of shop drawings, fastening details, stipulations as to the color of each panel, and final drawings showing where each panel would go....

For two reasons, we find unpersuasive Newcourt's ... argument that insufficient evidence supported the jury's finding that Newcourt breached its contract with Crest Ridge. First, the phrase "subject to credit department approval" does not constitute a refusal to grant credit. Indeed, the requirement of credit department approval would be unnecessary unless the parties contemplated some form of credit. Second, because Newcourt and Crest Ridge left the terms of payment blank in their exchange of price quotation and purchase order, payment was due either upon delivery, or perhaps according to "general usage." In either case, Newcourt breached the agreement by demanding full payment in advance....

Affirmed.

Questions for Analysis

1. The appeals court affirmed that a contract existed, even though a specific term had been ignored. Did Newcourt have good reason to worry about the ability of a little company like Crest Ridge to pay its bill?

2. Suppose a credit search found that Crest Ridge had serious financial problems; could Newcourt have ended the deal then?

An Indefinite Offer

Under Article 2, if parties intended to enter into an agreement on the basis of the offer, a contract exists. This can be the case even though some of the offer's major terms—such as price, delivery, or payment terms—are omitted or are left open for later determination. UCC 2–204(3) states that a contract does not fail for indefiniteness "if the parties have intended to make a contract and there is a reasonably certain basis for giving an appropriate remedy." When terms are left open by the parties, Article 2 has rules for determining the terms.

Merchant's Firm Offer

Article 2 modifies the contract rules governing when an offer may be revoked. Under the common law, an offer can be revoked anytime before acceptance. The main common-law exception is the option contract, under which the offeree gives consideration for the offeror's promise to keep the offer open for a stated time period. Section 2–205 provides another exception: If a merchant-offeror gives assurances in a signed writing that the offer will remain open for a given period, the merchant's *firm offer* is irrevocable. No consideration is needed. If the period is not stated in the offer, it stays open for a reasonable time not to exceed three months.

Acceptance

Article 2 modifies the common-law rules for acceptance in several important ways. To bring the rules of acceptance more in line with business practices, the

UCC provides greater flexibility in the way acceptance can be communicated. If the offeror does not clearly demand a particular method of acceptance, §2–206 holds that a contract is formed when the offer is accepted in any reasonable manner under the circumstances. This flexibility allows the legal rules governing acceptance to adapt to new methods of communication, such as the Internet.

The UCC provides that an acceptance may be valid even if the offeree includes additional terms or changes existing terms in an offer. Under the common law, an acceptance cannot deviate from the terms of the offer without being considered either a rejection or a counteroffer. Article 2 makes an acceptance valid when the parties intend to form a contract—even though the offeree's acceptance contains different terms from those in the offer.

Conflicting Terms

It is not uncommon for an offeror to send an offer on a standard company form that lists standard terms, such as when payment is due. The offeree may accept the offer but send acceptance on its own standard form that does not contain all the terms that were stated in the offer. UCC §2–207(1) states that in such cases there is a valid acceptance. However, the contract is based on the offeror's terms. The different terms contained in the acceptance become a part of the contract only if the offeror accepts the terms posed by the offeree in acceptance.

When terms in contracts conflict, it is called the "battle of the forms." Each company sent pieces of paper in the other direction that differed with what the other company's form said, but no one cared until a dispute arose, as we see in the *Axelson* case.

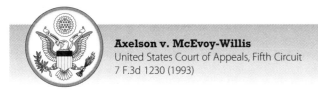

Axelson v. McEvoy-Willis
United States Court of Appeals, Fifth Circuit
7 F.3d 1230 (1993)

Case Background *McEvoy was hired to build oil rigs in the North Sea. It contacted Axelson about building actuators, complex pieces of equipment, for the rigs. Axelson sent a price quote with terms good for 60 days. McEvoy said it needed more time and accepted no deviations from its standard form contract. Axelson granted more time. The parties dickered for months, until McEvoy sent a "letter of intent" that spelled out terms but said it needed to see technical specifications to finalize the deal. Axelson did not want to provide all details without a firm order, because the specs included trade secrets, but it was assured the order was a done deal, so it sent the specs. Months later, after work started, McEvoy sent a form purchase order that stated it contained all terms of the contract and nothing else applied. One term was that McEvoy had the right to cancel the order at any time and was not liable for losses.*

After Axelson sent 28 actuators and had eight more ready for shipment, McEvoy cancelled the contract, which called for delivery of another 40. Axelson sued. The trial

court found McEvoy in breach, holding that earlier discussions, not the final contract, applied. Damages were $684,905 plus interest. McEvoy appealed.

Case Decision Duhè, Circuit Judge

* * *

Under the Code, "A contract for sale of goods may be made in any manner sufficient to show agreement, including conduct by both parties which recognizes the existence of such a contract.... even though the moment of its making is undetermined." In the present case, it is hard to tell exactly when the contract was perfected. The quotation from Axelson can be construed as an offer. An offer is an act that leads the offeree reasonably to believe that assent (i.e., acceptance) will conclude the deal....

That the [letter] of intent said the form purchase order was to follow in due course does not avail

McEvoy. Because the parties had a meeting of the minds months before, the additional terms on the June form purchase order never became part of the contract.

The result is no different even if the writings of the parties did not constitute a contract. The drafters of the UCC had this situation in mind when they wrote subsection 2.207(c):

> Conduct by both parties which recognizes the existence of a contract is sufficient to establish a contract for sale although the writings of the parties do not otherwise establish a contract. In such case the terms of the particular contract consist of those terms on which the writings of the parties agree, together with any supplementary terms incorporated under any other provisions of this title.

The conduct of the parties here recognizes the existence of a contract. The parties' writings do not agree on a particular cancellation provision, so the law provides one.... Affirmed.

Questions for Analysis

1. The appeals court affirmed that the parties had formed a contract prior to the final form contract sent by McEvoy, so its terms did not control the agreement. Hence, the rules of the UCC would settle the dispute and allow damages to be paid. What is the rationale in the UCC for not allowing the final form, as in this case, to control?

2. How did the court determine when the contract came into being?

Contract Modifications

Under the common law, contract modifications must be supported by new consideration to be binding on the parties. The UCC §2–209 makes a significant change in the common-law rule by providing that the parties need not provide new consideration to modify an existing sales contract. A modification to a sales contract, however, must meet the UCC's test of good-faith dealing and usually must be in writing.

Statute of Frauds

Article 2 §2–201 provides a *statute of frauds* provision. The basic rule is that a contract for the sale of goods for $500 or more is not enforceable unless it is in writing and signed by the party against whom enforcement is sought. Compared to the common law, the UCC relaxes the requirements for the sufficiency of a writing to

INTERNATIONAL PERSPECTIVE

How to Assure Foreign Buyers of Product Quality

Reputation in business is critical for a company to be accepted into commerce. When a firm is unknown, especially when it moves into foreign markets, it needs to demonstrate that its goods are of a quality worthy of consideration.

One way to make this demonstration is by obtaining certification from a private organization that has global acceptance as a measure of quality assurance. For many buyers, such certification is much better information than a statement by the company itself—or a government agency promoting the company—that its goods are of high quality.

Many companies seek certification from the International Standards Organization (ISO), headquartered in Geneva, Switzerland. The ISO is a network of national standards institutes, in 130 countries, that coordinates the system and sets standards. ISO certification is required by many firms before they will even consider buying goods from a supplier.

Firms apply for ISO certification, are visited by a certified registrar, and follow a complex procedure to document and organize production procedures. Firms are audited for compliance to ensure that they follow their own proper procedures. See http://www.iso.org/iso/home.htm for more details. ISO does not tell firms how to implement all aspects of the program; rather, firms must demonstrate that they know and follow quality-assurance procedures.

Getty Images

satisfy the Statute of Frauds. Under Article 2, the writing need not list every material term in the contract. The key element is that there is some basis for believing that the parties made a contract for the sale of goods, as we saw in the *Axelson* case.

Failure to Respond to a Writing

The UCC recognizes that it is not uncommon in business for contract writings to be incomplete. This is especially the case when parties discuss a deal, and one sends a writing to confirm what was discussed, but the other party does not send a written reply. However, even when there is a failure to respond to a writing signed by the other party, there may be a good contract.

Section 2–201(2) states: "Between merchants, if within a reasonable time a writing in confirmation of the contract and sufficient against the sender is received and the party receiving it has reason to know its contents, it satisfies the [writing] requirements … against such party unless written notice of objection to its contents is given within ten days after it is received." This only applies to contracts between merchants; the writing must be complete as to essential terms; and the writing must be sent soon, and received, after the contract has been formed.

Parol Evidence

Since the UCC is more generous than common-law contract law in presuming contracts to exist when terms are not all set, oral testimony is more likely to be needed to clarify disputes over terms of a contract subject to the UCC. Section 2–202 states that written documents may not be contradicted by oral testimony, but that such testimony may be used to explain customary trade dealings or the meaning of certain terms. Parol evidence may not be used "if the court finds the writing to have been intended also as a complete and exclusive statement of the terms of the agreement."

Filling the Gaps

Courts try to make sense out of contracts to keep commerce going. This is especially true under the UCC, which fills in parts of sales contracts that are left open, are unclear, or otherwise must be settled to make a contract complete. This handles the reality of business dealings where contracts are often not complete or circumstances force changes to occur. The UCC instructs the courts how to resolve uncertain terms.

In §1–205, the Code states that when parties have had regular dealings, their previous conduct will be looked to as the basis for resolving the current situation. Further, the courts will look to *trade usage—the* regular practice and methods of dealings in a given trade—to resolve an unsettled transaction.

We see an example of the court filling the gaps in the *Clear Lakes Trout* case.

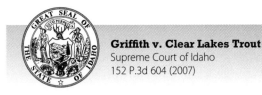

Griffith v. Clear Lakes Trout
Supreme Court of Idaho
152 P.3d 604 (2007)

Case Background *Clear Lakes, a fish hatchery, had a deal with Griffith, a trout grower, under which Griffith would buy small trout from Clear Lakes and sell them back when they had grown to "market size." Trout were priced at a set rate per pound. The deal* *was to be for six years. After three years, Clear Lake's customers began to demand larger fish than the 12- to 16-ounce fish delivered by Griffith. Clear Lakes began to take fewer fish and waited longer to get them, leaving Griffith with too many fish. Some adjustments were* *made, but Griffith was deeply in debt and could not easily change operations.*

He sued Clear Lakes for breach for "refusing to accept and purchase in a timely manner the trout that Griffith had grown to market size." Clear Lakes claimed no contract ever existed, because they differed as to what was market size. The district court found for Griffith, holding that the parties knew that market size was 12 to 16 ounces. The holding was appealed by Clear Lake.

Case Decision Schroeder, Chief Justice

* * *

Under the Uniform Commercial Code, "a contract for sale does not fail for indefiniteness if the parties have intended to make a contract and there is a reasonably certain basis for giving an appropriate remedy." Thus, "in order to have an enforceable contract, the UCC does not require a document itemizing all the specific terms of the agreement. Rather, the UCC requires a determination whether the circumstances of the case, including the parties' conduct, are 'sufficient to show agreement.'"…

The district court found that "the parties undoubtedly intended to make a contract and there is a 'reasonably certain basis for giving an appropriate remedy.'" The district court's statement is consistent with UCC § 2–204(3):

> Even though one or more terms are left open, a contract for sale does not fail for indefiniteness if the parties have intended to make a contract and there is a reasonably certain basis for giving an appropriate remedy.

Substantial evidence supports the district court's conclusion. The fact that the parties' interpretations coincided during the first three years of the contract is persuasive.…

The district court found that at the time of contract formation "Clear Lakes and Griffith had an understanding about what fish were 'market size.'" Specifically, "as between Griffith and Clear Lakes, the term is suggestive of a trout approximating one pound as the parties had considered it over the years." This finding is significant in determining whether Clear Lakes breached and negates the contention that there was no meeting of the minds as to the meaning of the term.

The district court found that the course of performance between the parties over the first three years of the contract, as well as their course of dealing prior to executing the Agreement, confirmed that the parties intended market size to indicate trout approximating one pound live weight. Griffith also presented evidence of similar trade usage predating the contract.…

The evidence cited by the district court is sufficient to support its finding that both parties understood the term "market size" to refer to a fixed range approximating one pound live weight.…

Affirmed.

Questions for Analysis

1. The Idaho high court held that by their actions the parties understood the meaning of "market size," so there was an agreement. How could Clear Lakes have avoided this problem?
2. Since market conditions changed, and customers began to want bigger fish, how could Clear Lakes and Griffith have adjusted in a friendly manner?

Price

While price is usually specified, in some contracts it is not clear or is to be set over time as the parties work together. If price is unclear when a contract is found to exist, §2–305 directs the courts to determine "a reasonable price." Reasonable price may or may not be "fair market value," depending on the past dealings and conduct of the parties. If the price referred to in the contract relies on benchmarks, such as "the price of wheat on August 15" or "cost plus 10 percent," disputes may arise as to whether the price of wheat included delivery or the cost was determined in good faith. In such cases, the courts attempt to determine what the parties intended when they formed the contract and what would be the most reasonable method, given usual business practices, to determine the price to fulfill the contract.

Quantity

The UCC generally requires that a contract specify the quantity to be bought. However, §2–306(1) recognizes requirements contracts and output contracts, in which the quantities may not be clear. A *requirements contract* is one in which a seller agrees to provide all of a certain good that a buyer needs. For example, Goodyear may agree to provide Ford all of the tires it needs to install on all new models of the Ford Explorer it produces next year. Ford is not certain how many that will be, but Goodyear says it will produce whatever is required. An *output contract* is when a buyer agrees to take all of the output of a certain seller. If The Gap wants to push a hot line of shoes made by Avia, it could agree to take all that Avia can produce next year. In both cases, the law imposes a duty to act in good faith. The buyer and seller are expected to act in a reasonable manner, given the customs of their industry.

ISSUE SPOTTER
Gouge the Wholesaler

Your chain of six gas stations has a requirements contract with a gasoline wholesaler. The wholesaler promised to deliver to you all the gasoline you need for two years at a price of $1.13 per gallon. After several months, because the price of oil has shot up, the wholesaler is losing 30 cents on every gallon he delivers to you. You are making so much money on every gallon you sell, that you begin to order more tanker loads and resell it to other gas stations. This practice may be unethical, but does it violate the requirements contract?

Getty Images

Delivery Terms

Most sales contracts specify how goods are to be delivered and who is responsible for the cost of transportation. At some point, responsibility for transportation and control of the goods switches from the seller to the buyer. Sections 2–319 to 2–324 detail the definition of delivery terms, such as "free on board" (F.O.B.), often used in contracts. If delivery is not specified, the UCC fills the gap so long as a contract exists. Section 2–309 states that the time for delivery is to be a "reasonable time."

What is reasonable depends, of course, on factors such as trade custom, the apparent intentions of the parties, and the availability of transportation services. If the parties do not state what is to determine the time of delivery, §2–311 states that "specifications or arrangements relating to shipment are at the seller's option." Section 2–308 presumes that delivery is to be at the seller's place of business. When the seller turns goods over to a shipping company, §2–504 holds that it has a duty to assure that the carrier is competent and that all parties understand who bears the risk of loss at various points before the buyer gets possession of the goods.

Performance and Obligations

Both parties must perform their obligations under that contract or risk being found in breach. The general duties and obligations assumed by each party to a contract for the sale of goods include those specified by the contract, imposed by the UCC, and, where necessary, provided by trade custom.

Seller's Rights and Obligations

The seller's basic obligation under the UCC is to transfer and deliver conforming goods to the buyer. The seller must be concerned about the appropriate manner and timeliness of delivery, the place of tender, and the quality of tender. The proper tender of goods to, and their acceptance by, the buyer entitles the seller to be paid according to the contract.

Under the common law, a seller's delivery was supposed to conform to all terms of the agreement. In practice, so long as there is substantial performance by the seller, it is likely that contract obligations have been met. The UCC expects parties to meet obligations but provides greater flexibility. UCC §2–601 states: "if the goods … fail in any respect to conform to the contract, the buyer may: (a) reject the whole; (b) accept the whole; or (c) accept any commercial unit or units and reject the rest." This modifies the common-law rule by allowing the buyer to accept less than the entire shipment.

On the other hand, allowing a buyer to reject a shipment when the problems are slight would allow the buyer to escape payment obligations. This is a problem particularly when the market price of the goods is falling. The buyer finds some minor problem, cancels the contract, and buy the goods at a lower price from another seller. Article 2's policy of enforcing contracts when performance is reasonable discourages such behavior.

Right to Cure by the Seller

UCC §2–508 provides some opportunities for a seller to *cure* an improper tender of goods that have been rejected by the buyer. After the buyer a rejected a shipment as not conforming to the contract, the seller may cure the defective tender or delivery if

- the time for the seller's performance under the contract has not yet passed.
- the seller notifies the buyer in a timely manner of an intent to cure the defect.
- the seller properly repairs or replaces the defective goods within the time allowed for his performance.

Buyer's Rights and Obligations

In general, a buyer's obligations begin when the seller delivers goods that conform to the contract. The buyer is required by §2–507 to accept conforming goods and to pay for them according to the contract. If the buyer accepts the goods, the seller awaits payment. If the buyer rejects the goods as nonconforming, the seller may need to remedy the problem or may have to sue for breach of contract.

Buyer's Right of Inspection

Unless the parties have otherwise agreed, under §2–513 the buyer has a right to inspect the goods before accepting them. Inspection allows the buyer to verify that the goods received are those the seller had agreed to deliver. The buyer must pay for any expenses associated with an inspection. However, the expenses can be recovered from the seller as damages if the goods do not conform to the contract.

Buyer's Right of Rejection

According to §2–601 and §2–602, a buyer who receives goods that are nonconforming may reject them as a breach of contract and withhold payment. The buyer may also cancel the contract and recover from the seller any prepayments made. The buyer must notify the seller of a rejection in a timely manner to allow the seller to either cure the nonconformity, if realistic, or reclaim the goods.

Buyer's Duty of Acceptance

When the seller has delivered conforming goods, the buyer has a duty to accept them. That is, under §2–606 and §2–607, the buyer has a duty to become the owner of goods. If the goods are nonconforming but have been accepted under §2–608, the buyer may later revoke acceptance only if the nonconformity "substantially impairs" the value of the goods. Of course, if the buyer is willing to accept nonconforming goods, they must be paid for.

Obligation of Payment

Unless otherwise agreed, §2–507 requires payment when and where the buyer receives the goods. Even when the contract calls for the seller to deliver the goods to a transportation company for shipment to the buyer, the buyer's payment for the goods is not due until the goods are received. Payment upon receipt gives the buyer a chance to inspect the goods before paying for them.

Sales Warranties

A *warranty* is a statement or representation made by a seller that goods conform to certain standards of quality, safety, performance, and title. If the goods do not conform to the standards created by the warranty, the seller can be held liable for damages for breach of warranty. Article 2 provides various types of warranties, which are summarized in Exhibit 11.3.

Warranty of Title

Under §2–312, a seller warrants that good title is being transferred to the buyer and that goods will be delivered free of any claims against them, such as liens, unless those have been revealed to the buyer. As the UCC explains in its official comments, the purpose of this is that a buyer gets "a good, clean title" and that the buyer "will not be exposed to a lawsuit in order to protect it." This means that a seller is responsible to the buyer if the seller innocently sells a good that does not have good title, such as a stolen property.

Warranty of title also means that the seller warrants that goods being sold are free of any claim of infringement. If a seller has infringed on a trademark, copyright, or patent owned by a third party, the seller is responsible for expenses incurred by a buyer who is ignorant of the infringement. For example, a department store was sued by a producer, because the store was selling goods that infringed on the producer's trademarks. The department store sued its supplier for violating the trademarks and was awarded damages to cover costs incurred.

Exhibit 11.3
Summary of Warranties under the UCC

Warranty to Title $2–312	Seller is the rightful owner of the goods, the goods are free of any lines, and there are no infringements
Express Warranty $2–313	Seller's promise as to quality, safety, or performance; may be created by the seller's statements, description, or models
Implied Warranties	Imposed on the seller by the UCC
Merchantability $2–314	Requires that the goods are reasonably fit and safe for the purposes they are being sold for; also applies to packaging and labeling
Fitness for a Particular Purpose $2–315	If the buyer relies on the seller's skill or judgment in selecting goods for a particular purpose, the goods must be able to perform that purpose.

Express Warranties

An *express warranty* is created by a seller's promise or guarantee as to the quality, safety, performance, or durability of goods being sold. During negotiations, a seller may induce a buyer to purchase goods by making representations about the goods, which become warranties. Section 2–313 lists three circumstances where an express warranty may be created:

1. A seller provides a sample or model of the good that the buyer relies upon as evidence of what the goods will be like.
2. A seller describes attributes about the goods to the buyer.
3. A seller makes specific oral or written statements or promises to the buyer about the goods that are a part of the basis of the bargain.

Statements about goods are more likely to be express warranties when the claims are specific, rather than general statements about "how nice" the goods are or other happy talk (puffery). Similarly, an express warranty is created if statements are made about attributes of the goods that are not obvious, such as claims about the quality of steel used in production of a good, or if it is a case in which the buyer has good reason to rely on the expertise of the seller. Obviously, when statements are made in writing, they are more likely to be held to be express warranties. It does not matter that a seller does not intend to create an express warranty by making claims about a product; if it is reasonable that the buyer rely on the seller's claims, then they are likely to be express warranties. This is particularly the case for goods sold to consumers.

Implied Warranties

An *implied warranty* is a quality and safety standard that is imposed by Article 2. This part of the UCC has important implications, for it establishes a standard similar to that imposed by product liability law in tort. Implied warranties exist at law. Unlike express warranties, which are based on representations made by the seller, implied warranties are automatically imposed on sellers unless they specifically disclaim them.

Implied Warranty of Merchantability

Section 2–314 states that unless the parties to the contract expressly agree otherwise, an *implied warranty of merchantability* accompanies every sale by a merchant. This provision of the UCC applies to sellers who are merchants of the goods of the kind in question. That is, it applies to those who routinely deal in such goods or offer their expertise to others about such goods, such as jewelers selling jewelry and restaurants serving food and drink.

Merchantable means that the good "must be of a quality comparable to that generally acceptable in that line or trade." That is, industry standards must be met. Obviously, for such things as jet engines, industry standards are very high, and any seller must offer products of current standards. If the product is a common one, such as bushels of #2 winter wheat, the quality must be average; one cannot pass off a load of bottom-of-the-silo, moldy, rat-dropping-infested wheat. Further, the goods must be able to do the tasks expected of them. If the goods are one-ton trucks, they must be able to carry the loads expected of such trucks. Also, goods must be adequately packaged and labeled and be in conformance with claims made on labels or sales materials.

ISSUE SPOTTER

How Much Advice Should Retailers Give?

At self-service home-center stores, where you can buy plumbing, electrical, and other supplies, the employees usually try to be helpful in giving advice. You explain the problem, and they point you to the supplies you need to fix the problem. Can the retailers be setting themselves up to be sued for breach of implied warranty of fitness for a particular purpose? That is, if you go into the store, tell an employee what is wrong with your sink—or at least what you think is wrong—and the employee advises you to change a fitting, and shows you what to buy, and the result is you flood your kitchen, could you have a suit against the retailer for the damages you suffered? Is it a good idea for store employees to give a lot of advice?

Implied Warranty of Fitness for a Particular Purpose

In some situations, a buyer orders a good with a special use in mind. Section 2–315 is more demanding of a seller who had reason to know the buyer's particular purpose for purchasing certain goods. If the buyer relies on the seller's skill or judgment to select the goods for that purpose, an implied warranty that the goods are suited for that purpose is created.

The buyer is required to demonstrate "actual reliance" on the seller's expertise. The buyer must also show that the seller had "reason to know" of the buyer's purpose. Suppose that Oprah needs to paint a metal barn. She tells the paint store salesperson what she needs. She is concerned about chipping and peeling and asks for a recommendation. The salesperson recommends Pittura Exterior. If Oprah buys Pittura based on the salesperso's recommendation, and the paint chips and peels the next year, there is a breach of implied warranty of fitness for a particular purpose.

Warranty Disclaimers

The warranty requirements imposed on sellers by the UCC are a form of strict liability under contract law. Because it is a tough standard, sellers may wish to reduce their liability by issuing *disclaimers*. If a seller has made an express warranty, the courts do not want to see disclaimers that are inconsistent with the promises made in that warranty. Under §2–316, boilerplate language that attempts to dismiss an express warranty is not allowed when the disclaimer is inconsistent with the warranty. The parol evidence rule generally prevents oral promises that have been made from being a part of the warranty, when the oral statement contradicts the written warranty.

Disclaimers of implied warranties of merchantability and of fitness for a particular purpose are permitted if the disclaimer uses the word "merchantability" and the disclaimer is conspicuous. Under UCC §1–201, conspicuous means that it is written so that a reasonable person would notice it, such as written in all capital letters or in a different color than the rest of the text. Further, a seller is more likely held to have disclaimed warranties if there is a conspicuous notice that the goods are being sold "as is." As the *Lee* case indicates, disclaimers mean consumers should beware.

Lee v. R & K Marine
Court of Appeals of North Carolina
598 S.E.2d 683 (2004)

Case Background *Lee bought a new boat from R & K Marine and signed a standard purchase agreement. On the agreement, all in capital letters, it stated: "EXCEPT TO THE EXTENT REQUIRED BY STATE LAW, SELLER EXPRESSLY DISCLAIMS ALL WARRANTIES, EXPRESS OR IMPLIED, INCLUDING ANY IMPLIED WARRANTY OF MERCHANTABILITY OR FITNESS FOR A PARTICULAR PURPOSE." Three years later, Lee took the boat in for repairs, when cracks and extensive deterioration were discovered in the hull. An appraiser determined that the problems were due to defects in manufacturing, and the boat was a complete loss. The manufacturer had gone out of business and was bankrupt, so Lee sued the retailer who sold him the boat, claiming breach of warranties of merchantability and fitness for a particular purpose. Defendant was granted summary judgment. Lee appealed.*

Case Decision Tyson, Judge.

* * *

[UCC §2–316(2)] provides, "to exclude or modify the implied warranty of merchantability or any part of it, the language must mention merchantability and in case of a writing must be conspicuous, and to exclude

or modify any implied warranty of fitness the exclusion must be by a writing and conspicuous." [UCC §1–201(10)] defines the term "conspicuous" as:

> A term or clause is conspicuous when it is so written that a reasonable person against whom it is to operate ought to have noticed it. A printed heading in capitals (as: NONNEGOTIABLE BILL OF LADING) is conspicuous. Language in the body of a form is "conspicuous" if it is in larger or other contrasting type of color.…

The disclaimer here met all the requirements and was conspicuous. Defendant effectively disclaimed any and all warranties of merchantability and fitness for a particular purpose. The trial court did not err in granting defendant's motion for summary judgment on plaintiff's breach of warranty claim.

Questions for Analysis
1. The appeals court affirmed that the *warranty disclaimer* was valid. There was no evidence that the retailer knew that the boat was junk, but suppose that could have been shown. How might that have changed the case?
2. Would there be any reason to sue the boat manufacturer?

LIGHTER SIDE OF THE LAW
Does It Come with a Warranty?

The inventor of the Quadro Tracker said that the device could locate drugs, bombs, and just about anything else, whether behind walls, inside cars, on persons, or out in fields. A brochure claimed that it could even detect drugs in a person's bloodstream just by being pointed at a person. An MIT physics professor said that the chances of the Quadro Tracker's working were slim to zero and that there are many hoaxes involving such incredible devices.

Nevertheless, dozens of law enforcement agencies and schools bought the device, also called the Positive Molecular Locator, for prices ranging from $400 to $8,000. Over 1,000 of the plastic boxes were sold, taking in more than $1 million, before a federal judge issued an injunction banning the sale or distribution of the product. An FBI agent said, "The only thing this accurately detects is your checkbook."

Source: The Herald (Rock Hill, SC) and *The Atlanta Journal and Constitution*

Getty Images

Remedies and Damages

When a buyer or seller breaches a contract for the sale of goods, the UCC provides the nonbreaching party with a number of remedies. The remedies are intended to place the nonbreaching party in the same position as if the contract had been performed according to its terms. In applying its remedies, §1–106 of the UCC directs the courts to interpret the remedies liberally.

Seller's Remedies

The buyer may default on contractual obligations by rejecting a tender of goods that conform to the contract, wrongfully revoking an acceptance, repudiating the contract, failing to make a payment, or failing to complete some other performance required by the contract. In each situation, the UCC provides the seller with remedies. As Exhibit 11.4 indicates, the seller is not restricted to any one remedy. Rather, §2–703 states that the seller may use several remedies at the same time.

The remedies available to the seller depend on whether the buyer breached before or after receiving the goods (see Exhibit 11.4). When the buyer breaches before receiving the goods, the seller may elect to cancel the contract, resell or salvage (recycle) the goods, and withhold or stop delivery. If the buyer breaches after receiving the goods, the remedies available to the seller depend upon whether the seller reclaims the goods. If unable to reclaim the goods, the seller may sue the buyer to recover the purchase price and any resulting incidental damages. If the goods are reclaimed by the seller, the seller may use any of the same remedies available had the buyer's breach occurred before receiving the goods.

Seller's Damages

When reclaiming and reselling the goods does not fully compensate the seller for the buyer's breach, damages are the proper remedy. UCC's damage measures are designed to put the seller in as good a position as if the buyer had performed

Exhibit 11.4
Summary of Seller's Rights and Remedies

Status of the Goods	Seller's Rights and Remedies
Buyer breaches before receiving the goods	The seller may: 1. Cancel the contract 2. Identify the goods; minimize losses if necessary by stopping production and salvaging the goods 3. Withhold delivery or, if needed, stop delivery 4. Resell the goods in a reasonable manner 5. Sue the buyer to recover the loss suffered by having to resell the goods and related costs

Buyer breaches after receiving the goods	The seller may:
	1. If buyer does not pay, sue to recover the purchase price and resulting *incidental damage*
	2. Be entitled to remedies if the buyer wrongfully rejects the goods, depending on:
	  a. Whether the seller reclaims the goods; if so, the remedies are the same as if the buyer had breached before receiving the goods
	  b. Whether the seller does not reclaim the goods; if not, the seller can sue to recover the purchase price and any related costs

contractual obligations. The seller is also allowed to seek incidental damages. Under §2–710, such costs may include expenses associated with stopping delivery, transporting and taking care of the goods after the breach, returning or reselling the goods, and taking any other necessary action.

Buyer's Remedies

A seller usually breaches a sales contract in one of the following ways:

1. The seller repudiates the contract before tendering the goods.
2. The seller fails to make a scheduled delivery on time.
3. The seller delivers nonconforming goods.

The buyer's remedies vary somewhat depending on the type of breach by the seller. In any case, the buyer may respond by canceling the contract, arranging to obtain the goods from another supplier, and suing the nonperforming seller for damages. The buyer's rights and remedies are summarized in Exhibit 11.5.

Buyer's Damages

Like the seller's damage provisions, the buyer's damage provisions under the UCC are designed to put the buyer in as good a position as if the seller had performed according to the contract. The terminology for damages is a bit different under the UCC than in the common law, so we consider the primary types of damages specified in the UCC.

Cover When a seller fails to deliver goods, either by being too late to be useful or because the goods are nonconforming, the buyer is entitled to buy substitute goods and recover the price difference. This is referred to as *cover* in §2–712 of the UCC. The cover price is what is paid for the substitute goods, or the market price may be used to measure the damages. Of course, if similar goods are available at the same or a lower price, then the breaching seller does not have to provide cover.

Status of the Goods	Buyer's Rights and Remedies
Seller repudiates the contract before delivery	The buyer may: 1. Cancel the contract 2. Obtain goods from another supplier 3. Sue the seller for damages and to recover advance payments
Seller fails to deliver	The buyer may: 1. Cancel the contract 2. Obtain goods from another supplier 3. Sue the seller for damages
Seller delivers nonconforming goods; buyer rejects them	The buyer may: 1. Cancel the contract 2. Obtain goods from another supplier if goods are rejected 3. Sue the seller for damages 4. Sell rejected goods to recover advance payments 5. Store or reship goods, if no advance payment was made
Seller delivers noncomforming goods; buyer accepts them	The buyer may: 1. Deduct damages from the price of goods 2. Sue the seller for damages 3. Sue for breach of warranty

Exhibit 11.5
Summary of Buyer's Rights and Remedies

The UCC does not permit overcompensation for losses by requiring the seller to pay the full cost of substitute goods.

Incidental Damages When the buyer properly rejects a delivery or does not receive the goods, incidental damages, under §2–710, include the reasonable costs of inspecting, receiving, transporting, and taking care of the goods while they remain in her possession. If there was no delivery at all, or if delivery is late, §2–715 states that the buyer's incidental damages include all reasonable costs or direct expenses associated with the delay in receiving the goods or in tracking down substitute goods.

Consequential Damages Consequential damages are foreseeable damages that result from the seller's breach. They differ from incidental damages in that consequential damages may result from the buyer's relations with parties other than the seller; that is, the breach may cause the buyer to lose sales and, most importantly, profits.

In sum, the UCC provides more structure to the measure of damages in commercial settings than may occur in the case of common law contracts; and tort claims are difficult to bring. Parties to commercial contracts are expected to allocate the risks carefully among themselves and not hope that claims of fraud will later allow for generous damage awards. This fact is emphasized in the *Grams* case.

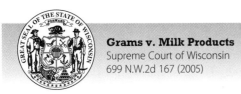

Grams v. Milk Products
Supreme Court of Wisconsin
699 N.W.2d 167 (2005)

Case Background *The Grams raise calves commercially. They buy them when they are 3 to 5 days old and raise them until they are about 4 months old, when they resell them. They feed the calves a "milk replacer" sold by Milk Products. The product provides nutrition and medications to keep calves healthy. The Grams asked if there was a cheaper product they could use instead, and they were told they could buy the same product without medications for about half the price. They did, and the mortality rate of the calves tripled as many became sick. They blamed the inferiority of the lower-cost product on their high loss rate and sued for breach of contract and for the tort of intentional misrepresentation. The district court held for Milk Products on all counts. The Grams appealed.*

Case Decision Prosser, Justice

* * *

Wisconsin has recognized the superior ability of contract law, and in particular the Uniform Commercial Code (UCC), to deal with certain kinds of disputes.... The UCC provides a "comprehensive system for compensating consumers for economic loss arising from the purchase of defective products." When a product proves to be defective, the UCC allows the aggrieved buyer to sue for breach of warranty or (under certain circumstances) to return the goods and sue for breach of contract.

Concern about duplicating or overriding UCC provisions was an important reason this court chose to adopt the economic loss doctrine in the first place. In [an earlier] case, we refused to allow the plaintiff to circumvent a warranty through a tort claim, reasoning that the "protections granted by the [UCC] are not to be buttressed by tort principles and recovery."

In addition, contract law and tort law embody distinctly different approaches to risk sharing. The UCC provides a structure that encourages parties to a contract to allocate the economic risks of a given transaction between or among themselves. This is especially true when a manufacturer produces a part or component that can be used in a variety of ways. In that case, a party down the supply chain—often the ultimate purchaser—may be best situated to assess the risk and guard against it by securing a warranty, buying insurance, or allocating risk in other ways....

The Grams urge this court to ... [adopt a new rule] that physical damage to anything other than the product itself would be ... subject to suit in tort....

We decline to adopt such a rule. The proposed rule would reject inquiry into the scope of the bargain and replace it with an overly formalistic distinction based on the kind of property harmed. Such a distinction would inevitably cause the erosion of the UCC. The "fundamental distinction" between contract and tort espoused in our cases would be lost....

Affirmed.

Questions for Analysis

1. The Wisconsin high court held that a tort claim could not be added on to the damage claims for breach that are allowed under the UCC. What would be the consequence of such a change?
2. If the calves became sick because they did not get the medicine that was in the more expensive milk replacer, why did the seller tell the Grams they could buy the product?

International Sales

Global commerce has expanded rapidly, so businesses must deal with the laws and customs of more countries. Litigation everywhere is costly, and people are often suspicious about the fairness of legal rules and procedures in other nations. So there are strong reasons to give partners around the world reasons to believe that we will all play by the same "rules of the game," and that those who serve as "referees" to disputes are qualified and impartial. Effective legal rules substantially reduce the cost of doing international business. While we discuss other aspects of international law in detail in Chapter 22, here we focus on how the law of the international sale of goods has been developing.

General Principles

Parties who make contracts for the sale of goods that cross international boundaries are generally free, given limits set by nations' domestic laws, to choose the law they want to apply to their contract. That is, if a company in Tennessee is buying toys from Bangladesh, the two parties can specify the law that governs their contract. They can specify that the Uniform Commercial Code of Tennessee will govern the contract and that disputes will be resolved by the arbitration rules of the International Chamber of Commerce. If the parties do not specify how contract disputes are to be govern, conflict-of-law rules will determine what law will resolve govern a dispute and what court system or arbitrator will govern the matter. Most people prefer to control their legal destiny, so most contracts for the sale of goods specify what governs the contract and where disputes must be resolved. Alternatively, as we see next, many are now governed by a common set of rules.

The Convention on Contracts for the International Sale of Goods

The *Convention on Contracts for the International Sale of Goods (CISG)* was adopted by the United Nations to have a commercial code that parties would think unbiased. It has been ratified by most major nations, including the United States. Since the CISG is a treaty adopted by Congress, it prevails over state laws, such as the UCC. Contracts for the sale of goods that fall under the coverage of the CISG between a party in, for example, Florida and in another nation that has adopted the CISG are resolved by the CISG. Hence, if an auto parts company in the United States buys parts from a German company, the contract is automatically governed by the CISG—unless the parties specify that they want to exclude application of the CISG, or some parts of it, and choose another law to govern. That is, the parties could specify German law or Florida law, but if not, the CISG automatically governs the contract.

Sales Covered by the CISG

The CISG applies to contracts for commercial sale of goods made by parties who have *places of business* in different countries that have ratified the CISG. It does not matter what the citizenship of the parties is; it is the location of the businesses that matters. Unlike the UCC, which applies to goods sold to the consuming public, contracts under the CISG only apply to commercial sales or sales between merchants. Even among merchants, certain sales are excluded from the CISG:

- Auction sales
- Consumer goods bought for personal or household use
- Contracts that are primarily for the supply of labor or of other services

Certain goods are excluded from the CISG:

- Electricity
- Ships and aircraft
- Securities such as stocks, negotiable instruments, and money

Again, parties to contracts that would normally be covered by the CISG can pick another law to govern their contract for the sale of goods, if they so desire.

Similarities to UCC

The CISG is not a great deal different from the UCC or the commercial civil codes used in most nations. It is based on the business reality that many deals are not based on detailed contracts that account for all possibilities. It instructs judges to look at the plain meaning of words and to look for consistency.

Formality Contracts need not be formal; the CISG states that "A contract of sale need not be concluded in or evidenced by writing and is not subject to any other requirements as to form. It may be proved by any means, including witnesses." Judges are told to look at the circumstances of past dealings, such as the negotiations, the practices of the parties in dealing with each other, and "any practices which they have established between themselves." However, if parties to a contract made under the CISG desire, they can insert a statement that judges are not to consider parol evidence and should not look beyond the words in the contract.

ISSUE SPOTTER

What Law Applies, and Where, to Your Contract?

Your store buys interesting articles from around the world, and you try to track down unusual items that are not found in major retail chains. So you are in international commerce. You have a line of credit at a bank. It makes payments to the sellers once the goods have been accepted in the United States. But what if something goes wrong? You accept a shipment of bamboo furniture from Borneo. It looks great, the bill is paid, but three months later, the furniture falls apart due to low humidity. You complain and get the runaround. The contract said nothing about jurisdiction or law. Can you sue? Where? What are you likely to do? What can you do to minimize such problems?

Getty Images

Offers Advertisements under the CISG are not offers that can be accepted to form a contract; they are only offers to enter into negotiations. However, offers made to "one or more specific persons" are valid offers to make a contract. Offers, become effective when they reach the offeree but can be revoked any time before acceptance is communicated.

Much like the UCC, the CISG holds that an offer "is sufficiently definite if it indicates the goods and expressly or implicitly fixes or makes provision for determining the quantity and price." When a contract does not expressly include the price, the parties are held "to have impliedly made reference to the price generally charged at the time of the conclusion of the contract for such goods sold under comparable circumstances in the trade concerned." Similarly, if there is uncertainty over a term, the courts will look to the practices "in the particular trade concerned." For example, in one case, the parties argued about what was meant by "chicken." One party claimed it meant young fryers, but the court found that industry practice meant any size cooking chicken.

Acceptance Acceptance of an offer must be made within the time stated in the offer, or, if not stated, within a reasonable time. Acceptance can be sent by any reasonable means. Any statement or conduct by the offeree to indicate acceptance is sufficient to form the contract. The acceptance is effective when it is received by the offeror, so an offer may be withdrawn up to the point the offeror receives acceptance. As with the UCC and common law, silence is normally not acceptance, but many contracts are formed by performance without stating that there will be performance. For example, if an offeror sends an order asking for 500 boxes of fried grasshoppers, the acceptance occurs when the requested act is performed.

Battle of the Forms It is common in business for orders (offers) to be sent that are accepted by the seller (offeree) returning a different standard form. When a dispute arises, the contract is based upon two forms with different terms. The CISG holds that if the differences are "material" then the second form is a counteroffer, not an acceptance, so there was no contract. Terms that are not "material" are a part of the contract unless specifically rejected by the offeror. In this sense, the CISG is less flexible than the UCC and more like the common law of contracts. Under the UCC, courts are more likely to fill in material terms than they are under the CISG.

Duties of the Parties The obligations that parties to a contract have under the CISG are very similar to those under the UCC. The seller must fulfill the obligation to deliver the goods with good title according to the terms specified, given reasonable commercial practices. If there is a problem, the buyer must notify the seller of defects "within as short a period as is practicable" after delivery. The seller may cure any defects in the delivered goods, so long as it is not costly to the buyer. If the goods are delivered properly, the buyer must take delivery and pay the price specified.

Remedies In the event of a breach of contract, parties are expected to behave in a reasonable manner and give the breaching party a notice of the alleged breach and an opportunity to cure the defect. In this sense, the CISG is like German commercial law, which requires a Nachfrist notice—a notice of the problem and a chance to perform properly—be given to the nonconforming party before suit for breach is filed. As under the common law and the UCC, if there is a failure to perform, there is an obligation to try to minimize the damages and make the best out of a bad situation so that the waste is minimized. If damages must be paid, they are usually the difference between the contract price and the value or cost incurred at the time of the breach.

The *Treibacher Industrie* case discusses some of these issues.

Treibacher Industrie, A.G. v. Allegheny Technologies
United States Court of Appeals, Eleventh Circuit
464 F.3d 1235 (2006)

Case Background *Treibacher of Austria sells hard metal powders. TDY, a subsidiary of Allegheny, ordered certain quantities of tantalum carbide (TaC) for delivery "on consignment" to be used at a plant in Alabama to make tungsten-graded carbide powders. After TDY received the first of several shipments due, it cancelled the order, as it found a cheaper source of TaC. Treibacher had to sell the powder at a lower price; it sued TDY for damages.*

At trial, TDY argued that "on consignment" meant the common usage of the term—no sale occurred unless and until TDY actually used the TaC. Treibacher argued that over seven years of previous dealings, the parties understood the term to mean that TDY had an obligation to pay for all TaC ordered, but Treibacher delayed billing until TDY actually used the powder. The trial court held that under the CISG, evidence of the parties' interpretation of the term in their dealings trumped evidence of the term's customary use. Hence, a sale had occurred, and TDY was liable for the $5 million plus loss suffered by Treibacher. TDY appealed.

Case Decision Tjoflat, Circuit Judge

* * *

Article 9 of the CISG provides the rules for interpreting the terms of contracts. Article 9(1) states that, "parties are bound by any usage to which they have agreed and by any practices which they have established between themselves."… Article 8 of the CISG governs the interpretation of the parties' statements and conduct. A party's statements and conduct are interpreted according to that party's actual intent "where the other party knew … what that intent was," CISG, art. 8(1).… To determine a party's actual intent, or a reasonable interpretation thereof, "due consideration is to be given to all relevant circumstances of the case including the negotiations, any practices which the parties have established between themselves, usages and any subsequent conduct of the parties." CISG, art. 8(3).…

[The] interaction—evidencing TDY's acquiescence in Treibacher's interpretation of the contract—along with TDY's practice, between 1993 and 2000, of using and paying for all of the TaC specified in each contract, amply support the district court's finding that the parties, in their course of dealings,

construed their contracts to require TDY to use and pay for all of the TaC specified in each contract.

With respect to damages, the district court did not commit clear error in finding that Treibacher reasonably mitigated its damages. Article 77 of the CISG requires a party claiming breach of contract to "take such measures as are reasonable in the circumstances to mitigate the loss." Article 77, however, places the burden on the breaching party to "claim a reduction in the damages in the amount by which the loss should have been mitigated." Treibacher's Commercial Director … testified that Treibacher sought to mitigate damages as soon as possible and ultimately obtained the highest prices possible for the quantity of TaC that TDY refused; their first sale in mitigation occurred on September 9, 2001, seventeen days after the date of TDY's letter denying its obligation to purchase all of the TaC. TDY, the party carrying the burden of proving Treibacher's failure to mitigate, presented no evidence showing that Treibacher did not act reasonably. The district court therefore had no basis upon which to find that Treibacher did not take reasonable steps to mitigate its losses.

In sum, the district court properly determined that, under the CISG, the meaning the parties ascribe to a contractual term in their course of dealings establishes the meaning of that term in the face of a conflicting customary usage of the term. The district court was not clearly erroneous in finding that Treibacher and TDY understood their contracts to require TDY to purchase all of the TaC specified in each contract and that Treibacher took reasonable measures to mitigate its losses after TDY breached. Accordingly, the judgment of the district court is affirmed.

Questions for Analysis

1. The appeals court affirmed that the buyer was liable for damages due to breach as their previous dealings established the terms of their relationship. Is this CISG case more like the common law of contracts or the UCC?

2. If TaC could be found on the market so much cheaper than Treibacher was selling it to TDY, why does TDY not have the right to demand the lower price?

International Sales Disputes: The Dominance of Arbitration

There are not many cases in the courts ruling upon disputes that occur under the CISG, because most commercial sales contracts specify arbitration as the required method of dispute resolution. The United Nations encourages the use of arbitration in commercial dealings through the *Convention on the Recognition and Enforcement of Foreign Arbitrable Awards*. If a country has adopted the Convention, as the United States has, then courts are bound to recognize and enforce arbitration decisions that have followed proper procedure, unless it is in conflict with the law of the nation of one of the parties or has gone beyond the scope of the matter covered by arbitration. Hence, as with domestic contracts in the United States, the parties to a contract written under the CISG who mandate arbitration have little reason ever to be in court, as it is the duty of the arbitrators to resolve the dispute under the rules of the CISG.

Full Circle

Centuries ago, when merchants could not rely upon public courts for resolution of disputes and commercial law was not well developed, the law merchant developed. It was a voluntary set of rules by which merchants across national boundaries could solve disputes under a common set of rules. It was based upon the way most business was done. Disputes were resolved by a process similar to arbitration: private dispute resolution.

Over many decades, nations adopted commercial law based upon business practices. Public courts were used to resolve some disputes. As international trade has grown, the basic rules of law under which most contracts are formed is much the same, whether it is the law of a particular nation, such as the UCC, or the civil code of a nation such as France, or the CISG. The rules do not vary radically from country to country.

Increasingly, merchants have turned to private dispute resolution. As with contracts made in the United States, parties know that arbitration is quicker and cheaper than court litigation. In international dealings, parties worry that they may suffer discrimination—intentional or not—if they litigate disputes in the home courts of the other parties, so neutral arbitrators are again preferred. Courts around the world have come increasingly to enforce arbitration decisions, so parties have confidence in the integrity of the international legal system.

Summary

- To make contract law more consistent with business practices, the Uniform Commercial Code was developed. Article 2 of the UCC governs contracts for the sale of goods. Goods are tangible things that are movable at the time of the identification of the contract. Real estate, services, stocks, bank accounts, patents, and copyrights are not goods under the UCC. Transactions involving those things are under the common law of contracts.

- Under the UCC, merchants are subject to a higher standard of conduct than are nonmerchants. A person is a merchant if she deals, holds herself out as having special knowledge, or employs an agent, broker, or other intermediary who holds himself out as having special knowledge of the goods involved in the transaction. Merchants are required to conduct their activities in good faith and must follow business practices common in the trade.

- The common law governs a transaction unless the UCC modifies or specifically changes the effect of the common law. Generally, when the UCC modifies the common law, the effect is usually to be less demanding than the common law. An acceptance under the UCC, for example, does not have to be unequivocal to form a contract. An indefinite offer can form the basis of a contract (even with open price, quantity, delivery, or payment terms) under the UCC but not under the common law.

- The basic obligation of the seller is to transfer and deliver the goods. The buyer is obligated to accept and pay for them. In performing their obligations, in contract performance and enforcement, the parties are required by the UCC to act in good faith.

- In delivering conforming goods to the buyer, the seller is concerned with the appropriate manner and timeliness of delivery, place of tender, and the quality of tender. The UCC instructs the courts to provide such terms according to the apparent intent of the parties or the trade custom.

- The common law's *perfect tender rule* requires that the seller's tender of delivery conform in detail to the terms of the contract. The UCC modifies the buyer's common-law right to reject the goods by providing the seller with the right to cure defects within the time frame of the contract.

- The UCC obligates the seller to warrant title to goods being sold. The seller warrants good title, the absence of any interests or liens on the goods, and that the goods are free of any patent, copyright, or trademark infringements.

- A seller may create an express warranty under the UCC by making a statement to the buyer about the goods or by providing the buyer with a description of the goods or a sample or model of the goods.

- The UCC provides an implied warranty of merchantability and an implied warranty of fitness for a particular purpose. The good must conform to the contract description; be fit for the purposes for which it is intended; be of even kind, quality, and quantity; be adequately labeled; and conform to label descriptions. If a seller knows a buyer has a particular purpose for a good, and the buyer relies on the seller's skill or judgment in selecting a good, an implied warranty of fitness for a particular purpose may be created.

- The UCC extends to designated third parties any express warranty made by the seller to a buyer. To be consistent with other third-party beneficiary rules within a state, the UCC provides alternative rules.

- When a buyer or seller breaches a contract for the sale of goods, the UCC provides the nonbreaching party with remedies designed to place them in the same position as if the contract had been performed. The seller may recover for losses suffered due to buyer's failure to accept goods or to pay for goods. Buyer may recover the difference between what had to be paid to obtain substitute goods and the contract price. The seller and the buyer may seek incidental damages for recovery of costs resulting from the breach. The buyer is also allowed to recover consequential damages suffered, usually lost profits.

- The UN Convention on Contracts for the International Sale of Goods applies to contracts for commercial sale of goods by parties who have places of business in different countries that have ratified the CISG. Most major nations, including the United States, have ratified it. Such sales are covered by the CISG unless the parties specify that they want some other law to govern the contract.

- The CISG applies only to goods in commercial sales, that is, between merchants. Like the UCC, it does not require contracts to be formal writings, but gives priority to written terms in case of dispute. When terms are unclear, the courts are to look to the intent of the parties and to trade usage.

- In the event of a battle of the forms, under the CISG, when there are differences in material terms, no contract is formed; when changes are to minor terms, they may become incorporated into the contract unless objected to by a party.
- As with commercial contracts in the United States, most international commercial sale contracts include an arbitration clause. Many nations have adopted the Convention on the Recognition and Enforcement of Foreign Arbitrable Awards, so courts will uphold arbitration clauses and enforce arbitration results unless it conflicts with national policy or there was a serious problem with the arbitration process.

Terms to Know

You should be able to define the following terms:

merchant, 253	output contract, 262	warranty of disclaimer, 267
goods, 254	warranty, 264	incidental damage, 268
sales contract, 254	warranty of title, 264	cover, 269
statute of frauds, 259	implied warranty of	CISG, 271
trade usage, 260	merchantability, 265	
requirements contract, 262	fitness for a particular purpose, 267	

Discussion Question

1. What is the advantage of the UCC compared to the common law of contracts? Are there disadvantages to the adoption of a statute such as the UCC?

Case Questions

1. Cal-Cut had dealt with Idaho Pipe for years. In response to one of its ads, Idaho Pipe requested 30,000 feet of steel pipe from Cal-Cut. After phone conversations, Cal-Cut sent a written offer in August. Idaho Pipe accepted the offer by return mail, changed the delivery date from October 15 to December 15, and sent a check for $20,000 in partial payment, which Cal-Cut deposited. Cal-Cut returned confirmation of the order and did not change the October 15 delivery date, but wrote, "We will work it out" on the contract. Cal-Cut delivered 12,937 feet of pipe before October 5, which Idaho Pipe accepted. Then Cal-Cut refused to deliver any more pipe. The sale had become unprofitable, as the price of pipe had risen quickly. Was this deal enforced? Could Idaho Pipe recover any damages? [*Southern Idaho Pipe and Steel* v. *Cal-Cut Pipe and Supply* 567 P.2d 1246 Sup. Ct., Id. (1977)]

2. Polygram, a French company, makes records, tapes, and CDs. Defendant 32–03, a New York distributor, ordered goods from Polygram that were delivered in four shipments with written invoices. The invoices noted that payment was due in sixty days and that claims about problems with the goods must be made within three months after delivery. The companies had done business this way for years. 32–03's objections to the terms of sale arose for the first time in this incident, and 32–03 refused to pay, claiming that there was no written contract in violation of the statute of frauds and that it was trade custom in the industry for distributors to be allowed to return any defective goods for credit. Polygram claims that the terms of the agreement were violated and sued for payment. Who was right? [*Polygram* v. *32–03 Enterprises*, 697 F. Supp. 132 E.D. NY (1988)]

3. Marquette agreed to provide all cement that Norcem would need for over two years. The quantity and sales price for the first two shipments were specified in the contract.

The third shipment, according to the contract, was to be negotiated for a price "not to exceed $38 per short ton." At the time of the third shipment, Marquette told Norcem the price would be $38; Norcem responded that Marquette's insistence on the maximum price was not in good faith and refused to buy the cement. Marquette sued for breach of contract. Was Marquette right? [*Marquette v. Norcem* 494 N.Y.S.2d 511 Sup. Ct., App. Div., NY (1985)]

✓ **Check your answer at http://academic.cengage.com/blaw/meiners**

4. In January, T. W. Oil purchased fuel oil at sea on the tanker Khamsin. After the purchase, T. W. Oil contracted to sell the oil to Consolidated Edison (ConEd). The contract called for delivery between January 24 and 30 and for the oil to have a sulfur content of 0.5 percent. During negotiations with ConEd, T. W. Oil learned that ConEd was authorized to use oils with sulfur contents up to 1.0 percent. The Khamsin arrived on time. However, the oil tested at 0.92 percent sulfur, 0.42 percent higher than specified in the contract. On February 14, ConEd rejected the shipment. T. W. Oil offered ConEd a reduced price. ConEd rejected the lower price offer. T. W. Oil offered to cure by providing a substitute due to arrive on February 28. ConEd rejected T.W. Oil's offer to cure. Was T. W. Oil's offer to cure properly rejected by ConEd? Was ConEd required to accept the substitute shipment tendered by T. W. Oil? [*T. W. Oil* v. *Consolidated Edison*, 443 N.E.2d 932 Ct. App., NY (1982)]

5. Community Television Services (CTS) hired Dresser to design and build a 2,000-foot antenna tower in South Dakota for $385,000. The contract contained technical specifications warranting that the tower would withstand winds of 120 mph. During negotiations, Dresser had given CTS a sales brochure that stated:

"Wind force creates the most critical loads to which a tower is normally subjected. When ice forms on the tower members, thereby increasing the surface area resisting the passage of wind, the load is increased. Properly designed towers will safely withstand the maximum wind velocities and ice loads to which they are likely to be subjected. Dresser … can make wind and ice load recommendations to you for your area based on U.S. Weather Bureau data. In the winter, loaded with ice and hammered repeatedly with gale force winds, these towers absorb some of the roughest punishment that towers take anywhere in the country … yet continue to give dependable, uninterrupted service."

The tower was built according to the contract's technical specifications. Six years later, the tower collapsed during an 80-mph blizzard. Is Dresser liable for breach of an express warranty? [*Community Television Services* v. *Dresser* 586 F.2d 637 8th Cir. (1978)]

✓ **Check your answer at http://academic.cengage.com/blaw/meiners**

6. Hartwig Farms bought seed potatoes from Pacific, which bought them from Tobiason. The seed potatoes were stated to be "blue tag certified," meaning they were certified by the North Dakota State Seed Department not to have more than 1 percent infection with a disease that ruins potatoes. Hartwig planted the seeds, but almost the entire crop turned out to be infected. Hartwig sued for damages from the loss of the crop. Tobiason defended, noting that when the seeds were shipped the invoice had a disclaimer: "Tobiason … gives no warranty, express or implied, as to description, variety, quality, or productiveness, and will not in any way be responsible for the crop. All claims must be reported immediately on receipt … or no claim will be allowed." Hartwig claimed that this was not a part of the contract, since nothing before the actual shipment of the seeds with the invoice said anything about a disclaimer. Is the disclaimer a part of the contract? [*Hartwig Farms* v. *Pacific Gamble Robinson*, 625 P.2d 171 Ct. App., Wash. (1981)]

7. Leavitt bought a new motor home. He told the dealer he would be driving in the mountains and wanted to be sure to have sufficient engine and brake power, which he was assured he would. He contended that there was not enough power to go uphill and the brakes overheated going downhill. Despite many warranty repairs, Leavitt concluded that the engine and brakes were not suitable, and he sued for breach of implied warranty of fitness for a particular purpose under the UCC. The jury awarded Leavitt

$33,730 (the vehicle was worth about $80,000). The judge also awarded Leavitt attorney's fees under the Magnuson-Moss Warranty Act. Defendant appealed. Was the award justified under the UCC? [*Leavitt* v. *Monaco Coach* 616 N.W.2d 175 Ct. App., Mich. (2000)]

✓ **Check your answer at http://academic.cengage.com/blaw/meiners**

8. In 1975, NDI contracted to manufacture 1,180 metric tons of ½-inch steel strand for Grand Pre-Stressed at a price of $675 per ton. The strand is used to reinforce concrete. NDI was to deliver the strand over a seven-month period, and Grand agreed to pay for each shipment. Grand accepted deliveries of 221.1 tons and still owed $57,960 for them when it repudiated the contract in May 1976. Of the 958.9 tons of strand that remained for delivery under the contract, NDI had already produced 317.9 tons and later sold them privately to other customers at prices averaging $608.47 per ton. At all times, NDI had sufficient capacity to produce 12,500 tons of strand annually at an average cost of $394.57 per ton. NDI sued Grand for breach of contract and won. Can you calculate the damages under the UCC? [*Nederlandse Draadindustrie NDI B.V.* v. *Grand Pre-Stressed* 466 F.Supp. 846 E.D. NY (1979)]

9. On August 20, 1983, Elmer and Martha Bosarge purchased from J&J Mobile Homes Sales in Pascagoula a furnished mobile home manufactured by North River Homes, an Alabama corporation. The Bosarges were extremely proud of their new home—described by a J&J salesman as the "Cadillac of mobile homes." This "Cadillac," which cost the Bosarges a whopping $23,900, turned out to be a jalopy. That is, upon moving into their new home, the Bosarges immediately discovered defect after defect after defect. After arguing with North River for a year, during which time only a few repairs were made, the Bosarges refused to make further monthly payments and sued North River for selling a mobile home of unmerchantable quality. North River countered that the Bosarges could not claim to reject the mobile home when they continued to live in it. Who was right? [*North River Homes* v. *Bosarge*, 594 So.2d 1153 Sup. Ct., Miss. (1992)]

10. Anhui, a Chinese company, contracted to sell dyed yarn to Hart, an American company. The contract contained a clause requiring arbitration of disputes before the China Council for the Promotion of International Trade in Beijing. When a dispute arose and Hart refused to pay Anhui, it began arbitration proceedings. Hart did not respond but sued Anhui in federal court in the United States. Hart claimed the arbitration clause was not enforceable, because arbitration in Beijing would be a hardship and, even if it were not, the dispute was over the validity of the contract itself, an issue of contract law, not a payment dispute. Since that was a legal matter, it could be litigated. What resulted in federal court? [*Hart Enterprises Intl.* v. *Anhui Provincial Import and Export*, 888 F.Supp. 587 (S.D. NY (1995)]

11. A textile mill in Bangladesh bought a large quantity of cotton from a broker in Tennessee. The contract stated that any problems with quality had to be resolved by arbitration at the Liverpool Cotton Association in England. Complaints had to be filed within two months, or the matter would not be heard. The buyer did not realize that the cotton was lower quality than paid for until six months had passed. Could it then sue under the CISG in federal court in Tennessee? [*Quasem Group, Ltd.* v. *W.D. Mask Cotton*, 967 F. Supp. 288 W.D. Tenn. (1997)]

Ethics Question

1. Many U.S. retailers include in their contracts with suppliers domestic and foreign, a requirement that the supplier agree not to violate any local labor laws or the contract can be terminated. Yet the illegal use of child labor is common in many countries, especially in carpet making in Pakistan and in sewing operations in many countries. The retailers have been criticized as using the codes of conduct for publicity purposes, since enforcement is difficult and rare. Should such codes be used, and if so, how can they be enforced?

Internet Assignment

http://www.uncitral.org/uncitral/en/index.html
http://www.cisg.law.pace.edu/
http://www.asil.org/resource/iel1.htm

These three Web sites are related to the United Nations Convention on Contracts for the Internationl Sale of Goods (CISG). Which Web site would you choose to:

1. find in-depth research materials related to the CISG?
2. broaden your research to additional topics related to the CISG?
3. find official documents, texts, and background information related to the CISG?

Explain your choices.

Negotiable Instruments, Credit, and Bankruptcy

Chapter 12

As students, you know about student loans. Credit has never been as extensive as it is now. What's a little more debt? Some students have used student loans to finance vacations to the Caribbean and help pay for weddings. After all, when you graduate, the income will roll in to cover all that. And, if worse comes to worst, you can just file bankruptcy! But if you buy that car on time payments, and use the credit cards that you are offered, what's the downside?

Credit and its opposite, debt, are contractual relationships. Many such contracts are common-law contracts, but some fall under the UCC. Real property, such as an office building, is usually purchased by using debt. Most companies rely on debt to get operations going or to expand. When in business, most firms extend credit to their customers. Sometimes the promises to pay are negotiable instruments that can be traded, which happens to most mortgages on property.

The downside is that each year over one million individuals and many businesses file for bankruptcy. These are debtors with financial problems that overwhelm them. Their creditors, other individuals and businesses, share the pain by being forced to absorb well over $20 billion a year in unpaid debt.

Just as managing personal finances is important, balancing the cost of carrying debt and minimizing the losses from bad credit is critical. Most businesses operate on thin profit margins, so decisions about borrowing and issuing credit are important to survival. This chapter considers the legal aspects of debt obligations and the financial instruments often used to evidence the granting of credit; it ends with a look at the major parts of the federal bankruptcy code. ∎

Getty Images

Negotiable Instruments

Like much law in the United States, the law of negotiable instruments has its origins in England. Five hundred years ago, the right to payment was a contract right that could not be sold to another. This inhibited trade because of the difficulty it created for merchants who worked on credit. Traders had to wait until they were paid by the buyer before they would have more cash to acquire more goods to sell.

To resolve this problem, laws developed that allowed traders to *assign* a promise to pay to a third party. Typically, a merchant would sell a third party, at a discount, his right to payment. The trader could then buy more goods without waiting for the debtor to pay. The third party made her profit by collecting the amount owed from the debtor.

Gradually, the law recognized assignments of promises to pay, and contractual promises to pay became tradable. Negotiable instruments became something that could be bought and sold. The law of negotiable instruments became more responsive to the needs of business, and they are now a part of the commercial law through Article 3 of the UCC.

The Functions of Negotiable Instruments

The *negotiable instrument* began as a written promise or order to pay a certain sum of money. It functions as a substitute for cash. Few businesses today require cash in payment for all purchases. Because the law recognizes their validity, negotiable instruments such as checks are accepted as a substitute for cash for the payment of goods and services.

Negotiable instruments also provide a way for credit to be extended to debtors. Suppose Lynex wants to purchase new computers for its management information systems department but needs to borrow money to finance the purchase. Lynex may borrow the money from a financial institution by signing a negotiable instrument called a *promissory note*. In that note, Lynex promises to repay the money it borrows, probably with interest, to make the purchase. The financial institution usually has the right to sell the note, or assign the obligation, to another party.

Major Types of Negotiable Instruments

UCC §3–104 identifies four types of negotiable instruments: *drafts, checks, notes,* and *certificates of deposit*. These instruments can be separated into two categories: *orders to pay* and *promises to pay*. Orders to pay, which include drafts and checks, are three-party instruments used instead of cash and as credit devices. Promises to pay, which include notes and certificates of deposit, are two-party instruments used as credit devices.

Before we look at the major forms of negotiable instruments, there is some common terminology to get down first. The *drawer* is the one who issues or creates the document that requests payment, probably from a bank, but it could be from another party. The *drawee* is the party who agrees to make the payment, such as the bank making a payment based on a document presented to it. The drawee owes money to the drawer, such as the bank owing you the money you have deposited in it, and will follow the wishes of the drawer of pay a third party. The party who is to receive payment is the *payee* or *beneficiary* who will be paid by the drawee.

For example, if you import a load of furniture from Thailand, you must pay for it; so you will be the drawer, because you need to draw on money you have available, perhaps at a bank. You will instruct the bank—the drawee—to make payment to the Thai company that sends you the furniture, the payee or beneficiary. Not all transactions are quite that simple, so various instruments are used in business to make payments. We start with the one most people are used to.

Orders to Pay: Checks

According to UCC §3–104(2), a check is a "draft drawn on a bank and payable on demand." The check is the most commonly used form of draft. However, unlike a draft—which may be payable at a later date and may have a bank, an individual, or a corporation as a drawee—the check must be paid *on demand* and must have a bank as its drawee.

Cashier's Check A *cashier's check* is one form of check in which the bank is both the drawer and the drawee. The customer gives money to the bank and designates a payee. The bank then writes a check on itself as drawee, with the check payable on demand to that payee. Cashier's checks are frequently used in transactions where the seller demands guaranteed payment.

An example is the purchase of real estate, where the owner/seller of the property requires that a guarantee of payment occur when title to the property is to pass to the buyer. To meet this requirement, a buyer gives the seller a cashier's check. Because the check is drawn by the bank ordering itself to pay, the seller can be secure that the bank will honor the check when it is presented.

What happens if someone forges the signature on checks printed to contain the correct information for a checking account? The court considers this in the *Lor-Mar* case.

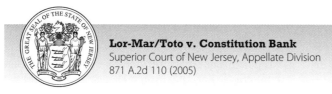

Lor-Mar/Toto v. Constitution Bank
Superior Court of New Jersey, Appellate Division
871 A.2d 110 (2005)

Case Background *Lor-Mar had a business checking account at First Constitution Bank. The resolution between Lor-Mar and the bank allowed checks to be honored if they contained the signature of either Van Middlesworth or Toto. The bank was given samples of their stamped signatures. Five bogus checks, totaling $24,350, were written against the account in one week and were paid by the bank. Lor-Mar saw the problem when reviewing its monthly statement.*

The bad checks contained all the correct information, but were on a different paper stock and color than the kind used by Lor-Mar. The checks contained some different "security features" than standard checks, and had signatures that looked like Van Middlesworth's stamped signature. The bank noted that customers were free to use checks not provided by the bank, and since the signature appeared the same, it held the payment to be proper. Lor-Mar sued and the trial court held in its favor. The bank appealed.

Case Decision Alexrad, Judge

* * *

The UCC specifies, in pertinent part, when a bank may charge its customer's account:

(a) A bank may charge against the account of a customer an item that is properly payable from that account even though the charge creates an overdraft. An item is properly payable if it is authorized by the customer and is in accordance with any agreement between the customer and bank.

(b) A customer is not liable for the amount of an overdraft if the customer neither signed the item nor benefited from the proceeds of the item. [§ 4–401]

Thus an instrument is "properly payable" if it is authorized by the customer and is in accordance with any agreement between the customer and bank. An item presented for payment is only "properly payable" if it is properly signed or adopted "with a present intention to authenticate [the] writing." Since the holding of the "intent" must be considered delegated

continues

to the individual authorized to apply the stamp, any use by unauthorized personnel would create an unauthorized signature.

An instrument, however, is not properly payable if it contains a forged drawer's signature or forged endorsement.

The bank's duty to charge its customer's account only for "properly payable" items under [§4–401] imposes standards of strict liability.

Fault occupies a secondary role in the treatment of UCC forgery losses.… Thus an analysis of whether the Bank exercised "ordinary care" in paying the instrument, as utilized in sections 3–406 and 4–406, is not relevant to the inquiry on appeal.

Our focus is whether the fraudulent checks were authorized by Lor-Mar and in accordance with any agreement between the customer and Bank. Through no negligence on the part of the customer, Van Middlesworth's stamped signature was identically duplicated on computer-generated checks.… The Bank … argues that by express contractual agreement and specific instructions from Lor-Mar, it was authorized to honor each of the checks, which purported to contain an authorized facsimile signature.…

The UCC as adopted by New Jersey permits a bank and its customer to modify the bank's strict liability under Section 4–401, and shift the risk of loss to the customer, provided the bank does not attempt to disclaim its statutory duty of good faith. Thus, the parties can agree for the bank to honor and charge its customer for all checks bearing a facsimile signature resembling the specimen on file, even if it is created by a forgery or the stamp is affixed by an unauthorized person. Such a risk-shifting agreement, however, must contain clear and unambiguous language defining the scope of the bank's obligation, identifying the customer's responsibility, and expressly shifting the risk of loss to the customer for a forged facsimile signature resembling the specimen on file. That did not occur here. Such an intent is not clearly stated in the documents. The sole document executed by Lor-Mar's representative pertaining to facsimile signatures is a facsimile cover sheet which just contains an imprint of the two stamped signatures. Even when that paper is read with the previously executed Resolution, the Bank is only authorized to honor a check bearing Van Middlesworth's or Toto's stamped signature. Lor-Mar did not expressly recognize and assume all risks involved in the unauthorized use of its officer's facsimile signature. Accordingly, there was no meeting of the minds between the Bank and its customer as to a modification of the Bank's responsibilities and its customer's rights under Section 4–401.…

Accordingly, the Bank is held to strict liability to Lor-Mar.… The forged checks were not authorized under Section 4–401; they are not "properly payable" by the Bank. Accordingly, they are not chargeable to Lor-Mar's account, so summary judgment was properly granted in favor of the customer on its collection case against the Bank.…

Affirmed.

Questions for Analysis

1. The appeals court affirmed that the bank was liable for cashing the forged checks. How could the bank have avoided liability?
2. It is common for businesses to use stamped signatures on checks. Anyone can make checks with any numbers on them, so forgery is not difficult. How could a business best avoid possible losses from such an occurrence?

LIGHTER SIDE OF THE LAW
Bounce My Check, Will You?

The Royal Bank of Scotland irritated the holders of checking accounts by charging high fees for account holders' mistakes, such as overdrafts or late payments. The charges were many times the cost of handling the mistake. Account holder Declan Purcell sued the bank for charging him what he believed to be excessive fees.

The bank failed to respond, so Purcell won a default judgment. The judgment entitled him to $6,600. To enforce the judgment, he had a bailiff escort him to a Royal Bank branch, where he seized four computers, two fax machines, and cash to fulfill the judgment.

Source: *This Is London*

Getty Images

Exhibit 12.1 A Sample Note

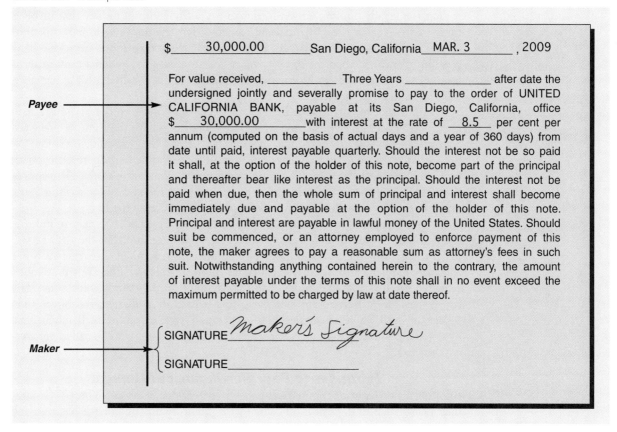

Promises to Pay: Notes

Another classification of commercial paper is *notes*. A note is a promise—not an order—by one party, called the *maker*, to pay a certain sum of money to another party, the *payee*. Usually called *promissory notes*, these instruments involve two parties—the maker and the payee—rather than three parties (a drawer, a drawee, and a payee) required for a draft or check. An example of a simple promissory note is provided in Exhibit 12.1.

Notes can have different forms, depending upon the transactions. Most notes are promissory notes—a promise by one party to pay money to another. Hundreds of billions of dollars worth of promissory notes have been issued by businesses to help raise capital. These notes are registered securities (see the chapter on Securities Regulation) and are often traded in the open market. But promissory notes are used in many other ways. When personal property is used as collateral to back up a loan, the note created is a *collateral note*. The party seeking the loan (the maker) promises to pay the party giving the loan (the payee) according to the loan agreement. If repayment is not made, the payee has certain rights to the personal property of the maker to help repay the loan. When real estate is used as collateral to secure the loan, the note is a *real estate mortgage note*. When the maker promises to repay the note in specified installments, the note is an *installment note*. A *balloon note* provides for installment payments but with a required final payment more than double that of the installment payments, or for one final payment of all principal.

Orders to Pay: Drafts

A *draft* is a legally binding written order to pay a fixed sum of money that involves three parties. It is created by the drawer, who orders the drawee—usually a bank— to pay a certain sum to the payee. If you transfer your own funds from one bank account to another, then the drawer and payee are the same. When a draft guarantees payment for goods in international trade, the draft is called a *bill of exchange*. This is the most common use of drafts.

A draft that requires immediate payment by the drawee to the payee is a *sight draft*. Most checks are considered sight drafts. Banks do have the right to check the legitimacy of a draft presented for payment, but usually they are paid "on sight."

Other drafts hold the payment until later, so there is time to make sure the goods ordered have been delivered. These are called *time drafts* or *term drafts*. They specify payment to be made in the future, such as 60 days from the date of the writing of the draft. The drafts are said to mature on the payment date set in the future.

When a payee is concerned about whether a draft is good, she may submit the draft to the drawee for confirmation that it is legitimate and that the drawee will make payment by the date specified. This confirmation is called an *acceptance*. Since it usually happens at a bank, it is called a *bankers' acceptance*. The draft is stamped accepted by the bank, making it good for payment on the date it comes due. The payee may sell a draft to another party to get cash immediately; the buyer then cashes the draft when it becomes due. To get cash for the draft immediately instead of at some point in the future, an interest rate must be paid. This is called *discounting* the draft.

Promises to Pay: Certificates of Deposit

Another major form of commercial paper is a *certificate of deposit*. The UCC states that a certificate of deposit is an "acknowledgment by a bank" that it has received money from a customer with a promise by the bank that it will repay the money received at a date specified or, in some instances, on demand. The bank as maker creates the certificate and acknowledges receipt of the customer's money, promising to repay the customer as payee plus a certain rate of interest. Most large certificates of deposit (CDs) are negotiable, which allows them to be sold, used to pay debts, or used as collateral for a loan. Most are insured by the Federal Deposit Insurance Corporation (FDIC) for up to $100,000.

The Concept of Negotiability

Negotiable instruments are flexible in how they are used in business. Once issued, a negotiable instrument can be transferred to another party. If the instrument is *assigned*, the assignee has the same contract rights and responsibilities as the assignor. If the instrument is *transferred by negotiation*, the transferee takes the instrument free of any of the transferor's contract obligations. This way, the transferee may have more rights than the transferor.

If an instrument is made "to bearer," the party in possession is required only to deliver the instrument to transfer it. Note that *bearer instruments* can be created in different ways. For example, the maker (drawer) may create a bearer instrument by stating: "to bearer," "to the order of bearer," "payable to bearer," "to cash," or "pay to the order of cash." Bearer instruments are risky, because mere delivery creates a negotiation or transfer. Suppose a buyer of a car pays the seller with a check made out "to the order of cash." Later, the seller loses the check. The check is found by Dr. Dre, who uses it to buy goods from Outkast Appliances. The check has been negotiated, because delivery is sufficient for the transfer of a bearer instrument.

Requirements for Negotiable Instruments

To be negotiable, a commercial instrument must meet the requirements of a negotiable instrument as provided by the UCC. Although commercial paper may be *negotiable* or *nonnegotiable*, only negotiable instruments fall under the UCC. If the instrument is nonnegotiable, the common law of contracts applies. The assignee is subject to the assignor's contract responsibilities under the instrument. If the commercial instrument is negotiable, the UCC governs the resolution of the dispute.

The UCC Requirements

According to UCC §3–104, to be negotiable, an instrument must meet certain requirements. It must

1. be written.
2. be an unconditional order or promise to pay.
3. be signed by the maker or drawer.
4. be payable on demand or at a specified time.
5. be made out "to order" or "to bearer."
6. state a certain sum of money.

The UCC requires commercial instruments to be in writing for practical reasons. Oral promises would be nearly impossible to transfer to third parties. Under UCC §3–105, the writing must be signed and unconditional, so the terms of payment are easily determined and not subject to the occurrence of another event or agreement. It must contain a clear statement of an order or promise to pay. UCC §3–106 requires that it must state a specific sum of money. If the instrument stated that payment was to be made in goods, for example, it would be too difficult for third parties to determine its market value. The UCC also requires that it be payable on demand or at a definite time. It must be clear when payment is to be made and received. Finally, the instrument must be "payable to order" (called *order paper* under UCC §3–110), or "to bearer" (called *bearer paper* under UCC §3–111), to ensure

INTERNATIONAL PERSPECTIVE

Mixing Religion and Finance

Getty Images

Laws limiting high interest rates (usury) in the United States can be traced to Christian views that the practice is sinful. Even more stringent are Islamic limits on interest. Islamic countries have hundreds of billions in wealth, but some prohibit banking as usual, such as charging interest on loans and paying interest to depositors. Many believers in the Koran hold that to be *haram,* or banned by Islam. Malaysian banks have been leaders in developing financial instruments that bring modern finance in line with Islamic rules.

In Malaysia and other countries, banks consult with advisers on Islamic law (*Shariah*) about what form of loans and repayments are acceptable. The result is that modern financial instruments are much more widely available than before, but the presentation is different from traditional financial institutions.

For example, in conventional finance, a company may borrow $100 million from a bank for expansion and pay 6 percent interest ($6 million) per year on a 10-year note and then repay the principal. Under rules permitted (*halal*) by some Muslims, the borrowing company transfers assets, such as buildings, to a legal entity something like a trust (*ijara sukuk*). The company leases the assets back for payments of $6 million per year. The borrower also pledges to buy back the assets at the end of 10 years for $100 million. Not all Muslims agree that this is acceptable, but banks using such instruments have exploded in growth.

that it is freely transferable. With this language, or its equivalent, the parties acknowledge that a third party, who currently may be unknown, could become the owner of the instrument.

A negotiable instrument may be transferred in two basic ways according to UCC §3–202(1). If the instrument is made "to the order" of the payee, the payee must 1) endorse and 2) deliver the instrument to a third party. Endorsement without delivery cannot bring about a transfer. Therefore, if a check is made "to the order of Johnny Depp," and Depp endorses the check but keeps it, there has not been a transfer.

Requirements for Holders in Due Course

If an instrument is negotiable under the UCC, it may be freely traded in the market without concern for other contract responsibilities—if the instrument is in the possession of a holder in due course. The person in possession of a negotiable instrument may be a *holder in due course* or an *ordinary holder*. An ordinary holder has the same contract responsibilities as an assignee under a nonnegotiable instrument. UCC §3–302 states that to be a holder in due course, the transferee must

1. give value for the negotiable instrument.
2. take the instrument without knowledge that it is overdue or defective.
3. take the instrument in good faith.

Thus, a transferee may be an ordinary holder who transforms her position to that of a holder in due course by meeting these three requirements of the UCC. The courts will require the drawer or maker to pay the instrument once it is in the possession of a holder in due course. This is the case even when a hardship may be imposed.

Suppose Pam is negotiating with Tommy to buy the rights to a J-Right Car Wash distributorship. Pam agrees to pay $50,000 by cashier's check to Tommy for the distributorship. After sending the check, Pam learns that Tommy is going bankrupt. She then tries to stop payment on the check. However, Tommy has already transferred the check to a third party, who meets the UCC's requirements for a holder in due course. Tommy declares bankruptcy, so J-Right is worthless. The bank pays the third party upon proper presentation of the check. The third party is a holder in due course and, despite the fact that Tommy defrauded Pam, the third party has no legal obligation to repay Pam. This is why the business community has confidence in negotiable instruments as a substitute for cash.

Credit

Not all promises to pay are negotiable instruments. There are many other payment arrangements. Whether a person or a business, a *creditor* is one who lends money to, or allows goods or services to be purchased on credit by, another party, the *debtor*. Credit terms must specify the interest rate, if any, that applies to the sum owed, the *principal* of the debt, and payment dates, such as in 30 days for materials or over 30 years for land. As discussed below, creditors want evidence of debt, such as a signed loan agreement, and may attach terms to debt that increase the chance it will be repaid.

While large corporations raise much of their funding by *equity financing*—that is, the sale of stock in the company (which we discuss in Chapter 21) or the sale of negotiable instruments—on securities regulation, smaller businesses tend to rely on *debt financing*, which usually means borrowing money evidenced by a contract.

Customer Financial Statements   It is normal practice to require a credit applicant to supply financial information. Individuals normally will be asked to provide financial statements, whereas business applicants may also be asked to provide audited balance sheets and income statements.

Banks   Banks may provide credit information about a customer. Credit departments of banks often share information about loan payment histories and related credit information about their customers.

Credit Reporting Agencies   Credit reporting agencies such as Dun & Bradstreet specialize in providing credit reports and credit ratings on companies. Credit histories of individuals and businesses can be purchased from reporting agencies such as Experian, Trans Union, and Equifax.

Trade Associations   A growing number of trade associations provide information about the credit experiences of its members. The typical information provided deals with the credit obtained from suppliers and lists the amount of credit and the repayment history.

Exhibit 12.2
Sources of Credit Information

The debt incurred by business includes long-term debt (such as financing of a building) and short-term debt (for inventory). Often, creditors want to see debt backed by something more solid than a promise to repay the money plus interest, so we discuss some of the devices used to strengthen the position of the parties.

Credit Policy

Some businesses, such as banks, are in the credit business. Other businesses extend credit as a part of operations, whether the purpose of the business is to provide accounting services or sell bricks. Since many businesses do not demand cash at the time of the sale of services or products, they have policies for credit standards and terms as well as a collection policy. Credit policy focuses on such characteristics as the following:

1. Capacity (the debtor's ability to pay)
2. Capital (the debtor's financial condition)
3. Character (the debtor's reputation)
4. Collateral (the debtor's assets to secure debt)
5. Conditions (the economic situation affecting debtor's business)

Since few lenders know all there is to know about a party seeking debt, sources are available to provide information about a potential borrower (see Exhibit 12.2). Most creditors use credit reporting agencies that sell reports for business purposes about individuals and companies. Some consumers' rights with respect to credit reports are specified by the Fair Credit Reporting Act (discussed in Chapter 19). For our discussion here, which focuses on business debt, an important point is that credit reports are not always accurate. Mistakes are made, so one should make sure credit histories are accurate.

Credit Accounts

When a company gives credit to its customers, it usually offers credit terms according to the size of the account and the importance of the customer. Many accounts do not charge interest if the debt is paid within a certain time. Exhibit 12.3 lists some basic credit accounts offered by many companies.

In most cases, credit terms are determined by competitive conditions or industry standards. For credit under an *open account*, for example, the terms define the

Exhibit 12.3
Common Types of Credit
Accounts

> **Open Account**   The most common form of credit. Goods are sold on an invoice that
>   provides evidence of the transaction. Full payment is expected within a fixed time.
> **Installment Account**   Generally used by consumers for the purchase of durable goods such
>   as automobiles. Debtors repay by regular (generally monthly) payments.
> **Revolving Account**   Similar to the installment account except that the debtor makes a mini-
>   mum monthly payment, which is generally a fraction of the oustanding balance. More
>   debt can be added to the account over time.

credit period available to the customer and any discounts offered for early payment. A typical industry standard is net 60 days from the date of invoice with a discount of 2 percent if paid within ten days of invoice. Consumer credit accounts—installment and revolving accounts—state the interest rate to be paid and the timing of the payments.

Collections Policy

Most bills are paid on time. However, a collections policy is needed for debtors that fail to make timely payments. This usually begins with a letter stating that the account is past due. A telephone call or a second letter may follow. Depending on the relationship, letters may be followed by a personal visit.

At times, additional action is necessary to protect the creditor's rights. The alternatives depend on whether the business is an unsecured or a secured creditor. In most transactions, the lender is an *unsecured (general) creditor.* There is little more than the customer's promise to pay. If the customer proves to be *insolvent*, or unable to pay, the business receives nothing. If the customer simply will not pay, legal action must be considered. Next, we look at ways to make more formal credit agreements.

Credit with Security

In contrast to being an unsecured creditor, a business is a *secured creditor* when it has the ability to take the nonpaying customer's property to satisfy the debt. The law provides two avenues through which the creditor can obtain the customer's property (referred to as *security* or *collateral):*

1. By agreement with the debtor
2. By operation of law, and without an agreement between the lender and the borrower

ISSUE SPOTTER
Helping a Dream?

Your sister has opened her own store, fulfilling her dream. The store looks great and customer traffic seems good, but the up-front costs are high. She is deep in debt and needs more credit to keep the store stocked well. The cash flow looks good and she believes, based on the trend and revenues, that within a year she will be turning a profit. To get more credit at a decent interest rate, she needs help. She asks you and your parents to cosign for an extension on her line of credit from a bank. She will sign a contract holding herself primarily liable on the debt and liable to you in case anything goes wrong. Is there much of a risk here? What is the downside?

Getty Images

By Agreement

The nature of the credit agreement depends upon whether the debtor's property is *real property* (real estate or other immovable property) or *personal property* (movable goods such as vehicles and supplies). The distinction between real and personal property is important for several reasons. The sale of goods is usually governed by the Uniform Commercial Code (discussed in Chapter 11). The sale of personal property can take place with relatively little or no formal documentation. On the other hand, real property is governed by contract and property law and requires documentation before a sale can be finalized. The agreement providing security in real property is a *mortgage*, and it is examined later.

Suretyship

Businesses often need to raise working capital to operate and expand. The owners of small businesses frequently must provide a *guaranty* or *suretyship* for major debts. If a business has a poor credit history, it may be required to provide a guaranty or suretyship for virtually any borrowing it would like to do.

For most small businesses, such a guaranty may be a pledge of personal assets by the owners. In addition, a third party may provide the guaranty or suretyship. In either case, a promise is made to pay a debt of a business in the event the business does not pay. In this way, a suretyship or guaranty is created, and the credit of the party providing it becomes the security for the debt owed.

LIGHTER SIDE OF THE LAW
So, Do We Write This Off as a Bad Loan?

Clancy and Ken Smith, newly married, bought a car. Since their credit was limited, Clancy's father cosigned the car loan from Trustmark Bank in Laurel, Mississippi. The couple fell behind on the loan, and the bank sent a tow truck to repossess the car. Clancy's parents made the needed payments to cover the loan to get the car back.

After five years, the loan was paid. But then the Smiths received a bill for $9,500. The bank had bought car insurance for them—at three times the normal price—when they let their insurance lapse in violation of the terms of the loan.

The Smiths and Clancy's father sued the bank. The jury awarded the Smiths and Clancy's father $19 million each. "We wanted to send a message to the insurance companies and financial institutions to straighten their act up," the jury foreman said.

Source: *The Wall Street Journal*

Getty Images

Surety Defined A contract for *suretyship* is a promise by a third party (the *surety*) to be responsible for the borrower's payment obligations, or performance, to a creditor. The borrower or debtor is referred to as the *principal*. In addition to being a party providing a suretyship for a fee (or out of kindness), the surety could be an owner or shareholder in the business. A suretyship can be created only by a contract between the surety and the creditor. The surety is obligated to pay the creditor if the principal fails to pay the debt, or provide performance, to the creditor. A common form of suretyship is a cosignature on a bank loan.

A *guarantor* provides a guarantee of payment to another and therefore is the same as a surety; that is, to guarantee is to assume the obligation of a surety. In some states, the distinction between a guaranty and a surety is that a surety is primarily liable after the debtor, whereas the guarantor is secondarily liable. Generally, one contract binds both the surety and the borrower, and the creditor is not obligated to exhaust legal remedies before demanding payment by the surety. In other states, the guarantor can be obligated to pay only after the creditor has exhausted legal remedies against the borrower and any surety.

Defenses of Sureties Any contract defenses available to the principal also are available to the surety, including impossibility, illegality, duress, and fraud—but not bankruptcy, because the surety is providing financial protection to the creditor for just such an event. A surety also is released when the creditor releases the borrower without the surety's consent. Similarly, the surety is released if material changes are made to the original contract between the creditor and the debtor without the surety's consent.

It must be emphasized that when one guarantees a loan, liability is imposed according to the terms of the documents signed, as the *Beal Bank* case discusses.

Beal Bank, SSB v. Biggers
Court of Appeals of Texas, Houston
227 S.W.3d 187 (2007)

Case Background *Glenda Biggers was sole shareholder and corporate secretary of Clark Warehouses, and Alton Biggers was president. In January 1993, Clark executed a note to the Small Business Administration (SBA) for $70,800. The Biggers both executed an SBA guaranty as sureties on the note. Later that year, the promissory note was modified and increased to $130,800. The Biggers signed, in their corporate capacity, to execute the loan to Clark, but did not sign the guaranty agreement on the increase in the loan principal. Four years later, Clark Warehouses filed for bankruptcy.*

The SBA sold the note. Beal Bank moved to enforce it against the Biggers personally. The trial court awarded Beal $87,862 in principal and interest on the original loan and $7,500 in attorney's fees. The bank appealed, contending it should also have been awarded the extra $60,000 principal and interest from the increase in the loan amount.

Case Decision Nuchia, Justice

* * *

Texas case law recognizes that a guaranty may be continuing or specific. A continuing guaranty contemplates a future course of dealing between the lender and debtor, and the guaranty applies to other liabilities as they accrue. A specific guaranty applies only to the liability specified in the guaranty contract. A guarantor may require that the terms of his guaranty be followed strictly, and the guaranty agreement

may not be extended beyond its precise terms by construction or implication. The questions, then, in this appeal are (1) what liabilities did appellees agree to guarantee and (2) did they agree to extend their obligation to the modified promissory note.

The guaranties executed by appellees granted to the lender the power to modify or change the terms of the note or the interest rate on the loan. However, the guaranties specifically excluded the power "to increase the principal amount of the note of the Debtor to Lender." The guaranties contain no language that contemplates a future course of dealing between the debtor and the lender. Thus, appellees executed specific guaranties. Although appellees later sought to increase the principal amount of the loan from $70,800 to $130,800, agreed and consented to that amount, and signed the note twice—once in their corporate capacities and once as "Borrower"—they did not sign in the spaces provided for "endorsers, guarantors, and/or sureties on the above described Note." Their consent to the additional $60,000 cannot be construed or implied to be a guaranty of the additional sum....

We hold that, under the facts of this case, appellees did not agree to be liable for the increased principal under the modified promissory note. Accordingly, we overrule the Bank's sole issue.

We affirm the judgment.

Questions for Analysis

1. The appeals court affirmed that the Biggers had to guaranty payment on the original amount of the loan but not on the additional amount. Why were they not liable for that?

2. The business, Clark Warehouses, was bankrupt and could not make good on the loan. Why are the Biggers, who lost their investment in Clark, liable for the loan to Clark?

Surety's Rights against the Principal If the principal (borrower) does not pay the creditor, and the surety has to satisfy the debt, the principal is obligated to repay the surety. If the borrower could pay the creditor but refuses to, the surety is entitled to *exoneration*, a court order requiring the principal to pay. The surety is also entitled to be *subrogated* to the rights of the creditor against the debtor. This generally occurs when part of the debt was paid by the surety. In seeking repayment from the principal, the surety may assert any rights the creditor could have asserted against the debtor, including taking any security interests the creditor obtained from the borrower.

Secured Transactions

The law governing the financing of commercial sales of goods is Article 9 of the UCC. When a good is sold to a customer, either a person or a business, the UCC provides that the goods may secure the debtor's obligation to pay. Called a *secured transaction*, it occurs when a buyer wants a good and does not pay cash and the seller is leery of an unsecured debt. By meeting the requirements of the UCC, the seller obtains a *perfected security interest* in the goods sold to the customer as collateral to help secure payment in the event of default.

Attachment To make a security interest more enforceable, the seller must create the interest, or legal right, and make sure that the interest is *attached* and *perfected*. According to the UCC, for a security interest to attach, the security agreement must be signed by the customer; the seller must have provided value; and the customer must have legal, transferrable rights in the collateral. If the customer is unable to pay, the seller has rights against the customer that are superior to unsecured creditors but not necessarily superior to other secured creditors.

Perfection To establish superior rights—that is, to *perfect* the security interest—the creditor must give notice of the existence of the security interest. The perfection of the interest establishes the date priority took effect. This way, when multiple creditors have claims, the priority order will be clear. The primary way to perfect is to file the financing statement with the secretary of state or other relevant official as required by state law, so it is available for public inspection.

This process must be followed, unless the goods being sold are consumer goods. Under the UCC, a security interest for consumer goods is perfected without filing. Normally, the financing statement contains little more than the names and addresses of the firm and the customer, a description of the product, and the signature of the customer. The details of the credit transaction—including the amount financed, the payment schedule, interest rate, and other such matters—are left to the security agreement.

Interests in Inventory As collateral, supplies such as equipment, inventory, and raw materials can be classified as *tangible property*—goods that are movable at the time a security interest *attaches*, or begins. To protect its interests, the lender

Exhibit 12.4
Security Interest Under
the UCC

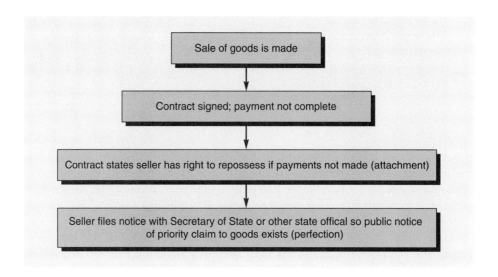

extending credit to a business obtains a security interest, sometimes called a *purchase money security interest*. The procedure is nearly the same as the procedure followed by the business when it extends credit to customers buying its product. As in that case, the security interest gives the lender rights against the borrower—rights that are superior to other creditors in the event the borrower fails to meet debt obligations.

A "Floating Lien" for Inventory Under the UCC, *inventory* includes goods held for sale as well as raw materials. Inventory is constantly changing. This could create a problem for a creditor that provides financing to a business with inventory as collateral. To avoid the need to renew the financing contract every time something is sold or used, the UCC allows a perfected security interest in property acquired after the security agreement is formed. This permits a *floating lien*. The security interest in any specific item of inventory ends upon the item's sale or use, but attaches to new inventory.

Default by the Debtor

A security interest helps to protect the interests of the seller in the event the customer *defaults*, that is, cannot or will not meet its payment obligations. Because the seller has a security interest in the product, it has *priority* to the collateral over all unsecured creditors and, depending on the priorities of other secured creditors, perhaps over them as well.

The UCC provides that when repossessing goods, "a secured party may proceed without judicial process if this can be done without breach of peace." That is, if you do not make payments on your car, it can be repossessed. In taking possession, the seller is not obligated to notify other parties who also may have a security interest in the product. The creditor may keep the product or resell it. If the product is resold, it must be sold in a "commercially reasonable manner." Any proceeds above what is owed must be returned to the customer.

Default by a debtor often affects more than one party. Repossession may or may not be possible, and in searching for funds to repay the debt, creditors commonly argue over who is eligible for whatever funds are available. The UCC and state laws governing liens determine who gets what, when a debtor cannot satisfy all creditors.

Like anything else, a perfected security interest may not work as hoped, as the *Fordyce Bank* case illustrates.

Fordyce Bank and Trust v. Bean Timberland
Supreme Court of Arkansas
369 Ark. 90 (2007)

Case Background *Fordyce Bank made several loans to Bean Timberland so it could buy timber from landowners. Bean would cut timber from owners' lands and sell the logs to Potlatch and Idaho Timber, which milled the logs into lumber. Bean gave the bank security interests in the timber, and the proceeds from its sale were to repay the loans. The bank perfected its interests by filing UCC financing statements with the Secretary of State's office.*

Bean sold the timber but failed to repay the loans and went bankrupt. The bank sued Potlatch and Idaho because the bank had priority interest in the timber sale proceeds. The bank alleged that Potlatch and Idaho were negligent in their dealings for failing to do a lien search and "failed to exercise good faith" as required by the UCC. The trial court held for Potlatch and Idaho, ruling that they were not negligent. They were not required to perform a security interest search in the ordinary course of business. The bank appealed.

Case Decision Glaze, Justice

* * *

Under [Arkansas UCC 4–9–320], a buyer in the ordinary course of business "takes free of a security interest created by the buyer's seller, even if the security interest is perfected and the buyer knows of its existence." Thus, if Potlatch and Idaho were buyers in the ordinary course of business, they would be under no duty to perform a lien search, because even if they knew of a lien and had performed a lien search, they could nonetheless take free of the Bank's security interest....

Evidence presented at trial clearly showed that Potlatch and Idaho's practices were "usual or customary" in the timber business.

Bean sold timber to various mills as "gatewood." Gatewood is severed timber that is brought to a lumber mill's front gate by a logger; the wood is weighed and inventoried, and if the timber meets the mill's specifications, the mill will purchase it. If the wood does not meet specifications, the mill will not buy it. Numerous witnesses testified that purchases of gatewood are common in the Arkansas logging industry....

The procurement manager for Potlatch's Prescott mill, Jim Cornelius, testified that nothing in Potlatch's gatewood purchases from Bean did "anything to cause alarm." Cornelius also stated that he had no actual knowledge that the Bank had a security interest in Bean's inventory. He also declared that, in his 30 years in timber procurement, he had "never undertaken a search for security interests in gatewood," and that Potlatch "does not perform lien searches in any other state, either."...

In sum, the trial court had before it abundant evidence that purchasing gatewood without performing a lien search was the standard practice in the timber industry. Clearly, Bean's sales to Potlatch and Idaho, and Potlatch's and Idaho's practice of not conducting lien searches, "comported with the usual or customary practices in the kind of business in which the seller is engaged or with the seller's own usual or customary practices." [UCC § 4–9–320(a)] As such, the trial court correctly determined that Potlatch and Idaho were buyers in the ordinary course of business. Further, because the mills were buyers in the ordinary course of business, they owed the Bank no duty to conduct a lien search. With no duty, there could be no breach of any duty....

Affirmed.

Questions for Analysis

1. The high court affirmed that the buyers of the timber had no duty to do a search for a security interest on the timber and were not liable to the bank, which lost its potential collateral. What is the logic of not having buyers in the ordinary course of business not do a search?

2. What could the bank have done to protect itself against this sort of outcome?

Property Exempt from Attachment

As discussed, it is not uncommon for business owners to pledge personal assets as security for the debts of the business (for example, as a surety). If the business is not able to pay, the creditor may have assets pledged as collateral that may be seized and sold to repay the debt. If the debt is not fully paid after the sale, the creditor may sue the owners for the rest of the debt. To protect its interests, the creditor may ask the court for an attachment. After the judgment has been rendered and the owner is unable or unwilling to pay, the creditor may ask the court for a writ of execution.

The creditor moves against the owner's *nonexempt property*. That is, certain real and personal property is *exempt* from attachment proceedings. In the interest of ensuring that a debtor has housing, for example, states provide a *homestead exemption*, which allows the debtor to retain the family home up to a specified amount free from creditors' claims. With regard to personal property, state statutes provide limited exemptions for, among other things, furniture, clothing, automobiles, and tools used in the debtor's trade or business.

Real Estate Financing

For most businesses and individual house buyers, buying real estate involves a large outlay of money. Normally, much of the purchase price is borrowed. The real estate itself is used to secure the debt obligation and is evidenced by a *mortgage*. The mortgage is a lien that gives the lien holder the right to sell the property and repay the debt from sale proceeds in the event the borrower defaults. The debtor is the *mortgagor*, and the creditor is the *mortgagee*. Such transactions are governed by state common law and real estate statutes, because the UCC does not apply to real estate.

The Mortgage

According to the Statute of Frauds, a mortgage must be in writing. In most states, a form such as that shown in Exhibit 12.5 is recognized by statute. In meeting the requirements of such documents, the mortgage contains a description of the property, sets forth any warranties relative to the property, states the debt, and states the mortgagor's duties concerning taxes, insurance, and repairs. To protect the mortgagee's rights against other creditors, the mortgage should be *recorded*. State statutes typically require that the mortgage be placed in a county office, often called the recorder's office, clerk of the court, county clerk, or the register of deeds.

Default by the Mortgagor

If the borrower is unable to pay the mortgage, the mortgagee has the right to foreclose on the property. Foreclosure may be by judicial sale. As in all such situations, if the proceeds of the sale are sufficient to cover the costs of the foreclosure and the debt, any surplus must be returned to the mortgage holder. If the proceeds are not sufficient, the mortgagee can seek to recover the remainder from the debtor by obtaining a *deficiency judgment*, obtained in a separate legal action after the foreclosure. In many states, a mortgagor has the right to redeem the property by paying the debt within the *statutory redemption* period, normally within six months to a year after the default.

Liens

Security obtained by a creditor through the operation of law is called a *lien*. Because it may be obtained by the seller without a specific agreement with the customer, the security may be called a *nonconsensual lien*. The term *lien* is derived

Mortgage

(New York Statutory Form)

This mortgage, made the _____ day of _____ , 20_____ , between_____ , [*insert residence*], the mortgagor, and _____ [*insert residence*], the mortgagee.

Witnesseth, that to secure the payment of an indebtedness in the sum of _____ dollars, lawful money of the United States, to be paid on the _____ day of _____ , 20 _____ , with interest thereon to be computed from _____ at the rate of _____ per centum per annum, and to be paid _____ , according to a certain bond or obligation bearing even date herewith, the mortgagor hereby mortgages to the mortgagee [*description*].

And the mortgagor convenants with the mortgagee as follows:

1. That the mortgagor will pay the indebtedness as hereinbefore provided.
2. That the mortgagor will keep the buildings on the premises insured against loss by fire for the benefit of the mortgagee; that he will assign and deliver the policies to the mortgagee; and that he will reimburse the mortgagee for any premiums paid for insurance made by the mortgagee on the mortgagor's dafault in so insuring the buildings or in so assigning and delivering the policies.
3. That no building on the premises shall be removed or demolished without the consent of the mortgagee.
4. That the whole or said principal sum and interest shall become due at the option of the mortgagee; after default in the payment of any installment of principal or of interests for _____ days; or after default in the payment of any tax, water rate or assessment for _____ days after notice and demand; or after default after notice and demand either in assigning and delivering the policies insuring the buildings against loss by fire or in reimbursing the mortgagee for premiums paid on such insurance, as hereinbefore provided; or after default upon request in furnishing a statement of the amount due on the mortgage and whether any offsets or defenses exist against the mortgage debt, as hereinafter provided.
5. That the holder of this mortgage, in any action to foreclose it, shall be entitled to the appointment of a receiver.
6. That the mortgagor will pay all taxes, assessments, or water rates, and in default thereof, the mortgagee may pay the same.
7. That the mortgagor within _____ days upon request in person or within _____ days upon request by mail will furnish a written statement duly acknowledged of the amount due on this mortgage and whether any offsets or defenses exist against the mortgage debt.
8. That notice and demand or request may be in writing and may be served in person or by mail.
9. That the mortgagor warrants the title to the premises. In witness whereof, this mortgage has been duly executed by the mortgagor.

Exhibit 12.5
Sample Mortgage Agreement

from the French language and means "tie" or "string." The legal meaning for lien is the legal right the seller has to the product now held by a customer. The lien helps to secure payment for goods or services, such as repairs.

The procedures for using liens are mostly determined by state statutes. The most common liens are the mechanic's lien (applicable to real property), the possessory lien (applicable to personal property), and court-decreed liens. In each case, a creditor may obtain the lien without the debtor's consent by following statutory procedures. An additional remedy, *garnishment*, is a statutory procedure under which a creditor gains the right to attach up to 25 percent of a customer's net wages to be applied to an outstanding debt.

Getty Images

ISSUE SPOTTER
Lean on a Lien?

Your concrete company is offered a chance to get in on a huge construction project at a new shopping center. If it goes as planned, you will be able to double the size of your operation, allowing you to compete for more large-scale jobs. The builder will hire you as a subcontractor, and the price offered is fair. But the builder will not pay you, or the other subcontractors, until he is paid. So you will have to carry some debt as the project goes along. The contractor points out that the risk to you is minimal, since the scale of the project is huge and you are involved in only a small part of the total cost. Besides, he says, if there is a problem in your getting paid, you can slap a lien on the whole project. Would this action give you adequate protection? Is the gamble worth it?

Mechanic's Lien

A *mechanic's lien* is the most common lien for work performed on real property. The party that furnished material, labor, or services for the construction or repair of a building or other real property can place a lien on the property for unpaid bills. The creditor must follow the steps the law requires be taken within a certain time. The requirements vary from state to state; some states require preliminary notice to the debtor before the lien is filed, but many do not. Upon filing the lien, the creditor obtains security for the debt.

If the owner of the real property does not pay the lien, the creditor can move to force the sale of the property to satisfy the debt. Obviously, the debtor must be notified that the property is going to be sold, that is, that there will be a foreclosure. In some states, such a sale must take place within 12 months of the original filing. If no action is taken within 12 months, the lien expires and cannot be revived.

Possessory Lien

The *possessory lien* or *artisan's lien* is the most common lien on personal property. It provides a security interest for creditors that add value to or care for personal property. This lien offers the right to continue to hold goods on which work has been done, or for which materials have been supplied, until the customer pays. The business doing the work must have the property in its possession, and it must have agreed to provide the work on a cash basis. The lien stays in existence as long as the creditor retains possession, unless the lien is filed according to the requirements of a state's lien and recording statutes. In that way, the creditor gives notice of the existence of the lien to others and protects its interests if the customer is in possession of the property.

If the customer does not pay for the work or supplies, the creditor can force the sale of the property to fulfill payment of the debt. As with the mechanic's lien, the debtor must have prior notice of the sale. Having a valid lien does not always mean payment can be extracted, because liens are costly to enforce, as we saw in the *Fordyce Bank* case, where the lien provided no real protection for the lender.

Court-Decreed Liens   When a debt is past due, the creditor may sue the debtor. Creditors prefer alternatives to litigation for collections because of the time and expense involved. If it is necessary to use the court system, creditors will find attachment and judgment liens as judicial means to try to protect their interests.

An *attachment lien* is a court-ordered seizure of goods from the customer to prevent the customer from disposing of it during the lawsuit. Under state statute, the requirements imposed on the creditor are specific and limited. To obtain an attachment lien, the business must show that the debtor is likely to dispose of the product. If the court concurs, it issues a *writ of attachment* directing the sheriff to seize the good. It is important for the creditor to follow state attachment procedures closely, or it could be liable for damages for wrongful attachment.

If the creditor is successful in an action against the debtor, the court awards a *judgment lien.* No lien is created simply by the rendering of a court judgment. Rather, the creditor must obtain an *abstract of judgment,* which, when prepared, recorded, and indexed creates a lien against the debtor's real property and provides notice to potential purchasers of the property of the existence of the judgment and lien. Normally, a lien holds for 10 years.

If the debtor does not pay the judgment, the creditor asks the court to issue a *writ of execution.* The writ is issued by the clerk of the court and directs the sheriff to seize and sell any of the debtor's nonexempt real or personal property within the court's jurisdiction.

Bankruptcy

Financial ruin comes to many in the marketplace. Some consumers and businesses engage in fraud, causing financial messes that others pay for, but most bankruptcies are due to bad luck or unintentional mismanagement. A person or a business is not able to pay debts that are due, usually because liabilities exceed assets, and at least some creditors will not extend the time for payment, so something must be done to resolve the financial mess. Bankruptcy is not a new issue; the framers of the Constitution thought it such an important issue that they specifically made bankruptcy a matter of federal law.

The *bankruptcy code* has been amended many times. The most recent major revision was the Bankruptcy Abuse Prevention and Consumer Protection Act of 2005. The code states how matters are resolved when debts are greater than assets available. Since over one and one-half million people file for bankruptcy each year, and over 35,000 businesses file bankruptcy, it is a significant issue. We review the major types of bankruptcy and then discuss nonbankruptcy choices for distressed debtors.

Personal Bankruptcy

While our focus is on business bankruptcy, because most bankruptcies involve individuals, and their bankruptcies often mean businesses do not get paid, we consider some of the steps in bankruptcy.

Before a person may file for bankruptcy, they must complete a debtor education course. The Department of Justice's U.S. Trustee Program approves organizations to provide the mandatory credit counseling and debtor education (see www.usdoj.gov/ust/). There are many in every state. Credit counseling and predischarge debtor education may not be provided together. A person must take credit counseling before filing bankruptcy. Debtor education is taken after filing.

Prebankruptcy counseling includes an evaluation of a person's financial situation, a discussion of alternatives to bankruptcy, and a personal budget plan. This usually takes about an hour. A certificate of credit counseling completion is provided and one must have it to be able to file bankruptcy. The purpose is to try to head people off from filing bankruptcy, as the number doing so is large. But if one does file, then there must be postfiling debtor education about budgeting, use of credit, and related issues.

Income and Means Testing

If a person wishes to file bankruptcy, there is an income test that will help determine if one files under Chapter 7 (liquidation) or Chapter 13 (reorganization of debts). If a person's monthly income is more than the state median income, then Chapter 13 is more likely. That is, people with higher income are less likely to have debts extinguished. Further, there is a test of income against reasonable expenditures for a person of a certain income level; that is, living above average for a given income level will be held to be evidence that expenses can be cut and debts repaid under Chapter 13. Both of these tests are complicated, but the intent is to shuffle people in one direction or the other at this point. It is intended to reduce the number of higher-income people who file Chapter 7, which traditionally was chosen about two to one over Chapter 13, and to force more repayments of debt.

Chapter 13

About one-half million personal bankruptcies are handled under Chapter 13 each year. There is only a voluntary option under Chapter 13, which is filed like a Chapter 7 bankruptcy, and it is available only for individuals. Because a sole proprietorship is a business owned by an individual, it may be handled under the Chapter 13 option.

In this proceeding, the debtor files a plan for payment of creditors over five years. This is an installment repayment plan. Unlike Chapter 7, where the debtor is relieved of all property except that protected by state statute, in Chapter 13, the debtor keeps the estate's property and shares administration of the bankrupt estate with a court-appointed trustee. The trustee collects income from the debtor and makes payments to creditors as called for by the *confirmation plan* that was approved. The trustee is there to make sure that payments are made and to approve any changes in the debt and credit position of the debtor.

Unlike Chapter 7, the debts of the bankrupt are not discharged. Chapter 13 is a court-protected change of debt repayment that usually must be accomplished within five years. Long-term, secured debt, such as a house mortgage, is treated differently. If the plan fails to work, it is possible to shift to a Chapter 7 bankruptcy and have the financial decks cleared by discharge.

While some people not familiar with bankruptcy have the impression it can mean a return to living the high life, the *Darby* case indicates that is hardly so.

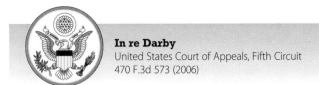

In re Darby
United States Court of Appeals, Fifth Circuit
470 F.3d 573 (2006)

Case Background *After Darby filed for Chapter 13 bankruptcy, Time Warner canceled his cable service. Darby filed a motion with the bankruptcy court to compel Time Warner to reinstate his service upon the offering of assurances of future payments. The bankruptcy court and district court held that cable service was not a utility that had to be provided as a necessity under the law. Darby appealed.*

Case Decision Stewart, Circuit Judge

* * *

The word "utility" as it is used in [the bankruptcy code] is not defined within the statute, but some guidance is provided by the legislative history of the provision. Both the House Judiciary Report and the Senate Report on the provision state in relevant part:

> This section gives debtors protection from a cut-off of service by a utility because of the filing of a bankruptcy case. This section is intended to cover utilities that have some special position with respect to the debtor, such as an electric company, gas supplier, or

telephone company that is a monopoly in the area so that the debtor cannot easily obtain comparable service from another utility....

The bankruptcy court did not err in determining that cable service is not a necessity. Therefore, cable service is not covered by [the bankruptcy code], and Time Warner is not required to reinstate Darby's service despite his offer of adequate assurances of future payment....

Even if Darby were correct in his assertion that he could not obtain an alternative to cable television, the fact that Time Warner is not a necessity is enough to exempt it from the requirements of [the bankruptcy code]....

Affirmed.

Questions for Analysis

1. The appeals court affirmed that a cable television company need not provide cable service to a person in bankruptcy. Would you think Internet service and television service is a necessity?

2. How could Time Warner assure itself of payment from Darby?

Chapter 7

Chapter 7 of the bankruptcy code was the most commonly used alternative, accounting for over one million bankruptcies filed per year (that is, Chapter 7 was the most common form of bankruptcy filing). But the 2005 reforms have forced many people into Chapter 13 instead. Chapter 7 means liquidation and fair distribution of the debtor's assets for the creditors. Liquidating bankruptcy under Chapter 7 is available for businesses, but only individuals can use Chapter 7 to obtain discharge.

Most Chapter 7 bankruptcies are filed voluntarily by the debtor. A petition is filed with the bankruptcy court, which may be the federal district court or a federal bankruptcy court. The filing is a statement of the financial affairs of the debtor, including a listing of all assets and liabilities, using specific forms. The petition provides the following:

- Statement of the financial affairs of the debtor
- List of all creditors and their addresses, with amounts owed
- List of properties owned by debtor
- Statement of current income and expenses of debtor

The filing of this petition means that an immediate freeze, an automatic stay, is made against all actions against the debtor or a debtor's property by any creditors. A temporary *trustee* is appointed to administer the debtor's estate. The trustee meets with the creditors within about a month to review the accuracy of the information provided by the debtor. The creditors usually approve formal appointment of the temporary trustee as the trustee. In an *involuntary bankruptcy*, creditors file a petition with the court, forcing the declaration of bankruptcy and the beginning of proceedings.

ISSUE SPOTTER

Credit for the Bankrupt?

Some credit issuers have a policy of offering credit to people who have just gone through bankruptcy. Having had their debts cleared, they are not allowed to file for bankruptcy again for years. Are these folks in fact good credit risks because they cannot file for bankruptcy?

Getty Images

The Bankruptcy Proceeding

A key feature of bankruptcy is the emphasis on creditors' receiving fair treatment. Under the federal system, once bankruptcy has been declared, a creditor cannot improve its position by getting to the debtor's property first. Nor can the debtor improve a favored creditor's position by transferring property to that creditor. It is the trustee's job to assure that no creditor has improved its relative position. Some creditors may have learned of the debtor's financial plight and then gained control of some of the debtor's property. Hence, bankruptcy proceedings hold that such transfers of debtor's property within 90 days of bankruptcy are void.

Role of the Trustee

The trustee's objective is to maximize the amount of the debtor's assets available for distribution to the creditors. However, as noted earlier, some of the debtor's property is *exempt* from bankruptcy. The equity in one's house (homestead) is protected up to $125,000. Also exempt are minimal household furnishings, a car, and tools of trade. The trustee is required to liquidate all the debtor's nonexempt property. The *liquidation* takes place through a sale at a public auction unless otherwise ordered by the court. After the property has been sold, the proceeds are disbursed among the creditors. All creditors holding a claim against the debtor are entitled to share in the distribution of the sales proceeds.

Priority Classes of Creditors

Bankruptcy law states that certain creditors take priority over other creditors in receiving shares of the debtor's assets to pay for the debts owed them. Standing first in line are *secured creditors*. As discussed previously, these creditors have a written security agreement that describes the property (collateral) that stands behind a particular debt. For a consumer, the most common would be a home mortgage or an automobile loan. In bankruptcy, the secured creditor may request that the court grant permission for it to take possession of the property covered by the debt. The *priority classes* in bankruptcy usually are as follows:

1. Secured creditors
2. Costs of preserving and administering the debtor's estate
3. Unpaid wage claims
4. Certain claims of farmers and fishermen
5. Refund of security deposits
6. Alimony and child support
7. Taxes
8. General (unsecured) creditors who can file a proof of claim

All the creditors of a particular class must be paid before the next-lower-priority creditors can be paid anything. Rarely is enough money received from the sale to pay general creditors what they are owed.

Discharge in Bankruptcy

The final stage of the bankruptcy proceeding for individuals is the *bankruptcy discharge*. Discharge means that the nonexempt assets are liquidated and the proceeds distributed among the creditors, who may not ask for more. The claimants are paid according to their priority, so unsecured credits are rarely paid, and even secured creditors may get very little. The books have been cleared, and the debtor gets a fresh start. However, a declaration of bankruptcy remains on a person's credit history for 10 years and the debtor may not seek another discharge for eight years.

INTERNATIONAL PERSPECTIVE

Bankruptcy Efficiency around the World

Critics of the Bankruptcy Code in the United States assert that the process is too slow and costly. If so, then perhaps the practices of other countries should be studied for ideas on reform. A study sponsored by the World Bank, completed by a group at Harvard University, looked at business bankruptcy practices.

As the table shows in the first column, the authors measured the average time that bankruptcy lawyers estimate is necessary to complete a procedure. In the second column, lawyers estimated the average cost of bankruptcies as a percent of the value of the bankrupt estate—including court costs, lawyer fees, accounting fees, and other direct costs. The last column documents the recovery rate, which calculates how many cents on the dollar

claimants (creditors, tax authorities, and employees) recover from an insolvent firm. Singapore is ranked one of the most efficient in the world by these standards.

Country	Time in Years	Cost as Percentage of Estate	Recovery Rate (cents on the dollar)
Singapore	0.8	1	91.3
United Kingdom	1.0	6	85.8
United States	1.5	7	77.0
Mexico	1.8	18	63.2
France	1.9	9	48.0
China	2.4	22	31.5
India	10.0	9	13.0

Source: *http://rru.worldbank.org/doingbusiness*

Getty Images

Some debts are not discharged by bankruptcy proceedings. The reason for these exceptions is to discourage the use of bankruptcy to evade certain responsibilities. The following are among the debts not extinguished by bankruptcy:

- Alimony and child support payments
- Back taxes
- Most student loans
- Some debts incurred immediately before filing bankruptcy
- Debts incurred by fraud against the creditors
- Fines owed to the government

Chapter 11

A portion of the bankruptcy code with a very different intent is Chapter 11, which applies to businesses that wish to remain in operation and not be liquidated. Many businesses are worth more if they can be kept alive, generating revenue, than if they are liquidated when debts are greater than assets. About 10,000 businesses each year use this option. The difference between the value of a business as a going concern compared with what is collected from selling the assets of the company is known as a "going concern surplus." It is that surplus that the creditors hope to capture by allowing the business to remain in operation so that they have a greater chance of full repayment. There is a risk, of course, that keeping the business in operation will only worsen things, in which case the creditors lose even more. It is a judgment call.

Although Chapter 11 has been used to restructure some multibillion-dollar businesses, such as in the airline and asbestos industries, most companies that file have assets worth less than $1 million. Well-planned Chapter 11 cases have much better track records and involve fewer legal fees than those done in haste. But many businesses are in dire straits, before a reorganization plan is rushed to court, to try to salvage operations as the creditors are pressing in.

Reorganization

As with Chapter 7, the filing under Chapter 11 automatically stays further action by any parties involved. An initial hearing with the trustee determines whether the plan should be allowed to proceed, or whether some creditors are due immediate payment or return of property. In most cases, the debtor is allowed by the court to continue operating the "reorganized" business. Thus, the debtor acts as trustee of the operation, called a *debtor in possession,* running the business for the benefit of all parties. This means that the debtor now owes an extra duty of care, because the debtor's duty is to act in the best interest of all, not just the owners of the business.

Watching over the debtor is the unsecured creditors' committee, composed of several creditors with the largest claims. These creditors are often the largest suppliers to the business. The committee supervises the management of the reorganized business, cooperating with the debtor to try to make a success of the operation. Any unusual actions by the debtor must be reviewed by the committee in advance; if the creditors object, the court will review the matter. As with Chapter 7, creditors must be satisfied by class in order of priority of claims. However, unlike Chapter 7, where discharge of debts is the goal, under Chapter 11, the purpose is to have the business emerge as a profitable venture or to see it sold for its greatest value. But Chapter 11 proceedings mean many issues are fought in court, which is costly and adds significant time delays to getting on with business. Judges and trustees end up running companies. The *Kmart* case illustrates the kind of issues that arise, and this is just one of many rulings involving that one company.

In the Matter of Kmart Corporation
United States Court of Appeals, Seventh Circuit
359 F.3d 866 (2004)

Case Background *Kmart consists of the parent company and 37 affiliates and subsidiaries. When it filed bankruptcy, it requested to pay, in full, the claims of all "critical vendors." The request stated that some suppliers would be unwilling to do business in the future if past debts were not paid. To stay in operation, it needed to continue to receive supplies. If it did not receive supplies, its ability to pay other creditors would be further impaired.*

The bankruptcy judge agreed and granted the order, without notifying the disfavored creditors. The judge held that its decision was in the best interest of the debtors and creditors. Kmart was allowed to determine who were critical vendors. Kmart paid about $300 million to 2,330 suppliers. Another 2,000 vendors were not paid. They and 43,000 additional unsecured creditors got about 10 cents on the dollar, mostly in stock of the reorganized company.

Some of the creditors appealed. The district court reversed the order authorizing payments to critical vendors. Judge Grady concluded that neither the Bankruptcy Code nor the "doctrine of necessity" supported the order. That decision was appealed.

Case Decision Easterbrook, Circuit Judge

* * *

Appellants insist that, by the time Judge Grady acted, it was too late. Money had changed hands and we are told, cannot be refunded. But why not? Reversing preferential transfers is an ordinary feature of bankruptcy practice, often continuing under a confirmed plan of reorganization....

Section 105(a) [of the Bankruptcy Code] allows a bankruptcy court to "issue any order, process, or judgment that is necessary or appropriate to carry out the provisions of" the Code. This does not create discretion to set aside the Code's rules about priority and distribution.... this statute does not allow a bankruptcy judge to authorize full payment of any unsecured debt, unless all unsecured creditors in the class are paid in full....

So does the Code contain any grant of authority for debtors to prefer some vendors over others? Many sections require equal treatment or specify the details of priority when assets are insufficient to satify all claims.… Filing a petition for bankruptcy effectively creates two firms: the debts of the prefiling entity may be written down so that the postfiling entity may reorganize and continue in business if it has a positive cash flow. Treating prefiling debts as … claims against the postfiling entity would impair the ability of bankruptcy law to prevent old debts from sinking a viable firm.…

The foundation of a critical-vendors order is the belief that vendors not paid for prior deliveries will refuse to make new ones.… For the premise to hold true, however, it is necessary to show not only that the disfavored creditors *will* be as well off with reorganization as with liquidation—a demonstration never attempted in this proceeding—but also that the supposedly critical vendors would have ceased deliveries if old debts were left unpaid while the litigation continued.…

Some supposedly critical vendors will continue to do business with the debtor because they must. They may, for example, have long term contracts, and the automatic stay prevents these vendors from walking away as along as the debtor pays for new deliveries.…

Doubtless many suppliers fear the prospect of throwing good money after bad. It therefore may be vital to assure them that a debtor will pay for new deliveries on a current basis. Providing that assurance need not, however, entail payment for prepetition transactions.…

Even if [the Code] allows critical-vendors orders in principle, preferential payments to a class of creditors are proper only if the record shows the prospect or benefit to the other creditors. This record does not, so the critical-vendors order cannot stand.

Affirmed.

Questions for Analysis

1. Assuming a vendor has no long-term obligation, would it continue to sell to Kmart if past debts were not paid?

2. Some critics of Chapter 11 contend that firms should be liquidated under Chapter 7, not operate under court supervision. Can you think of the reasons for that argument?

LIGHTER SIDE OF THE LAW
Home Sweet Home

Paul Bilzerian, a noted "corporate raider," was ordered to jail for contempt of court for allegedly hiding assets. He was being sued by the government, which was trying to collect a $62 million judgment against Bilzerian for securities fraud. Filing for bankruptcy protection against the judgment, Bilzerian claimed only $15,800 in assets, including a watch worth $5.

Fortunately for the destitute Bilzerian, Florida law allows bankrupts to keep their homes. He lived in a 37,000-square-foot residence, which had an indoor basketball court, movie theater, nine-car garage, and an elevator. He offered to rent the home for $600,000 a week during the Super Bowl in Tampa.

Source: *St. Petersburg Times*

Getty Images

Summary

- Negotiable instruments are flexible commercial instruments because of their ability to be transferred. Once issued, a negotiable instrument can be transferred by assignment or by negotiation. If the instrument is assigned, the assignee has the same contract rights and responsibilities as the assignor. If the instrument is transferred by negotiation, the transferee takes the instrument free of the transferor's contract responsibilities.

- To be negotiable, a commercial instrument must meet the general requirements of a negotiable instrument as provided by the UCC. It must be written, be an unconditional order or promise to pay, be signed by the maker or drawer, be payable on demand or at a specified time, be made out "to order" or "to bearer," and state a certain sum of money.

- If an instrument is negotiable under the requirements of the UCC, the instrument may be freely traded in the marketplace without concern for existing contract responsibilities as long as the instrument is in the possession of a holder in due course.

- As a creditor, a business monitors its credit extension and debt collection policies. As a debtor, a business borrows to pay for equipment, inventory, land, and buildings. Creditors are interested in being protected in the event a debtor is unable or unwilling to pay.

- A secured creditor has the right to take specific property of an insolvent debtor to satisfy the debt. The law provides two ways the creditor can obtain a debtor's property, referred to as security or collateral: 1) by agreement with the debtor or 2) by operation of law and without an agreement between the lender and the borrower.

- A lender may require that a financially strong third party guarantee a loan. Such a guaranty may be a pledge of personal assets by business owners or from a third party. A promise is made to pay a particular debt of the business in the event it does not pay. A suretyship or guaranty is created, and the credit of the party providing it is the security for the debt owed.

- When a product is sold to a customer, Article 9 of the UCC provides that the product itself may secure the customer's obligation to pay. When credit is extended this way, the sale is called a *secured transaction*. By meeting the requirements of the UCC, the creditor obtains a security interest in the product to secure payment.

- To make a security interest enforceable, the lender must create the interest and make sure the interest is attached and perfected. When a creditor has a security interest in the product, it has priority to the product over some other and unsecured creditors. The lender can sue the debtor to recover the debt or repossess the product and resell it.

- In most credit transactions, except mortgages, creditors require that a security agreement and a financing statement be accepted and signed by the borrower. When money is borrowed for the purchase of real estate, the real estate itself secures the obligation and is evidenced by a mortgage. In most states, the mortgage is a lien, giving the holder the right to sell the property and repay the debt from proceeds in the event of default.

- Security obtained by a creditor through the operation of law is called a *lien*. The procedures for using liens are determined by state law. The most common liens are the mechanic's lien (applicable to real property), the possessory lien (applicable to personal property), and court-decreed liens. In each case, the lender may obtain the lien without the borrower's consent by following statutory procedures.

- The bankruptcy code governs bankruptcy procedure. There are several approaches to bankruptcy, including Chapter 7 (providing for liquidation and fair distribution of the debtor's assets for creditors), Chapter 11 (allowing businesses to reorganize rather than being liquidated), and Chapter 13 (personal bankruptcy for individuals that reorganizes debts, but does not discharge them).

- The trustee (or debtor in possession) is the person in charge of the bankruptcy. It is the trustee's objective, under bankruptcy court supervision, to maximize the amount of the debtor's assets available for distribution to the creditors.
- Bankruptcy law states that certain creditors take priority over other creditors in receiving shares of the debtor's assets. Secured creditors take priority over unsecured creditors.

Terms to Know

You should be able to define the following terms:

negotiable instrument, 282	holder in due course, 288	mechanic's lien, 298
draft, 286	secured creditor, 290	attachment, 298
bill of exchange, 286	suretyship, 291	trustee, 301
sight draft, 286	guarantor, 291	secured creditors, 302
certificate of deposit, 286	perfected security interest, 293	

Discussion Question

1. What are the basic differences between Chapters 7, 11, and 13 bankruptcy?

Case Questions

1. Chung was at Belmont Park, a racetrack operated by the New York State Racing Association. He bought a gambling voucher for use in SAMS, which are "automated machines which permit a better to enter his bet by inserting money, vouchers, or credit cards into the machines, thereby enabling him to select the number or combination he wishes to purchase. A ticket is issued showing those numbers." The money credited to a voucher can be bet at once or can be used over time to make bets on SAMS. Chung forgot his voucher in a SAMS machine; it had several thousands of dollars credit on it. Someone found the voucher and traded it in for cash. The betting system does not link a person to a voucher, so the thief is unknown. Chung sued, contending that the racetrack should be liable for failing to check the identity and ownership of vouchers prior to their use. Is the racetrack liable or is Chung out of luck? [*Chung v. New York State Racing Assn.*, 42 UCC Rep.Serv.2d 867 Dist. Ct., City of N.Y., NY (2000)]

   ✓ **Check your answer at http://academic.cengage.com/blaw/meiners**

2. Chrysler Credit Corporation (CCC) had a security interest in a Dodge pickup truck that had been purchased by Robert Keeling. After Keeling defaulted on his payments, CCC tried to repossess the vehicle but could not locate it for some time. The truck was found in the storage lot of Highway Tow Service. It had been towed there from an apartment complex at the request of the manager of the complex. CCC requested that Highway deliver the truck to it, but Highway refused, requesting payment of its towing and storage charges. CCC sued to gain possession. Is Highway entitled to an artisan's or possessory lien on the truck? [*Chrysler Credit Corp. v. Keeling*, 793 S.W. 2d 222 Ct. App., Mo. (1990)]

3. McDowell owned and operated Big River Harley Davidson in Wapello, Iowa. As required by law, McDowell took out a retail motor vehicle dealer's surety bond for $35,000 with United Fire and Casualty Insurance. The bond protects retail customers who get stuck when a motor vehicle dealer, because of fraud or some other reason, does not deliver a vehicle that has been paid for. The surety bond was in force when Big River went out of business and McDowell left the state. While in business, Big River sold two Harleys wholesale to Elworth Harley Davidson Sales and Service in Norfolk, Nebraska. Only one of the two Harleys was delivered; the second Harley, for which Elworth paid $12,000, was

not delivered. Elworth sued United Fire as surety for the $12,000. Can Elworth recover? [*United Fire and Casualty* v. *Acker*, 541 N.W.2d 517 Sup. Ct., Iowa (1995)]

✓ **Check your answer at http://academic.cengage.com/blaw/meiners**

4. Bussewitz borrowed money from Citibank and signed a promissory note. Pitassi also signed the promissory note as co-maker of the note. When Bussewitz failed to make payments and defaulted on the note, Citibank, under the terms of the note, declared the entire unpaid balance due and sued both makers. Pitassi defended that he should not be liable, because he signed the note only as a favor to Bussewitz and, furthermore, the note did not state when the first installment payment was due; that term had been left blank. Is Pitassi liable? [*Citibank* v. *Pitassi*, 432 N.Y.S.2d 389 Sup. Ct., App. Div., NY (1980)]

5. Moody and three other people bought a business together and executed promissory notes for $8.17 million to be repaid on a certain schedule. For his contribution, Moody owned 20 percent of the business; the other three owned the other 80 percent of the business. Moody was unable to make several payments on schedule. The other owners covered the payments he was supposed to make so that the notes would not go into default. Moody was sued by the other three for his contribution. He asserted that he was the same as a surety. Since they made the payments that were due, he was no longer obligated on those payments. Is that correct? [*Krumme* v. *Moody*, 910 P.2d 993 Sup. Ct., Ok. (1996)]

✓ **Check your answer at http://academic.cengage.com/blaw/meiners**

6. Mollinedo's home was damaged by fire. Her insurance company, Sentry, recommended ServiceMaster as a good repair company. An adjuster for Sentry visited the home with the home contractor from ServiceMaster and approved $30,000 worth of work, which Service Master did with Mollinedo's approval. Sentry was suspicious about the origins of the fire and gave the payment of $30,000 to Mollinedo's mortgage company. Mollinedo filed for bankruptcy. ServiceMaster, which got nothing, sued Sentry for breach of contract and unjust enrichment. Did ServiceMaster, which never filed a lien, have a claim? [*Service-Master of St. Cloud* v. *GAB Business Services*, 544 N.W.2d 302 Sup. Ct., Minn. (1996)]

7. The Boggses were declared bankrupt under Chapter 13. Shortly after their discharge, Somerville Bank and Trust contended that the Boggses did not pay off the interest on a loan secured by a mortgage on their principal residence. The bank had not raised the issue until after the bankruptcy court had issued its discharge order covering the indebtedness. The bank attempted to collect the debt as though there had been no discharge. Is the bank entitled to collect the interest? [*Boggs* v. *Somerville Bank and Trust*, 51 F.3d 271 6th Cir. (1995)]

8. Noggle borrowed $1,005.72 from Beneficial Finance Company to finance a small business project. To obtain the loan, he gave Beneficial a security interest in certain specified household goods: a camera, some household appliances, and a Winchester rifle. Beneficial filed a financing statement to perfect its security interest in the property. Shortly thereafter, Noggle filed a voluntary petition in bankruptcy under Chapter 13. During the administration of the case, Noggle claimed the Winchester rifle as exempt household property. Using the federal list of exemptions, is the rifle exempt from the reach of the bankruptcy proceeding? [*Matter of Noggle*, 30 Bankr. 303 E.D. Mich. (1983)]

9. Globe Building went into Chapter 7 bankruptcy, so a trustee was appointed to control the bankrupt estate. As a number of Globe employees had not been paid when the company went under, the state of Wisconsin, where Globe was located, filed a lien for wages against all property owned by Globe. Could the lien be enforced? [*In re: Globe Building Materials*, 463 F.3d 631, 7th Cir. (2006)]

✓ **Check your answer at http://academic.cengage.com/blaw/meiners**

10. Strumpf was in default on a loan with a balance of $5,069 owed to Citizens Bank. When Strumpf filed for bankruptcy under Chapter 13, the bank put a hold on his checking account at the bank so that he could not write checks and leave less than $5,069 in the account. Strumpf complained to the bankruptcy court that the bank's action was illegal, because it gave the bank a setoff against the debt, rather than preserving the checking account on behalf of all creditors. Could the bank place a hold on the checking account? [*Citizens Bank of Maryland* v. *Strumpf*, 116 S. Ct. 286 (1995)]

Ethics Question

1. Should a small business be allowed to seek discharge of debts through bankruptcy, when those debts were incurred as a consequence of an automobile accident caused by one of its drivers who was legally drunk at the time of the accident? [See *Matter of Wooten*, 30 Bankr. 357 N.D. Ala. (1983)]

Internet Assignment

1. Using any Internet search engine, find the official Web site for the National Conference of Commissioners on Uniform State Laws.
2. What is the URL for the Pre-Final Official Draft, as approved, NCCUSL, July 30, 1998, of the UCC Revised Article 9, Secured Transactions?
3. Search your library's online public access catalog to find the call number for the following title, if available: *The ABCs of the UCC: (Revised) Article 9 Secured Transactions*, by Russell A. Hakes (2000).

Business Organizations

Getty Images

Chapter 13

Three chums from school, who have all worked as employees at different companies for the past five years, decide to join together to start their own firm, a partnership developing real estate. They consult a lawyer in drawing up the paperwork for the new partnership, knowing that legal form is important for any venture. They also know that good intentions at the beginning of an operation often disappear later when issues arise; and this is what happens to them. The business does not do well, and the chums turn on each other. One partner does not do much work. Another partner charges personal expenses to the partnership. They cannot agree on how to split the income. Could they have headed these problems off by forming the right kind of organization at the outset?

Unfortunately, no. While form is important, managing an organization requires a complex set of abilities. Many people, report that they would like to be their own boss some day. It is a great goal, but there is no magic key. You are often on your own, since you cannot afford a team of lawyers, accountants, and other experts to guide you. This chapter examines the relative merits of different forms of organizations.

There are over 27 million businesses in the United States. Sole proprietorships—often small businesses, such as computer repair stores, dry cleaners, and restaurants—account for about three quarters of the total. Proprietorships take in about 4 percent of all business revenues but 20 percent of all business profits. Corporations are fewer in number—20 percent of the total—but account for 87 percent of all revenues and 65 percent of profits. Partnerships take in 11 percent of business receipts while making up 8 percent of all businesses.

We begin with a discussion of different types of business organizations, including sole proprietorships, partnerships, corporations, and limited liability companies. Every state has laws concerning some aspects of corporation and partnership formation, operation, and dissolution, but organizations are primarily created by actions and contracts. The statutory requirements regarding business formation are not burdensome, but each form has advantages and disadvantages. This chapter considers factors that may influence a business's choice of organization. Finally, we look at franchises, a form of business that continues to grow. ■

Sole Proprietorships

A person doing business for himself or herself is a *sole proprietor;* the business organization is a *sole proprietorship.* The sole proprietorship is the oldest and simplest form of business organization. As a proprietor, a person may simply begin to do business without formality in enterprises that do not require a government license or permit, although most states require business names to be registered if a fictitious business name is used. The proprietor generally owns all or most of the business property and is responsible for the control, liabilities, and management of the business.

In a sole proprietorship, legally and practically, *the owner is the business;* capital must come from the owner's own resources or be borrowed. Perhaps the greatest disadvantage of the sole proprietorship is the fact that limited alternatives exist for raising capital. Because the profits of the business are taxed to the owner personally, a tax return in the business's name is not required so long as records of income and expenses are kept. The operational and record-keeping formalities of the business are at the owner's discretion as long as various taxing authorities are satisfied.

Partnerships

A *general partnership* is defined as an association of two or more persons to carry on a business as co-owners for a profit. The *partners* or *general partners* share control over the business's operations and profits. Many attorneys, doctors, accountants, and retail stores are organized as partnerships. A "person" in a partnership may be another partnership or a corporation.

At common law, a partnership was not treated as an independent legal entity. As a consequence, a case could not be brought by or against the business. The partners had to sue or be sued individually. State law now provides that, for many purposes, a partnership may be treated as an independent entity. Thus, a partnership may sue or be sued and collect judgments in its own name. The federal courts also provide that, in most circumstances, a partnership is treated as a legal entity.

Partnership law originated in the common law but is now codified in the *Uniform Partnership Act (UPA).* The UPA has been adopted in every state except Louisiana and governs partnerships and partnership relations. The UPA determines the operation of partnerships when the partnership agreement is silent or where there is no formal agreement among the partners.

Forming a Partnership

A partnership can begin with an oral agreement between two or more persons to do business as partners or with an implied agreement that may be inferred from the conduct of the partners as they do business together. Typically, the parties formalize their relationship by a written agreement likely to cover the following key points:

Basics—name of the partnership, name of the business, place and date of formation; state law that applies to the partnership

Finances—contributions of the partners (which may be money, facilities, or expertise); when payments are due; how additional capital contributions will be handled; the allocation of ownership shares; accounting rules; the distribution of profits; and priority rights in payments

Management—voting rights of partners; appointment of managing partners; and, in some cases, a compensation committee

Dissolution—procedures to be followed if the partnership is terminated; rights of partners to leave the partnership; how partnership shares will be valued; limits on transfers of partnership shares; requirement to go to arbitration in case of dispute among partners

In the absence of a specific agreement, the UPA specifies and governs the relationship of the parties. Since the law does not require that a partnership have a name or that it be registered, outsiders might not know of its existence or who is involved.

Partnerships may be informal, and some come about by oral agreement; but courts prefer to follow documentary evidence of a partnership to make sure the parties have followed the requirements of state law, as the *Brown* case discusses.

Brown v. Swett and Crawford of Texas
Court of Appeals of Texas, Houston
178 S.W.3d 373 (2005)

Case Background *Brown was a wholesale insurance broker, a middleman between retail insurance agents and insurance companies. He worked closely with Galtney for a company in which they shared commissions in an agreed-upon proportion. A Dallas company, IBS, asked Galtney to open a Houston office for it. Galtney wanted Brown to be with him, so the two were hired as "Houston Team One" for IBS. They shared a base salary on a 42:58 basis (Brown got 42 percent and Galtney 58 percent) and they shared commissions similarly; the ratio adjusted annually based on performance.*

IBS fired Brown after a year, claiming he mishandled accounts. He was offered severance pay, but rejected it. He sued, contending that he had been wrongfully expelled from the Houston Team One partnership. The district court held for IBS and Galtney; Brown appealed.

Case Decision Radack, Chief Justice

* * *

The Texas Revised Partnership Act ("TRPA") sets forth five factors to consider in determining whether a partnership has been created. Those factors include (1) the receipt or right to receive a share of profits of the business; (2) the expression of an intent to be partners of the business; (3) the participation or right to participate in control of the business; (4) the sharing of or agreement to share losses of the business or liability for claims by third parties against the business; and (5) the contribution of or an agreement to contribute money or property to the business.

The Supreme Court of Texas has held that, to establish a partnership or joint venture, a plaintiff must show (1) a community of interest in the venture, (2) an agreement to share profits, (3) an agreement to share losses, and (4) a mutual right or control or management of the enterprise.

IBS and Galtney contend that Brown's partnership claims fail as a matter of law, because the evidence conclusively establishes that he had no right to receive a share of the profits of the business, because his salary and bonus compensation package was merely compensation for the services of an at-will employee. We agree.

The TRPA provides that "sharing or having a right to share gross returns or revenues" is not indicative of a partnership arrangement. Additionally, the supreme court has held that an essential element of a partnership is "a community of profit, an interest in the profits as profits, as distinguished from an interest therein as compensation."…

The undisputed evidence in this case shows that Brown was entitled to receive a base salary plus 42 percent of … commissions attributable to business written out of IBS's Houston office. Brown's base salary … cannot be considered a share of profits. Similarly, Brown's portion of the gross commissions … was compensation for services rendered to IBS, not an interest in the overall profits of IBS. That IBS agreed to divide Brown's and Galtney's portion of gross commissions in a proportion that Brown and

Galtney had agreed was appropriate does not change the nature of the bonus from compensation to profits.

Because there was no evidence that Brown shared, or had the right to share profits, IBS and Galtney negated an essential element of Brown's partnership claims. Accordingly, the trial court did not err in granting Galtney's and IBS's motion for summary judgment on these claims....

Questions for Analysis

1. The appeals court affirmed that no partnership was ever created; Brown was an employee. Since Brown and Galtney made up the Houston office and operated on a commission basis, why would Brown not have a partnership claim, even though he shared in profits?

2. How could Brown have made sure he was considered a partner?

Duty of Partners

A partnership is a relationship based on extraordinary trust and loyalty. Partners owe a *fiduciary duty* to one another. A fiduciary relationship requires that each partner act in good faith for the benefit of the partnership. The partners must place their personal interests beneath those of the partnership. The Supreme Court stated the duty of partners as follows in *Latta* v. *Kilbourn*, 150 U.S. 524 (1893):

> It is well settled that one partner cannot, directly or indirectly, use partnership assets for his own benefit; that he cannot, in conducting the business of a partnership, take any profit clandestinely for himself; that he cannot carry on the business of the partnership for his private advantage; that he cannot carry on another business in competition or rivalry with that of the firm, thereby depriving it of the benefit of his time, skill, and fidelity without being accountable to his copartners for any profit that may accrue to him....

Control by Partners

Unless otherwise specified in the partnership agreement, which can allocate control any way that the partners want, the presumption is that each partner has an equal voice in partnership management. Regardless of the size of the interest in the part-

---

INTERNATIONAL PERSPECTIVE

Small Is Not So Beautiful in Japan

Each year about 700,000 new businesses are started in the United States. In Japan, adjusting for population, the number of new businesses would run about 190,000 per year—less than one third the rate in the United States. Attitudes seem very different in the two countries; in the United States, small businesses are looked on with favor and are exempted from compliance with some laws; in Japan, they are discriminated against by government policy and are considered less desirable places to work.

Tetsu Anzai owns a few stores selling CDs with revenues of $12 million a year. He reports that qualified people do not answer his job ads even though unemployment is at the highest level in decades. Worker wariness of small firms reflects government policy.

Government banking regulations favor big businesses. Small firms without large sums of cash to bankroll their operations, which includes paying large deposits to rent office space, are usually out of luck. Since tax rates run as high as 65 percent, it is hard for entrepreneurs to reinvest their earnings. The stock market is of limited help, as regulations make it difficult for newer firms to be able to offer stock.

Because the Japanese economy has hit hard times, consideration is being given to rules that would help small businesses stimulate the growth that was for so many years generated by the big firms smiled upon by public policy.

Getty Images

nership, each partner has one vote in managerial decisions. Except in the case of major decisions that require consent of all partners—such as decisions to change the nature of the partnership's business, to admit new partners, or to sell the business—a majority vote is controlling. In most large partnerships, the partners usually delegate most management responsibilities to one person or group, often referred to as the managing partner or partners.

Regardless of who runs a partnership, the partners have a duty to one another to disclose all financial aspects of the business and to be completely honest, regardless of personal differences.

Termination of the Partnership

A change in the relationship of the partners that shows an unwillingness or an inability to continue with business may bring about *termination* of the partnership. By agreement, partners can allow partnership interests to be sold or assigned, usually with approval of existing partners. A complete termination comes about only after the partnership has been dissolved and its affairs have been wound up. The *dissolution* of the partnership occurs when an event takes place that precludes the partners from engaging in any new business. The *winding up* of partnership affairs involves completing any unfinished business and then collecting and distributing the partnership's assets.

Dissolution can come about in several ways. Change in the composition of the partners results in a new partnership and dissolution of the old one. Thus, the withdrawal or death of a partner causes the partnership to be dissolved. Similarly, the partnership is dissolved if a partner is bankrupt. Since it would be expensive and disruptive for partnerships to be terminated and re-formed because of the withdrawal, death, or bankruptcy of one partner, many agreements have provisions to allow the partnership to continue despite such events.

Limited Partnership

A limited partnership is a special form of a general partnership. Like a general partnership, a *limited partnership* is a business organization made up of two or more persons (*partners*) who have entered into an agreement to carry on a business venture for a profit. Unlike in a general partnership, however, not all partners in a limited partnership have the right to participate in the management of the enterprise.

Forming a Limited Partnership

All states except Louisiana use some form of the *Uniform Limited Partnership Act* or the *Revised Uniform Limited Partnership Act*. Partners must execute a written agreement, called a *certificate of limited partnership*, and file it with the appropriate state official, often the secretary of state. The Uniform Act requires that certificates contain the following information:

1. Name of the business
2. Type or character of the business
3. Address of an agent who is designated to receive legal process
4. Names and addresses of each general and limited partner
5. Contributions (cash, work, and property) of each partner
6. Duration of the limited partnership

7. The rights for personnel changes in the partnership and the continuance of the partnership upon those changes
8. The proportion of the profits or other compensation that each partner is entitled to receive

In addition, the parties to the limited partnership agreement may agree to bind themselves in ways not required by the certificate.

Relationship of the Parties

A limited partnership has at least one *general partner* and one or more *limited partners*. The general partners are treated in the same manner as partners in a general partnership. They have responsibility for managing the business and are personally liable to the partnership's creditors.

Limited partners are investors who may not participate in managing the business. Although they have the right to see the partnership books and to participate in the dissolution of the business, limited partners are not liable for the debts or torts of the limited partnership beyond their capital contributions. Limited partners lose their limited liability and become general partners if they take an active role in managing the business. To avoid an inference of managerial control, limited partners may not take control of the firm, contribute services to the business, or allow their names to appear in the name of the business.

ISSUE SPOTTER
Brotherly Love?

You and your brother start a small business. You rent a space in a mall and start teaching judo and yoga classes. You have customers who pay fees, which you deposit into a joint checking account, from which you pay your bills. After six months, things are going pretty well; but you notice that a chunk of money seems to be missing and your brother is driving a new car. It turns out that he made the down payment out of the joint account. You get into a fight about that. Whose money was it? Did he have the legal right to take it? As you think about things, it occurs to you, the yoga teacher, that one of your brother's judo clients could get injured and sue. Who could be liable for that? What else have you not thought about that you should?

Getty Images

Terminating a Limited Partnership

A limited partnership is terminated in much the same way as a general partnership. Events that affect a general partner and would bring about the dissolution of a general partnership also dissolve a limited partnership. While the bankruptcy of a general partner dissolves a limited partnership, the bankruptcy of a limited partner usually does not.

The business continues to operate while it is winding up, but it may not enter into any new commitments. In the final dispersal of the assets of the limited partnership, creditors' rights precede partners' rights. The limited partners receive their share of the profits and their capital contributions before general partners receive anything, unless the limited partnership agreement holds otherwise.

Corporations

When most people think of a business, they think of a *corporation*. A corporation is an artificial person, or legal entity, created under state law. Most large, well-known businesses—such as Coca-Cola, General Motors, and Microsoft—are corporations. Although businesses have produced and traded goods for thousands of years, the modern corporation developed in the United States during the late 1700s. State governments issued *corporate charters* to selected businesses. Because the charter often granted special privilege, there was intense competition to receive charters. A charter might, for example, give a business the exclusive privilege of having the only bank in a town. In this way, monopoly power was often associated with early corporate charters.

In the late 1800s, the first liberal *general incorporation statutes* were enacted. Those statutes established a simple procedure for incorporating a business. Incorporation is now available to businesses regardless of their field of operation, size, or political influence.

Creating a Corporation

Every state has a general incorporation statute that sets the procedure for incorporation. Although that varies across the states, the basic requirements are similar. In general, a corporation's *articles of incorporation*, along with an application, must be filed with the appropriate state office, along with payment of a fee. As Exhibit 13.1 shows, the articles of incorporation usually provide the following:

1. Name and address of the corporation
2. Name and address of the corporation's registered agent
3. Purpose of the business
4. The class(es) of stock to be issued and their par value
5. Names and addresses of the incorporators

After reviewing the corporation's application for completeness, the state issues a *certificate of incorporation*. As a rule, the incorporators wait until the state has issued the certificate before holding their first formal organizational meeting. At that meeting, the incorporators elect a board of directors, enact the corporation's bylaws, and issue the corporation's stock. The *bylaws* are the "rules" that regulate and govern the internal operations of the corporation. The shareholders, directors, and officers of the corporation must follow the bylaws in conducting corporate activities.

Legal Entity Status

Unlike sole proprietorships, the corporation is a *legal entity* with rights and responsibilities separate from the owners. It is recognized under both federal and state law as a "person" and enjoys some of the same rights and privileges accorded U.S. citizens. Corporations are thus entitled to many constitutional protections, including free speech, equal protection under the law, and protections against unreasonable searches and seizures. As a "person," a corporation has the right of access to the courts as an entity that may sue and be sued. However, although the officers and employees of a corporation enjoy the privilege against self-incrimination under the Fifth Amendment, the corporation itself does not.

Close and Public Corporations

Corporations are often referred to as being a *close corporation* or a *closely held corporation* as compared to a *public corporation* or a *publicly held corporation*. A close corporation is one whose shares are held by one shareholder or a small group of shareholders.

Exhibit 13.1 Example of Certificate of Incorporation

Certificate of Incorporation

of _____ **Corporation**

1. Name. The name of the Corporation is _____ Corporation.

2. Registered Office and Registered Agent. The address of the Corporation's registered office in Delaware is _____ Street in the City of _____ and Country of _____, and the name of its registered agent at such address is _____.

3. Purposes. The purpose of the Corporation is to engage in any lawful act or activity for which Corporations may be now or hereafter organized under the General Corporation Law of Delaware.

4. Capital Stock (providing for Two Classes of Stock, One Voting and One Nonvoting). The total number of shares for all classes of stock the Corporation shall have authority to issue is _____, all of which are to be without par value. _____ of such shares shall be Class A voting shares and _____ of such shares shall be Class B nonvoting shares. The Class A shares and the Class B shares shall have identical rights except that the Class B shares shall not entitle the holder thereof to vote on any matter unless specifically required by law.

5. Incorporators. The names and mailing addresses of the incorporators are

Name	**Mailing Address**
_____	_____
_____	_____
_____	_____

6. Regulatory Provisions. [The Corporations may insert additional provisions for the management of the business and for the conduct of the affairs of the Corporation, and creating, defining, limiting, and regulating the powers of the Corporation, the Directors and the Stockholders, or any class of Stockholders.]

7. Personal Liability. The Stockholders shall be liable for the debts of the Corporation in the proportion that their stock bears to the total outstanding stock of the Corporation.

8. Amendment. The Corporation reserves the right to amend, alter, change or repeal any provision contained in the Certificate of INCORPORATION, in the manner now or hereafter prescribed by statute, and all rights conferred upon Stockholders herein are granted subject to this reservation.

We, the undersigned, being all of the incorporators above named, for the purpose of forming a Corporation pursuant to the General Corporation Law of Delaware, sign and acknowledge this Certificate of Incorporation this _____ day of _____, 20_____.

Acknowledgment

State of _____

County of _____

On this _____ day of _____, 20_____, before me personally came _____, one of the persons who signed the foregoing certificate of incorporation, known to me personally to be such, and acknowledged that the said certificate is his act and deed and that the facts stated therein are true.

_____
Notary Public

[seal]

There are no public investors; that is, the stock is not actively traded, unlike publicly held corporations. Most corporations are closely held; that is, they have a few stockholders and the stock is not traded on a stock exchange. The parties who form a corporation need not draft long documents, but they will be held to the agreements they make and must follow state law as the *Ironite* case discusses. It also illustrates how friends setting up a business can have a falling out, often with serious consequences.

The rules of the Securities and Exchange Commission, as we will see in Chapter 21, help determine such status. Some closely held corporations, such as Cargill

Ironite Products Co. v. Samuels
Missouri Court of Appeals, Eastern District
985 S.W.2d 858 (1998)

Case Background *In 1972, Irwin Fox and Alvin Samuels established Ironite. The articles of incorporation set forth the guidelines for operation. Irwin and Alvin agreed verbally on additional decisions about the company and shared equally. They later formed another company, Sweet Gas, run under the same rules. In 1989, they invited their sons, Richard Fox and Mark Samuels, to join them. Richard and Mark would eventually take control from their fathers.*

In 1990, Richard drafted new bylaws. Alvin made hand-written changes on the draft bylaws and all agreed to the new bylaws. In 1993, Irwin died and Richard took control of his half of the company. An outsider was invited to join the board to provide an independent tie-breaker vote. There were fights over who should be paid how much and who should control what. Richard and the independent director voted to pay Richard more than Mark. The Samuels then sued Richard, Ironite, and Sweet Gas, contending that the original agreement of equal shares should apply. Defendants contended that the board, under the new bylaws, would determine compensation; and it need not be the same. The trial court held that the proceeds from operations would be shared equally, by the terms of the original agreement. Richard and the companies appealed.

Case Decision Pudlowski, Presiding Judge

* * *

In the 1972 Oral Agreement, as testified to by Alvin, he and Irwin were to take equally from the Companies. However, when the written documents were drafted, discussed, and signed by all of the parties, the compen-sation for the officers was clearly stated to be at the discretion of the Board of Directors.... Since the 1972 Oral Agreement directly contradicts the terms of the bylaws, the prior agreement violated the parol evidence rule and, accordingly, that evidence must be ignored. We agree with the Companies' point....

We look to the Companies' bylaws to determine the authority granted to their Board of Directors. Article III, Section One of the Companies' bylaws clear-ly sanctions the Board of Directors to manage the business and affairs of the Companies.... We will not interfere with the decisions of the Board of Directors absent fraud, illegal conduct, or an irrational business judgment. In making decisions, the Board of Direc-tors is required to use its best independent discretion and judgment....

There is no allegation that the Board of Direc-tors perpetrated fraud or made an irrational business judgment.... Clearly, the Board of Directors may decide all aspects of the Companies' business affairs unless prohibited by the bylaws....

The judgment of the trial court is reversed.

Questions for Analysis

1. The appeals court held that it would uphold the bylaws, not oral testimony, about how company revenues would be shared. Does this mean the Samuels were cheated, because the oral agree-ment was not followed?

2. If the parties cannot stand to work with each other now, how do they sell out of the compa-nies, given that they own it 50–50?

---

and Koch, would be among the largest firms\ in the world if their stocks were public; there is no size limit. Publicly held corporations are those with stock traded on a stock exchange and, therefore, are likely to have many shareholders. Some corporations "go public" at the start of operations, which may be quite small, so that outside investors can help bankroll the new business. Whether a corporation is close or public, the basic rules are much the same.

Relationship of the Parties

A corporation consists of three major groups: the *shareholders*, the *board of directors*, and the *managers*. Each shares specific duties and responsibilities to the other groups, to the corporation, and to third parties.

Shareholders

The *shareholders* own the corporation. Evidence of ownership may be in the number of shares shown on a *stock certificate*, but, as a practical matter, most parties just keep electronic records of who owns how many shares. Shareholders have the right to buy any additional stock issued by the corporation, before it is offered to the public. Shareholders have a limited right to inspect the corporation's books and records. As a rule, inspection is provided to shareholders if it is for a proper purpose and a request is made in advance. Finally, unless stated to the contrary on the stock certificate or the bylaws, shareholders are not restricted from selling or giving the stock to someone else.

The shareholders are not responsible for managing the corporation. Shareholders elect the board of directors and vote on matters that change the corporation's structure or existence (such as a merger with another firm or an amendment to the corporation's articles of incorporation).

LIGHTER SIDE OF THE LAW
Your Honor, I'll Turn Rocks into Gold

Marinov, a Russian immigrant, formed Amrox Corporation. He gave himself one-half of the stock for his secret knowledge and equipment. Four investors bought the rest of the stock for $330,000.

Marinov claimed to have a Ph.D. in physics from Russia and medical degrees from Bulgaria, Sweden, and Germany. He told investors that this education taught him how to turn corundum, which is cheap, into high-quality rubies and sapphires that would be certified by the American Gemological Institute.

Nothing was ever produced, and the investors sued Marinov. The district court ruled for the investors; Marinov appealed. The appeals court upheld the verdict. Marinov told the court that "he is developing a linear accelerator which he wishes to sell to the United Nations." The court found that claim and others "absolutely incredible." Marinov was held to have breached his fiduciary duty to the investors.

Source: *Gizzi v. Marinov*, 79 F.3d 1148

Getty Images

Elections take place at shareholder meetings, which are usually held annually. Notice of shareholder meetings must be provided in advance, and a *quorum*—usually more than half of the total shares—must be represented at the meeting. Most shareholders give third parties their *proxy*, a written authorization to cast their vote so that they do not have to attend the meeting. The proxy is often solicited by the corporation's management.

At the meeting, important corporate business is presented to the shareholders in the form of *resolutions*, which shareholders vote to approve or disapprove. The articles of incorporation establish voting rules. They usually require more than a simple majority for resolutions for actions such as amendments to the articles of incorporation and the bylaws or the dissolution or merger of the corporation.

The shareholder has no legal relationship with creditors of the corporation. A shareholder's obligation to creditors is limited to capital contributions, usually the amount paid to buy stock. A shareholder, however, may become a creditor of the corporation—for example, by supplying needed material or by working for the business—and will enjoy the same rights of recovery against the corporation as any other creditor.

Board of Directors

The initial *board of directors*, the governing committee of a corporation, is specified in the articles of incorporation or chosen by the incorporators at the first corporate meeting. Thereafter, the selection of directors is a shareholder responsibility. Once elected, directors serve terms for a time specified in the articles, although the shareholders can remove a director from office *for cause* (generally for a *breach of duty* or *misconduct*).

Legally, the board is the *principal* of a corporation; that is, on behalf of the corporation, it sets corporate policy and decides corporate business, such as the sale of corporate assets, entrance into new product lines, major financing decisions, and appointment and compensation of corporate officers. The directors act, usually by majority vote, to exert managerial authority. Directors are under a *duty of care* to conduct themselves on behalf of the corporation as a reasonably prudent person in the conduct of personal business affairs. Honest mistakes in judgment not resulting from negligence do not result in personal liability for the directors. The *business judgment rule* makes directors and managers immune from liability when problems result from honest mistakes in judgment, so long as they had a reasonable basis for their decisions.

Directors are subject to a *fiduciary duty of loyalty*. This requires that directors place the interests of the corporation before their own interests. Directors have great leeway in making decisions. The courts understand that hindsight is better than foresight, so the business judgment rule protects directors against suits by shareholders claiming that the directors missed profit opportunities that they should have taken. However, if directors clearly fail to let shareholders profit from obvious opportunities, then liability may be assigned. In many corporations, it is common for shareholders to be directors and managers, giving them several roles to play. The kind of conflict that can arise from this practice is discussed in the *Storetrax* case.

Storetrax.com v. Gurland
Court of Appeals of Maryland
915 A.2d 991 (2007)

Case Background *Gurland founded Storetrax.com, an Internet-based commercial real estate listing service, in Maryland in 1998. He incorporated it as a Delaware corporation in 1999. He then agreed for a group of investors to buy a majority share, and he became president and a member of the board. An employment contract spelled out some terms of employment, including a year's worth of pay in case he was fired. Two years later, he was removed as president, but stayed on the board for another year. He requested severance pay, but it was denied. He sued.*

The board claimed he was not due severance pay, because his job duties, titles, and salary changed while he worked at Storetrax. Further, as a board member, it was a breach of fiduciary duty to sue the company. The lower court held for Gurland; Storetrax appealed.

Case Decision Harrell, Justice

* * *

It is well settled that directors of a corporation "occupy a fiduciary relation to the corporation and its stockholders." This fiduciary relationship requires that a director "perform his duties ... (1) in good faith; (2) in a manner he reasonably believes to be in the best interests of the corporation; and (3) with the care that an ordinarily prudent person in a like position would use under similar circumstances."

As such, directors of a corporation "are entrusted with powers which are to be exercised for the common and general interest of the corporation, and not for their own private individual benefit."...

This fiduciary duty, furthermore, is not intermittent or occasional, but instead "the constant compass by which all director actions for the corporation and interactions with its shareholders must be guided."…

Situations may arise where a corporate director, despite the requirement that a director adhere strictly to his or her fiduciary obligations, may proceed with an individual plan of action even though the director's interests conflict directly with those of the corporation on whose board he or she sits.…

When a member of a corporation's board of directors conducts business with his or her own corporation, as was the case here, there is an appreciable possibility that, at some point, the director's interests will diverge from the interests of the corporations. Where such a conflict of interest arises, courts scrutinize closely those dealings in order to ensure that the transaction is carried out consistent with notions of good faith and fair dealing on the part of the director. With this in mind … the director may find "safe harbor" by disclosing to the corporation the conflict of interest and pertinent facts surrounding the conflict so that a majority of the remaining disinterested shareholders or directors may ratify the transaction or, as the case may be, otherwise take action to protect the corporation's financial interests.…

In the present case, there existed a conflict between Respondent's interests as an aggrieved former employee and his duty as a director of the corporation. His personal interests were adverse to those of the corporation, because threatened or actual litigation is adversarial in nature. While Gurland endeavored to obtain severance payment under the employment agreement, he held at the same time a position of trust with Storetrax and was impressed with an obligation to act in the best interests of the corporation. Gurland's seeking severance pay from Storetrax in the amount of $150,000 clearly was not in the corporation's best interests. Under the circumstances, however, we believe that [Gurland] notified sufficiently [Storetrax] of the imminence of a lawsuit such that he may claim the protections of the "safe harbor" annunciated above.…

Affirmed.

Questions for Analysis

1. The Maryland high court held that a director did not breach his fiduciary duty by suing his own company board to fulfill a contractual obligation. Would it be good to have a rule that directors cannot do business with companies when they are board members?

2. Is there some way Gurland could cheat the company in this situation in a way that he could not had he not been on the board?

Managers

The corporation's board of directors hires *managers* to run the business. The extent of managerial control and the compensation enjoyed by managers are matters of contract and agency between the board and the managers. Once hired, managers have the same broad duties of care and loyalty as the directors.

Terminating the Corporation

The termination of a corporation, like the termination of a partnership, is conducted in two parts: the dissolution phase and the winding-up phase. *Dissolution* may be voluntary or involuntary and marks the end of the corporation. Upon dissolution, the corporation may not take on any new business. A *voluntary dissolution* involves approval of the shareholders and the board of directors. *Involuntary dissolution* usually occurs because of bankruptcy, but it can also occur as a result of fraud in the establishment of the corporation.

When a corporation is dissolved voluntarily, the board of directors is responsible for *winding up* the affairs of the corporation. After the corporation's affairs have been completed, the assets are liquidated. The proceeds of the liquidation are first used to satisfy creditors, and any remainder goes to the shareholders.

LIGHTER SIDE OF THE LAW
Mad at Each Other? Sue the Insurance Company

Soon after Truck Insurance sold a liability insurance policy to Marmac, an engineering company, Marmac's board members fell to fighting among themselves. Amey, a board member, 40 percent stockholder, and executive vice president, was demoted by the other board members. He sued Marmac and its officers for breach of fiduciary duty, intentional infliction of emotional distress, and other complaints.

Marmac insisted that Truck Insurance pay for the company and its officers' defense against Amey. Truck refused. The insurance policy covered torts inflicted by Marmac on outsiders; it did not provide coverage for torts board members commit against each other. The jury did not agree, awarding Marmac and its board members $61 million in damages from the insurer.

The Supreme Court of California noted that "the Amey lawsuit sets forth nothing more than a business dispute." The court tossed out the damage award; the board members would have to carry on their fight without their insurer.

Source: *Waller v. Truck Insurance Exchange*, 44 Cal.Rptr.2d 370

Getty Images

Professional Corporations

Many professional associations, such as groups of doctors in practice together, used to be partnerships. In recent decades, all states have enacted statutes to allow *professional corporations (PCs)* to be formed. One reason for this is so that the liability of the members of the group, such as the doctors, would be limited to what is invested in the PC. Each doctor is not personally liable for the debts of all others, which would most likely arise from a costly malpractice judgment against one doctor in the group. A doctor who loses a malpractice case does not have limited liability due to the fact that the practice is a PC, but other members of the practice are protected.

INTERNATIONAL PERSPECTIVE
Abuses of Shell Corporations from Afar

After 9/11 the federal government began to increase controls on the flow of funds in and out of the country. The Patriot Act gave strong powers to the Justice Department and other agencies to look around at transactions and require banks and other institutions to report many transactions. But it turns out that a simple tool for facilitating criminal activity of all kinds is the simplicity of incorporation.

Each year about 300,000 shell corporations are formed, usually as limited liability companies. Many states allow anyone to register one; it can be done on the Internet in some states. Delaware, Nevada, and Oregon are among the states used most frequently. Hence, someone can use false information about who is setting up the company and then have a legal entity in the United States for laundering drug money or for some other illegitimate purpose.

One LLC in Nevada received 3,774 wire transfers for $81 million from Russia and other places. But Immigration and Customs Enforcement was unable to determine who was involved. Other countries have complained that the United States is insistent that foreign banks and other institutions must provide information to U.S. authorities, but U.S. authorities often have no idea who is involved in foreign transactions that run money through U.S. operations.

Senator Levin of Michigan said "You have to supply more information to get a driver's license than you do to form one of these nonpublicly traded corporations." Concern over the issue could lead to federal controls on an area traditionally left to state discretion.

Getty Images

In most states, the owners of a PC can only be the professionals involved in the firm itself, that is, the doctors whose practices are tied together to some extent. Stock cannot be sold to outside investors. The tax treatment of PCs is complicated, but tax considerations are why many professionals choose this form of organization.

Limited Liability Companies

Compared with partnerships and proprietorships, the corporate form of organization presents entrepreneurs with a disadvantage—*double taxation* of profits—and an advantage—*limited liability*. The profits of corporations are taxed at the corporate level. They must pay federal taxes and, in some states, state taxes. Then, if the remaining profits are paid to the shareholders, the shareholders must pay income taxes on the earnings. This double taxation discourages the use of the corporate form of organization, especially for smaller businesses. But if a business chooses not to incorporate, it gives up the advantage of limited personal liability of the corporate form. This protection means the shareholders can lose the amount they have invested in the company, but are not personally liable for sums beyond that in the event the business collapses.

These concerns have not escaped the attention of state legislatures. To encourage small business ventures in the early 1990s, most states enacted statutes authorizing limited liability companies. A *limited liability company (LLC)* is a business organization that is treated like a corporation for liability purposes but like a partnership for federal tax purposes.

Although limited liability companies have been common in Latin America, Asia, and Europe for some time (for example, the GmbH in Germany), they were not of interest to U.S. entrepreneurs until the Internal Revenue Service ruled that it would treat LLCs like partnerships for federal tax purposes. The profits are taxed only once, as the earnings of the owners or shareholders. As a result, LLC activity increased markedly, and the states enacted statutes allowing the formation of limited liability companies. Most states adopted at least parts of the *Uniform Limited Liability Company Act*.

Method of Creation

As in the case of corporations, state laws provide the procedure to be followed in the creation of an LLC. The organizers file a document referred to as *articles of organization*, which are similar to a corporation's articles of incorporation and contain basic information:

1. Company name (must include "Limited Liability Company" or "LLC")
2. Address of the company or its registered agent
3. Whether the LLC is to be managed by its members or by a manager
4. Names and addresses of company members
5. Date (or event) upon which the company will be dissolved, if any
6. Whether any members are to be liable for company debts

Personal Liability

After reviewing the application, the state issues a certificate allowing the business to operate as an LLC. Most LLC statutes state that no member or manager will be personally liable for the debts of an LLC. However, members may agree by contract to be personally liable for the company's debts.

Relationship of the Parties

An LLC usually is formed by two or more *members* having equal status. (In Texas and Florida, it is possible to form an LLC with just one member.) The members have a *membership interest* in the company, somewhat like owning stock in a corporation or being a limited partner in a limited partnership. There are generally no restrictions on the number of members, but in practice the number is usually under 30. Individuals, corporations, partnerships, and other LLCs may be members. Unless the agreement says otherwise, members may not transfer membership interests without the consent of the other members.

The members sign an *operating agreement*. Similar to the bylaws of a corporation, the agreement provides rules about the operation of the company and the relationships of the members. It establishes the company's method of management, allocation of profits and losses among members, restrictions on the transfer of membership interests, and the process to be followed in dissolving the company. State statutes provide default provisions to cover issues not stated in the agreement.

The LLC agreement may give each member an equal voice in management regardless of ownership percentage. More typically, the agreement provides that members may hire a manager to run the LLC. The manager need not be a member. The right to set management policy can be delegated to a group of members based on the members' percentage ownership or on any other basis to which the members agree.

The Continuity-of-Life Factor

Unlike a corporation, an LLC is not allowed "perpetual" life. This means that a change in the relationship of the LLC members is determined under state law. Although death, bankruptcy, retirement, resignation, or expulsion of any member terminates the membership of a member, like a partnership, the LLC itself can continue if all remaining members give their consent. In this way, although the company continues to exist, the relationship of the members has changed, which satisfies the IRS regulations regarding continuity of life and the application of partnership taxation. The ability of the members to consent to the continuation of the LLC must be set out in the articles of organization.

Termination

A limited liability company is dissolved and its affairs are wound up usually because of the occurrence of an event specified in the articles of the organization to bring about the dissolution of the company or by the consent of all the members.

In some states, if there is no event or time specified in the articles of organization, the LLC is dissolved by statute 30 years after its formation. When dissolved, the LLC must wind up its affairs, defend itself against legal actions, and dispose of its property. The company may not take on any additional business. After the LLC has wound up its affairs, its assets are liquidated, first to satisfy creditors and then to satisfy the members. Usually, the company files a certificate of cancellation of articles of organization with the appropriate state office.

Key Organizational Features

Several factors influence the choice of business organization, including the potential liabilities imposed on the owners, the transferability of ownership interests, the ability of the business organization to continue in the event of the death or

Exhibit 13.2 Comparing Characterstics of Major Forms of Business Organization

	Proprietorship	Partnership	Corporation	Limited Liability Company
Method of Creation	Owner begins business operations	Created by agreement of parties; statutes may apply	Chartered under state statute	Created under statute by agreement of members
Entity Status	Not separate from owner	Separate from owners for some purposes	Legal entity distinct from owners	Separate from owners for some purpose
Liability of Owners	Owner personally liable for debts	Unlimited liability except for limited partner in a limited partnership	Shareholders liable only to the extent of paid-in capital	Members liable to the extent of paid-in capital
Duration	Same as owner	Ended by agreement or by death or withdrawal of a partner, but easily re-created	May have perpetual existence	Company dissolves after fixed time or the occurrence of a specific event
Transferability of Ownership Interests	May be sold at any time; new proprietorship formed	Generally, sale of partnership interest terminates partnership	Shares of stock can be transferred unless restricted by contract	Other members must consent to transfers
Control	Determined by owner	Partners have equal control unless otherwise agreed to; limited partners have no management rights	Shareholders elect board of directors who set policy and appoint officers to manage	Operating agreement specifies management control
Capital	Limited to what owner can raise	Limited to what partners contribute or can borrow	Sale of more shares increases capital; may also borrow	Limited to what members contribute; may also borrow
Taxation	Profits taxed to owner as individual	Profits taxed to each owner as agreed upon or all share equally	Double taxation; profits of corporation and shareholders' share of profits are taxed	If IRS conditions are met, same as a partnership

withdrawal of one or more of the owners, the capital requirements of the business, and the tax rate applicable to the business organization selected. Exhibit 13.2 summarizes the differences between the major forms of business discussed so far. The following subsections review some of these factors in more detail.

Limited Liability

Limited liability allows persons to invest in a business without placing their personal wealth at risk. Limited liability can also allow investors to be passive toward the internal management of the business.

Businesses incur debts by contract—for example, by borrowing money and buying supplies on credit—and they may incur liability arising from tort suits, such as for having sold asbestos in the past. Limited liability means that if the sums owed are so large that the organization must go into bankruptcy, the owners—the shareholders—could lose their investments but cannot be held personally liable. No creditor of the business can come after the owners for their personal assets.

Entities with Unlimited Liability

Sole proprietors and general partners have unlimited personal liability for the debts of the business, including its torts. Some states require that creditors exhaust the business partnership property before moving against the personal property of the partners. After those assets are exhausted, however, the creditor may require any of the partners to pay the entire remaining debt.

Entities with Limited Liability

The liability of a limited partner is limited to the capital the partner has contributed to the limited partnership. Like the limited partner, the shareholders of a corporation and the members of a limited liability company risk only their capital investment if the corporation fails. They are not personally liable for the business debts or torts of the firm unless they contract to make themselves personally liable.

In certain circumstances, the court will "pierce the corporate veil" and hold shareholders personally liable. That is, the court disregards the corporate entity by finding that the corporation is a sham and that the owners actually intend to operate the business as a proprietorship or partnership. Although not common, and usually only involving close corporations, the court can impose liability on shareholders in instances of fraud, undercapitalization, or failure to follow corporate formalities. As the following case illustrates, when the court pierces the veil, the corporate form of business organization may not be used to avoid obligations.

Miner v. Fashion Enterprises
Appellate Court of Illinois, First District, Second Division
794 N.E.2d 902 (2003)

Case Background *Miner, representing a trust, gave Karen Lynn, a corporation, a 10-year lease for space for a ladies' apparel store in Chicago. Several years later, Lynn was in default due to unpaid rent and the court issued a default judgment for $22,162. The trust moved to enforce the judgment, but Lynn had insufficient assets. The trust sued Lynn's parent corporation and the owners of that corporation, requesting the court to hold them liable for the debt. The trial court dismissed the suit. The trust appealed.*

Case Decision McBride, Justice

* * *

A corporate veil will be pierced where (1) there is such unity of interest and ownership that the separate personalities of the corporation and the individual are nonexistent, and (2) the circumstances are such that adherence to the fiction of a separate corporate existence would promote injustice or inequitable consequences. To determine whether a unity of interests

exists to the extent that the corporate veil should be pierced, courts will look to a number of factors, including whether there is inadequate capitalization, failure to observe corporate formalities, insolvency of the debtor corporation, and absence of corporate records....

We agree with the trust's assertion that a judgment creditor may choose to file a new action to pierce the corporate veil of a judgment debtor in order to hold individual shareholders and directors liable for a judgment against the corporation.

Questions for Analysis

1. The appeals court held that the parent corporation or shareholders and directors could be held liable for the debt owed by the insolvent company. None of those parties had a contract with the trust (Miner), so how could they be held liable?

2. Does not the application of the doctrine of piercing the veil defeat the purpose of limited liability?

Transferability of Ownership Interests

The *transferability of ownership interests* refers to the ability of an owner in a business venture to sell or pass that interest to others. The ability of owners to transfer ownership interests differs among the various forms of business organizations.

Nontraded Entities

The proprietor of a sole proprietorship is, in essence, the business. A decision to sell the business ends the existing proprietorship and means the creation of a new one. Selling proprietorships, partnerships, and other small businesses can be expensive (relative to the value of the business), because such businesses can be hard to price. Often, specialists are required to help determine the market value of the business.

If a partner sells or assigns his interest in a partnership, the partnership continues, but the new person does not automatically become a partner. The person is entitled to receive the share of profits the partner would have received, but she gains neither the right to participate in the management of partnership affairs nor continuous access to partnership information, as would the partner. As with sole proprietorships, the sale of partnerships or partnership shares often requires specialists to assist in determining the value of the business.

The sale of shares in a close corporation is similar to the sale of a sole proprietorship or an interest in a partnership or an LLC. Because the price of the share is not determined on a stock exchange, the parties themselves, often with the help of a specialist, must determine the market value of the corporation and its shares.

ISSUE SPOTTER

Keeping Things in Order

You have a small company. Whether it is a corporation or a limited liability company, you know there is always a chance that, should something go wrong, you can be sued by a supplier, customer, employee, or someone else for some problem. What steps should you take to ensure that your company will keep limited liability status?

Getty Images

Publicly Traded Corporations

The stock of public corporations may be traded on a stock exchange such as the New York Stock Exchange; the transfer of ownership of shares is simple and is done at very low cost. Since the price of the shares is determined by the many buyers and sellers of the stock, no specialists need be hired to estimate the market value. Thus, the transfer of ownership shares in complex corporations, such as HP, is far easier than the transfer of ownership in sole proprietorships and partnerships.

Duration

A business's *duration* refers to its ability to continue to operate in the event of the death, retirement, or other incapacity of an owner of the business. The ability of a business to continue under such circumstances can depend on the form of business organization.

Limited Life

A sole proprietorship terminates with the death or incapacity of the proprietor. Similarly, at common law, a partnership is dissolved by the death, retirement, or other incapacity of a partner, but it is not necessarily terminated. To avoid liquidation, partners usually agree in advance to a continuation agreement. The same is true of LLCs.

Perpetual Existence

Unless its articles of incorporation provide for a specified period of duration, a corporation has *perpetual existence*. With perpetual existence, the death or retirement of a shareholder does not bring about the termination of the corporation. In most corporations, the death of a shareholder has no impact on the operations of the business.

On the other hand, in a close corporation or an LLC with few members, the death of a shareholder can have an impact on the business. Although the business need not terminate with the shareholder's death, if the shareholder is also a key officer in the company, it may be difficult for the business to continue. Suppose Midstates Construction is a close corporation with five shareholders and 50 employees, including Mertz, the president. If Mertz dies, the company will not legally be terminated, but in practice it may be forced to liquidate, because Mertz was the key employee.

Other Business Organizations

In addition to the most common forms of business organization reviewed so far, other forms are available, including joint ventures, cooperatives, and syndicates. These alternative business organizations are generally used as vehicles to manage a specific project or business concept.

Joint Ventures

The Supreme Court has defined a *joint venture* as a general partnership for a limited time and purpose. Generally, a joint venture has several characteristics of a general partnership, including the same rights of control, risks of loss, and manner in which profits are taxed. It usually involves two or more persons who agree to join in a specific project and to share in the losses or profits.

A joint venture is not usually considered a legal entity and therefore may not sue or be sued in its own name. In addition, the members of a joint venture usually have limited authority to bind each other to matters not directly related to the project. Joint ventures vary in size and are most popular as an international business organization.

Cooperatives

A *cooperative* is an association, which may or may not be incorporated, organized to provide an economic service non-profit to its members. Cooperatives are usually formed by people who want to pool their purchasing power. They may obtain lower product prices for their members by buying products in large quantities at a discount.

Cooperatives that are not incorporated are usually treated as partnerships; the members are jointly liable for the acts of the cooperative. If the cooperative is formed as a corporation, it must follow state laws governing nonprofit corporations. In contrast to corporate dividends, however, cooperative dividends are provided on the basis of a member's transactions with (purchases from) the cooperative, rather than on the basis of capital contributed.

Syndicates

A *syndicate* is the name given to a group of who join together to finance a specific project. Syndicates are commonly used in financing real estate developments, such

INTERNATIONAL PERSPECTIVE

The Difficulty of Starting a Business

How tough is it to establish a new business? A World Bank study looked at that issue. It presumed a business owned by five citizens wants to become a limited liability company in the largest city of a country. The owners contribute cash equal to 10 times the average income per capita in the country. It will have 50 employees, does no foreign trade, seeks no special benefits from the government, and rents the place of operation.

As the table shows, the measures considered were: 1) the number of procedures to be completed; 2) the number of days to complete those procedures if done by an experienced attorney; 3) the cost of the procedure as a percent of per capita income (excluding bribes); and 4) the minimum capital required as a percent of per capita income (many countries require capital to be deposited in a bank account prior to doing business). The longer and more costly the process of starting a business, the fewer

opportunities there will be for ordinary people to try to fulfill their dreams.

Country	Number of Procedures	Number of Days	Cost (percent of per capita income)	Minimum Capital Required (percent of per capita income)
U.S.	5	5	0.7	0.0
Canada	2	3	0.9	0.0
Mexico	8	27	14.2	12.5
Brazil	17	152	9.9	0.0
Japan	8	23	7.5	0.0
China	13	35	9.3	231.1
India	11	35	73.7	0.0
Egypt	10	19	68.8	694.7
Indonesia	12	97	86.7	83.4

Source: *http://rru.worldbank.org/doingbusiness*

Getty Images

as shopping centers or office buildings. Although their specific structure varies considerably, such organizations may exist as general partnerships, limited partnerships, or corporations. It is not uncommon for the members of a syndicate simply to own property together with no other formal business organization.

Franchises

About one third of retail sales—or more than $1 trillion per year—takes place in franchise operations, which employ 10 million people, so franchises are a major form of business enterprise. Nationwide, there are about 3,000 franchises and more than half a million franchise outlets. Before the 1950s, only automobile manufacturers, soft-drink companies, and oil companies used franchising to market and distribute their goods. In the 1950s and 1960s, however, many of today's most recognized companies began franchising. Among others, they include Holiday Inn, TGI Friday's, The Gap, H & R Block, Baskin-Robbins, and McDonald's.

Generally a *franchise* exists whenever a *franchisee*, in return for payment of a *franchise fee*, is granted the right to sell goods or services by a *franchisor* according to a marketing plan. The plan must be substantially associated with the franchisor's trademark, trade name, or trade dress. As a rule, a franchisee operates as an independent business, usually as a corporation subject to the standards specified by the franchisor. Successful franchises have two characteristics in common: a trademark, conveying authenticity and exclusivity, and a uniform product or service. For example, as consumers travel throughout the country, they recognize the Burger King name and expect the product to taste the same in California as it does in South Carolina.

Types of Franchises

Franchises may be separated into three basic categories: 1) product distributorships, such as a car dealership, in which the franchisee has the right to sell the product of the parent company; 2) trademark or trade-name licensing, in which the franchisee has a license to market the company's brands, such as Coca-Cola; and 3) business format franchising, in which the franchisee follows the business model set out by the parent company, such as McDonald's.

In business format franchising, the franchisor provides the franchisee with everything needed to begin the business, demanding that the franchisee operate the business according to fixed standards and procedures. These have been responsible for franchising growth in recent years. Included in this category are restaurants, nonfood retailers, business services, rental companies, and motels.

The Law of Franchising

Federal and state laws are intended to protect investors from crooked or unethical operators. Franchise scams have defrauded investors of hundreds of millions of dollars. In response, federal and state regulations require franchisors to register the franchise and to disclose all relevant information necessary for franchisees to make informed investment decisions.

The FTC Franchise Rule

Federal statutory protections can be found in the Federal Trade Commission's *franchise rule*, which requires the franchisor to give prospective franchisees an *offering circular*—a detailed disclosure document—at least 10 days before any money changes hands, or before a franchisee is committed to a purchase. The franchise rule's disclosure document must provide the following important information about the business:

- Names, addresses, and telephone numbers of other franchisees
- An audited financial statement of the franchisor and its financial history
- The background and experience of the business's key executives
- The responsibilities that the franchisor and the franchisee will have to each other once the contract is signed
- The number of franchisees and how many have gone out of business

This document enables prospective investors to learn about the background of the business. If the information provided is not true, it affords a legal basis for the franchisee to attempt recovery directly from, or for the FTC to bring an action against, the franchisor. See http://www.ftc.gov for more details about franchises and the franchise rule.

State Regulation

California was the first state to regulate franchises. It requires franchisors to register with the state and to provide prospective franchisees with a prospectus disclosure document before selling any franchises. The document must detail all important facts about the franchise transaction. California's registration and disclosure law seeks to prevent misrepresentation in the offering of franchises to prospective franchisees and to force the disclosure of information important for making investment decisions. Other states, including Illinois and New York, have enacted similar laws. Some states have more limited business opportunity disclosure laws. In each case, the requirements imposed go beyond those imposed by the FTC franchise rule (see the FTC web site for a list of the states).

Most states have agencies, such as the attorney general, that have the authority to monitor franchises. The power to investigate franchise fraud is usually very broad. If franchise administrators find fraud, they can institute a civil lawsuit seeking damages, injunctions, and fines. In some cases, criminal liability may be imposed.

ISSUE SPOTTER

The Road to Riches?

You are offered a chance to have your own business: a franchise that would be the only one formed in your city for a new business that would deliver auto parts to auto repair shops in the city. The franchise promoter tells you great stories about the operation in other cities. For only $25,000 you can be your own boss and soon be living well. This is not an uncommon situation. Facing this wonderful opportunity, what sorts of questions do you need good answers to? Is the information provided via the FTC offering requirements a good guarantee of security?

Getty Images

The Franchise Agreement

The *franchise agreement* sets forth the rights and obligations of the franchisor and franchisee. Key elements that might be included in a business format franchise are shown in Exhibit 13.3. They include, among other things, the rights and limits associated with the use of the franchise trademarks or trade names, the use of the franchise operating manual, the location and designated territory of operation, fee and royalty payments, the advertising commitment, and termination.

Trade Name and Procedure

The agreement grants the franchisee the right to use the franchisor's name and identifying trademarks and trade dress. The franchisee normally must undergo training and will be given the use of the franchisor's confidential operating manual. The franchisor may specify requirements regarding record keeping, advertising, hours of operation, hiring and training practices, and other details of the franchise's operations.

Territorial Rights

The agreement may impose limits on the territorial rights of the franchisee and the franchisor. For example, the franchisor may not be allowed to operate additional outlets in the territory, unless the franchisee does not live up to certain performance standards. The franchisee may be limited to operating only one unit within the territory. The agreement also states which party has the responsibility to select the site and to construct the facility.

Franchise Fees and Royalties

Naturally, the initial franchise fee or up-front payment is specified. Once the business is operating, the franchisor may require a continuing royalty—generally a percentage of annual sales. The franchisor may also require payments for advertising. The advertising fees depend on whether the franchisor does local or national advertising on behalf of its franchises. To protect the trade name, most franchise agreements prohibit franchisees from engaging in any advertising or promotional programs not approved by the franchisor.

Despite the various federal and state regulations, most cases of conflict between franchisors and franchisees involve litigation over violations of the terms of the agreement.

Exhibit 13.3　The Franchise Agreement between Franchisor and Franchisee

Franchisor's Duties and Responsibilities	Franchisee's Duties and Responsibilities
Grants franchisee the right to • Operate a franchised unit • Use all of the franchisor's know-how related to the product • Use trademarks or trade dress of the franchise • Use franchise for a fixed period of time, perhaps with options for renewal **Furnishes franchisee with** • Manual setting forth the franchise's operating procedures, including employee training • Specifications regarding the building, accounting, advertising, and other procedures • Training for how franchisee is to operate the business • Company image **May provide franchisee with** • Territorial exclusivity • Source of product supply • A regional or national advertising program • Quality control inspections • Group purchasing power	**Promises to the franchisor to** • Pay an initial franchise fee • Pay a continuing royalty fee • Pay an advertising fund contribution (1–4 percent of sales) • Conduct the business according to the franchisor's standards • Take the franchisor's training program • Keep franchise information confidential • Prepare franchise's books and records as franchisor requires • Purchase certain products from franchisor • Comply with employee hiring and training requirements **May promise the franchisor to** • Build a facility to franchisor specifications • Sell only the products of the franchisor • Pay for national advertising • Purchase supplies only from approved suppliers • Exercise personal supervision of franchise operations • Maintain facilities according to franchisor's requirements • Maintain specified hours of operation • Consent to periodic inspections

Because most franchise agreements have arbitration clauses, disputes are handled in that manner, but some end up in court. The *Coffee Beanery* case illustrates some of the many things that can go wrong when as those excited by a new venture proceed without caution.

Coffee Beanery v. Albert
Court of Appeals of Michigan
2006 WL 1330326 (Not Reported in N.W.2d)

Case Background *Yurick was developing a site for a coffeehouse. Shaw approached him about doing it as a Coffee Beanery (CB) franchise and said that he had close ties to CB. Shaw got copies of business pro formas that projected sales, costs, income, and other statistics for new franchises.*

Yurick thought it was a good deal and convinced Albert to join. The three of them established Hartland LLC to run the franchise, and Yurick paid a $25,000 franchise fee. A month later, Shaw brought a franchise agreement for each of them to sign. They backdated the document to indicate

that they had received franchise disclosure documents from CB prior to signing. Shaw did not return copies of the documents for months.

Plans for the coffeehouse moved ahead, but Albert and Yurick had a falling out with Shaw for not working as hard as he should and for sexually harassing an employee. They bought out his share of the company. Shaw then pressed for payment on some equipment he had purchased but had not been paid for. At that point, Albert and Yurick quit making payments to CB and claimed the franchise agreement was void. CB sued for payments due and a declaration that the contract was valid. Shaw ended up out of the litigation. The trial court held the franchise agreement valid; Albert and Yurick were liable for royalties due CB. They appealed.

Case Decision Per Curiam

* * *

Defendants rely primarily on the Michigan Franchise Investment Law (MFIL) for their claims of rescission and damages. Under the MFIL, a franchisor must make certain mandatory disclosures at least 10 days before receiving any money from or entering a contract with a prospective franchisor. It also contains a provision that forbids persons from making material misrepresentations or employing deceptive practices to sell a franchise. Although defendants provided evidence that plaintiff technically violated the MFIL, a violation of the MFIL does not render the contract void and unenforceable. On the contrary, the MFIL only expressly permits two types of remedies for a violation, damages and rescission. Defendants failed to tender back the benefits of the contract (the signs, trademarks, equipment, location, and proceeds), so rescission is not available to them as a remedy. Nevertheless, our Supreme Court has traditionally found that a defrauded individual may continue under the contract and claim damages for the difference between the contract actually entered and the contract as represented. The difference in this case, however, is that defendants have continued with the contract

and have failed to tie any damages to a legally recognizable MFIL violation.

Defendants fail to point to any information contained in the disclosure documents that, because of their untimely presentation, caused them damage. Although defendants point to several unsavory and unanticipated contract provisions, defendants have failed to demonstrate that plaintiff has ever sought to enforce any of them. The only contractual elements to which defendants objected after Shaw returned all the signed documentation were those related to franchise renewal, management review, and a non compete clause. Without evidence that plaintiff has sought to enforce these provisions, however, damages are wanting....

Yurick and Albert argue that Shaw duped them into signing the franchise agreement and its attached "Guarantee" as individuals, thereby defrauding them out of the insulation from liability that they expected to enjoy through Hartland, LLC. The record demonstrates, however, that the individual defendants knew that they were signing a franchise agreement in their individual capacities.... Moreover, defendants only suggest that it was the *understanding* of the partners that Hartland, LLC would accept sole responsibility as the franchisee, and the documents do not refer to Hartland, LLC at all. The documents containing defendants' signatures as individuals and guarantors clearly indicate a direct legal relationship with plaintiff. Therefore, defendants failed to support their claim that, through an untrue material representation or deceptive practice, they were defrauded into believing that the franchise agreement only covered Hartland, LLC...

Affirmed.

Questions for Analysis

1. The appeals court affirmed that an enforceable franchise agreement was in place despite some violations of the state franchise law. Why would the court allow the contract to be valid despite such conflicts?

2. How could Albert and Yurick have avoided this outcome?

Termination

Franchise agreements are usually explicit about events that bring about the franchise's termination. Some have a fixed expiration time, such as twenty years. Typical provisions give the franchisor the right to terminate upon the occurrence of events, ranging from the bankruptcy of a franchisee to the failure of a franchisee to submit to inspection by the franchisor. Notice of termination must be given to the franchisee. In some states, franchisors must give the franchisees reasonable time to

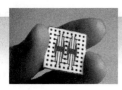

CYBER LAW

Offering Franchises on the Internet

The FTC has ruled that franchises can be marketed through the Internet. So long as a franchisor satisfies the disclosure requirements of the Franchise Rule (16 Code of Federal Regulations 436), such as spelled out in the Uniform Franchise Offering Circular (58 Federal Register 69, 224), it does not matter if a prospective franchisee gets the offering on paper or on the Internet. The entire transaction can be carried out on the Internet. The FTC and the National Fraud Information Center's Internet Fraud Watch (see http://www.fraud.org) will look for evidence of investment scams run on the Internet.

Getty Images

correct problems. In addition, several states have laws that restrict a franchisor's ability to terminate a franchise unless there is good cause. Upon termination, the franchisee loses all rights to the franchisor's trade name.

Summary

- The most prominent forms of business organization are the sole proprietorship, partnership, limited partnership, corporation, and limited liability company.
- Sole proprietorships automatically come into existence whenever people begin to do business for themselves. Legally, the sole proprietor is the business, responsible for business's debts and torts, liable for its taxes, and in control of its operation and its transfer.
- General partnerships are composed of two or more people, general partners, who agree to carry on a business for profit. Partnerships may be structured in almost any way desired by the partners. When an agreement does not specify what happens in some instance, such as death of a partner, the law of partnership, codified in the Uniform Partnership Act, determines the result. In general, partners share in the managerial control, debts, tort liability, and profits of the business. They are taxed personally on partnership profits.
- Limited partnerships are governed by state law. They must have at least one general partner. The limited partners are investors who may not share in managerial control of the business. Their liability is limited to the amount they invest, unless they try to exercise managerial control and become general partners, who are fully liable.
- Corporations are created under state law and are recognized as legal entities. They have their own legal life, which is potentially perpetual. They are responsible for their own debts and tort liabilities. Shareholders, investors in corporations, are liable only to the amount they invest in the corporation.
- Shareholders vote to elect the board of directors and must vote on major issues such as selling the corporation. The board of directors is the principal of a corporation. It has responsibility for determining how the company is to be operated and for hiring and instructing the management. Managers are agents of the board and respond to the board's instructions.
- A limited liability company (LLC) provides limited liability for its members (investors) and is taxed as a partnership. Members are thus taxed on the income, rather than being subject to the double taxation of a corporation and its shareholders. An LLC must restrict the transfer of member interests and is intended to operate for a fixed or definite time period, rather than have perpetual life.

- A key factor in the choice of business form is limited liability, which investors in corporations, limited partnerships, and limited liability companies have but proprietors and general partners do not have. Transfer of ownership interests is easiest in corporations with publicly traded stock. In other organizations, the value of interests is often not known, and often restrictions are placed on transfers. A corporation may have perpetual existence as a legal entity, but in practice, other organizations can last for very long times under contracts that control what happens in case of death or retirement of an investor or partner.
- A franchise exists when a franchisee pays a fee and is granted the right to sell a franchisor's goods or services. Marketing is associated with the franchisor's trade name or trademark. The relationship is defined by a franchise agreement that sets forth the rights and duties associated with the use of the franchise marks or names, the use of the franchise operating manual, designated territory of operation, royalty payments, advertising commitment, and termination.

Terms to Know

You should be able to define the following terms:

sole proprietorship, 311	breach of duty, 320	limited liability company, 323
partnership, 311	principal, 320	joint venture, 328
dissolution, 314	business judgment rule, 320	cooperative, 328
winding up, 314	fiduciary duty of loyalty, 320	syndicate, 328
limited partnership, 314	dissolution, 321	franchise, 329
corporation, 316	professional corporations, 322	
proxy, 319	limited liability, 323	

Discussion Question

1. Four people jointly own a summer cottage and use it solely for their personal enjoyment. Is this a partnership? What if they rent the cottage to other people for part of the year? Suppose a renter dies in the cottage due to a gas leak. Could all owners be liable?

Case Questions

1. Dr. Citrin had an agreement for Dr. Mehta to work in Citrin's medical offices to see his patients when he was on vacation. When Citrin was on vacation, Mehta saw a patient and misdiagnosed the problem; the patient died. The heirs of the patient sued Citrin, claiming that Citrin and Mehta were partners. Were they? [*Impastato* v. *DeGirolamo*, 459 N.Y.S.2d 512 N.Y. Sup. Ct., Special Term (1983)]
2. Covalt owned 25 percent and High owned 75 percent of CSI, a corporation that they operated together. They also entered into a partnership to build an office building that they leased to CSI. Covalt resigned from CSI and went to work for a competitor. When the lease on the office building expired, Covalt demanded that High raise CSI's rent in a new lease, from $1,850 to $2,850 per month. High signed CSI to a new lease in the building at the old rent. Covalt sued High for breach of fiduciary duty to the partnership. Who was right? [*Covalt* v. High, 675 P.2d 999 Ct. App., NM (1983)]

   ✓ Check your answer at http://academic.cengage.com/blaw/meiners
3. Bane was a partner in a Chicago law firm before he retired in 1985. The law firm had a retirement plan funded by current income, not by partners' contribution during their working lives. Retired partners were to be given a pension based on their income before

retirement. The law firm merged with another law firm. The merger did not work, and the new firm was dissolved in 1988, which left no retirement funds for Bane. Bane sued the managing partners of the law firm, claiming that their mismanagement was responsible for the loss of his pension. Did he win? [*Bane* v. *Ferguson*, 890 F.2d 11, 7th Cir. (1989)]

4. When Dr. Witlin died, his wife inherited his 2.654 percent share of a partnership that owned a hospital. As the partnership agreement called for, the dead partner's share was paid off. The amount paid was based on the financial records at the time of the payment. The other partners did not reveal that they were in the process of selling the hospital, which soon happened, and more than tripled the value of the partners' shares. Was Mrs. Witlin due the sale price of the hospital or its value based on financial records at the time of her husband's death? [*Estate of Witlin*, 83 Cal.App.3d 167 Ct. App., Calif. (1978)]

✓ Check your answer at http://academic.cengage.com/blaw/meiners

5. A law firm, organized as a general partnership, signed a 10-year lease for office property with Sheehan, who was a partner in the law firm. Sheehan withdrew from the law firm and assigned his partnership interest to the remaining partners. Nothing was done at that time to change the lease of the office property. Five years later, the law firm defaulted on the lease and filed for bankruptcy. Sheehan sued all past and present law firm partners for past due rent and other damages from the default on the lease. The trial court held that the personal assets of the original partners who signed the lease were not at stake, only the assets of the bankrupt partnership, and that none of the later joining partners were liable. Is that correct? [*8182 Maryland Assoc. L.P.* v. *Sheehan*, 14 S. W.3d 576 Sup. Ct., Mo. (2000)]

6. The Haffs were sole shareholders of a restaurant supply wholesale business that often bought supplies from Cosgrove. When Haff ceased operations, it owed Cosgrove $9,000. Cosgrove sued the Haffs personally for the amount owed, contending that the corporate shield should be pierced. The two companies had done business for 10 years. Cosgrove testified that it did not know what legal form Haff had. The phone was answered "J. Haff." The invoices sent from Cosgrove were made out to "J.A. Haff and Sons, Inc." Checks came from "J.A. Haff and Sons." The evidence was that Haff followed proper corporate procedures for annual meetings and separate accounts. Was the veil to be pierced? [*Cosgrove Distributors, Inc.* v. Haff, 798 N.E.2d 139 App. Ct., Ill. (2003)]

✓ Check your answer at http://academic.cengage.com/blaw/meiners

7. Rust and Kelly each contributed half the price of a plot of land they intended to subdivide and sell. Rust gave Kelly his share of the purchase price. When Kelly bought the land, he put the title to it in his name only. Several years later, Rust found out that Kelly had left him off the deed on the property and sued for his share of the purchase price plus interest. Kelly claimed that Rust had abandoned the property, and so he did not owe him anything. Rust claimed they had a joint venture. Was there a joint venture? [*Rust* v. *Kelly*, 741 P.2d 786 Sup. Ct., Mont. (1987)]

8. Beracha, CEO of Campbell, which operated a bread plant in North Carolina, told the employees in a meeting in August that the plant was profitable and their jobs were secure. In December, the employees were told that the plant would be closed in February and their jobs lost. Some employees sued Beracha and the company for negligent misrepresentation. The trial court dismissed the suit; the employees appealed. Do they have a claim? [*Jordan* v. *Earthgrains*, 576 S.E.2d 336 Ct. App., N.C. (2003)]

✓ Check your answer at http://academic.cengage.com/blaw/meiners

9. Domino's Pizza sold two franchises to experienced Domino's managers. The agreement stated that the franchisees agreed to "operate the Store in full compliance with all applicable laws, ordinances, and regulations." If not, Domino's had the right to terminate the franchise if problems were not corrected within thirty days of notification. Later, the franchisees' books were a mess, reports were not filed on time, and the franchisees failed to pay city, state, or federal payroll, income, and sales taxes. After six months of the franchisees' not correcting the problems, Domino's gave 30 days' termination notice. The

franchisees put the stores up for sale. When prospective buyers asked Domino's about the history of the stores, Domino's told the truth, which led to the sale price falling below what would have been offered if Domino's had not said anything and let the franchisees sell on their own. The franchisees sued Domino's; a jury awarded the franchisees over $2 million damages. Did this decision stand? [*Bennett Enterprises* v. *Domino's Pizza*, 45 F.3d 493 D.C. Cir. (1995)]

10. Several investors, organized through corporations, owned several Burger King restaurants in Wisconsin. The franchise agreement stated that franchise owners could not own competitor franchises. The investors formed other corporations and then obtained Hardee's franchises. Burger King terminated its franchise agreements with the owners for violating the franchise agreements. The owners argued that since the Burger King and Hardee's franchises were owned by different corporations the agreement had not been breached. Is that correct? [*Deutchland Enterprises* v. *Burger King*, 957 F.2d 449, 7th Cir. (1992)]

Ethics Question

1. Cook and Smith formed a limited partnership, called Trinty Development, to develop a shopping center. Adjacent to the shopping center was a 10-acre tract of undeveloped land that came up for sale after the limited partnership had begun its operations. Cook, the general partner, purchased the property from McCade, but only after McCade had refused to sell the property to Trinty. McCade stated that he did not want to do business with Smith. Cook then sold the property to another developer for a $60,000 profit. If Cook had sold the property to Trinty, Trinty could have profited. Smith objected to the purchase and sale by Cook. What alternatives did Cook have? With regard to his employment with Trinty, what was the ethical choice? How was Trinty damaged? With regard to Cook's relationship with McCade, what were Cook's alternatives?

Internet Assignment

http://en.wikipedia.org/wiki/Business_entity
http://jurist.law.pitt.edu/sg_bus.htm

Review these two Web sites. One is a widely-used public site, the other a more formal legal site. What features do you like or dislike? Which Web site do you think would link to a more reliable source?

Agency and the Employment Relationship

Chapter 14

The Levine Cancer Institute, like most health care facilities, is concerned about cost control. Proposals are submitted for possible cost reductions. One proposal recommends reducing the number of doctors and nurses employed directly by the hospital. It recommends that nurses and doctors be encouraged to form a company to provide professional medical services—their services—to the hospital. The hospital would contract with the company to obtain the services of the nurses and doctors it needs as independent contractors. While hospital administrators believe that the plan could reduce costs, they are concerned about several legal matters. Would the new company be an agent of the hospital? Would the hospital's liability change? By using the new company, is it possible to designate the doctors and nurses as independent contractors, rather than as employees, and thus reduce potential liability?

Another proposal recommends having an outsider do all buying for the hospital, rather than have an employee do the supply purchasing. One manager thinks that, this way, if the buyer makes a mistake in product choice or if a patient is asserted to have been injured due to the use of an inappropriate product, then the buyer will be liable for the mistake instead of the hospital. Is that right?

These are among the subjects discussed in this chapter, which considers the range of employment relationships that are possible, how they are created, and the legal constraints on their formation and functions. We begin by considering agency relationships, which are often part of an employment relationship but can be more limited in purpose. They are often critical in the formation of contracts, because businesses must assign various people to perform assorted services. ■

Getty Images

Agency Relationships

According to *Black's Law Dictionary*, an *agency relationship* is

> An employment [of an agent] for the purpose of representation in establishing relations between a principal and third parties.

That is, an agency is created when a person or company—the *agent*—agrees to act for, or in place of, another person or company—the *principal*. The agent represents the principal. An agent may negotiate and legally bind a principal to contracts with third parties as long as he acts within the scope of authority granted by the principal. In dealing with third parties, normally the customers or suppliers, the agent is granted certain authority to act for the principal. The typical agency relationship is compared with the typical two-party business transaction in Exhibit 14.1.

A principal's purpose for developing agency relationships is to expand business opportunities and use the expertise of an agent. For example, Don Reid Ford dealership in Orlando employs managers and sales agents to make decisions about ordering cars and selling them to customers. Don Reid and his customers enjoy business dealings that would not be possible without the ability to use agency relationships, since Reid personally could not directly run everything needed in a large business.

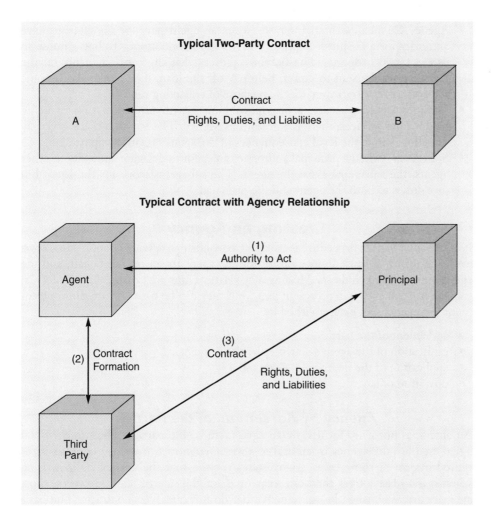

Exhibit 14.1
A Contract and an Agency Relationship

Similarly, the board of directors of a corporation enters into agency relationships with officers of the corporation who are charged with the authority to manage the corporation. The managers represent the directors—the principals of the corporation—and have the authority to bind the principals to contracts. The agency relationship is essential to business.

Classification of Agents

An agent's *authority* is the power to change the principal's legal obligations. That is, when an agent uses authority, say, by making a contract with a third party, new rights and duties are created for the principal. The principal controls this by establishing the extent and scope of the agent's authority to act on the principal's behalf.

Agents can have whatever duties they agree to accept, so the classes of agents are nearly unlimited. Some major ones are:

- Universal Agent—someone designated to do all acts that can be legally granted to an agent. The agent is usually given a general power of attorney to do all business transactions on behalf of the principal.
- General Agent—a person authorized to execute all transactions connected with a business, such as a manager who runs all aspects of a hotel. The principal may limit the extent of the general agent's authority to a portion of the business.
- Special Agent—an agent with authority to represent the principal only for a specific transaction, usually for a limited time.
- Agency Coupled with an Interest—when an agent pays for the right to have authority for a business. Suppose you lend someone money to buy a house to use as rental property. The borrower agrees that the rent payments on the property will be sent to you to help pay off the loan. The lender has become the agent of the borrower for the purpose of collecting rent.
- Gratuitous Agent—when a person volunteers with no expectation of being paid for her services, there is a gratuitous agency. The fact that there is no pay does not change the legal consequences of the agency relationship itself.
- Subagents—when a principal authorizes an agent to delegate authority to other agents, the subagents assist the agent. The subagents work for the agent but owe duties to both the agent and the principal.

Creating an Agency

No particular formal procedure is needed to establish an agency relationship. However, the principal must show a desire for the agent to act on her behalf, and the agent must consent to do so. Most agency relationships are created without formal statements such as "I will represent you," but they can be based on a written agreement. An agency can be established by

- agreement of the parties.
- ratification of the agent's activities by the principal.
- application of the doctrine of estoppel.
- operation of law.

Agency by Agreement of the Parties

An agency is normally formed by an agreement of the parties. The principal and agent establish the agency by an oral or a written contract. A written contract is required by law in some cases. Many states require that the agency be in writing when it is to last longer than one year or is for the sale of land. However, most agencies are established by agreements that do not qualify as contracts. The basis of the agency, its own area of law, is that the agent acts for the benefit of the principal and is subject to the principal's control.

One legal document that establishes an agency is the power of attorney, which authorizes a person or a company to act as an agent for a principal. The power of attorney can be general, or it can provide the agent with limited authority to act for the principal for one deal. The term *power of attorney* describes the document itself and does not mean that the agent, who may be called an *attorney-in-fact*, is actually an attorney.

Implied or Express Ratification by the Principal

An agency relationship also may be created by the principal's ratification—or acceptance of responsibility—of the agent's activities. This arises when a person who is not an agent, or an agent who is acting beyond her authority, enters into a contract on behalf of a third party—the alleged principal. In such circumstances, the alleged principal is ordinarily under no obligation to be bound by the person's actions. However, the alleged principal may become bound to the contract. By ratifying the agreement, the alleged principal becomes the real principal and is bound by the contract as if it had been negotiated by an agent with the authority to enter into the contract.

Suppose you advertised your car for sale for $9,000. A prospective buyer came to look at it while you were gone and offered $8,500, which your roommate accepted, thinking you would be happy to sell it for that. Since your roommate was not your agent, you would not be obligated to go through with the deal. However, you could also ratify the deal by selling for that price.

Ratification can be express or implied. An *express ratification* is a principal's clear signal to be bound to the otherwise unauthorized agreement. *Implied ratification* takes place when the principal behaves as if he has the intent of ratifying an unauthorized agreement. It usually occurs when the principal accepts the benefits of the agreement.

Express or implied, a ratification has limits as to what it covers. A principal can ratify only agreements when he knows the important facts. Further, an agreement can be ratified only if the agent purported to act for the principal. The principal must ratify the agreement before the third party involved withdraws. Finally, if the agreement between the agent and the third party was required by law to be in writing, such as a sale of real estate, the ratification must be in writing. In the *Hardcore Concrete* case, we see what happens when parties do not carefully read the details of contracts.

Hardcore Concrete, LLC v. Fortner Insurance Services
Missouri Court of Appeals, Southern District
220 S.W.3d 350 (2007)

Case Background *Hardcore pours concrete foundations and other structures. It bought a set of aluminum concrete forms for $33,000. Seeking theft insurance to cover the forms, it contacted Fortner about a policy. Fortner contacted Med James, a managing general insurance agency, and explained what was needed. Med James obtained a quote from Lloyd's of London. Hardcore completed an application, and the policy was sent from Med James to Fortner. The*

concrete forms were stolen from a construction site two months later. Hardcore filed a claim with Lloyd's, which denied payment.

The claim was denied because Med James had attached the wrong endorsement to the policy, which said it covered theft due to forcible entry into a vehicle. That was the policy Lloyd's issued. What Hardcore needed was a policy for "all risks" for a contractor. Hardcore sued Fortner
continues

and Med James. The jury held Med James liable for damages for breach of contract, negligence, and negligent misrepresentation. Med James appealed.

Case Decision Per Curiam

* * *

"Agency is the fiduciary relationship which results from the manifestation of consent by one person, a principal, to another, an agent, that the agent shall act on the principal's behalf and subject to the principal's control and consent by the agent so to act." (quoting *Restatement [Second] of Agency § 1 [1958]*). Actual "authority is the power of the agent to affect the legal relations of the principal by acts done in accordance with the principal's manifestations of consent to him." (*quoting Restatement [Second] of Agency § 1 [1958]*). Actual authority may be express or implied. Express authority is created when the principal explicitly tells the agent what to do, and implied authority consists of those powers incidental and necessary to carry out the express authority. Absent an express grant of authority, the relationship may result from implied or apparent agency. An agent for a disclosed principal is not a party to a contract and is not liable for its nonperformance.

In an action for negligence, plaintiff must establish that defendant had a duty to plaintiff, that defendant failed to perform that duty, and that defendant's breach was the proximate cause of plaintiff's injury....

In the instant matter, Hardcore maintains Med James was acting as an agent for Hardcore, because its representative and Mr. Fortner communicated via telephone with Med James's representative ... concerning Hardcore's insurance needs. Further, as additional proof that Med James was acting as Hardcore's insurance agent, Hardcore points to the fact that the completed policy in question from Lloyd's was sent by Med James to Fortner Insurance, and the claim of loss denial letter came from Med James as well.

However, the record clearly shows Hardcore initially contacted Fortner Insurance to obtain coverage and, in turn, Mr. Fortner acted as Hardcore's insurance agent by contacting Med James. Indeed, throughout the entire telephone discussion between Med James and Mr. Fortner, Med James did not speak directly with Hardcore or its representative. Instead, Med James, through its representative ... spoke directly with Mr. Fortner of Fortner Insurance. It was Fortner Insurance, not Med James, which was attempting to procure insurance for Hardcore. Ultimately, the record shows it was Lloyd's, not Med James, that ordered the issuance of the insurance policy.

Furthermore, Mr. Fortner testified that he understood Med James was acting as a managing general agent and that a managing general agent acts on behalf of an insurance company exclusively. Med James, as a managing general agent, was merely the conduit through which this was performed....

Likewise, Fortner Insurance and Mr. Fortner are not agents of Med James. Mr. Fortner related that he had submitted Hardcore's application for insurance to at least two separate managing general agencies, and the record shows that as a managing general agency, Med James is in the business of "underwriting" insurance policies for several insurance companies. Med James acts as a middleman between an insurance agent representing a client on the one hand and various insurance companies with which Med James has a contractual relationship on the other hand.

A representative of Med James testified that Med James, as an "underwriter for a company ... will look at an application for insurance" it receives from an insurance agent and it will "do an analysis on it...." Then, Med James "determines which company it would place it in."...

Also, the record clearly shows Med James exerts no control over Fortner Insurance nor holds any interest in Fortner Insurance. Mr. Fortner testified that he considered himself to be Hardcore's insurance agent, and a representative from Hardcore agreed that Mr. Fortner was its insurance agent. Indeed, Hardcore paid its insurance premiums to Fortner Insurance not to Med James. There is nothing in the record which would suggest Fortner Insurance had the authority to act as an agent for Med James.

Here, the evidence clearly shows Lloyd's was Med James's principal and that Med James was an agent of Lloyd's. As such, there was a contract between Lloyd's and Med James, which provided Med James would act as a managing general agent for Lloyd's. Similarly, there was a contract between Lloyd's and Hardcore, which provided that Hardcore would pay insurance premiums and Lloyd's would issue insurance coverage.

Additionally, Med James, who contracted with Lloyd's, owes no contractual duty to Hardcore in that Hardcore is not a party to Med James's contract with Lloyd's. Likewise, Med James is not a party to the contract for insurance between Hardcore and Lloyd's. It has long been held that a defendant who has contracted with another generally owes no duty to a plaintiff who is not a party to the contract, nor can a non party sue for negligent performance of the contract. Accordingly, since Med James was not acting as an agent of Hardcore, it had no legal duty to protect Hardcore's interests. It follows that Med James breached no contractual duty to Hardcore....

The judgment of the trial court is reversed.

Question for Analysis

1. The appeals court held that there was no agency relationship between Hardcore and Med James, so Med James was not liable for any problems here. Then who was Med James an agent for?

2. Who, if anybody, may be liable here?

Agency by Estoppel

Very similar to implied ratification, and legally identical in some states, is an *agency by estoppel*. There, an agency is created by the words or actions of a principal. Although no formal agency exists, the actions of the principal may lead one to reasonably believe that the presumed agent has the authority to act for the principal. When the agent enters into a contract with a third party for the principal, the principal is bound to the contract and will be *estopped* to deny the existence of the agent's authority.

Agency by Operation of Law

The courts may impose an agency relationship when an emergency exists. Suppose a hurricane is headed for Florida. Unable to talk to the boss, an employee buys $500 worth of plywood to protect the windows and other business property. That purchase is beyond delegated authority, but the situation required a decision. The agent, although acting beyond the authority granted by the principal, is provided the authority to do so in emergencies by *operation of law* and must be compensated.

LIGHTER SIDE OF THE LAW

Is Slavery an Employment Relationship?

Ruiz, a 60-year-old former schoolteacher from the Philippines, worked as a domestic servant for James Jackson and his wife. She claimed she was paid $300 a year for working 18 hours a day. She said she was hit and slept in a dog bed. She was told she would go to jail and never see her family again if she told anyone.

After she escaped and sued, a Los Angeles jury awarded her $825,000 damages for involuntary servitude and false imprisonment. She was helped by the Coalition to Abolish Slavery and Trafficking, which estimates that 15,000 people a year are brought to the United States and kept in such conditions.

Jackson, who knows the law, filed for bankruptcy right before the trial began. When he lost the suit, his employer fired him from his position as vice president for legal affairs for Sony Pictures Entertainment.

Source: *Associated Press*

Getty Images

Acts for the Principal

An agent's ability to transact business for a principal depends upon the scope of authority given to the agent. Authority is determined by statements of the principal, the principal's conduct, or the trade customs in business. An agent can have two general classes of authority: *actual authority* and *apparent authority*. If an agent claims to have authority but in fact has none, the principal is not responsible for the agent's dealings with third parties who have no reason to think the agent has authority.

Actual Authority

Actual authority, sometimes called *real authority*, is the authority given by the principal to the agent. Actual authority can come from express and implied authority. It confers upon an agent the power and the right to change the principal's legal status.

Express authority consists of oral or written instructions given by the principal to an agent. Suppose the owner of an apartment complex hires a leasing agent and tells the agent to rent apartments at a certain price. The agent would have express authority to rent the apartments as instructed.

Often, when an agent receives express authority, he also receives *implied authority* to do whatever is reasonable to carry out the agency purpose. Suppose a landowner authorizes a real estate agent to find a buyer for some acreage. The landowner does not describe to the agent every step that could be taken. Even though the parties may not discuss the matter, the agent would have implied authority to post a "For Sale" sign on the property, advertise the offer for sale in a newspaper, and take possible buyers to the property. The agent would have implied authority to use normal business practices unless instructed not to by the principal.

Apparent Authority

A principal can be bound by unauthorized acts of an agent who appears to have authority to act. *Apparent authority* arises when the principal creates an appearance of authority in an agent that leads a third party to conclude reasonably that the agent has authority to act for the principal.

Apparent authority commonly arises when a principal hires a business manager as an agent. As a rule, the authority to manage a business gives the agent the implied authority—or the appearance of authority, as we see in the *Town Center* case—to undertake usual business activities.

Town Center Shopping Center v. Premier Mortgage Funding
Court of Appeals of Kansas
148 P.3d 565 (2007)

Case Background *Town Center (TC) owns a shopping center in Derby, Kansas. It leased space to Empire Lending for a two-year term (Lease 1). The space could not be sublet without permission of TC. Bayer, a branch manager for Premier Mortgage, executed a lease of the premises from Empire that stated the lease could be ended at any time on five days' notice (Lease 2). TC was unaware of that arrangement.*

Bayer's employment contract stated that she could not enter into a lease without permission of the company president. The president of Premier approved the lease of the space from Empire and signed it. Later, someone at Premier's central office told Bayer the lease needed to be directly between Premier and TC, not with Empire. Bayer then signed a lease on behalf of Premier with TC (Lease 3). She sent the lease to TC with a general letter from Premier's

headquarters, stating that Premier had a branch office in good standing on the TC property. The lease Bayer signed was for a three-year term, not one that could be cancelled on five days' notice. Bayer did not send the new lease to the company president.

A year later, Premier gave TC five days' notice of intent to vacate and left. TC sued for breach. The district court held for TC and awarded $13,493 in damage as allowed in Lease 3. Premier appealed, contending Bayer had no authority to sign the lease with TC. She only was given authority for the first sublease with Empire.

Case Decision Green, Judge

* * *

Because both parties admit that Bayer did not have actual authority to bind Premier under the lease, the question is whether Bayer had apparent authority. In cases where actual authority is absent, Kansas recognizes the doctrine of apparent or ostensible agency: "An ostensible or apparent agency may exist if a principal has intentionally or by want of ordinary care induced and permitted third persons to believe a person is his or her agent even though no authority, either express or implied, has been actually conferred upon the agent." In determining whether an apparent agency existed, the court will look to the intentional acts or words of the principal to a third party and if those acts or words reasonably induced the third party to believe that an agency relationship existed. Therefore, the question in this case is whether the acts and words of Premier induced Town Center to enter into Lease 3 and whether that inducement was reasonable.…

Though Premier makes some legitimate arguments, we are not persuaded that the trial court erred in rejecting these arguments and concluding that Bayer had the apparent authority to sign Lease 3 on behalf of Premier and that Town Center was reasonably induced to enter into the lease.…

Premier and Town Center did not conduct business through a series of meetings and personal encounters; rather, the interaction between Premier and Town Center was limited to the letter and the lease. Lack of an ongoing relationship between Premier and Town Center, however, was sufficiently overcome by the letter that seemed to give Bayer limitless authority to conduct business on behalf of Premier.…

Town Center also notes the definition of the word "manager." Black's Law Dictionary 979 (8th ed., 2004) defines manager as "a person who administers or supervises the affairs of a business, office, or other organization."… Though referring to Bayer as a manager was probably not alone sufficient to establish apparent authority, the commonly understood meaning of that word in conjunction with the surrounding circumstances provided a sufficient basis to induce Town Center to sign the lease.

Based on the facts and circumstances of this case, Town Center established by clear and satisfactory evidence that Premier's letter induced Town Center to believe Bayer had apparent authority to act on behalf of Premier. Therefore, the district court properly concluded that Premier was bound to the lease executed by Bayer.…

Question for Analysis

1. The appeals court affirmed that Bayer, as branch manager for Premier, had apparent authority to enter into a lease with Town Center for office space. How could Premier have avoided the outcome?
2. Did Bayer breach a duty she owed to Premier? Do you think it was intentional?

Duties of the Agency Parties

Within an agency relationship, the parties have duties that govern their conduct. For example, each party is required to act in good faith toward the other and to share information having an important effect on the relationship. In addition, as Exhibit 14.2 summarizes, there are duties that each party owes the other.

Principal's Duties to an Agent

The law of agency emphasizes the duties an agent owes to his principal. This is understandable, since the acts central to the agency relationship are to be performed by the agent. Nevertheless, the principal owes the agent certain duties.

The principal has a *duty to cooperate* with her agent by performing responsibilities defined in the agreement forming the agency. If relevant, the principal must provide a safe working environment and warn the agent of any unreasonable risk associated with the agency. In addition, the principal must not furnish goods of inferior quality to the agent, if the agreement calls for the sale of goods of a specific quality.

Unless the agent agreed to work for free, the principal is under a *duty to compensate* her agent. If the agency does not specify the compensation, the principal has a duty to pay for the reasonable value of the services provided. In such circumstances, the agent is paid the "customary" rate for services provided.

Exhibit 14.2
Duties in an Agency
Relationship

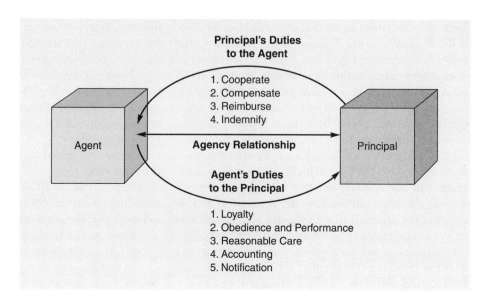

A principal has a duty to pay the reasonable expenses incurred by an agent. The principal would be expected, for example, to pay travel and lodging expenses. Hence, the principal is under a *duty to reimburse* authorized payments the agent makes to third parties on behalf of the principal. The agent cannot recover expenses incurred as a result of his misconduct or negligence.

The principal is under a *duty to indemnify*—to pay for damages or to insure the agent against losses suffered while undertaking authorized transactions. Suppose the principal has goods that belong to someone else and directs the agent to sell them. The agent sells the goods, believing they are the property of the principal. Later, if the agent is sued by the legal owner, the principal has a duty to indemnify the agent for losses incurred in the lawsuit.

Agent's Duties to the Principal

The agent's duties to the principal arise because an agent is a *fiduciary* of the principal. That is, the agent occupies a position of trust, honesty, and confidence for the principal. In addition to responsibilities the principal and agent agree upon in establishing the agency relationship, the law automatically imposes certain duties upon an agent.

The *duty of loyalty* requires an agent to place the principal's interests before the agent's personal interests or those of any third party. That is, the agent may not compete with the principal while working for the principal, unless the principal approves. It would be a violation of this duty if the agent also represented another party whose interests were in conflict with those of the principal.

Don Reid Ford in Orlando had a manager named Southern who handled inventory at Reid's "Get Ready Department." He received fake invoices from Stafford, who ran an operation that sold supplies to Reid. Southern would order the invoices paid and then Stafford and Southern would split the cash—about $300,000 over a two year period. The actions were criminal but also violated Southern's duty to Reid. He was ordered to pay restitution.

An agent must perform instructions provided by the principal. The agent violates this *duty of obedience and performance* by ignoring the principal's instructions and is liable to the principal. However, an agent has no obligation to engage in acts that could lead to personal liability.

An agent is required to exercise *reasonable care* and skill in the performance of duties. The duty is to perform responsibilities with the degree of care that a reasonable person would exercise under the circumstances. An accountant hired to prepare an income tax return who failed to take advantage of a legal tax deduction would violate this duty of reasonable care.

An agent has a *duty to account* for the funds and property of his principal that have been entrusted to him or have come into his possession. The agent must be able to show where money or property comes from and goes to. An agent must also avoid mixing personal funds with funds belonging to the principal.

Finally, an agent is under a duty to keep her principal informed of all facts relevant to the agency. Suppose Limbeck hires Airdate as her agent to sell some farmland at a given price. Airdate learns that in the next several months, the farmland will likely increase in value because of a new highway to be built nearby. Airdate is under a *duty to inform* Limbeck of this information so that she can decide whether she still wants Airdate to sell according to her original instructions. We see an example of an agent violating duties to a principal in the *Bearden* case.

Bearden v. Wardley
Court of Appeals of Utah
72 P.3d 144 (2003)

Case Background *Bearden decided to sell some rental property she owned. She listed the property with real estate agent Gritton, who worked for Wardley Corporation, a real estate brokerage firm. Soon after listing the property, Gritton told Bearden that he wanted to buy the property for $89,000. She agreed and allowed Gritton to take over the property. The contract called for him to pay Bearden $400 a month followed by a one-time balloon payment at the end of five years. Bearden would keep title to the property until the balloon payment was made.*

Unknown to Bearden, when Gritton gave her assorted documents to sign, one was a warranty deed that transferred title to Gritton. He had the signature improperly notarized and then recorded the deed. When he did not keep up on his payments to Bearden, she hired a lawyer to help her. He discovered that Gritton had fraudulently obtained the warranty deed, that he had borrowed money against the property, and that the property was in foreclosure because he had not made payments on the loan. Bearden paid $60,000 to keep the property from being lost.

She sued Gritton and Wardley for breach of contract, fraud, and breach of fiduciary duty. The jury awarded Bearden $75,000 in damages, plus $25,000 punitive damages, plus $50,000 attorney fees, plus costs and interest. Since the judgment was against both Gritton and Wardley, Wardley was stuck with paying the judgment. It appealed.

Case Decision Thorne, Judge

* * *

Wardley argues that the trial court erred ... because Bearden did not introduce evidence regarding Wardley's duty to Bearden or the resulting breach. Bearden introduced into evidence a listing contract drafted by Wardley and signed by Gritton, individually and as Wardley's agent. The listing Contract provided:

> Wardley Better Homes and Gardens and the Agent agree to act as agent for the seller and will work diligently to locate a Buyer for the Property. As the Seller's agent, they will act consistent with their *fiduciary duties to the Seller of loyalty, full disclosure, confidentiality, and reasonable care.* (Emphasis added.)

Bearden also introduced evidence that it was Wardley's policy to have management or a supervisor review the documents in its transition files and that Wardley had an internal policy that prohibited agents from purchasing properties that an agent listed. From this evidence, the jury could have found that Wardley owed Bearden the fiduciary duties of "loyalty, full disclosure, confidentiality, and reasonable care."

... Bearden introduced evidence that (1) Gritton was employed by Wardley, (2) Wardley was aware that Gritton had executed a listing agreement and a

continues

real estate purchase agreement with Bearden wherein Gritton acted as buyer and seller's agent and the purchaser of the property, (3) Wardley never questioned Gritton about violating its internal policy against an agent purchasing property listed by that agent, (4) Wardley never asked Gritton to stop representing Bearden, and (5) Wardley never informed Bearden of Gritton's violations of the internal policy. This evidence is sufficient for the jury to find that Wardley breached its duty of care to Bearden....

Affirmed.

Question for Analysis

1. The appeals court affirmed that the principal was liable for damages incurred by fraud of one of its agents. Since there was no evidence that Wardley participated in Gritton's fraud, why should it be liable?

2. Suppose Gritton had told Wardley he wanted to buy the property he had listed. What should Wardley have done?

Liability for Contracts

The primary purpose of agency relationships is to help principals expand business activities. Agents enter into contracts on behalf of the principal. The rights and liabilities of the principal and agent may be determined by whether the principal is disclosed or undisclosed.

Disclosed Principals

According to the *Restatement (Second) Agency*, a *disclosed principal* is one whose identity is known by the third party at the time a contract is entered into with an agent.

A disclosed principal is liable to a third party for a contract made by an agent who had *actual authority* to act on behalf of the principal. Suppose Thalia instructs Chan, her agent, to buy her a car. Chan contracts for a car with a seller who knows that Chan is acting as an agent. Thalia is bound by the contract and must honor it. The third-party seller may sue Thalia if she fails to perform according to the agreement made for her by Chan.

The principal is also liable if a third party enters into a contract with an agent with *apparent authority*. However, an agent who violates the duty of obedience to the principal is liable to the principal for any losses. To illustrate, suppose Thalia did not give Chan authority to buy a car, but Thalia's conduct in the past led the seller

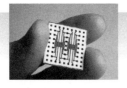

CYBER LAW

Computer Abuse by Employees

Citrin worked for a real estate development company to help identify properties that the company could buy. He decided to go into business for himself in competition with his employer. To cover his tracks, he installed a program to scrub his company computer clean of all information. Some of the files would have shown how he was collecting information for himself; others were company files he developed. His computer had the only copy, so valuable information was destroyed.

The company sued him for violating the Computer Fraud and Abuse Act, which holds it illegal to intentionally damage a protected computer. The federal appeals court held that Citrin breached his duty of loyalty. Once he breached that duty by planning to use company resources for his own gain, he no longer had an agency relationship that gave him the right to access company files. He then was liable for destroying files by accessing a computer he had no right to use (*International Airport Centers* v. *Citrin*, 440 F.3d 418). The Act gives employers additional legal weapons to go after those who damage company machines or files.

Getty Images

to believe that Chan had authority. If Chan contracts for a car, Thalia is bound by it. However, Chan must indemnify Thalia for losses incurred as a result.

Undisclosed Principals

An *undisclosed principal* is one whose identity is unknown by the third party. The third party has no knowledge that the agent is acting for another when a contract is made. Thus, the third party is unaware of both the identity of the principal and of the agency relationship. In this situation, the agent is liable to the third party for the principal's nonperformance of the contract.

If the agent had authority to make a contract, the undisclosed principal is bound to the obligations formed with third parties by the agent just as if the identity had been disclosed.

If the agent is found liable to the third party, because the principal failed to perform and the third party sues the agent, the agent is entitled to be indemnified by the principal. However, the agent must have been operating within the scope of his authority. If the agent acted outside his authority, the undisclosed principal is under no obligation to accept responsibility for the agent's actions. The *Dana* case provides an example of the intentional use of an undisclosed principal.

Dana v. Boren
Court of Appeals of Washington, Division Two
135 P.3d 963 (2006)

Case Background *Dana and Kupers were members of The Maple Mill, LLC, a business that buys and sells specialty wood products for musical instruments. The members of the LLC began to fight with each other, and a court ordered the LLC to stop all sales until matters were resolved.*

Dana suspected that Kupers was selling wood on the side. He hired Wilson, a private investigator, to see what was going on. Wilson discovered that Boren, a friend of Kupers, was selling wood on the Internet. Wilson sent Boren a bid and he accepted. Two days later, Wilson showed up at Boren's house to buy the wood. Dana then sued Boren and Kupers for breach of contract and fraud for selling wood in violation of the court order. The trial court dismissed the suit, holding that the contract for sale of the wood was with an undisclosed principal who was not a party to the matter. Dana appealed.

Case Decision Quinn-Brintnall, Chief Judge

* * *

It is a well established general rule that, where an agent on behalf of his principal enters into a simple contract as though made for himself, and the existence of the principal is not disclosed, the contract inures to the benefit of the principal, who may appear and hold the other party to the contract made by the agent. By appearing and claiming the benefit of the contract, it thereby becomes his own to the same extent as if his name had originally appeared as a contracting party, and the fact that the agent has made the contract in his own name does not preclude the principal from suing thereon as the real party in interest....

An undisclosed principal's right to enforce the contract is subject to some exceptions, none of which applies here. He or she may not enforce a contract if: (1) recovery by the principal is excluded by the form or terms of the contract; (2) the parties intended to exclude an undisclosed principal; (3) the third party's rights would be impaired by the principal's recovery; (4) the principal's existence is fraudulently concealed; (5) the agent expressly and falsely asserts that he is the principal or that he does not represent a certain principal with whom the third party does not wish to deal; or (6) the agent fails to disclose the principal's existence knowing that the third party would not enter into transactions with the principal. These exceptions are largely fact specific and a [motion to dismiss] will rarely, if ever, be appropriate....

continues

Generally, an undisclosed principal can sue to enforce a contract entered into by his agent. The superior court thus erred in granting Boren and Kupers's motion to dismiss.

Reversed and Remanded.

Question for Analysis

1. The appeals court held that in most circumstances, the contract made by an agent for an undisclosed principal is valid. Does this seem like an unethical practice?

Terminating an Agency

The agency relationship is voluntary. Thus, when a party leaves or when the consent comes to ends, the agency is *terminated*. The agent's authority to act for the principal ends. It may be necessary to give notice of the termination to third parties to end the agent's apparent authority.

Parties may set a specific date for an agency to end. If no time is set, the agency ends when its purpose, such as the sale of real estate, is fulfilled. The parties may agree to end the agency or to extend it beyond its original time and scope of duties. An agency can be ended upon reasonable notice by either the agent or the principal.

Certain events automatically terminate an agency. Termed *termination by operation of law*, an agency ends without any action by the principal or the agent. For example, if the principal or the agent dies, the agency ends. It also ends if the subject matter is destroyed, for example, when a house for sale burns down.

The Essential Employment Relationship

Many agent relationships involve people hired to perform specific tasks. A professional baseball player hires an agent to negotiate salary. A homeowner hires an agent to market and sell a house. You hire an accountant to prepare an annual audit

INTERNATIONAL PERSPECTIVE

Principals and Agents under a Civil-Law System

Comparing the common-law and civil-law traditions, it becomes apparent that agency relationships differ in important ways. For example, under the common law, an undisclosed principal is bound to contracts with third parties if the agent forming the contract has actual authority to enter into those contracts. The principal is able to hold the third party to the contract. In this situation, the common-law and the civil-law traditions can reach different conclusions. Under civil law, the "principle of lack of communication among parties that have no knowledge of each other's existence" prevails, and the principal is not bound. The principal is not able to hold the third party to the contract unless the third party had knowledge of the principal's existence.

Consider a situation where the principal and the agent have decided to establish their agency relationship on the basis of a written contract. With that contract, the agent has actual authority to act on behalf of the principal. The agent enters into a contract with a third party, and then the agency contract is found to have been invalid. Under the common-law tradition, the principal is not liable to the third party (unless through her actions she had created apparent authority in the agent.) In most countries with a civil-law tradition, the agent's power to perform is independent of the validity of the agency contract. Thus, under civil law, the principal is liable to the third party.

Getty Images

Types of Relationships	Characteristics
Principal–Agent	Agent acts on behalf of or for the principal, with a degree of personal discretion.
Master–Servant (Employer-Employee)	The servant is an employee whose conduct is controlled by the employer. A servant can also be an agent.
Employer–Independent Contractor	An independent contractor is not an employee, and the employer does not control the details of the independent contractor's performance. The contractor is usually not an agent.

Exhibit 14.3
Distinguishing Legal Relationships

statement for a business and do a tax return. All of these people may be employees, but they are not employees of the person who hired them to perform a certain job.

The employment relationship involves many aspects of agency. As we saw in the *Town Center* case, an employee—the branch manager—went beyond her authority and entered into a lease on behalf of her employer. Because of her employment situation, it was reasonable for the landlord to presume she had authority as an agent.

When someone is only an agent for a specific task, the authority is usually clear. When we get into employment situations, the issues are more complex, because there many possible relationships. Traditionally the *employer–employee* relationship was called, at law, a *master–servant* relationship. We next look at that and also at the *employer–independent contractor* relationship, which is more limited in scope. As Exhibit 14.3 shows, there are key differences in the major relationship categories.

Employer–Independent Contractor

The employer–independent contractor relationship differs from the agency and employee–employer relationships in several ways. Consider how *independent contractor* is defined by the *Restatement (Second) Agency:*

> An independent contractor is a person who contracts with another to do something for him but who is not controlled by the other nor subject to the other's right to control with respect to his physical conduct in the performance of the undertaking.

As this definition implies, the independent contractor is distinguished by the extent of control the employer retains over work performance. The more control the employee retains, the more likely the employee will be characterized as an independent contractor. As a rule, the employer is not liable for the torts of an independent contractor. In the chapter on employment law, we will see how a determination of employer or contractor status is likely to be determined by state or federal law.

Contractors as Agents

Some independent contractors are also agents. Contractors authorized to enter into contracts for the principal are agents. This often includes attorneys, auctioneers, and other such persons who conduct business on behalf of the principal. Some contractors do not have authority to enter into contracts for the principal and so are not agents. This would usually include building contractors and others hired to perform certain tasks for an employer.

Master–Servant or Employer–Employee

Master–servant is an old term still often used in law that means the same as employer–employee. The *servant* (employee) is hired by a *master* (employer). Traditionally, servants or employees did manual labor; they were not in a position to act on behalf of the master or employer when dealing with third parties. The master–servant rules apply when an employee is under the direct control of an employer, such as a food service or road maintenance worker. When the employee does not have authority to represent the employer in business dealings, no agency exists, but a master–servant relationship exists. Since employers are presumed to be in control of their employees, employers may be liable for the torts committed by employees in the course of employment.

Employees as Servants and Agents

Many employees now are agents and servants, that is, many of us work under the control of employers, but in some capacities, act as agents, in which case the employers are also principals. Employees often make business decisions that affect their employer. Sales representatives at Don Reid Ford dealership who are authorized to sell cars within certain price ranges without permission of a supervisor are employees with certain agency powers to make contracts for their employer.

The distinction between agent-principal and master–servant is often blurred. Most employers do not specify to their employees that they are agents in certain matters and employees in others. What matters is what legal authority or responsibility exists when questions arise about the validity of a contract or the responsibility for a tort.

Employment at Will

At common law, employees are presumed to work at will. That is, employers are free to discharge employees for any reason at any time, and employees are free to quit their jobs for any reason at any time. The *employment-at-will* doctrine is now affected by many statutes that control certain aspects of the employment relationship. Employers and employees can agree, by contract, to move away from employment-at-will. In the employment law chapter, we get into the ways we deviate from the presumption of at-will, but here we must stress that the employment-at-will doctrine is very strong. The common law rules of employment are generally a different matter

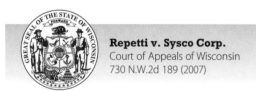

Repetti v. Sysco Corp.
Court of Appeals of Wisconsin
730 N.W.2d 189 (2007)

Case Background *Repetti worked his way up at Sysco over the course of 11 years. Part of his job was reporting income and expenses for the logistics department. While performing his duties, he learned that "a corporate officer was altering numbers in an attempt to falsely show profit or larger profits in the Operations Department by moving income from the Logistics Department into the Operations Department for purposes of financial reporting."*

Repetti complained about these falsifications to the company comptroller and the president. The president told him more than once to drop the matter. Repetti was concerned that he could personally face civil or criminal penalties for improper revenue reporting. He continued to complain about the accounting practices of some company officers and was fired.

He sued Sysco for wrongful discharge. He claimed his discharge violated public policy, because he refused to violate a specific law, the Sarbanes–Oxley Act, which requires accurate financial reporting. The trial court dismissed Repetti's complaint. He appealed.

Case Decision Anderson, Judge

* * *

Repetti was an at-will employee of Sysco. Generally, at-will employees may be terminated "for good cause, for no cause, or even for cause morally wrong, without being thereby guilty of legal wrong." Despite statutory modification of the at-will doctrine "to curb harsh applications and abuse of the rule," our supreme court recognized, as have other state courts, "the need to protect workers who are wrongfully discharged under circumstances not covered by any legislation or whose job security is not safeguarded by a collective bargaining agreement or civil service regulations." Therefore, our supreme court adopted a "narrow public policy exception" to the employment-at-will doctrine. The exception provides that "an employee has a cause of action for wrongful discharge when the discharge is contrary to a fundamental and well-defined public policy as evidenced by existing law." Existing law includes constitutional, statutory, and administrative provisions.

However, … our supreme court observed that "the legislature has enacted a variety of statutes to prohibit certain types of discharges" and "where the legislature has created a statutory remedy for a wrongful discharge, that remedy is exclusive." Our supreme court made clear that if the legislature creates a remedial process, the court will not override that process with the judicially-created public policy exception. The narrow public policy exception simply

recognizes that "the legislature has not and cannot cover every type of wrongful termination that violates a clear mandate of public policy." It applies where an employee has no other recourse to regain a former position or receive redress for a wrongful termination.

The Sarbanes–Oxley whistleblower provision … prohibits companies from discharging an employee because of any lawful act done by the employee to provide information … regarding any conduct which the employee reasonably believes constitutes a violation of … any rule or regulation of the Securities and Exchange Commission, or any provision of Federal law relating to fraud against shareholders, when the information or assistance is provided to … a person with supervisory authority over the employee.

[Sarbanes–Oxley] creates a procedure whereby wrongfully discharged employees can seek redress first through the Department of Labor and then through the courts.…

Even if we assume that Repetti has established that his discharge contravened a fundamental and well-defined public policy found in Sarbanes–Oxley, that act itself provides the remedies for violations of that policy. We affirm the order granting Sysco's motion to dismiss.

Question for Analysis

1. The appeals court affirmed that Repetti has no case for wrongful termination based on the at-will doctrine of employment, even if his being fired was related to his employer being involved in violations of federal law. Does Repetti have no legal protection?

2. Why does the court not allow Repetti to sue, because Sysco's actions may have violated a federal statute, which is part of public policy?

than laws passed by legislatures that control certain aspects of employment, as we see in the *Repetti* case.

Contracting to Limit At-Will Employment

As we have discussed, employment-at-will means an employee may be dismissed at any time without reason or cause. The employment contract only exists so long as the employee works and the employer pays. The arrangement can end at any time, unless the parties have agreed to a contract that goes beyond at-will.

We will see in later chapters that there are statutory grounds for employees to sue for improper dismissal or treatment on the job, but suits claiming that the employment contract was violated by termination are not generally successful.

INTERNATIONAL PERSPECTIVE

Flexibility in Labor Markets

The ability of labor markets to respond to changing conditions in a rapidly changing global economy means flexibility is more important than ever. A group of researchers from Harvard, Yale, and the World Bank looked at labor laws in many nations to see how they compare.

The authors constructed a number of measures. In all indexes, the lower the score, the greater the flexibility in the labor market. The higher the score, the greater the regulatory barriers faced by an employer. The first measure, the Difficulty of Hiring Index, includes the ability to hire part-time labor and use other nontraditional labor terms. The second measure, the Difficulty of Firing Index, includes the difficulties and expense of terminating a worker no longer needed. The third measure, the Rigidity of Employment Index, is a general measure that includes the first two measures and other factors, such as the ability to change the number of hours a worker provides. The fourth column, Firing Costs, is the average number of weeks of wages incurred by an employer in severance pay and other costs that are incurred in the dismissal process. Notice that many poor countries have the most restrictions on labor markets. How beneficial are the regulations for ordinary workers?

Country	Difficulty of Hiring Index	Difficulty of Firing Index	Rigidity of Employment Index	Firing Costs (weeks' wages)
U.S.	0	0	0	0
Singapore	0	0	0	4
Denmark	0	10	17	10
Canada	11	0	4	28
Mexico	33	40	38	74
Pakistan	78	30	43	90
Ukraine	44	80	55	13
Venezuela	67	100	76	47

Source: *http://rru.worldbank.org/doingbusiness*

Getty Images

Nevertheless, suits claiming breach of an employment contract are brought. They can be summarized into three general categories, although other claims may be made:

1. An *express contract* exists when the employer and employee agree on employment for a certain time or that job security is provided. The terms of the contract must be considered if the employee is fired. Suppose a company sends an employee to Mexico City on a three-year assignment. The person moves there and a month later is told the job no longer exists. In such cases, there is probably an express contract. Dismissing the employee without just cause (e.g., evidence of incompetence or proof of financial crisis) could be a breach of contract. This cause of action is not common.

2. An *implied contract*, based on written or oral statements, may restrict the grounds for termination or require specific procedures to be followed in a dismissal. Evidence includes the policies and past practices of the employer. Courts expect employers to behave consistently in such matters, not just follow procedure when the mood strikes.

   For example, the supreme court of Connecticut found an implied contract was breached in *Coelho* v. *Posi-Seal International* (544 A.2d 170). An employee was fired without good cause, despite statements by the company president that he had job security and that the president supported him in conflicts with other employees. The court stated that "there was sufficient evidence to permit the jury to find that the parties had an implied agreement that, so long as he performed his job properly, the plaintiff would not be terminated...." Employers must be cautious about the statements they make to employees, because what they say may be held as part of an employment contract.

3. Similarly, contracts contain an implied covenant of *good faith and fair dealing* that can be extended to employment contracts. The Montana supreme court took that position in *Flanigan* v. *Prudential Federal Savings and Loan* (720 P.2d 257), when it upheld a jury verdict of $1.5 million for a bank employee dismissed after 28 years of service. No good cause for the discharge was provided; it was found to be a breach of the implied covenant of good faith in employment dealings. Similarly, some successful suits have been brought against employers who misrepresented employment conditions to attract an employee, only to soon fire them with no good reason. This is not a common basis for successful suit.

LIGHTER SIDE OF THE LAW
Don't Rat Out Your Boss

Vernon Blake worked for the Alabama Department of Transportation (ALDOT) for 21 years. He was the computer system administrator. Among his duties was "to confirm and document" computer abuse. He thought he was doing that when he created a log to show that his supervisor was spending significant time at work playing computer games and surfing the web.

When this information was reported, his supervisor was given a private reprimand and Blake was fired. He says ALDOT "silenced the whistleblower." Displaying managerial excellence, his superiors also ordered all games removed from ALDOT computers.

Source: *http://www.ALDOTwaste.com*

Getty Images

Employee Handbooks

Many employers issue *employee handbooks* or *manuals* to explain company policies, benefits, and procedures. The handbooks often discuss grounds for discipline and dismissal. Some explain policy about how such matters will be handled; some assert that employees will be dismissed only for good cause and that certain dismissal safeguards exist, such as review by a committee or managerial supervisor. Courts can hold that such handbooks create express or implied contracts that limit the presumption of employment at will.

As the Supreme Court of California noted in *Foley* v. *Interactive Data* (765 P.2d 373), "breach of written 'termination guidelines' implying self-imposed limitations on employer's power to discharge at will may be sufficient to state a cause of action for breach of employment contract." That is, in California and other states, the courts will look to employment practices, including statements in a handbook, as limits on dismissal at will.

Even if the handbook states that employment is at-will, if other provisions of the handbook or company practice indicate otherwise, the employer may have to show that dismissal was for good cause and that promised procedure was followed. Hence, managers should be sure that handbooks and policies are procedures actually followed by the company, or suits for damages for wrongful dismissal are likely to be filed (see Exhibit 14.4).

Despite cases that have been brought under theories of wrongful discharge that limit employment-at-will, or that personnel policies in employee handbooks limit the right of employers to dismiss employees, unless specific steps to limit the right to fire employees have been taken, the likelihood of a successful claim by an employee is small, as indicated in the *Guz* case.

Guz v. Bechtel National
Supreme Court of California
24 Cal.4th 317, 8 P.3d 1089 (2000)

Case Background *Guz worked for Bechtel (BNI) for 22 years. He had a good employment record. Bechtel's personnel policy stated that its employees were at-will. It also stated that employees could be terminated for unsatisfactory performance or because of a reduction in workload or a reorganization. Management decided to cut the budget for Guz's division. Guz and others were fired. This occurred at a time of good profits for the company. The duties Guz performed were shifted to other employees. He applied for other positions at BNI, but he was rejected without reason.*

Guz sued, alleging breach of an implied contract to be terminated only for good cause and for breach of the implied covenant of good faith and fair dealing. The trial court dismissed the suit, holding that Guz was an at-will employee. The appeals court reversed, holding that "Guz's longevity, promotions, raises, and favorable performance reviews, together with Bechtel's written progressive discipline policy and Bechtel officials' statements of company practices, raised a triable issue: that Guz had an implied-in-fact contract to be dismissed only for good cause."

Bechtel appealed.

Case Decision Baxter, Judge

* * *

While the statutory presumption of at-will employment is strong, it is subject to several limitations. For instance, as we have observed, "the employment relationship is fundamentally contractual."…

Among the many available options, the parties may agree that the employer's termination rights will vary with the particular circumstances. The parties may define for themselves what cause or causes will permit an employee's termination and may specify the procedures under which termination shall occur. The agreement may restrict the employer's termination rights to a greater degree in some situations, while leaving the employer freer to acts as it sees fit in others.

The contractual understanding need not be express, but may be *implied in fact*, arising from the parties' *conduct* evidencing their actual mutual intent to create such enforceable limitations.… These factors might include "the personnel policies or practices of the employer, the employee's longevity of service, actions or communications by the employer reflecting assurances of continued employment, and the practices of the industry in which the employee is engaged."…

We did not suggest, however, that every vague combination of … factors, shaken together in a bag, necessarily allows a finding that the employee had a right to be discharged only for good cause, as determined in court.

On the contrary, "courts seek to enforce the *actual* understanding" of the parties to an employment agreement. Whether that understanding arises from express mutual words of agreement, or from the parties' conduct evidencing a similar meeting of minds, the exact terms to which the parties have assented deserve equally precise scrutiny.…

We see *no* triable evidence of an implied agreement between Guz and Bechtel on *additional, different, or broader* terms of employment security. As Bechtel suggests, the personnel documents themselves did not restrict Bechtel's freedom to reorganize, reduce, and consolidate its workforce for whatever reasons it wished. Thus, contrary to the Court of Appeals' holding, Bechtel had the absolute right to eliminate Guz's work unit and to transfer the unit's responsibilities to another company entity, even if the decision was influenced by dissatisfaction with the eliminated unit's performance, and even if the personnel documents entitled an individual employee to progressive discipline procedures before being fired for poor performance.

* * *

Guz insists his own undisputed long and successful service at Bechtel constitutes strong evidence of an implied contract for permanent employment except upon good cause. Guz argues that by retaining him for over twenty years, and by providing him with steady raises, promotions, commendations, and good performance reviews during his tenure, Bechtel engaged in "actions … reflecting assurances of continued employment."…

An employee's *mere* passage of time in the employer's service, even where marked with tangible indicia that the employer approves the employee's work, cannot *alone* form an implied-in-fact contract that the employee is no longer at-will. Absent other evidence of the employer's intent, longevity, raises, and promotions are their own rewards for the employee's continuing valued service; they do not, *in and of themselves*, additionally constitute a contractual guarantee of future employment security. A rule granting such contract rights on the basis of successful longevity alone would discourage the retention and promotion of employees....

Guz points to the deposition testimony of Johnstone, BNI's president, who stated his understanding that Bechtel terminated workers only with "good reason" or for "lack of [available] work." But there is no evidence that Bechtel employees were aware of such an unwritten policy, and it flies in the face of Bechtel's general disclaimer. This brief and vague statement, by a single Bechtel official, that Bechtel sought to avoid arbitrary firings is insufficient as a matter of law to permit a finding that the company, by an unwritten practice or policy on which employees reasonably relied, had contracted away its right to discharge Guz at will.

In sum, if there is any significant evidence that Guz had an implied contract against termination at will, that evidence flows exclusively from Bechtel's written personnel documents. It follows that there is no triable issue of an implied contract on terms *broader than the specific provisions of those documents....*

Bechtel's written personnel documents—which, as we have seen, are the sole source of any contractual limits on Bechtel's rights to terminate Guz—imposed no restrictions upon the company's prerogatives to eliminate jobs or work units, for any or no reason, even if this would lead to the release of existing employees such as Guz.

The Judgment of the Court of Appeals is reversed.

Question for Analysis

1. The high court held that employment-at-will is difficult to overcome by a claim of implied contract. Is there an incentive for employers to make it clear to employees that they are strictly at-will and there is no assurance of continued employment?

2. Is there an employment contract? Guz had to follow the requirements of his employer; what consideration did the employer give?

Tort Liability for Employers and Principals

Besides creating contractual liability, agents and employees can create tort liability. The principal or employer is liable for the tort of an agent or employee if the tort was authorized by the principal or, more commonly, if the tort occurred within the scope of employment. If the agent or employee commits an unauthorized tort outside the scope of employment, the agent or employee is liable to the third party for damages incurred, and the principal or employer is usually not liable.

Principal's Liability

It is obvious that a principal or employer is liable for torts committed by an agent or an employee following orders. But it is not often that an employer tells an employee, or a contractor, to commit a tort and the order is followed. Rather, liability tends to come from actions taken by agents or employees that the principal should have

---

- Using boilerplate forms that include material not relevant to the employer
- Making promises about discipline procedures that are not followed consistently
- Creating probationary periods that imply permanent status once probation has ended
- Failing to change the handbook to comply with state and federal laws as they change
- Listing specific offenses for which people may be fired can create the impression those are the only offenses that matter
- Not giving a clear at-will employment statement and failing to specify that the employer has the right to change the terms at any time without notice

Exhibit 14.4
Common Problems with Employee Handbooks

prevented so that injury would not have been inflicted. Liability may be imposed on the employer under the rule of vicarious liability or for a tort of *negligent hiring*.

ISSUE SPOTTER

Can You Be Too Encouraging to Employees?

Your company is an at-will employer that has a handbook that makes clear the legal status of employees. But no one likes to think he or she is always on the verge of being fired, or there will be little reason for loyalty. To encourage employee retention, it is not uncommon for supervisors to approach employees whose personal problems have begun to affect their job performance to say that the company "wants you to stay" and "will provide help for you". Does this kind of supportive talk set the company up for a suit for violation of an implied contract if the employee is later fired? Would it be better to say nothing, if it is clear there are problems? How are such matters best handled?

Getty Images

Vicarious Liability

Under the rule of *vicarious liability*, a principal or employer can be liable for the unauthorized intentional or negligent torts of agents and employees who were acting within the scope of employment. It is rare for an employee to be liable for a tort committed by an independent contractor. Courts consider many factors in determining whether an act was within the scope of employment. Some of the most important are whether

- the act was of the same general nature as those authorized by the principal.
- the agent was authorized to be where he was at the time the act occurred.
- the agent was serving the principal's interests at the time of the act.

The rule of law imposing vicarious liability upon an innocent principal is known as *respondeat superior* (let the master answer). This doctrine has been justified on the grounds that the principal is in a better position to protect the public from such torts, by controlling the actions of its agents, and to compensate those injured. This rule also means that employers may be liable for torts of employees that can be attributed to negligent hiring or supervision.

This is one of the most difficult areas of agency and employment law. The line between when an employer may or may not be liable for torts or criminal acts committed by employees, agents, or independent contractors is hard to draw. The *Armstrong* case reviews some of the issues.

ISSUE SPOTTER

Use of Company Cars

Your organization provides company cars for many sales reps so that they can present the proper image for the organization. Occasionally, accidents happen. The company has insurance for the cars, but that rate goes up every time there is an accident. Should an accident be severe, there could be liability in the millions. Sometimes employees are in accidents when they are running personnel errands in the company cars. What is a sensible way to handle this liability that the employer faces?

Getty Images

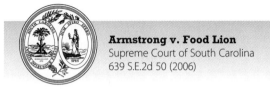

Armstrong v. Food Lion
Supreme Court of South Carolina
639 S.E.2d 50 (2006)

Case Background *Ronnie Armstrong went to a Food Lion store in Winnsboro with his mother, Tillie, to buy groceries. Three men in Food Lion uniforms approached Ronnie. One, Brown, had been in a fight with Ronnie two years before. He attacked Ronnie with a box cutter used to open cases of food. Another employer, Cameron, also attacked Ronnie. When Tillie came to help Ronnie, Cameron punched her and knocked her down. Another shopper, Loner, helped Tillie and called for assistance.*

The Armstrongs sued Food Lion for numerous torts. The trial court held for Food Lion and the appeals court affirmed. The Armstrongs appealed.

Case Decision Moore, Justice

* * *

Petitioners contend Food Lion is legally responsible to them for the acts of its employees, Brown and Cameron. The doctrine of *respondeat superior* rests upon the relation of master and servant. A plaintiff seeking recovery from the master for injuries must establish that the relationship existed at the time of the injuries and also that the servant was then about his master's business and acting within the scope of his employment. An act is within the scope of a servant's employment where reasonably necessary to accomplish the purpose of his employment and in furtherance of the master's business. These general principles govern in determining whether an employer is liable for the acts of his servant.

The act of a servant done to effect some independent purpose of his own and not with reference to the service in which he is employed, or while he is acting as his own master for the time being, is not within the scope of his employment so as to render the master liable therefor. Under these circumstances the servant alone is liable for the injuries inflicted. If a servant steps aside from the master's business for some purpose wholly disconnected with his employment, the

relation of master and servant is temporarily suspended; this is so no matter how short the time, and the master is not liable for his acts during such time.

The trial court appropriately granted a directed verdict, because petitioners failed to produce any evidence that the Food Lion employees were acting within the scope of their employment or in furtherance of Food Lion's business when they attacked petitioners.…

Two cases that have previously found an employer liable for its employee's assault of another person are distinguishable from the instant case. In *Crittenden* … an employee assaulted another person in an attempt to collect a debt of the business. In *Jones* … a dairy farm's general manager assaulted the owner of a company contracted to provide a refrigerating system. The assault resulted from a dispute arising over problems with the system. The factor that distinguishes these cases from the instant case is that the assaults in *Jones* and *Crittenden* occurred, not merely in connection with the master's business, but with the purpose of in some way furthering the master's business. Here, there is no evidence that Brown and Cameron were furthering Food Lion's business in any manner. Accordingly, the trial court properly granted Food Lion's motion for a directed verdict. Therefore, the decision of the Court of Appeals is affirmed.

Question for Analysis
1. The high court held that the attack by the employees on customers would not result in liability for the employer, because the acts of the employees were not related to business. What if the employees had criminal records? Should employers place ex-felons in contact with the public?
2. Suppose a Food Lion employee carelessly dumps a heavy box on a customer and injures the customer. Would liability likely be imposed in that case?

Negligent Hiring

An employer may be held liable for negligence in hiring and for putting in a position of trust or responsibility a person who could be expected to possibly cause problems. This is similar to respondeat superior. Most negligent hiring cases involve intentional torts committed by an employee who is not acting in the scope of employment.

The *Restatement (Second) of Agency § 213* states: "A person conducting an activity through servants or other agents is subject to liability for harm resulting from his conduct if he is negligent or reckless … in the employment of improper persons … in work involving risks of harm to others." That is, we may have an obligation to check the background of an employee or independent contractor to see if there is a history that makes hiring doubtful.

If a person has a history as a child molester, they should not be hired for a job in which they will be in routine contact with children. There would be an obligation to do a background check when hiring for such positions. A bad driving record would be irrelevant in that situation. However, if a company is hiring someone to drive a truck, driving history would be relevant. Employers must use good judgment or face possible liability. Since background searches are not costly to perform, employers have an obligation to use such services.

LIGHTER SIDE OF THE LAW
Who, Him? Must Be an Independent Contractor

Martinez worked for Singh at Singh's Donuts R' More shop in Sacramento. If Martinez was recognized as Singh's employee, Singh would be required to pay payroll taxes, such as workers' compensation and social security. Singh was not paying these taxes.

After Martinez was shot by gunmen who robbed Singh's store, Singh dragged him outside and told police Martinez was a customer. Singh then told an insurance agent that Martinez was a friend who had dropped by to watch him make doughnuts. Singh was fined $1,000 for falsifying information at a crime scene but was also sued by Martinez, who was, in fact, his employee.

Source: *Sacramento Bee*

Getty Images

Summary

- An agency relationship is created when an agent agrees to act on behalf of, and to be subject to the control of, the principal. As the principal's representative, the agent may bind the principal to contracts with third parties. By using agents, a principal can expand business activities.
- No formal procedure exists for the creation of an agency relationship. There must, however, be an affirmative response on the part of the parties, with the principal manifesting a desire that the agent act on her behalf.
- Agents' authority can range from the extensive powers of a universal agent or the broad business powers of a general agent to the more limited powers of a special agent, a gratuitous agent, or a subagent.
- Agency relationships can be established by agreement of the parties, ratification of the agent's activities by the principal, application of the doctrine of estoppel, or operation of law.
- The agent's ability to act on behalf of the principal depends on the scope of authority granted by the principal. An agent can have actual authority and apparent authority.
- The agent has actual authority if the principal has given the agent authority to act. For such actions, the principal is liable for contracts entered into by the agent on her behalf.

- Once an agency is created, the parties have the duty to share information and to act in good faith. The principal owes the agent the duties to cooperate, compensate, reimburse, and indemnify. The agent owes the principal the duties of loyalty, obedience and performance, reasonable care, accounting, and notification.
- The agent has apparent authority if the principal created the appearance of authority in the agent. While the principal is generally liable for the contracts of an agent with apparent authority, the agent may be obliged to indemnify the principal for losses incurred.
- Agency relationships may terminate through the activities of the parties or by operation of the law. Once an agency relationship is terminated, the agent's authority to act for the principal ceases. It may be necessary to notify third parties to end an agent's authority.
- Agency is distinguishable from master–servant (employer–employee) and employer–independent contractor relationships. Servants and independent contractors do not have authority to represent the employer in business dealings unless they are also authorized to be agents.
- An employer is not liable for the torts of an independent contractor but may be liable for the torts of an employee or agent if the act is committed in the course of business or if the employer failed to screen out employees who could pose a danger to others in certain situations.
- Employment is presumed to be at-will, but the contract may extend beyond that based on oral or written promises that extend the relationship. An employment handbook may also establish terms of the employment relationship that prevent termination without cause.

Terms to Know

You should be able to define the following terms:

agency relationship, 339	duty to compensate, 345	independent contractor, 351
agent, 339	duty to reimburse, 346	master–servant, 352
principal, 339	duty to indemnify, 346	employment-at-will, 352
power of attorney, 341	duty of loyalty, 346	employee handbook, 355
ratification, 341	duty to account, 347	negligent hiring, 358
agency by estoppel, 343	duty to inform, 347	vicarious liability, 358
actual authority, 344	apparent authority, 348	respondeat superior, 358
express authority, 344	undisclosed principal, 349	

Discussion Question

1. An agent embezzles funds from his principal and uses the funds to buy a car. What duties has the agent violated? Who is entitled to ownership of the car?

Case Questions

1. Zimmerman, a real estate salesman, asked Robertson if she was interested in selling her property. Robertson said she might be. Zimmerman came to Robertson with an offer by Velten to buy the property. After some negotiations, both sides signed a contract for sale. Zimmerman told Robertson he was being paid a commission by Velten. Before the deal on the property was to close, Robertson asked for a copy of the agreement between

Zimmerman and Velten, but they refused. Robertson refused to go through with the deal. Velten sued, claiming there was a valid contract. Robertson said that Zimmerman violated his fiduciary duty to her to disclose his interests. Is the deal valid? [*Velten* v. *Robertson*, 671 P.2d 1011 Ct. App., Colo. (1983)]

2. Hunter Mining hired Hubco Data to customize computer equipment specific to Hunter's needs. Before the job was done, Hubco went out of business. Hunter sued MAI, the company that made the computer products that Hubco sold to Hunter, for breach of contract. Hubco was a licensed distributor of MAI when it sold Hunter the computer package. Was MAI liable as principal for Hubco's failure? [*Hunter Mining* v. *Management Assistance, Inc.*, 763 P.2d 350 Sup. Ct., Nev. (1988)]

   ✓ Check your answer at http://academic.cengage.com/blaw/meiners

3. Ruppert owned a construction supply business in Sparks, Nevada. He sold the company to White Cap. The sales agreement contained a clause that Ruppert would not go into competition in Sparks and that he would serve as district manager. One of the employees, Harmon, was unhappy with White Cap's new management. He told Ruppert he was going to quit and start a competing company, which he did. Ruppert did not reveal his conversation with Harmon to White Cap. White Cap sued Ruppert for breach of fiduciary duties for failure to tell White Cap about Harmon's plans. Was that a breach of his duty? [*White Cap Industries* v. *Ruppert*, 67 P.3d 318 Sup. Ct., Nev. (2003)]

4. Guardsmark, a private security company, hired Kadah as a security guard. His record was fine, until one day he was accused of sexually assaulting Plancarte, a janitor at the office building where Kadah worked. No one witnessed the event, but one woman saw Plancarte running away hysterically. Plancarte sued Kadah in tort and sued Guardsmark based on respondeat superior, because the attack occurred while Kadah was on duty. Guardsmark paid for Kadah's attorney. Did that payment imply Guardsmark's ratification of Kadah's wrongful actions? [*Plancarte* v. *Guardsmark*, LLC, 13 Cal.Rptr.3d 315 Ct. App., Calif. (2004)]

   ✓ Check your answer at http://academic.cengage.com/blaw/meiners

5. Two stockbrokers, in clear violation of the rules of their employer, sold worthless stocks to unsuspecting customers. There was no question that the brokers did not have actual or implied authority to sell the stock. The customers who lost money sued the brokerage firm, contending it was liable for their losses because the brokers had apparent authority. Did they? [*Badger* v. *Paulson Investment Co.*, 803 P.2d 1178 Sup. Ct., Ore., (1991)]

6. Picard was a security guard for National Detective Agency. In violation of company rules, he had his own trained German shepherd dog with him while on duty. Meyers, a passerby, stopped to talk to Picard about the dog, which was in the back of a marked company car. Picard said he could show Meyers how well the dog was trained. When he took the dog from the car, it attacked and injured Meyers. Meyers sued National Detective, which argued that Picard's actions were outside the scope of his employment because he was violating company policy. Could the employer be liable? [*Meyers* v. *National Detective Agency*, 281 A.2d 435 Ct. App., D.C. (1971)]

   ✓ Check your answer at http://academic.cengage.com/blaw/meiners

7. While working for Lubrizol Corporation, Occhionero was injured by a fellow employee, Edmundson, who assaulted Occhionero. Occhionero sued Lubrizol for intentional tort and on the basis of respondeat superior—"the legal theory that an employer is derivatively responsible for the torts of his employee committed within the scope of employment." The trial court dismissed the suit; Occhionero appealed. Could Lubrizol be liable? [*Occhionero* v. *Edmundson*, 2001 WL 314821 Ct. App., Ohio, (2001)]

8. When Norton was hired in 1978, he signed an "Employment Agreement" that stated that his employment could be terminated at any time. Several years later, his employer issued a "Work Rule Policy and Handbook" that established policies for discipline and dismissal. Steps for notifying an employee about unsatisfactory performance were described. Norton was fired in 1989, because his boss was unhappy with sales in the office that Norton ran. Norton sued for violation of his employment contract, because the company did not follow

the steps in the handbook. A jury awarded him $305,000 in back pay for breach of contract. Was the award upheld on appeal, or was Norton an at-will employee? [*Norton* v. *Caremark*, 20 F.3d 330, 8th Cir. (1994)]

9. Meyers, an at-will employee, complained to his employer that he was not being paid overtime when he should have been. He was fired, he claimed, for making that complaint. He sued for improper discharge, because he claimed to have a right to overtime pay. What basis would he have for that claim, and do you think it would stand? [*Meyers* v. *Meyers*, 861 N.E.2d 704 Sup. Ct., Ind. (2007)]

10. Vermeulen booked a trip to Machu Picchu in Peru through Worldwide Holidays travel agency in Florida. Worldwide received a commission from the Peruvian tour agency, Chasquitur. When in Peru, the driver of a Chasquitur van rear-ended another vehicle and Vermeulen was injured. He sued Worldwide on the theory of vicarious liability for hiring unsafe drivers. Could he have a case? [*Vermeulen* v. *Worldwide Holiday*, 922 So.2d 271 Ct. App., Fla.(2006)]

Ethics Question

1. Clarence has been released from prison after a six-year term for armed robbery and assault. Having "paid his debt to society" for his crimes, he is now looking for work. You are advertising to hire workers for furniture-moving crews. Normally, two people work together all the time, so you know Clarence would be accompanied by another employee when on the job. However, you know of recent cases in which employers have been held liable for employees who have gone astray while on the job and have committed crimes. Since Clarence would be in people's homes, it is not impossible that this could happen. Should you not hire Clarence because of this worry?

Internet Assignment

ftp://www.ca6.uscourts.gov/opinion.asc/99a0220p.06(registration not required)
http://caselaw.lp.findlaw.com/scripts/getcase.pl?court=6th&navby=year&year=1999-6
(registration required)

1. For over twenty-five (25) years, the Dupont Shoe Company has catered to female clients who prefer conservative and professional shoes. However, one of its hotshot new buyers just went to a shoe trade show and purchased a truckload of loud, brassy, high-heeled shoes and sandals from a newcomer called Trendy Footwear, Inc. On the purchase agreement, the buyer signed as "John F. Marsh, on behalf of the Dupont Shoe Company." He also requested that the shoes be delivered to Dupont's corporate headquarters. When the shoes arrived, Dupont called Trendy in an attempt to return the shoes for a full refund, claiming that Marsh had no authority to order them. When Trendy refused, Dupont refused to pay, and Trendy was forced to file an action on its account.

2. Will Dupont have to pay for the shoes? Can Trendy prove that Marsh was an agent for his disclosed principal Dupont? Is Marsh personally liable on the contract? To answer these question, see the following case from the Sixth Circuit:

Soberay Machine & Equipment Company, Inc. v. *MRF Limited, Inc.*

Pulling It Together

We have covered a number of key concepts in chapters 5 through 14. Here we consider some cases that bring in legal issues from more than one area for you to identify.

Part 2 of the text reviewed the major areas of the common law that affect business. There is some statutory law in the chapters we covered, but most of the cases tended to reflect the way business practices were viewed, rather than being highly regulatory. Here, we consider cases that overlap more than one area that we covered and those that may raise issues going back to Part 1 of the text.

1. Two Men and a Truck (TMT) is a Michigan company that sells moving service franchises around the country. Mayes bought a TMT franchise in Indiana that operated under the TMT name. TMT sued Mayes for failure to pay royalties and advertising fees and for failure to file monthly sales reports for the franchise. TMT also terminated the franchise relationship, but Mayes continued to operate the franchise under the TMT name.

   Where would the suit be likely to be filed? What causes of action might TMT have against Mayes? Having read the material about franchises, take a guess what Mayes's likely defense may be with respect to the purchase of the franchises. List the possible actions TMT might file.

2. Miller was eating a Big Mac at a McDonald's franchise restaurant in Oregon, when she bit into a sapphire stone and injured her teeth. She sued. Where could she file suit? Who would she sue? What would she sue them for? What defenses do you think may be relevant?

3. The Center for Behavioral Health rented a building for six years from Priskos. One day a water pipe burst, flooding much of the building. The Center hired Advanced Restoration to do repair work, and the bill was $9,300. Priskos was aware the work was being done but did not participate. The Center's insurer said it was not responsible for paying for such damage to the building. The Center gave the bill to Priskos, who contacted his insurance company. It paid the bill minus a $1,000 deductible. Priskos offered the $8,300 check to Advanced for the work as payment in full. Advanced filed a mechanics' lien for the full amount. Priskos demanded a lien waiver from Advanced in exchange for the $8,300 as payment in full. Advanced sued Priskos and the Center for payment in full. Where would suit be filed? Did the tenant (the Center) have the right to have the work done and then expect the landlord to pay the bill, or is the tenant liable, because it called Advanced to do the work? Was the tenant an agent authorized to call Advanced and thereby commit the principal, the landlord, to the contract? What kind of an agent would the Center be for Priskos, if there was an agency relationship?

4. Barry and Sandra Erlich hired Menezes to build their dream house on an ocean-view lot in California. They moved into the house in December 1990. Two months later, in the rainy season, "the house leaked from every conceivable location." Walls were so saturated that the plaster fell off, most windows leaked, and there was three inches of water in the living room. Despite various repair efforts by Menezes, water continued to leak in all parts of the house. Another contractor and an engineer found serious defects in the roof, walls, windows, and waterproofing, as well as structural problems with the walls, roof, and foundation. The Erlichs sued Menezes and testified that the problems with their house made them sick. Barry Erlich said that the distress worsened his heart condition, forcing him to resign from his job. Sandra was afraid the house might collapse on the family, especially in an earthquake. Their suit sought recovery on several theories, including breach of contract, fraud, negligent misrepresentation, negligent construction, emotional distress, and pain and suffering. Which of their tort and contract claims would seem most likely to stand?

5. Landham played the role of Billy, the Native American Tracker, in the 1987 Fox film called *Predator* starring Arnold Schwarzenegger. In 1995, Fox licensed to Galoob Toys the right to produce and market a line of its "Micro Machine" toys based on *Predator*. One of three sets of toys contained a "Billy" action figure. It is 1.5 inches tall and bears no personal resemblance to Landham. Landham sued Galoob and

Fox for false endorsement under the Landham Act and for violating his right of publicity (a part of the right to privacy). The district court dismissed the suit. Landham appealed. Does he have a suit in tort for the violation of his right of publicity and/or a suit for trademark infringement?

6. Barber erected a sign on his property facing Interstate 20 in west Texas. The sign said "Just Say NO to Searches" and gave a phone number. Callers received information about a citizen's constitutional rights regarding police searches of automobiles. The Texas Department of Transportation sent Barber a letter telling him that the sign violated the Highway Beautification Act and that he must remove the sign or obtain a permit from the Department to have a sign that complies with Department regulations. The trial court ordered Barber to remove the sign and to pay the Department's attorney's fees. He appealed.

7. Gateway 2000 sells computers and related products by mail, Internet, and telephone. With each PC, Gateway sent a "Standard Terms and Conditions Agreement" including a "Dispute Resolution" clause, stating that any dispute would be settled by arbitration under the rules of the International Chamber of Commerce (ICC) in Chicago. Several buyers of computers and software from Gateway sued for breach of contract and breach of warranty, contending the company falsely stated that technical support for products was available when in fact, the plaintiffs claimed, it was almost impossible to get technical support by phone. The trial court dismissed the suit, holding that the parties had to go to arbitration. The plaintiffs appealed, contending that the arbitration clause violated UCC §2–302 as an unconscionable contract, because ICC rules require payment of a $4,000 advance fee when a claim is filed, of which $2,000 is nonrefundable regardless of outcome, and each plaintiff would have to bear the cost of travel to Chicago. These expenses are greater than the value of most of the products purchased. Is the arbitration clause valid under the UCC?

8. The Maretts owned Marett Properties, LLC. They hired Brice Building to work on two commercial real estate buildings that they intended to lease. The Maretts signed guaranties agreeing to be personally liable for Marett Properties' debt tio Brice, but the construction contracts were never signed. After some time, Brice had been paid nothing for the $337,800 worth of work he had completed. The two properties were not leased and were unfinished. Because there was no completed contract, Brice sued the Maretts in quantum meruit, an equity claim, and also to enforce their personal guaranty. The Maretts defended that there was a failure to complete a contract and that without a contract, the guaranty was not valid. Would Brice win the case?

9. Three accountants formed a partnership. Deodati was a client of McCreight, one of the partners. Deodati authorized McCreight to buy and sell certificates of deposit on his behalf. McCreight stole Deodati's money, generating fictitious income statements to conceal the fraud. The other partners knew nothing about the fraud. Deodati paid the partnetship $3,500 for accounting services. When another partner uncovered the fraud, he notified Deodati, who sued the partnership for his losses. The trial court awarded Deodati $290,000 and imposed joint and several liablility against the partnership and the individual partners. The innocent partners then filed for backruptcy. Deodati sought to prevent them from discharging the debt, because it arose from fraud. The trial court held for the innocent partners. Deodati appcaled. Are the innocent partners liable?

10. Elliott contracted with the Army to install a freezer at Fort Bliss, Texas. The contract required Elliot to install the freezer and provided that Elliott was "fully responsible for the actions of all employees and contracted representatives" and that Elliott would indemnify the Army for damages "and injury to person or property proximately caused by action or inaction attributable" to Elliott. Elliott subcontracted with Lingle to install the unit, which was done. Later, the Army hired IAS to do some construction work. When IAS employee Diaz was installing a sink, a panel from the Elliott freezer, installed by Lingle, fell and injured Diaz, who sued Elliott for negligence. The trail court dismissed the suit, but the appeals court reversed; Elliott petitioned the Texas high court for review. What controls here—contract law, tort law, or agency law?

Getty Images

PART 3: The Regulatory Environment of Business

OVERVIEW

Decades ago, business was almost entirely governed by private relationships based upon common-law principles. Now the legal environment is much more complex. Federal regulation has expanded, often in bursts, over the past century. Regulation is now so common that businesses actively participate in the political process that determines the extent of regulations and how they are enforced.

Why did these laws come about? A century ago, there was concern about the monopoly power of large corporations. After much political agitation, antitrust laws were passed. During the Great Depression, workers believed that they were denied the right to band together to promote their interests. Labor's political influence grew, and the National Labor Relations Act emerged. The 1960s saw social problems, such as race discrimination, that were not being resolved. The civil rights movement helped to promote the attitude that limits on discrimination must be put into place. Pollution became a major issue in the early 1970s, when most of the environmental statutes emerged. Today, as international trade expands, businesses must manage complexities in the law that were not imagined in times past.

Getty Images

Chapter 15: *The Regulatory Process* Regulatory agencies grow ever more important as a source of substantive law. Legislatures grant agencies the power to make and enforce laws. The processes that agencies and parties responding to them must follow are considered.

Chapter 16: *Employment Law and Labor Relations* Major laws regarding labor unions were passed in the 1930s and have been important since then. Over time, other statutes—such as substance abuse controls, workplace safety, and family leave policies—have come to change traditional employment relationships.

Chapter 17: *Employment Discrimination* Specific legal protections for person—based on race, sex, religion, national origin, age, and disability—were first passed in the 1960s. This now constitutes a major legal consideration for business managers.

Chapter 18: *Environmental Law* Before the 1970s, there were common-law restraints on abuse of air, water, and land. Passage of major environmental statutes has resulted in pervasive regulation of most parts of the environment, and, recently, global environmental issues have come to be of concern to many business operations.

Chapter 19: *Consumer Protection* Food and drug regulations were the first major area of federal consumer safety protection to develop. Over the years, the Federal Trade Commission and other agencies have been given expanded control over other areas of consumer concern, including consumer credit.

Chapter 20: *Antitrust Law* Federal antitrust law is over a century old. First established to burst the big trusts that dominated some areas of industry, antitrust law has evolved under Supreme Court direction to limit price fixing, market sharing, boycotts, and other business practices believed harmful to competition and consumers.

Chapter 21: *Securities Regulation* Federal supervision of the securities markets began in the 1930s. Trillions of dollars of wealth are held in securities, and billions of dollars in securities are traded daily on securities markets. The markets and the professionals who work in the securities industry are subject to federal oversight.

Chapter 22: *The International Legal Environment of Business* The globalization of business means that managers face an ever-greater range of legal issues. This chapter focuses on domestic controls on international trade and on some of the major international legal rules that often come into play in international business.

The Regulatory Process

Getty Images

Chapter 15

The Kopczynski family has run a construction company in Washington for many years. Chris, now the head of the company, deals with a more complex set of regulations than his father faced decades ago. Safety and environmental inspectors from assorted federal and state agencies are likely to show up at building sites at any time. Permits may be required from the Army Corps of Engineers and the Soil Conservation Service, among others. Local zoning rules and construction codes must be followed. The state requires the company to pay workers' compensation and unemployment insurance taxes and to file numerous regular and special reports. The IRS requires tax filings on all employees and documentation of work eligibility for every employee. Special labor regulations must be followed on all projects involving government money. Such rules add greatly to the cost and complexity of operations.

Administrative agencies have a huge impact on the legal environment of all businesses. Regulations concerning worker safety, discrimination, pollution, and many other activities have expanded significantly in recent decades. Some regulations, such as those on transportation, have been reduced, but others arise to deal with new enterprises, such as online businesses. Managers must stay abreast of regulatory developments in their areas if business.

Before we begin to look at major areas of business regulation, this chapter reviews the development of administrative agencies. It then considers the powers delegated to the agencies by Congress, including their legislative, investigative, adjudicatory, and enforcement powers. The last part of the chapter turns to the concept of *judicial review*, which is the power of the judicial branch of government to review agencies' actions or decisions. ∎

Administrative Agencies

Administrative agencies are a major part of government. They are the primary tool through which local, state, and federal governments perform regulatory functions. In the words of the Supreme Court in *F.T.C. v. Ruberoid Company* (1952):

> The rise of administration bodies probably has been the most significant legal trend of the last century and perhaps more values today are affected by their decisions than by those of all the courts.... They have become a veritable fourth branch of the government....

The first federal agency was the Interstate Commerce Commission (ICC), created in 1887 to regulate railroads. Early in the 1900s, the Federal Trade Commission (FTC), which handles antitrust cases, and the Food and Drug Administration (FDA) were created. During the Great Depression in the 1930s, many agencies were created, such as the Securities and Exchange Commission (SEC) and the Federal Communications Commission (FCC). In the late 1960s and early 1970s, a number of agencies were created, including the Environmental Protection Agency (EPA) and the Equal Employment Opportunity Commission (EEOC). Today, more than 50 independent agencies and the 14 cabinet departments issue tens of thousands of pages of regulations each year. Exhibit 15.1 is a list of a few agencies and their Web site addresses. Almost all agencies can be easily found on the Web.

Creating an Administrative Agency

An *administrative agency* is an authority of the government, other than a legislature or a court, created to administer a particular law. Congress gives an agency power and authority through a *legislative delegation*. It delegates to an agency the power to perform its regulatory purpose, which is to formulate, implement, and enforce policy relevant to its area of authority. A statute delegating those powers to the agency is an *enabling statute*.

Why Create an Agency?

Administrative agencies are created when a problem requires expertise and supervision. By 1970, for example, Congress decided the federal government should address the issue of air quality. But as an institution, Congress has neither the time nor the expertise to determine how the law might be applied to thousands of different sources emitting air pollutants. Congress also lacks the ability to handle law enforcement and compliance directly. Hence, when Congress passed the Clean Air Act, it delegated primary responsibility to the Environmental Protection Agency

Commodity Futures Trading Commission (CFTC); *http://www.cftc.gov*

Consumer Product Safety Commission (CPSC); *http://www.cpsc.gov*

Department of Commerce (DoC); *http://www.doc.gov*

Department of Labor (DoL); *http://www.dol.gov*

Equal Employment Opportunity Commission (EEOC); *http://www.eeoc.gov*

Food and Drug Administration (FDA); *http://www.fda.gov*

Federal Trade Commission (FTC); *http://www.ftc.gov*

Health and Human Services (HHS); *http://www.hhs.gov*

Occupational Safety and Health Administration (OSHA); *http://www.osha.gov*

Securities and Exchange Commission (SEC); *http://www.sec.gov*

Exhibit 15.1
Selected Federal Administrative Agencies and Web Sites

(EPA). The EPA has the legislative, investigative, adjudicatory, and enforcement powers to accomplish the task. The EPA can consider technical details more effectively than can Congress and can continuously monitor industry. Congress closely monitors the EPA, and all other agencies, and can change how those agencies operate if it is not satisfied with the results.

LIGHTER SIDE OF THE LAW
Give Us All Your Imported Goods So We Can "Protect" Consumers

Jenny Wang owns six small grocery stores in Beijing. Every year she must take one of each imported food product she sells to the Bureau of Quality and Technical Supervision. A box of Kellogg's Froot Loops goes in with a slice of Danish blue cheese. The couple thousand goods are worth over $1,000. The Bureau keeps it all.

The goods all passed customs and quarantine, but the government still demands that every small entrepreneur comply with this regulation, which is clearly designed to drive up the cost of buying imported goods, as no such "safety inspection" is imposed on goods produced in the country.

Source: *Wall Street Journal*

Getty Images

Administrative Law

Administrative law consists of legal rules that define the authority and structure of administrative agencies. The primary sources of *administrative law* include:

1. The enabling statutes of administrative agencies
2. The Administrative Procedures Act
3. Rules issued by administrative agencies
4. Court decisions reviewing the validity of agency actions

The primary structure of administrative law is determined by the *Administrative Procedures Act (APA)*. Enacted by Congress in 1946, the APA defines the *procedural rules* and formalities for federal agencies. An agency must abide by APA requirements, unless Congress specifically imposes different requirements on the agency.

Congress has authority under the commerce clause and the necessary and proper clause in the Constitution to create regulatory agencies and give them powers to enact rules. Agencies are also granted authority to investigate violations of rules the agency creates and to prosecute violators. Although specific powers differ from agency to agency, we can generalize a "typical" administrative agency. A summary of agency regulatory powers is provided in Exhibit 15.2.

Rule Making

Most agencies are authorized to engage in *rule making*. By this process, an agency develops administrative rules and regulatory policy. Agencies use their own terminologies. The Treasury Department, for example, calls its rules *decisions;* other agencies refer to their rules as *standards, guidelines, regulations,* or *opinions.*

Regulartory Power	Definition	Advantages of Agencies
Legislative or Rulemaking Power	Develop rules to implement the agency's regulatory policies	Uses experts to consider technical details
Investigative Power	Obtain needed information to ensure that the statute and agency rules are observed	Can monitor regulated industries continuously, whether or not there has been a violation
Adjudicatory Power	Resolve disputes and violations through a judicial type of proceeding	Can bring actions quickly and enjoy flexibility and informality in their procedures
Enforcement Power	Impose sanctions to encourage compliance with statutes, an agency's rules, and an agency's adjudicatory outcomes	Flexibility to impose sanctions such as fines, prohibitions, restrictions on licenses, and threat of public exposure

Exhibit 15.2
Administrative Agencies:
Summary of Regulatory
Powers

Types of Rules

The Administrative Procedures Act defines an agency rule as

> The whole or part of an agency statement of general or particular applicability and future effect designed to implement, interpret, or prescribe law or policy describing the organization, procedure, or practice requirements of an agency.

In general, administrative rules are classified as substantive (legislative), interpretative, or procedural.

Substantive or Legislative Rules

Substantive or *legislative rules* are administrative laws with the same force of law as statutes enacted by Congress; that is, when an agency issues a substantive rule or regulation, under its grant of authority by Congress, the rule is federal law. Contrary to popular misunderstanding, regulations are not a "lower form" of law than the laws written directly by Congress. Before issuing such rules, an agency is generally required by the APA to provide public notice and the opportunity for interested parties to comment in writing for the public record.

Interpretative Rules

Interpretative rules are statements issued by an agency to provide its staff and the public with guidance regarding the interpretation of a substantive rule or a congressional statute. Interpretative rules range from informal policy statements to authoritative rulings that are binding on the agency.

In contrast to legislative rules, interpretative rules are exempt from the notice and comment requirements of the APA. As a consequence, an agency may issue interpretative rules without inviting input from interested parties. However, parties affected by rules may challenge an agency's interpretative rule by arguing that it is really a legislative rule. If the challenge is successful, the agency must go through a more complex process to adopt the rule.

While some disputes about regulations are at the national level, many are at the state level, where the same procedures are in place, as we see in the *Association of Washington Business* case.

Association of Washington Business v. State of Washington, Department of Revenue
Supreme Court of Washington
120 P.3d 46 (2005)

Case Background *The Association of Washington Business (AWB) sued the state Department of Revenue (DOR) for publishing interpretive regulations concerning how it would handle certain tax matters under the state tax code. The AWB contented that DOR did not have authority to issue such regulations. The trial court agreed and ordered DOR to not adopt the interpretive rules. The court of appeals reversed in favor of DOR. AWB appealed.*

Case Decision Sanders, Justice

* * *

The party challenging a rule has the burden to prove it is invalid. This court may declare an agency rule invalid if it: (1) violates constitutional provisions, (2) exceeds statutory authority of the agency, (3) was adopted without compliance to statutory rule-making procedures, or (4) is arbitrary and capricious. Determining the extent of DOR's rule-making authority is a question of law which is reviewed de novo. AWB only alleges the rules exceed DOR's statutory authority.

Administrative agencies have those powers expressly granted to them and those necessarily implied from their statutory delegation of authority. DOR argues it has both express and implied authority to adopt interpretive rules, citing various statutes to support its position....

Legislative rules must be consistent with the statutes DOR is charged with administering and have the "same force and effect" as the statutes themselves. Such rules clearly cannot be merely interpretive, which by definition means nonbinding in the sense that violating the rule does *not* result in sanctions. [A state statute] *expressly* authorizes ... legislative rules....

One [state] statute ... grants agencies the authority to adopt interpretive statements, which are advisory only. The statute says, "To better inform and involve the public, an agency is encouraged to convert long-standing interpretive and policy statements into rules." Further, the statute allows a person to petition the agency to turn interpretive statements into rules. Clearly, the legislature intended agencies to adopt interpretive rules, or they simply could not comply with this statute....

Legislative rules ... have greater finality than interpretive rules, because courts are bound to give some deference to agency judgments embodied in the former, but they need not defer to agency judgments embodied in the latter....

Technically, interpretive rules are not binding on the public. They serve merely as advance notice of the agency's position should a dispute arise and the matter result in litigation. The public cannot be penalized or sanctioned for breaking them. They are not binding on the courts and are afforded no deference other than the power of persuasion. Accuracy and logic are the only clout interpretive rules wield. If the public violates an interpretive rule that accurately reflects the underlying statute, the public may be sanctioned and punished, not by authority of the rule, but by *authority of the statute*. This is the nature of interpretive rules....

Affirmed.

Questions for Analysis

1. The Washington high court held that state agencies have the right to issue nonbinding interpretive rules. If the rules are nonbinding, unlike legislative rules, what is their purpose?

2. Why do you suppose the AWB, a group representing business interests, would oppose interpretive rules?

Procedural Rules

Procedural rules detail an agency's structure and describe its method of operation and its internal practices. The power to enact such rules is authorized by the agency's enabling statute. Once procedural rules are issued, the agency is bound by them. A challenge to an agency decision is usually upheld if the challenging party can show that the agency did not comply with its own procedural rules in reaching a decision.

Rulemaking Procedure

Substantive rules are usually the most important. An agency lays out the requirements of how a statute is to be applied in practice and what regulations will have to be followed. Proposed rules are drafted by agency staff, reviewed internally, and approved by the head of the agency.

After the rule is approved and published in the *Federal Register* for public inspection, interested parties may submit written comments about the rule. The public comment period is usually 60 to 90 days, after which the agency reviews the comments and finalizes the rule. Most comments are contributed by trade associations and other professional organizations that assist members of an affected industry. These comments, which tend to be technical, are important, because they form the basis of most legal challenges to rules. Submitting the comments is proof that the agency was on notice of alleged defects in a rule.

Some statutes require that rule making must be "on the record." In these cases, statute requires an agency to hold hearings, at which witnesses appear to testify about the proposed rule. This is done for only a small fraction of all rules issued. In any case, once the agency issues the final rule, it may be appealed to the agency itself, after which appeal is made to the U.S. Court of Appeals. The appeals court ensures that the agency has not exceeded its authority or violated proper procedure, as we see in the *Harvey* case.

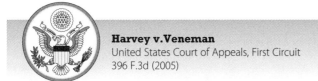

Harvey v. Veneman
United States Court of Appeals, First Circuit
396 F.3d (2005)

Case Background *Congress passed the Organic Foods Production Act (OFPA) in 1990 to "establish national standards governing the marketing" of organically produced agricultural products to "assure consumers that organically produced products meet a consistent standard." It establishes a national certification program. The U.S. Department of Agriculture (USDA) was given authority to issue regulations to make the law effective. The National Organic Program Final Rule became effective in 2002 and was challenged by Harvey, a producer of organic crops. He contended that some provisions of the organic foods regulations were inconsistent with the OFPA. The district court dismissed his suit. He appealed.*

Case Decision Schwarzer, Senior District Judge

* * *

Harvey ... challenges two parts of the Rule permitting synthetic substances to be used in processed organic foods. [One part] provides that synthetic substances may be used "as a processing aid or adjuvant" if they meet six criteria; [another part] lists 38 synthetic substances specifically allowed in or on processed products labeled as organic. These provisions,

Harvey contends, contravene the plain language of OFPA, which provides that certified handling operations "shall not, with respect to any agricultural product covered by this title ... add any synthetic ingredient during the processing or any postharvest handling of this product." Harvey is correct; the challenged regulations lie outside of the scope of authority granted the Secretary by OFPA....

The challenged regulations are contrary to the plain language of OFPA and therefore exceed the Secretary's statutory authority. We therefore reverse the District Court's grant of summary judgment to the Secretary on this count. [The case also had challenges to other parts of the Rule—some were upheld as proper, others were stricken.]

Questions for Analysis

1. The appeals court struck part of the substantive rule issued by USDA as in conflict with the statute passed by Congress and, therefore, invalid. What does USDA do next?

2. Why would an agency write a regulation inconsistent with a statute?

Enforcing Rules

The main job of most agencies is to enforce laws written by Congress or by the agencies under the authority granted them by Congress. Enforcement means that agencies must gather information and investigate. Agencies have various ways of doing this. While this chapter focuses on agency actions, many regulatory statutes give private parties the right to sue for violations of the law. In the following chapters, we will see many examples of such litigation.

Investigative Powers

Information about compliance with federal laws is obtained in three basic ways:

1. Regulated businesses are required to self-report.
2. Direct observation determines if a business is following the law.
3. Agency subpoena power is used to require a business to produce documents.

Monitoring and Self-Reporting Requirements

Agencies may require businesses to monitor their own behavior. Those subject to a regulation can be required to report certain information to an agency at set times, such as monthly, or when certain events—often a violation—occur. The Clean Air Act, for example, requires businesses to monitor air pollution emissions and report the data to the Environmental Protection Agency:

> The Administrator may require any person who owns or operates any emission source ... to A) establish and maintain such records, B) make such reports, C) install, use, and maintain such monitoring equipment or methods, D) sample such emissions, and E) provide such other information as the Administrator may reasonably require....

Reporting information on violations can lead to punishment. If, for example, the information reported shows that a firm has emitted too much pollution, the EPA can impose a fine. Businesses have contested fines resulting from mandatory *self-reporting* of violations, arguing that the reporting of self-incriminating evidence violates the Fifth Amendment. However, as pointed out in Chapter 4, the Supreme Court has ruled that the self-incrimination privilege of the Fifth Amendment does not provide strong protection for corporations. Failing to report violations or reporting false information almost always leads to heavier penalties than when a party volunteers violations.

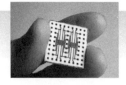

CYBER LAW

Do Old Regulations Apply to New Forms of Competition?

The growth of Internet-related technology raises tricky issues for regulators. If a new form of technology competes with existing regulated firms, and the new technology is not covered in the regulations that govern existing competitors, are the new competitors covered?

Bandwidth expansion allows Internet telephony and video, new forms of communication not covered by existing regulations. Existing firms want new competitors to be subject to rules so that they cannot expand so quickly.

Even if the regulators agree with existing competitors, the way the laws were written, and the regulations that implement the statutes, they did not envision the new inventions.

In many cases, if regulation is to be maintained, Congress will have to act. Such actions—as in the case of the Communications Decency Act of 1996, which was unanimously struck down by the Supreme Court as unconstitutional—indicate that Congress must not act too hastily lest it be defeated in its intent to control a new medium.

Getty Images

Direct Observation by Agencies

Agencies also acquire information by *direct observation.* Examples include on-the-spot worksite safety inspections by OSHA inspectors and testing by the EPA for excessive air pollution emissions. As discussed in Chapter 4, the Supreme Court has imposed limits on warrantless searches by administrative agencies, but the warrants are simple to obtain. However, no warrant is required if an agency's evidence is obtained from an "open-field" observation, that is, if the evidence is gathered by an inspector through observations from areas where the public has access.

In *Dow Chemical* v. *United States* (476 U.S. 227), the Supreme Court held it was legal for the EPA to fly over a Dow facility and take photographs for evidence of regulatory violations. Since the airspace over the facility was open to the public, there was no improper search in violation of the Fourth Amendment by this method of observation.

Agency Subpoena Power

An agency may also obtain information by issuing a *subpoena,* a legal instrument that directs the person receiving it to appear at a specified time and place to testify or to produce documents. The Clean Air Act provides an example of a congressional authorization of the power to issue subpoenas and the procedure for enforcing them:

> For purposes of obtaining information … the Administrator may issue subpoenas for the attendance and testimony of witnesses and the production of relevant papers, books, and documents, and he may administer oaths.… In case of … refusal to obey a subpoena served upon any person … the district court … shall have jurisdiction to issue an order requiring such person to appear and give testimony before the Administrator … and any failure to obey such an order may be punished by such court as a contempt thereof.

Unless the request for information by the agency is vague, or if the burden imposed on the business outweighs the possible benefits to the agency, a business must comply with the subpoena. If a business asserts that the information requested by a subpoena deserves confidential treatment, an agency usually respects the request, or the business may seek a court order providing such protection.

Enforcement Power

Congress grants agencies many enforcement tools. The EPA, for example, can ensure compliance with air pollution control requirements by seeking civil and criminal penalties and injunctions if necessary.

In addition to having the authority to sue in federal court to seek civil and criminal penalties, agencies have authority to impose other sanctions. Consider the examples offered by the APA in its definition of *sanction:*

1. Prohibition, requirement, limitation, or other condition affecting the freedom of a person
2. Withholding of relief
3. Imposition of a penalty or fine
4. Destruction, taking, seizing, or withholding of property
5. Assessment of damages, reimbursement, restitution, compensation, costs, charges, or fees
6. Requirement, revocation, or suspension of a license
7. Taking other compulsory or restrictive action

Enforcement methods vary among agencies. Most rely on a mix of formal and informal ways to obtain compliance with regulatory requirements. Our discussion focuses on agency procedures, but when an agency brings criminal charges against a party, it works with the Department of Justice (the Attorney General), which usually handles the prosecution of criminal cases that are heard in federal court.

Informal Agency Procedures

Agencies rely heavily on *informal procedures* that allow leeway in forcing compliance. Since informal procedures generally require less time and cost than formal procedures, agencies prefer to use them when possible.

Informal procedures include tests and inspections, processing applications and permits, negotiations, settlements, and advice in the form of advisory opinions. Publicity, or the threat of it, can also be considered an informal procedure for an agency to get industry to comply with its rules.

Various agencies engage in information campaigns to get the message out about some problem area and the possibility of agency assistance; but those affected may not like it, as the *Invention Submission* case illustrates.

Invention Submission v. Rogan
United States Court of Appeals, Fourth Circuit
357 F.3d 452 (2004)

Case Background *Congress passed the Inventors' Rights Act of 1999 to protect inventors from invention promotion scams. The Act authorized the Patent and Trademark Office (PTO) to publicize complaints it receives against promoters who tell inventors to bring their inventions to be marketed on behalf of the inventor—for a fee, of course.*

The PTO began public ads to alert the public to "invention promotion scams." One stated, "Make sure your ideas—and your money—don't wash away. To learn more, call the U.S. Patent and Trademark Office toll free." One had a testimonial from a person named Lewis who spent $13,000 with an invention promoter who produced nothing.

Newspapers interviewed Lewis, who told of his fruitless involvement with Invention Submission Corporation (ISC). It had been sued before passage of the Act by the FTC for "patent-marketing schemes" and had paid a $1.2 million settlement. ISC responded to Lewis's claims by saying it "did nothing wrong" and had not "misled Lewis or any other inventor." It settled with Lewis, and he withdrew his complaint with the PTO.

ISC then sued the PTO, contending that its advertising campaign violated the Administrative Procedure Act (APA) and that the ad campaign improperly singled out the company. The district court granted the PTO's motion to dismiss the suit. ISC appealed.

Case Decision Niemeyer, Circuit Judge

* * *

The Administrative Procedure Act does not provide judicial review for everything done by an administrative agency, and the PTO's advertising campaign, including its conduct in giving a journalist Lewis's telephone number, is not the type of conduct that constitutes agency action that is reviewable in court under the APA. Other than the administrative decision to conduct an advertising campaign at all—a decision that Invention Submission has not challenged—the content of the campaign was not the consummation of any decision-making process that determined rights or obligations or from which legal consequences flowed. Moreover, by looking at the campaign material, the public would see only that a consumer complained about an invention promoter and that invention promotion scams are causing the public $200 million in losses every year. Surely Invention Submission would not suggest that the attribution in the advertisements of $200 million in losses to patent scams was in any respect focusing the public's eye on it. The text of the advertising material can only be construed to be an effort by the PTO to inform inventors of the perils and potential scams that they might encounter during the patent process. Such advertising did not create "legal consequences" for Invention Submission or any other member of the public cognizable as final agency action, and the campaign itself did not determine any right or obligation of any party....

In short, the PTO's advertising campaign warning the public about invention promotion scams was consistent with the PTO's commission granted by the Inventors' Rights Act of 1999, and in the circumstances of this case, the decision to pursue such a campaign, as well as its content, did not create a final agency action that is reviewable in court. As we said in [an earlier case], this type of a campaign is "properly challenged through the political process and not the courts."

Because the conduct of the PTO that is the subject of this action did not constitute "final agency action" as used under the APA, the district court did not have subject matter jurisdiction to evaluate the complaint.... We therefore vacate its order ... as well as the supporting opinion, and remand with instructions to dismiss this case....

Questions for Analysis

1. The appeals court held that the courts do not have jurisdiction to review matters such as advertising campaigns by agencies that highlight legal issues. Why did it instruct the district court to vacate its order?

2. Why does the court say this belongs in the political arena and not the courts?

In some cases, agencies may act on the spot. For example, an OSHA inspector, upon finding a situation that endangers workers, may order immediate changes. Many such incidents are handled this way, rather than involving formal procedures. Similarly, manufacturers "voluntarily" withdraw products from the shelves and destroy them, when a problem is discovered that would likely result in formal action by an agency.

Review of Informal Procedure Decisions A business unhappy with an agency sanction resulting from informal procedures may seek review. The decision is first reviewed by the agency head. If dissatisfied with the agency's final decision, parties may seek review by the federal court. In reviewing agency procedures, the courts are generally most concerned with whether the agency procedure was fair and whether the decision was consistent with the legislative intent of Congress.

Formal Agency Procedures

Among the *formal procedures* used by most regulatory agencies are quasi-judicial powers, especially adjudicatory hearings. How hearings are conducted is dictated by the APA. In some instances, an agency's enabling statute may require procedures that differ somewhat from those provided by the APA.

Adjudicatory Hearings An *adjudicatory hearing* is a formal agency process under APA rules, which are similar to those followed in a trial. As Exhibit 15.3 illustrates, an adjudicatory hearing is initiated by the agency filing a complaint. The business must respond to the complaint that alleges violation of the law enforced by the agency. If the matter is not settled by negotiation, a hearing may be necessary.

ISSUE SPOTTER
Contest a Regulatory Order?

The Department of Labor contends that your firm has not been counting overtime work by employees properly. Labor demands the firm pay some back wages to employees to correct the calculation, pay a $1,000 fine, and promise not to violate the law concerning overtime work again. The matter can be settled quietly by accepting the Labor offer. One senior manager thinks Labor is wrong, and the matter should be contested. He suggests not only contesting the finding of Labor in this particular case, but contesting the validity of the regulation enforcing the overtime provisions of the Fair Labor Standards Act as written by the Department of Labor.

Would it make sense to contest Labor's administrative decision? What are the pros and cons of a challenge?

Getty Images

Exhibit 15.3
Formal Agency Procedure:
Adjudicatory Hearing

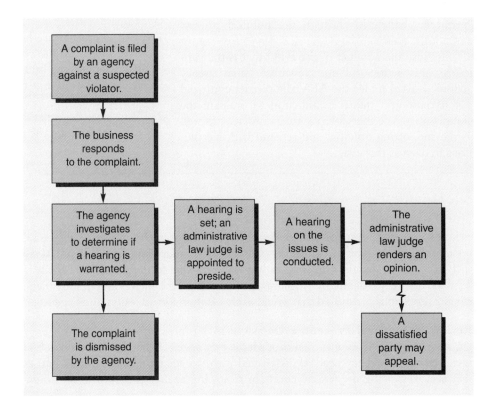

An *administrative law judge (ALJ)* from the agency presides over the hearing. The ALJ is a civil service employee of the agency, usually a staff attorney. The agency is represented by its counsel, who presents the agency's evidence in support of the complaint; the business presents its evidence. Witnesses may be cross examined, but the procedure is less formal than a court trial. The hearing must meet the due process guarantees of the Constitution, but there is no right to a jury trial, because these are not criminal or common-law causes.

After a hearing, the ALJ issues a written decision. If the business does not object to the decision, the agency normally adopts it. If the business is dissatisfied with the ALJ's decision and seeks review, the agency head (commissioners or administrator) reviews the decision. If the business is dissatisfied after this final agency review, it may then proceed to the federal courts for further review.

Judicial Review

The APA sets the procedural requirements for a party seeking court of appeals review of an agency decision. Most appeals concern the legitimacy of regulations and whether a penalty issued by an agency for a violation was justified. That appeal is referred to as *judicial review*, an external check on agency power. This ensures that agencies follow required procedures, do not go beyond the authority granted them by Congress, can justify their actions, and respect constitutional rights.

When Judicial Review Can Occur

Before a court accepts an appeal to review an agency's action, the party making the request must satisfy procedural requirements. Without such requirements, the

Getty Images

INTERNATIONAL PERSPECTIVE

Administrative Agencies in Japan

One of the most worrisome areas of Japanese legal culture for foreign companies is the body of administrative "law" known as "administrative guidance" (*gyosei shido*). This includes all procedural tools Japanese agencies can use to exert regulatory authority over businesses. An administrative agency, for example, may issue guidance by direction (*shiji*), request (*yobo*), warning (*keikoku*), encouragement (*kansho*), or suggestion (*kankoku*).

The power basis of administrative guidance is in the government's control of foreign trade. In theory, businesses are not forced to comply with guidance. But a business that ignores a suggestion might find that its quota of imported materials has been reduced, that it is being denied government financing for expansion, or that some other sanction is imposed.

The Foreign Exchange Control and Foreign Investment Acts, for example, require that any agreement involving expenditures abroad must be approved by the Foreign Investment Council. A business that has not complied with an agency's request that a pollution control device be installed might find that a contract requiring expenditures abroad has not been approved.

The Japanese judiciary has taken a hands-off policy toward administrative guidance. As long as the agency action is within its discretion, the action will not be reviewed unfavorably, even if it is abusive. This gives Japanese administrative agencies considerably more power than U.S. agencies.

---

courts could intrude into areas of agency responsibility, and they would be flooded with more cases. The most important of these procedural requirements are summarized in Exhibit 15.4.

Jurisdiction

As in any lawsuit, the party challenging an agency action must select a court that has authority to hear the case. Most regulatory statutes declare which court has *jurisdiction* to review agency actions. Suppose, for example, that the EPA enacts a new regulation. The Clean Air Act states the following:

> A petition for review of an action of the Administrator in promulgating any national ambient air quality standard ... may be filed only in the United States Court of Appeals for the District of Columbia.

Exhibit 15.4
Judicial Review of Agency Actions: Procedural Requirements

Procedural Requirement	Definition
Jurisdiction	The complaining party may seek judicial review only in courts that have power to hear the case. Most statutes specify which courts have jurisdiction to hear appeals of agency actions.
Reviewability	An appellate court has the ability to reconsider an agency decision to determine whether correction or modification is needed.
Standing	A party seeking judicial review must demonstrate that it incurred an injury recognized by law as a result of the agency's action.
Ripeness	There can be no judicial review until the agency's decision is final so that the court will have the final issues in the case before it and not hypothetical questions or unresolved disputes.
Exhaustion	This is a "gatekeeping" device, requiring that a party seeking judicial review must have sought relief through all possible agency appeal processes before seeking review by the courts.

Reviewability

An agency action that is challenged must be *reviewable* by the courts. Administrative agencies must follow required procedure rules or risk being found by the reviewing courts to have acted arbitrarily. Further, agencies may not exceed their regulatory objectives or risk being found to have violated the duties they were assigned by Congress. For these reasons, the APA authorizes the courts to review most agency actions. However, judicial review is not available if judicial review is prohibited by statute or the agency action is committed to agency discretion.

Review Prohibited by Statute Just as Congress may specify in a statute which court has jurisdiction for judicial review, it can prohibit certain judicial review. Consider, for example, the following statutory provision regarding the authority of the Secretary of Veteran Affairs:

> The decisions of the Secretary on any question of law or fact under any law administered by the Department of Veterans Affairs providing benefits for veterans and their dependents or survivors shall be final, and no other official or any court of the United States shall have the power or jurisdiction to review any decision.

LIGHTER SIDE OF THE LAW
Regulators Protecting Consumers?

Like most countries, Japan has regulations claimed to protect consumers that appear to do the opposite.

Japan's antitrust "watchdog," the Fair Trade Commission, does not allow retailers to give discounts below the listed price on CDs, books, or magazines. Discount coupons may not be issued, because they might "confuse" consumers. One Japanese retailer tried to import small, plastic food containers from Thailand. The customs agency required every carton to be opened and the containers and their lids tested to make sure they worked. Now the company buys containers made in Japan. They do not have to be tested; and they cost consumers three to four times as much as the "untrustworthy" imports.

Source: *The Wall Street Journal*

Getty Images

Thus, a party may not seek review of an administrative decision from the Department of Veteran Affairs in court. Congress can include such an exception in a statute as long as the exception does not violate constitutional rights.

Agency Action Committed to Agency Discretion In addition to statutory exceptions to judicial review, there are also exceptions for actions committed to agency discretion for practical reasons. Some agency actions require speed, flexibility, and secrecy in decision making. For example, decisions affecting national defense and foreign policy have been found to be committed to agency discretion and are therefore nonreviewable. Such agency actions cannot be challenged through the courts.

Standing

A party seeking to challenge an agency action in court must have *standing* to seek judicial review. Section 2 of Article III of the Constitution limits the judicial power to *actual cases or controversies*. Federal courts cannot hear complaints from parties who have no direct stake in a real dispute or who raise only hypothetical questions. Administrative law generally restricts the right of review to parties who can show an injury recognized by law as being entitled to protection.

The U.S. Supreme Court addressed the standing issue in *Lujan* v. *Defenders of Wildlife* (504 U.S. 555). In that case, environmental groups argued that U.S. aid to Egypt to build dams on the Nile River endangered the rare Nile crocodile. Plaintiffs asserted that the agencies providing the aid should comply with the Endangered Species Act. The Court refused to hear the challenge, because the plaintiffs lacked standing—they had suffered no "injury in fact." Concern about crocodiles in Egypt was too remote. Disagreement with an agency's policy is not the same as showing a concrete injury to the complaining party resulting from the policy.

Ripeness

The *ripeness doctrine* concerns whether an agency action is final so as to allow judicial review. That is, agency decisions that are not finalized are not ripe for review, because they could be changed. According to the Supreme Court in *Abbott Labs* v. *Gardner* (387 U.S. 136), the doctrine is designed "to protect agencies from judicial interference until an administrative decision has been formalized and its effects felt in a concrete way by the challenging parties."

Exhaustion

The *exhaustion doctrine* requires a party to complete all agency appeals procedures before turning to a court for review. That is, parties may not go to the courts until they have exhausted all agency review procedures regarding a new rule or a disciplinary action. An action must be considered final by an agency before proceeding to court.

Scope of Judicial Review

When all procedural requirements have been met, the court of appeals can review an agency action. The court's *scope of review* determines how far it can go in examining the action. The scope of review depends on whether the issue before it involves a question of substantive law, statutory interpretation, or procedure. Each imposes different requirements on the reviewing court.

Review of Substantive Determination

A court's review of an agency's substantive determination generally gets the lowest scope of judicial review. As a rule, the courts yield to the agency's judgment in technical and scientific matters in working out the details of regulations. The courts generally will not find that an agency's actions or decisions are *arbitrary, capricious, or an abuse of discretion* if the following are true:

1. The agency has sufficiently explained the facts and its policy concerns.
2. Those facts have some basis in the agency's record.
3. On the basis of those facts and concerns, a reasonable person could reach the same judgments the agency has reached.

We saw an example of a court review of an agency regulation in the *Harvey* case.

Review of Statutory Interpretation

A court's review of an agency's statutory interpretation is given a greater scope of review. In contrast to the technical judgments required of the agency in implementing a statute, the courts have responsibility for the interpretation of the meaning of statutes enacted by Congress; that is, the courts determine whether an agency has gone beyond the authority it was granted by Congress. Although the courts give great weight to the interpretation of a statute by the agency responsible for its implementation, they will reject that interpretation if it does not comply with interpretations by established principles of statutory construction.

Review of Procedural Requirements

The court's review of an agency's procedural requirements is provided the most intense scope of review. The court is responsible for ensuring that the agency has not acted unfairly or in disregard of statutorily prescribed procedures. The courts are regarded as the authority on procedural fair play. The rules of judicial review make clear that the administrative process must be completed, with no further administrative processes available, before turning to the courts. But at that point, the courts usually have control, as the *Bolser Enterprises* case shows.

Bolser Enterprises v. Arizona Registrar of Contractors
Court of Appeals of Arizona, Division 1
139 P.3d 1286 (2006)

Case Background *Bolser, a licensed contractor, built a garage for the Fords. They were unhappy with his work and filed complaints with the Registrar of Contractors (ROC). The ROC sent an inspector, Prince, who issued citations and complaints against Bolser.*

An administrative law judge (ALJ) held a hearing in the Office of Administrative Hearings (OAH). He ruled that Bolser made several construction mistakes. The ROC adopted that decision and ruled that Bolser's license would be revoked unless he corrected the problems. Bolser was also fined $200.

Bolser did repair work and notified ROC. The Fords were supposed to accept or reject the work within 10 days, but waited much longer than that to complain about the repair work. The ROC sent Prince again to look, and he again listed problems with the work. Bolser complained to ROC that the process was not proper, because Prince used to work for Bolser and did not like him. Prince did another inspection, found fault, and the ROC would not hold another hearing and revoked Bolser's contractor license. Bolser sued the ROC and the Fords, contending the administrative process was defective. The trial court held it did not have jurisdiction to review the matter. Bolser appealed.

Case Decision Timmer, Judge

* * *

[Arizona law] requires the ROC to conduct a hearing before revoking or suspending a license or imposing any other penalty for a specified number of acts or omissions committed by a contractor. Such hearings were held before issuance of the [order to repair the garage properly. The law does not require] that a hearing be held before an ROC decision can be considered a final administrative decision. Moreover, we discern no reason for requiring a hearing before an ROC deci-

sion can be subject to *judicial review*. If, as in this case, the ROC refuses a request for a hearing, it could ensure that a decision that otherwise fits the definition set forth in [the statute governing the ROC] would avoid review if we adopt the Fords's argument. We decline to interpret the law in such an unjust manner.

The Fords next argue that the ... disciplinary notice is not a final administrative decision, because the ROC did not place it in the form of an "order," which is described by the ROC's Web site as a signed document stating the ROC's decision, informing the parties if the case is closed or if the contractor has violated relevant statutes, specifying corrective work, and identifying a future effective date. We disagree. The definition of an administrative decision is not confined to orders and can consist of decisions and determinations, as long as they affect contractors' rights, duties, and privileges and terminate proceedings before the ROC....

In summary, we hold that the ROC's ... disciplinary notice revoking Bolser's license constituted a final administrative decision subject to *judicial review*....

For the foregoing reasons, the superior court erred by dismissing Bolser's complaint for lack of subject matter jurisdiction. We therefore reverse and remand for further proceedings consistent with this decision.

Questions for Analysis
1. The appeals court held that the trial court did have jurisdiction to review the determination made by the Registrar of Contractors, because a final determination had been made. Apparently there was no written decision by the ROC to justify revoking the license. Could that be proper procedure?
2. Why were the Fords involved in this matter?

Controls on Agencies

In addition to having checks imposed on them by judicial review, agencies are checked by Congress. Since it delegates powers to an agency, Congress may revoke those powers. This section discusses various measures that Congress uses, or has considered using, in providing those checks.

Direct Controls on Agencies

Public awareness and concern about the costs and effectiveness of regulation, as well as pressure from special interest groups, prompts responses from Congress. The most immediate control mechanism enjoyed by Congress is the ability to control agency activity through the budget process. The president, appointing top agency officials, helps control agency agendas. In addition, members of Congress have proposed bills calling for, among other things, mandatory cost-benefit analysis.

Agency Appropriations and Executive Orders

Administrative agencies depend on public funding to support their activities. Congress requires agencies to report on programs and activities on a regular basis, and congressional committees frequently hold oversight hearings. Administrative agencies submit budget requests annually for review by the president and by Congress. The president or Congress can recommend cuts in an agency's budget if either is opposed to some of the agency's activities. The final budget, which is very detailed, is agreed upon by the House, the Senate, and the president. Through budget appropriations, Congress can mandate that an agency address specific issues. In the *Harvey* case, we saw that Congress ordered a new regulation for organic foods. Congress can also prohibit an agency from working on other specific issues. Budget control gives the president, and especially Congress, the ability to control details of agency regulatory policy.

Presidents have used Executive Orders to instruct administrative agencies to undertake certain tasks. Presidents issue several dozen Executive Orders each year (see http://www.nara.gov/fedreg/eo.html). Many are trivial, but some have major policy implications, such as President Johnson's order that affirmative action programs in hiring are required of all companies that contract with the federal government. Congress can pass legislation to undo an Executive Order, or it may be challenged and stricken by the courts as an abuse of executive power, but it remains a strong tool for the president to allocate agency resources.

Cost-Benefit and Risk Analysis

Mandatory cost-benefit analysis requires agencies to weigh the costs and benefits of new regulations. When the costs exceed the benefits derived from a regulation, the regulation is more easily challenged for reasonableness. The same holds true for risk-assessment requirements that estimate the risk reduction achieved by regulations that affect health and safety.

The Data Quality Act, passed in 2000 and enforced by the Office of Management and Budget (OMB), requires agencies to ensure the quality of the analysis done to support regulations. If scientific, technical, and economic information standards are not met, affected parties may challenge a regulation for not being supported by adequate analysis. OMB, reviewing proposed regulations, can also send a proposed regulation back to an agency for not having met sufficiently strong scientific standards.

Indirect Controls on Agencies

Congress has passed several laws that can have the effect of indirectly controlling the power of administrative agencies. Through those acts, which include the Freedom of Information Act, the Privacy Act, and the Government in the Sunshine Act, Congress made it easier for parties outside an agency to obtain information in the possession of the agency.

Freedom of Information Act

The *Freedom of Information Act (FOIA)* makes most documents held by federal agencies available to the public. Unless the document falls within certain exempted categories, it must be released upon a request by a citizen. Exempted are trade secrets, documents related to national security, and documents that would, if disclosed, invade personal privacy.

Privacy Act

The *Privacy Act* is intended to give citizens more control over what information is collected about them and how that information is used. It requires that unless an exception applies, notice and prior consent are required before an agency can disclose information that concerns and identifies an individual. Individuals are given the right to access agency records and to request amendments to correct inaccuracies. The Act provides that individuals can enforce their rights in federal district courts.

Government in the Sunshine Act

Congress enacted the *Government in the Sunshine Act* to limit secret meetings by agencies. Under the Act, the public is entitled to at least one week's notice of the time, place, and subject matter of any agency meeting. The agency must specify whether the meeting is to be open or closed to the public. An agency action taken at a meeting in violation of the Act is not invalid because of the violation; some other basis for overturning an agency action would have to be established. A court may grant an injunction against future violations of the Act.

The Act lists situations in which meetings may be closed. An open meeting is not required, for example, when the meeting might concern matters to be kept secret in the interest of national defense or when there may be disclosure of trade secrets or protected financial information.

Summary

- Administrative agencies are created by Congress and granted legislative, investigative, adjudicatory, and enforcement powers.
- The first federal agency was the Interstate Commerce Commission, established by Congress in 1887 to regulate railroads. The most significant growth periods of agencies took place during the Great Depression of the 1930s and the "social reform" era of the 1960s and 1970s.
- Administrative law consists of legal rules defining the authority and structure of administrative agencies, specifying procedural requirements, and defining the roles of government bodies, particularly the courts, in their relationship with agencies. The primary administrative law is the Administrative Procedures Act (APA).
- Administrative regulations are classified as legislative (substantive), which are major regulations issued under grants of power from Congress; interpretative, which help to explain legislative regulations and statutes; and procedural, which detail the steps an agency uses in its rule-making procedures and enforcement.

- Agencies may require businesses that are subject to regulation to volunteer information related to the regulations on a regular basis, including reporting violations.
- Agencies may also watch for violations, including inspecting business property, and can gather information that is provided when requested or can force information from a business by use of subpoena.
- Agencies perform regulatory responsibilities by the use of informal and formal procedures. Informal procedures, which consist of tests and inspections, are not subject to the procedural requirements of the APA. Formal procedures, which include adjudicatory hearings, must meet the APA's procedural requirements.
- Agencies may issue fines, citations, or other penalties to rule violators. The violators can accept a penalty or contest it at an agency hearing before an administrative law judge, whose decision can be reviewed by the head of an agency and then by the federal courts of appeals. Criminal charges by an agency must be filed in federal court.
- Judicial review imposes a check on agency actions. To obtain review, the party challenging the action must meet the procedural requirements of jurisdiction, reviewability, standing, ripeness, and exhaustion.
- Congress provides direct and indirect checks on the administrative agencies. The direct checks provided by Congress include control over agency appropriations, reporting requirements, and cost-benefit analysis. Indirect checks include such acts as the Freedom of Information Act, the Privacy Act, and the Government in the Sunshine Act.

Terms to Know

You should be able to define the following terms:

judicial review, 368	interpretative rules, 371	standing, 380
administrative agency, 369	substantive rules, 373	exhaustion, 381
enabling statute, 369	self-reporting, 374	ripeness, 385
procedural rules, 370	adjudicatory hearing, 377	
rulemaking, 371	administrative law judge, 378	

Discussion Question

1. What advantages does an agency have over the judicial system in monitoring business behavior?

Case Questions

1. Dewey owned a mine in Wisconsin. He refused to allow agents of the Department of Labor to inspect the mine without a search warrant. The Department of Labor wanted to determine whether violations discovered in a previous search had been corrected. The Federal Mine Safety and Health Act authorizes a specific number of warrantless inspections, but it does not dictate the procedures that inspectors must follow. Did the warrantless search violate Dewey's Fourth Amendment rights? [*Donovan* v. *Dewey*, 452 U.S. 594, 101 S. Ct. 2534 (1981)]
2. Prison inmates sentenced to die by lethal injection sued the Food and Drug Administration for refusing to take action against the makers and users of the drugs used for lethal

injection. That is, the prisoners claimed that the drugs violated FDA standards and thus should be subject to an enforcement action to prevent violations of FDA rules. The FDA claimed that it did not have to review drugs or undertake enforcement actions that it did not think necessary. The prisoners claimed that the FDA had to hold all drugs to the same standards and that enforcement action had to be taken. Were the prisoners correct? [*Heckler* v. *Chaney*, 470 U.S. 821, 105 S. Ct. 1649 (1985)]

✓ **Check your answer at http://academic.cengage.com/blaw/meiners**

3. OSHA issued a directive establishing a "Cooperative Compliance Program" directed at workplaces with worse-than-average safety records. Companies that "volunteer" to comply with the requirements of the directive will be removed from the primary inspection list and have a much lower chance of inspection. The Chamber of Commerce petitioned for review, contending that OSHA should have published the directive for public comment, as it does for most new rules before they are issued. OSHA contended that the directive was not a rule subject to public comment and inspection before publication. Is that correct? [*Chamber of Commerce* v. *Dept. of Labor*, 174 F.3d 206 D.C. Cir. (1999)]

4. Congress passed a law that would force automakers to deal with the problem of under inflated tires. The law said "the Secretary of Transportation shall complete a rulemaking for a regulation to require a warning system in new motor vehicles to indicate to the operator when a tire is significantly underinflated." The rule the agency wrote said that automakers would be in compliance if they put a low-pressure sensor on any tire on a vehicle, not all four tires. This was contested as improper stating that Congress meant for a sensor to be on every tire. How would you think the courts viewed the rule given the wording of the statute? [*Public Citizen* v. *Mineta*, 340 F.3d 39, 2nd Cir. (2003)]

✓ **Check your answer at http://academic.cengage.com/blaw/meiners**

5. The Sierra Club sued the Secretary of the Interior for allowing the lease of federal land to be used for a ski resort. The secretary studied the issue and decided such use was appropriate. The Club claimed that the change in the use of the land would adversely change the area's aesthetics and ecology. The court of appeals held that the Club did not have standing to sue. Was that correct? [*Sierra Club* v. *Morton*, 405 U.S. 727, 92 S. Ct. 1361 (1972)]

6. A freedom of information request was filed with the Nuclear Regulatory Commission for information about nuclear plant operations that had been provided voluntarily by the plants to the commission on the agreement that the information be kept confidential, even though it did not involve trade secrets. The commission refused to release the information, claiming it would injure its working relationship with the plant operators. Was this a proper reason to refuse the information request? [*Critical Mass Energy Project* v. *Nuclear Regulatory Comm.*, 731 F.2d 554 D.C. Cir. (1990)]

Ethics Questions

1. Most regulatory matters are settled informally; only a small number result in litigation. When a company is in a dispute with a federal agency, it knows that if it does not reach a settlement, there can be costly litigation. From the perspective of the government agency, the litigation is costless—the taxpayers foot the bill. Agencies know that the threat of costly litigation enhances their chance of extracting a settlement from the company. Should the government use this leverage to extract more in a settlement than it knows it would be likely to get in a court-resolved dispute?

2. Suppose you are an administrator at the Environmental Protection Agency. It has been reported that a plant in a small town is in violation of the environmental laws. If you enforce the laws' requirements, the plant will be forced to shut down. The plant is the major source of employment for the town, and its closure would impose severe economic hardships. Should that fact play a role in regulatory enforcement?

Internet Assignment

http://www.access.gpo.gov
http://www.usa.gov
http://www.nass.org/acr/html/internet.html

Federal agencies, and the regulations they impose, often have a significant impact upon industry and commerce. The Internet exercises for other chapters will address agencies, such as the Securities and Exchange Commission, which regulate particular industries. Agencies, pursuant to their Congressional mandates, issue regulations that are proposed and first published in the *Federal Register;* final regulations are incorporated into the *Code of Federal Regulations.* Information about federal agencies is published annually in the *United States Government Manual.* The U.S. Government Printing Office offers an electronic resource, *GPO Access.* Recently the federal government launched *USA.gov,* which includes an A to Z Agency Index. Information exclusively about the administrative law of individual states can be found at the Web site of the National Association of Secretaries of State.

Find the federal agency of your choice using *USA.gov.* Use the *United States Government Manual,* or the agency's Web site, to find which statute created the agency.

Find the URL for the administrative code of the state in which you live, if it is available online.

Getty Images

Employment and Labor Regulations

Chapter 16

Thirty years ago, anyone hired by IBM believed they had a job for life. The company had grown for years and found ways even to care for employees who were not quality performers. But "Big Blue," once the biggest firm in the computer world, was cut down by tough new competitors, and job security went out the window as the company cut back and changed in order to survive in the world of global competition that arose from firms that did not even exist a few years ago.

Like other firms in today's rapidly changing economy, IBM must deal with drug problems, family leave issues, and a generation of workers that understand the lack of job security but are more likely to challenge decisions to fire employees. The strict chain of command that existed in most firms is being changed by a labor market that is more diverse in terms of race, sex, ethnicity, and employee expectations that employers will accept more flexible working arrangements. Changes in the law reflect the changes in society, and managing people is more complex than in the days when most workers had assembly-line jobs that changed slowly.

In this chapter, we look at how statutes passed by legislatures and interpreted by courts have affected the nature of the employment relationship. We look at modern employment law and practice, such as substance abuse policy and other rules imposed on employers. The last part of the chapter looks at labor law, which is the law that mostly concerns labor unions but which also can affect nonunion employees. ■

Public Policy Limits to At-Will Employment

As we saw in Chapter 14, the common law presumes that employers may hire and fire at will, and employees may quit at will. Those two parties to the employment relationship may contract around that presumption by an agreement that limits the ability to dismiss an employee without consequences.

Besides contractual agreements that place limits on the employment relationship, there are public policy exceptions that have arisen over the years. Most of these come from statutes, but some come from the application of common law rules.

Statutory Exceptions

States have statutes that impose *public policy exceptions* to the general rule of at-will discharges. Employers violate public policy if they fire or punish an employee for certain actions. The most common of these are:

- refusing to commit an illegal act, such as falsifying reports required by a government agency or refusing to commit perjury (lie) at trial.
- performing a public duty, such as reporting for jury duty or military service.
- exercising a public right, such as filing a claim for workers' compensation or filing for bankruptcy.

These issues do not arise all that often, but firing workers for filing workers' compensation claims is not uncommon. It rarely results in litigation, because it mostly affects low-wage workers who are not sophisticated about their rights and, even if they did act, the damages are usually small, because another job at about the same wage is usually available.

An exception to the rule that gets a lot of attention, because it has involved some notable cases, is the *whistle-blower* exception. This occurs when an employee reports an employer's illegal act. The general test of when this applies is that the whistle-blowing is primarily for the public good—to help law enforcement or to expose unsafe conditions—rather than for private gain. This exception is more likely to apply to public-sector employees than to private-sector employees. For example, a government employee who was punished for revealing bribes being taken by her supervisors could be due a reward for having taken that action, if her charges are shown to be true.

When a firm dismisses an employee in violation of a public policy exception to the right of at-will discharge, the employee may sue *for wrongful discharge* or *retaliatory discharge*, which are torts. Most courts limit the public policy exceptions to cases in which there is a clear constitutional or statutory basis. That is, the wrongful discharge suits exist because the state wants to enforce and protect certain public goals, such as reporting for jury duty and reporting health violations, not because there is a desire to control the employment relationship.

However, it must be emphasized that these cases are not very common or easy to win. For example, in *Fox* v. *MCI Communications* (931 P.2d 857), the supreme court of Utah held that firing an employee to punish him for reporting alleged violations of the law—slamming long-distance phone accounts—was not in violation of public policy. On the other hand, the Washington supreme court, in *Gardner* v. *Loomis Armored* (913 P.2d 377), held that it violated public policy for an armored car company to fire an employee who, in violation of company policy, abandoned his vehicle to save a person from a life-threatening hostage situation during a bank robbery.

Contracts in Violation of Public Policy

As we saw previously, some contracts are not enforceable, because they violate public policy; that same principle also applies to employment contracts. One part of the employment relationship not looked on with favor by the courts are *exculpatory agreements*. These are clauses in contracts in which one party promises not to sue another in case of an injury caused by a tort or some other event. As we see in the *Brown* case, the Connecticut high court disapproves of these as part of an employment agreement.

Brown v. Soh
Supreme Court of Connecticut
909 A.2d 43 (2006)

Case Background *Brown worked for the Skip Barber Racing School. The school offered advanced driving classes for the public that focused on accident avoidance. Driving took place in a restricted area and everyone, including instructors, signed a liability waiver holding the school harmless for any injuries incurred. The agreement stated: "In consideration of being permitted to … work … [the employee] hereby releases, waives, discharges, and covenants not to sue the promoters, participants … track owners, officials, car owners, drivers … from all liability…. "*

A client, Soh, driving with an instructor in the passenger seat, ran into Brown, who was in a restricted area, waving a flag to signal drivers. Brown sued the school and others involved for his injuries. The trial court granted the school summary judgment because of the liability waiver Brown had signed. He appealed.

Case Decision Borden, Justice

* * *

Exculpatory agreements are "almost universally rejected in the employment context, where exculpatory agreements exempting an employer from all liability for negligence toward his employees are void as against public policy." …

First, we note that workplace safety and compensation for workplace injuries are areas subject to public regulation….

We further note that an employer, in this case the racing school, possesses a decisive advantage of bargaining strength against the plaintiff employee….

It is also highly significant that, in exercising this superior bargaining power, the racing school con-

fronted the plaintiff with a standardized adhesion contract of exculpation. The agreement signed by the plaintiff was "offered … on a 'take it or leave it' basis." …

Another important consideration in deciding if an exculpatory agreement violates public policy is whether the signatory will be under the control of the person seeking exculpation from negligence and subject to the risk of that person's carelessness. By definition, an employee agrees to be under the control of the employer and is therefore exposed to the employer's carelessness. In the employment context, the employer generally has the greater ability to avoid harm, because the employer chooses the workplace and assigns tasks to the employees…. If employers were permitted to obtain broad waivers of their liability, an important incentive to manage risk would be removed. It would be unwise, in these circumstances, to undermine the public policy underlying the allocation of risk in tort law by allowing employees to bear risks they have no ability or right to control….

Judgment is reversed and the case is remanded. …

Questions for Analysis

1. The Connecticut high court held that exculpatory contracts in employment are in violation of public policy and cannot be enforced. In the case here, does it mean Brown will win his suit?
2. What does the court mean when it states that such contracts do away with the incentive for employers to make the workplace safe?

Anti-Raiding Covenants

Another area in which the law varies from state to state is the enforceability of *anti-raiding covenants;* that is, employees are required to sign, as a condition of employment, an agreement that they will not recruit fellow employees for another company when they leave their current place of employment.

Some courts have held such clauses to be in violation of public policy as an illegal restraint on competition; others have held it to be enforceable. For example, a New York court held that once an employee leaves a place of employment, continued restraints are not favored except to protect such things as trade secrets. Other states, including California and Texas, have held that such covenants—if limited in time and coverage—are enforceable. In Missouri, the legislature specifically held such covenants to be legal. So as in other policy areas, employers must be sure to consult state law.

LIGHTER SIDE OF THE LAW
Good Reasons Not to Come to Work

The following collection of excuses from workers as to why they could not come to work were reported by managers from Accountemps:

"I just got a new tattoo, and I need a few days to recover."

"I'm taking a few days off to start my own business."

"I need time to find myself."

"I'm going to be in a kick-boxing tournament."

"I need a leave of absence to try another job. But if it doesn't work out, I'd like to come back."

"I'm going to jail."

"My cat has hairballs."

Source: *Inc. Magazine*

Getty Images

Noncompete Agreements

It is not uncommon for employers to ask employees in certain positions to sign *noncompete agreements,* that is, the employee cannot leave and go directly into competition against the employer and will not go to work for a competitor for a certain time, usually one to three years. In states where such clauses are legal, some employers use them aggressively to discourage other companies from hiring their employees. They threaten suit against the employee and the new employer if there is such a move. The cost of fighting the litigation is often enough to discourage hiring people away from a competitor.

In some states, common law governs such covenants. So long as the restraints are reasonable in time and extent of coverage, they will be upheld. Other states have restrictions on agreements or covenants not to compete. For example, the California Business and Professions Code Section 16600 states that, with few exceptions, every contract that restrains anyone from engaging in a lawful profession, trade, or business is void. So this is an area where employers must pay careful attention to state law.

Substance Abuse

Some abused substances, such as cocaine, are illegal; others, like OxyContin, are legal but can be obtained illegally. The most commonly abused substance, alcohol, is usually legal. The Department of Health and Human Services reports that about 8 percent of the working population are serious alcohol abusers. Add to this the estimated 3 to 8 percent of the adult population who abuse or are addicted to illegal drugs or improperly dispensed drugs, such as OxyContin, and it means that as many as one in eight working-age people has a substance abuse problem. This issue provides an example of how employers may change the employment relationship in response to a problem.

A Costly Issue for Business

Substance abuse directly affects employers, because it can mean reduced productivity and higher medical insurance costs. The total economic cost is over $250 billion per year. The National Institute on Alcoholism and Alcohol Abuse estimates that health care (insurance) costs for families with an alcoholic are double the average. The huge cost of substance abuse does not include costs that arise from another widely used, highly addictive legal drug, nicotine, which also reduces productivity and increases medical expenses.

The oil spill caused by the wreck of the *Exxon Valdez* off the Alaska coast raised issues beyond environmental liability. The captain was found guilty of operating the ship under the influence of alcohol, which was, of course, in violation of company policy. While he suffered a small legal penalty for his action, Exxon suffered billions in costs. The company subsequently announced that all known alcohol and other drug abusers, even after treatment, would not be allowed to return to critical duties, such as piloting a ship or operating a refinery. Such workers would be given less sensitive—and less productive—assignments.

The U.S. Chamber of Commerce reports that workers under the influence of alcohol or other drugs are 3.6 times more likely to suffer an injury or cause one than someone else. The Federal Railroad Administration found that over 10 years, 48 railroad accidents that killed 37 people and caused millions of dollars in damages were caused by alcohol or other drug-impaired workers. The National Transportation Safety Board found alcohol or other drugs to be a factor in one third of all accidents involving truck drivers killed in highway accidents.

ISSUE SPOTTER
What Attitude toward Drinking and the Office?

Many employers have office parties, either at the workplace or at a location picked by the employer. Such events can help build morale. Having alcoholic beverages makes it a more festive event for those who enjoy a few drinks. What legal issues can you see emerging from this? If a worker appears at any time, perhaps after lunch, to have consumed too much alcohol, or to otherwise be impaired, what should be done? Should the person be sent home?

Getty Images

Legal Issues in Drug Testing

The discussion here largely concerns nonunionized places of employment, because companies that are unionized cannot impose a drug-testing program unless approved by the union in collective bargaining. Further, a substance abuser has certain rights under disabilities laws, an issue discussed in the next chapter.

Drug-Free Workplace Act

The *Drug-Free Workplace Act* requires all companies with more than $25,000 worth of business with the federal government, which includes all companies of any size, to certify that they will provide a "drug-free" workplace. The main requirements are that the employer

- Publish and distribute a statement notifying employees that the use, distribution, or possession of drugs in the workplace is prohibited.
- State what action will be taken against employees who violate the policy, which may range from completion of a rehabilitation program to dismissal.
- Establish a drug-free awareness program and make an effort to make it work.
- Notify employees that as a condition of employment, the employer must be notified of any drug-related convictions that occur, and the employer must notify the federal government.

Employers that fail to comply may lose their business with the federal government. In practice, this statute has been simple to deal with and is not regarded as having a significant effect in curtailing substance abuse.

Federal Requirements

Federal employees in certain positions, such as drug agents, are required to participate in drug-testing programs. The Omnibus Transportation Employee Testing Act requires employers who operate aircraft, public transportation, or commercial motor vehicles to test their employees for use of alcohol and illegal drugs. The tests include preemployment testing, random testing during employment, and testing after any accident. Confidentiality of test results is maintained, and the laboratory procedures used are highly accurate.

State Standards

Several states—Connecticut, Maine, Minnesota, Rhode Island, and Vermont—have statutes that impose specific restrictions on employee substance abuse testing. For example, in Minnesota, only employees in safety-sensitive positions may be drug tested. In Maine, an employee must be notified about failing a drug test and must be given another test before an employer can be notified. Firms must always ensure compliance with rules that may be peculiar to a state.

ISSUE SPOTTER

How Does an Employer Handle an Employee Who Flunks a Drug Test?

Company policy requires random drug testing of all employees. One employee, given a random test, tests positive for illegal drugs. Employees have been told that anyone flunking the test will be fired. Assuming you are in a state where that policy is allowed, as it is in most states, what steps should be in place to be sure the matter is handled properly?

Getty Images

Employee Substance Abuse Policies

Court cases give guidance as to what private employers can do in response to substance abuse. Because the elements listed here may not be treated the same in all states, managers are advised to seek counsel or to employ an experienced drug-testing firm.

1. Preemployment screening of job applicants for substance abuse is usually legal.
2. Testing of employees on an annual basis, or as a part of occasional physical examinations, is generally legal. However, physical examinations must be voluntary or directly related to the ability to perform the job. Drug tests are upheld when a job is safety sensitive or when the policy is announced and applied consistently.
3. Random drug tests, when announced as a condition of employment, are upheld for jobs where safety is an issue, such as for truck drivers and pipeline welders. Drug tests for employees not in sensitive positions, such as a vegetable stocker at a grocery store, are more likely to be subject to challenge.
4. Drug tests after accidents have been upheld, again because public safety issues generally outweigh the employee's right to privacy.
5. Substance tests given because of "reasonable suspicion" of improper usage are likely to be upheld, when there is an announced policy of such tests and when safety is an issue. Testing an employee because someone reported that the employee was seen in the company of drug users is less likely to be upheld, unless the person is in a position of sensitivity or safety.
6. Use certified labs to give and process drug tests.
7. Give all employees a copy of the company policy and keep a signed receipt from the employee.

In all cases, a *substance abuse policy* should be clear and must ensure that the testing is neither discriminatory nor done carelessly. The policy should state why the tests are done, what is being tested for, what will be done with the results, and what will be the consequences of the test results. To eliminate the chance of a false test result, employees should be given an opportunity to have a second, high-quality test if they challenge the results of a positive test result.

Worker Health and Safety

Concern about worker health and safety dates to the 1800s. Federal regulations of coal mines were first enacted in the late 1800s. Early legislation concentrated on the major issues of job safety—accidents, injuries, and deaths. Between 1890 and 1920, most states enacted job safety laws, although many of the laws were weak and poorly enforced. Over the years, laws have imposed more requirements on employers to provide certain levels of safety and health protection.

Occupational Safety and Health Act

Congress enacted the Occupational Safety and Health Act of 1970 (OSHAct), which created the *Occupational Safety and Health Administration (OSHA)*, a federal administrative agency. The Act states that employers must provide employees a workplace "free from recognized hazards that are causing or are likely to cause death or serious physical harm" and that employers must "comply with occupational safety and health standards" issued by OSHA under the statute (see http://www.osha.gov).

Inspections

OSHA inspectors visit workplaces and respond to workers calling with concerns. But since there are 7 million workplaces under OSHA jurisdiction, only a small fraction are inspected annually. In *Marshall* v. *Barlow's* (436 U.S. 307), the Supreme Court held that the Fourth Amendment prohibits warrantless searches. But because OSHA inspectors routinely obtain administrative warrants that do not require a showing of probable cause, unlike the requirement for obtaining a criminal search warrant, the warrant requirement is not problematic.

Since OSHA cannot inspect all workplaces, it focuses on those with the greatest dangers: where conditions are known to be dangerous, where employees have called to complain, where accidents have occurred, or where other agencies have noted problems. When an inspection occurs, credentials are presented. An employer can refuse admission without a warrant, but that is probably not wise, the inspector will get a warrant and is likely to be ticked by the time he returns, so things are unlikely to go as smoothly. In practice, inspectors can be lenient or take a hard line, so unless there is something that needs to be corrected quickly, most employers allow inspectors in without warrants.

Inspectors explain the purpose of the inspection and the procedures involved. The employer sends a representative to accompany the compliance officer on the walkaround, and the inspector looks for evidence of health or safety hazards. Some problems may be noted casually and not put in the formal report. At the end, the officer meets with the employer and employee representative to discuss findings. Violations may be handled in an informal manner, to allow corrections, or a citation may be issued as part of a formal report. The employer may contest the findings, as we see in the *Williams* case.

R. Williams Construction v. Occupational Safety and Health Review Commission
United States Court of Appeals, Ninth Circuit
464 F.3d 1060 (2006)

Case Background *Williams dug a 12-foot-deep trench at a construction site. Employees regularly cleaned a submersible pump used at the bottom of the trench to keep water out. Palomar and Aguiniga entered the trench—which had no supports in it—to work on the pump, when one side collapsed, killing Aguiniga and seriously injuring Palomar. OSHA inspected and cited the company for failing to instruct employees about safety and for failing to build and maintain the trench properly. Three serious violations, $7,000 each, and one willful violation of $70,000 were imposed for a total of $91,000 in fines.*

An administrative law judge (ALJ) held a hearing. Employees testified that they received minimal safety training and that there was little control over the trench; but managers claimed there was adequate safety. The ALJ downgraded the willful violation to a serious one and reduced the total fines to $22,000, because the company had a good history. Williams appealed, but the Commission denied the appeal. Williams then took the action to the appeals court.

Case Decision Fletcher, Circuit Judge

* * *

Williams violated [an OSHA regulation] for failing to instruct each employee in the recognition and avoidance of unsafe conditions and for failing to eliminate other hazards: Williams provided no training in trenching hazards to at least the two employees working in the trench; moreover, no Williams supervisor was familiar with OSHA regulations....

The Company also violated [another regulation] for failing to protect employees from cave-ins: Williams had reason to know that its employees would enter the trench on the day of the cave-in and had actual knowledge that two of its employees entered the trench prior to the cave-in. It is unavailing for Williams to argue that *employees* must take greater care to avoid placing themselves in harm's way or that management can "expect an employee ... not [to] intentionally place himself in danger." Such a claim misconstrues the purpose of the OSHA safety standards.

Williams failed to instruct its employees in proper safety measures and made no effort to ensure that employees not enter the trench on the day of the

continues

collapse. The ALJ findings, and the reasonable infer- ences drawn from them, easily satisfy the substantial- evidence standard. Consequently, the ALJ's decision affirming the citations is affirmed.

Questions for Analysis

1. The appeals court upheld the fine imposed by OSHA on the construction company for failing to follow OSHA training and construction safety rules. Since the fine was only $22,000, why would the company spend probably more than that on legal fees to contest the fine?

2. Williams argued that experienced people have good sense about dangers and that should be sufficient. Why does that argument fail?

Penalties

Based on inspections by compliance officers, citations may be issued for violations of OSHA rules or for failure to meet the general standard of a workplace free of preventable hazards that could cause injury or death. Penalties may be imposed under Section 17 of OSHAct for the following:

- A willful or repeated violation—up to $70,000 per violation
- A serious violation—up to $7,000 per violation
- A nonserious violation—up to $7,000 per violation
- Failure to correct a violation—or for knowingly making false statements in OSHA records up to $7,000 per day
- A willful violation resulting in the death of an employee may result in criminal penalties being imposed.

Because fines are often multiplied when violations continue over time, the total fine can be high. For example, Bridgestone/Firestone was fined $7.5 million for willful safety violations related to the death of a worker at an Oklahoma City plant.

LIGHTER SIDE OF THE LAW

Heal My Sensitive Heart

A 49-year-old high school teacher in Sydney, Australia, was fired when he was caught in a "romantic relationship" with a 15-year-old student. His wife divorced him. A workers' compensation commission awarded him $19,000 for his "psychological injury" plus $215 a month for as long as his "injury" continues.

Source: *Sydney Morning Herald*

Getty Images

Workers and Toxic Substances

Most OSHA standards concern safety, and they include specifications for machine design and placement, stairway design, and height of fire extinguishers. Health standards have been issued, some of which have had a major impact. Protection from exposure to asbestos was one of the first health standards developed; compliance has cost billions of dollars. Other standards have been issued for exposure to vinyl chloride, coke-oven emissions, and other industrial carcinogens.

OSHA must issue standards that "most adequately assure, to the extent feasible ... that no employee will suffer material impairment of health or functional

Exhibit 16.1
Biggest Mistakes

Ten Most Common Workplace Safety Violations

1. No written hazard communication program
2. No information or training on hazardous chemicals
3. Electrical conductors not protected when entering boxes or fittings
4. Electrical covers missing
5. Guards missing on grinding wheels or spinning machinery
6. Hard hats not worn on construction sites
7. No fall protection for workers on elevated work surfaces
8. No portable fire extinguishers
9. Improper use of electrical cords
10. Not maintaining OSHA Injury and Illness Log

Source: *National Federation of Independent Business*

capacity even if such employee has regular exposure to the hazard ... for the period of his working life."

Hazard Communication Standard

Besides exposure limits for some specific toxic substances, the *hazard communication standard (HazCom)* covers employees exposed to hazardous chemicals. Chemical producers and users must conduct a "hazard determination" of each chemical they produce or use. Information about chemical hazards must be updated as new evidence becomes available. Where hazardous chemicals are used, employers must have all of the following:

1. A written hazard communication program that includes
   - a list of hazardous chemicals in the workplace
   - the manner in which safety data sheets, chemical labels, and worker training about chemical safety will be handled
   - a description of how employees will be trained for nonroutine tasks, such as chemical spills or explosions
2. Labels for hazardous chemical containers that identify the chemical, hazard warnings, and the name and address of the producer or seller
3. Material safety data sheets provided by chemical distributors with every container; the data sheets identify the chemical, its characteristics, its physical hazards (such as fire) and health hazards, its primary route of entry (such as skin contact), exposure limits, cancer dangers, precautions for safe handling and use, control measures in the work place, emergency procedures, date of issue, and the identity of the person who can provide more information
4. Programs to inform employees of the HazCom requirements; to train employees to detect hazards; to inform employees of the consequences of the chemicals, how to protect themselves, and certain actions to take in an emergency

Workers' Compensation

In 1911, Wisconsin enacted the first *workers' compensation* law to require employers to pay insurance premiums for injury and death benefits for employees.

Other states followed quickly. The benefits are paid regardless of the cause of a work-related injury; that is, workers' comp is no-fault insurance. Workers' compensation benefits are set by state law. In exchange for paying premiums, employers become immune from employee damage suits (torts) arising from on-the-job accidents. The objectives are to

1. provide sure, prompt, and reasonable income and medical benefits to work-accident victims or income benefits to their dependents, regardless of fault.
2. provide a certain remedy and reduce court costs and time delays associated with tort litigation.
3. prevent public and private charities from incurring the financial strains that would accompany uncompensated accidents.
4. reduce payment of fees to lawyers and expert witnesses.
5. encourage employer interest in safety and rehabilitation of workers through an insurance scheme that bases rates on the accident rating of the employer.
6. promote open discussion of the causes of accidents rather than encourage concealment of fault, thus helping to reduce accidents and health hazards.

Compensation Claims

Most workers are covered by workers' compensation laws. To have a claim, workers must generally show that they have 1) a personal injury, 2) as a result of an accident or occupational disease, 3) that arose out of and in the course of employment. The negligence or fault of the employer in causing the injury is not an issue, and coverage is broad. Compensable injuries can include mental and nervous disorders and heart attacks that occur on the job.

Most courts are strict in interpreting state statutes that clearly state that the liability coverage of workers' compensation "shall be exclusive in place of any and all other liability to such employees … entitled to damages in any action at law or otherwise on account of any injury or death." The actions of the employer, employee, or third person become relevant only if there was intentional infliction of harm, that is, an intentional tort. The employee may then file a civil action for damages outside the workers' compensation system. As we noted earlier, employers are forbidden by public policy from punishing employees who seek compensation by filing claims.

Benefits and Incentives

Workers' compensation usually has five benefit categories: *death*, *total disability*, *permanent partial disability*, *temporary partial disability*, and *medical expenses*. Most states do not restrict the amount or length of medical benefits. While some injuries require only medical assistance, others take the worker out of the workplace for a recovery period, sometimes for life. Workers usually receive about two thirds of their gross wages as disability income, up to a state-imposed weekly maximum—as low as $400 in some states to over $1,000 in others.

Premiums Tied to Safety

Generally, workers' compensation provides employers with financial incentives to invest in safety at the worksite. Insurance premiums are based on injury claims records. Hence, firms with the lowest number of injuries, and therefore the fewest claims, will have the lowest premiums. Different states have different systems, different rules, and different payout histories. Some states run the system directly, others allow private insurers to compete.

Premiums vary widely: North Dakota has the lowest rates in the nation at about $1 per $100 payroll; Alaska and California have the highest rates at about $4 to $5 per $100 payroll. The national average is around $2 to $2.40 per $100 payroll. Rates vary within a state according to the type of occupation. For example, in Connecticut the rate is $0.33 per $100 payroll for clerical workers and $16.46 per $100 payroll for carpenters. Because of the cost, some employers would like to not pay for workers' compensation, or other obligations for employees, as we see in the *Juarez* case.

There are tax and insurance obligations that an employer has for an employee that do not exist for an independent contractor. Besides workers' compensation premiums, an employer must pay FICA (Social Security and Medicare) taxes, state unemployment taxes, and must with hold federal income taxes. That is not the case when employers hire contractors, who may be paid a lump sum. Both the Internal Revenue Service (IRS) and state agencies look closely at employer practices of declaring employees to be independent contractors rather than employees. In this case, we can see some consequences of failing to follow the law.

Juarez v. CC Services
United States District Court, District of Arizona
434 F.Supp.2d 755 (2006)

Case Background *Juarez worked for Westarz Homes at construction sites for five years. Bever was a superintendent at construction sites, supervising sub contractors and moving trash from sites to landfills. He presented himself as an independent contractor under the name T. Bever Construction. Westarz provided Bever a truck for moving trash. The truck was insured by Westarz's insurance company, Country Insurance.*

When Bever was backing the truck up at a construction site, he hit Juarez, crushing his left arm and shoulder, leaving him unable to work. Juarez filed for workers' compensation. Westarz paid no workers' compensation premiums, because it claimed it only used independent contractors. The state investigated and determined that Juarez was an employee, since he worked under the direct control of Westarz for years. It awarded him workers' compensation benefits from a Special Fund maintained for such instances.

Juarez also sued Bever Construction for negligence for Bever hitting Juarez with the truck. Country Insurance was then brought in, because it insured the truck. Country claimed that Bever and Juarez were both employees of Westarz, and it had insured the truck on that basis, so workers' compensation was the exclusive remedy. But the jury held that Bever was an indepen-

dent contractor and awarded Juarez $600,000 for negligence by Bever, all of which was covered by the insurance policy on the truck. Country moved for summary judgment on its behalf.

Case Decision Silver, District Judge

* * *

Country wishes to establish Bever and Juarez were co-employees, because the workers' compensation statutes bar Juarez from recovering anything from a co-employee.... The parties agree on the factors relevant to the determination of Bever's employment status pursuant to the workers' compensation statutes. Those factors include

1) The extent of control exercised by the master over details of the work and the degree of supervision;
2) The distinct nature of the worker's business;
3) Specialization or skilled occupation;
4) Materials and place of work;
5) Duration of employment;
6) Method of payment;
7) Relationship of work done to the regular business of the employer;
8) Belief of the parties....

continues

In light of all these factors, "the inference … is clear that a master–servant relationship existed." Westarz exercised ultimate control over all of Bever's activities, Bever's activities were meant to further the interests of Westarz, Westarz provided materials necessary for Bever's job, Westarz dictated where Bever would work, Bever and Westarz had a four-year exclusive relationship, Bever was paid a set amount each week, and Bever provided a vital service to Westarz' business. These facts are very similar to the facts Juarez argued to the Special Fund, when he sought to obtain workers' compensation benefits. Thus, just as Juarez was found to be an employee, Bever was also an employee at the time of the accident.

Juarez and Bever were co-employees, and Juarez has already sought workers' compensation benefits for his injury. Accordingly, Arizona law precluded Juarez from bringing suit against Bever for additional compensation. The fact that Bever eventually allowed judgment be taken against him does not control here. Country's policy was not implicated by the accident and the Court need not address the viability of the policy exclusions.

Therefore, it is ordered that defendant's Motion for Summary Judgment is granted.

Questions for Analysis

1. The court held that Bever and Juarez were both employees, not independent contractors; so workers' compensation was the remedy for the injury, and there would be no damages in tort. Where did Westarz end up in all this?

2. Why should Juarez not get to collect both workers' compensation benefits and sue for the injury caused by Bever's negligence?

A Flawed System?

Employers complain that workers' compensation insurance is too expensive; employers pay premiums of about $100 billion per year. Despite rising premiums, many compensation systems have run in the red. One reason for the expense appears to be that too many awards are given for permanent partial disability, which results in lifetime payment awards, when the worker is in fact not permanently disabled. Fraud and dubious claims plague many state workers' compensation systems.

On the other side, consider the amounts paid for losses suffered from injuries that are usually fixed by a schedule. Suppose a worker loses the use of an arm. Medical expenses and lost work time aside, how much is an arm worth? In the preceding case, Juarez is likely to receive less than the $600,000 from workers' compensation than the jury awarded him to tort damages. So in practice, it is unlikely that employers would prefer to operate under the tort system, rather than under this system of awards determined by statute.

ISSUE SPOTTER
Reducing Risks and Improving Looks

To prevent workers from being injured, which reduces the likelihood of an OSHA safety violation, as well as the number of workers' compensation claims, you would like to impose a dress code for employees that covers both safety and looks. You believe such a code would also improve professionalism in the workplace. Can you do what you want in this regard? Does a new dress code change the nature of the work contract you have with the workers? Must the workers to agree to the new dress code?

Getty Images

Getty Images

LIGHTER SIDE OF THE LAW
Donuts Are Not Healthy

David Howard was snacking on donuts and coffee while driving a truck in Oklahoma. He stated that he choked on a donut bite, which caused him to sneeze, which caused pain in his lower back. After chiropractors could not solve the problem, Howard had surgery to remove a hermated disk.

Howard applied for disability benefits, testifying that eating donuts and drinking coffee is customary in the truck-driving business. The trucking company argued that sneezing is a "personal internal weakness not related to his employment."

A Missouri workers' compensation administrative law judge sided with Howard and awarded him $18,542 in permanent partial disability benefits. The award was upheld by the Missouri Labor and Industrial Relations Commission. A dissenting commissioner said that he had "serious doubts" about a "donut disability."

Source: *National Law Journal*

Family and Medical Leave

The *Family and Medical Leave Act (FMLA)* applies to private employers with 50 or more employees and applies to all governmental units. Employers must grant workers up to 12 weeks of unpaid leave after childbirth or adoption; to care for a seriously ill child, spouse, or parent; or in case of an employee's own serious illness.

A "serious health condition" that qualifies for *FMLA leave* includes illness, injury, a physical or mental condition that involves in patient care (an overnight stay in a medical facility), or continuing treatment by a health care provider, which includes at least one of these:

a. More than three consecutive days of incapacity and treatment for a condition that involves two or more treatments, including exams, by a health care provider; or one treatment with continuing prescription medicine or special equipment;

b. Incapacity due to pregnancy;

c. Incapacity or treatment for a chronic, serious health condition; or

d. Any absence for multiple treatments and recovery for surgery or a condition that would likely result in more than a three day period of incapacity if left untreated.

While on leave, health care benefits, if provided, must remain in place. When employees return from leave, they must be returned to the same job or a comparable position.

Integration with Employment Rules

While the law does not seem that complicated, it has resulted in a lot of litigation, so employers should have clear policies. In general, an employer should have a manager who is knowledgeable about the law to ensure compliance. Individual managers should not make determinations of eligibility, because liability for FMLA violations may be imposed on individual managers as well as on the employing organization. As the *Callison* case indicates, employers can have policies to ensure such leave is not abused.

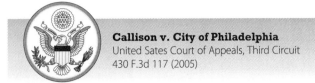

Callison v. City of Philadelphia
United Sates Court of Appeals, Third Circuit
430 F.3d 117 (2005)

Case Background *Callison had worked for the city for two years when he was diagnosed with deep anxiety reaction caused by stress at home and on the job. He used a lot of sick leave and was put on a Sick Abuse List. Empoyees on the list were required to get medical certification for all sick days and were subject to penalties for violations of the policy. Employees on sick leave were to call a hotline to report when they left home. A sick leave investigator would call homes to see if employees were there or not. Callison took three months FMLA leave; the city checked on him, and he was often not home. He was suspended for failure to follow policy.*

Callison sued, contending he should not be subject to discipline while on FMLA leave and that to discipline him was retaliation in violation of the statute. The trial court held for the city. Callison appealed.

Case Decision Cowen, Circuit Judge

* * *

The FMLA is meant to prohibit employers from retaliating against employees who exercise their rights, refusing to authorize leave, manipulating positions to avoid application of the Act, or discriminatory applying policies to discourage emloyees from taking leave. In the instant case, the City did not engage in any of these prohibited acts. The City provided Callison with the entitlements set forth in the FMLA (e.g., a 12-week leave and reinstatement after taking medical leave).

Callison's contention that the FMLA's anti abuse provisions ... preempt the City's procedures is merit-

less. The anti abuse provisions in the FMLA permitting employers to request second opinions and certifications does not conflict with the City's provision requiring employees on medical leave to call in when leaving their home during business hours. These "certification" provisions merely outline some of the employer's rights and employee's corresponding obligations...

Contrary to Callison's assertion there is no right in the FMLA to be "left alone." Nothing in the FMLA prevents employers from ensuring that employees who are on leave from work do not abuse their leave, particularly those who enter leave while on the employer's Sick Abuse List....

Because the City's internal call-in policy neither conflicts with nor diminishes the protections guaranteed by the FMLA, it is not invalidated by the Act. Accordingly, Callison was required to comply with the policy, and the City did not abrogate his FMLA rights by placing him on suspension for the violations.

For the foregoing reasons, the judgment of the District Court ... will be affirmed.

Questions for Analysis
1. The appeals court affirmed that the employer had the right to be sure an employee was in fact at home while taking FMLA leave. Why would the employer care where the employee is?
2. Is it not an invasion of privacy to call employees on sick leave to check on them?

FMLA coverage may be denied, on a case-by-case basis, to "key" employees. This may only include employees among the 10 percent highest paid, whose leave would cause "substantial and grievous economic injury to the operations of the employer." Also not covered are employees who have not worked for at least one year and who have not worked at least 1,250 hours in the past year. Employees are required to notify employers at least 30 days in advance for foreseeable leave, such as for birth, adoption, or planned medical treatment.

General Regulation of Labor Markets

Besides the major laws already discussed, a variety of other laws restrict the labor market. Immigration laws limit who is allowed to work in the country. The minimum wage law sets a lower limit on what employees may be paid. States restrict entry into occupations by licensing requirements. Employers must warn employees of pending plant closings and must provide family-leave opportunities. Employee pensions are also subject to federal regulation.

Hiring Immigrants

The United States is a nation of immigrants and is the most popular destination for people from many countries. Millions of undocumented immigrants work in the country with large concentrations in California, Arizona, New Mexico, Texas, and Florida. To be hired legally in the United States, a person must present certain documents to show identity and authorization to work. Such documentary proof is required even if a person is a U.S. citizen.

Since violations of the law can mean criminal penalties, employers must be sure to meet the basic requirements. Employers must collect evidence of citizenship or of legal work status for all new employees. For every person hired, the employer must have an I-9 form on file. Further, the following documents are some that are used as proof of personal identity and of employment eligibility:

- U.S. passport
- Unexpired employment authorization card
- Unexpired temporary resident card
- Foreign passport with employment authorization
- Alien registration card with photograph

Combinations of other documents, such as a driver's license, school ID card, original Social Security card, or birth certificate, may provide satisfactory proof to the Immigration and Naturalization Service of identity and employment eligibility requirements. See the Citizenship and Immigration Services Web site for details (www.uscis.gov).

Federal Minimum Wage Requirements

Federal *minimum wage* requirements were initiated in 1938 as part of the Fair Labor Standards Act. Over the years, the minimum wage has averaged about 50 percent of the average manufacturing wage. The minimum wage was raised to $7.25 in 2009. Some states, such as California, have higher minimum wages. Employers must also pay Social Security (FICA) tax $7.65 percent, workers' compensation insurance, and unemployment insurance taxes. Unemployment tax rates vary by state and by rates assigned to an employer. The maximum tax per employee in Florida, for example, is about $450, but it is less for most employers.

Supporters of the minimum wage contend that the law requires employers to pay a fair wage to employees and will not allow workers to be paid so little that they have trouble buying the necessities of life. Critics argue that the law results in lower demand for workers in the minimum wage category—usually young people, often minorities, with little education or job experience. The result is high unemployment among persons in those groups, who never get the chance to work to develop skills that will command higher wages.

Occupational Licensure and Regulation

Entry into many occupations is controlled by various regulations or *licensing requirements*. In such occupations, a person cannot simply set up and begin to operate a business. Rather, permission from the regulating agency is required. Such permission usually requires some demonstration of competency or payment of a high entry fee. The purpose of these labor restrictions is to protect the consumer, and the restrictions are supposed to help guarantee that businesses will provide service of a certain quality, so that fewer unscrupulous people will operate in those professions.

Regulations Set by State Law

Although entry controls for a few occupations are set at the federal level, most restrictions are set at the state level. In most states, a person must receive a license or certificate from the state to practice as a lawyer, doctor, dentist, nurse, veterinarian, optometrist, optician, barber, cosmetologist, or architect. In various states, an individual must be licensed to be a dog groomer, beekeeper, industrial psychologist, building contractor, electrician, plumber, or massage parlor operator. Usually, a state commission determines the entry criteria for a person to be licensed to practice. In most cases, there is a formal education requirement; in some cases, an apprenticeship period is required or a test of knowledge about the profession must be passed.

Warning Employees of Plant Closings

The *Worker Adjustment and Retraining Notification Act (WARN)* requires employers with 100 or more full-time employees to give advance notice of a plant closing or mass layoff if 50 or more employees will be affected. The notice must be given directly to each affected employee 60 days in advance of the closing or layoff. Notices must also be sent to collective bargaining agents, local elected officials, and state labor department officials. Such notices must be given for permanent terminations and reduction in work time of 50 percent or more for six months or longer.

Employees who do not receive proper notice of a plant closing or mass layoff may sue for up to 60 days' back pay and fringe benefits, interest, and attorney's fees. If the local government has not been properly notified, it may sue the company for up to $500 per day for each day there was no notice. If a firm fails to comply with WARN, it may not be ordered to not cut its labor force. In several states—including Connecticut, Maine, Massachusetts, and Wisconsin—state plant closing requirements go beyond the federal requirements. This statute has not generated much litigation.

Employee Retirement Plans

The most important legislation regulating private employee retirement plans is the *Employee Retirement Income Security Act (ERISA)*. The main objective of ERISA is to guarantee the expectations of retirement plan participants and to promote the growth of private pension plans. ERISA was prompted by horror stories about employees who made years of contributions to retirement funds only to receive nothing when their employer went bankrupt.

ERISA is directed at most employee benefit plans, including medical, surgical, or hospital benefits; sickness, accident, or disability benefits; death benefits; unemployment benefits; vacation benefits; apprenticeship or training benefits; day-care centers; scholarship funds; prepaid legal services; retirement income programs; and deferred income programs.

Vesting Requirements

The law establishes vesting requirements. It guarantees that plan participants will receive some retirement benefits after a certain length of employment. All plans must be adequately funded to meet their expected liabilities. A termination insurance program is to be provided in case of the failure of a plan. The law provides standards of conduct for trustees and fiduciaries of employee benefit plans.

The major problem addressed by ERISA was that of the loss of all benefits by employees who had many years of service with a company and then either quit or were fired. The law makes all full-time employees over the age of 25 with one year of service eligible for participation in employee benefit plans.

Mandatory *vesting*—when the employee becomes the owner of the retirement proceeds—was established by ERISA. It provides the employee with three options: 1) to have 100 percent vesting after 10 years of employment; 2) to have 25 percent vesting after five years, then 5 percent vesting a year for five years, then 10 percent vesting a year for five years, to achieve 100 percent vesting in 15 years; and 3) vesting under the rule of 45. Under the rule of 45, if the age and years of service of an employee total 45, or if an employee has 10 years' service, there must be at least 50 percent vesting. Each added year of employment provides 10 percent more vesting so that an employee will be fully vested within 15 years.

ISSUE SPOTTER
How Do You Count Hours for Telecommuters?

Working at home has become more common. There are over 10 million full-time telecommuters and 45 million more employees who do some work at home. This has raised problems in compliance with the Fair Labor Standards Act and other employment laws. How do you know for sure if an employee put in an 8-hour day? What if they claim a 10-hour day and expect overtime? What if they work through mandated break and meal times?

Getty Images

Major Labor Relations Acts

The federal labor code, generally called the *National Labor Relations Act (NLRA)* was enacted by Congress in three major phases: the Wagner Act in 1935, the Taft-Hartley Act in 1947, and the Landrum–Griffin Act in 1959. The only major labor law passed before the NLRA was the Norris–La Guardia Act of 1932. While much of labor law deals with unions, the laws are broader than that, and the rules can apply to all workers. We first review the major acts and then discuss the key aspects of labor law in practice.

Norris–La Guardia Act

Before passage of the *Norris–La Guardia Act* in 1932, there was little federal legislation that specifically addressed labor issues. Some courts held union activities to be criminal conspiracies, while others upheld similar activities as legal. The most common tactic of employers was to plead for an injunction to stop strikes and other union activities as a violation of antitrust law. The Norris–La Guardia Act ended such court intervention. The Act declared that every worker should "have full freedom of association, self-organization, and designation of representatives of his own choosing, to negotiate terms and conditions of his employment."

Injunctions Prohibited

Norris–La Guardia prohibits federal courts from issuing injunctions in nonviolent *labor disputes*. Hence, management must deal with the union or begin administrative proceedings involving the National Labor Relations Board (discussed later).

Specific acts not subject to court intervention include *striking*, belonging to a union, paying strike or unemployment benefits to labor dispute participants, publicizing a labor dispute, picketing, peacefully assembling, and advising others to do any of these acts without violence or fraud. The Act also prohibits employers from requiring employees to sign *yellow-dog contracts*. Under such contracts, employees agree not to join a union or risk being fired if they do.

Wagner Act of 1935

The basic goal of the *Wagner Act* of 1935—the first phase of the NLRA—was to ensure workers the right to "self-organization, to form, join, or assist labor organizations, to bargain collectively through representatives of their own choosing, and to engage in other concerted activities for the purpose of collective bargaining or other mutual aid or protection…." The *National Labor Relations Board (NLRB)* was created to monitor *unfair labor practices* and assure that union representation elections are fair. The NLRB does not regulate the substance of bargaining, the actual terms and conditions of employment between employers and employees; its concern is mostly about proper procedure and review of claims that the NLRA has been violated.

LIGHTER SIDE OF THE LAW
Rules Are Rules

A 73-year-old man had a heart attack in London. An ambulance was called. The nearest crew could not be disturbed, because European Union labor rules prohibit disturbing a crew for any reason during the first 20 minutes of their scheduled half-hour break. A more distant crew had to be called. The man died.

Source: *Daily Telegraph (London)*

Getty Images

The Taft-Hartley Act of 1947

The *Taft–Hartley Act* of 1947—the Labor–Management Relations Act—which amended the NLRA, marked a change in federal policy from actively encouraging labor union formation to a more balanced approach. Employers could also file charges with the NLRB for unfair labor practices. The Act prohibits unions from the following activities:

1. Coereing employees to support the union
2. Refusing to bargain in good faith with employers about wages and working conditions
3. Carrying out certain kinds of strikes, such as secondary boycotts; charging "excessive" union initiation fees or dues; or engaging in featherbedding (making employers pay for work not performed)
4. Going on strike during a 30-day "cooling-off" period or during a 60-day period ordered by the president

The Landrum–Griffin Act of 1959

The *Landrum–Griffin Act* of 1959—Labor–Management Reporting and Disclosure Act—which amended the NLRA, increased regulation of internal union affairs. Senate investigations revealed the improper use of union funds by union leaders and election fraud. The Act was intended to assure that union members are protected from improper actions by union leaders.

Monitoring Leadership

Union finances are subject to federal review, and a report is to be available to union members so that they know how their dues are used. Union officials who betray the trust of their office are subject to prosecution. Penalties exist to reduce employer wrongdoing, such as bribing union officials or attempting to hold off union activities by other illegal means. Employers must report annually to the Secretary of Labor about expenditures to attempt to influence collective bargaining activities.

Union Member Bill of Rights

A "bill of rights" for union members is included in the Landrum–Griffin Act. The Act ensures members the right to nominate candidates for union offices, maintains fair election procedures—such as the use of secret ballots in union elections—and allows members to participate in union business, subject to "reasonable" union rules. Union dues and fees are to be set by majority vote of the members. If a union member is to be disciplined by the union, procedural safeguards protect the member's rights, and punishment may not be inflicted on members who challenge union leadership or its actions.

The National Labor Relations Board

The NLRB is an administrative agency charged with overseeing the National Labor Relations Act. It has five board members, a general counsel, regional directors, and administrative law judges. The board reviews unfair labor practice case decisions by regional directors and administrative law judges. The general counsel oversees the investigation and prosecution of unfair labor practice charges and represents the NLRB in court. The NLRB has regional and field offices throughout the country (see http://www.nlrb.gov).

The NLRB has jurisdiction over all employers and all employees in labor disputes that affect interstate commerce. Certain classes of employees are not covered by the NLRA—federal, state, and municipal employees (the public sector), supervisors, managers, independent contractors, domestic servants, and agricultural laborers. Airline and railroad employees are covered by the Railway Labor Act, which is similar to the NLRA.

Unfair Labor Practice Complaints

In general, *unfair labor practices* are actions by employers or unions that impair the goals of the NLRA.

Examples of employer conduct that violates the NLRA:

- Threatening employees with loss of jobs or benefits if they join or support a union
- Threatening to close a plant if employees vote for unionization
- Questioning employees about union activities
- Promising benefits to employees if they do not support a union
- Giving employees worse assignments for participating in protected activities

Examples of union conduct that violates the NLRA:

- Threatening employees with loss of a job if they do not support the union
- Refusing to help employees with grievances who have criticized union leaders
- Engaging in picket line misconduct, such as threatening non strikers
- Striking over issues unrelated to employment terms and conditions

About 30,000 cases are filed each year with the NLRB. Most are charges of unfair labor practice. Charges filed against employers outnumber charges filed against unions about two to one. Each case must be filed by a private party, such as a worker, a union, or an employer.

Most casework is done in the field through the regional offices and involves the following process: Charges of unfair labor practices are filed at field offices that do investigations. If the investigation shows the case has merit, the regional director files a *complaint*. Many charges filed do not lead to a complaint being filed; they are either dismissed by the regional director or withdrawn by the complaining party when they are informed of their likely lack of success. Of the charges that do lead to a complaint, most are settled before a hearing takes place.

Hearing Complaints

An administrative law judge (ALJ), an employee of the NLRB, presides over complaints that are to be resolved at an administrative hearing. After taking evidence and receiving briefs, the ALJ issues a decision and order. The order either sets out the appropriate remedy or recommends that the complaint be dismissed. Unless one of the parties involved files an *exception*, the decision is final.

If an exception to the decision is filed, the appeal is heard in Washington by a panel of three NLRB members, if the case is routine, or by the entire board, if the case is considered important. Board members hear no evidence and see no witnesses; in that sense, they are similar to an appellate court.

If one of the parties refuses to accept the board's decision, the case will be referred to the U.S. Court of Appeals for enforcement or review of the order. Most decisions of the board that are referred to the Court of Appeals are upheld. In rare instances, the case may be taken for final review by the U.S. Supreme Court.

Pivotal Role of NLRB

The NLRA gives the NLRB great leeway to make policy and remedies regarding unfair labor practices. Its determinations are not to be reversed unless they are arbitrary, capricious, or manifestly contrary to the NLRA.

Because of the board's powers to determine much of the substance of labor law in practice, appointment to the NLRB is politically sensitive. Presidents sympathetic to labor unions because of political support appoint "pro-labor" members; presidents who are more sympathetic to the interests of employers appoint "pro-management" members. As the composition of the NLRB changes, its rulings tend to swing in one direction or another.

Remedies

If the NLRB finds that an employer has engaged in an unfair labor practice, the remedies it may impose include

- posting a notice in the workplace.
- issuing a cease and desist order.
- providing back pay for lost wages.
- reinstating dismissed workers.
- issuing an order to bargain with the union.

Unionization

A major responsibility of the NLRB is to determine whether employees want to be represented by a union. The NLRA focuses on the rights of employees to "self-organization; to form, join, or assist labor organizations." To ensure that the employees' right of self-organization can be exercised effectively, the NLRB has rules governing employer and union conduct.

Unionization Process

If employees are not represented by a union, a move to unionize might come about by some interested employees who contact a union for assistance, or by a union organizer who contacts employees to determine whether interest exists. The union starts an organization drive. An employee committee is formed and, with the help of the organizer, calls informational meetings and distributes information.

Representation Elections

If a union organizer collects *authorization cards*—signed by 30 percent or more of the employees—asking for an election to be held to determine whether the union should represent them (the cards are kept secret from the employer), the organizer turns the cards over to the NLRB and requests a *representation election.* The election determines whether a majority of employees in a *bargaining unit* want the union as their agent. A bargaining unit may be all workers at a company, the workers at one plant, or workers in certain skills at one or more work sites, such as nurses at a hospital or at several hospitals. Managers may not be in the bargaining unit.

Before the election, a campaign is held. The union tells the workers of the benefits of unionization and management tells the workers the benefits the company provides without a union. The company is prohibited from threatening those who favor unionization, nor may it promise, say, a 10 percent pay raise if the workers defeat the union. The company can argue about real problems it sees from unionization. For example, if the union tells workers it will get them a 25 percent raise, the company may explain the likely consequences of such an event.

The NLRB and the courts protect the interests of the employees, so they have access to union information, and it protects the employers, interest in controlling business without interference. As a rule, the NLRB and the courts do not permit access to company property by outside organizers. Like any other private property, the owner can control who comes on the property.

INTERNATIONAL PERSPECTIVE

The Power of German Unions

The competitive nature of the U.S. economy has always limited the strength of employee unions. If a union representing workers at one firm gets a generous package that makes the firm less cost competitive than other firms in the industry, the firm and its employees both lose. In Germany, competition among firms has been limited, because the majority of workers belong to trade unions, and most employers belong to industry associations.

Since all autoworkers belong to the same union, and automakers belong to the same industry association, one collective bargaining agreement traditionally covers all employees and all firms, so that wages and conditions are the same at all firms. German workers have enjoyed higher wages and shorter work hours than any major nation in the world. But the high costs have made German products less price competitive in the international market, putting pressure on the system.

German companies have begun to build more plants in lower-cost countries, including the United States. Persistent high unemployment in Germany also put pressure on the system to become more flexible and allow more workers to find employment. Increased flexibility has been demanded by German auto producers, to keep more jobs from leaving the country.

Getty Images

Union Certification

NLRB agents supervise the election, which is often held at the workplace. There are about 2,500 such elections around the country each year. After the election, the NLRB certifies the results. If more than 50 percent of the employees vote for the union, then *union certification* is granted by the NLRB. Unions win about 55 percent of the elections. The union is declared the *exclusive bargaining agent* for all employees in the bargaining unit and must be recognized by the company. All employees in the bargaining unit, even those who do not want the union, are bound by the recognition of the union as the exclusive bargaining agent. Exhibit 16.2 illustrates the process.

On the other side of the coin, 60 to 90 days before the expiration of a collective bargaining agreement, 30 percent of the workers can call for an election to attempt to *decertify* a union, that is, to get a majority of employees to vote to remove the union as bargaining agent. The number of such elections has increased over the years.

Agency Shops

When a union is selected to be the collective bargaining agent, the workers who join the union must pay *union dues*. What about the workers who do not want to be union members?

The NLRA prohibits *closed shops*, in which an employee must be a union member before going to work at a unionized worksite. It also prohibits *union shops*—worksites where being a member of the union is a condition of employment. *Agency shops*—places of employment where a majority of employees have voted to be represented by a union in a collective bargaining agreement—are legal. In an agency shop, employees who belong to the union pay union dues, while employees who do not want to join the union pay *agency fees*. That is, nonunion employees are represented by the union and have fees deducted from their paychecks that go to cover the costs of union services, including collective bargaining and enforcing the bargain. Agency fees are a little lower than union dues.

Political Action

The use of agency fees to support union political activities not directly related to the union's duties as a bargaining representative raises concerns about the constitutional rights of employees who are forced to provide financial support for political action. That is, unions devote significant sums to support favored political candidates. That money comes from union dues and may also come from agency fees. A number of Supreme Court cases have been heard on this issue. In *Chicago Teachers Union* (106

Exhibit 16.2 Unionization Process

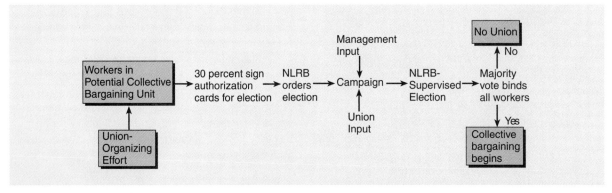

S.Ct. 1066), the Court listed four requirements regarding agency fees paid by non-union workers to unions at unionized workplaces. There must be

1. an adequate explanation of the basis for the fee.
2. a reasonably prompt explanation of the basis for the fee.
3. an opportunity to challenge the fee before an impartial decision maker.
4. an escrow account for the amounts in dispute while challenges are pending.

ISSUE SPOTTER
Moves to Help Keep Unions Out

Since most employers have little desire to see any of their workers unionize, employers generally are vigilant to indications that employees may be trying to generate interest in a union, or that a union is actively seeking to get workers to sign authorization cards to force an election on unionization. What moves can a company make if it detects interest in unionizing among its employees? Prohibit distribution of all union material by e-mail or in employee boxes? Fire employees who are ringleaders? Make clear the company's total opposition to unionization? What is fair game?

Getty Images

In the *Beck* decision (108 S.Ct. 2641), the Supreme Court found that 79 percent of the agency fees paid by Beck and other non union AT&T employees represented by a union went to political action. The Court ordered the union to cut its agency fees, refund the excess fees collected from nonunion workers, and keep clear records about union expenditures by category. Justice Brennan noted that unions are not "free to exact dues equivalents from nonmembers in any amount they please, no matter how unrelated those fees may be to collective bargaining activities."

In practice, the Supreme Court decisions have been difficult to enforce. About two million workers are represented by unions but do not belong to the unions, and so they pay agency fees. Most agency fees, like union dues, go to support political action and other union activities not related to the expenses of collective bargaining at a workplace. Unions generally ignore the *Beck* ruling, forcing employees to go to the expense of litigation to enforce their rights.

Right-to-Work Laws

A feature of the Taft–Hartley Act that is still politically controversial is the provision that allows states to pass *right-to-work* laws that prohibit agency shops. In right-to-work states, if a majority of the employees vote for union representation and pay union dues, the union is the collective bargaining agent for all employees. However, no employees can be required to pay agency fees, even though their wages and working conditions are determined by the collective bargaining agreement. Since some employees receive the benefits of the union without paying union dues or agency fees, unions claim they are free riders. Right-to-work laws, in effect in 22 Southern and Western states, clearly retard the effectiveness of unions in such states.

Collective Bargaining

Once employees choose a bargaining representative, that representative—the union—becomes the legal representative of the employees. The employer must bargain with the union. *Collective bargaining* refers to the process by which the employer and the union, on behalf of all employees in a collective bargaining unit, negotiate a contract, setting forth the terms and conditions of employment for a given time period. Collective bargaining is more than the initial contract negotiation; it is the entire process of contract administration, resulting in a continuous relationship between an employer and the employee representative.

Good-Faith Bargaining

The NLRA defines the duty to bargain in good faith as follows:

> To bargain collectively is the performance of the mutual obligation of the employer and the representative of the employees to meet at reasonable times and confer in good faith with respect to wages, hours, and other terms and conditions of employment, or the negotiation of an agreement, or any question arising thereunder, and the execution of a written contract incorporating any agreement reached if requested by either party, but such obligation does not compel either party to agree to a proposal or require the making of a concession....

Essentially, *good faith* means an obligation to meet and be willing to present proposals and explain reasons, to listen to and consider the proposals of the other party, and to search for some common ground that can serve as the basis for an agreement—but with no legal requirement that agreement be reached.

The Supreme Court has indicated that the NLRB and the courts should not become too involved in the details of the bargaining process, since Congress did not intend for direct intervention in the substance of labor bargains. Rather, Congress took the position that the parties should be free to reach an agreement of their own making.

Mandatory Subjects of Bargaining

The NLRA states that bargaining in good faith must occur with respect to "wages, hours, and other terms and conditions of employment." These are *mandatory subjects* about which employers and unions must bargain in good faith. However, either party may insist on its position and back that up with a strike or a lockout.

Employers and unions are free to bargain over any topics they agree to discuss. Among the topics that may be placed on the bargaining table because they have been determined by the NLRB or the courts to be subject to mandatory bargaining are the following:

- Pay rate
- Insurance plans
- Holidays
- Overtime pay
- Vacations
- Retirement plans
- Work hours
- Individual merit raises
- Breaks and lunch periods
- Safety practices
- Seniority rights
- Discipline procedures
- Termination procedures
- Layoff procedures
- Recall rights
- Union dues collection

- Grievance procedures
- Arbitration procedures
- No-strike clauses
- Drug testing

There is no requirement that every such issue be covered in a collective bargaining contract, only that the employer must consider demands about such issues raised by the union. In case the employer and the union cannot reach an agreement, an arbitrator may be called in to help get the talks going, or either party may request help from the Federal Mediation and Conciliation Service. These mediators have no authority to impose a settlement but often help the parties reach an agreement.

Arbitration Clauses

Under *grievance arbitration* clauses defined in collective bargaining agreements, disputes between employers and unions are resolved by an internal grievance procedure. If the results are not satisfactory, disputes are heard by an outside labor arbitrator. If an arbitration decision is violated, the aggrieved party may then sue for enforcement.

Almost all collective bargaining agreements contain such dispute-resolution clauses. The federal courts encourage the use of the grievance arbitration process. This helps prevent the federal court system from being clogged with thousands of disputes.

Concerted Activities

For productive collective bargaining, an employer and a union must be able to back up their positions. A union can do so with a strike, an employer can lock out the workers, or each side may use some other activity that puts pressure on the other party to settle. To promote productive collective bargaining, Congress provided that certain activities would be protected so that the parties could back up bargaining demands.

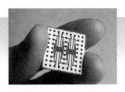

Getty Images

CYBER LAW

Employee Blogs

Most large employers use controls on e-mail. They have policies making clear that the organization has the right to access all e-mails that come to company computers or accounts. Software scans e-mails for red flag words—*sex, guarantee, social security number,* and so on. These controls help companies reduce lost work time, litigation from employees who claim harassment from e-mails with sexual content, and loss of information that should be secure.

Blogs have now become a concern. Some employees have been *dounced, or* fired, as a result of blogging activity. Since blog comments can be posted anonymously, it can be difficult and costly to track down who contributed to a negative blog. If a firm can show that defamation or trade secrets are involved, then it may obtain the right of discovery from a court to uncover the trail of the blogger, but courts do not wish to issue injunctions against blogs, because that gets into suppression of speech issues.

If a blog is dedicated to complaining about company employment policies, the speech may be protected as a part of concerted activity under the National Labor Relations Act. Some firms have announced policies about blogs. This can make clear that it is illegal to discuss financial information (securities laws or fiduciary obligations), personnel matters (employee privacy rights), proprietary information (trade secrets), and that employees who make negative comments about other employees, managers, or customers will be fired.

Protected Activities

The NLRA protects the rights of employees, individually or in groups, to engage in *concerted activities* for mutual aid or protection. Protected concerted activity includes most union organizing efforts. It also involves actions by employees, unionized or not, such as a refusal to work because of unreasonable hazards or other working conditions that endanger health or safety.

Unprotected Activities

If workers engage in threats or acts of violence, they will not be protected by the law. The Supreme Court has held that employers may fire employees for insubordination, disobedience, or disloyalty, unless the reason for such activity involves protected concerted activity. That is, a worker may not be fired for engaging in a union organizing activity that the employer thinks is disloyal.

Strikes and Boycotts

A *primary boycott*—a strike by a union against an employer whose collective bargaining agreement is in question—is clearly legal. The law restricts *secondary boycotts*, which occur when a union uses economic pressure to try to force others to stop doing business with an employer not directly involved in a primary labor dispute. The following secondary boycotts are illegal:

- A strike against an employer other than the one involved in the primary labor dispute, such as a strike against the steel companies that sell steel to the automakers if a strike is going on against the automakers.
- Refusal to handle goods or perform services for a secondary employer, such as refusing to carry steel from the steel companies to the automakers during a strike against the automakers.
- Threats, coercion, or restraints against any person engaging in commerce— usually an employee—in an effort to spread the dispute beyond the primary employer. For example, in a strike against the food manufacturer Hormel, the union picketed local banks, some of which did business with Hormel, others of which did not. The NLRB ruled that the union could not picket any of the banks, since they were not directly involved with Hormel products. The picketing was an unfair labor practice, an illegal secondary boycott.

Employer Economic Responses

Although employers may not retaliate against employees for engaging in protected activities, they have the right to use economic pressure. As previously noted, an employer may lock out the employees, or refuse to let them work until the dispute with the union is settled.

Lockouts are legal if evidence of bad intent is not shown, such as trying to break the union. A lockout is usually defensive—in response to a strike, to prevent a sit-down strike in the plant, or to prevent some other activity that would be destructive to the plant or its materials. So long as the lockout is seen as promoting the settlement of the collective bargaining process, it is most likely legal.

Replacement Workers

A tactic successfully used by companies in recent years is the hiring of nonunion workers to replace striking workers. Once a collective bargaining agreement expires, if the union and the employer have not agreed to a new contract, and the union calls for a strike, the employer may hire new workers and keep using existing workers who will cross the picket line (crossovers). In some cases, there were enough replacement workers and crossovers that the union disappeared or lost substantial strength by the time a new agreement was signed.

Summary

- There are public policy restrictions on employment at-will, either by statute or by court determination. These include a right not to be fired or disciplined for refusing to commit an illegal act, for performing a public duty, or for exercising a public right. In limited circumstances, there is an exception for whistle-blowers.

- State law varies on employment contracts that may be in violation of public policy. Exculpatory agreements waiving tort rights or other causes of action are not looked on with favor. Anti-raiding covenants and noncompete agreements are allowed in many states, if reasonable, but are prohibited in some states.

- Most companies have policies regarding testing for substance abuse and steps that must be taken by an employee if abuse is detected. Generally, companies are free to require drug tests of job applicants and of employees in positions that impact health, safety, or large sums of money. Companies may wish to control substance abuse to reduce medical expenses, improve worker productivity, and reduce accidents.

- OSHA may impose work safety and health regulations. If a company fails to meet minimal safety standards, workers have the right to walk off the job to protect their health. OSHA regulations must be justified by documented health or safety needs, but there is no requirement that they be cost effective. OSHA HazMat rules regard worker handling of hazardous chemicals.

- Most employers must pay for workers' compensation insurance to ensure that injured employees, regardless of fault, have medical expenses covered and receive partial compensation for lost wages. Workers' compensation prohibits tort suits except in cases of intentional infliction of injury.

- Labor regulations require employers to collect evidence that all new employees are U.S. citizens or are noncitizens with legal work status. Employers must also comply with federal minimum wage requirements. Under the WARN Act, employers of more than 100 employees must notify employees at least 60 days in advance of any plant closings or layoffs that will affect 50 or more employees. Employers with 50 or more employees must allow employees to take up to 12 weeks unpaid leave for family or medical reasons under the FMLA.

- The Employee Retirement Income Security Act (ERISA) gives employees the right to their pension benefits after a certain time of service and provides federal inspection and guarantee of the solvency of pension funds.

- Under the Norris–La Guardia Act, federal courts may not issue injunctions against unions in labor disputes. Employers must bargain with unions according to the terms of the collective bargaining agreement, rather than seek relief in federal court.

- The National Labor Relations Act (NLRA) originated with the Wagner Act in 1935. Employees may organize unions and bargain collectively through representatives of their choosing. Employers may not interfere in the exercise of those rights, and employee actions may not interfere with the employer's interest in plant safety and efficiency. The Act created the National Labor Relations Board (NLRB), which is responsible for resolving unfair labor practice complaints and supervising matters of union representation.

- The Landrum–Griffin Act, a part of the NLRA, regulates internal union affairs. The law was intended to make union procedures and elections democratic. It covers the election of union leadership, protects the right of union members to speak out about union matters, and assures union members the right to see the books of the union, which are audited by the Department of Labor.
- If more than 30 percent of the workers at a work place petition for a union representation election, the NLRB holds an election to determine whether a majority of the workers want union representation. Workers can also vote to end union representation. The employer and the union debate the pros and cons of union representation before workers vote.
- When a majority of the workers at a work place vote for union representation, all workers are covered by the collective bargaining agreement settled by management and the union, and all workers must follow the procedures established for handling complaints. Workers who are not union members must follow the rules set by the collective bargaining contract.
- Workers who work at a unionized workplace must either join the union and pay dues or, if they do not want to join the union, pay agency fees to the union. Agency fees should not include money used for union political purposes; they are to cover the cost of union representation. In the 22 right-to-work states—which are allowed under the Taft–Hartley Act—workers at unionized work places cannot be forced to pay agency fees, making unions less effective in such states.

Terms to Know

You should be able to define the following terms:

whistle-blower, 389	FMLA leave, 401	agency fees, 410
exculpatory agreement, 390	licensing requirements, 403	right-to-work laws, 411
exculpatory clause, 390	vesting, 405	collective bargaining, 412
anti-raiding covenant, 391	yellow-dog contracts, 406	mandatory subjects of bargaining, 412
noncompete agreement, 391	unfair labor practices, 406	concerted activities, 414
substance abuse policy, 394	authorization cards, 409	secondary boycott, 414
hazard communication standard, 397	union certification, 410	lockout, 414
workers' compensation, 397	agency shops, 410	

Discussion Question

1. Do firms have the right to test all job applicants and refuse to hire applicants who test positive for drug use, even if the job in question has no safety or sensitivity concerns?

Case Questions

1. Barbara Reynolds and Jason Stephens were at-will truck drivers for Ozark Motor Lines. They were fired when they refused to begin a trip from Memphis to Chicago without having adequate time to inspect the truck as required by safety provisions of the Tennessee Motor Carriers Act. The jury found this to be wrongful dismissal, because Ozark violated statutory public policy. Was this upheld on appeal? [*Reynolds* v. *Ozark Motor Lines*, 887 S.W.2d 822 Sup. Ct., Tenn. (1994)]
2. Rowan worked for TSC. She believed that her manager, Snider, and other employees were embezzling money from TSC. When Rowan expressed her concern to Snider, he twised her arm and pushed her. Rowan reported the matter to Snider's supervisor,

Carter, who told her to "keep her mouth shut." Rowan sued Snider for assault and was awarded $1,500 in damages. She also reported the assault to the police and charges were filed against Snider. A TSC manager told Rowan to drop the criminal charges. She refused and was fired. Snider was convicted of criminal assault and battery. Rowan sued TSC for wrongful termination in violation of public policy. The federal district court certified a question to the Virginia supreme court, asking if the public policy exception to the employment-at-will doctrine applied in this case. Do you think it does? [*Rowan* v. *Tractor Supply* 559 S.E.2d 709 Sup. Ct., Va. (2002)]

✓ Check your answer at http://academic.cengage.com/blaw/meiners

3. Tanks was a bus driver for the Greater Cleveland Rapid Transit Authority (GCRTA). The GCRTA had a substance abuse policy to protect public safety that required drivers to be tested after accidents. Tanks ran into a pole. As required, she submitted blood, saliva, and urine samples, which tested positive for cocaine. Under the terms of the policy, Tanks was fired. She sued, claiming that the drug test was an unreasonable search in violation of the Fourth Amendment to the Constitution. Did she have a case? [*Tanks* v. *GCRTA*, 930 F.2d 475, 6th Cir. (1991)]

4. A group of Boeing workers sued for injuries and disabilities from their four-year exposure to toxic chemicals. There was evidence that Boeing had known of the problem but did nothing about it. Boeing asserted that the employees could collect, if anything, under workers' compensation; the employees sued for intentional tort. Could they bring such an action? [*Birklid* v. *Boeing*, 904 P.2d 278 Wash. Sup. Ct. (1995)]

✓ Check your answer at http://academic.cengage.com/blaw/meiners

5. Nastasi drove a propane gas truck for Synergy Gas. He had been active in getting a union certified as the bargaining agent for fellow employees. The unionization fight was bitter, and the company was cited by the NLRB for five unfair labor practices. Soon after the unionization fight, Nastasi was in an accident in his truck. Synergy fired him, claiming that it fired all drivers in serious accidents, because of the danger involved in driving such trucks. The union protested that the firing was because of Nastasi's union leadership. The NLRB ordered Nastasi reinstated to his job; Synergy appealed. What would you think was the result was? [*Synergy Gas* v. *NLRB*, 19 F.3d 649 D.C. Cir. (1994)]

6. During a unionization campaign, a company told workers that no materials related to the union effort could be posted on employee bulletin boards. A supervisor told a union supporter that "if we got a union in there, we'd be in the unemployment line." The union claimed these were unfair labor practices. The NLRB agreed; did the court? [*Guardian Industries* v. *NLRB*, 49 F.3d 317, 7th Cir. (1995)]

✓ Check your answer at http://academic.cengage.com/blaw/meiners

7. WinCo operates a grocery store in Chico, California. It sits on a 10-acre parcel of land. Except for allowing Girl Scouts to sell cookies on the premises, WinCo has allowed no other solicitors. Union organizers came on the premises and passed out handbills purported to be from "Mothers Against WinCo," urging shoppers not to patronize the store. WinCo kicked the organizers off the premises. The union complained and the NLRB held that WinCo violated the NLRA when it prohibited non employee union representatives from giving handbills to customers. WinCo petitioned for review of the NLRB order. Was the NLRB correct? [*Waremart Foods* v. *NLRB*, 354 F.3d 870 D.C. Cir. (2004)]

8. When a collective bargaining agreement with IMT expired, the workers went on strike. The company announced it would take crossovers and then hire replacement workers, which it did. After the strike was settled, the union claimed the company had to take back all strikers in place of the replacement workers. Is that position correct? [*Iowa Mold Tooling Co.* v. *Teamsters Local Union No. 828.*, 16 F.3d 311, 8th Cir. (1994)]

Ethics Question

1. Contemplating the opening of a factory, you discover that it appears to be a toss-up between building a plant that uses cheaper machinery and hiring 200 workers who will

earn an average of $8 an hour and building a plant that uses more expensive, sophisticated machinery and hiring 70 workers likely to earn about $20 an hour. Is it more responsible to build one kind of factory than another? What if you know that the first kind of factory will probably never be unionized, but the second kind of factory is more likely to be unionized?

Internet Assignment

http://www.nlrb.gov
http://www.dol.gov
http://www.osha.gov

1. What is the policy stated in the National Labor Relations Act (Wagner Act, 1935), 29 U.S.C. 151 *et sequitur?*
2. What is the URL for decisions (Vol. 255–) of the National Labor Relations Board?
3. What is the URL for the Fair Labor Standards Act (FLSA) Advisor? (Hint: Wage and Hour Division)
4. What is the finding stated in the Occupational Safety and Health Act (OSHA, 1970), 29 U.S.C. 553, 651 *et sequitur?*
5. According to the OSHA Web site, what are the three forms of anthrax infection?

Employment Discrimination

Chapter 17

The owner of an Iowa electronics company made sexual advances to an employee after she posed nude in a nationally distributed magazine. Was he guilty of violating the law that limits sex discrimination in employment? "John Doe" worked as an engineer at Boeing aircraft. After six years at Boeing—under the supervision of his physician—he decided to become "Jane Doe." Prior to sex-transformation surgery, he began to live the social role of a woman. Boeing fired Doe for using the women's restroom and dressing as a woman despite company orders not to do so prior to sex-change surgery. Was Boeing guilty of disability discrimination?

These cases illustrate the wide range of employment issues that arise today. Years ago, neither of these cases would have emerged, but now the law restricts employment practices with respect to discrimination based on personal characteristics. In this chapter, we focus on the Civil Rights Act of 1964, which is the primary basis of modern employment discrimination law, the statutes that have been added over the years, and the cases that have helped to define the rights and duties of employees and employers in dealing with race, sex, color, religion, national origin, age, and disability.

The answer to the first question, was the owner guilty of sex discrimination, is yes; the answer to the second question, was Boeing guilty of disability discrimination, is no. ■

Getty Images

Origins of Discrimination Law

Discrimination in employment is a fact that occurs in varying degrees everywhere. More than 40 years after passage of the most important antidiscrimination legislation in history, discrimination in employment still exists, but it is not as overt as it was in earlier times.

Some of the differences in wages between men and women and between people of different races are due to voluntary choices by individuals, but the impact of subtle discriminatory decisions is significant. Studies indicate a persistent discrimination in favor of white job candidates over black job candidates, when qualifications are held to be equal.

Many of the differences between men and women and between racial and ethnic groups may be unintentional and attributable to employment patterns. Some of the "wage gap" is attributed to differences in education, training, family demands, and years of experience in the workforce. Careful stastical analysis shows that the wage gap for younger men and women with similar education, experience, and life situations has nearly disappeared. Still, some disparity is probably due to stereotyped assumptions about productivity and to preferences for associating with "one's own kind" in the workplace.

The Civil Rights Movements

Historically, employers could hire and fire at will, subject to the limits we covered in the last chapter. Employers could discriminate because of race, sex, or any other personal characteristics. Similarly, labor unions could impose discriminatory membership rules. The situation was worsened by federal and state laws—Jim Crow laws—that supported segregation and labor market discrimination.

The drive for civil rights in employment and other aspects of life became a national movement in the early 1960s. Rising public concern provided support for the first federal employment discrimination statute in 1963, the Equal Pay Act, followed by the Civil Rights Act of 1964, which is the cornerstone of federal employment discrimination law.

The Equal Pay Act of 1963

The *Equal Pay Act of 1963* was the first federal law to address employment discrimination. It prohibits pay discrimination on the basis of sex. It is illegal to pay men and women employees different wages when a job requires equal skill, effort, responsibility, and the same working conditions. Job titles are not relevant; job content is reviewed. The Equal Pay Act allows differences in wages if they are due to "(i) a seniority system; (ii) a merit system; (iii) a system which measures earnings by quantity or quality of production; or (iv) a differential based on any factor other than sex." Pay differentials on the basis of sex are to be eliminated by raising the pay of the women employees, not by lowering the pay of the men employees. Some sex discrimination suits are brought based on the 1963 statute, but the vast majority of discrimination suits are brought under Title VII of the Civil Rights Act.

Title VII of the 1964 Civil Rights Act

The most important antidiscrimination employment law is *Title VII of the Civil Rights Act of 1964.* The Act was amended in 1972 by the *Equal Employment Opportunity Act* to give the *Equal Employment Opportunity Commission (EEOC)* the power to enforce the Act, by the *Pregnancy Discrimination Act* in 1978, and by the *Civil Rights Act of 1991*. Title VII makes it illegal for an employer of fifteen or more workers

> (1) to fail or refuse to hire or to discharge any individual, or otherwise to discriminate against any individual with respect to his compensation, terms, conditions, or privileges of employment; or
>
> (2) to limit, segregate, or classify his employees or applicants for employment in any way which would deprive or tend to deprive any individual of employment opportunities or otherwise adversely affect his status as an employee because of such individual's race, color, religion, sex, or national origin.

Protected Classes

Title VII applies to employers, employment agencies, and labor unions in the private and public sectors. In general, it forbids *discrimination* in all aspects of employment on the basis of *race, color, religion, sex, or national origin*. The Supreme Court has stated that law firms and other partnership organizations are covered by the law, but that the law does not apply to business relationships or to the selection of independent contractors.

Title VII requires *equal employment opportunity* regardless of race, color, religion, sex, or national origin. Congress sought to protect certain classes of people who had a history of discriminatory treatment in employment relationships. Race, color, national origin, religion, and sex are the characteristics that determine *protected classes* for purposes of Title VII coverage.

Race

The courts have little difficulty in determining racial class. Federal law recognizes five major racial groupings: black or African American, white, American Indian or Alaska Native; Native Hawaiian or other Pacific Islander, Asian, and the ethnic category Hispanic or Latino.

Contrary to some claims that have been made, whites are protected under Title VII. That was made clear by the Supreme Court in *McDonald* v. *Santa Fe Trail Transportation* (96 S.Ct. 2574). In *McDonald*, an African-American employee and a white employee had stolen property from their employer. The African-American employee was reprimanded but allowed to keep his job, but the white employee was fired. The Court stated:

> Title VII prohibits racial discrimination against the white petitioners.... While Santa Fe may decide that participation in a theft of cargo may render an employee unqualified for employment, this criteria must be applied alike to members of all races.

Reverse discrimination—preferential treatment to members of protected classes—is illegal, but if minorities or women are *underrepresented* in a certain job category, it is legal for an employer to see that more minorities or women are hired to increase their share of the jobs. Affirmative action programs, which we will discuss later, designed to remedy discrimination against minorities or women may be adopted but may not violate the rule against reverse discrimination. Race is the most common basis for a discrimination complaint. It is the claim in about 36 percent of the charges filed, or 27,000 per year.

Color

Under Title VII, the term *color* refers generally to discrimination claims based on shade of skin. A small number of discrimination cases are in this category only, some brought by dark-skinned blacks against light-skinned blacks. Another example would be for a department store to refuse to hire a Hispanic woman to work at a cosmetics counter, because they would prefer to have a blue-eyed blonde with light skin in that position.

National Origin

According to the Supreme Court in *Espinoza* v. *Farah Manufacturing* (94 S.Ct. 334), the term *national origin* is to be given its ordinary meaning:

> [The term national origin] refers to the country where a person is born or … the country from which his or her ancestors came.

Discrimination has been held to exist where a person has a physical, cultural, or speech characteristic of a national origin group. Hispanics bring most suits under this category. For example, it may be discrimination to require that English be spoken at all times in the workplace. However, if business necessity requires that English be spoken, such as for reasons of safety or productivity, it may be a legitimate job requirement. Employment discrimination can take place when an employer allows ethnic slurs to occur and does not take steps to prevent such actions.

This protection is not provided to noncitizens (aliens) employed or seeking employment in this country. However, while an employer may discriminate against aliens, the employer may not discriminate on the basis of different origins. For example, an employer may not accept aliens from Italy but reject all aliens from Mexico.

Religion

Title VII does not define the term *religion* but states that "religion includes all aspects of religious observances and practice." This includes strong believers and atheists. The courts have defined the term broadly. According to the Court in *United States* v. *Seeger* (380 U.S. 163):

> [All that is required is a] sincere and meaningful belief occupying in the life of its possessor a place parallel to that filled by the God of those [religions generally recognized].

The employer is required to provide *reasonable accommodation* for an employee's religious practices. The employer may discriminate, however, if the accommodation will impose an *undue hardship* on the conduct of business. The Court has stated that undue hardship is created by accommodations that would cost an employer more than a minimal amount. For example, if an employer has a strict dress code so that the company gives a certain "look" to the public, the code need not be modified to allow certain employees to wear religious garb, such as a headdress. But if an employer does not have a strict code, then it could not tell an employee not to wear religious garb.

Further, an employer need not make other employees change their work schedule to accommodate the religious holiday preferences of an employee. But if such accommodation can be made at no cost other than giving employees the opportunity to switch work days, then only a minimal cost is incurred.

A religious institution, such as a seminary training ministers or mullahs, may legally hire only members of a particular religion for jobs in which that is critical. For example, Baylor University, a Baptist school, may wish to hire only Baptists to teach in its seminary. But it could not require that math instructors be Baptist, because there is no religious purpose in teaching math, unlike teaching religion.

INTERNATIONAL PERSPECTIVE

EEOC Impact on Global Operations

American firms have operations in other countries, and foreign firms have operations in the United States. Americans work for American firms in other countries; foreign citizens work for American firms in the United States and in other countries. When does Equal Employment Opportunity (EEO) law apply? This is not a trivial matter, because EEO law in the United States is much tougher than in most nations.

Sayaka Kobayashi was a personal assistant in New York to Hideaki Otaka, president of Toyota's North American operations. She complained that Otaka groped her and made numerous sexual advances. When she complained, she was told she should meet with Otaka privately to discuss the matter, or she could quit. She sued in federal court, because U.S. law applied to foreign operations in

the United States that employed foreign citizens. The president resigned and returned to Japan.

In general, U.S. law applies to anyone working for a company located in the United States and to U.S. citizens working for U.S. companies in other countries. But EEO does not apply to non-U.S. citizens working for U.S. companies in other countries. So, for example, when the Michigan company, Lear, ran an ad for a secretary for its operation in Mexico, it stated it wanted a woman, aged 20 to 28, unmarried, with "excellent presentation," and stated that she should submit a photo. Similarly, a large U.S. law firm, Baker and McKenzie, ran an ad for an attorney in Mexico. It wanted a man, the firm said, because Mexican clients expect to see a man. Those ads were legal in Mexico but probably were not good for public relations in the United States.

Getty Images

Discrimination because of religion is the charge in a little over 3 percent of the complaints filed annually, about 2,500 per year. Discrimination includes harassment based on religion. As with other protected classes, an employer must take steps to stop other employees from harassing an employee because of religion. It should be noted that *intersectional discrimination* is charged in a number of complaints filed; that is, a person may claim to suffer discrimination because of race (Asian) *and* because of religion (Buddhist).

LIGHTER SIDE OF THE LAW

A New Protected Class?

Curt Storey sued Burns International Security Services for wrongful discharge. He claimed he was fired for refusing to remove Confederate flags from his lunchbox and pickup truck.

A lifelong resident of Pennsylvania, Storey claims protection to display such items, because he is a "Confederate Southern American." Title VII does not recognize loyalty to the Confederacy as a protected class.

Source: *Observer-Reporter* (Washington, PA.)

Getty Images

Sex

The courts hold that the term *sex* should be given its ordinary meaning. Thus, Title VII prohibits sex discrimination simply on the basis of whether a person is male or female. This is the basis for complaints in about 31 percent of the cases, or 23,000 per year. Discrimination on the basis of sexual preference or sexual identity is not protected by Title VII, although the law in some states prohibits discrimination on the basis of sexual orientation. Title VII does not prohibit discrimination on the basis of marital status, as long as an employer applies employment rules evenly to employees of both sexes. However, many states prohibit discrimination on the basis of marital status.

Obvious examples of sex discrimination, or discrimination based on race or some other protected class, would include an employer allowing one protected class to work overtime but not another. It would be discrimination to hire men to be sales representatives but to hire women only for office-based positions. It would be discriminatory to require women to wear a uniform, while allowing men to wear what they want.

Pregnancy Discrimination Title VII was amended by the *Pregnancy Discrimination Act.* It states that an employer may not discriminate against women because of pregnancy, childbirth, or related medical conditions. Women affected by these conditions "shall be treated the same for all employment-related purposes, including receipt of benefits under fringe benefit programs." Examples of pregnancy discrimination include:

- Denying a woman a job, assignment, or promotion because she is pregnant or has children
- Requiring a pregnant woman to go on leave when she is able to do her job
- Treating maternity leave differently than other leaves for temporary disabilities
- Discriminating in fringe benefits, such as health insurance, to discourage women of childbearing age from working

Sexual Harassment A sexually hostile work environment is a form of sex discrimination. *Sexual harassment* is defined by the EEOC in the *Code of Federal Regulations* as unwelcome sexual advances, requests for sexual favors, and other verbal or physical conduct of a sexual nature ... when

(1) submission to such conduct is made either explicitly or implicitly a term or condition of an individual's employment,
(2) submission to or rejection of such conduct by an individual is used as a basis for employment decisions affecting such individual, or
(3) such conduct has the purpose or effect of unreasonably interfering with an individual's work performance or creating an intimidating, hostile, or offensive working environment.

CYBER LAW

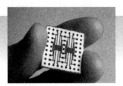

Your E-mail Is Your Boss's E-mail

In general, e-mail that is sent at work on company computers is available for company inspection. Whether the employee is told or not, employers have the right to monitor employee e-mail. A class-action suit by Epson employees against their employer for routinely reading employee e-mail was dismissed by the court, because there was no right-of-privacy issue.

A sports writer for a Chicago newspaper was told by his employer to quit sending unwanted e-mail to a female co-worker. When he did not quit sending her e-mail, the employer transferred the writer to another department. A federal court held that the paper was within its rights to do so; the employee could not complain about the interference with his e-mail, nor could he claim sex discrimination. The employer "was obviously trying to make the best of a difficult situation." See *Greenslade* v. *Chicago Sun-Times* (112F.3d 853).

Why do employers care so much about e-mail transmissions at work? Chevron paid $2.2 million to settle sexual harassment claims of women employees for dirty jokes

Getty Images

In practice, sexual harassment has been put in two major categories. The first is *quid pro quo*, or "this for that," where there is a promise of reward—such as promotion or pay raise—for providing sexual favors, or there is a threat of punishment for not going along with sexual requests. The second form is a *hostile environment* created at work by others (obviously a hostile environment can exist because of race or some other characteristic). An abusive work environment is created by words or acts related to a person's sex. Examples are

- Discussing sexual activities
- Commenting on physical attributes
- Unnecessary touching or gestures
- Using crude, demeaning, or offensive language
- Displaying sexually suggestive pictures

Trivial and isolated incidents usually are not sufficient grounds for a sexual harassment suit. The courts look to factors such as how often such conduct occurred; whether the harassment was by a supervisor who could control progress, pay, and working conditions or by a co-worker; whether there was talk or actual touching; and whether more than one person was involved. The Supreme Court offered guidance in the *Harris* case about what constitutes a hostile work environment in general. Again, this analysis would apply if the situation were based on race or other protected class.

Harris v. Forklift Systems
United States Supreme Court
510 U.S.17, 114 S.Ct.367 (1993)

Case Background *Harris worked as a rental manager for two years for Forklift Systems. Her boss, Hardy, often insulted her in front of others and made her the target of sexual slurs and suggestions. He said, "We need a man as the rental manager," and "you're a woman, what do you know?" He told her she was "a dumb-ass woman," and that they should "go to the Holiday Inn to negotiate her raise." Hardy asked Harris and other women employees to get coins from his front pants pocket, throw things on the ground and ask women to pick them up, and make sexual comments about their clothing.*

Harris complained to Hardy about his comments. Hardy said that he was only kidding. When Harris arranged a deal with a customer, Hardy asked her, "What did you do, promise the guy sex Saturday night?" Harris quit and sued, claiming that Hardy's conduct created a hostile work environment. The district and appeals courts ruled against her. She appealed.

Case Decision O'Connor, Justice

* * *

When the workplace is permeated with "discriminatory intimidation, ridicule, and insult" that is "sufficiently severe or pervasive to alter the conditions of the victim's employment and create an abusive working environment," Title VII is violated.

This standard … takes a middle path between making actionable any conduct that is merely offensive and requiring the conduct to cause a tangible psychological injury.… Conduct that is not severe or pervasive enough to create an objectively hostile or abusive work environment—an environment that a reasonable person would find hostile or abusive—is beyond Title VII's purview. Likewise, if the victim does not subjectively perceive the environment to be abusive, the conduct has not actually altered the conditions of the victim's employment, and there is no Title VII violation.

But Title VII comes into play before the harassing conduct leads to a nervous breakdown. A discriminatorily abusive work environment, even one that does not seriously affect employees' psychological well-being, can and often will detract from employees' job performance, discourage employees from remaining on the job, or keep them from advancing in their careers. Moreover, even without regard to these tangible effects, the very fact that the discriminatory conduct was so severe or pervasive that it created a work environment abusive to employees because of their race, gender, religion, or national origin offends Title VII's broad rule of workplace equality.…

continues

This is not, and by its nature cannot be, a mathematically precise test.... But we can say that whether an environment is "hostile" or "abusive" can be determined only by looking at all the circumstances. These may include the frequency of the discriminatory conduct; its severity; whether it is physically threatening or humiliating, or a mere offensive utterance; and whether it unreasonably interferes with an employee's work performance. The effect on the employee's psychological well-being is, of course, relevant to determining whether the plaintiff actually found the environment abusive. But while psychological harm, like any other relevant factor, may be taken into account, no single factor is required.

* * *

We therefore reverse the judgment of the Court of Appeals, and remand the case for further proceedings consistent with this opinion.

Questions for Analysis

1. The court held that the actions must be severe enough to created a hostile work environment to a reasonable person. If this issue were left to a jury, might not some people on the jury, especially men, be likely to think that Harris overreacted?
2. Two concurring opinions indicated that another standard that might be focused on is whether the abusive actions are sufficient to affect work performance. Would that provide better guidance?

The Supreme Court further clarified the law in *Oncale* v. *Sundowner Offshore Services* (118 S. Ct. 998). In that case, a male worker sued his employer because he suffered verbal and physical abuse of a sexual nature by other male workers. The Court held that same-sex harassment is prohibited by Title VII. The law:

> does not reach genuine but innocuous differences in the ways men and women routinely interact with members of the same sex and of the opposite sex. The prohibition of harassment ... forbids only behavior so objectively offensive as to alter the "conditions" of the victim's employment.... the objective severity of harassment should be judged from the perspective of a reasonable person in the plaintiff's position, considering "all the circumstances." ... Common sense, and an appropriate sensitivity to social context, will enable courts and juries to distinguish between simple teasing or roughhousing among members of the same sex, and conduct which a reasonable person in the plaintiff's position would find severely hostile or abusive.

Age Discrimination

Enacted in 1967 and amended since, the *Age Discrimination in Employment Act (ADEA)* prohibits discrimination in employment against persons over age 40. All employers who have 20 or more employees must comply. The ADEA generally parallels Title VII in its prohibitions, exceptions, remedies, and enforcement. So, while the ADEA is a separate statute, we presume it acts the same way as Title VII unless specifically noted. The law prohibits failing or refusing to hire or promote because of age, terminating employees because of age, or other discrimination in the terms of employment. About 22 percent of the discrimination claims, or 17,000 a year, are in this category.

Often the courts must, as in cases of race or sex discrimination, look to see whether age discrimination can be inferred by studying practices at the place of employment. The following are examples of age discrimination:

- Forcing retirement because of age
- Requiring older workers to pass physical examinations as a condition of continued employment
- Indicating an age preference in advertisements for employees, such as "young, dynamic person wanted"

- Choosing to promote a younger worker rather than an older worker, because the older worker may be retiring in several years
- Cutting health care benefits for workers over age 65 because they are eligible for Medicare

Bringing a Charge of Discrimination

If someone believes they have suffered a discriminatory act in employment under Title VII, the ADA, or the Disabilities Act we will look at later, a charge may be filed by mail or in person at an EEOC office or a similar state agency. For example, in Illinois, the complaint could be filed at the Illinois Department of Human Rights. The EEOC and state agencies, referred to as *Fair Employment Practices Agencies*, share the workload, because most actions can be under state or federal law. Under federal law, a charge must be filed within 180 days of an alleged discriminatory event, but state law extends this to 300 days in most instances.

Steps in the Process

The EEOC receives about 75,000 charges a year, so it must sort them based on an initial evaluation. If the charges appear to be particularly strong, then the case may get priority for staff investigation. When a claim seems more dubious, it is likely to sit on the back burner awaiting investigation.

As Exhibit 17.1 indicates, the EEOC investigates claims. This may involve interviews, requests for documents, and visits to places of employment. At any point, the EEOC can seek to settle a charge by mediation if the parties agree; otherwise, the investigation continues to completion.

The majority of charges are dismissed by the EEOC because, in the agency's judgment, no violation is likely to have occurred; that is, no reasonable cause exists. The party who brought the charge may still file suit, but that is not common. If the agency determines that a violation may have occurred, it can offer a settlement to the parties, besides mediation, or issue the plaintiff a *right to sue letter* that can be used in proceeding to court; the agency essentially bows out of the matter. The plaintiff, through a private attorney, proceeds to state or federal court.

Exhibit 17.1 Usual steps in a Discrimination Complaint to EEOC

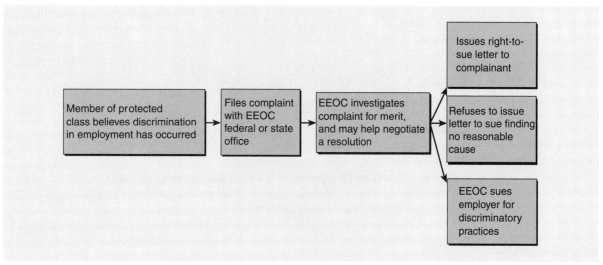

In some instances, but only in a small percentage of cases, the agency sues on behalf of the complaining party or on behalf of that party and others who are similarly affected, creating a class of plaintiffs. EEOC resources for such cases tend to be reserved for those in which a pattern of discriminatory behavior is believed present, not just for discrimination against one party.

Forms of Discrimination

The laws against discrimination in employment cover most of the conditions of the employment process: hiring, promotion, transfers, discipline, pay raises, benefits, opportunities, and termination. When employers impose *differential standards* on the basis of a protected class status, a violation of the law may have occurred.

As we saw in the *Harris* case, discrimination can also involve making life miserable for an employee, which is illegal *harassment*. Even if there was no discrimination on the basis of pay, employees need not tolerate abusive behavior that is related to protected class status. If an employee quits because of harassment, as in the *Harris* case, then there was a *constructive discharge*. That is, the employee was driven from the job by harassment. There is no obligation to stay and take abuse. However, as we will see, internal company policy makes a big difference in this regard.

Since employees have the right to make complaints about discrimination, if they are punished for doing so, then there is a basis for suit for *retaliation*. If workers are punished for participating in an official proceeding, such as filing a complaint or giving testimony in a discrimination investigation, they would have grounds for suit based on retaliation for a violation of a protected right.

Traditionally, cases have been broken down into two major groups: *disparate treatment* and *disparate impact*. While the Supreme Court seems to be gradually moving away from this categorization, it is still common in use. Disparate treatment cases are the vast majority of cases, so we will spend the most time on those and then return to disparate impact.

Disparate Treatment

To recover for illegal discrimination—whether for race, color, religion, sex, national origin, or age—in a claim of *disparate treatment*, the plaintiff must prove that the employer *intentionally* discriminated. That is, a member of a protected class claims an employer treated the plaintiff differently than other employees because of the plaintiff's personal characteristics. Next, we go through the key steps of such a case.

Plaintiff Must Establish a Prima Facie Case The Supreme Court established a four-part test in the *McDonnell–Douglas* decision (93 S.Ct. 1817), that the plaintiff in a disparate treatment case must meet to provide a *prima facie discrimination case*. Exhibit 17.2 lists the four steps that must be met for a case to go forward. This test holds for all aspects of employment—hiring, promotion, compensation, conditions, discipline, and termination. In *Swierkiewicz* v. *Sorema* (122 S.Ct. 992), the Supreme Court made clear that only a "short and plain statement of the claim" is needed. Once the plaintiff meets the McDonnell–Douglas test, the case goes forward and the burden shifts to the defendant to overcome the presumption of discrimination.

Burden Shifts to Defendant After a plaintiff shows a prima facie case of employment discrimination, the plaintiff wins unless the employer provides a successful defense; that is, the burden shifts to the defendant to present evidence that the claim is untrue or that there was a legal reason for the employment decision. The employer must show a legitimate, nondiscriminatory, clear, and reasonably specific

Exhibit 17.2 Initial Steps in Disparate Treatment Cases

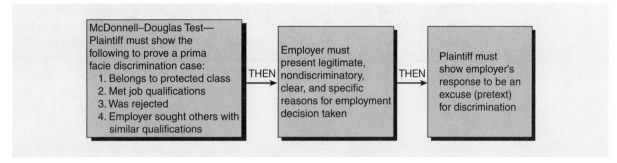

McDonnell–Douglas Test—Plaintiff must show the following to prove a prima facie discrimination case:
1. Belongs to protected class
2. Met job qualifications
3. Was rejected
4. Employer sought others with similar qualifications

THEN

Employer must present legitimate, nondiscriminatory, clear, and specific reasons for employment decision taken

THEN

Plaintiff must show employer's response to be an excuse (pretext) for discrimination

reason for its decision to overcome the presumption of discrimination. The courts prefer clear standards for employment decisions, rather than vague claims that amount to "I felt like it." Legitimate reasons include, as we will see, such factors as seniority, education, performance, and experience.

LIGHTER SIDE OF THE LAW
Modify Your Body in Private

Cloutier worked for Costco for four years. While she was there, she kept adding to her collection of body piercings, tattoos, cuttings, and scars. She is a card-carrying member of the Church of Body Modification (see its Web site at www.uscobm.com). Costco's dress code requires such personal decorations to be covered or removed. Cloutier refused to hide or remove some new facial piercings, so she was fired.

The EEOC tried to negotiate a compromise, but Cloutier refused to cover her piercings. She sued Costco for $2 million, claiming religious discrimination. The federal court held that while it would presume her religious beliefs were sincere, Costco had the right to a dress code so that customers see the workers as "reasonably professional in appearance."

Source: *Cloutier* v. *Costco,* 311 F.Supp.2d 190 (2004)

Getty Images

Burden Shifts to Plaintiff to Attack Defense After the employer offers a non-discriminatory reason for the employment decision, the burden shifts back to the plaintiff to show that the defendant had an illegal motive. A plaintiff must show that the rationale offered by the employer was just *pretext*, or unacceptable excuses amounting to cover ups, for disparate treatment. Such evidence can take many forms, such as showing inconsistency in decisions made by the employer, giving different reasons at different times for the decision, and presenting statistical evidence of discrimination based on sex or race. While discrimination is clear in some cases, it often requires a review of the entire situation and testimony from witnesses, usually other employees.

Complicating Factor: Mixed Motives

Many discrimination cases are not clear cut. The employee claiming discrimination was not the most wonderful employee, but the employer's story is not fully convincing either. The courts recognize the fact that mixed motives may exist in employment decisions. A plaintiff need not prove that discriminatory intent was the reason for the decision that was made; that is often nearly impossible to do. As the Supreme Court has held, a plaintiff need not have direct evidence of discrimination. Rather, the plaintiff needs to show, even if by circumstantial evidence, that discrimination played *some* role in the employer's decision. It is for a jury to weigh the evidence. We see a discussion of this in the *Machinchick* case. This is an age discrimination case, but the analysis would be the same for other protected classes.

Machinchick v. PB Power
United States Court of Appeals, Fifth Circuit
398 F.3d 345 (2005)

Case Background *Machinchick was hired by PB Power (PB) in 1996 to develop new clients in Houston. He received excellent evaluations and was promoted in 1998. In December 2001, Knowlton became his new supervisor. In January 2002, PB changed its business development tactics. The plan stated that it would "hand-pick employees whose mindset resides in the twenty-first century." On April 7, Knowlton e-mailed his plans to "strategically hire some younger engineers and designers" to execute the new plan. On April 9, he e-mailed PB's human resources department, explaining why Machinchick had problems.*

On April 17, Knowlton told Machinchick he was fired due to poor performance. This ignored PB's written policy that supervisors would engage in discussions with employees who had problems. Machinchick was given no warning. At age 63, he was replaced by Betz, age 42. Machinchick sued for age discrimination in Texas state court. PB moved the case to federal district court, which granted summary judgment in favor of PB. Machinchick appealed.

Case Decision Higginbotham, Circuit Judge

* * *

Direct evidence of discrimination is not necessary in order for a plaintiff to receive a mixed-motive analysis for an ADEA [age discrimination] claim....

Under this ... approach, a plaintiff relying on circumstantial evidence has two options for surviving summary judgment in an ADEA case: (1) the plaintiff may offer evidence showing that the defendant's proffered nondiscriminatory reasons are false; or (2) the plaintiff may offer evidence showing that his age was a motivating factor for the defendant's adverse employment decision.

Applying [this] approach, we first find that Machinchick met his initial burden of establishing a prima facie case of age discrimination. He produced uncontroverted evidence that he was qualified for his job, was terminated, and was a member of the protected class at the time of his termination....

[First,] Knowlton's e-mail and PB Power's business plan provide evidence that PB Power intended to assemble a younger workforce, creating an inference that Machinchick's age was a factor in his termination.

Second, Machinchick points to Knowlton's use of "age stereotyping remarks" as evidence that he was terminated because of his age. In his e-mail to [human resources] describing Machinchick's shortcomings, Knowlton claimed that Machinchick had a "low motivation to adapt" to change. Knowlton expounded upon this claim in his deposition, describing Machinchick as "inflexible," "not adaptable," and possessing a "business-as-usual attitude." We have found that purely indirect references to an employee's age, such as comments that an employee needed to look "sharp" if he were going to seek a new job, and that he was unwilling and unable to "adapt" to change, can support an inference of age discrimination. Thus, Knowlton's description of Machinchick in both his e-mail and deposition gives rise to an inference that Machinchick was terminated because of his age.

Third, Machinchick produced evidence that PB Power treated him in a disparate manner by terminating him while retaining the younger, similarly situated Mike Betz....

Fourth, Machinchick presented evidence that, immediately following his first meeting with Knowlton, he was asked by Knowlton when he planned on retiring. This inquiry, although potentially innocuous, constitutes some evidence giving rise to an inference of discriminatory motivation behind Machinchick's termination.

By presenting evidence sufficient to establish a prima facie case of age discrimination, Machinchick shifted the burden of production to PB Power to articulate a legitimate, non discriminatory reason for its decision to terminate him. PB Power met this burden by alleging that Machinchick was terminated due to his inadequate performance under the new "cradle-to-grave" business plan, his refusal to adapt and modify his personal marketing plan in order to implement the cradle-to-grave strategy, and his "business-as-usual" attitude after the new strategy was implemented....

In a mixed-motive case involving an employment decision based on a "mixture of legitimate and illegitimate motives," the plaintiff need only prove that the illegitimate motive was a motivating factor in the decision. Once the plaintiff meets this burden, the employer may seek to avoid liability by proving that it would have made the same employment decision in the absence of the illegitimate discriminatory motive. The employer's burden on this score is effectively that of proving an affirmative defense.

When considered as a whole, we find that the evidence presented by Machinchick would allow a reasonable jury to find that his age was a motivating factor in PB Power's decision to terminate him....

Reversed and remanded for trial.

Questions for Analysis

1. The appeals court held that the age discrimination claim would go to trial on a mixed-motive basis. Given the age-related evidence, how can PB overcome the presumption of discrimination?
2. If Knowlton had been more careful in his statements about Machinchick, might this case have been avoided?

Key Defense for Employers

In the *Ellerth* case, the Supreme Court made clear how important it is for an employer to have clear, effective policy and procedures to reduce the likelihood of discrimination cases. Going to the roots of the employment relationship, agency law, the Court notes that without policies that can be shown to be meaningful, an employer is likely to have a more difficult defense and be more likely to incur vacarious liability for the actions of employees who engage in discriminatory behavior. It also means there is a greater likelihood of punitive damages being imposed if the employer loses, because it is less likely to be able show good-faith efforts to prevent discrimination.

Burlington Industries v. Ellerth
Supreme Court of the United States
524 U. S. 742 118 S. Ct. 2257 (1998)

Case Background *Ellerth worked for 15 months in sales at Burlington. One of her supervisors was Slowik, a mid-level manager with authority to hire, promote, and fire employees, subject to higher approval. Ellerth quit, claiming she was subject to sexually offensive remarks by Slowik and that his comments could be taken as threats to deny her job benefits. She refused his advances, did not suffer retaliation, and was promoted once. She did not tell anyone at Burlington about the problem until after she quit and filed suit. The district court granted Burlington summary judgment. The appeals court reversed, ordering a trial. Burlington appealed.*

Case Decision Justice Kennedy delivered the opinion of the court

* * *

When we assume discrimination can be proved ... the factors we discuss below, and not the categories *quid pro quo* and hostile work environment, will be controlling on the issue of vicarious liability. That is the question we must resolve.

We must decide, then, whether an employer has vicarious liability when a supervisor creates a hostile work environment by making explicit threats to alter a subordinate's terms or conditions of employment, *continues* based on sex, but does not fulfill the threat. We turn to principles of agency law, for the term "employer" is defined under Title VII to include "agents."...

Section 219(1) of the Restatement (Second) of Agency sets out a central principle of agency law:

> A master is subject to liability for the torts of his servants committed while acting in the scope of their employment.

An employer may be liable for both negligent and intentional torts committed by an employee within the scope of his or her employment. Sexual harassment under Title VII presupposes intentional conduct. While early decisions absolved employers of liability for the intentional torts of their employees, the law now imposes liability where the employee's "purpose, however misguided, is wholly or in part to further the master's business." In applying scope of employment principles to intentional torts, however, it is accepted that "it is less likely that a willful tort will properly be held to be in the course of employment and that the liability of the master for such torts will naturally be more limited."...

In order to accommodate the agency principles of vicarious liability for harm caused by misuse of supervisory authority, as well as Title VII's equally basic policies of encouraging forethought by employers and saving action by objecting employees, we adopt the following holding.... An employer is subject to vicarious liability to a victimized employee for an actionable hostile environment created by a supervisor with immediate (or successively higher) authority over the employee. When no tangible employment action is taken, a defending employer may raise an affirmative defense to liability or damages, subject to proof by a preponderance of the evidence. The defense comprises two necessary elements: (a) that the employer exercised reasonable care to prevent and correct promptly any sexually harassing behavior, and (b) that the plaintiff employee unreasonably failed to take advantage of any preventive or corrective opportunities provided by the employer or to avoid harm otherwise. While proof that an employer had promulgated an antiharassment policy with complaint procedure is not necessary in every instance as a matter of law, the need for a stated policy suitable to the employment circumstances may appropriately be addressed in any case when litigating the first element of the defense. And while proof that an employee failed to fulfill the corresponding obligation of reasonable care to avoid harm is not limited to showing any unreasonable failure to use nay complaint procedure provided by the employer, a demonstration of such failure will normally suffice to satisfy the employer's burden under the second element of the defense. No affirmative defense is available, however, when the supervisor's harassment culminates in a tangible employment action, such as discharge, demotion, or undesirable reassignment....

Given our explanation that the labels *quid pro quo* and hostile work environment are not controlling for purposes of establishing employer liability, Ellerth should have an adequate opportunity to prove she has a claim for which Burlington is liable.

Although Ellerth has not alleged she suffered a tangible employment action at the hands of Slowik, which would deprive Burlington of the availability of the affirmative defense, this is not dispositive. In light of our decision, Burlington is still subject to vicarious liability for Slowik's activity, but Burlington should have an opportunity to assert and prove the affirmative defense to liability....

The judgment of the Court of Appeals is affirmed.

Questions for Analysis
1. The majority held that if a company has an effective in-house program to deal with discrimination complaints, it presents a strong defense for the employer if not used by the employee. The dissent in this case argued that it opened the door to cases that employers cannot defend themselves against—such as this case, where the company had a policy against discrimination that was apparently violated, but the injured employee did not take advantage of company policy. Is that likely to happen?
2. What steps should an antidiscrimination policy include?

Justice Ginsburg repeated the key point of the *Ellerth* case in *Pennsylvania State Police* v. *Suders* (124 S.Ct. 2342). Suders claimed she was subject to sexual harassment by her supervisors, which caused her to resign. She sued, claiming constructive discharge based on hostile environment. The employer responded that it had an affirmative defense. It should not be held vicariously liable for the supervisors' conduct, because Suders did not take advantage of the internal anti-harassment procedures before she quit.

The Court held that when harassment is "so intolerable as to cause a resignation" the employee need not "remain on the job while seeking redress." In such cases, constructive discharge is the same as being fired for an illegal reason. It is possible for an employer to establish the affirmative defense that it had a proper anti-harassment procedure in such a case, but it would be difficult.

Disparate Impact

Liability for employment discrimination may be based on a claim of *disparate impact* or *adverse impact*, which means that the employer used a decision rule that caused discrimination in some aspect of employment based on protected class status. The discrimination may have been unintentional, but the effect of the employer's action was to limit employment opportunities for a person or group of persons based on race, color, religion, sex, or national origin. In practice, few age discrimination suits fall into the disparate impact category. In fact, there are many fewer disparate impact cases than disparate treatment cases, because they are complex. But when they occur, they can be very costly to an employer, because it often involves a class of employees.

These cases involve employment practices that appear to be neutral but in fact have a disproportionately adverse impact on an employee or group of employees who are members of a protected class. Proof of intent to discriminate is not required, but the plaintiff must prove that the employment practice adversely impacts employment opportunities for members of a protected class. Hence, the key issues are:

1. Does an employer have rules or practices that affect members of a protected group differently than other workers?
2. Are the rules or practices justified by business necessity, or because they relate to valid job requirements?

ISSUE SPOTTER
Effective Sexual Harassment Policy

As the Supreme Court made clear in the *Ellerth* case, a critical part of a defense for an employer to avoid liability in a suit for sexual harassment is an effective in-house procedure to try to prevent such behavior and then deal with it should it arise. What steps would be reasonable to take to implement such a policy in an organization?

Getty Images

For example, employment procedure often requires that applicants have a high school diploma, achieve a minimum score on a specified test, or meet some other standard. If it is asserted that the employer's hiring or promotion practices have a discriminatory impact on an applicant, the employer must show that the applicant was rejected not because of personal characteristics, but because the qualification requirements of the job were not met. The impact of employment rules must be neutral—that is, the rules must not have a disparate impact on a protected class. We see an example of an employment rule that fails to meet the test in the *Dial* case.

Equal Employment Opportunity Comm. v. Dial Corporation
United States Court of Appeals, Eighth Circuit
469 F.3d 735 (2006)

Case Background *Workers at the Dial plant in Iowa needed to be able to lift about 35 pounds of sausage at a time to a height between 30 and 60 inches. Doing this over and over meant injuries to workers, so the company began a Work Tolerance Screen (WTS) test for potential employees. Candidates had to demonstrate certain strength ability. For years, the workforce was about half men and half women. After the WTS was introduced, the number of women hired dropped to 15 percent. One applicant took the test and passed it, but was not hired. She complained to the EEOC.*

The EEOC brought suit on behalf of 54 women who had applied for work at Dial but were rejected despite passing the WTS. The trial court held that Dial had not demonstrated that the WTS was a business necessity, nor had it shown that it was valid. It awarded back pay to the women, ranging from over $120,000 to a low of $920. Dial appealed, contending that disparate impact had not been shown at trial.

Case Decision Murphy, Circuit Judge

* * *

Dial objects to the district court's findings of disparate impact and its conclusion that the company failed to prove the WTS was necessary to establish effective and safe job performance.... In a disparate impact case, once the plaintiff establishes a prima facie case, the employer must show the practice at issue is "related to safe and efficient job performance and is consistent with business necessity." An employer using the business necessity defense must prove that the practice was related to the specific job and the required

skills and physical requirements of the position. Although a validity study of an employment test can be sufficient to prove business necessity, it is not necessary if the employer demonstrates the procedure is sufficiently related to safe and efficient job performance. If the employer demonstrates business necessity, the plaintiff can still prevail by showing there is a less discriminatory alternative....

The district court was persuaded by EEOC's expert in industrial organization and his testimony "that a crucial aspect of the WTS is more difficult than the sausage making jobs themselves" and that the average applicant had to perform four times as many lifts as current employees and had no rest breaks....

Although Dial claims that the decrease in injuries shows that the WTS enabled it to predict which applicants could safely handle the strenuous nature of the work, the sausage plant injuries started decreasing before the WTS was implemented. Moreover, the injury rate for women employees was lower than that for men in two of the three years before Dial implemented the WTS....

Affirmed.

Questions for Analysis

1. The appeals court affirmed that the strength test discriminated against women job candidates. Since the job required strength, what could Dial have done to evaluate job candidates better?
2. Was the discrimination here intentional or unintentional?

Statutory Defenses under Title VII

As we saw in cases of disparate treatment, the employer must present a legitimate, nondiscriminatory, clear, and specific reason for the employment action taken. Certain business practices are specifically protected by Title VII. Other defenses are more general and have been determined by the courts as they have evaluated cases and considered the evidence presented.

Business Necessity

If employment practices can be shown to discriminate against some employees, the burden is on the employer to prove that the challenged practices are justified as a *business necessity* and are *job related*, as was claimed in the *Dial* case. Business necessity is evaluated with reference to the ability of the employee to perform a certain job. Written tests, no matter how objective, must meet this business necessity test.

Experience and skill requirements, frequently measured by seniority, are often accepted as necessary. For example, to be a skilled bricklayer generally requires experience gained only by long practice. To require such experience for certain positions is not a violation of Title VII. Similarly, if a job requires certain abilities of strength and agility, tests for such ability are legitimate.

Selection criteria for professional, managerial, and other "white-collar" positions must also meet the business necessity test. When objective standards (such as two years' brick-laying experience) cannot be used, subjective evaluations—such as impressions made by job interviews, references, and job performance evaluation—are recognized as necessary in hiring and promoting professional personnel. Similarly, positions may have an education requirement as long as it is, in fact, job-performance related. For example, to work as a CPA, one must have a degree in accounting.

Professionally Developed Ability Tests

Tests are often used by employers to determine whether applicants for a job possess the necessary skills and attributes. According to Title VII:

> It shall not be an unlawful employment practice for an employer to give and to act upon the results of any professionally developed ability test provided that such test, its administration, or action upon the results is not designed, intended, or used to discriminate because of race, color, religion, sex, or national origin.

Such tests must be shown to predict the work ability required for the job. Employers are usually required to supply statistical validation of the tests. Expert testimony from educational and industrial psychologists is often used to interpret the results.

ISSUE SPOTTER
Dealing with Discrimination Complaints

Companies need internal policies to deal with discrimination and harassment complaints raised by employees. Having a policy is not very hard, but dealing with incidents that arise can be difficult. When a complaint of sexual harassment or racial discrimination arises, what steps would you think important in handling the matter in an effective way?

Getty Images

Bona Fide Seniority or Merit Systems

Employers often use differential treatment based on seniority or merit. Title VII requires the courts to uphold *bona fide seniority or merit systems*. Seniority is usually the length of time an employee has been with an employer and can be used to determine such things as eligibility for pension plans, length of vacations, security from layoffs, preference for rehire and promotion, and amount of sick leave.

The effects of seniority systems come under attack most often in cases involving layoffs on the basis of seniority. Many employers hold that in the event of a cutback in the workforce, workers with the most seniority have the most job protection—last hired, first fired. This means that minorities may suffer a greater share of the layoffs in a workforce cutback because they have less seniority than white workers who were hired when discrimination was practiced. The Supreme Court recognizes this fact, but seniority rights are protected by statute.

The Bona Fide Occupational Qualification (BFOQ)

Another defense is a *bona fide occupational qualification (BFOQ)*. Title VII states that discrimination is permitted in instances in which sex, religion, or national origin—but not race—is a BFOQ "reasonably necessary to the normal operation of that particular business." The employer has the burden of persuasion to establish the necessity of the BFOQ.

The EEOC has given this defense a narrow interpretation. Just because certain jobs have been traditionally filled by men does not mean that a legitimate defense exists for not hiring women for such positions. Simply because people were used to seeing, and may have preferred, female flight attendants did not mean that airlines could refuse to hire male flight attendants. No BFOQ on the basis of race is allowed. For example, an employer cannot assert that the business must have a white person for a particular job.

Generally, the increased cost of hiring members of the opposite sex may not be used to justify discrimination. The fact that separate bathroom facilities will have to be constructed is not a BFOQ.

A BFOQ exists where hiring on the basis of a personal characteristic is needed to keep the "authenticity" of a position. For example, a topless bar can argue that the cocktail servers should be female, since customers expect that as a part of the service. Male clothing is expected to be modeled by a male model. In some medical care situations, hospitals may restrict the sex of attendants for the comfort of patients or to protect sexual privacy.

Early Retirement Plans

The ADEA was amended by the *Older Workers Benefit Protection Act*, which states that an employer may "observe the terms of a bona fide employee benefit plan … that is a voluntary early retirement incentive plan consistent with the relevant purpose … of this Act." That is, employers are not supposed to force "involuntary retirement," but if early retirement incentive plan (ERIP) benefits are so generous that an employee chooses to retire, the employee cannot claim to have been forced to retire. Employers may ask employees to sign "knowing and voluntary waivers" of age discrimination claims when they agree to retire early in response to an ERIP. The ADEA also exempts senior executives in high-level policy positions who are at least age 65 and are entitled to a company pension.

Remedies in Discrimination Cases

Title VII gives the courts leeway in the kinds of damages and equitable remedies that may be imposed when discrimination is found. The focus, as in most damage measures, is to try to put the plaintiff in the position he or she would have enjoyed but for the discrimination. Specific remedies include:

- Back pay—to the date discrimination began, either the entire pay that would have been earned or the difference between pay received and what should have been received, including fringe benefits.
- Front pay—if an employee was unlawfully fired, they may be ordered to be reinstated, or the plaintiff may be ordered to be hired if improperly not hired or, if fitting, given a sum to compensate for longer-term damage to a career for not having gained the experience or seniority of the position.
- Compensatory damages for emotional distress, inconvenience, and loss of reputation. This is not available in ADEA cases.
- Punitive damages may be granted to punish the employer for wrongdoing, because the employer acted with malice or in reckless disregard for protected

rights. This is not available in ADEA cases. These damages are capped by federal law to a maximum of $300,000 for employers with more than 500 employees.

- Attorney's fees may be recovered, as well as "costs" such as filing fees, expert witness fees, and transcripts. Plaintiffs who win usually get this; defendants who win rarely do.

Affirmative Action

An *affirmative action program* is a deliberate effort by an employer to remedy discriminatory practices in the hiring, training, and promotion of protected class members, when a particular class is underrepresented in the employer's workforce. Such programs have been adopted based only on race or sex.

After finding that members of a protected class are underrepresented in the company's workforce, an employer may voluntarily start an affirmative action program to ensure that the company provides more opportunities for women or minorities in certain job categories. An involuntary program may be imposed by the courts as a remedy to correct past discriminatory employment practices by the company or, in the special case of government contractors, by the federal government as a requirement to enter into a government contract. This is now quite rare.

Executive Order 11246

As the chief executive officer of the United States, the president has the authority to determine certain conditions for government business that are issued in *executive orders* by the president. Referred to as *government contractors*, businesses must abide by the executive orders when they contract with the government. In 1965, President Johnson issued Executive Order 11246, a requirement that government contractors adopt *affirmative action*.

Enforced by the Office of Federal Contract Compliance Programs (OFCCP), the order requires companies with federal contracts totaling $10,000 per year to take affirmative action. Those with $50,000 in contracts and 50 or more employees must have a written affirmative action plan, which requires a contractor to conduct a *workforce analysis* for each job within the organization. Jobs are studied by rank, salary, and the percent of those employed on the basis of race and sex.

The contractor must do an *underutilization analysis*, comparing the percent of minorities and women in the community in each job category with the percent employed by the contractor. If underutilization is found—say because 19 percent of the lab technicians are women compared with 41 percent of the lab technicians available in the community—the contractor must establish an affirmative action plan to increase the number of women in these positions. The program may require efforts to hire more women or to invest in training women to improve their qualifications for certain jobs.

Affirmative Action as a Remedy

Title VII provides that in the event an employer is found to have engaged in illegal discrimination, "the court may … order such affirmative action as may be appropriate." Courts may require an offending employer to begin an affirmative action program. The court could require the employer to hire qualified employees in the protected class to make up for past discriminatory activities. The action may be oriented at new employee recruitment, or it could be directed at using more resources

INTERNATIONAL PERSPECTIVE

Employment Discrimination in Europe and Japan

Europeans often are portrayed as more sophisticated than Americans with regard to social legislation. However, in many respects, they are years behind the United States in their treatment of minorities and women in the labor force. Most European countries and Japan have antidiscrimination statutes on the books, but the laws are not nearly as strict as the U.S. laws.

Employees in Europe can be forced to retire between ages 55 and 65, depending on the country. Europeans over age 45 who lose their jobs have a harder time finding employment again than do their counterparts in the United States.

The first sexual harassment case in Japan was not decided until 1992. A woman who was harassed by her boss for two years was fired for complaining. She was awarded $12,500 in damages. While small by American standards, the case was a landmark in Japan.

Minority immigrants are treated as second-class citizens in most countries. In general, it is much harder for a noncitizen, especially a member of a racial minority, to obtain work and citizenship in Japan and most of Europe than it is in the United States. Immigrants in France face blatant discrimination in the job market, reducing opportunities and economic integration.

Where affirmative action exists, it tends to be weak or even overtly discriminatory in favor of male-citizen workers who already dominate the labor force. Women are kept out of many higher-level jobs and are not paid as much as men for equal work—especially in Japan.

European countries and Japan appear to treat women better in certain respects, such as by mandating generous maternity benefits, but one effect of those laws is to encourage employers not to hire women because of the high cost of the benefits to which women are entitled if they have children.

Getty Images

to train current minority or women employees to become qualified candidates for promotion into positions in which they are underrepresented.

In recent years, as the worst vestiges of overt discrimination have been reduced, court-ordered affirmative action programs have become less common than voluntary affirmative action programs. Most employers adopt a program before one is forced upon them. The Supreme Court has approved mandated programs where a pattern of intentional discrimination makes it clear that a strong remedy is required under the flexible powers granted courts by the Civil Rights Act. In *United States* v. *Paradise* (107 S.Ct. 1053), the Court upheld a court-ordered hiring and promotion goal program for the Alabama Department of Public Safety, which had failed to hire African-American troopers for years after passage of Title VII. Consistent with the state population, the Court upheld an ordered goal that 25 percent of all employees at all ranks should be qualified African Americans.

Employers may voluntarily implement an affirmative action program. They may do so to be sure they are in compliance with Executive Order 11246. Employers often implement a program after determining that a protected class is underrepresented in its workforce in certain job categories. An affirmative action program allows an employer to correct for underrepresentation.

Disability Discrimination

The *Rehabilitation Act* of 1973 provides protection for disabled persons seeking employment with, or who are currently employed by, employers that receive federal funds. The Act tends to follow the steps in Title VII employment discrimination suits. Section 503 of the Act is most important. It holds that all companies with federal contracts of $2,500 or more have a duty to ensure the disabled an opportunity in the workplace by providing reasonable accommodations.

The *Americans with Disabilities Act (ADA)* of 1990 expanded the rights of persons with disabilities in employment and supplements access rights to public accommodations, such as hotels, restaurants, theaters, public transportation, telecommunications, and retail stores. The ADA incorporates most remedies and procedures set out in Title VII. The ADA applies to all employers with 15 or more employees.

Definition of Disabled

The Rehabilitation Act and the ADA define *a person with disabilities* as

> any person who (i) has a physical or mental impairment which substantially limits one or more of such person's major life activities, (ii) has a record of such an impairment, or (iii) is regarded as having such an impairment.

The Supreme Court has recognized regulations by the Department of Health and Human Services as a guide to determining what is a disability. The regulations define "major life activities" as "functions such as caring for one's self, performing manual tasks, walking, seeing, hearing, speaking, breathing, learning, and working." Examples of disabilities covered by the statutes include people:

- With a history of alcohol or other drug abuse
- With a severe disfigurement
- Who have had a heart attack
- Who must use a wheelchair
- Who are hearing- or vision-impaired

LIGHTER SIDE OF THE LAW

Addicted to Not Working?

Pacenza was fired from his job at an IBM research facility in New York. He kept logging on to Internet chat rooms despite being told not to do that at work.

He sued IBM for $5 million for disability discrimination. He claimed he was "addicted" to chat rooms. They were "self-medication" for his Vietnam-based post-traumatic stress disorder. IBM responded that it does accommodate disabilities but had never heard of this one.

Source: *Information Week*

Getty Images

Even if a person is not actually impaired, if other people think the person is impaired, the person is considered disabled. For example, former cancer patients have found that some people are afraid to hire them, because they think cancer is contagious. As a result, even though no impairment exists, and even though doctors may say there is no disease present, bias against the person who had the disease makes the person disabled for purposes of this law.

ADA cases often involve individual evaluation of circumstances of what constitutes disability in relationship to particular employment. The courts have been clear that disabilities are major life conditions. Even if a person is partly impaired, it need not mean that person is considered disabled. It is a tough standard to meet, and for those who are disabled, employers need only to make reasonable accommodations. Employers need not keep in place an employee who can no longer perform their job. For example, one dock worker whose weight rose to over 400 pounds was dismissed. He sued, claiming disability protection. The appeals court held (463 F.3d 436) that morbid obesity was not an impairment. Since his weight prevented him from going up and down ladders as needed, he could be terminated and had no grounds for suit. The point of how difficult it can be to qualify as disabled is emphasized in the *Gretillat* case.

Gretillat v. Care Initiatives
United States Court of Appeals, Eighth Circuit
481 F.3d 649 (2007)

Case Background *Gretillat worked in food service at a nursing home. Her duties stated that she would, at times, have to cover every aspect of operations. At times she might have to stoop, kneel, crouch, or crawl as part of needed physical movements. After 10 years, she began to suffer pain from osteoarthritis in her right knee, which made it hard to walk much. Her supervisor told her she would no longer have to make rounds at the home to reduce her walking. Three years later she had knee replacement surgery.*

After the surgery, but she reported a lot of pain from standing for long periods. She said she could not squat, kneel, crouch, crawl, or stand for long times. Her manager told her she could resign or be terminated, since she could no longer do physical acts needed for the job. She resigned and sued for disability discrimination for failure to accommodate her disability. The district court held for the nursing home. Gretillat appealed.

Case Decision Wollman, Circuit Judge

* * *

[As the Supreme Court has stated] the terms "major life activities" and "substantial limitation" must be "interpreted strictly to create a demanding standard for qualifying as disabled...." Major life activities include "functions such as caring for one's self, performing manual tasks, walking, seeing, hearing, speaking, breathing, learning, and working." More generally, they include "activities that are of central importance to daily life." A court should consider the nature, severity, duration, and long-term impact of the impairment when deciding whether that impairment substantially limits a major life activity. The

impairment must be of an extended or permanent duration, and should be considered substantially limiting only if "an individual is 'significantly restricted as to the condition, manner, or duration under which ... the average person in the general population can perform that same major life activity.' Furthermore, merely demonstrating that an impairment prevents one from performing job functions in the absence of accommodations does not suffice to demonstrate a disability....

Walking and standing are major life activities. Nevertheless, nothing presented by Gretillat concerning her walking and standing limitations suggests to us that she was substantially limited in these activities.... A limited standing limitation does not amount to a disability....

After Gretillat's departure from Care Initiatives, [her doctor stated] that (1) she considered Gretillat disabled both before and after the knee surgery; (2) Gretillat's ability to kneel, crouch, squat, and crawl is significantly worse than that of average individuals of her age and sex; (3) Gretillat is permanently restricted in kneeling, crouching, squatting, and crawling; and (4) she had not previously indicated these restrictions on forms provided to Care Initiatives, because she had misunderstood the physical requirements of Gretillat's job. A medical diagnosis of an impairment cannot qualify as a disability *per se*; instead, a plaintiff "must satisfy the ADA's demanding standard in each individual case in the context of the major life activity asserted."

Even accepting that Gretillat's impaired knee substantially and permanently restricts her ability to crawl, kneel, crouch, and squat, these functions cannot meet the demanding standard required … for us to consider them major life activities.…

Nor is there any indication that Gretillat's limitations, taken together, severely limit any major life activity.… Her testimony also indicated that she is fully capable of creatively mitigating the effects of her impairment. Accordingly, the district court properly concluded that Gretillat's limitations do not render her disabled under the ADA and that Care Initiatives is thus entitled to summary judgment as a matter of law.

The judgment is affirmed.

Questions for Analysis

1. The appeals court affirmed that Gretillat's physical impairments did not rise to the level of a disability, so she had no case. Although she was "impaired," why was she not considered "disabled"?
2. Suppose Gretillat's condition was severe enough to be a disability. What would the employer have needed to do then?

Compliance Process

Suits under the ADA arise the same way that discrimination suits brought under Title VII come about—by filing complaints with the EEOC. About 20 percent of the charges filed with the EEOC are disability complaints. They proceed much the same way as do Title VII charges.

Reasonable Accommodation

Employers are obliged to make *reasonable accommodations* for persons with disabilities and are expected to incur expenses in making a position or workstation available to qualified disabled applicants and employees. Exactly where the line is drawn is not clear. Ford does not have to redesign its assembly line at high cost so that a worker in a wheelchair could work on the assembly line, because that would impose an *undue hardship* on business operations. However, when a workstation can be redesigned for several thousand dollars to accommodate a person with a disability, that must be done. The Department of Labor estimates that in most cases, the cost of accommodation is under $500. Firms are also expected to provide special equipment and training for the disabled and to allow modified work schedules.

EEOC Guidance

The EEOC has issued *ADA Enforcement Guidance: Preemployment Disability-Related Questions and Medical Examinations.* The guidelines note that the ADA prohibits employers from asking disability-related questions or requiring medical exams before a job is offered. Hence, employers cannot ask questions about the nature or severity of a disability. The following are examples of questions that are illegal to ask during a job interview:

- Do you have AIDS?
- Have you ever been treated for mental health problems?
- Have you ever filed for workers' compensation benefits?
- Do you have a disability that would interfere with your ability to perform the job?
- How many sick days were you out last year?
- Have you ever been unable to handle work-related stress?
- Have you ever been treated for drug addiction or drug abuse?

In the case of drugs, past addiction is treated as a disability, but current use of illegal drugs is not, so applicants may be asked about current use and may be given a drug test. However, current alcoholism is a protected disability, and applicants may not be asked questions about drinking habits, although it is permissible to ask whether an applicant has been arrested for driving under the influence of alcohol.

If a disability is obvious, or if an applicant volunteers a disability, some questions may be asked about the need for reasonable accommodation. For example, if an applicant discloses that she needs to take breaks to take diabetes medication, the employer may ask how often such breaks are needed and how long they would be. Employers may make clear the requirements needed to perform a job, and if it is dubious that someone could perform a job function, an applicant may be asked to demonstrate how he or she could accomplish the task.

ISSUE SPOTTER
Accommodating Disabilities

The Americans with Disabilities Act does not give "bright lines" for exactly what accommodations are reasonable for employees with disabilities. Proper accommodations must be determined case-by-case. The key terms are "reasonable" and "undue hardship." What guidelines would you set for an organization in developing an accommodation policy?

Getty Images

Once a job offer has been made, an employer may ask for documentation of a disability and may ask more questions about the reasonable accommodation needed for the employee. If a physical exam is given to new employees, similar exams must be given to all employees in the same job category and the results must be kept confidential. Such exams can be given so long as they are related to the ability to do the job, and not because an employer is trying to screen out employees with potential health problems.

Violations by Employers

As in the case of discrimination based on race, sex, or age, the law is broken if a qualified person is denied an opportunity primarily because of disability. However, in the case of disabilities, besides not discriminating, an employer must also make reasonable accommodations and go the extra mile to make adjustments for disabilities. In this sense, there is an affirmative action requirement, but it is not one tied to specific goals. This requirement works on a case-by-case basis. Employment situations that have been in violation of the law include

- using standardized employment tests that tend to screen out people with disabilities.
- refusing to hire applicants because they have a history of alcohol abuse, rather than because they are currently alcohol abusers.
- rejecting a job applicant because he or she is HIV-positive.
- asking job applicants if they have disabilities, rather than asking if they have the ability to perform the job.
- limiting advancement opportunities for employees because of their disabilities.
- not hiring a person with a disability, because the workplace does not have a bathroom that can accommodate wheelchairs.

LIGHTER SIDE OF THE LAW
Get the Women Out of My Classes

Winston was fired after 19 years as an English teacher in the Maine Technical College System. While complaints had been made of sexual misconduct, he was dismissed after a sexual harassment complaint was filed after he kissed a female student "after a sexually suggestive conversation."

Winston sued, "claiming that he was terminated because of his 'mental handicap of sexual addiction.'" His expert witness testified that this disorder, which had led to his seeking the services of prostitutes, was a permanent condition but that Winston could perform his job as a teacher.

The supreme court of Maine tossed out the complaint, noting that the ADA specifically excludes "sexual behavior disorders" from the term *disability*.

Source: *Winston v. Maine Technical College System* (631 A.2d 70)

Getty Images

Summary

- Title VII of the Civil Rights Act and the Age Discrimination in Employment Act require employers not to discriminate on the basis of sex, race, color, religion, national origin, or age. This applies to all aspects of the employment process—hiring, promotion, discipline, benefits, and firing. The laws are enforced by the EEOC and private party suits.

- Legally, race means black or African American, White, American Indian or Alaska Native, Native Hawaiian or Other Pacific Islander, Asian, and the ethnic category Hispanic or Latino. Under federal law, *sex* means male or female. There is no consideration for sexual preference.

- Sex discrimination specifically includes discrimination with respect to childbearing plans, pregnancy, and related medical conditions. Sexual harassment now poses a legal challenge for managers, who must take steps to inform employees of the seriousness and the consequences of harassment and establish internal procedures to allow claims to be investigated with an assurance of confidentiality.

- Key tests that the courts use to look for discrimination are disparate treatment, where, everything else being equal, employment decisions are illegally motivated by discrimination based on race, sex, national origin, religion, or age; and disparate impact, where the effect of hiring or promotion standards is to discriminate, even if unintentionally, on the basis of protected class status.

- A charge of discrimination must be filed at a federal or state EEO office within 180 days (300 under state law) of a discriminatory event. The EEOC may dismiss a charge, offer to mediate a dispute, file suit on behalf of an employee or group of employees, or give the employee a right to sue letter to go forward with litigation with their own attorney.

- An employee bringing suit must meet the *McDonnell–Douglas* test, which applies to all aspects of the employment process, to show that they 1) belong to a protected class; 2) met the qualifications of the job in question; 3) were rejected for the job, or suffered some other adverse job action; and 4) the employer sought other persons with similar qualifications or otherwise treated the employee differently.

- When employers are sued under the discrimination laws, they must present a preponderance of evidence that the practices they engage in are not discriminatory. The practices must be related to legitimate business necessity. Practices that, when properly designed, are allowed to stand include professionally developed ability tests, bona fide seniority and merit systems, and bona fide occupational qualifications that provide a rationale for personnel decisions.
- Employers may have affirmative action plans imposed on them by court order as a remedy for discrimination. Federal contractors must have affirmative action plans in place. These plans are designed to increase minority or female representation in certain job categories. This may be done by setting goals to be met within certain time frames.
- The Rehabilitation Act of 1973 and the Americans with Disabilities Act of 1990 require employers to take positive steps to make accommodations for disabled workers. Court decisions have broadened the definition of a disabled person to include alcohol and other drug addicts as well as persons with serious diseases such as AIDS.
- A disability under the ADA means a limitation of a major life activity, such as walking, breathing, seeing, and hearing. It does not mean an impairment that a person can adjust to and not suffer a serious limitation on a major activity. The standard for disability is strict; the test is whether the disabled person can do the job in question with reasonable accommodation.

Terms to Know

You should be able to define the following terms:

equal employment opportunity, 420	sex, 423	prima facie discrimination case, 428
discrimination, 421	harassment, 424	pretext, 429
race, 421	hostile environment, 425	seniority or merit system, 435
color, 421	age, 426	bona fide occupational qualification, 436
religion, 421	constructive discharge, 428	affirmative action, 437
national origin, 421	retaliation, 428	disability, 443
protected classes, 421	disparate treatment, 428	
reasonable accommodation, 422	disparate impact, 428	

Discussion Question

1. Would a dress code that required men to wear three-piece suits, but stated only that women had to "look professional," be discriminatory against the male employees? What differences would be considered discriminatory?

Case Questions

1. Wise was fired for getting into a fight with another employee during lunch at the company lunchroom. She kicked and scratched the other employee and used abusive language. She claimed sex discrimination under Title VII, because male employees who had been in fights had not been fired. Was this sex discrimination? [*Wise* v. *Mead*, 614 F.Supp. 1131 (1985)]
2. Parr applied for a position as an insurance representative, for which he was well qualified and had experience. The manager who interviewed Parr told him he would probably be hired and also told him the company did not sell insurance to African Americans. Parr

told the employment service that set up the interview of the manager's remarks and told the service that he was married to an African-American woman. The employment service told the insurance company of Parr's interracial marriage, at which point they declined to hire him. Was that a violation of Title VII? [*Parr* v. *Woodmen of the World Life Insurance*, 791 F.2d 888, 11th Cir. (1986)]

✓ **Check your answer at http://academic.cengage.com/blaw/meiners**

3. Quinones worked as a technician for Houser Buick. He learned that his hourly pay, which amounted to about $30,000 per year, compared poorly to another employee, Barnes, who was paid a "flat rate" of $52,000 per year. Quinones asked to be paid on a "flat rate" pay scale, rather than on an hourly basis, but was rejected. He sued, contending that the pay difference was based on his Hispanic origin. Houser defended that the "flat rate" system allows employees who are highly productive to earn more as pay and is computed for each repair job completed. Quinones worked slowly; Barnes worked quickly and did high-quality work. The district court held that Houser offered a nondiscriminatory reason for the pay differential and held for the defendant. Quinones appealed. Does he have a case? [*Quinones* v. *Houser Buick*, 436 F.3d 284 1st Cir. (2006)]

4. Friedman applied for employment at a pharmaceutical warehouse. He was offered a position and told that, as a condition of employment, he would have to be vaccinated against the mumps. He refused to be vaccinated, because the vaccine is grown in chicken embryos. He said that it would violate his system of beliefs as a vegan, which prohibits the use of any animal-related product. The employment offer was withdrawn; he sued for discrimination based on religion. The district court dismissed the case, holding that veganism is not a religion. Friedman appealed. Does he have a case? [*Friedman* v. *So. Cal. Permanente Medical Group*, 102 Cal.App.4th 39 Ct. App., Calif. (2002)]

✓ **Check your answer at http://academic.cengage.com/blaw/meiners**

5. Lack sued his former employer, Wal-Mart, and his former supervisor, Bragg, for sexual harassment. He contended that Bragg made "inappropriate and demeaning statements … of a sexual nature" and told vulgar jokes in front of Lack and others. When Lack complained, he suffered retaliation as Bragg made "his work scheduled more burdensome and inconvenient." Wal-Mart ignored the problem. Other employees testified as to Bragg's behavior. The jury found for Lack and awarded him $80,000 in damages. Wal-Mart appealed. Did Lack have a case? [*Lack* v. *Wal-Mart Stores*, 240 F.3d 255 4th Cir. (2001)]

6. Breeden worked for a school district in Nevada. She attended a meeting with two male workers. One of the men made a sexist joke to the other male, but it was not directed at Breeden, who complained to her supervisor about the incident. Breeden filed a sexual harassment complaint with the EEOC. Soon after, she was transferred to another position, a move that she had known for some time might occur. She added a charge of retaliation to her complaint. The district court dismissed the case. The court of appeals reversed for Breeden. The school district appealed to the Supreme Court. Does Breeden have a good case? [*Clark County School District* v. *Breeden*, 121 S.Ct. 1508 Sup. Ct. (2001)]

✓ **Check your answer at http://academic.cengage.com/blaw/meiners**

7. Grosjean worked for First Energy since 1970. In 1997 he was promoted to a supervisory position. Two years later, when he was 54, his boss, Dressner, who was 41, removed Grosjean from his position, stating that he was not performing adequately. Grosjean kept the same pay, but had less status. The position was given to Riley, who was 51. Grosjean sued for age discrimination for being denied promotion to a supervisory position. The trial court dismissed the suit. Grosjean appealed. Does he have a case? [*Grosjean* v. *First Energy*, 349 F.3d 332, 6th Cir. (2003)]

8. The Jackson, Michigan, Board of Education had a rule that in the event of a cutback in teachers, the layoffs would be proportional on the basis of race. That way, students would be guaranteed more minority teachers as role models. This was done because

more of the older teachers were white; if the layoff was based on seniority only, more minority teachers would be laid off in proportion to the white teachers. The district court and court of appeals agreed with the school board, saying the rule helped to remedy past discrimination. What did the Supreme Court say? [*Wygant* v. *Jackson Board of Education*, 106 S.Ct. 1842 (1986)]

✓ Check your answer at http://academic.cengage.com/blaw/meiners

9. Medina Rene, who is openly gay, worked for the MGM Grand Hotel in Las Vegas for two years. During his employment, he contends that his male supervisor and co-workers subjected him to a hostile work environment on a daily basis. He was subject to crude jokes, name-calling, and unwelcome physical touching. He sued the hotel for sexual harassment, noting that the reason for the harassment was his sexual orientation. The district court dismissed the suit, holding that his claim of sexual orientation discrimination is not recognized under Title VII. Rene appealed. Does he have a case? [*Rene* v. *MGM Grand Hotel*, 305 F.3d 1061, 9th Cir. (2002)]

10. J. B. Hunt Transport would not hire truck drivers who used prescription medications with side effects that might impair their driving ability. The EEOC sued Hunt, contending that this practice violated the Americans with Disabilities Act, because Hunt discriminated against those with perceived disabilities. The district court held for Hunt; the EEOC appealed. [*EEOC* v. *J.B. Hunt Transport*, 321 F.3d 69, 2nd Cir. (2003)]

11. Bolton worked in a grocery warehouse for two years when he suffered a work-related injury that required medical leave. Under company policy, an employee on medical leave could not return until the company doctor certified that the employee was fit to resume work. When Bolton wanted to return, the doctor declared him unable to perform his work in the warehouse, which refused to rehire him. Bolton sued, claiming disability discrimination. Did he have a case? [*Bolton* v. *Scrivner*, 36 F.3d 939, 10th Cir. (1994)]

Ethics Question

1. You are a supervisor at a company that does not have an affirmative action program. In looking to hire a new person for a certain position, the person who best fits the job criteria is a white male, age 30. Two other candidates are also well qualified for the position but just slightly less so than the top candidate. One of the other candidates is African American; the third is a white woman, age 63. You believe that, in general, there is societal discrimination against minorities and older people. Should you give a little extra credit to the candidates who are in protected classes, given that you can justify whatever choice you make? How would you decide between the African-American man and the older white woman? Should you take into account that the man supports a wife and three children, whereas the woman has an employed husband and no children?

Internet Assignment

http://eeoc.gov/
http://eeoc.gov/abouteeo/overview_practices.html
http://eeoc.gov/abouteeo/overview_laws.html

1. Briefly describe the role of the U.S. Equal Employment Opportunity Commission (EEOC) in enforcing federal equal employment laws.
2. Search your institution's Web site to see if it makes reference to compliance with federal equal opportunity laws.

Environmental Law

Chapter 18

Some years ago, the Environmental Protection Agency (EPA) and Amoco Corporation cooperated on a four-year project to study pollution-control effectiveness. The EPA listened to company experts; the company revealed operation details to the EPA. The study showed that EPA regulations required Amoco to spend $41 million a year to trap air pollution from one refinery system, when the same control, using a better technology, could be achieved for $11 million. The regulations did not allow the cheaper control methods. The study also showed that no controls were required on another part of the refinery that emitted five times as much pollution as the pollution being controlled at a cost of $41 million. EPA was as frustrated as Amoco by the results, but both were trapped by inflexible regulations that are slow to change.

More than $250 billion per year is spent on pollution controls in the United States. Because pollution controls are so costly, there has often been a fight between industry and regulators. Some expensive pollution controls achieve little, while some major sources of pollution go largely uncontrolled. Whether recognition of this will translate into more cost-effective pollution controls that deliver better environmental quality at a lower price remains to be seen.

This chapter reviews the major federal laws providing environmental protection, but it begins with a discussion of common-law rules that regulate environmental quality, such as the application of nuisance law. The chapter then discusses the creation of the EPA and the most important environmental statutes, including the Clean Air Act, the Clean Water Act, the Resource Conservation and Recovery Act, the Superfund, and the Endangered Species Act. ∎

Getty Images

Environmental Regulation

During the 1960s, the environment became a major issue. Books such as Rachel Carson's *Silent Spring*, which discussed problems such as the effects of heavy pesticide use on birds, brought attention to environmental concerns. Since that time, there has been strong support for federal legislation to improve environmental quality. Whether the legislation has been effective in reducing pollution, or is cost-effective in getting the most protection for the money spent, is beyond the scope of what we study here.

Federal control of the environment essentially began in 1970. Before then, some pollution laws were on the books, but they meant little in practice. Since 1970, an explosion of federal legislation has affected most aspects of the environment. Exhibit 18.1 lists only a fraction of the environmental statutes on the books now, but those statutes are the ones that have the greatest effects.

To implement and enforce federal environmental mandates, Congress created the EPA in 1970. Today, the EPA is one of the largest federal agencies, with almost 18,000 employees and a budget of about $8 billion. Add to that the state environmental agencies that are required to help enforce the federal and state environmental

Exhibit 18.1   Federal Regulation of Environmental Pollution

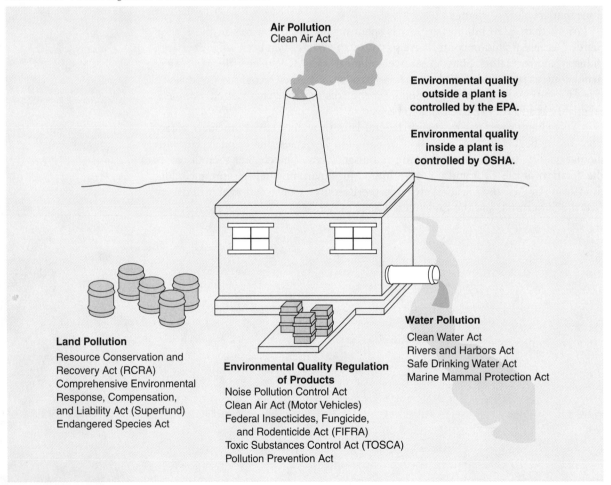

laws. The EPA has primary responsibility for four major external environmental problems: air pollution, water pollution, land pollution, and pollution associated with certain products (see www.epa.gov). This chapter reviews the key features of the major federal mandates, but before we get to the regulations, we will review an important contribution of the common law, historically and today, that helps to protect environmental quality.

Pollution and the Common Law

Before 1970, pollution was a problem handled by the states. State statutes dealt with some of the worst problems, such as automobile emissions in California, but citizens primarily relied on the common law, especially nuisance and trespass.

Nuisance, Trespass, and Pollution

As we saw when we studied property and torts, nuisances may be public or private. A *public nuisance* is an unreasonable interference with a right held in common by the public. In a pollution case, the right held in common is a community's right to a reasonably clean and safe environment. As a rule, a public nuisance case will be brought against the polluter by a city or state attorney. A *private nuisance* is a substantial and unreasonable interference with the use and enjoyment of the land of another. It generally involves a polluter who is injuring one person or a group of people.

For example, in the 1907 case *Georgia* v. *Tennessee Copper Company* (206 U.S. 230), the Supreme Court reviewed a complaint by the state of Georgia that a copper smelter in Tennessee was discharging gases that killed vegetation in Georgia and threatened human health. The Court held that an injunction against the smelter to shut it down could be issued, if the smelter could not control the pollution enough to stop the damage.

A *trespass* is an unauthorized breach of the boundaries of another's land. The main difference between trespass and nuisance is that a trespass occurs whenever there is physical invasion of a plaintiff's property. A nuisance requires proof that interference with property is substantial and unreasonable. In practice, nuisance and trespass are difficult to distinguish in many pollution cases.

Negligence, Strict Liability, and Pollution

Both *negligence* and *strict liability for abnormally dangerous activities* may apply in pollution cases. Tort liability may be due to negligence, which is failure to use reasonable care to prevent pollution from causing a foreseeable injury. Strict liability for abnormally dangerous activities applies to businesses that produce or emit toxic pollutants. In imposing strict liability, the courts emphasize the risks created by the toxic pollutant and the location of the business relative to where people live. Courts have found crop dusting, the leakage of chemicals into groundwater, the storing of flammable liquids in quantity in a populated area, and the emitting of noxious gases by factories all to be abnormally dangerous.

Water Rights and Pollution

There is no common-law right to pollute water. Most states rely on *riparian water law*, although the western states have a variety of other water rights. Riparian water law holds that people who live along rivers and other bodies of water have the right to use the water in reasonable amounts but must allow the water to flow downstream in usable form. People have no right to pollute the water so that it is not usable downstream. Hence, along with nuisance and other common-law rights, enforcement of riparian water rights has long been a basis for suing polluters. The *Whalen* decision illustrates how the law works to protect water quality in the absence of any regulation. Note the New York high court's classic statement about how rights are to be protected.

Whalen v. Union Bag and Paper
Court of Appeals of New York
208 N.Y.1, 101 N.E.805 (1913)

Case Background *Whalen owned a farm on a creek in New York. He used water from the creek to water plants and livestock. Union Bag built a pulp mill upstream, employing about 500 people. The mill polluted the creek so that Whalen could not use the water.*

Whalen sued Union Bag for damages and requested that the court issue an injunction to stop the pollution. The trial court (special term) awarded damages of $312 per year and issued an injunction to take effect in one year. Either the pollution had to be stopped or the mill was to be shut down. The appellate court eliminated the injunction and reduced damages to $100 per year. Whalen appealed to the highest court in New York.

Case Decision Werner, Justice

* * *

The setting aside of the injunction was apparently induced by a consideration of the great loss likely to be inflicted on the defendant by the granting of the injunction as compared with the small injury done to the plaintiff's land by that portion of the pollution which we regarded as attributable to the defendant. Such a balancing of injuries cannot be justified by the circumstances of this case.

... Although the damage to the plaintiff may be slight as compared with the defendant's expense of abating the condition, that is not a good reason for refusing an injunction. Neither courts of equity nor law can be guided by such a rule, for if followed to its logical conclusion, it would deprive the poor litigant of his little property by giving it to those already rich. It is always to be remembered in such cases that "denying the injunction puts the hardship on the party in whose favor the legal right exists, instead of on the wrongdoer."...

The fact that the appellant has expended a large sum of money in the construction of its plant, and that it conducts its business in a careful manner and without malice, can make no difference in its rights to the stream. Before locating the plant, the owners were bound to know that every riparian proprietor is entitled to have the waters of the stream that washes his land come to it without obstruction, diversion, or corruption, subject only to the reasonable use of the water, by those similarly entitled, for such domestic purposes as are inseparable from and necessary for the free use of their land; they were bound also to know the character of their proposed business, and to take notice of the size, course, and capacity of the stream, and to determine for themselves at their own peril whether they should be able to conduct their business upon a stream of the size and character of Brandywine creek without injury to their neighbors; and the magnitude of their investment and their freedom from malice furnish no reason why they should escape the consequences of their own folly....

The judgment of the Appellate Division, insofar as it denied the injunction, should be reversed, and the judgment of the special term in that respect reinstated, with costs to the appellant.

Questions for Analysis

1. The New York high court held that the polluter must stop the damaging pollution or cease operation. If the common law was this tough, why would we need federal regulation of water pollution?

2. Should damages be the only resort in such cases? Assuming that the real loss to Whalen was $312 per year, why should he be able to get an injunction that would put hundreds of people out of work?

This decision contrasts sharply with a famous decision years later by the same court, *Boomer* v. *Atlantic Cement Company*, 1970 (257 N.E.2d 870). The air pollution, noise, and vibration from a cement plant created a nuisance for nearby homes. The court refused to issue an injunction, only awarding damages to the homeowners. The court reasoned that the value of the cement plant was higher than the cost suffered by the homeowners, so no injunction should be issued. Unlike in the *Whalen* case, where no price tag was put on rights, and where costs and benefits were not compared, the *Boomer* court compared costs and benefits and made the economically "efficient" decision, rather than simply ordering the nuisance to be stopped. This kind of decision played a role in the push for federal regulation of pollution.

Clean Air Act

The *Clean Air Act of 1970*, which had major amendments in 1977 and 1990, established federal authority to control air pollution. In the words of the Supreme Court, Congress intended to "take a stick to the states" with this law. The Act requires the EPA to set pollution standards and, through forced cooperation of the states, to enforce the standards across the country.

National Ambient Air Quality Standards

The key regulatory program to achieve air quality is the *National Ambient Air Quality Standards (NAAQS)*. The EPA determines NAAQS for air pollutants that, in its judgment, "arise or contribute to air pollution which may reasonably be anticipated to endanger public health and welfare." The NAAQS set limits on how much of a pollutant is allowed to be found in the air outside—ambient air—as its quality is measured at hundreds of sites around the country.

The primary factors for a pollutant's NAAQS are the public health effects. Secondary factors are its considerations of public welfare effects (impact on plants, animals, soil, and constructed surfaces). The EPA has national standards for sulfur dioxide, particulates, ozone, carbon monoxide, nitrogen oxide, and lead. Exhibit 18.2 summarizes the principal characteristics, health effects, and sources of those major air pollutants.

State Implementation Plans

When EPA sets limits for the NAAQS, each state develops a *State Implementation Plan (SIP)*. The SIPs define the control efforts to be used in each state to achieve the national standards. In theory, if each emission source in a state met its pollution control requirements, the state's air quality would meet the national standards. The Act requires that regulated emission sources meet pollution control requirements as set by the SIP by a certain date.

The Clean Air Act, like some of the other major pollution statutes, places the primary enforcement burden on the states. The EPA is the oversight agency that sets limits on what the states may do and sets the minimum regulations they must impose. Whenever the EPA changes air pollution standards, states must revise their SIPs, which are then reviewed by the EPA. If a state does not submit an adequate plan, the EPA writes one for it. All SIPs must include the following:

- Enforceable emission limits
- Schedules and timetables for compliance

- Measures for monitoring air quality and emissions from pollution sources
- Adequate funding, personnel, and authority for implementing and enforcing the SIP

The Permit System

The Clean Air Act sets rules for the construction of new industrial plants or for major renovations of existing facilities. The standards imposed on plant owners depend on the air quality of the area in which a plant is built. One set of rules applies if the plant is built in a "clean air area," and another set applies if a plant is built in a "dirty air area." In either case, the plant owner is required to obtain a preconstruction permit from the EPA or the state agency that enforces the Act.

Clean Air Areas

Areas with clean air—air of better quality than required by the NAAQS—are called *attainment areas* or *prevention of significant deterioration (PSD) areas*. PSD areas include national parks, wilderness areas, and other areas where the air quality is better than the national standards. Because of the sensitive nature of those areas, only a slight increase in pollution is allowed from new construction. That slight increase is called the *maximum allowable increase*. Any activity, including the construction or expansion of a plant, that will cause the maximum allowable increase to be exceeded is prohibited in a PSD area.

Exhibit 18.2   Major Air Pollutants Subject to NAAQS

Pollutant	Characteristics	Sources	Health Effects
Sulfur Dioxide (SO_2)	Colorless gas with pungent odor; oxidizes to form sulfur trioxide, which forms acid rain	Power and industrial plants that burn sulfur-containing fossil fuels; smelting of sulfur-bearing ores	Causes and aggravates respiratory ailments, inducing asthma, chronic bronchitis, emphysema
Particulates (PM)	Any particle dispersed in the atmosphere, such as dust, ash, and various chemicals	Wind erosion; stationary sources that burn solid fuels; agricultural operations	Chest discomfort; throat and eye irritation; respiratory problems
Ozone (O_3)	A gas formed from hydrocarbon vapors and nitrogen oxides in sunlight; smog	Mostly from vehicle exhaust, refineries, and chemical plants	Aggravates respiratory ailments; causes eye irritation
Carbon Monoxide (CO)	Colorless, odorless gas	Motor vehicle exhaust and other carbon-containing materials; natural sources	Reduces oxygen-carrying capacity of blood; impairs heart function, visual perception, and alertness
Nitrogen Oxide (NO_x)	Brownish gas with pungent odor; component in photochemical oxidants	Motor vehicle exhaust; power plants	Aggravates respiratory ailments
Lead (Pb)	Heavy metallic chemical element; often occurs as lead oxide or dust	Nonferrous metal smelters; motor vehicle exhaust	Can cause mental and physical disabilities (lead poisoning)

New construction is allowed in PSD areas if two basic requirements are met: First, the owner must agree to install the *best available control technology (BACT)*—as determined by the EPA—on the new plant to control its air pollution. Second, the owner must show that the pollution from its plant will not cause the maximum allowable increase in the area to be exceeded. The maximum allowable increase in the various forms of air pollution depends upon the classification of an area and the effect a particular pollutant would have on the air there. Some PSD classes, such as wilderness areas, are subject to much stricter controls than are less sensitive PSD areas.

Dirty Air Areas

Dirty air areas are called *nonattainment areas*, meaning that they have not met the NAAQS. Businesses wanting to build in nonattainment areas are required to meet more restrictive standards than are imposed in PSD areas. The *emissions offset policy* imposes three requirements on owners of new or expanded plants:

1. A new plant's pollution must be controlled to the maximum degree possible. The plant must use the *lowest achievable emissions rate (LAER) technology*. LAER can be a cleaner technology than the BACT requirement. Generally, the EPA designates the LAER as the cleanest emission technology in use by any similar plant.
2. New plant owners must certify that any other plants they have in the area meet SIP requirements.
3. A new plant can be built in a nonattainment area only if any increase in air pollution from the new plant is *offset* by reductions in the same pollutants from other plants in the area. That is, when the new plant is operating, the area must enjoy an overall air quality improvement.

Suppose Polo Automotive wants to build a new plant in Detroit, a nonattainment area for sulfur dioxide. Polo must obtain a preconstruction permit from the EPA. The EPA will require Polo to show that it will apply the LAER technology and that any other plants it owns in the area are in compliance with Michigan's SIP. Polo must also obtain an emissions offset by reducing pollution in other plants by buying them and closing them or by paying for their pollution controls. That is, if Polo's new plant will add ten units of pollution to the air, Polo must reduce pollution elsewhere in the area by more than ten units. When the plant begins operation, air quality in the area should improve.

Expanding Need for Air Quality Permits

While we hear most about air pollution permit issues from big projects, such as coal-fired electricity plants, air pollution policies are built in to state environmental policy at a much lower level than that.

Many construction projects require environmental impact reports to be prepared that consider a wide range of effects of new projects. For example, suppose Wal-Mart wishes to build a new store in California. The California Environmental Quality Act requires an environmental impact report that considers the air pollution consequences of the change in traffic flows given the existence of a new store. The impact on air quality is an issue even for an agricultural facility in rural Mississippi, as the *Sierra Club* case discusses.

Sierra Club v. Mississippi Environmental Quality Permit Board
Supreme Court of Mississippi
943 So.2d 673 (2006)

Case Background *Bill Cook owns a large swine facility in Oktibbeha County. Eight barns hold up to 7,000 pigs. It is a concentrated animal feeding operation (CAFO) subject to water and air pollution controls. When Cook built the facility in 1996, no air pollution permit was required. A new state law required him to apply for an air pollution permit, which he did in 1999. Under new rules, the state Permit Board issued Cook a permit in 2002 that approved his current methods of operation, which included fans and a windbreak wall to help disperse odor.*

The Sierra Club challenged the permit process as inadequate, contending that the odors from the operation should be subject to more stringent air pollution rules. That challenge was considered by the Permit Board. Expert testimony was heard from the Mississippi Department of Environmental Quality (MDEQ) and others. The Board affirmed Cook's permit. The Club challenged that determination in state court. The court held that the Permit Board properly granted Cook the permit in compliance with the ambient air quality regulations (Mississippi Air Quality Standard APC–S–4) and was not an arbitrary or capricious decision. The Club appealed that decision.

Case Decision Dickinson, Justice

* * *

Based on the amended statute, the Commission adopted the current version of APC–S–4, which provides:

There shall be no odorous substances in the ambient air in concentrations sufficient to adversely and unreasonably: (1) affect human health and well-being; (2) interfere with the use of enjoyment of property; or (3) affect plant or animal life. In determining that concentrations of such substances in the ambient air are adversely and unreasonably affecting human well-being or the use or enjoyment of property of plant or animal life, the factors to be considered by the Commission will include, without limiting the generality of the foregoing, the number of complaints or petitioners alleging that such a condition exists, the frequency of the occurrence of such substances in the ambient air as confirmed by the Department of Environmental Quality staff, and the land use of the affected area....

Faced with conflicting yet credible testimony, the Permit Board made the following observation:

Put bluntly, if the Permit Board accepts only the testimony of [the Club's] witnesses, then the permit recommendations of MDEQ are not sufficient. But if the Permit Board accepts only the testimony of Cook's witnesses, then the Permit Board has no justification for requiring the additional odor and emission control elements of the … permit. The Permit Board finds that the objective truth, if such a state exists with odor, is somewhere in the middle.

After evaluating the evidence presented by both sides, the Permit Board arrived at a decision imposing several air quality control requirements on Cook's facility. We agree … that the Permit Board's decision was supported by substantial evidence and may not be disturbed on appeal....

Affirmed.

Questions for Analysis

1. The Mississippi high court held that the state properly issued an air quality permit for the swine operation. The operation did not emit the pollutants under the NAAQS, so why would there be an issue here?
2. Does the extent of the Mississippi air rule, APC–S–4, indicate that almost anything can be pulled in under it?

Mobile Sources of Pollution

Since the Clean Air Act was passed, some major air pollutants, such as lead, have nearly disappeared from the atmosphere. Large reductions have occurred in particulates and carbon monoxide. But ozone at lower levels of the atmosphere has changed little; it is mostly produced by the imperfect burning of petroleum products. Since vehicles are the primary source, the law has tightened controls on cars and trucks. While vehicles produce fewer hydrocarbons that help form ozone than they did when the Clean Air Act was passed, many more miles are driven by more vehicles today, keeping ozone emissions up.

The level of ozone allowed is determined by the NAAQS, but the law also imposes direct controls on certain emission sources. Tailpipe exhaust standards for cars, trucks, and buses have become tougher. Where ozone pollution is worst, in most major cities, SIPs impose tougher vehicle emission inspections, vapor recovery systems at gas stations, reformulated gasoline, and alternative fuel sources.

The law allows states to impose emissions standards that go beyond the federal requirements. California has set tougher auto emissions standards and requirements for cleaner-burning gasoline and has forced use of alternative-fuel and electric-powered cars. The regulations are supposed to cut auto pollution 50 percent more than do the federal standards. New York, New Jersey, Pennsylvania, Massachusetts, Virginia, Maryland, Delaware, New Hampshire, Maine, Rhode Island, and Vermont have adopted the California standards, which means that some California standards will become the national standard.

Toxic Pollutants

As amended in 1990, the Clean Air Act lists 191 substances declared to be hazardous air pollutants. The EPA sets *maximum emission rates (MERs)* for pollutants. The goal is a 90 percent reduction in emissions for the pollutants and a 75 percent reduction in cancer caused by air pollution. If the EPA determines that a pollutant is a threat to public health or the environment, tighter control standards are to be imposed without regard to such economic factors as cost or technological feasibility. Tough standards for many pollutants, such as emissions from dry-cleaning establishments and commercial bakeries, have been issued by the EPA. These rules are highly technical.

Enforcement

The EPA and state environmental agencies have primary authority to enforce the Clean Air Act and other environmental statutes. Citizens, including environmental groups, have rights to bring *citizen suits* to enforce environmental statutes when

---

INTERNATIONAL PERSPECTIVE

Industrialization Brings Environmental Problems to China

The pollution that afflicts the poorest people—breathing smoke-filled air from cooking fires in their living huts and drinking contaminated water—is reduced when industrialization occurs and economic conditions improve. But then pollutants from rising industrial production create problems.

As the economy of China has grown rapidly in the past two decades, environmental damage has increased rapidly. The government of China understands the magnitude of the problem and has laws and agencies to deal with pollution. On the books, the structure looks much like the EPA. In practice, there is little enforcement.

At least 70 percent of the water in major rivers is rated as "severely polluted." The China National Environmental Monitoring Center reports that no major city has good air quality. Waters around coastal cities are badly polluted. The State Oceanographic Administration Marine Environment Protection Department warns that marine ecological systems near Shanghai and other major cities are "dangerously close to collapse."

Rules that have weak enforcement mean little. When a fertilizer plant dumped large quantities of ammonia and nitrate into a river, killing tons of fish and poisoning drinking water for downstream cities, nothing much happened. An official from the State Environmental Protection Administration said that there is no authority to shut down the worst offenders: "We can only fine them, and such a small amount at that. They basically decide it's a cost that doesn't matter."

Source: *China Daily News* and *The Wall Street Journal*

Getty Images

government agencies fail to do so. A large number of such suits are brought every year. The environmental statutes list the penalties that may be imposed on violators.

Some environmental offenses are prosecuted as criminal matters, which means more than 100 criminal indictments per year. EPA and state environmental agencies collect hundreds of millions of dollars per year in fines.

Carrot-and-Stick Approach

Enforcement uses a carrot-and-stick approach. The U.S. Sentencing Guidelines, punishment for environmental crimes holds that the penalties imposed on a company and its executives should take into account several factors. Punishment is reduced for companies that

- cooperate with the government in investigations.
- voluntarily report illegal actions.
- educate their workforce about environmental standards.
- assist those who suffer from environmental wrongdoing.
- have a strong internal environmental compliance program.

Clean Water Act

Federal authority over water pollution goes back to the Rivers and Harbors Act of 1886 and 1899. But like the Federal Water Pollution Control Act of 1948, there was little effective federal control. Primary responsibility was left with the states. By 1970, marine life in Lake Erie was almost gone, and many rivers were unfit for drinking water or recreation.

The Clean Water Act (CWA) was passed in 1972 and was substantially amended in 1977 and 1986. The objective of the Clean Water Act is to "restore and maintain the chemical, physical, and biological integrity of the Nation's waters." The Act has five main elements:

1. National *effluent* (pollution) standards set by the EPA for each industry
2. Water quality standards set by the states under EPA approval
3. A *discharge permit* program that sets water quality standards to limit pollution
4. Special provisions for toxic chemicals and oil spills
5. Construction grants and loans from the federal government for *publicly owned treatment works (POTWs)*, such as sewage treatment plants

The CWA makes it unlawful for any person, business, or government to dump pollutants into navigable waters without a *permit*. Although the Act does not define "navigable waters," it is broadly interpreted for regulatory purposes. Except for isolated small bodies of water, all waters are considered to be under federal jurisdiction. National Pollution Discharge Elimination System (NPDES) permits are required not only for dumping waste water into water, but even for moving water from one place to another.

Cleaning the nation's waters has been much more expensive and has taken longer than was anticipated when the Clean Water Act was passed in 1972. At that time, Congress said that the discharge of pollutants into any waters would be eliminated by 1985. That was an impossible goal. As it stands, discharges have probably dropped to about half of what they were when the Act was passed. But since pollutants that are easiest to eliminate have been attacked first, the cost of removing more pollutants will be much higher.

Point Source Pollution

The water pollution that is easiest to identify comes out of a pipe. We can see it, measure it, and, given technical knowledge, treat the discharge. Control of such *point source pollution* has been the primary focus of federal law since 1972. Sewage from homes and industrial sources (point sources) is often treated at publicly owned treatment works (POTWs). Billions are spent every year to improve existing POTWs (sewage treatment plants). Since most effluents treated at POTWs are not toxic, the *sludge*—the glop that is removed during sewage treatment—is often used for fertilizer. The treated water is pumped back into rivers or lakes. Exhibit 18.3 illustrates primary water effluent sources.

Under the Clean Water Act, states must designate all surface water as to intended use. If the use is drinking water, treated water dumped into a bay, lake, or river must be quite pure; if the body of water is designated for recreation, the treated water must be clean enough not to contaminate swimmers or fish.

Industrial Permits

Industrial discharges are subject to a permit process. As we have seen already, the EPA and state environmental agencies, under the National Pollutant Discharge Elimination System (NPDES), require industrial polluters to list the amount and type of their discharges. The polluters are issued permits to release various pollutants in certain quantities.

Control Technology Each firm in an industry must meet the effluent (pollutant) limits set by the EPA for each chemical dumped into wastewater. The list of

Exhibit 18.3 Primary Sources of Water Effluents

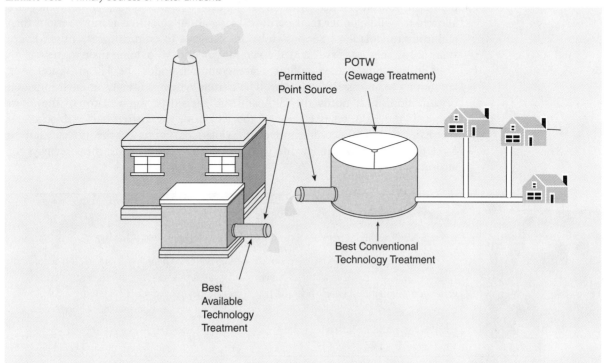

controlled substances is expanding, and the degree to which the substances must be controlled grows gradually tighter. Conventional pollutants, like human waste, are controlled by the *best conventional technology (BCT)*. Congress ordered the EPA to consider cost-effectiveness when setting such standards.

Cost considerations are not as important for toxic or unconventional pollutants, which are subject to tighter control, called *best available technology (BAT)*—defined by the EPA as the "very best control and treatment measures that have been or are capable of being achieved." Hence, as better technology is invented to control pollutants, polluters must use it to reduce their pollution. Regardless of the kind of pollutants, if a polluter is located on a particularly sensitive waterway, even more stringent controls may be ordered.

When a new plant is built or a new source of pollution is created, it is subject to even tighter controls—called *new source performance standards (NSPS)*. The law says that the standard is "the greatest degree of effluent reduction … achievable through application of the best available demonstrated control technology, processes, operating methods, and other alternatives, including, where practicable, standards permitting no discharge of pollutants." Using BAT controls for the pollution produced is not enough; the entire production process must use the best technology that exists to minimize pollution output.

Enforcement

Since point-source water pollution control is based on a permit system, the permits are the key to enforcement. Under the NPDES, the states have primary responsibility for enforcing the permit system, subject to EPA monitoring and approval.

Operating without a permit or discharging more pollution than is allowed under a permit violates the law. Firms that have pollution permits must monitor their own performance and file *discharge monitoring reports (DMRs)*, available for public inspection. Hence, firms must report violations of the amount they are allowed to pollute under their permits. Lying about violations is more serious than admitting to violations. Serious violations can lead to criminal prosecution. Every year, prison sentences are handed down for violators who dump toxic wastes.

Citizen suits against polluters are common under the Clean Water Act, amounting to at least 200 per year. The citizen, which is usually an environmental organization, must notify the EPA and the alleged permit violator of the *intent to sue*. If the EPA takes charge of the situation, the citizen suit is blocked. If the EPA does not act diligently, and violations continue, the private suit to force enforcement of the law may proceed. If the plaintiff wins, the loser pays for attorneys' fees.

ISSUE SPOTTER

Does Obeying EPA Regulations Eliminate Litigation?

Your company's production facility produces certain water pollutants that are treated according to EPA standards. You have all the EPA permits that are required. Does this mean the treated water you pump into the river near the plant has no legal consequence? Are there legal problems that you could face even if EPA has no complaints about your operations? How can you be sure?

Getty Images

Nonpoint Source Pollution

About half of all water pollution is from nonpoint sources—it is runoff from construction sites, logging and mining operations, streets, and agriculture. Pollutants are washed by rain into streams and lakes and seep into groundwater. Much *nonpoint source pollution* has only recently come under control efforts. The complexity of the problem requires multiple solutions.

Because runoff from streets usually occurs during rainstorms, when sewage treatment plants do not have the capacity to treat all runoff water, holding tanks may have to be built to allow the water to be treated later. Since a lot of pollution is due to air pollution that settles on the ground or is washed from the atmosphere by rain, tighter air pollution rules result in less nonpoint source water pollution.

The consequences of groundwater pollution that comes from agricultural fertilizers and sprays are considered by various agencies under statutes in addition to the Clean Water Act. These include the Safe Drinking Water Act; the Federal Insecticide, Fungicide, and Rodenticide Act; the Toxic Substances Control Act; and other laws that deal, one way or another, with pollution that shows up in water from nonpoint sources. Although regulations to reduce runoff have been gradually tightened, runoff pollution remains a problem that is difficult to resolve technologically or politically.

Wetlands

In years past, *wetlands* were seen as nuisances to be drained and filled with dirt. Wetlands destruction was subsidized by agencies such as the Army Corps of Engineers. Now that the environmental value of wetlands is better known, developers and others must protect wetlands. The EPA defines wetlands as

> Those areas that are inundated or saturated by surface or groundwater at a frequency and duration sufficient to support, and that under normal circumstances do support, a prevalence of vegetation typically adapted for life in saturated soil conditions. Wetlands generally include swamps, marshes, bogs, and similar areas.

This definition includes mangrove swamps of coastal saltwater shrubs in the South; prairie potholes in the Dakotas and Minnesota, where shallow depressions that hold water during part of the year are visited by migrating birds; and playa lakes in the Southwest that are rarely flooded basins. Wetlands can be small holes or large areas and may contain one plant or dozens of important species.

Permit System

Under the CWA, anyone wanting to change a wetland must receive a §404 permit from the Army Corps of Engineers. The EPA may block an Army Corps permit to prevent environmental damage. About 10,000 permits are issued each year to allow dredging or filling of wetlands. Often, a permit to dredge wetlands will include a requirement that other land be restored to wetland status in exchange. Another 75,000 permits are issued each year for activities that "cause only minimal adverse environmental effects" to wetlands. Hence, businesses in construction or other activities that disturb earth must make sure wetlands requirements have been met. Permits have become standard practice, even for ordinary building projects, as the *Responsible Economic Development* case illustrates.

Responsible Economic Development v. S.C. Department of Health and Environmental Control
Supreme Court of South Carolina
641 S.E.2d 425 (2007)

Case Background *Wal-Mart intended to build a new store in Florence, South Carolina. Because the store would have a parking lot, it needed a permit that determined how stormwater runoff would be handled. The parking lot was designed to make water flow in the direction of a detention (holding) pond. It could accommodate 100-year frequency storm events. From the pond, water would flow into assorted creeks. The South Carolina Department of Health and Environmental Controls (DHEC) granted a stormwater permit.*

The Responsible Economic Development (RED) group challenged the permit. RED claimed that the stormwater runoff would degrade creek water and then flow into Jeffries Creek, an impaired body of water. An administrative law judge for DHEC ruled that the permit had been properly granted. RED challenged that ruling, but it was upheld first by the DHEC board and then by the circuit court. RED appealed to the state high court.

Case Decision Burnett, Justice

* * *

Appellants contend the circuit court erroneously affirmed the issuance of a stormwater permit in this case. Appellants allege Regulation 72–305(B)(4) requires the denial of the stormwater permit, because stormwater runoff from Wal-Mart's proposed development will further depress oxygen levels in the unnamed tributary and Jeffries Creek and thus violates the antidegradation rules....

The Stormwater Management and Sediment Reduction Act (Stormwater Act) requires a person who intends to engage in a land disturbing activity to submit a stormwater management and sediment control plan to the appropriate agency and obtain a permit before engaging in the activity, unless an exemption applies. The Stormwater Act further requires DHEC to promulgate regulations for the "types of activities that require a stormwater ... permit" and for "permit

application and approval requirements." DHEC fulfilled that duty by promulgating, in relevant part, Regulations 72–305 and –307. Regulation 72–305 outlines the permit application and approval procedure, and Regulation 72–307 sets forth the minimum standards and specifications and the specific design criteria for projects requiring a stormwater management and sediment control plan....

The ALJ determined the requirements of Regulations 72–305 and –307 applied to this case, because Wal-Mart's proposed development involves a land disturbing activity.... He found the stormwater runoff from Wal-Mart's development would not flow directly into Jeffries Creek, an impaired water body, but would flow directly into an unnamed tributary, which is an unimpaired water body. Then the stormwater would flow for one-half mile before converging with Jeffries Creek, and he determined the stormwater runoff would obtain re-aeration properties before converging with Jeffries Creek. The ALJ found stormwater runoff from three other commercial developments flowed into the unnamed tributary before converging with Jeffries Creek without negatively affecting the water quality of Jeffries Creek. He also found there was no significant evidence that quantified the inadequate measures alleged by Appellants. Based on the totality of the circumstances, the ALJ ... upheld the issuance of the stormwater permit to Wal-Mart....

Affirmed.

Questions for Analysis
1. The South Carolina high court upheld the issuance of the stormwater runoff permit, because it met state standards. RED claimed that the state permitting process was flawed and favored land developers. Could that be the case?
2. What alternative would Wal-Mart have to building a parking lot?

Wetlands Takings

The wetlands permit system can result in prohibitions on building or modifying land that was purchased with the expectation that certain uses were allowed. Some landowners have discovered their land to be worthless, because they cannot get a permit for the land to be modified. Several cases, such as *Loveladies Harbor* v. *United*

States (28 F.3d 1171 [1994]), have resulted in decisions that the government must pay for land it forces out of circulation for wetlands protection.

In *Loveladies*, a New Jersey coastal development that had been under construction for 30 years was halted when the Army Corps prohibited any further construction. Fifty acres of wetlands fell from $2.66 million in value to nearly nothing. The Federal Circuit Court of Appeals ordered the government to pay the developer for the land as a taking for public benefit.

Land Pollution

Millions of tons of hazardous waste are disposed of each year. Some waste is stored in drums and deposited in clay-lined dumps, injected deep underground between layers of rock, or illegally abandoned in vacant lots, lagoons, and landfills. Some storage methods fail as containers corrode and rain washes the wastes from storage sites. Hazardous waste can make its way into lakes, streams, and groundwater.

To reduce the amount of toxic substances that are dumped and to limit exposure to chemicals that are toxic to people or animals, controls are imposed on the production, distribution, use, and disposal of toxic chemicals. Careless disposal of chemicals in the past means that billions are now being spent to clean up waste sites. As Exhibit 18.4 indicates, managers must be aware of the liability that can arise from use of chemicals today and from ownership of property that may contain toxic wastes.

Toxic Substances Control Act

More than 70,000 chemicals are in commercial use. Under the *Toxic Substances Control Act (TOSCA)* passed in 1976, the EPA controls and keeps track of chemicals. Because chemicals can cause health hazards, accurate information about their possible effects is vital.

When a producer wants to sell a new chemical, it must notify the EPA, which studies the substance and its proposed uses to determine environmental hazards. Producers may be required to run tests for toxicity and other effects so that the EPA can determine whether any restrictions should be placed on the chemical. Restrictions may be just labeling requirements; some chemicals are allowed in restricted uses, and some are banned.

Exhibit 18.4 Regulation of Hazardous Substance

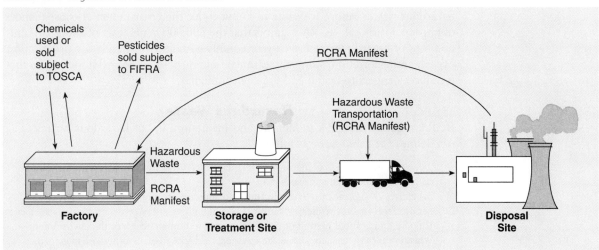

Biotechnology, the manipulation of biological processes to produce chemicals or living organisms for commercial use, is subject to TOSCA. Since the results may be eligible for patents, this is a field with valuable products worth tens of billions of dollars. Genetic engineering produces such things as enzymes that can purify water and consume the oil in oil spills. The EPA monitors efforts to use natural organisms in new ways and to use genetically altered microorganisms.

Pesticides

Pesticides are used to prevent, kill, or disable pests, including undesirable plants, insects, rodents, fungi, and molds. Most pesticides are toxic to people and the environment if improperly used. Congress originally passed the *Federal Insecticide, Fungicide, and Rodenticide Act (FIFRA)* in 1947 and has amended it several times since.

The EPA has registered more than 20,000 products under FIFRA. Registration means that before a pesticide is sold, the EPA has examined scientific data about the product's effects and the label on the product is accurate as to proper use and precautions. Registration is approved for five years at a time for pesticides that meet these conditions:

1. The product does what the producers claim it will do.
2. The registration materials and the label are accurate as to proper use.
3. The product, when used properly, will not have "unreasonable adverse effects on the environment."

FIFRA requires that the economic and environmental costs and benefits of each product be considered. The EPA tries to determine what risk—such as groundwater contamination or skin irritation—might be posed by a pesticide so that it can limit how the product is used and who may use it. Since some products pose a danger to certain species, the EPA may restrict use to locations that minimize exposure for those who could be harmed. Working with the Food and Drug Administration, the EPA sets usage requirements to take into account the residues that remain in food products to ensure that consumers are not exposed to unsafe levels of pesticides.

Resource Conservation and Recovery Act

TOSCA and FIFRA are primarily concerned with controlling toxic substances before they get to the market. How toxic substances are handled once they are in the market, or when they are being disposed of, is the concern of the *Resource Conservation and Recovery Act (RCRA)* passed in 1976 and amended in 1984.

"Out of sight, out of mind" was standard procedure for the disposal of many hazardous wastes before we came to know about the environmental consequences of improper disposal. RCRA requires that the 500,000 generators of about 200 million tons of hazardous waste each year comply with an EPA regulatory program for over the transportation, storage, treatment, and disposal of hazardous waste, so that it reduces dangers to health and the environment.

Hazardous Waste

RCRA requires the EPA to identify and maintain a list of hazardous wastes. The Act defines *hazardous waste* as follows:

> … a solid waste … which because of its quantity, concentration, or physical, chemical, or infectious characteristics may—
> (a) cause, or significantly contribute to, an increase in mortality or an increase in serious irreversible, or incapacitating reversible, illness; or,
> (b) pose a substantial present or potential hazard to human health or the environment when improperly treated, stored, transported, or disposed of, or otherwise managed.

The characteristics of hazardous waste are ignitability, such as gasoline; corrosivity, such as acids; reactivity, such as unstable chemicals; and toxicity, where ingredients threaten groundwater. Wastes like that, such as batteries and unused pesticides, may be stored or disposed of only at sites whose owners or operators have obtained a permit from the EPA. To get the permit, the owners of the *treatment, storage, and disposal (TSD) sites* agree to meet all regulations regarding the handling of hazardous wastes.

Regulation of TSD Sites

RCRA requires the EPA to regulate TSD sites. Certain hazardous wastes must be treated prior to disposal. A treatment facility is where there is a change in the physical, chemical, or biological character of hazardous waste to make it less hazardous or to recover energy or materials from it. A storage facility or where waste is held, such as in storage tanks, until it can be disposed of or treated. A disposal facility is where hazardous wastes are placed into water or land, such as sealed landfills.

The Manifest System

RCRA forces compliance by hazardous waste generators, transporters, and TSD-site owners by a *manifest system.* The producer of a hazardous waste must complete a *manifest*—a form that states the nature of the hazardous waste and identifies its origin, shipping route, and final destination. The waste must be packaged in appropriate and properly labeled containers.

Generators must give transporters of hazardous waste a copy of the manifest. Transporters, such as trucking companies, must sign the manifest and, upon delivery, provide a copy to the owner of the TSD site, who must return a copy of the manifest to the generator, thereby closing the circle. If a generator is not informed of the proper deposit of the waste, it notifies the EPA. This reporting system provides regulators with the ability to track hazardous waste through its generation, transportation, and disposal phases.

LIGHTER SIDE OF THE LAW

Environmental Harmony

China has experienced a rapid growth in many pollutants to accompany its economic growth. But that does not mean steps are not being taken to do something about problems. In Fumin county in the southwest, Laoshou mountain had been mined and was an ugly scar.

Rather than plant trees to reclaim the hillside, it was spray painted green. Officials declared that this was a proper use of *feng shui*. Wikipedia describes feng shui as "the ancient practice of placement and arrangement of space to achieve harmony with the environment".

Source: *Globe and Mail (Toronto)*

Getty Images

Superfund

Congress enacted the Comprehensive *Environmental Response, Compensation, and Liability Act (CERCLA)* in 1980. Called the *Superfund,* the Act provides the authority to clean up abandoned hazardous sites. Congress amended the Superfund program in 1986 with the *Superfund Amendments and Reauthorization Act (SARA),* which imposes a tax on the petroleum and chemical industries. Some of the $1 billion to $2 billion per year in revenues go to Superfund cleanups. However, private parties are incurring substantial costs.

Over the years, the EPA has evaluated about 6,000 sites and has put about 2,000 of them on the *National Priority List (NPL)*. Those are the locations that receive the most attention and federal resources. EPA is responsible for cleanups at federal facilities, which make up about 10 percent of the sites. Some sites cost a few million dollars to clean up; others run as high as a half billion dollars. The EPA has deleted over 300 sites from the NPL, stating these have been successfully cleaned; that number rises each year, but of course other sites can be added to the list, so the number of sites continually changes, but it is usually around 1,700. Details and state maps may be found at www.epa.gov/superfund/about.htm.

Responsible Parties

An abandoned dump site might contain hazardous wastes contributed by many waste generators. In addition, the dump site may have been operated by different parties over the years. Under the law, there may be multiple *potentially responsible parties (PRPs)*. CERCLA defines PRPs, who can be held liable for both cleanup costs and damages to natural resources:

1. Current owners of a hazardous waste site
2. Prior owners of a site at the time of hazardous waste disposal
3. Any hazardous waste generator who arranged for disposal at the site
4. Any transporter of hazardous waste who selected the site for disposal

The parties may be held *strictly and jointly and severally liable* for these costs; that is, each party can be liable for the entire cleanup cost regardless of the size of its contribution to the hazardous waste at the site. As a result, each party has a strong incentive to identify other PRPs, which often results in lengthy, expensive litigation.

Practical Problems

The EPA may begin a cleanup if there is a threat to public health or the environment if cleanup is delayed. Later, the government can try to recover expenses by suing PRPs, if they can be located. More commonly, the EPA orders private parties to pay to clean up the site under EPA supervision. This generates a lot of expensive litigation.

So, an important issue to consider when buying property is whether it contains toxic wastes that may have been buried years ago or, when buying a business, whether the business was involved in handling toxic materials. If so, the new owner may be held responsible for cleanup costs. Some new owners have been handed cleanup bills for more than the property is worth, even though the new owners did not generate the waste. If they cannot find other PRPs capable of paying the bill, the new owners are stuck. As a result, property buyers often have an *environmental audit* performed for property they intend to purchase.

LIGHTER SIDE OF THE LAW
Honor Your Local Superfund Site

The Department of Interior declared the Fresno, California, municipal landfill to be a historical landmark listed on the National Register, because it pioneered certain methods of disposal. Upon being informed that the landfill was on the National Priority List of Superfund sites, the Department decided to rescind the honor.

Source: *New York Times*

Getty Images

Because of the nearly unlimited liability for unknown cleanup costs, useful property sits abandoned. The Cleveland *Plain Dealer* built a new plant for the newspaper on farmland out of the city. The abandoned urban site it had originally chosen was found to have chemicals in the soil from years before. Such old sites are referred to as *brownfields*. Since the newspaper could not risk Superfund liability, it moved out of town rather than help restore downtown Cleveland. Bringing brownfields back into use has been helped by the Brownfields Revitalization Act of 2002. It limits the liability to purchasers of contaminated sites for previous improper dumping of toxic wastes on the land.

Species Protection

Most environmental laws are written with primary concern for the effect of pollutants on human health. But some laws address environmental protection for wildlife or, more broadly, for all species. The most important of these laws is the *Endangered Species Act (ESA)*, enacted in 1973 and amended several times. In some respects, the ESA is the toughest environmental statute of all.

The Act recognizes the value of species habitat. It authorizes designation of critical habitat—areas needed to preserve endangered species—and calls for recovery plans for listed species. The Department of the Interior has estimated that a recovery program for the approximately 1,900 recognized threatened and endangered species in the United States (see http://www.fws.gov/endangered/) would cost billions of dollars. Funding from Congress has often been a few hundred million dollars per year.

Habitat Protection

The ESA authorizes the Secretary of the Interior to declare species of animal or plant life endangered and to establish the critical habitat of such species. An *endangered species* is defined as "any species which is in danger of extinction throughout all or a significant portion of its range." When a species is *listed* as endangered or threatened by the Interior Department, the Act imposes obligations on private and public parties. Under the ESA, no person may "take, import, or conduct commercial activity with respect to any endangered species." In most disputes involving an endangered species, parties generally agree that the species deserves protection; the conflict centers on how protection is provided.

LIGHTER SIDE OF THE LAW

Protect Truly Rare Species

An office in the Parliament of Sweden was searching environmental records. It discovered a 1986 regional environmental court order from Jaemtland. The court had denied a resort-development permit to a builder because it could interfere with the "Storsjoe monster." The Storsjoe monster is something like the Loch Ness monster, with a serpent's body and cat like head. It was first "seen" in 1635.

The court held that "it is prohibited to kill, hurt, or catch animals of the Storsjoe monster species" or to "take away or hurt the monster's eggs, roe, or den."

Source: *Washington Post*

Getty Images

The ESA states that projects may not "result in the destruction or modification of habitat of [endangered] species." The full impact of that statement was not clear for years. But in 1991, a federal court ordered logging stopped on federal lands in Oregon, Washington, and northern California. Environmental groups had sued to stop logging to protect the habitat and nesting areas of the spotted owl, a bird on the endangered species list. In 1995, the Supreme Court, in *Babbitt* v. *Sweet Home* (515 U.S. 2407), held that habitat protection is a key part of the ESA, so the termination of logging until a habitat protection plan was put in place was proper. The reduction in logging on behalf of the spotted owl is estimated to have cost about $25 billion.

Controversy and Uncertainty

Endangered species protection joins wetlands in being one of the most controversial environmental issues. There is no clear legal definition of *endangered* or *species* or *habitat*. The legal requirements for adding a species to the list are minimal. Because listing a species can lead to very tight controls on private property use,

Exhibit 18.5 Threatened and Endangered Species

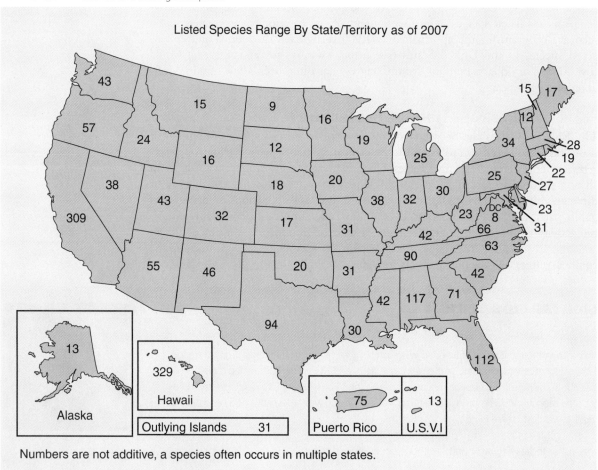

Source: *Fish and Wildlife Service*

landowners fear having their land removed from use resulting from uncompensated habitat protection. In response, Congress has encouraged a limit on ESA listings while pondering alternatives.

Of all species listed, habitats have been clearly defined for only a fraction. The Fish and Wildlife Service devotes most of its resources to protecting the most "popular" species, such as the manatee. Creatures like the Alabama cave fish and the red hills salamander are largely ignored. With limited resources, environmental agencies cannot address all problems. Citizen groups play a large role in pressing for enforcement of environmental statutes. The following case illustrates that and how it is not uncommon for more than one statute to come into play.

ISSUE SPOTTER
Picking a Sweet Spot

Your firm develops resort spots. Nice pieces of land are found for developing a hotel and a golf course and other facilities. Sometimes houses are also built for permanent residents. The plots of land purchased run between 100 and 600 acres. In considering land for development, what environmental issues should be considered before buying the property?

Getty Images

Center for Biological Diversity v. Marina Point Development Associates
United States District Court, Central District California
434 F.Supp.2d 789 (2006)

Case Background *A condo project on the shoreline of Big Bear Lake, California, began in the early 1980s. Developers obtained multiple construction permits from the Big Bear Municipal Water District, the County of San Bernardino, the California Regional Water Quality Control Board, the California Department of Fish and Game, and the Army Corps of Engineers, among others. After 20 years of background work, permits were in place and construction began.*

The Center for Biological Diversity and other opponents of the project watched the process, took photos, and complained to the Corps and other agencies that the construction process violated terms of some permits. There was improper dredging along the lake, improper rock movement, improper use of silt screens along the lake edge, and disturbance of trees used as habitat by bald eagles on the endangered species list. The Corps ordered corrective actions. The Center kept gathering evidence of violations and sued to enjoin further work on the project.

Case Decision Real, District Judge

* * *

Congress enacted the ESA in an attempt to preserve endangered species and the ecosystems upon which they depend....

Bald eagles in particular have been protected by the ESA for decades. One of the primary threats to their continued survival is the destruction or degradation of their habitats. Habitat destruction occurs through (1) the direct cutting of trees for shoreline development; (2) human disturbance associated with the recreational use of shorelines and waterways; and (3) the contamination of those waterways as a result of pollution....

To obtain injunctive relief, a plaintiff need only show that the defendants' activities are likely to cause a take [taking an endangered species] in the future....

continues

In this case, construction on the Project site so far has already caused a "take" by harassing the bald eagle population by modifying and disturbing its habitat....

The text of the Clean Water Act creates an express right of action for any citizen to file suit on her own behalf against any person who is alleged to be in violation of (1) an effluent standard or limitation; or (2) an administrative order issued with respect to the standard or limitation....

Section 402 of the CWA provides a permit regime for stormwater discharges. But the Defendants were never issued a 402 permit and only applied for one in January 2005, after this suit had commenced....

Without the appropriate permit, the Defendants' point source discharges violated the CWA. Point sources include not only the sources that generate pollutants but also the conveyances—such as gullies and ditches—that transfer them to protected waters....

Section 404 [of the CWA] authorizes a permit regime for discharges of dredge and fill material. Discharges of dredged and fill material into the lake or subject wetlands violate the CWA....

[Defendants] ignored their 404 permit's clear prohibition against the deposit of fill in the wetlands when they bulldozed the site. They then went ahead with the bulldozing despite repeated admonitions that doing so would create fill and thus violate the CWA....

The Court finds that the Defendants are in continuing violation of both ... the ESA and ... the CWA and that there is a significant likelihood of future violations.

Therefore, it is ordered that the Defendants pay a statutory penalty of $2,500 for each day of violation, totaling $1,312,500.00 from October 7, 2002 to April 16, 2004.

In addition, it is further ordered that the Defendants be enjoined from any development on the Project site without the prior authorization of this Court.

Finally, it is ordered that the Defendants immediately take all remedial measures prescribed by the [Army Corps] to repair and restore the integrity of the shoreline and the wetlands.

The Court retains jurisdiction over this matter to ensure the Defendants' full compliance with the terms of this order and the dictates of the Army Corps of Engineers.

Questions for Analysis

1. The court found the developer in violation of the ESA and CWA. It imposed a fine and ordered construction stopped without court permission. Do you think the developer knew it was likely in violation of some environmental rules?

2. Why do you suppose the Army Corps or some other agency did not step in earlier, rather than wait for a private party to enforce the law?

Global Environmental Issues

Some of the biggest environmental issues—the ozone layer, global climate change, habitat destruction, and the marine environment—must be dealt with on an international scale. Even if the United States did not contribute to global environmental problems, the consequences would still be borne here, so the United States must work with other countries to decide what to do about such issues. The ozone issue provides a good example of an international legal solution to an environmental problem.

The Ozone

While too much ozone (O_3) in the air we breathe is a problem caused largely by vehicle exhaust and is a localized problem, ozone depletion at high levels in the atmosphere is caused by chemicals called *chlorofluorocarbons* (CFCs), known popularly by such brand names as Freon. CFCs were widely used as refrigerants in air-conditioning systems, in making computer chips, and in some plastics products. In the stratosphere, CFCs are presumed to eat away at the ozone layer, which protects life on earth from ultraviolet radiation. The effect on humans would be an increase in skin cancer, more eye cataracts, and injury to the immune system.

Evidence of a "hole" in the ozone layer over Antarctica in 1985 convinced industry and the government that CFCs could pose a serious problem. Ozone loss could cause tens of thousands of deaths per year from skin cancers. In the United States, the makers of CFCs, which produced one third of the world supply, agreed with the EPA that CFC production had to be eliminated.

The producers supported the *Montreal Protocol* of 1987, which the United States signed. Under the protocol, an international treaty, nations that produced CFCs agreed to cut production by 50 percent by 1998. The protocol was revised by the London treaty of 1990, requiring production of CFCs and halon (the best firefighting chemical) to be eliminated by 2000.

A solution was achieved that resulted in producers giving up a multibillion-dollar-per-year market. Producers' cooperation was hastened by the promise from the government that the existing producers would have a monopoly over the product during its final years. The total cost to the world's economy of the CFC phase-out was about $200 billion.

International Cooperation

CFC production was largely in the United States, Japan, and European nations—countries that could essentially force the decision on this issue. Other international environmental issues require more cooperation from less-developed nations, since those nations will bear more of the effects of changes in policies that would reduce environmental problems.

The Montreal Protocol provided a fund, set up by wealthier nations, to pay poorer nations to sign the agreement to ban CFCs. That is, the United States paid for environmental cooperation from other nations. Similarly, the United States helps to pay the cost of water treatment plants in Mexico located near the U.S. border to reduce pollution of the Rio Grande and the Pacific Ocean.

There is little doubt that if the United States and other nations are concerned about species preservation and other environmental issues, they must pay less-developed nations to protect species and to cover the costs of some pollution controls.

INTERNATIONAL PERSPECTIVE

Exporting Hazardous Waste

You see Hazardous Waste signs on assorted collection boxes, and it is important that such materials do not end up in landfills, where they can pollute groundwater or be burned and emitted into the air. So toxics are often separated into separate waste categories. But where does the stuff go?

Mercury as a liquid metal is not particularly harmful. But emitted into the atmosphere, it returns to lakes and oceans, contaminates fish, and then poisons humans who eat the fish. At sufficient levels, it causes numerous, serious health problems, especially for children.

Products containing mercury, such as switches and batteries, often must be collected as a hazardous waste

under laws designed to protect air and water. But such waste from the United States and other countries may be sold and end up in primitive gold mines, where it is used to leach gold from ore. From there it returns to the atmosphere, which means it can end up anywhere in the world when it comes back down.

In 2004, the United States exported almost 300 tons of mercury to Mexico, Vietnam, Peru, and other countries that have few controls on its use. The European Union has promised to ban mercury exports in the future. In the United States, some states have regulations to limit where the waste goes. But until there is widespread agreement on controls of mercury, the recycling program in the United States does not give the environmental value expected.

Getty Images

Global Warming

Greenhouse gases that many scientists link to global warming are the basis of the current major environmental issue. A treaty drafted in Kyoto, Japan, in 1997 contains assertions by most nations that they will take steps to substantially reduce certain gas emissions—such as carbon dioxide—by 2008–2012. The Clinton administration signed the treaty in 1998 but did not submit it to Congress for ratification, because it would not have passed. A Senate resolution passed 95 to 0 indicating opposition. The Bush administration dropped the treaty and proposed alternative plans.

The Kyoto Treaty may be more symbolic than a real commitment. Greenhouse gas emissions have increased faster in some signing nations in Europe than they have in the United States. As the economies of the most populous nations, China and India, grow quickly, their emissions are rising quickly. If there is a consensus that the emissions must be addressed, it will require international action. Poor nations cannot afford advanced technology, so the United States, the European Union, and Japan may have to offer some solutions. The Supreme Court chipped in on the issue in 2007, which may be a signal of new trends in environmental law in the years to come.

Massachusetts v. Environmental Protection Agency
Supreme Court of the United States
127 U.S. 1438 (2007)

Case Background *Twelve states, some local governments, and private organizations sued the EPA, contending that it did not live up to its obligation under the Clean Air Act to regulate greenhouse gases that result from vehicle emissions. EPA responded that its regulations were sufficient and that it need not design more stringent regulations. The appeals court agreed; plaintiffs appealed.*

Case Decision Stevens, Justice

* * *

Congress has ordered EPA to protect Massachusetts (among others) by prescribing standards applicable to the "emission of any air pollutant from any class or classes of new motor vehicle engines, which in [the Administrator's] judgment cause, or contribute to, air pollution which may reasonably be anticipated to endanger public health or welfare." Congress has moreover recognized a concomitant procedural right to challenge the rejection of its rulemaking petition as arbitrary and capricious. Given that procedural right and Massachusetts' stake in protecting its quasi-sovereign interests, the Commonwealth is entitled to special solicitude in our standing analysis....

EPA's steadfast refusal to regulate greenhouse gas emissions presents a risk of harm to Massachusetts that

is both "actual" and "imminent." There is, moreover, a "substantial likelihood that the judicial relief requested" will prompt EPA to take steps to reduce that risk.

The harms associated with climate change are serious and well recognized. Indeed, the National Research Council Report itself—which EPA regards as an "objective and independent assessment of the relevant science," identifies a number of environmental changes that have already inflicted significant harms, including "the global retreat of mountain glaciers, reduction in snow-cover extent, the earlier spring melting of rivers and lakes, [and] the accelerated rate of rise of sea levels during the twentieth century relative to the past few thousand years...." (NRC Report 16....)

EPA does not dispute the existence of a causal connection between man-made greenhouse gas emissions and global warming. At a minimum, therefore, EPA's refusal to regulate such emissions "contributes" to Massachusetts' injuries.

EPA nevertheless maintains that its decision not to regulate greenhouse gas emissions from new motor vehicles contributes so insignificantly to petitioners' injuries that the agency cannot be haled into federal court to answer for them. For the same reason, EPA does not believe that any realistic possibility exists that the relief petitioners seek would mitigate global climate change and remedy their injuries. That is especially so, because predicted increases in greenhouse gas emissions from developing nations, particularly China and India, are likely to offset any marginal domestic decrease....

And reducing domestic automobile emissions is hardly a tentative step. Even leaving aside the other greenhouse gases, the United States transportation sector emits an enormous quantity of carbon dioxide into the atmosphere … more than 1.7 billion metric tons in 1999 alone. That accounts for more than 6 percent of worldwide carbon dioxide emissions....

While it may be true that regulating motor-vehicle emissions will not by itself *reverse* global warming, it by no means follows that we lack jurisdiction to decide whether EPA has a duty to take steps to *slow* or *reduce* it....

In sum—at least according to petitioners' uncontested affidavits—the rise in sea levels associated with global warming has already harmed and will continue to harm Massachusetts. The risk of catastrophic harm, though remote, is nevertheless real. That risk would be reduced to some extent if petitioners received the relief they seek. We therefore hold that petitioners have standing to challenge the EPA's denial of their rule-making petition....

Because greenhouse gases fit well within the Clean Air Act's capacious definition of "air pollutant," we hold that EPA has the statutory authority to regulate the emission of such gases from new motor vehicles....

Questions for Analysis

1. The Supreme Court held that the EPA has authority to regulate greenhouse gases, such as carbon dioxide emissions from vehicles. If Massachusetts and other states feel strongly about it, why do those states not address the matter?

2. Does the Supreme Court have the authority to order EPA to control such emissions?

Summary

- Before passage of federal environmental laws, environmental protection relied on common-law remedies, including private and public nuisance actions, trespass, negligence, strict liability for hazardous activities, and riparian water rights. Actions could result in damages or an injunction ordering the offender to cease damaging activities. The EPA is the key regulator of the environment. It works with environmental agencies in all states to enforce federal requirements.

- The Clean Air Act sets air quality standards for several major pollutants: sulfur dioxide, particulates, ozone, carbon monoxide, nitrogen oxide, and lead. These standards are constantly tightened. New polluters must use the best pollution control technology available. In some areas, if a business is to produce any new air pollution, it must buy pollution rights from existing polluters, who are paid either to quit polluting or to install better pollution-control equipment.

- The Clean Water Act focuses on point source pollution, which comes out of pipes from factories or sewer systems. Point sources must have permits that allow them to discharge certain amounts of pollution into water bodies. States must declare what standards all bodies of water in the state will meet according to the use (e.g., drinking versus swimming quality). Nonpoint source pollution—runoff from farms, streets, construction sites, mining, and logging—is just beginning to be addressed.

- Wetlands are lands saturated with water at least part of the year. Prior to building on or disturbing a wetland, developers must obtain a permit from the Army Corps of Engineers. The EPA has final say on wetlands use.

- The Toxic Substances Control Act and the Federal Insecticide, Fungicide, and Rodenticide Act require EPA review and approval of toxic substances before they are sold. The EPA may restrict product usage and keep track of evidence of harm from such products.

- The Resource Conservation and Recovery Act requires comprehensive paperwork, called *manifests*, to follow the production, distribution, and disposal of hazardous substances. Hazardous waste treatment, storage, and disposal facilities are subject to strict licensing and regulatory control.
- The Superfund program provides federal support to clean up abandoned hazardous waste sites. Any parties who contribute to the disposal of the wastes, even if legal at the time, may be held liable for part or all of the cleanup costs. Land purchasers should consider an environmental audit to check for possibilities of hazardous wastes, wetlands, or endangered species.
- The Endangered Species Act can block any economic activity, without compromise, if the activity can harm the habitat of an endangered species. Compromises that demonstrate habitat protection may allow a project to go forward as approved by the Fish and Wildlife Service.
- Some environmental controls are imposed by international agreements. The Montreal Protocol required the production of chlorofluorocarbons (CFCs) and halon—chemicals used in refrigeration systems, plastics production, and fire-fighting chemicals—to be eliminated. Protection of biological diversity and reduction of greenhouse gases are other international issues that require the United States and other advanced nations to pay for environmental protection in poor nations.

Terms to Know

You should be able to define the following terms:

public nuisance, 449

private nuisance, 449

trespass, 449

abnormally dangerous activities, 449

riparian water law, 449

National Ambient Air Quality
   Standards (NAAQS), 451

State Implementation Plan, 451

prevention of significant deterioration
   (PSD) areas, 452

nonattainment areas, 453

citizen suits, 455

point source pollution, 457

nonpoint source pollution, 459

wetlands, 459

manifest system, 463

Superfund, 463

National Priority List, 464

endangered species, 465

Discussion Question

1. Were common-law actions—such as nuisance, trespass, and strict liability—against pollution too weak? That is, was federal statutory intervention needed to prevent serious environmental damage?

Case Questions

1. A land developer started a retirement village in an area known for its large cattle feedlots. Later, after much of the village was built and sold, the developer brought an environmental nuisance action against the largest feedlot owner in the area. The developer claimed that the feedlot was polluting the air with terrible odors, causing discomfort to the residents of the village and reducing the value of the remaining lots. Assume the court found the feedlot to be a nuisance. What should be the remedy? Could the feedlot be a nuisance in one location and acceptable in another? [*Spur Industries* v. *Del Webb Development*, 108 Ariz. 178, 494 P.2d 700 Sup. Ct., Ariz. (1972)]

2. For ten years, a company dumped millions of gallons of chemical wastes on its property in Tennessee. The state shut down the site. Residents around the property sued the company, claiming that their drinking water was contaminated. What basis for suit did they have, and could they win? [*Sterling* v. *Velsicol Chemical*, 647 F. Supp. 303 W.D. Tenn. (1986)]

   ✓ Check your answer at http://academic.cengage.com/blaw/meiners

3. The EPA set emission standards for vinyl chloride, a toxic substance that is carcinogenic to humans. The Clean Air Act says such standards must be "at the level which … provides an ample margin of safety to protect the public health." The exact threat from vinyl chloride was not known. The EPA said that the proper emissions requirement is the lowest level attainable by best available control technology. The Natural Resources Defense Council sued, contending that since there was uncertainty about the danger, the EPA had to prohibit all emissions. Which position was held correct? [*NRDC* v. *EPA*, 824 F.2d 1146 D.C. Cir. (1987)]

4. As required by the Clean Water Act, the EPA issued standards for discharges from hundreds of sources. Despite the standards, the EPA issued on a case-by-case basis variances to some water polluters, allowing them to exceed the discharge standards. The Natural Resource Defense Council sued to oppose such variances; the Chemical Manufacturers Association defended the variances. Who won? [*Chemical Manufacturers Assn.* v. *NRDC*, 470 U.S. 116, 105 S.Ct. 1102 (1985)]

   ✓ Check your answer at http://academic.cengage.com/blaw/meiners

5. Congress gave the EPA the power in RCRA to regulate "solid wastes." The EPA declared that this includes materials that are being recycled. This was challenged as incorrect, that Congress meant the regulation of materials being discarded or disposed of, not materials being reused. Which position would seem logical? [*American Mining Congress* v. *EPA*, 824 F.2d 1177 D.C. Cir. (1987)]

6. The City of Cochran, Georgia, operated a wastewater treatment facility under an NPDES (Clean Water Act) permit. Treatment water is dumped into Jordan Creek, a tributary of the Ocmulgee River in the Altamaha River basin. For five years, the city regularly exceeded the effluent limitations in its NPDES permit. The Altamaha Riverkeeper (ARK), a nonprofit environmental organization founded to protect and restore the Altamaha River, sued Cochran under the citizen suit provision of the Clean Water Act. ARK sought injunctive relief against the pollution as well as civil penalties and attorney fees. ARK moved for partial summary judgment. Does the citizen group have the right to bring such a suit? [*Altamaha Riverkeepers* v. *City of Cochran*, 162 F.Supp.2d 1368 M.D. Ga. (2001)]

   ✓ Check your answer at http://academic.cengage.com/blaw/meiners

7. A South Carolina company ran a hazardous waste disposal and recycling operation. Several companies sent their hazardous wastes to the site. The facility was improperly managed: waste was dumped on the ground, chemicals were mixed, and records were not kept about what was there. The EPA cleaned up the site under Superfund and sued the companies that sent their waste to the site, since the owners of the site could not pay the bill. The companies responded that they were not liable under CERCLA, because there was no evidence that the particular waste they sent had been improperly disposed of. Were they right? [*U.S.* v. *S.C. Recycling and Disposal*, 653 F.Supp. 984 Dist. S.C. (1984)]

8. Georgoulis was sole shareholder and president of TICI, which owned White Farm Equipment (WFE) from 1980 to 1985. During those years, WFE dumped its hazardous waste in a dump in Iowa owned by another company. The EPA declared the dump to be a Superfund site. It claimed Georgoulis was a responsible party and should have to contribute personally to the cleanup costs. The court found that Georgoulis did not "have any personal knowledge of the disposal practices at the dump site, or was in any way directly involved in waste disposal matters. However … Georgoulis had authority to control, and did in fact exert direct control, over many significant aspects of the ongoing operations and management of WFE." Could Georgoulis be liable? [*U.S.* v. *TIC Investment*, 68 F.3d 1082, 8th Cir. (1995)]

Ethics Question

1. You are an executive with a leading manufacturing company, and one aspect of your business pollutes heavily. You know that you can build a plant in a third world country to handle that aspect without pollution control. This would mean that for the same amount of production, you would add 10 times as much pollution to the world's environment as you do now, but it would be more profitable for the company. Can you legally move the plant? Should you?

Internet Assignment

http://www.epa.gov
http://www.vermontlaw.edu/library/envlawresources.cfm
http://www.topix.net/law/environmental

The Environment Protection Agency (EPA) is an authoritative source of official agency information related to the environment.

1. What is the URL for the EPA's summary of the Clean Air Act?
2. What title of the *Code of Federal Regulations (CFR)* addresses the protection of the environment?

Note that the Internet can be a good way to find specialists. The Vermont Law Library, for example, has an environmental law librarian on staff.

Topix is an example of a Web 2.0 application, which strives to maintain the best information possible by allowing anyone to post information. The many are thought to be smarter than one specialist, however dedicated and knowledgeable. Wikipedia is another obvious example. Contrast Topix to Wex (Chapter 10 Internet exercise), which only allows certain authorized users to post information.

Consumer Protection

Chapter 19

People suffering from AIDS and other deadly diseases are willing to try new drugs before the drugs are fully tested, because they see no advantage in waiting. However, under Food and Drug Administration supervision, drug manufacturers engage in years of tests on animals and limited tests on humans before marketing drugs, so that the public is protected from defective drugs and manufacturers can reduce expensive liability suits for selling drugs with undesirable side effects.

Abbott Laboratories was working on a drug, HIVIG, for HIV-infected people. The National Institutes of Health and various private groups wanted Abbott to begin tests on people right away. Abbott was concerned that the drug could increase the risk that a baby born to a mother who used the drug would be more likely to become AIDS-infected. Abbott refused to go ahead with human tests, unless it was granted immunity from liability for such side effects. The American Civil Liberties Union sued, claiming Abbott had a duty to test the drug. Abbott walked away from all rights to the drug, giving up its investment. The government ordered the drug turned over to a small company that had little to lose if liability problems arose.

Drug regulation, like other forms of consumer protection covered in this chapter, such as credit regulation, affects liability and the decisions made by consumers and producers. Regulations can protect consumers but can also prevent parties from entering into contracts to which they might otherwise agree. Should the government prohibit voluntary agreements among informed, consenting parties? As we discuss various regulations, consider whether producers such as drug makers should be allowed to avoid government regulation and deal directly with consumers. ■

Getty Images

The FDA: Food and Drug Regulation

The Food and Drug Administration (FDA), an agency of the federal government, is charged with monitoring food and drug safety (see www.fda.gov). About one third of its nearly $2 billion budget is devoted to food safety, sanitation, and processing. One third of the budget is devoted to the study of the quality of marketed drugs and new-drug evaluations. The rest of the budget supports the study of biological products, veterinary products, medical devices, radiological products, cosmetics, and the National Center for Toxicological Research. Besides a large research staff, every year, more than a thousand FDA inspectors inspect thousands of establishments that have annual sales of over $1.5 trillion and their products, which amounts to 20 percent of all consumer expenditures.

Food Safety

The control of safety in commercial food, drink, drugs, and cosmetics affects a large sector of the economy. It began with the Pure Food and Drug Act of 1906. For years the primary concern was food safety. This was triggered by several events:

- More soldiers in the American army during the Spanish-American War were reputed to have died from impure food than from enemy bullets.
- Upton Sinclair's *The Jungle*, while failing to stir the public to support socialism as Sinclair had hoped, caused concern about food safety with its graphic description of food processing.
- The chief chemist of the U.S. Department of Agriculture studied the safety of certain food preservatives and determined that some were harmful to human health.

The 1906 Act concerned sanitation and misbranding of food and drug products. The Bureau of Chemistry of the Department of Agriculture performed food analyses for identification of misbranded or impure foods. The Bureau of Chemistry of the Department of Agriculture administered the Food and Drug Act until the FDA was created as a separate unit in 1927.

FDA and USDA Standards and Inspections

After a drug disaster in which many people were poisoned by a nonprescription medicine, Congress passed the *Federal Food, Drug, and Cosmetic Act* in 1938. The Act greatly expanded the regulatory reach of the FDA by providing the agency with the power not only to extend the standards for foods beyond canned goods but also to prohibit false advertising of drugs, classify unsafe food, add new enforcement powers, form inspection systems, and set the safe levels of additives in foods.

The U.S. Department of Agriculture has primary responsibility for sanitation of meat, poultry, and eggs. It works closely with the FDA and Centers for Disease Control (CDC) and the EPA on food safety issues (see www.fsis.usda.gov). The FDA and USDA have detailed regulations concerning inspection of foods and both agencies inspect food processors. The agencies have the power to bring criminal charges against those who do not comply with the safety standards of the agencies, as the *LaGrou* case shows.

Food Quality Protection

The Food Additives Amendment, known as the Delaney Clause, was added to the Food, Drug, and Cosmetic Act in 1958. It gave the FDA authority to set the

United States v. LaGrou Distribution Systems
United States Court of Appeals, Seventh Circuit
466 F.3d 585 (2006)

Case Background *LaGrou's cold storage warehouse in Chicago kept raw, fresh, and frozen meat, poultry, and other food products. LaGrou did not own the food, but stored products for customers. About two million pounds of food went in and out daily. The manager became aware, when hired, that there were rats. He talked to the company president, Stewart, about the problem. Rats were caught daily and food the rats had gnawed on was thrown away. Customers were not told of the rats; they were told food damaged in shipment was destroyed. An expert said there needed to be many structural changes to eliminate holes in the building for the rats. Stewart thought it was too expensive to fix.*

Two USDA inspectors saw rodent droppings and other problems. The next day, 14 USDA inspectors came as well as inspectors from the FDA and the Illinois Department of Public Health. That night, before the inspectors came, LaGrou threw away a lot of food and did a thorough cleaning, but employees told inspectors what had gone on. A huge number of violations were found. The warehouse was ordered closed and 22 million pounds of food destroyed. LaGrou was convicted of three felonies, put on probation for five years, and ordered to pay $8.2 million in restitution and $2 million in fines. The president and manager of the company were also convicted. LaGrou appealed.

Case Decision Bauer, Circuit Judge

* * *

While LaGrou argues that the infested area was limited to the warehouse basement, the evidence illustrated that the situation at the warehouse was dire. The USDA and other government agencies found dangerous conditions *throughout* the ... facility. Dr. Rose testified that LaGrou's warehouse was the "worst case" she had seen in her 28 years with the USDA. She further explained that given the ventilation system in the warehouse, the pathogens and viruses could have become airborne. In addition, the leaking roofs, condensation from overhead pipes and ceilings, and dripping pipes found throughout the warehouse could have also carried food-borne pathogens.

Affirmed.

Questions for Analysis

1. The appeals court affirmed the conviction of the company for violating food sanitation rules. People, not companies, make decisions; so what sense does it make to convict a company?
2. Who would restitution be paid to in such a case?

safe-use level of food additives. It was so strict (a "zero risk" standard) that it was replaced by the more flexible Food Quality Protection Act of 1996, which states that the FDA is to ensure a "reasonable certainty of no harm" (meaning no more than a one-in-a-million lifetime chance of cancer) from any source that affects foods, raw or processed, whether added directly, such as food coloring, or indirectly, such as pesticide residues. The Food Quality Protection Act expanded FDA jurisdiction to thousands of pesticides used in food production.

Nutrition Labeling

The FDA began issuing regulations for *nutrition labeling* in 1973. The *Nutrition Labeling and Education Act* of 1990 required the FDA to issue new nutrition labeling regulations in 1994. These requirements apply to more than 250,000 products. The Department of Agriculture, which regulates meat and poultry, works with the FDA to have regulations for those foods that are consistent with the FDA rules. The intent is to prevent misleading product claims and to help consumers make informed purchases.

Getty Images

LIGHTER SIDE OF THE LAW
Food Fraud Everywhere

The Hufulou restaurant, located near a tiger reserve in Hailin, China, advertised stir-fry tiger meat with chilies for $98 and a liquor flavored with tiger bones for $74 a bottle. The restaurant advertised raw tiger meat for $864 per kilogram.

Since tigers are protected, meat or parts are not to be sold. Authorities investigated, and the restaurant owner admitted it was not tiger meat, but donkey meat flavored with tiger urine to give the dish a special flavor. The owners was required to pay a $296 fine plus give up some profits.

Source: *Associated Press*

Nutrients by Serving Size

FDA regulations list over 100 categories of food, from soup to nuts, whose nutrients must be listed by standard serving size. The following must be listed per serving portion on nutrition labels:

- Total calories and calories from fat
- Total fat and saturated fat
- Carbohydrates (sugar and starch separately)
- Cholesterol
- Calcium
- Fiber
- Iron
- Sodium
- Protein
- Vitamins A and C

Producers may list other nutrients, such as potassium, other essential vitamins and minerals, and polyunsaturated fat. Vitamins that are so common that there is no shortage in American diets like thiamin, riboflavin, and niacin do not have to be listed.

Standards for Health Claims

Since many consumers know little about the details of nutrition, labels must meet standards for words commonly used so that consumers can learn more about what they are buying. For example, "fresh" refers to raw food that has not been processed, frozen, or preserved; "low fat" means 3 or fewer grams of fat per serving and per 100 grams of the food; "low calorie" means fewer than 40 calories per serving and per 100 grams of food; and "light" or "lite" may be used on foods that have one-third fewer calories than comparable products.

Further, health claims that are not well established, such as the claim that fiber reduces heart disease and cancer, may not be made unless sufficiently documented by the seller. The food health claims that may be noted on labels involve the health connection between calcium and the prevention of osteoporosis (weak bones), sodium (salt) and high blood pressure, fat and heart disease, and fat and cancer.

Drug Safety

Until 1938, drug control existed to protect the public against quacks, false claims, mislabeling, and the sale of dangerous drugs. The Food, Drug, and Cosmetic Act provided federal regulators with new powers in 1938 and has been added to since then. The Act prohibits the sale of any drug until the FDA approves the application submitted by the manufacturer. The applicant must submit evidence that the drug

INTERNATIONAL PERSPECTIVE

Drug Controls and Uncontrols

In many ways the United States sets the international standard for drugs. FDA standards are generally tougher than in Europe or Japan, so anything that has made it through the process is likely to be accepted worldwide. Foreign producers who wish to sell in the United States must meet FDA standards and allow inspection of facilities.

FDA-approved drugs are the gold standard. Development costs are so high that producers must charge high prices to cover investments. People in low-income countries cannot pay U.S. prices, so the firms sell for less in such places. Some nations, such as Canada, buy all drugs for their market and bargain with the drug companies, so their drug prices are a little lower (but not much; drug sales from Canada to the United States are trivial).

The drug market is becoming more fragmented. The high cost of development and approval in the United States is driving firms overseas where costs are lower and marketing may be allowed, even if the drugs do not meet U.S. standards.

Foreigners expect drugs that carry the name of a U.S. maker to be high quality, but forgery is common. Some forgeries are good-quality illegal copies, but others are random ingredients mashed together and sold as the real thing. Over 50 people in Panama died from a cough syrup from China that contained a chemical like antifreeze.

People waste money and injure their health taking worthless drugs they think are real. Some drug makers in China send the Chinese FDA real U.S. drugs, claiming they represent their product. The agency knows there are big problems, but can do little to control all 170,000 products on the market, especially when the agency is known to take bribes to grant approval for products to enter the market.

is *safe* for its intended use. This prevents the sale of untested drugs in a market that generates over $250 billion per year in sales.

A critical issue for a seller is whether or not its product is classified as a drug. This has become a major issue for the nutrition supplement industry. Its sales, over $20 billion a year, are largely unregulated. If a dietary supplement seller goes too far in its claims, then the FDA may classify the product as a drug, which makes it subject to significant regulations. If the FDA thinks a dietary supplement is dangerous, it may ban it from the market, as we see in the *Nutraceutical* case.

Nutraceutical Corp. v. Von Eschenbach
United States Court of Appeals, Tenth Circuit
459 F.3d 1033 (2006)

Case Background *Nutraceutical makes Ephedra, a product containing ephedrine-alkaloid dietary supplements (EDS). In 2004, the FDA banned EDS sales. Nutraceutical sued the agency, claiming the action was unlawful.*

The district court found that the risk-benefit analysis used by the FDA to support the ban was contrary to the intent of Congress. The agency failed to prove by a preponderance of the evidence that the EDS posed an unreasonable risk of injury at 10 milligrams (mg) or less per day. The court held for Nutraceutical. The FDA appealed.

Case Decision Eagan, District Judge

* * *

In 1994, Congress amended the Food Drug and Cosmetic Act with the Dietary Supplement Health and Education Act ("DSHEA"). Under DSHEA, the FDA regulates vitamins, minerals, herbs, amino acids, and other dietary substances. Dietary supplements are generally regulated in a manner similar to food, and the FDA is authorized to prevent adulterated products from entering the market. Congress declared that a dietary supplement is "adulterated": If it is a dietary supplement or contains a dietary ingredient that (A) presents a significant or unreasonable risk of illness or injury under (i) conditions of use recommended or suggested in labeling, or (ii) if no conditions of use

continues

are suggested or recommended in the labeling, under ordinary conditions of use …

The FDA argues that EDS are adulterated and points to the "unreasonable risk of illness or injury" provision of DSHEA as the primary source of statutory authority for its EDS ban.…

In determining that EDS pose an "unreasonable risk of illness or injury," the FDA found that the weight loss and other health benefits possible from the use of EDS were dwarfed by the potential long-term harm to the user's cardiovascular system. The agency went on to enact a complete ban on the product after making a finding that any amount of EDS had negative ramifications on the cardiovascular system and, based on the FDA's analysis, EDS provided no benefits so great as to justify such risk.…

We find that the FDA correctly followed the congressional directive to analyze the risks and bene-fits of EDS in determining that there is no dosage level of EDS acceptable for the market. Summary judgment for plaintiffs was therefore improper, and summary judgment for defendants should have been entered. Accordingly, the district court's decision is reversed, and we remand for entry of judgment in favor of defendants.

Questions for Analysis

1. The appeals court held that FDA had sufficient evidence to allow it to ban the sale of EDS. Nutraceutical claimed it was a dietary supplement, not a drug; if so, why should it be regulated like a drug?

2. Do you think preponderance of the evidence is a sufficient standard, or should it be beyond a reasonable doubt?

Designation of Prescription Drugs

Before the 1938 Act, no drugs were designated as *prescription drugs*—that is, drugs that may be used only with the permission of a physician. Drugs were either legal or illegal. Since 1938, the FDA has determined which drugs will be prescription drugs, which are sold by pharmacies only with a physician's permission.

Drug Effectiveness Testing

The *Kefauver Amendment* of 1962 requires the FDA to approve drugs based on their proven effectiveness—not just on their safety. The FDA must approve testing of drugs on humans and may specify the details of the testing. The FDA has strict regulations concerning testing and adoption of new drugs. It now costs almost $1 billion and takes 12 to 15 years to develop a new drug and to clear all FDA hurdles before marketing the product. As a result of the high cost, drug companies produce only half (about 23) as many new drugs each year compared to previous decades.

To earn approval for a drug to go to market, a new substance—which is seven years in the making on average (only 1 in 6,000 new compounds gets this far)—goes to Phase I tests on 100 or fewer patients to determine the maximum tolerated dosage and likely side effects. If that works, in Phase II, several hundred patients are tested to identify stages of the disease affected by the therapy. Then, if approved, it goes to Phase III for testing on several thousand patients so comparisons can be made to existing drugs and to placebos. Ninety percent of drugs do not then make it to final FDA approval, meaning only 1 in 60,000 new compounds initially tested in the lab make it to market.

Medical Devices

The FDA also has responsibility for oversight of medical devices. Each one is assigned to a class based on the level of control needed to assure safety. Class I devices are things such as bandages and gloves; Class II devices include surgical equipment and power wheelchairs; Class III is the most controlled, and it includes artificial hearts and pacemakers. The FDA must give approval prior to marketing, and it then tracks the devices once on the market to watch for problems that may require recalls.

Liability for Problems

Does FDA approval of a drug reduce the liability of the producers if the drug creates problems? The courts give weight to the protection offered by the regulatory process. The number of liability suits from consumers injured by side effects of a drug is reduced, because some effects are not preventable given the state of technology. But FDA approval is only evidence of safety, not a shield against liability.

What if a drug was improperly administered? The drug companies are not likely to be liable, assuming they have given proper dosage instructions. If a physician ignores the instructions and changes the recommended dosage, resulting in an injury, the drug manufacturer is shielded from liability by the *learned intermediary doctrine*. That is, the learned intermediary—the doctor—would be liable for misuse of the product.

Enforcement Activities

Besides deciding when drugs will be allowed to be marketed, the FDA can force existing products, including food, cosmetics, and medical devices, to be removed from the market if their claims appear to be misleading or if new information becomes available that indicates the product was not as safe as previously thought. The FDA forces hundreds of products off the market each year and seizes thousands of import shipments.

For example, the FDA seized shipments of Citrus Hill Fresh Choice orange juice, because the juice was made from concentrate and not "fresh" from oranges. The agency ordered vegetable oil manufacturers to remove "no cholesterol" from the labels of their product. The no-cholesterol claim was not false, but the FDA said it was misleading, since many consumers think cholesterol is the same as fat, which is not the case.

While enforcement has become tougher, the FDA has been allowing quicker approval for drugs that show some promise in life-threatening diseases such as AIDS. Rather than require the full, lengthy review process before the drugs are allowed to be sold to informed patients, the FDA allows the drugs to be carefully distributed.

ISSUE SPOTTER

How Much Can You Hype Health Supplements?

Your store sells "health foods" and many "health supplements," such as vitamins and herbs. It is common for new claims to be made about products. Several years ago, shark cartilage (ground up shark bones) was touted as preventing cancer. Many products grow popular at first, then fall by the wayside when the alleged benefits become less clear. For example, if the media is reporting that eating seaweed from the coast of Brazil is believed to prevent senility, can you repeat such a claim? Do you have the right to advertise a product for having such a benefit? Can you get in trouble for going too far to promote a product?

Getty Images

The FTC and Consumer Protection

The Federal Trade Commission (FTC) was established in 1915 to help enforce the antitrust laws (Chapter 20), but the FTC also devotes resources to its Bureau of Consumer Protection, which handles matters such as deceptive business advertising and marketing practices (see www.ftc.gov). Some responsibilities are specifically ordered by Congress, such as the consumer credit statutes. But most consumer protection efforts evolve as the FTC decides what Congress meant when it amended the FTC Act in the 1930s and said, in Section 5, that "unfair and deceptive acts or practices in or affecting commerce are hereby declared unlawful."

Based on its experience, and in response to pressure from Congress, the FTC investigates practices said to be *unfair and deceptive*. The FTC staff proposes complaints to the five commissioners, who decide by majority vote whether to issue a complaint. The complaint begins legal proceedings against a business engaged in practices the commission would like to see ended or modified.

Many complaints are settled by a *consent decree* agreed upon by the parties charged in an FTC complaint. Consent decrees contain the terms of a settlement and frequently include prohibition of certain practices, redress for consumers, and payment of civil penalties. Some cases result in administrative trials at the FTC. If the accused party or the FTC attorneys are not satisfied with the decision of the administrative law judge, they may appeal to the commissioners for review. An accused party who is not satisfied with the decision of the commissioners may appeal to a federal court of appeals.

Unfair and Deceptive Acts or Practices

Congress ordered the FTC to fight "unfair and deceptive acts or practices." The lack of a clear legal definition for those terms means that the FTC has considerable leeway in deciding what cases to bring—what advertising is deceptive and what sales practices are unfair. The key term has always been *deceptive*. Essentially, things held to be deceptive are also unfair, a term we define below.

Policy Statement on Deception

To give the FTC staff guidance, the commissioners adopted a *deception policy statement* that summarizes a three-part test for deciding whether a particular act or practice is deceptive. There is *deception* if the following are true:

1. There is a misrepresentation or omission of information in a communication to consumers.
2. The deception is likely to mislead a reasonable consumer.
3. The deception is material; that is, it is likely to be misleading to the detriment of consumers.

Some points help make clear the elements of deception. First, not all omissions are deceptive. Omissions, or failure to reveal information, is not deceptive if there is no affirmative misrepresentation (false statement) or practice that takes advantage of consumer misunderstanding. Second, to decide whether an omission or representation (claim or statement) is deceptive, the FTC looks at what has been presented to consumers. The words in an advertisement are examined in the context of the entire ad, and consideration is given to evidence about what consumers think the ad means. Third, a reasonable consumer is an "ordinary person" in the target audience of the ad. For example, ads directed at children or ill people are held to a tougher standard. Fourth, the representation or omission must be likely to affect a consumer's product choice. Fifth, no proof of injury to consumers— usually financial loss—is needed if there is evidence that such injury is likely to occur, given the practice in question.

Defining Unfairness

Section 5 of the FTC Act says that "unfair or deceptive acts or practices in or affecting commerce, are declared unlawful." The word *unfairness* is usually added to a charge of deception. The FTC has given operational meaning to unfair acts or practices in business by issuing a policy statement that gives a consumer injury standard:

1. It causes substantial harm to consumers.
2. Consumers cannot reasonably avoid injury.
3. The injury is harmful in its net effects.

The following are examples of FTC enforcement actions and an Internet-based scam.

Telemarketing Fraud The FTC obtained an injunction against five telemarketing firms for making misrepresentations in the sale of water purifiers and home security systems. The FTC charged that the companies mailed postcards telling consumers they had won valuable awards, including $5,000 worth of merchandise. In fact, the awards consisted only of certificates that required payment of large sums of money to get the goods. The telemarketers also made charges against consumers' credit cards without permission and billed customers for goods never sent.

Telemarketers are subject to the Telephone Consumer Protection Act and the Telemarketing and Consumer Fraud and Abuse Prevention Act, which resulted in the FTC's Telemarketing Sales Rule. These laws allow consumers to sue telemarketers if they make telemarketing calls in violation of consumer instructions to be removed from call lists.

Oil and Gas Well "Investments" Several companies were involved in oil and gas well lease scams. They persuaded more than 8,000 people to invest $5,000 to $10,000 each in application fees to participate in a lottery for oil and gas rights on federal lands. The FTC obtained $47 million in refunds. Not only were the promoters sued, so were all the companies that worked with them in the scheme, such as insurance companies, banks, and accounting firms.

LIGHTER SIDE OF THE LAW
Protecting Consumers

A group that calls itself Common Good listed the most useless warning labels that are put on products, supposedly to help consumers. Winners include labels on

- a bottle of drain cleaner: "If you do not understand, or cannot read, all directions, cautions and warnings, do not use this product."
- a snow sled: "Beware: sled may develop high speed under certain snow conditions."
- a 12-inch rack for storing CDs: "Do not use as a ladder."
- a fishing lure with a three-prong hook on the end: "Harmful if swallowed."
- a smoke detector: "Do not use the Silence Feature in emergency situations."
- on a children's scooter: "This product moves when used."

Getty Images

Work-at-Home Opportunities A federal appeals court upheld a $16 million judgment against a company and its officers in *FTC* v. *Febre* (128 F.3d 530) for deceptive practices in four work-at-home "opportunities." This included mailing postcards, which supposedly could earn someone up to $15,000 per day. Almost 200,000 consumers had paid the promoters over $13 million, which was ordered rebated to the consumers, plus $3 million in damages.

Invention-Promotion Scams The FTC sued 12 companies that raked in $90 million by claiming that they were consultants who help people make deals for valuable new inventions. "Project Mousetrap" discovered that people paid between $10,000 and $20,000 each to get "expert advice" in licensing and marketing such things as a toothbrush with bristles at both ends and a device that collects the shavings scratched off lottery tickets. While the operations were closed, only $250,000 remained for consumer redress.

Federal Trade Commission v. Cyberspace.com LLC
United States Court of Appeals, Ninth Circuit
453 F.3d 1196 (2006)

Case Background *Cyberspace.com was a venture run by EPV. Mailings were sent to 4.4 million individuals and small businesses offering Internet access service. In the mailing was a check for $3.50. On the back of the check, in fine print, it said that if you cashed the check, you subscribed to the access service and agreed to be billed monthly by a charge added to your phone bill. About a quarter million people cashed the check. Less than one percent of them ever logged on to the access service. Most did not read the fine print.*

The FTC sued for unfair and deceptive trade practice. The district court issued a permanent injunction against EPV and its owners not to engage in such practices and ordered consumer redress of $17.7 million. EPV appealed.

Case Decision O'Scannlain, Circuit Judge

* * *

In this case, [the owners] contend that the fine print notices they placed on the reverse side of the check, invoice, and marketing insert preclude liability under FTCA § 5. We disagree. A solicitation may be likely to mislead by virtue of the net impression it creates even though the solicitation also contains truthful disclosures....

We agree with the district court that no reasonable fact finder could conclude that the solicitation was not likely to deceive consumers acting reasonably under the circumstances.

Our conclusion is bolstered by undisputed evidence indicating that [EPV's] solicitation actually deceived nearly 225,000 individuals and small businesses. [EPV] billed each of these consumers for a service that less than one percent of them ever attempted to use. It is reasonable to infer that most of the remaining 99 percent did not realize they had

contracted for Internet service, when they cashed or deposited the solicitation check....

We further conclude that the solicitation was likely to mislead in a way that is material. A misleading impression created by a solicitation is material if it "involves information that is important to consumers and, hence, likely to affect their choice of, or conduct regarding, a product." ...

In sum, the district court properly granted summary judgment to the FTC on the FTCA § 5 violation, because no reasonable fact finder could conclude that the solicitation was not likely to mislead consumers acting reasonably under the circumstances in a way that is material....

We next address [an owner's] contention that the district court erred by finding, as a matter of law, that he is liable in his individual capacity. An individual is personally liable for a corporation's FTCA § 5 violations if he "participated directly in the acts or practices or had authority to control them" and "had actual knowledge of material misrepresentations, was recklessly indifferent to the truth or falsity of a misrepresentation, or had an awareness of a high probability of fraud along with an intentional avoidance of the truth."...

Affirmed.

Questions for Analysis

1. The appeals court affirmed the judgment against a firm and its owners for deceptive acts. Why are the owners of such businesses personally liable in such instances, rather than just the company?

2. Most business owners favor this sort of regulation. Why would that be?

Regulating Advertising Claims

About $300 billion is spent on advertising each year. The *advertising substantiation program* requires advertisers and advertising agencies to have a reasonable basis before they make claims. When advertisers claim that "studies show" or "tests prove," they must actually have evidence that provides a reasonable basis for the claims. The FTC considers the following factors to determine what is a reasonable basis:

- The product
- The type of claim
- The consequences of a false claim and the benefits of a truthful claim
- The cost of developing substantiation for the claim
- The amount of substantiation that experts believe is reasonable

What Advertising Is Deceptive?

Years ago, the FTC commissioners said: "Perhaps a few misguided souls believe … that all 'Danish pastry' is made in Denmark. Is it therefore an actionable deception to advertise 'Danish pastry' when it is made in this country? Of course not." The point is that some people may misunderstand certain advertisements, but that does not mean that the FTC will be concerned. For example, if a hair dye is advertised as "permanent" and someone thinks it means that their hair will be the color of the dye forever, no deception is involved. Most consumers know what is meant, and those who do not understand do not incur significant injury.

Some ads that reach a small number of people, such as pamphlets handed out door-to-door, may deceive many who read it because the claims are false and likely to deceive. Other ads may reach a large number of people, deceive very few, yet be held to be deceptive. For instance, if a small number of consumers lose a lot of money because they believe a deceptive claim, the FTC may act because of the seriousness of the injury.

Examples of Deceptive Ad Cases

Gateway Educational Products settled FTC charges that the claims about the ability of its "Hooked on Phonics" program to teach reading, including those with learning disabilities, were unsubstantiated. The FTC contended that consumer testimonials did not represent typical experiences. Experts on reading disability said that phonics instruction may not help people with dyslexia or other reading disabilities. The producer promised to stop the challenged claims and to make no other claims without substantiation.

The FTC helps enforce FDA definitions of food terms. The FTC sued Häagen-Dazs about the fat and calorie claims on its frozen yogurt products: "And each with just 1 gram of fat and 100 calories." In fact, the products contained up to 12 grams of fat per serving (compared to the FDA definition of low fat as three grams or less) and up to 230 calories per serving. The company agreed to meet FDA standards for labeling food products and not to misrepresent the amount of fat or calories.

Quaker State agreed to stop running unsubstantiated ads for Slick 50, an engine treatment. Similarly, Ashland Oil agreed to end a major ad campaign that touted Valvoline TM8 Engine Treatment. The ads claimed, without substantiation, that the additive would reduce wear on some engine parts by as much as 75 percent.

Most deceptive advertising cases are settled in a similar manner—the advertiser agrees to stop making false claims. In some cases, a civil penalty is imposed, but large sums are not common. In rare instances, the FTC orders a company to engage in corrective advertising to make up for past false claims. The *Telebrands* case illustrates FTC action.

Telebrands Corp. v. Federal Trade Commission
United States Court of Appeals, Fourth Circuit
457 F.3d 354 (2006)

Case Background *Telebrands direct markets assorted products, including the Audubon Singing Bird Clock, the Magic Hanger, Ambervision Sunglasses, and the Better Pasta Pot. Its strategy is to compare its product to similar ones and note that its product costs less. Here the product was Ab Force, an electronic muscle stimulation (EMS) abdominal belt. Like other such products, it sends a small electric current into the abdominal muscles. It was careful not to say directly that Ab Force did anything useful, but said it was part of "the latest fitness craze to sweep the country" and that other such belts "promise to get our abs into great shape fast—without exercise." Well-muscled models were used on TV to demonstrate the product.*

The FTC sued for false and misleading advertising claims. Telebrands had made unsubstantiated claims that Ab Force caused loss of weight, inches of fat, well-defined abs, and was an effective alternative to exercise. The Commission issued an order that included a "fencing-in" provision on Telebrands ads. It stated that Telebrands "in connection with the manufacturing, labeling, advertising, promotion, offering for sale, sale, or distribution of Ab Force and any other EMD device or any food, drug, dietary supplement, device, or any other product, service, or program, shall not make any representation, in any manner … about weight, inch, or fat loss, muscle definition … unless, at the time the representation is made, Telebrands possesses and relies upon competent and reliable evidence … that substantiates the representation." Telebrands appealed.

Case Decision Duncan, Circuit Judge

* * *

The FTC considers three factors in determining whether order coverage bears a reasonable relationship to the violation it is intended to remedy: "(1) the seriousness and deliberateness of the violation; (2) the ease with which the violative claim may be transferred to other products; and (3) whether the respondent has a history of prior violations."…

Substantial evidence supports the FTC's finding that Telebrands's violations of [the FTC Act] were serious.… the violations involved claiming, with no substantiation, that the Ab Force could deliver certain results that Telebrands later admitted were beyond the device's capabilities. Telebrands [admitted] that "the Ab Force does not cause loss of weight, inches, or fat."…

Moreover, Telebrands mounted an expensive, nationwide advertising campaign for the Ab Force that was highly successful. Telebrands spent over four million dollars on the multimedia advertising campaign for the Ab Force, which included spots that aired more than 10,000 times on cable, satellite, and broadcast television outlets in major national markets. That campaign resulted in the sale of approximately 747,000 units with gross sales, including accessories, exceeding 19 million dollars. These facts militate in favor of a finding that the violations were serious.…

Telebrands's assertion that … it did not intend for consumers to believe that the Ab Force provided those same benefits strains credulity. In fact, Telebrands calculatedly fostered such beliefs through its choice of visual images for the television advertisements.…

The FTC found that the marketing strategy for the Ab Force has potential applicability to almost any kind of product or service, including many that Telebrands already markets. Indeed, the compare and save strategy is one of Telebrands's standard marketing tools. An unfair practice is transferable when other products can be marketed using similar techniques.…

The order is enforced.

Questions for Analysis

1. The appeals court upheld the FTC order that restricted the advertising practices of Telebrands for a range of consumer products. Is this not a restriction of free speech?
2. Suppose some doctor endorses such a product. Is that enough to substantiate claims about the benefits of the product?

False Advertising and the Lanham Act

Another way that false advertising claims may be struck down, and one that can yield far more expensive results than most FTC advertising cases, is when a private party brings a suit under the *Lanham Act*. Section 43 of the Act states:

Getty Images

INTERNATIONAL PERSPECTIVE

Foreign Advertising Regulation

Advertising is subject to different controls around the world. Most countries impose fewer regulations on ads than is the case in the United States. In Europe, ad regulations tend to be tightest in northern Europe and loosest in the Mediterranean countries.

Britain has an Office of Fair Trading that operates somewhat like the FTC with respect to ad regulation. The general standard is that an ad is illegal if it misrepresents a product, whereas in the United States it may be illegal if it simply misleads. For an ad to misrepresent a product, there must be an estimation that consumers suffer damages because they have not been told the truth in the ad. For example, a soup ad in the United States was held to be illegal by the FTC because the soup was photographed to look as though it had more chunky bits in it than a random bowl of the soup really would have. In most of Europe and Japan, that ad would not be illegal because, while it misleads, it does not injure consumers.

Beer ads in Japan promote the "extra strong" alcohol content, a practice that would be illegal in the United States under the alcohol advertising rules of the Bureau of Alcohol, Tobacco, and Firearms. As the chairman of a Japanese advertising firm explained, "When you come to Japan, you have to do as the Japanese do, especially in advertising."

Any person who, or in connection with any goods or services, or any container for goods, uses in commerce any word, term, name, symbol, or device … or any false designation "of origin, false or misleading description of fact, or any false or misleading representation" of fact, which 1) is likely to cause confusion, or to cause mistake, or to deceive as to the affiliation, connection, or association of such person with another person, or as to the origin, sponsorship, or approval of his or her goods, services, or commercial activities by another person, or 2) in commercial advertising or promotion, misrepresents the nature, characteristics, qualities, or geographic origin of his or her or another person's goods, services, or commercial activities, shall be liable in a civil action by any person who believes that he or she is or is likely to be damaged by such act.

When private cases claiming misleading advertising are brought under the Lanham Act, the courts generally consider the meaning of "deceptive" the same as does the FTC. Most cases result in injunctions against further false advertising claims, much like most FTC advertising cases. But plaintiffs also may recover damages, as in *U-Haul International* v. *Jartran* (793 F.2d 1034), where the appeals court upheld an award of $40 million. The Act allows injured parties—the plaintiff who is a competitor—to collect double the value of the profits that the defendant earned from false advertising by luring business away.

ISSUE SPOTTER

How Aggressive Can You Be in Advertising?

Different advertising tactics seem to work for various products and in different markets. Some small firms, to get noticed, directly take on the big firms in the industry by calling their products by name and saying that the small firm has a better product or service. If you really believe your product is better for the price, how explicit can you be in comparing it to your competitor without violating false advertising rules? How much risk is there in calling your competitor names to draw attention to yourself?

Getty Images

Trade Regulation Rules

Under Section 18 of the FTC Act, the Commission may issue *trade regulation rules* that set boundaries for practices when problems are common. Because many trade regulation rules are on the books—most dealing with narrow areas—here we consider only a few major rules.

As with most regulations, a proposed rule must be published in the *Federal Register* so that interested parties may comment on it before it is finalized. When the rule is finalized, it becomes part of the Code of Federal Regulations. It gives the FTC grounds for charging that violators of the rule are committing an unfair and deceptive act, since firms in an industry are required to know about rules that apply to them. Rules may limit certain contracts, as in the case of the rule that allows buyers to cancel contracts they agreed to in certain door-to-door sales.

The Insulation R-Value Rule

The FTC's Trade Regulation Rule Concerning the Labeling and Advertising of Home Insulation (the *R-value Rule)* was written because of problems consumers had understanding insulation claims. By standardizing R-values, the FTC requires insulation manufacturers and installers to use the same terminology and measures of R-values.

The rule provides a standard to evaluate home insulation products. If a company claims that it provides R-19-value insulation and it has not, there is a standard to measure the R-value. For example, the FTC sued Sears for violating the R-value Rule. Sears advertised the thickness and price of an insulation product but failed to disclose the R-value. In the settlement, Sears agreed to pay a civil penalty, to comply with the rule in the future, and to pay for advertisements to educate consumers about home insulation and R-values.

The Mail-Order Rule

One of the best-known trade regulation rules is the *Mail-Order Rule.* If a company sells merchandise by mail, it must ship goods in the time stated in its ads. Shipping dates must be stated on the offers (such as "allow five weeks for shipment") or shipment must be within 30 days of receipt of an order. If the goods cannot be shipped on time, customers must be sent a notice allowing them to cancel the order or to

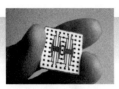

CYBER LAW

Regulating Cyberspace Advertising

The FTC has prosecuted dozens of cases involving alleged online scams and false advertising. One company paid $195,000 in consumer redress in response to an FTC challenge to its claims for "self-improvement" products. In another case, the FTC charged that Fortuna Alliance collected more than $6 million based on false claims that "investors" could easily earn large sums in what amounted to a pyramid scheme. The FTC seized Fortuna's assets and obtained a court order

that a notice of the FTC's action be placed on Fortuna's Web site.

The FTC pushed for Congress to pass the Children's Online Privacy Protection Act, which requires the FTC to adopt rules requiring Web sites that appeal to children under age 13 to provide parents with notice of information that is being collected and how the Web site uses the information. Such sites must obtain "verifiable parental consent" regarding the collection, distribution, and use of their children's information, and parents must be able to withdraw consent.

Getty Images

agree to a new shipping date. The rule gives the FTC a simple basis for issuing complaints against companies that fail to live up to the terms of their offers.

The Used Car Rule

The FTC *Used Car Rule* requires dealers to give consumers clear information on who pays for repairs after a sale. A Buyer's Guide must be put in the window of used cars offered for sale. The guide must contain

1. A statement of the terms of any warranty offered with the car
2. A prominent statement of whether the dealer is selling the car "as is" and, if so, that the consumer must pay for any repairs needed after buying the car
3. A warning that oral promises are difficult to enforce, with a suggestion to get all promises in writing
4. A suggestion that the consumer ask for an independent inspection of the car

---

LIGHTER SIDE OF THE LAW

Make Granny Pay More

Raj Bhandari had a good idea for his BP station—he would offer a 2-cent per gallon discount to senior citizens and discount cards that gave a 3-cent discount to sports boosters. The 3 cents per gallon would support a local youth hockey program.

   The Wisconsin Department of Agriculture, Trade, and Consumer Protection swiftly moved in and ordered him to stop the discounts and raise prices. The Wisconsin Unfair Sales Act *requires* gas stations to mark up gasoline at least 9.2 percent over wholesale price. Bhandari was engaged in "unfair sales," because he was not marking up his gasoline as much as required.

Source: *Associated Press*

Getty Images

State Deceptive Practices Laws

We have focused on the FTC here, but the states play similar roles. All states give their attorneys general powers similar to the FTC to bring suit against those involved in scams or dubious business practices. Most states have some kind of business code or consumer protection act that restricts deceptive trade practices. These statutes can be applied to a wide range of activities.

   Besides the state attorney general having power to sue, consumers have private causes of action. For example, the Texas Business and Commerce Code states (§ 17.50):

   A consumer may maintain an action where any of the following constitute a producing cause of economic damages or damages for mental anguish:

1. the use or employment by any person of a false, misleading, or deceptive act or practice that is:
   a. specifically [listed later]; and
   b. relies on by a consumer to the consumer's detriment;
2. breach of an express or implied warranty;
3. any unconscionable action or course of action by any person; or
4. any [violation of the Insurance Code].

As the *Schuchmann* case indicates, these state codes provide a statutory basis for a cause of action that goes beyond what may exist under contract law.

Schuchmann v. Air Services Heating and Air Conditioning
Missouri Court of Appeals, Southern District
199 S.W.3d 228 (2006)

Case Background *Schuchmann bought a heating and air conditioning unit for his house with a "lifetime warranty" from Air Services in 1998. Up to 2003, Air services worked on the system when needed, but then refused to honor the warranty, saying it was too costly. Schuchmann sued and argued that Air's action violated the Missouri Merchandising Practices Act (MMPA). The court awarded Schuchmann $1,047 plus costs. Air appealed.*

Case Decision Shrum, Judge

* * *

Defendant is simply wrong, however, when it says we must reverse because Plaintiff did not prove Defendant intended from the beginning to default at some time on its promise of a lifetime warranty. Such an intent is not an element of an MMPA case. This follows from a reading of the last sentence of section 407.020.1: "Any act, use, or employment declared unlawful by this subsection violates this subsection *whether committed before, during, or after the sale*, advertisement, or solicitation." Thus, the fact that Defendant's refusal to honor the warranty came after the sale is of no consequence....

An unfair practice is defined as a practice that either: (1) offends any public policy as it has been established by the Constitution, statutes, or common law of this state, or by the Federal Trade Commission, or its interpretive decisions *or* (2) is unethical, oppressive, or unscrupulous; *and* (3) presents a risk of, or causes, substantial injury to consumers. Due to the unrestricted and all-encompassing nature of … the MMPA, the Supreme Court of Missouri, in speaking of the statute, has stated that "the literal words cover *every practice imaginable and every unfairness to whatever degree.*"

"The purpose of Missouri's Merchandising Practices Act is to preserve fundamental honesty, fair play, and right dealings in public transactions." As stated above, the MMPA supplements the definition of common law fraud, eliminating the need to prove an intent to defraud or reliance. The statute and the regulation paint in broad strokes to prevent evasion thereof due to overly meticulous definitions....

Affirmed.

Questions for Analysis

1. The court affirmed that the seller violated the state deception law by refusing to honor the warranty on a product. The air conditioner was more than five years old. Is it reasonable to expect "lifetime" service?

2. What does the court mean that the state statute uses "broad strokes" to prevent evasion "due to overly meticulous definitions"?

Consumer Credit Protection

Congress first involved the federal government in the direct regulation of consumer credit with the *Consumer Credit Protection Act* (CCPA) of 1968. At that time, there was about $100 billion worth of consumer credit outstanding; now the figure is about $2.5 trillion. The CCPA is an umbrella law containing several credit-related laws. The laws provide rights for consumers and put requirements on creditors, including the following:

- Creditors must disclose all relevant terms in credit transactions (truth in lending).
- Procedures for correcting inaccurate and disputed bills and charges must be provided (fair credit billing).
- Credit-reporting agencies must provide accurate information in consumer reports (fair credit reporting).
- Creditors may not use certain personal characteristics, such as sex or race, in determining a person's creditworthiness (equal credit opportunity).
- Abusive debt collection techniques are prohibited (fair debt collection practices).

Exhibit 19.1 The Major Elements of Consumer Credit Legislation

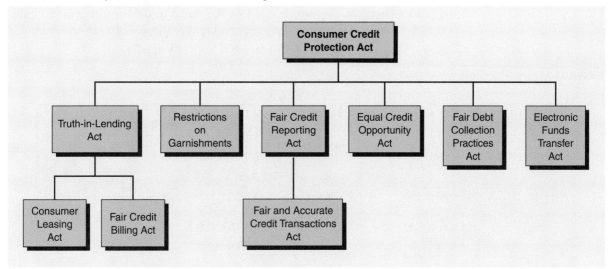

Truth-in-Lending Act

As Exhibit 19.1 shows, the first law to come under the CCPA was the *Truth-in-Lending Act* (TILA), which requires creditors in consumer transactions to disclose basic information about the cost and terms of credit to the consumer-borrower. By standardizing credit terms and methods of calculation, it helps people to shop for the most favorable credit terms.

Finance Charge Disclosures

Until TILA was passed, creditors quoted interest in many ways. For example, an 8 percent "add-on interest rate" is the same as a 15 percent "simple interest rate." This is because an add-on rate calculates interest on the initial amount of the loan regardless of the outstanding principal. The simple interest rate calculates interest only on the outstanding principal. Both methods are legitimate, but standardized terms let consumers make better comparisons.

TILA does not control interest rates; it requires standardized loan terms. TILA covers only consumer credit transactions, since the debtor must be a "natural person," not a business organization. Since the creditor must be in the credit business, TILA does not apply to transactions such as loans to friends. The law does not apply if the credit transaction does not include a finance charge, unless the consumer repays the creditor in more than four installments. Finally, the Act does not apply to consumer credit transactions for more than $25,000, except real estate purchases.

Credit Cost Disclosure

Transactions covered by TILA must disclose the credit costs in dollars (the *finance charge)* and the interest rate of that finance charge (the *annual percentage rate*, or *APR)*. These items must be disclosed prominently in the agreement. *Regulation Z,* written by the Federal Reserve Board to implement the Truth-in-Lending Act, specifies items that must be listed if part of the finance charge:

1. Service, activity, carrying, and transaction charges
2. Loan fees and points
3. Charges for credit life and credit accident and health insurance
4. In non-real-estate transactions, the fees for credit reports and appraisals

Certain other items, such as licenses and fees imposed by law, are not part of the finance charge if they are itemized and disclosed to the consumer in the transaction. Exhibit 19.2 shows the disclosure required in the sale of a car on credit.

Exhibit 19.2 Sample Credit Sale Disclosure Form

Big Wheel Auto				Alice Green
ANNUAL PERCENTAGE RATE The cost of your credit as a yearly rate.	FINANCE CHARGE The dollar amount the credit will cost you.	Amount Financed The amount of credit provided to you or on your behalf.	Total of Payments The amount you will have paid after you have made all payments as scheduled.	Total Sale Price The total cost of your purchase on credit, including your down-payment of $ 1500—
14.84%	$ 1496.80	$ 6107.50	$ 7604.30	$ 9129.30

You have the right to receive at this time an itemization of the Amount Financed.
☐ I want an itemization.   ☒ I do not want an itemization.

Your payment schedule will be:

Number of payments	Amount of Payments	When Payments Are Due
36	$211.23	Monthly, beginning 6-1-09

Insurance:
Credit life insurance and credit disability insurance are not required to obtain credit and will not be provided unless you sign and agree to pay the additional cost.

Type	Premium	Signature	
Credit Life	$120—	I want credit life insurance.	*alice Green* Signature
Credit Disability		I want credit disability insurance.	Signature
Credit Life and Disability		I want credit life and disability insurance.	Signature

Security: You are giving a security interest in:
☒ the goods being purchased.
☐ _____.

Filing Fees $_____   Non filing insurance $_____

Late Charge: If a payment is late, you will be charged $10.

Prepayment: If you pay off early, you
☐ may   ☐ will not   ☐ have to pay a penalty.
☒ may   ☐ will not   ☐ be entitled to a refund of part of the finance charge.

See your contract documents for any additional information about nonpayment, default, any required repayment in full before the scheduled date, and prepayment refunds and penalties.

I have received a copy of this statement.

____*alice Green*_____   5-1-09
Signature   Date

_____
e means an estimate

Enforcement and Penalties

TILA provides for both civil and criminal penalties. The creditor can avoid liability for a violation, such as a failure to specify all finance charges, if the violation is corrected within 15 days from the time it is discovered by the creditor and before the consumer gives written notification of error.

Consumers may sue creditors who violate TILA disclosure rules for twice the amount of the finance charge (up to $1,000), court costs, and attorney's fees. A creditor who willfully or knowingly gives inaccurate information or fails to make proper disclosures is subject to criminal liability.

Consumer Leasing Act

The *Consumer Leasing Act* does for consumer leases, such as for automobiles, what the Truth-in-Lending Act does for consumer credit; that is, it provides standard terms for leases. The Act applies to leases of personal property for personal or household purposes, not for business use. The lease must be longer than four months and have an obligation of less than $25,000. Apartment leases are not covered by the Act because the property leased is real, not personal. Most car rentals are not covered, because the term of the agreement is too short.

Disclosure Requirements

The Consumer Leasing Act specifies information that must be given. The required disclosures include the following:

- Number, amount, and period of the payments and the payment total
- Express warranties offered by the leasing party or the manufacturer of the leased property
- Identification of the party responsible for maintaining the leased property
- Whether the consumer has an option to buy the leased property and, if so, the terms of that option
- What happens if the consumer terminates the lease before it expires

Fair Credit Billing Act

TILA includes the *Fair Credit Billing Act* (FCBA). Before the Act, some consumers complained they were unable to get creditors to correct inaccurate or unauthorized charges that appeared on their bills. Another problem was that credit cards were sent to people who did not request them. Some cards were lost or stolen, and consumers who never requested the cards were billed for unauthorized purchases. The FCBA addresses these problems:

1. In case of a *billing error*, a consumer must notify the creditor in writing within 60 days of the billing of a disputed charge. The creditor must answer the complaint within 30 days of receipt and has 90 days to resolve the problem and notify the consumer.
2. It prohibits the mailing of unsolicited credit cards.
3. It establishes procedures to report lost or stolen credit cards. Liability for unauthorized charges is $50.

Enforcement

Most billing disputes are resolved through the procedures established by the FCBA. Dissatisfied consumers can also sue for civil penalties for FCBA violations. In successful actions, creditors are liable for twice the amount of the finance charge plus attorney's fees and court costs.

The FTC is a major FCBA enforcement agency, with jurisdiction over department stores, gasoline retailers, and non-bank-card issuers, such as American Express. Other federal agencies enforce the credit statutes for other credit-granting institutions. Most banks are regulated by the Federal Reserve Board.

Fair Credit Reporting Act

The *Fair Credit Reporting Act* (FCRA) regulates *credit bureaus* (consumer reporting agencies). It focuses on confidentiality and accuracy in *consumer credit reports*. No limit is placed on the information that consumer reporting agencies may include in their files, such as information on political beliefs or sexual practices, so long as the information is accurate.

Agencies may sell consumer reports only for business needs, such as to evaluate an applicant for credit, insurance, or employment. Any other use requires a court order or the consumer's permission.

Consumer Rights

The FCRA gives consumers the right to see information reported about them to a creditor that results in credit being denied. Further, credit bureaus must

- respond to consumer complaints about inaccurate information within 30 days.
- tell consumers, on request, who has asked for copies of their credit history in the past year.
- provide a toll-free consumer service number.
- get the consumer's permission before giving a report to an employer or before releasing a report containing medical information.

When a consumer tells a reporting agency about incorrect information, the information must be deleted or changed or a statement from the consumer about the problem must be put in the file.

INTERNATIONAL PERSPECTIVE

Credit Around the World

The United States has many laws governing credit, but how does it compare to other countries? The World Bank research, in the project called Doing Business, looks at that (www.doingbusiness.org).

Here we see four measures related to credit. The first, Legal Rights Index, measures the degree to which collateral and bankruptcy laws assist the lending process. The second, Credit Information Index, measures rules that affect the scope, access, and quality of credit information. Third is the percent of adults in a country covered by a public credit registry which does not exist in the United States and some other countries; so the fourth measure is the percent of adults in a country covered by private credit bureaus.

Country	Legal Rights Index	Credit Information Index	Public Registry	Private Bureau
Brazil	2	5	0.0	43.2
Canada	7	6	0.0	100.0
China	2	4	10.2	0.0
France	5	4	12.3	0.0
Germany	8	6	0.5	93.9
India	5	3	0.0	6.1
U.K.	10	6	0.0	86.1
U.S.	7	6	0.0	100.0

Getty Images

Enforcement and Penalties

The FTC has responsibility for enforcing the FCRA. The Act provides civil remedies to injured consumers, who may recover actual damages when noncompliance is negligent. When the credit agency is in willful noncompliance, the consumer may recover actual damages and a punitive penalty. In one suit, TRW was ordered to pay $290,000 in damages—of which $275,000 was punitive damages—for ignoring a consumer's attempt to correct errors in his credit report.

Fair and Accurate Credit Transactions Act

The Fair and Accurate Credit Transaction Act (FACT Act) amended the Fair Credit Reporting Act in 2003. It requires the major credit reporting services (Experian, TransUnion, and Equifax) to allow consumers to see their credit reports annually for free. That allows consumers to correct bad information in the report as well as to think of ways to improve their credit score.

The primary concern of the FACT Act was to help deal with identity theft, which impacts millions of people annually. The Act has numerous requirements, such as a rule that credit and debit card receipts may not include more than the last five digits of the card number, nor may the card's expiration date be printed on the cardholder's receipt.

The FTC followed up with a regulation, the Disposal Rule, that requires consumer information to be properly disposed of to protect against unauthorized access. The FTC coordinates with the Federal Reserve Board and other financial regulators to have consistent rules about information disposal and protection. Such information does not belong in a dumpster outside of a business. Rules also govern the disposal of information stored electronically. Since hard drives are difficult to erase, they must be given particular care.

ISSUE SPOTTER
Dealing with Customer Records

Identity theft affects about eight million people annually and costs about $50 billion. Businesses are becoming more sophisticated in the handling of information, so the volume of fraud has been dropping. If the information that a criminal has comes from your company records, you can be liable. What practical steps should be considered to help protect your customers and your business reputation?

Getty Images

Equal Credit Opportunity Act

The *Equal Credit Opportunity Act (ECOA)* was added to the CCPA to prohibit *credit discrimination* on the basis of race, sex, color, religion, national origin, marital status, receipt of public benefits, the good-faith exercise of the applicant's rights under any part of the CCPA, or age (provided the applicant is old enough to sign a contract). Creditors are prohibited from using such criteria, known as *prohibited bases*, in determining creditworthiness.

Unlawful Credit Discrimination

The guiding law for ECOA compliance is simple:

> A creditor shall not discriminate against an applicant on a prohibited basis regarding any aspect of a credit transaction.

Because this provision is broad, *Regulation B*, issued by the Federal Reserve Board, provides rules explaining what is unlawful discrimination.

- A creditor may not make statements related to a prohibited basis to discourage a person from applying for credit.
- A creditor may not use information concerning the likelihood that the applicant may have children or that the applicant is likely, for that reason, to have reduced or irregular income.
- Credit history must, at the applicant's request, consider not only the applicant's direct history but also the applicant's indirect credit history (for example, accounts that the applicant was liable for and accounts listed in the name of a spouse or former spouse that reflect his or her credit history).
- A creditor may not request information about a spouse or former spouse of the applicant unless (a) the spouse will use the account or will be liable for the debt; (b) the applicant is relying on the spouse's income or on alimony or child support from the former spouse; or (c) the applicant lives in a community property state.

A violation of ECOA exists if a creditor used a factor prohibited by the Act. The consumer can sue the creditor for ECOA violations. If successful, the creditor is liable to the consumer for actual damages, punitive damages up to $10,000, attorney's fees, and court costs, whether the discrimination was intentional or not.

ECOA Notification Requirements

When a consumer's credit application is denied or accepted at less favorable terms, the creditor must provide *written notification* containing the following:

1. The basic provisions of ECOA
2. Name and address of the federal agency regulating the creditor
3. Either a statement of the reasons for the action taken or a disclosure of the applicant's right to receive a statement of reasons

The first and second requirements tell rejected applicants that it is against the law to discriminate on a prohibited basis and point them to the federal agencies that enforce the Act. The third requirement is the most significant. By knowing why they were rejected, applicants can reapply when their situation changes, or they can correct any misinformation. By knowing the reasons for credit denial, applicants can better understand how credit decisions are made.

LIGHTER SIDE OF THE LAW

Watch Who You Nickle and Dime

Wendy Ehringer bounced a check for $15.02. She got a notice from a debt collector (ACS) demanding the $15.02 plus $40 in fees, so she sent a money order for $55.02. Months later, she received notice of a lawsuit. Her payment was late, ACS claimed, so she was being sued for 18 cents—the interest on the original amount she owed because her payment arrived two days late—plus $311.26 in attorney fees.

Ehringer, a paralegal, knew her rights under the FDCPA and countersued. The court threw out ACS's claim and awarded Ehringer $500 damages plus $7,000 for attorney's fees.

Source: *Seattle Times*

Getty Images

Fair Debt Collection Practices Act

Creditors have the right to collect debts they are owed. If not repaid, under state law they may go to court and ask for an order to *garnish* (set aside a portion of) the wages of the debtor to pay the debt, but that is a costly process. If unsuccessful in collecting a debt, a creditor can sell the debt to a *debt collection agency* and pay the agency a commission for the funds it collects. Agencies handle about $40 billion in claims each year.

To collect accounts, debt collectors advise consumers by telephone or letter of the outstanding debt and urge them to pay. Sometimes, consumers are subjected to phone calls in the middle of the night, obscene language, and other harassment and abusive tactics. The *Fair Debt Collection Practices Act (FDCPA)* helps reduce unfair, deceptive, and abusive collection techniques used by some debt collectors.

Restrictions Imposed

The FDCPA regulates the conduct of about 5,000 independent debt collection agencies that collect billions of dollars each year from consumers. In *Heintz* v. *Jenkins* (115 S. Ct. 1489) the Supreme Court held that the FDCPA "applies to attorneys who regularly engage in consumer-debt collection activity." The law does not apply to creditors attempting to collect their own debts, such as a department store trying to collect from a customer. The Act makes abusive debt collection practices illegal and contains a list of required actions.

Harassing, deceptive, and unfair debt collection practices—including threats of violence or arrest, obscene language, the publication of a list of delinquent consumers, and harassing phone calls—are prohibited. Debt collectors may not discuss the debts with other people, including the debtor's employer. The Act prohibits the use of false or misleading representations in collecting a debt.

Getty Images

ISSUE SPOTTER

How Should You Handle Unpaid Accounts?

Your company sells furniture mostly to low-income people who buy on credit provided by your company. You know that the default rate, which is pretty high in your business, can determine whether the store is profitable or not. Should you sell or assign the debt to a debt collector or handle the collection internally? What difference is there legally? Are there advantages of going one way or another?

What Must Be Communicated

The FDCPA requires the debt collector to send certain information to the consumer within five days of the initial communication:

- Amount of debt
- Name of the creditor to whom the debt is owed
- A statement that unless the consumer disputes the validity of the debt within 30 days, the debt collector will assume the debt is valid
- A statement that the debt collector must show proof of the debt if the consumer advises the debt collector within 30 days of the notification that the consumer disputes the debt

Contact with the consumer must end when the collector learns that the consumer is represented by an attorney or when the consumer requests in writing that contact end. The debt collector then waits for payment or sues to collect the debt. Most cases that arise under the FDCPA concern improper language in debt collection letters. As the *Chuway* case shows, debt collectors must be precise in their language.

Chuway v. National Action Financial Service
United States Court of Appeals, Seventh Circuit
362 F.3d 944 (2004)

Case Background *National Action, a debt collector, mailed Chuway, a debtor, a letter which identified a creditor (a credit card company) and stated that the "balance" on the debt was $367.52. The letter said that the creditor "has assigned your delinquent account to our angency for collection. Please remit the balance listed above in the return envelope provided. To obtain your most current balance information, please call 1-800-916-9006. Our friendly and experienced representatives will be glad to assist you and answer any questions you have."*

Chuway sued National Action for violating the FDCPA because the communication was not proper under the Act. The district court granted summary judgment for National Action because the letter stated "the amount of the debt" and so did not violate the statute. Chuway appealed.

Case Decision Posner, Circuit Judge

* * *

Here ... the *entire* debt that the defendant was hired to collect was the $367.42 listed as the "balance."

So if the letter had stopped after the "Please remit" sentence, the defendant would be in the clear. But the letter didn't stop there. It went on to instruct the recipient on how to obtain "your most current balance information." If this means that the defendant was dunning her for something more than $367.42, it's in trouble, because the "something more" is not quantified.... The credit card company, which is to say the creditor, not the debt collector, may charge the plaintiff interest on the $367.42 between when the debt accrued and when the plaintiff finally pays and may add the interest accruing in the interim to the plaintiff's current balance. But that would not be a part of "the amount of the debt" for which the *defendant* was dunning her....

It is not enough that the dunning letter state the amount of the debt that is due. It must state it clearly enough that the recipient is likely to understand it. Otherwise the collection agency could write the letter in Hittite and have a secure defense....

If the debt collector is trying to collect only the amount due on the date the letter is sent, then he complies with the Act by stating the "balance" due, stating that the creditor "has assigned your delinquent account to our agency for collection," and asking the recipient to remit the balance listed—and stopping there, without talk of the "current" balance. If, instead, the debt collector is trying to collect the listed balance plus the running interest on it or other charges, he should use the safe-harbor language [established in an earlier case]: "As of the date of this letter, you owe $____[the exact amount due]. Because of interest, alter charges, and other charges that may vary from day to day, the amount due on the day you pay may be greater. Hence, if you pay the amount shown above, an adjustment may be necessary after we receive your check, in which event we will inform you before depositing the check for collection. For further information, write the undersigned or call 1-800-[phone number]."

Reversed and remanded.

Questions for Analysis
1. The appeals court held the debt collection letter to violate the FDCPA. How could Chuway afford to sue National Action over such a small sum of money?
2. Why did National Action not use the language the court cited as providing a safe harbor, because the words meet the specific requirements of the FDCPA?

Enforcement

Consumers subjected to collection abuses enforce compliance by suing. A collector who violates the FDCPA is liable for actual damages caused, as well as any additional damages (not over $1,000). Consumers bringing action in good faith will have their attorney's fees and court costs paid by the collector. The FTC can sue collectors that violate the act, as can state attorneys general in states with similar laws.

When debt collection practices go overboard, the debtor may, of course, sue in tort, as well as for violations of the FDCPA. In a case in El Paso, Texas, a jury awarded debtors $11 million in damages against Household Credit Services, their creditor, and Allied Adjustment Bureau, a collection agency used by Household Credit. Attempting to collect a $2,000 debt, death threats and numerous other violations of the debtor's rights were made. Damages under the FDCPA were a tiny fraction of the jury tort verdict.

Electronic Fund Transfer Act

Many *electronic fund transfer* (EFT) services are available to consumers. Such transfers are larger in volume than funds transfers by check and cash. They include:

- ATM deposits or other transactions
- Direct deposits of paychecks
- Debit cards used to buy goods or services
- Automatic bill-paying services
- Telephone transfers to credit cards (presuming a written agreement exists)

As electronic innovations developed, Congress became concerned about the rights and liabilities of the consumers, financial institutions, and retailers who use electronic fund transfer systems. *The Electronic Fund Transfer Act* was passed and required the Federal Reserve Board to write *Regulation E* to implement the Act.

Liability for Stolen Cards

One important protection provided by the Act is the liability limit when a consumer's ATM card is stolen and an unauthorized user drains the account. Unlike the Fair Credit Billing Act's $50 limit on liability for lost or stolen credit cards, the Electronic Fund Transfer Act's limit on liability is potentially greater.

Regulation E provides that the consumer's liability is no more than $50 if the financial institution is notified within two days after the consumer learns of the theft. The consumer's liability becomes $500 as long as the financial institution is notified within 60 days. If the consumer does not report the theft within 60 days after receiving the first statement containing unauthorized transfers, the consumer is liable for all amounts after that.

Liability for Mistakes

The Act makes financial institutions liable to consumers for damages caused by failure to make electronic transfers. However, liability is limited to actual damages proved, such as costs incurred by a consumer if a car is repossessed for failure to make a required payment.

Consumers are to receive a monthly statement from financial institutions. Consumers have 60 days to report errors. When a consumer reports an error, the institution must resolve the dispute within 45 days. If an investigation takes more than ten business days to complete, the institution must recredit the disputed amount to the consumer's account; the consumer has use of the funds until the complaint is resolved. Failure to undertake a good-faith investigation of an alleged error makes the institution liable for triple the consumer's actual damages.

Summary

- The Food, Drug, and Cosmetic Act, enforced by the FDA, imposes liability on companies and persons involved in the production and distribution of food and drug products. The primary concern for food is safety. The FDA is helped by the U.S. Department of Agriculture in food sanitation inspection.
- Food additives must be approved by the FDA before being sold to the public. Nutrition labels on processed foods must list by standard consumer portions fat, carbohydrates, cholesterol, and other nutrients, as well as certain vitamins and minerals and total calories.
- The FDA determines when drugs are safe and effective for sale and whether drugs will be sold by prescription only or over the counter. Food, drugs, cosmetics, and medical devices that the FDA determines to be unsafe may be ordered off the market or seized.
- The FTC has broad authority to attack unfair or deceptive business practices. The consumer protection mission includes the advertising substantiation program, which requires advertisers to be able to demonstrate the truth of product claims.
- The FTC issues trade regulation rules to govern business practices that have raised problems. The rules fix standards that businesses must meet, which makes prosecution for rule violations quite simple.
- The attorney general of a state has the authority to sue sellers involved in deceptive business practices. Most states have statutes that give consumers broad rights to sue for unfair and deceptive business practices. These statutes can provide legal rights beyond those provided by contract.
- The Truth-in-Lending Act, which applies to most consumer loans, requires that lenders meet requirements on how the details of loan amounts, interest charges, and other items are calculated and stated to the borrower. There is no defense for certain violations of this statute. The Consumer Leasing Act sets similar standards for consumer leases.
- The Fair Credit Billing Act details the rights of consumers to resolve billing errors. Creditors must follow requirements on how long they have to respond to the consumer and what they must do to resolve the dispute. As under other parts of the credit statutes, violations mean double damages, plus attorney's fees, for the plaintiff.
- Credit bureaus sell lenders the credit history about consumers seeking credit. The Fair Credit Reporting Act specifies consumers' rights to challenge the accuracy of reports issued by these bureaus. Credit bureaus must respond to inquiries from consumers about errors in credit reports.
- Under the Equal Credit Opportunity Act, creditors may not consider the following factors in determining who will be granted credit: race, sex, age, color, religion, national origin, marital status, receipt of public benefits, or the exercise of legal rights. Specific regulations govern how lenders must comply with this statute.
- Debt collectors may not abuse the rights of debtors granted by the Fair Debt Collection Practices Act. They may not make abusive phone calls, threats, or claims of legal action not actually underway or use other forms of harassment. A debt collector informed by any debtor that no further contact is desired may not contact the debtor except for notice of legal action.
- Consumer rights and responsibilities for credit cards and ATM cards that have been stolen are spelled out in the law. To limit liability for unauthorized charges, the consumer must notify the card issuer of the theft of the card.

Terms to Know

You should be able to define the following terms:

learned intermediary doctrine, 481

consent decree, 482

deception, 482

unfairness, 482

advertising substantiation program, 485

trade regulation rules, 488

consumer credit reports, 494

debt collection agency, 497

Discussion Question

1. If consumers think agencies such as the FTC prevent unfair and deceptive practices, will they become less careful in watching out for themselves, thereby encouraging more bad business practices?

Case Questions

1. Laetrile is a drug not approved by the FDA for sale. Some people believed it helped fight certain cancers. Some People with cancer went to Mexico to be treated with Laetrile. Some sued the FDA, saying they had a constitutional right to privacy that was being denied by the FDA's refusal to let them have access to Laetrile. A court of appeals held that it is not reasonable to apply the FDA's drug safety and effectiveness standards to dying cancer patients. The Supreme Court reviewed the case. What do you think the result was? [*United States* v. *Rutherford*, 99 S. Ct. 2470 (1979)]

2. Heath took Ortho-Novum oral contraceptives from 1967 to 1974, when, at age 28, she suffered kidney failure that required a kidney transplant. She sued, claiming the kidney failure was caused by Ortho-Novum, which did not warn physicians to monitor blood pressure or watch for signs of kidney problems. Ortho defended that it was in compliance with FDA regulations in marketing the product, so it should not be subject to common-law strict liability or negligence. Could the case go to the jury, or did federal regulation of the drug remove common-law liability? [*Ortho Pharmaceutical* v. *Heath*, 722 P.2d 410 Colo. Sup. Ct. (1986)]

   ✓ Check your answer at http://academic.cengage.com/blaw/meiners

3. Buckingham Productions sold various diet plans, such as the Freedom Diet. It claimed that dieters could eat almost anything they wanted for four days each week and lose weight if during the other three days they followed a low-calorie diet and took the company's vitamin supplements. The company reported that the average monthly weight loss was 8 to 20 pounds for women and 12 to 25 pounds for men. What government agency would likely sue the company, and on what grounds? What would be the likely result?

4. A store constantly has big signs in its windows and puts ads in the newspapers that take different approaches. For a month the store advertised "Gigantic Savings of 75 percent" and similar claims. The next month it advertised "Going-Out-of-Business Clearance Sale." The next month it advertised "Distress Sale Prices—Everything Must Go." In fact, the store is not going out of business, and most of its prices are always the same. The prices are competitive, but not 75 percent off normal retail. Is this deceptive advertising?

   ✓ Check your answer at http://academic.cengage.com/blaw/meiners

5. Dr. Amrani performed two major back surgeries on Williamson to try to resolve a major back problem. After the surgeries, which were apparently not as successful as hoped, Williamson sued Amrani under the Kansas Consumer Protection Act. She claimed that Amrani made representations to her about the benefits of the surgery that were not true. He told her the surgery worked well, when in fact the record was not so good. She claimed this was deception to induce her to undergo the surgery. Could she use a consumer deception statute to bring an action for a medical procedure? [*Williamson* v. *Amrani*, 152 P.3d 60 Sup. Ct., Kan. (2007)]

6. Procter and Gamble sold a detergent, *Ace con Blanqueador*, in Puerto Rico. It advertised that *"Mas blanco no se puede"* (Whiter is not possible). Clorox, a bleach maker, sued Procter and Gamble, contending that the ad was false and misleading in violation of the Lanham Act. The district court dismissed the suit; Clorox appealed. Did it have a suit for false advertising against its competitor under the Lanham Act? [*Clorox Company Puerto Rico* v. *Procter and Gamble*, 228 F.3d 24 1st Cir. (2000)]

   ✓ Check your answer at http://academic.cengage.com/blaw/meiners

7. Fairbanks Capital acquired 12,800 mostly delinquent mortgages from a mortgage company, including a mortgage owned by the Schlossers. Identifying itself as a debt collector, Fairbanks sent the Schlossers a letter asserting that their mortgage was in default. In fact, the Schlossers were not in default and sued Fairbanks for failure to notify the debtors of their right to contest the debt as required by the Fair Debt Collections Practices Act (FDCPA). The district court held that since the Schlossers were not in default, there was no debt to collect, so the FDCPA did not apply. The Schlossers appealed. Do they have a case? [*Schlosser* v. *Fairbanks Capital*, 323 F.3d 534 7th Cir. (2003)]

8. Pfennig sued Household Credit Services for violations of the Truth-in-Lending Act. She contended that she was extended credit but was then charged a fee of $29 a month when she went over the $2,000 limit on her credit card. The fee was not listed in the finance charges disclosed on her monthly statements, but was listed as a new purchase on which additional finance charges were calculated. Does she have a case? [*Pfennig* v. *Household Credit Services*, 295 F.3d 522, 6th Cir. (2002)]

9. Sarah Grendahl moved in with Lavon Phillips and was planning to marry him. Mary Grendahl, Sarah's mother, believed Phillips was lying about his background, so she hired a private investigator to check him out. Using consumer reports, the investigator determined that Phillips had been convicted for writing bad checks, sued for paternity in one state, and was delinquent in child support in another state. When Phillips learned that the truth about his background had been revealed, he sued Mary Grendahl, the detective agency, and the consumer reporting agency for violating the Fair Credit Reporting Act. Does he have a case? [*Phillips* v. *Grendahl*, 312 F.3d 357 8th Cir. (2002)]

Ethics Question

1. The FDA, FTC, or some other agency is proposing a regulation that would hurt the sales of one of the products your company produces. The agency believes that there is a long-run consumer health issue that it should address. You estimate the regulation will cost your company $20 million a year in sales and $2 million a year in profits. The three other firms in the industry that make a similar product will likewise be hurt. Your Washington representative tells you that if all four firms are willing to spend $5 million in lobbying efforts it can get Congress to kill the proposed regulation. All other firms agree to help foot the bill. This kind of lobbying is common. Should you pay to help get the regulation killed?

Internet Assignment

http://www.consumer.gov
http://www.ftc.gov/bcp/consumer.shtm
http://www.bbb.org

In addition to finding resources from federal agencies devoted to helping protect America's consumers, you can use the Internet as a self-help tool to avoid purchasing problematic products in the first place. You can check the Better Business Bureau in your area. You can search for product specifications on a company's Web site. You can check the Internet for "gripe sites" related to the product you are considering purchasing. If purchasing items online, you may be able to access reviews of the products posted by other customers. Information about product recalls is likely to be available on the Internet, as well.

Antitrust Law

Chapter 20

Because of the downturn in housing construction, your building supply company is suffering. Trying to stay in business, you have cut prices to the bone, leaving no profit. Your competitors are doing the same thing. In fact, you know that some are selling certain supplies at less than cost, just to keep some cash flowing in. If this continues, some, suppliers in your area will be out of business.

Stability would be better if you and the other suppliers agreed not to sell supplies at a loss. Housing construction is always boom-and-bust. If all the suppliers just hold on for a while, everyone can stay in business and be ready to serve clients when things pick up again. Your clients will be better served at that time than if a number of suppliers go broke now and only a few competitors remain in business to serve the market when things pick up.

What happens if you discuss this idea—not selling supplies at a loss—with your competitors to try to get an agreement? What kind of agreement among competitors will not cause antitrust-law violations?

The antitrust statutes written by Congress do not tell us whether that would be legal. Instead, the courts must interpret the very general language in the statutes to determine what activities are prohibited and what activities are allowed. Antitrust law, therefore, refers to the antitrust statutes, the interpretation of the statutes by the courts, and the enforcement policies of administrative agencies, especially the Department of Justice and the Federal Trade Commission. This chapter reviews the antitrust statutes and looks at how antitrust law is applied to both horizontal and vertical business arrangements. ∎

Getty Images

Antitrust Statutes

The growth of large corporations in the late nineteenth century led to calls for constraints on business. The result was the passage of federal antitrust legislation: the Sherman Act, the Clayton Act, and the Federal Trade Commission (FTC) Act. The key parts of these broadly written statutes are excerpted in Appendix H. Except for some actions that are clearly illegal under the statutes, it has been left largely to the federal agencies and courts to determine how the laws will be applied in practice.

The Sherman Act

The *Sherman Antitrust Act* was passed by Congress in 1890 in response to the unpopularity of large business organizations. The most famous was the Standard Oil Trust, John D. Rockefeller's company, which had about 90 percent of the oil sales in the country. The word *antitrust* comes from Standard Oil, which was organized in the form of a trust. The sponsors of the Act saw it as a way to reduce concerns that some industries were dominated by a few large firms. The major sections of the Sherman Act are so broad that one could find almost any business activity to be illegal:

> Sec. 1: Every contract, combination in the form of trust or otherwise, or conspiracy, in *restraint of trade* or commerce among the several States, or with foreign nations, is hereby declared to be illegal.
>
> Sec. 2: Every person who shall *monopolize*, or *attempt to monopolize*, or combine or conspire with any other person or persons, to monopolize any part of the trade or commerce among the several States, or with foreign nations, shall be deemed guilty of a felony.

The Clayton Act

Enacted in 1914, the *Clayton Act* was meant to add to the Sherman Act. The Clayton Act is intended to stop a business practice early in its use to prevent a firm from becoming a *monopoly* by making practices that "substantially lessen competition or tend to create a monopoly" illegal.

Under the antitrust laws, what is a monopoly? There is no exact answer. In general, a monopoly exists in a market when one firm or only a few dominate the sales of a product or service. As we will see in this chapter, the fact that a company obtains such a position is not necessarily illegal. The laws focus more on certain actions that show an effort to eliminate competition. The Clayton Act holds some specific actions to be illegal. The most important sections of the Act include:

> Sec. 2: It shall be unlawful for any person engaged in commerce ... to discriminate in price between different purchasers of commodities of like grade and quality ... where the effect of such discrimination may be substantially to lessen competition or tend to create a monopoly in any line of commerce ... [This section was added by the Robinson–Patman Act of 1936 and restricts price discrimination in the sale of goods. As we will see, this means when a producer sells the same good at different prices to different buyers.]
>
> Sec. 3: It shall be unlawful for any person engaged in commerce ... to lease or make a sale ... on the condition ... that the lessee or purchaser thereof shall not use or deal in the goods ... or other commodities of a competitor ... where the effect ... may be to substantially lessen competition or tend to create a monopoly.... [This is a restriction on *tying sales*, where the sale of one good is tied to the sale of another good, and *exclusive dealing*, when a company is forbidden from dealing with other possible buyers or sellers.]

Sec. 7: No corporation … shall acquire the whole or any part of the assets of another corporation engaged also in commerce, where … the effect of such acquisition may be substantially to lessen competition, or to tend to create a monopoly. [This restricts mergers of competitors, such as McDonald's and Burger King.]

Sec. 8: No person at the same time shall be a director in any two or more corporations … if such corporations are or shall have been … competitors, so that the elimination of competition by agreement between them would constitute a violation of … the antitrust laws. [This restricts interlocking directorates, such as the same people sitting on the boards of directors of both Ford and GM.]

The Federal Trade Commission Act

In addition to the Clayton Act, in 1914 Congress enacted the *Federal Trade Commission Act.* It established the FTC as an agency to investigate and enforce violations of the antitrust laws. Although most of the Act provides for the structure, powers, and procedures of the FTC, it also provides a major addition to antitrust law:

Sec. 5: Unfair methods of competition in or affecting commerce, and unfair or deceptive acts or practices in commerce, are hereby declared unlawful.

The *unfair methods of competition* referred to in the FTC Act have been interpreted by the courts as any business activity that may tend to create a monopoly by unfairly eliminating or excluding competitors from the marketplace.

Exemptions

Not all business activities are subject to the antitrust laws. In some cases, successful lobbying of Congress resulted in statutory exemptions from the antitrust laws. The following activities and businesses are provided exemptions:

- The Clayton Act exempts some activities of nonprofit organizations and of agricultural, fishing, and some other cooperatives.
- The Export Trading Company Act allows sellers of exports to receive limited antitrust immunity. For example, a group of domestic producers may be allowed to join together to improve their ability to sell their products in other countries.
- The *Parker doctrine*, or *state action doctrine*, allows state governments to restrict competition in industries such as public utilities (e.g., cable television), professional services (e.g., nursing), and public transportation (e.g., taxicabs). However, the Supreme Court has held that for the doctrine to protect parties from antitrust actions, the state must play "a substantial role in determining the specifics of the economic policy." That is, the state must have intended to restrict competition and perhaps fix prices.
- The McCarran–Ferguson Act exempts the insurance industry from federal antitrust laws so long as the states regulate insurance.
- Under the Noerr–Pennington doctrine, lobbying to influence a legislature is not illegal. This is because the First Amendment gives persons the right to petition their government, even if the purpose is anticompetitive.
- Most labor unions' activities are exempt. The National Labor Relations Act protects collective bargaining to set conditions of employment.

Enforcement

Individuals and businesses have the right to sue for the violations of the antitrust laws. The Antitrust Division of the Justice Department brings dozens of criminal antitrust suits each year. For a civil lawsuit under the Sherman Act or Clayton Act, a choice must be made as to whether the Justice Department or the FTC will bring the case. The agencies have agreed to divide the cases by industry, but may consult to decide which agency will handle a particular case. State attorneys general may also bring antitrust cases under federal or state law.

Sherman Act

Violations of the Sherman Act carry the most severe penalties of the antitrust statutes. Most of the criminal cases involve price fixing or bid rigging by competitors.

- Violations of Sections 1 and 2 of the Sherman Act can be *criminal felonies*. Individuals found guilty of violating the Act face up to 10 years in prison, a fine of $1 million, or both. Corporations found guilty can be fined up to $100 million. Criminal cases are brought by the Antitrust Division of the Department of Justice. Some years, fines totaling over $1 billion have been collected.
- Private parties or the government can seek injunctive relief under the Act in a civil proceeding. An *injunction* is an order to a defendant (the party who may have violated the Act) to stop the illegal acts.
- Private parties harmed by a violation of the Sherman Act can sue for *treble damages*; if they win, they get three times their actual money damages, plus court costs and attorney's fees.

Clayton Act

The Department of Justice or private parties may bring civil proceedings under the Clayton Act, but the normal procedure has been for the FTC, which shares jurisdiction with the Justice Department, to issue cease and desist orders, prohibiting further violation. The FTC has the authority to investigate suspect business dealings, hold hearings (rather than trials), and issue administrative orders approved in federal court that require parties to stop or change certain business acts. When these orders are ignored there may be criminal penalties.

FTC Act

Violations of the FTC Act carry a variety of penalties, ranging from an order preventing a planned merger to substantial civil penalties. It is much easier for the FTC to bring administrative actions against a company than for the Justice Department to bring a criminal suit under the Sherman Act, so the agencies decide which route is most appropriate to take in each case.

Remedies Available

Whether an antitrust suit is brought by a private plaintiff or by the government, the courts can provide a number of remedies, besides monetary damages, including the following:

- Restrain a company or individuals from certain conduct
- Force a company to sell part of its assets (break up the company)
- Force a company to let others use its patents or facilities (licensing)
- Cancel or modify existing business contracts

For a firm to recover damages under the antitrust laws, the harm suffered by the plaintiff must be the kind of harm that the antitrust laws are meant to avoid. A firm that loses profits because a new competitor enters its market cannot sue for damages, because increased competition is favored by antitrust law. Only plaintiffs suffering injuries caused by the *anti*competitive behaviors of defendants can recover damages under antitrust law.

Per Se Rule and the Rule of Reason

As we will see as we look at antitrust cases, one question the courts must address is whether, as a matter of policy, a certain business practice will be held to be illegal *per se* or whether a *rule of reason* is appropriate.

A *per se rule* means that some business agreements or activities will automatically be held to be illegal. The classic example of a per se violation of antitrust law is a group of competitors agreeing on the prices they will charge for their goods so as to eliminate price competition. In discussing per se illegality, the Supreme Court in *Northern Pacific Railway Co.* v. *United States* (356 U.S. 1) stated that there are certain activities that

> because of their pernicious effect on competition and lack of any redeeming virtue are conclusively presumed to be unreasonable and therefore illegal without elaborate inquiry as to the precise harm they have caused or business excuse for their use.

A rule of reason, in contrast, means that the court looks at the facts surrounding business practice before deciding whether it helps or hurts competition. The court considers such factors as the business reasons for the restraint, the restraining business's position in its industry, and the structure of the industry.

If the court concludes that the business practice promotes competition, the court dismisses the case. But if the court finds that the practice on net reduces competition, the court rules that it violates the antitrust laws.

Monopolization

The Sherman Act and Clayton Act are concerned with monopolization of markets but provide little guidance as to what behavior crosses the line of illegal monopoly practices. Therefore, antitrust law has been built on many court cases over the years. The courts usually consider the structure of a market and the nature of the behavior that is attacked. The focus of the law is on business practices that can lead to a monopoly. The law does not restrict the size of firms. The concern is to protect competition in a given market, not just to protect individual competitors who complain about another competitor's behavior. In the *Spanish Broadcasting* case we see a discussion of the factors that courts consider in a monopolization case brought under the Sherman Act.

Spanish Broadcasting System of Florida v. Clear Channel Communications
United States Court of Appeals, Eleventh Circuit
376 F.3d 1065 (2004)

Case Background *Spanish Broadcasting System (SBS) owns 14 Spanish-language stations, including five stations in top-ten markets. Hispanic Broadcasting Corporation (HBC) owns 55 Spanish-language stations and is in all top-ten markets. Clear Channel (CC) owns the largest English-language radio network in the United States, with 1,200 stations, and it owns 26 percent of HBC.*

SBS sued CC and HBC, claiming they conspired to drive SBS out of the Spanish-language radio market by practices that violate the Sherman Act. SBS claimed that the two stations discouraged advertisers from placing ads with SBS and induced SBS employees to quit to join HBC. SBS contended that the stations made it difficult for SBS to enter new markets by bidding up prices and taking away

continues

business opportunities, and interfered with SBS's ability to raise money in capital markets. The district court dismissed the suit, holding that SBS did not meet the standards necessary to maintain an antitrust suit under the Sherman Act; SBS appealed.

Case Decision Barkett, Circuit Judge

* * *

Because the Sherman Act contains only general language, courts have played an extremely important role in shaping the reach of the Act and the requirements for stating a cause of action under each section. Critically, under both sections, an antitrust plaintiff must show harm to competition in general, rather than merely damage to an individual competitor.... This case turns in large part on whether SBS has met its obligation to allege facts that would support a showing of this harm to competition, rather than merely to itself....

SBS alleged that the practices [described above] constituted an agreement between CC and HBC to restrain trade in violation of Section One of the Sherman Act as well as attempted monopolization by both CC and HBC of the major Spanish-language radio markets in violation of Section Two of the Act....

Section One of the Sherman Act ... prohibits combinations and conspiracies the restrain interstate or foreign trade. This provision applies both to agreements between companies that directly compete with one another, called "horizontal" agreements, and to agreements between businesses operating at different levels of the same product's production chain or distribution chain, known as "vertical" agreements. In addition, although some restraints on trade remain illegal per se, such as certain agreements to fix prices, most asserted antitrust violations now require "the finder of fact [to] decide whether the questioned practice imposes an *unreasonable* restraint on competition, taking into account a variety of factors, including specific information about the relevant business, its condition before and after the restraint was imposed, and the restraint's history, nature, and effect." Section One claims that do not allege per se antitrust violations are analyzed under this "rule of reason," and the claims fail if the restraint on trade is reasonable. Both parties accept that the rule of reason applies to the Section One claims raised by SBS in this case....

Even if we were to assume that CC and HBC acted in concert for purposes of Section One, however, we would still affirm here, given that SBS failed to allege sufficient anticompetitive effect, a critical component of any antitrust claim....

Anticompetitive effects are measured by their impact on the market rather than by their impact on competitors.... In order to prove this anticompetitive effect on the market, the plaintiff "may either prove that the defendants' behavior had an actual detrimental effect on competition, or that the behavior had the potential for genuine adverse effects on competition."

In an attempt to meet this burden, SBS focuses upon the harm it allegedly suffered at the hands of HBC and CC, such as weakened stock prices, restricted access to capital markets, loss of employees, damaged reputation, and loss of advertising revenue. None of these allegations assert damage to competition itself rather than damage to SBS, one competitor in the Spanish-language advertising market....

Section Two makes it a crime to monopolize, to attempt to monopolize, or to conspire to monopolize any part of interstate or foreign trade. This provision covers behavior by a single business as well as coordinated action taken by several businesses.

The ... complaint alleged only attempted monopolization, which involves three distinct elements: "(1) the defendant has engaged is predatory or anticompetitive conduct with (2) a specific intent to monopolize and (3) a dangerous probability of achieving monopoly power."

Like claims under Section One, Section Two claims require harm to competition that must occur within a "relevant," that is, a distinct market, with a specific set of geographical boundaries and a narrow delineation of the products at issue.... SBS explained that it considered the relevant market to be advertising purchased in the top-ten Spanish-language markets and HBC earned 51 percent of the advertising revenue in that market....

There is no question that CC does not participate in the Spanish-language radio market. Thus, CC cannot attempt to monopolize that market. SBS attempted to overcome this hurdle by pointing out that CC owned 26 percent of HBC, implying that this either makes CC an effective participant in the relevant market or at least gives CC sufficient control over HBC to permit attempted monopolization. We reject this contention. Absent allegations of significant control over the policies of a subsidiary, a minority ownership share does not convert a parent corporation into a competitor.... To be a competitor at the level of the subsidiary, the parent must have substantial control over the affairs and policies of the subsidiary.

As with Section One claims, conduct that injures individual firms rather than competition in the market as a whole does not violate Section Two. The

Supreme Court has explained that "even an act of pure malice by one business competitor against another does not, without more, state a claim under the federal antitrust laws."…

Because SBS has not alleged any harm to competition in the market, nor explained how any of the actions taken by HBC could lead to monopolization of that market, SBS has not alleged anticompetitive conduct and thus has not stated a claim against HBC under Section Two.…

Affirmed.

Questions for Analysis

1. The appeals court affirmed that no antitrust violation occurred. The court focused on damage to competition in the market. What is the relevant product market that was under consideration?
2. If it is true that HBC lured away SBS employees, which weakend SBS's ability to compete, why was the court not concerned?

Mergers

Mergers are a source of monopolization concern. If competitor companies in a market merge, will competition be significantly injured? A *merger* involves two or more firms coming together to form a new firm. The combination can be created by one firm's acquiring all or part of the stock or the assets of another firm. A merger is termed a *horizontal merger* when the two firms were competitors before they merged (e.g., Exxon and Mobil). One of the most famous merger decisions, *Standard Oil*, established the rule of reason as the approach the courts use in judging merger activities.

In the 1911 case, *Standard Oil* v. *United States* (221 U.S. 1), the Supreme Court ordered the breakup of the Standard Oil Trust, which was a combination of 72 companies that had joined to control as much as 90 percent of the production, shipping, refining, and selling of oil products. The court held that such a combination was a violation of Section 1 of the Sherman Act, which prohibits monopolization by a combination. Since that time, government authorities have challenged a number of mergers in part or in whole.

Premerger Notification

Before two firms merge, the Hart–Scott–Rodino Antitrust Improvements Act (HSR) requires the firms to notify the Antitrust Division of the Department of Justice or the Federal Trade Commission at least one month before the planned merger, if there is more than $50 million involved. The *premerger notification* requires payment of a filing fee.

Of all the HSR notices filed each year, about 100 to 150 are subject to detailed examination by antitrust authorities, which may put the merger on hold while it is studied. The result may be that the merging firms agree to sell certain assets to allow the merger to go forward. For example, in several mergers of gasoline producers, the merged company was required to sell gas stations in some parts of the country, where it would have had too much market power. Very few merger cases go to the courts for review. Most that are opposed, such as the proposed merger of Staples and Office Depot, are called off.

Determining Market Power

To help businesses and regulators assess the antitrust implications of a merger, over the years the Department of Justice has issued *merger guidelines.* Revised by Justice and the FTC in 1982, 1992, and 2000, the guidelines discuss factors that will be considered in determining whether a merger will likely be challenged (http://www.ftc.gov). Many of the factors considered important by the Supreme Court in merger cases over the years have been incorporated into the guidelines, which place particular importance on the notion of *market power:*

The unifying theme of the Guidelines is that mergers should not be permitted to create or enhance *market power* or to facilitate its exercise.… The ability of one or more firms profitably to maintain prices above competitive levels for a significant period of time is termed *market power.*

Product and Geographic Markets

To assess a firm's market power in antitrust cases, the courts determine the *market share* held by the firms involved in the merger. A firm's market share refers to the percentage of the relevant market controlled by the firm.

Recall that the Clayton Act states that the legality of a merger between two firms rests on whether "in any line of commerce in any section of the country, the effect of such acquisition may be substantially to lessen competition, or tend to create a monopoly." The phrase "in any line of commerce" refers to the particular *product market* in which the firms operate. For example, banks may be both in the credit market and the checking account market. The phrase "in any section of the country" has reference to a *geographic market.* The relevant area may be one city or may be the nation. Therefore, in determining the *relevant market*, the courts and antitrust authorities take into account the appropriate product and geographic markets.

After determining the relevant market, a firm's market share can be determined by dividing the firm's sales by total sales within that market. In a merger case, the court will often consider whether the combined market share of the merging firms will exceed some maximum market share and will, therefore, "substantially … lessen competition" within the relevant market. The determination of the product and geographic markets can be very complex.

Potential Competition

Ordinarily one thinks of competitors as offering similar products in the same market area. If the companies do not compete in this sense, should the courts be concerned about a merger? The Supreme Court has stated that the *potential competition* (the possibility that two companies will become *competitors*) may be enough to stop a merger.

LIGHTER SIDE OF THE LAW

Didn't We Just Sue Them Eighty Years Ago?

Kodak lost an antitrust case in 1915 that found the company "had monopolized the amateur camera, film, and photofinishing industries" by anticompetitive practices. The matter was resolved in 1921 when Kodak signed a consent decree. The company sold some of its assets and agreed not to sell "private-label" film, that is, film under any name besides Kodak.

Years later, in 1995, Kodak was arguing to a federal court that it should be freed from the 1921 decree and allowed to sell private-label film. The government opposed releasing Kodak from the decree, arguing that Kodak may still be benefiting from "its illegal monopoly ninety years ago." The court found, however, that the film market is competitive. Kodak has 36 percent of world sales, followed by Fuji at 34 percent, Konica at 16 percent, Agfa at 10 percent, and 3M at 4 percent. Since Kodak "lacks market power" in the film market, it was released from the 1921 decree. It has since quit the film market.

Source: *United States v. Kodak*, 63 F.3d 95 (1995)

Getty Images

For example, in *United States* v. *El Paso Natural Gas* (376 U.S. 651), a gas pipeline company with a large share of the natural gas market in California wanted to merge with a pipeline company that operated in the Northwest. The Court blocked the merger, because the possibility that the northwestern company could move into California served as a check on El Paso's operations in California. The Court wanted El Paso to have the threat of strong potential competition that would be eliminated by the merger.

The idea of potential competition was also used in *FTC* v. *Procter and Gamble* (386 U.S. 568), in which Procter and Gamble, a large household products maker, wanted to merge with Clorox, the leading maker of liquid bleach. After finding that bleach was the relevant product market, the Supreme Court held that even though Procter and Gamble did not make bleach, it could not merge with Clorox, because Procter and Gamble could make bleach in the future. The Court wanted Clorox to face the threat of potential competition by a company like Procter and Gamble.

When Mergers Are Allowed

The Supreme Court has noted that if one of the firms involved in a merger is facing bankruptcy or other circumstances that threaten the firm, the Court will look more favorably upon the merger. This is called the *failing firm defense*. That defense was created by the courts. To use the defense, the merging firms must establish that

1. the firm being acquired is not likely to survive without the merger.
2. either the firm has no other prospective buyers or, if there are other buyers, the acquiring firm will affect competition the least.
3. other alternatives for saving the firm have been tried but have not succeeded.

The merger guidelines also note that a major defense to a merger is the demonstration that it will enhance efficiency in the market, benefiting consumers by a better allocation of resources.

Considering Business Realities

The courts weigh economic evidence and, like the FTC and Justice Department, often find that mergers are not harmful to consumers. One defense used recently is the *power buyer defense*. Under this defense, a merger that increases concentration to high levels can be defended by showing that the firm's customers are sophisticated and powerful buyers. If the court finds that powerful buyers have sufficient bargaining power to ensure that the merged firm will be unable to charge monopoly prices, the merger might be allowed.

For example, in *United States* v. *Baker Hughes* (908 F.2d 981), the D.C. Circuit Court of Appeals denied the government's attempt to stop a merger of manufacturers of hard-rock hydraulic underground drilling rigs. Even though this industry had few sellers, the court found that the sophisticated and powerful buyers of such drilling rigs—oil companies—had sufficient bargaining power to ensure that the merged firm would be unable to charge monopoly prices for its rigs.

Horizontal Restraints of Trade

When businesses at the same level of operation, such as retailers of a common product or producers of a raw material, come together in some manner—through contract, merger, or conspiracy—they risk being accused of restraining trade. A *horizontal restraint of trade* occurs when the businesses involved operate at the same

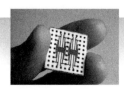

CYBER LAW

B2B Antitrust Concerns

Selling goods on the Internet has increased competition; retailers located anywhere have the potential to reach customers they could not have reached before. There are few antitrust issues in that regard. However, the growing use of the Internet for large buyers, such as Ford and Boeing, to obtain supplies in highly competitive markets has raised some concerns.

Many buyers use reverse auctions. The bidders post the lowest price at which they are willing to sell to the buyer who has announced how much of what is needed by when. The bidders see each others' bids and can change their bids up to the last second of the auction.

The result has been some substantial reductions in prices, and competition is very strong.

The FTC and the Department of Justice have stressed the need for competitors to use effective firewalls to prevent them from learning each other's sensitive information. Another issue has been the open nature of such bidding—where all bidders see each other's bids. The open records can increase the ability to collude, since all buyers or sellers can know what everyone else is bidding and thereby know if someone is willing to sell for less than the colluders' agreed-upon price. Such information was much harder for colluders to obtain when bids were all sealed.

Getty Images

level of the market and generally in the same market. It is easy to visualize a horizontal arrangement among competitors by examining the diagram in Exhibit 20.1. For example, think of three manufacturers of lightbulbs who agree to charge the same price for bulbs or to split the market on a geographical basis.

The diagram could also show an arrangement among wholesalers or among retailers of a certain product. A collection of rival firms that come together by some form of agreement in an attempt to restrain trade by restricting output and raising prices is called a *cartel*. The most famous cartel of our day is the Organization of Petroleum Exporting Countries *(OPEC)*, the group of oil-producing nations that banded together for the express purpose of controlling the output of oil and raising its price. Since that cartel consists of sovereign nations, American antitrust laws do not affect it. When private firms in the United States attempt to cartelize an industry, however, they are subject to antitrust law.

When firms selling the same product agree to fix prices, they are in a conspiracy and the agreement will almost certainly violate the Sherman Act. One question the Supreme Court must decide as a matter of policy is whether price fixing is illegal per se or whether a rule of reason may be applied.

Price-Fixing

Many antitrust cases have concerned price fixing. When firms sell the same product and agree to fix the price, they have formed a conspiracy that will likely violate the Sherman Act. Price fixing has usually been held to be the worst violation of the antitrust laws. In a 1927 case, *United States* v. *Trenton Potteries* (276 US 392), the

Exhibit 20.1
Horizontal Business
Relationships

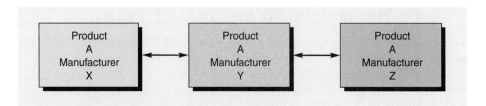

Supreme Court held that when competitors get together to fix prices, there is a violation of the Sherman Act, whether the prices they set are reasonable or not. The Court decision held that agreements to set prices "may well be held to be in themselves unreasonable or unlawful restraints, without the necessity of minute inquiry whether a particular price is reasonable or unreasonable." That is, most price fixing is a horizontal arrangement that is illegal per se. In the *Freeman* case, we see a modern application of this principle.

Freeman v. San Diego Association of Realtors

United States Court of Appeals, Ninth Circuit
322 F.3d 1133 (2003)

Case Background *In most cities, a Multiple Listing Service (MLS) is used by real estate agents to share information about properties on the market via a computerized database. Agents subscribe to the MLS to list the properties they represent, as well as to see information about other properties on the market.*

Before 1992, there were 12 such MLS associations in San Diego, California. The associations bought data services from four different database operators. Eleven of the MLS associations decided to combine so that all subscribing agents would have access to all San Diego properties; the combined database would also cost less to maintain than separate database. The new entity, owned by the 11 MLS associations, was called Sandicor. The 11 associations continued to sign up agents and collect subcription fees, but Sandicor set the rules. No price cutting was allowed. When the MLSes compared costs, they discovered that the largest MLS spent $10 per month per subscriber, while two small ones spent $50 per month per subscriber. The fee for all was set at $44 per subscribing agent, paid to Sandicor. That price was less than the $50 cost per subscriber that the small operators incurred, so the lower-cost MLSes agreed to cover the losses that the smaller MLS associations incurred.

Freeman and other San Diego real estate agents who subscribed to MLSes sued. They contended that Sandicor's central database was beneficial and efficient, but that the price of Sandicor's services was inflated. A service that had cost $10 a month at some MLSes was now $44. Plaintiffs contended that Sandicor was charging excessive service fees, allowing Sandicor to profit millions. Freeman offered Sandicor the opportunity to market the MLS information to subscribers through a new service center at lower prices than the existing associations charged, but Sandicor refused. Freeman sued for Sherman Act violations for a conspiracy in restraint of trade by fixing prices, a violation of Section 1. The district court dismissed the suit; plaintiffs appealed.

Case Decision Kozinski, Circuit Judge

* * *

No antitrust violation is more abominated than the agreement to fix prices. With few exceptions, price-fixing agreements are unlawful *per se* under the Sherman Act and ... no showing of so-called competitive abuses or evils which those agreements were designed to eliminate or alleviate may be interposed as a defense." The dispositive question generally is not whether any price fixing was justified, but simply whether it occurred....

Sandicor charges subscribers for their use of the MLS; its MLS fee includes the support services provided by the associations. The support fee Sandicor pays the associations for support services was fixed at a level more than twice what it cost the most efficient association to provide them....

Were we to grant immunity from Section 1 merely because defendants nominally sell services through another entity rather than to consumers directly, we would risk opening a major loophole for ... retailer collusion.... Sandicor charges MLS subscribers $44 per month; an association collects this fee from each subscriber and hands it over to Sandicor, which then returns $22.50 to the association as the support fee.... Defendants can't turn a horizontal agreement to fix prices into something innocuous just by changing the way they keep their books....

Reversed and remanded.

Questions for Analysis

1. The appeals court held that competitors improperly rigged prices. Sandicor claimed that the quality of its data was better, because all associations contributed data, and the subscribers got

continues

superior service. Why did that argument not matter?

2. Sandicor claimed that it helped competition because the smallest, highest-cost associations were kept in business, because they were subsidized by the larger ones. Why was that argument rejected?

While the courts take a hard line against collusion for the purpose of rigging prices, any one company has the right to charge whatever price it wishes for its products or services. The courts also recognize that certain organizations, such as joint ventures, may help markets to work better. In some cases, a joint venture helps to set market prices, and if a court finds that a good reason exists for this, it will allow the practice to stand.

Consider the problem faced by the thousands of artists and owners of music copyrights, who have the right to earn royalties when their music is played by thousands of radio stations and other commercial music users. Because the artists could not possibly contract with every user of their music, they join organizations such as Broadcast Music, Inc. (BMI) or the American Society of Composers, Authors and Publishers (ASCAP), which issue "blanket licenses" that set the fees to be paid by any commercial users of the music. In *Broadcast Music, Inc.* v. *CBS* (441 U.S. 1), the Court held that blanket licensing in such situations is not illegal price fixing, because there is no other way for this market to work. Since the market works better than it would if BMI and ASCAP did not exist, the "price fixing" is not illegal. But, in general, price fixing is rarely found to be legal.

Exchanges of Information

One problem in antitrust law is deciding whether the trading of information among businesses helps or restrains the competitive process. Some business information is collected and shared by the government, but many exchanges are done by private organizations, such as trade associations of firms in the same industry. If a business knows its competitors' sales, production, planned or actual capacities, cost accounting, quality standards, and research developments, is competition enhanced or is the information likely to be used to restrain trade?

Information Sharing

The Supreme Court considered the issue of the sharing of information by competitors in *United States* v. *United States Gypsum* (438 U.S. 422). Six major producers of gypsum called each other to determine the price being offered on gypsum products to various customers. That is, a buyer would tell Company B that Company A had offered to sell gypsum board at a certain price. Company B would call Company A to confirm the offer to make sure the buyer was telling the truth. The gypsum companies defended the practice as a good-faith effort to meet competition.

The Court said that a rule of reason may be applied, but the practice was not defensible. In an industry with few producers, an exchange of price information by competitors would most likely help to set prices and so could not be justified. The Court did not apply a per se rule against such price information exchanges. Instead, it warned that such exchanges would be examined closely and would be allowed in limited circumstances.

We see an example of illegal information sharing by competitors in the *Todd* case.

Todd v. Exxon Corporation
United States Court of Appeals, Second Circuit
275 F.3d 191 (2001)

Case Background *Fourteen large companies in the oil industry organized a system to conduct surveys of the salaries they each paid to managerial, professional, and technical (MPT) employees. They used a "Job Match Survey" to be sure that the jobs at each company were compared properly. Representatives of the companies met to discuss job classifications and other data issues. A consultant then analyzed, refined, and distributed the data to the 14 firms. The firms used the data in setting the salaries of MPT employees.*

Todd and other employees sued, contending that the sharing of information was done to hold down MPT salaries. Plaintiffs contended this violated Section 1 of the Sherman Act. They did not claim that the companies conspired to fix wages, but that the sharing of information allowed the employers to control wages more than they could have without such information. The district court dismissed the suit. Plaintiffs appealed.

Case Decision Sotomayor, Circuit Judge

* * *

Information exchange is an example of a facilitating practice that can help support an inference of a price-fixing agreement....

The [Supreme Court has explained]: "The exchange of price data and other information among competitors does not invariably have anticompetitve effects; indeed such practices can in certain circumstances increase economic efficiency and render markets more, rather than less, competitive." ...

Plaintiff argues that the relevant market in this case is the market for "the services of experienced, salaried, non-union, managerial, professional, and technical (MPT) employees in the oil and petrochemical industry, in the continental United States and various sub-markets therof." If the market is defined in this way, defendants would have a substantial market share of 80 to 90 percent....

The traditional horizontal conspiracy case involves an agreement among sellers with the purpose of raising prices to supracompetitve levels. The Sherman Act, however, also applies to abuse of market power on the buyer side—often taking the form of monopsony or oligopsony. Plaintiff is correct to point out that a horizontal conspiracy among buyers so stifle competition is as unlawful as one among sellers.... There is thus no reason to doubt that a ... data exchange claim—a close cousin of traditional price fixing—can be brought against a group of buyers....

If ... the plaintiff in this case could prove that (1) defendants engaged in information exchanges that would be deemed anticompetitive ... and (2) such activities did in fact have an anticompetitive effect on the market for MPT labor in the oil and petrochemical industry, we would not deny relief.... On remand, therefore, the court should consider whether plaintiff has demonstrated anticompetitive effects as part of the court's assessment of defendant's market power....

Another important factor to consider in evaluating an information exchange is whether the data are made publicly available. Public dissemination is a primary way for data exchange to realize its procompetitive potential.... Access to information may better equip buyers to compare products, rendering the market more efficient while diminishing the anticompetitive effects of the exchange. A court is therefore more likely to approve a data exchange where the information is made public.

In the instant case, dissemination of the information to the employees could have helped mitigate any anticompetitive effects of the exchange and possibly enhanced market efficiency by making employees more sensitive to salary increases. No such dissemination occurred, however. The information was not disclosed to the public nor to the employees whose salaries were the subject of the exchange....

Remanded.

Questions for Analysis
1. The appeals court held that the information sharing could violate the Sherman Act. Wage information is often gathered and published. Why is it normally legal?
2. The district court held that the oil companies did not control the MPT market, but that contention was rejected by the appeals court. Why might that court see it differently?

Conspiracy to Restrict Information

Although the courts have indicated that it is generally legal to share price information in an open manner, and it is illegal to share information secretly among competitors or for the purpose of constructing a common price list for competitors, it may also be illegal to band together to restrict certain nonprice information.

In the Supreme Court decision *FTC* v. *Indiana Federation of Dentists* (476 U.S. 447) the Court held that the FTC justifiably attacked the policy of an Indiana dentists' organization requiring members to withhold X rays from dental insurance companies. Insurance companies sometimes required dentists to submit patient X rays to help evaluate patients' claims for insurance benefits. The X rays helped the companies eliminate insurance fraud and make sure that dentists did not prescribe dental work not required. The FTC attack on this policy was upheld under a rule of reason analysis that showed the dentists' policy to be a conspiracy in restraint of trade. The Court noted that no procompetitive reason for the anti–X-ray-sharing rule was found.

LIGHTER SIDE OF THE LAW
We're Lawyers, and We're Here to Help You

Nineteen lawyers teamed together to bring a class-action antitrust suit on behalf of consumers against three gasoline retailers in Dothan, Alabama. In a trial that lasted six weeks in federal court, the jury found that there was a conspiracy to fix gasoline prices. Damages were found to be $1. However, under the law, the guilty party is also responsible for attorney's fees. The judge granted the attorneys $2 million in legal fees for their diligent efforts.

Source: *Associated Press*

Getty Images

Exhibit 20.2
Avoiding Antitrust
Problems at Trade
Meetings

Antitrust Reminder

Competitors often meet when attending industry conventions. This means firms could share information improperly and even plan to act together. Because of this possibility, it is common for meeting organizers to remind participants of antitrust problems that could emerge from their being together. Here is a list from one trade association meeting.

DON'T

- Discuss with other members your own, or your competitors', prices or anything that might affect prices, such as costs, discounts, terms of sale, or profit margins.
- Make public announcements or statements about your own prices or those of competitors.
- Talk about what your company, or any other company, plans to do in particular geographic or product markets or with particular customers.
- Disclose to others at meetings any competitively sensitive information.
- Stay at a meeting where any such price, or competitively sensitive, talk occurs.

DO

- Always look for and adhere to a written agenda, and limit discussion to agenda or non business topics.
- Consult your corporate counsel in case of doubt about the propriety of a topic of discussion.
- State any reservations you have concerning remarks or discussion at a meeting; if the discussion is not terminated or resolved satisfactorily, leave the meeting.
- Avoid "rump sessions" involving the discussion of business matters.

Territorial Restrictions

A horizontal market division occurs when firms competing at the same level of business reach an agreement to divide the market on geographic or other terms. The effect of the agreement is to eliminate competition among those firms. Firms competing in a national market, for example, may reach an agreement to divide the market into regional markets, with each firm being assigned one region. Each firm can then exercise monopoly power within its region.

Agreements intended to provide horizontal *customer allocations* or *territorial allocations* are often held to violate antitrust law. When the agreement does not involve price fixing by the firms participating in the agreement, the case may be considered under a rule of reason; that is, each challenged agreement will be evaluated in light of its effect on consumer welfare. This has not been a common basis for antitrust cases in recent years.

ISSUE SPOTTER

Share and Share Alike

Your customers, retail housing construction supply firms, tell you that the price your pipe production company is asking for PVC pipe is too high and that they will be taking their business elsewhere. The profit margins are thin, and you are not interested in cutting prices unless it is absolutely necessary to retain business. When you go to the annual PVC pipe makers convention, how might you legally find out what your competitors are charging? What type of action would be most likely to get you into trouble with the antitrust authorities?

Getty Images

Vertical Restraint of Trade

Until now, we have considered antitrust law mostly as it applies to horizontal restraints of trade. We now turn to antitrust issues such as vertical restraint of trade, exclusionary practices, and price discrimination. *Vertical restraint of trade* concerns relationships between buyers and sellers, such as between the manufacturer and its wholesalers or the wholesalers and retailers. A key subject of this part of the chapter is how firms deal with each other along the business chain. We look at how producers', distributors', and retailers' dealings are controlled by antitrust law.

Vertical business arrangements govern relationships in the different stages of the production, distribution, and sale of the same product, as we see in Exhibit 20.3. For example, think of a manufacturer that imposes resale restrictions on the retailers. The producer tells the retailer the price it must set at retail (the resale price), the area in which there may be resales, or who the retailer's customers may be. Since these arrangements may restrain competition, they may be challenged as being contrary to the goals of antitrust law.

A company that does more than one function internally, such as manufacturing and distribution, is not constrained by the antitrust laws. However, a group of firms doing business at different levels in a given product are prohibited from engaging in certain practices.

Vertical Price Fixing

Vertical price-fixing arrangements involve agreements between a manufacturer, its wholesalers, its distributors or other suppliers, and the retailers that sell the product

Exhibit 20.3
Vertical Business
Relationships

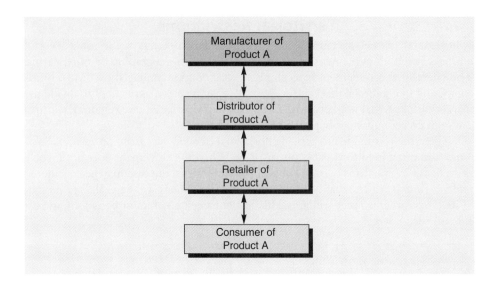

to consumers. As a rule, these are intended to control the price at which the product is sold to consumers. In many cases, it has been the retailers that approach the manufacturer and request a price agreement. In other instances, the manufacturer requires the wholesaler (supplier) to control the price being charged by retailers. Agreements can call for the retailer to fix minimum prices or maximum prices.

Resale Price Maintenance

Resale price maintenance (RPM) is an agreement between a manufacturer, a supplier, and retailers of a product under which the retailers agree to sell the product at not less than a minimum price. One purpose of these arrangements is to prevent retailers from cutting the price of a brand-name product. Although manufacturers contend that such arrangements make product distribution more efficient, such arrangements can be an illegal restraint of trade.

Dr. Miles Case In 1911 the Supreme Court pronounced a basic rule about RPM. It stated that once a producer or supplier sells a product to a retailer, it cannot control the price the retailer will charge consumers. In *Dr. Miles Medical* v. *John D. Park and Sons* (220 U.S. 373), the court held that a manufacturer can, of course, sell its product for whatever it wants, but it cannot "fix prices for future sales." That is, it cannot set prices further down the sales chain.

Pros and Cons of Resale Price Maintenance RPM has been the subject of political wrangling in Congress and of debate by lawyers and economists since the time of *Dr. Miles.* The groups favoring the ability to control resale prices have been the producers of quality, well-known products and small retailers. Opponents have been mass retailers and producers of lesser-known products.

Many small retailers favor RPM. They cannot match Wal-Mart prices, so they would like to see all retailers forced to offer goods at the same prices. Even in the absence of competition from discount retailers, if the retailers are strong enough, they band together to demand that the producer impose RPM so that retailers will not compete with each other by price cutting. RPM thus prevents cheating by members of the retail cartel.

Producers of well-known, established products (such as Sony televisions) may favor RPM, because it allows retailers to earn higher profits from the sale of their products. These higher retail profits, in turn, encourage retailers to advertise the products more to customers and to give good service.

Mass retailers oppose RPM, because they have grown large by slashing retail prices and taking customers away from smaller stores. The mass retailers often offer little point-of-sale service; their concern is selling a large volume of products at lower markup. Similarly, the producers of lesser-known brands want to compete on the basis of price, so they like the chance to be on the mass retailers' shelves with the best-known products. They have not incurred the high costs of establishing a good reputation, so their prices are lower, even if the quality is good. If the result is that fewer full-service stores can afford to stay in business, RPM advocates claim that consumers and well-established brands may be worse off by the disappearance of the information and service that would be provided under an RPM arrangement.

Vertical Maximum Price-Fixing

The Supreme Court has held that some price fixing in vertical relationships is acceptable.

In *State Oil Co.* v. *Khan* (118 S.Ct. 275), a gasoline distributor controlled the maximum gasoline sales markup that its gasoline station dealers could charge customers. One gas station owner wanted to charge more for retail gasoline than the distributor would allow and sued, claiming this was illegal price fixing. The Supreme Court upheld the maximum-price controls, noting that low prices benefit consumers regardless of how the prices are set. A rule of reason will be applied in such cases.

Vertical Minimum Price-Fixing

After 96 years the Supreme Court limited the rule from the *Dr. Miles* case by holding that vertical minimum price-fixing, or resale price maintenance, was no long per se illegal. Since the *Leegin* case, it has been subject to a rule of reason analysis. That is, when a manufacturer imposes resale prices, such as retail prices to be set by stores on certain products, the courts will look to see if the practice, in a particular case is destructive to competition or not. As the Court explained, intrabrand competition must be considered as well as interbrand competition.

Leegin Creative Leather Products v. PSKS
United States Supreme Court
127 S.Ct. 2705 (2007)

Case Background *Leegin designs, makes, and distributes leather goods. Most popular are belts with the brand name "Brighton." It is sold across the country in over 5,000 stores, that are mostly independent, small boutiques and specialty stores. Leegin refused to sell to retailers that discounted Brighton goods below suggested prices. Products not selling well that the retailer did not plan on reordering could be discounted.*

Leegin told the stores that bought from it: "In this age of mega stores like Macy's ... consumers are perplexed by promises of product quality and support of product which we believe is lacking in these large stores. Consumers are further confused by the ever popular sale, sale, sale, etc." The Leegin policy was consistent prices that allowed selected retailers to earn good profits so they would support the Brighton brand.

Leegin discovered that Kay's Kloset, a retail store in Texas, was consistently discounting Brighton-brand products by 20 percent. It requested Kay's stop the price cutting below suggested retail prices, but it did not, so Leegin quit selling to it. Kay's then sued Leegin for violating Section 1 of the Sherman Act. At trial, the court would not allow expert testimony about the economic benefits of the Leegin policy, holding that resale price maintenance was a per se violation. The
continues

jury awarded Kay's $1.2 million damages, which were tripled. The appeals court affirmed. Leegin appealed.

Case Decision Kennedy, Justice

* * *

Though each side of the debate can find sources to support its position, it suffices to say here that economics literature is replete with procompetitive justifications for a manufacturer's use of resale price maintenance....

Minimum resale price maintenance can stimulate interbrand competition—the competition among manufacturers selling different brands of the same type of product—by reducing intrabrand competition-the competition among retailers selling the same brand. The promotion of interbrand competition is important because "the primary purpose of the antitrust laws is to protect [this type of] competition." A single manufacturer's use of vertical price restraints tends to eliminate intrabrand price competition; this in turn encourages retailers to invest in tangible or intangible services or promotional efforts that aid the manufacturer's position as against rival manufacturers. Resale price maintenance also has the potential to give consumers more options so that they can choose among low-price, low-service brands; high-price, high-service brands; and brands that fall in between.

Absent vertical price restraints, the retail services that enhance interbrand competition might be underprovided. This is because discounting retailers can free ride on retailers who furnish services and then capture some of the increased demand those services generate. Consumers might learn, for example, about the benefits of a manufacturer's product from a retailer that invests in fine showrooms, offers product demonstrations, or hires and trains knowledgeable employees....

Resale price maintenance, in addition, can increase interbrand competition by facilitating market entry for new firms and brands....

While vertical agreements setting minimum resale prices can have procompetitive justifications, they may have anticompetitive effects in other cases; and unlawful price fixing, designed solely to obtain monopoly profits, is an ever present temptation. Resale price maintenance may, for example, facilitate a manufacturer cartel....

To the extent a vertical agreement setting minimum resale prices is entered upon to facilitate a ... cartel, it would need to be held unlawful under the rule of reason....

For these reasons the Court's decision in *Dr. Miles Medical Co. v. John D. Park & Sons Co.*, 220 U.S. 373, 31 S.Ct. 376 (1911), is now overruled. Vertical price restraints are to be judged according to the rule of reason....

The judgment of the Court of Appeals is reversed, and the case is remanded for proceedings consistent with this opinion.

Questions for Analysis

1. Assuming resale price maintenance to be generally legal, what kind of companies do you think would benefit the most from the practice?
2. This overturned a rule set in a case almost 100 years ago. Should courts overturn old rulings?

Vertical Nonprice Restraints

Manufacturers frequently impose nonprice restraints on their distributors and retailers. Such vertical arrangements often take the form of territorial or customer restrictions on the sale of the manufacturer's products. Coca-Cola and PepsiCo, for example, set *territorial restrictions* on their bottlers. Each bottler is permitted to sell and deliver the product within its designated territory. Delivery outside that territory—that is, delivery in competition with another bottler—is grounds for loss of the franchise agreement.

Customer restrictions may be imposed on distributors and retailers when the manufacturer sells directly to a certain customers. A construction materials manufacturer, for example, may deal directly with large commercial accounts but allow distributors to deal with smaller accounts. The courts apply the rule of reason in such cases.

In most territorial restraint cases, the plaintiff is a retailer or distributor that has been terminated by a manufacturer changing its product distribution strategy.

The manufacturer often eliminates some distributors so that the remaining distributors have the necessary territorial or customer base to be successful.

Exclusionary Practices

A principal concern of the antitrust laws is the extent to which firms with market power can control the markets in which they do business. Various business practices are designed to make it more difficult for competitors to challenge the market dominance of the firm using such tactics. Such practices, which include tying arrangements, exclusive-dealing agreements, and boycotts, can come under antitrust attack if the courts find them to be anticompetitive. Section 3 of the Clayton Act applies to tying arrangements and exclusive-dealing agreements involving goods, while Section 1 of the Sherman Act, which covers goods and services, governs the antitrust aspects of group boycotts.

Tying Arrangements

In *Northern Pacific Railway Company* v. *United States* (356 U.S. 1), the Supreme Court defined a *tying arrangement* or *tie-in sale* as

> an agreement by a party to sell one product [the tying product] but only on the condition that the buyer also purchases a different [complementary or tied] product, or at least agrees that he will not purchase that product from any other supplier.

The Supreme Court holds that where monopoly power exists, tying arrangements violate the antitrust laws; the arrangement extends a firm's market power over the tying product into the market for the tied product. The courts apply either Section 1 of the Sherman Act—viewing tying arrangements as an unreasonable restraint of trade—or Section 3 of the Clayton Act—viewing tying arrangements as a sales contract that may substantially lessen competition or tend to create a monopoly.

The practice of tying products together is found in other, generally legal, business practices. A grocery store, for example, that offers Brand A flour at half price when a buyer purchases a bag of Brand A sugar is conducting a legal tie-in sale, because Brand A and the grocery store have no monopoly power over either product.

Rule of Reason Applied to Tie-In Cases The Supreme Court has held that tie-ins meet a rule of reason test so long as competitive alternatives exist. That is, if a tie-in creates a monopoly, when there are no or few good alternatives, it is likely illegal; but if products or services are tied together when there are competitors, the tie-in will likely pass the rule of reason test, as the Court held in *U.S. Steel* v. *Fortner Enterprises* (429 U.S. 610).

U.S. Steel produced mobile homes. Fortner needed $2 million to develop land on which to place mobile homes that he promised to buy from U.S. Steel if it would loan him the money. U.S. Steel made the loan. Later, Fortner's venture failed, and he claimed the contract with U.S. Steel violated antitrust law because there was a tie-in between the purchase of homes and the financing. The mobile homes were the product tied to U.S. Steel's alleged power over the credit market. The Court rejected that argument, holding that U.S. Steel, while large, had no monopoly power over credit or over mobile homes, which are in highly competitive markets. Since the tie-in did not exploit any monopoly power, the actions of U.S. Steel did not violate the antitrust law under a rule of reason analysis.

Getty Images

INTERNATIONAL PERSPECTIVE

European Antitrust

The European Union (EU) is gradually developing a common antitrust policy for EU countries. It is taking decades, because each country has economic interests they wish to protect against increased competition. Nevertheless, a set of rules rather similar to U.S. antitrust law is emerging. Since most large companies are global in operations, they would prefer similar rules in all countries, so they can adapt policies to all operations.

Traditionally there have been a trivial number of antitrust actions in Europe. One study found only 12 successful antitrust actions in Europe from 1962 to 2004. The United States has had much tougher

competition policies—and hundreds of antitrust cases every year—but now U.S. antitrust lawyers are moving in to help craft cases in Europe based on U.S. experience.

Leading the way are legal actions in the EU that are based in the United Kingdom. The legal system in the U.K. gives plaintiffs a more favorable base for an antitrust case than do most countries in Europe. It allows pretrial discovery to obtain evidence from corporate defendants. Firms can invest in cases in exchange for a percentage of awards, thereby bankrolling cases that look like good bets. Victims of price-fixing schemes can sue in the U.K. to recover losses that occurred throughout the EU. And, being based in the U.K., all the lawyers can speak English, making it much easier for U.S. litigators to bring their skills to the table.

Vertical Restraint Guidelines

The Department of Justice's *Vertical Restraint Guidelines* claim that the Supreme Court is likely to impose a per se rule of illegality only when three conditions are met:

1. The seller has market power in the tying product.
2. Tied and tying products are separate.
3. There is evidence of substantial adverse effect in the tied product market.

In other situations, the rule of reason approach is to be employed. The Justice Department said that in such cases, the following test would hold:

> The use of tying will not be challenged if the party imposing the tie has a market share of 30 percent or less in the market for the tying product. This presumption can be overcome only by a showing that the tying agreement unreasonably restrained competition in the market for the tied product.

The Supreme Court found an illegal tie-in arrangement in *Eastman Kodak* v. *Image Technical Services* (504 U.S. 451). Kodak, a maker of complex equipment, refused to sell replacement parts for its machines to independent companies that offered repair and maintenance service on the machines. Kodak required buyers of its machines to use its repair personnel in order to obtain Kodak replacement parts. Independent repair companies lost business, and some went out of business. The Court held that Kodak used its market power over the machines to extend the power to replacement parts. That would not be allowed unless Kodak could show that the practice promoted competition in the market for the machinery.

Boycotts

A *boycott* occurs when a group conspires to prevent the carrying on of business or to harm a business. It can be promoted by any group—consumers, union members, retailers, wholesalers, or suppliers—who, when acting together, can inflict economic damage on a business. The boycott is used to force compliance with a price-fixing scheme or some other restraint of trade. Boycott cases usually fall under the per se rule against price fixing.

Unlike other vertical restrictions in which one manufacturer negotiates with individual dealers about terms of trade for its goods, boycotts involve either all manufacturers getting together to tell dealers what they must do, or all dealers getting together to tell manufacturers what they must do. The Supreme Court has made clear that when horizontal competitors use a boycott to force a change in the nature of a vertical relationship, there is a per se violation of the law. These cases are not common.

LIGHTER SIDE OF THE LAW
Give Us What We Want, or We Will Throw a Tantrum

Where a Web site shows up in a Google or Yahoo! search depends on many factors. The formula is complex, but it is partly a function of how many other searchers have looked at a Web site. The algorithm is secret to try to reduce the gaming that Web site owners engage in to try to get a higher ranking for their sites than they earn otherwise.

KinderStart.com is a specialty search engine designed for "children zero to seven." Google gave KinderStart.com a low Page Rank (PR) based on the formula it uses. The low PR meant little traffic.

So KinderStart.com sued Google for being anti competitive in its PR system. It accused Google of Sherman Act violations and, of course, demanded money and demanded that Google reveal its trade secrets about how it sets PRs.

Source: *True Stella Awards*

Getty Images

The Robinson–Patman Act

The Robinson–Patman Act, enacted in 1936, amends the Clayton Act. Section 2(a) states that "it shall be unlawful for any person engaged in commerce … to discriminate in price between different purchasers of commodities of like grade and quality … where the effect of such discrimination may be substantially to lessen competition or tend to create a monopoly in any line of commerce." Thus, a seller is said to engage in *price discrimination* when the same product is sold to different buyers at different prices.

Section 2(a) is perhaps the most controversial part of antitrust law, as the reason for its passage was to limit the ability of chain stores to offer merchandise at a price lower than their single-store competitors. The intent of the Act is to deny consumers the benefits from lower prices that result from mass merchandising. As a consequence, the Department of Justice and the FTC have been reluctant to enforce the Act. Most cases brought under the Robinson–Patman Act are private actions.

Price Discrimination

Many cases brought under the Robinson–Patman Act concern a firm charging different prices in different markets or offering bulk sale discounts to larger volume retailers. To illustrate, suppose that two sellers—Simpson's Wholesale and South Park Distributors—sell the same product in competition with each other in San Francisco. Simpson's also sells the product in Oakland, but South Park does not. If Simpson's reduces its price levels in San Francisco but not in Oakland, that price cut may violate the Robinson–Patman Act. Simpson's is engaging in price discrimination—charging different prices in different markets to the detriment of a competitor, which in this case is South Park.

Predatory Pricing

The business practice just described is sometimes called *predatory pricing*. That is, Simpson's attempts to undercut South Park in San Francisco and sells the product for a higher price in other markets in which it does not compete with South Park. Presumably, Simpson's intends to drive South Park from the San Francisco market and then raise prices there when South Park goes out of business.

Firms can file suits alleging predatory pricing under both the Robinson–Patman Act and Section 2 of the Sherman Act. However, because it is difficult to distinguish predatory prices from prices driven low by competition, the Supreme Court today is reluctant to rule in favor of plaintiffs alleging predation.

To win, a plaintiff must present strong evidence showing that

1. the defendant priced below cost.
2. the defendant's below-cost prices created a genuine prospect that the defendant would monopolize the market.
3. the defendant would enjoy its monopoly at least long enough to recoup the losses it suffered during the price war.

The Court puts this heavy burden on predatory-pricing plaintiffs because it understands that firms might otherwise sue their price-cutting rivals for no reason other than to keep these rivals from lowering prices to competitive levels. As the Court said in *Brooke Group* (113 S.Ct. 2578), "It would be ironic indeed if the standards for predatory pricing liability were so low that antitrust suits themselves became a tool for keeping prices high." In the *Weyerhaeuser* case, the Supreme Court extended the analysis to include what some have called *predatory bidding*—when a strong firm can outbid rivals.

Weyerhaeuser v. Ross–Simmons Hardwood Lumber
Supreme Court of the United States
127 S.Ct. 1069 (2007)

Case Background *Ross–Simmons sued Weyerhaeuser for antitrust violation for driving it out of business. The claim was that Weyerhaeuser consistently outbid Ross for logs to process into lumber. Ross contended this was predatory behavior—Weyerhaeuser bid higher to get control of the logs, so Ross could not compete in the lumber market. Weyerhaeuser used state-of-the-art technology to increase efficiency and captured 65 percent of the red alder log market in the area around Longview, Washington. The jury held for Ross, awarding it $26 million. The appeals court affirmed. Weyerhaeuser appealed, claiming the holding violated the Supreme Court's previous decision in the* Brooke Group *case.*

Case Decision Thomas, Justice

* * *

Predatory bidding, which Ross–Simmons alleges in this case, involves the exercise of market power on the buy side or input side of a market. In a predatory-bidding scheme, a purchaser of inputs "bids up the market price of a critical input to such high levels that rival buyers cannot survive (or compete as vigorously) and, as a result, the predating buyer acquires (or maintains or increases its) monopsony power." Monopsony power is market power on the buy side of the market. As such, a monopsony is to the buy side of the market what a monopoly is to the sell side and is sometimes colloquially called a "buyer's monopoly."

A predatory bidder ultimately aims to exercise the monopsony power gained from bidding up input prices. To that end, once the predatory bidder has caused competing buyers to exit the market for purchasing inputs, it will seek to "restrict its input purchases below the competitive level," thus "reducing the unit price for the remaining inputs it purchases." The reduction in input prices will lead to "a significant cost saving that more than offsets the profits that would have been earned on the output." If all goes as planned, the predatory bidder will reap monopsonistic profits that will offset any losses suffered in bidding up input prices.

Predatory-pricing and predatory-bidding claims are analytically similar....

Tracking the economic similarity between monopoly and monopsony, predatory-pricing plaintiffs and predatory-bidding plaintiffs make strikingly similar allegations. A predatory-pricing plaintiff alleges that a predator cut prices to drive the plaintiff out of business and, thereby, to reap monopoly profits from the output market. In parallel fashion, a predatory-bidding plaintiff alleges that a predator raised prices for a key input to drive the plaintiff out of business and, thereby, to reap monopsony profits in the input market. Both claims involve the deliberate use of unilateral pricing measures for anticompetitive purposes. And both claims logically require firms to incur short-term losses on the chance that they might reap supracompetitive profits in the future....

More importantly, predatory bidding mirrors predatory pricing in respects that we deemed significant to our analysis in *Brooke Group*.... Predatory pricing requires a firm to suffer certain losses in the short term on the chance of reaping supracompetitive profits in the future. A rational business will rarely make this sacrifice. The same reasoning applies to predatory bidding. A predatory-bidding scheme requires a buyer of inputs to suffer losses today on the chance that it will reap supracompetitive profits in the future....

A predatory-bidding plaintiff also must prove that the defendant has a dangerous probability of recouping the losses incurred in bidding up input prices through the exercise of monopsony power. Absent proof of likely recoupment, a strategy of predatory bidding makes no economic sense, because it would involve short-term losses with no likelihood of offsetting long-term gains.....

Ross–Simmons has conceded that it has not satisfied the *Brooke Group* standard. Therefore, its predatory-bidding theory of liability cannot support the jury's verdict.

For these reasons, we vacate the judgment of the Court of Appeals and remand the case for further proceedings consistent with this opinion.

Questions for Analysis

1. The Supreme Court held that there was no basis for an antitrust suit based on a claim of predatory bidding. Since Ross was driven from the market, why did its claim not hold?
2. If Weyerhaeuser was more profitable than Ross, why could Ross not show that Weyerhaeuser had an unfair advantage in the market?

Volume Discounts Legal?

The Robinson–Patman Act is also concerned with sales discounts given to large-volume retailers. To illustrate, suppose Simpson's and South Park both buy the same product from Myspace Distributors for the purpose of selling it retail. Because Simpson's is a larger-volume retailer, Myspace gives Simpson's a price discount on its larger bulk purchases. The price discount gives Simpson's a competitive advantage over South Park in the sale of the product to customers in the area. The alleged injury to competition is the price discount given to Simpson's, the larger purchaser. This type of action generates numerous private actions against producers who discriminate in pricing to wholesalers or retailers.

ISSUE SPOTTER
Who Do You Sell What to, and for How Much?

Your company sells appliances. You handle the selling of refrigerators to retailers. Your Big Box model has a wholesale price of $629, plus actual shipping cost. Home Depot calls and wants to buy 20,000 Big Box units over ten months. Bob's Home Store calls and wants to buy ten Big Box units over ten months. Home Depot wants a discount because of the size of its order. Can you give them a discount? What about Bob's? How might Robinson-Patman apply?

Getty Images

Defenses

A key defense for firms charged with violating the Robinson–Patman Act is to show a *cost justification* for different prices charged in different markets or to different buyers. An obvious cost-justification defense is a difference in transportation costs—it costs more to transport a refrigerator 300 miles than 50 miles. Similarly, on a per-unit basis, it is cheaper to deliver a thousand refrigerators than it is to deliver five refrigerators. The major problem with using the cost-justification defense is that it is virtually an accounting impossibility to assign specific costs of production to individual products. As a consequence, the cost-justification defense is rarely successful by itself.

The other defense that may be used is that of *meeting competition*. That is, a firm cuts its price in response to a competitor's cutting its price first. The problem with this defense can be that the original price cut will be held illegal under Robinson–Patman, which will mean that subsequent price cuts may also be illegal, at least at some point. Competitors must show that the meeting-competition price cut was done in good faith, not in an effort to injure competitors but to stay competitive.

Summary

- The three most important antitrust statutes—the Sherman Act of 1890, the Clayton Act of 1914, and the FTC Act of 1914—were enacted in response to concern about the economic power of the large industrial corporations and trusts that emerged during the late nineteenth century. Before the enactment of the statutes, common-law precedent was relied on to combat certain restraints on trade, but the government had little authority to intervene.
- Congress exempts labor unions and others from the antitrust laws. The state action doctrine allows states to regulate business in such a way as to fix prices or otherwise monopolize a market.
- Violations of the antitrust laws can expose defendants to criminal penalties, which can include prison sentences, as well as civil penalties. Defendants who lose antitrust suits in which damages are found must pay treble damages. The antitrust laws are enforced by the Antitrust Division of the Justice Department, the Federal Trade Commission, and private parties. Only the Justice Department can bring criminal charges for alleged antitrust violations.
- Most antitrust matters are determined by a rule of reason analysis, where the courts weigh the pros and cons of business practices alleged to be anticompetitive. Some practices, such as price fixing by competitors, are so clearly anticompetitive that they are declared to be illegal per se.
- Horizontal restraints of trade occur when business competitors at the same level of business, such as producers of similar products, agree to act together.
- Mergers of competitor companies are likely to be challenged only if the merger would significantly reduce competition in a market. The market is defined along both territory and product lines.
- Independent companies in the same industry are usually not allowed to agree to divide the market geographically, by type of customer, or in any other arrangement that reduces competition.
- Horizontal price fixing occurs when competitors agree to act together to set prices for their products or services. This can happen at any level of operation and is usually illegal per se.
- There is no defense for companies in the same industry that get together, by any means, to agree on product prices in the markets in which they operate.

Prices may not be fixed at any level by competitors unless there are special circumstances that make the arrangement procompetitive, which is rare.

- Companies in an industry may share price and other market information through a trade association so long as the information is not used to control the market, and the information is available to the public.

- Vertical relationships are between sellers and buyers at different levels of business, such as between manufacturer and distributor. Vertical restraints of trade occur when a firm at one level of business controls the practices of a firm at another level, such as a distributor telling a retailer what price to charge its customers for its products.

- Vertical price fixing, or resale price maintenance, in which the producer tells the retailers of its products the minimum prices at which to sell the products, is illegal per se. Suggested retail prices are legal but may not be enforced by a threat to cut off a retailer who will not adhere to them.

- Vertical nonprice restraints, such as granting exclusive territory to dealers, are viewed under a rule of reason. Manufacturers are given wide latitude in picking dealers and deciding the terms under which they will retain them. The producer may not conspire with a dealer against another dealer.

- Tie-in sales, where the sale of one product is tied to the sale of another, are judged under a rule of reason. For such a sale to be illegal, it must be shown that monopoly power in one product existed and was extended to the other product.

- When any organized group at one level of business (such as hardware store owners) gets together to agree to a joint action (such as refusal to deal) against one or more businesses at another level of business (such as a particular hardware supplier), such action is a boycott, which is usually illegal per se.

- The Robinson–Patman Act holds that price discrimination—selling the same product to different buyers at different prices—must be justified by differences in the cost of selling to the different buyers or because the price difference was required to meet competition. This is one of the most troublesome areas of law for producers, since hundreds of private lawsuits are filed each year by unhappy buyers (usually retailers) claiming they were discriminated against. The courts are not sympathetic to such cases, but they pose expensive problems that can be avoided by careful planning with legal counsel.

Terms to Know

You should be able to define the following terms:

injunction, 506	failing firm defense, 511	tying arrangement, 521
rule of reason, 507	horizontal restraint of trade, 511	boycott, 522
per se rule, 507	cartel, 512	price discrimination, 523
market power, 509	territorial allocations, 517	predatory pricing, 524
market share, 510	vertical restraint of trade, 517	predatory bidding, 524
potential competition, 510	resale price maintenance, 518	

Discussion Question

1. Why was the Sherman Act written in such broad language? Is it possible that Congress wrote the legislation in an unclear manner to give the courts broad leeway in attacking monopolistic business practices? Would it have been better for Congress to have specified more of the terms of antitrust violations?

Case Questions

1. Many professional engineers belong to a trade association called the National Society of Professional Engineers, which governs the nontechnical aspects of the practice of engineering. The canon of ethics adopted by the society held that engineers could not bid against one another for a particular job. The society claimed that this rule was to prevent engineers from engaging in price cutting to get engineering jobs, which could then give them incentives to cut corners on the quality of work to save time and resources. Such a practice could lead to inferior work that could endanger the public. The Justice Department sued, claiming that this was a violation of Section 1 of the Sherman Act. The government claimed that the ethical rule reduced price competition and gave an unfair advantage to engineers with well-established reputations. Who wins? [*National Society of Professional Engineers* v. *United States*, 98 S.Ct. 1355 (1978)]

2. Professional basketball players and their union sued the National Basketball Association (NBA) for various practices, such as the draft of college players and its salary-cap system. They claimed that this violated the antitrust law by restricting opportunities for professional basketball players. Could such practices survive a rule of reason analysis? [*NBA* v. *Williams*, 45 F.3d 684, 2nd Cir. (1995)]

   ✓ Check your answer at http://academic.cengage.com/blaw/meiners

3. Certified registered nurse anesthetists (CRNAs) sued a hospital and its doctors, claiming a violation of Section 1 of the Sherman Act, based on the hospital's staffing decision to terminate its contract with the CRNAs and instead use a group of physician anesthesiologists, a competitor, that would provide anesthesia services for the hospital at a lower cost. The district court dismissed the case. Was that the correct decision? [*BCB Anesthesia Care* v. *Passavant Memorial Area Hospital*, 36 F.3d 664, 7th Cir. (1994)]

4. Several companies operated downhill ski facilities in Aspen, Colorado. They all sold a joint ticket that allowed skiers to ski at all facilities; the receipts were later divided according to various use rates. Eventually, one firm owned all the ski areas but one. This firm stopped issuing the joint ticket and instead issued a ticket good for all of its ski areas. The firm that owned only one ski facility saw its market share fall from 20 percent to 11 percent over a four-year period. It sued, claiming that the larger firm violated Section 2 of the Sherman Act by attempting to monopolize skiing by ending the joint ticket arrangement. Is the sale of the joint ticket a violation of the antitrust law? [*Aspen Skiing Company* v. *Aspen Highlands Skiing Corporation*, 472 U.S. 585, 105 S.Ct. 2847 (1985)]

   ✓ Check your answer at http://academic.cengage.com/blaw/meiners

5. For years the American Medical Association (AMA) stated that chiropractors were unscientific cult members. The Principles of Medical Ethics of the AMA said that a "physician should practice a method of healing founded on a scientific basis; and she should not voluntarily associate with anyone who violates this principle." This was the basis of medical discrimination against chiropractic until the AMA dropped these statements in 1980. Five chiropractors sued the AMA after 1980, claiming that the effect of the past actions had "lingering effects" that injured their business in the medical market and that this was an illegal boycott. What resulted? [*Wilk* v. *AMA*, 895 F.2d 352, 7th Cir. (1990)]

6. Raymond Syufy bought all of Las Vegas's first-run movie theaters. The government sued Syufy for monopolization. While admitting that he had a substantial share of the market, Syufy defended his mergers by pointing out the following facts: first, movie prices in Las Vegas were no higher than movie prices in comparable cities; second, no sooner did Syufy acquire all of Las Vegas's first-run theaters than other competitors successfully entered the market; and third, movie studios (for example, Paramount Pictures) are such powerful firms with an interest in avoiding theater monopolization that they can be relied upon to ensure that Syufy does not abuse his market dominance. Evaluate Syufy's arguments. [*United States* v. *Syufy*, 903 F.2d 659, 9th Cir. (1990)]

   ✓ Check your answer at http://academic.cengage.com/blaw/meiners

7. Coca-Cola required independent food distributors (IFDs) that sold its fountain syrup to sign a loyalty agreement that they would not sell any Pepsi products so long as they were selling Coke products. Pepsi sued, contending that the loyalty agreement was monopolization and attempted monopolization of the IFD market. Is this monopolization, or are there adequate alternatives in the relevant markets? [*Pepsico* v. *Coca-Cola* 315 F.3d 102, 2nd Cir. (2002)]

8. Dr. Johnson joined the obstetrics practice of Dr. Fadel. Johnson soon became unhappy with the arrangement, contending she was not being given enough patients. She wanted to set up her own practice, so she met with the physician recruiter at the hospital used by their patients. Johnson claimed the recruiter promised her an $800,000 line of credit and guaranteed annual income of at least $200,000 a year. The hospital board voted not to make her such an offer. Fadel fired her; she moved to another city and sued for conspiracy to restrain trade in violation of the Sherman Act. The district court dismissed the suit; Johnson appealed. Did she have grounds for suit? [*Johnson* v. *University Health Services*, 161 F.3d 1334, 11th Cir. (1998)]

   ✓ **Check your answer at http://academic.cengage.com/blaw/meiners**

9. A maker of hamburger patty machines requires its dealers to also purchase its hamburger patty paper. A dealer that did not like this requirement was cut off by the manufacturer. The dealer sued, claiming that his was an illegal tie-in sale. The dealer was awarded $300,000 damages for the value of its lost sales, which were trebled. Was this the correct decision? [*Roy B. Taylor Sales* v. *Hollymatic*, 28 F.3d 1379, 5th Cir. (1994)]

10. The Utah Pie Company made and sold frozen pies in the Salt Lake City area. It was very successful and soon had two thirds of the frozen-pie market in that area. In response to the loss of their market shares, three large pie makers—Carnation, Pet, and Continental—cut their prices in the Salt Lake area but not elsewhere. As a result, their sales picked back up and Utah Pie's fell to 45 percent of the market. The result was lower frozen-pie prices for consumers in that market. Utah Pie sued the other three companies for violating what part of the antitrust law? Did it win? [*Utah Pie Co.* v. *Continental Baking Co.*, 87 S.Ct. 1326 (1967)]

Ethics Question

1. Your firm produces electric blenders. A certain popular model has a suggested retail price of $30. Your firm sells it wholesale for $18. Smaller stores tend to sell the blender at the suggested retail price. One large discount chain begins to sell the blender for $26 and asks you to cut the price to them to $17.50. Because of that chain's large sales, your production and profits are up. You will earn even higher profits if you cut the price to them to $17.50—a possible violation of the Robinson–Patman Act. Should you cut the price for the chain? What if the chain says that it will cut its retail price to $25.50 if you cut the price to $17.50?

Internet Assignment

http://www.alderantitrust.com
http://www.abanet.org/publiced/preview/briefs/home.html
http://supreme.lp.findlaw.com/supreme_court/docket/2006/november/05-381-weyerhauser-v-ross-simmons.html

The Internet can sometimes be a source for legal briefs related to a case. Briefs for *Weyerhaeuser Co.* v. *Ross–Simmons Hardwood Lumber Co.* (127 S.Ct. 1069 [2007]) are available for free on the Internet from a law firm (with exhibits), the American Bar Association, and a commercial Web site. As with all Internet resources, permanent access to such documents cannot be guaranteed.

Securities Regulation

Chapter 21

Several years ago, the collapse of Enron and Worldcom, each once valued in the tens of billions of dollars, was asserted to be the financial scandal of the ages. Thousands lost their jobs, and the retirement funds of even more people, were wiped out. Congress responded by toughening federal securities laws. But that was soon forgotten by most people, as it was followed by Martha Stewart, among others, being sent to prison for lying to federal investigators about possible insider trading.

Then it was revealed that hundreds of senior executives received huge gains in the value of stock they had in the companies they worked for, because they picked a date in the past when the value was low and took credit for having earned stock options at that point. The backdating of stock options resulted in many company heads resigning and some being convicted of financial manipulation.

Since securities markets handle tens of trillions of dollars in assets, perhaps there should be little surprise that there are cases involving huge sums of money put at risk. When that happens, confidence in securities is shaken. The Securities and Exchange Commission (SEC) is important as the primary regulator of U.S. securities markets. Other nations look to the SEC for leadership in how to regulate, but not damage the quality of, the major sources of support for financing business operations. This chapter looks at the workings and legal control of some of the key elements of the securities industry. ■

Getty Images

The Elements of Securities

Securities are the financial backbone of the U.S. economy, so the efficient operation of the securities market is critical to economic growth. Business operations, especially larger companies, rely on securities for financing operations. Those securities are the major form of investment for pension funds, so the financial future of most people is tied to securities.

Corporate Finance

A *security* is almost always one of two things: First, it may be *debt* of certain forms, primarily money borrowed by a corporation, usually a note or bond that can be traded. Second, it may be *equity*, the most famous being common stocks traded on the New York Stock Exchange and other stock exchanges. Securities provide *capital* for business operations, the money needed to get a business started or increased in size. Securities are represented by pieces of paper, or records in computers, that represent value in something real. This chapter opens with a look at the elements of debt and equity.

Debt

When bonds are sold, there is often an *issue* of a certain amount. For example, if General Motors issues 10,000 bonds that are each worth $10,000, the company raises $100 million to help pay for expansion of a factory. The bond issue means that GM has incurred debt that is to be repaid to the holders, or owners, of the bonds. The bonds are usually traded on the securities market, so they are securities. *Debt financing* may also be obtained by borrowing money from large lenders, such as banks and insurance companies. In that case, as we discussed in Chapter 12, a note may be issued to represent the debt. Since that note may be sold to other parties, it can also be a security. A debt instrument issued by a corporation, such as a bond, specifies:

1. Amount of the debt
2. Length of the debt period
3. Debt repayment method
4. Rate of interest charged to the sum borrowed

Most purchases and sales are handled by professional bond traders, such as Merrill Lynch, which earns a commission for handling the sales or trades of bonds by bond owners.

Equity

Equity financing is the raising of funds through the sale of company stock. It is called *equity* financing, because a purchaser of shares of stock gains an ownership interest, or equitable interest, in the corporation. Shareholders have a claim on a portion of the future profits (if any) of the corporation. Unlike with debt financing, a company has no liability to repay shareholders the amount they have invested. For example, when Google sold stock for the first time to the public, it sold 19.6 million shares at $85 a share, which raised $1.67 billion cash to finance Google operations. Each share represents a right to a tiny fraction of the future value of the corporation.

Investors buy shares in the corporation if they think the profits will be sufficient to provide them a competitive rate of return on their investment. The officers of the corporation are under an obligation to make reasonable efforts to earn a profit. As in the case of bonds, unless prohibited by contract, stock can be traded, usually through a stock exchange.

Origins of Securities Regulation

Concern with fraud in the sale of securities to the public led to state laws regulating the sale of securities. The first securities statute was enacted by the state of Kansas in 1911. State securities laws are called *blue sky laws.* That comes from a Supreme Court opinion describing the purpose of state securities laws as attempting to prevent "speculative schemes which would have no more basis than so many feet of blue sky." Promoters had gone door-to-door selling worthless securities to unsuspecting Kansas investors. Later, after their money and the promoters were gone the buyers found that the securities had nothing more backing them than the "blue sky."

Beginnings of Federal Regulation

Federal regulation of securities began during a time of economic catastrophe. The stock market crashed in 1929 and that crash was followed by the Great Depression. Over one quarter of all jobs disappeared, and national income fell by one third. Many people blamed the depression on the stock market crash. In fact, the market was correctly forecasting the coming depression. Nevertheless, there was a common belief that manipulators on Wall Street needed to be controlled and, indeed, there had been abusive practices.

Congress enacted a number of statutes. Most important were the Securities Act of 1933 and the Securities Exchange Act of 1934. The 1933 Act regulates the public offerings of securities, when they are first sold. The Act requires that investors be given material information about new securities, and if prevents misrepresentation in the sale of securities. The 1934 Act regulates trading in existing securities and imposes disclosure requirements on corporations that have issued publicly held securities. It also regulates securities markets and professionals.

The Securities and Exchange Commission

The *Securities and Exchange Commission* (SEC) is the agency charged with the responsibility for the enforcement and administration of the federal securities laws (see http://www.sec.gov). The SEC has five members appointed by the president for five-year terms. One is appointed as chairman. The SEC's staff is composed of attorneys, accountants, financial analysts and examiners, and other professionals. The staff is divided into divisions and offices, including regional offices around the country.

What Is a Security?

Although Congress often provides vague guidance to regulators, forcing the courts and the regulatory agencies to define the terms and the scope of the legislation, this was not the case in defining the term *security* in the 1933 Act. Congress provided a detailed definition. According to the 1933 Act, a *security* includes

> any note; stock; treasury stock; bond; debenture; evidence of indebtedness; certificate of interest or participation in any profit-sharing agreement; collateral-trust certificate; preorganization certificate or subscription; transferable share; investment contract; voting-trust certificate; certificate of deposit for a security; fractional, undivided interest in oil, gas, or other mineral rights; or, in general, any interest or instrument commonly known as a "security"; or any certificate of interest of participation in, temporary or interim certificate for, receipt for, guarantee of, or warrant or right to subscribe to or purchase any of the foregoing.

Despite this detailed definition of a security, both the courts and the SEC look to the economic realities of an investment transaction to determine whether it is a security. That is, just because something is called a stock does not mean it is a security that falls within the jurisdiction of the federal security laws. Similarly, other things with names not included in the list written by Congress may also be securities.

Supreme Court's Howey Test

If an investment instrument is a security, it must comply with the legal requirements imposed on securities issuers. Note that investors have incentives to sue to have the court declare that an investment instrument is a security. If an investment instrument is a security, investors have a higher degree of legal protection than that given to investments not qualifying as securities. In the 1946 case *Securities and Exchange Commission* v. *Howey*, the Supreme Court established a test to determine when an investment is a security for the purposes of federal regulation.

The test developed by the Court is still the critical test. It holds that for an investment to be classified as a security for the purpose of federal regulation, it must contain four basic elements:

1. The investment of money
2. In a common enterprise
3. With an expectation of profits
4. Generated by the efforts of persons other than the investors

The Four Elements

The first element, *the investment of money*, requires that an investor turn over money to someone else for an investment. The second element, *in a common enterprise*, means that the investment is not the property of an investor, such as an investor's house. Rather, an investor's capital has been pooled with other investors' money so that each investor owns an undivided interest in the investment. An investor who owns Ford stock, for example, does not have the right to go to a Ford factory and demand a truck or other property equal in value to the money the investor invested in the company. An investor has a claim only to a share of future earnings as established in the securities contract. Even though stock owners, or shareholders, own a portion of the company, they own an *undivided interest* in the company. That is, the shareholders cannot divide company property among themselves, unless they agree to liquidate (sell) the company.

The third and fourth elements, *the expectation that profits will be generated by the efforts of persons other than the investor*, require that an investor not have direct control over the work that makes the investment a success or failure. That is, a board of

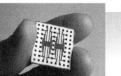

CYBER LAW

Securities Offerings on the Web

There is no technological reason why new securities offerings cannot be posted on the Web, and some have been. The Capital Markets Efficiency Act of 1996, which preempts state registration of offers to "qualified purchasers," provides an opportunity for such offerings to develop. They are much cheaper than the traditional offers presented on paper, but such offerings have been slow to come about.

Responding to an offering for a stock on the Internet, rather than through an established stock broker, still seems like an odd idea. The SEC sweeps the Internet looking for scams and finds plenty. Gullible investors are promised very high rates of return. While fools and their money are soon parted, one can at least also use the Web to check the SEC's EDGAR database (at www.sec.gov) to see if an investment is at least registered, or if the whole deal is fiction.

Getty Images

directors controls the future of the organization. They hire managers to run the company. The shareholders do not have direct control. If an investment meets this definition, it is a security, and must be registered with the SEC before it is sold to the public.

Securities Exempt from Regulation

Some new securities that are being sold to the public are exempt from regulation. The most important securities exempted by both the 1933 and the 1934 Acts are debts issued or guaranteed by a federal, state, or local government. The 1933 Act also provides an exemption for securities issued by banks, religious and charitable organizations, insurance policies, and annuity contracts. Since most of these securities are subject to control by other federal agencies, such as the Federal Reserve System, there is another regulatory scheme to protect investors.

In general, an exempted security is not subject to the registration requirements of the federal statutes. However, the security may be subject to the Acts' antifraud and civil liability provisions.

ISSUE SPOTTER
What Are You Selling?

Your family cattle business, like many, has had a hard time making a profit. Your idea is to let city folks buy a piece of a cattle herd. You will sell young cows to investors for the going market price. Your family will keep possession of the cattle, raise them, and then market them. After costs are deducted, such as food and transport, you will split any profit (per cow) 50-50 with its buyer. Since there are about 800 cattle in the herd at any time, that is the maximum number of cows you will sell. Investors may buy as many cows as they wish, up to the maximum, and they are welcome to come visit the herd. Assuming everything is done honestly, could there be any securities issues here?

Getty Images

Offering Securities to Investors

The 1933 Act, sometimes called the *truth-in-securities* law, requires that before a security is sold, the sellers *disclose* to prospective investors all material information about the security, its issuers, and the intended use of the funds raised. *Material information* is all relevant information that an investor would want to know about a company—its background, its executives, and its plan of operation. Disclosure is accomplished by filing a registration statement with the SEC.

Registration of securities provides investors with sufficient information about important facts regarding the security interest that a company is proposing to sell. With that information, investors can make an informed decision about the merits of new securities before buying them.

The Registration Statement

The *registration statement* for a new security offering has two parts: The first part is the *prospectus*, a document providing the legal offering of the sale of the security. The second part is detailed information required by the SEC.

The Prospectus

A prospectus (called a *Schedule A)* condenses the longer registration statement provided to the SEC and helps investors evaluate a security. The first version of the prospectus is called a *red herring*, because of the red ink used on the first page. It is used by securities brokers to interest potential investors in a forthcoming offering. Every prospectus provides material information about

- the security issuer's finances and business.
- the purpose of the offering.
- the plans for the funds collected.
- the risks involved in the business venture.
- the promoters' managerial experience and financial compensation.
- financial statements certified by independent public accountants.

Regulation S–K

The second part of the registration statement has more detailed information than the prospectus. The SEC spells out the requirements in *Regulation S–K*. More history on the financial background and past experience of the issuers is required. There is also more information about the proposed business and the issuers. This information may be used by investment analysts who want to see more detail, and the disclosure document is available for public inspection.

Review by the SEC

The SEC does not rule on the *merits* of an offering; that is, it does not give an opinion about the likelihood of success of a proposed business. But it can require issuers to make high-risk factors clear in the prospectus so as to put buyers on notice. The registration becomes effective 20 days after it is filed, but if the SEC issues a *deficiency letter*, the issuer needs time to amend the filing to provide more detail in the registration materials. The SEC can issue a *stop order* to prohibit the sale of securities until the registration statement is amended to satisfy the examiners, but this is not common.

The Costs of Registration

The registration process is expensive. The prospective issuer must hire professionals, including a securities attorney, a certified public accountant, and a printer for the prospectus. There is also the expense of hiring an *underwriter*—an investment banker, such as Morgan Stanley—that will market the securities.

Stock underwriting fees may be less than 1 percent of the value of a large stock offering sold to the public, but the fee may be as high as 10 percent for a small offering by an unknown company. To avoid such costs, one may consider selling through a transaction that makes the security exempt from the registration process.

Exemptions from Registration

Some securities, such as government bonds, are exempt from the securities laws. All other securities are subject to the securities laws, but they may qualify for an *exemption from registration*. Only the initial sale of the securities is exempt from registration; the securities are not exempt from other parts of the securities laws.

Private Placement

The 1933 Act provides that registration is not necessary for new securities not offered to the public. In some years, more money has been raised through *private placement securities* than through public offerings. The primary users of the exemption are those placing large blocks of securities with institutional investors, most often pension funds or insurance companies. For example, IBM might sell $250 million in new bonds directly to Prudential Insurance, rather than offering the bonds to the general public.

Rule 144A Private placements are most common for large security issues, mostly bonds, that are sold to qualified institutional buyers (QIBs). Rule 144A exempts U.S. and foreign security issuers from registration requirements for the sale of bonds and stocks to institutions with a portfolio of at least $100 million in securities. Further, securities issued to such large institutions may be traded among similar institutions without registration or disclosure requirements. Over one-fifth of all offerings have been sold under this registration exemption.

Regulation D To explain what qualifies as a private placement exemption, the SEC adopted *Regulation D*. Such offerings may only be made to *accredited investors*. These are investors presumed sophisticated and wealthy enough to evaluate investment opportunities without an SEC-approved prospectus. Only accredited investors may participate in private placement offerings of securities. Institutions, such as banks and insurance companies, are accredited investors. Individual investors must have an annual income of at least $200,000 ($300,000 for a couple) or a net worth of at least $2.5 million. Other investors are unaccredited.

The most common Regulation D offerings are called *Small Corporate Offering Registration (SCOR)*. This allows small companies to issue stock directly to the public, and it falls under Rule 504. A company may raise up to $1 million within 12 months with a minimum stock price of $5 per share. This can be done on the Internet, as can larger offers that fall under Rule 505 ($1 to $5 million) or Rule 506 (over $5 million). Most states similarly allow such offerings without going through the registration process. While the offering is not registered with the SEC, the SEC must be notified of the fact that this is occurring by filing Form D.

The rules about private placements are complex. Even though the offerings may be exempt from registration, there is usually a reporting requirement to the SEC about the offers, and the law requires that investors be given information— called a *private-placement memorandum*—similar to what they would have received in a prospectus. Also, restrictions are placed on the resale of securities bought by investors in private placements, which can reduce their value.

Most securities offerings are in compliance with the SEC rules and relevant state laws. That does not mean they will be profitable investments, but at least competent information has been provided to investors. But that is not always so, as the *Johnson* case illustrates.

United States v. Johnson
United States Court of Appeals, Eleventh Circuit
440 F.3d 1286 (2006)

Case Background *Johnson formed Link Express Delivery Solutions (LEDS) in 1997, claiming it would compete with FedEx. Over the years, he raised over $15 million from hundreds of investors in five private stock offerings. As the court explained, "Contrary to his representations to investors that their investments would be used exclusively for financing and operating LEDS, Johnson absconded with over $5.5 million, which he used to purchase homes, boats, cars, and plastic surgery for various girlfriends, as* well as to fund his extensive interest in gambling." *Johnson also used some money to start a nightclub that went under.*

He then closed LEDS and told investors that Link Worldwide Logistics (LWL) had taken its place. It was run under the same business plan as LEDS, with Johnson as president, chief executive officer, chairman, and majority shareholder. He then convinced investors to convert LEDS shares to LWL shares, for a fee of $5 per share, or *to exchange LEDS shares for LWL shares without fees, which required investing more money in LWL. He then bought Pony Express, an express delivery service, out of bankruptcy. It failed as a result of Johnson taking cash from the company prior to his arrest in 2002. He was convicted of securities fraud, perjury, and money laundering. He appealed.*

Case Decision Per Curiam

* * *

Having reviewed the record, we find more than sufficient evidence to support Johnson's convictions for perjury and securities fraud. We further find no reversible error in the district court's jury instructions, evidentiary rulings, and denial of Johnson's motion to suppress and motion for continuance. Finally, after due consideration, we affirm the money laundering convictions....

Questions for Analysis

1. The appeals court affirmed the conviction for securities fraud. Given the shady nature of the operation, why did hundreds of investors fall for the scam?

2. How could this stock offering go unnoticed by the SEC? Will investors get their money back?

WKSIs

Most securities are issued by *well-known seasoned issuers (WKSIs)*. Formally, these are issuers that have issued at least $1 billion in securities previously or have a public-equity market capitalization of at least $700 million. This includes most well-known securities firms. As of 2006, they can file registration statements the day they announce a new offering, rather than submitting it beforehand to the SEC; there is no need to wait for SEC staff review. This does not make their securities exempt, but simplifies the registration process and makes it consistent with EU securities rules for such issuers.

Further, WKSIs may use a *free-writing prospectus* that allows them to continuously update information, and it may be done on a Web site. The standards are the same as for a traditional formal prospectus, but this allows communication with potential buyers at any time. Such securities are said to be under a *shelf registration*. That is, once announced and registered, they may be sold at any time over the next three years. This helps firms market securities when conditions are favorable and when the firm needs the cash, rather than try to sell the entire issue immediately.

ISSUE SPOTTER
Can New Start-Up Firms Issue Securities?

We have heard of companies, such as Google, that came out of nowhere. Assume you are involved with a new, small company looking to expand. To do that, you need capital. A regular securities offering is complex and expensive. Without a reputation, it is highly unlikely to work. Would a private securities offering be likely to work?

Getty Images

Regulation of Securities Trading

While the 1933 Act imposes *disclosure requirements* on corporations issuing new securities, the 1934 Act imposes disclosure requirements on securities that are publicly traded. A security registered under the 1933 Act must be registered with the

SEC under the 1934 Act. Even if exempt from registration under the 1933 Act, a security must be registered under the 1934 Act if it is listed on a *securities exchange*, such as the New York Stock Exchange, or if it is traded *over the counter (OTC)*, and the company has $5 million or more in assets and 500 or more shareholders.

Any company that has issued securities that are traded is a *publicly held company* and is subject to reporting requirements. A company that has fewer than 500 shareholders and does not allow its securities to be openly traded is called a *private company*. Its financial information is not available to the public. A company can go from being publicly held to privately held by buying up its stock, so that it is held by fewer than 500 shareholders. Many multibillion-dollar corporations are in this category.

Disclosure requirements apply to more than 10,000 publicly held companies, most of which have securities traded in the OTC market. These companies must file reports on their securities. The most important report is the *10-K annual report*, an extensive audited financial statement similar in content to the information provided in the registration process under the 1933 Act. Companies must also file *quarterly 10-Q reports* with unaudited financial information and *8-K reports* whenever significant financial developments occur. The purpose of these reports is to ensure disclosure of financial information to investors. It must all be posted on company Web sites, and, as of 2007, it must include details about executive compensation.

LIGHTER SIDE OF THE LAW
Triple Your Money Overnight!

Ade Ogunjobi filed papers with the SEC to announce that he was offering to buy all of the stock in GM, GE, AOL Time Warner, AT&T, Hughes Electronics, and Marriott, which together were worth about $600 billion. He was offering three times the current value of the shares in the form of shares in his company, Toks, which had zero value. Ogunjobi asserted in the filing that the tripling in value would occur due to "synergies" and would allow "aggressive expansion of Toks into other industry sectors." The SEC accepted the filing, but response by investors to the offering was not good.

Source: *Chicago Tribune*

Getty Images

Regulation FD

The SEC adopted *Regulation Fair Disclosure (Reg FD)* to create a more "level playing field." It requires public companies to release material information to the public, rather than to reveal such information selectively. The primary purpose of Reg FD is to restrict the traditional practice of firms having executives give private briefings to big investors and favored securities analysts. Such meetings may occur, so that analysts can better understand company operations, but any material information provided at such meetings must also be released to the public. All securities traders are to have the same access to information, not just those who attend private briefings.

Firms are not required to provide more information; the regulation simply requires open disclosure of material information that is revealed to anyone outside the company. Public disclosure of material information can be made by filing Form 8-K or by distributing the information in a way "reasonably designed to provide broad, non-exclusory distribution of information to the public," such as by press release or on a company Web site.

Proxies and Tender Offers

Most shares of stock, besides representing a claim on a share of the future profits of a company, carry voting rights used to elect boards of directors and to determine major issues facing the company. Shares of stock carry extra value because of voting rights, especially when major events, such as a takeover, occur. The SEC ensures that fair voting procedures are followed.

Proxies

A *proxy* is permission given by a shareholder to someone else to vote his shares in the manner he instructs. Since it is not practical for many stock owners to attend corporate meetings at which shareholders vote to approve major decisions—such as whether to merge with another company, or to elect the board of directors—shareholders are sent proxies to be voted on their behalf. Firms must provide shareholders with proxy statements, information about major proposed changes in the business. SEC regulations spell out the form and timing that proxy solicitations must take.

While most proxies are routine, such as voting for boards of directors or amendments to company bylaws, proxy fights can be used in a struggle over the future of an organization. For example, a proxy fight was waged over the issue of whether Compaq Computer should be merged with Hewlett-Packard. Shareholders were offered the chance to stay with two independent companies or go with a different strategy of merging into one company. The board of directors was successful in getting approval, but the vote was close on the issue.

Tender Offers

When one company attempts to take over another, it often uses *a tender offer*. Stock owners in the target company are offered stock in the acquiring company or cash in exchange for their stock. If successful, the acquiring company obtains enough stock to control the target company. Tender offers must be registered with the SEC, and certain procedures must be followed.

Securities Fraud

Disclosure requirements do not prevent the sale or trading of securities in risky or poorly managed companies. Rather, the various Acts passed by Congress help ensure the adequate and accurate disclosure of material facts concerning the securities of a publicly traded company. Failure to follow the disclosure requirements may result in suits for *securities fraud*. Some securities fraud cases arise from false and misleading information in the registration materials, but most arise from information obtained during later disclosure, such as public statements made by corporate representatives.

Basis for Securities Fraud

Because obligations are created in the sale of a security, an investor can rely on common-law fraud standards for protection. Investors who think they have suffered a loss due to fraud and want to sue for damages often have difficulty establishing all elements of common-law fraud. Thus, injured investors generally rely on the antifraud provisions of the 1933 and 1934 Acts that hold that specific acts constitute statutory fraud.

Section 11 of the 1933 Act imposes civil liability for *misleading statements* or *material omissions* in securities registration material. Any person who buys a security covered by a registration statement that contains false or misleading information, or that omits information that was important to a decision to purchase, may sue to recover losses incurred in that purchase.

Rule 10b–5

Section 10(b) of the 1934 Act makes it illegal for any person "to use or employ, in connection with the purchase or sale of any security registered on a national securities exchange or any security not so registered, any manipulative or deceptive device or contrivance in contravention of such rules and regulations as the Commission may prescribe...." It provides the broadest base for bringing a securities fraud action, and it has come to be used in litigation more than any other part of the Act.

The SEC adopted *Rule 10b–5* to enforce Section 10(b) of the 1934 Act. The rule is broad in scope:

> It shall be unlawful for any person, directly or indirectly, by the use of any means or instrumentality of interstate commerce, or of the mails, or of any facility of any national securities exchange,
>
> 1. To employ any device, scheme, or artifice to defraud;
> 2. To make any untrue statement of a material fact or to omit to state a material fact necessary in order to make the statements made, in the light of the circumstances under which they were made, not misleading; or
> 3. To engage in any act, practice, or course of business which operates or would operate as a fraud or deceit upon any person, in connection with the purchase or sale of any security.

The rule applies to all securities, registered or not. Since the rule does not state specific offenses, it has been left to the SEC and the courts to decide how strict the standards will be.

Liability for Securities Law Violations

The law allows investors who lose in the purchase or sale of securities because of omission of material information or misleading statements to sue parties connected with the preparation of disclosure documents or other important information about the securities. This includes directors of the company; the chief executive, financial, and accounting officers of the company; and accountants, lawyers, and other experts who helped prepare disclosure material. All parties are held to high standards of professional care, which is one reason for the high cost of preparing disclosure materials.

SEC Action

The SEC may also sue those alleged to be violating securities law. Most SEC actions are remedial, such as an injunction ordering someone not to do something again or to direct a company to issue corrected financial statements. Since the SEC action is public, the parties involved are exposed to publicity. Injury to reputation in financial dealings can be costly as people are likely to shy away from future dealings. Further, SEC action may lead to private suits to recover losses attributed to the error in information.

The SEC can also recommend that the Department of Justice bring criminal charges against violators. To warrant a criminal action, the offender must have engaged in fraud related to securities. Penalties may involve fines and imprisonment.

Liability for Misstatements

Securities law imposes liability for *misstatements* or *omissions* about the financial status of a business that has issued securities. Misleading information that would reasonably affect investment decisions by securities owners includes misinformation about the present financial status or the future prospects of the enterprise that would affect the price of the security. For example, overly optimistic statements by executives can cause expectations of higher profits, leading investors to bid up the price of the stock. When the statements are found to be false, the stock price falls, imposing losses on those who bought the stock on the basis of the positive statements. This is one of the most common grounds for private suits seeking damages based on a claim of securities fraud.

Directors and senior managers of businesses know they may be responsible for the consequences of misstatements they make that cause the price of the securities issued by their company to rise or fall. Under the law of securities fraud, if investors lose money because of things not said (omissions) or because of misstatements that investors may reasonably rely on, then there was *material misinformation* that caused the loss.

Safe Harbor

The Securities Litigation Reform Act of 1995 amended the securities law to protect companies from liability for predictions about profits and the likely success of its products, so long as forecasts are accompanied by "meaningful cautionary statements identifying important factors that could cause actual results to differ materially from those in the forward-looking statement." This is called *a safe harbor*, because it gives greater immunity from suit for corporate forecasts that turned out not to be accurate after the fact.

Federal Exclusivity

The Securities Litigation Uniform Standards Act of 1998 requires securities suits involving nationally traded securities to be brought exclusively in federal court under federal law. The 1998 Act prohibits the pursuit of a class action suit under the law of any state if the suit alleges: (a) an untrue statement or omission of a material fact in connection with the purchase or sale of a covered security; or (b) that the defendant used or employed any deceptive device or contrivance in connection with the purchase or sale of a covered security. The Act was passed in an effort to reduce the huge number of securities suits brought claiming losses due to misrepresentation. The *Ray* case is an example of a securities class action suit. An average of about 200 such suits are filed every year, and settlements in recent years were almost $10 billion.

Ray v. Citigroup Global Markets
United States Court of Appeals, Seventh Circuit
482 F.3d 991 (2007)

Case Background *SmartServ Online (SSOL) was involved in the dot-com bubble. Shares that were worth less than $1 a share in 1999 were bid up to over $170 a share in early 2000. Citigroup stockbrokers recommended SSOL and over a hundred customers invested in it. The price collapsed, falling back to under $1 a share. The investors* *sued, claiming misrepresentation about SSOL by Citigroup stockbrokers. They also claimed violations of Illinois securities laws.*

The district court held that the Securities Litigation Uniform Standards Act preempted state law claims, so the issue was whether there was misrepresentation that
continues

constituted securities fraud under federal law. The district court held that there was not. Plaintiffs appealed.

Case Decision Wood, Circuit Judge

* * *

[The Supreme] Court summarized [fraud] elements as follows, for cases involving publicly traded securities and purchases or sales in public securities markets:

1. a material misrepresentation (or omission);
2. scienter (i.e., a wrongful state of mind);
3. a connection with the purchase or sale of a security;
4. reliance, often referred to in cases involving public securities markets (fraud-on-the-market cases) as "transaction causation," (presuming that the price of a publicly traded share reflects a material misrepresentation, and that plaintiffs have relied upon that misrepresentation as long as they would not have bought the share in its absence);
5. economic loss; and
6. "loss causation," (i.e., a causal connection between the material misrepresentation and the loss).

The loss causation element was the most obvious missing link, in the district court's view: plaintiffs had no evidence that ... would show that the particular misrepresentations they accused ... Citigroup of making had a causal connection with the loss in value of the SSOL shares....

There is no evidence in this record from which a jury could conclude that the drop in the value of the SSOL shares was attributable somehow to ... Citibank's alleged misrepresentations. The defendants introduced expert evidence that SSOL lost its value because of market forces, and the plaintiffs have offered nothing to rebut that theory—no expert testimony suggesting that the collapse was caused by the lack of the fraudulently promised contracts and financing, no evidence that companies similar to SSOL that had firm contracts survived....

We therefore affirm the judgment of the district court.

Questions for Analysis

1. The appeals court affirmed that the investors had no claim for securities misrepresentation by the stockbrokers. Since the investors said they relied on the advice of the brokers, why could they not recover their losses?
2. Why did the investors not sue SSOL instead of the brokers?

Sarbanes–Oxley Act Requirements

Congress added new requirements to the securities law in 2002 with the Sarbanes–Oxley Act. It requires that the Chief Executive Officer (CEO) and Chief Financial Officer (CFO) of large companies that have publicly traded stock personally certify that financial reports made to the SEC comply with SEC rules and that the information in the reports is accurate. Knowingly making a misstatement is a criminal offense with fines up to $5 million and up to 20 years in prison. The law also provides protection for corporate whistle-blowers who report securities violations and provides them a statutory basis for suing their employer if they suffer retaliation.

As with most newer statutes, Sarbanes–Oxley (SOX) is still being fleshed out by the SEC and the courts as to how it will work in practice. It established a Public Company Accounting Oversight Board that has authority to set accounting standards and discipline CPAs for misconduct. Accountants, who have been accused of being too passive regarding bad practices and for conflicts of interest in the firms they audit, now have a direct incentive to ensure comprehensive reporting of risks and costs. This has caused new tensions between firms and their auditors. Many financial reports have been delayed as accountants have insisted on digging deeper than usual; but new standards take time to settle in.

SOX has forced many firms to standardize procedures and accounting, which in some cases has benefited firms, because CEOs could better understand procedures in some areas that had been unclear before. An unexpected impact of the law was seen in the practice of backdating executive stock options, as noted before, when a favorable date of a low purchase price for stock is chosen after the fact. SOX revealed such dealings and forced many firms to reveal what had happened and, in most cases, firms discontinued this practice.

LIGHTER SIDE OF THE LAW

The Pay Is Okay, but the Food Is Terrible

Randall Hutchens was in federal prison for trying to cheat the IRS out of $300,000. A former investment adviser, he spent his time filing shareholder-fraud cases against companies in California small claims court, where the damages are limited to $5,000.

Rather than contest the claims, at least 17 companies paid settlements between $500 and $5,000, allowing Hutchens to collect over $300,000. His claims were bogus, especially since he never actually owned the stock involved. But the cost of hiring a California attorney to look into the securities fraud claims based on alleged misinformation was high enough that many companies just offered settlements.

Given that the prison provided Hutchens all the material he needed, his only expense was the small court filing fee.

Source: *The Wall Street Journal*

Getty Images

Insider Trading

Rule 10b–5 is used to prohibit *insider trading*—the buying or selling of stock by persons who have access to information affecting the value of the stock that has not yet been revealed to the public. As the Supreme Court has noted, misappropriation of private information gives insiders an unfair advantage in the market over investors who do not have the information. It is illegal for an insider to trade on inside information until that information has been released to the public, and the stock price has had time to adjust to the new information.

Executives are the ones most likely to be affected by the rule, as they have valuable information concerning the financial well-being of the company before the release of the information to the public. The SEC brings over 40 such cases each year.

In Rule 10b–5–1, the SEC defines insider trading to include trading "on the basis of" material, nonpublic information, which means that "the person making the purchase or sale was aware of the material, nonpublic information when the person made the purchase or sale." To be aware of the information means "having knowledge: conscious; cognizant." Executives in a firm, who almost always are aware of such information, may trade stock in their company and not be liable for insider trading if they contracted at an earlier date to have another person buy or sell the security at a specific time or on a "program" basis; that is, to make trades at specific time intervals.

SEC Prosecution

The SEC may prosecute insiders if they trade in the stock before the public has a chance to act on the information. For example, suppose an attorney working for General Electric found out that GE was about to announce the sale of $1 billion worth of jet engines to Boeing in two days. Knowing that this good news would make GE stock rise, the attorney buys some GE stock before the announcement. This is insider trading for which the attorney could be sued for all profits earned from the stock transaction.

Supreme Court Interpretation

The Supreme Court started to clarify the rules about insider trading in a 1980 case. A printer at a company that printed financial documents read some confidential information. The printer, Chiarella, traded in the stock of the company involved and made $30,000 in profits because of his access to inside information. The SEC charged Chiarella with securities fraud, but the Supreme Court reversed the lower court conviction.

In *Chiarella* v. *United States* (445 U.S. 222), the Court said that Chiarella was not a corporate insider who owed a *fiduciary duty* to the shareholders of his company. He was an outsider who was lucky enough to learn inside information. He could be responsible only if his position had a requirement that he could not use such information. He may have had an unfair advantage over other stock traders, but it did not constitute securities fraud.

In the 1983 case, *Dirks* v. *Securities and Exchange Commission* (463 U.S. 646), the Supreme Court held that not all breaches of fiduciary duty in a securities transaction indicate securities fraud. There must also be "manipulation or deception" and, in insider-trading cases, there must be "inherent unfairness involved, where one takes advantage of information intended to be available only for a corporate purpose and not for the personal benefit of anyone." An example of how the court applies the law to insider trading is seen in the *Ginsburg* case.

U.S. Securities and Exchange Commission v. Ginsburg
United States Court of Appeals, Eleventh Circuit
262 F.3d 1292 (2004)

Case Background *Scott Ginsburg was CEO of Evergreen Media, which owned radio stations. He met with the CEO of EZ Communication to discuss "strategic alternatives." Two days later, Ginsburg called his brother, Mark. The next day Mark bought 3,800 shares of EZ stock. Ginsburg also talked to his father, Jordan, who immediately bought 20,000 shares of EZ. The next day, Evergreen and EZ began discussing a merger under a confidentiality agreement. Scott called Mark and Jordan. The calls were followed by more purchases of EZ stock. When EZ's stock rose 30 percent, Mark made a profit of $413,000 and Jordan made $664,000.*

The SEC sued Ginsburg for securities violations for communicating material, nonpublic information to his brother and father. The jury found that Ginsburg violated the rule against insider trading and ordered him to pay $1 million in penalties. The trial judge set aside the verdict, holding

that the evidence was insufficient to find that Ginsburg had tipped off his brother and father. The SEC appealed.

Case Decision Carnes, Circuit Judge

* * *

The SEC must prove violations … by a preponderance of the evidence, and may use direct or circumstantial evidence to do so….

The district court stated that "the phone records are insufficient to compel an inference that Scott Ginsburg conveyed material, nonpublic information to Mark," but that is not the issue. The SEC did not have the burden of putting in evidence that compelled the inference Ginsburg conveyed nonpublic information to Mark. All it was required to do was put in evidence that reasonably permitted that inference. It did that. The call/trade pattern occurrences coupled with the jury's right to disbelieve the innocent explanations of the calls and trades are enough to support the verdict....

Ginsburg contends that the SEC did not provide sufficient evidence to permit a reasonable jury to find that the information tipped was material and nonpublic, as required by Rule 10b–5. "An omitted fact is material if there is a substantial likelihood a reasonable shareholder would consider it important in deciding how to vote." Materiality is proved by showing a "substantial likelihood that the disclosure of the omitted fact would have been viewed by the reasonable investor as having significantly altered the 'total mix' of information made available." ...

The jury could recognize as material ... nonpublic information about a private meeting between executives and the specific share price they discussed confidentially....

The district court's grant of judgment as a matter of law is reversed and the case is remanded with instructions that the court reinstate the civil penalty of $1,000,000, and enjoin Scott Ginsburg from future violations of the securities laws and regulations.

Questions for Analysis

1. The appeals court affirmed the conviction for insider trading. The Ginsburgs denied that the phone conversations were about a likely merger between Evergreen and EZ, and there is no recording of the conversations, so how could Ginsburg be found liable for insider trading for passing on private information?

2. Why was this a civil case and not a criminal case?

Insider Trading Sanctions Act

The *Insider Trading Sanctions Act* of 1984 gave the SEC a statutory basis for prosecuting insider trading. The law does not define insider trading, but it gives the SEC authority to bring enforcement actions, as in the *Ginsburg* case, against violators who trade in securities while in possession of material, nonpublic information. The courts may order violators to pay treble damages based on a measure of the illegal profit gained or the loss avoided by the insider trading. Those convicted of violations may also have to pay back illegal profits to those who suffered the losses, which effectively means quadruple damages. In addition, criminal penalties may be assessed.

This law was strengthened by the *Insider Trading and Securities Fraud Enforcement Act* of 1988, which increased the maximum fine to $1 million for persons convicted of violating the law against insider trading and set the maximum prison term at ten years per violation. The fine against corporations was raised to $2.5 million per violation, and the SEC is authorized to pay bounties—up to 10 percent of the penalty the government receives—to informants who give leads that produce insider trading convictions.

The Investment Company Act

The *Investment Company Act* (ICA) of 1940 gives the SEC control over the structure of investment companies. It requires investment companies to register as such with the SEC, which then makes the companies subject to regulations of their activities and holds them liable to the SEC, and to private parties, for violations of the ICA.

Investment Companies

An *investment company* invests and trades in securities. The ICA defines three types of investment companies: *face-amount certificate companies*, which issue debt securities paying a fixed return; *unit investment trusts*, which offer a fixed portfolio of securities; and *management companies*, the most important type of investment company.

Getty Images

INTERNATIONAL PERSPECTIVE

European Approaches to Insider Trading

The U.K. passed insider trading legislation in 1980 and brings about the same number of suits as the SEC does in the United States, given the size of the two nations.

After a scandal involving high-ranking government officials, France adopted insider trading rules in 1989, giving the *Commission des Operations de Bourse* stronger powers than it had under older statutes. However, there have been only a few administrative sanctions.

Italy enacted its first insider trading law in 1991. While the terms of the statute appear to be stringent, in practice, enforcement is minimal; and the law has significant loopholes. There were only two convictions in ten years, and in 2001, false accounting was reduced to a misdemeanor.

Germany did not pass a law against insider trading until 1994. The law is enforced by a new agency, the *Bundes aufsichtsamt für den Wertpapierhandel,* which obtained its first conviction in 1995.

Compared to the United States, where the SEC convicts an average of more than 50 defendants a year for insider trading, European nations still show minimal concern. The *Wall Street Journal* reports that the head of the German Association for Shareholder Protection says that the organization gives evidence of abuses to the authorities, but "more than 95 percent end up not being investigated. The cases are often too complicated for prosecutors to handle. They've not been trained in these matters."

Mutual Funds

The most common investment management company is the *open-end company*, or *mutual fund.* In 1980, $52 billion was invested in mutual funds. That has risen into the trillions. Most mutual funds are open-end companies that offer no specific number of shares and can expand as long as people invest with them. The money from these shares is invested in a portfolio of securities. The price of the shares is determined by the value of the portfolio divided by the number of shares sold to the public.

There are *load* and *no-load* mutual funds. The former are sold through a securities dealer and have a sales commission (load) of some percentage of the price. No-load funds are sold directly to the public through the mail or Internet with no sales commission. All funds charge an annual expense fee that covers costs of operation. The fee usually runs about 1 percent per year.

Investment companies that do not offer securities to the public but are involved in internal investing, such as banks and insurance companies, are exempt from the regulations imposed on investment companies that deal with the public.

ISSUE SPOTTER

Can You Exploit the Gossip?

Riding the elevator 42 floors in a New York City building, you overhear two people from the headquarters of a company located in the building discussing the fact that tomorrow they will announce that their company will be bought by another company. Price is not discussed, but you know that in such cases, the stock of the company being purchased often rises 20 to 30 percent when the announcement is made. You can immediately buy stock in that company and probably profit nicely from the information you overheard. Could you be accused of insider trading? Is there a breach of fiduciary duty if you trade?

Getty Images

Regulation of Investment Companies

Investment companies must register with the SEC, stating their investment policy and providing financial information. Annual reports and other information must be provided on a continuing basis. Capital requirements, including how much debt such companies may have, are set by the SEC. Payment of dividends to investors must equal at least 90 percent of the taxable ordinary income of the investment company. A company must invest in only those activities that it said it would in its sales literature and policy statements.

Registration and Disclosure

Since investment companies sell securities, such as shares in mutual funds, to buy securities for investment purposes, their securities must be registered with the SEC. Hence, companies under the ICA are subject to the *registration and disclosure* requirements of the SEC for publicly traded securities. The sales literature used by mutual fund companies to promote their investment strategies to the public must be filed with the SEC for review. In general, no share of stock in an investment company may be sold for more than its current net asset value plus a maximum sales charge (load) of 8.5 percent.

Limiting Conflicts of Interest

To reduce possible *conflicts of interest*, there are restrictions on who may be on the board of directors of an investment company. At least 40 percent of the members of the board must be outsiders; that is, persons with no direct business relationship with the company or its officers. The outsiders on the board are responsible for approving contracts with the investment advisers who are hired to manage the investment fund offered. Further, investment companies may not use the funds invested for deals with any persons affiliated with the company. All deals are to be "arm's length."

To reduce conflicts of interest, in 2001 Merrill Lynch became the first major brokerage firm to announce that it was prohibiting its research analysts from trading in the securities of the firms they cover. So a Merrill Lynch analyst who covers Intel may not buy and sell that company's stock while making recommendations about that stock to clients of Merrill Lynch.

Investment Advisers

Investment companies hire *investment advisers* to manage operations. Registered investment advisers manage pension funds and the portfolios held by insurance companies and banks. According to the ICA, investment advisers are "deemed to have a fiduciary duty with respect to the receipt of compensation for services" rendered to investment companies. The standard fee paid to advisers to manage an investment company fund is about 0.5 percent of the net assets of the fund each year.

The Investment Advisers Act

The *Investment Advisers Act* (IAA) defines *investment adviser* as a "person who, for compensation, engages in the business of advising others ... as to the advisability of investing in, purchasing, or selling securities." Investment advisers direct the investment strategies of mutual funds.

Brokers and Dealers

The IAA regulates *brokers*, persons who make transactions in securities for the account of others; *dealers*, persons who buy and sell securities for their own account;

and *advisers*, persons who charge fees for investment advice. They are all *securities professionals* and must be registered with the SEC. Violations of SEC rules can lead to suspension or loss of the right to do business in the industry, as happens hundreds of times a year.

LIGHTER SIDE OF THE LAW
Public Servants

An empirical study, headed by a Professor Ziobrowski of Georgia State University, looked at rates of return on stock transactions. The study showed that, over a five year period, members of the U.S. Senate beat the market by 12 percentage points a year on average. Corporate insiders only beat the market by 6 percentage points a year. A mutual fund manager is considered a genius if he beats the market by 2 percent a year.

The authors of the study concluded that the only way members of the Senate could achieve such high returns was by "trading stock based on information that is unavailable to the public." An office of the SEC said it reviewed the study but declined to follow up, because "it is hard to win insider-trading cases."

Source: *Securities Litigation Watch*

Getty Images

Professional Responsibility to Clients

Primary concerns of the SEC in regulating securities professionals are obligations to clients and conflicts of interest. The Supreme Court has held that broker-dealers must make known to their customers any possible conflicts or other information that is material to investment decisions. Professionals violate their duty when they charge excessive markups on securities above their market value to unsuspecting customers. Markups over 5 percent are difficult to justify, and those over 10 percent are not allowed under SEC guidelines.

Illegal practices include *churning*: when a broker who has control of a client's account buys and sells an excessive amount of stock to make money from the commissions earned on the transactions. Also illegal is *scalping*: when a professional buys stock for personal benefit, then urges investors to buy the stock so that the price will rise to the benefit of the professional.

Another concern of the SEC focuses on ensuring investors *adequate information* about available securities to make informed investment decisions. Generally, professionals violate the antifraud provisions of the regulations when they recommend securities without making adequate information available.

Stock Market Regulation

The volume and value of stock transactions have grown rapidly. They are more than 30 times higher than they were in 1970. Since trillions of dollars are changing hands on the New York Stock Exchange and the other securities markets, investors want to be assured that proper safeguards are in place.

Self-Regulation of Securities Markets

The 1934 Securities Exchange Act allows private associations of securities professionals to set rules for professionals dealing in securities markets. Congress gave the SEC the power to monitor these *self-regulating organizations*, which include the stock exchanges, such as the *New York Stock Exchange* (NYSE), the American Stock Exchange (AMEX), the regional exchanges, and the over-the-counter (OTC) markets, the most important of which is the NASDAQ.

Rules for Exchange Members

The stock exchanges have rules of conduct for their members. Rules govern the operation of an exchange; how securities are listed; obligations of issuers of securities, who may handle certain transactions; and how prices are set and reported. Other rules include how investors' accounts are to be managed and the qualifications of dealers and brokers. Governing the OTC market is the *National Association of Securities Dealers* (NASD), which sets rules of behavior for its traders similar to the rules of the NYSE for its members.

Liability and Penalties

Punishment for violating rules can include suspension or expulsion from the exchange. If an exchange knows that a member is violating the rules—or the law—and ignores such a violation, causing investors to lose money, it can be held liable for the losses. The potential liability and SEC pressure have given the exchanges an incentive to watch securities professionals for bad behavior.

Regulations of Securities Transactions

The SEC, with the NASD, regulates securities professionals who handle the actual trading of securities. To reduce problems, floor trading by professionals is limited to registered experts, as is off-floor trading. The difference between these two types of trading is that one is done on the floor of a securities exchange, while the other is done elsewhere, such as OTC. In either case, the professional securities dealers may not trade for their own advantage ahead of their customers.

Regulations also cover *specialist firms*. These firms generally do not deal directly with the public; rather, they handle transactions for brokers. Brokers may leave customers' orders with specialists to be filled. For example, if a stock is selling for $21 a share, and a stock owner is willing to sell at $22 dollars, the order may be left to be filled should the price rise to $22. SEC rules prohibit specialists from dealing for their own benefit in the orders they execute. Since they are the first to learn of price changes, they could buy and sell the stock left with them to take advantage of changes in stock prices.

Arbitration of Disputes

When investors establish accounts with investment firms or stockbrokers, they usually sign a standard form that states that disputes must be arbitrated, not litigated. SEC rules govern the arbitration process, which is the primary dispute resolution mechanism for brokers and investors. Although arbitration records are secret, the decisions are made public so that people have a better understanding of the process.

Supreme Court Support

The Supreme Court has upheld the arbitration agreements. It would be unusual for an investor to be allowed to litigate a dispute with a broker. The Court has held that the arbitration agreements apply to security fraud claims against brokers and that there is a "strong endorsement of the federal statutes favoring this method of resolving disputes."

Arbitration is generally less expensive than litigation. Most of the thousands of arbitration cases filed annually are resolved in favor of the client. For example, the New York Stock Exchange arbitration panel ordered Prudential Securities to pay \$11.8 million in damages, plus interest, for mismanaging an account.

Summary

- Securities include any 1) investment of money 2) in a common enterprise in which there is 3) an expectation of profits 4) from the efforts of persons other than the investors. This definition includes any investment device that meets these general criteria.

- Registration of new securities requires public disclosure of financial and managerial information and of future business plans with the SEC. Since the disclosure is complicated, and mistakes can lead to serious legal consequences, skilled counsel is required.

- Securities that are sold under a private placement exemption do not have to be registered with the SEC prior to sale. Most securities sold this way are large bond issues sold directly to institutional investors, such as insurance companies. Some smaller stock offerings are sold in limited numbers to accredited (wealthy and sophisticated) investors to avoid the cost of registration. These securities are subject to SEC regulation after their sale.

- Companies that have publicly traded securities must file financial disclosure information with the SEC, including quarterly and annual reports. Production of these reports is costly and exposes a company's finances to the public, including competitors.

- Takeover attempts and proxy battles for control of a company are subject to SEC regulations, as are certain voting rights of shareholders.

- All securities are subject to the law concerning securities fraud, which arises from the common law of fraud. They are also subject to the securities statutes that are expressed by the SEC in Rule 10b–5, which applies to a wide range of activities related to the handling of securities.

- Liability may be imposed on securities issuers or corporate officials for misstatements in corporate documents, including statements to the media. Material information that misleads investors about a company, and that causes profits in a security to be lost, may be the basis of legal action. Executives and those who work with sensitive financial matters must address company matters with a high degree of care.

- Insider trading can lead to criminal and civil prosecution under securities law as well as private liability. Liability is imposed when insiders violate a fiduciary duty. If one is in a position of trust that provides access to valuable information, one may not exploit the information for personal gain, since there exists a duty to protect the information and use it for the benefit of those to whom the duty is owed: the shareholders.

- Securities professionals—brokers, dealers, and financial advisers—are regulated by the SEC and must meet certain financial requirements. Those who give investment advice only through an investment newsletter are not subject to regulation.

- Firms that trade securities for investors (brokerage firms), firms that make investments for investors (investment companies, such as mutual funds), and the stock exchanges are regulated by the SEC. Self-regulatory organizations impose rules on industry members that are subject to SEC approval. Violations of regulatory requirements are subject to civil and criminal penalties.

Terms to Know

You should be able to define the following terms:

security, 531	registration statement, 534	securities fraud, 539
debt, 531	prospectus, 534	misstatements, 541
equity, 531	exemption from registration, 535	insider trading, 543
blue sky laws, 532	shelf registration, 537	investment company, 545
securities, 532	disclosure requirements, 537	mutual fund, 546
Howey test , 533	proxy, 539	investment advisers, 547
material information, 534	tender offer, 539	

Discussion Question

1. What is the difference in the legal protection for purchasers of registered versus unregistered securities?

Case Questions

1. A developer announced that a new apartment building was to be constructed. To have first chance at a unit in the building, you would have to deposit $250 per room. Each room was called a *share* of stock in the building. If you wanted a six-room apartment, you had to buy six shares of stock and later pay the sale price or rental rate. The stock price was to be refunded at the time you sold your apartment or quit renting and left the building. You could not sell the stock directly to another person. Is this stock a security? [*United Housing Foundation* v. *Forman*, 421 U.S. 837, 95 S. Ct. 2051 (1975)]

   ✓ Check your answer at http://academic.cengage.com/blaw/meiners

2. PTL (Praise the Lord, or People That Love) was a nonprofit ministry run by James Bakker. Bakker and his wife Tammy had a TV show on which they discussed, among other things, the availability of "Lifetime Partnerships" in PTL that cost from $500 to $10,000. About 153,000 people bought the partnerships, contributing $158 million to the construction of Heritage USA, a Christian retreat center for families. According to the level contributed, purchasers were promised a short annual stay at a hotel at Heritage USA. Contributors were told that the number of partnerships sold was limited. However, the partnerships were oversold, and much of the money was spent on other facilities and lavish living. Was the sale of the partnerships securities fraud? [*Teague* v. *Bakker*, 35 F.3d 978, 4th Cir. (1994)]

3. For ten years, a certified public accounting firm audited the books of an investment company to prepare disclosure documents required by the SEC. The head of the firm was stealing investors' funds and rigging the books, and the accountants never found out. One day the head of the firm disappeared, leaving behind a mess and many unhappy investors. The investors sued the accounting firm to recover the money they lost, claiming that the firm was liable for securities fraud. Who won? [*Ernst and Ernst* v. *Hochfelder*, 425 U.S. 185, 96 S. Ct. 1375 (1976)]

   ✓ Check your answer at http://academic.cengage.com/blaw/meiners

4. Novell merged with WordPerfect by issuing Novell stock in exchange for WordPerfect stock. After the merge, Novell's stock fell 7 percent. Grossman sued in a class-action suit alleging false and misleading statements and omissions from Novell, in the filing with the SEC related to the merger, that caused the stock price to be artificially inflated before the fall. Grossman cited statements from the company that the merger was "perhaps the smoothest of mergers in recent history" and that WordPerfect was "gaining market share … from less than 20 percent in 1992 to more than 40 percent today [1994]," and

that the merger created a "compelling set of opportunities." Did the case have merit? [*Grossman* v. *Novell*, 120 F.3d 1112, 10th Cir. (1997)]

5. Plains Resources' executives reported that the company found an unusually large natural gas field. As a result, the company's stock was bid up from $7.63 to $29 a share in a few months. Insiders were told that initial estimates were too high. They sold more than 30,000 shares of stock. Information about the lower estimates was then released, driving the price down to about $15. Shareholders sued, claiming that the executives traded on insider information and misled investors by not revealing bad information about the gas find more quickly. Was that securities fraud? [*Rubinstein* v. *Collins*, 20 F.3d 160, 5th Cir. (1994)]

    ✓ **Check your answer at http://academic.cengage.com/blaw/meiners**

6. SG ran "StockGeneration," a Web site offering the chance to buy shares in "virtual companies" listed on SG's "virtual stock exchange." SG arbitrarily set the buy and sell prices of each stock in the imaginary companies biweekly and allowed investors to buy and sell any quantity at posted prices. Millions of dollars had been collected by SG, and participants had trouble redeeming their shares. SG suspended operations and the SEC sued, contending that the sale of shares in a company that was claimed to be a "game without any risk" that had an average increase in value of 10 percent per month was in fact a sale of an unregistered security in violation of the Securities Exchange Act. The district court dismissed the complaint, holding that the shares were clearly marked and defined as a game lacking a business context. The SEC appealed. Were these unregistered securities? [*SEC* v. *SG Ltd.*, 265 F.3d 42, 1st Cir. (2001)]

7. Fleming, a publicly held company, and several officers of the company, were sued by various stockholders for securities fraud for filing documents that were materially false and misleading. The stockholders contended that information in various reports failed to discuss litigation lost by Fleming that resulted in a damage award of $200 million, which saw the company's stock fall by about 25 percent. The stock price recovered some, after part of the trial verdict was set aside, and Fleming settled the case by paying $20 million. Stockholders contended that failure to fully reveal the risks of that litigation caused losses to investors in Fleming stock. The district court dismissed the suit, because the plaintiffs failed to show that Fleming made deliberate and materially misleading statements or omissions. Stockholders appealed; did they have a case? [*City of Philadelphia* v. *Fleming Companies*, 264 F.3d 1245, 10th Cir. (2001)]

    ✓ **Check your answer at http://academic.cengage.com/blaw/meiners**

8. Plaintiffs owned stock in Dura. They sued, contending they lost money due to false statements by company executives about possible future profits and, especially, the financial benefits of possible approval by the FDA of a new medicine. FDA approval did not occur, and the stock fell. The suit claimed the losses were due to misstatements that the plaintiffs relied upon when they bought the stock. The district court dismissed, noting that plaintiffs failed to show causation between alleged misstatements and the losses suffered. The Court of Appeals reversed, holding that loss causation had been established, if plaintiffs owned stock during the time the events in question happened. Dura appealed. Do you think plaintiffs showed securities fraud? [*Dura Pharmaceuticals* v. *Broudo*, 125 S. Ct. 1627 (2005)]

Ethics Question

1. You started the Triangular Frisbee Company as a small operation. When the product went over big, you decided to seek outside funding to build a larger company. Your lawyer explained to you the costs of SEC registration and securities disclosure in the case of a public stock offering. Your lawyer also explained that you could avoid this by organizing as a corporation on the Caribbean island nation of Torlaga and selling stock in the corporation from there. U.S. investors would simply buy your stock through a Torlaga stockbroker. This would be much cheaper and quicker than U.S. registration. What are

the pros and cons of this arrangement? Is it ethical to avoid compliance with American laws in this manner?

Internet Assignment

1. What is the primary mission of the U.S. Securities and Exchange Commission (SEC)?
2. What are the six primary laws that govern the securities industry? Give the URLs of these documents, if available. Find an alternative, academic Web site featuring some of the same information in a Lawyer's Deskbook.
3. What is the EDGAR database?
4. What type of form is an EDGAR "DEF" form? What type of form is an EDGAR "486" form?

The International Legal Environment of Business

Chapter 22

Seawinds Limited was a Hong Kong corporation with its principal place of business in California. The shipping company owned three container ships that operated between Asia and the United States. Hoping to expand, the company entered into shipping contracts with companies from Hong Kong, Singapore, Great Britain, the Netherlands, and the United States. Its expectations were not met, and it sued the shippers for delivering only a small amount of goods for shipment, an alleged breach of contract. The contract specified that all disputes were to be brought before the Hong Kong courts and subject to the law of Hong Kong. However, the law of Hong Kong, compared to U.S. law, would not likely be favorable to Seawinds.

Was Seawinds obligated to bring the lawsuit in Hong Kong? Did all aspects of the dispute require the application of Hong Kong law? Was it possible to try some disputes in U.S. courts under U.S. law?

These are some of the issues that are the focus of this chapter on the international legal environment of business. We begin with a discussion of the nature of the international business environment. Then we consider the various ways that the U.S. government works to restrict imports and stimulate exports. The business organizations that may be considered before becoming involved in an international venture are then looked at. The constraints imposed by the Foreign Corrupt Practices Act are considered next. Finally, we discuss the nature of international contracting, insurance against loss, and procedures for the resolution of international disputes. ∎

Getty Images

International Law and Business

Faster and cheaper transportation and communications have changed the nature of business. The percentage of U.S. gross domestic product involved in international trade has tripled in recent decades. Most businesses are affected by events originating in other countries. Crop failures in Argentina, wars in the Middle East, currency devaluations in Mexico, and shipping strikes in England can all impact U.S. businesses.

The International Business Environment

International business includes all business transactions that involve entities from two or more countries. In addition to the movement of goods between countries, international trade includes the movement of services, capital, and personnel by multinational enterprises.

The *international business environment* includes business activities that are affected by international conditions and events. For example, U.S. businesses that operate only in the domestic market often find themselves in direct competition with foreign manufacturers. Initially, the main source of foreign competition came from imported products. However, foreign competitors now build factories in the United States to compete more effectively. Some Hondas are built more in the U.S. than some Fords.

A major difference between domestic and international businesses are the special financial, political, and regulatory risks in international enterprises. These arise from a variety of sources, including differences among countries in currencies, languages, customs, legal systems, social philosophies, and government policies.

Origins of International Law

Before the development of the modern international procedures we will focus on, nations and merchants involved in international commerce developed rules for trade. Early trade customs centered around the law of the sea. They provided, among other things, for rights of shipping in foreign ports, salvage rights, fishing rights, and freedom of passage.

International commercial codes date back as far as 1400 B.C. to Egyptian merchants involved in international trade. Merchants from various countries developed commercial codes to provide some legal certainty in international transactions. Greek and Roman civilizations both had well-developed codes of practice for international trade.

During the Middle Ages, principles embodied in the *lex mercatoria* (law merchant) arose from trading customs that governed commercial transactions throughout Europe. This law merchant conduct created a legal structure for the protection and encouragement of international transactions. Commerce codes in use today, such as those discussed in Chapter 11, are derived from codes dating back many centuries.

Sources of International Law

The main sources of international commercial law are the laws of individual countries, the laws defined by trade agreements between countries, and the rules enacted by worldwide or regional organizations, such as the United Nations or the European Union (EU). There is, however, no international system of courts generally accepted for resolving international conflicts between businesses. An overview of some international and U.S. organizations affecting the international legal environment is provided in Exhibit 22.1.

Exhibit 22.1   Selected Organizations Affecting the International Legal Environment

World Organizations

• United Nations (www.un.org)	Created as a peacekeeping body, the U.N. works to encourage international cooperation in a variety of areas. It has several departments that encourage world trade.
• World Bank (www.worldbank.org)	Promotes private foreign investment through loans and guarantees; also provides technical and managerial assistance on large capital projects.
• International Monetary Fund (IMF) (www.imf.org)	Responsible for promoting intenational trade by working to promote the stability of currency exchange rates.
• World Trade Oganization (WTO) (www.wto.org)	Promotes international trade by working to reduce trade barriers and to establish uniform tariff schedules.
• Commission on International Trade Law (www.un.org/law)	Promotes uniformity in laws; discourages legal obstacles to trade.
• World Intellectual Property Organization (www.wipo.org)	Promotes protection of intellectual property worldwide and promotes uniformity in laws.
• International Court of justice (www.icj-cij.org)	Principal court of the United Nations. Located in the Netherlands, it has jurisdiction over all cases brought to it, but only countries—not private parties—have standing.

United States Organizations

• International Trade Administration (ITA) (www.ita.doc.gov)	Part of the Department of Commerce. Developed to promote trade and to help American companies sell their products. Provides companies with data, foreign license requirements, and other information.
• International Trade Commission (ITC) (www.usitc.gov)	Independence agency responsible for recommending trade restrictions to the President. Examines the impact of a subsidized foreign import on domestic industry.
• Court of International Trade (www.uscourts.gov)	Has jurisdiction to review findings of the ITC or ITA. Has Jurisdiction over lawsuits against the United States regarding imports, tariffs, duties, or embargoes.
• Bureau of Export Administration (BEA) (www.bis.doc.gov)	Part of the Department of Commerce. Responsible for maintaining the Commodity Control List and goods subject to export controls.
• United States Export-Import Bank (Ex-Im Bank) (www.exim.gov)	Provides loans and loan guarantees to foreign purchasers of goods exported from the United States; mostly involved in heavy capital equipment projects and aircraft sales.
• Overseas Private Investment Corporation (OPIC) (www.opic.gov)	Provides insurance for U.S. projects that would be rejected by private insurers, largely projects in developing countries. Coverage protects against currency exchange problems, expropriation or confiscation, and war
• United States Trade Respresentative (USTR) (www.ustr.gov)	Appointed by the president. Has authority to negotiate trade agreements on the behalf of the United States to reduce trade barriers, including the WTO.

International Trade Agreements

Most countries seek to improve their economic relations through trade agreements. The intent is to improve investment and trade climates among countries. For example, most industrialized countries have tax agreements to prevent double taxation of individuals and businesses. Two particularly important trade agreements for U.S. businesses are the *North American Free Trade Agreement* (NAFTA) and the General Agreement on Tariffs and Trade, which created the World Trade Organization.

North American Free Trade Agreement

NAFTA was signed by the governments of Canada, the United States, and Mexico in 1992. After being ratified in each of those countries, it went into effect in 1994. NAFTA reduces or eliminates tariffs and trade barriers on most North American trade. Although some tariffs were eliminated immediately, most tariffs are being phased out through 2009. The industries most affected by NAFTA are agriculture, automobiles, pharmaceuticals, and textiles. In the end, the agreement creates a huge free trade area with over 400 million consumers.

NAFTA also provides for greater Mexican protection of U.S. and Canadian intellectual property. It calls for greater protection of the environment and ensures that the managers of U.S. companies do not use access to Mexico as a way to avoid U.S. environmental laws. NAFTA uses special panels to resolve disputes involving unfair trade practices, investment restrictions, and environmental issues. The activity spurred by NAFTA has generated interest to expand the reach of NAFTA to include other Latin American countries.

World Trade Organization

After World War II, the General Agreement on Tariffs and Trade (GATT) worked to reduce trade barriers. GATT focused on trade restrictions, including import quotas and tariffs. It published tariff schedules to which countries agreed. Tariff schedules were developed in trade negotiations, or *rounds*. In the most recent round (called the Uruguay Round), 124 nations participated.

GATT was replaced by the *World Trade Organization (WTO)*, one of the significant developments of the last round. Since 1995, the WTO has overseen trade agreements and has worked to set up a dispute-resolution system using three-person arbitration panels. The panels follow strict schedules for making decisions. WTO member nations agreed they should not veto WTO decisions.

The WTO trade agreements have lowered tariffs around the world. The United States, Japan, Canada, countries of the European Union, and other industrialized nations agreed to eliminate tariffs completely among themselves in ten industries:

Beer	Medical equipment
Construction equipment	Paper
Distilled spirits	Pharmaceuticals
Farm machinery	Steel
Furniture	Toys

As we saw in Chapter 9, the WTO also helps to provide worldwide protection for intellectual property. The WTO countries also agree to reduce or eliminate governmental subsidies on business research, civil aviation, and agriculture. Only in the film and television programming arena was the United States not able to gain reductions in trade barriers by the Europeans. France wanted to maintain the barrier because of its concerns about the domination of American films, music, and videos in Europe.

U.S. Import Policy

Countries have long imposed restrictions on the import and export of certain products and services. In addition, regulations are often enacted to encourage international business activity by domestic industries.

Taxes on Imports

Restrictions on imports are generally imposed to generate revenue for the government and to protect a country's domestic industries from foreign competition. Import licensing procedures, quotas, testing requirements, safety and manufacturing standards, government procurement policies, and complicated customs procedures are all ways to regulate imports.

Tariff Classes

A *tariff* is a duty or tax imposed by a government on an imported good. Tariffs can be classified into two categories: *specific* tariffs, which impose a fixed tax or duty on each unit of a product, and *ad valorem tariffs*, which impose a tax as a percentage of the price of the product. Domestic producers often argue that without a tariff, foreign products will force them out of the market. Workers will lose their jobs, and the country will grow dependent on foreign businesses for products. Those arguing against tariffs assert that only through free trade will countries exploit their comparative advantage and help consumers by lowering prices on many goods.

In the United States, the duty imposed is published in the *tariff schedules*, which are applied by the Customs and Border Protection (CBP) to all products entering U.S. ports. Customs officials classify products and determine the tariff rates when products enter the country. Any tariff must be paid before the goods enter the country.

Each year, importers file hundreds of requests with Customs for determination of the classification of goods. The Supreme Court stated, in *U.S. v. Mead Corp.* (121 S.Ct. 2164), that Customs is entitled to significant deference by the courts when it interprets the tariff laws passed by Congress.

An appeal of a Customs tariff determination goes first to the U.S. Court of International Trade and from there to the U.S. Court of Appeals for the Federal Circuit. Since classification greatly affects the tariff that is imposed on imports, companies argue to be classified in the most favorable category. As the *BASF* case shows, the law in this area is detailed and technical.

BASF v. United States
United States Court of Appeals, Federal Circuit
482 F.3d 1324 (2007)

Case Background *BASF imports a product, Lucarotin ® 1%, which contains 1% beta-carotene and is used as a food colorant. It is classified as 3204.19.35, Beta-carotene and other carotene coloring matter, under the Harmonized Tariff Schedule of the United States (HTSUS). As such, it is subject to a tariff.*

BASF argued that it should be duty-free, because beta-carotene is listed on the duty-free Pharmaceutical Appendix of the HTSUS. Beta-carotene is what makes carrots orange, and it plays a role in generating vitamin A.

Customs classified Lucarotin ® 1% under 2109.90.99, Food preparations not elsewhere specified or included: Other, which is subject to a tariff. BASF appealed this ruling to the Court of International Trade. It held that the product is only used as a food coloring, and so it is properly classified as 3204.19.35. BASF appealed.

Case Decision Newman, Circuit Judge

* * *

The methodology of tariff classification is established by the HTSUS, which consists of the General Notes, the General Rules of Interpretation (GRI), and the Additional United States Rules of Interpretation (USGRI), including all section and chapter notes and article provisions and the Chemical Appendix. The rules are applied in numerical order.

The HTSUS is a hierarchical classification system, which requires application of the most specific descriptive category in determining the applicable duty....

BASF states that the Court of International Trade erred in denying duty-free treatment, because beta-carotene is a provitamin and is listed on the Pharmaceutical Appendix....

The Court of International Trade applied the International Trade Commission's definition of a pharmaceutical product as "used in the prevention, diagnosis, alleviation, treatment, or cure of diseases in humans or animals." *Advice Concerning the Addition of Certain Pharmaceutical Products and Chemical Intermediates to the Pharmaceutical Appendix to the Harmonized Tariff Schedule of the United States*, USITA Pub. 3167, at 3 (April 1999), and found, without dispute, that "customers do not buy Lucrotin ® 1% for any purpose other than delivery of a beta-carotene colorant." Thus the court held that Lucrotin ® 1% is not eligible for duty-free importation despite the listing of beta-carotene on the Pharmaceutical Appendix....

Affirmed.

Questions for Analysis

1. The appeals court affirmed that the import product was properly classified by the lower court and was not duty free. Would you think Customs would be likely to apply the highest tariff possible to imported products, given that many can fit under more than one classification?

Harmonized Tariff Schedules

The United States uses a *harmonized tariff schedule*, developed by countries for the purpose of standardizing the ways in which goods are classified by customs officials worldwide. Each country uses the same codes to classify goods traded. The process streamlines trade by reducing language and usage differences among countries, but different countries may impose different tariffs.

Bans on Certain Products

Importing certain products may violate regulations. For example, some explosives and weapons cannot be imported. Illegal products, such as narcotics, violate domestic laws and cannot legally be imported. Products made from endangered species are prohibited. Other items may not meet safety regulations or pollution requirements and cannot be imported. Foreign vehicles that do not meet U.S. safety or pollution standards will not be cleared for importation.

ISSUE SPOTTER
Starting an Import Business

Having seen good quality wood furniture and handicrafts in Central America, you want to import it to the United States and try to develop a full-time business. Assuming you have some cash to get started, what key steps do you see in such a venture in terms of the international trade aspects?

Getty Images

Import Controls

Congress has given the Department of Commerce, through its *International Trade Administration* (ITA) and the *International Trade Commission* (ITC), the ability to restrict imports. These agencies are concerned with foreign companies that sell their products at prices lower in the U.S. market than in their home market—called dumping—or receive a subsidy from their government to lower costs of production, so they can produce more goods to sell in other countries.

Antidumping Orders

Under both the WTO and U.S. law, *dumping* "is the business practice of charging a lower price in the export market than in the home market, after taking into consideration important differences in the sale (such as credit terms and transportation) and the goods being sold."

If it is determined that goods from a country are being dumped, and domestic industries are losing sales as a result, an antidumping order may be issued. Under an order, the incoming goods will be subject to an *antidumping duty*, or tax. The amount of the duty is determined by comparing the market price in the home market with the price charged in the United States. The difference between the two prices determines the tariff to be applied to the price of the product.

Similarly, if the Commerce Department determines that a government is "providing, directly or indirectly, a subsidy with respect to the manufacture, production, or exportation of a class or kind of merchandise imported, or sold for importation into the United States," and the ITC determines that this injures U.S. producers, duties, called tariffs, are imposed in an amount equal to the net subsidy.

Duty orders generally remain in place until the importer can show three consecutive years of "fair market value" sales, and Commerce is convinced that there is little chance of "less than fair market value" sales in the United States in the future. Hundreds of antidumping requests are filed each year by companies hoping to impose taxes on their competitors' imports. After a decision is made by the

Huaiyin Foreign Trade Corp v. United States
United States Court of Appeals, Federal Circuit
322 F.3d 1369 (2003)

Case Background *Crawfish processors in the United States filed an antidumping petition with the Department of Commerce, claiming that freshwater crawfish tail meat from the People's Republic of China (PRC) was sold in the United States at less than fair market value. Commerce investigated. It sent questionnaires to various PRC freshwater crawfish tail meat exporters and producers.*

Commerce determined that most crawfish producers in the PRC were controlled by the government and were not market companies selling crawfish at market prices. Government-controlled processors are called non-market economy (NME) processors. Commerce imposed a dumping duty of 201.63 percent for all crawfish tail meat from NME processors and a duty of 91.5 percent for crawfish producers able to show they were not controlled by the government.

One exporter, Huaiyin, was accidentally classified as not under government control and so received the duty rate of 91.5 percent. U.S. competitors noticed that classification and complained that Huaiyin was under government control. Commerce then issued a Final Determination that changed the rate, which applied the higher duty to Huaiyin. That decision was upheld by the Court of International Trade. Huaiyin appealed.

Case Decision Clevenger, Circuit judge

* * *

As required by statute, we will sustain the agency's determinations unless they are "unsupported by substantial evidence on the record, or otherwise not in accordance with law." ...

First, Huaiyin had no entitlement to the lower duty margin.... Only entities able to demonstrate their independence from the PRC government were entitled to an individual rate as if they were part of a market economy. Based on the responses and evidence it received from participating companies during its investigation, the Department calculated company-specific rates from only eight entities. Beyond those eight specifically-named entities, the Department instructed Customs to apply the PRC-wide higher dumping duty margin of 201.63 percent to all exporters not specifically indentified in the *Final Determinations*. Since Huaiyin concedes that it neither participated in the initial investigation nor provided any evidence that it was independent from the PRC, it necessarily fell within the ambit of the NME presumption, and the Department justifiably determined the the PRC controlled its export activities. Subject to the presumption, Huaiyin received the default PRC-wide dumping duty margin; it could not and did not receive a lower rate....

Affirmed.

Questions for Analysis
1. Antidumping cases have steadily risen over the years. What might contribute to that increase?
2. When the United States imposes dumping duties on the sale of imports, how are other countries likely to respond?

Department of Commerce, the decision may be appealed to the Court of International Trade and then to the Court of Appeals for the Federal Circuit. We see an example in the *Huaiyin Foreign Trade* case.

When a dumping tarrif is imposed by the United States, or any other government, there may also be an appeal to the World Trade Organization, which hears hundreds of complaints each year. It does not have the power to force nations to change restrictions on imports, but it can allow other nations to retaliate without violating international trade treaties.

Foreign Trade Zones and Duty-Free Ports

Foreign trade zones are areas where businesses can import goods without paying tariffs. The zone is a secured area where goods may be processed, assembled, or warehoused. Tariffs are imposed only on the finished product, generally much less than those imposed on individual parts, and only when the product leaves the zone for sale in the domestic market. Products exported from the zone to other countries are generally not subject to tariffs.

Duty-free ports are ports of entry that do not assess duties or tariffs on products. They encourage the importation and sale of international goods within the country. Hong Kong is well known for such practices. Benefits to a country are the encouragement of trade with other countries and the attraction of businesses and tourists to the country to purchase products free of duties and other fees.

Export Regulation and Promotion

Most governments encourage the export of domestic products. They hope to stimulate employment and bring in foreign exchange from export sales. When the value of imports exceeds the value of exports, the country is said to be running a *trade deficit*. However, for reasons of national defense and foreign policy, governments may restrict exports of certain products.

ISSUE SPOTTER

Where to Produce?

Your company makes electric scooters for sale in the North American market. You import the motors from China, the tires from Brazil, the frames from the United States, and other parts come from suppliers around the world. Where might you consider building the scooters? What are the tradeoffs?

Getty Images

Federal Government Efforts

The Commerce Department is the major export-promotion agency. Primary responsibility for export promotion within Commerce falls upon the ITA. The ITA manages the U.S. Foreign Commercial Service, which has commercial officers at major cities around the world and export counselors in district offices around the United States. At its overseas offices, referred to as *Commercial Consulates*, it supplies U.S. product information, arranges business meetings with local firms, accompanies U.S. company representatives to meetings, and gathers local market information. The Commercial Consulates, for example, might assist a U.S. company in finding a foreign agent to distribute its products. They also lead trade missions overseas each year and participate in hundreds of trade expositions.

Export Restrictions

The U.S. government imposes some restrictions on exports. The sale of a certain good may 1) injure domestic industry (for example, exporting a raw material in short supply), 2) jeopardize national security (for example, selling military hardware to the wrong country), or 3) conflict with national policy (for example, selling goods to a country that supports terrorist activities). Restrictions are implemented through licensing requirements in the *Export Administration Act.*

Congress delegated the power to enforce export licenses to the Secretary of Commerce. It can do so only according to strict standards. The standards reflect the tension between a desire to control exports of strategic goods for security reasons and the desire to encourage exports to reduce the trade deficit.

LIGHTER SIDE OF THE LAW
A Bargain—Only $29.35 for a Razor Blade!

Finance professors Zdanowicz and Pak from Florida International University question whether the trade deficit numbers are not inflated as a result of global money laundering via fake import/export invoices.

They found ordinary telephones from Hong Kong "priced" at $2,400 each, salad dressing at $720 per bottle, smoke detectors at $653 each, and razor blades from Panama at $29.35 apiece. Similarly, they found underpriced export invoices: radial tires shipped to Colombia at $3.03 each, pianos to France at $38 each, and snowplows to Jamaica (!) at $267.70.

The professors' explanation is that the funds are transferred as the invoices assert, but the transferring is done for the purpose of money laundering to avoid paying income taxes. By making inflated payments to itself in another country, a business avoids taxes, and the transfer of funds is counted as a business expense. The professors estimate that the cost to the U.S. Treasury is about $40 billion a year in lost revenue. The Treasury "expressed interest" in the issue.

Source: *Forbes*

Commerce maintains a list—the *Commodity Control List*—of the goods subject to restricted licenses. The restrictions imposed depend upon the country to which goods are to be sent and the reason for the export restriction. Goods not on the list are subject to a general license, which requires little more than filing a Shipper's Export Declaration with Commerce.

Controls on Exports To determine if an export is subject to Export Administration Regulations, one must consult its database at http://www.access.gpo.gov/bis/ear/ear_data.html. If the item does not appear there, then it is not subject to special controls. If it is on the Commerce Control List, it will specify what the controls are and, if export is allowed, what sort of licensing is required. One can learn more about the process at the Bureau of Industry and Security at http://www.bis.doc.gov/licensing/exportingbasics.htm.

Application to Reexported U.S. Goods Commerce's export licensing requirements also apply to the *reexport* of U.S. goods. That is, an export license is needed to ship U.S.-origin controlled goods from, say, India to Iran. The intent is to prohibit the shipment of sensitive goods from the United States first to a "safe" country and then to a controlled country. In this way, the Export Administration Act reaches beyond U.S. boundaries.

Penalty Provisions Penalties for violations of Commerce's licensing provisions include criminal and civil penalties. For example, McDonnell Douglas, an aircraft maker, paid a $2.1 million fine for improper sale of sensitive equipment to China. Since the company reported the violation, there were no criminal penalties. An exporter who "knowingly" violates the Act can be fined up to $50,000 per violation. An exporter who "willfully" violates the Act can be fined more and may receive up to 20 years in prison. Penalties also can result in the suspension or revocation of an authority to export.

Business Structures in Foreign Markets

Businesses have two basic ways of selling products in foreign markets: They can either export products manufactured in this country to a foreign country or manufacture products in the foreign country for distribution there.

Foreign Manufacturing

Foreign manufacturing is motivated by a desire to reduce costs and expand. Costs reduced by foreign manufacturing may include shipping, labor expenses, and raw materials. Operating in another country may also help secure long-term contracts to supply goods to producers in that country. In addition, foreign manufacturing may be a way to avoid import restrictions or tariffs imposed by the host country.

Several leading Japanese companies decided to open manufacturing facilities in the United States. They feared that Congress might impose high tariffs on Japanese products. Since products made by a Japanese business located in the United States are made in America, they are not subject to duties. Businesses considering foreign manufacturing have several options, including

- A wholly owned foreign subsidiary
- A joint venture
- A licensing agreement
- A franchise agreement
- Contract manufacturing

Wholly Owned Subsidiary

By doing foreign manufacturing through a *wholly owned subsidiary*, a business owns the operation. A business may buy an existing facility or build a new one. Situations exist, however, in which complete ownership is not possible. Many countries impose limits on the percentage of ownership in a local enterprise by foreigners.

Joint Venture

A *joint venture* means sharing ownership with foreign partners. For example, one party may supply the facilities, and the other party may supply the technological skills required for the operation. Although a joint venture requires less investment by the company than does a wholly owned subsidiary, it can mean loss of managerial control.

Licensing Agreement

A *licensing agreement* is a contract. One business—the *licensor*—grants another business—the *licensee*—access to its patents and other technologies. The licensor is usually granted a royalty on sales. Allowing the licensee to use the business's trademark could help establish a worldwide reputation. However, the licensing company

INTERNATIONAL PERSPECTIVE

Controlling International Pirates

One of the most significant challenges facing a manager is deciding how to react to foreign manufacturers who pirate (copy) a company's product and then sell the product as authentic at lower prices than the real thing. Pirates cost U.S. industry more than $100 billion in lost sales every year.

Microsoft knows that pirates make copies of its Windows programs. After one three-month investigation, Microsoft led police to an apartment building in Taipei, Taiwan.

Police uncovered a sophisticated software pirating operation. In addition to finding the diskettes, they found flawless copies of the operation and installation manuals and of the hologram sticker intended to foil pirates. The number of copies on order at this one operation represented a lost revenue of $150 million to Microsoft, which sued the pirating company. In addition, the U.S. International Trade Commission issued a warning against Taiwan that Taiwan try to reduce pirating. If it fails, the United States could impose high tariffs on Taiwanese products entering the United States.

Getty Images

needs to make sure that the agreement is enforceable in the licensee's country or the technology and trademark may be easily stolen.

Franchise Agreement

Franchising is a popular vehicle for establishing a foreign market presence. Franchising is a form of licensing. The *franchisor* (the supplier) grants the *franchisee* (the foreign dealer) the right to sell products or services in exchange for a fee. The most visible franchises are fast-food restaurants: McDonald's, Pizza Hut, Coca-Cola, and KFC have made major inroads with franchises in China. The franchising company must work to make sure that the quality, and thus the reputation, of its products is maintained at overseas franchises.

Contract Manufacturing

Companies may contract for the production of certain products in foreign facilities. U.S. retailers, for example, contract for the production of clothing and shoes in Malaysia, India, and China, where labor costs are low. Contract manufacturing has the advantage of requiring limited investment in production facilities.

Nike has made contract manufacturing an important part of its operations. The company does not own the manufacturing plants that produce its shoes. When demand for the products slows, it can end a manufacturing contract. The company does not have to worry about making payments on a plant that is not producing.

Foreign Corrupt Practices Act

Governments in many countries are involved in business activity. Government permission often is required before business transactions can be completed, which increases the likelihood of bribery. Corruption is a global problem, but is more common in less-developed nations.

In the United States, the *Foreign Corrupt Practices Act* (FCPA) prohibits U.S companies and their agents from bribing foreign officials (www.usdoj.gov/

criminal/fraud/fcpa). The law was enacted in 1977 after exposure of cases in which U.S. corporations bribed foreign officials for favors. A study by the Securities and Exchange Commission found that the practice was widespread: more than 400 companies (117 of which were Fortune 500 companies) admitted to making substantial bribes to foreign officials.

Corruption

In many countries, corruption is so common that normal business is nearly impossible. It is a major barrier to economic development. There are measures of risk of investment around the world. One measure comes from Transparency International (TI) (see www.transparency.org), an organization in Berlin founded by a former World Bank director who was frustrated at the inability of countries to grow because of corruption. Exhibit 22.2 shows some of TI's Corruption Perception Index, which is based on numerous surveys. A score of 10 would indicate a corruption-free country.

Exhibit 22.2 Corruption Perception Index

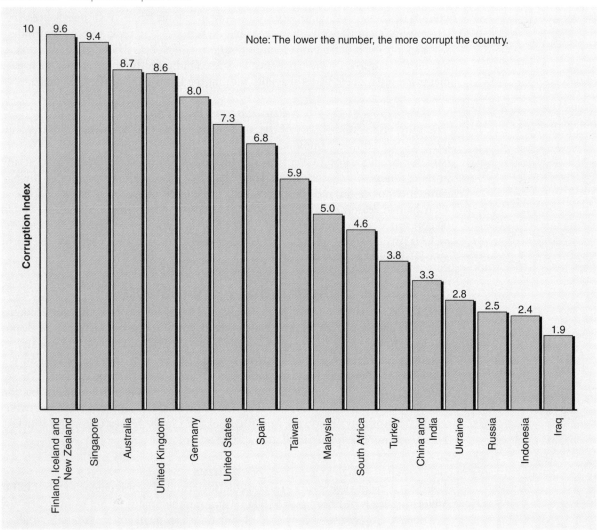

Note: The lower the number, the more corrupt the country.

Source: *Transparency International*

International Antibribery Movement

Recently, many nations signed a convention against corruption. All agreed to present legislation to their national legislatures that would make bribery a crime. In 1998, the U.S. Senate ratified the Convention on Combating Bribery of Foreign Officials in International Business Transactions. In 2006, Congress ratified the United Nations Convention Against Corruption (UNCAC). It is supposed to bring international cooperation to corruption enforcement actions. Some nations have not been quick to act, and enforcement remains another issue.

FCPA Antibribery Provisions

The antibribery provisions of the FCPA prohibit U.S. companies from "corruptly" paying or offering to pay a foreign official to gain assistance in obtaining or retaining business. The Act also prohibits payments to a person, such as a foreign agent, when the U.S. company knows that payment will go toward bribing a foreign official.

The Act recognizes that some payments are necessary and routine. An exception exists for a "facilitating or expediting payment … the purpose of which is to expedite or secure the performance of a routine government action." Such "routine actions" normally include bribes for services such as processing visas and providing utilities or transportation services. Guess wrong about what constitutes "necessary" or "routine," and the consequences could be serious. The basic test in determining whether a bribe is permissible focuses not on the person to whom payment is made, but on the purpose of the payment. This is complicated by the fact that such payments are often made by local agents without the knowledge of the U.S. manager.

Who Knows What?

The most controversial part of the antibribery law is the "knowing" requirement. Congress stated that "simple negligence" or "mere foolishness" should not be the basis for liability. The FCPA provides that the knowing requirement covers "any instance where any reasonable person would have realized the existence of the circumstances or result and the [individual] has consciously chosen not to ask about what he had reason to believe he would discover." For example, managers should be concerned about foreign agents who work on a commission basis. The government is particularly suspicious that large commissions may be a cover for the agent to make bribes.

Accounting Requirements

The FCPA requires companies to "make and keep books, records, and accounts which, in reasonable detail, accurately and fairly reflect the transactions and dispositions of [their] assets." The law also requires companies to "devise and maintain a system of internal accounting controls sufficient to provide reasonable assurances" that all transactions are authorized and that access to assets can be tracked. The accounting provisions were included in the Act in response to a study by the Securities and Exchange Commission that showed that many corporations maintained "slush funds" that were "off the books" to make bribes to foreign officials. The Act requires a "paper trail" to improve corporate accountability.

Penalties

The Department of Justice is responsible for criminal enforcement of the FCPA. A violation leads to fines up to $100,000 and imprisonment for up to five years for individuals. Corporations convicted of violations can incur fines of up to $2 million per violation. The *King* case is an example of an FCPA action.

United States v. King
United States Court of Appeals, Eighth Circuit
351 F.3d 859 (2003)

Case Background *The FBI investigated the dealings of Owl Securities and Investments (OSI), a Kansas City company that was raising funds for a large land development project in Costa Rica. The investigation focused on King, one of OSI's largest investors. The FBI obtained the cooperation of OSI executives, including Kingsley, OSI's president, who tape recorded conversations.*

King was convicted of planning to bribe senior Costa Rican officials to obtain the rights to the land to be developed. He was fined $60,000 and sentenced to 30 months in prison. He appealed.

Case Decision Beam, Circuit Judge

* * *

Viewing the evidence in the light most favorable to the verdict, there was ample evidence in the record to support the jury's conviction. The tape recordings, alone, support the jury's verdict. [Footnote, quoting King: "I think we could pay the top people enough, that the rest of the people won't bother us any. That's what I'm hoping this million and a half dollars does.

I'm hoping it pays for enough top people."] There was sufficient evidence to prove King's knowledge of the proposed payment long before Kingsley became an informant for the government. Moreover, the recordings show King's knowing participation in, approval of, and subsequent actions in furtherance of the conspiracy to offer the bribe. In addition, the testimony of six witnesses conducted over a five-day period, and the remaining exhibits, suppot the jury's conviction of King for conspiracy and substantive violations under the FCPA.…

Affirmed.

Questions for Analysis

1. The appeals court affirmed the conviction for the FCPA violation. King contended that since Kingsley was a conspirator, his testimony should not be allowed, because it could not be considered reliable. Is it?
2. Is it fair that King got prison time and Kingsley did not, because Kingsley cooperated with the FBI?

International Contracts

As in domestic business agreements, the basis for any international agreement is a contract. As we saw in Chapter 11, many sales of goods are under the CISG, but many contracts are not. Such contracts can differ from domestic contracts in complexity and use of unusual provisions. The distance between the parties often complicates contract negotiation, substance, and performance. The differing languages, currencies, legal systems, and business customs of parties can affect the nature of the contract and influence the way it is written.

Cultural Aspects

Sensitivity to cultural differences is important in international contracting. In Japan, for example, *meishi*, or business cards, are exchanged formally at a first meeting and treated with respect, while in the United States, business cards may be exchanged casually at any time. In many countries, including China, hours may go by before the details of the business are mentioned. This is different from the U.S. approach, where the parties usually get right to the point.

The attitude toward relationships is another difference. Many countries have a cultural expectation that a relationship will be long-term. As a result, the negotiation process may be long, since it is necessary for the parties to know one another before entering into a relationship. Contracts based on long-term expectations are often relatively short, with few contingencies expressly provided. The idea is that problems can be worked out as they arise, with the parties trying to maintain the relationship.

Language itself should not be a barrier to an international contract. However, it is important that the terms of the contract are clearly defined in a language that all parties understand. Interpreters can be an integral part of the negotiations and the final draft of the contract, where parties are not fluent in a common language.

Financial Aspects

To manage the financial risks that may arise in international contracts, care must be taken in specifying the method of payment. In addition, the parties may be concerned about removing profits from the countries in which they conduct their business.

Exchange Markets

In an international transaction, the seller often receives another country's currency. A business may want to exchange that currency into dollars, but the exchange is not always simple. Exchange risk is the potential loss or profit that occurs between the time currency is acquired and the time it is exchanged for another currency. Suppose, for example, that U.S. Wine Company buys French wines. The contract calls for the payment of three million Euros in 180 days. When the contract is signed, the exchange rate is 1 Euro to the dollar, or $3,000,000. Suppose that U.S. Wine waits 180 days before paying, and the exchange rate falls to .85 Euros to the dollar. U.S. Wine now must pay $3,530,000. Change in the exchange rate costs the company $530,000. To avoid such difficulties, businesses may require payment in dollars rather than in the currency of the other country.

Financial Instruments Used in International Contracts

International contracts often use special international financial devices. These assure later payment or allow for the arrangement of credit when buyers are otherwise unable to come up with the cash necessary for the transaction. One device commonly used is the letter of credit.

A *letter of credit* is an agreement or assurance by the bank of the buyer to pay a specified amount to the seller upon receipt of certain documents that prove that the goods have been shipped and that contractual obligations of the seller have been fulfilled. The usual documentation required includes a certificate of origin, an export license, a certificate of inspection, a bill of lading, a commercial invoice, and an insurance policy. Once the bank has received the required documentation, it releases payment to the seller. Exhibit 22.3 illustrates the route taken by a letter of credit and the documentation in an international business transaction between an Italian seller and an American buyer, each using its own bank.

Letters of credit can be either revocable or irrevocable. As the label attached to each implies, a *revocable letter of credit* may be withdrawn before the specific date stated on it, while an *irrevocable letter of credit* may not be withdrawn. Exhibit 22.4 is an example of an irrevocable letter of credit.

Repatriation of Monetary Profits

Repatriation is the ability of a business to return money earned in a foreign country to its home country. Some countries restrict the amount of currency that can be taken out of the country. The usual reason for restrictions on repatriation is the desire that money earned in the country be put back into the local economy.

Key Clauses in International Contracts

The contract is the foundation of any business venture. As with domestic contracts, care should be taken that the intent of the parties is fully represented by the

Exhibit 22.3 Letter of Credit in an International Transaction

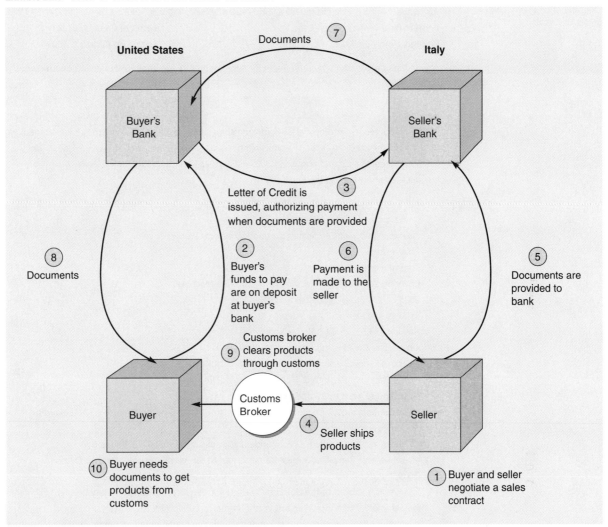

contract. International contracts should be in writing, even if they only state the positions and goals of the parties. Certain key clauses are generally considered critical in international deals.

Payment Clauses

The *payment clause* states the manner in which payment is to be received and the currency in which it is made. Since some nations restrict currencies from leaving the country, payments have special effects on the receiver of the currency that must be addressed. Problems with inflation and currency exchange risks, especially in unstable economies or in long-term agreements, should also be covered.

Choice of Language Clause

Even when parties speak the same language, complex contractual terms may exceed the understanding of one of the parties, when the contract is made in another country. A word or phrase in one language or country may not be readily translatable to another. Technical terms should be defined. A contract should have a *choice-of-language clause*, which sets out the official language by which the contract is to be interpreted, as seen in Exhibit 22.5.

Exhibit 22.4
Example of an Irrevocable
Letter of Credit

LETTER OF CREDIT—CONFIRMED, IRREVOCABLE

Western Reserve Bank   Letter of Credit #59723
Chicago, Illinois   Issued on August 1, 2009

To: Exotica Company   From: Tiramisu Import Company
Dallas, Texas   Rome, Italy

Gentlemen:

We are instructed by Commercial Bank of Italy, Rome, Italy, to inform you that they have opened their irrevocable credit in favor of Tiramisu Import Company, Rome, Italy, for the sum in U.S. dollars not exceeding a total of about $55,000.00 (Fifty-five Thousand and 00/100 Dollars), available by your drafts on us, to be accompanied by:

1. Full Set on Board Negotiable Ocean Bills of Lading, stating: "Freight Prepaid" and made out to the order of Commercial Bank of Italy.
2. Insurance Policy or Certificate covering Marine and War Risk.
3. Packing List.
4. Commercial Invoice in triplicate:
   Covering 200 Pcs. 1025 Electric Espresso Coffee Machines
   200 Pcs. 750 Stove-Top Espresso Coffee Makers
   350 Pcs. 420 Electric Pasta Makers

Total Value $54,702.75 C.I.F. Rome, Italy

Import Lic. No. 3792 Expires October 24, 2009

5. Shipper's Export Declaration.
   Partial Shipment Permitted. Transshipment Not Permitted.
   Merchandise must be shipped in SS Mercaso.
   All documents must indicate Letter of Credit No. 59723, Import License No. 3792, expires October 24, 2009.
   All drafts must be marked "Drawn under Letter of Credit No. 59723, issued by Western Reserve Bank. Drafts must be presented to this company not later than October 1, 2009."
   This credit is subject to the Uniform Customs and Practices for Documentary Credits (1984 Revision) International Chamber of Commerce Publication No. 400.
   We confirm the credit and thereby undertake that all drafts drawn and presented as above specified will be duly honored by us.

By

International Credit Department

Force Majeure Clause

Force majeure is a French term meaning a "superior or irresistible force." Thus, it protects contracting parties from problems beyond their control. Traditionally, this clause was used to protect the parties from the consequences of a natural disaster that interfered with performance. The clause also protects the parties against political upheavals. An illustration of a typical force majeure clause is given in Exhibit 22.5.

Forum Selection and Choice-of-Law Clauses

To reduce uncertainties in the event of a dispute, companies often put *forum selection* and *choice-of-law clauses* in their contracts. (Examples are given in Exhibit 22.5.) The forum may be in one place (Paris), and the law to be applied may be from another place (California).

Example of Choice of Language Clause with Arbitration Provision

This Agreement is signed in two (2) originals in the English language, which shall be regarded as the authoritative and official text. Any matters referred to arbitration will also be in the English language which will be the official language used in arbitration.

Example of Choice of Language with Translation Provision

This Agreement is signed in two (2) originals in the French language, which shall be regarded as the authoritative and official text. Parties hereto agree to provide an official translation of this Agreement in the English language. This translation will be ratified by both parties, and it may be relied upon as being an accurate representation of the official form.

Example of Force Majeure Clause

The parties hereto shall not be liable for failure of performance hereunder if occasioned by war, declared or undeclared; fire; flood; interruption of transportation; inflation beyond the expected rate; embargo, accident; explosion; inability to procure or shortage of supply of materials, equipment, or production facilities; prohibition of import or export of goods covered hereby; governmental orders, regulations, restrictions, priorities or rationing by strike or lockout or other labor troubles interfering with production or transportation of such goods; or with the supplies of raw materials entering into their production; or any other cause beyond the control of the parties.

Forum Selection and Choice-of-Law Clauses

All Claims and disputes arising out of or in relation to this contract shall be litigated before the courts of the city of Paris, France.

This contract shall be governed by the laws of the state of California, the country of the United States of America.

Exhibit 22.5
Choice of Language Clauses

By selecting the court or place of arbitration in which disputes must be resolved and which law that is to be applied, the possibility that the parties will go "forum shopping"—looking for the most favorable forum for the resolution of a dispute—is reduced.

Loss of Investment

Political upheavals, unstable monetary systems, and changes in laws are some of the risks encountered in other countries. In addition, businesses must be concerned about the loss of investment by nationalization, expropriation, and confiscation.

Nationalization

Nationalization is when a country takes over, or nationalizes, a foreign investment or, at times, an entire industry in a country. The compensation paid by the government is often less than the true value of the business. Nationalization has been seen in Iran, Russia, Saudi Arabia, and Venezuela. England has nationalized certain industries off and on over the years.

Expropriation

Expropriation, like nationalization, is the action of a country in taking foreign property in accordance with international law. Most countries agree that for a valid expropriation, there must be adequate compensation provided. International law recognizes a country's right to expropriate the property of foreigners within its jurisdiction, so long as payment is made. If a takeover is unlawful, it is a *confiscation*.

Getty Images

ISSUE SPOTTER

Making the Deal Stick

You have worked for a long time to attract a client and have finally won an order for your company to supply financial services to Glorious, a large Chinese company headquartered in Shanghai. Glorious sends you an agreement drawn up by its attorney. Chinese law governs in all respects. Are you sure you want to sign? What changes in the agreement would be high on your list?

Insuring against Risk of Loss

An all-risk insurance policy can provide financial relief in the event of nationalization, or if other problems occur. Short-term private insurance usually lasts from three to five years and is available for most investments. Risks such as currency blockages, embargoes, and a government's arbitrary decision to recall letters of credit may be insured by such major insurers as Lloyd's of London. In addition, sellers may obtain rejection insurance in the event that a buyer rejects a product for reasonable cause, such as spoilage at sea.

Some countries have government agencies to assist in insuring exporters from risk of loss. In the United States, for example, the *Overseas Private Investment Corporation (OPIC)* insures investors willing to invest in less-developed countries friendly to the United States. OPIC offers investors insurance against expropriation, currency inconvertibility, and damage from wars or revolutions.

International Dispute Resolution

World trade is in the trillions of dollars and growing rapidly. With that much commerce, disputes will arise. They may be due to unanticipated events, difficulties in performance, or changes in the political climate of a country that may affect a contract. Whatever the problem, parties to international contracts need help to try to resolve disputes and enforce their rights.

Litigation

Disputes often end up either in the court system at home or within the opposing party's country. Litigation is complicated, because evidence, witnesses, and documents central to resolving the dispute are often located in two or more countries. In some instances, these difficulties may be overcome by treaties or conventions between the two countries. These may allow for proper notice of the suit to the foreign party, appropriate service of process, issues of standing, methods for documentation certification, and procedures for taking evidence.

If the action is commenced in a foreign court, the U.S. participant often encounters a judicial system very different from that in this country. Courts in some countries are influenced more by political pressures than are U.S. courts. In addition, some courts will not enforce contract provisions that may be enforceable in the United States.

LIGHTER SIDE OF THE LAW
You Yanks Are Too Old for Us Hip Brits

Garland Denty worked for Smith Kline—a U.S. company—in Philadelphia, where he was director of manufacturing operations/technical services, international. The firm merged with Beecham and became SmithKline Beecham, a British corporation.

Denty was told he was to be promoted to vice president of technical services/plant operations and transferred to England. But the company reversed its decision and told Denty he would not get the job, because he was too old—at age 52. Denty sued for age discrimination.

The federal court tossed out Denty's suit. The Age Discrimination in Employment Act does not apply to employment decisions affecting U.S. employees that are made by foreign-owned companies regarding employment outside the United States.

Source: *Denty v. SmithKline Beecham* (907 F.Supp. 879)

Getty Images

Arbitration

Judicial forums are not very effective in resolving many international commercial disagreements. Cost considerations, jurisdictional barriers, the length of time to litigate, legal uncertainties, and the inability of judicial systems to fashion appropriate relief have encouraged the use of alternative dispute resolution techniques, especially *arbitration*.

Attempts to standardize arbitral rules and procedures have resulted in the creation of organizations such as the United Nations Commission on International Trade Law, the International Chamber of Commerce, and other arbitration organizations around the world. These organizations have rules to address issues concerning arbitration proceedings and awards. In many countries, including the United States, the enforcement of arbitral awards is facilitated by the United Nations Convention on the Recognition and Enforcement of Foreign Arbitral Awards. Federal district courts have jurisdiction to hear motions to confirm or challenge an international arbitration award involving a U.S. business.

The International Court of Justice

Contrary to common belief, there are no "international courts" to handle business disputes, but certain disputes may be taken to the *International Court of Justice (ICJ)* headquartered at The Hague, Netherlands, and part of the United Nations. The ICJ has 15 judges, representing all of the world's major legal systems, with no two judges from the same country.

Only nations have standing to go before the ICJ. Individuals and businesses have no standing to initiate a suit. Hence, countries—not the parties to a dispute—have complete discretion in deciding whether to pursue a claim. Suppose a country where an investor does business violates the law and damages the investor. The country in which the investor is a citizen has discretion to pursue or not to pursue the investor's claim by bringing suit against the other nation. This is rarely used.

Doctrine of Sovereign Immunity

In international law, the *doctrine of sovereign immunity* allows a court to give up its right to jurisdiction over foreign enterprises or countries. The doctrine is based on traditional notions that a sovereign should not be subject to litigation in a foreign court. As a result, investors may not be able to obtain relief in their country's court system.

Some countries restrict the doctrine's application in commercial circumstances. If a foreign nation does not do this when it enters into a contract with a private party, then there is no recourse to U.S. courts in case of breach. The *Foreign Sovereign Immunities Act* provides a uniform rule for the determination of sovereign immunity in legal actions in this country's courts. The Act provides the following:

> Under international law, [countries] are not immune from the jurisdiction of foreign courts insofar as their commercial activities are concerned, and their commercial property may be levied upon for the satisfaction of judgments rendered against them in connection with their commercial activities.

Doing business with foreign partners can result in special problems that are not as common in domestic business. Issues of jurisdiction, the effect of statutes and treaties, and the ability to obtain a judgment—and collect on one—are not unique to international business but are major concerns that should not be ignored in the rush to grab what may look like easy money.

Summary

- In contrast to the domestic market, the international market is characterized by additional financial, political, and regulatory risks. Those risks arise from differences among countries in currencies, language, business customs, legal and social philosophies, and national economic goals.
- The principal sources of international trade law are the laws of individual countries, the laws arising from trade agreements between countries, and the rules enacted by worldwide or regional trade organizations.
- To reduce trade barriers, most nations participated in General Agreement on Tariffs and Trade (GATT), which resulted in the World Trade Organization, which now oversees some trade disputes.
- Most countries have import and export regulations. Import restrictions include import licensing requirements, import quotas, safety standards, government procurement policies, and customs procedures. To standardize tariff schedules and their application, most countries have adopted the harmonized tariff schedule to classify goods.
- The United States imposes prohibitions on the export of certain technologies that could be used by hostile nations or terrorists. The exportation of weapons and computers is monitored by the government.
- The most common international business arrangements are wholly owned subsidiaries, joint ventures, licensing agreements, franchise agreements, and contract manufacturing. The choice of business organization is influenced by the laws of a country, the purposes of the commercial venture, the financial resources of the parties, and the degree of managerial control desired by the company.
- The Foreign Corrupt Practices Act (FCPA) prohibits U.S. companies and their agents from bribing foreign officials. The FCPA makes the bribery of foreign officials a criminal offense and requires U.S. companies to establish internal accounting mechanisms to prevent such bribery. It is a criminal offense to make payments to foreign officials for the purpose of gaining business favor in a foreign country.
- To create an effective international contract, a business should consider differences in business customs, attitudes toward the contractual relationship, and

languages. Specific clauses in international contracts worthy of special consideration are the payment, choice of language, force majeure, and forum selection and choice-of-law clauses.

- Business in foreign countries may face special risks. Political upheavals, unstable monetary systems, dramatic changes in laws, and other problems associated with doing business with a developing country must be considered. Losses may occur through nationalization, expropriation, or confiscation of the foreign investment.
- Although most international trade occurs without incident, disputes sometimes arise concerning contract performance. Various national and international institutions may assist a business in effective dispute resolution. Those institutions include judicial litigation in court systems and arbitration. The doctrine of sovereign immunity may create bars to recovery through the judicial system.

Terms to Know

You should be able to define the following terms:

World Trade Organization, 557	duty-free ports, 561	force majeure, 570
harmonized tariff schedule, 558	Commodity Control List, 562	forum selection, 570
tariff, 559	Foreign Corrupt Practices Act, 564	nationalization, 571
dumping, 559	letter of credit, 568	expropriation, 571
antidumping duty, 560	repatriation, 568	sovereign immunity, 573
foreign trade zones, 561	choice-of-language clause, 569	

Discussion Question

1. Compare the merits of arbitration and judicial litigation as methods of dispute resolution in international trade.

Case Questions

1. A Houston corporation contracted for a German corporation to tow a drilling rig from Louisiana to an area off the coast of Italy, where the Houston company was to drill wells. The contract provided that: "Any dispute arising must be treated before the London Court of Justice." While on its way to Italy, the rig was damaged by a severe storm. The German tug towed the rig to Tampa, Florida, the nearest port. The Houston company sued in the U.S. District Court at Tampa, seeking $3.5 million damages from the German company. Is the use of the American court proper in this situation? What effect would the contract clause have on the lawsuit? [*M/S Bremen* v. *Zapata Off-Shore*, 92 S.Ct. 1907 (1972)]

2. Seawinds, a shipping company, was incorporated in Hong Kong with its principal place of business in California. It contracted with Nedlloyd Lines, a shipping company in the Netherlands, to "establish a joint venture company to carry on a transportation operation." The agreement had the following choice-of-law provision:

   This agreement shall be governed by and construed in accordance with Hong Kong law, and each party hereby irrevocably submits to the non-exclusive jurisdiction and service of process of the Hong Kong courts.

   Later, Seawinds sued in California state court, asserting that Nedlloyd had breached its duties under the contract by engaging in activities that led to the cancellation of charter hires essential to the joint venture's business and by making and then reneging on commitments to contribute additional capital. Nedlloyd responded that Seawinds had failed to state causes of action, because Hong Kong law was to be applied. If the case is brought in California court, which law should be applied: that of Hong Kong or that of California? Does California have a substantial relationship to the parties or their transaction? Is there a reasonable basis for the selection of Hong Kong law by the parties in their original agreement? [*Nedlloyd Lines B.V.* v. *Superior Court* (Seawinds Limited), 834 P.2d 1148 Sup. Ct., Cal. (1992)]

✓ **Check your answer at http://academic.cengage.com/blaw/meiners**

3. Nettie Effron, a Florida resident, bought a 16-day cruise of the Brazilian coast from Sun Line Cruises. The cruise was on the Stella Solaris, owned by Sun Line Greece. The cruise ticket stated that "any action against the carrier must be brought only before the courts of Athens, Greece, to the jurisdiction of which the Passenger submits himself formally excluding the jurisdiction of all and other court or courts of any other country." Effron was injured when she fell while on the ship. She sued for damages in federal court in New York. Sun Line moved to have the case dismissed because of the forum selection clause in the ticket. The district court refused to dismiss; Sun Line appealed. What resulted? [*Effron* v. *Sun Line Cruises*, 67 F.3d 7, 2nd Cir. (1995)]

4. Farr, a U.S. company, contracted to buy sugar from CAV, a Cuban company owned by U.S. citizens. Because the government of Cuba nationalized its sugar industry, including CAV, it demanded that payments for sugar already shipped must be made to the Banco Nacional de Cuba. At CAV's insistence that it was the rightful owner of the sugar, and that the nationalization violated international law, Farr paid CAV. Banco Nacional sued to collect payment from Farr for the sugar delivered. The case went to the Supreme Court, where Banco Nacional was held to be correct. On what theory did the Supreme Court base this opinion? [*Banco Nacional de Cuba* v. *Sabbatino*, 84 S. Ct. 923 (1964)]

✓ **Check your answer at http://academic.cengage.com/blaw/meiners**

5. The *F/V Cape Cod*, a commercial fishing vessel and the only asset of R&M, sank in 1994; during the accident, DiMercurio, a fisherman, was injured. He sued the company for his injuries and was awarded $350,000. R&M, having no assets, assigned DiMercurio all rights it had against Sphere Drake, the London-based insurer of the boat. DiMercurio took his claim to Sphere Drake, but it denied the demand and invoked the arbitration process specified in the policy, which called for arbitration of all coverage disputes in London. DeMercurio then sued, contesting the validity of the arbitration provision. The district court held for Sphere Drake. DiMercurio appealed. Does he have a valid claim? [*DiMercurio* v. *Sphere Drake Insurance PLC*, 202 F.3d 71, 1st Cir. (2000)]

6. Chisholm and Company and the Bank of Jamaica agreed that Chisholm was to arrange lines of credit from a number of banks and was to obtain ExIm Bank credit insurance. The Bank of Jamaica then "went around" Chisholm and dealt with ExIm Bank directly. It excluded Chisholm from receiving any benefit from the credit insurance that ExIm Bank provided. Chisholm sued the Bank of Jamaica. In its defense, the bank asserted that its actions were protected by sovereign immunity and the act of state doctrine. Were the bank's assertions correct? [*Chisholm and Company* v. *Bank of Jamaica*, 643 F.Supp. 1393 S.D. Fla. (1986)]

✓ **Check your answer at http://academic.cengage.com/blaw/meiners**

7. Vance provides security services. The company was hired by the government of Saudi Arabia to help with security for Princess Anud, a wife of King Fahad, while she was undergoing medical treatment in California. Security was supervised by the Saudi military. Vance hired Butters as a part-time, at-will security agent in the team guarding the Saudi royal family. Vance recommended she serve a full rotation in the command post at the family's California residence. The Saudi officer in charge of security rejected that recommendation, saying it would violate Islamic law for a woman to be in a command position and that the Princess only wanted to speak to male officers when she called the command post. Butters quit and sued Vance for sex discrimination. The district court entered summary judgment for Vance. Butters appealed; does she have grounds? [*Butters* v. *Vance International*, 225 F.3d 462, 4th Cir. (2000)]

8. Robinson worked for the Shields Agency as a security guard at a building in New York owned by the government of Malaysia. While the building was being renovated, Robinson slipped and fell on some "white substance" that had been spilled on the floor. Contending that he suffered permanent injuries in the fall, he sued the Malaysian government in tort for his injuries. The district court dismissed the suit, holding that the government was immune due to the Foreign Sovereign Immunities Act. Robinson appealed. Does the Act bar his suit? [*Robinson* v. *Government of Malaysia*, 269 F.3d 133, 2nd Cir. (2001)]

   ✓ **Check your answer at http://academic.cengage.com/blaw/meiners**

Ethics Question

1. In some countries, it is expected that businesses will pay off officials. Suppose it makes the difference between getting the contract and not getting the contract? If a payoff is not made, because of the Foreign Corrupt Practices Act, a foreign competitor that will make the bribe will get the deal. The American company that loses the deal would have to close a factory, putting 500 people out of work. The law aside, can you justify a bribe in that instance?

Internet Assignment

http://www.loc.gov
http://www.llrx.com
http://www.wto.org
http://www.oecd.org/home/

1. Find the URL for a legal guide to Afghanistan by the Law Library of Congress.
2. Using http://www.llrx.com, find a research guide for the European Union.
3. Find the URL for the text of the Agreement Establishing the World Trade Organization. According to the Organization for Economic Cooperation and Development, what does the acronym *PPP* represent?

Pulling It Together

In the last section of the text, we focused on statutory law, the regulations that follow from them, and how the courts and agencies interpret the laws in practice. When a statute imposes a rule different from the traditional common law, the statute dominates. So in certain areas of law, administrative rules are of key importance. Here we consider some cases that cover at least two areas of law that we have considered in the text.

1. Morrison and Gugle opened a store together. The business was incorporated; each owned half the stock. Gugle was president; Morrison was secretary-treasurer. Both were employees of the corporation. They got into a dispute over money. Gugle did not trust Morrison and sent her a letter offering to buy her out. Morrison did not respond. Gugle fired her and denied her access to company records. Morrison sued Gugle for wrongful termination and defamation. The trial court held for Gugle. Morrison appealed. Does employment law, corporation law, or tort law control this matter?

2. Illinois Tool Works (ITW) has a patent on a printhead and ink container that use unpatented ink in printing. ITW required its customers to only buy ink from ITW to use with their printheads and containers. They could not buy refill ink from other suppliers, such as Independent Ink, which sued ITW for antitrust violation for improperly tying the sale of ink to the sale of printheads and containers. Did the fact that the printheads and containers were patented give ITW the right to require buyers to buy only their ink, or was that an abuse of the patents that created an antitrust violation?

3. A federal statute, the Magnuson-Moss Warranty Act, requires sellers of consumer products to meet certain standards in the warranties they place on goods. Many states have lemon laws that concern the rights of consumers if they buy a vehicle that turns out to have problems that cannot be fixed in a reasonable number of attempts. Sales of goods are also covered by the UCC or possibly by the common law. The Edwards bought a new Hyundai that had a six-year, 72,000 mile bumper-to-bumper warranty. It had multiple problems over the next two years plus and, despite many repair attempts, still had problems. The Edwards sued for breach of written warranty, breach of implied warranty of merchantability, violation of the federal Magnuson-Moss Warranty Act, and violation of the Missouri Lemon Law. Can all of these claims, based on different sources of law, be brought together?

4. Kossol was a partner in Continental Food Network, which sold food plans to consumers. Consumers signed contracts to pay thousands of dollars for a plan to provide them a certain quantity of food over several years and give them a "free" freezer. The plan cost much more than the food and freezer were worth, and the food was not the quality claimed. The Attorney General of Maryland sued under state consumer protection law. The court ordered the operation shut down and $6 million in restitution paid to consumers. Kossol was held jointly and severally liable for the payments. He appealed, contending that only the parent company could be held liable, and that he could not be held personally liable. Assuming there was consumer fraud, could liability go against both the owners of the business as well as the business itself?

5. Ravenscroft worked for Westvaco for years when he was fired for sexual harassment of a co-worker in violation of company policy. He challenged his discharge as improper, because he was represented in employment by a union. The collective bargaining agreement stated that the union could challenge discharges by arbitration. The arbitrator then held that Ravenscroft had harassed the woman, but ordered him reinstated in his job. The company sued, contending that the arbitrator exceeded his authority by substituting his judgment for that of management and that reinstatement violated public policy, because it prevented the company from dealing effectively with sexual harassment. Who prevails? Does labor law or discrimination law control?

Getty Images

Appendix A

Legal Research and the Internet

Legal Information

There are several good starting points for finding free legal information on the Internet. FindLaw (*http://www.findlaw.com*) has become the legal information portal for those lacking access to fee-based services, such as Westlaw and Lexis. The Legal Information Institute (LII) at Cornell (*http://www.law.cornell.edu*) also attempts to provide legal information to the world. WashLawWEB (*http://www.washlaw.edu*) provides many links through its no-nonsense menu. Hieros Gamos (*http://www.hg.org*) provides links for foreign and international legal research.

If these sites do not produce the results you want, try LawRunner at the Internet Legal Research Group (*http://www.lawrunner.com*), LawCrawler at FindLaw (*http://lawcrawler.findlaw.com/*), or a general search engine (*http://www.google.com*, *http://www.yahoo.com*, or *http://www.msn.com*). Obviously, it helps to know and use the advanced search techniques of whichever search engine you choose. Also, it helps to acquaint oneself with the area of law one's issue addresses. For topical legal research that includes topics such as business organizations, two Web sites, recommended by Internet experts Kathy Biehl and Tara Calishan in *The Lawyer's Guide to the Internet* (2000), still seem useful: FindLaw Legal Subjects (*http://www.findlaw.com/01topics/index.html*) and Legal Materials Organized by Topic (*http://www.law.cornell.edu/wex/index.php/Category:Overview*). LSU Libraries provides an Internet Searching page (*http://www.lib.lsu.edu/general/internet_search.html*), which links to a variety of search engines. Search Engine Showdown (*http://www.searchengineshowdown.com*) provides an excellent comparison of Internet search engines.

Students should become familiar with their institution's library Web site. Virtually every law school library and university has a Web site with links to relevant reference sources. In addition to providing access to the library's online catalog, the library or its consortium may allow affiliated students access to legal databases, full text journal databases, indexes to legal journals, and general reference databases. In addition, libraries are increasingly accommodating e-mail reference questions and virtual reference sessions. Many of these services are available to affiliated users remotely by the Internet. Public patrons may be able to access some of these services in the library itself.

Although there are a number of commercial sites that have free legal information, FindLaw (*http://www.findlaw.com*) has become the dominant provider of legal information to the public. Yahoo! offers an alternative index to governmental and legal information. For a fee, Westlaw and Lexis directly market their services to the public. Their citator services, Key-Cite and Shepard's, respectively—used to ensure that cited law is still "good"—are absent from free or less expensive legal databases. For legal newspapers via the Internet, visit Law.com (*http://www.law.com*).

Primary sources of law, in an American context, consist of cases, legislation (statutes), and administrative regulations. The Internet is a potential source for each type of law, though not every statute or case can be found for free on the Internet. Courts (e.g., the U.S. Supreme Court, federal appellate courts, and some federal district courts) have been releasing their opinions via the Internet in vendor-neutral formats since 1994. Government agencies, such as the Library of Congress and the Government Printing Office (GPO), have made available by the Internet—for free—sources such as federal legislative materials (since the 104th Congress), the *Federal Register*, and the *Code of Federal Regulations*.

Secondary sources—such as encyclopedias, treatises, and the *American Law Reports*—are not likely to be found for free on the Web. Only a fraction of published law review articles are available for free on the Internet, although recent international or technological law review articles may be available. One may search FindLaw, American Law Sources On-Line (*http://www.lawsource.com/also/usa.cgi?usj*), or the USC Law School's *legal journals* (*http://law-web.usc.edu/library/resources/journals.cfm*), to see if a given law review article is available in full-text via the Internet. The savvy legal researcher realizes that consulting a relevant secondary source at the outset, even one not available on the Internet, may save time and effort in the long run.

Supreme Court opinions are available at FindLaw and LII publishers opinions from May 1990—going back as far as 1893—and selected previous ones. The U.S. Supreme Court also has its own Web site (*http://www.supremecourtus.gov*). Federal appellate courts began to place their opinions on the Internet in the early 1990's. For information and statistics pertaining to the federal courts, see *http://www.uscourts.gov*. For an interactive map that links to opinions and related information about the U.S. federal appellate courts, visit the Emory Law Library's Federal Courts Finder (*http://www.law.emory.edu/FEDCTS*). Federal district court opinions may or may not be available; try searching FindLaw's index (*http://www.find-law.com/10fedgov/judicial/district_courts.html*). For coverage of state courts, a good starting point is the National Center for State Courts (*http://www.ncsconline.org/D_KIS/info_court_web_sites.html*) or FindLaw (*http://www.findlaw.com/11stategov*).

The *U.S. Code* is available at GPO Access (*http://www.gpoaccess.gov*). The Thomas database (*http://thomas.loc.gov*) in the Library of Congress allows users to access federal legislative information, such as Bill Summary and Status (93rd Congress to present), Bill Text (101st to present), Public Laws By Law Number (93rd to present), *Congressional Record* (101st to present), *Congressional Record Index* (194th to present), Roll Call Votes (101st to present), Committee Reports (194th to present) and House and Senate Committee information. The Government Printing Office's GPO Access database also hosts *Public Laws* back to 1994, and the *Congressional Record* back to 1995.

Administrative law resources are readily available on the Internet. The GPO provides access to the *Federal Register* stated twice, the *Code of Federal Regulations*, the *List of CFR Sections Affected (LSA)*, the *United States Government Manual*, and other administrative law databases. Most, if not all, federal administrative agencies have Web pages that allow access to pertinent statutory and regulatory sources, as well as agency-specific information. USA.gov (*http://www.usa.gov*, formerly *firstgov.gov*) is a good starting point for access to federal agency information on the Internet. A Spanish-language version of the portal is available at *http://www.usa.gov/gobiernousa/index.shtml*.

Availability of state administrative law sources via the Internet varies; the Web site of the National Association of Secretaries of State (*http://nass.org/acr/html/internet.html*) provides comprehensive links to state administrative materials, where available.

Researching a new topic? Visit LLRX.com (*http://www.llrx.com*) and see if any of the research guides are relevant. Or, if you are unfamiliar with both the jurisdiction and the legal issue or process you are researching, search for a research guide from a library in that jurisdiction. For example, the New York State Library has a very useful guide to research legislative history in New York available at *http://www.nysl.nysed.gov/leghist/*. Similarly, the Law Librarians' Society of Washington D.C. provides an excellent guide to federal legislative history research (*http://www.llsdc.org/sourcebook/fed-leg-hist.htm*).

The Internet now boasts so-called Web 2.0 features, such as blogs—expert and non expert commentary on any topic under the sun; RSS, a format for syndicating Internet content, such as news; and wikis, collaborative work areas, such as Wikipedia. While these tools may help manage your research and access background research information, remember that such Internet resources are tools and unlikely to be the best for accurate, in-depth legal research.

Try to find statutes from the official Web site of the jurisdiction you are researching. Likewise, try to find court opinions (cases) from official court Web sites. Remember the fee-based services, such as Westlaw, Lexis, LoisLaw, and VersusLaw, and databases licensed by your institutional or public library may be a more appropriate starting point. Westlaw and

Lexis are especially valuable in providing trustworthy sources and tools called *citators*—such as KeyCite and Shepard's—that help you confirm that the statute or case you are citing is still "good law." Many academic and public libraries allow patrons working in the library to access Westlaw, Lexis, or some version thereof.

Business Information

Academic institutions offer the starting point for effective business research via the Internet. Most business school Web sites offer a mix of proprietary information accessible only to currently affiliated members of their communities, as well as an assortment of generally accessible Web sites. Academic institutions that offer extensive business research guides—with selected, related websites—include the Jackson Library at Stanford University (*http://www.gsb.stanford.edu/jacksonlibrary/research*) and the Lippincott Library of the Wharton School at the University of Pennsylvania (*http://gethelp.library.upenn.edu/guides/business/businesswebsites.html*). Ohio State University provides the Virtual Finance Library (*http://fisher.osu.edu/fin/cerns.htm*), which provides, among other information, a Finance Site List for researchers. As previously mentioned, it is key that the business researcher become familiar with the online subscription databases, such as ABI/Inform and Business Sources Premier, to which he or she has access via affiliation with an institutional or public library.

The Securities and Exchange Commission's EDGAR database (*http://www.sec.gov*) is a major governmental source for finding such information as registration statements and periodic reports on large public companies. Another non profit, human-edited source of business information links is the Librarian's Index to the Internet (*http://lii.org*).

Companies, big and small, have Web pages offering their mission statements, product descriptions, and annual reports. Larger companies, such as IBM (*http://www.ibm.com*), also post press releases and messages from company executives. Corporate Web sites, while primarily marketing tools, may shed light on corporate America's reaction to and opinions regarding specific government policy measures or rules of law. Many corporate sites provide an e-mail address for a company official. With a little creativity, one can often acquire information unavailable through traditional research methods. Yahoo! (*http://www.yahoo.com*) and Yahoo! Finance (*http://finance.yahoo.com*) provide access to information about businesses, finances, and stock prices.

The commercial providers of business information by the Internet include BRINT.com, The BizTech Network (*http://www.brint.com*). The site claims to be "the premier business and technology knowledge portal and global community network for the new world of business." It features a searchable news section, an e-business and e-commerce section, featured articles and books, a knowledge-management section, and a new economy business technology section. CEOExpress (*http://www.ceoexpress.com*), "designed by a busy executive for busy executives," provides links to daily news and information, as well as business research. Hoovers Online (*http://www.hoovers.com*), "The Business Network," features sections about companies, IPOs, free newsletters, small businesses, business links, and a portfolio tool.

News Information

Keeping up on recent news developments is easy. For breaking news, visit ABC News (*http://www.abcnews.go.com*), CBS News (http://www.cbsnews.com), CNN Interactive (*http://www.cnn.com*), MSNBC (*http://www.msnbc.com*), or Fox News (*http://www.foxnews.com*). Some prefer more independent sources, such as the Drudge Report (*http://www.drudgereport.com*), and various *blogs*, or *weblogs*. Blogs related to law are sometimes called *blawgs*. In addition to news updates via Web browsers, most newspapers have a Web site with at least some free content. The *Wall Street Journal* (*http://www.wsj.com*) still limits access to its online content to current print subscribers. Access to current articles in the *New York Times* (*http://www.nyt.com*) is free with registration as of this writing. Articles from its archives are not. Additional Web sites of major newspapers include the *Boston Globe* (*http://www.boston.com/globe*), the

Chicago Tribune (*http://www.chicagotribune.com*), and the *Washington Post* (*http://www.washingtonpost.com*) includes a searchable database of the previous two weeks' issues. The extent of archival coverage on newspapers' Web sites varies, so those doing in-depth news research may wish to use an index of newspaper articles, which are readily available from most libraries for registered patrons. Newspapers.com (*http://www.newspapers.com*) is the place to see if one's local newspaper has an Internet presence.

Case Analysis and Legal Research

The legal environment of business is often one's first encounter with the law and the legal process in detail. Legal citations, the organization of legal materials, and opinion analysis can be bewildering at first. This appendix provides a look at the structure of a court opinion, plus a bit more detail on legal sources.

Reading a Legal Opinion

In resolving disputes, courts often report their decisions in written opinions. Decisions of appellate courts are most frequently reported. Usually only important decisions at the trial court level are reported. Through a written opinion, a judge explains the legal basis for the decision reached. Published opinions provide legal precedents in the common law.

An opinion can exceed one hundred pages and involves several complex issues. To help analyze an opinion, law students often prepare a summary of the opinion, called a case *brief*, essentially an abstract of the opinion setting forth its most essential parts. Attorneys often write case briefs in researching a legal problem, particularly when a case involves a complicated situation or the dispute requires the court to consider several legal questions in reaching a resolution.

To brief an opinion, there is no formal or standard procedure. Here, we provide a basic approach to assist in briefing the opinions excerpted in this text. It is an effective way to study legal opinions.

Before you brief an opinion, read it carefully. Then separate the opinion into its five fundamental parts by asking yourself questions about those parts:

(1) A Statement of the Significant Facts
Who is the plaintiff? The defendant?
Who did what to whom?
What relief is being sought from the court?

(2) A Statement of the Relevant Procedural History
Who prevailed in the lower court?
Which party is appealing?

(3) A Statement of the Legal Issue in the Dispute
What are the specific legal questions the court is being asked to address?

(4) A Statement of the Court's Decision
How did the court respond to the question(s) posed to it?
Did the plaintiff or the defendant prevail on the appeal?

(5) An Explanation of the Court's Reasoning
What is the legal basis for the court's decision?

This basic procedure is illustrated and described in the following opinion. Before examining the brief, read the actual opinion of the court in the right-hand column. In the left-hand column is a commentary on the case opinion. Although an understanding of the law and legal terms used in the opinion is not essential to an understanding of the briefing process, most legal terms used in the opinion are defined in the glossary at the back of this text. As in the text, this opinion has been shortened by inserting * * * or … where material has been deleted. The essence is retained in the material that remains.

Dallas Parks v. George Steinbrenner and New York Yankees, Inc.
New York Supreme Court, Appellate Division, First Department
520 N.Y. 2d 374 (1987)

Brief and Explanation Begin by summarizing the essential facts in the opinion. In the text, the facts and procedural history are summarized for you in the Case Background section provided with each opinion.

1. Facts Dallas Parks, the plaintiff, alleges that he was defamed by the defendant, George Steinbrenner, owner of the New York Yankees. The alleged defamation occurred when the defendant issued a press release criticizing Park's abilities as a baseball umpire. The plaintiff seeks damages on the grounds that the press release falsely attacked his abilities as an umpire.

> Note: The procedural history summarizes how the lower court(s) ruled on the dispute. In the text, the procedural history is summarized in the Case Background section.

2. Procedural History The defendant argued that the press release represented a constitutionally protected expression of opinion. The Special Term (the lower court) disagreed, finding that although the press release expressed an opinion, it was not backed up by an adequate statement of the facts to support that opinion. The defendant appealed to the New York Supreme Court.

> Note: The legal issue in the opinion is the question the parties are asking the court to resolve. Some opinions state exactly what the issue is that the court is being asked to resolve. In the text, the issue is generally found in our summary of the lower court's decision or from the stated contentions of the parties. In analyzing an opinion in the text, state the issue in your own words to aid your understanding of the opinion. Next we see the names of the four appeals judges who heard the appeal. Then we see the first part of their decision.

Before Carro, J. P., and Kassal, Ellerin, Wallach, JJ.

Memorandum Decision This action for defamation brings into play one of the most colorful of American traditions—the razzing of the umpire.

The Plaintiff, Dallas Parks, served as an American League baseball umpire from 1979 through 1982. He alleges that he was defamed by George Steinbrenner, principal owner of the New York Yankees, when Steinbrenner, on August 29, 1982, issued a press release, excerpts of which were published in newspapers throughout the United States, criticizing Park's abilities as an umpire. The press release, which was issued after the Yankees had played a two-game series with the Toronto Blue Jays in Toronto, Cananda, on August 27th and 28th, at which Parks officiated, reads as follows:

> Judging on his last two days' performance, my people tell me that he is not a capable umpire. He is a member of one of the

finest crews umpiring in the American League today, but obviously he doesn't measure up.

We are making no excuse for the team's play this season, but this weekend our team has had several key injuries and for umpire Dallas Parks to throw two of our players out of ballgames in two days on plays he misjudges is "ludicrous."

This man, in my opinion, has had it in for the Yankees ever since I labeled him and several of the umpires as "scabs" because they worked the American League games in 1979 during the umpires' strike.

Parks must learn that the word *scab* is a commonly used phrase. It is in no way meant as a personal insult. However, because he worked during the strike for baseball management does not mean he should be protected by them and annually given a job is not capable of handling.

3. Issue Does the press release constitute a constitutionally protected statement of pure opinion?

> Note: After stating the issue, state the court's decision, both procedural (e.g., judgment for the defendant) and substantive (a yes or no response to the issue presented).

4. The Court's Decision Yes, the press release is a constitutionally protected expression of pure opinion. Judgment for the defendant; the Special Term's trial court's decision is reversed.

> Note: The court's rationale is the heart of the opinion. The court will generally discuss the relevant law surrounding the question presented to it. Then the court will apply that law to the facts of the dispute before it. In reaching its decision, the court will explain its rationale—why and how it reached the conclusion that the facts in this dispute do or do not fall within the existing law. In the text, the court's rationale is presented in excerpts from the actual opinions in the Case Decision section.

5. Court's Reasoning Quoting the court: A statement of pure opinion is a statement that is accompanied by the facts upon which it is based, or it does not imply that it is based on undisclosed facts.

Statements that constitute pure opinion whether false or libelous may not serve as the basis for an action for defamation.

In determining whether a statement is fact or opinion, consideration is given to what an average person hearing or reading the statement will take it to mean, the circumstances surrounding its use, and the way it is written.

The press release must be evaluated within the broader social context of baseball. It is an American tradition to verbally abuse umpires. In this context, the average reader would perceive the release as opinion and not fact. The release is the kind of statement that generally accompanies a voicing of displeasure at an umpire's calls.

The statement by the defendant represents the view of an owner of a baseball team that is doing poorly and who has chosen to vent his frustration by baiting the umpire.

There is no indication that defendant's opinions are based on some other undisclosed facts unknown to the reader.

This less than complimentary critical assessment appears to have been the "final straw" in the rhubarb that had long simmered between the umpire and the owner and resulted in commencement of the instant action, against Steinbrenner and the Yankees, wherein plaintiff seeks damages for defamation on the ground that the press release falsely impugned his ability, competence, conduct, and fairness as a baseball umpire.

In subsequently moving to dismiss the complaint for failure to state a cause of action, defendants argued that the press release represented a nonactionable, constitutionally protected expression of opinion. While Special Term [lower court] found that the statement was "clearly expressed as an opinion," it nevertheless held that the complaint sufficiently pleaded a cause of action in defamation because the press release did not set forth an adequate statement of fact contained in the statement—i.e., that Parks expelled two Yankee players from the game—did "not in any way support the opinions proffered" that plaintiff was incompetent and biased and, further, that no factual basis was set forth for the conclusory assertion that plaintiff misjudged plays.

We disagree with Special Term's assessment of the press release in question and find that it constituted a constitutionally protected expression of pure opinion.

In all defamation cases, the threshold issue which must be determined, as a matter of law, is whether the complained of statements constitute fact or opinion. If they fall within the ambit of "pure opinion," then even if false and libelous, and no matter how perjorative or pernicious they may be, such statements are safeguarded and may not serve as the basis for an action in defamation. A nonactionable "pure opinion" is defined as a statement of opinion which either is accompanied by a recitation of the facts upon which it is based, or, if not so accompanied, does not imply that it is based upon undisclosed facts. Alternatively, when a defamatory statement of opinion implies that it is based upon undisclosed detrimental facts which justify the opinion but are unknown to those reading or hearing it, it is a "mixed opinion" and actionable. Similarly actionable as a "mixed opinion" is a defamatory opinion which is ostensibly accompanied by a recitation of the underlying facts upon which the opinion is based, but those underlying facts are either falsely misrepresented or grossly distorted.

Determining whether particular statements, or particular words, express fact or opinion is ofttimes an exercise beset by the uncertainties engendered by the imprecision and varying nuance inherent in language. While mechanistic rules and rigid sets of criteria have been eschewed as inappropriate vehicles for the sensitive process of separating fact from opinion, reference to various general criteria has been found helpful in resolving the issue. Predominant among these is that the determination is to be made on the basis of what the average person hearing or reading the communication would take it to mean, and what significance is to be accorded the purpose of the words, the circumstances surrounding their use and the manner, tone, and style with which they are used. An approach which was favorably commented upon in the *Steinbrenner* case is that set forth by Judge Starr in his plurality opinion in *Ollman* v. *Evans* which enunciates four factors which should generally be considered in differentiating between fact and opinion. They are summarized … as follows:

1) an assessment of whether the specific language in issue has a precise meaning which is readily understood or whether it is indefinite and ambiguous;
2) a determination of whether the statement is capable of being objectively characterized as true or false;
3) an examination of the full context of the communication in which the statement appears; and
4) a consideration of the broader social context or setting surrounding the communication including the existence of any applicable customs or conventions which might signal to readers or listeners that what is being read or heard is likely to be opinion, not fact.

These factors have particular relevance to the statement here in issue, which must be evaluated within the broader social context of a baseball club owner versus an umpire, and special attention should be accorded to whether there exist any customs and conventions regarding the status of an umpire in the great American pastime which would signal to readers that what is being read is likely to be opinion not fact.

* * *

From the late nineteenth century on, the baseball umpire has come to expect not only verbal abuse, but in many cases, physical attack as well, as part of the "robust debate" ingrained in the profession. …

Judges, too, have expressed their acceptance of this American tradition. In dimissing a minor league general manager's defamation action on other grounds, a federal court noted that harsh insults, especially those directed at an umpire, are accepted commonplace occurrences in baseball.

* * *

When Steinbrenner's remarks are viewed in this context, it is clear that they would be perceived by the average reader as a statement of opinion, and not fact. The negative characterizations of the plaintiff umpire as "not capable," that "he doesn't measure up," that he "misjudges" plays and that his decision to "throw two of our players out of ball games" was "ludicrous" are readily understood to be the kind of "rhetorical hyperbole" that generally accompany the communication of displeasure at an umpire's "calls." While the subjective and emotional character of such sentiments is commonly

continues

recognized and construed as "opinion" rather than fact, that view is expressly emphasized upon a reading of the entire press release with its qualifying phrases of "my people tell me" immediately evident that the statement represents the view of the owner of an embattled baseball team who is obviously chafing at "the team's (poor) play this season," which has been exacerbated by a weekend of injuries and ejections of players, and who is venting his frustrations in the venerated American tradition of "baiting the umpire." Indeed, even if the assertions in the statement implying that plaintiff was incompetent and biased in performing his duties were to be viewed as statements of fact, it is questionable whether they could be construed as defamatory, i.e., exposing the plaintiff to public contempt, ridicule, aversion, and disgrace and inducing an evil opinion of him in the minds of right thinking persons—in light of the generally "critical" attitudes which baseball umpires, in any event, ordinarily inspire in both the game's fans and its participants.

Although acknowledging that the statement in issue was "clearly expressed as opinion," Special Term held that it was actionable, because the accompanying underlying facts were found by Special Term not to adequately support the opinions proffered. That one may dispute the conclusions drawn from the specified facts is not, however, the test. So long as the opinion is accompanied by a recitation of the facts upon which it is based, it is deemed a "pure opinion" and is afforded complete immunity even though the facts do not support the opinion. The rationale for this broad protection of an expression of opinion accompanied by a recitation of the facts upon which it is based is that the reader has the opportunity to assess the basis upon which the opinion was reached in order to draw his or her own conclusions concerning its validity.

* * *

The reverence which the First Amendment accords to ideas has properly resulted in the determination that, "however pernicious an opinion may seem, we depend for its correction not on the conscience of judges and juries but on the competition of other ideas." Those competing ideas about baseball's arbiters will undoubtedly continue to abound aplenty both on the playing fields and in the sports columns, albeit not in the courtroom.

Accordingly the Order, Supreme Court, Bronx County (Alfred J. Callahan, J.), entered May 9, 1986, which denied the defendants' motion to dismiss the complaint and supplemental complaint for failure to state a cause of action, should be reversed, on the law, and the complaint dismissed, without costs.

Major Sources of the Law

There are several important sources of law in the United States, including the U.S. Constitution; case law established by the written opinions of judges; statutes enacted by legislative bodies; regulatory agency orders, opinions, and regulations; treatises; law reviews; and Restatements of Law. At one time or another, we reference these sources in explaining the laws making up the legal environment of business. This section provides a guide to reading a citation to a source of law. If you decide to study an aspect of the legal environment in more detail, this section provides guidance in locating appropriate material.

Case Law

The published judicial opinions of all federal courts and the appellate state courts are available in court reporters. As a rule, opinions appear in hardback volumes of the reporters about a year after a court has delivered its decision. The opinions are available more quickly in paperback volumes published shortly after the case is decided, even more quickly through computer research services (such as Westlaw and Lexis), and in the form of *slip opinions*, copies of a decision as soon as it is made public by the court. Appendix A discussed which of these are available for free on the Internet.

Supreme Court decisions are published in *United States Reporter* (U.S.), *Supreme Court Reporter* (S.Ct.), *Lawyers' Edition of Supreme Court Reports* (L.Ed.), and *U.S. Law Week*. A citation reads as follows: *Arnett v. Kennedy*, 416 U.S. 134, 94 S.Ct. 1633 (1974). This tells us that Arnett appealed a decision of a lower court to the U.S. Supreme Court. In 1974, the Supreme Court decided the case (which was argued in 1973), and its decision is reported in volume 416 of *United States Reporter* beginning on page 134 and in volume 94 of *Supreme Court Reporter* beginning on page 1633. A reference to a point cited on a particular page in that opinion might read 416 U.S. 134, 137, which means that the case begins on page 134 and the particular point referenced is on page 137. Decisions of U.S. Circuit Courts of Appeals are reported in *Federal Reporter* (F.), now in its third series (F.3d). The following is an example of a citation: *Easton Publishing Co.* v. *Federal Communications Commission*, 175 F.2d 344 (1949). The decision in this case can be found in volume 175 of *Federal Reporter* (second series), page 344. The decision was issued by the court in 1949.

Opinions of U.S. district courts that the judges decide to publish are reported in *Federal Supplement* (F.Supp.) now in its second (2d) series. An example *is Amalgamated Meat Cutters* v. *Connally*, 337 F.Supp. 737 S.D. NY (1971). The decision can be found in volume 337 of *Federal Supplement* beginning on page 737. The case was decided by the federal district court in the southern district of New York in 1971.

State appellate court decisions are reported in regional reporters published by West Publishing Company. Decisions of the state supreme courts and courts of appeals for Arkansas, Kentucky, Missouri, Tennessee, and Texas, for example, are reported in *South Western Reporter* (S.W.). As shown in Exhibit A.1, other state court opinions are reported in *Atlantic Reporter* (A.), *North Eastern Reporter* (N.E.), *North Western Reporter* (N.W.), *Pacific Reporter* (P.), *South Eastern Reporter* (S.E.), and *Southern Reporter* (S.), all of which are in the second series (2d). Because they handle so many cases, California and New York have individual reporters, *New York Supplement* and *California Reporter*. Some states publish their own reporters in addition to the West series.

Statutory Law

Statutes, laws passed by Congress, are published in the *United States Code* (U.S.C.) and printed by the U.S. Government Printing Office. The U.S.C. contains the text of all laws passed by Congress and signed by the president. A reference to this source might read 40 U.S.C. §13.1 (volume 40, *United States Code*, section 13.1). As noted in Appendix A, these are available on the Internet.

A very popular source of statutory law is the *United States Code Annotated* (U.S.C.A.). In the U.S.C.A., each section of a statute contains helpful annotations that provide references to the legislative history of the section and to court decisions using and interpreting it. A reference to this source might read 14 U.S.C.A. §45.3 (volume 14, *United States Code Annotated*, section 45.3). In both the U.S.C. and the U.S.C.A., the laws are organized and integrated into a pattern that makes them relatively easy to find and to read.

The U.S. Government Printing Office also publishes *Statutes at Large*, a chronological list of all laws enacted by Congress. This list is not often used unless it is necessary to look up a law that has just been passed by Congress but that is not yet reported in the U.S.C. or U.S.C.A. A full citation might read: Voting Rights Act of 1965, Pub.L. No. 89–110, 79 Stat. 437, 42 U.S.C. §§1971, 1973. The Voting Rights Act of 1965 was the 110th *Public Law* enacted by the 89th Congress and appears in volume 79 of *Statutes at Large*, page 437. In addition, it appears in volume 42 of the U.S.C., sections 1971 and 1973. Also, remember that there is often a difference between the number of the section in the statute as written by Congress and the number of the section in the Code. For example, the "National Environmental Policy Act of 1969, §102, 42 U.S.C. §4332" means that section 102 of the statute as passed by Congress is found in section 4332 of volume 42 of the U.S.C.

Regulatory Law

Regulations, rules passed by agencies subsequent to a congressional statute, are published in the *Code of Federal Regulations* (C.F.R.). These regulations are intended to implement a particular statute enacted by Congress. The C.F.R., revised annually, is organized by subject matter and contains the text of regulations in effect as of the date of publication. A citation reading 7 C.F.R. §912.65 refers to Title 7 of the *Code of Federal Regulations*, section 912.65. Different titles refer to different government agencies. These are all available on the Internet.

To keep up-to-date on new and proposed regulations, one needs to consult the *Federal Register* (Fed.Reg.). Printed five days a week by the U.S. Government Printing Office, the *Federal Register* lists all proposed regulations and all new and amended regulations. A citation might read 46 Fed.Reg. 26,501 (1981). This refers to volume 46 of the *Federal Register*, published in 1981, page 26,501, which has to do with a new environmental standard.

Agency Orders and Opinions

Agency orders and opinions are official regulatory materials that go beyond the regulations. Orders may be issued by the top officials (e.g., the commissioners) of a regulatory agency, while opinions are generally issued by an agency's administrative law judge in adjudicatory hearings (discussed in Chapter 15). While agencies usually have official publications published on the Internet, the agency materials are also published by private companies such as Commerce Clearing House, Bureau of National Affairs, and Prentice-Hall. Each reporter covers a single topic, such as environmental law or federal tax law. The reporters are up-to-date and contain new regulations, orders, opinions, court decisions, and other materials of interest to anyone following regulations in a certain area. These reporters, which are usually large loose-leaf binders, cover hundreds of topics, such as chemical regulations, hazardous materials, transportation, noise regulations, collective bargaining negotiations, securities regulations, patents, and antitrust laws.

Treatises, Law Reviews, and Restatements of the Law

Important secondary sources of law are legal treatises, law reviews, and Restatements of Law. Most of these are not freely available on the Internet. Treatises generally cover one area or topic of law, summarizing the principles and rules dealing with the topic. An example of a treatise is W. Jaeger, *Williston on Contracts* (3d ed. 1957).

Law reviews, published by law schools and edited by law students, contain articles written by legal scholars, judges, law students, and practitioners on virtually all aspects of the law. An example of a legal citation to a law review is Mark J. Roe, "Corporate Strategic Reaction to Mass Tort," 72 *Virginia Law Review* 1 (1986), which means that the article "Corporate Strategic Reaction to Mass Tort" written by Mark J. Roe can be found in volume 72 of *Virginia Law Review* beginning on page 1.

Like a treatise, a Restatement is limited in its coverage to a single area of law. Restatements are the consequence of intensive study on a specific topic by legal scholars, culminating in a written statement of the law. That statement will include rules stated in bold type—often referred to as *black-letter law*—along with explanatory comments. The rules presented are usually synthesized from opinions of the courts in all jurisdictions. An example is *Restatement (Second) of Torts*.

The Constitution of the United States of America

Preamble

We the People of the United States, in Order to form a more perfect Union, establish Justice, insure domestic Tranquility, provide for the common defence, promote the general Welfare, and secure the Blessings of Liberty to ourselves and our Posterity, do ordain and establish this Constitution for the United States of America.

Article I

Section 1. All legislative Powers herein granted shall be vested in a Congress of the United States, which shall consist of a Senate and House of Representatives.

Section 2. The House of Representatives shall be composed of Members chosen every second Year by the People of the several States, and the Electors in each State shall have the Qualifications requisite for Electors of the most numerous Branch of the State Legislature.

No Person shall be a Representative who shall not have attained to the Age of twenty five Years, and been seven Years a Citizen of the United States, and who shall not, when elected, be an Inhabitant of that State in which he shall be chosen.

Representatives and direct Taxes shall be apportioned among the several States which may be included within this Union, according to their respective Numbers, which shall be determined by adding to the whole Number of free Persons, including those bound to Service for a Term of Years, and excluding Indians not taxed, three fifths of all other Persons. The actual Enumeration shall be made within three Years after the first Meeting of the Congress of the United States, and within every subsequent Term of ten Years, in such Manner as they shall by Law direct. The number of Representatives shall not exceed one for every thirty Thousand, but each State shall have at Least one Representative; and until such enumeration shall be made, the State of New Hampshire shall be entitled to chuse three, Massachusetts eight, Rhode Island and Providence Plantations one, Connecticut five, New York six, New Jersey four, Pennsylvania eight, Delaware one, Maryland six, Virginia ten, North Carolina five, South Carolina five, and Georgia three.

When vacancies happen in the Representation from any State, the Executive Authority thereof shall issue Writs of Election to fill such vacancies.

The House of Representatives shall chuse their Speaker and other Officers; and shall have the sole Power of Impeachment.

Section 3. The Senate of the United States shall be composed of two Senators from each State, chosen by the Legislature thereof, for six Years; and each Senator shall have one Vote.

Immediately after they shall be assembled in Consequence of the first Election, they shall be divided as equally as may be into three Classes. The Seats of the Senators of the first Class shall be vacated at the Expiration of the second Year, of the second Class at the Expiration of the fourth Year, and of the third Class at the Expiration of the sixth Year, so that one third may be chosen every second Year; and if Vacancies happen by Resignation, or otherwise, during the Recess of the Legislature of any State, the Executive thereof may make temporary Appointments until the next Meeting of the Legislature, which shall then fill such Vacancies.

No Person shall be a Senator who shall not have attained to the Age of thirty Years, and been nine Years a Citizen of the United States, and who shall not, when elected, be an Inhabitant of that State for which he shall be chosen.

The Vice President of the United States shall be President of the Senate, but shall have no Vote, unless they be equally divided.

The Senate shall chuse their other Officers, and also a President pro tempore, in the Absence of the Vice President, or when he shall exercise the Office of President of the United States.

The Senate shall have the sole power to try all Impeachments. When sitting for that Purpose, they shall be on Oath or Affirmation. When the President of the United States is tried, the Chief Justice shall preside: And no Person shall be convicted without the Concurrence of two thirds of the Members present.

Judgment in Cases of Impeachment shall not extend further than to removal from Office, and disqualification to hold and enjoy any Office of honor, Trust or Profit under the United States: but the Party convicted shall nevertheless be liable and subject to Indictment, Trial, Judgment and Punishment, according to Law.

Section 4. The Times, Places and Manner of holding Elections for Senators and Representatives, shall be prescribed in each State by the Legislature thereof: but the Congress may at any time by Law make or alter such Regulations, except as to the Places of chusing Senators.

The Congress shall assemble at least once in every Year, and such Meeting shall be on the first Monday in December, unless they shall by Law appoint a different Day.

Section 5. Each House shall be the Judge of the Elections, Returns and Qualifications of its own Members, and a Majority of each shall constitute a Quorum to do Business; but a smaller Number may adjourn from day to day, and may be authorized to compel the Attendance of absent Members, in such Manner, and under such Penalties as each House may provide.

Each House may determine the Rules of its Proceedings, punish its Members for disorderly Behaviour, and, with the Concurrence of two thirds, expel a Member.

Each House shall keep a Journal of its Proceedings, and from time to time publish the same, excepting such Parts as may in their Judgment require Secrecy; and the Yeas and Nays of the Members of either House on any question shall, at the Desire of one fifth of those Present, be entered on the Journal.

Neither House, during the Session of Congress, shall, without the Consent of the other, adjourn for more than three days, nor to any other Place than that in which the two Houses shall be sitting.

Section 6. The Senators and Representatives shall receive a Compensation for their Services, to be ascertained by Law, and paid out of the Treasury of the United States. They shall in all Cases, except Treason, Felony and Breach of the Peace, be privileged from Arrest during their Attendance at the Session of their respective Houses, and in going to and returning from the same; and for any Speech or Debate in either House, they shall not be questioned in any other Place.

No Senator or Representative shall, during the Time for which he was elected, be appointed to any civil Office under the Authority of the United States, which shall have been created, or the Emoluments whereof shall have been encreased during such time; and no Person holding any Office under the United States, shall be a Member of either House during his Continuance in Office.

Section 7. All Bills for raising Revenue shall originate in the House of Representatives; but the Senate may propose or concur with Amendments as on other Bills.

Every Bill which shall have passed the House of Representatives and the Senate, shall, before it become a Law, be presented to the President of the United States; If he approve he shall sign it, but if not he shall return it, with his Objections to that House in which it shall have originated, who shall enter the Objections at large on their Journal, and proceed to reconsider it. If after such Reconsideration two thirds of that House shall agree to pass the Bill, it shall be sent, together with the Objections, to the other House, by which it shall likewise be reconsidered, and if approved by two thirds of that House, it shall become a Law. But in all such Cases the Votes of both Houses shall be determined by Yeas and Nays, and the

Names of the Persons voting for and against the Bill shall be entered on the Journal of each House respectively. If any Bill shall not be returned by the President within ten Days (Sundays excepted) after it shall have been presented to him, the Same shall be a Law, in like Manner as if he had signed it, unless the Congress by their Adjournment prevent its Return, in which Case it shall not be a Law.

Every Order, Resolution, or Vote to which the Concurrence of the Senate and House of Representatives may be necessary (except on a question of Adjournment) shall be presented to the President of the United States; and before the Same shall take Effect, shall be approved by him, or being disapproved by him, shall be repassed by two thirds of the Senate and House of Representatives, according to the Rules and Limitations prescribed in the Case of a Bill.

Section 8. The Congress shall have Power to lay and collect Taxes, Duties, Imposts and Excises, to pay the Debts and provide for the common Defence and general Welfare of the United States; but all Duties, Imposts and Excises shall be uniform throughout the United States;

To borrow Money on the credit of the United States;

To regulate Commerce with foreign Nations, and among the several States, and with the Indian Tribes;

To establish an uniform Rule of Naturalization, and uniform Laws on the subject of Bankruptcies throughout the United States;

To coin Money, regulate the Value thereof, and of foreign Coin, and fix the Standard of Weights and Measures;

To provide for the Punishment of counterfeiting the Securities and current Coin of the United States;

To establish Post Offices and post Roads;

To promote the Progress of Science and useful Arts, by securing for limited Times to Authors and Inventors the exclusive Right to their respective Writings and Discoveries;

To constitute Tribunals inferior to the supreme Court;

To define and punish Piracies and Felonies committed on the high Seas, and Offenses against the Law of Nations;

To declare War, grant Letters of Marque and Reprisal, and make Rules concerning Captures on Land and Water;

To raise and support Armies, but no Appropriation of Money to that Use shall be for a longer Term than two Years;

To provide and maintain a Navy;

To make Rules for the Government and Regulation of the land and naval Forces;

To provide for calling forth the Militia to execute the Laws of the Union, suppress Insurrections and repel Invasions;

To provide for organizing, arming, and disciplining, the Militia, and for governing such Part of them as may be employed in the Service of the United States, reserving to the States respectively, the Appointment of the Officers, and the Authority of training the Militia according to the discipline prescribed by Congress;

To exercise exclusive Legislation in all Cases whatsoever, over such District (not exceeding ten Miles square) as may, by Cession of particular States, and the Acceptance of Congress, become the Seat of the Government of the United States, and to exercise like Authority over all Places purchased by the Consent of the Legislature of the State in which the Same shall be, for the Erection of Forts, Magazines, Arsenals, dock-Yards, and other needful Buildings;—And

To make all Laws which shall be necessary and proper for carrying into Execution the foregoing Powers, and all other Powers vested by this Constitution in the Government of the United States, or in any Department or Officer thereof.

Section 9. The Migration or Importation of such Persons as any of the States now existing shall think proper to admit, shall not be prohibited by the Congress prior to the Year one thousand eight hundred and eight, but a Tax or Duty may be imposed on such Importation, not exceeding ten dollars for each Person.

The Privilege of the Writ of Habeas Corpus shall not be suspended, unless when in Cases of Rebellion or Invasion the public Safety may require it.

No Bill of Attainder or ex post facto Law shall be passed.

No Capitation, or other direct, Tax shall be laid, unless in Proportion to the Census or Enumeration herein before directed to be taken.

No Tax or Duty shall be laid on Articles exported from any State.

No Preference shall be given by any Regulation of Commerce or Revenue to the Ports of one State over those of another; nor shall Vessels bound to, or from, one State, be obliged to enter, clear, or pay Duties in another.

No Money shall be drawn from the Treasury, but in Consequence of Appropriations made by Laws; and a regular Statement and Account of the Receipts and Expenditures of all public Money shall be published from time to time.

No Title of Nobility shall be granted by the United States: And no Person holding any Office of Profit or Trust under them, shall, without the Consent of the Congress, accept of any present, Emolument, Office, or Title, of any kind whatever, from any King, Prince, or foreign State.

Section 10. No State shall enter into any Treaty, Alliance, or Confederation; grant Letters of Marque and Reprisal; coin Money; emit Bills of Credit; make any Thing but gold and silver Coin a Tender in Payment of Debts; pass any Bill of Attainder, ex post facto Law, or Law impairing the Obligation of Contracts, or grant any Title of Nobility.

No State shall, without the Consent of the Congress, lay any Imposts or Duties on Imports or Exports, except what may be absolutely necessary for executing its inspection Laws: and the net Produce of all Duties and Imposts, laid by any State on Imports or Exports, shall be for the Use of the Treasury of the United States; and all such Laws shall be subject to the Revision and Controul of the Congress.

No State shall, without the Consent of Congress, lay any Duty of Tonnage, keep Troops, or Ships of War in time of Peace, enter into any Agreement or Compact with another State, or with a foreign Power, or engage in War, unless actually invaded, or in such imminent Danger as will not admit of delay.

Article II

Section 1. The executive Power shall be vested in a President of the United States of America. He shall hold his Office during the Term of four Years, and, together with the Vice President, chosen for the same Term, be elected, as follows:

Each State shall appoint, in such Manner as the Legislature thereof may direct, a Number of Electors, equal to the whole Number of Senators and Representatives to which the State may be entitled in the Congress: but no Senator or Representative, or Person holding an Office of Trust or Profit under the United States, shall be appointed an Elector.

The Electors shall meet in their respective States, and vote by Ballot for two Persons, of whom one at least shall not be an Inhabitant of the same State with themselves. And they shall make a List of all the Persons voted for, and of the Number of Votes for each; which List they shall sign and certify, and transmit sealed to the Seat of the Government of the United States, directed to the President of the Senate. The President of the Senate shall, in the Presence of the Senate and House of Representatives, open all the Certificates, and the Votes shall then be counted. The Person having the greatest Number of Votes shall be the President, if such Number be a Majority of the whole Number of Electors appointed; and if there be more than one who have such Majority, and have an equal Number of Votes, then the House of Representatives shall immediately chuse by Ballot one of them for President; and if no Person have a Majority, then from the five highest on the List the said House shall in like Manner chuse the President. But in chusing the President, the Votes shall be taken by States, the Representation from each State having one Vote; a quorum for this Purpose shall consist of a Member or Members from two thirds of the States, and a Majority of all the States shall be necessary to a Choice. In every Case, after the Choice of the President, the Person having the greatest Number of Votes of the Electors shall be the Vice President. But if there should remain two or more who have equal Votes, the Senate shall chuse from them by Ballot the Vice President.

The Congress may determine the Time of chusing the Electors, and the Day on which they shall give their Votes; which Day shall be the same throughout the United States.

No Person except a natural born Citizen, or a Citizen of the United States, at the time of the Adoption of this Constitution, shall be eligible to the Office of President; neither shall any Person be eligible to that Office who shall not have attained to the Age of thirty five Years, and been fourteen Years a Resident within the United States.

In Case of the Removal of the President from Office, or of his Death, Resignation, or Inability to discharge the Powers and Duties of the said Office, the Same shall devolve on the Vice President, and the Congress may by Law provide for the Case of Removal, Death, Resignation or Inability, both of the President and Vice President, declaring what Officer shall then act as President, and such Officer shall act accordingly, until the Disability be removed, or a President shall be elected.

The President shall, at stated Times, receive for his Services, a Compensation, which shall neither be encreased nor diminished during the Period for which he shall have been elected, and he shall not receive within that Period any other Emolument from the United States, or any of them.

Before he enter on the Execution of his Office, he shall take the following Oath or Affirmation:—"I do solemnly swear (or affirm) that I will faithfully execute the Office of President of the United States, and will to the best of my Ability, preserve, protect and defend the Constitution of the United States."

Section 2. The President shall be Commander in Chief of the Army and Navy of the United States, and of the Militia of the several States, when called into the actual Service of the United States; he may require the Opinion, in writing, of the principal Officer in each of the executive Departments, upon any Subject relating to the Duties of their respective Offices, and he shall have Power to grant Reprieves and Pardons for Offences against the United States, except in Cases of Impeachment.

He shall have Power, by and with the Advice and Consent of the Senate, to make Treaties, providing two thirds of the Senators present concur; and he shall nominate, and by and with the Advice and Consent of the Senate, shall appoint Ambassadors, other public Ministers and Consuls, Judges of the supreme Court, and all other Officers of the United States, whose Appointments are not herein otherwise provided for, and which shall be established by Law: but the Congress may by Law vest the Appointment of such inferior Officers, as they think proper, in the President alone, in the Courts of Law, or in the Heads of Departments.

The President shall have Power to fill up all Vacancies that may happen during the Recess of the Senate, by granting Commissions which shall expire at the End of their next Session.

Section 3. He shall from time to time give to the Congress Information of the State of the Union, and recommend to their Consideration such Measures as he shall judge necessary and expedient; he may, on extraordinary Occasions, convene both Houses, or either of them, and in Case of Disagreement between them, with Respect to the Time of Adjournment, he may adjourn them to such Time as he shall think proper; he shall receive Ambassadors and other public Ministers; he shall take Care that the Laws be faithfully executed, and shall Commission all the Officers of the United States.

Section 4. The President, Vice President and all civil Officers of the United States, shall be removed from Office on Impeachment for, and Conviction of, Treason, Bribery, or other high Crimes and Misdemeanors.

Article III

Section 1. The judicial Power of the United States, shall be vested in one supreme Court, and in such inferior Courts as the Congress may from time to time ordain and establish. The Judges, both of the supreme and inferior Courts, shall hold their Offices during good Behaviour, and shall, at stated Times, receive for their Services, a Compensation, which shall not be diminished during their Continuance in Office.

Section 2. The judicial Power shall extend to all Cases, in Law and Equity, arising under this Constitution, the Laws of the United States, and Treaties made, or which shall be made, under their Authority;—to all Cases affecting Ambassadors, other public Ministers and Consuls;—to all Cases of admiralty and maritime Jurisdiction;—to Controversies to which the United States shall be a Party;—to Controversies between two or more States;—between a State and Citizens of another State;—between Citizens of different States;—between Citizens of the same State claiming Lands under Grants of different States, and between a State, or the Citizens thereof, and foreign States, Citizens or Subjects.

In all Cases affecting Ambassadors, other public Ministers and Consuls, and those in which a State shall be Party, the supreme Court shall have original Jurisdiction. In all the other Cases before mentioned, the supreme Court shall have appellate Jurisdiction, both as to Law and Fact, with such Exceptions, and under such Regulations as the Congress shall make.

The Trial of all Crimes, except in Cases of Impeachment, shall be by Jury; and such Trial shall be held in the State where the said Crimes shall have been committed; but when not committed within any State, the Trial shall be at such Place or Places as the Congress may by Law have directed.

Section 3. Treason against the United States, shall consist only in levying War against them, or in adhering to their Enemies, giving them Aid and Comfort. No Person shall be convicted of Treason unless on the Testimony of two Witnesses to the same overt Act, or on Confession in open Court.

The Congress shall have Power to declare the Punishment of Treason, but no Attainder of Treason shall work Corruption of Blood, or Forfeiture except during the Life of the Person attainted.

Article IV

Section 1. Full Faith and Credit shall be given in each State to the public Acts, Records, and judicial Proceedings of every other State. And the Congress may by general Laws prescribe the Manner in which such Acts, Records and Proceedings shall be proved, and the Effect thereof.

Section 2. The Citizens of each State shall be entitled to all Privileges and Immunities of Citizens in the several States.

A Person charged in any State with Treason, Felony, or other Crime, who shall flee from Justice, and be found in another State, shall on Demand of the executive Authority of the State from which he fled, be delivered up, to be removed to the State having Jurisdiction of the Crime.

No Person held to Service or Labour in one State, under the Laws thereof, escaping into another, shall, in Consequence of any Law or Regulation therein, be discharged from such Service or Labour, but shall be delivered up on Claim of the Party to whom such Service or Labour may be due.

Section 3. New States may be admitted by the Congress into this Union; but no new State shall be formed or erected within the Jurisdiction of any other State; nor any State be formed by the Junction of two or more States, or Parts of States, without the Consent of the Legislatures of the States concerned as well as of the Congress.

The Congress shall have Power to dispose of and make all needful Rules and Regulations respecting the Territory or other Property belonging to the United States; and nothing in this Constitution shall be so construed as to Prejudice any Claims of the United States, or of any particular State.

Section 4. The United States shall guarantee to every State in this Union a Republican Form of the Government, and shall protect each of them against Invasion; and on Application of the Legislature, or of the Executive (when the Legislature cannot be convened) against domestic Violence.

Article V

The Congress, whenever two thirds of both Houses shall deem it necessary, shall propose Amendments to this Constitution, or, on the Application of the Legislatures of two thirds of the several States, shall call a Convention for proposing Amendments, which, in either Case, shall be valid to all Intents and Purposes, as Part of this Constitution, when ratified by the Legislatures of three fourths of the several States, or by Conventions in three fourths thereof, as the one or the other Mode of Ratification may be proposed by the Congress; Provided that no Amendment which may be made prior to the Year One thousand eight hundred and eight shall in any Manner affect the first and fourth Clauses in the Ninth Section of the first Article; and that no State, without its Consent, shall be deprived of its equal Suffrage in the Senate.

Article VI

All Debts contracted and Engagements entered into, before the Adoption of this Constitution, shall be as valid against the United States under this Constitution, as under the Confederation.

This Constitution, and the Laws of the United States which shall be made in Pursuance thereof; and all Treaties made, or which shall be made, under the Authority of the United States, shall be the supreme Law of the Land; and the Judges in every State shall be bound thereby, any Thing in the Constitution or Laws of any State to the Contrary notwithstanding.

The Senators and Representatives before mentioned, and the Members of the several State Legislatures, and all executive and judicial Officers, both of the United States and of the several States, shall be bound by Oath or Affirmation, to support this Constitution; but no religious Test shall ever be required as a Qualification to any Office or public Trust under the United States.

Article VII

The Ratification of the Conventions of nine States, shall be sufficient for the Establishment of this Constitution between the States so ratifying the Same.

Amendment I [1791]

Congress shall make no law respecting an establishment of religion, or prohibiting the free exercise thereof; or abridging the freedom of speech, or the press; or the right of the people peaceably to assemble, and to petition the Government for a redress of grievances.

Amendment II [1791]

A well regulated Militia, being necessary to the security of a free State, the right of the people to keep and bear Arms, shall not be infringed.

Amendment III [1791]

No Soldier shall, in time of peace be quartered in any house, without the consent of the Owner, nor in time of war, but in a manner to be prescribed by law.

Amendment IV [1791]

The right of the people to be secure in their persons, houses, papers, and effects, against unreasonable searches and seizures, shall not be violated, and no Warrants shall issue, but upon probable cause, supported by Oath or affirmation, and particularly describing the place to be searched, and the persons or things to be seized.

Amendment V [1791]

No person shall be held to answer for a capital, or otherwise infamous crime, unless on a presentment or indictment of a Grand Jury, except in cases arising in the land or naval forces, or in the Militia, when in actual service in time of War or public danger; nor shall any person be subject for the same offence to be twice put in jeopardy of life or limb; nor shall be compelled in any criminal case to be a witness against himself, nor be deprived of life, liberty, or property, without due process of law; nor shall private property be taken for public use, without just compensation.

Amendment VI [1791]

In all criminal prosecutions, the accused shall enjoy the right to a speedy and public trial, by an impartial jury of the State and district wherein the crime shall have been committed, which district shall have been previously ascertained by law, and to be informed of the nature and cause of the accusation; to be confronted with the Witnesses against him; to have compulsory process for obtaining witnesses in his favor, and to have the Assistance of counsel for his defence.

Amendment VII [1791]

In Suits at common law, where the value in controversy shall exceed twenty dollars, the right of trial by jury shall be preserved, and no fact tried by a jury, shall be otherwise re-examined in any Court of the United States, than according to the rules of the common law.

Amendment VIII [1791]

Excessive bail shall not be required, nor excessive fines imposed, nor cruel and unusual punishments inflicted.

Amendment IX [1791]

The enumeration in the Constitution, of certain rights, shall not be construed to deny or disparage others retained by the people.

Amendment X [1791]

The powers not delegated to the United States by the Constitution, nor prohibited by it to the States, are reserved to the States respectively, or to the people.

Amendment XI [1798]

The Judicial power of the United States shall not be construed to extend to any suit in law or equity, commenced or prosecuted against one of the United States by Citizens of another State, or by Citizens or Subjects of any ForeignState.

Amendment XII [1804]

The Electors shall meet in their respective states and vote by ballot for President and Vice President, one of whom, at least, shall not be an inhabitant of the same state with themselves; they shall name in their ballots the person voted for as President, and in distinct ballots the person voted for as Vice President, and they shall make distinct lists of all persons voted for as President, and of all persons voted for as Vice President, and of the number of votes for each, which lists they shall sign and certify, and transmit sealed to the seat of the government of the United States, directed to the President of the Senate;—The President of the Senate shall, in the presence of the Senate and House of Representatives, open all the certificates and the votes shall then be counted;—The person having the greatest number of votes for President, shall be the President, if such number be a majority of the whole number of Electors appointed; and if no person have such majority, then from the persons having the highest numbers not exceeding three on the list of those voted for as President, the House of Representatives shall choose immediately, by ballot, the President. But in choosing the President, the votes shall be taken by states, the representation from each state having one vote; a quorum for this purpose shall consist of a member or members from two-thirds of the states, and a majority of all the states shall be necessary to a choice. And if the House of Representatives shall not choose a President whenever the right of choice shall devolve upon them, before the fourth day of March next following, then the Vice President shall act as President, as in the case of the death or other constitutional disability of the President. The person having the greatest number of votes as Vice President, shall be the Vice President, if such number be a majority of the whole number of Electors appointed, and if no person have a majority, then from the two highest numbers on the list, the Senate shall choose the Vice President; a quorum for the purpose shall consist of two-thirds of the whole number of Senators, and a majority of the whole number shall be necessary to a choice. But no person constitutionally ineligible to the office of President shall be eligible to that of the Vice President of the United States.

Amendment XIII [1865]

Section 1. Neither slavery nor involuntary servitude, except as a punishment for crime whereof the party shall have been duly convicted, shall exist within the United States, or any place subject to their jurisdiction.

Section 2. Congress shall have power to enforce this article by appropriate legislation.

Amendment XIV [1868]

Section 1. All persons born or naturalized in the United States, and subject to the jurisdiction thereof, are citizens of the United States and of the State wherein they reside. No State shall make or enforce any law which shall abridge the privileges or immunities of citizens of the United States; nor shall any State deprive any person of life, liberty, or property, without due process of law; nor deny to any person within its jurisdiction the equal protection of the laws.

Section 2. Representatives shall be appointed among the several States according to their respective numbers, counting the whole number of persons in each State, excluding Indians not taxed. But when the right to vote at any election for the choice of electors for President and Vice President of the United States, Representatives in Congress, the Executive and Judicial officers of a State, or the members of the Legislature thereof, is denied to any of the male inhabitants of such State, being twenty-one years of age, and citizens of the United States, or in any way abridged, except for participation in rebellion, or other crime, the basis of representation therein shall be reduced in the proportion which the number of such male citizens shall bear to the whole number of male citizens twenty-one years of age in such State.

Section 3. No person shall be a Senator or Representative in Congress, or elector of President and Vice President, or hold any office, civil or military, under the United States, or under any State, who, having previously taken an oath, as a member of Congress, or as an officer of the United States, or as a member of any State legislature, or as an executive or judicial officer of any State, to support the Constitution of the United States, shall have engaged in insurrection or rebellion against the same, or given aid or comfort to the enemies thereof. But Congress may by a vote of two-thirds of each House, remove such disability.

Section 4. The validity of the public debt of the United States, authorized by law, including debts incurred for payment of pensions and bounties for services in suppressing insurrection or rebellion, shall not be questioned. But neither the United States nor any State shall assume or pay any debt or obligation incurred in aid of insurrection or rebellion against the United States, or any claim for the loss or emancipation of any slave; but all such debts, obligations and claims shall be held illegal and void.

Section 5. The Congress shall have power to enforce, by appropriate legislation, the provisions of this article.

Amendment XV [1870]

Section 1. The right of citizens of the United States to vote shall not be denied or abridged by the United States or by any State on account of race, color, or previous condition of servitude.

Section 2. The Congress shall have power to enforce this article by appropriate legislation.

Amendment XVI [1913]

The Congress shall have power to lay and collect taxes on incomes, from whatever source derived, without apportionment among the several States, and without regard to any census or enumeration.

Amendment XVII [1913]

The Senate of the United States shall be composed of two Senators from each State, elected by the people thereof, for six years; and each Senator shall have one vote. The electors in each State shall have the qualifications requisite for electors of the most numerous branch of the State legislatures.

When vacancies happen in the representation of any State in the Senate, the executive authority of each State shall issue writs of election to fill such vacancies; Provided, That the legislature of any State may empower the executive thereof to make temporary appointments until the people fill the vacancies by election as the legislature may direct.

This amendment shall not be so construed as to affect the election or term of any Senator chosen before it becomes valid as part of the Constitution.

Amendment XVIII [1919]

Section 1. After one year from the ratification of this article the manufacture, sale, or transportation of intoxicating liquors within, the importation thereof into, or the exportation thereof from the United States and all territory subject to the jurisdiction thereof for beverage purposes is hereby prohibited.

Section 2. The Congress and the several States shall have concurrent power to enforce this article by appropriate legislation.

Section 3. This article shall be inoperative unless it shall have been ratified as an amendment to the Constitution by the legislatures of the several States, as provided in the Constitution, within seven years from the date of the submission hereof to the States by the Congress.

Amendment XIX [1920]

The right of citizens of the United States to vote shall not be denied or abridged by the United States or by any State on account of sex.

Congress shall have power to enforce this article by appropriate legislation.

Amendment XX [1933]

Section 1. The terms of the President and Vice President shall end at noon on the 20th day of January, and the terms of Senators and Representatives at noon on the 3d day of January, of the years in which such terms would have ended if this article had not been ratified; and the terms of their successors shall then begin.

Section 2. The Congress shall assemble at least once every year, and such meeting shall begin at noon on the 3d day of January, unless they shall by law appoint a different day.

Section 3. If, at the time fixed for the beginning of the term of the President, the President elect shall have died, the Vice President elect shall become President. If a President shall not have been chosen before the time fixed for the beginning of his term, or if the President elect shall have failed to qualify, then the Vice President elect shall act as President until a President shall have qualified; and the Congress may by law provide for the case wherein neither a President elect nor a Vice President elect shall have qualified, declaring who shall then act as President, or the manner in which one who is to act shall be selected, and such person shall act accordingly until a President or Vice President shall have qualified.

Section 4. The Congress may by law provide for the case of the death of any of the persons from whom the House of Representatives may choose a President whenever the right of choice shall have devolved upon them, and for the case of the death of any of the persons from whom the Senate may choose a Vice President whenever the right of choice shall have devolved upon them.

Section 5. Sections 1 and 2 shall take effect on the 15th day of October following the ratification of this article.

Section 6. This article shall be inoperative unless it shall have been ratified as an amendment to the Constitution by the legislatures of three-fourths of the several States within seven years from the date of its submission.

Amendment XXI [1933]

Section 1. The eighteenth article of amendment to the Constitution of the United States is hereby repealed.

Section 2. The transportation or importation into any State, Territory, or possession of the United States for delivery or use therein of intoxicating liquors, in violation of the laws thereof, is hereby prohibited.

Section 3. This article shall be inoperative unless it shall have been ratified as an amendment to the Constitution by conventions in the several States, as provided in the Constitution, within seven years from the date of the submission hereof to the States by the Congress.

Amendment XXII [1951]

Section 1. No person shall be elected to the office of the President more than twice, and no person who has held the office of President, or acted as President, for more than two years of a term to which some other person was elected President shall be elected to the office of the President more than once. But this Article shall not apply to any person holding the office of President when this Article was proposed by the Congress, and shall not prevent any person who may be holding the office of President, or acting as President, during the term within which this Article becomes operative from holding the office of President or acting as President during the remainder of such term.

Section 2. This article shall be inoperative unless it shall have been ratified as an amendment to the Constitution by the legislatures of three-fourths of the several States within seven years from the date of its submission to the States by the Congress.

Amendment XXIII [1961]

Section 1. The District constituting the seat of Government of the United States shall appoint in such manner as the Congress may direct:

A number of electors of President and Vice President equal to the whole number of Senators and Representatives in Congress to which the District would be entitled if it were a State, but in no event more than the least populous State; they shall be in addition to those appointed by the States, but they shall be considered, for the purposes of the election of President and Vice President, to be electors appointed by a State; and they shall meet in the District and perform such duties as provided by the twelfth article of amendment.

Section 2. The Congress shall have power to enforce this article by appropriate legislation.

Amendment XXIV [1964]

Section 1. The right of citizens of the United States to vote in any primary or other election for President or Vice President, for electors for President or Vice President, or for Senator or Representative in Congress, shall not be denied or abridged by the United States or any State by reason of failure to pay any poll tax or other tax.

Section 2. The Congress shall have power to enforce this article by appropriate legislation.

Amendment XXV [1967]

Section 1. In case of the removal of the President from office or of his death or resignation, the Vice President shall become President.

Section 2. Whenever there is a vacancy in the office of the Vice President, the President shall nominate a Vice President who shall take office upon confirmation by a majority vote of both Houses of Congress.

Section 3. Whenever the President transmits to the President pro tempore of the Senate and the Speaker of the House of Representatives his written declaration that he is unable to discharge the powers and duties of his office, and until he transmits to them a written declaration to the contrary, such powers and duties shall be discharged by the Vice President as Acting President.

Section 4. Whenever the Vice President and a majority of either the principal officers of the executive departments or of such other body as Congress may by law provide, transmit to the President pro tempore of the Senate and the Speaker of the House of Representatives their written declaration that the President is unable to discharge the powers and duties of his office, the Vice President shall immediately assume the powers and duties of the office as Acting President.

Thereafter, when the President transmits to the President pro tempore of the Senate and the Speaker of the House of Representatives his written declaration that no inability exists, he shall resume the powers and duties of his office unless the Vice President and a majority of either the principal officers of the executive department or of such other body as Congress may by law provide, transmit within four days to the President pro tempore of the Senate and the Speaker of the House of Representatives their written declaration that the President is unable to discharge the powers and duties of his office. Thereupon Congress shall decide the issue, assembling within forty-eight hours for that purpose if not in session. If the Congress, within twenty-one days after receipt of the latter written declaration, or, if Congress is not in session, within twenty-one days after Congress is required to assemble, determines by two-thirds vote of both Houses that the President is unable to discharge the powers and duties of his office, the Vice President shall continue to discharge the same as Acting President; otherwise, the President shall resume the powers and duties of his office.

Amendment XXVI [1971]

Section 1. The right of citizens of the United States, who are eighteen years of age or older, to vote shall not be denied or abridged by the United States or by any State on account of age.

Section 2. The Congress shall have power to enforce this article by appropriate legislation.

Amendment XXVII [1992]

No law varying the compensation for the services of the senators and representatives shall take effect, until an election of representatives shall have intervened.

Appendix D

The Uniform Commercial Code (Excerpts)

Article 1. General Provisions

Section 1–101. **Short Title.**

This Act shall be known and may be cited as Uniform Commercial Code.

Section 1–102. **Purposes; Rules of Construction; Variation by Agreement.**

(1) This Act shall be liberally construed and applied to promote its underlying purposes and policies.

(2) Underlying purposes and policies of this Act are

(a) to simplify, clarify and modernize the law governing commercial transactions;

(b) to permit the continued expansion of commercial practices through custom, usage, and agreement of the parties;

(c) to make uniform the law among the various jurisdictions.

(3) The effect of provisions of this Act may be varied by agreement, except as otherwise provided in this Act and except that the obligations of good faith, diligence, reasonableness and care prescribed by this Act may not be disclaimed by agreement but the parties may by agreement determine the standards by which the performance of such obligations is to be measured if such standards are not manifestly unreasonable.

(4) The presence in certain provisions of this Act of the words "**unless otherwise agreed**" or words of similar import does not imply that the effect of other provisions may not be varied by agreement under subsection (3).

(5) In this Act unless the context otherwise requires

(a) words in the singular number include the plural, and in the plural include the singular;

(b) words of the masculine gender include the feminine and the neuter, and when the sense so indicates, words of the neuter gender may refer to any gender.

Section 1–106. **Remedies to Be Liberally Administered.**

(1) The remedies provided by this Act shall be liberally administered to the end that the aggrieved party may be put in as good a position as if the other party had fully performed but neither consequential or special nor penal damages may be had except as specifically provided in this Act or by other rule of law.

(2) Any right or obligation declared by this Act is enforceable by action unless the provision declaring it specifies a different and limited effect.

Section 1–201. **General Definitions.**

Subject to additional definitions contained in the subsequent Articles of this Act which are applicable to specific Articles or Parts thereof, and unless the context otherwise requires, in this Act:

(1) **"Action"** in the sense of a judicial proceeding includes recoupment, counterclaim, set-off, suit in equity, and any other proceedings in which rights are determined.

(2) **"Aggrieved Party"** means a party entitled to resort to a remedy.

(3) **"Agreement"** means the bargain of the parties in fact as found in their language or by implication from other circumstances including course of dealing or usage of trade or course of performance as provided in this Act (Sections 1–205 and 1–206). Whether an agreement has legal consequences is determined by the provisions of this Act, if applicable; otherwise by the law of contracts (Section 1–103). (Compare "Contract".)

(4) **"Bank"** means any person engaged in the business of Banking.

(5) **"Bearer"** means the person in possession of an instrument, document of title, or certificated security payable to bearer or endorsed in blank.

(6) **"Bill of lading"** means a document evidencing the receipt of goods for shipment issued by a person engaged in the business of transporting or forwarding goods, and includes an airbill. "Airbill" means a document serving for air transportation as a bill of lading does for marine or rail transportation, and includes an air consignment note or air waybill.

(7) **"Branch"** includes a separately incorporated foreign branch of a bank.

(8) **"Burden of establishing"** a fact means the burden of persuading the triers of fact that the existence of the fact is more probable than its nonexistence.

(9) **"Buyer in ordinary course of business"** means a person who in good faith and without knowledge that the sale to him is in violation of the ownership rights or security interest of a third party in the goods buys in ordinary course from a person in the business of selling goods of that kind but does not include a pawnbroker. All persons who sell minerals or the like (including oil and gas) at wellhead or minehead shall be deemed to be persons in the business of selling goods of that kind. "Buying" may be for cash or by exchange of other property or on secured or unsecured credit and includes receiving goods or documents of title under a preexisting contract for sale but does not include a transfer in bulk or as security for or in total or partial satisfaction of a money debt.

(10) **"Conspicuous":** A term of clause is conspicuous when it is so written that a reasonable person against whom it is to operate ought to have noticed it. A printed heading in capitals (as: Non-Negotiable Bill of Lading) is conspicuous. Language in the body of a form is "conspicuous" if it is in larger or other contrasting type or color. But in a telegram any stated term is "conspicuous". Whether a term or clause is "conspicuous" or not is for decision by the court.

(11) **"Contract"** means the total legal obligation which results from the parties' agreement as affected by this Act and any other applicable rules of law. (Compare "Agreement".)

(12) **"Creditor"** includes a general creditor, a secured creditor, a lien creditor and any representative of creditors, including an assignee for the benefit of creditors, a trustee in Bankruptcy, a receiver in equity, and an executor or administrator of an insolvent debtor's or assignor's estate.

(13) **"Defendant"** includes a person in the position of defendant in a cross-action or counterclaim.

(14) **"Delivery"** with respect to instruments, documents of title, chattel paper, or certificated securities means voluntary transfer of possession.

(15) **"Document of title"** includes bill of lading, dock warrant, dock receipt, warehouse receipt, or order for the delivery of goods, and also any other document which in the regular course of business or financing is treated as adequately evidencing that the person in possession of it is entitled to receive, hold, and dispose of the document and the goods it covers. To be a document of title, a document must purport to be issued by or addressed to a bailee and purport to cover goods in the bailee's possession which are either identified or are fungible portions of an identified mass.

(16) **"Fault"** means wrongful act, omission, or breach.

(17) **"Fungible"** with respect to goods or securities means goods or securities of which any unit is, by nature or usage of trade, the equivalent of any other like unit. Goods which are not fungible shall be deemed fungible for the purposes of this Act to the extent that under a particular agreement or document unlike units are treated as equivalents.

(18) **"Genuine"** means free of forgery or counterfeiting.

(19) **"Good faith"** means honesty in fact in the conduct or transaction concerned.

(20) **"Holder"** with respect to a negotiable instrument means the person in possession if the instrument is payable to bearer or, in the case of an instrument payable to an identified person, if the identified person is in possession. "Holder" with respect to a document of title means the person in possession if the goods are deliverable to bearer or to the order of the person in possession.

(21) To **"honor"** is to pay or to accept and pay, or where a credit so engages to purchase or discount a draft complying with the terms of the credit.

(22) **"Insolvency proceedings"** include any assignment for the benefit of creditors or other proceedings intended to liquidate or rehabilitate the estate of the person involved.

(23) A person is **"insolvent"** who either has ceased to pay his debts in the ordinary course of business or cannot pay his debts as they become due or is insolvent within the meaning of the federal bankruptcy law.

(24) **"Money"** means a medium of exchange authorized or adopted by a domestic or foreign government and includes a monetary unit of account established by an intergovernmental organization or by agreement between two or more nations.

(25) A person has **"notice"** of a fact when
    (a) he has actual knowledge of it; or
    (b) he has received a notice or notification of it; or
    (c) from all the facts and circumstances known to him at the time in question, he has reason to know that it exists.

    A person **"knows"** or has **"knowledge"** of a fact when he has actual knowledge of it. "Discover" or "learn" or a word or phrase of similar import refers to knowledge rather than to reason to know. The time and circumstances under which a notice or notification may cease to be effective are not determined by this Act.

(26) A person **"notifies"** or "gives" a notice or notification to another by taking such steps as may be reasonably required to inform the other in ordinary course whether or not such other actually comes to know of it. A person "receives" a notice or notification when
    (a) it comes to his attention; or
    (b) it is duly delivered at the place of business through which the contract was made or at any other place held out by him as the place for receipt of such communications.

(27) Notice, knowledge, or a notice or notification received by an organization is effective for a particular transaction from the time when it is brought to the attention of the individual conducting that transaction, and in any event from the time when it would have been brought to his attention if the organization had exercised due diligence. An organization exercises due diligence if it maintains reasonable routines for communicating significant information to the person conducting the transaction, and there is reasonable compliance with the routines. Due diligence does not require an individual acting for the organization to communicate information unless such communication is part of his regular duties or unless he has reason to know of the transaction and that the transaction would be materially affected by the information.

(28) **"Organization"** includes a corporation, government or governmental subdivision or agency, business trust, estate, trust, partnership or association, two or more persons having a joint or common interest, or any other legal or commercial entity.

(29) **"Party,"** as distinct from **"Third Party,"** means a person who has engaged in a transaction or made an agreement within this Act.

(30) **"Person"** includes an individual or an organization (Section 1–102).

(31) **"Presumption"** or **"presumed"** means that the trier of fact must find the existence of the fact presumed unless and until evidence is introduced which would support a finding of its non existence.

(32) **"Purchase"** includes taking by sale, discount, negotiation, mortgage, pledge, lien, issue or reissue, gift, or any other voluntary transaction creating an interest in property.

(33) **"Purchaser"** means a person who takes by purchase.

(34) **"Remedy"** means any remedial right to which an aggrieved party is entitled with or without resort to a tribunal.

(35) **"Representative"** includes an agent, an officer of a corporation or association, and a trustee, executor, or administrator of an estate, or any other person empowered to act for another.

(36) **"Rights"** includes remedies.

(37) **"Security interest"** means an interest in personal property or fixtures which secures payment or performance of an obligation. The retention or reservation of title by a seller of goods notwithstanding shipment or delivery to the buyer (Section 2–401) is limited in effect to a reservation of a "security interest." The term also includes any interest of a buyer of accounts or chattel paper which is subject to Article 9. The special property interest of a

buyer of goods on identification of those goods to a contract for sale under Section 2–401 is not a "security interest," but a buyer may also acquire a "security interest" by complying with Article 9. Unless a consignment is intended as security, reservation of title thereunder is not a "security interest," but a consignment in any event is subject to the provisions on consignment sales (Section 2–326).

Whether a transaction creates a lease or security interest is determined by the facts of each case; however, a transaction creates a security interest if the consideration the lessee is to pay the lessor for the right to possession and use of the goods is an obligation for the term of the lease not subject to termination by the lessee, and

(a) the original term of the lease is equal to or greater than the remaining economic life of the goods,

(b) the lessee is bound to renew the lease for the remaining economic life of the goods or is bound to become the owner of the goods,

(c) the lessee has an option to renew the lease for the remaining economic life of the goods for no additional consideration or nominal additional consideration upon compliance with the lease agreement, or

(d) the lessee has an option to become the owner of the goods for no additional consideration or nominal additional consideration upon compliance with the lease agreement.

A transaction does not create a security interest merely because it provides that

(a) the present value of the consideration the lessee is obligated to pay the lessor for the right to possession and use of the goods is substantially equal to or is greater than the fair market value of the goods at the time the lease is entered into,

(b) the lessee assumes risk of loss of the goods, or agrees to pay taxes, insurance, filing, recording, or registration fees, or service or maintenance costs with respect to the goods,

(c) the lessee has an option to renew the lease or to become the owner of the goods,

(d) the lessee has an option to renew the lease for a fixed rent that is equal to or greater than the reasonably predictable fair market rent for the use of the goods for the term of the renewal at the time the option is to be performed, or

(e) the lessee has an option to become the owner of the goods for a fixed price that is equal to or greater than the reasonably predictable fair market value of the goods at the time the option is to be performed.

For purposes of this subsection (37):

(x) Additional consideration is not nominal if (i) when the option to renew the lease is granted to the lessee the rent is stated to be the fair market rent for the use of the goods for the term of the renewal determined at the time the option is to be performed, or (ii) when the option to become the owner of the goods is granted to the lessee, the price is stated to be the fair market value of the goods determined at the time the option is to be performed. Additional consideration is nominal, if it is less than the lessee's reasonably predictable cost of performing under the lease agreement if the option is not exercised;

(y) **"Reasonably predictable"** and **"remaining economic life of the goods"** are to be determined with reference to the facts and circumstances at the time the transaction is entered into; and

(z) **"Present Value"** means the amount as of a date certain of one or more sums payable in the future, discounted to the date certain. The discount is determined by the interest rate specified by the parties, if the rate is not manifestly unreasonable at the time the transaction is entered into; otherwise, the discount is determined by a commercially reasonable rate that takes into account the facts and circumstances of each case at the time the transaction was entered into.

(38) **"Send"** in connection with any writing or notice means to deposit in the mail or deliver for transmission by any other usual means of communication with postage or cost of transmission provided for and properly addressed and in the case of an instrument to an address specified thereon or otherwise agreed, or if there be none to any address reasonable under the circumstances. The receipt of any writing or notice within the time at which it would have arrived if properly sent has the effect of a proper sending.

(39) **"Signed"** includes any symbol executed or adopted by a party with present intention to authenticate a writing.

(40) **"Surety"** includes guarantor.

(41) **"Telegram"** includes a message transmitted by radio, teletype, cable, any mechanical method of transmission or the like.

(42) **"Term"** means that portion of an agreement which relates to a particular matter.

(43) **"Unauthorized"** signature means one made without actual, implied, or apparent authority and includes a forgery.

(44) **"Value."** Except as otherwise provided with respect to negotiable instruments and bank collections (Sections 3–303, 4–208 and 4–209), a person gives "value" for rights if he acquires them

(a) in return for a binding commitment to extend credit or for the extension of immediately available credit whether or not drawn upon and whether or not a charge back is provided for in the event of difficulties in collection; or

(b) as security for or in total or partial satisfaction of a preexisting claim; or

(c) by accepting delivery pursuant to a preexisting contract for purchase; or

(d) generally, in return for any consideration sufficient to support a simple contract.

(45) **"Warehouse receipt"** means a receipt issued by a person engaged in the business of storing goods for hire.

(46) **"Written"** or **"writing"** includes printing, typewriting, or any other intentional reduction to tangible form.

Section 1–202. **Prima Facie Evidence by Third-Party Documents.**

A document in due form purporting to be a bill of lading, policy or certificate of insurance, official weigher's or inspector's certificate, consular invoice, or any other document authorized or required by the contract to be issued by a third party shall be prima facie evidence of its own authenticity and genuineness and of the facts stated in the document by the third party.

Section 1–203. **Obligation of good faith.**

Every contract or duty within this Act imposes an obligation of good faith in its performance or enforcement.

Section 1–204. **Time; Reasonable Time; "Seasonably."**

(1) Whenever this Act requires any action to be taken within a reasonable time, any time which is not manifestly unreasonable may be fixed by agreement.

(2) What is a reasonable time for taking any action depends on the nature, purpose, and circumstances of such action.

(3) An action is taken **"seasonably"** when it is taken at or within the time agreed or if no time is agreed at or within a reasonable time.

Section 1–205. **Course of Dealing and Usage of Trade.**

(1) A course of dealing is a sequence of previous conduct between the parties to a particular transaction which is fairly to be regarded as establishing a common basis of understanding for interpreting their expressions and other conduct.

(2) A usage of trade is any practice or method of dealing having such regularity of observance in a place, vocation, or trade as to justify an expectation that it will be observed with respect to the transaction in question. The existence and scope of such a usage are to be proved as facts. If it is established that such a usage is embodied in a written trade code or similar writing, the interpretation of the writing is for the court.

(3) A course of dealing between parties and any usage of trade in the vocation or trade in which they are engaged, or of which they are or should be aware, give particular meaning to and supplement or qualify terms of an agreement.

(4) The express terms of an agreement and an applicable course of dealing or usage of trade shall be construed wherever reasonable as consistent with each other; but when such construction is unreasonable, express terms control both course of dealing and usage of trade, and course of dealing controls usage of trade.

(5) An applicable usage of trade in the place where any part of performance is to occur shall be used in interpreting the agreement as to that part of the performance.

(6) Evidence of a relevant usage of trade offered by one party is not admissible unless and until he has given the other party such notice as the court finds sufficient to prevent unfair surprise to the latter.

Article 2. Sales

Part 1 **Short Title, General Construction and Subject Matter**

Section 2–101. **Short Title.**
This Article shall be known and may be cited as Uniform Commercial Code–Sales.

Section 2–102. **Scope; Certain Security and Other Transactions Excluded from This Article.**
Unless the context otherwise requires, this Article applies to transactions in goods; it does not apply to any transaction which, although in the form of an unconditional contract to sell or present sale, is intended to operate only as a security transaction, nor does this Article impair or repeal any statute regulating sales to consumers, farmers, or other specified classes of buyers.

Section 2–103. **Definitions and Index of Definitions.**
(1) In this Article, unless the context otherwise requires,
> (a) "Buyer" means a person who buys or contracts to buy goods.
> (b) "Good faith" in the case of a merchant means honesty in fact and the observance of reasonable commercial standards of fair dealing in the trade.
> (c) "Receipt" of goods means taking physical possession of them.
> (d) "Seller" means a person who sells or contracts to sell goods.

Section 2–104. **Definitions: "Merchant"; "Between Merchants"; "Financing Agency."**
(1) "Merchant" means a person who deals in goods of the kind or otherwise by his occupation holds himself out as having knowledge or skill peculiar to the practices or goods involved in the transaction or to whom such knowledge or skill may be attributed by his employment of an agent or broker or other intermediary who by his occupation holds himself out as having such knowledge or skill.

(2) "Financing agency" means a bank, finance company, or other person who in the ordinary course of business makes advances against goods or documents of title or who by arrangement with either the seller or the buyer intervenes in ordinary course to make or collect payment due or claimed under the contract for sale, as by purchasing or paying the seller's draft or making advances against it or by merely taking it for collection whether or not documents of title accompany the draft. "Financing agency" includes also a bank or other person who similarly intervenes between persons who are in the position of seller and buyer in respect to the goods (Section 2–707).

(3) "Between merchants" means in any transaction with respect to which both parties are chargable with the knowledge or skill of merchants.

Section 2–105. **Definitions: Transferability; "Goods"; "Future" Goods; "Lot"; "Commercial Unit."**
(1) "Goods" means all things (including specially manufactured goods) which are movable at the time of identification to the contract for sale other than the money in which the price is to be paid, investment securities (Article 8), and things in action. "Goods" also includes the unborn young of animals and growing crops and other identified things attached to realty as described in the section on goods to be severed from realty (Section 2–107).

(2) Goods must be both existing and identified before any interest in them can pass. Goods which are not both existing and identified are "future" goods. A purported present sale of future goods or of any interest therein operates as a contract to sell.

(3) There may be a sale of a part interest in existing identified goods.

(4) An undivided share in an identified bulk of fungible goods is sufficiently identified to be sold although the quantity of the bulk is not determined. Any agreed proportion of such a bulk or any quantity thereof agreed upon by number, weight, or other measure may to the extent of the seller's interest in the bulk be sold to the buyer who then becomes an owner in common.

(5) "Lot" means a parcel or a single article which is the subject matter of a separate sale or delivery, whether or not it is sufficient to perform the contract.

(6) "Commercial unit" means such a unit of goods as by commercial usage is a single whole for purposes of sale and division of which materially impairs its character or value on the market or in use. A commercial unit may be a single article (as a machine) or a set of articles (as a suite of furniture or an assortment of sizes) or a quantity (as a bale, gross, or carload) or any other unit treated in use or in the relevant market as a single whole.

Part 2 Form, Formation, and Readjustment of Contract

Section 2–201. Formal Requirements; Statute of Frauds.

(1) Except as otherwise provided in this section, a contract for the sale of goods for the price of $500 or more is not enforceable by way of action or defense unless there is some writing sufficient to indicate that a contract for sale has been made between the parties and signed by the party against whom enforcement is sought or by his authorized agent or broker. A writing is not insufficient because it omits or incorrectly states a term agreed upon, but the contract is not enforceable under this paragraph beyond the quantity of goods shown in such writing.

(2) Between merchants if within a reasonable time a writing in confirmation of the contract and sufficient against the sender is received and the party receiving it has reason to know its contents, it satisfies the requirements of subsection (1) against such party unless written notice of objection to its contents is given within ten days after it is received.

(3) A contract which does not satisfy the requirements of subsection (1) but which is valid in other respects is enforceable

(a) if the goods are to be specially manufactured for the buyer and are not suitable for sale to others in the ordinary course of the seller's business and the seller, before notice of repudiation is received and under circumstances which reasonably indicate that the goods are for the buyer, has made either a substantial beginning of their manufacture or commitments for their procurement; or

(b) if the party against whom enforcement is sought admits in his pleading, testimony, or otherwise in court that a contract for sale was made, but the contract is not enforceable under this provision beyond the quantity of goods admitted; or

(c) with respect to goods for which payment has been made and accepted or which have been received and accepted (Sec. 2–606).

Section 2–202. Final Written Expression: Parol or Extrinsic Evidence.

Terms with respect to which the confirmatory memoranda of the parties agree or which are otherwise set forth in a writing intended by the parties as a final expression of their agreement with respect to such terms as are included therein may not be contradicted by evidence of any prior agreement or of a contemporaneous oral agreement but may be explained or supplemented

(a) by course of dealing or usage of trade (Section 1–205) or by course of performance (Section 2–208); and

(b) by evidence of consistent additional terms unless the court finds the writing to have been intended also as a complete and exclusive statement of the terms of the agreement.

Section 2–203. Seals Inoperative.

The affixing of a seal to a writing evidencing a contract for sale or an offer to buy or sell goods does not constitute the writing of a sealed instrument, and the law with respect to sealed instruments does not apply to such a contract or offer.

Section 2–204. Formation in General.

(1) A contract for sale of goods may be made in any manner sufficient to show agreement, including conduct by both parties which recognizes the existence of such a contract.

(2) An agreement sufficient to constitute a contract for sale may be found even though the moment of its making is undetermined.

(3) Even though one or more terms are left open, a contract for sale does not fail for indefiniteness if the parties have intended to make a contract and there is a reasonably certain basis for giving an appropriate remedy.

Section 2–205. **Firm Offers.**

An offer by a merchant to buy or sell goods in a signed writing which by its terms gives assurance that it will be held open is not revocable, for lack of consideration, during the time stated or if no time is stated for a reasonable time, but in no event may such period of irrevocability exceed three months; but any such term of assurance on a form supplied by the offeree must be separately signed by the offeror.

Section 2–206. **Offer and Acceptance in Formation of Contract.**

(1) Unless otherwise unambiguously indicated by the language or circumstances
> (a) an offer to make a contract shall be construed as inviting acceptance in any manner and by any medium reasonable in the circumstances;
> (b) an order or other offer to buy goods for prompt or current shipment shall be construed as inviting acceptance, either by a prompt promise to ship or by the prompt or current shipment of conforming or nonconforming goods, but such a shipment of nonconforming goods does not constitute an acceptance if the seller seasonably notifies the buyer that the shipment is offered only as an accommodation to the buyer.

(2) Where the beginning of a requested performance is a reasonable mode of acceptance, an offeror who is not notified of acceptance within a reasonable time may treat the offer as having lapsed before acceptance.

Section 2–207. **Additional Terms in Acceptance or Confirmation.**

(1) A definite and seasonable expression of acceptance or a written confirmation which is sent within a reasonable time operates as an acceptance even though it states terms additional to or different from those offered or agreed upon, unless acceptance is expressly made conditional on assent to the additional or different terms.

(2) The additional terms are to be construed as proposals for addition to the contract. Between merchants such terms become part of the contract unless:
> (a) the offer expressly limits acceptance to the terms of the offer;
> (b) they materially alter it; or
> (c) notification of objection to them has already been given or is given within a reasonable time after notice of them is received.

(3) Conduct by both parties which recognizes the existence of a contract is sufficient to establish a contract for sale although the writings of the parties do not otherwise establish a contract. In such case the terms of the particular contract consist of those terms on which the writings of the parties agree, together with any supplementary terms incorporated under any other provisions of this Act.

Section 2–208. **Course of Performance or Practical Construction.**

(1) Where the contract for sale involves repeated occasions for performance by either party with knowledge of the nature of the performance and opportunity for objection to it by the other, any course of performance accepted or acquiesced in without objection shall be relevant to determine the meaning of the agreement.

(2) The express terms of the agreement and any such course of performance, as well as any course of dealing and usage of trade, shall be construed whenever reasonable as consistent with each other; but when such construction is unreasonable, express terms shall control course of performance, and course of performance shall control both course of dealing and usage of trade (Section 1–205).

(3) Subject to the provisions of the next section on modification and waiver, such course of performance shall be relevant to show a waiver or modification of any term inconsistent with such course of performance.

Section 2–209. **Modification, Rescission, and Waiver.**

(1) An agreement modifying a contract within this Article needs no consideration to be binding.

(2) A signed agreement which excludes modification or rescission except by a signed writing cannot be otherwise modified or rescinded, but except as between merchants such a requirement on a form supplied by the merchant must be separately signed by the other party.

(3) The requirements of the statute of frauds section of this Article (Section 2–201) must be satisfied if the contract as modified is within its provisions.

(4) Although an attempt at modification or rescission does not satisfy the requirements of subsection (2) or (3), it can operate as a waiver.

(5) A party who has made a waiver affecting an executory portion of the contract may retract the waiver by reasonable notification received by the other party that strict performance will be required of any term waived, unless the retraction would be unjust in view of a material change of position in reliance on the waiver.

Section 2–305. **Open Price Term.**

(1) The parties if they so intend can conclude a contract for sale even though the price is not settled. In such a case the price is a reasonable price at the time for delivery if

(a) nothing is said as to price; or

(b) the price is left to be agreed by the parties and they fail to agree; or

(c) the price is to be fixed in terms of some agreed market or other standard as set or recorded by a third person or agency, and it is not so set or recorded.

(2) A price to be fixed by the seller or by the buyer means a price for him to fix in good faith.

(3) When a price left to be fixed otherwise than by agreement of the parties fails to be fixed through fault of one party, the other may at his option treat the contract as cancelled or himself fix a reasonable price.

(4) Where, however, the parties intend not to be bound unless the price be fixed or agreed, and it is not fixed or agreed, there is no contract. In such a case, the buyer must return any goods already received or, if unable so to do, must pay their reasonable value at the time of delivery, and the seller must return any portion of the price paid on account.

Section 2–309. **Absence of Specific Time Provisions; Notice of Termination.**

(1) The time for shipment or delivery, or any other action under a contract if not provided in this Article or agreed upon, shall be a reasonable time.

(2) Where the contract provides for successive performances but is indefinite in duration, it is valid for a reasonable time but unless otherwise agreed may be terminated at any time by either party.

(3) Termination of a contract by one party except on the happening of an agreed event requires that reasonable notification be received by the other party, and an agreement dispensing with notification is invalid if its operation would be unconscionable.

Section 2–311. **Options and Cooperation Respecting Performance.**

(1) An agreement for sale which is otherwise sufficiently definite (subsection 3 of Section 2–204) to be a contract is not made invalid by the fact that it leaves particulars of performance to be specified by one of the parties. Any such specification must be made in good faith and within limits set by commercial reasonableness.

(2) Unless otherwise agreed specifications relating to assortment of the goods are at the buyer's option, and except as otherwise provided in subsections (1)(c) and (3) of Section 2–319, specifications or arrangements relating to shipment are at the seller's option.

(3) Where such specification would materially affect the other party's performance but is not seasonably made or where one party's cooperation is necessary to the agreed performance of the other but is not seasonably forthcoming, the other party in addition to all other remedies

(a) is excused for any resulting delay in his own performance; and

(b) may also either proceed to perform in any reasonable manner or after the time for a material part of his own performance treat the failure to specify or to cooperate as a breach by failure to deliver or accept the goods.

Section 2–312. **Warranty of Title and Against Infringement; Buyer's Obligation Against Infringement.**

(1) Subject to subsection

(2) there is in a contract for sale a warranty by the seller that

(a) the title conveyed shall be good, and its transfer rightful; and

(b) the goods shall be delivered free from any security interest or other lien or encumbrance of which the buyer at the time of contracting has no knowledge.

(3) A warranty under subsection (1) will be excluded or modified only by specific language or by circumstances which give the buyer reason to know that the person selling does not claim title in himself or that he is purporting to sell only such right or title as he or a third person may have.

(4) Unless otherwise agreed a seller who is a merchant regularly dealing in goods of the kind warrants that the goods shall be delivered free of the rightful claim of any third person by way of infringement or the like, but a buyer who furnishes specifications to the seller must hold the seller harmless against any such claim which arises out of compliance with the specifications.

Section 2–313. **Express Warranties by Affirmation, Promise, Description, Sample.**

(1) Express warranties by the seller are created as follows:

(a) Any affirmation of fact or promise made by the seller to the buyer which relates to the goods and becomes part of the basis of the bargain creates an express warranty that the goods shall conform to the affirmation or promise.

(b) description of the goods which is made part of the basis of the bargain creates an express warranty that the goods shall conform to the description.

(c) Any sample or model which is made part of the basis of the bargain creates an express warranty that the whole of the goods shall conform to the sample or model.

(2) It is not necessary to the creation of an express warranty that the seller use formal words such as "warrant" or "guarantee" or that he have a specific intention to make a warranty, but an affirmation merely of the value of the goods or a statement purporting to be merely the seller's opinion or commendation of the goods does not create a warranty.

Section 2–314. **Implied Warranty: Merchantability; Usage of Trade.**

(1) Unless excluded or modified (Section 2–316), a warranty that the goods shall be merchantable is implied in a contract for their sale if the seller is a merchant with respect to goods of that kind. Under this section the serving for value of food or drink to be consumed either on the premises or elsewhere is a sale.

(2) Goods to be merchantable must be at least such as

(a) pass without objection in the trade under the contract description; and

(b) in the case of fungible goods, are of fair average quality within the description; and

(c) are fit for the ordinary purposes for which such goods are used; and

(d) run, within the variations permitted by the agreement, of even kind, quality, and quantity within each unit and among all units involved; and

(e) are adequately contained, packaged, and labeled as the agreement may require; and

(f) conform to the promises or affirmations of fact made on the container or label if any.

(3) Unless excluded or modified (Section 2–316) other implied warranties may arise from course of dealing or usage of trade.

Section 2–315. **Implied Warranty: Fitness for Particular Purpose.**

Where the seller at the time of contracting has reason to know any particular purpose for which the goods are required and that the buyer is relying on the seller's skill or judgment to select or furnish suitable goods, there is unless excluded or modified under the next section an implied warranty that the goods shall be fit for such purpose.

Section 2–316. **Exclusion or Modification of Warranties.**

(1) Words or conduct relevant to the creation of an express warranty and words or conduct tending to negate or limit warranty shall be construed wherever reasonable as consistent with each other; but subject to the provisions of this Article on parol or extrinsic evidence (Section 2–202), negation or limitation is inoperative to the extent that such construction is unreasonable.

(2) Subject to subsection (3), to exclude or modify the implied warranty of merchantability or any part of it, the language must mention merchantability and in case of a writing must be conspicuous, and to exclude or modify any implied warranty of fitness the exclusion must be by a writing and conspicuous. Language to exclude all implied warranties of fitness is sufficient if it states, for example, that "There are no warranties which extend beyond the description on the face hereof."

(3) Notwithstanding subsection (2)

    (a) unless the circumstances indicate otherwise, all implied warranties are excluded by expressions like "as is," "with all faults," or other language which in common understanding calls the buyer's attention to the exclusion of warranties and makes plain that there is no implied warranty; and

    (b) when the buyer before entering into the contract has examined the goods or the sample or model as fully as he desired or has refused to examine the goods, there is no implied warranty with regard to defects which an examination ought in the circumstances to have revealed to him; and

    (c) an implied warranty can also be excluded or modified by course of dealing or course of performance or usage of trade.

(4) Remedies for breach of warranty can be limited in accordance with the provisions of this Article on liquidation or limitation of damages and on contractual modification of remedy (Sections 2–718 and 2–719).

Part 4 Title, Creditors, and Good Faith Purchasers

Section 2–401. Passing of Title; Reservation for Security; Limited Application of This Section.

Each provision of this Article with regard to the rights, obligations, and remedies of the seller, the buyer, purchasers, or other third parties applies irrespective of title to the goods except where the provision refers to such title. Insofar as situations are not covered by the other provisions of this Article and matters concerning title became material, the following rules apply:

(1) Title to goods cannot pass under a contract for sale prior to their identification to the contract (Section 2–501), and unless otherwise explicitly agreed, the buyer acquires by their identification a special property as limited by this Act. Any retention or reservation by the seller of the title (property) in goods shipped or delivered to the buyer is limited in effect to a reservation of a security interest. Subject to these provisions and to the provisions of the Article on Secured Transactions (Article 9), title to goods passes from the seller to the buyer in any manner and on any conditions explicitly agreed on by the parties.

(2) Unless otherwise explicitly agreed, title passes to the buyer at the time and place at which the seller completes his performance with reference to the physical delivery of the goods, despite any reservation of a security interest and even though a document of title is to be delivered at a different time or place; and in particular and despite any reservation of a security interest by the bill of lading

    (a) if the contract requires or authorizes the seller to send the goods to the buyer but does not require him to deliver them at destination, title passes to the buyer at the time and place of shipment; but

    (b) if the contract requires delivery at destination, title passes on tender there.

(3) Unless otherwise explicitly agreed, where delivery is to be made without moving the goods,

    (a) if the seller is to deliver a document of title, title passes at the time when and the place where he delivers such documents; or

    (b) if the goods are at the time of contracting already identified and no documents are to be delivered, title passes at the time and place of contracting.

(4) A rejection or other refusal by the buyer to receive or retain the goods, whether or not justified, or a justified revocation of acceptance revests title to the goods in the seller. Such revesting occurs by operation of law and is not a "sale".

Part 5 Performance

Section 2–507. Effect of Seller's Tender; Delivery on Condition.

(1) Tender of delivery is a condition to the buyer's duty to accept the goods and, unless otherwise agreed, to his duty to pay for them. Tender entitles the seller to acceptance of the goods and to payment according to the contract.

(2) Where payment is due and demanded on the delivery to the buyer of goods or documents of title, his right as against the seller to retain or dispose of them is conditional upon his making the payment due.

Section 2–508. **Cure by Seller of Improper Tender or Delivery; Replacement.**

(1) Where any tender or delivery by the seller is rejected because non conforming and the time for performance has not yet expired, the seller may seasonably notify the buyer of his intention to cure and may then within the contract time make a conforming delivery.

(2) Where the buyer rejects a non conforming tender which the seller had reasonable grounds to believe would be acceptable with or without money allowance, the seller may if he seasonably notifies the buyer have a further reasonable time to substitute a conforming tender.

Section 2–513. **Buyer's Right to Inspection of Goods.**

(1) Unless otherwise agreed and subject to subsection (3), where goods are tendered or delivered or identified to the contract for sale, the buyer has a right before payment or acceptance to inspect them at any reasonable place and time and in any reasonable manner. When the seller is required or authorized to send the goods to the buyer, the inspection may be after their arrival.

(2) Expenses of inspection must be borne by the buyer but may be recovered from the seller if the goods do not conform and are rejected.

(3) Unless otherwise agreed and subject to the provisions of this Article on C.I.F. contracts (subsection 3 of Section 2–321), the buyer is not entitled to inspect the goods before payment of the price when the contract provides

    (a) for delivery "C.O.D." or on other like terms; or

    (b) for payment against documents of title, except where such payment is due only after the goods are to become available for inspection.

(4) A place or method of inspection fixed by the parties is presumed to be exclusive, but unless otherwise expressly agreed, it does not postpone identification or shift the place for delivery or for passing the risk of loss. If compliance becomes impossible, inspection shall be as provided in this section, unless the place or method fixed was clearly intended as an indispensable condition failure of which avoids the contract.

Part 6 **Breach, Repudiation, and Excuse**

Section 2–601. **Buyer's Rights on Improper Delivery.**

Subject to the provisions of this Article on breach in installment contracts (Section 2–612) and unless otherwise agreed under the sections on contractual limitations of remedy (Sections 2–718 and 2–719), if the goods or the tender of delivery fail in any respect to conform to the contract, the buyer may

    (a) reject the whole; or

    (b) accept the whole; or

    (c) accept any commercial unit or units and reject the rest.

Section 2–606. **What Constitutes Acceptance of Goods.**

(1) Acceptance of goods occurs when the buyer

    (a) after a reasonable opportunity to inspect the goods signifies to the seller that the goods are conforming or that he will take or retain them in spite of their non conformity; or

    (b) fails to make an effective rejection (subsection 1 of Section 2–602), but such acceptance does not occur until the buyer has had a reasonable opportunity to inspect them; or

    (c) does any act inconsistent with the seller's ownership; but if such act is wrongful as against the seller, it is an acceptance only if ratified by him.

(2) Acceptance of a part of any commercial unit is acceptance of that entire unit.

Section 2–607. **Effect of Acceptance; Notice of Breach; Burden of Establishing Breach After Acceptance; Notice of Claim or Litigation to Person Answerable Over.**

(1) The buyer must pay at the contract rate for any goods accepted.

(2) Acceptance of goods by the buyer precludes rejection of the goods accepted and if made with knowledge of a non conformity cannot be revoked because of it, unless the acceptance was on the reasonable assumption that the non conformity would be seasonably cured but acceptance does not of itself impair any other remedy provided by this Article for non conformity.

(3) Where a tender has been accepted

(a) the buyer must within a reasonable time after he discovers or should have discovered any breach notify the seller of breach or be barred from any remedy; and

(b) if the claim is one for infringement or the like (subsection 3 of Section 2–312) and the buyer is sued as a result of such a breach, he must so notify the seller within a reasonable time after he receives notice of the litigation or be barred from any remedy for liability established by the litigation.

(4) The burden is on the buyer to establish any breach with respect to the goods accepted.

(5) Where the buyer is sued for breach of a warranty or other obligation for which his seller is answerable over

(a) he may give his seller written notice of the litigation. If the notice states that the seller may come in and defend, and that if the seller does not do so he will be bound in any action against him by his buyer by any determination of fact common to the two litigations, then unless the seller after seasonable receipt of the notice does come in and defend hc is so bound.

(b) if the claim is one for infringement or the like (subsection 3 of Section 2–312) the original seller may demand in writing that his buyer turn over to him control of the litigation including settlement or else be barred from any remedy over, and if he also agrees to bear all expense and to satisfy any adverse judgment, then unless the buyer after seasonable receipt of the demand does turn over control, the buyer is so barred.

(6) The provisions of subsections (3), (4) and (5) apply to any obligation of a buyer to hold the seller harmless against infringement or the like (subsection 3 of Section 2–312).

Section 2–608. **Revocation of Acceptance in Whole or in Part.**

(1) The buyer may revoke his acceptance of a lot or commercial unit whose non conformity substantially impairs its value to him if he has accepted it

(a) on the reasonable assumption that its non conformity would be cured and it has not been seasonably cured; or

(b) without discovery of such non conformity if his acceptance was reasonably induced either by the difficulty of discovery before acceptance or by the seller's assurances.

(2) Revocation of acceptance must occur within a reasonable time after the buyer discovers or should have discovered the ground for it and before any substantial change in condition of the goods which is not caused by their own defects. It is not effective until the buyer notifies the seller of it.

(3) A buyer who so revokes has the same rights and duties with regard to the goods involved as if he had rejected them.

Part 7 **Remedies**

Section 2–703. **Seller's Remedies in General.**

Where the buyer wrongfully rejects or revokes acceptance of goods or fails to make a payment due on or before delivery or repudiates with respect to a part or the whole, then with respect to any goods directly affected and, if the breach is of the whole contract (Section 2–612), then also with respect to the whole undelivered balance, the aggrieved seller may

(a) withhold delivery of such goods;

(b) stop delivery by any bailee as hereafter provided (Section 2–705);

(c) proceed under the next section respecting goods still unidentified to the contract;

(d) resell and recover damages as hereafter provided (Section 2–706);

(e) recover damages for non-acceptance (Section 2–708) or in a proper case the price (Section 2–709);

(f) cancel.

Section 2–710. **Seller's Incidental Damages.**

Incidental damages to an aggrieved seller include any commercially reasonable charges, expenses, or commissions incurred in stopping delivery; in the transportation, care, and custody of goods after the buyer's breach, in connection with return or resale of the goods or otherwise resulting from the breach.

Section 2–711. **Buyer's Remedies in General; Buyer's Security Interest in Rejected Goods.**

(1) Where the seller fails to make delivery or repudiates, or the buyer rightfully rejects or justifiably revokes acceptance then with respect to any goods involved, and with respect to the whole if the breach goes to the whole contract (Section 2–612), the buyer may cancel and, whether or not he has done so, may in addition to recovering so much of the price as has been paid

    (a) "cover" and have damages under the next section as to all the goods affected whether or not they have been identified to the contract; or

    (b) recover damages for non delivery as provided in this Article (Section 2–713).

(2) Where the seller fails to deliver or repudiates, the buyer may also

    (a) if the goods have been identified recover them as provided in this Article (Section 2–502); or

    (b) in a proper case obtain specific performance or replevy the goods as provided in this Article (Section 2–716).

(3) On rightful rejection or justifiable revocation of acceptance, a buyer has a security interest in goods in his possession or control for any payments made on their price and any expenses reasonably incurred in their inspection, receipt, transportation, care, and custody and may hold such goods and resell them in like manner as an aggrieved seller (Section 2–706).

Section 2–712. **"Cover"; Buyer's Procurement of Substitute Goods.**

(1) After a breach within the preceding section, the buyer may "cover" by making in good faith and without unreasonable delay any reasonable purchase of or contract to purchase goods in substitution for those due from the seller.

(2) The buyer may recover from the seller as damages the difference between the cost of cover and the contract price together with any incidental or consequential damages as hereinafter defined (Section 2–715), but less expenses saved in consequence of the seller's breach.

(3) Failure of the buyer to effect cover within this section does not bar him from any other remedy.

Section 2–715. **Buyer's Incidental and Consequential Damages.**

(1) Incidental damages resulting from the seller's breach include expenses reasonably incurred in inspection, receipt, transportation, and care and custody of goods rightfully rejected, any commercially reasonable charges, expenses, or commissions in connection with effecting cover and any other reasonable expense incident to the delay or other breach.

(2) Consequential damages resulting from the seller's breach include

    (a) any loss resulting from general or particular requirements and needs of which the seller at the time of contracting had reason to know and which could not reasonably be prevented by cover or otherwise; and

    (b) injury to person or property proximately resulting from any breach of warranty.

Article 3. Negotiable Instruments

Part 1 **General Provisions and Definitions**

Section 3–104. **Form of Negotiable Instruments; "Draft"; "Check"; "Certificate of Deposit"; "Note".**

(1) Any writing to be a negotiable instrument within this Article must

    (a) be signed by the maker or drawer; and

    (b) contain an unconditional promise or order to pay a sum certain in money and no other promise, order, obligation, or power given by the maker or drawer except as authorized by this Article; and

    (c) be payable on demand or at a definite time; and

    (d) be payable to order or to bearer.

(2) A writing which complies with the requirements of this section is

    (a) a "draft" ("bill of exchange") if it is an order;

    (b) a "check" if it is a draft drawn on a bank and payable on demand;

(c) a "certificate of deposit" if it is an acknowledgment by a bank receipt of money with an engagement to repay it;

(d) a "note" if it is a promise other than a certificate of deposit.

(3) As used in other Articles of this Act, and as the context may require, the terms "draft," "check," "certificate of deposit," and "note" may refer to instruments which are not negotiable within this Article as well as to instruments which are so negotiable.

Section 3–105. **When Promise or Order Unconditional.**

(1) A promise or order otherwise unconditional is not made conditional by the fact that the instrument

(a) is subject to implied or constructive conditions; or

(b) states its consideration, whether performed or promised, or the transaction which gave rise to the instrument, or that the promise or order is made, or the instrument matures in accordance with or "as per" such transaction; or

(c) refers to or states that it arises out of a separate agreement or refers to a separate agreement for rights as to prepayment or acceleration; or

(d) states that it is drawn under a letter of credit; or

(e) states that it is secured, whether by mortgage, reservation of title, or otherwise; or

(f) indicates a particular account to be debited or any other fund or source from which reimbursement is expected; or

(g) is limited to payment out of a particular fund or the proceeds of a particular source, if the instrument is issued by a government or governmental agency or unit; or

(h) is limited to payment out of the entire assets of a partnership, unincorporated association, trust, or estate by or on behalf of which the instrument is issued.

(2) A promise or order is not unconditional if the instrument

(a) states that it is subject to or governed by any other agreement; or

(b) states that it is to be paid only out of a particular fund or source except as provided in this section.

Section 3–106. **Sum Certain.**

(1) The sum payable is a sum certain even though it is to be paid

(a) with stated interest or by stated installments; or

(b) with stated different rates of interest before and after default or a specified date; or

(c) with a stated discount or addition if paid before or after the date fixed for payment; or

(d) with exchange or less exchange, whether at a fixed rate or at the current rate; or

(e) with costs of collection or an attorney's fee or both upon default.

(2) Nothing in this section shall validate any term which is otherwise illegal.

Section 3–110. **Payable to Order.**

(1) An instrument is payable to order when by its terms it is payable to the order or assigns of any person therein specified with reasonable certainty, or to him or his order, or when it is conspicuously designated on its face as "exchange" or the like and names a payee. It may be payable to the order of

(a) the maker or drawer; or

(b) the drawee; or

(c) a payee who is not maker, drawer, or drawee; or

(d) two or more payees together or in the alternative; or

(e) an estate, trust, or fund, in which case it is payable to the order of the representative of such estate, trust, or fund or his successors; or

(f) an office, or an officer by his title as such, in which case it is payable to the principal, but the incumbent of the office or his successors may act as if he or they were the holder; or

(g) a partnership or unincorporated association, in which case it is payable to the partnership or association and may be endorsed or transferred by any person thereto authorized.

(2) An instrument not payable to order is not made so payable by such words as "payable upon return of this instrument properly endorsed."

(3) An instrument made payable both to order and to bearer is payable to order unless the bearer words are handwritten or typewritten.

Section 3–111. **Payable to Bearer.**

An instrument is payable to bearer when by its terms it is payable to

    (a) bearer or the order of bearer; or

    (b) a specified person or bearer; or

    (c) "cash" or the order of "cash", or any other indication which does not purport to designate a specific payee.

Part 2 **Negotiation, Transfer, and Endorsement**

Section 3–201. **Negotiation.**

(1) (a) "Negotiation" means a transfer of possession, whether voluntary or involuntary, of an instrument by a person other than the issuer to a person who thereby becomes its holder.

(2) (b) Except for negotiation by a remitter, if an instrument is payable to an identified person, negotiation requires transfer of possession of the instrument and its endorsement by the holder. If an instrument is payable to bearer, it may be negotiated by transfer of possession alone.

Section 3–202. **Negotiation Subject to Rescission.**

(1) (a) Negotiation is effective even if obtained (i) from an infant, a corporation exceeding its powers, or a person without capacity, (ii) by fraud, duress, or mistake, or (iii) in breach of duty or as part of an illegal transaction.

(2) (b) To the extent permitted by other law, negotiation may be rescinded or may be subject to other remedies, but those remedies may not be asserted against a subsequent holder in due course or a person paying the instrument in good faith and without knowledge of facts that are a basis for rescission or other remedy.

National Labor Relations Act (Excerpts)

* * *

Rights of Employees

Section 7. Employees shall have the right to self-organization, to form, join, or assist labor organizations, to bargain collectively through representatives of their own choosing, and to engage in other concerted activities for the purpose of collective bargaining or other mutual aid or protection, and shall also have the right to refrain from any or all of such activities requiring membership in a labor organization as a condition of employment as authorized in section 8(a)(3).

Unfair Labor Practices

Section 8. (a) It shall be an unfair labor practice for an employer—

(1) to interfere with, restrain, or coerce employees in the exercise of the rights guaranteed in section ;

(2) to dominate or interfere with the formation or administration of any labor organization or contribute financial or other support to it: *Provided*, That ... an employer shall not be prohibited from permitting employees to confer with him during working hours without loss of time or pay;

(3) by discrimination in regard to hire or tenure of employment or any term or condition of employment to encourage or discourage membership in any labor organization....

(4) to discharge or otherwise discriminate against an employee because he has filed charges or given testimony under this Act;

(5) to refuse to bargain collectively with the representatives of his employees, subject to the provisions of section 9(a).

(b) It shall be an unfair labor practice for a labor organization or its agents—

(1) to restrain or coerce (A) employees in the exercise of the rights guaranteed in section 7: *Provided*, That this paragraph shall not impair the right of a labor organization to prescribe its own rules with respect to the acquisition or retention of membership therein; or (B) an employer in the selection of his representatives for the purposes of collective bargaining or the adjustment of grievances;

(2) to cause or attempt to cause an employer to discriminate against an employee ... or to discriminate against an employee with respect to whom membership in such organization has been denied or terminated on some ground other than his failure to tender the periodic dues and the initiation fees uniformly required as a condition of acquiring or retaining membership;

(3) to refuse to bargain collectively with an employer, provided it is the representative of his employees subject to the provisions of section 9(a);

(4) (i) to engage in, or to induce or encourage any individual employed by any person engaged in commerce or in an industry affecting commerce to engage in, a strike or a refusal in the course of his employment to use, manufacture, process, transport, or otherwise handle or work on any goods, articles, materials, or commodities or to perform any services; or (ii) to threaten, coerce, or restrain any person engaged in commerce or in an industry affecting commerce, where in either case an object thereof is—

(A) forcing or requiring any employer or self-employed person to join any labor or employer organization or to enter into any agreement which is prohibited by section 8(e);

(B) forcing or requiring any person to cease using, selling, handling, transporting, or otherwise dealing in the products of any other producer, processor, or manufacturer, or to cease doing business with any other person, or forcing or requiring any other employer to recognize or bargain with a labor organization as the representative of his employees unless such labor organization has been certified as the representative of such employees under the provisions of section 9: *Provided,* That nothing contained in this clause (B) shall be construed to make unlawful, where not otherwise unlawful, any primary strike or primary picketing;

(C) forcing or requiring any employer to recognize or bargain with a particular labor organization as the representative of his employees if another labor organization has been certified as the representative of such employees under the provisions of section 9;

(D) forcing or requiring any employer to assign particular work to employees in a particular labor organization or in a particular trade, craft, or class rather than to employees in another labor organization or in another trade, craft, or class, unless such employer is failing to conform to an order or certification of the Board determining the bargaining representative for employees performing such work:

Provided, That nothing contained in this subsection (b) shall be construed to make unlawful a refusal by any person to enter upon the premises of any employer (other than his own employer), if the employees of such employer are engaged in a strike ratified or approved by a representative of such employees whom such employer is required to recognize under this Act: *Provided further,* that for the purposes of this paragraph (4) only, nothing contained in such paragraph shall be construed to prohibit publicity, other than picketing, for the purpose of truthfully advising the public, including consumers and members of a labor organization, that a product or products are produced by an employer with whom the labor organization has a primary dispute and are distributed by another employer, as long as such publicity does not have an effect of inducing any individual employed by any person other than the primary employer in the course of his employment to refuse to pick up, deliver, or transport any goods, or not to perform any services, at the establishment of the employer engaged in such distribution:

(5) to require of employees covered by an agreement authorized under subsection (a)(3) the payment, as a condition precedent to becoming a member of such organization, of a fee in an amount which the Board finds excessive or discriminatory under all the circumstances. In making such a finding, the Board shall consider, among other relevant factors, the practices and customs of labor organizations in the particular industry, and the wages currently paid to the employees affected;

(6) to cause or attempt to cause an employer to pay or deliver or agree to pay or deliver any money or other thing of value, in the nature of an exaction, for services which are not performed or not to be performed; and

(7) to picket or cause to be picketed, or threaten to picket or cause to be picketed, any employer where an object thereof is forcing or requiring an employer to recognize or bargain with a labor organization as the representative of his employees, or forcing or requiring the employees of an employer to accept or select such labor organization as their collective bargaining representative, unless such labor organization is currently certified as the representative of such employees:

(A) where the employer has lawfully recognized in accordance with this Act any other labor organization and a question concerning representation may not appropriately be raised under section 9(c) of this Act;

(B) where within the preceding twelve months a valid election under section 9(c) of this Act has been conducted, or

(C) where such picketing has been conducted without a petition under section 9(c) being filed within a reasonable period of time not to exceed thirty days from the commencement of such picketing. . . .

Nothing in this paragraph (7) shall be construed to permit any act which would otherwise be an unfair labor practice under this section 8(b).

(c) The expressing of any views, argument, or opinion, or the dissemination thereof, whether in written, printed, graphic, or visual form, shall not constitute or be evidence of an unfair labor practice under any of the provisions of this Act, if such expression contains no threat of reprisal or force or promise of benefit.

(d) (i) For the purposes of this section, to bargain collectively is the performance of the mutual obligation of the employer and the representative of the employees to meet at reasonable times and confer in good faith with respect to wages, hours, and other terms and conditions of employment, or the negotiation of an agreement, or any question arising thereunder, and the execution of a written contract incorporating any agreement reached if requested by either party, but such obligation does not compel either party to agree to a proposal or require the making of a concession. . . .

(e) It shall be an unfair labor practice for any labor organization and any employer to enter into any contract or agreement, express or implied, whereby such employer ceases or refrains or agrees to cease or refrain from handling, using, selling, transporting, or otherwise dealing in any of the products of any other employer, or to cease doing business with any other person, and any contract or agreement entered into heretofore or hereafter containing such an agreement shall be to such extent unenforceable and void. . . .

Representatives and Elections

Section 9. (a) Representatives designated or selected for the purposes of collective bargaining by the majority of the employees in a unit appropriate for such purposes, shall be the exclusive representative of all the employees in such unit for the purposes of collective bargaining in respect to rates of pay, wages, hours of employment, or other conditions of employment: *Provided,* That any individual employee or a group of employees shall have the right at any time to present grievances to their employer and to have such grievances adjusted, without the intervention of the bargaining representative, as long as the adjustment is not inconsistent with the terms of a collective-bargaining contract or agreement then in effect: *Provided further,* That the bargaining representative has been given opportunity to be present at such adjustment.

(b) The Board shall decide in each case whether, in order to assure to employees the fullest freedom in exercising the rights guaranteed by this Act, the unit appropriate for the purposes of collective bargaining shall be the employer unit, craft unit, plant unit, or subdivision thereof. . . .

(c) (1) Whenever a petition shall have been filed, in accordance with such regulations as may be prescribed by the Board—

(A) by an employee or group of employees or an individual or labor organization acting in their behalf, alleging that a substantial number of employees (i) wish to be represented for collective bargaining and that their employer declines to recognize their representative as the representative defined in section 9(a), or (ii) assert that the individual or labor organization, which has been certified or is being currently recognized by their employer as the bargaining representative, is no longer a representative as defined in section 9(a); or

(B) by an employer, alleging that one or more individual or labor organizations have presented to him a claim to be recognized as the representative defined in section 9(a); the Board shall investigate such petition and if it has reasonable cause to believe that a question of representation affecting commerce exists shall provide for an appropriate hearing upon due notice. Such hearing may be conducted by an officer or employee of the regional office, who shall not make any recommendations with respect thereto. If the Board finds upon the record of such hearing that such a question of representation exists, it shall direct an election by secret ballot and shall certify the results thereof.

(2) In determining whether or not a question of representation affecting commerce exists, the same regulations and rules of decision shall apply irrespective of the identity of the persons filing the petition or the kind of relief sought and in no case shall the Board deny a labor organization a place on the ballot by reason of an order with respect to such labor organization or its predecessor not issued in conformity with section 10(c).

(3) No election shall be directed in any bargaining unit or any subdivision within which, in the preceding twelve-month period, a valid election shall have been held. Employees engaged in an economic strike who are not entitled to reinstatement shall be eligible to vote under such regulations as the Board shall find are consistent with the purposes and provisions of this Act in any election conducted within twelve months after the commencement of

the strike. In any election where none of the choices on the ballot receives a majority, a run-off shall be conducted, the ballot providing for a selection between the two choices receiving the largest and second largest number of valid votes cast in the election.

(4) Nothing in this section shall be construed to prohibit the waiving of hearings by stipulation for the purpose of a consent election in conformity with regulations and rules of decision of the Board.

(5) In determining whether a unit is appropriate for the purposes specified in subsection (b) the extent to which the employees have organized shall not be controlling.

(c) Whenever an order of the Board made pursuant to section 10(c) is based in whole or in part upon facts certified following an investigation pursuant to subsection (c) of this section and there is a petition for the enforcement or review of such order, such certification and the record of such investigation shall be included in the transcript of the entire record required to be filed under section 10(e) or 10(f), and thereupon the decree of the court enforcing, modifying, or setting aside in whole or in part the order of the Board shall be made and entered upon the pleadings, testimony, and proceedings set forth in such transcript.

(d) (1) Upon the filing with the Board, by 30 per centum or more of the employees in a bargaining unit covered by an agreement between their employer and a labor organization made pursuant to section 8(a)(3), of a petition alleging they desire that such authority be rescinded, the Board shall take a secret ballot of the employees in such unit, and shall certify the results thereof to such labor organization and to the employer.

(2) No election shall be conducted pursuant to this subsection in any bargaining unit or any subdivision within which, in the preceding twelve-month period, a valid election shall have been held.

* * *

Title VII of Civil Rights Act of 1964 (Excerpts)

Definitions

Section 701. (j) The term "religion" includes all aspects of religious observance and practice, as well as belief, unless an employer demonstrates that he is unable to reasonably accommodate to an employee's or prospective employee's religious observance or practice without undue hardship on the conduct of the employer's business.

(k) The terms "because of sex" or "on the basis of sex" include, but are not limited to, because of or on the basis of pregnancy, childbirth or related medical conditions; and women affected by pregnancy, childbirth, or related medical conditions shall be treated the same for all employment-related purposes, including receipt of benefits under fringe benefit programs, as other persons not so affected but similar in their ability or inability to work, and nothing in Section 703(h) of this title shall be interpreted to permit otherwise. This subsection shall not require an employer to pay for health insurance benefits for abortion, except where the life of the mother would be endangered if the fetus were carried to term, or except where medical complications have arisen from an abortion: *Provided*, That nothing herein shall preclude an employer from providing abortion benefits or otherwise effect bargaining agreements in regard to abortion.

Discrimination Because of Race, Color, Religion, Sex, or National Origin

Section 703. (a) It shall be unlawful employment practice for an employer—

(1) to fail or refuse to hire or to discharge any individual, or otherwise to discriminate against any individual with respect to his compensation, terms, conditions, or privileges of employment, because of such individual's race, color, religion, sex, or national origin; or

(2) to limit, segregate, or classify his employees or applicants for employment in any way which would deprive or tend to deprive any individual of employment opportunities or otherwise adversely affect his status as an employee, because of such individual's race, color, religion, sex, or national origin.

(b) It shall be unlawful employment practice for an employment agency to fail or refuse to refer for employment, or otherwise to discriminate against, an individual because of his race, color, religion, sex, or national origin, or to classify or refer for employment any individual on the basis of his race, color, religion, sex, or national origin.

(c) It shall be an unlawful employment practice for a labor organization—

(1) to exclude or to expel from its membership, or otherwise to discriminate against, any individual because of his race, color, religion, sex, or national origin;

(2) to limit, segregate, or classify its membership or applicants for membership or to classify or fail or refuse to refer for employment any individual, in any way which would deprive or tend to deprive any individual of employment opportunities, or would limit such employment opportunities or otherwise adversely affect his status as an employee or as an applicant for employment, because of such individual's race, color, religion, sex, or national origin; or

(3) to cause or attempt to cause an employer to discriminate against an individual in violation of this section.

(d) It shall be an unlawful employment practice for any employer, labor organization, or joint labor-management committee controlling apprenticeship or other training or retraining, including on-the-job training programs to discriminate against any individual because of his race, color, religion, sex, or national origin in admission to, or employment in, any program established to provide apprenticeship or other training.

(e) Notwithstanding any other provision of this title, (1) it shall not be an unlawful employment practice for an employer to hire and employ employees, for an employment agency to classify, or refer for employment any individual, or for any employer, labor organization, or joint labor-management committee controlling apprenticeship or other training or retraining programs to admit or employ any individual in any such program, on the basis of his religion, sex, or national origin in those certain instances where religion, sex, or national origin is a bona fide occupational qualification reasonably necessary to the normal operation of that particular business or enterprise, and (2) it shall not be an unlawful employment practice for a school, college, university, or other educational institution or institution of learning to hire and employ employees of a particular religion if such school, college, university, or other educational institution or institution of learning is, in whole or in substantial part, owned, supported, controlled, or managed by a particular religion or by a particular religious corporation, association, or society, or if the curriculum of such school, college, university, or other educational institution or institution of learning is directed toward the propagation of a particular religion.

* * *

(h) Notwithstanding any other provision of this title, it shall not be an unlawful employment practice for an employer to apply different standards of compensation, or different terms, conditions, or privileges of employment pursuant to a bona fide seniority or merit system, or a system which measures earnings by quantity or quality of production or to employees who work in different locations, provided that such differences are not the results of an intention to discriminate because of race, color, religion, sex, or national origin; nor shall it be an unlawful employment practice for an employer to give and to act upon the results of any professionally developed ability test provided that such test, its administration or action upon the results is not designed, intended, or used to discriminate because of race, color, religion, sex, or national origin. It shall not be an unlawful employment practice under this title for any employer to differentiate upon the basis of sex in determining the amount of wages or compensation paid or to be paid to employees of such employer if such differentiation is authorized by the provision of Section 6(d) of the Fair Labor Standards Act of 1938 as amended (29 U.S.C. 206(d)).

(i) Nothing contained in this title shall apply to any business or enterprise on or near an Indian reservation with respect to any publicly announced employment practice of such business or enterprise under which a preferential treatment is given to any individual because he is an Indian living on or near a reservation.

(j) Nothing contained in this title shall be interpreted to require any employer, employment agency, labor organization, or joint labor-management committee subject to this title to grant preferential treatment to any individual or to any group because of the race, color, religion, sex, or national origin of such individual or group on account of an imbalance which may exist with respect to the total number or percentage of persons of any race, color, religion, sex, or national origin employed by any employer, referred or classified for employment by any employment agency or labor organization, admitted to membership or classified by any labor organization, or admitted to, or employed in, any apprenticeship or other training program, in comparison with the total number or percentage of persons of such race, color, religion, sex, or national origin in any community, State, section, or other area, or in the available work force in any community, State, section, or other area.

Other Unlawful Employment Practices

Section 704. (a) It shall be an unlawful employment practice for an employer to discriminate against any of his employees or applicants for employment, for an employment agency, or joint labor-management committee controlling apprenticeship or other training or retraining, including on-the-job training programs, to discriminate against any individual, or for a labor organization to discriminate against any member thereof or applicant for membership, because he has opposed any practice, made an unlawful employment practice by this title, or because he has made a charge, testified, assisted, or participated in any manner in an investigation, proceeding, or hearing under this title.

(b) It shall be an unlawful employment practice for an employer, labor organization, employment agency, or joint labor-management committee controlling apprenticeship or other training or retraining, including on-the-job training programs, to print or cause to be printed or published any notice or advertisement relating to employment by such an employer or membership in or any classification or referral for employment by such a labor organization, or relating to any classification or referral for employment by such an employment agency, or relating to admission to, or employment in, any program established to provide apprenticeship or other training by such a joint labor-management committee indicating any preference, limitation, specification, or discrimination, based on race, color, religion, sex, or national origin, except that such a notice or advertisement may indicate a preference, limitation, specification, or discrimination based on religion, sex, or national origin when religion, sex, or national origin is a bona fide occupational qualification for employment.

Americans with Disabilities Act (Excerpts)

Title I—Employment Section 101. Definitions.

(8) Qualified individual with a disability. The term "qualified individual with a disability" means an individual with a disability who, with or without reasonable accommodation, can perform the essential functions of the employment position that such individual holds or desires. For the purposes of this title, consideration shall be given to the employer's judgment as to what functions of a job are essential, and if an employer has prepared a written description before advertising or interviewing applicants for the job, this description shall be considered evidence of the essential functions of the job.

(9) Reasonable Accommodation. The term "reasonable accommodation" may include—

(A) making existing facilities used by employees readily accessible to and usable by individuals with disabilities; and

(B) job restructuring, part-time or modified work schedules, reassignment to a vacant position, acquisition or modification of equipment or devices, appropriate adjustment or modifications of examinations, training materials or policies, the provision of qualified readers or interpreters, and other similar accommodations for individuals with disabilities.

(10) Undue Hardship.

(A) In general: The term "undue hardship" means an action requiring significant difficulty or expense, when considered in light of the factors set forth in subparagraph (B).

(B) Factors to be considered: In determining whether an accommodation would impose an undue hardship on a covered entity, factors to be considered include—

(i) the nature and cost of accommodation needed under this Act;

(ii) the overall financial resources of the facility or facilities involved in the provision of the reasonable accommodation; the number of persons employed at such facility; the effect on expenses and resources, or the impact otherwise of such accommodation upon the operation of the facility;

(iii) the overall financial resources of the covered entity; the overall size of the business of a covered entity with respect to the number of its employees; the number, type, and location of its facilities; and

(iv) the type of operation or operations of the covered entity, including the composition, structure, and functions of the workforce of such entity; the geographic separateness, administrative, or fiscal relationship of the facility or facilities in question to the covered entity.

Section 102. Discrimination.

(a) General Rule. No covered entity shall discriminate against a qualified individual with a disability because of the disability of such individual in regard to job application procedures, the hiring, advancement, or discharge of employees, employee compensation, job training, and other terms, conditions, and privileges of employment.

(b) Construction. As used in subsection (a), the term "discriminate" includes—

(1) limiting, segregating, or classifying a job applicant or employee in a way that adversely affects the opportunities or status of such applicant or employee because of the disability of such applicant or employee;

(2) participating in a contractual or other arrangement or relationship that has the effect of subjecting a covered entity's qualified applicant or employee with a disability to the discrimination prohibited by this title (such relationship includes a relationship with an employment

or referral agency, labor union, an organization providing fringe benefits to an employee of the covered entity, or an organization providing training and apprenticeship programs);

(3) utilizing standards, criteria, or methods of administration—

    (A) that have the effect of discrimination on the basis of disability; or

    (B) that perpetuate the discrimination of others who are subject to common administrative control;

(4) excluding or otherwise denying equal jobs or benefits to a qualified individual because of the known disability of an individual with whom the qualified individual is known to have a relationship or association;

(5) (A) not making reasonable accommodations to the known physical or mental limitations of an otherwise qualified individual with a disability who is an applicant or employee, unless such covered entity can demonstrate that the accommodation would impose an undue hardship on the operation of the business of such covered entity; or

    (B) denying employment opportunities to a job applicant or employee who is an otherwise qualified individual with a disability, if such denial is based on the need of such covered entity to make reasonable accommodation to the physical or mental impairments of the employee or applicant;

(6) using qualification standards, employment tests or other selection criteria that screen out or tend to screen out an individual with a disability or a class of individuals with disabilities unless the standard, test or other selection criteria, as used by the covered entity, is shown to be job-related for the position in question and is consistent with business necessity; and

(7) failing to select and administer tests concerning employment in the most effective manner to ensure that, when such test is administered to a job applicant or employee who has a disability that impairs sensory, manual, or speaking skills, such test results accurately reflect the skills, aptitude, or whatever other factor of such applicant or employee that such test purports to measure, rather than reflecting the impaired sensory, manual, or speaking skills of such employee or applicant (except where such skills are the factors that the test purports to measure).

Section 104. Illegal Use of Drugs and Alcohol.

    (b) Rules of Construction. Nothing in subsection (a) shall be construed to exclude as a qualified individual with a disability an individual who—

(1) has successfully completed a supervised drug rehabilitation program and is no longer engaging in the illegal use of drugs, or has otherwise been rehabilitated successfully and is no longer engaging in such use;

(2) is participating in a supervised rehabilitation program and is no longer engaging in such use; or

(3) is erroneously regarded as engaging in such use, but is not engaging in such use; except that it shall not be a violation of this Act for a covered entity to adopt or administer reasonable policies or procedures, including but not limited to drug testing, designed to ensure that an individual described in paragraph (1) or (2) is no longer engaging in the illegal use of drugs.

The Antitrust Statutes (Excerpts)

Sherman Act
Restraints of Trade Prohibited

Section 1—Trusts, etc., in restraint of trade illegal; penalty. Every contract, combination in the form of trust or otherwise, or conspiracy, in restraint of trade or commerce among the several States, or with foreign nations, is declared to be illegal. Every person who shall make any contract or engage in any combination or conspiracy declared by sections 1 to 7 of this title to be illegal shall be deemed guilty of a felony, and, on conviction thereof, shall be punished by fine not exceeding $10,000,000 if a corporation, or if any other person, $350,000, or by imprisonment not exceeding three years, or both said punishments, in the discretion of the court.

Section 2—Monopolizing trade a felony; penalty. Every person who shall monopolize, or attempt to monopolize, or combine or conspire with any other person or persons, to monopolize any part of the trade or commerce among the several States, or with foreign nations, shall be deemed guilty of a felony, and, on conviction thereof, shall be punished by fine not exceeding $10,000,000 if a corporation, or, if any other person, $350,000, or by imprisonment not exceeding three years, or by both said punishments, in the discretion of the court.

Clayton Act
Refusals to Deal

Section 3—Sale, etc., on agreement not to use goods of competitor. It shall be unlawful for any person engaged in commerce, in the course of such commerce, to lease or make a sale or contract for sale of goods, wares, merchandise, machinery, supplies, or other commodities, whether patented or unpatented, for use, consumption, or resale within the United States or any Territory thereof or the District of Columbia or any insular possession or other place under the jurisdiction of the United States, or fix a price charged thereof, or discount from, or rebate upon, such price, on the condition, agreement, or understanding that the lessee or purchaser thereof shall not use or deal in the goods, wares, merchandise, machinery, supplies, or other commodities of a competitor or competitors of the lessor or seller, where the effect of such lease, sale, or contract for sale or such condition, agreement or understanding may be to substantially lessen competition or tend to create a monopoly in any line of commerce.

Private Suits

Section 4—Suits by persons injured; amount of recovery. Any person who shall be injured in this business or property by reason of anything forbidden in the antitrust laws may sue therefor in any district court of the United States in the district in which the defendant resides or is found or has an agent, without respect to the amount in controversy, and shall recover threefold the damages by him sustained, and the cost of suit, including a reasonable attorney's fee....

Mergers

Section 7—Acquisition by one corporation of stock of another. No corporation engaged in commerce shall acquire, directly or indirectly, the whole or any part of the stock or other share capital and no corporation subject to the jurisdiction of the Federal Trade Commission shall acquire the whole or any part of the assets of another corporation engaged also in commerce, where in any line of commerce in any section of the country, the effect of such acquisition may be substantially to lessen competition, or to tend to create a monopoly.

No corporation shall acquire, directly or indirectly, the whole or any part of the stock or other share capital and no corporation subject to the jurisdiction of the Federal Trade Commission shall acquire the whole or any part of the assets of one or more corporations engaged in commerce, where in any line of commerce in any section of the country, the effect of such acquisition, of such stocks or assets, or of the use of such stock by the voting or granting of proxies or otherwise, may be substantially to lessen competition, or to tend to create a monopoly.

This section shall not apply to corporations purchasing such stock solely for investment and not using the same by voting or otherwise to bring about, or in attempting to bring about, the substantial lessening of competition. Nor shall anything contained in this section prevent a corporation engaged in commerce from causing the formation of subsidiary corporations for the actual carrying on of their immediate lawful business, or the natural and legitimate branches or extensions thereof, or from owning and holding all or part of the stock of such subsidiary corporations, when the effect of such formation is not to substantially lessen competition.

Interlocking directorates

Section 8—Interlocking directorates and officers. No person at the same time shall be a director in any two or more corporations, any one of which has capital, surplus, and undivided profits aggregating more than $1,000,000, engaged in whole or in part in commerce, other than banks, banking associations, trust companies, and common carriers subject to the Act to regulate commerce approved February fourth, eighteen hundred and eighty-seven, if such corporations are or shall have been theretofore, by virtue of their business and location or operation, competitors, so that the elimination of competition by agreement between them would constitute a violation of any of the provisions of any of the antitrust laws. The eligibility of a director under the foregoing provision shall be determined by the aggregate amount of the capital, surplus, and undivided profits, exclusive of dividends declared but not paid to stockholders, at the end of the fiscal year of said corporation next preceding the election of directors, and when a director has been elected in accordance with the provisions of this Act it shall be lawful for him to continue as such for one year thereafter.

Federal Trade Commission Act
Unfair Methods of Competition Prohibited

Section 5—Unfair methods of competition unlawful; prevention by Commission— declaration. Declaration of unlawfulness; power to prohibit unfair practices.

(a) (1) Unfair methods of competition in or affecting commerce, and unfair or deceptive acts or practices in or affecting commerce, are declared unlawful. . . .

(b) Any person, partnership, or corporation who violates an order of the Commission to cease and desist after it has become final, and while such order is in effect, shall forfeit and pay to the United States a civil penalty of not more than $5,000 for each violation, which shall accrue to the United States and may be recovered in a civil action brought by the Attorney General of the United States. Each separate violation of such an order shall be a separate offense, except that in the case of a violation through continuing failure or neglect to obey a final order of the Commission each day of continuance of such failure or neglect shall be deemed a separate offense.

Robinson-Patman Act (an Amendment to the Clayton Act)
Price Discrimination; Cost Justification; Changing Conditions

Section 2—Discrimination in price, services, or facilities.

(a) Price; selection of customers.

It shall be unlawful for any person engaged in commerce, in the course of such commerce, either directly or indirectly, to discriminate in price between different purchases of commodities of like grade and quality, where either or any of the purchasers involved in such discrimination are in commerce, where such commodities are sold for use, consumption, or resale within the United States or any Territory thereof or the District of Columbia or any insular possession or other place under the jurisdiction of the United States, and where the effect of such discrimination may be substantially to lessen competition or tend to create a monopoly in any line of commerce, or to injure, destroy, or prevent competition with any person who either grants or knowingly receives the benefit of such discrimination, or with customers of either of them: *Provided*, That nothing herein contained shall prevent differentials which make only due allowance for differences in the cost of manufacture, sale, or delivery resulting from the differing methods or quantities in which such commodities are to such purchasers sold or delivered: *Provided*, however, That the Federal Trade Commission may, after due investigation and hearing to all interested parties, fix and establish quantity limits, and revise the same as it finds necessary as to particular commodities or classes of commodities, where it finds that available purchasers in greater quantities are so few as to render differentials on account thereof unjustly discriminatory or promotive of monopoly in any line of commerce; and the foregoing shall then not be construed to permit differentials based on differences in quantities greater than those so fixed and established: And provided further, That nothing herein contained shall prevent persons engaged in selling goods, wares, or merchandise in commerce from selecting their own customers in bona fide transactions and not in restraint of trade: And provided further, That nothing herein contained shall prevent price changes from time to time where in response to changing conditions affecting the market for or the marketability of the goods concerned, such as but not limited to actual or imminent deterioration of perishable goods, obsolescence of seasonal goods, distress sales under court process, or sales in good faith in discontinuance of business in the goods concerned.

Meeting Competition

(b) Burden of rebutting prima-facie case of discrimination.

Upon proof being made, at any hearing on a complaint under this section, that there has been discrimination in price or services or facilities furnished, the burden of rebutting the prima-facie case thus made by showing justification shall be upon the person charged with a violation of this section, and unless justification shall be affirmatively shown, the Commission is authorized to issue an order terminating the discrimination: *Provided*, however, That nothing herein contained shall prevent a seller rebutting the prima-facie case thus made by showing that his lower price or the furnishing of services or facilities to any purchaser or purchasers was made in good faith to meet an equally low price of a competitor, or the services or facilities furnished by a competitor.

Brokerage Payments

(c) Payment or acceptance of commission, brokerage or other compensation.

It shall be unlawful for any person engaged in commerce, in the course of such commerce, to pay or grant, or to receive or accept, anything of value as a commission, brokerage, or other compensation, or any allowance of discount in lieu thereof, except for services rendered in connection with the sale or purchase of goods, wares, or merchandise, either to the other party to such transaction or to an agent, representative, or other intermediary therein where such intermediary is acting in fact for or in behalf, or is subject to the direct or indirect control, of any party to such transaction other than the person by whom such compensation is so granted or paid.

Promotional Allowances

(d) Payment for services or facilities for processing or sale.

It shall be unlawful for any person engaged in commerce to pay or contract for the payment of anything of value to or for the benefit of a customer of such person in the course of such commerce as compensation or in consideration for any services or facilities furnished by or through such customer in connection with the processing, handling, sale, or offering for sale of any products or commodities manufactured, sold, or offered for sale by such person, unless such payment of consideration is available on proportionally equal terms to all other customers competing in the distribution of such products or commodities.

Promotional Services

(e) Furnishing services or facilities for processing, handling, etc.

It shall be unlawful for any person to discriminate in favor of one purchaser against another purchaser or purchasers of a commodity bought for resale, with or without processing, or by contracting to furnish or furnishing, or by contributing to the furnishing of, any services or facilities connected with the processing, handling, sale, or offering for sale of such commodity so purchased upon terms not accorded to all purchasers on proportionally equal terms.

Buyer Discrimination

(f) Knowingly inducing or receiving discriminatory price.

It shall be unlawful for any person engaged in commerce, in the course of such commerce, knowingly to induce or receive a discrimination in price which is prohibited by this section.

Predatory Practices

Section 3—Discrimination in rebates, discounts, or advertising service charges; underselling in particular localities; penalties.

It shall be unlawful for any person engaged in commerce, in the course of such commerce, to be a party to, or assist in, any transaction of sale, or contract to sell, which discriminates to his knowledge against competitors of the purchaser, in that, any discount, rebate, allowance, or advertising service charge is granted to the purchaser over and above any discount, rebate, allowance, or advertising service charge available at the time of such transaction to said competitors in respect of a sale of goods of like grade, quality, and quantity; to sell, or contract to sell, goods in any part of the United States at prices lower than those exacted by said person elsewhere in the United States for the purpose of destroying competition, or eliminating a competitor in such part of the United States; or, to sell, or contract to sell, goods at unreasonably lower prices for the purpose of destroying competition or eliminating a competitor.

Appendix I

Securities Statutes (Excerpts)

Securities Act of 1933

Definitions

Section 2. When used in this title, unless the context requires—

(1) The term "security" means any note, stock, treasury stock, bond, debenture, evidence of indebtedness, certificate of interest or participation in any profit-sharing agreement, collateral-trust certificate, preorganization certificate or subscription, transferable share, investment contract, voting-trust certificate, certificate of deposit for a security, fractional undivided interest in oil, gas, or other mineral rights, any put, call, straddle, option, or privilege on any security, certificate of deposit, or group or index of securities (including any interest therein or based on the value thereof), or any put, call, straddle, option, or privilege entered into on a national securities exchange relating to foreign currency, or, in general, any interest or participation in, temporary or interim certificate for, receipt for, guarantee of, or warrant or right to subscribe to or purchase, any of the foregoing.

Exempted Securities

Section 3. (a) Except as hereinafter expressly provided the provisions of this title shall not apply to any of the following classes of securities:

* * *

(2) Any security issued or guaranteed by the United States or any territory thereof, or by the District of Columbia, or by any State of the United States, or by any political subdivision of a State or Territory, or by any public instrumentality of one or more States or Territories, or by any person controlled or supervised by and acting as an instrumentality of the Government of the United States pursuant to authority granted by the Congress of the United States; or any certificate of deposit for any of the foregoing; or any security issued or guaranteed by any bank; or any security issued by or representing an interest in or a direct obligation of a Federal Reserve Bank....

(3) Any note, draft, bill of exchange, or banker's acceptance which arises out of a current transaction or the proceeds of which have been or are to be used for current transactions, and which has a maturity at the time of issuance of not exceeding nine months, exclusive of days of grace, or any renewal thereof the maturity of which is likewise limited;

(4) Any security issued by a person organized and operated exclusively for religious, educational, benevolent, fraternal, charitable, or reformatory purposes and not for pecuniary profit, and no part of the net earnings of which inures to the benefit of any person, private stockholder, or individual;...

Exempted Transactions

Section 4. The provisions of section 5 shall not apply to—

(1) transactions by any person other than an issuer, underwriter, or dealer.

(2) transactions by an issuer not involving any public offering.

(3) transactions by a dealer (including an underwriter no longer acting as an underwriter in respect of the security involved in such transactions), except—

> (A) transactions taking place prior to the expiration of forty days after the first date upon which the security was bona fide offered to the public by the issuer or by or through an underwriter,

(B) transactions in a security as to which a registration statement has been filed taking place prior to the expiration of forty days after the effective date of such registration statement or prior to the expiration of forty days after the first date upon which the security was bona fide offered to the public by the issuer or by or through an underwriter after such effective date, whichever is later (excluding in the computation of such forty days any time during which a stop order issued under section 8 is in effect as to the security), or such shorter period as the Commission may specify by rules and regulations or order, and

(C) transactions as to the securities constituting the whole or a part of an unsold allotment to or subscription by such dealer as a participant in the distribution of such securities by the issuer or by or through an underwriter.

With respect to transactions referred to in clause (B), if securities of the issuer have not previously been sold pursuant to an earlier effective registration statement the applicable period, instead of forty days, shall be ninety days, or such shorter period as the Commission may specify by rules and regulations or order.

(4) brokers' transactions, executed upon customers' orders on any exchange or in the over-the-counter market but not the solicitation of such orders.

(6) transactions involving offers or sales by an issuer solely to one or more accredited investors, if the aggregate offering price of an issue of securities offered in reliance on this paragraph does not exceed the amount allowed under section 3(b) of this title, if there is no advertising or public solicitation in connection with the transaction by the issuer or anyone acting on the issuer's behalf, and if the issuer files such notice with the Commission as the Commission shall prescribe.

Prohibitions Relating to Interstate Commerce and the Mails

Section 5. (a) Unless a registration statement is in effect as to a security, it shall be unlawful for any person, directly or indirectly—

(1) to make use of any means or instruments of transportation or communication in interstate commerce or of the mails to sell such security through the use or medium of any prospectus or otherwise; or

(2) to carry or cause to be carried through the mails or in interstate commerce, by any means or instruments of transportation, any such security for the purpose of sale or for delivery after sale.

(b) It shall be unlawful for any person, directly or indirectly—

(1) to make use of any means or instruments of transportation or communication in interstate commerce or of the mails to carry or transmit any prospectus relating to any security with respect to which a registration statement has been filed under this title, unless such prospectus meets the requirements of section 10, or

(2) to carry or to cause to be carried through the mails or in interstate commerce any such security for the purpose of sale or for delivery after sale, unless accompanied or preceded by a prospectus that meets the requirements of subsection (a) of section 10.

(c) It shall be unlawful for any person, directly, or indirectly, to make use of any means or instruments of transportation or communication in interstate commerce or of the mails to offer to sell or offer to buy through the use or medium of any prospectus or otherwise any security, unless a registration statement has been filed as to such security, or while the registration statement is the subject of a refusal order or stop order or (prior to the effective date of the registration statement) any public proceeding of examination under section 8.

Securities Exchange Act of 1934
Definitions and Application of Title

Section 3. (a) When used in this title, unless the context otherwise requires—

* * *

(4) The term "broker" means any person engaged in the business of effecting transactions in securities for the account of others, but does not include a bank.

(5) The term "dealer" means any person engaged in the business of buying and selling securities for his own account, through a broker or otherwise, but does not include a bank, or any person insofar as he buys or sells securities for his own account, either individually or in some fiduciary capacity, but not as part of a regular business.

* * *

(7) The term "director" means any director of a corporation or any person performing similar functions with respect to any organization, whether incorporated or unincorporated.

(4) The term "issuer" means any person who issues or proposes to issue any security; except that with respect to certificates of deposit for securities, voting-trust certificates, or collateral-trust certificates, or with respect to certificates of interest or shares in an unincorporated investment trust not having a board of directors or the fixed, restricted management, or unit type, the term "issuer" means the person or persons performing the acts and assuming the duties of depositor or manager pursuant to the provisions of the trust or other agreement or instrument under which such securities are issued; and except that with respect to equipment-trust certificates or like securities, the term "issuer" means the person by whom the equipment or property is, or is to be, used.

(8) The term "person" means a natural person, company, government, or political subdivision, agency, or instrumentality of a government.

Regulation of the Use of Manipulative and Deceptive Devices

Section 10. It shall be unlawful for any person, directly or indirectly, by the use of any means or instrumentality of interstate commerce or of the mails, or of any facility of any national securities exchange—

(a) To effect a short sale, or to use or employ any stop-loss order in connection with the purchase or sale, of any security registered on a national securities exchange, in contravention of such rules and regulations as the Commission may prescribe as necessary or appropriate in the public interest or for the protection of investors.

(b) To use or employ, in connection with the purchase or sale of any security registered on a national securities exchange or any security not so registered, any manipulative or deceptive device or contrivance in contravention of such rules and regulations as the Commission may prescribe as necessary or appropriate in the public interest or for the protection of investors.

Sarbanes-Oxley Act of 2002

(Public Company Accounting Reform and Corporate Responsibility Act)

Title 15, Ch. 98, United States Code

Sec. 7241.—Corporate responsibility for financial reports

(c) Regulations required

(d) The Commission shall, by rule, require, for each company filing periodic reports under section 78m (a) or 78o (d) of this title, that the principal executive officer or officers and the principal financial officer or officers, or persons performing similar functions, certify in each annual or quarterly report filed or submitted under either such section of this title that—

(1) the signing officer has reviewed the report;

(2) based on the officer's knowledge, the report does not contain any untrue statement of a material fact or omit to state a material fact necessary in order to make the statements made, in light of the circumstances under which such statements were made, not misleading;

(3) based on such officer's knowledge, the financial statements, and other financial information included in the report, fairly present in all material respects the financial condition and results of operations of the issuer as of, and for, the periods presented in the report;

(4) the signing officers—

(A) are responsible for establishing and maintaining internal controls;

(B) have designed such internal controls to ensure that material information relating to the issuer and its consolidated subsidiaries is made known to such officers by others within those entities, particularly during the period in which the periodic reports are being prepared;

(C) have evaluated the effectiveness of the issuer's internal controls as of a date within 90 days prior to the report; and

(D) have presented in the report their conclusions about the effectiveness of their internal controls based on their evaluation as of that date;

(5) the signing officers have disclosed to the issuer's auditors and the audit committee of the board of directors (or persons fulfilling the equivalent function)—

(A) all significant deficiencies in the design or operation of internal controls which could adversely affect the issuer's ability to record, process, summarize, and report financial data and have identified for the issuer's auditors any material weaknesses in internal controls; and

(B) any fraud, whether or not material, that involves management or other employees who have a significant role in the issuer's internal controls; and

(6) the signing officers have indicated in the report whether or not there were significant changes in internal controls or in other factors that could significantly affect internal controls subsequent to the date of their evaluation, including any corrective actions with regard to significant deficiencies and material weaknesses.

Glossary

A

Abnormally dangerous activity *see* ultrahazardous activity.

Absolute liability liability for an act or activity that causes harm or injury even though the alleged wrongdoer was not at fault.

Absolute privilege a defense in a defamation suit affirming that the defendant had an unconditional right to make the statements in question and be free from litigation. This most often applies to statements made by members of a legislature as part of the deliberation process.

Acceptance the offeree's notification or expression to the offeror that he agrees to be bound by the terms of the offeror's proposal, thereby creating a contract. The trend is to allow acceptance by any means that reasonably notifies the offeror of the acceptance.

Accord in a debtor/creditor relationship, an agreement between the parties to settle a dispute for some partial payment. The creditor has a right of action against the debtor.

Accord and satisfaction in a debtor/creditor relationship, an agreement between the parties to settle a dispute and subsequent payment. The agreement is an accord because the creditor has a right of action against the debtor. Accord and satisfaction are complete when payment has been tendered.

Account receivable a debt that arises in the course of business that is not supported by negotiable paper; for example, the charge accounts at a department store.

Actual authority power of an agent to bind a principal; the power is from an express or implied agreement between principal and agent.

Actus reus in Latin, "guilty act"; the wrongful deed that constitutes the physical component of a crime; usually must be joined with *mens rea* to establish criminal liability.

Adjudication the legal process of resolving a dispute.

Adjudicatory hearing in administrative law, a formal process involving a regulatory agency and the private parties involved in a complaint; procedures are more informal than a court trial but protect due process rights.

Administrative agency a governmental bureau established by Congress (or the president) to execute certain functions of Congress. Agencies transact government business and may write and enforce regulations under the authority of Congress or the president.

Administrative law rules and regulations established by administrative agencies to execute the functions given them by Congress or the president; also the law that governs how agencies must operate.

Administrative law judge a person appointed to conduct an administrative hearing about a regulatory matter. Usually attorneys who work for the administrative agency, such as the Federal Trade Commission, serve in this capacity. They run a trial-like proceeding and issue a decision in the matter based on the facts determined at the hearing.

Adversary system of justice a legal system in which the parties to a dispute present their own arguments and are responsible for asserting their legal rights.

Adverse possession (easement by prescription) a method by which one obtains the right to property by following specific rules under which a non owner may be declared to be the lawful owner. This normally requires open possession of the property and restraining others from use of the property for a period of time required by state law and may require payment of property taxes.

Advertising substantiation program a policy of the Federal Trade Commission to review advertisements for content to ensure they are not deceitful.

Affirm in a court of appeals, or supreme court, a decision to declare that a judgment entered by a lower court is valid and will stand as decided.

Affirmative action employment programs, often mandated by federal law, to remedy discriminatory employment practices affecting racial minorities and women. Programs seek to remedy past patterns of discrimination and discrimination that results from facially neutral employment practices.

Affirmative defense defendant's response to plaintiff's claim that attacks the plaintiff's legal right to bring the action rather than attacking the truth of the claim. An example of an affirmative defense is the running of the statute of limitations.

Age under federal employment discrimination law, all persons over age 40 are covered.

Agency a relationship between two persons, by explicit or implicit agreement, where one (the agent) may act on behalf of the other (the principal) and bind the principal by words and actions.

Agency by estoppel an agency created by operation of law that arises when the principal, by failing to properly supervise the agent, allows the agent to exercise too many powers, thereby allowing others to be justified in thinking that the agent possesses the powers the agent claimed to have.

Agency coupled with an interest when an agent has an interest in the subject matter that is relevant to the agency relationship; this is often an interest in a specific piece of property.

Agency fees in labor law, the right of a union to charge fees to employees who are not union members, instead of union dues, to cover the cost of representing such employees; such fees are illegal in right-to-work states.

Agency order in administrative law, a statement by a regulatory agency, under its powers granted by Congress and subject to procedural requirements, to inform parties subject to the rules what they must do to comply with a rule they are violating.

Agency regulation in administrative law, a rule issued by a regulatory agency under its powers granted by Congress and subject to procedural requirements that detail the legal obligations of affected parties.

Agency shop in labor law, a unionized workplace where employees who are not union members must pay agency fees to the union for being the sole bargaining agent for all employees; illegal in states that have right-to-work laws.

Agent a person authorized to act for or to represent another, called the principal.

Agreement a "meeting of the minds"; a mutual understanding between the parties as to the substance of a contract.

Agreement (U.C.C.) means the bargain of the parties in fact as found in their language or by implication from other circumstances including course of dealing or usage of trade or course of performance as provided in the U.C.C.

Alternative dispute resolution a process by which the parties to a dispute resolve it through a mechanism other than litigation in court. Alternative dispute resolution includes arbitration, negotiation, and mediation.

Ambient air under the Clean Air Act, ambient air is the air outside of buildings or other enclosures.

Amicus curiae a party not directly involved in the litigation but who participates as a friend of the court, usually by submitting briefs in favor of one position at the appellate level.

Amount in controversy the damages claimed or the relief demanded by the injured party in a dispute.

Answer the response of a defendant to the plaintiff's complaint, denying in part or in whole the charges made by the plaintiff.

Anticipatory breach the assertion by a party to a contract that she will not perform a future obligation as required by the contract.

Antidumping duty a tariff to equalize the difference between the price at which the product is sold in the exporting country and the price at which the importer will sell the product in the importing country; designed to prevent foreign businesses from artificially lowering their prices and gaining unfair advantages outside their home market.

Anti raiding covenant in employment law, when employees are required to sign, as a condition of continued employment, an agreement that in the future, should they no longer work for the employer, they will not attempt to hire away other employees from the company; these are looked at closely by the courts as possible restraints of trade.

Antitrust federal and state statutes to protect commerce from certain restraints of trade, such as price fixing and monopolization.

Apparent authority that authority a reasonable person would assume an agent possesses in light of the principal's conduct.

Appeal requesting removal from a court of a decided or an adjudicated case to a court of appellate jurisdiction for the purpose of obtaining a review of the decision.

Appellant the party, either the plaintiff or the defendant, who invokes the appellate jurisdiction of a superior court.

Appellate courts courts with jurisdiction to review cases decided in trial courts to ensure that the law was properly applied.

Appellate jurisdiction the power of a court to revise or correct the proceedings in a case already acted upon by a lower court or administrative agency.

Appellee the party against whom an appeal is taken.

Arbiter in an arbitration proceeding, the person granted the authority to decide a controversy.

Arbitrary and capricious a judgment or decision, by an administrative agency or judge, which is without basis in fact or in law. Such a decision is often referred to as being without a rational basis.

Arbitrary and fanciful mark the most favored trademark, because it is distinctive and either made up or a word not related to the product it represents.

Arbitration a means of settling disputes between parties when they submit the matter to a neutral third party of their choosing, who resolves the dispute by issuing a hinding award. A popular alternative to the court system for resolving disputes due at lower cost and greater speed.

Arraignment this is the initial step in a criminal prosecution; the defendant is brought before the court to hear the charges and enter a plea.

Articles of incorporation under state law, a document that every new corporation must file providing information about the name, address, and purpose of the corporation, as well as a statement about the stock that may be issued and the names of the principal officers.

Artificial seniority in employment discrimination law, a remedy that may be granted giving minority or women workers extra years of work credit to make up for past acts of discrimination by their employer.

Artisan's lien a possessory lien given as security for payment to a person who has made improvements to another person's property. The statutory right of an artisan to keep possession of the object that she has worked on until paid for the work.

Assault any word or action intended to cause another to be in fear of immediate physical harm.

Assault and battery intentionally causing another to anticipate immediate physical harm through some threat and then carrying out the threatened activity.

Assignment a transfer of one's interest in property or a contract to another person.

Assumption of risk common-law doctrine under which a plaintiff may not recover for the injuries or damages that result from an activity in which the plaintiff willingly participated. A defense used by the defendant in a negligence case, when the plaintiff had knowledge of the danger, voluntarily exposed himself to the danger, and was injured.

Attachment the legal process of seizing another's property in accordance with a writ or judicial order for the purpose of security satisfaction of a judgment to be rendered.

Attachment (U.C.C.) when the requirements of a security interest (agreement, value, and conveyable rights in the collateral) exist, the security agreement becomes enforceable between parties and is said to attach.

Attainment areas under the Clean Air Act, areas that meet federal standards for major pollutants; they are designated "prevention of significant deterioration areas," because they are not allowed to become more polluted.

Authorization card a card signed by an employee at a worksite targeted for possible unionization; the card authorizes the union to request that an election be held to determine if all workers will be represented by the union.

Award the decision that settles an arbitration proceeding. It is normally the determination of a single arbiter, but it can be the decision of the panel of arbitrators that heard the dispute. The decision may be in writing but need not give a rationale.

B

Back pay compensation for past economic losses (lost wages and fringe benefits) caused by an employer's discriminatory employment practices, such as limiting promotion opportunities for older workers.

Balance of payments an official accounting that records a country's foreign transactions; exports are recorded as credits and imports as debits.

Bankruptcy a proceeding under the law that is initiated by an insolvent individual or business (a voluntary bankruptcy) or by creditors (an involuntary bankruptcy) seeking to have the insolvent's assets distributed among the creditors and to then discharge the insolvent from further obligation or to reorganize the insolvent's debt structure.

Bankruptcy trustee in bankruptcy proceedings, the person given authority to manage the assets of the bankrupt for the benefit of the creditors.

Bargaining agent the union recognized and certified by the National Labor Relations Board, upon election by a majority of the workers, to be the exclusive representative of employees in a bargaining unit (work site) to determine working conditions and wages.

Battery the intentional unallowed touching of another. The "touching" may involve a mere touch that is offensive or an act of violence that causes serious injury.

Bearer (U.C.C.) the person in possession of an instrument, document of title, or certificated security payable to bearer or indorsed in blank.

Bearer instrument an instrument payable to bearer (the person in possession); it must specify that it is payable to bearer, to cash, or to a specific bearer.

Beyond a reasonable doubt in criminal law, the general rule that for a judge or jury to find a defendant guilty, there can be no significant doubt that the defendant violated a criminal statute.

Bilateral contract a contract formed by the mutual exchange of promises of the parties.

Bill of exchange an unconditional order in writing, addressed by one person to another, signed by the person giving it, requiring the person to whom it is addressed to pay on demand, or at a fixed or determinable future date, a certain sum of money. Same as a draft under the U.C.C.

Bill of lading (U.C.C.) a document evidencing the receipt of goods for shipment issued by one engaged in the business of transporting goods; includes an airbill.

Blue Sky laws name given to state laws that regulate the offer and sale of securities.

Board of directors the principals of a corporation, elected by shareholders, responsible for governing the business, especially as to major decisions; directors appoint corporate officers and agents to act on their behalf in running the business day to day. Boards are usually composed of inside directors, such as the president of the company, and outside or independent directors, who have no employment relationship with the company.

Bona fide occupational qualification (BFOQ) employment in particular jobs may not be limited to persons of a particular sex or religion, unless the employer can show that sex or religion is an actual qualification for performing the job. Not permitted on the basis of race.

Bond an evidence of debt carrying a specified amount (principal), schedule of interest payments, and a date for redemption of the face value.

Bondholders creditors of a business whose evidence of debt is a bond issued by the business.

Boycott an effort to organize a group to not deal with some party, such as a group of retailers refusing to buy products from manufacturers who do certain things not liked by the retailers, or a group of labor unions agreeing not to handle any products made by a certain company.

Breach of contract failure, without a legal excuse, of a promisor to perform the terms agreed to in a contract.

Bribery the offering, giving, receiving, or soliciting of something of value for the purpose of influencing the action of an official in the discharge of public or legal duties.

Brief an appellate brief is a written document, prepared by an attorney, to be the basis for an appeal of a case to an appellate court. It contains the points of law the attorney wants to establish, with the arguments and authorities to support that view.

Business judgment rule a principle of corporate law under which a court will not challenge the business decisions of a corporate officer or director made with ordinary care and in good faith.

Business necessity justification for an otherwise prohibited discriminatory employment practice based on employer's proof that 1) the otherwise prohibited employment practice is essential for the safety and efficiency of the business, and 2) no reasonable alternative with a lesser impact exists.

Business tort a noncontractual breach of a legal duty by a business resulting in damages or injury to another; includes certain torts that can only occur in business situations.

Bylaws in corporation law, the rules that regulate and govern the internal operations of a corporation with respect to directors, shareholders, and officers rights and duties.

C

Cartel a combination of independent producers in an industry attempting to limit competition by acting together to fix prices, divide markets, or restrict entry into the industry.

Cashier's check a bank's check, drawn on itself, signed by the cashier of the bank or other bank official obligating the bank to pay the payee a certain sum of money on demand.

Cause in fact an act or omission without which an event would not have occurred. Courts express this in the form of a rule commonly referred to as the "but for" rule: the injury to a person would not have happened but for the conduct of the wrongdoer.

Cause of action the facts that give rise to a person's legal right of redress against another.

Caveat emptor Latin for "let the buyer beware."

Cease and desist order an order by an administrative agency or a court prohibiting a firm from conducting activities that the agency or court deems illegal.

Certificate of deposit a written bank document that provides evidence of a deposit made at a bank, for a certain time, that pays a certain rate of interest that is promised to be paid to the depositor or to another party as ordered.

Certificate of incorporation *see* corporate charter.

Certification mark in trademark law, any symbol, name, or word used to identify the location or other aspect of the origin of a product.

Challenge for cause challenge by an attorney to a prospective juror for which some cause or reason is asserted.

Charges *see* Instructions to jury.

Charter *see* corporate charter.

Chattel in property law, an article of personal property but not real property; things that are movable.

Check a draft or order drawn upon a bank, payable on demand, signed by the maker or drawer, that is an unconditional promise to pay a certain sum of money to the order of the payee named on the instrument. It normally must say "pay to the order of" on the face of the check.

Choice-of-language clause in international contracts especially, a clause that specifies the language that will apply to the contract between parties in the event of a dispute, so that there will be an official version in one language only.

Choice of laws *see* Conflict of laws.

Citizen-suit provisions in regulatory law, a right provided by Congress for private citizens to bring a suit before a federal court to force compliance with a law passed by Congress; in some instances, the cost of the suit is borne by the government or the defendant if the private party wins the case.

Civil law 1) laws, written or unwritten, that specify the duties that exist between and among people, as opposed to criminal matters. 2) Codified or statutory law, used in many Western European countries and Japan, as distinguished from the common or judge-made law used in England and the United States.

Close corporation a closely held corporation; a corporation that has stock that is not allowed to be widely held; the number of shareholders is limited and usually, unlike a publicly held corporation, the shareholders are active in oversight of the firm.

Closed shop a work site where one must be a union member before obtaining work.

Closing argument oral presentation to the jury by the attorneys after the plaintiff and defendant have stated their cases and before the judge charges the jury.

Collateral property pledged as a secondary security for the satisfaction of a debt in the event the debtor does not repay as expected.

Collective bargaining the process by which a union and an employer arrive at and enforce agreements regarding employment of workers represented by a union.

Collective mark a trademark or service mark used by the members of a cooperative association to identify the goods and services they produce.

Color under federal employment discrimination law, the shade of one's skin.

Commerce clause that part of the U. S. Constitution that gives Congress the power to regulate interstate commerce; the basis of much federal regulation.

Commercial speech expressions made by businesses about commercial matters or about political matters; the First Amendment protects most truthful speech in this category.

Commodity Control List a list maintained by the Department of Commerce that classifies restrictions on the exportation of certain goods to certain nations.

Common law law developed by American and English courts by decisions in cases. Unlike statutes, it is not passed by a legislative body and is not a specific set of rules; rather, it must be interpreted from the many decisions that have been written over time.

Common stock the shares of ownership in a corporation having the lowest priority with regard to payment of dividends and distribution of the corporation's assets upon dissolution.

Community property property owned in common by husband and wife.

Comparative negligence a defense to negligence whereby the plaintiff's damages are reduced by the proportion his fault bears to the total injury he has suffered.

Compensatory damages a sum awarded to an injured party that is equivalent to her actual damages or injuries sustained. The rationale is to restore the injured party to the position she was in before the injury.

Complaint the initial pleading by the plaintiff in a civil action that informs the defendant of the material facts on which the plaintiff bases the lawsuit.

Compliance program under the federal Sentencing Guidelines, a company that maintains a compliance program with regulations that apply to the company will be subject to less punishment in case of violations of the law than if there is no good-faith effort to have internal procedures to help ensure that the law is followed within the organization.

Concentration in antitrust law, the percent of market share, usually sales volume, that one or more firms control in a given product or geographic market; used as a measure of the degree of competition within a market.

Concentration ratio fraction of total market sales made by a specified number of an industry's largest firms. Four-firm and eight-firm concentration ratios are the most frequently used.

Concerted activity in labor law, actions by employees, such as a strike or other mutual activity that furthers their employment interests, protected by the National Labor Relations Act.

Concurrent jurisdiction when two different courts are each empowered to deal with the subject matter at issue in a dispute.

Concurring opinion at the appellate court level, an opinion filed by one or more of the justices in which the justices agree with the majority opinion but state separate views or reasons for the decision.

Condition a provision in a contract providing that upon the occurrence of some event the obligations of the parties will be set in motion, suspended, or terminated.

Condition precedent in a contract, a condition that must be met before the other party's obligations arise.

Condition subsequent in a contract, a condition which, if met, discharges the obligations of the other party.

Conditional privilege a defense in defamation cases affirming that the defendant published in good faith or as part of a duty to publish; it protects the defendant in a case that may otherwise be actionable.

Confiscation the act whereby a sovereign takes private property without a proper public purpose or just compensation.

Conflict of interest a real or seeming incompatibility between one's private interests and one's public or fiduciary duties; for example, in securities, when a broker has a personal stake in an investment that is promoted to clients.

Conflict of laws body of law establishing the circumstances in which a state or federal court shall apply the laws of another state, rather than the laws of the state in which it is sitting, to decide a case before it.

Conglomerate merger a merger between two companies that do not compete with or purchase from each other.

Consent a voluntary agreement, implied or expressed, to submit to a proposition or act of another.

Consent decree a judgment entered by consent of the parties and approval of a court, whereby the defendant agrees to stop alleged illegal activity without admitting guilt or wrongdoing. Often used to settle complaints by regulatory agencies.

Consequential damages under the U.C.C., losses that do not flow directly from a breach of contract but that result indirectly from the act and should have been foreseeable by the seller.

Consideration in a contract, the thing of value bargained for in exchange for a promise; the inducement or motivation to a contract; the element that keeps the contract from being gratuitous and, therefore, makes it legally binding on the parties.

Consignment the act or process of depositing goods to be sold in the custody of a third party.

Constitution the fundamental law of a nation; a written document establishing the powers of the government and its basic structure; the controlling authority over all other law.

Constructive discharge under federal employment discrimination law, when an employee quits employment due to pervasive abuse or discriminatory treatment in violation of Title VII.

Constructive notice information or understanding that is equivalent to a formal notice of facts that a person using proper diligence would be expected to know.

Consumer expectation test in tort law, as applied to products, the level of safe performance an ordinary consumer could expect from a product under the circumstances.

Consumer reports often called *credit reports;* files maintained by companies concerning consumers' credit history and evidence of income and debt; sold for legitimate business purposes.

Contempt of court any act that obstructs a court in the administration of justice or that is calculated to lessen the court's authority.

Contract a legal relationship consisting of the rights and duties of contracting parties; a promise or set of promises constituting an agreement between the parties that gives each a legal duty to the other and also the right to seek a remedy for the breach of those duties. The elements of a contract include agreement, consideration, legal capacity, lawful subject matter, and genuine consent.

Contract (U.C.C.) the total legal obligation which results from the parties' agreement as affected by the U.C.C. and any other applicable rules of law.

Contract clause the statement in the constitution that "No State shall . . . pass any . . . Law impairing the Obligation of Contracts. . . ." Arises primarily when a state attempts to reduce its obligations created by contracts with private parties.

Contractual capacity the mental capacity required by law for a party entering into a contract to be bound by that contract. Minors, intoxicated persons, and the insane generally lack capacity to contract.

Contributory negligence as a complete defense to negligence, an act or a failure to act that produces a lack of reasonable care on the part of the plaintiff that is the proximate cause of the injury incurred.

Conversion the unauthorized taking of property, permanently or temporarily, that deprives its rightful owner of its lawful use.

Cooperative two or more persons or enterprises that act through a common agent to achieve a common objective.

Copyright a grant to an author or a publisher of an exclusive right to print, reprint, publish, copy, and sell literary work, musical compositions, works of art, and motion pictures for the life of the author plus an additional 50 years.

Corporate charter a certificate issued by a state government recognizing the existence of a corporation as a legal entity; it is issued automatically upon filing the information required by state law and payment of a fee.

Corporate social responsibility the belief that businesses have a duty to society that goes beyond obeying the law and maximizing profits.

Corporation a business organized under the laws of a state that allow an artificial legal being to exist for purposes of doing business in its name.

Cost-benefit analysis computing the costs of an activity compared to the estimated monetary value of the benefits from the activity.

Cost justification in antitrust law, a defense available in price discrimination (Robinson–Patman) cases to show that a buyer was offered a good at a lower price than another buyer because of differences in the costs of serving the two customers.

Counterclaim a claim a defendant asserts against the plaintiff.

Counterfeiting to imitate, forge, or copy without authority and to pass off as original with an intent to deceive. This may be done for money, securities, copyrights, patents, trademarks, and other protected property.

Counteroffer an offeree's response to an offeror rejecting the offeror's original offer and at the same time making a new offer.

Court of appeals courts with the power to review cases decided in trial courts; in the federal court system and in about half the states, these are intermediate courts between trial courts and supreme courts.

Court of original jurisdiction *see* original jurisdiction.

Covenant an agreement between two or more parties in which one or more of the parties pledges that some duty or obligation is or is not to be done.

Covenant in property law, an agreement by two or more parties, in writing, that places certain restrictions on the use of property or obligates the owner of the property to take specific actions with respect to the land. These obligations normally go with the property as it passes from owner to owner over time.

Covenant not to compete part of an agreement in the sale of a business for the seller not to compete with the buyer for a given time in a given market; in employment law, it is an agreement, not enforceable in all states, for an employee not to go to work for a competitor for a certain time after leaving current employment.

Cover   under the U.C.C., the buyer can recover from the seller the difference between the cost of the substituted goods and the original contract price. It is the purchase on the open market, by the buyer in a breach-of-contract case, of goods to substitute for those promised but not delivered.

Craft union   a union organized on the basis of a specified set of skills or occupations.

Credit rating   an opinion as to the reliability of a person in paying debts.

Credit report   a report made by a consumer reporting agency concerning the financial condition and credit character of a person or business.

Creditor   a person to whom a debt is owed by a debtor.

Crime   a violation of the law that is punishable by the state or nation. Crimes are classified as felonies and misdemeanors.

Criminal law   governs or defines legal wrongs, or crimes, committed against society. Wrongdoers are punished for violating the rules of society. A person found guilty of a criminal offense is usually fined or imprisoned.

Criminal negligence   this is gross negligence so extreme that it is punishable as a crime. For example, involuntary manslaughter can be based on criminal negligence, such as when an extremely careless automobile driver kills someone.

Cross complaint   during the pleadings, a claim the defendant asserts against the plaintiff. *See also* counterclaim.

Cross examination   examination by the attorney representing the adverse party after the other party has examined her witness.

Cruel and unusual punishment   punishment that is disproportionate to the offense and is a shock to the moral sense of the community; prohibited by the Eighth Amendment.

Cure   under the U.C.C., the right of a seller to make good on an improper delivery of goods if done within the time allowed by contract and with notification to the buyer in a timely manner.

Cybersquatting   when a trademark is improperly used in a domain name; this is in violation of federal law that extends trademark protection to include domain name usage.

D

Damages   money compensation sought or awarded as a remedy for a breach of contract or for tortious acts.

Debt   a sum of money due by an express agreement.

Debt collection agency   a business that is paid to or buys the right to collect the debts owed by consumers to a business.

Debt securities   an obligation of a corporation, usually in the form of a bond, issued for a certain value at a certain rate of interest to be repaid at a certain time.

Debtor   a person who owes a debt to a creditor.

Debtor in possession   in bankruptcy law, the debtor in Chapter 11 bankruptcy who remains in control of a business or assets or the trustee appointed to control a business or assets.

Deception   in consumer protection law, a claim, practice, or omission likely to mislead a reasonable consumer and cause the consumer to suffer a loss.

Decertification   a process by which employees vote to withdraw their consent to union representation; an election is conducted by the National Labor Relations Board.

Deed   a conveyance of realty; a writing signed by a grantor, whereby title to realty is transferred from one to another.

Defamation   an intentional false communication, either published or publicly spoken, that injures another's reputation or good name.

Default   the omission or failure to perform a contractual duty to fulfill a promise or discharge an obligation to pay interest or principal on a debt when due. Under the U.C.C., when default occurs may be defined by the parties to the agreement.

Default judgment   judgment entered against a party who failed to appear in court to defend against a claim brought by another party.

Defendant   the party against whom an action or lawsuit is brought.

Defense   that offered and alleged by a defendant as a reason in law or fact why the plaintiff should not recover or recover less than what she seeks.

Delaney clause   the portion of the Food, Drug, and Cosmetic Act that any food additive that is found to cause cancer in animals may not be marketed.

Delegation   the legal transfer of power and authority to another to perform duties.

Delegation of powers   the constitutional right of Congress to authorize government agencies to perform certain legal duties.

Demurrer   an older term for a motion to dismiss a claim for failure to state a cause of action. *See* motion to dismiss.

Deposition   sworn testimony, written or oral, of a person taken outside the court.

Descriptive mark   a mark not favored at law, because it describes the good or service in question; a mark must have strong market recognition to receive legal protection.

Design defect in product liability litigation, a claim that a consumer suffered an injury because a safer product design was not used.

Detrimental reliance *see* promissory estoppel.

Differential standard in federal employment discrimination law, when an employer sets rules to make it more difficult for a person who is a member of a protected class to meet job requirements than for similarly situated employees.

Dilution a violation of trademark rights that occurs by blurring or tarnishing a famous mark regardless of intent on the part of the violator; specific rights are provided by federal law for strong marks.

Direct examination the initial examination of a witness by the party on whose behalf the witness has been called.

Directed verdict verdict granted by the court on the grounds that the jury could reasonably reach only one conclusion on the basis of the evidence presented during the trial.

Directors *see* board of directors.

Disability under the Americans with Disabilities Act, a physical or mental condition that affects a major life activity that limits the ability of a person to perform a particular job function.

Discharge the termination of one's obligation. Under contract law, discharge occurs either when the parties have performed their obligations in the contract, or when events, the conduct of the parties, or the operation of law releases parties from performing.

Discharge monitoring reports (DMRs) under the Clean Water Act, firms with pollution permits must file these reports with the EPA and have them available for public inspection to show the level of emissions actually dumped into bodies of water or treatment facilities.

Disclosure requirements in securities law, the revealing of financial and other information relevant to investors considering buying securities; the requirement that sufficient information be provided prospective investors so that they can make an informed evaluation of a security.

Discovery the process by which the parties to a lawsuit gather information from each other to reduce the scope of what will be presented in court; process is determined by rules of procedure and may be limited by the court hearing the case.

Discrimination illegal treatment of a person or group (intentional or unintentional) based on race, color, national origin, religion, sex, disability, or age. This includes the failure to remedy the effects of past discrimination.

Disparagement a false communication that injures a person in his business or profession.

Disparate impact in employment discrimination law, when an apparently neutral rule regarding hiring or treatment of employees works to discriminate against a protected class of employees.

Disparate treatment differential treatment of employees or applicants on the basis of their race, color, religion, sex, national origin, or age; for example, when applicants of a particular race are required to pass tests not required of other applicants.

Dissenting opinion an opinion written by one or more appellate judges or justices explaining why they disagree with the decision of the majority of the court in a given case.

Dissolution the process of terminating or winding up a corporation or partnership that changes the nature of the organization or ends it completely. This may come about involuntarily, such as through forced bankruptcy, or may be voluntary, as when a board of directors approves the end of the life of a company.

Diversity jurisdiction when parties to a suit are from different jurisdictions (states or nations), it may create a basis for having a case heard in federal court.

Diversity of citizenship an action in which the plaintiff and the defendant are citizens of different states.

Dividend a distribution to corporate shareholders in proportion to the number of shares held.

Domain name a unique electronic address assigned to a particular user of the Internet; it receives legal protection against infringement much like a trademark.

Draft a written order signed by a party (the drawer), instructing another party (the drawee, usually a bank) to pay a certain sum of money, on demand, to a third party (the payee).

Due care the degree of care that a reasonable person can be expected to exercise to avoid harm reasonably foreseeable if such care is not taken.

Due process constitutional limitation requiring that a person not be deprived of life, liberty, or property without a fair and just hearing.

Dumping when a seller provides a large quantity of goods at less than fair market value or less than the cost of production; selling goods in another country for less than the market price at home.

Duress when coercion or threats are used to get another person to act in a way, such as sign a contract, that the person would not otherwise agree to.

Duty-free port a special economic zone in a nation where goods may be imported or exported without being subject to usual tariffs; often done for transshipment of goods or to encourage processing in a country.

Duty of loyalty in agency law, the obligation an agent has to put the interests of the principal before the interests of the agent in matters related to the agency relationship.

Duty to account in an agency relationship, the obligation of an agent to report with accuracy about all financial matters related to the relationship, including expenditures and revenues.

Duty to compensate in an agency, the obligation of a principal to pay an agent a reasonable fee for services performed or to pay the amount agreed upon by the parties.

Duty to indemnify in an agency, the obligation of a principal to pay for damages or losses suffered by an agent in the execution of transactions allowed under the relationship.

Duty to inform in an agency relationship, the legal requirement an agent has to inform a principal of any matters related to the agency that can affect its success.

Duty to reimburse in agency law, the obligation a principal has, unless otherwise agreed upon, to pay the agent for reasonable expenses incurred in carrying out agency obligations.

E

Easement the right to use the property of another in a particular manner. Most commonly, this is a right of access to cross one piece of property to reach another piece of property or the right to have utilities go across, on, or under property. It is a right that is said to "run with the land."

Easement by prescription *see* adverse possession.

Economic espionage when commercial trade secrets are stolen for use by a competitor; this is specifically in violation of federal law.

Economic loss rule the principle that a plaintiff cannot sue in tort to recover for purely monetary loss (damages) that occur in breach of contract instances. An exception to this rule is when the defendant commits fraud or negligent misrepresentation, which brings in a tort cause of action to what would otherwise only be a contract matter.

Effluent charge a fee, fine, or tax imposed on a polluting activity.

Electronic fund transfer (EFT) monetary transactions made electronically, usually by telephone or computer.

Embezzlement statutory offense when a person fraudulently appropriates for her own use the property or money entrusted to her by another.

Eminent domain the power of the government to take private property for public use for fair compensation.

Emission offset under the Clean Air Act, a requirement that for a polluting facility to be built or expanded, the owner must reduce certain pollutants by as much or more than the new pollution to be generated; this may be done by paying other polluters to reduce emissions.

Emotional distress a tort action for damages to compensate a person for mental injury suffered due to another's actions.

Employee a person who works in the service of another person (the employer) under an express or implied contract of hire, usually at-will, under which the employer has the right to control the details of work performance.

Employee handbooks manuals issued by employers to inform employees of their duties and rights as employees; often used as evidence of an employment contract that must be followed by both parties.

Employment-at-will a doctrine under the common law providing that unless otherwise explicitly stated, an employment contract was for an indefinite term and could be terminated at any time by either party without notice.

Enabling statute legislative enactment granting power to an administrative agency.

En banc legal proceedings before or by the court as a whole rather than before or by a single judge or a panel of judges.

Endangered species in environmental law, a list of animals and plants declared by the government to be in danger of becoming extinct; violators may be prosecuted for killing endangered animals or plants or injuring their habitat.

Entrapment a law-enforcement officer's inducement of a person to commit a crime, by fraud or undue persuasion, in an attempt to bring a criminal prosecution against that person. It provides an affirmative defense that the crime would not have been committed but for the set up.

Environmental Impact Statement statements required of agencies by the National Environmental Protection Act when they make recommendations concerning proposed legislation or other federal activity that significantly affects the quality of the environment.

Equal protection clause Section 1 of the Fourteenth Amendment to the Constitution, providing that states treat all persons subject to state laws in a similar manner. "No State shall . . . deny to any person within its jurisdiction the equal protection of the laws."

Equitable remedy the means by which a court enforces a right adjudicated in equity or prevents or redresses the violation of such a right. Remedies include specific performance, injunction, recission, reformation, and declaratory judgment.

Equity 1) in securities law, an ownership claim on a business interest, usually a security with no repayment terms; 2) a legal system that operates alongside the "law," and is concerned with achieving justice in cases when courts of law are incompetent to act.

Error of law a determination by an appeals court that a lower court, usually a trial court, made a mistake in applying the law to the facts that were established at trial.

Estoppel a principle that provides that a person is barred from denying or alleging certain facts because of that person's previous conduct, allegation, or denial.

Ethics the duties which a member of society owes to other members.

Evidence in procedural law, the legal matters—oral, written, or physical testimony—that may be presented at a trial or at other legal proceeding for use in resolving a dispute.

Excessive fine an excessive penalty that is held to violate the Eighth Amendment. This occurs when a fine or penalty, such as a prison term, is too large relative to the legal violation that occurred.

Excise tax a tax on the sale of a good. A specific tax is a fixed tax per unit of the good sold. An *ad valorem* tax is a fixed percentage of the value of the good. *See* tariff.

Exclusionary rule under the Fourth Amendment, as interpreted by the courts, evidence that has been gathered in violation of the search-and-seizure rules cannot be used against a defendant at trial.

Exclusive dealing contract an agreement between two firms to deal only with each other for certain products or services.

Exclusive jurisdiction the power of a court over a particular subject matter as provided by statute to the exclusion of other courts.

Exculpatory clause a part of a contract that releases one of the parties from liability for their wrongdoings; not favored at laws; *See also* liability waiver.

Executed contract a contract that has been fully performed by the parties.

Executive order under powers granted by the Constitution, or by Congress in legislation, an order by the president to establish or enforce a legal requirement.

Executory contract a contract that has not been performed by the parties.

Exemplary damages *see* punitive damages.

Exemptions from registration in securities law, provisions that allow certain securities to be sold without meeting the usual registration requirements with the Securities and Exchange Commission; does not exempt the securities from other aspects of securities laws.

Exhaustion of administrative remedies a doctrine providing that in instances when a statute provides an administrative remedy, relief must be sought through all appropriate agency channels before a court can act to consider other relief.

Ex parte Latin for "by one party."

Expert witness a witness with professional training or skill in helping evaluate evidence in a case.

Export products manufactured in one country and then shipped and sold in another.

Express authority in agency law, when an agent has clear authority, verbal or written, to act on behalf of a principal for certain matters.

Express contract a contract that is oral or written, as opposed to being implied from the conduct of the parties (*see* implied contract).

Express warranty a promise, in addition to an underlying sales agreement, that goes beyond the terms of the sales agreement and under which the promisor assures the description, performance, or quality of the goods.

Expropriation the taking of a privately owned property by a government. Governments are required to, but at times do not, pay compensation for such takings.

Ex rel (Ex relatione) Latin for "by the relation of information."

Externalities effects, good or bad, on parties not directly involved in the production or use of a product. Pollution is an example of a bad effect, or negative externality.

F

Failing firm defense in antitrust law, a rule that firms may be allowed to merge that would not be allowed to do so otherwise, because one of the firms is in danger of going out of business anyway.

Failure to warn in product liability cases, when a producer is found liable in tort for not warning consumers of dangers the producer knew existed or should have known existed.

Fair use the right of persons other than the owner of copyrighted material to use it in a reasonable manner without the consent of the owner; factors include the purpose of the use, the extent of the use, and the economic effect of the use.

False imprisonment (false arrest) the intentional detention or restraint of an individual by another.

Featherbedding a practice, under a union rule, in which the number of employees used, or the amount of time taken, to perform a job is unnecessarily high.

Federal question a question in a case in which one of the parties, usually the plaintiff, is asserting a right based on a federal law.

Federal Rules of Civil Procedure govern civil procedures in federal courts; written by a committee appointed by the Chief Justice in 1935, Congress adopted the rules as federal law in 1938. Many state court systems use very similar rules.

Fee simple in property law, an absolute ownership interest in an estate (real property) without restrictions; the strongest form of property ownership.

Fellow-servant rule a rule that precludes an injured employee from recovering from his employer when the injury results from the negligent conduct of a fellow employee.

Felony a serious class of crime—such as rape, murder, or robbery—that may be punishable by imprisonment in excess of one year or death.

Fiduciary a person having a duty, generally created by his own undertaking, to act in good faith for the benefit of another in matters related to that undertaking. A fiduciary duty is the highest standard of duty implied by law.

Firm offer (U.C.C.) a signed writing by a merchant promising to keep an offer open. In contrast to an option, a firm offer does not require consideration to make the offer irrevocable.

Fitness for particular purpose under the U.C.C., a buyer may rely on a seller's skill or judgment in selecting goods for a special use, thereby creating a warranty that the goods are fit for the intended use.

Floating lien a security interest retained in collateral even when the collateral changes in character, classification, or location. An inventory loan in which the lender receives a security interest or general claim on a company's inventory. Under the U.C.C., such security is not only in inventory or accounts of the debtor at the time of the original loan, but also in inventory or accounts acquired after the loan.

Foreign exchange rate the price of a country's currency stated in terms of the currency of another country.

Foreseeable dangers in tort law, the duty to reasonably anticipate when an injury is likely to result from certain acts or failure to act to protect others.

Forgery the false making, or the material altering, of a document with the intent to defraud.

Forum non conveniens a rule that allows a court, in equity, to decline jurisdiction over a case when it believes that the matter would be better resolved in another forum. Usually this is invoked when most of the parties and witnesses to a case are in another location, making it more convenient for the trial to be held there, rather than where the case was filed.

Forum-selection clause a contractual provision in which the parties establish the place—such as the country, state, or type of court—for specified litigation or arbitration in the event of a dispute.

Franchise a contract between a parent company (franchisor) and an operating company (franchisee) to allow the franchisee to run a business with the brand name of the parent company, so long as the terms of the contract concerning methods of operation are followed.

Fraud an intentional misrepresentation of a material fact designed to induce the person receiving the miscommunication to rely upon it to her detriment, so that a loss is suffered.

Free trade when all goods and services can be freely imported and exported without special taxes or restrictions being imposed.

Free-trade zone areas where foreign merchandise may be brought without formal customs entry and payment of duty for most legal purposes including storage, grading, sampling, manufacturing, cleaning, or packaging. Duties are paid when the products enter the domestic market.

Freedom of speech a First Amendment protection of expression of all forms; it is strongest in the political arena, but increasingly protected in the commercial arena (*see* commercial speech), giving the United States some of the strongest speech protections in the world.

Fringe benefits medical, accident, and life insurance; retirement benefits; profit sharing; bonus plans; leave; and other terms and conditions of employment other than wage or salary compensation.

Frustration a doctrine in contract law that allows a party to be relieved of a duty to perform because the purpose of the contract no longer exists. Circumstances occurred after the contract was formed that make performance irrelevant or impossible.

Full warranty defined by the Magnuson–Moss Warranty Act as an unlimited warranty for repairs or product replacement for problems that arise with a product within the warranty period.

G

Garnishment a legal process by which a creditor appropriates a debtor's wages or property in the hands of a third party.

General agent a person serving as an agent who is authorized to act for the principal in all matters relating to a particular business or employment relationship.

General creditor a lender with no lien or security to assist in the payment of his debt or claim.

General jurisdiction a power of a court to hear all controversies that may be brought before it.

General partner a partner in a limited partnership or any partner in a general partnership who accepts, or has imposed by law, personal liability for all debts of the partnership.

General verdict a verdict whereby the jury finds either for the plaintiff or the defendant in general terms.

Generic mark a mark used to identify a good that has no legal protection; it may have been a valid trademark at one time, but was not protected against common use.

Genuine consent *see* reality of consent.

Geographic market in antitrust law, the area in the country in which a business has market power.

Golden parachute a severance agreement a manager of a corporation negotiates in return for withdrawing opposition to a tender offer.

Good faith (U.C.C.) honesty in fact in the conduct or transaction in question.

Goods under the U.C.C., manufactured things (not services) that are movable and have physical existence (not intangible).

Goodwill an intangible property that is generally considered to be the expected continued business that will come due to the existing reputation of a firm.

Gratuitous agent an agent who volunteers services without an agreement or expectation of compensation, but whose voluntary consent creates the rights and liabilities of the agency relationship.

Grievance in labor law, a complaint filed by an employer or a union regarding failure to comply with terms of a collective bargaining agreement or to negotiate in good faith; also a dispute resolution procedure that workers must follow if represented by a union.

Guarantor one who makes a guaranty. Person who becomes secondarily liable for another's debt; in contrast to a surety, who is primarily liable with the debtor. One who promises to answer for the debt in case of default.

Guaranty a collateral agreement for performance of another's undertaking. An agreement in which the guarantor agrees to satisfy the debt of a debtor, only if the debtor fails to repay the debt (secondary liability).

Guardian a person appointed to act on behalf of a person lacking ability to perform legal acts, acquire legal rights, or incur legal liabilities.

H

Harmonized tariff schedule a set of definitions to classify goods; adopted by many countries so that they share common terminology when setting tariffs.

Hazard communication standard or HazCom in employment law; the requirement that an employer provide training and information about hazardous chemicals employees will be exposed to on the job.

Hazardous waste a substance that may cause or contribute to an increase in mortality or pose a hazard to human health or the environment when improperly treated.

Hearsay evidence not derived from the personal knowledge of the witness, but from what the witness has heard others say. Hearsay evidence is allowed only in special cases.

Hispanic legally, a person of Mexican, Puerto Rican, Cuban, Central or South American, or other Spanish culture or origin, regardless of race.

Holder in due course (U.C.C.) a holder of an instrument who took it for value in good faith and without any notice of any claim against the instrument; the holder is free of any claims against the instrument.

Horizontal business arrangement an agreement among firms operating at the same level of business in the same market.

Horizontal merger a merger between two companies that compete in the same product market.

Horizontal price fixing price fixing among competitors; an agreement among competitors to charge noncompetitive prices.

Horizontal restraint of trade anticompetitive action by businesses at the same level of operation. Rival firms that come together by agreement in an attempt to restrain trade by restricting output and raising prices is called a *cartel.*

Hostile environment in federal employment discrimination law, creating or allowing to exist a climate at work that is abusive to a person based on their protected class status.

Hot cargo agreement an agreement between an employer and a union in which the employer agrees to refrain from handling, using, selling, transporting, or dealing in any products of an employer the union has labeled as unfair, or "hot."

Howey test the rule established by the Supreme Court to determine what a security is under the federal securities law: an investment of money in a common enterprise with the expectation that profits will be generated by the efforts of others.

Hung jury a jury so divided in opinion that it cannot agree upon a verdict.

I

Identification (U.C.C.) the process of specifying the actual goods that are covered by a contract.

Implied authority in agency law, when the right of an agent to act on behalf of a principal is inferred from past actions or from the current position of the agent.

Implied contract a contract formed on the basis of the conduct of the parties.

Implied warranty an unwritten, unexpressed promise or guarantee that a court infers to exist and that accompanies a good.

Import a product manufactured in another country then shipped to and sold in this country.

Impossibility of performance a doctrine used to discharge the obligations of parties to a contract when an event—such as a law being passed that makes the contract illegal or the subject matter of the contract is destroyed (called *objective impossibility*)—makes performance impossible for one or both parties.

Impracticability an interpretation of the doctrine of impossibility in contracts that allows a party to a contract to be relieved of the duty to perform, when the basis of the contract no longer exists due to unforeseen events.

Incidental damages under the U.C.C., losses that are reasonably related to actual damages, such as a seller's commercially reasonable expenses incurred in stopping delivery or in transporting and caring for goods after a buyer's breach.

Independent contractor one who provides service in the course of an occupation, who follows the employer's direction as to the result of the work but does the work according to her own methods, unlike a servant or employee, who is subject to detailed control in the performance of work.

Indictment a formal written charge issued by a grand jury asserting that the named person has committed a crime.

Infringement in patent, copyright, and trademark law, the unauthorized use or imitation of another's recognized right to the property involved.

Injunction an order issued by a court that restrains a person or business from doing some act or orders the person to do something. May be permanent or temporary.

In personam jurisdiction the power the court has over the person(s) involved in the action.

In rem jurisdiction an action taken by a court against the property of the defendant.

Insider an officer or other person who has information not yet available to the general public concerning the future profits or losses of a corporation.

Insider trading the buying or selling of securities of a firm by persons who have information about the firm not yet available to the public and who expect to make a profit through those transactions.

Insolvency the financial state of a person or business when debts and liabilities exceed the value of assets.

Intangible asset property that is a "right," such as a patent, copyright or trademark, or an asset that is lacking physical evidence, such as goodwill in a firm.

Intangible property property that has no value because of its physical being but is evidence of value, such as securities, promissory notes, copyrights, patents, and certain contracts.

Intellectual property property recognized at law that arises from mental processes, such as inventions and works of art.

Intentional misrepresentation *see* fraud.

Intentional tort a wrong committed upon the person or property of another, where the actor is expressly or impliedly judged to have intended to commit the act that led to the injury.

Interbrand competition competition among various brands of a particular product.

Interference with business relationship a tort in which a defendant commits an intentional and unjustified interference with a plaintiff's valid business dealings that inflicts monetary damage.

Interference with contractual relationship a tort in which there is a valid contract, and the defendant knew of the contract but intentionally caused a breach of the contract, resulting in damages to the plaintiff.

Interference with prospective advantage (or with a business relationship) a tort where there is an intentional and unjustified intervention with a relationship that a party had been developing with others in an effort to obtain new business or more business.

International law those laws governing the legal relations between nations.

Interpretative rules statements issued by administrative agencies that explain how the agency understands its statutory authority to operate; these may be *advisory* or *binding.*

Interrogatories in the discovery process, a set of written questions for a witness or a party for which written answers are prepared with assistance of counsel and signed under oath.

Interstate commerce the carrying on of commercial activity that affects business in more than one state.

Intervening conduct in tort, an independent cause that comes between the original wrongful act and the injury that relieves liability that would otherwise exist for the original act; a legal break in the causal connection.

Intrabrand competition competition among retailers in the sales of a particular brand of product.

Invasion of privacy in tort, the encroachment on the right of a person to their solitude, the appropriation of a person's reputation for commercial purposes, or the public disclosure of facts that the person had a legal right to keep private.

Investigatory hearing in administrative law, when an agency uses rulemaking authority granted by Congress to gather information, on the public record, needed to determine the desirability of proposed rules.

Investment adviser under securities law, a person who, for compensation, engages in the business of advising others as to the advisability of investing in, purchasing, or selling securities. This includes securities brokers and dealers.

Investment company any corporation in business to own and hold the stock of other corporations.

Involuntary bankruptcy a bankruptcy proceeding against an insolvent debtor that is initiated by creditors.

J

Jeopardy a person is said to be in jeopardy when she is charged with a crime before a court. The constitutional doctrine of *double jeopardy* prohibits a person from being prosecuted twice in the same court for the same offense.

Joint and several liability liability that a person or business either shares with other tortfeasors or bears individually.

Joint liability liability that is owed to a third party by two or more other parties together.

Joint stock company a partnership in which the capital is divided, or agreed to be divided, into shares so as to be transferable without the express consent of the other partners.

Joint tenancy a tenancy with two or more co-owners who take identical interests by the same instrument and with the same right of possession. It differs from a tenancy in common in that each joint tenant has a right of survivorship to the other's share.

Joint venture the participation of two companies jointly in a third enterprise. Generally, both companies contribute assets and share risks.

Judgment the official decision of a court of law upon the rights and claims of the parties to an action litigated in and submitted to the court for its determination.

Judgment as a matter of law *see* directed verdict.

Judgment lien a lien binding the real estate of a judgment debtor, in favor of the judgment holder, and giving the latter a right to levy on the property for the satisfaction of his judgment to the exclusion of others.

Judgment notwithstanding the verdict judgment entered by the court for a party following a jury verdict against the party.

Judicial review authority of a court to reexamine a dispute considered and decided previously by a lower court or by an administrative agency.

Junior creditor a creditor whose claim against a debtor arose at a later date than that of the claim held by another creditor with the same or superior priority. A creditor whose claim ranks below other creditors with regard to priority to the debtor's property.

Jurisdiction the right of a court or other body to hear a case and render a judgment.

Jurisdiction over the person power of a court to lawfully bind a party involved in a dispute before it.

Jurisdiction over the subject power of a court to lawfully affect the thing or issue in dispute.

Jurisprudence the science or philosophy of law.

Jury a body of people selected to hear the evidence in a case presented in court and who are given the power to apply the law to the facts established at trial in determining which party prevails in the matter in dispute, whether civil or criminal.

Jury instruction sometimes called the *charge* to the jury; it is the direction or guideline that a judge gives a jury concerning the law of the case being deliberated.

Just compensation clause the portion of the Fifth Amendment that states "nor shall private property be taken for public use, without just compensation." The requirement that when the government uses its power to force a private party to give up a property interest, fair market value should be paid.

K

Kefauver Amendment the portion of the Food, Drug, and Cosmetic Act that requires the Food and Drug Administration to approve drugs only after their safety and effectiveness have been established.

L

Labor dispute under labor law, specific actions by employers, a union, or employees that are subject to coverage by standards set by the National Labor Relations Act.

Laissez faire French for "let do"; a policy implying the absence of government intervention in a market economy.

Landlord the owner of real property (an estate) that has been leased to another party, the tenant.

Latent defect *see* unknown hazard.

Law enforceable rules of conduct set forth by a government to be followed by the citizens of the society.

Law merchant in commercial law, the rules devised by merchants in Europe over several centuries to govern their trade; many of these rules were formally adopted into law.

Leading question a question by an attorney in a trial that instructs the witness how to answer or provides the desired answer.

Learned intermediary doctrine the rule that a physician or other qualified medical professional will be held liable for misapplication of a prescription medication if ordered for a use not recommended by the producer, who is relieved of liability in such instances when a patient is injured by the medicine.

Lease an agreement, usually a contract, that gives the right to a party to take exclusive possession of property for a specific time for a certain payment. This normally creates a landlord and tenant relationship.

Leasehold refers to the real property, an estate, that is under the lawful control of a tenant for the term of the lease agreed to with the landlord.

Legal capacity the right to be able to enter into legal matters that may be restricted by age, mental ability, or other requirements established at common law or by statute.

Legal cause *see* proximate cause.

Legal detriment when a promisee gives up the right to retain control of something he was entitled to keep, or to give up the right to do something, in exchange for a promise by the other party to the contract.

Legal entity the existence of a thing, other than a natural person, that has legal existence so that it can function in a legal capacity, such as a corporation doing business.

Legal ethics practices and customs among members of the legal profession, involving their moral and professional duties toward one another, clients, and the courts.

Legislative history the history of a statute consisting of the legislative committee reports and transcripts of debates in the legislature. Often used by a court in interpreting the terms and provisions of a statute.

Legislative rule *see* substantive rule.

Letter of credit a written document in which the party issuing the document—usually a bank—promises to pay third parties in accordance with the terms of the document.

Levy a seizure; the process by which a state official is empowered by writ or other court directive to seize or control a judgment debtor's property to satisfy a judgment.

Lex loci delecti the place where the wrong, such as a tort, was committed.

Liability a general term referring to possible or actual responsibility; when one is bound by law or equity to be accountable for some act; in product liability, it is in reference to the obligation to pay for damages for which the manufacturer has been held responsible.

Liability waiver similar to an exculpatory clause, in that a party contracts to waive certain tort rights that may otherwise exist against another party; these can be valid if limited in scope and the risks involved are clearly understood by the party who agrees to the waiver, which is found to be reasonable by the court.

Libel a defamation that is in the form of a printing, a writing, pictures, or a broadcast on radio or television.

Lien a claim or encumbrance on property for payment of some debt, obligation, or duty. Qualified right that a creditor has in or over specific property of a debtor as security for the debt or for performance of some act. Right to retain property for payment of a debt.

Lien creditor a creditor who has acquired a lien on certain property by attachment, levy, or other judicial means.

Life estate in property law, when a life tenant (the beneficiary of the arrangement) has the right to occupy a piece of property for life or earn income from a piece of property for life, after which control of the property passes to the designated owner.

Limited jurisdiction also called *special jurisdiction*; the power of a court to hear cases only of particular types—such as small claims courts or family courts—where judgments may be issued that only cover certain kinds of disputes.

Limited liability the fact that shareholders of a corporation are not liable for the debts of the corporation beyond the amount of money they have invested in the corporation.

Limited liability company or LLC, is a form of organization authorized by statute at the state level that is characterized by limited liability, management by members or managers, and limitations on ownership transfer.

Limited partner a partner in a limited partnership whose liability for partnership debts is limited to the amount of his contribution to the partnership.

Limited partnership a business organization consisting of one or more general partners, who manage and contribute assets to the business and who are personally liable for the debts of the business, and one or more limited partners, who contribute assets only and are liable only up to the amount of that contribution.

Limited warranty under the Magnuson–Moss Warranty Act, any product sold with less than a full warranty has what is defined as a limited warranty, the terms of which must be explained in writing.

Liquidated damages amounts specified in a contract to be paid in the event of a breach. They represent a reasonable estimation by the parties of the damages that will occur in the event of breach.

Liquidated debt a debt for a known or determinable amount of money that can not be disputed by either the debtor or the creditor.

Liquidation the sale of the assets of a debtor, the proceeds from which are distributed to the creditors, with any remaining balance going to the debtor.

Lockout refusal by an employer to allow employees to work.

Long-arm statute a state statute permitting courts to obtain personal jurisdiction over nonresidents as long as the requirements of the statute are met.

M

Mail fraud an act of fraud using the Postal Service, as in making false representations through the mail to exploit another party.

Majority opinion when an appeals court issues an opinion in a case that affirms or reverses the decision of the lower court, a majority of the judges join in an opinion that expresses the legal rationale for the decision of the court. If all judges agree, it is a unanimous opinion.

Malice the intentional doing of a wrongful act, without a legal excuse, with the intent to inflict injury.

Malicious prosecution bringing a criminal or civil case for an improper purpose and without probable cause. It is a tort that requires four elements: 1) bringing a lawsuit; 2) lack of probable cause; 3) malice; and 4) favorable end to the lawsuit.

Mandatory subjects of bargaining under the National Labor Relations Act, all terms and conditions of employment that must be discussed by employers and unions or an unfair labor practice occurs.

Manifest system in environmental and occupational safety law, the requirement that certain chemicals have documentation concerning their production, distribution, and disposal to ensure proper handling and disposal of toxic substances.

Margin requirement the fraction of a price of a stock that must be paid in cash, while putting up the stock as security against a loan for the balance.

Market failure failure of an unregulated market to achieve socially optimal results. Sources include monopolies and externalities.

Market power in antitrust law, the ability to raise prices significantly above the competitive level without losing much business.

Market share the percentage of a market, by sales volume of a product nationally or in a geographic area, that is controlled by a firm.

Market share liability when plaintiff is unable to determine which manufacturer of a product caused her injury, the court may assign liability to all firms in the industry on the basis of their shares of the product market.

Master a principal who hires another to perform services and who has the right to control the conduct of that person in the performance of the service; more commonly, an employer.

Material breach *see* breach of contract.

Material fact information that is substantially relevant to the consideration of a contract or to securities or to the decision made in a trial.

Material information *see* material fact.

Maturity the due date of a financial instrument.

Mechanic's lien a claim under state law to secure priority of payments for the value of work performed and materials supplied in building on or improving land and buildings.

Mediation a form of alternative dispute resolution in which a third party is hired by parties to a dispute with the intent to persuade them to settle their dispute.

Mediator a neutral person, usually paid, who attempts to help other parties reach an agreement to resolve a dispute.

Meeting competition in antitrust law, a defense in price discrimination (Robinson–Patman) cases in which a firm shows that prices were cut to meet the prices of competitors.

Meeting of minds a key element of a contract; it means that there has been agreement by both parties to the substance of the agreement.

Mens rea Latin for "the state of mind" of the actor.

Mental distress *see* emotional distress.

Merchant under the U.C.C., one who regularly deals in goods covered by contract for sale, who holds himself out as having specialized knowledge about particular goods; held to a standard of good-faith dealing.

Merchantability in commercial law, the notion that goods are reasonably fit for the ordinary purposes for which such goods are used.

Merger a contract through which one firm acquires the assets and liabilities of another firm.

Merit regulations state securities law provision that in some states allows a securities commissioner to decide if a proposed security offering is too risky to be sold to the public in that state.

Merit system in employment discrimination law, the right of an employer to have a system to reward employees based on performance; often used an as affirmative defense in discrimination cases.

Mineral rights also called *subsurface rights;* in property law, an interest in minerals in land, usually underground, that is separate from ownership of the surface of the land. There is a right to take the minerals from the land or to receive a royalty from the sale of minerals.

Minimum contacts a due process doctrine that requires an out-of-state defendant in a civil suit to have sufficient contacts in a state to make the party subject to the jurisdiction of the state courts.

Minitrial a voluntary form of alternate dispute resolution in which attorneys for both sides make a presentation to a neutral third party, who plays the role of judge. The person who hears the matter gives an opinion that is often the basis of a settlement negotiated without a trial in court.

Minorities persons classified as black (not of Hispanic origin), Hispanic, Asian, Pacific Islander, American Indian, or Alaskan native.

Miranda rights from a 1966 Supreme Court case, the doctrine that a criminal suspect in police custody must be informed of certain constitutional rights before interrogation. The suspect must be advised of the right to remain silent, the right to have an attorney present during questioning, and the right to have an attorney appointed if he cannot afford one. If not advised of these rights, evidence obtained from the suspect during the interrogation cannot be used.

Misappropriation an unauthorized taking of another's property that denies the rightful owner the full use an benefit of the property.

Misdemeanor a lesser crime that is neither a felony nor treason, punishable by a fine and/or imprisonment in other than state or federal penitentiaries.

Misrepresentation words or conduct by a person to another that, under the circumstances, amount to a false statement.

Misstatements in securities law, liability may be imposed on those responsible for issuing information about securities that misleads a reasonable investor in investment decisions to her detriment.

Mistrial a trial that cannot stand in law because the court lacks jurisdiction, because of juror misconduct, or because of disregard for some other procedural requirement.

Mitigation of damages doctrine that imposes a duty upon an injured party to exercise reasonable diligence in attempting to minimize damages after being injured.

Mobile source under the Clean Air Act, a pollution source such as automobiles, trucks, and airplanes.

Modify in an appeals court, to change some detail of a lower court holding, but to leave the primary finding in place. For example, the decision of the lower court is likely to be affirmed, but the legal reasoning for the decision is amended.

Monetary damages *see* damages.

Money laundering is the act of transferring illegally obtained money through legitimate people or accounts so that its original source cannot be traced; a federal crime that is often involved in illegal international transactions.

Monopoly a market structure in which the output of an industry is controlled by a single seller or a group of sellers making joint decisions regarding production and price.

Moral principles social rules that categorize different actions as right or wrong.

Morals generally accepted standards of right and wrong in a society.

Mortgage an interest in real property created by a written instrument providing security for the payment of a debt. In many states, a mortgage is a lien; it is a pledge or security of particular property to help ensure payment of a debt or other obligation.

Mortgagee party who holds or receives a mortgage; the creditor.

Mortgagor one who, having all or part of a title to real property, pledges the property in writing for a particular purpose, such as to secure a debt; the party who mortgages property; the debtor.

Motion the formal way an attorney submits a proposed measure for the consideration and action of the court.

Motion to dismiss a request that a complaint be dismissed, because it does not state a claim for which the law provides a remedy or is in some other way legally deficient.

Mutual consent *see* consent.

Mutual fund an investment vehicle regulated by the Investment Company Act, where many investors pool their money to be managed by a professional staff.

N

National Ambient Air Quality Standards (NAAQS) federal standards under the Clean Air Act that set the maximum concentration levels in the atmosphere for several air pollutants.

National origin under federal employment discrimination law, the country a person or a person's ancestors are from.

National Priority List contaminated sites, as determined by the Environmental Protection Agency under the Superfund law, that must be cleaned up and returned to nearly original condition.

National Uniform Effluent Standards federal standards under the Clean Water Act that set the water pollution effluent standards for every industry that discharges liquid wastes into the nation's waterways.

Nationalization the act of bringing an industry under governmental control or ownership; often this is applied to foreign-owned firms.

Natural monopoly an industry characterized by economies of scale so large that one business can supply the entire market most efficiently.

Necessary and proper clause the part of the U.S. Constitution that gives Congress the authority to use various powers to execute its functions under the Constitution.

Negligence the failure to do something that a reasonable person, guided by the ordinary considerations that regulate human affairs, would do or the doing of something that a reasonable person would not do.

Negligent hiring a basis for tort that may arise from an employer's lack of care in selecting an employee who the employer knew or should have known was unfit for the position, thereby creating an unreasonable risk of harm to others.

Negotiable instrument a signed, written, unconditional promise to pay, to the bearer of the instrument or to order of a certain party, a specific sum of money on demand or on a certain date.

Negotiation voluntary discussion of the terms and conditions of a proposed agreement or a form of alternative dispute resolution to resolve a dispute and avoid litigation; under the U.C.C., the transfer of an instrument to another party who becomes the holder, or the act of putting into circulation a check or promissory note.

Nolo contendere is Latin for "I do not wish to contend"; that is, a party pleads no contest. It is often shortened to *nolo*.

Nominal damages a damage award whereby a court recognizes that the plaintiff has suffered a breach of duty but has not suffered any actual financial loss or injury as a result. Plaintiff's recovery for such breaches is often as little as one dollar.

Nonattainment area under the Clean Air Act, an area in which the air quality for certain pollutants fails to meet the National Ambient Air Quality Standards.

Noncompete agreement in employment law, when an employer requires an employee, as a condition of employment, to agree not to compete with the employer in the future for a certain time and in a certain location; such agreements are not favored in some states.

Nonpoint sources under the Clean Water Act, sources of pollution that are diverse, such as urban and agricultural runoff from rainstorms.

Novation an agreement between the parties to a contract to discharge one of the parties and create a new contract with another party to be responsible for the discharged party's obligations.

Nuisance an unreasonable and substantial interference with the use and enjoyment of another's land (*private nuisance*); an unreasonable or substantial interference with a right held in common by members of the general public (*public nuisance*).

O

Occupational licensure requirement at the state level that for one to practice a certain profession, one must meet certain educational or experience guidelines, pass an entry examination, and show evidence of continuing educational accomplishments.

Offer a proposal to do or refrain from doing some specified thing by a party, called the *offeror*, to another party, called the *offeree*. The proposal creates in the offeree a legal power to bind the offeror to the terms of the proposal by accepting the offer.

Offeree the party to whom an offer is made.

Offeror the party making an offer to another party to enter into a contract.

Open account credit extended by a seller to a buyer that permits buyer to make purchases without security.

Opening statement or argument oral presentations made to the jury by the attorneys before the parties present their cases.

Option contract in contract law, an offer that is included in a formal or informal contract that creates an obligation to keep an offer open for a specified period, so that the offeror cannot revoke the offer during that period. To be valid, the option must be supported by consideration.

Oral argument presentations made in an appeals court or supreme court, usually by attorneys, in support of or objecting to the decision of a lower court as part of the appeals process.

Order for production of documents when a court requires certain documents or other things to be produced for examination; it may be done by issuance of a subpoena *duces tecum*, which is a court order to appear and produce evidence for use at a hearing or at trial.

Ordinary care *see* due care.

Original jurisdiction power of a court to take a lawsuit at its beginning, try it, and pass judgment upon the law and facts.

Out-of-court settlement an agreement by the parties in a case to resolve the matter before a determination by the court.

Over-the-counter market a stock market for securities generally not sold in large daily volumes so that they are not listed on a stock exchange, such as the New York Stock Exchange; a securities market created by stockbrokers who relay information to a central location about offers to buy or sell certain amounts of a stock.

P

Parol in French and Latin, "spoken" or "oral."

Parol evidence rule a rule that prohibits the introduction into a lawsuit of oral evidence that contradicts the terms of a written contract intended to be the final and complete expression of the agreement between the parties.

Partnership a business owned by two or more persons that is not organized as a corporation.

Par value stock stock that has been assigned a specific value by the corporation's board of directors.

Patent a grant from the government conveying and securing for an inventor the exclusive right to make, use, and sell an invention for 20 years from the time of application.

Per curiam opinion Latin for "by the court." A per curiam opinion expresses the view of the court as a whole in contrast to an opinion authored by one member of the court.

Perfect tender rule at common law, seller's offer of delivery must conform to every detail of contract with buyer; under the U.C.C., parties may agree to limit the operation of this rule, or the seller may cure a defective tender if the time for performance has not ended; the seller notifies the buyer quickly of intent to cure defect, or the seller repairs or replaces defective goods within performance time limits.

Perfection of security interest in a secured transaction, the process by which a security interest is protected against competing claims to the collateral. It usually requires the secured party to give notice of the interest by filing it in the appropriate government office, usually the secretary of state.

Performance in contract law, the fulfilling of obligations or promises according to the terms agreed to or specified by parties to a contract. Complete performance of those obligations or promises by both parties discharges the contract.

Periodic disclosure in securities law, requirements that issuers of most publicly held securities file monthly, quarterly, and annual reports with the Securities and Exchange Commission.

Permanent injunction *see* injunction.

Per se Latin for "in itself" or "taken alone"; as in the per se rule in antitrust, whereby the facts alone are enough to lead to conviction of the defendants.

Per se rule in antitrust, a violation held to be so pernicious as to have no defense if a violation is shown to have occurred.

Personal jurisdiction *see* jurisdiction over the person.

Personal property physical, movable property other than real estate.

Personal service in the pleadings stage, personal service of the complaint is accomplished by physically delivering it to the defendant.

Piercing the corporate veil a court's act of ignoring the legal existence of a corporation and holding the corporation's officers personally liable for their wrongful acts done in the name of the corporation.

Plaintiff the party who initiates a lawsuit.

Plea bargain or *negotiated plea;* a negotiated agreement between a prosecutor and a criminal defendant for the defendant to plead guilty to a lesser offense or to only one of multiple charges in exchange for concessions such as a lighter sentence or a dismissal of the other charges.

Pleadings statements of the plaintiff and the defendant that detail their facts, allegations, and defenses, which create the issues of the lawsuit.

Point source under the Clean Water Act, any definitive place of discharge of a water pollutant, such as pipes, ditches, or channels.

Police power a general power of the states to enact laws to protect public safety, health, and order so long as due process and equal protection are not violated.

Political speech in constitutional law, speech that concerns political, as opposed to commercial, matters; given a high level of protection by the First Amendment.

Pollution the release of substances into the air, water, or land that cause physical change.

Possessory lien (artisan's lien) a lien in which the creditor has the right to the possession of specific property until a debt is satisfied or an obligation is performed.

Potential competition in antitrust law, consideration given to the degree of competitiveness that exists in a market because of the possibility that firms not now in the market will enter it and compete with existing producers.

Power of attorney a document authorizing another person to act as one's agent or attorney with respect to the matters stated in the document.

Precedent a decision in a case that is used to guide decisions in later cases with similar fact situations.

Predatory bidding in antitrust law, similar to predatory pricing; when a dominant firm bids up the price of an input to get sufficient control of it to be able to dominate a market that relies on the input, so as to drive out competitors and then be able to raise prices later.

Predatory pricing in antitrust law, pricing below an accepted measure of cost (such as average variable cost) to drive competitors from the market in the short run to reduce competition in the long run.

Pre existing duty in common-law contracts, the rule that when a party promises to do something she was already obligated to do, there is not sufficient consideration to support a new contract.

Preferred stock class of stock that has priority over common stock both as to payment of dividends and to distribution of the corporation's assets upon dissolution.

Pregnancy discrimination under federal employment discrimination law, treating an employee differently because of pregnancy or related conditions, such as having children, is illegal.

Premises liability an intentional tort, or a tort based on negligence, when the owner or party with responsibility for maintaining certain property fails to provide adequate safety for visitors to the property against criminal attacks or accidents.

Preponderance of the evidence in civil trials, the burden of persuasion to win a verdict requires that the plaintiff prove its claim by having the majority or bulk of the evidence on its side.

Presumption means the trier of fact must find the existence of the fact presumed, unless and until evidence is introduced that would support a finding of its nonexistence.

Pretext under federal employment discrimination law, an attack made by a plaintiff against a defense offered by an employer to a charge of discrimination, holding that the rationale given is a false excuse to cover discriminatory treatment.

Prevention of significant deterioration (PSD) area under the Clean Air Act, an area where the air quality is better than required by the national ambient air standards, such as national parks and wilderness areas. Air quality is not allowed to fall.

Price discrimination in antitrust law, charging different prices to different customers for the same product without a cost justification for the price difference.

Prima facie Latin for "at first sight." Something presumed to be true until disproved by contrary evidence.

Prima facie case in federal employment discrimination law, the requirement that a plaintiff show they are a member of a protected class, met relevant job qualifications, suffered some adverse job action, and was treated differently with respect to the same issue by an employer.

Primary boycott in labor law, a union action that tries to convince people not to deal with an employer with which the union has a grievance.

Principal in an agency relationship, a person who, by explicit or implicit agreement, authorizes an agent to act on his behalf and perform acts that will be binding on the principal.

Principal (credit transactions) an amount of money borrowed or invested. The capital sum of a debt or obligation, distinguished from interest or other additions to it.

Principal (suretyship) the person primarily liable, for whose performance of her obligation the surety has become bound.

Privacy a right that has been expanded over time by the courts based on a belief in the existence of the right to be free from governmental intrusion to a particular place or thing.

Private law a classification of law, generally denoting laws that affect relationships between people.

Private nuisance in tort law, when an activity reduces the right of one person, or a small number of persons, to enjoy property without unreasonable interference.

Private property right an individual economic interest supported by the law.

Privilege in tort law, the ability to act contrary to another's legal right without that party having legal redress for the consequences of that act; usually raised as a defense.

Privity a legal relationship between parties, such as between parties to a contract.

Privity of contract the immediate relationship that exists between the parties to a contract.

Probable cause reasonable ground to believe the existence of facts warranting the undertaking of certain actions, such as the arrest or search of a person.

Procedural law the rules of the court system that deal with the manner in which lawsuits are initiated and go forward. Court systems generally have rules regarding pleadings, process, evidence, and practice.

Product abuse (product misuse) a defense in a product liability suit where the producer or seller accused of marketing a defective product that caused an injury can show that the user of the product abused or misused the product in such a way as to be the primary cause of the injury that occurred.

Product liability a general category of cases in which the producer or seller of products may be held responsible to buyers, users, or innocent third parties, who suffer injuries due to defects in the goods.

Product market in antitrust law, the product market includes all products that can be reasonably substituted by consumers for the product of the business under investigation.

Professional corporation in most states, a category of corporations that may be used by those providing a personal service that require a license, such as physicians, dentists, architects, and accountants. The primary reason to adopt this status is for tax benefits.

Profit a servitude that gives the right to pasture cattle, dig for minerals, or otherwise take away some part of the soil.

Program trading the trading of stock on stock exchanges through the use of computers programmed to buy and sell at specified prices and other conditions.

Promise a statement or declaration that binds the party making it (the promisor) to do or refrain from doing a particular act or thing. The party to whom the declaration is made (the promisee) has a right to demand or expect the performance of the act or thing.

Promissee party to whom a promise is made.

Promisor party who makes a promise.

Promissory estoppel a doctrine that allows promises to be enforced in the absence of consideration, if a promise is made which the promisor reasonably expects will induce action or forbearance on the part of the promisee and, which in fact, does cause such action or forbearance to the detriment of the promisee.

Promissory note an unconditional promise, in writing, to pay a certain sum at a specific time, or on demand, to a person named on the instrument or to the bearer of the instrument; such notes are negotiable.

Promulgation an administrative order that causes an agency law or regulation to become known and obligatory.

Proprietorship a business owned by a person who is not organized as a corporation.

Prospectus under securities law, a pamphlet that must be produced for distribution to prospective buyers of securities that contains information about the background of the security being offered.

Protected class under Title VII of the Civil Rights Act of 1964, those groups the law seeks to protect, including groups based on race, sex, national origin, religion, and color.

Protective order a decree by a court to protect a person or a legal entity against harassment by another person or to protect certain documents, such as trade secrets, against discovery in the litigation process.

Proximate cause in tort law, the action of the defendant that produces the plaintiff's injuries, without which the injury or damage in question would not have existed.

Proxy giving another person the right to vote on one's behalf; in stock votes, when a person gives another the right to vote in a certain manner, such as for candidates for board of directors.

Public corporation or publicly held corporation; while this can refer to a corporation established by the government for a specific purpose, it generally means a private corporation that has stock that is actively and openly traded.

Public law a classification of law, generally denoting laws that affect relationships between people and their governments.

Public nuisance in tort law, when an activity reduces the right of the public in general to enjoy property without unreasonable interference.

Public policy exception in employment law, statutory or court-mandated exceptions to the presumption of employment-at-will that goes beyond contract issues in employment; for example, it is illegal for an employer to dismiss an employee for reporting for jury duty.

Publicly owned treatment works (PTOWs) under the Clean Water Act, a heavily funded federal program to bring local water treatment facilities up to federal standards, usually the best conventional technology level.

Punitive damages compensation awarded to a plaintiff beyond actual damages; awarded to punish the defendant for doing a particularly offensive act.

Purchase money security interest a secured interest created when a buyer uses the money of a lender to make a purchase and gives the lender a security interest in the property purchased.

Q

Quantum meruit a concept in equity that a party should not be unjustly enriched by not paying for goods or services received that do not clearly fall under a contract; it is the recovery a plaintiff is allowed to be granted under an implied contract to pay for the reasonable value of services provided.

Quasi-contract a contract imposed by law, in the absence of an actual contract, to prevent unjust enrichment. A contract implied in law.

Quasi in rem jurisdiction a proceeding brought against the defendant personally, when the defendant's interest in property serves as the basis of the court's jurisdiction.

Quid pro quo "what for what," or "something for something"; the giving of something valuable for something valuable, such as consideration in a contract. Also refers to sexual discrimination, when sexual favors are exchanged for employment favors.

Quitclaim deed a deed that conveys the grantor's complete interest or claim in real property but that does not warrant that the title is valid.

R

Race under federal employment discrimination law: black, white, American Indian or Alaska Native, Native Hawaiian or Other Pacific Islander, Asian, and Hispanic or Latino.

Racketeer Influenced and Corrupt Organizations Act (RICO) a law designed to attack organized criminal activity by prosecuting persons who participate or conspire to participate in racketeering. The federal RICO statute of 1970 applies to activity involving interstate or foreign commerce. Many states have adopted laws—"little RICO" acts—based on the federal statute. The federal and most state RICO acts provide for enforcement not only by criminal prosecution but also by civil lawsuit, in which plaintiffs can sue for treble damages.

Ratification in contract law, the act of accepting responsibility for a previous act that would not constitute an enforceable contractual obligation but for the ratification. Ratification causes the obligation to be binding as if it were valid and enforceable in the first place.

Real property land, the products of land (such as timber), and property that cannot be moved (such as houses).

Reality of consent in contract law, a contract must have been entered into freely based upon correct information about the matter to be valid; if duress, misrepresentation, or fraud was present when the agreement was made, there is no contract.

Reasonable accommodation in employment discrimination law, the requirement that employers take steps that are not very costly to make employment possible for persons with disabilities.

Reasonable care the degree of care that a person of ordinary prudence would use in the same or similar circumstances or in the same line of business.

Reasonable person the standard which one must observe to avoid liability for negligence; often includes the duty to foresee harm that could result from certain actions.

Rebuttal during the trial stage, when evidence is given by one party to refute evidence introduced by the other party.

Red herring in securities law, a prospectus that has not yet been approved by the Securities Exchange Commission. It has a red border on its front to signal to interested parties that it is not yet approved for final distribution; used as an advertising device.

Reformation when a court orders a correction to a contract so that its true intention will be met; it is a remedy in equity that allows a court to correct mistakes the parties did not intend or to correct fraud that occurred.

Registration statements in securities law, the financial information that must be filed with the Securities and Exchange Commission for review prior to the sale of securities to the public.

Regulation Z a rule issued by the Federal Reserve Board to implement the Truth-in-Lending Act requiring systematic disclosure of the costs associated with credit transactions.

Regulatory taking when a government action results in a reduction in the value of private property; such instances are usually not subject to compensation under the Constitution, unless most of the value of property is destroyed.

Rejoinder during the trial stage, the defendant's answer to the plaintiff's rebuttal.

Reliance when the tort of fraud or deceit occurs, the plaintiff must show that she relied on the false information that was provided, and that such reliance was reasonable under the circumstances.

Religion under federal employment discrimination law, any sincere and meaningful belief a person possesses.

Remand the act of an appellate court in sending a case back to a trial court ordering it to take action according to the appellate court's decision. The order usually requires a new trial or limited hearings on specified subject matter.

Remedy the legal means by which a right is enforced or the violation of a right is prevented or compensated.

Removal jurisdiction the power to remove a case from one court system or location to another.

Repatriation the process used to transfer assets or earnings from a host nation to another nation.

Reply during the pleading stage, plaintiff's response to the defendant's answer to the plaintiff's original complaint.

Representation election in labor law, when at least 30 percent of workers in a current or proposed bargaining unit sign a request to have an election to determine if all workers in that workplace will be represented by a particular union.

Repudiation a rejection, disclaimer, or renunciation of a contract before performance is due, but which does not operate as an anticipatory breach, unless the promisee elects to treat the rejection as a breach and brings a suit for damages.

Request for admission a statement of facts about a case that the other party to a case is asked to admit are facts so that they need not be proved at trial.

Res Latin for "a thing" or "things."

Resale price maintenance when a manufacturer or wholesaler sets the price of a good at the next level, such as at the retail level; if the price set is not charged by the retailer, the manufacturer or wholesaler will no longer sell the good to the retailer.

Rescission to cancel or nullify a contract; it is the unmaking of a contract, as if it never existed. It may occur because both parties agree to avoid the contract, or because one party gives the other party grounds for canceling the contract, such as by an act that would create grounds for not fulfilling the obligations.

Res ispa loquitor Latin for "the thing speaks for itself;" given the facts presented, it is clear that the defendant's actions were negligent and were the proximate cause of the injury incurred.

Res judicata a rule that prohibits the same dispute between two parties from being relitigated by a court after final judgment has been entered and all appeals exhausted.

Respondeat superior doctrine of vicarious liability under which an employer is held liable for the wrongful acts of his employees committed within the scope of their employment.

Respondent the party, plaintiff, or defendant who won in a lower court but must now respond to the appeal of the case by the losing party, the appellant.

Restatement of Law a series of books sponsored by the American Law institutes that explain the current state of the law in different areas (contracts, property, agency, torts, etc.) and the direction the law is moving. As the books are authored by leading scholars in their respective fields, they are often looked to for authority on points of law by courts in interpreting the law as it applies to a case.

Restitution a remedy in equity to restore a person to his original position had there been no loss or injury or to the position he would have enjoyed had there been no breach of contract.

Restraint of trade any contract, agreement, or combination that eliminates or restricts competition.

Retaliatory discharge *see* wrongful discharge.

Reverse a decision by an appellate court that overturns or vacates the judgment of a lower court.

Reverse discrimination when discrimination is employed against majority groups so as to favor certain minority groups, often in affirmative action programs.

Revocation the recall of some power, authority, or thing granted; in contract law, the withdrawal by the offeree of an offer that had been valid until withdrawn.

Right-to-work law state laws that prohibit unions from forcing employees who do not want to pay union dues or agency fees to pay such dues or fees even if the employees are represented by the union under a collective bargaining agreement.

Riparian at common law, relating to the bank of a river or stream; the owner of land bounded by a river or body of water has the right to reasonably use the water next to the land or that passes over the land.

Ripeness in administrative law, a doctrine that before a matter may be appealed to the court system, an agency must have finalized its decision, so the matter is ready for court review.

Rule making in administrative law, the procedures that agencies must follow when issuing rules to interpret or enforce the statutory authority they were granted by Congress.

Rule of reason in antitrust law, the court considers all facts and decides whether what was done was reasonable and did not harm competition in net; compare to the per se rule.

S

Sale under the U.C.C., when there is a passing of title of a good from the seller to the buyer for a price.

Sales contract under the U.C.C., "the passing of title from the seller to the buyer for a price."

Sanctions the penalty imposed, or threatened to be imposed, by a court on a party to litigation that is not complying with some aspect of the process, such as refusing to provide documents requested by the opposing party and approved by the court.

Satisfaction the performance of a substituted obligation in return for the discharge of the original obligation.

Search and seizure in criminal law, an examination of a person's body or property, that the person would reasonably be expected to consider as private, conducted by a law-enforcement officer for the purpose of finding evidence. The Fourth Amendment prohibits unreasonable searches and seizure; a search cannot usually be conducted without probable cause.

Scienter Latin for "knowingly;" usually meaning that the defendant knew that the act in question was illegal.

Second lien a lien that ranks after a first lien on the same property (such as a second mortgage) and is entitled to satisfaction out of the proceeds of the sale of the property after the first lien is satisfied.

Secondary boycott a union's refusal to handle products of or work for a secondary company with whom the union has no dispute; to force that company to stop doing business with another company with which the union has a dispute.

Secondary meaning when a mark or trade dress is distinctive and receives public recognition by itself, not just as a means of identifying the origins of the good or service it represents.

Secured creditors a person who has loaned money to another and has a legally recognized interest in the property of the debtor until fulfillment of the terms of the debt agreement.

Secured transaction any transaction, regardless of form, intended to create a security interest in personal property, including goods, documents, and other intangible property.

Securities in securities law, debt or equity instruments that are evidence of a contribution of money by a group of investors into a common enterprise that will be operated for profit by professional managers.

Securities fraud in securities law, the statutory basis for charging anyone involved in the issuance or trading of securities with fraud, which is usually due to misleading issuance of information or failure to disclose material information that causes investors to suffer losses.

Security interest interest in property obtained under a security agreement. An interest in property that allows the property to be sold on default to satisfy the obligation for which the security interest is given. A mortgage grants a security interest in real property.

Self-defense generally, a legal excuse for the use of force to resist an attack on one's person or to defend another person who is under attack or property that is under attack. This defense may apply in common-law cases and in criminal cases.

Self-incrimination the rule that a witness is not bound to give testimony that would incriminate him with respect to a criminal act.

Self-reporting the requirement under many laws that one subject to the law must volunteer certain matters, including violations, that have occurred to the relevant regulatory agency.

Seniority in employment, a system that recognizes length of service in deciding promotions, layoffs, and other job actions, in which preference is given to the worker with more years of employment and/or more time in a particular position.

Sentencing Guidelines a federal statute that provides detailed instructions for judges to determine appropriate sentences for federal crimes; it includes factors such as the nature of the crime and the history of the defendant.

Separation of powers governments at the state and federal level in the United States are divided into the legislative, executive, and judicial branches, which each have certain duties and powers. This division of authority was designed to restrain the power of any one branch.

Servant *see* employee.

Service mark under trademark law, any symbol, word, or name used in the sale of goods to distinguish the services available from a particular source; service marks apply to services; trademarks apply to goods.

Service of process in the pleadings stage, the delivery of the complaint to the defendant either to her personally or, in most jurisdictions, by leaving it with a responsible person at her place of residence.

Servitude a burden that rests on one estate for the benefit of another. Servitudes on land may impose obligations on the owner of land to permit something to be done on the property by another, or it may be a restriction on the use of property that would normally be permitted.

Sex under federal employment discrimination law, male and female; under some state laws, sexual orientations may be recognized categories.

Sexual harassment discrimination in employment in violation of Title VII of the 1964 Civil Rights Act that may be evidenced by sexual advances, requests for sexual favors, and other conduct of a sexual nature.

Shareholder the owner of one or more shares of stock in a corporation.

Shelf registration a Securities and Exchange Commission rule that allows certain companies to file a single registration statement for the future sale of securities. This registration allows the company to react quickly to favorable market conditions.

Short-swing profits profits made by an insider on the purchase and sale of stock of a corporation within a six-month period.

Sight draft a draft payable upon proper presentment.

Sine qua non rule *see* cause in fact.

Slander an oral defamation of one's reputation or good name.

Sole proprietorship *see* proprietorship.

Sophisticated user in tort law, a defense that when a manufacturer sells a product to a sophisticated buyer, such as another manufacturer, the purchaser is responsible for instructing its employees about the dangers in using the product.

Sovereign a person, body, or nation in which independent and supreme authority is vested.

Sovereign immunity the doctrine under which a nonsovereign party is precluded from engaging in a legal action against a sovereign party, unless the sovereign gives its consent.

Special agent one employed as an agent to conduct a specific transaction or business act for a principal; while there may be more than one action involved, it is not expected to be a continuous relationship.

Special damages in contract law, damages not contemplated by the parties at the time the contract is made. To be recoverable, they must flow directly and immediately from the breach of contract and must be reasonably foreseeable.

Specific performance an equitable remedy, whereby the court orders a party to a contract to perform his duties under the contract. Usually granted when money damages are inadequate as a remedy, and the subject matter of the contract is unique.

Standing the right to sue in a particular court.

Stare decisis the use of precedent by courts; the use of prior decisions to guide decision making in cases before the courts.

State implementation plans under the Clean Air Act, a requirement that each state prepare, under Environmental Protection Agency supervision, a plan to control certain air pollutants by certain dates to meet national air quality standards.

Stationary sources under the Clean Air Act, a nonmoving source of pollution, such as a factory or an electrical power plant.

Statute a law enacted by a legislative body.

Statute of frauds a statutory requirement that certain types of contracts be in writing to be enforceable.

Statute of limitations a statute setting maximum time periods from the occurrence of an event, during which certain actions can be brought or rights enforced. If an action is not filed before the expiration of that time period, the statute bars the use of the courts for recovery.

Statutory law laws enacted by a legislative body.

Stock equity securities that evidence an ownership interest in a corporation.

Strict liability a legal theory that imposes responsibility for damages regardless of the existence of negligence; in tort law, any good sold that has a defect that causes injury leads to the imposition of liability.

Strike a work stoppage by employees for the purpose of coercing their employer to give in to their demands.

Subagent one authorized by an agent to help perform agency duties for a principal. When an agent has authority to appoint a subagent, he is subject to control by both the agent and the principal.

Subject-matter jurisdiction *see* jurisdiction over the subject.

Subpoena an order by a court or other legal authority empowered to require a person to appear to give testimony about a certain civil or criminal matter. A subpoena *duces tecum* orders the production of documents.

Subrogation the substitution of one party in place of another with respect to a lawful claim, so that the party substituted succeeds to the rights of the other in relation to the debt or claim and its rights and remedies.

Subsidy a government monetary grant to a favored industry.

Substance-abuse policy in employment law, workplace rules adopted by an employer with respect to any required tests and the consequences of abuse of drugs, alcohol, or other substances; must comply with certain federal and state laws.

Substantial factor test a standard adopted in several states in place of proximate cause; a jury may hold a defendant liable in tort if it finds that defendant's conduct was a major cause of the injury in question.

Substantial performance a doctrine that recognizes that a party that performs a contract, but with a slight deviation from the contract's terms, is entitled to the contract price less any damages caused by the deviation.

Substantive law law that defines the rights and duties of persons to each other, as opposed to procedural law, which is law that defines the manner in which rights and duties may be enforced.

Substantive rules administrative rulings based on statutory authority granted an agency by Congress; the rules have the same legal force as statutes passed by Congress.

Substituted service a form of service other than personal service, such as service by mail or by publication in a newspaper.

Suggestive mark a trademark which, by its name, suggests the use or purpose of the good it represents; legal protection is due such marks but can be more difficult to establish than for arbitrary and fanciful marks.

Summary judgment a judgment entered by a trial court as a matter of law, when no genuine issue of law is found to exist.

Summary jury trial a form of alternate dispute resolution in which both parties give a brief presentation of their argument in a courtlike setting in which a mock jury may be used; the decision of the jury need not be binding but often helps the parties negotiate a settlement based on the information learned from the proceedings.

Summons process through which a court notifies and compels a defendant to a lawsuit to appear and answer a complaint.

Sunset laws a statute that requires periodic review for the continued existence of an administrative agency; the legislature must take positive steps to allow the agency to continue to exist by a certain date.

Superfund in environmental law, the Comprehensive Environmental Response, Compensation, and Liability Act (CERCLA); it concerns requirements about when hazardous waste sites must be cleaned up and who is liable for the costs.

Superseding cause the act of a third party, or an outside force, that intervenes to prevent a defendant from being liable for harm to another due to negligence.

Supremacy Clause article VI, paragraph 2 of the U.S. Constitution, which states that the Constitution and federal laws are supreme over the laws of all states.

Supreme courts in the federal and state court systems, the highest court of appeal or the court of last resort; such courts are established by federal and state constitutions.

Surety one who undertakes to pay money or otherwise act in the event that her principal fails to pay or act as promised. A surety is usually bound with her principal by the same contract, executed at the same time and for the same consideration. Under the U.C.C., this includes a guarantor. However, liability of guarantor, depending on state law, is secondary and collateral, whereas liability of surety is primary and direct.

Suretyship the relationship among three parties in which one party, the surety, guarantees payment of a debtor's debt owed to a creditor or acts as a co debtor.

Syndicates a business association made of parties for the purpose of carrying out some particular business transaction in which the members are mutually interested.

T

Takings clause *see* just compensation clause.

Tangible property property that has physical form and substance, such as real estate and goods.

Tariff a tax imposed on imported goods by the government to encourage domestic industry or to raise revenues. *See* excise tax.

Tax incentive a government taxing policy intended to encourage a particular activity.

Temporary injunction *see* injunction.

Tenancy in common an ownership interest in which each tenant (owner) has an undivided interest in property. More than one party owns the property in joint possession, but there are separate titles so that when an owner dies, her interest passes to her heirs.

Tenant one who possesses (rents) real property for a period of time, usually under a lease. The property or estate is normally owned by the landlord.

Tender offer an offer open to current stockholders to buy a stock at a certain price; offer may be contingent upon receiving a certain amount of stock before any purchase is completed or may be an open offer; a method used to obtain enough stock to control a corporation.

Termination in contract law, the ending of an offer or contract, usually without liability.

Territorial allocation in antitrust law, the boundaries specified by contract or other agreement in which a wholesaler or retailer may sell a product.

Territorial jurisdiction territory over which a court has jurisdiction. The authority of any court is generally limited to its territorial boundaries. *See* long-arm statute.

Tie-in sale in antitrust law, the requirement that if one product or service is purchased then another product or service must also be purchased, even if it is not desired by the customer.

Title generally, the legal right of ownership; under the U.C.C., title is determined by rules regarding identification of goods, the risk of loss of goods, and insurable interest in the goods.

Tort an injury or wrong committed with or without force against another person or his property; a civil wrong that is a breach of a legal duty owed by the person who commits the tort to the victim of the tort.

Tortfeasor an individual or business that commits a tort.

Toxic pollutants a pollutant that may cause an increase in mortality or serious illness.

Trade acceptance a draft drawn by a seller that is presented for acceptance to the buyer when goods are purchased; it is a negotiable instrument that the seller can use to raise funds.

Trade dress intellectual property protected by trademark law and the Lanham Act that concerns the total appearance and image of products and of service establishments, including shape, size, graphics, and color.

Trademark a distinctive design, logo, mark, or word that a business can register with a government agency for its exclusive use in identifying its product or itself in the marketplace.

Trade name a word or symbol that has become sufficiently associated with a product over a period of time that it has lost its primary meaning and has acquired a secondary meaning; once so established, the company has a right to bring a legal action against those who infringe on the protection provided the trade name.

Trade regulation rules administrative rulings by the Federal Trade Commission or other agencies that hold certain practices to be illegal or create standards that must be met by sellers of certain products or services.

Trade secret in tort law, valuable, confidential data—usually in the form of formulas, processes, and other forms of information not patented or not patentable—that are developed and owned by a business.

Treatment, storage, and disposal (TSD) sites under the Resource Conservation and Recovery Act, a requirement that producers, transporters, and disposers of hazardous wastes keep records (manifests) and meet federal standards in all phases of such operations.

Treble damages a money damage award allowable under some statutes that is determined by multiplying the jury's actual damage award by three.

Trespass an unauthorized intrusion upon the property rights of another.

Trespass to personal property an unlawful interference with the rights of another person to possess their personal property, such as movable objects.

Trial a judicial examination of a dispute between two or more parties under the appropriate laws by a court or other appropriate tribunal that has jurisdiction.

Trial de novo Latin for "a new" trial, or retrial at an appellate court in which the entire case is examined as though no trial had occurred.

Trustee a person who has legal title in some property, such as the property of a bankrupt business, held in trust for the benefit of another person (the beneficiary).

Tying arrangements an agreement between a buyer and a seller in which the buyer of a specific product is obligated to purchase another good. *See* tie-in sale.

U

Ultrahazardous activity in tort law, a rule that when an activity "necessarily involves a risk of serious harm," such as the use of explosives or toxic chemicals, strict liability will be imposed when any harm is caused to other persons or property.

Unconscionable contract a contract, or a clause in a contract, that is grossly unfair to one of the parties because of stronger bargaining powers of the other party; usually held to be void as against public policy.

Underwriter a professional firm that handles the marketing of a security to the public; it either buys all of a new security offering and then sells it to the public, or it takes a commission on the securities it actually sells.

Undisclosed principal when the identity of a principal is unknown to a third party, so that the third party is unaware that the agent being dealt with is representing the agency.

Undue influence the misuse of one's position of confidence or relationship with another individual to overcome that person's free will thereby taking advantage of that person to affect decisions.

Unenforceable contract a contract that was once valid but, because of a subsequent illegality, will not be enforced by the courts.

Unfair labor practice in labor law, a wide range of actions that violate the rights of workers to organize and engage in collective activities or that violate the rights of employers to be free from practices defined as illegal under the National Labor Relations Act.

Unfair methods of competition under the Federal Trade Commission Act, a range of business practices found to violate the public interest; they may be based on fraud, deception, or a violation of public policy, because competition is injured.

Unfairness in a consumer protection law, a charge under Section 5 of the Federal Trade Commission Act that a business practice causes harm that consumers cannot reasonably avoid.

Uniform Commerical Code (U.C.C.) a statute passed in similar form by the states that sets many rules of commercial sales agreements and negotiable debt instruments.

Unilateral contract an offer or promise of an offeror that is binding only after completed performance by the offeree. The offeree's completed performance serves as acceptance of the offer and performance of the contract.

Union an association of workers that is authorized to represent them in bargaining with their employers.

Union certification in labor law, when a majority of the workers at a workplace vote to have a union be their collective bargaining agent, the National Labor Relations Board certifies the legal standing of the union for that purpose.

Union shop a place of employment where one must be a union member before obtaining employment or must become a union member after obtaining employment.

Universal agent one serving as an agent who is authorized to conduct every transaction that can be lawfully delegated by a principal to an agent.

Unknown hazard in products liability, a claim that tort liability should be assigned to a producer for injuries suffered by a consumer due to a defect or hazard in a product that was not known by the producer at the time the product was made.

Unliquidated debt a disputed debt; a debt that has not been reduced to some specific amount.

Unsecured creditor a party owed money but who has no collateral, lien, or other security to secure the debt or claim in the event of default by the debtor.

Usury laws statutes that prohibit finance charges (interest and other forms of compensation for loaning money) above a certain level for debt.

V

Valid contract a contract in which all of the elements of a contract are present and is, therefore, enforceable at law by the parties.

Venue the geographic area in which an action is tried and from which the jury is selected.

Verdict from a Latin term meaning "a true declaration." It is the formal finding of a jury in a case, determining which party prevails and, depending on the case, awarding damages or imposing a criminal penalty.

Vertical merger a merger of two business firms, one of which is the supplier of the other.

Vertical price fixing an agreement between a supplier and a distributor relating to the price at which the distributor will resell the supplier's product.

Vertical restraint of trade in antitrust law, contracts or combinations which reduce or eliminate competition among firms in the production, distribution, and sale of some good.

Vesting under the Employee Retirement Income Security Act, the requirement that pension benefits become the property of workers after a specific number of years of service to an employer.

Vicarious liability liability that arises from the actions of another person who is in a legal relationship with the party upon whom liability is being imposed.

Void contract a contract that does not exist at law; a contract having no legal force or binding effect.

Voidable contract a contract that is valid but which may be legally voided at the option of one of the parties.

Voidable preference a preference given to one creditor over another by a bankrupt person or business, usually manifested by a payment to that creditor just prior to the bankruptcy declaration that may be set aside by the trustee in bankruptcy.

Voir dire to "speak the truth." In the trial stage, preliminary examination of a juror in which the attorneys and the court attempt to determine bias, incompetency, and interest.

Voluntary bankruptcy a bankruptcy proceeding that is initiated by the debtor.

W

Waiver an express or implied relinquishment of a legal right.

Warrant a judicial authorization for the performance of an act that would otherwise be illegal.

Warrantless search a search by law enforcement authorities, generally not permitted in cases involving persons, but allowed for closely regulated businesses.

Warranty an assurance or guaranty, either expressed in the form of a statement by a seller of goods or implied by law, having reference to and ensuring the character, quality, or fitness of purpose of the goods.

Warranty deed a deed containing one or more covenants of title; a deed that expressly guarantees good, clear title and that contains covenants concerning the quality of title, including defense of title against all claims.

Warranty disclaimer under the U.C.C., the ability of goods to be sold as is, or with fewer warranty rights that would normally exist, based upon clear communication to the buyer that warranty rights are reduced or eliminated at the time of sale.

Warranty of title in general, the duty of a seller to provide good title or legal right of ownership of goods to the buyer; under the U.C.C., specific warranty rights are provided when title to goods passes.

Wetlands in environmental law, land covered by water at least part of the year; exact coverage by various environmental statutes is still unresolved.

Whistle-blower an employee who alerts the authorities to the fact that her employer is undertaking an activity that is contrary to the law.

White-collar crime a wide range of nonviolent crimes, often involving cheating or dishonesty in commercial matters. Examples would be fraud, embezzlement, and insider trading.

Winding up process of settling the accounts and liquidating the assets of a partnership or corporation for the purpose of dissolving the concern.

Wire fraud fraud involving the use of electronic communications, such as by making false representations on the telephone or the Internet to obtain money. The federal Wire Fraud Act holds that any fraud by wire or other electronic communications, such as radio or television in foreign or interstate commerce is a crime.

Worker's compensation laws state statutes that provide for awards to workers or their dependents if a worker incurs an injury or an illness in the course of employment. Under such laws, the worker is freed from bringing a legal action to prove negligence by the employer.

World Trade Organization an international organization to which most nations belong that works to open markets to free trade and protect property rights.

Writ a mandatory precept issued by a court of justice.

Writ of certiorari an order by an appellate court used when the court has discretion whether to hear an appeal from a lower court. If appeal is granted, the writ orders the lower court to certify the record and send it to the higher court, which then has the discretion to hear the appeal. If the writ is denied, the judgment of the lower court stands.

Writ of execution a writ to put into force the judgment of a court.

Written brief *see* brief.

Written interrogatories *see* interrogatories.

Wrongful discharge a cause of action an employee may have if dismissed for an improper reason, such as exercising a public right or other interest protected in the employment relationship, such as protected class status under Title VII.

Y

Yellow-dog contract an agreement between an employer and an employee under which the employee agrees not to join a union, and that if he joins a union, there is a breach of contract and the employee is dismissed.

Z

Zoning when the land in an area, usually a city, is divided into categories according to the kinds of structures that may be built, the purposes of the use of the land, and other regulations that may apply to different parcels of property.

Index

8-K reports, 538

A

Abbott Labs v. Gardner, 381
ability tests, 435
absolute privilege, 146–147
abstract of judgment, 299
abuse of discretion, 381
acceptance
  under CISG, 273
  of draft, 286
  of offer, 257–258
  proper communication of, 228–229
  unconditional, 227
  unequivocal, 228
accommodation, reasonable, 422, 441
accord, 242
accredited investors, 536
activities, protected, 414
actual authority, 344, 348
actual damages, 245
actual malice, 147
actus reus, 105
ad valorem tariffs, 558
ADA (Americans with Disabilities Act of 1990), 439
ADA Enforcement Guidance: Preemployment Disability-Related Questions and Medical Examinations, 441
ADEA (Age Discrimination in Employment Act), 426–427
adequacy of consideration, 229–230
adequate information, 548
adjudicatory hearing, 377–378
administrative agencies, 7
  controls on, 383–384
  creation of, 369–370
  in Japan, 379
  and regulations, 10
Administrative Dispute Resolution Act, 71
administrative law
  rule making, 370–371, 373

types of rules, 371–372
administrative law judge (ALJ), 378, 408
Administrative Procedures Act (APA), 370
admissions, requests for, 56
ADR (alternative dispute resolution), 64, 70–71
adversary system of justice, 49
adverse impact, 431
adverse possession, 179
advertising
  claim regulation, 485–486
  false, 486–489
  international regulation, 487
  online regulation, 488
  substantiation program, 485
  unfair and deceptive practices, 482
affirm (judgment), 62
affirmative action, 437–438
affirmative defense, 51
age discrimination, 426–427
Age Discrimination in Employment Act (ADEA), 426–427
agency, 382. *See also*
  administrative agencies
  by agreement of the parties, 340–341
  appropriations, 383
  classification of, 340
  coupled with an interest, 340
  creation of, 340–343
  definition, 339
  disclosed principals, 348–349
  discretion, 380
  duties of agency parties, 345–348
  by estoppel, 343
  fees, 410
  implied or express ratification by principal, 341
  liability for contracts, 348–350

by operation of law, 343
  shops, 410
  termination of, 350
  undisclosed principals, 349
agent, 339
  acts for the principal, 343–345
  duties of agency parties
    agent's duties to principal, 346–347
    principal's duties to agent, 345–346
  general, 340
  gratuitous, 340
  universal, 340
Agriculture, U.S. Department of (USDA), 476
air pollutants, 452. *See also*
  Clean Air Act; pollution
Akin v. Ashland Chemical, 170
ALJ (administrative law judge), 378, 408
Alternative Dispute Resolution Act of 1998, 70
alternative dispute resolution (ADR), 64, 70–71
America Online (AOL), 146
American Arbitration Association, 64
American Civil Liberties Union of Georgia v. Miller, 86
American Law Institute, 103, 161, 162
American Society of Composers, Authors and Publishers (ASCAP), 514
American Stock Exchange (AMEX), 549
Americans with Disabilities Act (ADA) of 1990, 439
AMEX (American Stock Exchange), 549
amount in controversy, 33
analysis, cost-benefit, 383
annual 10-K report, 538
annual percentage rate (APR), 491
answer, 51
antibribery movement, 566
anticipatory breach, 242

anticompetitive conduct, 110
Anticybersquatting Consumer Protection Act, 205
antidumping duty, 560
antidumping orders, 559–561
anti-raiding covenants, 391
Antitrust Division, Justice Department, 505–506
antitrust law, 110, 503–527
  in European Union, 522
  horizontal restraints of trade, 511–517
  monopolization, 504, 507–511
  online issues, 512
  Robinson-Patman Act, 523–526
  statutes, 504–507
    (*See also* Clayton Act; Federal Trade Commission Act; Sherman Antitrust Act)
  enforcement, 505–506
  exemptions, 505
  per se rule, 507
  remedies, 506
  rule of reason, 507
  vertical restraints of trade, 517–523
AOL (America Online), 146
APA (Administrative Procedures Act), 370
apparent authority, 344, 348–349
appellate courts, 26, 27–28, 30–31, 62
appellate jurisdiction, 26, 30–31
application to reexported U.S. goods, 562
APR (annual percentage rate), 491
arbitrary and fanciful trademarks, 200
arbitrary decisions, 381
arbitration, 63, 573
  award, 65–66
  clauses, 413
  and domain name disputes, 67, 202

global acceptance of, 68
grievance, 413
hearing procedure, 65
international, 275
negotiation, 66–68
process of, 64–66
and public sector
  employment, 66
voluntary vs. compulsory,
  66
arbitrator/arbiter, 64–65
*Armstrong v. Food
  Lion*, 358–359
arraignment, 108–109
articles of incorporation, 316
articles of organization, 323
artisan's lien, 298–299
Ashland Oil, 485
assault, 137
assault and battery, 138
assign, 282
assigned instrument, 286
assignment, 241
*Association of Washington
  Business v. State of
  Washington, Department of
  Revenue*, 371–372
assumption of risk, 134, 169
*Atkinson v. City of
  Pierre*, 190–191
attachment, 293
attachment lien, 298
attainment areas, 452
attorney-in-fact, 341
Audi AG v. D'Amato,
  205–207
*Austin v. Michigan Chamber of
  Commerce*, 86
authority, 340
  actual, 344, 348
  apparent, 344, 348–349
  implied, 344
  real, 344
authorization cards, 409
*Axelson v. McEvoy-
  Willis*, 258–259

B

Babbitt v. Sweet Home, 466
Baccus Imports v. Dias, 82
BACT (best available control
  technology), 453
bailiff, 58
balloon note, 286
bankers' acceptance, 286
bankruptcy, 299–305
  Chapter 11, 303–305
  Chapter 13, 300
  Chapter 7, 301
  discharge of, 302–303
  and fraud, 110

internationally, 303
involuntary, 301
personal, 299–300
proceedings, 302–303
Bankruptcy Abuse Prevention
  and Consumer Protection
  Act of 2005, 299
bans, on certain products, 559
bargaining unit, 409
BASF v. United States, 558–559
BAT (best available
  technology), 458
battery, 137
Baxter v. Ford Motor, 160
BCT (best conventional
  technology), 458
*Beal Bank, SSB v.
  Biggers*, 292–293
Bearden v. Wardley, 347–348
bearer instruments, 286
bearer paper, 287
Beck decision, 411
beneficiaries, third-party, 241
beneficiary, 282
best available control
  technology (BACT), 453
best available technology
  (BAT), 458
best conventional technology
  (BCT), 458
beyond a reasonable doubt,
  15
BFOQ (bona fide occupational
  qualification), 436
Bigelow v. Virginia, 86
bilateral contracts, 227
bill of exchange, 286
Bill of Rights, 75
  excessive fines, 93–94
  just compensation, 91–93
  right to trial, 93
  self-incrimination, 90–91
  unreasonable search and
    seizure, 89–90
billing error, 493
biotechnology, 462
Black's Law Dictionary, 5, 103,
  106, 339
Blackstone, William, 223
Blackwell, Roger, 112
blanket licenses, 514
*Blimka v. My Web Wholesalers,
  LLC*, 36–37
blogs, 413
blue sky laws, 532
board of directors, 318, 310
*Board of Trustees of the State
  University of New York v.
  Fox*, 88
*Bolser Enterprises v. Arizona
  Registrar of
  Contractors*, 382

BOMA (Building Owners and
  Managers
  Association), 184
bona fide occupational
  qualification (BFOQ), 436
bona fide seniority, 435
*Boomer v. Atlantic Cement
  Company*, 451
*Bose Corp. v. Consumers
  Union*, 88–89
boycotts, 414, 522–523
Bradkin v. Leverton, 248
Braswell v. United States, 91
breach of contract, 241–242
breach of duty, 320
bribery, 110
*Broadcast Music, Inc. v.
  CBS*, 514
brokers, 547
Brooke Group case, 524
Brown v. Soh, 390
*Brown v. Swett and Crawford of
  Texas*, 312–313
brownfields, 465
Brownfields Revitalization Act
  of 2002, 465
Building Owners and
  Managers Association
  (BOMA), 184
bulk-supplier doctrine, 170
burden of persuasion, 58
Burke v. McKee, 248
*Burlington Industries v.
  Ellerth*, 431–432
business ethics, 15–20
  definition, 18
  and law, 19–20
  online, 18
  perceptions of, 17
  and regulation, 19
business necessity, 434–435
business
  organizations, 310–335
  comparison of major
    forms, 325
  cooperatives, 328
  corporations, 316–323
  in foreign markets,
    563–564
  franchise, 329–334
  joint ventures, 328, 563
  key features, 324–328
  limited liability companies
    (LLC), 323–324
  limited partnership,
    314–315
  obstacles to starting, 329
  partnership, 311–314

sole proprietorship, 311
  syndicates, 328–329
business torts, 151–156
  See tort law
but for rule, 130
buyer
  remedies, 269–270
  rights and obligations,
    263–264
Buyer's Guide, 489
bylaws, 316

C

*Caley v. Gulfstream Aerospace
  Corp.*, 230
*Callison v. City of
  Philadelphia*, 401–402
*Campisi v. Acme Markets,
  Inc.*, 193
capacity, 231–232
capital, 531
Capital Markets Efficiency Act
  of 1996, 533
capricious decisions, 381
Cardozo, Benjamin N., 5
care
  ordinary, 128
  reasonable, 159, 347
*Carrel v. National Cord and
  Braid*, 170
Carson, Rachel
  Silent Spring, 448
cartel, 512
case law, 10–12
case reporters, 10
cashier's check, 283
causation, 130
cause in fact, 130
caveat emptor, 157
CBP (Customs and Border
  Protection), 558
CDC (Center for Disease
  Control), 476
*Center for Biological Diversity v.
  Marina Point Development
  Associates*, 467–468
Center for Disease Control
  (CDC), 476
*Central Hudson Gas and Electric
  Corporation v. Public
  Service Commission of New
  York*, 86–88, 94
certificate of
  incorporation, 316, 317
certificate of limited
  partnership, 314
certificates of deposit, 282, 286
certification mark, 208
CFCs
  (chlorofluorocarbons), 468
Chad, legal system of, 6, 7

change of venue, 43
chat rooms, and privacy, 92
checks, 282
Chemical Waste Management v. Hunt, 80
Chiarella v. United States, 544
Chicago Teachers Union case, 410–411
child pornography, 92
Children's Online Privacy Protection Act, 488
China, environmental issues in, 455
chlorofluorocarbons (CFCs), 468
choice of language clause, 569–570
choice-of-law clause, 570
choice-of-law rules, 41
churning, 548
Chuway v. National Action Financial Service, 498
CISG (Convention on Contracts for the International Sale of Goods), 13, 271–273
civil law, 14–15, 52, 103, 350
civil litigation, 59–62
civil procedure, 31
Civil Rights Act of 1964, 77–78. *See also* Title VII, Civil Rights Act of 1964
Civil Rights Act of 1991, 421
Civil Rights Movement, 420
civil wrong, 15
Clayton Act, 110, 504–505, 506, 510
Clean Air Act
    attainment areas, 452
    clean air areas, 452–453
    enforcement of, 455–456
    and Environmental Protection Agency (EPA), 369, 374
    expanding need for air quality permits, 453–454
    and jurisdiction, 379
    mobile sources of pollution, 454–455
    National Ambient Air Quality Standards (NAAQS), 451
    nonattainment areas, 453
    permit system, 452–453
    State Implementation Plan (SIP), 451–452
    and subpoena power, 375
    toxic pollutants, 455
Clean Water Act, 8
    control technology, 457–458
    elements of, 456

enforcement of, 458
    industrial permits, 457–458
    nonpoint source pollution, 459
    point source pollution, 457–458
    wetlands, 459–461
        permit system, 459
        wetlands takings, 460–461
Cleveland *Plain Dealer*, 465
close corporation, 316
closed shops, 410
closely held corporation, 316
"closely regulated" businesses, 90
closing arguments, 58
Club Italia Soccer and Sports Organization, Inc. v. Charter Township of Shelby, Michigan, 97–98
Coca-Cola Company, 213, 215, 520
Code of Federal Regulations, 424, 488
Coelho v. Posi-Seal International, 354
Coffee Beanery v. Albert, 332–333
collateral, 290
collateral note, 286
collections policy, 290
collective bargaining, 411
    concerted activities, 413–414
    employer economic responses, 414–415
    good faith, 412
    mandatory subjects, 412–413
collective mark, 208
commerce among several states, 77
Commerce Clause
    among several states, 77
    federal and state regulatory relations, 78–81
    interstate commerce, 77, 79–81
    necessary and proper clause, 76
Commerce Control List, 562
Commercial Consulates, 561
commercial law, history of, 253
commercial leases, 184–185
commercial speech, 86, 88–89
commercial symbol, 207
Commission on International Trade Law, United Nations, 573

Commodity Control List, 562
common law, 10–12, 449–451
common law of contracts, vs. Uniform Commercial Code, 255
Communications Decency Act of 1996, 86, 374
comparative negligence, 135
compensation, just, 91–93
compensatory damages, 59–60, 245
competition, potential, 510–511
complaint, 49, 50, 408
compliance committees, 117
compliance program, 17
composition of matter, 213
Comprehensive Environmental Response, Compensation, and Liability Act (CERCLA). *See* Superfund
computer fraud, 111
Computer Fraud and Abuse Act, 348
concerted activities, 413–414
concurrent jurisdiction, 39–40
concurring opinion, 62
conditional privilege, 147
condominiums, and property law, 178–179
confirmation plan, 300
confiscation, 572
conflict resolution, 6. *See also* dispute resolution
conflicting terms, 258
conflict-of-law rules, 41
conflicts of interest, 547
Congress, U.S., 8, 10
consent, 138, 236–238
consent decree, 482
consequential damages, 270
consideration
    adequacy of, 229–230
    enforceable promises without, 231–232
Consolidated Edison Company v. Public Service Commission of New York, 84–85
conspiracy to restrict information, 516
Constitution, U.S., 8, 75–99
    Bill of Rights, 75, 89–94
    business and free speech under, 84–89
    Commerce Clause, 76–81
    Eighth Amendment, 93
    Fifth Amendment, 90–91, 94, 107, 186–187
    First Amendment, 94
    Fourteenth Amendment, 37, 89, 94–98

Fourth Amendment, 89, 90, 107
    Seventh Amendment, 57, 93
    Sixth Amendment, 57, 93
    and taxing power, 82–84
constitutional privilege, 147
constitutions, 7–8
constructive discharge, 428
consumer credit protection, 490–499. *See also* consumer protection
    Consumer Credit Protection Act (CCPA) of 1968, 490
    Consumer Leasing Act, 493
    credit reports, 494
    Electronic Fund Transfer Act, 499
    Equal Credit Opportunity Act (ECOA), 495–496
    Fair and Accurate Credit Transactions Act (FACT Act), 495
    Fair Credit Billing Act (FCBA), 493–495
    Fair Credit Reporting Act (FCRA), 289, 494–495
    Fair Debt Collection Practices Act (FDCPA), 497–499
    internationally, 494
    Truth-in-Lending Act (TILA), 491–493
Consumer Leasing Act, 493
consumer protection, 475–489. *See also* advertising; consumer credit protection
    Federal Trade Commission (FTC) (*See* Federal Trade Commission (FTC))
    Food and Drug Administration (FDA), 369, 476–481
    negligence, 157–159
Consumer Reports, 88–89
contempt of court, 55
continuity-of-life factor, 324
contract manufacturing, 564
contracts
    assignment and delegation, 241
    contrary to public policy, 234–236
    definition, 223
    and digital signatures, 239
    discharge of, 240–243

by agreement of the
parties, 242–243
by breach, 241–242
by impossibility,
impracticality, or
frustration, 243
elements of, 223–239
capacity to contract,
232–233
consent, 236–238
consideration,
229–232
contracts in writing
and the Statute of
Frauds, 238–239
legality, 233–236
offer and acceptance,
224–229
express, 223, 354
formality of, 272
and fraud, 110–116, 152,
236–238
freedom to, 222
intent, 256–257
interference with,
153–154
international, 567–572
international enforcement
of, 233
with Japanese companies,
244
law of, 222
and minors, 233
misrepresentation, 238
modifications, 259
nonvoidable, 233
option, 226
output, 262
parol evidence rule, 239,
260
performance, 227,
240–241, 291
privity of, 157
quasi, 248
remedies
damages, 243–247
quasi contracts, 248
restitution, 233, 247
requirements, 262
in restraint of trade,
234–236, 504
(*See also* restraint of
trade)
sales contracts, 256–262
and Statute of Frauds, 238
sufficiency of the writing,
238–239
unconscionable, 234
unenforceable, 234
unilateral, 227
void and voidable, 232
yellow-dog, 406

contractual capacity, 232–233
contractual relations,
interference with, 153–154
contrary to public
policy, 234–236
contributory negligence, 135.
See also negligence-based
torts
Convention Against
Corruption
(UNCAC), 566
Convention on Combating
Bribery of Foreign
Officials in International
Business
Transactions, 566
Convention on Contracts for
the International Sale of
Goods (CISG), 13,
271–273
Convention on the
Recognition and
Enforcement of Foreign
Arbitral Awards, 13, 68,
275, 573
conversion, 191–192
convicted, 103
Cooling-Off Rule, 236
*Cooper Tire & Rubber v.
Mendez*, 54–55
cooperatives, 328
copyright, 209–212
Copyright Act of
1976, 210–211
corporate charters, 316
corporate finance, 531
corporations
creation of, 316–318
professional, 322–323
public, 316
publicly traded, 327
relationship of the parties,
315–318
termination of, 321
types of, 316–318
corruption, 565–566
Corruption Perception
Index, 565
cost justification, 526
cost-benefit analysis, 383
counterclaim, 51
counterfeiting, 110, 203, 207
counteroffer, 226
Court of Appeals for the
Federal Circuit, 28
Court of International
Trade, 560
court-decreed lien, 298–299
courts
appellate, 62
concurrent jurisdiction,
39–40

exclusive jurisdiction,
38–39
federal, 26–30
appellate courts,
27–28
applying the
appropriate law in,
40
Court of Appeals for
the Federal Circuit,
28
district courts, 27
specialized courts, 28
subject-matter
jurisdiction, 32–33
Supreme Court,
28–30
French system, 28
judges, 25–26
municipal, 30
organization of, 26
relations between, 37–43
small claims, 30
state
appellate jurisdiction,
26, 30–31
applying the
appropriate law in,
41–42
original jurisdiction,
30
venue, 43
covenants, 181–182
not to compete, 234, 391
running with the land, 181
cover, 269
coverage, extent of, 203–204
CPR Institute for Dispute
Prevention and
Resolution, 67. *See also*
dispute resolution
credit, 288–290
collections policy, 290
credit policy, 289–290
with security, 290–299
by agreement,
290–296
types of accounts, 290
credit bureaus, 494, 495
credit card fraud, 111
credit cost disclosures, 491–492
credit discrimination, 495–496
creditor, 288, 290, 302
*Crest Ridge Construction v.
Newcourt*, 256–257
crime, 114. *See also* criminal
law; white-collar crime
categories of, 103–104
prosecution of, 105–106
victimless, 104
criminal intent, 105
criminal law, 14–15, 102–118

categories of, 103–106
vs. civil law, 103
(*See also* civil law)
defenses, 106–107
(*See also* defenses)
evidence, 107
international, 113
procedural steps, 109
prosecution, 108–109
sentencing guidelines and
compliance, 116–118
white-collar crime, 104,
110–116
criminal negligence, 106
criticism, freedom of, 88–89
cross examination, 58
cure, 263
customer allocations, 517
customer restrictions, 520
Customs and Border
Protection (CBP), 558
cybersquatting, 205

D

Daanen v. Cedarapids, 243–244
damages, 237, 243
actual, 245
buyer's, 269–270
calculating, 244–245
compensatory, 59–60, 245
consequential, 270
exemplary, 60, 247
expectancy, 245
federal statutory limits on,
151
incidental, 270
liquidated, 246
mitigation of, 247
monetary, 59–60
nominal, 60, 246–247
punitive, 60, 247
and sales, 268–271
seller's, 268–269
Dana v. Boren, 349–350
danger invites rescue, 133
Data Quality Act, 383
*Davis v. Baugh Industrial
Contractors, Inc.*, 12
*Davis v. Michigan Dept. of
Treasury*, 82
*DCS Sanitation Management v.
Castillo*, 235–236
De Soto, Hernando, 179
dealers, 547
death of the offerer or
offeree, 227
debt
collection agency, 496
financing, 289, 531
debtor, 288, 294–295
debtor in possession, 304

deceit, 152
deception policy
    statement, 482
deceptive practices laws,
    state, 489–490
decertify, 410
deeds, 177
defamation, 143–147
defamation per se, 144
default by debtor, 294–295
default judgment, 33, 55
defendants, 31
defendants, out-of-state, 34–36
defenses
    affirmative, 51
    criminal, 106–107
    for employment
        discrimination,
        431–433, 434–436
    failing firm, 511
    insanity, 106
    for intentional torts
        against persons,
        138–139
    intoxication, 106
    for invasion of privacy,
        143
    for a negligence action,
        134–135
    power buyer, 511
    in product liability,
        168–170
    self-defense, 106–107,
        138–139
    sophisticated user, 170
    of suretyship, 292
    under Title VII, 434–436
    against torts, 138–139
    truth as, 146
    valid, 134
    for workplace defamation,
        146–147
deficiency judgment, 296
deficiency letter, 535
definite terms and
    conditions, 225
Delaney Clause, 476
delegation, 240
delivery terms, 262
demurrer, 49
deposition, 53
Derry v. Peek, 152
DES (diethylstilbestrol), 168
descriptive trademarks, 203
design defects, 165–166
detrimental reliance, 231
detriment-benefit test, 229
Die Stern, 84
differential standards, 428
digital signatures, 239
dilution, 204–205
direct examination, 58

direct observation, 375
direct testimony, 58
*Dirks v. Securities and Exchange
    Commission*, 544
dirty air areas, 453
disability
    Americans with
        Disabilities Act (ADA)
        of 1990, 439
    categories of, 398
    definition, 439–440
    discrimination, 437–442
        compliance process,
        441–442
        EEOC guidance,
        441–442
        violations by
            employers, 442
discharge monitoring reports
    (DMRs), 458
discharge of contracts,
    241–243
discharge permit, 456
discharge, wrongful, 389
disclaimers, 266
disclosed principal, 348
disclosure, 534
disclosure requirements, 537,
    548
discounting, 286
discovery stage, 51, 53–56
discretion, abuse of, 381
discrimination.
    See employment
        discrimination
discrimination,
    intersectional, 423
disparate impact, 428, 433
disparate treatment, 428–429
Disposal Rule, 495
dispute resolution
    Administrative Dispute
        Resolution Act, 71
    Alternative Dispute
        Resolution Act of 1998,
        70
    alternative dispute
        resolution (ADR), 64,
        70–71
    internationally, 572–574
disputes, 6
dissenting opinion, 62
dissolution, 314, 321
district courts. *See* courts
diversity jurisdiction, 33
diversity-of-citizenship
    jurisdiction, 32
Doe v. Cahill, 146
Doing Business project, 494
domain name disputes, 67, 204
double jeopardy, 109
double taxation, 323

*Dow Chemical v. United
    States*, 375
*Dr. Miles Medical v. John D.
    Park and Sons*, 518
drafts, 282, 286
drawee, 282
drawer, 282
drug safety, 478–481
Drug-Free Workplace Act, 393
due care, 128
due process, 94–96
Due Process Clause, 37
dumping, 559
duration, 327
duress, 235
duty
    of acceptance, 263–264
    to account, 347
    of care, 128–129, 320
    to compensate, 345
    to cooperate, 345
    fiduciary, 313, 346, 544
    to indemnify, 346
    to inform, 347
    of loyalty, 346
    of obedience and
        performance, 346
    of ordinary care, 128
    to reimburse, 346
duty-free ports, 561

E

early retirement plans, 436
easement by prescription, 180
easements, 179–180
easements, negative, 179
*Eastman Kodak v. Image
    Technical Services*, 522
ECOA (Equal Credit
    Opportunity
    Act), 495–496
economic development, and
    eminent domain, 91–92.
    See also eminent domain
economic espionage, 111, 217
Economic Espionage Act of
    1996, 217
economic loss rule, 243–244
EDGAR database, 533
EEOC (Equal Employment
    Opportunity
    Commission), 369,
    420–421
    filing a charge with,
        427–428
    global impact, 423
    guidance on disability
        discrimination, 441–442
effluent standards, 456
EFT (electronic fund
    transfer), 499

Eighth Amendment, 93
election, representative, 409
electronic fund transfer
    (EFT), 499
Electronic Signatures in Global
    and National Commerce
    Act (E-Sign), 239
e-mail, 424
embezzlement, 111
eminent domain, 91–92, 186
emissions offset policy, 453
emotional distress, infliction
    of, 140
employee blogs, 413
employee e-mails, 424
employee handbooks, 355, 357
Employee Retirement Income
    Security Act
    (ERISA), 404–405
employment discrimination,
    419–444. *See also*
    employment law
    affirmative action,
        437–438
    and age, 426–427
    Americans with
        Disabilities Act (ADA)
        of 1990, 439
    and disabilities, 437–442
    employer defenses,
        431–433
    in European Union, 438
    filing a charge, 427–437
    forms of, 428–434
    in Japan, 438
    origins of discrimination
        laws, 420
    prima facie case, 428
    remedies, 436–437
    reverse, 421
    statutory defenses,
        434–436
    Title VII, Civil Rights Act
        of 1964, 420–427
    types of, 428–434
employment law, 388–416.
    See also employment
    discrimination
    collective bargaining,
        411–415
    employees
        employer-employee
            relationship,
            351–355
        as servants and
            agents, 352
    employer-independent
        contractor relationship,
        351
    employment-at-will
        doctrine, 352, 352–355,
        389–391

contracting to limit,
353–355
statutory exceptions,
389–390
in violation of public
policy, 390–391
Fair Employment
Practices Agencies, 427
Family and Medical Leave
Act (FMLA), 401–402
health and safety, 394–397
labor relations acts,
405–407
National Labor Relations
Board (NLRB), 406,
407–408
negligent hiring, 359–360
plant closings, 404
regulation of labor
markets, 402–405
substance abuse, 391–394
unfair labor practices,
407–408
unionization, 408–411
workers' compensation,
397–401
workplace defamation,
145–147
workplace safety
violations, 397
wrongful discharge, 389
employment relationships,
350–357
employee handbooks, 355
employer-employee,
351–355
employer-independent
contractor, 351
master-servant, 352–355
enabling statute, 369
Endangered Species Act
(ESA), 177, 465
enforcement, of regulatory
rules
enforcement power,
375–378
investigative power,
374–375
Enron, 116
enterprise liability, 168
entrapment, 107
environmental audit, 464
environmental issues. *See also*
pollution
global warming, 470–471
international cooperation,
469
ozone, 468–469
environmental law, 447–472.
See also Clean Air Act;
Clean Water Act;
pollution

global issues, 468–471
land pollution, 461–465
liability, 392
pollution and common
law, 449–451
regulations, 448–449
species protection,
465–468
violations, 111–112
Environmental Protection
Agency (EPA), 10,
448–449
and Clean Air Act, 369,
374
creation of, 369–370
and Superfund, 463–465
Equal Credit Opportunity Act
(ECOA), 495–496
Equal Employment
Opportunity Act, 420
Equal Employment
Opportunity Commission
(EEOC), 369, 420–421
filing a charge with,
427–428
global impact, 423
guidance on disability
discrimination,
441–442
*Equal Employment Opportunity
Comm. v. Dial
Corporation*, 434
Equal Pay Act of 1963, 420
equal protection, 94, 96–97
Equifax, 495
equitable remedies, 59–60,
61–62, 247
equity, 531
equity financing, 288–289, 531
*Erichsen v. No-Frills
Supermarkets of
Omaha*, 194–195
*Erie Railroad Co. v.
Tompkins*, 40–41
ERISA (Employee Retirement
Income Security
Act), 404–405
ESA (Endangered Species
Act), 177, 465
*Espinoza v. Farah
Manufacturing*, 422
estate, 178
estoppel, 343
ethics. *See* business ethics
European Union
antitrust law in, 522
employment
discrimination in, 438
insider trading, 546
and product liability, 169
evidence, 107
evidence, gathering of, 90

examinations, mental and
physical, 56
exceptions, 408
excessive fines, 93–94
exchange market, 568
exchanges of
information, 514–516
exclusionary practices,
521–523
exclusionary rule, 90, 107
exclusive bargaining agent, 410
exclusive dealing, 504
exclusive jurisdiction, 38–39
exculpatory agreements, 234,
390
exculpatory clause, 134
executive branch, 13
Executive Order 11246, 437
executive orders, 13, 383
exemplary damages, 60, 247
exemption from
registration, 535–537
exhaustion doctrine, 381
exoneration, 293
expectancy damages, 245
Experian, 495
expert witnesses, 54–55
Export Administration Act, 562
Export Administration
Regulations, 562
Export Trading Company
Act, 505
exports
controls on, 562
regulation and promotion,
561–563
restrictions, 561–563
express contract, 223, 354
express ratification, 341
express warranty, 160, 265
expropriation, 571–572
extent of coverage, 203–204
Exxon Valdez oil spill, 392

F

face-amount certificate
companies, 546
FACT Act (Fair and Accurate
Credit Transactions
Act), 495
failing firm defense, 511
failure to respond to a
writing, 260
failure to warn, 164–165
Fair and Accurate Credit
Transactions Act (FACT
Act), 495
Fair Credit Billing Act
(FCBA), 493–495
Fair Credit Reporting Act
(FCRA), 289, 494–495

Fair Debt Collection Practices
Act (FDCPA), 497–499
Fair Employment Practices
Agencies, 427
fair use, 210–211
false advertising, 486–489
false arrest and
imprisonment, 139
Family and Medical Leave Act
(FMLA), 401–402
FCBA (Fair Credit Billing
Act), 493–495
FCPA (Foreign Corrupt
Practices Act), 564–567
accounting requirements,
566–567
antibribery provisions, 566
corruption, 565–566
FCRA (Fair Credit Reporting
Act), 289, 494–495
FDA (Food and Drug
Administration), 369
drug safety, 478–481
enforcement activities,
481
food safety, 476–477
nutrition labeling, 478
FDCPA (Fair Debt Collection
Practices Act), 497–499
Federal Arbitration Act
(FAA), 64, 66, 71
Federal Communications
Commission (FCC), 369
federal courts. *See* courts
federal exclusivity, 541
Federal Food, Drug, and
Cosmetics Act, 476
Federal Insecticide, Fungicide,
and Rodenticide Act
(FIFRA), 462
federal jurisdiction, 39–40
Federal Mediation and
Conciliation Service,
69, 413
federal questions, 32, 39
Federal Register, 373, 488
Federal Regulations, Code
of, 424, 488
Federal Reserve Board, 491,
495, 496
Federal Rules of Civil
Procedure, 31, 51, 53
federal supremacy, 76
federal taxation, 82
Federal Trade Commission
Act, 505
Federal Trade Commission
(FTC), 369, 481–490, 506
advertising claim
regulation, 485–486
false advertising, 486–489
and Ford Motor Co., 56

franchise rule, 330
trade regulation rules, 488–489
unfair and deceptive practices, 482
unfairness, 482–484
Federal Trade Commission v. Cyberspace.com LLC, 484
Federal Water Pollution Control Act of 1948, 456. *See also* environmental law; pollution
fee simple, 178–179
fee simple absolute, 178
Feist Publications v. Rural Telephone Service Co., 210
felony, 14–15, 103–104, 506
fiduciary duty, 313, 346, 544
Fifth Amendment, 90–91, 94, 107, 186–187
finance, and religion, 287
finance charge disclosures, 491
financial fraud, 112
financial instruments, used in international contracts, 568
firm offer, 257
First Amendment, 94
First National Bank of Boston v. Bellotti, 84
Flanigan v. Prudential Federal Savings and Loan, 355
floating lien for inventory, 294
FOIA (Freedom of Information Act), 384
Foley v. Interactive Data, 355
Food Additives Amendment, 476
Food and Drug Administration (FDA), 369
drug safety, 478–481
enforcement activities, 481
food safety, 476–477
nutrition labeling, 478
Food, Drug, and Cosmetic Act, 478
Food Quality Protection Act of 1996, 476–477
food safety, 476–477
for cause, removal, 320
force majeure clause, 570
Force v. Ford Motors, 166–167
Ford Motor Co., 56, 70, 160, 166–167
Fordyce Bank and Trust v. Bean Timberland, 295, 298
Foreign Corrupt Practices Act (FCPA), 564–567
accounting requirements, 566–567
antibribery provisions, 566
corruption, 565–566

foreign manufacturing, 563–564
foreign markets, business structures in, 563–564
Foreign Sovereign Immunities Act, 574
foreign trade, and state taxes, 83
foreign trade zones, 561
foreseeable events, 131
forfeiture, 93
formal procedures, 377–378
formal rules, 6
formality, of contracts, 272
forms, 273
Fortuna Alliance, 488
forum non conveniens, 43
forum selection, 570
Fourteenth Amendment, 37, 89
due process, 94–96, 94–96
equal protection, 94, 96–97
Fourth Amendment, 89, 90, 107
fourth branch. *See* administrative agencies
Fox v. MCI Communications, 389
France, 28, 128
franchise
agreement, 331–334, 564
fee, 329, 331
franchisee, 329, 564
franchisor, 329, 564
law of, 330–331
marketing online, 334
rule, 330
state regulation, 330–331
termination of, 333–334
types of, 330
fraud, 152
and bankruptcy, 110
computer, 111
Computer Fraud and Abuse Act, 348
and consent, 236–238
and contracts, 110–116, 152, 236–238
credit card, 111
financial, 112
government, 112
healthcare, 112
Insider Trading and Securities Fraud Enforcement Act of 1988, 545
insurance, 112
Internet, 111
mail, 112–113
securities regulation, 115, 539–543

basis for, 539–540
liability for misstatements, 541–542
liability for securities law violations, 540
Sarbanes-Oxley Act requirements, 542–543
statute of frauds, 223, 259–260
Telemarketing and Consumer Fraud and Abuse Prevention Act, 483
telemarketing fraud, 115, 483
and white-collar crime, 110–116
wire, 115–116
Frederick, William, 17
freedom of contract, 222
freedom of criticism, 88–89
Freedom of Information Act (FOIA), 384
freedom of speech
and business, 84–89
commercial speech, 86, 88–89
and criticism, 88–89
internationally, 84, 89
and the Internet, 86
and political speech, 84, 86, 89
Freeman v. San Diego Association of Realtors, 513–514
free-writing prospectus, 537
frustration, 243
FTC (Federal Trade Commission). *See* Federal Trade Commission (FTC)
FTC v. Febre, 483
FTC v. Indiana Federation of Dentists, 516
FTC v. Procter and Gamble, 511
FTC v. Ruberoid Company, 369
fiduciary duty of loyalty, 320
Fuerschbach v. Southwest Airlines, 137–138

G

Gardner v. Loomis Armored, 389–390
garnishment, 63, 297, 497
Gateway Educational Products, 485
GATT (General Agreement on Tariffs and Trade), 557
general agent, 340

General Agreement on Tariffs and Trade (GATT), 557
general incorporation statutes, 316
general jurisdiction, 30
General Motors, 60
general partnership, 311
generic trademarks, 203
genuine consent, 236–238
geographic market, 510
Georgia v. Tennessee Copper Company, 449
Germany, 63, 409
Getty Oil, 126
Gibbons v. Ogden, 77
global warming, 470–471
Goldberg v. Florida Power and Light, 131–132, 133
Goldberg v. Sweet, 83
good faith, 241, 254, 412
good faith and fair dealing, 355
goods, 254
goodwill, 207
government contractors, 437
government fraud, 112
Government in the Sunshine Act, 384
government, U.S., 9
Grams v. Milk Products, 270–271
gratuitous agent, 340
Great Chicago Fire of 1871, 131
greenhouse gases, 470
Greenman v. Yuba Power Products, 161
Greenslade v. Chicago Sun-Times, 424
Gretillat v. Care Initiatives, 440–441
grievance arbitration, 413
Griffith v. Clear Lake Trout, 260–261
gross leasable, 183
Growth of Law, 5
guarantor, 291–292
guaranty, 291
guilty mind, 105
Guz v. Bechtel National, 355, 356–357

H

Häagen-Dazs, 485
habitat protection, 465–468. *See also* environmental law
handbooks, employee, 355
harassment, 428
Hardcore Concrete, LLC v. Fortner Insurance Services, 341–342
hardship, undue, 422, 441

harmonized tariff schedule,
    559
*Harris v. Forklift
    Systems*, 425–426, 428
Hart-Scott-Rodino Antitrust
    Improvements Act
    (HSR), 509
Harvey v. Veneman, 373
hazard communication
    standard (HazCom), 397
hazardous waste, 462–463, 469
HazCom (hazard
    communication
    standard), 397
health and safety, worker
    Occupational Safety and
        Health Act of 1970
        (OSHAct), 394–396
    toxic substances, 396–397
    workplace safety
        violations, 397
health care costs, 392
health claims, standards
    for, 478
healthcare fraud, 112
hearing, adjudicatory, 377–378
hearings, 65
Heintz v. Jenkins, 497
*Henningsen v. Bloomfield
    Motors*, 160
*Hicklin Engineering v. R.J.
    Bartell*, 215–217
*Hinson v. N&W Construction
    Company*, 230–231
holder in due course, 288
Holmes, Oliver Wendell, 5,
    84, 135
Holocaust denial, 89
home solicitation statutes, 236
homestead exemption, 296
Hooked on Phonics, 485
horizontal merger, 509
horizontal restraints of trade,
    511–517. *See also*
    restraint of trade
    exchanges of information,
        514–516
    price-fixing, 512–514
    territorial restrictions,
        517, 520
hostile environment, 425
hostile use, 180
House of Representatives,
    U.S. *See* Congress, U.S.
Howey Test, 533–534
HSR (Hart-Scott-Rodino
    Antitrust Improvements
    Act), 509
*Huaiyin Foreign Trade Corp v.
    United States*, 560
Hughes v. Oklahoma, 80–81
hung jury, 58

Hurricane Katrina, 112
Hyundai Motor Company, 116

I

IAA (Investment Advisers
    Act), 547–548
ICA (Investment Company Act
    of 1940), 545–547
ICC (Interstate Commerce
    Commission), 369
ICJ (International Court of
    Justice), 573. *See also* courts
illegal agreement, 233–234
illegal bargain, 233
immigrants, hiring, 403
impact, adverse, 433
impact, disparate, 428, 433
implicit rules, 6
implied authority, 344
implied contract, 223, 354
implied ratification, 341
implied warranty, 160, 265, 266
imports
    controls on, 559–561
    export regulation and
        promotion, 561–563
    taxes on, 557–559
    U.S. policy, 557–563
impossibility, 243
impracticality, 243
in defense of others, 139
in defense of property, 139
in personam jurisdiction, 33
In re Darby, 300–301
in rem jurisdiction, 37
*In the Matter of Kmart
    Corporation*, 304–305
incapacity, mental or
    physical, 227
incidental damages, 270
income and means testing, 300
incorporation
    articles of, 316
    certificate of, 316, 317
indefinite offer, 257
indefiniteness, 225
independent contractor, 351
indictment, 108
industrial permits, 457–458
infliction of emotional
    distress, 140
influence, undue, 236
informal procedures, 376–377
informal rules, 6
information, adequate, 548
information, exchanges
    of, 514–516
information sharing, 514
infringement, 200, 204
injunction, 61–62, 246,
    405–406, 506

insanity, as defense, 106
insider trading, 112
    in European Union, 546
    SEC prosecution, 543–544
    Supreme Court
        interpretation, 544
Insider Trading and Securities
    Fraud Enforcement Act of
    1988, 545
Insider Trading Sanctions Act
    of 1984, 545
insolvent, 290
installment note, 286
instruments, negotiable.
    See negotiable instruments
insulation r-value rule, 488
insurance fraud, 112
insuring against risk of
    loss, 572
intangible goods, 254
intangible property, 200
intellectual property, 200–219
    copyright, 209–212
    definition, 188, 200
    internationally, 203, 215
    patents, 213–215
    trade secrets, 213,
        215–218
    trademarks, 201–209
intent
    to contract, 256–257
    establishing, 135–136
    manifestation of, 225
    to sue, 458
intentional misrepresentation,
    152
intentional torts against
    persons, 135–147. *See also*
    tort law
    assault and battery,
        137–138
    categories of, 139
    defamation, 143–144
    defenses, 138–139
    establishing intent, 135–136
    false imprisonment, 139
    infliction of emotional
        distress, 140
    invasion of privacy,
        142–143
    shoplifting, 140
    workplace defamation,
        145–147
interests in inventory, 293–294
interference
    with contractual relations,
        153–154
    with prospective
        advantage, 155
    with prospective
        contractual relationship,
        155

with prospective economic
        advantage, 155
*International Airport Centers v.
    Citrin*, 348
international business
    environment, 555,
        567–568
International Centre for
    Dispute Resolution, 68
International Chamber of
    Commerce, 573
international contracts,
        567–572
    cultural aspects, 567–568
    financial aspects, 568
    key clauses in, 568–572
    loss of investment,
        571–572
International Corporation for
    Assigned Names and
    Numbers (ICANN), 204
International Court of
    Arbitration, 68. *See also*
    courts
International Court of Justice
    (ICJ), 573. *See also* courts
international dispute
    resolution, 572–574
    arbitration, 573
    doctrine of sovereign
        immunity, 573–574
    International Court of
        Justice (ICJ), 573
    litigation, 572–573
international law
    and commercial speech,
        89
    and consumer credit
        protection, 494
    and criminal law, 113
    dispute resolution,
        572–574
    drug safety, 479
    financial instruments, 568
    freedom of speech, 84, 89
    global environmental
        issues, 468–471
    intellectual property, 203,
        215
    land ownership, 179
    libel, 146
    origins of, 555
    patents, 215
    pirates, 564
    political speech, 89
    sources of, 13, 555–556
    trade agreements,
        556–557
    and white-collar crime,
        116
international sales, 271–275
    and arbitration, 275

Convention on Contracts for the International Sale of Goods, 271–273
International Shoe Company v. Washington, 35
International Standards Organization (ISO), 259
International Trade Administration (ITA), 559
international trade agreements, 556–557
International Trade Commission (ITC), 559
Internet
  blogs, 413
  cybersquatting, 205
  domain name disputes, 67, 204
  Electronic Signatures in Global and National Commerce Act (E-Sign), 239
  e-mail, 424
  fraud, 111
  and freedom of speech, 86
  liability, 146
  sales, 34
  security of, 239
  speech, 146
  top-level domain (TLD) system, 204
Interpol, 113
interpretive rules, 371
interrogatories, 54
intersectional discrimination, 423
interstate commerce, 77, 79–81
Interstate Commerce Commission (ICC), 369
intervening conduct, 132–133
intervening illegality, 226
intoxication, as defense, 106
invasion of privacy, 142–143
Invention Submission v. Rogan, 376–377
invention-promotion scams, 484
inventory, 294
inventory, interests in, 293–294
investigative power, 374–375
investment
  advisers, 547
  companies, 547
  loss of, 571–572
  of money, 533
Investment Advisers Act (IAA), 547
Investment Company Act (ICA) of 1940, 545–547
investors, accredited, 536
involuntary bankruptcy, 301
involuntary dissolution, 321

Ironite Products Co. v. Samuels, 317–318
irrevocable letter of credit, 568, 570
Islamic law, 287
ISO (International Standards Organization), 259
ITA (International Trade Administration), 559
ITC (International Trade Commission), 559

J

James v. Bob Ross Buick, 142–143
Japan
  administrative agencies in, 379
  contracts with, 244
  employment discrimination in, 438
  small businesses in, 313
  sources of law in, 16
  tort law in, 157
Japan Line, Ltd. v. County of Los Angeles, 83
"Jim Crow" laws, 97
job related, 434–435
Johnson, Lyndon, 437
joint and several liability, 168
joint tenancy, 178
joint ventures, 328, 563
Juarez v. CC Services, 399–400
judges, 25–26
judgment, 63
judgment, abstract of, 299
judgment lien, 299
judgment rule, 320
Judicial Improvements Act, 71
judicial review, 378–382
judiciary, 10–12
Jungle, The (Sinclair), 476
jurisdiction
  appellate, 26, 30–31
  based on power over property, 37
  concurrent, 39–40
  definition, 31–32
  diversity, 33
  diversity-of-citizenship, 32
  exclusive, 38–39
  federal question, 39–40
  general, 30
  judicial review, 379
  limited, 30
  original, 26, 30
  original and exclusive, 29
  out-of-state business defendants, 35–36
  out-of-state defendants, 34–36

personal, 33, 34
  in personam, 33
  quasi in rem, 37
  in rem, 37
  standing, 380–381
  subject-matter, 32–33
jury, 57–58
just compensation, 91–93
Justinian's Institutes, 5

K

Kafauver Amendment of 1962, 480
Katzenbach v. McClung, 77–78
Kelo v. City of New London, Connecticut, 91–92
King, Martin Luther, Jr., 19
Kohl v. U.S., 186
Kyoto Treaty, 470

L

L&L Doc's v. Florida Division of Alcoholic Beverages and Tobacco, 237–238
labor disputes, and injunctions, 405–406
labor law. *See* employment law
labor markets, 354, 402–405
labor relations acts, 405–407
Labor-Management Reporting and Disclosure Act. *See* Landrum-Griffin Act of 1959
LAER (lowest achievable emissions rate technology), 453
land ownership. *See* real property
land pollution. *See also* pollution
  pesticides, 462
  Resource Conservation and Recovery Act (RCRA), 462–463
  Superfund, 463–465
  Toxic Substances Control Act (TOSCA), 461–462
land, trespass to, 188
landlords, 182–185
Landrum-Griffin Act of 1959, 405, 406–407
land-use rules, 93
Lanham Act
  and counterfeit goods, 207
  and false advertising, 486–489
  and service marks, 208
  and trademarks, 201, 202, 204
lapse of time, 226

Latta v. Kilbourn, 313
law. *See also specific types*
  classification of, 13–15
  and constitutions, 7–8
  definition, 5
  and ethics, 19–20
  and the executive, 13
  and judiciary, 10–12
  and legislatures, 8, 10
  sources of, 7–13, 555–556
  sources of in Japan, 16
law merchant, 253, 555
law of contracts, 222
learned intermediary doctrine, 481
leasehold, 182
leases, 183
Lee v. R & K Marine, 267
Leegin Creative Leather Products v. PSKS, 519–520
legal benefit, 229
legal cause rule, 132
legal detriment, 229
legal entity status, 316
legal system, 5–8. *See also* law
legislative delegation, 369
legislative rules, 371
legislatures, 8, 10
Letter from Birmingham Jail (King), 19
letter of credit, 568–570
lex mercatoria, 253, 555
liability. *See also* product liability
  for employers and principals, 357–360
  enterprise, 168
  environmental, 392
  joint and several, 168
  limited, 325–326
  market share, 168
  for misstatements in securities, 541–542
  for mistakes in electronic funds transfers, 499
  personal, 323
  premises, 192–194
  of principal, 357–358
  releases, 133
  for securities law violations, 540
  for stolen ATM cards, 499
  strict
    for abnormally dangerous activities, 449
    based on warranty, 160
    under contract law, 159–163
    in tort, 160–163
  unlimited, 326

vicarious, 358
waivers, 136
libel, 143, 146
licensee, 563
licensing agreements, 563
licensing requirements, 403–404
licensor, 563
liens, 186, 297
   artisan's, 298–299
   attachment, 298
   court-decreed, 298–299
   floating, 294
   judgment, 299
   mechanic's, 298
   nonconsensual, 296
   possessory, 298–299
life estate, 178
Lightle v. Real Estate Commission, 153
limited jurisdiction, 30
limited liability, 325–326
limited liability companies (LLC), 323–324
limited life, 327
limited partnership, 314–315
liquidated damages, 245
liquidation, 302
litigation, 59–62, 572–573. *See also* courts; dispute resolution
litigation, cost of, 151–152
Livedoor, 116
LLC (limited liability companies), 323–324
Llewellyn, Karl N., 6
load mutual funds, 546
lockouts, 414
Logan v. D.W. Sivers, 245–246
long-arm statute, 35
Lor-Mar/Toto v. Constitution Bank, 283–284
loss of investment, 571–572
Loveladies Harbor v. United States, 460–461
lowest achievable emissions rate (LAER) technology, 453
Lujan v. Defenders of Wildfire, 381

M

Machinchick v. PB Power, 430–431
Macon-Bibb County Planning and Zoning v. Vineville Neighborhood, 187–188
MacPherson v. Buick Motor Company, 158–159
Madrid System, 202
mail fraud, 112–113

Mail-Order Rule, 488–489
majority opinion, 62
maker, 285
malice, actual, 147
management companies, 546
managers, 318, 321
mandatory subjects, 412–413
manifest system, 463
manifestation of intent, 225
manslaughter, 103
manufacture, 213
manufacturing defect, 163–164. *See also* product liability
market power, 509–510
market share, 510
market share liability, 168
Marshall, John, 76
Marshall v. Barlow, 90, 395
Martin v. Hunter's Lessee, 75
Massachusetts v. Environmental Protection Agency, 470–471
master, 352
master-servant relationship, 352–355
material breach, 241
material information, 534
material misinformation, 541
material omissions, 539–540
Matrix Group Limited v. Rawlings Sporting Goods, 154–155
maximum allowable increase, 452
maximum emission rates (MERs), 455
Mazetti v. Armour, 160
McCarran-Ferguson Act, 505
McCulloch v. Maryland, 76
McCune v. Myrtle Beach Indoor Shooting Range, 134–135
McDonald v. Santa Fe Trail Transportation, 421
McDonnell-Douglas decision, 428
MDM Group Associates v. CX Reinsurance Company, 155–156
mechanic's lien, 298
media, 84
mediation, 68–70
medical devices, 480
meeting competition, 526
members, in limited liability company, 324
membership interest, 324
mens rea, 105
merchantable, 265
merchants, 254
merchant's firm offer, 257
mergers, 509–511
merit systems, 435

merits, 535
Merrill Lynch, 547
MERs (maximum emission rates), 455
Metro-Goldwyn-Mayer Studios v. Grokster, 211–212
Mexico, property law in, 184
Microsoft Corp., 564
Miller v. Pilgrim's Pride Corporation, 42–43
Miner v. Fashion Enterprises, 326
mineral rights, 178
minimum contacts, 35
minimum wage, 403
minorities, underrepresented, 421
minors, 233
Miranda rights, 107
mirror image, 227
misappropriation, 192
misconduct, 320
misdemeanor, 15, 103, 104. *See also* criminal law
misleading statements, 539–540
misrepresentation, 152, 159, 160, 236
misrepresentation, intentional, 152
Missouri System, 25
misstatements, 541–542
misstatements of material fact, 236
mistrial, 58, 109
Mitchell v. Gonzales, 132
mitigation of damages, 246
mixed motives, 429–430
Model Penal Code, 103
modify (judgment), 62
monetary damages, 59–60
money laundering, 113–114
monitoring requirements, 374
monopolization, 504, 507–511
Montreal Protocol of 1987, 469
moral rights, 210
Morales v. Trans World Airlines, 80
morals, 18
Moran v. Sims, 180–181
mortgage, 290, 296, 297
motions
   for a directed verdict, 59
   to dismiss, 49
   for a judgment as a matter of law, 59
   for a judgment notwithstanding the verdict, 59
municipal courts, 30
mutual funds, 546

N

NAAQS (National Ambient Air Quality Standards), 451
NAFTA (North American Free Trade Agreement), 556–557
NASD (National Association of Securities Dealers), 65–66, 549
NASDAQ, 549
National Ambient Air Quality Standards (NAAQS), 451
National Association of Securities Dealers (NASD), 65–66, 549
National Center for Toxicological Research, 476
National Conference of Commissioners on Uniform State Laws, 10, 253
National Labor Relations Act (NRLA), 405, 505
National Labor Relations Board (NLRB), 406, 407–408
national origin, 422
National Pollutant Discharge Elimination System (NPDES), 457
National Priority List (NPL), 464
nationalization, 571
Nazi artifacts, 89
necessary and proper clause, 76
negative easements, 179
negligence, criminal, 106
negligence in tort, 158–159
negligence-based torts, 127, 449
   causation, 130
   cause in fact, 130
   contributory, 135
   defenses to, 134–135
   duty of care, 128–129, 320
   elements of, 133
   intervening conduct, 132–133
   proximate cause, 128, 130–132, 236
   res ipsa loquitur, 130
   substantial factor, 132
negligent hiring, 359–360
negotiability, 286
negotiable instruments
   functions of, 282
   requirements for, 287–288
   types of, 282–286
negotiation, 66–68, 225, 286

net leasable, 184

new source performance standards (NSPS), 458

New York Stock Exchange (NYSE), 549

New York Times v. Tasini, 211

New York v. Burger, 90

Nielsen v. Gold's Gym, 185

Nike Shox trademark, 203

NLRA (National Labor Relations Act), 405, 505

NLRB (National Labor Relations Board), 406, 407–408

Noerr-Pennington doctrine, 505

Nollan v. California Coastal Commission, 93

no-load mutual funds, 546

nominal damages, 60, 246–247

nonattainment areas, 453

noncompete agreements, 234, 391

nonconsensual lien, 296

nonexempt property, 296

nonnegotiable instruments, 287. *See also* negotiable instruments

nonpoint source pollution, 459. *See also* pollution

nontraded entities, 327

nonvoidable contracts, 233

Norris-La Guardia Act, 405–406

North American Free Trade Agreement (NAFTA), 556–557

Northern Pacific Railway Co. v. United States, 507, 521

Northwestern States Portland Cement Co. v. Minnesota, 82

notes, 282, 283

novation, 242

NPDES (National Pollutant Discharge Elimination System), 457

NPL (National Priority List), 464

NSPS (new source performance standards), 458

nuisance, 189–190, 449

Nutraceutical Corp. v. Von Eschenbach, 479–480

nutrition labeling, 477

Nutrition Labeling and Education Act of 1990, 477

NYSE (New York Stock Exchange), 549

Nystrom v. Trex Company, 214

O

obligation of payment, 264

obligations, 262–264

occupational licensure and regulation, 403–404

Occupational Safety and Health Administration (OSHA), 90, 394–396

OFCCP (Office of Federal Contract Compliance Programs), 437

offer, 224–227, 272–273

offerer/offeree, death of, 227

offering circular, 330

offerings, of securities, 533–537

Office of Federal Contract Compliance Programs (OFCCP), 437

Office of Management and Budget (OMB), 383

oil and gas well investments, 483

Old Island Fumigation v. Barbee, 171

Older Workers Benefit Protection Act, 436

OMB (Office of Management and Budget), 383

omission, 128, 541–542

Omnibus Transportation Employee Testing Act, 393

on demand, 283

Oncale v. Sundowner Offshore Services, 426

OPEC (Organization of Petroleum Exporting Countries), 512

open account, 290

open-and-obvious doctrine, 170

open-end company, 546

opening statements, 58

operating agreement, 324

operation of law, 343

OPIC (Overseas Private Investment Corporation), 572

option contract, 226

oral arguments, 62

order paper, 287

orders
to pay, 282, 283, 286
for production of documents, 55–56

ordinances, 104

ordinary care, 128

ordinary holder, 288

organization, articles of, 323

Organization of Petroleum Exporting Countries (OPEC), 512

organized crime, 114. *See also* criminal law

original and exclusive jurisdiction, 29

original jurisdiction, 26, 30

OSHA (Occupational Safety and Health Administration), 90, 394–396

OTC (over the counter), 538

out-of-state defendants, 34–36

output contract, 262

over the counter (OTC), 538

Overseas Private Investment Corporation (OPIC), 572

owner is the business, 311

ownership, forms of, 178

ownership interests, transferability of, 327

ozone, 468–469

P

Parish v. ICON, 164–165

Parker doctrine, 505

Parker v. Glosson, 227–228

parol evidence rule, 239, 260

partial capacity, 232

partnerships
control by partners, 313–314
duties of partners, 313
formation of, 311–314
general, 311
termination of, 314

Pasquantino v. U.S., 116

Patent and Trademark Office, U.S., 200

patents, 211–213

payee, 282, 285

payment clause, 569

payment, obligation of, 264

PC (professional corporation), 322–323

penalty, 246

Pennsylvania State Police v. Suders, 432–433

Pennzoil, 126

People v. Salas, 105–106

PepsiCo, 520

per se rule, 507

perfection, secured transactions, 293

performance, 227, 240–241, 262–264, 291

permanent injunction, 61

perpetual existence, 328

personal jurisdiction, 33, 34

personal liability, 323

personal property, 188, 191, 290

personal service, 33

persuasion, burden of, 58

pesticides, 462

Philip Morris USA v. Williams, 95–96

pierce the corporate veil, 326

piracy, 564

pirates, international, 564

places of business, 272

plaintiff, 31

plant closings, warning employees, 404

plea bargain, 109

pleadings, 49

point source pollution, 457–458. *See also* pollution

police powers, 186–187

political action, by unions, 410–411

political speech, 84, 86, 89

pollution. *See also* Clean Air Act; Clean Water Act; environmental law
air pollutants, 452
in China, 455
and common law, 449–451
of land, 461–465
mobile sources of, 454–455
nonpoint source pollution, 459
point source pollution, 457–458
toxic pollutants, 455
and water rights, 449–451

positive easements, 179

Posner, Richard, 11

possession, adverse, 180

possessory lien, 298–299

potential competition, 510–511

potentially responsible parties (PRPs), 464

POTWs (publicly owned treatment works), 456, 457

Powell v. Washburn, 182

power buyer defense, 511

power of attorney, 341

precedent, 11

predatory bidding, 524–525

predatory pricing, 524

Preemployment Disability-Related Questions and Medical Examinations, 441

preferential treatment, 421

Pregnancy Discrimination Act, 421, 424. *See also* employment law

preliminary negotiations, 225

premerger notification, 509
premises liability, 192–194
preponderance of the
        evidence, 15, 58
prescription drugs, 480
pretext, 429
pretrial conference, 56
prevention of significant
        deterioration (PSD)
        areas, 452
price, 262
price discrimination, 523–525
price-fixing, 512–514, 517–520
prima facie discrimination
        case, 428. *See also*
        employment
        discrimination
primary boycott, 414
principal
        in agency relationship,
                339
        of corporation, 320
        of debt, 288
        disclosed, 348
        liability of, 357–358
        in suretyship, 291
        undisclosed, 349
priority classes, 302
priority, secured
        transactions, 294
Privacy Act, 384
privacy, right of, 92
private company, 538
private disputes, 6
private enforcement, 207
private law, 14
private nuisance, 189–190, 449
private placement
        securities, 535–536
privilege, 138, 146–147
privity, 237
privity of contract, 157
probable cause, 107
procedural law, 15
procedural requirements,
        review of, 382
procedural rules, 370, 372
process, 213
product defect law, 163.
        See also product liability
product liability,157–171.
        See also tort law
        categories of product
                defect, 162–163
        consumer products and
                negligence, 157–159
        defenses, 168–170
        design defects, 165–166
        in European Union, 169
        need for reform, 171
        primary areas of,
                163–168

*Restatement (Third) of
        Torts*, 162–163, 164–165
        statutory limits on, 170
        strict liability under
                contract law, 159–163
        ultrahazardous activity,
                170–171
Product Liability
        Directive, 169
product market, 510
product misuse, 169
professional corporation
        (PC), 322–323
professionally developed ability
        tests, 435
profit, 179
prohibited bases, 495
Project Mousetrap, 484
promisee, 229
promises, 223
promises to pay, 282, 285
promisor, 229
promissory estoppel, 231
promissory note, 282, 285
property. *See also* real property
        exempt from attachment,
                296
        interests, 177
        ownership, 179
        torts against owners,
                192–195
        (*See also* tort law)
Property Restatement, 178
prosecution, criminal, 108–109
prospective advantage,
        interference with, 155
prospectus, 534–535
protected activities, 414
protective order, 56
proximate cause, 128, 130–132,
        236
proxy, 319, 539
PRPs (potentially responsible
        parties), 464
PSD (prevention of significant
        deterioration areas), 452
Public Citizen case, 383
public corporation, 316
public disputes, 6
public law, 14
public nuisance, 190, 449
public policy exceptions, 389
public sector employment, 66
publicly held company, 538
publicly held corporation, 316
publicly owned treatment
        works (POTWs), 456, 457
publicly traded
        corporations, 327
punitive damages, 60, 246
purchase money security
        interest, 293

Pure Food and Drug Act of
        1906, 476

Q

QIBs (qualified institutional
        buyers), 536
Quaker State, 485
qualified institutional buyers
        (QIBs), 536
quality assurance, 259
quantity, 262
quantum merit, 248
quarterly 10-K reports, 538
quasi contracts, 247–248
quasi in rem jurisdiction, 37
quid pro quo, 425
*Quill Corp. v. North
        Dakota*, 82–83
quitclaim deed, 177
quorum, 319

R

*R. Williams Construction v.
        Occupational Safety and
        Health Review
        Commission*, 395–396
Racketeer Influenced and
        Corrupt Organizations
        (RICO) Act, 114
ratification, 233, 341
*Ray v. Citigroup Global
        Markets*, 541–542
RCRA (Resource Conservation
        and Recovery Act),
        462–463
real authority, 344
real property, 177–185, 290
        and condominiums,
                178–179
        deeds and titles, 177
        definition, 188
        fee simple, 178–179
        financing, 296
        historical origins, 177
        landlords and tenants,
                182–185
        in Mexico, 184
        mortgage note, 286
        public control of,
                186–188
                eminent domain,
                        91–92, 186
                police powers,
                        186–187
                zoning, 187
        servitudes, 179–182
reality of consent, 236–238
reasonable accommodation,
        422, 441
reasonable care, 159, 347

reasonable person
        standard, 128–129
re-cross examination, 58
red herring, 535
redirect examination, 58
reexport, 562
registration, exemption
        from, 535–537
registration requirements, 547
registration statement, 534–535
regulations
        and ethics, 19
        federal and state relations,
                78–81
        Regulation B, 496
        Regulation D, 536
        Regulation E, 499
        Regulation Fair Disclosure
                (Reg FD), 538
        Regulation S-K, 535
        Regulation Z, 491
        regulatory process,
                368–385
                administrative
                        agencies
                        (*See* administrative
                        agencies)
                administrative law,
                        370–373
                as applied to new
                        technologies, 374
                controls on agencies,
                        384–385
                enforcement,
                        374–378
                judicial review,
                        378–382
        takings, 93
Rehabilitation Act of
        1973, 438–439
relevant market, 510
religion, and finance, 287
remand (case), 62
remedies, 273
        and antitrust laws, 506
        buyer's, 269–270
        in civil litigation, 59–62
        and contracts, 243–248
        for discrimination,
                436–437
        equitable, 59–60, 61–62,
                247
        in equity, 61–62
        and sales, 268–271
        seller's, 268–269
        under Title VII, 436–437
        for unfair labor practices,
                408
*Reno v. American Civil Liberties
        Union*, 86
repatriation of monetary
        profits, 568

Repetti v. Sysco Corp., 352–353
replacement workers, 414–415.
    See also employment law
reply, 51
representative election, 409
*Republic Tobacco v. North
    Atlantic Trading*, 144–145,
    147
repudiation, 242
requests for admissions, 56
requirements contract, 262
res ipsa loquitur, 130
res judicata, 63, 66
resale price maintenance
    (RPM), 518–519
rescission, 242
resolutions, 319
Resource Conservation and
    Recovery Act (RCRA),
    462–463
respondent superior, 358
*Responsible Economic
    Development v. S.C.
    Department of Health and
    Environmental Control*, 460
Restatement of Torts, 170
Restatement (Second) Agency,
    348, 351
*Restatement (Second) of
    Agency*, 360
*Restatement (Second) of
    Contracts*, 223, 224, 231,
    243
*Restatement (Second) of
    Torts*, 159, 161–162, 215
*Restatement (Third) of
    Torts*, 162–163, 164–165
restitution, 233, 247
restraint of trade, 234–236, 504
    horizontal, 511–517
    vertical, 517–523
retaliation, 428
retaliatory discharge, 389
retirement plans, 404–405
reverse discrimination, 421
reverse (judgment), 62
reviewability, 380
Revised Uniform Limited
    Partnership Act, 314
revocable letter of credit, 568
revocation, 226
*Reynolds v. Ethicon
    Endo-Surgery*, 140–141
RICO (Racketeer Influenced
    and Corrupt
    Organizations Act), 114
right to sue letter, 427–428
rights
    to cure, 263
    of inspection, 263
    of rejection, 263
    to trial, 93

right-to-work laws, 411
riparian water law, 449–450
ripeness doctrine, 381
risk analysis, 383
risk, assumption of, 134, 169
Rivers and Harbors Acts, 456
Robinson-Patman Act
    defenses, 526
    price discrimination,
        523–525
Rockefeller, John D., 504
royalties, 331
RPM (resale price
    maintenance), 518–519
Rule 10b-5, 540
Rule 144A, 536
rule of reason, 507, 521
rulemaking procedure, 373
*Russell v. Kinney
    Contractors*, 139–140
R-value Rule, 488
Rylands v. Fletcher, 170

S

safe harbor, 541
sales, 252–276
    forming a sales contract,
        256–262
    international, 271–275
    performance and
        obligations, 262–264.
        (*See also* performance)
    remedies and damages,
        268–271
    Uniform Commercial
        Code (UCC)
        (*See* Uniform
        Commercial Code
        (UCC))
    warranties, 264–267
sanctions, 375
SARA (Superfund
    Amendments and
    Reauthorization Act), 463
Sarbanes-Oxley Act, 542–543
satisfaction, 243
scalping, 548
Schedule A, 534–535
Schench v. U.S., 84
*Schuchmann v. Air Services
    Heating and Air
    Conditioning*, 490
scienter, 152, 236
scope of review, 381–382
SCOR (Small Corporate
    Offering Registration),
    536
search and seizure, 89–90
SEC (Securities and Exchange
    Commission), 369, 532,
    535, 543–544

secondary boycott, 414
secondary meaning, 208
Section 402A, 161–162
secured creditor, 290
secured creditors, 302
secured transactions, 293–294
Securities Act of 1933, 532
Securities and Exchange
    Commission (SEC), 369
    prosecution by, 543–544
    review of offerings, 535
    and securities regulation,
        532
*Securities and Exchange
    Commission v.
    Howey*, 533–534
securities exchange, 538
Securities Exchange Act of
    1934, 534, 548–549
Securities Litigation Reform
    Act of 1995, 541
Securities Litigation Uniform
    Standards Act of
    1998, 541
securities offerings
    exemptions from
        registration, 535–537
    online, 533
    registration statement,
        534–535
    review by SEC, 535
securities professionals, 548
securities regulation, 530–550
    definition, 532–534
    elements of, 531–532
    exempt securities, 534
    fraud, 115
        basis for, 539–540
        liability for
            misstatements,
            541–542
        liability for securities
            law violations, 540
        Sarbanes-Oxley Act
            requirements,
            542–543
    insider trading, 112,
        543–546
    Investment Advisers Act
        (IAA), 547
    Investment Company Act
        (ICA), 545–547
    offerings to investors,
        534–537
    origins of, 532
    proxies, 539
    Regulation Fair Disclosure
        (Reg FD), 538
    stock market regulation,
        548–550
    tender offers, 539
    trading regulation, 537–539

security, 290, 531
security interest, 293
self-defense, as defense,
    106–107, 138–139
self-incrimination, 90–91
self-regulating organizations,
    549
self-regulation of securities
    markets, 548–549
self-reporting requirements,
    374
sellers
    damages and remedies,
        268–269
    rights and obligations,
        262–263
Senate, U.S *See* Congress, U.S.
sentencing guidelines and
    compliance, 17, 116–118
separation of powers, 8
servant, 352
service marks, 206
service of process, 33, 49
servitudes, 179–182
Seventh Amendment, 57, 93
sexual harassment, 424–425.
    See also employment law
*Shapero v. Kentucky Bar
    Association*, 88
shareholders, 318–319
shatterproof windshield, 160
shelf registration, 537
shell corporations, 322
Sherman Antitrust Act, 110,
    504, 506
shoplifting, 140
Siemens, 116
*Sierra Club v. Mississippi
    Environmental Quality
    Permit Board*, 454
sight draft, 286
significant interest, 41
Silent Spring (Carson), 448
Simpson, O.J., 127
Sinclair, Upton
    The Jungle, 476
*Sindell v. Abbott
    Laboratories*, 168
sine qua non rule, 130
SIP (State Implementation
    Plan), 451–452
Sixth Amendment, 57, 93
Skeel, David, 19
*Skinner v. Railway Labor
    Executives' Association*, 90
slander, 143
slavery, 94
Slick 50, 485
sludge, 457
small claims court, 30
Small Corporate Offering
    Registration (SCOR), 536

Smith v. Kulig, 189
social stability, 6–7
Society of Professionals in
   Dispute Resolution, 69
sole proprietorship, 311
*Sony v. Universal City
   Studios*, 211
Sonzinsky v. U.S., 82
sophisticated user defense, 170
*South-Central Timber
   Development v.
   Wunnicke*, 81
*Southern Railway Co. v.
   Arizona*, 79–80
sovereign immunity, doctrine
   of, 573–574
*Spanish Broadcasting System of
   Florida v. Clear Channel
   Communications*,
   507–509
special agent, 340
special jurisdiction, 30
specialist firms, 549
specialized courts, 28
species protection, 465–468
specific performance, 61, 247
specific tariffs, 558
spotted owl, 465. *See also*
   habitat protection
*Squish La Fish v. Thomco
   Specialty Products*, 129–130
Standard Oil Trust, 504, 509
*Standard Oil v. United
   States*, 509
standing, 380–381
stare decisis doctrine, 11
state action doctrine, 505
state courts. *See* courts
State Implementation Plan
   (SIP), 451–452
state of mind, 135–136
State Oil Co. v. Khan, 519
state taxation, 82–83
statute of frauds, 223, 259–260
statute of limitations, 106, 180
statutory interpretation, review
   of, 381
statutory law, 8
statutory redemption
   period, 296
*Stewart v. Federated Department
   Stores*, 194
stock certificate, 319
stock market regulation,
   548–550
Stop Counterfeiting in
   Manufactured Goods Act
   of 2006, 203
stop order, 535
*Storetrax.com v.
   Gurland*, 320–321
strict liability. *See also* liability

for abnormally dangerous
   activities, 449
based on express warranty,
   160
based on implied
   warranty, 160
under contract law,
   159–163
in tort, 160–163
strictly and jointly and
   severally liable, 464
strikes, 405–406, 414
Stuntz, William, 19
subagents, 340
subject matter is
   destroyed, 227
submission, 64
subpoena power, 375
subrogated surety, 293
subsidiary, wholly owned, 563
substance abuse, 391
   costs for businesses, 392
   drug testing, legal issues
      in, 393
   employee policies,
      393–394
substantial factor, 132
substantial performance,
   240–241
substantive determination,
   review of, 381
substantive law, 15
substantive rules, 371
suggestive trademarks, 203
summary judgment, 56
summary jury trial, 70–71.
   See also trials
summons, 33–34, 49
Superfund, 463–465
Superfund Amendments and
   Reauthorization Act
   (SARA), 464
superseding cause, 132–133
supremacy clause, 76
Supreme Court, 28–30
   on arbitration agreements,
      549–550
   on insider trading, 544
suretyship, 291–293
Swierkiewicz v. Sorema, 428
Swift v. Tyson, 40
syndicates, 328–329

T

Taft-Hartley Act of 1947, 405,
   406, 411
takings clause. *See* just
   compensation
tangible goods, 254
tangible property, 293
tariffs, 558–559

tax evasion, 115
taxation
   double, 323
   federal, 82
   on imports, 557–559
   state, 82–83
taxing power, 82–83
technology, regulation of
   new, 374
*Telebrands Corp. v. Federal
   Trade Commission*, 486
Telemarketing and Consumer
   Fraud and Abuse
   Prevention Act, 483
telemarketing fraud, 115, 483
Telemarketing Sales Rules,
   483
Telephone Consumer
   Protection Act, 483
temporary injunction, 61
tenancy in common, 178
tenants, 182–185
   for life, 178
   rights and duties of,
      183–184
tender offer, 539
term draft, 286
termination
   by operation of law,
      226–227, 350
   by the parties, 226
   of partnership, 314
territorial allocations, 517
territorial restrictions, 517, 520
territorial rights, 331
terrorism, 113
Texaco, 126
Texas Business and Commerce
   Code, 489
the thing speaks for itself.
   See res ipsa loquitur
theft, 192
third-party beneficiaries, 241
TI (Transparency
   International), 565
tie-in sale, 521
TILA (Truth-in-Lending
   Act), 491–493
Tillack, Hans, 84
time draft, 286
time, lapse of, 226
Title VII, Civil Rights Act of
   1964, 420
   protected classes
      color, 421–422
      national origin, 422
      race, 421
      religion, 422–423
      sex, 423–427
   remedies, 436–437
   statutory defenses,
      434–436

titles, 177, 255–256
TLD (top-level domain
   system), 204
Todd v. Exxon Corporation, 515
toll, 106
top-level domain (TLD)
   system, 204
tort law, 126–147
   business torts, 151–157
      cost of litigation,
         151–152
      and fraud (*See* fraud)
      interference with
         contractual
         relations, 153–154
      interference with
         prospective
         advantage, 155
      in Japan, 157
   classification of, 127
   definition, 127
   in France, 128
   intentional torts against
      persons, 135–147
      assault and battery,
         137–138
      categories of, 139
      defamation, 143–144
      defenses, 138–139
      establishing intent,
         135–136
      false imprisonment,
         139
      infliction of
         emotional distress,
         140
      invasion of privacy,
         142–143
      shoplifting, 140
      workplace
         defamation,
         145–147
   and the legal system, 127
   liability for employers and
      principals, 357–360
   liability for Internet
      servers, 146
   negligence-based, 127,
      449
      causation, 130
      cause in fact, 130
      contributory, 135
      defenses to, 134–135
      duty of care,
         128–129, 320
      elements of, 133
      intervening conduct,
         132–133
      proximate cause, 128,
         130–132, 236
      res ipsa loquitur, 130
      substantial factor, 132

against property
 conversion, 191–192
 misappropriation, 192
 nuisance, 189–190
 trespass to land, 188
 trespass to personal
  property, 189
against property
 owners, 192–195
tortfeasors, 135
TOSCA (Toxic Substances
 Control Act), 461–462
*Town Center Shopping Center v.
 Premier Mortgage
 Funding*, 344–345, 351
toxic pollutants, 455
toxic substances, 396–397
Toxic Substances Control Act
 (TOSCA), 461–462
trade agreements, 556–557
trade deficit, 561
trade dress, 207–208
trade names, 208–209, 331
Trade Regulation Rule
 Concerning the Labeling
 and Advertising of Home
 Insulation, 488
trade regulation rules, 488–489
trade secrets, 213, 215–218
trade, unfairness in, 482–484
trade usage, 260
Trademark Dilution Act of
 1995, 204–205
Trademark Revision Dilution
 Act of 2006, 205
trademarks, 201–209
 arbitrary and fanciful, 202
 certification mark, 208
 classification of, 202–203
 collective mark, 208
 counterfeiting, 110, 203,
  207
 cybersquatting, 205
 descriptive, 203
 dilution, 204–205
 extent of coverage,
  203–204
 generic, 203
 goodwill, 209
 infringement, 200, 204
 registration, 202
 service marks, 208
 suggestive, 203
 trade dress, 207–208
 trade names, 208–209, 331
training, online, 18
transferability of ownership
 interests, 327
transferred by negotiation, 286
Transparency International
 (TI), 565
TransUnion, 495

treatment, disparate, 428–429
treatment, storage, and disposal
 (TSD) sites, 463
treble damages, 506
*Treibacher Industrie, A.G. v.
 Allegheny Technologies*, 274
trespass, 188, 191, 449
trial de novo, 30
trials
 appellate stage, 62
 complaint, responses to,
  49, 51
 criminal, 109
 discovery stage, 51
  impact on business,
   56
  sanctions for failing
   to respond, 55
  tools of, 53–56
 enforcement stage, 63
 in Germany, 63
 pleadings stage, 49
 pretrial stage, 56
 summary jury trial, 70–71
 trial stage, 56–59
 voir dire, 57
trustee, 301, 302
truth, as defense, 146
Truth-in-Lending Act
 (TILA), 491–493
"truth-in-securities" law, 534.
 See also securities
 regulation
TSD sites (treatment, storage,
 and disposal sites), 463
Two Pesos v. Taco Cabana, 208
tying arrangements, 521
tying sales, 504

U

UAA (Uniform Arbitration
 Act), 64
UCC (Uniform Commercial
 Code). *See* Uniform
 Commercial Code (UCC)
UDRP (Uniform Dispute
 Resolution Policy), 67
*U-Haul International v.
 Jartran*, 487
ultrahazardous
 activity, 170–171
UNCAC (Convention Against
 Corruption), 566
unconscionable contracts, 234
underrepresented
 minorities, 421
underutilization analysis, 437
underwriter, 535
undisclosed principals, 349
undivided interest, 533
undue hardship, 422, 441

undue influence, 236
unenforceable contracts, 234
unfair and deceptive
 practices, 482
unfair labor practices, 407–408.
 See also employment law
unfair methods of
 competition, 505
unfairness, in trade, 482–484
Uniform Arbitration Act
 (UAA), 64
Uniform Commercial Code
 (UCC), 10, 223, 253
 application of, 254
 vs. common law of
  contracts, 255
 delivery terms, 262
 filling the gaps of sales
  contracts, 260–262
 and goods, 254
 and merchants, 254
 and price, 261
 and quantity, 261–262
 requirements for
  negotiable instruments,
  287–288
 and sales, 255
 security interest under,
  294
 similarities with CISG,
  272–273
 and titles, 255–256
 and warranties, 264–267
Uniform Dispute Resolution
 Policy (UDRP), 67
Uniform Electronic
 Transactions Act, 239
Uniform Limited Liability
 Company Act, 323
Uniform Limited Partnership
 Act, 314
Uniform Partnership Act
 (UPA), 10, 311
Uniform Residential Landlord
 and Tenant Act, 183–184
unilateral contracts, 227
unilateral mistake, 236
unions, 408
 certification, 410
 dues, 410
 in Germany, 409
 member bill of rights, 407
 political action by,
  410–411
 process of unionization,
  409–410
 shops, 410–411
unit investment trusts, 546
United Nations
 Convention Against
  Corruption (UNCAC),
  566

Convention on
 Combating Bribery of
 Foreign Officials in
 International Business
 Transactions, 566
Convention on Contracts
 for the International
 Sale of Goods (CISG),
 13, 271–273
Convention on the
 Recognition and
 Enforcement of Foreign
 Arbitral Awards, 13, 68,
 275, 573
*United States v.
 Bajakajian*, 93–94
*United States v. Baker
 Hughes*, 511
*United States v. El Paso Natural
 Gas*, 511
*United States v.
 Johnson*, 536–537
United States v. Kahriger, 82
United States v. King, 567
*United States v. LaGrou
 Distribution Systems*,
 476, 477
*United States v. Mead
 Corp.*, 558
United States v. Paradise, 438
United States v. Seeger, 422
United States v. Stanley, 19–20
*United States v. Trenton
 Potteries*, 512–513
*United States v. United States
 Gypsum*, 514
United States v. Virginia, 97
United States v. Yang, 217–218
United States v. Young,
 107–108, 117–118
universal agent, 340
unjust enrichment, 247
unknown hazards, 167–168
unlimited liability, 326
unprotected activities, 414
unreasonable risk of harm, 128
unreasonable search and
 seizure, 89–90
unsecured creditor, 290
UPA (Uniform Partnership
 Act), 10, 311
*U.S. Securities and Exchange
 Commission v.
 Ginsburg*, 544–545
*U.S. Steel v. Fortner
 Enterprises*, 521
USDA (U.S. Department of
 Agriculture), 476
Used Car Rule, 489
usefulness, 213
usury, 234, 286
utility patents, 213

V

valid defense, 134
Valvoline TM8 Engine
    Treatment, 485
venue, 43
verdict, 58–59
Verisign, 239
vertical nonprice
    restraints, 520–521
vertical price fixing, 517–520
Vertical Restraint
    Guidelines, 522
vertical restraints of trade,
    517–523. *See also*
    restraint of trade
    exclusionary practices,
        521–523
    vertical nonprice
        restraints, 520–521
    vertical price fixing,
        517–520
vesting requirements, 404–405
Veterans Affairs, Department
    of, 380
vicarious liability, 358
victimless crime, 104
*Virginia State Board of
    Pharmacy v. Virginia
    Citizens Consumer
    Council*, 86
void/voidable contract, 232
voir dire, 57. *See also* trials
volume discounts, 525
voluntary dissolution, 321

W

Wagner Act of 1935, 405, 406
*Wal-Mart Stores v. Samara
    Brothers*, 208

*Ward v. Rock Against
    Racism*, 84
WARN (Worker Adjustment
    and Retraining
    Notification Act), 404
warrant, 107
warranties, 159
    deed, 177
    definition, 264
    disclaimers, 266
    express, 160, 265
    implied, 160, 265–266
    and sales, 264–267
    of title, 264
warrantless searches, 90
Washington, George, 75
Wassell v. Adams, 135
water rights, and
    pollution, 449–451
well-known seasoned issuers
    (WKSIs), 537
wetlands, 459–461
*Weyerhaeuser v. Ross-Simmons
    Hardwood Lumber*,
    524–525
*Whalen v. Union Bag and
    Paper*, 450
whistleblower exception, 389
whistleblower hotlines, 117
white-collar crime, 104
    antitrust violations, 110
    bankruptcy fraud, 110
    bribery, 110
    computer and internet
        fraud, 111
    counterfeiting, 110
    credit card fraud, 111
    economic espionage, 111
    embezzlement, 111
    environmental law
        violations, 111–112

financial fraud, 112
government fraud, 112
healthcare fraud, 112
insider trading, 112,
    543–546
insurance fraud, 112
internationally, 116
mail fraud, 112–113
money laundering,
    113–114
RICO violations, 114
securities fraud, 115
tax evasion, 115
telephone and
    telemarketing fraud, 115
wire fraud, 115–116
wholly owned subsidiary,
    563
Wickard v. Filburn, 77
willful acts, 136
winding up
    corporations, 321
    partnerships, 314
Windows program, 564
WIPO (World Intellectual
    Property Organization),
    67, 202, 204, 215
wire fraud, 115–116
WKSIs (well-known seasoned
    issuers), 537
work-at-home
    opportunities, 483
Worker Adjustment and
    Retraining Notification
    Act (WARN), 404
workers' compensation, 397.
    See also employment law
    benefits and incentives,
        398–401
    compensation claims, 398
    flaws in, 400

workforce analysis, 437
workplace defamation,
    145–147. *See also*
    employment law
workplace safety violations,
    397. *See also*
    employment law
World Customs
    Organization, 203
World Intellectual Property
    Organization (WIPO), 67,
    202, 204, 215
World Trade Organization
    (WTO), 557
WorldCom, 116
Worthington Foods, 112
writs
    of attachment, 299
    of certiorari, 29
    of execution, 63, 299
written briefs, 62
wrongful discharge, 389
WTO (World Trade
    Organization), 557
Wynn, Steve, 49
Wynn v. Lloyd's of London, 244
Wyoming v. Oklahoma, 80

Y

Yahoo!, 89
yellow-dog contracts, 406

Z

Zeran v. America Online, 146
zoning, 186